Middle East
Geophysical

Sandy Desert
Elevations to 6,000 ft.
Elevations to 12,000 ft.
Elevations to 18,000 ft.

200 Miles   450 Miles
500 Kilometers

Black Sea

Aral Sea

Caspian Sea

Rud-e Aras (Araks)

Amu Darya (Oxus)

Cyprus

MESOPOTAMIA

Nahr Dijlah (Tigris)

Nahr al Furat (Euphrates)

Elburz Mountains

Hindu Kush

GREAT SALT DESERT

GREAT SAND DESERT

Jordan River

Dead Sea

Zagros Mountains

IRANIAN PLATEAU

Suez Canal

Sinai

SYRIAN DESERT

Indus River

Hejaz

NAFUD

ARABIAN PENINSULA

Persian Gulf (Arabian Gulf)

Gulf of Oman

Nile River

Red Sea

Lake Nasser

NUBIAN DESERT

NEJD

RUB AL KHALI

Arabian Sea

Nahr 'Atbara

Blue Nile

White Nile

Gulf of Aden

Socotra

Ethiopian Highlands

Albert Nile

INDIAN O

Victoria Nile

Lake Victoria

45°

60°

75°

ENCYCLOPEDIA
OF THE
MODERN
MIDDLE EAST

ENCYCLOPEDIA
OF THE
MODERN
MIDDLE EAST

VOLUME 2

Edited by

Reeva S. Simon
Philip Mattar
Richard W. Bulliet

MACMILLAN REFERENCE USA
SIMON & SCHUSTER MACMILLAN
NEW YORK

SIMON & SCHUSTER AND PRENTICE HALL INTERNATIONAL
LONDON   MEXICO CITY   NEW DELHI   SINGAPORE   SYDNEY   TORONTO

Simon & Schuster Macmillan
1633 Broadway
New York, NY 10019-6785

PRINTED IN THE UNITED STATES OF AMERICA

printing number

1   2   3   4   5   6   7   8   9   10

LIBRARY OF CONGRESS CATALOGING-IN-PUBLICATION DATA

Encyclopedia of the Modern Middle East / edited by Reeva S. Simon,
    Philip Mattar, Richard W. Bulliet.

     p.   cm.

  Includes bibliographical references (p.   ) and index.

   ISBN 0-02-896011-4 (set : lib. bdg. : alk. paper). — ISBN
0-02-897061-6 (v. 1 : lib. bdg. : alk. paper). — ISBN 0-02-897062-4
(v. 2 : lib. bdg. : alk. paper). — ISBN 0-02-897063-2 (v. 3 : lib.
bdg. : alk. paper). — ISBN 0-02-897064-0 (v. 4 : lib. bdg. : alk.
paper).

   1. Middle East—Encyclopedias.   2. Africa, North—Encyclopedias.
I. Simon, Reeva S.   II. Mattar, Philip, 1944–   III. Bulliet,
Richard W.
DS43.E53   1996
956'.003—dc20   96-11800
                                                                CIP

ENCYCLOPEDIA
OF THE
MODERN
MIDDLE EAST

D

Dab'a Nuclear Power Station

Egyptian nuclear power station.

As part of a plan to build several nuclear power plants in the early and mid-1980s, Egypt signed a deal to construct the first such plant at Dab'a, 160 kilometers west of Alexandria. While the deal initially benefited from French and Italian financial backing, the Italians backed away from the plan in 1987.

Michael R. Fischbach

Dabbas, Charles   [?–1935]

President of Lebanon.

Dabbas (also Debbas), born to a Greek Orthodox family, earned a law degree. His close association with French interests in the Middle East led France to select him to be the first "elected" president of Lebanon before independence. He assumed the presidency in 1926, during the French mandate. The selection of a Greek Orthodox as president was intended to appease the Muslims, who were displeased with the idea of Lebanon's separation from Syria.

Dabbas's judicial and administrative background and his French wife made him extremely acceptable to the French mandate authorities. His rule was facilitated by his strong alliance with the SUNNI Muslim speaker of the Senate, Shaykh Muhammad al-Jisr. Dabbas worked to extend the authority of the government to areas outside of Beirut. He made trips to the Shuf and to the south, and he criticized the low standard of state services—or their absence in some cases. Ultimately disillusioned, he resigned in 1933 and moved to Paris, where he died two years later.

BIBLIOGRAPHY

Awad, Walid. *Ashab al-Fakhama* (Their Excellency). Beirut, n.d.

As'ad AbuKhalil

Dadaloğlu

Turkish poet and musician.

Although no definite biographical information is known about Dadaloğlu, it is believed that he lived between 1785 and 1868, that his original name was Veli, and that he was the son of a minstrel. In his poetry, he often celebrated the resistance of nomadic tribes to the settlement policies of the Ottoman authorities. He wrote in a simple proselike style that distinguished his work from the elegant, stylized court poetry. A collection of his poetry was published in 1940.

BIBLIOGRAPHY

ÖZKIRIMLI, ATILLA. *Türk Edebiyati Ansiklopedisi*, vol. 2. Istanbul, 1982, pp. 337–338.

David Waldner

Daddah, Mokhtar Ould   [1924–   ]

Former president of the Islamic Republic of Mauritania.

Born December 25, 1924 in Boutilimut Tarza District, Mokhtar Ould Daddah attended the Madrasa (Qur'anic school), Sons of Chiefs School, and interpreters schools in St. Louis, Dakar, and Nice. He received his LL.B. and B.A. from the Faculty of Law at the University of Paris. Elected as a member of the Territorial Assembly in 1957, Daddah became the vice president of the governing council, minister of Youth Sports and Education, and founded the Parti du Regroupement Mauritanien (PRM) in 1958. He was elected to the national assembly the following year, becoming both the prime minister and the minister of the interior. In 1960 he was elected the president of the republic and remained until July 10, 1978, when he was overthrown. In 1961, he founded the Mauritanian People's Party (PPM). Daddah was elected the chairman of the Organization of African Unity in 1971. After his overthrow, he was arrested and then subsequently released.

BIBLIOGRAPHY

Who's Who in the Arab World, 1993–94, 11th ed. Lebanon, 1994, p. 183.

Mia Bloom

Daftari, Ahmad Matin   [1896–1971]

Iranian politician.

The son-in-law of Mohammad MOSSADEGH and father of the cleric Hedayatollah Matin Daftari (a leading member of MOJAHEDIN-E KHALQ, the Baghdad-based opposition group), Ahmad Matin Daftari was born to an Iranian vizierial family. In 1929, he was sent to Europe by the Iranian government to study law. He was Reza Shah Pahlavi's minister of justice in 1936 and prime minister in 1939. Throughout his political career, Daftari also taught at Tehran University, as a member of the faculty of law, and wrote several books on the subject of law. His participation in politics was stalled in 1962 because of his opposition to the price hikes imposed by Mohammad Reza Shah Pahlavi's government and the political activism of his two sons, who opposed the shah's regime. Daftari died in Tehran.

BIBLIOGRAPHY

AQELI, BAQER. *Iranian Prime Ministers from Moshir al-Dowleh to Bakhtiyar.* Tehran, 1991. In Persian.

Neguin Yavari

Daghistani, Ghazi al-

Iraqi military officer.

General Ghazi al-Daghistani served as deputy chief of staff for the Iraqi army in 1954. Opposed to Plan X, the Iraqi invasion-of-Syria scheme drawn up by his predecessor, he sought to encourage a pro-Iraq coup instead. He was thus a major conspirator in Adib Shishakli's attempted return to power in Syria, in 1956, pledging Iraqi support to Shishakli at an April meeting in Switzerland.

BIBLIOGRAPHY

Who's Who in the Middle East, 1967–1968.

Charles U. Zenzie

Dağlarca, Fazıl Hüsnü   [1914–   ]

Prolific Turkish poet.

The son and grandson of army officers, Dağlarca was educated at the Küleli Military Lycée in Istanbul. He won his first poetry prize at age thirteen. From 1933 his poems appeared in leading journals and newspapers, and his first collection was published the day of his graduation from Mekteb-i Harbiye (the war academy) in Ankara (1935). He continued publishing during fifteen years as an army officer and seven as a Ministry of Labor inspector. In 1959 he became a bookstore owner and publisher in Istanbul and edited a monthly literary journal between 1960 and 1964. His shop was a gathering place for leading literary figures until he closed it to devote himself fully to literature (1970). He has won numerous Turkish and foreign awards. In 1967 a five-man jury of Turkish writers named him Turkey's leading poet, and he received the International Poetry Forum's Turkish Award in 1968.

In general, critics connect him to no literary school (Turkish or foreign), noting his highly developed individuality and originality, even in the formative years. Some liken his method to that of free association. His profound influence led to a new Turkish surrealism. He has written in diverse forms, from epic to quatrain, and his verses range from lyric and inspirational to satire and social criticism.

Among the themes in the poetry that built his reputation are the individual's relationship to God, the cosmos, nature, and fellow human beings; the beginnings of the Ottoman Empire; Turkish heroism at the Turkish Straits and in the war of independence; and praise of Mustata Kemal ATATÜRK. In the 1950s, Dağlarca turned to social and political criticism, protesting the plight of the Turkish villager over the centuries and denouncing the West for colonialism and exploitation, taking up, for example, events in ALGERIA, the atom bomb, and in *Vietnam Savaşımız* (Our Vietnam War, 1966), expressing the strong anti-American feelings of the day.

Some have taken him to task for sacrificing his art to politics, arguing that his social and political poetry lacks the significance of his earlier work. In all, Dağlarca has published some fifty books, including a number for children.

BIBLIOGRAPHY

HALMAN, TALÂT SAIT. *Fazıl Hüsnü Dağlarca: Selected Poems*. Pittsburgh, 1969.
MENEMENCIOĞLU NERMIN, ed. (in collaboration with Fahir İz). *The Penguin Book of Turkish Verse*. Harmondsworth, U.K., 1978.

Kathleen R. F. Burrill

Dahir

Moroccan decree of appointment.

In traditional Moroccan administration, a dahir is given by the sultan to administrators of the state and to local authorities in cities and tribes. The sultan used to send a dahir to some QA'ID chiefs as a sign of recognition of their authority over a tribe or a confederation of tribes. Today, ministers, ambassadors, governors of *wilaya*s (provinces) qa'ids, presidents of universities, and other officials are appointed by dahir from the king.

Rahma Bourqia

Daim, Abdullah   [1924–   ]

Syrian politician.

Born in Aleppo. Daim holds a doctorate in education from the Sorbonne (1956). He also studied at the University of Damascus and the Lebanese University. He has held several political positions, such as minister of education and minister of information in Syria. He has also held several positions at UNESCO. He is a member of the Arab Language Council in Damascus.

George E. Irani

Dajani, Arif al-   [1856–1928]

Palestinian politician.

Dajani, who hailed from a notable family from Jerusalem, was a key figure in the early phase of the Palestinian national movement. He held a number of senior positions in the Ottoman imperial bureaucracy, including mayor of Jerusalem during World War I. Dajani led a number of Palestinian political bodies, including the Jerusalem branch of the Muslim–Christian Association (1918–1920), and the Third Palestinian Arab Congress, which convened in Haifa in December 1920. Dajani belonged to an older generation of Palestinian politicians who sought to achieve the goals of Palestinian nationalism through legalistic measures, most notably through petitions to the British authorities.

Muhammad Muslih

Dajani, Hasan Sidqi al-   [?–1938]

Palestinian politician.

A lawyer and journalist from Jerusalem, Dajani helped found the Literary Club in 1918. He became involved in Palestinian politics in the 1920s and was a leading member of the opposition faction led by the NASHASHIBI FAMILY. In 1927, he helped found the LIBERAL PARTY, which strove to distance itself from the bitter factional rivalry characterizing the relationship between the opposition and the "councilists," led by the HUSAYNI FAMILY, and tried to promote nationalist unity.

Dajani helped precipitate the 1936 general strike in Palestine when, as leader of the Arab Car Owners' and Drivers' Association, he led a transportation workers' strike in the spring of that year. The strike evolved into three years of Palestinian guerrilla actions against British and Zionist targets. Dajani was assassinated in 1938 during violence among Palestinian factions.

Michael R. Fischbach

Dajani Family, al-

Prominent Palestinian family.

Two Palestinian families bear the name Dajani. The more prominent is a leading Jerusalem family that has held important political positions since the Ottoman era, including Arif al-DAJANI, mayor of Jerusalem during World War I. During the British Mandate, Arif was involved in the early Palestinian nationalist movement. He and others in the family later became leading members of the opposition faction, led by the NASHASHIBI FAMILY, which was locked in a bitter rivalry with the "councilist" faction, led by the HUSAYNI FAMILY. Family members like Sa'id Wafa and Ali later held positions in the Jordanian government, and Ahmad Sidqi was a leading figure in the Palestine Liberation Organization.

The other Dajani family hailed from Jaffa, and produced the academician Burhan al-Dajani, among other figures.

Michael R. Fischbach

Dakhla Oasis

Oasis in Egypt.

Dakhla is one of the oases in Egypt's Western Desert. Al-Qasr (ancient Castrum) is its main city, located in New Valley governorate (province), where the NEW VALLEY DEVELOPMENT SCHEME is being carried out.

BIBLIOGRAPHY

Webster's New Geographical Dictionary. Springfield, Mass., 1984.

Arthur Goldschmidt, Jr.

Damanhur

City of the Nile delta.

This is the capital of BUHAYRA (Beheira) governorate; it is southeast of Alexandria, Egypt. Its original name was Timinhur (city of Horus), and it was called Hermopolis Parva in Byzantine times. It has been the seat of a COPTIC bishop since the fourth century C.E. It became a commercial center during the early spread of Islam and was made the residence of a senior MAMLUK officer—because it commanded the entire Nile delta region and was a major stage on the post road from Alexandria on the Mediterranean Sea to Cairo on the Nile River. In April 1799, its inhabitants destroyed a company of Napoleon's troops.

Now a major station on the railroad and the center of a network of secondary rail routes within the delta, it is an important market center for cotton and rice. Its population was estimated at about 226,000 in 1986.

BIBLIOGRAPHY

ATIYA, AZIZ S., ed. *The Coptic Encyclopedia.* New York, 1991.
Encyclopaedia of Islam, 2nd ed.

Arthur Goldschmidt, Jr.

Damascus

Syria's capital and largest city.

Damascus is situated on the edge of an ancient oasis, al-Ghuta, where the Barada River runs along the eastern base of the Anti-Lebanon mountains. The city is mentioned by name as early as the fifteenth century B.C., when it was captured by the Egyptian pharaoh Thutmoses III. It was subsequently occupied by the Israelites, Assyrians, Babylonians, Greeks, and Nabataeans before being conquered by Rome, whose governors constructed the network of streets, plazas, walls, and gates that continues to define the contours of the Old City. When the Byzantines took charge of Damascus around 395 C.E., they consecrated the massive temple to Jupiter in the center of the city as the Church of Saint John the Baptist. The largely Monophysite population remained hostile to the Melkite rulers of Byzantium and welcomed the Sassanid army that occupied the city in 612.

Byzantine forces retook Damascus around 627, but after a brief siege the city opened its gates to the Arab Muslims led by Khalid ibn al-Walid in September 635. Byzantium's counterattack was crushed on the banks of the Yarmuk River the following summer, and in December 636 an Arab/Muslim army commanded by Abu Ubaida ibn al-Jarrah marched into the city once again. Upon the death of the governor Yazid ibn Abi Sufyan three years later, Yazid's brother Mu'awiya assumed command of the Arab Muslim forces based in Damascus. Mu'awiya succeeded Ali as caliph, or leader, of the Muslims after a series of confrontations in 658–661 and designated the city as the capital of the new Umayyad dynasty.

During the Umayyad era from 661 to 750, Damascus constituted the center of a political and eco-

Tagiyya mosque in Damascus, Syria, 1954. (D.W. Lockhard)

View of Damascus. (David Rewcastle)

Street scene in Damascus. (David Rewcastle)

nomic domain stretching from Spain in the west to Khorasan in the east. The third Umayyad ruler, al-Walid, transformed the comparatively modest mosque that had been built on the grounds of the Church of Saint John into a much grander structure, known as the UMAYYAD Mosque. This building and other monuments constructed by the Umayyads were ransacked when an Abbasid army occupied the city in the spring of 750. Damascus fell into relative obscurity after the Abbasid dynasty transferred the Muslim capital to Iraq; its inhabitants repeatedly rose in revolt, but Abbasid forces crushed each of these insurrections. The powerful governor of Egypt, Ahmad ibn Tulun, incorporated Damascus into his domain in 878, as did a powerful Turkic confederation, the Ikhshidids, sixty years later.

By the late tenth century, Damascus stood at the intersection of conflicts involving the Fatimid rulers of Egypt, the Hamdanids of Aleppo, the Byzantines to the west, various Turkoman tribes from the north, and the collapsing Abbasid empire in the east. Continual raids and occupations severely disrupted the city's trade and destroyed whole commercial and residential districts. A series of Saljuq governors struggled to gain control of the city during the last quarter of the eleventh century, but it was only when the

military commander (*atabeg*) Zahir al-Din Tughtaqin seized power in 1104 that a modicum of order returned. Tughtaqin's successors, the Burids, oversaw a marked recovery of the Damascene economy and the establishment of several new suburbs, although the dynasty faced a combination of internal challenges from the Batiniyya and external threats from the Crusaders and the Zangids of Aleppo until the last Burid ruler was supplanted by Nur al-Din MAHMUD in 1154.

Nur al-Din reestablished Damascus as the capital of Syria. New fortifications were constructed; religious schools and foundations proliferated. The city fell into the hands of Nur al-Din's former lieutenant, Salah al-Din ibn al-Ayyubi, in 1176 and remained an important Ayyubid center for the next half century. During these decades, European merchants turned the silk brocade, copper wares, and leather goods manufactured in the city into lucrative items of international commerce. Profits generated by the burgeoning trade with Europe enabled the court to patronize large numbers of prominent scholars and artisans. This illustrious era ended only when the Mongols overran the city in the spring of 1260. In the wake of the Mongol defeat at Ayn Jalut, Damascus became subordinated to the Mamluk rulers

Azm Palace in Damascus. (Walton Chan)

of Egypt, for whom it served first as a forward base of operations against Mongol incursions and later as a provincial capital.

Damascus put up little resistance to the Ottomans, who occupied the city in September 1516. When Sultan Selim I died five years later, however, the long-standing governor Janbirdi al-Ghazali declared the city independent. Janissaries quickly suppressed the revolt, pillaging and burning whole neighborhoods. Thereafter, Damascus lost much of its political and economic importance and became the seat of one of three Ottoman governorates (*vilayets*) in Syria. The city's fortunes rose whenever local families captured the office of governor, most notably during the period of al-Azm rule in the early eighteenth century, but fell when such families relinquished power to outsiders. Throughout the Ottoman era, Damascus served as a key way station along the pilgrimage route between Anatolia and Mecca. The governor of the city assumed the office of commander of the pilgrimage (emir al-hajj) for the arduous trip south across the Syrian desert, a position from which both his administration and his fellow Damascenes derived considerable revenue. The link to the Hijaz was reinforced with the opening of a railway line between Damascus and Medina in 1908.

By the first years of the twentieth century, Damascus had become a major center of agitation against the Ottoman regime. The reformist governor MIDHAT Paşa not only tolerated the growth of Arab nationalist sentiment, but also inaugurated improvements in the city's roads and commercial districts that strengthened the local bourgeoisie. The liberal atmosphere encouraged Damascenes to demonstrate in support of the 1908 revolution in Istanbul, but the outbreak of World War I brought a reassertion of Ottoman authority. The wartime governor Cemal Paşa cracked down on Arab nationalists, most famously by hanging twenty-one prominent leaders in the main squares of Damascus and Beirut on 6 May 1916. The Ottoman troops did not withdraw from Damascus until the end of September 1918, and on 1 October Arab forces led by Emir Faisal ibn Husayn of the Hijaz marched into the city alongside British imperial units.

Faisal immediately set up a military government in Damascus then supervised the formation of a general Syrian congress, which on 7 March 1920 declared Syria a sovereign state with Faisal as king. When the establishment of the new civilian administration went unacknowledged by the European powers meeting in San Remo the following month, and France was given charge of the country's affairs by way of a mandate from the League of Nations to prepare the country for eventual independence, Damascus exploded in rioting; the general congress declared a state of emergency and ordered the formation of a militia to assist in restoring order. Despite the efforts

Passageway at the Azm Palace in Damascus. (Walton Chan)

of the Syrian authorities, popular unrest persisted, prompting the French army to occupy the city at the end of July 1920 and exile King Faisal. Strikes and demonstrations continued throughout the mandate period; the rebel Druze leader Sultan al-Atrash managed to gain a foothold in the southern suburbs during the revolt of 1925. French commanders responded by bombarding Damascus twice, in October 1925 and April 1926. Nineteen years later, on the eve of France's final evacuation and Syria's independence, the city was bombarded yet again.

Contemporary Damascus is not only the largest city and capital of the Syrian Arab republic, but also a major industrial and commercial center. Damascus University, founded in 1923, remains the country's most prestigious institution of higher education, and al-Asad Library houses Syria's largest collection of printed materials. An annual international trade fair, initiated in 1954, promotes a wide range of Syrian-made goods, while encouraging the city's influential business community to establish closer connections with the outside world.

Fred H. Lawson

Damascus Affair of 1840

Blood libel.

On February 5, 1840, a Capuchin friar named Thomas disappeared with his Muslim servant, Ibrahim. Their whereabouts were never discovered. The friar was under the jurisdiction of the recently appointed French consul, Count Ratti-Menton, who supported the accusation of local Christians that the Jews were responsible for the alleged murders in order to obtain blood to make their matzoth for Passover. Several prominent Jews of Damascus were thereupon rounded up and subjected to torture; several died, one converted to Islam, and a confession of guilt was extracted.

In March, the Jews of Istanbul, alarmed at the libel of Damascus and a simultaneous libel in Rhodes, alerted western Jewish leaders to the events. An international campaign to rescue the Jews of Damascus and to pressure the Egyptian governor of Damascus, Sharif Paşa was organized in England. The defense efforts were spearheaded by Moses Montefiore of England and Albert Crémieux of France. Press coverage and parliamentary condemnations of injustices in the East heightened public interest in the Jewish plight in general and Ottoman judicial malpractice in particular. Interventions by Queen Victoria, Lord Henry Palmerston, American Secretary of State John Forsyth, and Klemens von Met-

ternich of Austria to obtain a release of the victims were of no avail.

In the summer of 1840, Montefiore and Crémieux set off for Egypt and Syria to win the freedom of the Jews of Damascus. The fate of the delegation was monitored by the European press as the Damascus affair became a cause célèbre. Newly emancipated European Jewry was haunted by the specter of a return to medieval anti-Jewish prejudice. British parliamentary liberals were also concerned about the continued use of torture and the need for Ottoman judicial reform. Great Britain, additionally, expressed an interest in protecting the Jews of the East as a counterbalance to French and Russian protection of Roman Catholics and Orthodox Christians in the Muslim world.

In August, Montefiore and Crémieux won the release of the tortured Jews of Damascus, but Muhammad Ali refused to exonerate them. Montefiore then proceeded to Istanbul to obtain imperial condemnation of the libel and future protection for Ottoman Jewry. The FERMAN of Abdülmecit of 6 November 1840 denounced the blood libel and stressed "that the charges made against them and their religion are nothing but pure calumny." He further specified that Jews were to be specifically included in the reforms embodied in the Hatt-i Şerif of Gülhane and that "the Jewish nation shall possess the same advantages and enjoy the same privileges as are granted to the numerous other nations who submit to our authority. The Jewish nation shall be protected and defended."

Despite Montefiore's success and the imperial rescript, blood libel recurred throughout the Middle East. Libels in Damascus (nine occurred there between 1840 and 1900), Aleppo, Beirut, Chios, Safad, the Dardanelles, Gallipoli, Cairo, Alexandria, Dayr al-Qamar, Hamadan in Iran, Salonika, Smyrna, and elsewhere were instigated by Armenians and Greeks as well as Muslims. The havoc wrought by these repeated accusations was partially responsible for the decline and emigration of Ottoman Jewry beginning in the late nineteenth century. The vulnerability of Ottoman Jewry led as well to the formation of the Alliance Israélite Universelle in 1860.

BIBLIOGRAPHY

GERBER, JANE S. "The Damascus Blood Libel: Jewish Perceptions and Responses In." *Proceedings of the Eighth World Congress of Jewish Studies.* Jerusalem, 1982, pp. 105–111.

PARFITT, TUDOR. " 'The Year of the Pride of Israel': Montefiore and the Blood Libel of 1840." In *The Century of Moses Montefiore,* ed. by Sonia Lipman and V. D. Lipman. Oxford, 1985, pp. 131–148.

Jane Gerber

Damascus University

Oldest of the present four universities in Syria.

The other three are the University of ALEPPO, the University of TISHRIN (at LATAKIA), and the University of the BA'TH (at HOMS). The earliest institutions of higher learning in Ottoman Syria were the Institute of Medicine (Ma'had al-Tibb) established in Damascus in 1903 and the School of Law (Madrasa al-Huquq) established in Beirut in 1913. After the end of Ottoman rule in Syria in 1918 and the establishment of the Arab government of King Faisal in Damascus (1918–1920), the Institute of Medicine and the School of Law, which had experienced difficulties and closures during World War I, were newly opened in Damascus in 1919. The Institute of Medicine was then renamed the Arab Institute of Medicine (al-Ma'had al-Tibbi al-Arabi) and was headed by Dr. Rida Sa'id, who became president of the newly established Syrian University from 1923 to 1936.

On June 15, 1923, the head of the Union of Syrian States, created by the mandatory authorities of France, issued a decree establishing the Syrian University (al-Jami'a al-Suriyya) which was to include medicine and law in addition to the Arab Scientific Academy (al-Majma al-Ilmi al-Arabi), and the Arab Directorate of Antiquities (Dar al-Athar al-Arabiyya). On March 15, 1926, the Academy and the Antiquities were removed from the Syrian University. A School of Higher Literary Studies (Madrasa al-Durus al-Adabiyya al-Ulya) was established in 1928 and attached to the university. The school taught Arabic language and literature and Arabic philosophy and sociology over a period of three years. In 1929, it was renamed the School of Higher Letters (Madrasa al-Adab al-Ulya); between 1935 to 1956, it was closed.

The number of students in medicine and law rose from 180 (1919–1920) to 1,094 (1944–1945). Women first enrolled in medicine and law from 1922 to 1923. Their numbers in 1945 were 72 in medicine and 12 in law.

After Syria became independent in 1945, faculties of sciences and arts and a Higher Institute for Teachers were established the following year in the Syrian University. A Faculty of Engineering was opened in Aleppo the same year as part of the Syrian University. This faculty later became the nucleus of the University of Aleppo, established in 1958. In 1954, a Faculty of Islamic Law (*Shari'a*) was established in the Syrian University. In 1956, the Institute of Commerce was established and attached to the Faculty of Law, becoming the Faculty of Commerce (1959–1960).

On October 19, 1958, during the union between Syria and Egypt, a new law was issued regulating the affairs of the universities. The Syrian University changed its name to Damascus University. Two new faculties for engineering and dentistry were added to it from 1959 to 1960.

Under the Ba'th party, which has been ruling Syria since 1963, and especially after the Correctionist Movement of President Hafiz al-Asad in 1970, university education expanded tremendously. The University of Tishrin was established in 1971 and the University of the Ba'th in 1979. Damascus University by 1982 included fifteen faculties and institutions of higher learning. It started offering M.A. and Ph.D. programs in the early 1970s. Dormitories for students multiplied, the number of faculty increased, and students' numbers soared.

BIBLIOGRAPHY

Dalil Jami'at Dimashq, 1989–1990 (the catalogue of the Damascus University, 1989–1990).

FARES, KHALED. "Jami'at Dimashq fi amiha al-thamanin min 1903 ila 1983" (the University of Damascus on its eightieth anniversary, 1903–1983). In *al-Majalla al-Arabiyya li-Buhuth al-Ta'lim al-Ali* (June–July, 1984).

Abdul-Karim Rafeq

Damavand

The highest mountain in the Alburz mountain range in northern Iran.

Damavand is an extinct volcano, about 50 miles (80 km) northeast of Tehran. It is rich in minerals such as anthracite and sulphur. Its height is 18,934 feet (35,711 m). The first European to reach the summit was W. Taylor Thomson in 1837. In the Iranian national epic of the *Book of Kings* (*Shahnameh*) many events take place on Damavand. One Persian legend says it was the resting place of Noah's ark.

There were many fortified places on the slopes and in the valleys of the mountain in former times. Now, however, the most important place is the small town of Damavand on the southwestern slopes. Due to elevation its climate is very pleasant, and therefore it is a favorite resort. Its name appears in different ways in various Persian and Arabic sources, e.g., Danbawand, Damawand, Demawand, and Dunbawand.

BIBLIOGRAPHY

Lewis, B., C. Pellat, and J. SCHACHT, eds. *The Encyclopaedia of Islam*, vol. 2. Leiden, 1965, pp. 106–107.

Parvaneh Pourshariati

Damiyat

Eastern branch of Nile river in Egypt.

Damiyat (also, Damietta) is one of two principal branches of the northern Nile river. North of Cairo, the Nile river splits in two as it runs through the Delta and flows into the Mediterranean Sea. Damiyat, the eastern branch, is 110 miles (177 km) long and terminates at the port of Damiyat. The western branch is the Rosetta.

BIBLIOGRAPHY

NYROP, RICHARD F., ed. *Egypt: A Country Study,* 4th ed. Washington, D.C., 1983.

David Waldner

Dammam, al-

A city on Saudi Arabia's Gulf coast.

Capital of the Eastern Province since 1952, Dammam was transformed by the discovery of oil at nearby Dhahran. Al-Dammam boasts a major port (built in 1950) and the terminus of the Riyadh railroad. An Anglo-Saudi conference in al-Dammam (1952) failed to produce agreement on Saudi–Qatar and Saudi–Abu Dhabi frontiers.

John E. Peterson

Dance

[This entry includes the following articles: Belly Dance; Debka; Hora; *and* Israeli Dance.*]*

Belly Dance

Popular form of entertainment, probably derived from the traditional birth dance practiced by women in the Middle East.

The movements of the belly dance, the rib slide and the belly roll, are traditional techniques for inducing and easing labor; however, when Europeans first saw belly dancing in the mid-nineteenth century, they focused solely on the sexual aspects of the dance. Belly dancing became a symbol of the decadent, sensual Middle East, a dance performed by HAREM girls or by prostitutes.

Today, women still perform the belly dance as a birth dance in many parts of the Middle East. It is also a major form of entertainment in expensive nightclubs and hotels throughout the Middle East. Yet, in between these extremes, the belly dance re-mains a part of popular culture and occupies a position in the Middle East similar to that of the tango and other dances in the Western world.

BIBLIOGRAPHY

KABBANI, RANA. *Europe's Myths of the Orient.* London, 1986.

Zachary Karabell

Debka

Popular Arabic dance.

In the *debka* (also, *dabka*), performed on joyous occasions in Greater Syria, dancers (traditionally young men) join hands in an open circle and move slowly in step to drumbeats. The steps become faster at specific intervals. The dancers are usually accompanied by a single dancer waving a cloth or a stick.

Michael R. Fischbach

Hora

Israeli folk dance in the round.

The hora's origins can be traced back to the Balkans, but it was brought to Palestine after World War I by Baruch Agadati, an actor of Romanian origin. Many Israeli composers have written music using the rhythm of the hora.

Bryan Daves

Israeli Dance

Folk dance, dance companies, and schools.

Jews moving to Palestine/Israel during the twentieth century brought with them a variety of folk dances, both of national and local origin. These include, for example, the dances of Yemenite Jews and HASIDIM, while the HORA, introduced from Romania, became Israel's national dance. The dances of the local DRUZE population and those of the Arabs of Israel also had considerable influence.

Jewish pioneers in dance of the 1920s and 1930s included Rina Nikova, who founded the Biblical Ballet; Gertrude Kraus, who came from Vienna and introduced European impressionist styles; and Gurit Kadman, who choreographed new folk dancing forms based on the immigrant traditions.

The first permanent company after the establishment of the State of Israel (1948) was the Inbal Dance Theater, founded in 1949 by Sara Levi-Tannai, a dance group based in Yemenite ethnic roots. The outstanding patron of dance is the Baroness Batsheva de Rothschild, who established both the Batsheva Dance Company in 1964 and the Bat-Dor Company in 1968. These were the leading modern dance companies—the Batsheva working closely with Martha Graham in its early stages and the Bat-Dor directed by Jeannette Ordman, which also has a studio enrollment of some four hundred students. Both companies are centered in Tel Aviv but tour Israel and also appear frequently abroad.

Dancing, with a strong folk emphasis, is a popular recreation on kibbutzim (collective settlements); the Kibbutz Dance Company, all of whose members live on kibbutzim, is centered in Kibbutz Gaaton in western Galilee, where its dance studio is attended by some five hundred children. An unusual professional company is Kol Demama (Sound of Silence), established and directed by Moshe Ephrati and composed of both deaf and hearing dancers, the former trained by a system based on vibration. Degrees in dance are awarded by Jerusalem's Music Academy in association with the Hebrew University.

BIBLIOGRAPHY

DORA SOWDEN has written extensively on dance in Israel in the journal *Ariel*, from 1972 onward, covering the companies discussed and the folk tradition.

Geoffrey Wigoder

Danesh Publishers

Iranian publishing company.

Danesh publishing house, one of the oldest and most prestigious publishing houses in Iran, was founded in Tehran in 1935. Danesh collaborated in the publication of the first encyclopedia compiled in Iran, by Ali Akbar DEHKHODA. In 1956, Danesh also published a journal under the same name, but the project was terminated that same year. It is now directed by a grandson of the founder, Sa'id Iranparast.

Neguin Yavari

Daneshvar, Simin   [1921–   ]

The most prominent Iranian woman writer of prose fiction.

Born in Shiraz, Iran, Simin Daneshvar taught art history at Tehran University from the mid-1950s to 1979. She was also the wife of prominent author and social critic Jalal AL-E AHMAD (1923–1969).

Daneshvar published the first collection of short stories by an Iranian woman in 1948. Two other collections followed through the 1980s. Translations of five stories, together with an assessment by the author of her own career appear in *Daneshvar's Playhouse* (1989).

Daneshvar's fame in Persian literature, rests primarily on a novel called *Savushun* (Mourners of Siyavosh, 1969), twice translated into English: *Savushun* (1990) and *A Persian Requiem* (1992). It was the first published novel by an Iranian woman and became Iran's best-selling Persian novel ever; *Savushun* treats a family's life in World War II Shiraz. After the assassination of the anti-establishment husband, his wife emerges from self-doubts and years of conventional wifely behavior to take her fallen husband's place in opposing local tyranny and foreign oppression.

Michael C. Hillmann

Daniel Family

Eminent family of Baghdad Jewry.

The Daniels had great wealth as owners of large tracts of land in Iraq and extensive estates, especially in and around Hilla, Kifil, Musayyab, and Baghdad. They had been tax farmers (ILTIZAM) in the province (VILAYET) of Baghdad and had gained the concession for the collection of the consumption tax on grain and other agricultural produce that were destined for the Baghdad market. They were also the custodians of the Tomb of the Prophet Ezekiel (al-Nabi Heskel) in Kifil, which was equally revered by both Islam and Judaism.

After the establishment of the State of Israel in 1948, Ezra Daniel (1874–1951) believed that there was still a future for Jews in Iraq and that he still had a duty toward them. In March of 1950, he defended Iraqi Jews in the senate with two speeches considered outspoken and courageous. He died soon after and was, like the rest of his family, buried in Kifil, within the precincts of Ezekiel's tomb.

BIBLIOGRAPHY

BEN YAAKOV, ABRAHAM. *A History of the Jews in Iraq: End of the Gaonic Period, 1038 C.E. to the Present Time.* Jerusalem, 1965. In Hebrew.
STILLMAN, NORMAN N. *The Jews of Arab Lands.* Philadelphia, 1979.
UDOVITCH, A., and M. COHEN. *Jews among Arabs: Contacts and Boundaries.* Princeton, N.J., 1989.

Sylvia G. Haim

Daqhaliya

Province (governorate) on the Egyptian delta.

Daqhaliya was named for the coptic Christian village of Tkehli, known in times past for its paper mills. Located in the Nile delta, the province has an area of some 1,340 square miles (3,470 sq km). Its 1986 population was estimated at some 3.5 million. The capital and chief city is al-MANSURA.

BIBLIOGRAPHY

Encyclopaedia of Islam, 2nd ed. Leiden, 1993.

Arthur Goldschmidt, Jr.

Dar al-Da'wa wa-al-Irshad

Shaykh Rashid Rida opened this Institute of Propaganda and Guidance in Cairo, Egypt, in 1912 as a reformist Islamic school.

As a youth in Tripoli (now in Lebanon), Rashid RIDA had seen American missionaries use a bookshop to proselytize, and his master, Muhammad ABDUH, had commented similarly on a Capuchin monastery-school in Sicily. Egypt's higher state schools ignored Islam, and Abduh was unable to reform the mosque-university of al-Azhar. When he died in 1905, Abduh was trying to found his own reformist Islamic school.

Rida's efforts to found such a school in Constantinople (now Istanbul) in 1909 fell through. The Cairo Dar al-Da'wa offered free room, board, and tuition to Muslims aged twenty to twenty-five, with preference to students from distant lands. Three years of study were to qualify one as a guide (*murshid*) fit to preach and teach among Muslims; six years were to qualify one as a missionary (*da'i*) to non-Muslims. Although World War I closed the school, its example was presumably not lost on Rida's later admirers among the Muslim Brotherhood.

BIBLIOGRAPHY

ADAMS, CHARLES C. *Islam and Modernism in Egypt: A Study of the Modern Reform Movement Inaugurated by Muhammad 'Abduh.* New York, 1968. Reprint of 1933 ed.

Donald Malcolm Reid

Dar al-Fonun

One of the first secular institutions of higher education, established on the European model, in Iran.

The Dar al-Fonun (Abode of Arts) was founded in 1851 in Tehran, Iran, by Mirza Taqi Khan AMIR KABIR, one of the chief reform-minded ministers of the long-ruling Qajar dynasty king, Naser al-Din Shah.

As elsewhere in the Middle East, the establishment of the school was stimulated by the desire to import European science and technology, especially military technology, and to train army officers and civil servants. Dar al-Fonun's teachers were usually Europeans. Its first cadre included seven Austrians who were hired to give military training in the cavalry, infantry, and artillery divisions, and courses in engineering, medicine, pharmaceuticals, agriculture, and mineralogy, as well as foreign languages. The first efforts at translation of Western books into Persian as well as the publication of the first Persian textbooks is also associated with the Dar al-Fonun. The students of the Dar al-Fonun were usually sons of the aristocracy, some of whom, upon graduation, were sent to Europe to pursue further education, and who came to assume important positions later in their careers.

BIBLIOGRAPHY

KEDDI, N. *Roots of Revolution: An Interpretive History of Modern Iran.* New Haven, Conn., 1981.
MUSAHIB, GHULAMHUSAYN. *Da'irat al-Ma'arif Farsi.* Tehran and New York, 1967.

Parvaneh Pourshariati

Dar al-Islam

An abode, country, territory, or land where Islamic sovereignty prevails.

In *Dar al-Islam,* the citizenry abide by the ordinances, rules, edicts, and assembly of Islam. The Muslim state guarantees the safety of life, property, and religious status (only if the religion is not idolatrous) of minorities (*ahl al-dhimma*) provided they have submitted to Muslim control.

Dar al-Harb (the abode of war) provides the contrast to Dar al-Islam. *Shari'a* law (Islamic) divides the world into these two abodes. Dar al-Harb denotes territory which is not governed by the assembly of Islam, and is directly contiguous to the abode of Islam. Warfare (*jihad*) can be invoked in order to convert the abode of war into the abode of Islam, or to rescue the bordering abode. Theoretically, an abode of war can extend ad infinitum. Muslim states, in order to avoid conditions requiring constant jihad, yield to the decision of legal experts (*ulama*), who, based on certain criteria, accept or reject the notion that an area has converted from, or needs to be reconfigured into, Dar al-Islam. These are as follows: 1) the edicts of unbelievers have gained ascendancy;

2) unprotected Muslims and peoples of the book must be rescued; 3) territorial proximity to unbelievers has become repugnant.

Of the above conditions, the first is probably the most important since even if a single edict of Islam is observed, a territory cannot be deemed Dar al-Harb. Further, jihad can be invoked for the sole purpose of turning Dar al-Harb into Dar al-Islam—in other words, to allow for the prevalence of Islamic edicts and the protection of Muslims.

Cyrus Moshaver

Dar al-Kuttub al-Misriyya

The Egyptian national library.

The library was founded in 1870 in Cairo as the Khedivial Library by Ali Mubarak, Khedive Isma'il's minister of education. German orientalists directed the library until World War I, when Egyptians took over. In 1904, along with the Museum of Arab Art, the Dar was installed in a neo-Islamic-style building. The Dar was moved again in the 1970s to new quarters on the Nile in Bulaq. In addition to the main library, there are now a dozen branches.

BIBLIOGRAPHY

CRABBS, JACK A., JR. *The Writing of History in Nineteenth-Century Egypt.* Cairo, 1984.

Donald Malcolm Reid

Dar al-Mo'allamin

Teacher-training school in Afghanistan.

The first Dar al-Mo'allamin (House of Teachers) teacher-training school was established in Kabul by Emir Habibollah in 1914. Emir Habibollah was interested in Western education and he sought to bring the secular European pedagogy and curriculum to Afghanistan. (At that time the French system of education was popular.) Habibollah therefore created the Dar al-Mo'allamin as a pedagogical school in which teachers were introduced to the new secular curriculum. Initially, the students entered the school and received three years of instruction after having had six years of primary-school education, but the system was changed during the reign of King Amanollah so that students entering the Dar al-Mo'allamin did so after having had nine years of primary school.

Eventually Dar al-Mo'allamins were established in other major provincial centers besides Kabul. Be-cause most of the Dar al-Mo'allamins are boarding schools, they have played an important part in educating rural youth sent to provincial centers to be educated. They have also served an important political function in Afghanistan, since public school teachers, as an important segment of the Afghan intelligentsia, have been an influential political force.

BIBLIOGRAPHY

ADAMEC, LUDWIG. *Historical Dictionary of Afghanistan.* Metuchen, N.J., 1991.

Grant Farr

Dar al-'Ulum

Teacher-training school in Egypt

Khedive Isma'il Pasha and Minister of Education Ali Mubarak opened Dar al-'Ulum in 1871 to train teachers of Arabic for Egypt's new state schools. Its mixed curriculum included both the religious subjects of Islam taught at al-AZHAR and "modern" subjects such as history, geography, and mathematics. Since 1946, Dar al-'Ulum has been a college of CAIRO UNIVERSITY.

BIBLIOGRAPHY

AROIAN, LOIS A. *The Nationalization of Arabic and Islamic Education in Egypt: Dar al-Ulum and al-Azhar. Cairo Papers in Social Science,* vol. 6, monograph 4. Cairo, 1983.

Donald Malcolm Reid

Darazi

See Druze

D'Arcy, William Knox   [1849–1917]

A British born entrepreneur who procured the concession to explore for and extract oil in Iran and who later established the Anglo-Persian Oil Company (APOC).

D'Arcy was considered to be a mining entrepreneur, but had actually been trained as a solicitor. He began his connection with mining in 1882, as a member of a syndicate which funded the purchase of gold mining concessions from the Morgan brothers in Rockhamton, Queensland. His shares in the mine would pay off later and would enable him to move back to Britain, ostensibly to establish himself in English upper-class society. When, in 1900, a former British minister to Iran proposed that he should invest in Iranian oil exploration, D'Arcy sent his agent to the court. His representative obtained a concession to search for oil in an area of land covering 480,000 square miles (12,432 sq km); vast expenditures of money had, by 1905, produced no finds and proved to be taxing on D'Arcy's estate. In 1905, D'Arcy, on the verge of bankruptcy, made over his right to Burma Oil, in return for 170,000 barrels of Burma Oil discovered in D'Arcy's old concession, the biggest oil field yet known in the world. In 1909, APOC was formed, taking the place of Burma Oil, which was to eventually evolve into British Petroleum (BP), with D'Arcy as a member of the board. D'Arcy died in 1917 of bronchial pneumonia, leaving behind a legacy of nearly one million pounds sterling to his descendants.

BIBLIOGRAPHY

BLAINEY, G. *The Rush That Never Ended*. Melbourne, 1963.

Cyrus Moshaver

D'Arcy Concession

Oil concession granted by the Persian government to William Knox D'Arcy in 1901.

D'Arcy (1849–1917) was a British entrepreneur from Australia. The concession gave him the right to explore for PETROLEUM and produce oil in all provinces of Persia (now Iran) except Azerbaijan, Gilan, Mazandaran, Astrabad, and Khorasan for sixty years beginning in 1901. The Persian government received 20,000 British pounds in cash, paid-up shares of an equal value, and 16 percent of the annual net profits. The latter were to be determined by the company formed to administer the concession, but the Persian government was never given the opportunity to audit the books to verify the company's figures. D'Arcy solicited the help of the Burma Oil Company for exploration, and oil was discovered in 1908. The Anglo-Persian Oil Company was formed the following year with a capital of two million British pounds. The conversion of the British navy from coal to oil led to increased interest in Persian oil, and the British invested a further two million pounds in the company. The concession was highly successful, especially for Great Britain. Until nationalization in 1951, the company paid the equivalent of 610 million U.S. dollars in profits, most to the British government. It also paid 700 million U.S. dollars in corporate taxes to the British government. Royalties to Tehran were 310 million U.S. dollars.

After receiving the oil concession for Persia, D'Arcy tried to obtain a comparable concession in Mesopotamia (now Iraq) from the government of the Ottoman Empire. The British government supported his efforts but lost out to Germany in 1903. From 1904 to 1914, however, the Ottoman government continued to discuss oil concessions with D'Arcy, as well as with American and Dutch interests. These discussions led to a joint German–British concession agreed to in March 1914 but never formally executed. The beginning of World War I ended this effort.

BIBLIOGRAPHY

KENT, MARIAN. *Oil and Empire: British Policy and Mesopotamian Oil, 1900–1920*. New York, 1976.
SYKES, PERCY. *A History of Persia*, 3rd ed. London, 1930.

Daniel E. Spector

Dardanelles

See Straits, Turkish

Dardanelles, Treaty of the

Officially known as "The Treaty of Peace, Commerce, and Secret Alliance: Great Britain and the Ottoman Empire, 5 January 1809," with ratifications exchanged in Istanbul on July 27, 1809.

The Treaty of the Dardanelles grew out of the international rivalries surrounding the Napoleonic wars. The one constant rivalry during this period was that between Great Britain and France. The other European powers sided with one or the other as their military fortunes ebbed and flowed. Until 1805, Russia and France were allies. After Russia joined the Third Coalition against Napoleon, France endeavored to involve the Ottoman Empire in a war with Russia as a distraction. This war began in 1806 and lasted until 1812. Now allied with Russia, Britain sent a naval expedition against Istanbul in 1807; although Britain was able to force its way through the Dardanelles, the Ottomans pushed them back with a loss of two ships. Britain also occupied Alexandria but was forced to withdraw. Except for Britain, France was able to defeat the Third Coalition powers, and in 1807 Russia once more allied with France while continuing its war against the Ottomans. This set the stage for a change in British relations with the Ottomans, now fighting an ally of their perpetual enemy, France.

Sir Robert Adair led the British negotiations with the SUBLIME PORTE that led to the 1809 treaty. The treaty contained eleven articles to which were appended four "separate and secret articles" and one "additional and secret article." The basic articles addressed the recent war between the two powers. They provided for an end to hostilities between Great Britain and the Ottomans with the exchange of prisoners; restoration of any Ottoman fortresses in British possession; mutual restoration of the property of British and Ottoman citizens seized by either side during the war; continuation of the 1675 Treaty of Capitulations; mutual good treatment of the merchants of both countries; an Ottoman tariff set at 3 percent; customary honors to the ambassadors of each nation on the same basis as all other ambassadors; appointment of consuls to facilitate trade; British agreement not to appoint Ottoman subjects as consuls nor to grant patents of protection to Ottoman subjects; and recognition of Ottoman authority to prohibit ships of war passing through the straits in time of peace. This latter was of special significance as it marked Britain as the first European power to recognize this Ottoman prerogative. General recognition of this did not, however, occur until 1841.

The "separate and secret articles" dealt primarily with France and Russia. Britain pledged to support the Ottomans should France declare war on them, including sending a fleet to the Mediterranean for that purpose. Britain also agreed to provide military supplies if France threatened the Ottomans short of declaring war. Regarding Russia, Britain offered to help secure a peace with Russia should this be possible before the Ottomans were able to end their war. This part of the treaty also included a provision for adjudication of the claims of both parties surrounding the British invasion and retreat from Alexandria.

The "additional and secret article" promised 300,000 pounds sterling to the Ottomans as a confirmation of friendship. Although Britain ratified this article, it was not to be presented for exchange unless France began a war with the Ottomans, which never took place.

In addition to ending the war between Britain and the Ottomans, recognizing the right of the Ottomans to close the straits, creating an alliance against France, and reconfirming the capitulations, the treaty is of particular interest because of its language. Normally, treaties are drawn in the language of the parties negotiating them. Because the Ottomans had a limited knowledge of English, however, they insisted that the treaty be drawn in Turkish and French, with which they were much more comfortable. This was a matter of some discussion in the foreign office, but the Ottoman position prevailed.

BIBLIOGRAPHY

ADAIR, ROBERT. *Negotiations for the Peace of the Dardanelles*, 2 vols. 1808–1811.
HUREWITZ, J. C. *Diplomacy in the Near and Middle East: A Documentary Record, 1535–1914*. 1956. Reprint, 1972.

Daniel E. Spector

Darfur

Westernmost province of the Republic of the Sudan.

Darfur, land of the Fur, lies between the province of KORDOFAN and the Republic of CHAD. Much of it is an extension of the Kordofan plain over which the Arab tribesmen of the northern reaches move seasonally with their camels in search of *gizu*, a mixture of grass and plants upon which camels can survive without water. In the heartland of Darfur is Jabal Marra, a volcanic massif soaring to over 10,000 feet 3,050 meters) that extends to the western border. Here live the Fur, who for centuries have terraced and cultivated on the well-watered hillsides. In the south of the province live the Taisha and the Rizayqat of the cattle-owning Baqqara Arabs. The provincial capital El Fasher (al-Fashar), was founded about 1700 as a capital of the Fur sultanate, which ruled until ousted by forces of Egypt and Britain in 1916. East of El Fasher lie the *goz*, stabilized sand dunes. Nyala, in the south, and al-Geneina, forty miles (64 km) from the Chad border, are important towns whose inhabitants trade in livestock, agricultural produce, and gum arabic.

Robert O. Collins

Dari

See Tajik

Darülfünün

The Darülfünün (Imperial Ottoman University) was the first institution of higher learning in the Middle East modeled along Western lines.

As a prominent symbol of the Tanzimat reforms, it was the frequent victim of the Ottoman Empire's domestic politics in early years and suffered repeated closures. Its creation was first proposed in 1846 by MUSTAFA REŞID Paşa, but the school did not actually open until 1870, and then only for one year. On the impetus of the minister of education, Ahmed Cevdet Paşa, it was open again between 1874 and 1881.

Then it remained closed until opening permanently in the fall of 1900, largely because of the efforts of a leading Ottoman politician, Mehmet Küçük SAIT Paşa. Its curriculum included law, mathematics, chemistry, biology, philosophy, and the humanities, as well as courses on the Qur'an, the *hadith* (traditions of Muhammad), and other aspects of Islam. In 1933, the Darülfünün was renamed the University of Istanbul, and it remains one of the preeminent universities in the Middle East.

BIBLIOGRAPHY

LEWIS, BERNARD. *The Emergence of Modern Turkey.* New York, 1961.
SHAW, STANFORD, and EZEL KURAL SHAW. *History of the Ottoman Empire and Modern Turkey.* New York, 1977.

Zachary Karabell

Darwaza, Muhammad Izzat   [1889–1975]

Palestinian politician and historian.

Darwaza, born in Nablus, was an Ottoman bureaucrat in Palestine and Lebanon. He was a major figure in several Arab nationalist organizations, including al-FATH, during the waning years of the Ottoman Empire, and helped organize the first Arab Congress (Paris, 1913). A pan-Arab nationalist who believed in the unity of Greater Syria after the Ottoman defeat and the establishment of the British and French mandates, Darwaza was also concerned with resisting Zionism.

During the British mandate in Palestine, Darwaza became a leading figure in the ISTIQLAL (Independence) Party, a pan-Arab nationalist party reestablished in Palestine in 1932. When the PALESTINE ARAB REVOLT that began in 1936 flared up in 1937, Darwaza coordinated guerilla activities from Damascus for the Arab Higher Committee.

He was a member of the reconstituted Arab Higher Committee for one year in 1947, then retired from active politics to write on Arab, Islamic, and Palestinian history.

Michael R. Fischbach

Darwish, Ishaq   [1896–1974]

Palestinian politician.

The nephew of Jerusalem mufti Amin al-Husayni, Muhammad Ishaq Darwish was born in Jerusalem. He went to Beirut for his higher education, and was a soldier in the Ottoman army during World War I. Darwish's long career in politics began after the war, when he joined the Arab Club and supported PAN-ARABISM and the regime of King Faisal I in Damascus, Syria. With Faisal's fall, however, Darwish turned toward Palestine-centered nationalism and in the early 1920s became the first secretary of the Palestine-wide Muslim–Christian Association, headquartered in Jerusalem. He joined the Palestine Arab party after it was founded in 1923, and was one of the founders of the ISTIQLAL PARTY in 1932. Through most of these years, Darwish was an aide to his uncle, the mufti. In 1947, he was elected to the Fourth Arab Higher Committee, which that year staged a protest strike and boycotted UNSCOP, the UN committee researching plans for the partition for Palestine. Darwish lived with his uncle in Lebanon and London, England, briefly in the 1960s and returned to Jerusalem before his death.

BIBLIOGRAPHY

AL-HASHIM, ABD AL-HADI, ed. *Al-Mawsu'a al-filastiniyya* (The Palestinian Encyclopaedia). Damascus, 1984.
MUSLIH, MUHAMMAD. *The Origins of Palestinian Nationalism.* New York, 1988.
PORATH, Y. *The Emergence of the Palestinian-Arab National Movement 1918–1929.* London, 1974.

Elizabeth Thompson

Darwish, Mahmud   [1942–   ]

Palestinian poet.

Mahmud Darwish, recognized since the mid-1960s as the leading national poet of the Palestinian people, was born to a peasant family in al-Birwa, east of Acre, PALESTINE. In 1948, when several Arab states attacked the new State of Israel, Israeli troops took and destroyed the village. With other villagers, Darwish fled to Lebanon. After two years of hardship, Darwish and an uncle returned, but the Israelis had demolished al-Birwa, replacing it with a kibbutz and moshav. The family therefore resettled in Dayr al-Asad, where the breadwinner found work as a stonecutter.

As a refugee without legal status in his own country, Darwish began a life in hiding. While Hebrew had become Israel's official language, the boy was writing Arabic poems that amplified the collective voice of his compatriots. Darwish recited his poetry at festivals and rallies. Soon, he became the subject of ceaseless harassment by the Israeli military. Darwish continued to write, publishing his first collection of poems in 1960. The following year, he moved to Haifa, where for a decade he wrote for *al-Ittihad* and *al-Jadid,* periodicals of the Arab faction of the Israeli Communist party. He also published four more collections of poetry, two of them written in jail. He had been jailed because of his connection with the Palestine Liberation Organization (PLO). Translations of his poetry began reaching international audiences. In 1969, the Afro-Asian Writers Union awarded him its Lotus Prize.

After a year in Moscow, in 1971 Darwish settled in Cairo, Egypt, where he wrote for *al-Ahram.* He later went to Beirut, Lebanon, as editor of *Shu'un Filastiniyya.* Arab audiences in the thousands attended his recitals. By decade's end, Darwish had published four new collections of poetry and three volumes of prose. In 1980, he received the Mediterranean Award and in 1983 the Lenin Prize. After Israel's seige of Beirut in 1982, Darwish was evacuated with the Palestinian forces. From a new exile, in Paris, he wrote weekly columns for *al-Yawm al-Sabi* and started editing *al-Karmel.* During the 1980s, Darwish published five more collections of poetry and a book of prose. The unrivaled esteem with which his poetry has been received in and outside the Arab world has given Darwish legendary stature among his people, and his poetry wields powerful influence in modern Arabic letters.

Following the 1967 ARAB–ISRAEL WAR, Palestinian poetry written within Israel reached the Arab world as a revelation. It presented not only an unbroken continuity with poetry written in Palestine before 1948 but had an organic connection with issues central to the evolution of modern Arabic verse. Darwish's work was considered the vanguard of the "poetry of resistance." Over three decades, Darwish's work developed extensively. Moving from the instigational statement to the connotational image, his lines remain as refreshing to the connoisseur as they are appealing to the people in the street. Consistently lyrical, his is love poetry in the best SEMITIC tradition, borrowing erotic metaphors to express closeness to the homeland.

BIBLIOGRAPHY

BENNANI, BEN, tr. *Bread, Hashish and Moon: Four Modern Arab Poets.* Greensboro, N.C., 1982.
BOULLATA, ISSA J., tr. *Modern Arab Poets.* London and Washington, D.C., 1976.
JAYYUSI, SALMA K., tr. *Modern Arabic Poetry, an Anthology.* New York, 1987.
AL-NAQQASH, RAJA. *Mahmud Darwish: Sha'ir al-ard al-muhtalla* (Mahmud Darwish: Poet of the Occupied Land). Cairo, 1969.
AL-UDHARI, ABDULLA, tr. *Victims of a Map: Mahmoud Darwish, Samih al-Qasim.* London, 1984.

Kamal Boullata

Darwish, Sayyid   [1892–1923]

Egyptian composer and singer.

During his short life, Sayyid Darwish composed thirty musical plays and dozens of other songs, including light strophic tunes, virtuosic love songs, and religious songs. His work drew upon the language, songs, and images of working-class Egypt. He took Arabic song in a new direction by laying the foundation for Egyptian populist musical expression that has endured throughout the twentieth century and has been heard echoing in the compositions of Zakariyya Ahmad and Sayyid Makkawi. As a consequence, he remains a dominating figure in Egyptian cultural life.

He was born in Alexandria and around 1917 moved to Cairo, where he composed for the theatrical troupes of George Abyad, Ali al-Kassar, Munira al-Mahdiyya, the Ukkasha Brothers, and Najib al-Rihani, often in collaboration with his friend the poet Badi Khayri. Together they helped develop a colloquial comic theater based on indigenous language, music, and characters. Sayyid Darwish infused his compositions with the anti-imperialist political sentiments of his day and with pride in an Egyptian heritage. He and his music expressed sentiments widely shared by the Egyptian people at the time of the Revolution of 1919, and they remain identified with attitudes of popular resistance to the present day.

Among Sayyid Darwish's best-known works are "al-Ashara al-Tayyiba," a play mocking Turkish governance written by Muhammad Taymur, and songs such as "Zuruni Kull Sana Marra" (Visit Me Once Every Year). His "Biladi, Biladi" (My Country), with a text derived from a speech by nationalist leader Mustafa KAMIL and an arrangement by lyricist Yunis al-Qadi, was adopted as the Egyptian national anthem in 1977.

BIBLIOGRAPHY

AL-HIFNI, MAHMUD AHMAD. *Sayyid Darwish: His Life and the Signs of his Genius.* Cairo, 1974. In Arabic.
SAHHAB, VICTOR. *The Great Seven in Contemporary Arabic Music.* Beirut, 1987. In Arabic.

Virginia Danielson

Dashnak Party

Translated as the Armenian Revolutionary Federation, the Dashnak Party sought to improve the lives of Armenians in the Ottoman Empire, eventually embracing Armenian nationalism.

The Dashnak party was founded in 1890 by Armenians in Tbilisi, Georgia, then part of the Russian empire. The initial focus of its operations was western Armenia or so-called Turkish Armenia, the sector of historic Armenia in the OTTOMAN EMPIRE. In the early twentieth century, it also began to organize seriously in eastern Armenia in the Russian empire, as well as in Armenian communities across Russia, Turkey, and Iran. Between 1918 and 1920, during the period of the independent Republic of Armenia, its activities were centered in the new country. After Sovietization, the ARF moved abroad, first fleeing to Iran and eventually settling in Beirut, Lebanon, from where it guided Armenian political life in the Middle East until the Lebanese civil war.

The ARF was organized to gather and coordinate the efforts of numerous small groups of Armenians in the CAUCASUS region involved in revolutionary activity. Bringing together a literate elite, local activists, and peasant *fida'iyyuns* into a single party was probably its principal contribution. With its leadership schooled in the Russian educational system as well as current revolutionary doctrine, nationalist, populist, and socialist, the ARF articulated the goals of these numerous strands of Armenian society into coherent collective national objectives.

Relieving the plight of the Armenians in the Ottoman provinces as its primary objective, the ARF concentrated on arming the population in the countryside to resist the arbitrary rule of Ottoman administrators. Eventually it resolved to oppose despotism at its source by planning to assassinate Abdülhamit II. The overthrow of the sultan by the Young Turks and the restoration of the Ottoman constitution in 1908 seemed to affirm that the struggle against the sultan's regime, despite the increased brutalization of the Armenian population by the army, police, and the Hamidiye corps, had been worth the price.

Reluctant to divide its energy and its attention, the ARF had chosen to sidestep the problem of autocracy in the Russian empire. The events leading up to the 1905 revolution, however, precipitated the decision to oppose the czar also as a despotic ruler devising and implementing policies oppressive to the Armenians. Crossing that threshold proved decisive because the consequences of World War I compelled the ARF to reconsider its objectives. With the decimation of the Armenian population in the Ottoman Empire, the ARF goal of seeing a national home built out of the eastern provinces of Turkey was voided. The breakup of the czarist empire instead provided an opportunity to develop the former Russian province, which was declared an independent republic, into the nucleus of an Armenian state. ARF members virtually ran the entire government of the Armenian republic. This close association had its drawbacks for the Armenian state in that Western powers were unsympathetic

with a government run by a party whose platform advocated socialism. Conversely, its nationalist program made it a foe of Bolshevism and hence subjected it to the enmity of the Soviet regime. Banished from Soviet Armenia, the ARF assumed the mantle of a nationalist government-in-exile. When it reorganized in Diaspora, the ARF completely lost its Russian-Armenian character as it found a new basis for its existence among the exile communities in the Middle East, mostly composed of the survivors of the former Armenian population of the Ottoman state.

Part of the success of the ARF is explained by the fact that from 1890 to 1920 it attracted a sizable contingent of the Armenian intellectual elite. Whether as party members, advocates, or supporters, they created a huge body of literature. The practice was set by its founders, Kristopor Mikayelian (1859–1905), Stepan Zorian (1867–1919), known as Rostom, and Simon Zavarian (1866–1913). The party organ, *Droshak* (Banner), was the leading journal of Armenian political thought. During the independent republic, many distinguished figures from Russian-Armenian society became associated with it. Avetis AHARONIAN, famed as a writer, became president and traveled to Paris to negotiate with the Allies. Alexander KHATISIAN, one-time mayor of Tbilisi, also became president. Others who rose to prominence during this period, such as Simon VRATSIAN, Nigol Aghbalian, and Levon Shant, remained central figures in the Armenian diaspora and its endeavors to educate a new generation of Armenians in exile. The ARF also attracted numerous guerilla leaders and frontline revolutionaries into its ranks. Papken Suni led the capture of the Ottoman Bank in 1896 in Constantinople. Men like OZANIAN ANDRANIK, Aram Manoogian, and Drastamard Kanayan, called Dro, led organized armed defense of Armenian communities and of the Armenian republic. In diaspora, the ARF has been less successful in finding the kind of charismatic leadership that once distinguished it as the leading Armenian political organization. From this standpoint, the evocation of past leadership has become an important element sustaining the organization in the diaspora communities.

From an organizational standpoint, the ARF bridged two major gaps in late nineteenth- and early twentieth-century Armenian society: it created an alliance between Turkish Armenians and Russian Armenians, who had become divided by a boundary, and between the rural population and the urban population, who inhabited completely separate spaces as the Armenian bourgeoisie lived outside the Armenian heartland. To maintain a network that spanned so widely both socially and geographically, the ARF developed a highly decentralized organization, which empowered regional bureaus with the privilege of devising policy.

Throughout its existence, the ARF has relied on direct financial support from Armenian society. With a large following and popular base, the organization has maintained a substantial infrastructure. Despite the destruction of innumerable Armenian communities, the ARF continuously maintained its operations and reorganized its network as the Armenians migrated across the Middle East.

Though based in the urban Armenian communities and deriving support from the lower and middle classes, the ARF program addressed principally the condition of the Armenians in the Turkish provinces and of the agrarian population in general. Beyond equal treatment before the law and structural reform in the Ottoman government, the ARF placed great emphasis on improving the lot of Armenian farmers. An economic program therefore always formed a vital part of its doctrine. With many socialists among its ranks, the party as a whole was still slow to adopt socialism as party platform despite its ideological currency in Russia. Ideas of the kind seemed remote from Armenian reality in the distant provinces of the Ottoman and Russian empires. Consequently, despite its urban base, the ARF did not agitate as strongly among industrial workers, who tended to be drawn to social democratic groups, but rather concentrated on the program of national liberation.

As a subject minority unequipped to resolve its own problems in the judgment of the ARF, the Armenians depended on the attention of the European powers. Their sympathetic influence was required to compel the Ottomans to introduce reforms. This policy remained controversial throughout the period as outside powers involved themselves with the Armenian question on their own timetable of interests and as the Ottoman government in its state of weakness looked upon the strategy with enormous suspicion. The wholesale persecution of Armenians in the Ottoman Empire during World War I finally aligned the Western powers on the side of the Armenian republic. The Western failure to extend enough assistance to make a difference in preserving Armenian statehood, however, raised the question whether the ARF had not misplaced its trust.

The ARF regards itself a vanguard organization. In its early decades, its membership consisted of professional revolutionaries who published its papers, organized its cells, manufactured weapons, led guerilla operations, and briefly ran a government. Its constituency has not been restricted to any class because it derived its strength from its popular nationalist program. The ARF constituency remains the larger segment of the Armenian diaspora though it no longer draws the same level of critical support from the professional class as it once did.

With its political mission defused by 1920, the ARF began to devote considerable attention to resurrecting Armenian communal life among the exile settlements. In this regard, the ARF became the support system for a range of institutions that were formed in the diaspora to tend to the needs of the newly formed communities. Schools, youth groups, athletic and social service organizations, and even cultural societies emerged from this effort. To name a few, the Armenian Youth Federation, the Armenian Relief Society, the Hamazkayin Cultural Association, the Hairenik publishing house founded back in 1899 in Boston, Massachusetts, to circumvent censorship in the home countries, and the once most important educational institution in the diaspora, the Nishan Palanjian Academy in Beirut, Lebanon, are all the products of this undertaking.

The ARF has deep roots in the global Armenian community. Traditions built up over one hundred years of existence give it special strength as a binding force among a dispersed people. Its national program has been overtaken, superseded, and even defeated by the course of events. However, its organizational function in educating and socializing a politically conscious diaspora has remained continuous. The emergence of a new independent Republic of Armenia has posed special challenges to the organization, which for long sustained itself with the myth of national leadership. The rise of a major movement in Armenia independent of the ARF has left it somewhat stranded. These problems have combined with earlier difficulties when its principal base was destroyed by the civil war in Lebanon, where the largest and most dynamic diaspora community had provided the ARF a secure home in the post–World War II decades.

BIBLIOGRAPHY

ATAMIAN, SARKIS. *The Armenian Community: The Historical Development of a Social and Ideological Conflict.* New York, 1955.

Rouben P. Adalian

Dashti, Ali   [1886–1981?]

Iranian writer, member of parliament, and ambassador.

Born near Bushehr and trained in Muslim religious studies at Karbala, Iraq, Ali Dashti became a journalist upon his return to Persia (now Iran) in 1918. He established the paper *Shafaq-e Sorkh* in 1922, and his first book, a collection of articles called *Prison Days,* described several short stays in prison at this time. From 1928 to the end of his life, he spent many terms in the parliament, first as an elected deputy and from the mid-1950s as a senator appointed by the shah, Mohammad Reza PAHLAVI. In 1948 he was named Iranian ambassador to Egypt and Lebanon. In the 1950s, Dashti published several novels treating the plight of upper-class Iranian women. His book on Hafez's poetry, the first of a series of important impressionistic critiques of major classical poets of Persian LITERATURE, appeared in 1957.

Dashti's Pahlavi-era political career led to his harassment and incarceration (after the Iran Revolution) at the hands of the Islamic Republic.

BIBLIOGRAPHY

In Search of Omar Khayyam (1971) typifies ALI DASHTI's literary, critical, and scholarly work, while *Twenty-Three Years: A Study of the Prophetic Career of Mohammad* (1985) illustrates his secular concerns about Islam in the modern world.

Michael C. Hillmann

Dates

Throughout history, the date palm has satisfied the needs—from food to fuel to construction materials—of those who live in desert and tropical regions. Now, the importance of its cultivation is waning.

Since the dawn of recorded history, the date palm has been associated with the Middle East. It has featured prominently in the rituals of the religions of antiquity, Judaism, Christianity, and Islam. Perfectly

Harvesting dates from date palms in Gabès, Tunisia. (D.W. Lockhard)

suited to the climate of the region, the date palm can endure desert heat, withstand long periods of flooding, and tolerate high levels of salinity. In general, a plentiful supply of water together with prolonged periods of high temperatures are ideal for the growth of the tree and for the ripening of its fruit. An average tree will produce approximately fifty pounds of fruit each year. The date palm has been for the settled Arabs what the camel has been for the nomads, providing a commercial crop to exchange for imported necessities, material for construction, bedding, and an important source of fuel. Beneath its shade they can grow other fruit trees, vines, and aromatic plants, and beneath these cultivate vegetables, melons, and fodder crops. For many it provides a staple food, rich in calories and with appreciable amounts of vitamins. The fruit can be easily packed and transported, while the seeds are ground up and used as camel food.

Date-palm cultivation is labor intensive. Trees may be grown from seed but are usually grown from shoots, suckers, or buds. Soil preparation for date-palm cultivation involves a multistage process, and an elaborate system of irrigation requiring regular maintenance is essential. Because half of all trees grown from seeds are male and unproductive, sophisticated means of growing plants, relying most especially on artificial pollination, have been practiced from ancient times. Each tree requires special care and pruning for optimum yields. Harvesting of dates usually occurs in September and October but may begin as early as mid-August and continue until December, depending on the variety. In Iraq, the unique art of date cultivation has, since antiquity, been acknowledged legally by awarding to tenant cultivators hereditary property rights to the tree independent of the rights attached to the land on which it is grown. Contractual arrangements between cultivators and landowners vary according to differences in the inputs of skill and capital. Tenure practices and juristic ramifications associated with date cultivation are therefore complex.

Dates are most prolific in Iraq where there are 627 varieties. The groves along the SHATT AL-ARAB make up the largest single area of date cultivation, at one time covering over 100 square miles (260 sq km). Their harvest season long determined trade patterns in the Persian Gulf and much of the Indian Ocean. Until World War II, Iraq provided some 80 percent of the world's date crop, and dates constituted its largest export earnings. With the growth of the oil industry, the importance of dates in Iraq and elsewhere in the Middle East has declined. Greater oil earnings have reduced dependence on date palms for necessities, the attraction of other more remunerative and less arduous employments has depleted the pool of skilled cultivators, while the pollution associated with oil and modernization generally has had a detrimental effect on date palms.

BIBLIOGRAPHY

Dowson, V. H. W. "The Date and the Arab." *Journal of the Royal Central Asian Society* 36 (1949): 34–41.
Lennie, A. B. "Agriculture in Mesopotamia in Ancient and Modern Times." *The Scottish Geographical Magazine* 52 (1936): 33–46.

Albertine Jwaideh

Daud, Muhammad   [1909–1978]

President of Afghanistan, 1973–1978.

Daud, who earned the nickname of Sardar-i Diwana (the crazy Prince) because of his hot temper and ruthlessness, was born in Kabul. His father, Sardar (Prince) Muhammad Aziz Khan, was a half brother of King Mohammad NADIR BARAKZAI (1929–1933), the founder of the Musahiban ruling dynasty of the Muhammadzai clan, of the BARAKZAI FAMILY of the Pashtuns (or Pakhtun) who dominated national politics in Afghanistan since the early 1800s. Daud attended Habibia and Amania schools in Kabul before continuing his education in France from 1921 to 1930. He returned to Kabul and after a one-year course at the Infantry Officers School, was appointed a major general and commanding officer of the armed forces in Mashriqi province, eastern Afghanistan (1932–1935). In 1933, Daud's uncle, King Nadir Shah, and his father, the Afghan envoy in Berlin, were assassinated separately as a result of political and family feuds. Nadir Shah's son, Mohammad ZAHIR, assumed the Afghan throne, and in 1934 Daud married the sister of Zahir Shah. Between 1935 and 1953, Daud rose from governor and general commanding officer in the western provinces to minister of defense and interior.

Daud was prime minister from 1953 to 1963. An ardent secular nationalist, Daud made strong military and economic progress his top priority. Initially denied assistance by the United States and the West, he turned to the Soviets. With their help he created a mechanized military force and adopted an etatist (state socialist) economic policy that concentrated on transportation and communication infrastructures and the expansion of education. Exploiting Pakhtun Nationalism, Daud pursued an aggressive territorial claim (for Pakhtunistan) against Pakistan, which resulted in greater trade and with economic and military dependence on the Soviet Union. An alleged

rift within the royal household over this issue culminated in Daud's resignation as prime minister in March 1963. He spent the next decade in retirement, unhappy with the constitutional developments in 1964 that curtailed participation of royal family members in government and political processes. Assisted by a group of junior military officers active in the pro-Soviet PARCHAM (Banner) Communist party, Daud returned to power on July 17, 1973, and proclaimed himself president of the Republic of Afghanistan, thus ending the monarchy.

Shortly thereafter, Daud consolidated power by relying on his old networks and persecuting his perceived enemies, among whom were members of the Islamist political movements. Toward the end of his rule, he appeared to distance himself from his old ally, the Soviet Union, in favor of closer ties with Iran and the Gulf States, while striving to improve relations with Pakistan. In spite of these attempts, his presidency proved to be a period of confusion, contradictions, and indecision. In the end, Daud met his death at the hands of pro-Soviet Afghan communists, whom he had protected and nurtured during the previous decades.

In retrospect, some remember him as a patriot who singlehandedly sought, but failed, to bring about progress and economic development in Afghanistan. Although intelligent, he was also a stubborn dictator and was ill informed about Soviet thinking and long-term goals in the region. Thus, he allowed himself to be used as a conduit for Communism and Soviet influence, which led to ongoing strife.

BIBLIOGRAPHY

Arnold, Anthony. *Afghanistan: The Soviet Invasion in Perspective,* rev. ed. Stamford, Conn., 1985.
Dupree, Louis. *Afghanistan.* Princeton, N.J., 1980.

M. Nazif Shahrani

Da'ud Pasha   [1812–1872]

Ottoman official in Lebanon.

Da'ud Pasha was born in Constantinople (now Istanbul) (some sources say in 1816 and others say in 1818) to an Armenian Catholic family. He received his education at a French school and then attended a French college in Vienna, where he earned a law degree. He then entered the foreign service, and his first post was in Berlin. He wrote a book on Western jurisprudence and was known as a doctor of law. Da'ud Pasha also served as consul general in Vienna and later was director of publications and then director of post and telegraphic services in Constantinople. His French education brought him close to French circles in Constantinople. He was the first MUTASARRIF in Lebanon after the 1861 *mutasarrifiyya* order was designed for Lebanon by the Great Powers and the Ottoman Empire.

Before he began his mission in Lebanon, Da'ud Pasha was promoted to the rank of minister, thus becoming the highest-ranking Christian working for the Ottoman government. He improved tax collection in Lebanon and established public schools. He also founded a school for the Druze, in an attempt to appease that community after the end of the Druze–Maronite armed conflict. His mission was abruptly ended in 1868 after he became embroiled in the politics of Lebanon and tried to expand the area of "Lebanon." He then held various administrative positions in Constantinople. He died in Switzerland.

As'ad AbuKhalil

Davar

Hebrew newspaper founded in Tel Aviv in 1925 as the official journal of the Histadrut (workers' federation).

A daily paper, *Davar* always took the stand of the HISTADRUT majority, and by the 1960s, it had become an organ for the labor "establishment" in Israel. After the 1967 Arab–Israel War, *Davar* was one of the first Israeli papers to give frequent and critical attention to the issue of the territories occupied by Israel. Its current daily circulation is about forty thousand.

BIBLIOGRAPHY

ELON, AMOS. *The Israelis*. New York, 1981.
Encyclopedia Judaica. New York, 1971.
New Standard Jewish Encyclopedia. New York, 1977.

Zachary Karabell

Da'wa, al-

Egyptian magazine.

Al-Da'wa (The Call) was published in Cairo by the MUSLIM BROTHERHOOD in the years 1951 to 1954 and 1976 to 1981. Gamal Abdel Nasser's repression of the Muslim Brotherhood in 1954 ended the magazine's first phase. Anwar al-Sadat allowed it to reappear in 1976, with Umar al-Tilmisani as editor. *Al-Da'wa* criticized Sadat's domestic policies and his overtures toward Israel and the United States. Sadat

banned the magazine in the September 1981 crackdown just before his assassination. It has not been allowed to reappear.

BIBLIOGRAPHY

BAKER, RAYMOND WILLIAM. "Return to the Future: The Muslim Brothers." In *Sadat and After: Struggles for Egypt's Political Soul*. Cambridge, Mass., 1990, pp. 118–162.

Donald Malcolm Reid

Da'wa al-Islamiyya, al-

An underground Islamic group in Iraq.

Al-Da'wa, as al-Da'wa al-Islamiyya (Islamic Call Party) is commonly called, advocates a return to Islamic principles in government and social justice against government exploitation. It was organized mainly by Shi'ite clergy concerned about the decline of religious consciousness among the educated and urban Shi'ite masses in the 1950s. The party arose possibly in 1957 or in the early 1960s. There is a dispute concerning the role of Ayatollah Muhammad Baqir al-SADR. Some say he was the founding member; others say he was too young to be the founder. Regardless, Sadr was the driving force behind Da'wa.

In the late 1960s, Da'wa, along with other underground Islamic groups, gained some support among the Shi'tes in southern Iraq and in Madinat al-Thawra, a Baghdad suburb. Some reasons for its popularity were the Communist-Atheist ascendancy under Abd al-Karim KASSEM, the pronounced Sunnism of the Abd al-Salam ARIF regime of 1963–1966, and the secularly oriented policies of the BA'TH regime that came to power in 1968. Other reasons for the increased support were the arrival of Ayatollah Ruhollah KHOMEINI at al-Najaf and the low standard of living among the Shi'ite community.

The IRANIAN REVOLUTION of 1979 radicalized all Da'wa members toward militant tactics, including guerilla attacks on Ba'ath Party offices, the police, the People's Army, and communication networks. In 1979 the government prevented Sadr from leading a delegation to congratulate Khomeini on his return to Iran. This sparked riots in the Shi'ite community that led to Sadr's house arrest in June 1979. With the start of the Iran–Iraq war, several attempts were made by Da'wa members to assassinate officials including Foreign Minister Tariq Aziz. In response, the government rounded up hundreds of Da'wa members and supporters and executed several members, including Sadr. Iraq's government had feared Sadr's leadership, his close association with

Khomeini, and his influence among the common people.

In the 1980s, the Da'wa Islamiyya lost much of its Iraqi support because of the government's two-pronged policy of intimidation and enticement. The government banned the party and made membership in it a capital crime. Several members of Da'wa were executed, thousands of its members and supporters were imprisoned, and thousands of Iraqis of Persian origin were expelled to Iran. At the same time, Iraq's government went out of its way to lure the Shi'ite community to side with it. Millions of dollars were spent on improving Shi'ite shrines, mosques, and *husainiyah*. The birthday of Imam Ali was declared a national holiday. The government also spent tremendous amounts to improve the standard of living in the Shi'ite community by providing clean drinking water, sewer systems, and paved roads.

Another factor that contributed to the decline of Da'wa's support was the atrocities committed in Iran by the revolutionary government that dampened the early euphoria and sympathy among Iraq's Shi'ite community. Others include the execution of Sadr, which deprived the party of powerful guidance and a unifying symbol. In the 1980s, the Da'wa was forced to reorganize in Europe and Iran. In 1982, with the encouragement of Iran, the Da'wa, along with other Iraqi Shi'ite groups active in Iran, formed an umbrella organization known as the Supreme Assembly for the Islamic Revolution in Iraq (SAIRI), with headquarters in Tehran. The Da'wa and other Islamic Shi'ite groups took an active part in failed uprisings in the southern part of Iraq after the Gulf War. Neither Da'wa nor other Islamic groups were strong enough to topple Saddam's government.

Today, the Da'wa Islamiyya is headed by a council; among its prominent members are Muhammad al-Asafi (spokesman) and Muwaffaq al-Rubayi.

BIBLIOGRAPHY

BATATU, HANA. *Shiism Organization in Iraq: Al-Dawah, al-Islamia and al-Mujahidin in Shiism and Social Protest.* Ed. by Juan Cole and Nikki Keddie. New Haven, Conn., 1986.
WILEY, JOYCE N. *The Islamic Movement of Iraqi Shias.* Boulder, Colo., 1992.

Ayad al-Qazzaz

Dawalibi, Ma'ruf al-   [1908–   ]

Sunni Muslim Arab politician from Aleppo, Syria.

Born of a middle-class mercantile family, al-Dawalibi studied Islamic law in Paris. He was ac-tive in Syrian politics during the French mandate. In the mid-1930's he assisted Jamil Ibrahim Pasha in leading the Aleppo branch of the National Guard, an outfit of uniformed youth with sections in most of Syria. It was a nonsectarian organization with a militaristic orientation whose aim was to secure Syria's independence from the French. In addition to his political activities, al-Dawalibi practiced law in Aleppo. During World War II, he resided in Paris, where he joined a pro-Axis (anti-British government) association of Syrian students. After the war, he returned to Aleppo and reopened his law office. He was a member of the People's party, an organization that emerged in August 1948, representing business interests in Aleppo and the north. After the first coup of Colonel Adib al-SHISHAKLI (December 1949), al-Dawalibi served as minister of national economy. In 1951 he became president of the Syrian parliament. On November 28, 1951, he formed the Syrian cabinet, managing in the process to take over the defense ministry, and to give the People's party the greatest share of the other appointments.

Al-Dawalibi served as prime minister for a single day: on the night of November 28/29, 1951, barely ten days after his second coup, Shishakli ordered the arrest of al-Dawalibi and his government. Al-Dawalibi was among the progressive avant-garde in that he was an anti-Hashimite shaykh who at the time, called on the Arabs to forge a nonaggression pact with the Soviet Union to break the Western arms monopoly. However, al-Dawalibi opposed the growing influence of the al-Ba'th party and did not favor the Syrian–Egyptian union (1958–1961). During these years, he lived in Lebanon but returned after the breakup of the union to form a cabinet that reversed many of the socialist measures introduced by the United Arab Republic regime.

Since the pro-union coup that was staged by Colonel Abd al-Karim NAHLAWI on March 28, 1962, al-Dawalibi has lived in exile—first in Saudi Arabia as a legal adviser to the king and, after 1974, as president of the World Muslim Congress, head-quartered in Karachi, Pakistan. In general, al-Dawalibi opposed the army's dictation of policy in Syria, favored political and economic reform, and belonged to the mainstream current in the Arab world.

BIBLIOGRAPHY

KHOURY, PHILIP. *Syria and the French Mandate.* Princeton, N.J., 1990.
SEALE, PATRICK. *The Struggle for Syria.* London, 1965.

Muhammad Muslih

Dawasir Tribe

A sharif tribe of central Saudi Arabia, centered in the Wadi al-Dawasir south of Riyadh.

The Dawasir are notable for their great success as landowners and oil contractors and for their maintenance of tribal solidarity. The AL SUDAYRI FAMILY is the most famous to have come from the tribe; through it the tribe's influence has been felt throughout Saudi Arabia.

Eleanor Abdella Doumato

Dayan, Moshe   [1915–1981]

Israeli military leader and statesman.

Born at Kibbutz Degania, in the Jordan valley, his family left in 1920 to join the founders of Nahalal, the first *moshav* (cooperative settlement) in the Jezreel valley, where Dayan was educated at an agricultural school. During the Arab revolt, Dayan served in a Jewish patrol unit (*notrim*) of Britain's mandatory police in Palestine under the command of Capt. Charles Wingate. As a member of Haganah—the defense force of the Jewish National Institutions in Palestine—and a student of its officers' school, he was arrested in 1940 by the British. Released after fifteen months in jail, Dayan commanded an advance unit of the Haganah that was sent by the Allies into Syria, then controlled by Vichy France. It was here that he lost an eye in battle, and the black patch that he subsequently wore became his trademark. The injury put a temporary halt to Dayan's military career. In 1946, he received his first political assignment, representing the MAPAI (Labor) at the World Zionist Congress in Basel.

At the beginning of the ARAB–ISRAEL WAR of 1948, Dayan served as an officer for Arab affairs at Haganah headquarters. In May he was given his first combat position—organizing the defense of the kibbutzim on the Kinneret front. He next led a mobile commando regiment that captured the city of Lydda. In July 1948, Dayan was named commander of Jerusalem. In this position, he negotiated a cease-fire in the Jerusalem area and an armistice with Jordan. He and Reuven Shiloah drew up a draft of principles for a territorial agreement with King Abdullah of Jordan; it was not negotiated, however, because the king refused to be the only Arab ruler to sign a peace treaty with Israel.

Between 1949 and 1953, Dayan held several senior positions in Israel's army. Appointed chief of staff in December of 1953, he reshaped Israel's army as a fighting force. The greatest achievement of the army under Dayan's direct command was the Sinai campaign of 1956, in which it took over the entire Sinai peninsula in a week. Dayan objected to Prime Minister David BEN-GURION's decision to withdraw Israel's forces from all positions in Sinai in response to U.S. pressure and Soviet threats, and in return for Western guarantees of free passage in the Strait of Tiran and the placement of UN observers in Sharm al-Shaykh and Gaza. Dayan resigned from the army in January 1958. Following two years of study at the Hebrew University of Jerusalem, he was elected a MAPAI member of the Knesset and named minister of agriculture in Ben-Gurion's government (1959). With Shimon PERES, Dayan became prominent in MAPAI's young leadership club, which aspired to democratize the party and take over its leadership. Although Ben-Gurion had encouraged their entry into politics and the government, his veteran associates, including Levi Eshkol and Golda Meir, felt threatened by the younger group and were alienated by its criticism of the party. Eshkol succeeded Ben-Gurion as prime minister in June 1963. In November 1964, Dayan resigned from the Eshkol government to protest what he described as the prime minister's lack of confidence in him.

Prior to the 1965 elections, Dayan joined Ben-Gurion's RAFI PARTY. His greatest political hour came in the ARAB–ISRAEL WAR of 1967. Criticism of Eshkol's hesitancy to react forcefully to Egypt's blocking the Strait of Tiran to Israel's shipping and its rapid military buildup in Sinai created pressure for Dayan's appointment as defense minister and the formation of a national unity government. Dayan led the army as a civilian. He was reluctant to occupy the Golan Heights but succumbed to pressure from the government. He also did not want Israel's forces to reach the Suez Canal but did not prevent it. After the war, Dayan was put in charge of the territories occupied by Israel—the Golan Heights, the West Bank, and the Gaza Strip. He promulgated the economic integration of the territories, Israeli settlement there, and the maintenance of open bridges over the Jordan river.

The 1967 war and its aftermath made Dayan a leading, though controversial, national political contender. In 1968, Rafi joined MAPAI to form the LABOR PARTY. Dayan supported the merger but kept alive his option to run as an independent until the ARAB–ISRAEL WAR of 1973, which severely undermined his public support. The coordinated attack by Egypt and Syria, which caught Israel unprepared, shattered Dayan's leadership credibility and produced demands for his and Prime Minister Meir's resignations. The Labor party managed to win the next election (December 31, 1973), though with decreased representation. Although a state commission of inquiry (the Agranat commission) found no personal negligence in the conduct of the war, criticism did not wane. A large segment of the public was not prepared to put all the blame for the army's lack of preparedness on military officers. Israel's advantageous military position at the end of the war, and the beginning of diplomatic negotiations, did not put an end to criticism.

Prime Minister Meir resigned on January 18, 1974, and Dayan refused to serve in the Labor government headed by Yitzhak Rabin. In the 1977 elections, Dayan ran on the Labor party's Knesset list; he had first negotiated with the Likud and had contemplated an independent run. Following Likud's electoral victory, its leader, Menachem Begin, invited Dayan to serve as foreign minister in his government. In this position, Dayan launched the secret talks with Egypt that eventually led to President Anwar al-Sadat's visit to Jerusalem, and he is largely credited with playing a major role in the CAMP DAVID ACCORDS between Israel and Egypt (1978), and the subsequent peace treaty with Egypt (1979). Nevertheless, he resigned from the Begin government on October 23, 1979, criticizing its handling of the talks with Egypt on the implementation of the Camp David autonomy plan for the Palestinians in the occupied territories. He believed that Israel should have negotiated more vigorously, unencumbered by internal political restraints. Subsequently, Dayan advocated unilateral implementation of the autonomy plan. Under this banner he ran as an independent in the 1981 elections, but his list (Telem) received meager support. He died soon afterward. An accomplished amateur archaeologist, Dayan also was a prolific writer whose books include *Diary of the Sinai Campaign* (1967), *Story of My Life* (1976), *Vietnam Diary* (1977, in Hebrew), *Living with the Bible* (1976), and *Breakthrough* (1981).

BIBLIOGRAPHY

SLATER, ROBERT. *Warrior Statesman: The Life of Moshe Dayan.* New York, 1991.

Nathan Yanai

Dayr al-Zawr Province

Province in eastern Syria on the Euphrates river named after its major town, Dayr al-Zawr.

The name Dayr al-Zawr means literally the convent of the grove where clusters of tamarisks grow along-side the river. Apparently, a convent was originally established there. The town of Dayr al-Zawr is located on the right bank of the Euphrates river 640 feet (195 m) above sea level. The river is crossed by a suspension bridge 1,476 feet (450 m) long, completed in 1931.

The province of Dayr al-Zawr (or al-Furat), according to official data, in 1982 included 29 villages and 261 farms spreading over 3 *qadas* (subprovinces) currently referred to as *mintaqas*: Dayr al-Zawr, Abu Kamal, and al-Mayadin. They are divided into 14 *nahiyas* (smaller administrative units).

The total population of the province, according to the 1980 census, was 423,874, and of the town of Dayr al-Zawr, 92,091.

BIBLIOGRAPHY

Encyclopaedia of Islam, new ed.
al-Mu'jam al-Jughrafi li al-Qutr al-Arabi al-Suri (The Geographical Dictionary of Syria), vol. 1. Damascus, 1990.

Abdul-Karim Rafeq

Dayri, Akram al-

Syrian military officer.

Akram al-Dayri began his career as a captain in Syria's military police and rose to command the Homs military college as a lieutenant colonel. He headed a pro–Abd al-Hammid SARRAJ organization known as the Damascus group. He was one of twelve military officers sent to pledge Ba'th support to Egypt's President Gamal Abdel Nasser in January 1958, when Syria and Egypt formed the United Arab Republic (UAR). Dayri was then appointed chief of army intelligence by Sarraj and served as minister of labor and social affairs in 1960.

BIBLIOGRAPHY

SEALE, PATRICK. *The Struggle for Syria.* London, 1965.

Charles U. Zenzie

Dayr Yasin

Palestinian Arab village.

Dayr Yasin, on the outskirts of mandatory Jerusalem, was attacked by Jewish paramilitary units during the civil war between Palestinian Arabs and Jews in the period between announcement of the United Nations partition plan in November 1947 and proclamation of the state of Israel in May 1948. Although only one of several incidents in which Jewish forces attacked Arab civilians, Dayr Yasin became the most well-known and the longest remembered because of the unusually large number of deaths, Arab loss of the village, and the extent to which reports of the massive loss of lives circulated through the Arab community exacerbated fear leading to mass flight of Palestinian Arabs.

The attack on Dayr Yasin occurred on April 4, 1948, initiated by the Irgun Zva'i Le'umi, or Etzel (National Military Organization), and Lohamei Herut Yisrael, or Lehi (Fighters for the Freedom of Israel), which was also known as the Stern Gang. Etzel, headed by Menachem Begin, later to become Israel's prime minister, was a dissident faction of the Haganah, the quasi-official defense organization of the Palestinian Jewish community, or Yishuv. While the Haganah's official policy was to use military force primarily in response to Arab attacks, Etzel favored a more confrontational approach, taking the offensive against Arabs. Lehi, a faction that broke with Etzel over policy during World War II, adopted an even more aggressive policy.

Although Dayr Yasin had not been involved in any significant incident against the Yishuv, the leaders of Etzel and Lehi justified the surprise attack by charging that the village had been a base for Arab guerillas, which was not substantiated by the Haganah. During the attack, 200 to 250 men, women, and children were murdered; many bodies were mutilated and thrown into a well. There was little armed resistance to the attack.

The leaders of the Yishuv, including David Ben-Gurion, later to become Israel's first prime minister, strenuously denounced the attack and disclaimed any responsibility for it. However, the leaders of Etzel and Lehi maintained that the Haganah had been informed of the impending attack in advance and that a Haganah unit had provided covering fire for Etzel and Lehi. During the incident, residents of Dayr Yasin who were not slain were driven from the village, and most of it was destroyed. Later, the remains of the village were taken over and occupied by the Haganah.

Dayr Yasin symbolized the extent to which the struggle between Arab and Jewish communities in Palestine was becoming an all-out civil war without sparing the lives of civilians. It thus contributed to the panic that led to the collapse and mass flight of the Palestinian Arab community.

BIBLIOGRAPHY

BEGIN, MENACHEM. *The Revolt: Story of the Irgun.* New York, 1951.

KHALIDI, WALID. *From Haven to Conquest: Readings in Zionism and the Palestine Problem until 1948.* Beirut, 1971.

Don Peretz

Dead Sea

Salt lake situated between Jordan, the West Bank, and Israel.

The Dead Sea (Arabic, Bahr al-Lut; ancient Greco-Romano, Lacus Asphaltites), the lowest surface point on the planet (the actual lowest point is under the ocean), is situated in the 350-mile-long (560 km) Jordan–Dead Sea rift valley, bordered by the Hashimite Kingdom of Jordan to its east, the State of Israel to its southwest, and the West Bank to its northwest. The surface of the Dead Sea is 1,302 feet (397 m) below Mediterranean sea level, with an area of about 395 square miles (1,020 sq km). It is 51 miles (82 km) long.

This inland lake is the world's saltiest; its water contains about 25 percent solid concentrates, as compared to ocean concentrates of some 4 to 6 percent. The lake has no outlet and is fed from the north by waters of the Jordan river and *wadis* (streams that are usually dry but fill during the rainy season). In its middle, it is divided by the Lisan (tongue), which stretches across some 75 percent of the lake's width from Jordan toward Israel. Economically, the Dead Sea is important to the bordering regions, since each uses it for tourism—many visitors seek its purported medicinal properties and spas exist to allow such visits, especially in Israel. The land near its shores is also cultivated, with sweet irrigation water brought to those fields. From the Dead Sea's brine, both Jordan

View of the Dead Sea from the Judean hills. (Bryan McBurney)

and Israel extract potash, an important component of agricultural fertilizer.

BIBLIOGRAPHY

"Dead Sea." In *Encyclopaedia Britannica,* 1972.

Peter Gubser

Dead Sea Scrolls

Ancient religious documents.

The Dead Sea Scrolls are ancient manuscripts found at Khirbet Qumran, in caves in the Judean desert near the Dead Sea, 7.5 miles (12 km) from Jericho. The scrolls were uncovered in 1947. Archeologists later discovered a cemetery of over one thousand graves, a central building, and central caves containing fragments of old documents. The area was apparently destroyed by an earthquake in 31 B.C.E. and then rebuilt. The authors of the scrolls lived there until 68 C.E. The contents of the scrolls and other evidence show that the authors belonged to a Jewish sect. The scrolls or fragments include two complete copies of Isaiah and fragments of nearly every other book of the Bible. Their discovery advanced the study of the Hebrew Bible, since the earliest versions before the scrolls were discovered dated to the Middle Ages. Fragments of the Apocrypha and the Pseudepigrapha and other unknown books were also found, including the Book of Tobit, the Hebrew version of Jubilees, and the Aramaic version of the Book of Enoch. The scrolls include sectarian books as well, including a commentary on Habakkuk, parts of a commentary on Micah and Nahum, and others. These commentaries explain the prophetic writings in relation to the history of the sect. Other scrolls deal with the sect's organization and theological doc-

trines. They also contain fragments of the Zadokite documents which were found in Cairo. The Temple scroll minutely details the Temple. The sect responsible for the scrolls was assumed to have been the Essenes, but recent scholarship has placed this thesis in doubt. They beheld the power of good ruling in a world in opposition to the power of evil, and they saw themselves as the chosen "sons of light." Their apocalyptic circles, among whom Enoch was composed, probably influenced the beginnings of Christianity, especially those close to Paul and John the Evangelist.

Some of the scrolls came into the possession of Hebrew University through E. L. Sukenik, who was responsible for the first publication of selections. Others went to the United States where they were published by Burrows, Brownlee and were subsequently purchased for the government of Israel through the agency of Sukenik's son, Yigal Yadin. They are housed in the Shrine of the Book in the Israel Museum. The publication of the many fragments was entrusted to a group of scholars whose slow progress generated international controversy. In 1991, the system was overhauled to ensure speedy publication. The Huntington Library in San Marino, California, in the interim, published photographs of the collection and made them available without restrictions.

BIBLIOGRAPHY

REED, STEPHEN A. *The Dead Sea Scrolls Catalogue: Documents, Photographs and Museum Inventory Numbers.* Atlanta, 1994.

Mia Bloom

Dead Sea Works

An Israeli company that extracts minerals from the Dead Sea.

Located on the Dead Sea, the world's most saline lake, the Dead Sea Works Ltd. is responsible for the extraction of minerals of which phosphates and potash are the most important. The mainly state-owned Israel Chemical Industries Ltd. owns 88 percent of the shares in the company, and 12 percent are owned by the public.

Its origins date back to 1931, when the Potash Company Ltd. was set up by British and local Jewish investors, on the basis of plans drawn up by Moshe Novemeysky. This operated until 1948. A new, state-owned company was formed in 1952, and following the opening of the Sodom-Beersheva road in 1955, production began. In 1991, the Dead Sea

Shrine of the Book, in Jerusalem. (Mia Bloom)

Works had 1,110 employees and sales of 1.27 billion shekels ($550 million). Phosphates and potash remain the main products, and small quantities of copper and clays are also produced.

BIBLIOGRAPHY

NOVOMEYSKY, M. "The Dead Sea and the World Potash Industry." In *Palestine's Economic Future*. London, 1946.

Paul Rivlin

Debka

See Dance

De Bunsen, Maurice   [1852–1932]

British diplomat.

De Bunsen entered the diplomatic service in 1877 and helped settle the dispute between France and Spain over Morocco in 1911/12. In 1915, Prime Minister H. H. Asquith appointed him head of a committee to determine British wartime policy toward the Ottoman Empire in Asia. The resulting report of the De Bunsen committee established the foundation for British policy in the Middle East.

BIBLIOGRAPHY

Dictionary of National Biography, 1931–1940. London, 1949.
HUREWITZ, J. C., ed. *The Middle East and North Africa in World Politics*. New Haven, Conn., 1979.

Zachary Karabell

Decentralization Party

Political party of the Ottoman Empire from 1912 to 1916.

The Ottoman Administrative Decentralization party was founded in Egypt in December 1912 by Muslim and non-Muslim Syrian émigré intellectuals. Party leaders included Rafiq al-Azm (president), Iskandar Ammun (vice-president), Rashid Rida, and Muhibb al-Din al-Khatib. The party espoused a program of decentralization for the multiethnic and multireligious empire. But it formed branches only in Arab areas and lacked official status. Along with the empirewide Ottoman Liberty and Entente party, it sought wider powers for provincial councils in education, financial affairs, religious foundations, and public works. It advocated local military service and two official languages in each region, Turkish and the local language. The party maintained close links with the reform societies that emerged in Arab cities in 1912/13. Despite dissension in its ranks after the Arab Congress (June 1913), the party survived until World War I as the coordinator of Arab autonomist movements. The dominant Committee of Union and Progress implied that party members advocated separatism and pro-Western treason. CEMAL PAŞA sentenced prominent members to death in 1915/16.

BIBLIOGRAPHY

DURI, A. A. *The Historical Formation of the Arab Nation*. London, 1987.

Hasan Kayali

Declaration of La Celle St. Cloud

Agreement by France to allow Morocco independence.

In August 1953, France deposed the Moroccan sultan, Sidi Muhammad ben Yusuf. Until then, the Moroccan opposition had been divided, but the exile of the monarch united the country. A wave of strikes, violence, and disturbances swept the country, accompanied by demands for the sultan's return and the immediate independence of Morocco. The French government of Prime Minister Pierre Mendès-France finally recognized that Morocco would not be pacified, except at a cost far greater than the French were willing to pay. In October 1955, the exiled sultan went to France, and the Declaration of La Celle St. Cloud was issued by the French foreign minister, Antoine Pinay, on November 6. Under its terms, France agreed to grant Morocco independence in accord with the principle of Franco–Moroccan interdependence. This concept raised some concern in Morocco about the sincerity of the French, but in March 1956, the promise enshrined in the declaration became fact, with the former sultan becoming King MUHAMMED V, ruler of the new state.

BIBLIOGRAPHY

La grande encyclopedie du Maroc: Histoire. Rabat, 1987.
MANSFIELD, PETER. *The Arabs*. New York, 1985.

Zachary Karabell

Dede Zekai   [1825–1899]

Ottoman Turkish composer.

Dede Zekai, also known as Hoca Zekai Dede Efendi and Mehmet Zekai Dede, was born in the Eyub district of Istanbul. His father was a teacher and imam of the local mosque. As a child, he was schooled in singing, calligraphy, and memorization of the Qur'an; his music teachers included HAMMAMZADE ISMAIL DEDE and DELLALZADE İSMAIL. At the age of thirteen, he went to Egypt where he was a court musician in Cairo. He acquired the title "dede" after studying Sufism, and the title "hoca" for teaching music at the Darüşşafaka. Among his students were Subhi Ezgi, RAUF YEKTA Bey, and AHMET RASIM. Over 260 of his compositions survive today. Half of these are religious compositions; the other half were composed in the *beste, ağır semai, yürük semai,* and *şarkı* genres. Fifty-five of his pieces are melodies, and 182 of his compositions were published in a four-volume collection.

David Waldner

Deedes, Wyndham   [1883–1956]

British colonial official in the Middle East.

After serving in World War I, the British Brigadier General Sir Wyndham Henry Deedes was posted to Istanbul as a military attaché and to Cairo, then a British protectorate, as public security director. In 1920/22 he served as chief secretary to British High Commissioner Sir Herbert Samuel in Palestine, then under British mandate. Although known for his pro-Zionist sympathies, Deedes played a role in promoting the SUPREME MUSLIM COUNCIL as an Arab counterweight to the JEWISH AGENCY.

BIBLIOGRAPHY

INGRAMS, DOREEN. *Palestine Papers 1917–1922: Seeds of Conflict.* London, 1972.
PORATH, Y. *The Emergence of the Palestinian-Arab National Movement.* London, 1974.

Elizabeth Thompson

De Gaulle, Charles   [1890–1970]

President of France, 1958 to 1969; instrumental in ending French colonialism in the Middle East and North Africa.

Charles de Gaulle, one of republican France's great statesmen, earned his place in French history by the spirited exercise of leadership in the face of national adversity—first when he placed himself at the head of the Free French movement in 1940 to meet the challenges of the German occupation in World War

II, and again when he took the lead in reshaping French political institutions in 1958 to meet the challenges of the Algerian war of independence, European integration, and the Cold War. Faced, in both periods, with the contradiction of ensuring France's well-being in Europe and sustaining a precarious hold on remnants of the French empire, de Gaulle did not deviate from his primary objective for long. The relative ease, therefore, with which he could divest France of claims to empire helped pave the way for full independence in the Middle Eastern mandates of Lebanon and Syria by 1945 and for the decolonization of Algeria by 1962.

De Gaulle established this priority early in his military career when he reluctantly deferred his passionate interest in French defense strategies to complete a tour of duty in the Middle East from 1929 to 1931. While there, he hinted at the charismatic didacticism that was to become the hallmark of his speeches. This was when, overriding the contradictions that separated colonial administrators from the political aspirations of their subjects, he urged Lebanon's youth to build a progressive state with the help of France. Returning to the Middle East during World War II, after its liberation in 1941 by British and Free French forces, General de Gaulle was incensed when he saw how Britain, with tacit American backing, was exploiting French weaknesses to support the Lebanese and Syrian nationalist movements. Ultimately, however, he refrained from exerting what would have been a corrosive resistance to Allied demands for France's retreat from empire in the area.

When de Gaulle returned to power in 1958, he had to deal with the French army's repression of Algeria's nationalist struggle against a colonial social order. This morally and materially debilitating war also affected France's relations with neighboring Arab states as well as with the United States, Britain, and the international community. De Gaulle initially mapped out a progressive future for what was to be a felicitously integrated Franco–Algerian society. He concentrated, however, on turning the sometimes dangerously rebellious military around to building France up as a nuclear power independent of its erstwhile allies and able to lead with Germany in the development of the European community. With these priorities uppermost in his mind, de Gaulle agreed in 1962 to the nationalist demand for a fully independent Algeria, and France subsequently closed this chapter in the history of empire with the absorption of a massive flight of colonists from across the Mediterranean.

In the aftermath of the Algerian peace, de Gaulle favored a resolution with the Arab world to complement French links with Israel. In the last years before he resigned his presidency in 1969, he assumed France's heightened stature would justify the role of arbiter in the Arab–Israel conflict, but he failed to make allowances for the complexity of the problem and the greater involvement of the superpowers.

BIBLIOGRAPHY

JEAN LACOUTURE'S *De Gaulle* in two volumes translated by Patrick O'Brian and Alan Sheridan (London and New York, 1990–1991), is an excellent biography, while the general's own *Memoirs of Hope: Renewal and Endeavor*, translated by Terence Kilmertin (London and New York, 1971), illustrates the charisma with which he steered France away from the Algerian war to national and European commitments.

John P. Spagnolo

De Haan, Yaakov Yisrael   [1881–1924]

Dutch-born poet and journalist who was assassinated because of his anti-Zionist activities.

Yaakov de Haan was assassinated on June 30, 1924, near the Shaare Tsedek Hospital in Jerusalem by two members of the Haganah. He joined the Mizrachi Zionist movement early in his career, but after moving to Palestine he eschewed ZIONISM, joined the Agudat Israel, and became the spokesman for the Ashkenazi Council (see ASHKENAZIM). He wrote increasingly anti-Zionist articles and sent pro-Arab reports to the League of Nations and the British mandatory authorities. These activities made De Haan an enemy of the Yishuv leadership and led to his assassination.

Bryan Daves

Dehkhoda, Ali Akbar   [1880–1956]

A leading reformist voice during Iran's Constitutional Revolution, 1905–1911; lexicographer.

Dehkhoda's journalistic and satirical prose—for example, in *Charand Parand* (Balderdash) and in engagé (politically concerned) verse (collected in his *Divan*)—influenced later writers of Persian literature.

During the Pahlavi era (1925–1941), like some other literary intellectuals, Dehkhoda left politics to work on academic projects. In the early 1940s, he returned as an administrator to his old secondary school, which had become the Faculty of Law at Tehran University. With the approval and support of Iran's parliament, in 1945 he began work on his Persian encyclopedic dictionary called *Loghat'nameh* (Book of Words). Some twenty thousand pages later and years after his death, the work reached completion in 1980.

BIBLIOGRAPHY

P. LOSENSKY'S, "Inshallah Gurbah Ast: God Willing, It's a Cat." *Iranian Studies* 19 (1986), illustrates Dehkhoda's erudition, satirical writing style, and anticlerical views.

Michael C. Hillmann

Dellalzade İsmail   [1797–1869]

Ottoman Turkish singer and composer.

Dellazade İsmail, the son of a palace official, was born in the Fath district of Istanbul. Upon finishing primary school, his musical talents were noticed, and he became a student of the great DEDE ZEKAI Efendi. At the age of nineteen, he joined the palace orchestra as a singer; later, he became the companion and chief prayer caller of Sultan Mahmud II. In 1846, Sultan Abdülmecit appointed him singing instructor in the newly established Academy of Music. Dellalzade is considered one of the musical geniuses of a period in which the flowering of Turkish classical music was met by the increasing popularity of Western music. He composed more than seventy pieces, including solemn folk tunes (*semai*) and ballads (*şarki*). Among his most well known compositions are *Yegah Ağır Semai*, *Suznak Beste*, and *Şehnaz Şarki*.

David Waldner

Delouvrier, Paul   [1914–   ]

Delegate general of the French government in Algeria in the 1950s.

Born in Remiremont, Vosges, in France, Delouvrier was a financial specialist in the coal and steel industries. France's President Charles de Gaulle appointed him delegate general to Algeria, a most difficult position because of the ongoing ALGERIAN WAR OF INDEPENDENCE and France's complex internal politics. Delouvrier's chief task—where he had considerable success—was to supervise social and economic projects of the Constantine Plan (outlined by de Gaulle in October 1958), which aimed to accelerate Algeria's development as it headed toward independence in 1962. Nevertheless, his political and moral authority disintegrated during this fitful period of decolonization, resulting in his resignation in 1960. Returning to France, he became a prefect (a government administrator of a French department, 1966–1969) and then head of France's electricity board (*Président du Conseil d'Administration d'Electricité*, 1969–1979).

BIBLIOGRAPHY

HORNE, ALISTAIR. *A Savage War of Peace: Algeria, 1954–1962,* 2nd ed. New York, 1987.

Phillip C. Naylor

Delta

Often called Lower Egypt, the land between the mouths of the Nile.

The delta is a triangular area (shaped like the Greek letter Δ) that has been built up by the silt carried within the waters of the Nile. When the Nile approaches the Mediterranean, much of the solid wastes and organic matter picked up during its long trip to the sea is screened out at the marshy estuaries and left behind to build more delta land. Although in ancient Egypt the Nile delta had seven mouths, today it has two—the Damietta on the east and Rosetta on the west—and many small channels. The broad coastal rim of the delta measures about 150 miles (240 km) from Alexandria in the west to Port Sa'id in the east. It is about 100 miles (160 km) from the Mediterranean coast south to Cairo, Egypt's capital.

The delta landscape is flat and mostly fertile, but the area nearest the coast is marshy, dominated by brackish inlets and lagoons. Since the construction of the Delta Barrages in the early nineteenth century, most of the farmland has been converted from basin to perennial irrigation, which supports two or three crops per year instead of one. Almost half the inhabitants are small landowners, sharecroppers, or peasants working for wages who live in villages surrounded by the lands they till. The others live in towns or cities. Fruits, vegetables, and cotton are the important delta crops. Delta Egyptians have generally had more contact with the outside world than have Upper Egyptians and are therefore more Westernized.

BIBLIOGRAPHY

U.S. LIBRARY OF CONGRESS, FEDERAL RESEARCH DIVISION. *Egypt: A Country Study.* Washington, D.C., 1991.

Arthur Goldschmidt, Jr.

Delta Barrages

Dams designed to regulate the flow of water in the two branches of the Nile.

Construction of the Delta Barrages seventy miles (113 km) north of Cairo, Egypt, was begun by Muhammad Ali Pasha, viceroy of Egypt, in 1833 and completed in 1843. The completion of the barrages regulated the flow of water in the two branches of the Nile river, Damietta and Rosetta. This permitted the conversion of several hundred thousand *feddans* in the Nile delta to be converted from basin irrigation to perennial irrigation. The barrages were rebuilt in the early years of Britain's occupation, and by 1900, 725,000 feddans (753,000 a; 305,000 ha) were perennially irrigated. Later, two additional barrages were constructed; the first, at Idfina, was completed in 1915, and the second, at Zifta, in 1943.

BIBLIOGRAPHY

NYROP, RICHARD F., ed. *Egypt: A Country Study*, 4th ed. Washington, D.C., 1983.
WATERBURY, JOHN. *Egypt: Burdens of the Past, Options for the Future.* Bloomington, Ind., 1978.

David Waldner

De Menasce Family

Sephardic family who arrived in Egypt during the eighteenth century, via Palestine and Morocco.

The leading member of the family in the nineteenth century was Jacob De Menasce (1807–1887), who began his career in Cairo as a money changer (*sarraf*) and banker and gradually emerged as the private banker of the Khedive Isma'il. He was one of the earliest entrepreneurs in Egypt to recognize the opportunities offered by European trade and, with Jacob Cattaoui, opened the banking and trading establishment of J. L. Menasce et Fils with branches in England, France, and Turkey. In 1872 and 1873, De Menasce was granted Austro-Hungarian protection and subsequently was given the title of baron by the Austro-Hungarian Empire, along with Hungarian citizenship. In 1871, he moved to Alexandria, the new and permanent seat of the family. His son, Béhor Levi, continued in the family's financial enterprises, but his grandson, Baron Jacques Béhor De Menasce (1850–1916), deserted the banking profession in favor of the cotton and sugar businesses. In 1890, Jacques served as the president of Alexandria's Jewish community and remained in that capacity for about twenty-five years. His younger brother Félix Béhor (1865–1943) became concerned with Zionism and was a personal friend of Dr. Chaim Weizmann, then president of the World Zionist Organization. In September 1921, Félix represented the Egyptian Zionist organization in Carlsbad at the twelfth World Zionist Congress; in later years he served as Alexandria's Jewish community president. The De Menasce family was not merely wealthy. It was European-educated and Western-oriented and led the Alexandria community from the early 1870s into the 1930s.

BIBLIOGRAPHY

KRÄMER, GUDRUN. *The Jews in Modern Egypt: 1914–1952.* Seattle, 1989.

LANDAU, JACOB M. *Jews in Nineteenth-Century Egypt.* New York, 1969.

MAKARIYUS, SHAHIN. *Tarikh al-Isra'iliyyin.* Cairo, 1904.

MIZRAHI, MAURICE. "The Role of Jews in Economic Development." In *The Jews of Egypt: A Mediterranean Society in Modern Times,* ed. by Shimon Shamir. Boulder, Colo., and London, 1987.

Michael M. Laskier

Demetrius II   [?–1870]

111th Coptic patriarch of Egypt, 1862–1870.

Because Khedive Sa'id Pasha had likely ordered the murder of Demetrius II's predecessor, CYRIL IV (for his pursuit of closer associations with foreign churches without the viceroy's approval), Demetrius adopted a modest domestic agenda. His sometimes obsequious loyalty to the khedive guaranteed that his tenure was trouble-free but undistinguished. He continued Cyril's support of education for the clergy but had little of his interest in church reform, which was eagerly sought by the progressive laity, specifically in matters of finance and land management. As a result, the Coptic populace's long-held mistrust of the conservative clergy, having been suspended during Cyril's enlightened tenure, was renewed in intensity and has flared intermittently to the present. After Demetrius's death, the patriarchate went empty for almost five years.

[*See also:* Copts]

BIBLIOGRAPHY

ATIYA, AZIZ S. *A History of Egyptain Christianity,* rev. ed. Millwood, N.Y., 1980.

STROTHMANN, R. *Die koptische Kirche in der Neuzeit.* Tübingen, Germany, 1932.

Donald Spanel

Demirel, Süleyman   [1924–   ]

The Republic of Turkey's ninth president.

Born in Islamköy, a province of Isparta, Turkey, Demirel graduated from the Engineering School of Istanbul Technical University in 1949, whereupon he entered the Research Unit of the Istanbul Electricity Company. In 1954, Demirel journeyed to the United States, where he spent one year as an Eisenhower Fellow. After his return, Demirel was appointed general director of the State Irrigation Administration (1955–1960). During this period, he realized a series of dams inspired by the Tennessee Valley Authority. He also taught at the Middle East Technical University, Ankara, from 1962 through 1964.

In 1962, Demirel joined the Justice party (commonly known as the ADALAT PARTY; AP); upon the sudden death of its founder, Ragip Gümüşpala, he was elected chairperson on November 29, 1964. During the budget debate in parliament in 1964, the conservative parties forced Ismet INÖNÜ's government to resign. After an unsuccessful attempt to form an independent government under the leadership of Suat Hayri Ürgüplü, general elections were held in October 1965. The AP obtained, in spite of the proportional electoral system, an absolute majority—namely, 52.73 percent of the vote and over 200 seats in the National Assembly of 450 seats. By 252 votes to 172, Demirel became Turkey's twenty-ninth prime minister on November 11, 1965. Four years later, during the general elections of October 1969, Demirel's party gained 46.53 percent of the vote, 256 out of 450 seats. Thus, the AP retained its overwhelming position in parliament.

Demirel's budget proposal of 1970 was rejected on February 14, 1970. Nevertheless, he succeeded in organizing a new cabinet and obtained the required vote of confidence on March 15, 1970. But the domestic violence that had been brewing since 1968, paired with radical student movements, gained ground. The inability of the government to present efficient solutions led high-ranking military personnel—a chief of staff, and ground, air, sea commanders—to present the government with the so-called "March 12 Memorandum." As a result, Demirel resigned in March 1971. Parliament was not suspended; an "above the parties" government was formed, but it did not receive a vote of confidence.

Turkey again went to the polls in 1973. Although the Adalat party obtained fewer votes than the major opposition party, the Republican People's party (CHP), Demirel succeeded in spite of accusations of nepotism and misuse of power to form the first "National Front" government, composed of a coalition of several rightist parties. Due to hyper-inflation, escalating domestic strife, and the fast decrease of foreign currency, early elections were held on June 5, 1977. Although the CHP won 213 seats and the AP only 189, Bülent ECEVIT's attempt to form a minority government failed. Demirel succeeded once more in forming his second coalition government, composed of the AP, National Salvation Party (MSP) and National Action Party (MHP). The resignation of ten MP's from the AP resulted in a parliamentary confrontation in which Demirel was forced to resign (December 31, 1978). However, due to the CHP's losses in the by-elections of 1979, Ecevit's short-lived minority government was forced to resign and Demirel for the third time formed a minority government with the help of the MSP and MHP. With no end in sight to the growing internal conflicts, ethnic clashes, economic bottlenecks, and parliamentary immobility, resulting in its inability to elect a head of state, the armed forces intervened for the third time within two decades, on September 12, 1980. With Demirel's prime ministry at an end, he was taken, for his "personal safety," to Hamzaköy and consequently deprived of his political rights for ten years. All political parties were dissolved.

Upon Demirel's attempt to support the newly formed Great Turkey party, he together with its leading party members, was placed under compulsory residence in Zincirbozan for four months. In spite of the political ban, Demirel supported during the 1986 general elections the recently established TRUE PATH PARTY (DYP), and following the lifting of the political ban through the referendum of 1987, he returned to parliament and was elected chairman of the DYP. During the general elections of 1991, Demirel's party won the highest number of seats (178 out of 450) and formed with the SOCIAL DEMOCRATIC POPULIST PARTY (SHP) a coalition government, Turkey's first rightist/leftist coalition, on November 29, 1991. Upon the sudden death of President Turgut Özal (April 17, 1993), Demirel was elected by the parliament, during the third round of deliberation, with 244 votes as the Republic of Turkey's ninth president (May 16, 1993). Following Demirel's resignation as chairman of the True Path Party, Tansu Çiller became Turkey's first woman prime minister. During the GULF CRISIS, Demirel followed a cautious, noninterventionist policy, but he was unsuccessful in preventing Turgut Özal's parliamentary election as president of the republic.

Demirel is considered a shrewd negotiator, a man of action, and an influential orator capable of attracting large crowds. His major strengths have been his great skill in building and maintaining political organizations; his unrelenting support for the rank and file; and his remarkable memory concerning technical details related to Turkish economy and industry. He draws his major support from rural voters and the provincial bourgeoisie.

BIBLIOGRAPHY

Grolier International Americana Encyclopedia. Danbury, Conn., 1987.
Larousse encyclopédique. Paris, 1962.

Nermin Abadan-Unat

Democratic Movement for Change

Israeli political party.

Democratic Movement for Change (DMC) was founded in 1976 to consolidate movements of dissatisfaction in the aftermath of the Yom Kippur War. Best-known figures of DMC were Yigal YADIN, former armed forces chief of staff and archeology professor, and Amnon RUBINSTEIN, Tel Aviv University law professor. Dissidents in the Labor party helped DMC win fifteen seats in the KNESSET of 1977. The DMC's program included electoral reform, decentralization of government, reorganization of the educational system, increased emphasis on social integration, and simplification of the bureaucracy. In foreign policy, the DMC stressed the preservation of the Jewish character of the state and territorial compromise on the West Bank but opposed establishment of an independent state there. Divided over the issue of cooperation with the Likud, DMC members decided to join the Likud-led government in 1977 without winning any of the major concessions they had insisted on. This led to a loss of DMC's credibility as well as to splits in its organization, and the party did not put forward any candidates in the 1981 election.

Walter F. Weiker

Democratic Party of Azerbaijan

Political party that supported autonomy for Iranian Azerbaijan.

The Democratic Party of Azerbaijan (DPA) was created in September 1945 in Tabriz (Iranian AZERBAIJAN) under the leadership of Ja'far Pishevari. He and other DPA leaders were Azerbaijani Turks of middle-class or landowning origin. Earlier, many had been involved in communist movements (Gilan or Khiyabani revolts, 1920); some had lived or been educated in Soviet Azerbaijan or Moscow. DPA, however, was an independent organization established to secure autonomy for Azerbaijan within Iran. The local branch of the communist Tudeh party dissolved itself and joined DPA.

Reacting against the brutal policies of economic neglect and Persianization by Reza Shah PAHLAVI's dynasty, a DPA-led All Peoples Grand National Assembly (in Tabriz, November 1945, just after World War II) declared rights to national self-determination within sovereign Iran, to retain a just share of their tax revenues, and to use Azerbaijani TURKISH (called Türki) as the official language of an autonomous province of Azerbaijan. Elections in December produced an all-DPA *majles* (parliament); Pishevari formed a government that enfranchised women, began land reform, and established Azerbaijani Turkish as the official language.

The autonomy movement had the support of the occupying Soviet troops, which prevented the forces of Mohammad Reza Shah Pahlavi from entering the province to suppress it. Western observers interpreted the DPA, therefore, as a Soviet puppet. In June 1946, after Soviet forces were withdrawn, Tabriz and Iran signed an agreement that fulfilled most DPA demands. In December 1946, however, Iranian forces entered Azerbaijan and suppressed the DPA government and autonomy movement, so the June agreement was abrogated. Pishevari fled to Baku and died there the following year after mysterious complications from an automobile accident.

BIBLIOGRAPHY

ABRAHAMIAN, ERVAND. *Iran Between Two Revolutions.* Princeton, N.J., 1982.
EMAMI-YEGANEH, JODY. "Iran vs. Azerbaijan (1945–46): Divorce, Separation or Reconciliation?" In *Central Asian Survey.* Oxford, 1984.
FATEMI, FARAMARZ S. *The USSR in Iran.* New York, 1980.
SWIETOCHOWSKI, TADEUSZ. *Russia and a Divided Azerbaijan: Foreign Conquest and Divergent Historical Development.* New York, 1994.

Audrey L. Altstadt

Democratic Party of Kurdistan, Iran

Political party that backed 1945 revolt to form an independent republic for Kurds.

The Democratic Party of Kurdistan, Iran, was formed in 1945 by Kurdish nationalists, with Soviet support, in Mahabad of the Kurdistan region in northwest Iran. While declaring its desire to remain within the Iranian boundary, the party demanded the use of the Kurdish language in state schools and government offices in Kurdistan; the retention of tax revenues for the benefit of the region; and the establishment of provincial assemblies as upheld by the constitution. The party claimed for KURDS a "distinct national identity" based on language, history, and culture. Finding the government unresponsive to its demands, the party, with the help of the Soviet army and local tribes, launched a revolt and declared the formation of the Independent Republic of Kurdistan in December 1945. Under the central government's Royal Army attack, the Mahabad government fell in December 1946. In the revolutionary upheavals of 1979, Kurdish intellectuals from the Kurdish Democratic party formed councils (or *shuras*) that held local power in conjunction with the leading clergy in Mahabad—Shaykh Ezz al-Din Hosseini and his followers—and boycotted the referendum on the country's constitution. The party and its activities have been suppressed ever since the Iranian revolution.

BIBLIOGRAPHY

ABRAHAMIAN, E. *Iran between Two Revolutions.* Princeton, N.J., 1982.
KEDDI, N. *Roots of Revolution: An Interpretive History of Modern Iran.* New Haven, Conn., 1981.

Parvaneh Pourshariati

Democratic Party of Kurdistan, Iraq

Political party advocating the autonomy of the Iraqi Kurds.

The Kurdistan Democratic party (KDP) was founded on August 16, 1946, at the suggestion of Mullah Mustafa BARZANI, who was then in the Kurdish republic of Mahabad. Its creation sanctioned the split of the national movement of the KURDS into different, sometimes opposing, Iranian and Iraqi organizations.

In the absence of Barzani, who went into exile in the Soviet Union, KDP became a progressive party, led by Kurdish intellectuals quite close to the Iraqi Communist party. After he returned in 1958, the party was shaken by a severe crisis, opposing Barzani's acceptance to the political bureau, along with Ibrahim Ahmed and his son-in-law Jalal TALABANI. KDP never fully recovered from these events of 1964 and became a mere instrument of Barzani.

After the collapse of the Kurdish movement in 1975 and discredited by Barzani's decision to stop the resistance, KDP lost the monopoly it had enjoyed for thirty years. Today, the KDP led by Mas'ud al-Barzani must share leadership of the movement in

Iraq with its rival, Talabani's PATRIOTIC UNION OF KURDISTAN, and several smaller organizations.

BIBLIOGRAPHY

KUTSCHERA, CHRIS. *Le mouvement national kurde.* Paris, 1979.

Chris Kutschera

Democrat Party

Turkish political party.

Four members of the Republican People's party (RPP)—Celal BAYAR, Adnan MENDERES, Mehmet Fuat KOPRÜLÜ, and Refik Koraltan—founded the Democrat party (DP; Demokrat parti) on January 7, 1946. The immediate impetus for the establishment of the party was to oppose an RPP-sponsored land reform bill. More generally, the DP founders criticized the government for being authoritarian and arbitrary, and for its extensive control of the economy. The DP campaigned on a platform of economic, political, and cultural liberalism.

The DP participated in the elections of 1946, which were held before the party had a chance to build a national organization or make known its candidates. The party gained only 64 out of 465 seats. Over the next four years, party leaders built a strong organization and attracted the support of many groups that had become alienated from the RPP over the previous decade and a half. In the 1950 elections, the DP received 53.3 percent of the popular vote and 86.2 percent of the seats in the Grand National Assembly. On May 29, 1950, the DP formed its first government as the new assembly elected Bayar as president, Menderes prime minister, and Koprülü foreign minister. In the 1954 elections, the DP increased its share of the vote to 56.6 percent, capturing 408 out of 503 assembly seats. In the 1957 general elections, held in the context of growing economic crisis, the DP still managed to garner 325 seats.

Despite encouraging the private sector, DP policies maintained wide latitude for state control over the economy, particularly through investments in the state manufacturing sector. Between 1950 and 1953, inflows of foreign aid and high prices for agricultural goods induced the DP government to encourage agricultural production and exports. A diverse array of policies increased peasant incomes, helping to cement DP popularity in the countryside. After 1953, a combination of declining world prices and a growing shortage of foreign exchange led the DP to implement trade policies that encouraged import-substituting industrialization. Despite growing in-

vestment and manufacturing output, large government deficits and the lack of coherent policy led to severe economic problems, and by 1958, the government was forced to impose austerity measures.

The DP pursued a staunchly pro-West foreign policy, joining the North Atlantic Treaty Organization in February 1952 and, on several occasions, siding with the West, even at the expense of creating tensions with its neighbors. Turkey's support for the BAGHDAD PACT, for example, prompted the Egyptian government to label Turkey a Western surrogate in the region.

As economic conditions deteriorated, the DP became increasingly authoritarian. A series of antidemocratic laws, designed to cripple the RPP while muzzling dissent in the press and in universities, alienated the liberal intelligentsia and the liberal wing within the party. In early 1960, to stifle growing opposition, the government passed some unconstitutional measures. When these measures only catalyzed further opposition, the government declared martial law. At this point, the DP paid the price for never having established harmonious relations with the military: The combination of economic crisis and increasing authoritarianism triggered a military coup that deposed the DP government on May 27, 1960. The leading members of the DP were subsequently placed on trial for treason. On September 15, 1961, fifteen of them were sentenced to death. Twelve of these sentences were commuted, but Menderes and two of his top ministers were executed.

BIBLIOGRAPHY

AHMAD, FEROZ. *The Making of Modern Turkey.* London, 1993.
———. *The Turkish Experiment in Democracy.* London, 1977.
SARIBAY, ALI YASAR. "The Democratic Party." In *Political Parties and Democracy in Turkey,* ed. by Metin Heper and Jacob M. Landau. London, 1991.

David Waldner

Demography

See Population

Denktash, Rauf [1924–]

Turkish Cypriot statesman.

Rauf Denktash was born in Paphos, Cyprus, in 1924. His father was a judge. After graduating from the English school in Nicosia, he worked briefly as a columnist for *Halkın Sesi* (The People's Voice), a Turkish Cypriot newspaper founded in 1940 by Dr. Fazıl Küçük, the veteran leader of the Turkish Cypriot community. In 1944, Denktash went to study law in England, and in 1947, he was called to the bar.

Upon his return to Cyprus, which was then a British crown colony, Denktash became a barrister, serving from 1949 to 1957 as junior crown counsel, crown counsel, and acting solicitor general. During this time, he also embarked on a political career. He became Küçük's chief aide and served his community as a member of the Consultative Assembly (1948–1960) and as a member of the assembly's Turkish Affairs Committee. He was also elected president of the Federation of Turkish Cypriot Associations, a voluntary organization for the purpose of coordinating the social and economic life of the Turkish Cypriots and organizing their resistance to Greek Cypriot agitation for *enosis* (union of Cyprus with Greece).

In 1954, the efforts of the Greek Cypriot leaders, Archbishop MAKARIOS III and Georgios GRIVAS, to achieve enosis and hellenize Cyprus culminated in a full-fledged guerilla war against the British colonial administration and all those who opposed the Greek Cypriot aims. Denktash helped organize the Turkish resistance movement (TMT) to protect his community.

Küçük and Denktash represented the Turkish Cypriot community at the London Conference of 1959, which resulted in an agreement to establish an independent partnership state in Cyprus. Shortly thereafter, Denktash represented his community on the Constitutional Committee, which drafted a constitution for the new state, and at the Athens Conference, which specified how the Treaty of Alliance and the Treaty of Guarantee (which were to provide security for the new state) were to be implemented. Denktash, therefore, was one of the chief architects of the bicommunal Republic of Cyprus, which came into being in 1960. That year, Denktash was elected president of the Turkish Cypriot Communal Chamber.

In December 1963, Küçük (who had been elected vice president of Cyprus) and Denktash both opposed the proposal by Archbishop Makarios (who had been elected president of Cyprus) to amend the Constitution of 1960 on the grounds that the projected changes would pave the way for enosis. As a consequence, all Turkish Cypriot officials and parliamentary deputies were dismissed, attacks were carried out against Turkish Cypriot enclaves, and the Turkish Cypriots were forced to evacuate 103 villages.

Early in 1964, Denktash flew to New York to present his community's case before the UN Security Council, but he was not allowed to return to Cyprus and remained in what he termed "de facto banishment" for several years. In October 1967, when he returned to Cyprus secretly, he was arrested but then freed as a result of international pressure. After his release, he resumed his position as president of the Turkish Cypriot Communal Chamber (April 1968). Since the Turkish Cypriot community was no longer being represented in the national government, the Communal Chamber had become the backbone of what was gradually becoming an autonomous Turkish Cypriot administration.

Denktash was one of the founders of the provisional Turkish Federated State of Cyprus, which was established in northern Cyprus in February 1975, following the overthrow of the Makarios regime by the Greek junta and the military intervention of Turkey, which the overthrow precipitated (July–August 1974). In June 1976, Denktash was elected as the federated state's first president. In June 1981, he was reelected.

Denktash was also one of the founders of the secessionist Turkish Republic of Northern Cyprus, which was established in November 1983, following the collapse of negotiations with the head of the Greek Cypriot government, Spyros Kyprianou. In June 1985, Denktash was elected as the republic's first president; he was reelected to that position in June 1990.

Denktash has been a strong advocate of a federal solution to the Cyprus problem, championing the establishment of a bizonal, bicommunal partnership state on the island. He has also been one of the chief promoters of the UN-sponsored intercommunal talks, which have taken place at various intervals since 1975.

Denktash is the author of numerous articles and several books. His best-known work is *The Cyprus Triangle* (London, 1982).

BIBLIOGRAPHY

DENKTASH, R. R. "Karkot Deresi." *Cengel* (April–May 1988): 3–8; (June–July 1988): 14–23; (August–September 1988): 3–20; (October 1988): 2–21.

OBERLING, PIERRE. *The Cyprus Tragedy.* London, 1982.

———. *Negotiating for Survival.* Princeton, N.J., 1991.

———. *The Road to Ballapais.* Boulder, Colo., 1982.

Pierre Oberling

Dentz, Henri-Fernand

French high commissioner of Syria and Lebanon and Vichy commander of l'Armée du Levant.

Dentz's harsh treatment of the native population was one of the causes of the Syrian revolt of 1925/26.

The Vichy government appointed Dentz high commissioner in December 1940. On June 8, 1941, the British and their Free French allies launched an invasion from Palestine and Iraq. Dentz counterattacked fiercely at Marjayun, Sasa, and Mazzeh. He ultimately surrendered to the British alone after receiving guarantees that most of his army would be repatriated to France rather than be compelled to join Charles DE GAULLE.

BIBLIOGRAPHY

LAFFARGUE, ANDRÉ. *Servitude et grandeur militaire: Le Général Dentz.* Paris, 1940. Reprint, 1954.

Bassam Namani

Déracinement

The French term for "uprooted"; appears periodically in Algerian history.

Déracinement particularly refers to the expropriation and displacement (*refoulement*) of natives from their land during COLONIALISM in the MAGHRIB (North Africa). This often occurred after insurrections (e.g., the Kabyle Revolt of 1871) or legislation (e.g., the Warnier Law, 1873). It also related to the imposition of French culture and the policy of assimilation, which caused Algerians to lose their "roots," their sense of ethnic identity. Finally, it applies to displaced populations, such as the emigrant workers who left their families to find work in France, but also to French settlers (*pieds-noirs*) who fled Algeria during the trauma of decolonization in the late 1950s.

BIBLIOGRAPHY

BOURDIEU, PIERRE, and ABDELMALEK SAYAD. *Le déracinement: La crise de l'agriculture traditionelle en Algérie.* Paris, 1964.

Phillip C. Naylor

Derb

Traditional word for Moroccan street or neighborhood.

In Morocco, the cities were traditionally constituted of streets or neighborhoods, each called a *derb*. People belonging to the same derb shared an identity. A family often gave its name to the derb it inhabited. Today, the term is seldom used to designate a street, replaced by the term *zanga* or *shari*.

Rahma Bourqia

Derdli   [1772–1845]

Nineteenth-century Turkish Ottoman musician and poet.

The pen name of İbrahim, the son of an agricultural laborer who was born in the village of Sahneler. Using the pseudonym of Lutfi, Derdli (also spelled Dertli) earned his living as a traveling minstrel until his performances attracted the attention of Sultan MAHMUD II. Following an attempted suicide in 1840, he took the name Derdli (Sorrowful). Derdli's prose style was influenced by the great poet Fuzuli, while his compositions set to music were in the style of Aşık Ömer and Gevheri.

BIBLIOGRAPHY

ÖZKIRIMLI, ATILLA. *Türk edebiyatı Ansiklopedisi,* vol. 2. Istanbul, 1982, pp. 364–64.

David Waldner

Dergah

Turkish nationalist journal.

Published between 1921 and 1923, during the Turkish war of independence, *Dergah*'s editors sought a spiritual and mystical vision for the emerging nation of TURKEY. They took the name for their bimonthly journal from the word for lodges of Sufi mystics. Under the editorial management of Mustafa Nihat Özön, *Dergah* sought to prepare a new atmosphere of history, art, and culture, often preaching that the Turks must shake off the degeneration of their culture over the past century.

Simultaneously cosmopolitan and for NATIONALISM, *Dergah* published articles on a wide variety of topics under the editorial guidance of Yahya Kemal. It gathered contributions from the leading literary figures of the early republic, including Halide Edip, Yakup Kadri Karaosmanoğlu, Abddülhak Hamit Tarhan, and Falih Rıfkı Atay. When the Turkish war of independence ended in 1923, the group dissolved after publishing forty-two issues. *Dergah* represented a conservative current in Turkish journalism that has continued until today.

BIBLIOGRAPHY

KONGAR, EMRE. "Turkey's Cultural Transformation." In *The Transformation of Turkish Culture,* ed. by Günsel Renda and C. Max Kortepeter. Princeton, N.J., 1986.

Elizabeth Thompson

Dervish

See Sufism and the Sufi Orders

Desalinization

Removing salt from seawater is important throughout the Middle East as a supplement to scarce freshwater supplies.

Those parts of the Middle East without surface streams depend on fresh WATER pumped from deep aquifers or on desalinized water, whether from the sea or from brackish wells. To date, the cost of desalinizing techniques and of pumping desalinized water from sea level to elevations where it is needed has prohibited its use for agriculture. Nevertheless, the escalating demand for water in the Middle East ensures that desalinization activities will continue to grow.

Desalinization (or desalination) refers to the reduction of dissolved solids in brackish or saline waters by technical means. Four methods of accomplishing this exist: distillation, membrane processes, ion exchange, and freezing. The latter process has no commercial applications.

Distillation is based upon the boiling or vaporization of salty water and the condensation of pure water from the resulting vapors. Distillation methods include multistage flash distillation (MSF), multieffect distillation (MED), and vapor compression (VP). All these techniques require large amounts of energy to supply the latent heat of evaporation (580 calories/gram). However, multistage flash distillation is able to desalt saline waters as high as forty-five thousand parts per million of total dissolved solids (TDS) and has the greatest use. With this technique, heated seawater is led under pressure through a series of chambers, in each of which it expands rapidly (flashes), giving off water vapor while at the same time cooling. The water vapor in each chamber is then condensed and collected as fresh water.

Multieffect distillation operates by spraying seawater over horizontal tubes where some of it evaporates. The progressively concentrated brine is moved from one set of tubes to the next (effect to effect), each effect hotter in its turn. At the end, the brine is cooled and its heat returned to the system. The vapor meanwhile is condensed and saved, and the cooled brine returned to the sea.

Vapor compression relies on the mechanical compression of water vapor resulting from the boiling of seawater. This distillate is then condensed while the heat of compression is used to boil more seawater. This new method works best for operations needing less then 3,800 cubic meters of fresh water per day.

Dual-purpose plants combining power generation and one of the above distillation techniques are considered most efficient. Although low temperatures are required for distillation, the incremental price of raising the steam to temperatures suitable for supplemental power generation is less than the value of the electricity produced. Solar power and geothermal energy are being considered as inexpensive alternatives to conventional fuels for these installations.

Membrane processes depend on the flow of saline water through a semipermeable membrane, during which dissolved solids are left behind. The application of pressure to the solution being purified changes its chemical potential and results in reverse osmosis (RO). This results in the osmotic flow of water toward the pure water side, which has now achieved a lower solvent chemical potential. Reverse electrodialysis (ED) employs the passage of electric current through the membranes, thus enabling anions to pass in one direction and cations in the other. This latter technique is used most often with brackish waters, which have fewer parts per million of salt than does seawater.

Ion exchange consists of passing brackish water across the surface of synthetic organic resins, where the ions in the water are exchanged and the salts removed. These resins can be regenerated. At Eilat, Israel, this technique has been successfully combined with reverse osmosis, the resins being regenerated with latent heat from the RO plant.

Desalinization of any type is still relatively expensive. Brackish water (10,000 ppm TDS or less) desalinization costs about 30 U.S. cents per cubic meter using either RO or ED. Seawater purified in a dual-purpose plant can be produced at from 81 cents to 1.47 U.S. dollars per cubic meter. The cost is higher for a single purpose MSF or MED operation—1.06 to 1.74 U.S. dollars per cubic meter. Thus, this source of sweet water is at present used for municipal purposes but is too costly for agriculture. Regardless of cost, approximately 13 million cubic meters of potable water are produced daily by 4,000 plants worldwide.

Further problems include corrosion of equipment resulting from concentrations of briny solutions and the production of calcium carbonate and magnesium hydroxide precipitates (solids), which can clog the tubing in MSF and MED plants—this is counteracted by adding small amounts of acid to the water being desalted but, in turn, may cause additional corrosion.

During the GULF CRISIS of 1991, oil spills were a further threat to desalinization plants belonging to Saudi Arabia and other nations along the eastern shore of the Arabian peninsula. Saudi Arabia has turned to desalinizing brackish well water through reverse osmosis plants. U.S. troops in Operation

Desert Storm (1990/91) were almost entirely supplied with water produced from similar sources by military RO plants. Saudi Arabia has 30 percent of the installed world desalinization capacity: Seventeen plants with an annual production of about 628 cubic meters account for about 50 percent of the kingdom's domestic water use. Kuwait and the United Arab Emirates each account for about 11 percent of total world capacity (with the United States just below that amount). Israel as of December 1990 produced nearly 4 million cubic meters annually from 33 desalting units at 23 sites from brackish water, using reverse osmosis. The Middle East accounts for more than 67 percent of the world's desalinization effort.

BIBLIOGRAPHY

ABELSON, PHILIP H. "Desalination of Brackish and Marine Waters." *Science* 251, 4999 (1991): 1289.
ABU RIZAIZA, OMAR S., and MOHAMED N. ALLAM. "Water Requirements versus Water Availability in Saudi Arabia." *Journal of Water Planning and Management* 115, 1 (1989): 64–74.
AWERBUCH, LEON. "Desalination Technology: An Overview." In *The Politics of Scarcity: Water in the Middle East,* ed. by Joyce R. Starr and Daniel C. Stoll. Boulder, Colo., 1988.

John F. Kolars

Desert Mobile Force

Precursor to the modern Jordanian army.

The Desert Mobile Force was established in 1930 during the British mandate to provide law and order in the desert region. Commanded by John Bagot GLUBB, the force was composed primarily of bedouin tribesmen. The force built a number of police forts in the desert as command posts under Glubb's direction. Glubb also equipped it with armored cars and wireless sets. This was the seed for the enlarged, mechanized force that became the ARAB LEGION, and finally the Jordanian armed forces.

BIBLIOGRAPHY

GLUBB, SIR JOHN BAGOT. *A Soldier with the Arabs.* New York, 1957.

Jenab Tutunji

Deserts

Predominant landscape of the Middle East and North Africa.

The Grand Erg Occidental desert, part of the Algerian Sahara. (Richard Bulliet)

Stretching from the Atlantic coast in the west to Pakistan in the east, a band of arid land (15° and 30° north latitude) dominates this region. The North African expanse is generally known as the Sahara, although subdivisions within it have individual names indicating the nature of the surface. The terms *erg* (as in the Great Eastern Erg of Algeria) and *serir* (as the Serir of Kalanshu in Libya) indicate a region of sand dunes. Where the surface is rocky underfoot the terms used are *reg* or *hamada* (for example, the Hamada of Dra south of the Anti-Atlas mountains). Individual areas may also be given the name desert, the Western Desert and the Eastern Desert in Egypt, although they are smaller parts of the whole. On the peninsula of the same name, the Arabian Desert is an extension of the Sahara and is divided into the Rub al-Khali (Empty Quarter, a region of vast sand dunes) and the Nafud and Najd. To the north is the Syrian Desert, and to the east the two deserts of the Iranian plateau are known as the Dasht e Kavir and the Dasht-e Lut.

The term *desert* is one in common usage and therefore difficult to define. Most experts prefer to speak

Aerial view of Tidikelt plain in the Algerian Sahara.
(Richard Bulliet)

of "drylands" or "arid lands" and to define such places through various measures of the availability of WATER for plant growth (implying that not all deserts are hot.) A common definition of desert, however, is those regions of the earth's surface having less than ten inches (250 mm) of precipitation annually and extreme high temperatures. This classical approach relates such measures to areas with types of vegetation adapted to hot, arid conditions. In areas with much sunshine and small amounts of precipitation and/or natural moisture from the soil, only plants called *xerophytes* survive—those adapted to such conditions. In certain hyperarid locations, precipitation may be even less and no vegetation of any kind is found.

Desert rainfall is not only sparse but is also extremely variable in time and space as well as in quantity. Such variance means that human occupancy of the desert must depend for survival on reliable springs and rivers for irrigation rather than on precipitation. Traditional pastoral nomadism, located on the desert margins, was adapted to this environment by moving its productive units (i.e., herds and flocks) to where grass and water seasonally occurred. But even nomads ventured into the true desert only for travel as transporters and raiders. The few permanent inhabitants of the deserts were those oasis dwellers dependent upon perennial springs for intensive agriculture and the growing of date palms.

Desert soils are usually of poor quality except for those in the valleys of rivers where alluvial deposits have accumulated. True desert soils—called *aridisols*—have low biomass, very sparse or no organic acids and gases, few or no bacteria, and are essentially mineral in character. Any rain or sheet flooding and runoff that percolate beneath the surface rapidly evaporate. As a result, soluble salts are precipitated and redeposited, forming a crusty layer on the surface or just beneath it. Repeated leaching and deposition can result in concentrations of sodium chloride (NaCl), white alkali (salt), or similar deposits of sodium carbonate (Na_2CO_3), black alkali, which poison the soil and make agriculture impossible. Under desert conditions agriculture is extremely difficult, and even the use of irrigation water can cause salinity, through evaporation and the precipitation of the dissolved salts it may carry, which leads to the abandonment of such farmland.

The natural xerophytic vegetation found in deserts has adapted to conditions of high temperatures and scant and irregular amounts of precipitation. Xerophytes often occur as drought-resisting plants with heavy cuticles, which reduce transpiration, or with stomata, which can be closed for the same purpose. Other xerophytes reduce water use by shedding their leaves and remaining leafless during the dry season. Among these plants are the euphorbia and the cacti, the latter originally found only in the Western Hemisphere.

Phreatphytes constitute another class of desert vegetation, which includes palms. These plants have developed long tap roots, which reach the water table, allowing them to survive the driest of surface conditions. Other plants evade drought by flowering and seeding only during brief rainy periods. During the intervening months and years of drought, the seeds remain dormant.

Desert vegetation under such conditions is sparse, and soil-forming conditions (including the creation of humus) are poor. Rainstorms can be intense, although of short duration, and often soil particles are carried away from desert surfaces by sheet flooding. The result of these conditions is erosion—which results in hills lacking deep layers of soil. Their profiles are characteristically steep sided with thick strata forming cliff faces rising vertically from the surrounding plains. Flat-topped mesas and steep buttes dominate the landscape, while valleys are flat bottomed with vertical side slopes. Wind erosion and deposition are also significant factors in desert landscape formation. Crescent-shaped barchan dunes are found where sands are insufficient to completely mantle the underlying surface. Copious sands form "seas," with longitudinal sief dunes and star-shaped rhourd dunes. Such seas, however, are the exceptions and rocky desert surfaces are common.

In desert areas, underground supplies of water assume great importance. Porous and permeable strata deep beneath the surface sometimes contain large quantities of water. Such aquifers may have impervious layers (aquicludes) above and below them that confine the water and keep it from escaping except in limited amounts at oases. Other aquifers occur in unconsolidated alluvial materials in river valleys (Arabic, *wadis*). This water is recharged from river seepage and/or rainfall. In the Middle East, most of the major aquifers are nonrenewable and contain fossil water, which once used—extracted or mined—will not be replaced. Desert countries, such as Libya and Saudi Arabia, with few or no surface streams have in the last two decades turned to the exploitation of such aquifers as part of their economic development plans. An ambitious agricultural program in Saudi Arabia has utilized tube wells and central pivot irrigation to produce bumper wheat crops in an otherwise hostile desert environment. Libya is engaged in constructing a "Great Manmade River"—actually a gigantic system of pumps and pipelines—with which to bring water from aquifers beneath the central Sahara to coastal locations, for municipal and agricultural use. In both these cases and others, the critical element is the quantity of water available and whether it will last long enough to justify such expensive projects. Many experts counsel caution in undertaking such attempts to remake, or "green," the desert.

[*See also*: Climate, Desalinization, Geography]

BIBLIOGRAPHY

BEAUMONT, PETER. *Environmental Management and Development in Dry Lands.* London, 1989.
GOUDIE, ANDREW, and JOHN WILKINSON. *The Warm Desert Environment.* London, 1977.
WHITEHEAD, EMILY E., CHARLES F. HUTCHINSON, BARBARA N. TIMMERMAN, and ROBERT G. VARADY, eds. *Arid Lands Today and Tomorrow.* Proceedings of an International Research and Development Conference. Boulder, Colo., 1988.

John F. Kolars

Desert Shield

Name given to U.S. military operations carried out in response to the Iraqi invasion of Kuwait on August 2, 1990.

When Kuwait requested U.S. assistance, there were no immediate military options available for repelling the Iraqi attack. The United States moved two aircraft-carrier task forces to the area, held talks with Saudi Arabia about defending that nation from Iraqi attack, and dusted off U.S. Central Command plan 1002-90. According to this plan, 200,000 U.S. troops were to be sent to Saudi Arabia over the course of a number of months to defend that nation from Iraqi aggression.

Pending a Saudi request for help, the U.S. administration issued orders to General H. Norman Schwarzkopf, the commander of Central Command, to prepare to implement Plan 1002-90 immediately. The Saudi request came on August 6, and on August 7 elements of the 82nd Airborne Division and U.S. Air Force fighter planes were en route to Saudi Arabia, thus officially inaugurating Operation Desert Shield. Other nations had also pledged aid, and on August 8 President Bush announced the deployment of forces to defend Saudi Arabia.

Operation Desert Shield was paralleled by British Operation Granby, French Operation Daguet, and the deployment of Egyptian and Syrian troops, as well as smaller units contributed by other nations. The American contribution was, however, the largest and consisted initially of substantial air force, navy, and marine units, as well as the XVIII Army Airborne Corps; the latter included the 82nd and 101st Airborne Divisions, the 1st Cavalry Division, the 24th Mechanized Infantry Division, and the 3rd Armored Cavalry Regiment. By November 5—in a military movement not equaled since World War II—the XVIII had 763 tanks, almost 1,500 armored vehicles, over 1,000 pieces of artillery and antiaircraft artillery, about 1,000 helicopters, and almost 400 antitank vehicles in the theater. Total U.S. forces deployed 88 days after August 7 numbered 184,000, a number that was not reached for 12 months in the deployment to Vietnam.

The initial deployment was sufficient to defend Saudi Arabia from Iraqi attack, but not enough to push Iraq out of Kuwait. Opposition to the occupation of Kuwait had quickly solidified, and most nations of the world, including most Arab nations, demanded Iraqi withdrawal. This concerted opposition was reflected in UN resolutions, backed by the Soviet Union, and gained China acquiescence. By November, Pres. George Bush had decided to move from a defensive to an offensive posture in preparation for driving Iraqi forces from Kuwait. As a consequence of the change in strategy, the American commitment was doubled, and the president announced the decision on November 8. Additional air force, navy, and marine units were programmed for southwest Asia, and the U.S. Army VII Corps from Germany began to deploy.

By the time Operation Desert Shield had become Operation DESERT STORM in January 1991, the United States had over 500,000 men and women in the theater. The ground forces included the 1st and 2nd Marine Divisions, the previously described XVIII Army Corps, and the VII Corps, which consisted of the 1st Armored Division and the 3rd Armored Division, the 1st Infantry Division, the 2nd

Armored Cavalry Regiment, and brigades from the 2nd Armored Division and the 3rd Infantry Division. It was planned that by mid-January the air force would be contributing 195 air-to-air fighters, 477 air-to-ground aircraft, and 426 dual-purpose aircraft. The Navy deployed 6 aircraft carriers, 2 battleships, 13 cruisers, 20 destroyers and frigates, and 31 amphibious ships. The deployment to southwest Asia included large numbers of Reserve and National Guard forces in addition to the active forces.

[*See also:* Gulf Crisis]

BIBLIOGRAPHY

FREEDMAN, LAWRENCE, and EFRAIM KARSH. *The Gulf Conflict, 1990–1991: Diplomacy and War in the New World Order.* Princeton, N.J., 1993.
FRIEDMAN, NORMAN. *Desert Victory: The War for Kuwait.* Annapolis, Md., 1991.

Daniel E. Spector

Desert Storm

Military operation carried out by a U.S.-led and UN-supported international coalition to eject Iraq from Kuwait, 1991.

Sanctioned by the United Nations and carried out by the United States, this action began with an air offensive on January 17, 1991. On February 24, coalition forces began a land offensive, which ended in the liberation of Kuwait, and a temporary cease-fire on February 28. Iraq agreed to cease-fire terms on March 3 and formally accepted UN cease-fire conditions and resolutions on April 7.

After the Iraqi invasion of Kuwait on August 2, 1990, the United States, supported by the UN resolutions, formed a coalition to deter further aggression and, eventually, to push Iraq out of Kuwait (see DESERT SHIELD). The most extensive military buildup since World War II led to an overwhelming coalition force, which was arrayed against one of the largest third-world military forces. By the time it started the air offensive, the coalition had 1,820 combat aircraft in the theater, of which 1,376 were those of the United States. The rest came from Bahrain, Canada, France, Italy, Kuwait, Oman, Qatar, Saudi Arabia, the United Arab Emirates, and the United Kingdom. Opposing this force were approximately 660 Iraqi combat aircraft.

The coalition's naval superiority was even more marked. Iraq had 87 vessels, most of which were patrol and missile attack craft. Seventeen nations of the coalition contributed naval forces. The United States had 108 combat vessels in the theater at the beginning of the air war, including 6 aircraft carriers and 2 battleships; the British contributed 11 destroyers and frigates, as well as numerous other vessels; France had 13 ships in the theater, including an aircraft carrier; other nations with naval forces included Italy, Australia, Argentina, Belgium, Canada, Denmark, Germany, Greece, Kuwait, the Netherlands, Norway, Poland, Portugal, and Spain.

The Iraqi army consisted of approximately 56 divisions and 1,100,00 men, making it the world's fourth largest military power. In January 1991, an estimated 530,000 were in the Kuwaiti theater with about 4,300 tanks. Opposing this army were forces from 18 coalition nations. The United States contributed 532,000 and 2,000 tanks; other major forces were those of Saudi Arabia with 95,000 men and 550 tanks, Egypt with 40,000 men and 400 tanks, and Britain with 35,000 men and 292 tanks.

The air offensive that had been launched on January 17 began with a dramatic display of fireworks viewed by much of the world on the cable television station CNN. There were four phases in the air campaign. In the first, the coalition sought to destroy Iraq's offensive and defensive air capabilities; its national communications and transportation systems; its nuclear, biological and chemical research and production facilities; and its war production potential. In the second and third phases, the coalition sought to cut off Iraqi forces in the Kuwaiti theater and then destroy and demoralize those forces. The destruction of Iraq's Scud missiles, which Iraq had launched against both Saudi Arabia and Israel, in an attempt to bring Israel into the war and disrupt the coalition, was also an objective of this part of the campaign. The final phase involved winning the air and ground campaign by providing intelligence, massive firepower, and protective air cover for the ground forces. The effectiveness of the coalition's air offensive was enhanced by the stealth technology of U.S. aircraft, which allowed for undetected penetration of Iraqi air defenses and the use of smart weapons capable of destroying targets with great precision. This technology minimized civilian casualties, although they usually were significant nevertheless (the exact numbers may never be known). The destruction of Iraq's infrastructure also led to great suffering.

By mid-February, the air campaign had reached the point of diminishing returns and the attrition of Iraqi forces in the theater was such that a ground attack could be mounted with a high probability of success. The plan was to fix Iraqi forces in place with the threat of an amphibious assault on Kuwait City and an attack by U.S. Marines and coalition forces across the Saudi–Kuwait border approximately thirty-seven miles (59 km) west of the Persian Gulf at the "armpit" of the border northwest of the al-Jaber airfield. The main attack was to be executed by the U.S. VII and XVIII Corps, with coalition forces positioned further to the west across the Saudi–Iraqi border and the westernmost forces crossing the border about 240 miles (386 km) west of Kuwait City. Aimed at enveloping the Iraqi forces in the Kuwaiti theater by attacking them north toward the Euphrates river and then east to cut off their retreat into the interior of Iraq, the coalition attack was a success. Iraq sued for a cease-fire, which went into effect after 100 hours of fighting. At this point, coalition forces had wrested control of about 29,600 square miles (74,000 sq. km) of territory, including 15 percent of Iraq. The coalition's losses were about 240 killed in action and 775 wounded. Estimates of Iraqi losses were originally as high as 100,000 killed and wounded. Later estimates were as low as 10,000, but 35,000 is probably close to the correct figure. The coalition had won the war; it was now a question of whether it could win the peace as conclusively.

BIBLIOGRAPHY

FREEDMAN, LAWRENCE, and EFRAIM KARSH. *The Gulf Conflict, 1990–1991: Diplomacy and War in the New World Order.* Princeton, N.J., 1993.

FRIEDMAN, NORMAN. *Desert Victory: The War for Kuwait.* Annapolis, Md., 1991.

SCALES, ROBERT H., JR. *Certain Victory: The U.S. Army in the Gulf War.* Washington, D.C., 1993.

WATSON, BRUCE W., ed. *Military Lessons of the Gulf War.* Novato, Calif., 1991.

Daniel E. Spector

Destour Party

Tunisian political party that challenged French colonial rule.

This political party was founded by Abd al-Aziz THAALBI in 1920. It drew its primary support from the cautious anti-French bourgeoisie of Tunis. The name derived from the demand for the restoration of the 1861 constitution of Tunisia, which had been in force before the French established a protectorate in 1883. In the 1920s, the Destour called for the formation of a Tunisian government responsible to an elected assembly and guarantees of basic rights. The hesitancy of party leaders to go beyond petitioning French colonial authorities in Tunisia resulted in very limited success.

In the early 1930s, an outspoken group of Western-educated young men from the Sahil region achieved prominence in the party. One of them, Habib BOURGUIBA (Tunisian president, 1957–1987), assumed the editorship of the newspaper *L'Action Tunisienne* in 1932. His strong criticisms of the French protectorate opened a rift in the party by challenging the conservative approach of Destour leaders. When *L'Action Tunisienne* issued a call for independence in 1933, protectorate authorities ordered the dissolution of the Destour. Bourguiba was expelled because of his opposition to a French offer allowing the party to operate if it modulated its policies.

In March 1934, Bourguiba convened a meeting in Ksar Hellal at which the Neo-Destour party was born. Its founders included Bourguiba's brother Muhammad, Dr. Mahmoud Matari, Tahar SFAR, and Bahri Guiga. Independence, an end to colonialism, the granting of a constitution, and a larger role in the political process for Tunisians were its principal demands. The Destour never again played an important role in Tunisia, although it continued to exist until after independence (1956).

To create an effective countrywide organization, Neo-Destour established local cells linked to the party's central command in a pyramidal structure. Along with Destour malcontents, it attracted support in the rural regions the older party had ignored. Bourguiba and other Neo-Destour leaders were jailed between 1934 and 1936, but the structure sustained the party and enabled its leaders to resume their work immediately upon their release. Neo-Destour demonstrations in April 1938 led to the reimprisonment of party leaders and the disbanding of the organization.

At the outbreak of World War II, some Neo-Destour members advocated collaboration with the Axis (against the French), but from his prison cell Bourguiba denounced this tactic and urged Tunisian loyalty to France in its confrontation with fascism. Freed in 1943, Bourguiba set about strengthening Neo-Destour. By helping to organize the Union Générale des Travailleurs Tunisiens (General Union of Tunisian Workers), the party affirmed its already strong links with the workers' movement and assured itself of influence in an important interest group through which it could mobilize public opinion. When the war ended, Bourguiba left Tunisia to solicit support for Neo-Destour in the Middle East, Europe, and North America, while at home party Secretary-General Salah BEN YUSUF continued to stress the demand for complete and immediate independence.

Bourguiba returned in 1949 and resumed control of the party. In contrast with the less patient Ben Yusuf, he counseled a policy of negotiation and gradualism that became the Neo-Destour's approach to resolving conflicting French and Tunisian views on the country's future. In 1951, France recognized the party and prominent members served in Tunisian governments that searched, in vain, for an acceptable formula of cosovereignty. When the frustrated Neo-Destour tried to bring its grievances before the United Nations in 1952, the French authorities again arrested party leaders, triggering riots. After an abortive effort to find credible interlocutors among Tunisians not affiliated with Neo-Destour, the French government finally entered talks with Bourguiba that produced an accord granting internal autonomy in 1955. Party radicals, led by Ben Yusuf, denounced Bourguiba's willingness to compromise in these negotiations. The Neo-Destour Congress of October 1955 saw a bitter struggle between the two factions that ended in a victory for Bourguiba and the expulsion of Ben Yusuf.

Tunisia attained full independence in March 1956, and in the ensuing constituent assembly elections, the party won a comfortable victory. The pyramidal structure established during the colonial era remained in place, with regional coordinating committees supervising the activities of local cells. At periodic party congresses, delegates chose a central committee to formulate policy. This committee also selected the party's executive board, or political bureau, from among its members. The party apparatus included a secretary-general and a director to manage daily affairs, but real power lay with Bourguiba, who was its president. Bourguiba's personal popularity, his position as head of government (and head of state after the deposition of al-Amin Bey on July 25, 1957), and his leadership of the only legal political party, the practice of filling government jobs with Neo-Destour stalwarts, and the close conjunction between the party's organizational structure and the subdivisions of the new republic all contributed to blurring the distinctions between state and party.

With independence attained, the party's goals shifted to modernization through social change and economic development. The configuration of the Neo-Destour and the presence of a cadre of committed militants facilitated the dissemination of new ideas and the mobilization of mass support. The party also made good use of such auxiliary organizations as the Union Nationale des Femmes Tunisiennes (National Union of Tunisian Women) and the Union Générale des Etudiants Tunisiens (General Union of Tunisian Students) to promote its policies within special interest groups.

After several years of pursuing laissez-faire policies that had left the economy stagnant, the party inaugurated a new economic tack with the 1961 appointment of one of its most promising young leaders, Ahmed BEN SALAH, as minister of planning. Charged with designing a strategy to foster self-sufficiency and raise living standards, Ben Salah crafted a ten-year plan predicated on intensive government participation in the economy. Throughout the decade other socialist development schemes followed. In 1964, to underscore its dedication to this new philosophy, the party officially changed its name to the Parti Socialiste Destourien (PSD), the Destour Socialist party.

Following Ben Salah's downfall in 1969, prominent PSD leaders expressed dismay over the extensive powers Bourguiba had accorded him. Anxious to prevent a recurrence, they tried to reform party mechanisms to restrict the president's prerogatives. The adamant opposition of Bourguiba and his allies created disaffection, particularly among younger PSD members. After a period of relative political inactivity owing to ill health, during which the reformers achieved some gains, Bourguiba reasserted his control over the party's apparatus at its 1974 congress. He secured appointment as party president for life and assumed personal responsibility for appointing the political bureau, after which his critics were purged from the party. Several opposition parties crystallized at this time; nevertheless, the PSD remained the only legally recognized party in the country until 1981.

During these political controversies, the party steered a more liberal economic course encouraging private enterprise, although it did not abandon its advocacy of state control over crucial sectors of the economy. In social matters, it espoused progressive ideals, but was unable to implement them consistently. Large numbers of working-class Tunisians concluded that the party had lost interest in their problems, spawning serious social unrest, but also making it difficult to attract new party recruits, especially among the young. In an extremely youthful population, the aura and prestige attached to the PSD—as the party of those who had fought for and achieved independence—came to mean very little. The legalization of other parties theoretically ended the PSD's monopoly, but for as long as Bourguiba dominated the political scene, the opposition showed little enthusiasm for contesting elections whose impartiality was in doubt. By the mid-1980s, calls to create an Islamic society in Tunisia constituted another, and potentially more serious, challenge to the PSD.

After Bourguiba's removal as head of state in November 1987, the close ties between the government and the Destour Socialist party continued. His successor, Zayn al-Abidine BEN ALI, had served as secretary-general of the PSD since 1987, while the new prime minister, Hadi Bakkush, had been the party's director since 1984.

In February 1988, the name of the party was officially changed to the Rassemblement Constitutionnel Démocratique (RCD), the Democratic Constitutional Rally. Ben Ali explained that the renaming reflected the party's recognition of the need to broaden its appeal by democratizing its structures, but the RCD has exhibited very little willingness to embark on a course of political pluralism.

BIBLIOGRAPHY

JULIEN, CHARLES-ANDRÉ. L'Afrique du nord en marche: Nationalismes musulmans et souveraineté française. Paris, 1972.
LE TOURNEAU, ROGER. Evolution politique de l'Afrique du nord musulmane, 1920–1961. Paris, 1962.
MOORE, CLEMENT HENRY. Tunisia since Independence: The Dynamics of One-Party Government. Berkeley, Calif., 1965.
PERKINS, KENNETH J. Tunisia: Crossroads of the Islamic and European Worlds. Boulder, Colo., 1986.

Kenneth J. Perkins

Devrim, Izzet Melih　[1887–1966]

Turkish novelist.

Born in Jerusalem, the son of an Ottoman administrator, Devrim graduated from the prestigious Galatasaray School in Istanbul and worked at various commercial jobs. His first literary effort was a volume of prose poetry, entitled *Çocuklara Mahsus Gazete* (The Childrens' Newspaper), published in 1898, but he did not receive public recognition until 1905 when he was the runner-up in a competition sponsored by a French literary journal. Many of his subsequent works were published in French, and in 1938, he was awarded a doctorate from the Faculty of Letters in Paris. Among Devrim's principal works are *Leyla* (1912), *Sermed* (1918), and *Hüzün ve Tebessüm* (Sadness and a Smile, 1922).

BIBLIOGRAPHY

ÖZKIRIMLI, ATILLA. Türk Edebiyatí Ansiklopedisi, vol. 2. Istanbul, 1982.

David Waldner

Dewey, John　[1859–1952]

American philosopher and educator.

Dewey developed a philosophy of education that rejected the rigid formalism of American schools and called for "learning by doing." He saw the school as society in microcosm, wherein the child could be instilled with the basic values of society. After retiring from Columbia University in 1930, Dewey worked with the government of Turkey to establish a reformed Turkish education system that would embrace his conception of the school as inculcating the root values of society, in the Turkish case the secular-nationalist ethic developed by the president, Mustafa Kemal Atatürk. Dewey was a major influence on Muhammad Fadhil al-JAMALI in Iraq.

BIBLIOGRAPHY

EDWARDS, PAUL, ed. The Encyclopedia of Philosophy. New York, 1967.
SHAW, STANFORD, and EZEL KURAL SHAW. History of the Ottoman Empire and Modern Turkey. New York, 1977.

Zachary Karabell

Dey

Ottoman Turkish word (literally, maternal uncle) and rank of appointment.

Although initially the term *dey* was military in nature, by force of circumstances in some provincial areas of the Ottoman Empire it came to encompass executive control. The most specific historical examples of this occurred in the Maghrib (North Africa), from the late seventeenth through the early nineteenth centuries.

In Tunisia, the military-support functions of an original body of several dozen deys were overthrown in the seventeenth century by a line of individual deylical usurpers. They were, in turn, overthrown in 1710 by what became a quasi-autonomous dynasty of BEYS, who, although non-Tunisian in origin, based their ruling power throughout the province on alliances with indigenous tribal groups.

In Algeria, fractionalization of Ottoman authority created another pattern, where the transformed post of dey of Algiers remained in Algiers throughout the Ottoman period, supported by a symbolic retinue of subordinates of Turkish descent. Power in the Algerian hinterland, however, was in the hands of several beys, whose tribal supporters never really came under the control of the deys of Algiers.

Until their expulsion by French invasion, in 1830, the deys exercised symbolic sovereign Ottoman authority over those portions of land (mainly in Algiers province only) that could be clearly claimed as part of the *dar al-sultan* (the house or "realm" of the sultan). They also collected a certain number of taxes in the sultan's name and commanded a limited number of military garrisons, representing the by-then dispersed ranks of the former imperial JANISSARIES (military force abolished in 1826).

BIBLIOGRAPHY

ABUN-NASR, JAMIL M. *A History of the Maghrib in the Islamic Period.* Cambridge, Mass., 1987.
CHERIF, MOHAMMED HEDI. *Pouvoir et société dans la Tunisie de Husayn ibn 'Ali,* 2 vols. Tunis, 1984.
JULIEN, CHARLES-ANDRÉ. *Histoire de L'Algérie contemporaine.* Paris, 1964.

Byron Cannon

Dhahran

The site of Saudi Arabia's first oil strike in 1935, not far from the Gulf coast.

The resultant settlement became the headquarters of the Arabian American Oil Company (ARAMCO) as well as the location of the King Fahd University for Petroleum and Minerals and a major Saudi air base.

John E. Peterson

Dhimmi

A "pact" (dhimma) that designated "People of the Book" under Islamic rule as protected minorities, or dhimmis.

The agreement, attributed to the "Pact of Umar" came to mean that in exchange for paying a poll tax (*jizya*) and behaving as a subject population in relation to the dominant ruler, the designated minorities—which included Jews, Christians, and Zoroastrians—would have their lives and property safeguarded and be able to practice their religions freely. Sartorial distinctions and codes of behavior were introduced to stipulate the dominant/subordinate relationship between Muslim rulers and minority subjects. For the minorities these included wearing a certain color dress, prohibiting construction of new houses of worship, holding public religious processions, riding horses, or carrying arms. Enforcement of these discriminatory restrictions was harsh or lax according to the vagaries of circumstances and the security of the regime in power. During the reform era of the Tanzimat in the Ottoman Empire, minorities were granted citizenship in 1856 and the poll tax was dropped. Minorities were then subject to military conscription or the payment of the *bedel-e-askari*, which exempted them from military service.

BIBLIOGRAPHY

BOSWORTH, C. E. "The Concept of *Dhimma* in Early Islam." In *Christians and Jews in the Ottoman Empire: The Functioning of a Plural Society,* ed. by Benjamin Braude and Bernard Lewis. New York, 1982.

Mia Bloom

Dhow

A term, probably of Swahili origin, referring to several types of sailing vessels (many now outfitted with motors) common to the Gulf Arab states.

Arabs refer to dhows by names specific to each type, determined principally by size and hull design. Four kinds of dhow account for most of these vessels. The *sambuk* (or *sambook*), perhaps the most widely represented, is a graceful craft with a tapered bow and a high, squared stern; it was often used for pearling, and today is used for fishing and commerce. A larger vessel, the *boom*, is still common in the Gulf. It ranges from 50 to 120 feet in length, 15 to 30 feet in width, and up to 400 tons displacement. Like early Arab ships it is double-ended (pointed at both ends) with a straight stem post. It is important in Gulf commerce. Now rare is another large ship, the *baggala*, formerly an important deep-sea vessel. Sometimes over 300 tons and with a crew of 150, it was built with a high, squared poop, reflecting the influence of sixteenth- and seventeenth-century Portuguese vessels. Like the sambuk and baggala, it has two masts. The *jalboot*, a single-masted vessel and much smaller (20–50 tons), formerly was widely used on the pearling banks of the Gulf. Its name and its features, notably an upright bow stem and transom stern, indicate its probable derivation from the Brit-

A dhow in Abu Dhabi. (Richard Bulliet)

ish jolly boat. Other smaller craft, all single masted, occasionally found in Gulf or adjacent waters include the *bedan, shu'i,* and *zarook.*

Dhows were well adapted to Gulf waters because of their shallow draft and maneuverability. Their lateen sails, long stems, and sharp bows equipped them well for running before the monsoon winds of the Indian Ocean, toward India in summer and toward Africa in winter. Wood for planking and masts was imported from the Malabar Coast of India or from East Africa. Traditionally no nails were used; cord made from coconut husks was used to lash together the planks of the decks and gunwales. By the eighth century Arab fleets of such ships were part of a commercial maritime network not matched or superseded until the European circumnavigation of the globe. In the latter part of the eighteenth century, the QAWASIM EMIRATE of the lower Gulf created a maritime empire that displaced earlier Omani dominance. Their power rested on the large fleets of dhows and the skill and ferocity of their crews. The attacks of these "pirates" on Anglo–Indian shipping brought Britain's naval intervention in the early nineteenth century and the eventual establishment of a trucial system under Britain's oversight. Until the 1930s hundreds of dhows made up the fleets that remained over the pearling banks from June to September. Today a considerable number of commercial cargoes are carried in motorized dhows between Dubai, especially as a transshipment point, and Iran. Some dhows are used for recreational purposes. Traditionally the Gulf's most important manufacturing industry was the construction and outfitting of dhows. In the early twentieth century there were some 2,000 dhows in Bahrain alone, and 130 were built there yearly. Small numbers continue to be built in Bahrain and elsewhere in the Gulf, still with the planks of the hull formed into a shell and the ribs then fitted to them.

BIBLIOGRAPHY

KAY, SHIRLEY. *Bahrain: Island Heritage.* United Arab Emirates, 1989.
VINE, PETER. *Pearls in Arabian Waters: The Heritage of Bahrain.* London, 1986.

Malcolm C. Peck

Dhufar

Southernmost part of the Sultanate of Oman.

Dhufar is distinct from the rest of Oman in several ways. Its coastal plain and rugged, mountainous interior receive monsoon winds. The resulting moist climate sustains coconuts and bananas, and beef cattle are raised. Much of the population of about 50,000 speaks a South Arabian language that predates, but is close to, Arabic. Dhufar, which possesses several oil fields, is the only part of Oman to be headed by a governor except for the strategic Musandam peninsula.

The Al Bu Sa'id dynasty first asserted its claim to Dhufar in the 1820s, though often its authority was confined to the provincial capital of Salala and its environs. The ruler in the mid-1990s, Sultan Qabus, had to put down an externally supported rebellion that began during the 1960s, the last decade of his father's rule. By 1976 Dhufar was militarily secure; the sultan has since devoted considerable resources to the economic and social development of the province.

BIBLIOGRAPHY

ALLEN, CALVIN H., JR. *Oman: The Modernization of the Sultanate.* Boulder, Colo., 1987.

Malcolm C. Peck

Dhufar Rebellion

Campaign against ruler of Dhufar (c. 1960–1975).

About 1960, rebel groups initiated a sporadic campaign of violent acts against the rule of Sultan Sa'id bin Taymur of Oman, whose neglect of social and economic development in the Dhufar region was especially pronounced. At first the uprising was primarily a tribal separatist movement, organized as the Dhufar Liberation Front in a part of Oman never meaningfully integrated with the rest of the sultanate. It received encouragement from Egypt and from Saudi Arabia, which had previously backed the Ibadi leader, Imam Ghalib, against the sultan.

The course of the rebellion changed dramatically in 1967 with the emergence of a Marxist state in neighboring South Yemen (People's Democratic Republic of Yemen; PDRY). By 1968 the tribal leaders had yielded to a radical leftist command. The uprising now had a secure PDRY base and a steady flow of money and weapons from the Soviet Union, the People's Republic of China, and other Communist states that also offered training to the rebels. The movement's goals were reflected in its name, POPULAR FRONT FOR THE LIBERATION OF THE OCCUPIED ARABIAN GULF (PFLOAG). Its anti-Islamic character and its attempt to impose a collectivist, socialist regime denied it a large popular base, but extensive external support and Sa'id's ineffective response enabled to control most of Dhufar. When another rebel movement, the NATIONAL DEMOCRATIC FRONT FOR THE LIBERATION OF OMAN AND THE ARAB GULF (NDFLOAG), emerged in northern Oman in 1970, disaffected Omanis, including the sultan's exiled uncle, conspired with military advisers from Britain and with Qabus ibn Sa'id AL BU SA'ID, the sultan's son, to depose Sa'id. Qabus, who came to power in July 1970, made defeating the Dhufar rebellion his first priority.

Support from Britain, especially in the form of seconded and contract military officers, was crucial, and Iran's supplies of material and manpower were important in countering a determined insurgency in mountainous terrain where, for half the year, monsoon weather severely reduced visibility. Also significant were Jordan's loan of military officers and large financial infusions from the United Arab Emirates, Kuwait, and Saudi Arabia, all of which feared the radical leftist threat.

In 1971 PFLOAG and NDFLOAG merged, becoming the Popular Front for the Liberation of Oman and the Arab Gulf. The insurgency, however, succumbed over the next four years to Qabus' combined military, political, and economic initiatives. The success of the government's counteroffensive was reflected in the rebel movement's assumption of the more modest title POPULAR FRONT FOR THE LIBERATION OF OMAN (PFLO) in 1974. By the end of the following year, only isolated pockets of resistance remained in the rugged interior, and the rebellion was essentially over.

Qabus continued to promote significant social and economic development in Dhufar following its pacification. Indeed, for some time the province received a disproportionate share of central government investment to promote its prosperity and its integration with the rest of the sultanate.

[See also: Ibadiyya]

BIBLIOGRAPHY

ALLEN, CALVIN H., JR. Oman: The Modernization of the Sultanate. Boulder, Colo., 1987.
PETERSON, J. E. The Arab Gulf States: Steps toward Political Participation. New York, 1988.

Malcolm C. Peck

Diaspora

Dispersion of the Jewish people.

The Greek word meaning "dispersion" (*diasperein*), diaspora has been applied since classical times to the Jewish settlement outside Palestine after the Babylonian exile. Diaspora also refers to Jews living outside Israel as well as to any group living far from its ancestral homeland.

Since the dispersion of the Jews from Palestine by the Roman suppression of the Jewish revolts of the first and second centuries, the Jewish communities of Europe have kept alive the idea of a return to the Holy Land. Historical memories of the reigns of David and Solomon intermingled with the centrality of Jerusalem in Jewish religious belief and ritual have created a sustained vision of the ultimate redemption of the Jewish people by ending the Diaspora and returning to the Holy Land. Political Zionism uses the concept of return.

BIBLIOGRAPHY

EISEN, ARNOLD M. Galut: Modern Jewish Reflection on Homelessness and Homecoming. Bloomington, Ind., 1986.

Mia Bloom

Dib, Mohammed

Algerian novelist and poet.

Dib was born into a middle-class family in Tlemcen. He was educated there and in Oujda. Before devoting his time to a literary career, Dib was a teacher and journalist. He was forced to leave Algeria in 1959 and subsequently settled in France. Dib's works chronicle Algeria's decolonization and postcolonial periods. A theme in his writings is the search for authentic self or identity. Dib's body of work underscores the common pursuit of human dignity. He earned his literary reputation as a result of a remarkable series of novels: *La grande maison* (1952); *L'incendie* (1954); *Le métier à tisser* (1957); *La danse du roi* (1968); *Dieu en Barbarie* (1970); *Le maître de chasse* (1973); and *Habel* (1979). His poetry collections include *Ombre gardienne* (1961); *Omneros* (1975); *Feu beau feu* (1979); and *O vive, Paris* (1987). Dib is distinguished as a leading member of the Generation of 1954, composed of Kateb YACINE, Moulaoud MAMMERI, Malek HADDAD, and Mouloud FERAOUN.

BIBLIOGRAPHY

DÉJEUX, JEAN. Dictionnaire des auteurs maghrébins de langue française. Paris, 1984.

Phillip C. Naylor

Dickson, Harold Richard Patrick
[1881–1959]

British official in the Persian Gulf.

Dickson was born in Beirut, where his father served in the Foreign Office. After graduating from Oxford, he joined the army. During World War I he was sent to the Gulf, serving first as a political officer for the government of India and, after retirement in 1936, as an adviser to the Kuwait Oil Company. He wrote *The Arab of the Desert* (1949) and *Kuwait and Her Neighbours* (1956).

Benjamin Braude

Didouche, Mourad   [1922–1955]

A historic chief of the Algerian revolution (1954–1962).

Mourad Didouche was born into a relatively prosperous family in Algiers. He was a member of Messali Hadj's PARTI DU PEUPLE ALGÉRIEN (PPA; Algerian People's Party) and MOUVEMENT POUR LE TRIOMPHE DES LIBERTÉS DÉMOCRATIQUES (MTLD; Movement for the Triumph of Democratic Liberties). He became a leader in the north Constantine region of the *Organisation Spéciale* (OS; Special Organization). After the OS's suppression, he fled Algeria and collaborated with Mohamed BOUDIAF in Paris. He was a prominent member of the Committee of 22 and the COMITÉ RÉVOLUTIONNAIRE D'UNITÉ ET D'ACTION (CRUA; Revolutionary Committee for Unity and Action), earning his inclusion among the nine historic chiefs (*chefs historiques*) of the Algerian revolution. Didouche also edited the Front de Libération Nationale's (FLN; National Liberation Front) Proclamation of November 1, 1954, inaugurating the war of liberation. He died in combat. After the war, the Algerian government renamed rue Michelet in downtown Algiers as Didouche Mourad.

BIBLIOGRAPHY

STORA, BENJAMIN. *Dictionnaire biographique de militants nationalistes algériens.* Paris, 1985.

Phillip C. Naylor

Dilmun

Prehistoric society of about 2000 B.C.E. that existed in the Persian/Arabian Gulf region, especially on the island of Bahrain.

The search for Dilmun was undertaken by Dr. Geoffrey Bibby and his 1953 Danish archeological expedition to Bahrain. His excavation of 100,000 burial mounds yielded dates and documents about Dilmun as a rich seafaring civilization. It extended from Ku-wait in the north to Oman at the south end of the Persian/Arabian Gulf. Bahrain is believed to have been the center of that civilization.

BIBLIOGRAPHY

BIBBY, GEOFFREY. *Looking for Dilmun.* London, 1970.

Emile A. Nakhleh

Dimona

An Israeli city.

Located some twenty miles (32 km) southeast of Beersheba in Israel's southern Negev Desert, near the Sinai peninsula, Dimona is neither particularly large nor strategically located. It is, however, immensely important to Israel because it is home to scientists stationed at the nearby nuclear reactor and to the workers for the Potash mines at Sodom on the Dead Sea.

The Dimona reactor was built with the aid of the French and, during the mid-1960s, it became a source of concern to both the Arabs and the United States, who feared that the reactor would be used to produce nuclear-weapons-grade plutonium. The Israelis gave assurances that the Dimona reactor was for peaceful use, but suspicions remained. In 1980, the International Atomic Energy Agency confirmed that the Dimona reactor was capable of producing weapons-grade ore. Though it has never been publicly acknowledged, it is likely that the Israelis have used the Dimona reactor to help develop nuclear weapons.

BIBLIOGRAPHY

BUNDY, McGEORGE. *Danger and Survival.* New York, 1988.
SAFRAN, NADAV. *Israel: The Embattled Ally.* Cambridge, Mass., 1981.
SPIEGEL, STEVEN. *The Other Arab–Israeli Conflict.* Chicago, 1985.

Zachary Karabell

Din al-Tawhid

See Druze

Dinar

The name of the gold unit of currency in early Islam.

Now a basic currency unit in some countries, a dinar is the equivalent of 1,000 fils. The word derives from the Greek (*dinarion*) and the Latin (*denarius*). Currently it is the currency of Algeria, Bahrain, Iraq, Jordan, Kuwait, Libya, Tunisia, and the former Yugoslavia.

Mia Bloom

Dinka

A people of Sudan.

The Dinka are a Nilotic people in the Republic of Sudan. Numbering over two million, they are the most numerous ethnic group inhabiting about a tenth of its one million square miles. The land of the Dinka is rich savanna broken by the Nile, its tributaries, and the Sudd, the great swamps of the Nile that flood the grasslands during the rainy season (May to October) and fall during the dry season (November to April). The Dinka are separated by these rivers and swamps into some twenty-five independent groups. In the past they were governed by lineages rather than any single authority.

Their physical characteristics, ethnic pride, and striking cultural uniformity bind the Dinka together as one people, despite their widespread geographical dispersion. They call themselves not Dinka but *Monyjang*, which means "the man, or the husband of men." They are convinced of their superiority to all others, whom they call "foreigners" (*juur*, sing., *jur*).

The Dinka are devoted to their cattle, which provide them with many of their worldly and spiritual needs, from dairy products (supplemented by fish and grain) to protection against illness or death. Cattle are the social cement for "bride wealth" (for marriage) and "blood wealth" (to resolve disputes). The Dinka are a proud people who, despite the ravages of civil war in Sudan, will nevertheless continue to survive.

Robert O. Collins

Dinshaway Incident

British atrocity committed in June 1906 against Egyptian peasants accused of assaulting British officers.

Some British officers were hunting pigeons near Dinshaway village in Minufiyya province. One officer died, most probably of sunstroke, but the villagers were accused of assaulting him. As the news spread, the British assumed that a national insurrection might occur, so they called for exemplary punishment of the villagers. The accused assailants were arrested and hastily tried by a special tribunal; some were sentenced to death, some to public flogging or imprisonment.

Their sentences led to widespread protests in Europe and in Egypt. The summary public execution of the convicted peasants caused the rise of Egypt's NATIONAL PARTY and the retirement of Britain's consul general, Lord Cromer. For Egyptians, it remains a black mark against Britain's rule.

BIBLIOGRAPHY

BLUNT, WILFRID S. *Atrocities of Justice under British Rule in Egypt.* London, 1907.
AL-MASADDI, MUHAMMAD JAMAL AL-DIN. *Dinshaway.* Cairo, 1974.
AL-SAYYID, AFAF LUTFI. *Egypt and Cromer.* London, 1968.

Arthur Goldschmidt, Jr.

Dinur, Ben-Zion   [1884–1973]

Israeli statesman, author, and educator.

Dinur was born in the Ukraine and in 1921 emigrated to Palestine where he became a history teacher in Jerusalem. In 1947 he was appointed professor at Hebrew University, where he developed, in accord with Zionism, an interpretation of Jewish history as a constant tension between the Diaspora and the desire of Jews to return to Israel. Between 1949 and 1955, he sat in the Knesset (parliament) as part of Prime Minister David Ben-Gurion's MAPAI labor party, and he served as Ben-Gurion's minister of culture.

BIBLIOGRAPHY

Encyclopedia Judaica. New York, 1971.
ROLEF, SUSAN HATTIS, ed. *Political Dictionary of the State of Israel.* New York, 1987.

Zachary Karabell

Dirham

A standard monetary unit.

The dirham was the silver unit of the Arab monetary system from the rise of Islam until the Mongol period. It is currently used in Morocco, the United Arab

Emirates, and Libya. The rate of dirhams to dinars fluctuated between 10 and 50 dirhams to the dinar.

Mia Bloom

Disease

See Cholera; Malaria; Medicine and Public Health; Trachoma

Disengagement Agreements

After the 1973 war, agreements between Israel and Egypt and Israel and Syria.

The agreements were signed after back and forth trips between the countries' capitals by U.S. Secretary of State Henry Kissinger, in what became known as shuttle diplomacy, following the 1973 ARAB–ISRAEL WAR.

Under the disengagement agreement with Egypt, which was signed on January 18, 1974, Israel withdrew from Egyptian territory west of the Suez Canal, ended the siege of the Egyptian Third Army, and accepted the October 1973 cease-fire line in Sinai. A six-mile (10-km) buffer zone was set up under UN supervision, and the parties reduced forces and equipment along the borders of this zone.

Under the disengagement agreement with Syria, concluded on May 31, 1974, Israel withdrew from the town of Kuneitra and a nearby area that had been occupied since the 1967 Arab–Israel War, as well as from some other Syrian areas seized in October 1973. There too, a buffer zone with limitations on forces and equipment was set up and manned by UN forces.

BIBLIOGRAPHY

ROLEF, S. H., ed. *Political Dictionary of the State of Israel.* New York, 1987.

Benjamin Joseph

Dishdasha

A traditional loose-fitting, ankle-length robe with long sleeves worn by both men and women.

The woman's garment, sometimes called a kaftan, is usually embellished with embroidery, appliqué, or other decoration, and can be made of plain or colorful material. The man's garment, usually plain, may be embellished with same-colored braid. All

Omani children at play. The boy is wearing a dishdasha. (Sandra Batmangelich and the University of Chicago)

dishdashas are designed to provide total coverage and comfort.

Jenab Tutunji

Disraeli, Benjamin   [1804–1881]

English politician and author; British prime minister 1868; 1874–1880.

Disraeli (first earl of Beaconsfield) was born into a Jewish family, but he was baptized as an Anglican Christian at the age of thirteen. Inasmuch as Jews were denied full civil rights in Britain before 1858, his conversion, imposed on him by his father, Isaac, made a political career possible. In 1831, Disraeli made his only visit to the Middle East, touring Greece, the Aegean, Turkey, Palestine, and Egypt. During a long career as a novelist, 1825–1870, he frequently made romanticized reference to the region.

In his second term as Britain's prime minister (1874–1880), he revealed an interest in the Middle East that chiefly centered on excluding the Russians from bases in the Mediterranean and on gaining control for Britain of the Suez Canal and the island of Cyprus. At the Congress of Berlin (1878), he obtained a ninety-nine-year lease over Cyprus, in exchange for a pledge to guarantee Ottoman claims to their realm in Asia for that same period.

BIBLIOGRAPHY

MONYPENNY, WILLIAM FLAVELLE, and GEORGE EARLE BUCKLE. *The Life of Benjamin Disraeli, Earl of Beaconsfield,* 6 vols. New York, 1913–1920.

Arnold Blumberg

Divan-ı Humayun

See Ottoman Empire, Imperial Council

Divan Poetry

See Literature, Turkish

Diwan

Pronounced "divan" in Persian and Turkish; a term that has been used in a variety of senses.

The term *Diwan* has been used to mean all of the following:

- A collection of poetry or prose written by one author.
- A register of census, from the Arabic *awwana,* to collect. The first diwan was the "diwan al-jund," the register that covered the people of Medina, Medina's military forces, émigrés and their families during the time of Muhammad.
- Ministries from the Umayyad period onward in the Arab world and in India and Iran. Three basic diwans corresponded to the three essential needs of the state: chancellery and state secretariat (*diwan al-rasa'il*), finance (*diwan al-amal*), and the army (*diwan al-jaysh*).
- The imperial privy council of the Ottoman Empire.
- Place of meeting, understood as a separate apartment or sitting room
- A council chamber or a smoking room.
- A large couch or sofa without a back or arms, often used as a bed.

BIBLIOGRAPHY

CLEVELAND, WILLIAM L. *A History of the Modern Middle East.* Austin, Tex., 1993.

Mia Bloom

Diyarbekır

City and province in southeastern Turkey.

Known in former times as Amida and Kara-Amid, the city of Diyarbekır is now the capital of Diyarbekır province, populated mostly by KURDS. Located on the Tigris river, the city has grown rapidly since World War II, from a 1950 population of 45,495 to 235,617 people in 1980. It is an agricultural market center known also for its cotton textiles, leather products, and trade in grain, mohair, and wool. Linked to western Turkey by railroad, the city is also the site of an air base.

Diyarbekır province is bounded on the north by the Bitlis mountains and on the west by the Euphrates river. The region became a Roman colony in 230 C.E.; it was captured by the Persians in 363 C.E., and the city's distinctive black basalt fortification walls date from the fourth century. The city has long been known for its goldsmithing and silversmithing. In the Ottoman Empire it had strong economic links with cities now in Iraq and Iran.

BIBLIOGRAPHY

Chambers World Gazetteer. New York, 1988.

Elizabeth Thompson

Diyojen

Nineteenth-century Ottoman Turkish humor magazine.

First published on November 24, 1870, *Diyojen* was the first humor magazine in the Ottoman Empire. Owned by Teodor KASAP, it featured EBÜZZIYA TEVFIK, NAMIK KEMAL, and Ali Bey among its regular writers. Most of the articles were unsigned and written in simple, direct prose. Originally a weekly, *Diyojen* began to be published twice a week with issue 23 and three times a week with issue 148. The final issue, number 183, appeared on December 10, 1873.

BIBLIOGRAPHY

ÖZKIRIMLI, ATILLA. *Türk Edebiyatı Ansiklopedisi,* vol. 2. Istanbul, 1982, pp. 393–394.

David Waldner

Djaout, Taher [1954–1993]

Algerian poet, novelist, and journalist.

Djaout was born on January 11, 1954, in Azzefoun, Great Kabylia. After he studied political science and journalism, he worked at the weekly *Algérie-actualité* until his assassination in 1993.

Djaout, who wrote in French, was deeply anchored in his country's history. Algeria is always in the background of his writings, whether they evoke the growing pains of a poor boy during the colonial period in *Les Rets de L'Oiseleur* (1983; The Hunter's Net), or tackle the more complex situations of the postindependence years. Many of these themes are central to his first novel, *L'Exproprié* (1981; The Expropriated).

Djaout began his literary activity as a poet. His collection of poems, *Solstice barbelé* (1975; Thorny Solstice), revealed a solid poet who believed in creative freedom. He achieved fame, however, through his fiction, particularly *Les Chercheurs D'os* (1984; The Bones Seekers), which won the Duca Foundation Prize. Like other Algerian writers, in this work Djaout deplores the abuse of the martyrs' memory in postindependence Algeria. His next novel, *L'invention du Désert* (1987; Inventing the Desert), contracts history with present-day ordinary activities, particularly the problems of a journalist like himself. The novel raises questions dealing with the search for identity and the ordeal of exile.

It is in his last novel, *Les Vigiles* (1991; The Vigils), that Djaout steps into present-day Algeria, revealing the early signs of religious fervor as an escape and a solution to insurmountable daily problems on the administrative, political, and economic levels. There are also memories of the Algerian war of independence, which continue to haunt Algerian writers.

BIBLIOGRAPHY

ACHOUR, CHRISTINE. *Anthologie de la littérature algérienne de langue française*. Paris, 1990.
BONN, CHARLES. *Anthologie de la littérature algérienne*. Paris, 1990.
DÉJEUX, JEAN. *Dictionnaire des auteurs maghrébins de langue française*. Paris, 1984.
LIPPERT, ANNE. "Tahar Djaout." *CELFAN Review* 7, no. 3 (1989):1–5.

Aida A. Bamia

Djebar, Assia   [1936–   ]

Algerian writer and cinematographer.

Assia Djebar was born in Cherchell on the Mediterranean coast of Algeria. She was educated in Blida, Algiers, Paris, and Sèvres. During the war of independence, she participated in a hunger strike and later, when pursuing historical studies in Tunis, joined the staff of al-MOUDJAHID, newspaper of the FRONT DE LIBÉRATION NATIONALE (FLN; National Liberation Front). She taught at the University of Rabat and in 1962 joined the faculty at the University of Algiers. Her literary career began during the war with the publication of her first novel *La soif* (1957). Her other novels, some of which have been translated into English, are *Les impatients* (1958); *Les enfants du nouveau monde* (1962); *Les alouettes naïves* (1967); *L'amour la fantasia* (1985)/*Fantasia: An Algerian Cavalcade*; and *Ombre sultane* (1987)/*A Sister to Scheherazade*. A collection of short stories has also been translated (*Femmes d'Alger dans leur appartement* [1980]). Djebar's cinematographic production includes the acclaimed *La nouba des femmes du Mont Chenoua* (1979) and *La zerda et les chants de l'oubli* (1982). Her thematic interests generally relate to the social place and predicament of Algerian women.

BIBLIOGRAPHY

DÉJEUX, JEAN. *Dictionnaire des auteurs maghrébins de langue française*. Paris, 1984.
MORTIMER, MILDRED. *Journeys through the African Novel*. Portsmouth, N.H., 1990.

Phillip C. Naylor

Djema'a

Constituent assembly, usually regulating the village or clan but occasionally tribe or confederation; also the place where its members gather, usually daily.

The traditional form of governance in rural communities in North Africa, the djema'a consists of the heads of landholding families or lineages. Its head (AMGHAR in most Berber-speaking areas) is chosen, usually annually, on a rotating basis by the members. Decisions are made by consensus, typically after considerable consultation. Its responsibilities include maintaining roads and paths, water and irrigation systems, and the local mosque and its school; hiring the school's teacher; ensuring hospitality for visitors; organizing community support for families needing manpower (especially in plowing and harvesting); organizing community festivities; assigning communal land to families for cereal production; and setting times and rules for wood collection, grazing, and beginning the harvest. In the past, the djema'a had greater judicial functions: in accordance with the local QANUN—essentially a list of fines and punishments for a wide variety of misdeeds—it regulated community life and ensured equal justice, responsibility, and benefit.

[*See also:* Tiwizi]

Thomas G. Penchoen

Djerba

An island off the southeast coast of Tunisia, near the Libyan border.

The island of 198 square miles (514 sq km) is shaped like a molar tooth, connected to the mainland of TUNISIA on the southeast by a ferry at Adjim and on the southwest by a bridge that dates from the Roman Empire. Between Djerba and the mainland is the shallow inland sea of Bou Grara. The island's elevation is low—barely 188 feet (54 m) above sea level at its highest point—and is surrounded by shallow beaches of fine sand and palm trees, especially in the northeast. The principal population center is Houmt-Souk, a market and fishing port on the north coast. Since Tunisian independence in 1956, dozens of tourist hotels and an airport have been built on Djerba.

Djerba is reputed to be the island of the lotus eaters in Homer's *Odyssey*. Djerba's early history is one of contact with many peoples—Berbers, Carthaginians, Greeks, Romans, Vandals, Byzantines, and others. Companions of the Prophet Muhammad brought the ARABIC language and religion of ISLAM to Djerba in 665 C.E. BERBER Kharijites, considered heretics by many orthodox Muslims, took refuge in southern Djerba after the Almohads expelled them from western Algeria. Since then the southern part of the island has tended to be Berber and Kharijite, the northeast Arab and Malekite, and the center mixed in population.

During the Middle Ages, Djerba was the scene of continuous persecutions, conquests, revolts, reconquests, civil wars, and plagues. Spaniards, Sicilians, Hafsids, Corsairs, and Ottoman Turks controlled the island at various times. In the eighteenth century, Tunis eventually won the contest with Tripoli for jurisdiction under the OTTOMAN EMPIRE over Djerba.

Open air market in Djerba. (Mia Bloom)

Interior of a synagogue in Djerba, dating from the sixth century B.C.E. (Mia Bloom)

During the French protectorate, Djerba was under military administration from 1881 to 1890, then French civil administration until independence in 1956. The island is today part of the Tunisian Governorship of Medenine, and its population is a mix of Arab and Berber, plus elements of black African, Turkish, and Maltese origin.

The center and southeast of Djerba and portions of the nearby mainland are among the rare areas of Tunisia where a Berber language is spoken, although it is highly mixed with Arabic vocabulary. According to Arab historian Ibn Khaldun (1332–1406) "Djerba" originally referred to a branch of the Lemata Berbers.

Djerba is home to one of the few remaining Jewish communities in North Africa, the towns of Hara Sghira and Hara Kebira. According to local tradition, the Jewish community of Djerba dates from after the Babylonian captivity in 586 B.C.E.; others claim that Judeo-Berbers migrated to the island in the late eighth century C.E., following the Arab conquest of North Africa. The town of Hara Sghira is the site of the Ghriba—a Jewish synagogue, shrine, and site of a popular annual pilgrimage.

Djerba has low and irregular rainfall—averaging eight inches (21 cm) per year—and high humidity. The only freshwater sources on the island are a few wells in the northeast and rainwater captured by cisterns. This limits local agriculture to date palms of mediocre quality, olive trees, fruit trees, and some grains and legumes.

In the twentieth century, the pressures of increasing population on this ecologically marginal island have gradually forced people out of the traditional occupations of agriculture, fishing, weaving, and pottery-marking. As the island's population increased from 31,800 in 1906 to 62,445 in 1956 to more than

82,000 in 1991, Djerbians began to rotate between the island and the mainland as shopkeepers. In reaction to anticommercial policies of the Ben Salah government of the 1960s, Djerbians increasingly turned to international migration, and many of them have become successful shopkeepers and businessmen in the Paris area.

BIBLIOGRAPHY

MZABI, HASSOUNA. *La croissance urbaine accélérée à Jerba et ses conséquences sur la vie des relations avec l'extérieur: Etude géographique*. Tunis, 1978.
TLATLI, SALAH-EDDINE. *Djerba: L'île des lotophages*. Tunis, 1967.

Laurence Michalak

Dlimi, Ahmed   [1931–1983]

Moroccan military officer.

Ahmed Dlimi achieved dubious prominence during the BEN BARKA affair of 1965/66, when he was acquitted in a Paris trial. By the mid-1970s, he was King Hassan II's closest military adviser; as a colonel, he was given command of the military seizure of the contested former Spanish colony of Western Sahara in 1974/75. Promoted to general and given full control over theater operations, from 1979 to 1980 Dlimi oversaw the building of the "wall" in Western Sahara—a fortified sand barrier stretching across nearly 25 percent of the northern border. In early 1983, with relations souring between the military and the throne, Dlimi died in a mysterious auto accident.

BIBLIOGRAPHY

HODGES, TONY. *Western Sahara: Roots of a Desert War*. London, 1983.
Who's Who in the Arab World, 1990–1991.

Matthew S. Gordon

Do'ar Ha-Yom

Hebrew newspaper, 1919–1936.

In 1919, Ittamar Ben-Avi founded the Hebrew newspaper *Do'ar Ha-Yom* (Daily Mail). Published in Jerusalem, it was geared to the older Jewish settlers in Palestine as well as to Jews born there. *Do'ar Ha-Yom* opposed Zionism, and it ceased publication in 1936. It has been called the first modern Hebrew newspaper.

BIBLIOGRAPHY

Encyclopedia Judaica. New York, 1971.

Zachary Karabell

Dobbs, Henry   [1871–1934]

British diplomat.

Dobbs entered the Indian civil service and was a political officer in Iraq during World War I. In 1923, he succeeded Sir Percy COX as high commissioner to Iraq, remaining until January 1929. During his tenure, the question of MOSUL's inclusion in Iraq was finally settled with the League of Nations approving the inclusion, as Iraq gradually moved toward independence.

BIBLIOGRAPHY

Dictionary of National Biography, 1931–40. New York, 1949.
SLUGLETT, PETER. *Britain in Iraq, 1914–1932*. London, 1976.

Zachary Karabell

Doha

Capital and largest city of Qatar.

Situated at about the midpoint of the east coast of the Qatari Peninsula, Doha is the country's chief port and principal business center. The name reflects its location on a "branch" or inlet of the Persian/Arabian Gulf. (Earlier the town was also called al-Bida.) In the eighteenth century Doha was a tiny fishing village, but by the late nineteenth century it had become a substantial town of about 12,000. It was a major center for the pearling trade, with a fleet of 300 pearling dhows in 1939, just before the collapse of that industry. With the rapid accumulation of wealth that followed discovery of oil in the 1940s, Doha rapidly grew into a major city. Doha and its suburbs contain two-thirds of Qatar's 422,000 people (official 1989 estimate). The plan of the modern city generally reflects that of Kuwait City, with concentric ring roadways marking its growth.

BIBLIOGRAPHY

GRAZ, LIESL. *The Turbulent Gulf: People, Politics and Power*. London and New York, 1992.
ZAHLAN, ROSEMARIE SAID. *The Creation of Qatar*. London, 1979.

Malcolm C. Peck

Dolma

Stuffed vegetables.

Dolma are rice, meat, herb, and spice-stuffed vegetables found especially in Turkish cuisine but common to many Middle Eastern cuisines. The most popular vegetables for stuffing are zucchini, eggplant, peppers, tomatoes, and grape leaves.

Clifford A. Wright

Dolmabahçe Palace

Ottoman sultan's palace.

Built in 1853 by Sultan ABDÜLMECIT I, Dolmabahçe is located on the banks of the Bosporus in Beşiktaş, north of the centuries-old sultanic residence TOPKAPI. The new palace, built in a mixture of European styles, replaced an older one on the site, where Sultan Mahmud II had moved in 1815. While it was used for official functions through most of the nineteenth century, Dolmabahçe was the sultan's official residence for only a few years, as Abdülmecit soon moved to Çağiran Palace and Abdülaziz moved to a newer palace on the hill above it at Yildiz. Mustafa Kemal Atatürk died at Dolmabahçe on 8 November 1938.

BIBLIOGRAPHY

MANTRAN, ROBERT, ed. *Histoire de l'empire Ottoman.* Paris, 1989.
SHAW, STANFORD J., and EZEL KURAL SHAW. *History of the Ottoman Empire and Modern Turkey*, vol. 2. Cambridge, U.K., 1977.

Elizabeth Thompson

Dome of the Rock

See Temple Mount and Haram al-Sharif

Donanma

Ottoman Turkish magazine.

A publication of the Naval Association (Donanma Cemiyeti), *Donanma* first appeared in March 1910. The initial forty-nine issues were monthly; after this, the magazine appeared weekly until the last issue in Kasım, 1917. Although *Donanma*'s raison d'être was to cover naval issues and advocate the strengthening of the Ottoman navy, it also had a marked literary bent and added calls to modernize the Ottoman economy.

BIBLIOGRAPHY

Tanzimat'tan Cumhuriyet'e Türkiye Ansiklopedesi, vol. 1. Istanbul, 1984, pp. 124–125.

David Waldner

Dönme

A group in Turkey descended from followers of the mystical messiah Shabbetai Tzevi (1626–1676) who converted from Judaism to Islam.

Like many of his Jewish contemporaries, Shabbetai Tzevi was steeped in Lurianic cabala, whose doctrine of restoration of the universe, which called for simultaneous Jewish and universal redemption, is thought to have paved the way for his messianic claim. In addition the apocalyptic events of the early modern era (expulsions, persecutions, the rise and fall of empires) fired many Jews and Gentiles with the hope that they were witnessing the early stages of the Messiah's arrival. Shabbetai Tzevi's lieutenant, Nathan of Gaza, possessed profound ascetic beliefs, steadfast conviction, and great intellectual power to reinterpret well-known cabalistic texts to suit the needs of the moment. He brought Shabbetai Tzevi a following greater than any other Jewish messianic movement since Christianity.

In 1665, after Nathan's formal proclamation of Shabbetai Tzevi's messiahship, the emotional floodgates of centuries-old aspirations opened. Most of Ottoman Jewry and many other Jews believed in him. Two contradictory but equally profound trends then developed—one was an ascetic penitential movement of prayer, fasting, and self-mortification; the other involved the abrogation of Jewish law, sexual licentiousness, and the introduction of new rites that turned the old upside down. In 1666 Shabbetai Tzevi went to Constantinople to overthrow the sultan and inaugurate the first year of his kingdom. He was arrested. To avoid execution, he became a Muslim and took the name Mehmed Aziz Efendi. At this point most of his followers abandoned him, but a sizable minority did not. They were assuaged by a new theory that Nathan proclaimed: the exile of the messiah. Shabbetai Tzevi must assume the guise of a Muslim and banish himself among the nations in order to gather and liberate the sparks of holiness that had been scattered and lost outside of Israel, according to a widely accepted cabalistic notion, during the Creation. For the true believers the dilemma was which outward guise their own belief would now assume. Their inward, esoteric Sabbatean core would remain, but outwardly would they be pious Jews or good Muslims? Shabbetai Tzevi's own instructions were inconsistent. Nathan and most of the believers remained, at least outwardly, Jews, but a few converted.

During the ten last years of Shabbetai/Mehmed's life, the number of convert families was only about 200, but they included learned cabalists and rabbis whose descendants were to form the elite of Dönme ("converted to Islam") society and who continued to be respected by the more numerous Sabbatean Jews. This larger support system of secret allies within the Jewish community enabled the Dönme to survive and grow over the following centuries. They also benefited from ties with an important Sufi order, the BEKTASHIS, who promoted doctrines, notably *takiye* (religious dissimulation), that provided an Islamic rationale for the contradictions of Dönme beliefs.

After Shabbetai's death, the original converts flocked to the major Jewish center in the Ottoman Empire SALONIKA. Subsequently Jacob Querido, Shabbetai's brother-in-law, became the driving force behind a mass conversion of another 200 to 300 families who formed a second subsect, the Yakubi—the original sect was now called İzmirli. A few decades later a third group (the Karakaş) arose around Baruchiah Russo/Osman Baba, who was proclaimed the reincarnation of Shabbetai Tzevi and later the divine incarnation itself. Osman Baba's grave near the Bektashi monastery in Salonika became their shrine.

The new Muslims kept to themselves. They did not marry outsiders. Generally they maintained their own neighborhood—located between the Jewish and Muslim quarters. Although apparently good Muslims, with the greatest of secrecy and in the privacy of their homes they conducted Sabbatean prayers, initially in Hebrew and later in Judeo-Spanish, which remained their vernacular until late in the nineteenth century, when they adopted Turkish.

In the course of the eighteenth and nineteenth centuries the Dönme became a significant element in Salonika. They may have accounted for as much as half of its Muslim population. They were well represented in government administration, as well as in the professional classes and in more modest occupations. They were very active in textile manufacturing in the early Turkish Republic.

During the twilight of the Ottoman Empire, Salonika was the birthplace of the COMMITTEE OF UNION AND PROGRESS (CUP) and of Mustafa Kemal (ATATÜRK). The Dönme influenced both. Cavit Bey, a direct descendant of Baruchiah Russo/Osman Baba and a leader of his subsect, was an important minister in the CUP government. Atatürk had studied in a progressive school founded by a Dönme educator. Although the claim that Atatürk was a Dönme is untrue, their complex and sophisticated values shaped the environment of his youth. However, this tie did not keep Atatürk from executing Cavit along with other members of the CUP in 1926.

Two years earlier the death knell of the Dönme community as a whole had sounded. In 1924, following the Greco-Turkish war, the entire Muslim population of Salonika—including the Dönme—was deported to Turkey. In 1925 all Sufi orders were abolished. Now that the Dönme had been uprooted and shorn of their support system, intermarriage and assimilation took their toll. In 1924 Ahmed Emin Yalman, a prominent journalist, publicly renounced all ties to the sect and called for its complete integration into Turkish national life. Although some are still identified as Salonikli (a discrete term for Dönme), there is no evidence that they maintain their distinctive beliefs and practices.

BIBLIOGRAPHY

GEORGEON, FRANÇOIS. "Selanik musulman et deunmè." In *Salonique, 1850–1918*, edited by Gilles Veinstein. 1992.
SCHOLEM, GERSHOM, *The Messianic Idea in Judaism*. New York, 1971.

Benjamin Braude

Dor De'a

Jewish educational reform movement.

The Dor De'a (Hebrew, Generation of Knowledge) was a Jewish enlightenment movement founded by Hayyim HABSHUSH (?–1899) and Rabbi Yihye ben Solomon QAFIH (1850–1932) in San'a, Yemen, in the late nineteenth century. The two men were inspired in part by their personal contacts with the European Jewish academic scholars, Joseph Halévy and later Edouard Glaser, who explored Yemen.

Dor De'a aimed at reforming Jewish education by purging it of Cabalistic elements (a mystical interpretation of Scriptures) and by introducing a small amount of modern secular subjects and vocational training. From 1910 to 1915, Rabbi Qafih operated a modern school that included the Turkish language as well as Hebrew and Arabic. He was encouraged by the ALLIANCE ISRAÉLITE UNIVERSELLE, whose support he had sought. The movement faced strong opposition from conservative elements led by Rabbi Isaac Yiyha (?–1932), supported by the iman of Yemen. The community remained split into opposing factions, which called each other derisively the *Darade'a* (a mocking Arabic plural derived from Dor De'a) and the *Iggeshim* (the crooked ones) until their mass emigration to Israel.

BIBLIOGRAPHY

AHRONI, REUBEN. *Yemenite Jewry: Origins, Culture, and Literature*. Bloomington, Ind., 1968.

Norman Stillman

Dost Mohammad Barakzai   [1792–1863]

Emir of Afghanistan, 1826–1838, 1842–1863.

Dost Mohammad, also called the Great Emir (Amir Kabir), was born in Kandahar in the Mohammadzai branch of the Durrani Pushtun subtribe. Considered the founder of the Mohammadzai dynasty that ruled Afghanistan until 1973, Dost Mohammad first became ruler of Afghanistan in 1826 after a period of civil war. After battling even his own brothers for control, he gradually united the country. He also attempted to regain Afghan territory lost to the Sikhs, who ruled Peshawar at that time. Having defeated the Sikhs at the Battle of Jumrud (1837), he assumed the title Amir al-Mu'minin (Commander of the Faithful).

In the 1830s, Dost Mohammad began to turn away from the British and to make overtures to Persia and Russia. As a result the British invaded Afghanistan (1839) in the first Anglo–Afghan war. Once they had defeated Dost Mohammad and taken him as a hostage to India (1840), the British placed Dost Mohammad's rival Shah Shuja on the throne. The occupation of Afghanistan soon turned into a disaster for the British, however, and they were forced to retreat from Kabul in the winter of 1842, losing almost all of their troops in the process. In 1842, Dost Mohammad returned to the throne and ruled for another twenty years. Three of his twenty-seven sons became rulers of Afghanistan, although only Sher Ali ruled for a prolonged period.

BIBLIOGRAPHY

ADAMEC, LUDWIG. *Historical Dictionary of Afghanistan*. Methuchen, N.J., 1991.

Grant Farr

Dou'aji, Ali al-   [1909–1949]

Tunisian short story writer, dramatist, and painter.

Al-Dou'aji, born in Tunis, worked for literary journals, contributing articles mainly to *Al-Alam al-Adabi*. He joined the group of bohemian writers known as Jama'at Taht al-Sur (Group under the Wall), which was active between the two world wars. Many of them indulged in drinking and drugs to escape the harsh realities of their lives.

Al-Dou'aji's short stories and essays deal with the problems of the poor and struggling classes. The pessimism of the subjects is tempered by the subtle humor of the writer. He often used dialect in the dialogue of his short stories for a more truthful portrayal of life. His collection of short stories *Sahirtu minhu al-Layali* (1969; Sleepless Nights) concerns Tunisia's society and its social ills. His sketches *Jawlatun bayna Hanat al-Bahr al-Abyad al-Mutawassit* (1973; A Tour around the Bars of the Mediterranean) reveal his humor, his powers of observation, and his capacity to portray human ridicule.

[*See also*: Literature, Arabic, North African]

BIBLIOGRAPHY

BACCAR, TAOUFIK, and SALAH GARMADI. *Ecrivains de Tunisie: Anthologie*. Paris, 1981.
FONTAINE, JEAN. *Vingt ans de littérature tunisienne, 1956–1975*. Tunis, 1977.

Aida A. Bamia

Douar

Algerian term for an administrative jurisdiction.

From the Arabic *da'r* (pl. *dur*), this term used in an Algerian context can refer to a group of tents, a village, or an administrative unit.

BIBLIOGRAPHY

JULIEN, CHARLES-ANDRÉ. *Histoire de l'Algérie contemporaine: La conquête et les débuts de la colonisation (1827–1871)*, 2nd ed. Paris, 1979.

Phillip C. Naylor

Doughty, Charles   [1843–1926]

English author and traveler in Arabia.

Born in Suffolk to an Anglican cleric, Doughty studied at Cambridge. His travels among the bedouins were motivated by a desire to examine ancient inscriptions and to explore the origins of humanity—and the earth itself—in what he considered its primitive setting. The result, *Travels in Arabia Desert* (Cambridge, 1888), did not gain popular success until after World War I.

BIBLIOGRAPHY

HOGARTH, DAVID GEORGE. *The Life of Charles M. Doughty*. New York, 1929.

Benjamin Braude

Dowlatabadi, Mahmoud   [1940–   ]

Iranian novelist.

Dowlatabadi, born in Dowlatabad, Khorasan, was a popular novelist of the 1980s. His 3,000-page saga *Klidar* recounts the lives of Kurdish villagers in Khorasan in the mid-1940s. Dowlatabadi uses vernacular in his narratives to show the individuality of each character and to depict their emotions. He has published collections of stories and novels, and a volume of interviews, *Ma Niz Mardom Hastim* (We Are Also People, 1991).

BIBLIOGRAPHY

MOAYYAD, HESHMAT, ed. *Stories from Iran: A Chicago Anthology, 1921–1991*. Washington, D.C., 1991.

Pardis Minuchehr

Doğru Yol Partisi

See True Path Party

Dragomans

Translators of Turkish, Persian, and Arabic into European languages.

When the Ottoman Empire began commercial dealings with the Europeans, translators were employed by European agents and diplomats in the capital, Istanbul. As no business could be conducted without these translators, they fulfilled a vital intermediary role in European–Ottoman relations, both political and commercial. Known as dragomans, these translators were usually Christians and often Greeks from the Phanar district of Istanbul. By the nineteenth century, they occupied a position of power and influence in Istanbul.

The Ottoman ministry for foreign affairs employed an official dragoman, and many European diplomats dealt with him or his deputies rather than directly with Ottoman administrators. Ottoman embassies in Europe also employed dragomans. After the Greek revolt in 1821, part of the Greek War of Independence, Muslims and Turks began to act as dragomans, and some became important figures during the TANZIMAT reform period of the mid-1800s. One of the many Tanzimat reforms was the creation of a bureau of translation in the Ottoman Ministry of Foreign Affairs, which centralized and incorporated the dragomans.

BIBLIOGRAPHY

LEWIS, BERNARD. *The Emergence of Modern Turkey*. New York, 1961.

SHAW, STANFORD, and EZEL KURAL SHAW. *History of the Ottoman Empire and Modern Turkey*. Cambridge, U.K., 1977.

Zachary Karabell

Dreyfus Affair

Famous turn-of-the-century case of French anti-Semitism overturned by liberal politics and publicity.

It began in 1894 with the court-martial and conviction of the only Jewish officer on the general staff of the French army, Captain Alfred Dreyfus, on manufactured charges of espionage for Germany. Dreyfus was sentenced to life on Devil's Island (off the coast of French Guiana, South America), but in 1896 new evidence emerged to implicate an aristocrat, Major Ferdinand Esterhazy. Based on the persistence of Madame Dreyfus and the liberal intelligentsia (including Emile Zola's newspaper article "J'accuse"—an open letter to the president of France), a new court-martial was ordered and in 1899 Dreyfus was brought back to France. He was tried at Rennes but convicted again—to ten years—but ten days later was pardoned and reinstated in the army. Not until 1906 was he exonerated after long enquiries; by then he had become a symbol of injustice overturned by liberal determination. French politics was tainted by the competing factions for decades, including those who, with long-standing anti-Semitism, became Nazi collaborators in World War II.

The virulent anti-Semitic nature of the case against Dreyfus, an assimilated Alsatian Jew, led Theodor HERZL to conclude that Jewish emancipation in Europe was impossible and that only a Jewish state might ensure protection for Jewish life. Thus, the case became a turning point in Herzl's own career—his authorship of *Der Judenstaat* (1896), his agitation on behalf of Zionism, and his founding of the first Zionist congress, on August 29, 1897, in Basel, Switzerland.

BIBLIOGRAPHY

CHAPMAN, GUY. *The Dreyfus Case*. London, 1955.

Jon Jucovy

Drobles Plan

Zionist plan to settle the West Bank.

Named for its 1978 author, Matityahu Drobles of the WORLD ZIONIST ORGANIZATION, the Drobles plan called for a chain of eighty Jewish settlements in the WEST BANK along the mountain ridge from Nablus to Hebron for up to 120,000 settlers. Its intent was to create a barrier for Israel against an Arab uprising or invasion from east of the Jordan river and to forestall the rise of a separate state of Palestine.

With support from Israel's Likud government, Israeli settlement in the West Bank (excluding Jerusalem) rose from 3,000 in 1977 to 25,000 in 1981 and nearly 120,000 in 1992.

BIBLIOGRAPHY

BENVENISTI, MERON. *The West Bank Handbook: A Political Lexicon.* Jerusalem, 1986.
HIRST, DAVID. *The Gun and the Olive Branch.* London, 1977, 1984.

Elizabeth Thompson

Drugs and Narcotics

Drugs have long played a prominent role in the affairs of the Middle East.

The Middle East is ideally suited to profit from all phases of the drug trade. Climate, geography, and, more recently, politics have combined to make the region an important source and transit point of drugs destined for Europe, the United States, and many of the countries of the Middle East itself. Traditionally, the most important drugs in the Middle East have been opium and marijuana, which provide the raw material for the heroin and hashish that form the staple of the illicit drug trade in the region. Both the opium poppy (*Papaver somniferum*) and marijuana (*Cannabis sativa*) grow easily in many parts of the Middle East and North Africa, and the centuries-old trade routes that crisscross the region give illicit drug producers ready access to the major international drug markets. Although the drug trade is driven largely by the profits inherent in any lucrative criminal activity, in the Middle East it has taken on an important political dimension as rival groups have used enormous drug revenues to pay for the arms necessary to pursue their political ambitions. With a metric ton of heroin worth between $100 million and $600 million, retail, on the streets of the United States, drug sales are an appealing source of immediate, vast revenues for clandestine or criminal activities.

The importance of the Middle East in the international drug trade has varied according to the demand for certain illicit drugs. The taste for drugs is cyclical, alternating between periods of demand for stimulants such as cocaine and amphetamines, and times when the drug-abusing public seeks depressants such as opiates (e.g., morphine, heroin, and other opium derivatives) and hashish. Because the Middle East primarily produces depressants, its importance as a drug source increases when opiates are in demand, as in the 1930s, 1970s, and 1990s.

Opiates. Because *Papaver somniferum* grows best at higher altitudes, Turkey, Afghanistan, Iran, and more recently Lebanon, have at different times been major sources of heroin and other opiates. In the late 1960s and early 1970s, Turkey gained international notoriety as the principal source of the heroin that fed an epidemic of drug abuse in the United States and Europe. In 1973, as part of an agreement with the United States, Turkey first banned, then allowed only very restricted, cultivation of opium poppies for medicinal purposes. This is still the only successful drug crop-control program of its kind, with virtually no leakage into illicit channels.

With Turkey effectively eliminated as a source in the mid-1970s, the center of illicit opiate production shifted eastward to Afghanistan, Lebanon, and, to a lesser extent, Iran. In both Afghanistan and Lebanon, the chaos created by civil war, coupled with the absence of a strong central government and rival combatants' desire for a source of revenue for arms purchases, led to an explosion of opium cultivation. By 1992, Afghanistan had become second only to Myanmar (Burma) in the production of illicit opium. The U.S. government estimated that at the end of 1992, Afghanistan had nearly 19,500 hectares (over 48,000 acres) of opium poppy under cultivation, capable of producing 640 metric tons of opium or 64 metric tons of heroin. This would be enough to satisfy estimated heroin needs in the United States six times over and to pump between $6.4 billion and $38.4 billion into the underworld economy. While a large percentage of these opiates is probably consumed by addicts in Afghanistan, Iran, and Pakistan, the remainder flows into the international drug trade through Iran for transshipment to heroin refineries in Turkey and Lebanon. There is also evidence that Afghan opium is flowing northward into new routes opened in central Asia following the collapse of the Soviet Union in 1991.

Although not an opium producer on the scale of Afghanistan, Lebanon is an important country in the international heroin trade. Following Syria's occupation of the Biqa' valley in 1976, eastern Lebanon became a center of opium cultivation and heroin refining. The Lebanese government has blamed the Syrian military for the Biqa' valley drug trade, which in 1991 had the capacity to produce an estimated 34 metric tons of opium (or 3.4 metric tons of heroin) from an estimated 3,400 hectares (nearly 8,400 acres). Subsequently, a combination of harsh weather and joint Syrian–Lebanese eradication efforts have reduced cultivation to an estimated 440 hectares (slightly less than 1,100 acres) in late 1993, though clandestine laboratories may be refining more than 5 metric tons a year of heroin from Afghan opium.

Despite Iranian government efforts to ban the opium poppy in 1980, Iran in 1992 was still an important potential source of opium. The United States Government estimated that 3,500 hectares (nearly 8,650 acres) of *Papaver somniferum* were under cultivation at the end of the year. There are indications, however, that Iran's addicts consume most domestic opium production. Iran continues to be a conduit for Afghan and Pakistani opiates moving to Turkey and onward along the Balkan Route into Europe.

Hashish. Although there is cannabis cultivation in nearly every country of the Middle East, only Morocco and Lebanon are significant hashish producers and exporters. Hashish is simple to manufacture, requiring little of the intensive labor and none of the chemicals needed to refine opiates. And while it does not generate profits on the same scale as opiates, hashish production is a multimillion dollar criminal enterprise. In 1992, Morocco's 30,000 hectares (nearly 74,000 acres) of cannabis potentially yielded nearly 9,000 metric tons of hashish, most of which was destined for Europe. Lebanon, with an estimated 15,700 hectares (nearly 38,800 acres) of cannabis under cultivation in 1993, potentially had 565 metric tons of hashish available for export. Cannabis may be sold and used legally in many countries so most governments accord cannabis control a relatively low priority. The hashish trade is likely to remain steady therefore, even as the governments of the Middle East intensify efforts to suppress illicit opiates and stimulants.

BIBLIOGRAPHY

EHRENFELD, RACHEL. *Narco-Terrorism.* New York, 1990.
U.S. CONGRESS. SENATE. COMMITTEE ON THE JUDICIARY. *Poppy Politics. Hearings before the Subcommittee to Investigate Juvenile Delinquency.* Washington, D.C., 1975.
U.S. DEPARTMENT OF JUSTICE. DRUG ENFORCEMENT ADMINISTRATION. *Illegal Drug Price/Purity Report: January 1989–December 1992.* Washington, D.C., 1993.
———. *Illicit Drug Trafficking and Use in the United States.* Washington, D.C., 1993.
———. *The NNICC Report 1992: The Supply of Illicit Drugs to the United States.* Washington, D.C., 1993.
U.S. DEPARTMENT OF STATE. *International Narcotics Control Strategy Report, April 1993.* Washington, D.C., 1993.

W. Kenneth Thompson

Drummond-Wolff Convention

Abortive pact (1885) between Britain and the Ottoman Empire.

Sir Henry Drummond-Wolff negotiated an agreement with Sultan ABDÜLHAMIT II at the behest of British Foreign Secretary Lord Robert Salisbury; the pact was to terminate Britain's occupation of Egypt after a three-year period. Because the agreement would have empowered Britain to reenter Egypt under certain conditions, the French and Russian ambassadors in Istanbul persuaded the sultan to withdraw his approval. Consequently, the British occupation of Egypt was greatly prolonged.

BIBLIOGRAPHY

HORNIK, F. P. "Mission of Sir Henry Drummond-Wolff to Constantinople 1885–1887." *English Historical Review* 55 (1940): 598–623.

Arthur Goldschmidt, Jr.

Druze

Religious sect founded in the eleventh century derived from Islam.

Originating in the highly politicized theological circles of the court of the Fatimid imam-caliph al-Hakim ibn Amr Allah in late tenth-century Cairo, the Druze faith reflected an extreme movement of ISMA'ILI SHI'ISM that sought to bring about the long anticipated rule of the MAHDI. The leaders of this power struggle identified al-Hakim as this longed-for deliverer and, in a revolutionary twist, viewed him as an embodiment of the godhead, thus placing him above the prophet Muhammad, who never claimed any status other than that of a divinely inspired prophet.

Druze farmer on the slopes of Majdal Shams in the Golan Heights. (Bryan McBurney)

Druze wearing traditional garb in Lebanon, 1954. (D.W. Lockhard)

The chief advocate of al-Hakim's divinity was Hamza ibn Ali ibn Ahmad al-Zawzani, an Iranian Isma'ili theologian who came to Cairo in 1016 and quickly established himself as the leader among those who regarded al-Hakim as the promised redeemer. Perhaps in collusion with Hamza, the imam-caliph in 1017 issued a proclamation confirming himself to be indeed the final manifestation of the deity that his disciples had claimed him to be. With this powerful backing, Hamza pursued *da'wa* (divine call) of the Druze faith throughout the Fatimid territories; in this he was assisted by two main disciples, Baha al-Din al-Samuqi and Muhammad al-Darazi. The latter's name is generally regarded as having been given to converts to the new faith, and it is the name, (*Druzi*, sing., *Duruz,* pl.) by which they were to become popularly known.

Such was the fervor of Hamza and his followers that the Druze faith spread rapidly from Cairo to other areas of the empire, and even beyond its borders to Aleppo and Damascus. From the beginning, the movement did not see itself as yet another sect of Islam but rather as a new religion or even a perfected Islam whose aim it was to establish a new world order. Very early on, however, Hamza and al-Darazi fought over who was to exercise authority and how converts were to be brought into the community of believers. In 1019 Hamza declared his rival to be a

heretic; al-Darazi was assassinated in short order, and soon he was anathematized by the Druze faith as the devil incarnate. In the midst of political and religious anarchy brought about by Hamza and his *da'wa*, al-Hakim mysteriously disappeared in 1021. His son and successor, al-Zahir (he ruled from 1021 to 1035), denied his father's divine nature and ruthlessly stamped out the followers of Druzism in Egypt. He was unable, however, to stem the Druze tide in the remoter regions of his empire, notably southern Lebanon, and the areas outside Fatimid territory where it had taken root. Meanwhile, Baha al-Din began the important task of assembling the religious teaching of Druzism and nurturing the faith of those who had managed to survive persecution. For sixteen years (1027–1043), the missionary *da'wa* continued to gain adherents, during which time Baha al-Din arranged the 111 epistles and proclamations composed by al-Hakim, Hamza, and himself into the books of the *Hikmat al-Sharifa* (the Noble Knowledge), the so-called secret books of the Druze faith. The last of these is dated 1042 (434 A.H.), and in 1043 the da'wa was formally ended. From this time forward, no new members were allowed to join the religious community.

The followers of the Druze faith call themselves MUWAHHIDUN (or those who believe in absolute monotheism), a word drawn from the Arabic root *whd*, which means "to be one." Their faith itself is called the *tawhid*, again from the same root, which expresses the indivisible unity of God. Druze beliefs have been held in strict secrecy since 1043 and have been shared only by a small number of people within the community in each generation. These people are known as the *uqqal*, or initiates, and they have always included women in their ranks. The remainder are known as the *juhhal*, or the unknowing or uninitiated, and as members of a secret cult they have protected the sanctity of their faith through communal loyalty and have been encouraged to model their lives on the strict moral code and standard of behavior set by the *uqqal*. Although the Druze movement grew out of a branch of Islam, albeit an extreme and esoteric one, there is little in these people's theology, religious practices, or social behavior that would make them Muslim. Their faith is exclusive and secret rather than universal and freely accessible. Their belief in the transmigration of souls, which they share in part with the ALAWIZ and YAZIDIS, is anathema to Islam. Male circumcision is universal among Muslims but is a matter of choice among the Druze. While it is permitted or even encouraged by Islam, polygamy is forbidden to Druze, along with concubinage and the Shi'a tradition of temporary marriage. Divorce for the Druze is not the relatively easy procedure that it is for Muslims, and a Druze woman can begin the proceedings. The five pillars of Islam are not ritually observed or officially recognized among members of this sect. Absolute secrecy is required in all relations with people outside the sect, and to protect themselves and their families in times of great danger the Druze may outwardly reject their faith (the Shi'a practice of *taqiyya* or dissimulation). The Druze, unlike the Shi'ites, however, place no value on martyrdom, and, as believers in free will, they reject the Islamic concept of predestination. One central aspect of the Druze faith that is at total variance with Islam is its Neoplatonic doctrine of periodic appearances of the Universal Intelligence emanating from God. Finally, the Druze sever themselves irrevocably from Islam by declaring that the revelations of al-Hakim, Hamza, and Baha al-Din supersede those of the prophet Muhammad.

Druze worship services are held on Thursday evenings at a secluded place of prayer called a *khalwa* or sometimes a *majles*. The religious leadership of the community is conducted by the chief leaders of the *uqqal*, one of whom in any given area assumes the title of *Shaykh al-Aql*. Secular leadership is exercised by the traditional political figures who are not religiously initiated. The most prized attributes of the Druze are their personal honor and their hospitality. Over the centuries, European visitors to the Druze region have frequently referred to the munificence of the Druze as well as to their excellence as warriors. Unlike Muslim or Christian fighters, however, they are scrupulously circumspect in their dealings with the women of their enemies. Education and literacy have traditionally been widespread among both Druze men and Druze women, and it is today universal through at least the sixth year of school.

The Druze have historically maintained political autonomy in the areas of Lebanon where they were numerically dominant since the end of the *da'wa*. In the sixteenth and seventeenth centuries, however, they extended their political influence following the collapse of Mamluk power at the hands of the Ottomans. Under the rulers of the Ma'ni family—notably the emir Fakhr al-Din II, who governed from 1590 to 1635—Druze authority was expanded into Syria and Palestine. When the last Ma'nid emir died without male issue in 1697, the Chehab family came to power, but not without opposition. A challenge by the Yazbaki faction within the community led to an intercommunal struggle that, following the battle of Ayn Dara in 1711, forced the dispersal of many Druze to what is today the Jabal Druze region of southern Syria. In the meantime, many leading Druze families had begun to adopt Maronite Christianity (see MARONITES). After the fourth ruling

prince of the Chehab line, Mansur (ruled 1754–1770), the Druze political leadership passed to the JUMBLATT FAMILY, recent arrivals to Lebanon from Aleppo. Although reputed to be of Kurdish Muslim origin, they steadfastly maintained their ancestral Druze origins in the Jabal al-A'la region near Antioch, which is still dotted with Druze villages to this day. They established themselves firmly at al-Mukhtara in the Shuf region. The rivalry between the Chehab and the Jumblatt came to a head in 1825 at the battle of Simqaniya, near Mukhtara, after which the Druze entered a period of political decline. In 1860 when Druze–Maronite hostilities, exacerbated by Turkish machinations, once again surfaced, the French intervened and established an autonomous government for Mount Lebanon, which was largely Maronite with a Druze minority and ruled by a non-Maronite Christian. At the end of World War I, the French were given a League of Nations mandate in Syria, and they enlarged the boundaries of Mount Lebanon to the present-day borders of the state of Lebanon, in which the Druze, according to the census of 1932, accounted for only 6.7 percent of the total population.

When independence was achieved by Lebanon in 1943 on the basis of an unwritten constitutional agreement in which the Maronite Catholic and Sunni Muslim communities arranged to share power, the Druze were promised only proportional representation in parliament and at least one cabinet position in any given government. The Druze political leader during Lebanon's early days of independence until his assassination during the civil war in 1976 was Kamal Jumblatt; his only rival was the leading member of the Yazbaki faction and sometime minister of defense, Majid ARSLAN. Kamal Jumbalatt was succeeded by his only son, Walid JUMBLATT, who successfully led the Druze through the difficult years of fighting from 1976 to 1991, and who thereafter ruled with unquestioned authority over the political fortunes of the Lebanese Druze.

After Syria achieved independence in 1930, the Druze were briefly represented in parliament and the government until the rise to power of President Hafiz al-ASAD, who has traditionally favored his own Alawi community from the region of Latakia. Druze, however, were active in Asad's Ba'th party and shared power briefly following the Ba'th coup of 1965 until the war with Israel in 1967. The leading Druze family in Syria in this century has been the al-Atrash clan of Suwayda. In Israel the Druze, though numerically small (only 10 percent of the Arab population), have played an important strategic role owing to their close cooperation, since Israel's inception, with the Israeli government, which, unlike the British mandate and

Ottoman predecessors, recognized the Druze as a separate entity independent of the authority of Sunni religious law. Alone among the Arab communities of Israel, the Druze serve voluntarily in the Israeli Defense Forces and have been given minor posts in the government and diplomatic service. The leading Druze family in Israel is the Tarif clan, from the village of Julis in Galilee, from whom the Shaykh al-Aql of Israel has traditionally been drawn.

The Druze remain a rural-based community, and even today they are rarely found in communities of their own with populations exceeding 10,000; the exceptions are the towns of al-Suwayda in Syria and Ba'qlin in Lebanon. They number between 8 and 10 percent of a population of close to 4 million in Lebanon, and in Syria between 3 and 3½ percent of a population of over 12 million in Syria. Some 65,000 to 70,000 Druze live in Israel proper, and this figure has been augmented since 1967 by 15,000 coreligionists in four villages in the occupied Golan Heights. There are some 15,000 to 20,000 Druze in Jordan and as many as 100,000 living outside the Middle East in North and South America, Australia, and West Africa, for a total Druze population worldwide of about 1 million. The Lebanese Druze are located in the small towns and villages of the Shuf district on the western slope of Mount Lebanon from the Beirut-Damascus highway south to the Jazzin escarpment (plus a few settlements to the north in al-Matn), and in the southeastern part of the country in the western foothills of Mount Hermon around the towns of Hasbeya and Rashayya. A small number are permanently established in Beirut. In Syria 90 percent of the Druze live in the district of al-Suwayda (Jabal Druze) south of Damascus on the Jordanian border. A second, smaller concentration is found on the eastern slope of Mount Hermon in Damascus province and in the capital itself. A third and very historic center is in the Jabal al-A'la region to the west of Aleppo overlooking the Turkish frontier where some 30,000 to 40,000 Druze live in a dozen villages amid ruined Byzantine churches such as Qalb Lawza. Nearly all the Druze of Israel live in sixteen towns and villages in Galilee, nine of which are exclusively Druze, and two major settlements on Mount Carmel Southeast of Haifa. They show little inclination to move to nearby large, ethnically mixed urban centers, and even when they do, they maintain homes and firm roots in their historic rural settlements.

BIBLIOGRAPHY

ABU-IZZEDDIN, NEILA M. *The Druzes: A New Study of Their History, Faith and Society*. Leiden, 1984.
BETTS, ROBERT. *The Druze*. London and New Haven, Conn., 1988.
DE SACY, SILVESTRE. *Exposé de la religion des Druzes, tiré des livres religieux de cette secte*. 2 vols. Paris. 1838.
FIRRO, KAIS. *A History of the Druzes*. Leiden, 1992.
HODGSON, MARSHALL G. S. "Al-Darazi and Hamza in the Origin of the Druze Religion." *Journal of the American Oriental Society* 82 (1962): 5–20.
JOUMBLATT (JUMBLATT), KAMAL. *I Speak for Lebanon*. Tr. by Michael Pallis. London, 1982.
LAYISH, AHARON. *Marriage, Divorce and Succession in the Druze Family*. Leiden, 1982.
MAKAREM, SAMI N. *The Druze Faith*. Delmar, N.Y., 1974.
NAJJAR, ABDALLAH. *The Druze: Millennium Scrolls Revealed*. Tr. by Fred I. Massey (under the auspices of the American Druze Society). Cairo, 1965.

Robert Betts

Druze Revolts

Druze uprisings in Syria and Lebanon in the 1830s.

These large-scale revolts erupted among the DRUZE (particularly in Hawran) beginning in 1837, when Ibrahim Pasha sought to force conscription in the region to support his adventures and those of his father. The Egyptian force sent from Damascus to suppress the rebels was defeated. The Druze of Hawran were soon aided by those from Shuf and Wadi al-Taym, and by Muslims from Mount Nablus in Palestine, who also were subject to conscription. During the revolt, a Druze warrior named Shibli al-Aryan became a national hero. Ibrahim Pasha's frustration in dealing with Druze rebels led him to request Bashir II to send Christian fighters to quell the rebellion. The Christian soldiers were under the command of Bashir's son Khalil, which reinforced Druze suspicions about Bashir's sectarian biases. The revolt failed, but it resulted in intensified sectarian animosities in the mountain regions for years to come.

As'ad AbuKhalil

Dual Containment

U.S. Persian Gulf policy, 1993.

Dual containment was the name given by the Clinton administration in 1993 to its foreign policy in the Persian Gulf. The essence of dual containment was in American efforts to isolate the governments of both Iraq and Iran from political, military, and commercial contacts with the rest of the world. Through such isolation the Clinton administration hoped to force Iraq to abide fully by the United Nations resolutions imposed on it after its invasion of Kuwait in 1990, and to coerce Iran into abandoning a number of policies opposed by Washington, including its rearmament program, opposition to the Arab–Israeli peace process, and support for Islamic movements in other parts of the Middle East.

F. Gregory Gause, III

Dual Control

Joint British–French supervision of Egyptian government revenues and disbursements from 1878 to 1882, supplementing the supervision provided by the Caisse de la Dette Publique set up in 1876.

The first controllers were members of the so-called European cabinet, in which a British subject was finance minister and a Frenchman held the portfolio for public works. This cabinet, appointed by Egypt's Khedive Isma'il in August 1878, under pressure from his European creditors, lasted only six months because of its fiscal stringencies, which included placing many Egyptian army officers on half pay. Four months later Khedive Isma'il was deposed in favor of his son, TAWFIQ.

The British and French governments appointed their controllers: Sir Evelyn Baring (later Lord Cromer), who had served on the Caisse, and de Blignières, the former Egyptian works minister. They drew up what would become the 1880 liquidation law, which reduced Egyptian government indebtedness by strictly limiting government expenditure. This caused either antiforeign sentiment or feelings of nationalism among Egyptian officers and officials, leading to the 1881/82 Urabi revolution.

Once the cabinet headed by Mahmud Sami al-Barudi took control in February 1882, the controllers could no longer direct the budget. Dual Control was formally terminated when the British occupied Egypt in September of 1882. Without access to military force, which Britain and France refused to apply until the Urabi revolution, Dual Control could not impose its program on Egypt's economy and body politic.

BIBLIOGRAPHY

MARLOWE, JOHN. *Cromer in Egypt.* London, 1970.
SCHÖLCH, ALEXANDER. *Egypt for the Egyptians!* London, 1981.

Arthur Goldschmidt, Jr.

Dubai

The second largest (1,500 square miles; 3,885 square kilometers) and second wealthiest of the seven emirates in the United Arab Emirates (UAE); also its capital city.

Dubai became a significant settlement when the Al Bu Falasa clan broke away from the BANIYAS of ABU DHABI in 1833 and asserted their independence. Under the Al Maktum ruling family Dubai became an important commercial center by the early twentieth century. An influx of merchants from Iran, Baluchistan, and India gave it a cosmopolitan character. An enlightened laissez-faire spirit generated considerable prosperity and orderly development, most notably under Rashid ibn Sa'id al-MAKTUM (reigned 1958–1990), which accelerated with the addition of oil and gas income beginning in the 1960s. Among major recent initiatives is the creation of the world's largest artificial port at Jabal Ali.

Rashid and the ruler of rival Abu Dhabi, Zayid ibn Sultan al-NAHAYYAN, worked together to ensure the successful launching of the UAE in 1971. The price for Rashid's cooperation was Dubai's nearly equivalent status with that of Abu Dhabi in the federation, despite the disparity in size and wealth. Under Rashid and his son and successor, Maktum, Dubai has favored a loose structure, whereas Abu Dhabi has pressed for stronger central authority.

Dubai creek in the port of Dubai. (Richard Bulliet)

Princely palace in Dubai. (D. W. Lockhard)

BIBLIOGRAPHY

HEARD-BEY, FRAUKE. *From Trucial States to United Arab Emirates.* London and New York, 1982.
PECK, MALCOLM C. *The United Arab Emirates: A Venture in Unity.* Boulder, Colo., 1993.

Malcolm C. Peck

Dubs, Adolph   [1920–1979]

U.S. ambassador to Afghanistan, 1977–1979; assassinated in Kabul.

Ambassador Adolph ("Spike") Dubs was the American ambassador to Afghanistan at the time of the Saur Revolution in April 1978. On February 14, 1979, Dubs was kidnapped in Kabul and held hostage by unidentified people claiming to be opponents of the Afghan Marxist government. He was shot to death after a few hours by police allegedly trying to free him. His death had a deleterious effect on relations between Afghanistan and the United States.

BIBLIOGRAPHY

ARNOLD, ANTHONY. *Afghanistan's Two-Party Communism: Parcham and Khalq.* Stanford, Calif., 1983.

Grant Farr

Dufferin Report

Report commending reorganization of Egyptian government under British occupation.

Lord Dufferin, the British ambassador to the Ottoman Empire in Constantinople (now Istanbul), was sent to Egypt following the defeat of the Urabi revolt to recommend policies for the administration of Britain's occupation. His report on the reorganization of the Egyptian government was issued on February 6, 1883. Recognizing the importance of the rising tide of Egyptian nationalism, Lord Dufferin sought middle ground between the restoration of Egyptian sovereignty and full annexation by England. British officials were to take advisory positions in key offices within the Egyptian administration, including the ministries of finance, interior, public works and irrigation, justice, police, and the army. Other specific measures and reforms discussed in the report were the establishment of an elected government under the khedive (ruler of Egypt, viceroy of the sultan of the Ottoman Empire), the promulgation of civil and criminal codes for the Native Tribunals, the abolishment of forced labor, and putting an end to the use of whippings to collect taxes and obtain evidence of crimes. As a result of Dufferin's report, a Legislative Council and a General Assembly were established, changing the contours of Egyptian politics. Contrary to Dufferin's intention of minimizing British control over the Egyptian government, the reforms discussed in his report increased British presence in Egypt and enhanced Egyptian opposition to the occupation.

BIBLIOGRAPHY

GOLDSCHMIDT, ARTHUR, JR.. *Modern Egypt: The Formation of a Nation-State.* Boulder, Colo. 1988.
VATIKIOTIS, P. J. *A History of Modern Egypt,* 4th ed. London, 1991.
WUCHER KING, JOAN. *Historical Dictionary of Egypt.* Metuchen, N.J., 1984.

David Waldner

Dukan Dam

The dam was built on Iraq's Little Zab river to control flooding and to provide irrigation and hydroelectric power.

Severe, recurrent flooding of the Little Zab river to northeastern IRAQ was formerly commonplace. The rate of flow in this river as it passes through the Dukan gorge is about 34 cubic yards (26 cu. m) per minute during the dry season, rising to more than 4,000 cubic yards (3,000 cu. m) per minutes at flood time. Iraq's Development Board was already considering major flood control, drainage, and irrigation schemes throughout the country when the Little Zab gave rise to a series of major floods in 1941, 1946, 1949, 1953, and 1954. The highest flood levels were recorded in this latest year when the river's rate of flow reached 4,800 cubic yards (3,660 cu. m) per minute despite a normal average daily rainfall.

In 1954, to control further flooding of the Little Zab and to provide water for irrigation in northeastern Iraq, the Development Board awarded a contract to a French consortium for the construction of an arch dam at Dukan gorge on the Little Zab, some thirty-seven miles (60 km) northwest of SULAYMAN-IYA and sixty miles (100 km) northeast of KIRKUK. Between 1,000 and 1,200 families, representing the population of some fifty villages in the adjacent region, were moved and settled to the northwest at Sanga Sir. The Dukan dam and reservoir were completed in 1959 although structural problems necessitated ongoing repairs and further expense. As part of the Dukan project, a series of regulators and dams were built on the Little Zab and adjacent Udayn river, while a spillway conveying water from the Little Zab to the Udayn provided irrigation to the Ghurfa lands and the lands on the right bank of the Udaym river.

The project was tested almost immediately when the Little Zab flooded in 1959, depositing over 2.6 billion cubic yards (2 billion cu. m) of water into the reservoir. This allowed a constant runoff for irrigation during the dry season from August to November. Over 20 billion cubic yards (15 billion cu. m) of water were processed through the reservoir during the first six years of its operation.

The dam itself is an enormous structure, 382 feet (116.5 m) high and 1,180 feet (360 m) long. It is 20 feet (6.2 m) wide at the top and 107 feet (32.5 m) wide at its base. The reservoir behind it, covering an area of some 104 square miles (270 sq. km) or more, has an estimated usual capacity of 8.9 billion cubic yards (6.8 billion cu. m), but a maximum capacity of 10.9 billion cubic yards (8.3 billion cu. m). The complex serves multiple purposes including flood control, the provision of hydroelectric power (originally rated at 200,000 kilowatts), and the storage of water for lean periods when the Tigris is low. Indeed, the water contained in the reservoir is intended chiefly for the Kirkuk irrigation project whereby over 890,000 acres (360,000 ha) of land around Arbil, Kirkuk, and Diyala districts are to be brought under cultivation, almost 494,000 acres (200,000 ha) around Kurkuk alone.

BIBLIOGRAPHY

ALI, HASSAN MOHAMMAD. *Land Reclamation And Settlement In Iraq*. Baghad, 1955.
SALTER, LORD. *The Development of Iraq: A Plan of Action*. London, 1955.

Albertine Jwaideh

Dukhan

Part of a limestone escarpment in the center of Bahrain Island.

The name in full is Jabal al-Dukhan (Arabic for "mountain of smoke"). It is the site of Bahrain's principal onshore oil field of the same name. A similar geological structure near the west coast of Qatar bears the same name and also identifies a producing oil field.

BIBLIOGRAPHY

HELD, COLBERT C. *Middle East Patterns: Places, Peoples, and Politics*. Boulder, Colo., 1989.

Malcolm C. Peck

Dulles, John Foster   [1888–1959]

U.S. secretary of state, 1953–1959.

As President Dwight D. Eisenhower's secretary of state from 1953 to 1959, Dulles directed U.S. foreign policy in tandem with the president. The USSR was their focal concern, with communism considered an immoral and dangerous system. Concerned with the strategic northern tier of Middle Eastern countries that bordered on the USSR, Dulles supported conservative pro-U.S. rulers such as the Reza Shah PAH-LAVI in Iran, the Hashimites and Nuri al-Sa'id in Iraq, and Adnan MENDERES in Turkey.

When Iran's Prime Minister Mohammad MOS-SADEGH threatened to supplant the shah in 1953, Dulles advocated the removal of the prime minister. Dulles and his brother, CIA director Allen Dulles, organized Operation AJAX, which was significant to Mossadegh's fall in August 1953. In August 1955, Dulles proposed a solution to the Arab–Israel conflict based on resettlement of the Palestinian refugees, with treaties to establish permanent frontiers as well as guarantees of security for both sides. Although he supported the British-sponsored BAGHDAD PACT of 1955, he tried in vain to create a Middle Eastern version of the North Atlantic Treaty Organization (NATO), believing that such a security pact was vital to protect the region from the USSR. Dulles distrusted the attempts of various Middle Eastern states, particularly Egypt, to remain neutral in the Cold War between the superpowers.

In 1955, he responded favorably to Egypt's request for funding of the Aswan High Dam, but Egypt's new president Gamal Abdel Nasser made an arms deal with Czechoslovakia, a country under Soviet domination, in September of 1955, which dampened U.S. enthusiasm. Distrusting Nasser's overtures to the USSR, Dulles decided, with Eisenhower's approval, to revoke the funding offer in July of 1956. This initiated a series of events that began with Nasser's nationalization of the Suez Canal and culminated in the Suez crisis (Arab–Israel War) of October 1956. Dulles refused to support the actions of Israel, France, and Great Britain in their attempt to seize the canal.

In 1957, Dulles participated in the formulation of the Eisenhower Doctrine, which offered U.S. military aid to Middle East states threatened by the USSR. Invoking the doctrine, Dulles and Eisenhower decided to send U.S. troops to Lebanon in July 1958 in the wake of the revolution in Iraq.

BIBLIOGRAPHY

HOOPES, TOWNSHEND. *The Devil and John Foster Dulles.* Boston, 1973.
SCHOENEBAUM, ELEANORA, ed. *Political Profiles: The Eisenhower Years.* New York, 1977.
SPIEGEL, STEVEN. *The Other Arab–Israeli Conflict.* Chicago, 1985.

Zachary Karabell

Dunsterville, Lionel C.   [1865–1946]

British officer who led the Dunsterforce in World War I.

Major General Dunsterville commanded a small task force that was dispatched from Iraq in January 1918 to organize resistance against German and Turkish troops in the Caucasus mountains, after the beginning of the Russian revolution and the collapse of the Russian front in 1917. When he finally reached Baku in August, Turkish pressure forced his prompt withdrawal back to Qazvin, which remained a British outpost until 1921.

BIBLIOGRAPHY

WRIGHT, SIR DENIS. *The English amongst the Persians.* London, 1977.

Jack Bubon

Dunum

Unit of surface area.

The *dunum* is used to measure landholdings in successor states of the Ottoman Empire. During the late Ottoman period, it was 919 square meters (less than 0.25 acre). In the 1920s, the *dunum* was enlarged to 1,000 square meters (about 0.25 acre) in Lebanon, Syria, Palestine, and Transjordan. In Iraq, the *dunum* equals 0.618 acre.

Michael R. Fischbach

Durand, Henry Mortimer   [1850–1924]

British diplomat.

Durand was educated at Eton and entered the Bengal Civil Service in 1873. He was political secretary during the KABUL campaign in 1879 and became foreign secretary in India in 1884, a position he held until 1894. In 1893, he led a mission to Afghanistan to define the border between that country and British India. The line he negotiated came to be known as the DURAND LINE. The British wanted a border that would separate those tribes that looked to Kabul for leadership from those that looked to British India. Although the Durand Line is still the border between Afghanistan and Pakistan, it remains a matter of controversy; many Afghans believe that all ethnic Pakhtun areas should be part of that country. From 1894 to 1900, Durand was minister at Tehran, Iran. He then served as Britain's ambassador to Spain, 1900–1903, and to the United States, 1903–1906.

BIBLIOGRAPHY

DEPARTMENT OF THE ARMY. *Afghanistan: A Country Study.* Washington, D.C., 1986.

Daniel E. Spector

Durand Line

Afghanistan–Pakistan border.

The present border of approximately 1,500 miles (2,414 km) between Afghanistan and Pakistan was agreed upon in a treaty signed on November 12, 1893, in Kabul by Sir Mortimer Durand, representing British India, and Abd al-Rahman, emir of Afghanistan. Afghanistan has never accepted the legitimacy of this border, since it cuts through the Pushtun (or Pakhtun) area, leaving over half the Pushtun tribes in Pakistan. Afghans believe the area should be part of Afghanistan; therefore the "Pushtunistan question" has remained an obstacle to good relations between Pakistan and Afghanistan.

When the state of Pakistan was created in 1947, a plebiscite was held in the Pushtun area of Pakistan in which people were asked to vote whether they wanted to join Pakistan or India. Afghanistan did not accept the results of the plebiscite, since the choices given did not include Afghanistan. In 1979, the Afghan parliament formally repudiated the Durand agreement.

BIBLIOGRAPHY

DUPREE, LOUIS. *Afghanistan*. Princeton, N.J., 1980.

Grant Farr

Durrani Dynasty

Rulers of Afghanistan.

The Durrani dynasty (1747–1842) was founded in Kandahar, Afghanistan, in 1747, when a group of PAKHTUN elders elected AHMAD DURRANI to lead them. Members of the house of Ahmad Shah ruled over the empire he created until its collapse in 1818. A branch of the family maintained control over Herat and the northwestern region until 1842. A grandson of Ahmad Shah regained the Afghan throne in 1838 but was overthrown in 1842, in the course of a popular uprising against British forces.

The province of Kandahar had changed hands repeatedly between the Moghul and Safavid empires when, in 1708, a coalition of Pakhtun and non-Pakhtun elements under the leadership of Mir Wais Hotak freed the province from the Safavids. In 1722, the Pakhtuns conquered Isfahan, establishing a short-lived Ghilzai empire. By 1737, their capital in Kandahar was taken over by the Persian conqueror, Nadir Shah Afshar, whose death in 1747 provided Ahmad Shah with the opportunity to establish the Durrani empire.

Ahmad Shah belonged to the Saddozai lineage, which had provided the Abdali clan with its leaders for several centuries. On assuming power, Ahmad Shah changed the name of the clan from Abdali to Durrani (Pearl of Pearls). He bestowed special privileges on the Saddozai lineage but confined the kingship to his own house. The crown was hereditary in the house of Ahmad Shah. But in the absence of clear rules, every succession gave rise to an intense struggle for the throne. When Ahmad Shah died, two of his four sons emerged as contenders, but their conflict was quickly resolved in favor of the eldest, Timur Shah (ruled 1772–1793). When he died, the

continuous struggle among his numerous sons became a permanent feature of the politics of the dynasty, ultimately leading to its collapse. Three of his sons became rulers, Shah Zaman (ruled 1793–1800), Shah Mahmud (ruled 1800–1803; 1809–1818), and Shah Shuja (ruled 1803–1809; 1838–1842).

Under Ahmad Shah, foreign conquest was the main goal of the dynasty. To build himself a base of support at home and provide a force for conquest abroad, Ahmad Shah showered the Durrani clans with privileges, investing their leaders with the main offices of the empire. Most of the ministers and generals belonged to various branches of the Durrani clan, though rarely to the Saddozai lineage to which Ahmad Shah's house belonged. But near the end of his rule, changed regional conditions had rendered further conquests unprofitable. Timur Shah, who fought only defensive wars, rarely called the Durrani clans to action. To reduce the power of his ministers, he moved the capital from Kandahar, the heartland of Pakhtuns, to KABUL, a predominantly Persian (Farsi)-speaking city. He also created new offices, to which he appointed non-Durranis owing loyalty to his person.

The warring princes, however, not only had to reconfirm Durrani nobles in their privileges but had to concede to them new powers as well. The cumulative effect of these concessions resulted in the weakening of the crown to the point that ministers were in a position to depose rulers at will. Most of the rulers, however, managed to prevent members of a single lineage from monopolizing all official positions. But under Shah Mahmud, members of the BARAKZAI clan managed to gain control of the most important offices. When, in 1818, the crown prince blinded the powerful Barakzai chief minister, the latter's brothers, seeking revenge, overthrew the house of Ahmad Shah and brought about the collapse of the Durrani empire.

A civil war ensued. The Indian provinces of the Durrani empire gained their independence, and Afghanistan was divided into a number of independent principalities. A great-grandson of Ahmad Shah, Prince Kamran, gained control of the province of Herat, which he ruled until 1842. Shah Shuja, a grandson of Ahmad Shah and former ruler, mounted a number of expeditions from his exile in India to regain power but without success. Fearing the rising influence of Russia in Persia and Central Asia, British officials in India decided to extend their support to Shah Shuja. To help restore him to power, they sent forces simultaneously against the rulers of Kabul and Kandahar in 1838, thereby initiating the first Anglo-Afghan War. The house of Ahmad Shah still retained enough legitimacy, and Shah Shuja was welcomed by the people. Soon, however, he revealed himself to be no more than a stooge of British power. In 1841, anxious about their own loss of influence, Afghan notables led a popular revolt against the British forces. The British army was destroyed, and Shah Shuja was assassinated in 1842. His descendants fled to India, and from then on, no member of the house of Ahmad Shah ever played a prominent role in the politics of Afghanistan.

The advent of the Durrani dynasty transformed the Pakhtuns in general, and the Durrani clans in particular, into the dominant political force in Afghanistan. The dynasty, however, derived its model of power from the ancient Persian and Islamic theories of government. Persian was the language of bureaucracy, and it gradually became the language of the court.

BIBLIOGRAPHY

DUPREE, LOUIS. *Afghanistan*. Princeton, N.J., 1980.
FOFALZAI, A. W. *Timur Shah-e-Durrani* (Timur Shah Durrani). Kabul, 1967.
LEECH, R. "An Account of Early Abdalees." *Journal of the Asiatic Society of Bengal* 14 (11845): 445–470.
MONSHI, MAHMUD. *Tarikh Ahmad Shahi* (History of the Reign of Ahmad Shah). Moscow, 1974.

Ashraf Ghani

Dustur, al-

Jordanian newspaper.

Founded in 1967, *al-Dustur* (The Constitution) is an Arabic–language morning daily published by the Jordan Press and Publishing Company. In August 1988, the government dismissed the paper's board of directors, following a general crackdown on the press, and exercised editorial control over it until December 1989, when it relinquished its control. With a circulation of 60,000, it is one of Jordan's three major daily papers in Arabic.

BIBLIOGRAPHY

The Middle East and North Africa 1991, 37th ed. London, 1991.

Abla M. Amawi

E

Eastern and General Syndicate

Syndicate established to obtain oil concessions in Arabia (1920).

Major Frank HOLMES, a mining engineer from New Zealand, established the syndicate to obtain oil exploration concessions from Gulf Arab rulers. The syndicate failed, but Holmes's sale of a concession in Bahrain to Standard Oil of California (today Chevron) led indirectly to the ARABIAN AMERICAN OIL COMPANY (ARAMCO) concession in Saudi Arabia. Holmes represented Gulf Oil in securing a half share in the Kuwait Oil Company.

BIBLIOGRAPHY

YERGIN, DANIEL. *The Prize: The Epic Quest for Oil, Money, and Power.* New York, 1991.

Malcolm C. Peck

Eastern Desert

Also called the Arabian Desert; it makes up almost a quarter of Egypt's land surface, covering an area of 85,690 square miles (221,937 sq km).

The northern sector, from the Mediterranean coast to the latitude of Qena, is a limestone plateau marked by rolling hills. At Qena the Eastern Desert is marked by cliffs, some as high as 6,500 feet (2,000 m), and scored by deep *wadis* (dry stream beds or valleys) that are difficult to cross. Farther south the desert becomes a sandstone plateau broken by ravines, but some can be traversed easily, such as the ancient trade route from the Nile River to al-Quseir. In the eastern section of the desert, a chain of hills, more like a series of interlocking systems than a continuous range, runs from near Suez south to the border of the Sudan. At the foot of these hills lies the Red Sea coastal plain, which gradually widens as one moves south.

The sedentary population lives in towns and villages on the Red Sea coast; their main occupations are fishing, transport, and serving the growing Red Sea tourist trade. Nomadic pastoralists make up about 10 percent of the Eastern Desert's population. Pasture lands and water suffice to support small herds of sheep, goats, and camels. Arab tribes include the Huwaytat, Ma'aza, and Ababda. In the south are the Bisharin, part of the BEJA, a Hamitic ethnic group.

BIBLIOGRAPHY

Egypt: A Country Study. Washington, D. C., 1991.
Encyclopaedia Britannica, 15th ed.
HOBBS, JOSEPH J. *Bedouin Life in the Egyptian Wilderness.* Austin, Tex., 1989.
TREGENZA, L. A. *Egyptian Years.* London, 1958.

Arthur Goldschmidt, Jr.

Eastern Orthodox Church

Direct descendant of the Byzantine State Church; also includes a group of independent national Christian churches.

593

The Eastern Orthodox Church comprises a group of autonomous Christian churches united by doctrine, liturgy, and internal hierarchical organizations. The heads are patriarchs or metropolitans, with the patriarch of Constantinople only the first among equals. Orthodox churches represented in the Middle East include the Russian, the Balkan, the Greek; the churches of Antioch (now based in Damascus), Alexandria, Jerusalem, and the See of Constantinople (now Istanbul); and the old churches that date to the fifth century C.E., which emancipated themselves from the Byzantine State Church—the Nestorian Church in the Middle East and India (with a half million members) and the Monophysite churches (with some 17 million, including the Coptic of Egypt, the Ethiopian, the Syrian, the Armenian, and the Mar Thoma of India). There are also the Uniate churches, which, properly speaking, are not Orthodox churches because, though they retain traditional eastern liturgies, they acknowledge the primacy and authority of the pope in Rome. Orthodox Christians today number some 150 million or more worldwide—with 125 million in Europe, 25 million in Africa, 3.5 million in Asia, and about 1 million in North America.

Eastern Christianity, with its decentralized organization, diverged from the Western hierarchically organized Roman (Catholic) Church after the fourth century C.E., when Constantinople became the capital of the Roman Empire. The theological split between the Western and Eastern churches was formalized in the Schism of 1054. Rivalry between Rome and Constantinople, aided by longstanding differences and misunderstandings, led to the schism: The Eastern Orthodox churches recognize only the canons of the seven ecumenical councils (325–787 C.E.) as binding for faith, and they reject doctrines that have subsequently been added in the West.

After the fall of the Byzantine Empire in 1453 to the Ottoman Turks, the Orthodox patriarch was entrusted with full civil administration over all Orthodox Christians in the Ottoman Empire. This centralized administration contrasted with the Eastern church's traditional localist organization. Although the Ottomans granted Christians freedom of worship, the restrictions they imposed on the public profile of the church bred resentment and stagnation in theological scholarship.

In the nineteenth and twentieth centuries, the Ottoman Empire's Orthodox community once again splintered under the impact of European Catholics and Protestants and of emerging nationalism. The Russian Empire assumed a pan-Slavic stance in its attempts to expand south and east into warm-water ports during the nineteenth and early twentieth centuries; the affinity of Russian Orthodoxy with other Eastern Orthodox communities was stressed. World War I, the Russian Revolution, and the breakup of the Ottoman Empire ended that gambit, although Russian and Soviet interests in the Middle East never diminished.

Today in the Arab East, the Antioch (Melkite) church represents the largest Arab Christian group, with dioceses in Syria, Lebanon, and Iraq. The Alexandria church has become the center of emerging African Orthodox communities.

BIBLIOGRAPHY

BRAUDE, BENJAMIN, and BERNARD LEWIS, eds. *Christians and Jews in the Ottoman Empire.* New York, 1982.
HADDAD, ROBERT M. *Syrian Christians in Muslim Society.* Princeton, N.J., 1970.
SHAW, STANFORD J. *History of the Ottoman Empire and Modern Turkey,* vol. 1. New York, 1976.

Elizabeth Thompson

Eastern Province

See Hasa, al-

Eastern Question

A concept coined in the initial stage of the Greek War for Independence (1821–1829) to describe the territorial effect of the political decline of the Ottoman Empire on great-power diplomacy in Europe.

In the seventeenth century the Ottoman Empire, at its greatest extent, sprawled across southeast Europe (Hungary included), southwest Asia, and northern Africa (Morocco excluded). The weakening of the sultan's power began in the last decade of the reign of Sultan Süleyman (1520–1566). However, Europe remained paralyzed by religious wars until the Peace of Westphalia (1648), and the Sublime Porte (the Ottoman imperial government) did not admit its growing frailty vis-à-vis Europe until the end of the seventeenth century. Only then did it negotiate treaties and other international acts, chiefly with the great powers of Europe. In the Treaty of Karlowitz (1699), for the first time, the sultan ceded large tracts in Christian Europe—in this instance to Austria and Poland—which were never recovered.

For a century longer, Ottoman military might was still respected on the Continent. Tsar Peter I (1682–1725), the first European monarch to send troops into Ottoman Asia, occupied the Sea of Azov and its Crimean rim in 1696, only to lose the short-lived conquest along with a claim to power over the Black Sea after a disastrous defeat (1711) at the Prut River (later in Romania). The Ottoman recapture of the Crimea's Tatar khanates was ratified in 1713, in the Treaty of EDIRNE (Adrianople). That delayed for six decades—until Catherine II (1762–1796), after a six-year war with Turkey—Russia's taking the first solid step toward establishing itself as a Black Sea power through the treaty of KUÇUK KAYNARJA (1774), which detached the khanates from the sultan's realm by declaring them independent. Russia did not annex them until nine years later. Finally in 1792, after four more years of war, the Sublime Porte, in the treaty of peace at JASSY, the capital of the Ottoman province of Moldavia (later part of Romania), at last acknowledged this segment of the Black Sea coast as Russian. The victories set in motion Ottoman territorial attrition in southwest Asia; it spread to North Africa in 1830, when France began its conquest of Algeria.

Europe's expansion into the Ottoman Empire at times appeared to consist of predators rushing as far and as fast as they could, paying no heed to the risks of collision. Such a judgment, however, belies the realities. Contenders for the same or overlapping districts were sensitive to one another's interests. Avoidance of conflict became the name of the game as early as the Congress of Vienna (1814–1815). At the end of the Congress the conveners—Austria, Great Britain, Prussia, and Russia—styled themselves the Concert of Europe to act as a permanent executive for settling all their disputes by conference or consensual diplomacy.

In 1818, at Aachen, the four powers admitted France to their ranks and promptly instructed the restored Bourbon monarchy to join Britain, as the Concert's sole maritime powers, in suppressing the institutionalized piracy in the western Mediterranean, carried out by the sultan's autonomous *ocaklar* (garrisons) or provinces of Tripoli (Libya), Tunis, and Algiers. A dozen years elapsed before the Barbary garrisons of the Ottoman Maghrib were finally put out of the piracy business.

Only once between 1815 and 1914 did the great powers resort to war over a dispute arising from the Eastern Question. In that case Britain, France, and Russia were the Concert's belligerents in the CRIMEAN WAR (1854–1856); Austria served as mediator, and Prussia stayed aloof. The entry of the Kingdom of Sardinia, alongside Britain and France, as allies of the Sublime Porte against Russia served, in effect, as its application for membership in the Concert. Having led the Risorgimento for the political unification of the city-states in the Italian peninsula after 1848, Sardinia provided the monarchs follow-ing the emergence in 1861 of the kingdom of Italy, which was promptly made a member of the Concert.

The great-power contest for ownership or denial of the sultan's strategic realm reflects the pace and the modes of Europe's expansion into Asia and Africa. The Ottoman Empire spanned the heart of the eastern hemisphere by joining its three continents. The desire to control the Turkish Straits, which separate Asia and Europe while linking the Black and Mediterranean seas, became a fixed, if also thwarted, aim of Russia after 1774. The Black Sea remained closed to Russia's naval power while the tsardom was exposed to possible attack by hostile maritime powers, as occurred in the Crimean War.

Similarly, on occupying Egypt in 1798, Napoléon declared, in the name of France, his intention to construct and own a man-made waterway from the Mediterranean's landlocked southeast corner to the Red Sea. By cutting across Asia and Africa, such a canal would reduce the distance (and the time) of uninterrupted travel from western Europe, notably from Britain and France, to India by two-thirds, and by lesser amounts to all points along the African and Asian shores of the Indian Ocean.

Given the challenge of two rivals, the cautious shaping by Britain, as the world's foremost maritime and naval power, of its own strategy to deny Russia and France a naval presence on the Mediterranean's eastern littorals was remarkable.

As the decades passed, Saint Petersburg's aspiration became an obsession. In preparation for the expected takeover of the Turkish Straits, Russia continued swallowing Ottoman property that circled the Black Sea in both Europe and Asia, in the latter from the Crimea through the Caucasus; the last bit was the adjacent corner of Anatolia in 1878. To support the quest for the Turkish Straits even before the Crimean War, Russia established precedents to assert its right to protect the sultan's Orthodox subjects in Anatolia and Syria (including Lebanon and Palestine). In 1856, the Islahat Fermani (Reform Edict) of Sultan ABDÜLMECIT I (1839–1861), reinforced by Article 9 of the Treaty of Paris ending the Crimean War, briefly interrupted, but did not end, the Russian practice.

Meanwhile, over Britain's resolute opposition, French investors in the late 1850s launched the Suez Canal Company, which in 1869 completed the waterway. Backed by the government of France, these entrepreneurs also preempted Britain's moves to take control of the company's policy-framing executive before and after Britain's occupation of Ottoman Egypt in 1882. By 1914 Algeria and Tunisia were part of France's empire, although the Sublime Porte withheld formal recognition of the protectorate in

Tunisia. Of the surviving Ottoman provinces in Asia, France's interest centered on Lebanon and Syria from 1860 on. After a lapse of about a century, France in the 1840s had revived earlier treaty rights to custody of papal institutions and their members, covering affiliated eastern Uniate churches as well as Roman Catholicism. Finally, the financial community of France bankrolled railway, harbor, and other concessions in Syria, Lebanon, and Palestine and became the dominant shareholder in the Ottoman Imperial Bank, the Ottoman Empire's official agent.

But above all, the overseers of Britain's empire saw the shrinking Islamic state as both a continuing barrier and an unfolding passage to India. In both functions, the Ottoman Empire had grown into a major asset for Britain. Little wonder that, under Britain's persistent lead, the Concert of Europe in 1840 began nearly four decades as guarantor of the integrity of Ottoman Asia and Africa. The chosen formula was that of a self-denying protocol, first used in the Concert's convention of 1840 for "the Pacification of the Levant," which stated that "in the execution of the engagements resulting to the Contracting Powers from the . . . Convention, those Powers will seek no augmentation of territory, no exclusive influence, no commercial advantage for their subjects, which those of every other nation may not equally obtain." Even France, which had upheld Egypt in the crisis, rejoined the Concert in 1841.

Foreign Secretary Lord Palmerston, the strategy's author, saw in Egypt's threats to the Osmanlı dynasty's survival (1831–1833, 1839) a threat to the British Empire. With the appearance of the steamship in the 1820s, Britain belatedly discovered what the East India Company had begun learning under sail more than half a century earlier: that through the sultan's realm there ran developing routes of communication and transportation between the metropole and the empire in India. In the regional contest of the 1830s, Russia backed the sultan, and France, the viceroy. The main problem, in Palmerston's diagnosis, was to keep Russia and France apart, for if they joined forces, Britain would suffer along with the Osmanlı dynasty. Palmerston preferred a weak Ottoman Empire to a powerful Egypt. He thus responded favorably in 1839 and 1840 to the tsar's proposal for joint military intervention, with the cooperation of the Sublime Porte, to contain an ominous threat to the survival of the Ottoman Empire posed by MUHAMMAD ALI, the viceroy of Egypt, backed by France. Austria and Prussia adhered to this plan of action.

France returned to the fold in 1841, as part of the settlement of the regional crisis. It reduced Muhammad Ali from quasi-independence to Ottoman vassalage, but only upon his being recognized as the founder of a hereditary provincial dynasty with full domestic autonomy (though subject to Ottoman control of Egypt's foreign policy). "[A]ll the Treaties concluded and to be concluded between my Sublime Porte and the friendly Powers," read the Sultan's *ferman*, "shall be completely executed in the Province of Egypt likewise." This clause immediately imposed on Egypt the Porte's obligations to Britain, France, and the Netherlands to change the basis of Ottoman foreign commerce from protection to free trade. That deprived Muhammad Ali of the assured revenues from his commercial and industrial monopolies and put an early end to his integrated program of economic and military modernization. Those steps reduced the innovative, self-made, ambitious governor to manageable size. Later they enabled Palmerston, as foreign minister and prime minister, to delay for a dozen years execution of Egypt's grant of a ninety-nine year concession to a national of France to build and operate the Suez Canal.

In 1840/1841 the Concert had thus created a subsidiary system expressly to defuse crises in Europe arising from the rivalry over the Middle East (and North Africa) portions of the sultan's realm. For nearly forty years the great powers, with the Sublime Porte taking part and Britain playing the balancer in alternating alliances with Russia against France or the reverse, met five times—in London (1840/41, 1871), Paris (1856, 1860/61), and Berlin (1878)—and framed obligatory guidelines on policies toward the Ottoman Empire. Military occupation without time limit, commonly unilateral, was denied legitimacy; formal protectorates were legitimated by the powers, not by the Sublime Porte (in the end by the Turkish Republic); direct annexation was invariably solemnized by formal agreement with Constantinople. All three practices rested on general usage under (Western) international law.

Other styles of Europe's imperialism were particular to the Eastern Question. In the economic sphere the practices derived from the CAPITULATIONS (nonreciprocal commercial treaties that the Porte had concluded with Europe's governments from the fifteenth to the mid-nineteenth centuries), assured Western residents unilateral extraterritorial privileges. They and their enterprises—banks, railroads, harbors, the Suez Canal—were immune from sultanic and provincial laws and taxes, and subject only to those of home governments. To such built-in dominance by Europe over key developmental aspects of the Ottoman economy was added guardianship of selected religious communities, with Russia and France the leading practitioners. The prevalence in the same districts of resident missionaries and their many charitable, medical, and educational, as well as religious, institutions attested to this.

Strategy apart, Britain's most valuable interest was commerce. As the sole industrializing nation from the last third of the eighteenth century through the Napoleonic Wars, Britain speedily moved into first place in the foreign trade of the Ottoman Empire. By 1850, the Porte had become Britain's third-best customer. Britain clung to its commercial lead up to the outbreak of World War I. Financial investment by British nationals lagged far behind. The quest for oil in Ottoman Arab Asia quickened only when the Anglo–Persian Oil Company discovered commercial quantities in Persia in 1908, too late for the find to become practicable before the outbreak of war six years later. Still, the oil potential of the *vilayet* (province) of Mosul riveted the attention, during World War I and afterward, of Britain's companies and their bureaucratic supporters on the Sublime Porte's promise of a concession, in June 1914, to the Turkish Petroleum Company, a nonoperating international consortium of British, Dutch, and German interests registered in London.

Meanwhile, Italy, upon its unification in 1861, promptly entered the fray. After losing a bid for Tunisia in Berlin in 1878, Italy finally occupied Libya and the Dodecanese Islands in a lackluster war with the Ottoman Empire (1911–1912). One of Italy's primary aims in entering the war in 1915 was to legalize the titles to both and, if possible, enlarge its imperial holdings.

Upon replacing Continent-centered Prussia in 1871, unified Germany was the final entrant into the competition. BISMARCK moved into the role vacated by Disraeli. Germany centered its regional activity after 1882 on serving as military and naval adviser and supplier to Sultan ABDÜLHAMIT II (1876–1909). And from 1903, German entrepreneurs, with their government's encouragement and protection, sponsored the building of the Baghdad Railroad to link Europe, across Anatolia through the *vilayets* of Mosul, Baghdad, and Basra, to the head of the Persian Gulf, with Ottoman assurances of privileged investment rights along the way.

Britain's occupation of Egypt in 1882 helped draw Russia and France together, binding them twelve years later in a formal alliance. In all this time and for a decade longer, France kept urging Britain to fix a date for leaving Egypt, while Britain refused to ratify the 1888 Suez Canal Convention until France accepted, for the duration of the occupation, Britain's exercise of the supervisory powers of the projected international commission. Finally the two quarrelers signed an entente cordiale in 1904 that rested on a trade: Britain's responsibility for the canal's security

by occupation in return for France's creating a protectorate in Morocco. Before the year's end, the Concert ratified the amended convention that implied approval of Britain's military presence in Egypt. Finally, Britain and Russia reduced irritants in their relations in the Ottoman Empire by reaching an accord on Iran, Afghanistan, and Tibet in 1907.

The three bilateral instruments underlay the formation of the Triple Entente (Britain, France, and Russia) on the outbreak of war in 1914 against the Central powers (Germany and Austria). For the first time, the Sublime Porte, which entered World War I in November 1914 as an ally of the Central powers, placed itself simultaneously at war with the three countries that had territorial scores to settle with the sultan—Britain in Egypt (and Sudan), France in Tunisia, and Russia at the Turkish Straits. The secret accords of the Entente powers (the CONSTANTINOPLE AGREEMENT of 1915 and the SYKES–PICOT AGREEMENT of 1916) proposed assigning the Turkish Straits and eastern Anatolia to Russia, parceling the Fertile Crescent (later Iraq, Lebanon, Palestine, Syria, and Transjordan) under variable terms among the three allies, and declaring the Arabian peninsula a British sphere of influence.

In April 1915, Italy associated itself with the Entente for the express aim of legitimizing its occupation of Libya and the Dodecanese Islands. Two years later, after the overthrow of the tsarist regime, Italy concluded a separate agreement (treaty of SAINT-JEAN-DE MAURIENNE) with Britain and France, to become a party to the Entente plans for sharing in the Ottoman spoils; to the Sykes-Picot arrangement were added zones for Italy's administration and influence in southern and western Anatolia. But the instrument never won the requisite assent from the Bolshevik regime, which seized power in the fall of 1917. After the war the unratified draft did not deter Italy from trying—but failing—to anchor itself in Anatolia.

Meanwhile, the secret correspondence of Sir Henry MCMAHON (Britain's high commissioner for Egypt) with Sharif HUSAYN IBN ALI of Mecca (the Ottoman governor of the province of Hijaz) served as the basis for mounting an Arab rebellion against the sultan. Clearly, Britain perceived McMahon's exchanges with Husayn, which were started and finished (July 1915–March 1916) before the Sykes-Picot negotiations (December 1915–April 1916), as a solidifying step in the Arabian peninsula. They agreed on mutual military commitments but left unsettled their political differences that gave rise to bitter Anglo–Arab quarrels. The later conflicting Anglo–French–Arab claims in the Fertile Crescent were compounded by the Balfour Declaration: Britain's secret understanding with the Zionists and public declaration of sympathy for the formation in Palestine of a Jewish national home. This was the price that Britain's government had to pay for finally acquiring an exclusive mandatory presence in Palestine in defense of the Suez Canal.

The Eastern Question thus was not resolved until the defeat of the Ottoman Empire in World War I, the empire's formal dissolution in 1922, and the peace treaty of Lausanne—the only such settlement negotiated but not imposed after that war—that the entente and associated powers signed with the Republic of Turkey in 1923 and ratified a year later. Even then, Turkey's nationalist regime at Ankara contested the proposed transfer of two territorial slivers, losing one (the *vilayet* of Mosul to Iraq) in 1926 but winning the other (the return to Turkey by France, as mandatory of Syria, of the *sanjak* [provincial district] of Alexandretta) in 1939. In between, at Turkey's insistence, in the MONTREUX CONVENTION of 1936, the naval signatories of the Treaty of Lausanne restored to the Republic of Turkey full sovereignty over the Turkish Straits by dissolving the International Straits Commission.

BIBLIOGRAPHY

ANDERSON, M. S. *The Eastern Question, 1774–1923: A Study in International Relations.* London, 1966.
HUREWITZ, J. C. *The Middle East and North Africa in World Politics.* 2 vols. New Haven, Conn., 1975–1979.
MARRIOTT, J. A. R. *The Eastern Question: An Historical Study in European Diplomacy.* 4th ed. Oxford, 1940.

J. C. Hurewitz

East India Company

British trading firm doing business in the Middle East during the nineteenth and early twentieth centuries.

The East India Company was active on behalf of Britain in the Persian Gulf, from 1820 until World War I, to ensure the security of Britain's merchant vessels heading toward ports in southern Iraq and Iran. This was achieved by signing peace treaties with the shaykhs of the lower Gulf, the first in 1820 and two more in 1835 and 1853. The main objectives of these treaties were to put an end to piracy, to prevent traffic in slaves, to curb widespread smuggling of arms and other goods, and to promote peaceful trade. By 1869, Britain was able to conclude a treaty in which the Gulf rulers pledged to refrain from conducting foreign relations with powers other than Britain, in effect providing Britain with protectorate powers over those territories.

Britain's interests were represented in the Gulf by the government of India through the local political resident, headquartered in the coastal township of Bushehr in Iran (moved after World War II to Bahrain). The political resident had representatives, called political agents, posted in Kuwait, Qatar, and Bahrain, and political officers in the Trucial Coast.

Jenab Tutunji

Eban, Abba   [1915–   ]

Israeli politician; foreign minister, 1966–1974.

Born in Capetown, South Africa, Aubrey Eban was educated at Queen's College, Cambridge, where he specialized in Middle Eastern languages and literature. He received a master's degree in this field in 1938 and stayed on at Cambridge as a lecturer in Arabic, Persian, and Hebrew literature. After Cambridge, Eban joined the British army, and in 1941 he served as a British army major in Cairo. In the British army, he helped train Jewish volunteers to fight against a German invasion of Palestine.

Eban worked for the Jewish Agency in 1946, and in 1947 he was made a liaison officer to the UNITED NATIONS SPECIAL COMMITTEE ON PALESTINE. He also served as a member of the Jewish Agency's delegation to the General Assembly of the United Nations. After the creation of the State of Israel in 1948, Eban was appointed Israel's representative at the United Nations; he held that position from 1950 to 1959, during which time he also was Israel's ambassador to the United States.

In 1959, Eban was elected to the Knesset for the first time. From 1960 to 1963, he served in David Ben-Gurion's cabinet as minister of education and culture, and, from 1964 to 1965, he was deputy prime minister in the government of Levi Eshkol. During this time, from 1959 to 1966, Eban also was president of Israel's prestigious WEIZMANN INSTITUTE OF SCIENCE. He was foreign minister from 1966 to 1974, and it was during this period in 1967 that he achieved his greatest international visibility, when he presented the case for Israel's war policy before the UN Security Council.

While a member of the Israeli cabinet, Eban argued against the idea of Arab migrant labor, which Moshe Dayan and other cabinet members supported. Eban thought that Israel should not become dependent upon Arab labor, both for economic reasons and for more philosophical reasons relating to the pioneering character of Israel. He was in the minority on this question, however, and Arab day labor increased over time.

In 1974, when Golda Meir resigned, primarily because of political criticism of her government's handling of the Yom Kippur War (1973), Eban was mentioned by some as a possible successor to the prime minister, but his candidacy did not generate much excitement or support from either the public or from members of the MAPAI party. In many respects, Eban subsequently had a bigger following overseas than in Israel. To the surprise of many, he failed to win reelection to the Labor Party's list of nominees for the Knesset. He thereafter retired from politics and devoted himself to educational pursuits and to writing.

BIBLIOGRAPHY

EBAN, ABBA. *Abba Eban: An Autobiography*. New York, 1977.
SACHAR, HOWARD M. *A History of Israel: From the Rise of Zionism to Our Time*. New York, 1981.

Gregory S. Mahler

Ebüzziya Tevfik   [1848–1913]

Ottoman Turkish journalist.

The scion of a notable family; he was born and died in Istanbul. Despite his lack of a formal education, Ebüzziya Tevfik entered the finance ministry where he met and was tutored by Namık Kemal and Şinasi. Forced into exile in Europe, he wrote under the name Ebüzziya. Following the YOUNG TURK revolution, he was elected to parliament as a deputy from Antalya. His first articles appeared in 1868/69 in the newspaper *Terakki*. In 1872, he joined Namık Kemal in publishing *Ibret*. Later, he founded and published two popular literary reviews, *Mecmua-i Ebüzziya* and *Kütüphane-i Ebüzziya*. The latter series included the translation of 114 works of European literature. Among his many publications are *Numune-i Edebiyat-i Osmaniye*, an anthology of Ottoman literature, and *Yeni Osmanlılar Tarihi* (The History of the Young Ottomans).

BIBLIOGRAPHY

ÖZKIRIMLI, ATILLA. *Türk Edebiyati Ansiklopedisi*. Istanbul, 1982.
Yeni Türk Ansiklopedisi. Istanbul, 1985.

David Waldner

Ecevit, Bülent   [1925–   ]

Turkish politician and journalist; former prime minister.

Born in Istanbul, Ecevit graduated from Robert College, Istanbul, in 1944 and then attended English literature classes at Ankara University. Following his appointment to the Press General Directorate, he was sent as an assistant to the press attaché at the Turkish Embassy, London. After his return to Turkey, he worked for the *Ulus* and *Halkçi* newspapers. Ecevit received in 1957 a Rockfeller scholarship and spent one year at Harvard University. He was elected the same year as an MP (member of parliament) from Istanbul on a ticket of the Republican People's party (CHP).

Continuing his career in politics, Ecevit was reelected from Istanbul (1961) and then represented Zonguldak (1965, 1969). After the first military intervention of 1961, he participated actively in the Constituent Assembly (1961), served as the Minister of Labor in the CHP/Adalat Party (or Justice Party, AP) coalition government from 1961 to 1965, and was elected Secretary General of the CHP in 1966. As MP, he wrote a daily column in the *Milliyet* from 1961 to 1965. His political philosophy, best defined as "left of center," continued to gain weight inside the CHP.

Ecevit adopted a clear-cut negative attitude toward the military memorandum of March 12, 1971. As a reaction against İnönü's support of a "nonpartisan" government, he resigned from his post as Secretary General of the CHP. This crisis led to an extraordinary party convention, in which İnönü first resigned from the leadership of the CHP and consequently the party too. As a result, Ecevit was elected chairman of the CHP in 1972. He thus became, after Atatürk and İnönü, its third president.

During the general elections of 1973, the CHP gained the highest number of seats; however, this gain did not enable the party to form a government by itself. After long negotiations and an interim period, a coalition government between the left-of-center CHP and pro-religious National Salvation Party came about, with Ecevit named the prime minister and Turan Güneş the foreign minister. Under his leadership, the ban on the cultivation of poppy, which was imposed because of U.S. political pressure, was lifted and research in the Aegean Sea started. On the occasion of the fiftieth anniversary of the Republic of Turkey, October 29, 1973, general amnesty was pronounced. In order to bring an end to the Cyprus crisis, following the ouster of Archbishop Makarios, Ecevit's government, after exhausting all peaceful legal alternatives decided to initiate in July 1974 the "Cyprus Peace Action" in order to prevent the annihilation of the Turkish Cypriots. The sharp conflict between Ecevit and his coalition partner, Necmeddin ERBAKAN, led to the resignation of the former on September 17, 1974. Ecevit's proposal to go to the polls was rejected, and a government called the National Front was constituted between the AP, the Republican Reliance Party (CGP), the National Salvation Party (MSP), and the Nationalist Action Party (MHP).

Due to the continuous pressure of the opposition (this time the CHP), new elections were held on June 5, 1977. The CHP was able to increase the number of its parliamentary seats from 189 to 213. As a result, the CHP once more was entrusted to form a government. But Ecevit's attempt to establish a minority government failed. Thus, Demirel's second National Front government formed. This government fell by a vote of confidence on December 31, 1977. This time Ecevit formed a coalition government with the help of nine independent MPs. However, the serious defeat of the CHP in by-elections caused Ecevit's resignation and led to the return of Demirel's National Front. Due to escalating domestic violence and the parliament's inability to elect a new president for the republic, the army intervened for the third time in two decades. Ecevit was taken together with Demirel and other party leaders to Hamzaköy for "safety" reasons.

Ecevit labeled the new constitution of 1982 as undemocratic and was arrested twice in 1982 because of his declarations to representatives of the foreign press. Together with all previous Turkish political leaders, he was deprived of his political rights for ten years. During this period, his wife, Rabşan, founded the Democratic Left Party (DSP) and became its first chairperson. Ecevit regained his political rights in 1987 through a countrywide referendum. On September 13, 1987, he assumed leadership of the DSP. During the general elections of 1987, he was not re-elected because his party was unable to fill the 10 percent quota required nationwide. As an act of protest, Ecevit resigned as leader of the DSP and decided to withdraw from political life. However in January 1989, Ecevit changed his mind and resumed once more DSP leadership. In the general elections of 1991, his party with 10.75 percent of the vote nationwide was able to enter parliament with a gain of seven seats.

Ecevit is also a major literary figure, having published many poems as well as several works of political theory, including *Left of the Center* (1966); *This Order Must Change* (1968, 1970); *Atatürk and His Reforms* (1970). His interview with Saddam Hussein in Baghdad on behalf of the *Milliyet* newspaper was awarded the best interview prize in 1990. Ecevit is very critical of the present electoral system, maintaining that it favors only large parties.

BIBLIOGRAPHY

Grolier International Americana Encyclopedia. Danbury, Conn., 1987.
Larousse encyclopédique. Paris, 1962.

Nermin Abadan-Unat

Economic and Military Aid

Countries of the Middle East are prominent both as recipients and donors of foreign assistance.

Israel, Egypt, Turkey, Iraq, and Syria are major long-term recipients, but nearly every country in the region has, at one time or another, received economic and development aid as well as military assistance. The transfers have come in the form of grants and concessional loans for goods and services, for projects and programs, and for direct budgetary support. From the mid-1950s until 1991, the United States and the Soviet Union divided and sometimes shared the region's aid clients, providing most of the assistance to the region. France and Britain, along with other countries in the European community, have also been major benefactors, and, in recent years, Japan has provided direct assistance. Bilateral aid aside, many Middle East states have looked to regional and international lending institutions for financing.

In spite of suspicions about foreign interference, most governments in the region actively seek foreign aid in order to strengthen economies, improve technologies, and bolster military capabilities. The loans and grants are intended to overcome the constraints of insufficient capital investment resulting from limited savings and foreign exchange. Chronic domestic budget deficits—usually traceable to generous consumer subsidies and heavy outlays for arms—help to create and perpetuate a dependence on foreign aid.

Foreign aid to the Middle East often carries ideologies and philosophies of development. In the 1990s, the major donors have pressed liberal economic reforms in recipient countries, stressing export-led growth and expansion of the private sector at the expense of state-owned enterprises. Support for market-oriented economies is believed to enhance the possibility of increasing political pluralism and strengthening civil societies in the region. For the United States and others, the promotion of democratic institutions and human rights is increasingly stated as an objective in giving aid. Environmental and population concerns are also reflected in programs, and humanitarian assistance remains available in times of acute need. But, notably in aid to the Middle East, strategic political objectives overshadow other motives. Donors seek to reward political friends or woo others by improving the ability of governments to realize the demands and fulfill the expectations of their elites and wider publics. Political expediency can lead to minimizing developmental objectives, waiving economic reforms, and ignoring democratic-rights violations. Emphasis on political criteria by the more important donors has, moreover, resulted in the lion's share of foreign aid in the Middle

East, as elsewhere, going to middle-income countries rather than to the poorest, most needy ones.

U.S. economic aid obligated through the Economic Support Fund (ESF) is deemed specifically to be in the foreign-policy interests of the United States. Over the history of the program, aid to Israel and Egypt has dominated expenditures. With strategic concerns uppermost, regimes in Turkey, Jordan, and Morocco have also been amply rewarded. Proponents argue that U.S. economic and military aid to the Middle East contributes to cooperation and stability, and that, earlier, it helped to thwart communist penetration into the region. Thus, U.S. policymakers have at various times actively discouraged direct or indirect assistance to Libya, South Yemen, Syria, Afghanistan, and Iraq, all of them at one time beholden for aid to the Soviet Union. More recently, efforts to prevent technological assistance to Iran have figured strongly in U.S. policy.

U.S. assistance to the Middle East advanced dramatically with the Arab–Israel War of 1973 and its aftermath. Israel was first resupplied militarily and then helped to recover economically from the war. Egypt, which had been heavily dependent on the Soviet Union for aid, was supported in its decision to join the Western camp with promises of development, commodity, and military assistance. U.S. aid subsequently provided critical incentives for signing the Camp David Accords and a peace treaty. Since 1977, Israel and Egypt have received nearly 40 percent of all U.S. aid, more than seventy-five billion dollars in total. But unlike aid given to other countries, the three billion dollars Israel receives annually is not tied to specific projects and is allowed to accrue interest. Egypt, with annual aid at roughly $2.1 billion had, by the mid-1990s, received well over $35 billion from the United States—in the last decade, mainly in the form of grants rather than repayable loans. In reward for Egypt's helpful role in the 1991 Gulf War, the United States agreed to the cancellation of seven billion dollars in loans accumulated earlier for military assistance. Jordan, after concluding a peace agreement with Israel in October 1994, also came in line for debt relief and a major increase in weapons aid from the United States.

Creditors to the region also include the wealthier, oil-exporting states of the Persian Gulf, most notably Saudi Arabia, Kuwait, and the United Arab Emirates. They have assisted the Yemen Arab Republic, Jordan, Sudan, Egypt, and Syria, among others, in filling their investment-resource gap and relieving budgetary pressures. Arab aid has also been designed to buy off potential enemies. Before Saudi Arabia cut back on its foreign-aid programs in the 1990s, it was giving about 2.8 percent of its gross national product

as foreign aid—this compared with an average of 0.36 percent for all industrial countries. It ranked highest among the region's wealthier countries in providing assistance to less-developed nations, directly giving five billion dollars annually. Additionally, Saudi Arabia in the 1980s provided another $7.34 billion through the Saudi Development Fund, about half as grants, with long periods of repayment and very low interest rates. Israel has also been an aid giver with its development and military assistance aimed mainly at solidifying international support in Africa, Latin America, and Asia.

Whatever the drawbacks, politically motivated bilateral aid is less bound by stringent economic requirements set for loans by the International Monetary Fund (IMF) and its sister institution, the development-oriented World Bank. Middle East countries receiving aid from these multilateral-aid sources have been obliged to agree to comprehensive structural reforms of their economies in order to attain loans and reschedule previous debts. These may include the elimination of state subsidies and removal of other price distortions, reform of tax collection, reduction in imports, devaluation of currency, and unification of exchange rates—essentially deflationary policies aimed at greater adherence to free-market principles.

Demands for fiscal and monetary changes and revised development strategies have been widely resented and often resisted. Under pressure from the IMF and World Bank, governments that have accepted the conditions for aid have been forced to introduce economic reforms that bear down hardest on the least well-off in their societies. As a consequence, several countries in the region have had to contend with popular demonstrations against mandated changes. IMF austerity programs over the years have led to street violence in Egypt, Tunisia, and Morocco and contributed to antigovernment activities in Algeria and Sudan.

Among the regional multilateral-aid givers, the Arab Monetary Fund, the Islamic Development Bank, and the OPEC Fund for International Development are the most prominent. The Arab Monetary Fund assists members in balance-of-payments difficulties. It approved ninety-one loans between 1978 and 1993. The Islamic Development Bank offers interest-free loans (with a service fee), mainly for infrastructural financing, agricultural projects, and technical assistance, all of which are expected to have an impact on long-term social and economic development. Priority is given to the import of goods from other member countries of the bank. Major contributors to the bank are Saudi Arabia, Kuwait, and Libya. Loans have been made to several countries outside the region in Africa and Asia. The OPEC fund is a multilateral agency that seeks to reinforce financial cooperation between OPEC member countries and other developing countries. It provides concessional loans for balance-of-payments support, the implementation of development projects and programs, and technical assistance and research financing through grants. The OPEC fund, which has had recipients in Africa, Asia, and Latin America, gives priority to countries with the lowest income. Yet with heavy debts of their own owing to the Gulf War and low oil prices, the generosity, both bilaterally and multilaterally, of the once-cash-rich Arab states declined in the 1990s.

Foreign military credits and grants have greatly eased the burden of defense spending for many Middle East countries. The region is the largest arms market in the third world, accounting for 56 percent of all agreements from 1990 to 1993. With an average of some 30 percent of government expenditures for the military, the Middle East ranked ahead of any other region. In terms of the percentage of gross domestic product devoted to arms expenditures over the last two decades, nine of the top twelve countries—Iraq, Israel, Jordan, Oman, Syria, Egypt, Libya, the Yemen Arab Republic, and the Yemen People's Democratic Republic—have been in the Middle East. Among the leading recipients of major conventional weapons in the last decade are Saudi Arabia, Turkey, Afghanistan, Syria, Israel, and Iran. The major suppliers of arms to the region were the United States, the Soviet Union, France, Britain, and China.

U.S. military sales have been based in large part on a loan program set up in 1975 under which the U.S. Treasury, bypassing the U.S. Congress, provides credits from a special fund at prevailing commercial interest rates. Since most commercial lenders are reluctant to finance weapons purchases, these credits represent a form of foreign assistance. Several countries in the Middle East also received some or all of their arms from the United States on concessionary-loan terms or as outright grants. Beneficiaries through the mid-1990s have included Turkey, Morocco, and Jordan, but Israel and Egypt, assured $1.8 billion and $1.3 billion, respectively, in grants every year, virtually monopolize the most favorable military-assistance program.

The annual value of Russian arms to the Middle East, having fallen to only $1.7 billion by 1994, had been running to at least $20 billion annually during the 1980s. From 1987 to 1990, the Soviets accounted for 20 percent of all conventional weapons sold—mostly in grants, barter deals, or based on artificial exchange rates—while the United States provided 36 percent of all arms to the region over the same period. Much of this is apart from the covert assistance to the

belligerents in Afghanistan during the 1980s. As much as ten billion dollars was spent by the United States in supporting the Afghan resistance in a decade-long war that saw the completion of Soviet-troop withdrawals in early 1989. The Soviet Union is believed to have spent about three hundred million dollars monthly in direct aid to sustain the communist regime in Kabul that finally fell in 1992. During the subsequent civil war among victorious Islamic factions, the United States funded aid programs for returning Afghan refugees and grants for humanitarian assistance until these programs ended in 1995.

It is difficult to assess whether foreign aid has on balance improved the lives and increased the security of most people in the Middle East. Bilateral- and multilateral-aid programs have brought visible infrastructural improvements throughout the region. They have also addressed humanitarian needs, especially in areas of armed conflict, and induced estimable health and social gains. In recent years, foreign advisers have also succeeded in forcing national planners to rationalize strategies of economic growth and have promoted integration within the global economy.

Foreign aid has, however, disappointed both the recipient countries in the Middle East and their donors. Aid-giving countries and agencies have complained about the inefficiencies and domestic corruption that often accompany sponsored programs and doubt the will of national leaders fully to implement reforms. Critics point out that much foreign assistance never actually reaches those it was intended to help. Very modest success in slowing population growth has often wiped out domestic-production gains realized through aid programs. The region has lagged behind most of the world in expanding economic liberalization. Recipient-country industries and trade continue to be highly protected, and while donors applaud evidence of growing democratization in several Arab states, they are concerned about the likely political beneficiaries of free elections. Bilateral donors are also frequently left unsatisfied with the diplomatic cooperation they have extracted from policymakers in Middle East countries.

Aside from the political resentments it provokes, foreign aid is criticized by recipients for its failure to put development on a self-sustaining basis and for possible disincentive effects on domestic production. Although donors have made industrial growth and higher agricultural output high priorities, unemployment remains a serious problem, and appropriate technologies and training are sometimes withheld. Considerable foreign assistance for agriculture that began in the 1980s has neither paid off in terms of impressive export earnings nor greatly improved the capacity for food self-sufficiency in the region's less well-off countries. With the mandating of difficult economic reforms, foreign assistance is also seen as increasing inequities and exacerbating domestic class conflicts.

Most controversial is whether, by selling arms to the Middle East, the United States and other suppliers are reducing conflict by allowing countries to become better able to protect themselves, or whether weapons aid has stimulated defense spending and a regional arms race. Investment of borrowed money and domestic savings in weapons programs may also come at the expense of efforts to deal with severe economic problems and address the welfare of citizens. Accumulated loans have created considerable national debt and a long-term drain on national treasuries. Even so, while the end of the Cold War and the outcomes of recent regional wars have changed some of the sources and character of military and economic assistance, the quest for and dependence on foreign aid is unlikely to diminish any time soon.

BIBLIOGRAPHY

DILLER, DANIEL C. *The Middle East,* 8th ed. Washington, D.C., 1994.

RICHARDS, ALAN, and JOHN WATERBURY. *A Political Economy of the Middle East.* Boulder, Colo., 1990.

SADOWSKI, YAHYA. "The Political Economy of Arms Control in the Arab World." *Middle East Report* (July–August 1992): 3–13.

SIPRI 1994 Yearbook. Oxford, 1995.

SULLIVAN, DENIS J. "Extra-State Actors and Privatization in Egypt." In *Privatization and Liberalization in the Middle East,* ed. by Ilya Harik and Denis J. Sullivan. Bloomington, Ind., 1992.

TENDLER, JUDITH. *Inside Foreign Aid.* Baltimore, 1975.

WEINBAUM, MARVIN G. *Egypt and the Politics of U.S. Aid.* Boulder, Colo., 1986.

Marvin G. Weinbaum

Economics

The economies of the Middle East can be divided into oil producers and nonproducers.

The producers include Saudi Arabia, Iran, Kuwait, Iraq, Qatar, the United Arab Emirates (UAE), Oman, Algeria, and Libya. There are four marginal producers: Bahrain, Yemen, and Syria. The nonproducers or minimal producers are Egypt, Turkey, Jordan, Sudan, Tunisia, and Morocco.

Another taxonomic variable is population. The Middle East has countries with large populations—Iran, Egypt, Turkey, Morocco, and Algeria—and others with minimal indigenous populations—Qatar and the UAE.

The production of oil per capita tends to define the type of economy to which each Middle Eastern country belongs. Countries with oil production per capita of more than 0.25 barrels per day per person tend to emphasize the development of low-labor/high-capital industries. Saudi Arabia, UAE, and Qatar have sought to develop alternatives to their dependence on crude oil by investing heavily in industry, mainly in petrochemicals, which require large amounts of natural gas or crude oil, energy, and capital but minimum labor. Until 1995 most of the development in oil and petrochemicals was spearheaded by the governments, with some support of the private sector. Due to lessening income streams from lower oil prices, efforts are being made to include private industry more fully.

The nonoil economy in the countries with high per capita oil output is very liberal. Except in Libya,

Country	Population (nationals only)	Oil Production (b/d) 1993**	B/d per National	GNP (GDP) (millions of US$)
UAE	380,000	2,191,700	5.77	*$31,600*
Kuwait	606,000	1,852,800	3.06	$8,750
Qatar	160,000	416,400	2.60	$7,400
Saudi Arabia*	12,000,000	8,128,300	0.68	$111,000
Oman	1,900,000	780,000	0.41	*$12,680*
Libya	5,100,000	1,374,600	0.27	$26,100
Bahrain	385,000	38,000	0.10	*$4,000*
Iran	64,000,000	3,647,000	0.06	*$90,000*
Algeria	26,667,000	751,400	0.03	$54,000
Yemen	10,400,000	220,000	0.02	$8,000
Syria	13,500,000	580,000	0.04	$30,000
Iraq***	19,000,000	481,200	0.03	*$35,000*
Egypt	58,000,000	88,000	0.00	$39,200
Turkey	58,584,000	0	0.00	*$91,780*
Morocco	28,600,000	0	0.00	*$27,200*
Tunisia	8,554,000	0	0.00	$10,900
Israel	5,300,000	0	0.00	$57,400
Jordan	3,557,000	0	0.00	$4,400
Lebanon	3,439,000	0	0.00	$4,800
Total	320,132,000	20,549,400		

* The estimate of Saudi population is not based on the official figure of 17 million, but on an average of estimates of scholars.
** Figures from OPEC, Annual Report (1993); IMF, *International Statistics; American Encyclopedia;* Gregory Gause, *Oil Monarchies* (New York, 1994); J.-F. Seznec, *The Financial Markets of the Arabian Gulf* (London, 1988).
*** Should the UN embargo on Iraq be lifted, the production of Iraq could average 3 million b/d for a per capita average of 0.20 b/d/person.

all the countries in this group have no foreign-exchange controls, no restriction on import or export of capital by nationals, no limits on imports and exports (except pork products and alcohol), and most prices are set by supply and demand (although some food staples are subsidized by the governments).

The countries with production between zero and 0.25 b/d/person mostly have large populations (Iran, Syria, Iraq, Algeria). They emphasize centrally planned industrial growth with more labor content. They have very stringent regulations on investments and on foreign-exchange and capital export by residents. Large segments of their economy tend to be nationalized (banks, mining, large manufacturing plants). Their economic growth has been minimal, and most are attempting to deregulate their economies.

The final group (Turkey, Egypt, Morocco, Jordan, etc.), with very limited earnings from oil, relies on private local and foreign investment as well as foreign aid to fund their development.

A large segment of the population in the Middle East is active in agriculture (35.35 percent). However, this average is skewed by the large numbers of people employed in that sector in Egypt (43 percent) and Morocco (50 percent). Mining, manufacturing, and construction employs about 20.57 percent; public administration and services employs 23.54 percent; and trade, transport, and communication employs 9.27 percent.

Oil producers tend to have a much larger percentage of their population in public administration and services, suggesting that oil resources are down-streamed to the population through the creation of jobs in the civil service (34 percent in Saudi Arabia, 40 percent in Qatar, 39 percent in Iraq, 53 percent in Kuwait).

The balance of trade for the whole region is positive (see table above). However, the positive balance is due mainly to the oil producers, who collectively had a positive trade balance in 1991 of about $55 billion. The only nonoil producer with a positive trade balance is Israel.

BIBLIOGRAPHY

Arab Banking and Finance 1994/1995. Bahrain.

ARAB BANKING CORPORATION. *The Arab Economies: Structure and Outlook.* Bahrain, 1983.

GAUSE, GREGORY. *Oil Monarchies: Domestic and Security Challenges in the Arabian Gulf States.* New York, 1994.

INTERNATIONAL MONETARY FUND. *International Financial Statistics.* Washington, D.C.

SEZNEC, JEAN-FRANÇOIS. *The Financial Markets of the Arabian Gulf.* London, 1988.

WORLD BANK. *World Tables.* Baltimore, 1987.

Jean-François Seznec

Eczacıbaşı, Nejat   [1913–   ]

Turkish businessman.

Born in İzmir, Eczacıbaşı studied chemistry and related subjects in Heidelberg, Chicago, and Berlin before founding the various pharmaceutical, cosmetics, housecleaner, and ceramics companies that form the core of the Eczacıbaşı Holding Company. In the early 1990s, it was the fourth-largest conglomerate in Turkey. Eczacıbaşı joined the influential Turkish Industrialists and Businessmen's Association in 1971 and has long advocated land reform as the key to economic progress.

BIBLIOGRAPHY

SCHICK, IRVIN C., and ERTUĞRUL AHMET TONAK. *Turkey in Transition.* New York, 1987.

Elizabeth Thompson

Eddé, Emile

Maronite leader in Lebanon.

A controversial leader in modern Lebanon, Eddé was affiliated with ultranationalist views. After serving as president in the 1930s, he gave support to French policies and actions in the Middle East that discredited him especially in the 1940s, when independence

	Imports	Exports	Trade Balance
Algeria	$9,000	$11,700	$2,700
Bahrain	$3,700	$3,700	$0
Egypt	$11,700	$4,500	($7,200)
Iran	$15,900	$17,800	$1,900
Iraq	$6,600	$10,400	$3,800
Israel	$24,500	$27,800	$3,300
Jordan	$2,300	$1,000	($1,300)
Kuwait	$6,600	$11,400	$4,800
Libya	$8,660	$9,710	$1,050
Lebanon	$3,700	$490	($3,210)
Morocco	$7,600	$4,700	($2,900)
Oman	$3,000	$4,900	$1,900
Qatar	$1,500	$3,200	$1,700
Saudi Arabia	$21,500	$44,300	$22,800
Syria	$2,700	$3,600	$900
Tunisia	$4,900	$3,700	($1,200)
Turkey	$21,000	$13,600	($7,400)
UAE	$11,000	$21,300	$10,300
Yemen	$1,900	$720	($1,180)

sentiments were running high among the people of Lebanon. Muslims in Lebanon consider him hostile to them and reject his hostility to Arabism. Eddé headed the NATIONAL BLOC, which later became a political party under Raymond EDDÉ, his son.

As'ad AbuKhalil

Eddé, Henri [1923–   ]

Lebanese engineer and architect.

After leaving his native Cairo for studies at St. Joseph University of Beirut and the Higher School of Engineering of Beirut, Eddé served as president of the Engineers Association of Lebanon, as a member of the planning and development board, and as secretary-general of the International Architects Union. Eddé was public works minister for the Lebanese government from 1970 to 1971 and education minister briefly in 1972. He began serving as a technical adviser to the government in 1971.

BIBLIOGRAPHY

Who's Who in Lebanon, 1980–1981. Beirut, 1980.

Mark Mechler

Eddé, Raymond [1913–   ]

Lebanese politician and leader of the National Bloc party since 1949; minister of the interior, social affairs, and communications (1958–1959); minister of public works, hydraulic and electric resources, agriculture, and planning (1968–1969).

The eldest son of former president of Lebanon Emile EDDÉ, Raymond was trained as a lawyer at St. Joseph University in Beirut. Following his father's death in 1949, he took over the leadership of the NATIONAL BLOC party. A leader of the opposition to President Bishara al-KHURI, he was elected to parliament in 1953 from the Jubayl district. He was reelected in 1960, 1968, and 1972. Appointed minister following the 1958 civil war, Eddé soon broke with President Fu'ad CHEHAB over the latter's reliance on the Deux-ième Bureau (military intelligence) to implement his policies. In 1967, arguing that the growing influence of the military posed a threat to the open and democratic nature of Lebanon's society, he joined the Tripartite Alliance (with Pierre JUMAYYIL and Camille CHAMOUN), thus ensuring the defeat of the Chehabist candidate Ilyas Sarkis in the 1970 presidential elections.

By the time civil hostilities broke out in 1975, Eddé had become the most outspoken and prominent Christian opponent of the Phalange, which he described as a fascist organization. A representative of the more moderate Maronites, he warned about the potentially disastrous consequences of the growth of paramilitary organizations in Lebanon and strove to prevent the growing polarization in the country by reaching out to like-minded Muslim leaders. However, because he never was a grassroots organizer, lacked mass support within the Maronite community, and refused to organize a militia of his own, he was rapidly marginalized. In January 1977, after three attempts on his life, he went into exile in Paris. In 1989 he opposed the TA'IF ACCORD on the grounds that it institutionalized Syria's power in Lebanon, and expressed support for General Michel Aoun. Following the 1992 legislative elections, he refused to recognize the legitimacy of the new Parliament. Although he is widely respected as a man of principle and is often described as "the moral conscience of Lebanon," his long exile has cut him off from the realities in Lebanon, and his influence over politics there is very limited.

BIBLIOGRAPHY

GORIA, WADE R. *Sovereignty and Leadership in Lebanon, 1943–1976.* London, 1986.
RABINOVICH, ITAMAR. *The War for Lebanon, 1970–1985.* Ithaca, N.Y., 1985.

Guilain P. Denoeux

Edebiyat-i Cedide

See Literature, Turkish

Eden, Anthony [1897–1977]

British statesman; prime minister, 1955–1957.

Richard Anthony Eden, first earl of Avon, was elected a Tory member of Parliament between 1923 and 1957. As minister without portfolio for League of Nations affairs (1935) and as secretary of state for foreign affairs (1935–1938), he concluded the "gentlemen's agreement" with Italy's Count Ciano in 1937 concerning the Mediterranean, after negotiating the 1936 Anglo–Egyptian treaty and the MONTREUX CONVENTION with Turkey. He resigned in disagreement with the policy of Sir Neville Chamberlain concerning Hitler's ambitions for Nazi Germany and the Munich conference but returned as foreign secretary in the World War II governments of Prime Minister Winston S. Churchill.

After the war, he objected to the Labour party's conciliatory policy toward Iran's Prime Minister Mohammad MOSSADEGH. When he resumed office in 1951, he opposed Mossadegh's nationalization of the Anglo–Iranian Oil Company and worked with the United States to bring him down. In 1954, he negotiated an agreement with Egypt for the withdrawal of Britain's troops from the Suez Canal zone and, in the years following, hardened against Egypt's President Gamal Abdel Nasser.

As prime minister from 1955 to 1957, Eden was determined to maintain Britain's prestige in the Middle East. Convinced that Nasser was dangerous, Eden reacted quickly after Nasser nationalized the Suez Canal on July 26, 1956. With France and Israel as allies, Eden orchestrated the October attack on Suez—the ARAB–ISRAEL WAR of 1956—without informing his main ally, the United States. Furious, President Dwight D. Eisenhower and U.S. Secretary of State John Foster Dulles refused to support Eden in the United Nations, insisting on a withdrawal. Humiliated and ill, Eden resigned in January of 1957 and was replaced by Harold Macmillan. Eden was made first earl of Avon and Viscount Eden in 1961. He is the author of *Full Circle* (1960), *Facing the Dictators* (1972), and *The Reckoning* (1965).

BIBLIOGRAPHY

LOUIS, WILLIAM ROGER, and ROGER OWEN, eds. *Suez 1956*. London, 1991.

Zachary Karabell

Edirne

Turkish city on the Bulgarian border, 130 miles (209 km) northwest of Istanbul.

Formerly called Adrianople, the city's population as of 1980 was approximately 361,888. Adrianople dates from antiquity; between 1361 and 1453, it was the capital city of the Ottomans. In the nineteenth century, Edirne was occupied by various invaders of the Ottoman Empire. Given the gentle terrain between Edirne and Istanbul, once an army took Edirne, Istanbul was almost indefensible. The fall of Edirne thus represented a profound defeat for the Ottomans each time it was occupied. In 1829, it was captured by Russia, and the Treaty of Edirne signed soon after marked the temporary ascendancy of Russian influence in Istanbul. Edirne was taken by the Russians again in 1879, by the Serbians and Bulgarians during the First BALKAN WAR in 1913, and then retaken by the Ottoman Turks in the Second Balkan War, also in 1913. Occupied by the Greeks at the end of World War I, Edirne was restored to Turkey in the 1922/23 settlement negotiated in the Treaty of Lausanne.

BIBLIOGRAPHY

SHAW, STANFORD, and EZEL KURAL SHAW. *History of the Ottoman Empire and Modern Turkey*. New York, 1977.
Webster's New Geographical Dictionary. Springfield, Mass., 1988.

Zachary Karabell

Edot ha-Mizrah

The popular term used in Israel for Oriental Jews— those who came from the Islamic countries—now known as Middle Eastern Jews.

The Jewish population that emigrated to Israel from the Middle East, North Africa, India, and Central Asia were considered Oriental by those who had emigrated from northern Europe. The term is problematic, since it lumps SEPHARDIM (Jews expelled from Spain in 1492 to live in Christian Europe and the Islamic Middle East) with Jews who had lived among Muslims since the dispersal in Roman times. These two populations had, in 1,400 years, developed different languages, rituals, and social customs.

The term *Sephardim* had also been employed in Israel for all other Jews but the ASHKENAZIM (who had lived in and around medieval Germany); consequently another term was needed. In both popular and social science discourse, the accepted term is becoming *mizrahim* (literally, Orientals), while the term *edot ha-mizrah* is falling out of use. The customary English meaning of the term *Oriental* leads to another problem as it has the connotation of East Asia, where very few Jews lived and from where even fewer had emigrated to Israel. In English-language discourse, then, social scientists increasingly use the term *Middle Easterners* (which includes immigrants from India—so a problem remains).

Until the late nineteenth century in Palestine, Middle Easterners dominated Jewish society both politically and demographically. Thereafter, as a result of ZIONISM and the vigorous pioneer settlement movement of northern European Jewry, the Middle Easterners faltered. Some emigrated, others became absorbed among the Ashkenazim, and over all, they lost political predominance. In 1948, when the State of Israel was established, mass emigration from Islamic nations changed the demography; by about 1970, some 50 percent of Israeli Jews were of Middle

Eastern background. Since then, the rate of increase of Middle Easterners has lessened, but the inflow from the former Soviet Union has increased and will probably continue to increase as the new republics strike an economic and social balance in the new Europe. The former Soviet Jews are mostly Ashkenazim. In the long run, the reproduction rates of these two categories of Israeli Jews will probably equalize their populations.

It is notable that the marriages that link Israelis of Middle Eastern and European background amount to about 25 percent. Given the approximately even numbers of these two populations in Israel as of the 1990s, the data imply that the intermarriage rate is about 50 percent of the theoretical optimum, indicating social acceptance, at least on the individual level. In the 1950s and 1960s, both institutional and social discrimination had descended on Middle Eastern Jews to burden the economic plight of impoverished refugees, in many cases. The new state was struggling economically to cope with the flow of immigration, so many were housed in the tents and shacks of transit camps or taken to new settlements far from the cities and population centers—to the Galilee and Negev desert towns, to live in homogeneous settlements. Consequently, many only slowly acculturated to their emerging society.

In the 1970s, Middle Eastern Jews regained important political positions in an electoral shift that led to the ascendance of a LIKUD-led coalition government of right-wing and religious parties. The support of Middle Easterners for Likud is linked to their positive view of that party's long-time opposition to the Ma'arakh (Alignment) party. Ma'arakh had formerly dominated them; they are not necessarily in favor of Likud's right-wing politics.

Despite Israel's recent demographic and political developments, the Middle Easterners remain prominent in some of the problem areas of Israeli life. They are overrepresented among the poor, the undereducated, and the criminal fringe. These social problems are rooted partly in the handling of Israel's mass immigration of Middle Easterners in the early 1950s. Like most traditional Jews in the DIASPORA Middle Easterners had filled middleman positions in the economies of their host societies. Those who moved to Western countries soon filled their old economic roles; they did well. These who moved to Israel, however, encountered European immigrants of their own economic type who had arrived earlier, who were politically well connected, and who—crucially—already filled the few available middleman niches in Israel's small, underdeveloped economy; consequently, many Middle Eastern immigrants of the 1950s fell into social, economic, and cultural crises.

Israel's Middle Easterners are composed of ten major populations (listed here according to size): Morocco, Iraq, Yemen, Iran, Tunisia, Turkey, Libya, Egypt, Georgia, and India. According to 1988 figures, more than 600,000 Israelis originate (directly or through their parents) from North Africa; about 260,000 from Iraq; and 160,000 from Yemen. North Africans, the major groups of Middle Easterners, suffered most from the aforementioned travails of immigration. Since the 1950s, the North Africans have evolved certain ways to contend with their depressed condition, particularly through politics and through religio-cultural creativity. The Moroccans in particular have mobilized politically and captured positions within existing political parties dominated by European Israelis (but only secondarily are they engaging in political mobilization on a separatist base). On the religio-cultural plane, Moroccan Israelis have created new holy places to which mass pilgrimages converge, and they engage in the publication of religio-subethnic writings. In the pilgrimages, there figure motifs that enhance various depressed localities, linking them with general Israeli society; there has been a resurgence of interest in traditional religion and in Moroccan origins.

The other two major Middle Eastern groups have taken different paths in Israel. The Iraqis and Yemenis have kept a much lower profile than the Moroccans, both in politics and in religion. The Iraqis had a background of widespread modern education in Iraq, long before emigration. Consequently, once in Israel, the immigrants were better equipped to cope with the limited economic opportunities. Many moved into the professions. In fact, the Israeli Iraqis have done well socially and economically, in comparison with the Moroccans. The Yemenites, in contrast, were relatively less involved in trade but more in crafts in Yemen. Upon arrival in Israel they did not compete to enter trade niches but adapted themselves to opportunities, becoming skilled workers and craftsmen.

Since the 1970s, people of Middle Eastern background have attained many notable positions in Israel. There has been a state president (Yitzhak NAVON), two army chiefs-of-staff (David Elazar and Moshe Levy), and several cabinet ministers. Also in academics, there has been a Tel Aviv University president (Moshe Many) and several recipients of the prestigious Israel Prize for arts and science. No Middle Easterner has yet attained the pinnacle positions of prime minister or of minister of defense, although one did fill the crucial position of finance minister (Moshe Nissim). Typically, the single Middle Eastern figure who for several years was considered a serious contender for the position of prime minister is David Levy, whose main base of power is the Moroccan ethnic constituency. Although in the early 1990s the Middle Easterners have not succeeded in attaining the ultimate political prizes, two fundamental sociopolitical factors operate in their favor. One has been the long, slow resolution of the Palestinian problem (which has provided cheap labor for the Israeli market). The second is the early 1990s mass migration from the former Soviet Union, which has had a similar effect on the economic sector. The result is that Middle Easterners have become positioned well above the lowest rungs of the Israeli socioeconomic order—in contrast to conditions that existed before the 1970s.

BIBLIOGRAPHY

BEN-RAFAEL, E., and S. SHAROT. *Ethnicity, Religion and Class in Israeli Society.* Cambridge, U.K., 1991.
DESHEN, S., and M. SHOKEID, eds. *Jews of the Middle East: Anthropological Perspectives on Past and Present.* Tel Aviv, 1984.
INBAR, M., and C. ADLER. *Ethnic Integration in Israel: A Comparative Study of Moroccan Brothers Who Settled in France and Israel.* New Brunswick, N.J., 1977.
SCHMELZ, U. O., S. DELLA PERGOLA, and U. AVNER. *Ethnic Differences among Israeli Jews.* Jerusalem, 1991.
WEINGROD, A. *The Saint of Beersheba.* Albany, N.Y., 1990.

Shlomo Deshen

Effendi

A title of respect.

Effendi was an Ottoman title of Greek origin, meaning "lord" or "master," probably via a Byzantine colloquial form of *afendi* or the Greek *aphetes*, designating a man of property, authority, or education in the eastern Mediterranean. The term was used after the thirteenth century. The word became increasingly common in late Ottoman usage as a designation of certain middle classes. It was especially used to indicate important functionaries. The chief secretaries of the diwan were called effendis.

Mia Bloom

Ege University

Public university in İzmir, Turkey.

Founded in 1955, Ege (or Aegean) University now comprises faculties of medicine, dentistry, pharmacy, agriculture, science, engineering, and letters, as well as schools of journalism and broadcasting, water

products, nursing, a conservatory of Turkish music, and five vocational training schools, two of which are located in neighboring Manisa and Uşak provinces. English and Turkish are used in the programs in computer sciences, food engineering, and chemical engineering. In 1990, the university had about 1,650 teaching staff and 17,500 students (about half were female). In 1991, its state-funded budget amounted to 242 billion Turkish lire, of which about 50 billion was for capital investment.

Turkey's third-oldest university was established in response to growing demand for higher education in the prosperous region around İzmir, whose traditional agricultural and commercial potential led the way to rapid industrial development in the era of political and economic liberalization. As befits its name, the university has lately tried to establish programs emphasizing its relationship with the Aegean Sea and the rest of the Mediterranean area as a cultural and ecological region.

BIBLIOGRAPHY

Higher Education in Turkey. UNESCO, European Centre for Higher Education. December 1990.
World of Learning. 1990.

I. Metin Kunt

Egypt

Arab nation occupying northeastern Africa and the Sinai peninsula.

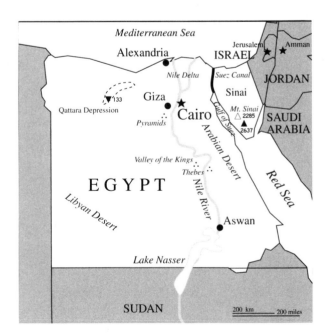

Egypt is bordered by the Mediterranean Sea on the north, Sudan on the south, the Red Sea on the east, and Libya on the west. It consists of three regions: (1) the Nile valley and Nile Delta (a little less than 4 percent of the total area), extending from Sudan north to the Mediterranean; (2) the eastern desert–Sinai peninsula (28 percent), extending from the Nile valley to the Red Sea east of the Suez Canal; and (3) the Western desert (68 percent), stretching from the Nile valley west to Libya.

Egypt's geographic position makes it an easy country to control and rule. Its society and polity are characterized by central rule and the absence of long-standing regional allegiances. Dependence on the Nile for irrigation has called for central administration and enabled the government to extend its authority to the distant parts of the land. And because the territory is mostly desert, 96 percent of Egyptians live on less than 5 percent of the total area of the country.

Population and Social Structure. Egypt is one of the oldest continuously settled lands in the world. Egyptians speak Arabic, with the exception of the Nubians (less than 1 percent). More than 90 percent of the population are Muslim, and ISLAM is the state religion. The COPTS are the largest non-Muslim religious group. Estimates of their numbers vary between 2.3 and 4 million. In 1992, the total population of Egypt was 58 million and was increasing by 1 million less than every ten months. The growth rate between 1966 and 1976 was about 65,000 persons each month.

Almost half of Egyptians are under twenty years of age; two-thirds are under thirty. Thus there is high dependency ratio (the number of dependents supported by working adults), a situation that severely strains the economy. The government is increasingly unable to meet the demands for food, education, and work opportunities. Thus some 3 million Egyptians migrate to other Arab countries, particularly the oil-producing states, in search of work. Their remittances constitute a major source of Egypt's hard currency.

In contrast to many developing countries, Egypt has a high degree of social and national integration. Presidents Gamal Abdel NASSER (1956–1970), Anwar al-SADAT (1970–1981), and Husni MUBARAK (1981–) have spoken proudly of Egypt's national unity. The one major area of anxiety is the Copts' concern about the implementation of Islamic law in Egypt and the status of Copts in an Islamic state.

Population growth has limited Egypt's development efforts by aggravating unemployment, increasing the dependency ratio, spurring rural migration to urban centers, and diverting resources from investment to consumption needs. Population is increasing at a rate far beyond the increase of arable crop land

Common motifs of the Egyptian landscape. (© Andrea C. Hoyer)

and far beyond educational and industrial development. Although the cropped area almost doubled between 1882 and 1970, population growth absorbed and exceeded the increase. Since the 1970s Egypt has had to import food. This has made it more dependent on the outside world and more vulnerable to the fluctuations of food prices.

Economy. Since the 1970s economic factors have played a crucial role in Egypt's politics. By 1991,

Bahriyya oasis, Egypt. (David Rewcastle)

One of the sixty gates of medieval Cairo, Bab al-Futuh, the Gate of Conquests, was built in 1087. (Richard Bulliet)

inflation was nearly 21.3 percent a year, the national debt was $25 billion, and the GNP per capita was $600. Indeed, since World War II, Egypt has had a balance-of-payments deficit that has had to be made up from other sources. From 1948 to 1958 it was accomplished through existing reserves; from 1958 to 1964, Egypt received foreign aid from Eastern and Western sources; from 1965 to 1971, the former Soviet Union shouldered most of the deficit; from 1971 to 1977, the aid was primarily from Arab nations; and since 1978, support has been from the United States and the West.

In 1974 Sadat inaugurated al-INFITAH, the open door economic policy (ODEP), to attract foreign investment. He justified it on the following grounds: (1) the failure of Nasser's socialist experience; (2) the availability of capital from Arab oil-producing countries; and (3) the international context of détente. From an economic standpoint, the two essential purposes of ODEP were (1) to attract export-oriented foreign enterprises by establishing duty-free zones and (2) to attract foreign capital through a liberal investment policy. However, the ultimate goal was to develop Egypt's economy through joint ventures and projects bringing together Egyptian labor, Arab capital, and Western technology and management expertise.

Egypt's policy of economic reform led to a restructuring of its economy. In the early 1990s, the government implemented financial stabilization (unifying the rate of exchange, reducing subsidies) and started a program of structural adjustment (privatization and trade liberalization).

History and Politics. On 1 July 1798 the people of ALEXANDRIA watched some three hundred French ships standing out to sea, preparing to invade Egypt. The expedition, led by Napoléon BONAPARTE, subjected Ottoman Egypt to a direct confrontation with the dynamic civilization of Europe.

In the wake of the popular uprising that followed France's withdrawal in 1801, Egypt forced the Ottoman Porte to accept MUHAMMAD ALI as *wali* of the country. Muhammad Ali (ruled 1805–1849) modernized Egypt's administrative, economic, and military structures by introducing Western methods and technologies.

By the 1880s, a succession of incompetent rulers had reduced Egypt to a state of anarchy and bankruptcy that culminated in the URABI revolt. The revolt was suppressed, and on 11 July 1882 Britain bombarded Alexandria, marking the start of an occupation that lasted for seventy-two years.

Britain took virtual control of Egypt's finances and foreign affairs, and the real ruler was Britain's consul general. In response, a national movement emerged with the objective of achieving Egypt's independence. The struggle of Mustafa KAMIL, Muhammad FARID, and Sa'd ZAGHLUL achieved success in 1922. On 28 February, Britain's declaration terminated the protectorate (declared in October 1914), proclaimed Egypt a sovereign, independent kingdom, and reserved four issues for future negotiations: imperial communication, defense, minorities, and the Sudan. On 15 March 1922, Ahmad FU'AD was proclaimed king; a constitution was issued on 9 April 1923.

From 1923 to 1936, negotiations took place on the four reserved points. The treaty of 1936 settled most of the issues and organized the presence of Britain's troops in the Suez Canal Zone. The treaty was opposed by a number of political forces, including the powerful MUSLIM BROTHERHOOD. On 15 October 1951, Egypt's government unilaterally abrogated the treaty, and Britain's soldiers and installations increas-

Landscape of Sakkara District in Egypt. (D.W. Lockhard)

ingly became targets of commando operations. Egypt's military defeat in the ARAB–ISRAEL WAR of 1948 coincided with social and political instability that had originated in the early 1940s as a result of increasing class disparities, uncontrolled urbanization, and labor unrest.

The monarchy violated or suspended the constitution and dissolved parliaments. During King Fu'ad's reign (1922–1936), the constitution was suspended three times. The WAFD, the most popular party, held power less than eight years (out of thirty). It was dismissed from office in 1928, 1931, 1937, and 1952. No Egyptian parliament ever completed its term of office, and the average life of a cabinet was less than eighteen months.

These tensions led to frequent demonstrations, widespread political alienation, and the growth of "system challenging organizations," such as the Muslim Brotherhood, the YOUNG EGYPT Party, Communist organizations, and the FREE OFFICERS group. The insistence of the palace on absolute rule, the opposition of the ruling class to reform, and the rigidity of Britain's position on withdrawal from the Suez Canal Zone gave rise to the belief that only revolution could bring about change. On 23 July 1952, the army intervened; three days later King FAROUK abdicated the throne to his infant son. In June 1953, the monarchy was abolished and a republic was declared.

From 1952 to 1970, the basic characteristics of the political regime in Egypt were absence of political competition, centralization of power, emphasis on mobilization rather than participation, and the supremacy of the executive branch. In the absence of political parties, three organizations became vehicles for political mobilization: the LIBERATION RALLY (1953–1956), the NATIONAL UNION (1956–1962), and the ARAB SOCIALIST UNION (1962–1977).

An imbalance clearly existed between politics and administration; the bureaucracy, police, and army far outgrew interest groups and political organizations. Whenever possible, the government attempted to penetrate and dominate intermediary associations and groups such as trade unions, professional associations, and religious institutions, bringing them under its legal and financial control. During the same period, the state controlled broad areas of the economy in the name of achieving rapid development and social justice.

In the 1970s there was increasing civilianization of the ruling elite and the development of political pluralism. Sadat professionalized the army, disengaged it from politics, and placed more reliance on civilians in high posts. For the first time since 1952, civilians held the posts of vice president (Mahmud FAWZI) and prime minister (Aziz Sidky, Mahmud

The Nile river at Luxor. (Richard Bulliet)

Fawzi, Abdel-Aziz Hegazi, and Moustafa Khalil). The gradual democratization of the political structure led in 1977 to the establishment of a controlled multiparty system. Domestically, Sadat was eager to establish his legitimacy independent from Nasser's. The failure of the Arab Socialist Union as a political institution was generally accepted, and an increasing number of intellectuals and professional associations advocated political pluralism. Externally, Sadat's rapprochement with the United States and his desire to project the image of a democratic Egypt reinforced this trend.

The judiciary, an independent and respected institution, referees many issues, including the establishment of new political parties. Applications for new parties are considered by a committee whose decisions are subject to judicial review. Since its establishment in 1977, the committee has not approved any new parties. Only through court verdicts overturning the committee's rejections have new parties been formed.

In 1993, there were twelve political parties in Egypt. The most important were the ruling NATIONAL DEMOCRATIC PARTY (NAP), headed by President Mubarak with 85 percent of parliamentary seats; the Labor Socialist Party (LSP), led by Ibrahim Shukry, which adheres to Islamic ideology and had formed a coalition with the Muslim Brotherhood; and the leftist NATIONAL PROGRESSIVE UNIONIST PARTY (NPUP), led by Khalid Mohie al-Din.

Throughout the 1980s and until 1993, political life in Egypt was dominated by the NAP, which could not make itself into a credible political force. All of Egypt's twelve political parties suffer from lack of a strong organization and/or a coherent ideology. The opposition parties have been unwilling to compromise and have shown little talent for coalition politics. Ideological cleavages, historical legacies, and leadership rivalries have kept them from working together to challenge the NAP.

Integrating Islamist groups into the political process remains a problem. Between 1987 and 1990, the Muslim Brotherhood, which wants the country to adopt Islamic law, had approximately fifty members in Parliament. Their boycott of the 1990 parliamentary elections and their opposition to the government during the second Gulf war have weakened their position, yet they remain the most influential Islamist group. Small, militant Islamist groups, such as al-Jihad, have resorted to violence. By 1992, the Islamic influence controlled most universities' student unions and professors' associations, as well as a number of professional associations (e.g., of engineers, physicians, pharmacists, and lawyers).

What is the balance sheet for the democratization process in Egypt? On the positive side are a liberal tradition, a strong sense of national identity, and a complex civil society. Another positive element is a middle class that has increasingly organized itself into a network of business associations, trade unions, and professional syndicates and thus contributed to consensus building outside the political process. On the negative side, Egypt has a tradition of authoritarianism. The ruling elite has grown up with and worked within a single-party system. Most parties, including those in opposition, have little internal democracy. And many parties have adopted ideologies that are incompatible with the working of democratic institutions. Ultimately, Egypt's democracy and political stability will rest on its ability to solve its acute economic troubles.

BIBLIOGRAPHY

BAKER, R. W. *Egypt's Uncertain Revolution under Nasser and Sadat.* Cambridge, Mass., 1983.
DEKMEJIAN, R. H. *Egypt under Nasser.* New York, 1974.
GOLDSCHMIDT, ARTHUR. *Modern Egypt: The Formation of a Nation-State.* Boulder, Colo., 1988.
HINNEBUSCH, R. A. *Egyptian Politics.* New York, 1985.
VATIKIOTIS, P. J. *The History of Egypt from Muhammad Ali to Mubarak.* London, 1985.
WATERBURY, J. *The Egypt of Nasser and Sadat: The Political Economy of Two Regimes.* Princeton, N.J., 1983.

Ali E. Hillal Dessouki

Egyptian Geographical Society

Group of geographers in Egypt.

Khedive Isma'il founded the Khedivial (later Royal, now Egyptian) Geographical Society in 1875 to promote and legitimize his empire in the Sudan and the

Horn of Africa. The society later shifted its concentration to Egypt itself and evolved from a foreign-dominated layman's society into the professional society of Egyptian geographers.

BIBLIOGRAPHY

REID, DONALD MALCOLM. "The Egyptian Geographical Society: From Foreign Layman's Society to Indigenous Professional Association." *Poetics Today.* 1993.

Donald Malcolm Reid

Egyptian–Israeli Peace Treaty

See Camp David Accords

Egyptian Museum

The world's finest collection of pharaonic antiquities is exhibited, stored, and studied here.

The Ottoman Empire's viceroy of Egypt, Sa'id Pasha, commissioned French Egyptologist Auguste

Sarcophagus of King Tut, made of gold and lapis lazuli. (David Rewcastle)

View of the Egyptian Museum in Cairo. (Laura Mendelson)

MARIETTE to create an antiquities service and a museum in 1858. In 1863, Khedive Isma'il inaugurated the Egyptian Museum in Cairo. Moved to Giza in 1891, the museum has occupied its present building in Tahrir Square in Cairo since 1902. Gaston MASPERO succeeded Mariette as director of the museum and the Antiquities Service in 1881. For ninety-four years, until the 1952 revolution, all directors of the service were French. In 1954, Mustafa Amir took over as the first Egyptian director. The museum gradually relegated subsidiary collections to the Greco-Roman, Arab (later called Islamic), and Coptic museums. Since the 1920s, the Tutankhamen collection has been the museum's greatest treasure. The present building has been overcrowded almost since it opened, but proposals for a new structure—ranging from a Rockefeller proposal in the 1920s to a recent Japanese overture—have yet to move forward.

BIBLIOGRAPHY

ABOUBAKR, ABDEL MONEIM. "Historique du musée égyptien à l'occasion du centenaire de sa création." *La Revue du Caire* 42 (January 1959): 1–30.

Donald Malcolm Reid

Egyptian–Syrian Defense Pact

Agreement for mutual defense against military aggression.

On November 7, 1966, following several months of rising tension between Israel and Syria, Egypt and Syria signed a five-year mutual defense pact requiring the two parties to come to each other's assistance in case of threat of military aggression. The two countries exchanged ambassadors for the first time since the dissolution of the United Arab Republic in 1961 and established a joint high command. The two countries had their own reasons for signing the pact: while Egypt's president, Gamal Abdel NASSER, hoped to gain some control over Syrian foreign policy, the Syrians were interested in mobilizing Egypt in support of their own policy of using Palestinian guerillas to harass Israeli operations in the demilitarized zone between Syria and Israel. The signing of the pact did not ease the escalation of tensions between Syria and Israel, and in May 1967, Syria charged Israel with mobilizing troops for an impending attack and requested Egypt to fulfill its obligations defined by the pact. The pact lapsed in 1971, though Syria and Egypt continued to coordinate military strategy through 1973.

BIBLIOGRAPHY

SEALE, PATRICK. *Asad: The Struggle for the Middle East.* Berkeley, Calif., 1988.

David Waldner

Egyptian Women's Union

Women's rights organization.

Often called the Egyptian Feminist Union, the Egyptian Women's Union was founded by Huda al-SHA'ARAWI in 1923 to demand voting rights for women in Egypt. It also spearheaded the rejection of the veil by Egyptian women as a step toward their emancipation. After opening a women's clubhouse in Cairo, the group published monthly journals in both French and Arabic, ran a clinic and a dispensary for poor women and children, and established childcare centers for working mothers. As a result of their actions, the government set a minimum marriage age and opened its first secondary school for girls. As the Palestine conflict intensified, the Egyptian Women's Union convened an Arab women's conference in 1938 and another in 1944; it thus laid the groundwork for the Arab Feminist Union, which elected Huda al-Sha'arawi as its first president. Following her death in 1947, the Egyptian Women's Union was eclipsed by other feminist groups that attracted younger women. After the 1952 Revolution, the union's functions were taken over by government ministries, and it faded away.

BIBLIOGRAPHY

KEDDIE, NIKKI, and BETH BARON, eds. *Women in Middle Eastern History.* New Haven, Conn., 1992.

AL-SABAQI, AMAL KAMIL. *Al-haraka al-nisa'iyya fi misr ma bayna thawratayn 1919 wa 1952.* Cairo, 1987. In Arabic.

SHAARAWI, HUDA. *Harem Years: The Memoirs of an Egyptian Feminist.* Tr. and intro. by Margot Badran. New York, 1987.

Arthur Goldschmidt, Jr.

Ehrlich, Simha   [1915–1983]

Israeli politician.

Born in Poland, Ehrlich was active with the youth movement of Zionism there before immigrating to Palestine in 1938. He made his political start in municipal politics in Tel Aviv, and then entered the Knesset (parliament) in 1969 as member of the Liberal party. He became minister of finance in Prime Minister Menachem Begin's 1977 Likud coalition, but he quickly fell victim to rising inflation and public outcry at his handling of the economy. Resigning as head of finance, he became deputy prime minister and oversaw the development of Galilee.

BIBLIOGRAPHY

ROLEF, SUSAN H., ed. *Political Dictionary of the State of Israel.* New York, 1987.

Zachary Karabell

Eisenhower, Dwight David   [1890–1969]

U.S. Army officer; president of the United States, 1953–1961.

Born in Denison, Texas, Eisenhower graduated from the U.S. Military Academy at West Point, New York, in 1915. During World War II, he was chief of the war plans division, U.S. general staff, before becoming commander in chief of U.S. forces, European theater, and commander of allied forces in Northwest Africa. In 1943, he was appointed general, supreme commander in North Africa and the western Mediterranean, and he planned the invasions of North Africa, Sicily, and Italy. He was made general of the army in 1944 and planned and commanded the European invasion at Normandy, France, called D-Day (June 6, 1944). After conquering Nazi Germany, Eisenhower remained in Europe as the U.S. member of the Allied Control Commission for Germany and chief of staff of the U.S. Army (1945–1948).

In 1948, Eisenhower returned to the United States and became the president of Columbia University (1948–1953) while remaining supreme commander

of the North Atlantic Treaty Organization (NATO) forces in Europe (1951/52). He was then persuaded to run for president of the United States on the Republican ticket, won, and served two terms (1953–1961). Along with his secretary of state, John Foster DULLES, he was concerned about preventing Soviet incursions in the Middle East, whether economic, political, or ideological. Careful to maintain good relations with the Arab states, he showed no undue favoritism to the new State of Israel. At first he was interested in funding the Aswan High Dam in Egypt, but President Gamal Abdel Nasser's 1955 arms deal with Czechoslovakia, a Soviet satellite country, led Eisenhower, on the advice of Dulles, to deny the loan. In the 1956 ARAB–ISRAEL WAR, when France, Britain, and Israel attempted to take back the SUEZ CANAL from Nasser's nationalization of it, Eisenhower angrily brought the matter to the United Nations, calling for a cease-fire and a withdrawal. This stance won him few friends in the Middle East—only Hashimite-ruled Iraq and Reza Pahlavi's Iran.

On January 5, 1957, Eisenhower proposed the policy that became known as the Eisenhower Doctrine, calling on Congress to provide military and economic aid to any Middle Eastern nation that believed itself under risk from "armed aggression from any country controlled by international communism." In July 1958, in the wake of the revolution in Iraq, President Camille Chamoun of Lebanon appealed to the United States for help. Believing that the security of Lebanon was endangered by Nasser and by communism, Eisenhower dispatched a contingent of U.S. Marines from the Sixth Fleet; they landed on July 15 to be greeted by astonished sunbathers but stayed for almost four months. Order was restored to Lebanon, and power passed from Chamoun to General Fu'ad Chehab.

BIBLIOGRAPHY

AMBROSE, STEPHEN. *Eisenhower: The President.* New York, 1984.

SCHOENEBAUM, ELEANORA, ed. *Political Profiles: The Eisenhower Years.* New York, 1977.

SPIEGEL, STEVEN. *The Other Arab–Israeli Conflict.* Chicago, 1985.

Zachary Karabell

Eitan, Rafael   [1929–   ]

Chief of staff of the Israeli military; member of Israel's Knesset.

Rafael Eitan was born in Israel, at Moshav Tel Adashim. He attended the University of Tel Aviv and Israel's National Security College. He joined the PALMACH in 1946 and fought in the Arab–Israel War of 1948. After serving in a number of high posts in the Israeli military, he became chief of staff in 1978, serving until 1983. As chief of staff, he worked with Defense Minister Ariel Sharon to plan and execute the invasion of Lebanon in the Arab–Israel War of 1982. In the aftermath of that war, he was criticized by the Kahan Commission, which investigated Israel's conduct in the war, for failing to prevent the mass killing of Palestinian civilians in the Sabra and Shatila refugee camps.

In 1983, Eitan entered politics, founding the right-wing nationalist Tzomet party, which united with the Tehiya party before the 1984 elections. Eitan has been a member of the Knesset (Israel's parliament) representing the Tzomet and Tehiya parties since 1984 and has been an unrelenting advocate of the annexation of the WEST BANK and GAZA STRIP. In the early 1990s, he rejected an offer to join the government under Yitzhak Rabin.

BIBLIOGRAPHY

ROLEF, SUSAN H., ed. *Political Dictionary of the State of Israel*. New York, 1987.

Martin Malin

Eldad, Israel   [1910–   ]

Israeli politician.

Born in eastern Galicia when it was part of the Austro-Hungarian Empire, Eldad (whose original name was Scheib) received a Ph.D. from the University of Vienna and graduated from the Vienna Rabbinical Seminary. He taught in Jewish schools in Poland during the 1930s and became a member of the REVISIONIST MOVEMENT, Betar, as a follower of Vladimir Jabotinsky, Menachem Begin, and Abraham Stern.

After emigrating to Palestine in 1941, he was a leader of the Stern Gang (LOHAMEI HERUT YISRAEL, Lehi), a militant group dedicated to the independence of Zionist Palestine. In 1944, he was arrested by the British (who held the mandate over Palestine from 1922 to 1948) for his missions against them. After Israel had become independent in May 1948 and Prime Minister David Ben-Gurion had dissolved Lehi in September of 1948, Eldad remained a prominent advocate of a GREATER ISRAEL, encompassing the land between the Nile and the Euphrates rivers.

Eldad became a lecturer of the Haifa Technion, and he edited the journal *Sulam* until 1964. In response to Eldad's inflammatory attacks, Prime Minister Ben-Gurion banned him from teaching. After the 1967 Arab-Israel War, when Israel took Jerusalem and the West Bank territory, Eldad's star rose. He became a hero of Israel's extreme right and made his views known as a columnist for Israel's daily newspaper *Haaretz*.

BIBLIOGRAPHY

ROLEF, SUSAN H., ed. *Political Dictionary of the State of Israel*. New York, 1987.

Zachary Karabell

Eldem, Sedad Hakki   [1908–1988]

Turkish architect.

Eldem was born into an artistic Istanbul family. His uncle was Osman Hamdi Bey, founder of the Istanbul Fine Arts Academy. Eldem went to school in Switzerland and Germany before studying architecture at his uncle's academy from 1924 to 1928; he remained a teacher at the academy until 1962. By age thirty-one, he had designed some of the major buildings in the new Republic of Turkey: the Yalova Termal Hotel (1937), the office building for the prime ministry (1938), and the Turkish pavilion at the New York World's Fair (1939). He became the most influential architect in mid-century Turkey.

Eldem wrote articles defending local architectural styles over international styles and, in a nationalist vein, argued that foreign architects should never be allowed to build in Turkey. Nonetheless, because of German influence and a shortage of materials in the 1940s, Elden built the faculties of arts at Ankara and Istanbul universities in a modern, monumental, streamlined style. His only gesture toward Turkish roots was ornamental detail. In 1954, he built the modern-style Istanbul Hilton Hotel. Eldem also served as president of Turkey's antiquities committee and wrote a book on Turkish domestic architecture.

BIBLIOGRAPHY

YAVUZ, YILDIRIM. "Turkish Architecture during the Republican Period (1923–1980)." In *The Transformation of Turkish Culture,* ed. by Günsel Renda and C. Max Kortepeter. Princeton, N.J., 1986.

Elizabeth Thompson

Elgin, Lord

See Bruce, Thomas

Elites

Small but powerful minorities with a disproportionate influence in human affairs.

Both tribal society and Islam have a strong egalitarian component, but early Islamic writers assumed a distinction between the few (*khassa*) and the many (*amma*) not unlike that in modern Western elite theory between the elite and the masses. Like the term *elite, khassa* had vague and various meanings. It was applied on occasion to the following: the early (661–750) Arab aristocracy under the Umayyads; the whole ruling class; the inner entourage of a ruler; educated people generally; and philosophers who pursued a rational (and sometimes a mystical) road to truth.

In the 1960s and 1970s, elite analysis—pioneered by V. Pareto and G. Mosca early in the century, partly as an alternative to Marxist class analysis—attracted many Western scholars of the Middle East. National political elites received much of the attention, although anthropologists continued their special interest in local elites. Economic, social, and cultural elites attracted notice particularly when they overlapped with political elites. Elite studies examine the background, recruitment, socialization, values, and cohesiveness of elites. They probe elite–mass linkages, circulation into and out of the elite, the effects of elite leadership on society, and the evolution of all these factors over time.

The Ottoman Empire, which ruled loosely over most of the Middle East in the late eighteenth century, conceived of society as divided into a ruling class of *askari*s (literally, "soldiers" but also including "men of the pen"—ULAMA [Islamic scholars] and scribal bureaucrats) and a ruled class of *re'aya* (subjects). "Ottomans" were the core elite among the askaris, presumed to be muslim, available for high state service, and familiar with the manners and language (Ottoman Turkish, which also entailed a knowledge of Arabic and Persian) of court. The recruitment of slaves into the elite was one mechanism that made for extreme upward social mobility.

Ever shifting social realities rarely match prescriptive theories. Although theoretically excluded from the askari elite, merchants, Coptic scribes, Jewish financiers, and Greek Orthodox patriarchs wielded considerable power in some times and places. Women attained such great informal power during one seventeenth-century period that the Ottomans called it "the sultanate of women." When central control weakened—as in the Fertile Crescent provinces in the eighteenth and early nineteenth centuries, a "politics of notables" mediated between the center and the provincial masses. Notable status often ran in families; the notables could include *ulama*,

tribal shaykhs, merchants, large landowners, and local military forces.

Since 1800, the Middle East and its elites have greatly changed under the impact of the Industrial Revolution, European conquest and rule, the breakup of the Ottoman Empire, NATIONALISM and independence struggles, the ARAB–ISRAEL CONFLICT, the petroleum and oil bonanza, secularist and Islamic ideologies, and the frustrations of continuing military, cultural, and economic dependency. Yet there has been continuity too.

In the countries where COLONIALISM prevailed, foreign elites forced the partially displaced indigenous elites to make the painful choice of collaboration or resistance. Collaboration was particularly tempting to some religious and ethnic minorities. In the Fertile Crescent, tribal shaykhs and large landowners functioned as notables mediating between the colonial power and the people, as they had once done with the Ottomans. Whether one collaborated or not, knowledge of the West and Western language became a career asset for officials and the emerging professional class. In the milieu of mandates and of party and parliamentary politics between the two world wars, lawyers flourished in both government and opposition. After World War II, as most Middle Eastern countries regained control of their affairs, landed elites and reactionary politicians in many cases still frustrated serious social reform. Pressure built, and army officers of lower-middle-class origin overthrew one regime after another. Was it a return to the praetorian politics of the Ottoman JANISSARIES and the MAMLUKS—the armed forces that early nineteenth-century rulers had destroyed to clear the way for Western-style armies? The new armies remained on the political sidelines for most of the nineteenth century, reemerging briefly in Egypt during Ahmad URABI's vain attempt to resist colonial control.

After 1900, armies reentered politics first in countries that had escaped colonial rule—Turkey with the YOUNG TURKS and Mustafa Kemal Atatürk and Iran with Reza Shah Pahlavi. Military coups in the Arab countries began later, following independence from colonial rule: Iraq in the 1930s and again in 1958, Syria in 1949, and Egypt in 1952. The regime of Gamal Abdel Nasser—with its Soviet alliance, single-party authoritarianism, and Arab socialism—became a prototype for many others. Hopes that the new military elites and their civilian technocratic allies—economists, engineers, scientists—represented the progressive vanguard of a new middle class soon proved to be overblown.

Patrilineal monarchies in Morocco, Jordan, Saudi Arabia, and elsewhere in the Arabian peninsula weathered the revolutionary Arab socialist challenge. Oil wealth helped rulers purchase political acquiescence, but it did not save the monarchs of Iraq, Libya, or Iran. In both the monarchies and their revolutionary challengers, patterns of authoritarian rule persisted. Family connections, old-boy networks, and patron–client relations still figure prominently in elite recruitment and perpetuation despite the widespread longing for a fair and open system.

Unlike the military, the *ulama* have lost much of the influence they had in 1800. During the nineteenth century, reforming rulers appropriated revenues from religious endowments, tried to turn the *ulama* into bureaucrats, and bypassed them with Western-style courts and state-school systems. In the *ulama*'s willingness to provide legitimation for almost any regime in power, they have jeopardized their moral authority. Engineers and others associated with the state schools, not the *ulama*, have been in the forefront of Islamic and Islamist protest since the late 1960s. Yet in contrast to the turbulent 1950s and 1960s, most Middle Eastern regimes proved remarkably durable in the 1970s and 1980s. In Iran, however, the distinctive tradition of SHI'ISM enabled a counterelite of *ulama* to lead a revolution against the shah and to consolidate its power as the core of a new ruling elite. Attempts to export the revolution to Sunni-dominated countries have met little success.

BIBLIOGRAPHY

For premodern Muslim conceptions, see "Al-Khassa wa'l-Amma" by M. A. J. BEG and "Askari" by B. LEWIS in *The Encyclopedia of Islam,* 2nd ed. (Leiden, 1954). ALBERT HOURANI's "Ottoman Reform and the Politics of Notables," reprinted in his *The Emergence of the Modern Middle East* (Berkeley, Calif., 1981), explores "the politics of notables." For nineteenth-century elites, see CARTER VAUGHN FINDLEY, *Ottoman Civil Officialdom: A Social History* (Princeton, N.J., 1989), and F. ROBERT HUNTER, *Egypt under the Khedives 1805–1879* (Pittsburgh, 1984). For the twentieth century, I. WILLIAM ZARTMAN, et al., *Political Elites in Arab North Africa* (New York, 1982), presents informed case studies. LEONARD BINDER, *In a Moment of Enthusiasm: Power and the Second Stratum in Egypt* (Chicago, 1978), argues for the long-term persistence of a second-level elite rooted in the provinces but with access to the center.

Donald Malcolm Reid

Elphinstone, Mountstuart   [1779–1859]

Envoy of the British East India Company to Afghanistan, 1808–1809.

Elphinstone traveled to Kabul in 1808 to negotiate an alliance of "eternal friendship" between the Afghans and British India. This was the first official contact between the British and the Afghans. While he was in Afghanistan, Elphinstone conducted a study of the Afghan people. He later wrote *An Account of the Kingdom of Caubul* (1815), the first comprehensive account of Afghan society.

BIBLIOGRAPHY

ADAMEC, LUDWIG. *Historical Dictionary of Afghanistan.* Metuchen, N.J., 1991.

Grant Farr

Emergency Regulations

During the British mandate of Palestine and as adopted by Israel, rules allowing the restriction of civil rights in emergencies.

On September 22, 1945, Britain's high commissioner in Palestine issued Defense Emergency Regulations that in turn were based on the 1937 Palestine (Defense) Order in Council. That order gave the commissioner broad powers to adopt measures needed in defense of "public safety" and to suppress mutiny. The regulations were originally enacted to subdue the PALESTINE ARAB REVOLT of 1936–1939. They were later used against Zionism's guerilla organizations fighting to remove British rule from Palestine.

The regulations were carried over after the State of Israel was established (May 15, 1948), under the 1948 Law and Administration Ordinance. On May 21, 1948, the Provisional State Council proclaimed a state of emergency that has never been revoked, although various sections have been amended or adapted. The regulations, consisting of 170 articles divided into fifteen sections, allow the government and the military to introduce extreme measures and abolish the most elementary rights, such as freedom of movement, travel, and work. Thus, between 1948 and 1966, approximately 90 percent of Israeli Arabs were placed under military administration, with military governors appointed directly by the defense minister. The governors drew their virtually unlimited powers from the Emergency Regulations. The regulations have also been widely used to detain Israeli Arabs and Palestinian refugees without trial, without formal charges, and without judicial or legislative review.

BIBLIOGRAPHY

LUSTICK, IAN. *Arabs in the Jewish State: Israel's Control of a National Minority.* Middle East Series, No. 6. Austin, Tex., 1980.
ROLEF, SUSAN H., ed. *Political Dictionary of the State of Israel.* New York, 1987.

Benjamin Joseph

Emin Nihat   [?–c. 1875]

Turkish Ottoman writer.

Almost no biographical information about Emin Nihat is available, other than that he worked as a civil servant in the foreign ministry and that he died sometime after 1875. He is known for his stories gathered in a volume entitled *Müsamaretname* (The Book of a Soirée). In this collection of seven stories, Emin Nihat combined the style of court literature with folk stories to create a new form of storytelling.

BIBLIOGRAPHY

EVIN, AHMET O. *Origins and Development of the Turkish Novel.* Minneapolis, Minn., 1983.

David Waldner

Emir

See Amir

Empty Quarter

See Rub al-Khali

ENA

See Star of North Africa

Enez–Midye Line

A border between Bulgaria and the Ottoman Empire.

The Enez–Midye line was suggested by the great powers at the LONDON CONFERENCE, 17 December 1912 to 6 January 1913, which was called to negotiate an end to the first Balkan war in 1912. The line was to run from Midye on the Black Sea to Enez at the mouth of the Maritsa River on the Aegean, and came within fifty miles of Istanbul. After Bulgarian victories, the Ottomans reluctantly accepted the border in the Treaty of London (1913). However, a boundary more favorable to them resulted from the second Balkan war in 1913.

BIBLIOGRAPHY

LEWIS, BERNARD. *The Emergence of Modern Turkey.* Oxford, 1965.

Justin McCarthy

ENI

See Ente Nazionale Idrocarboni

Enos Line

See Enez–Midye Line

Entebbe Operation

Israeli hostage rescue operation, code-named Kadoor Ha-Raam (Thunderbolt).

On June 27, 1976, two German nationals and two Palestinians boarded Air France Flight 139 en route from Tel Aviv to Paris during a stopover in Athens, and hijacked it first to Benghazi, Libya, then on to Entebbe Airport in Uganda. Following a plan masterminded by Dr. Wadi Haddad of the POPULAR FRONT FOR THE LIBERATION OF PALESTINE (PFLP) and which involved terrorists of varied affiliations (including the notorious "Carlos") the hijackers were there joined by a second team, the passengers divided into Jews and non-Jews, and the latter released. While feigning negotiation with the hijackers and with their host, President Idi Amin of Uganda, Israel made preparations for a military rescue mission. On the night of July 3, four Hercules transport jets carrying 150 Israeli commandos took off from SHARM AL-SHAYKH and flew 2,484 miles (4000 km) to Entebbe, evading detection throughout. Accompanied by diversionary measures, the paratroopers stormed the terminal where the 101 hostages were kept, killing 7 of their captors and numerous Ugandan soldiers. The Israeli commander, Lt. Col. Yonatan Netanyahu, and three hostages were killed during the operation, which lasted some forty-five minutes from landing to takeoff (an elderly Israeli woman who had been hospitalized was later murdered). The jets refueled at Nairobi and returned to a tumultuous welcome the following morning in Israel. Arab and African countries and the Communist bloc condemned the Israeli action, while in the West reaction was largely positive.

Zev Maghen

Ente Nazionale Idrocarboni

Italian oil company that sought access to Algeria's oil industry.

The multistate petroleum company was headed by Enrico Mattei, who promised both arms and money to Algeria's FRONT DE LIBÉRATION NATIONALE (National Liberation Front, FLN) during the Algerian

War of Independence (1954–1962) in return for unspecified future access to the oil and natural gas supplies discovered in Algeria's Saharan region. Mattei's private plane crashed under mysterious circumstances in October 1962, and Algeria nationalized its oil and gas industry after independence.

Dirk Vandewalle

Enver Paşa   [1881–1922]

Ottoman general and strongman of the Committee of Union and Progress.

Enver was born in Constantinople (now Istanbul) November 23, 1881. When his father, a railway employee, was transferred to Macedonia, Enver attended the Monastir military junior high school. He graduated from the War Academy (Mekteb-i Harbiye) as staff corporal in 1902 and was posted to the Third Army in Macedonia.

In 1906 Enver joined the Ottoman Liberty Society in Salonika, a constituent group of the reorganized COMMITTEE OF UNION AND PROGRESS (CUP). He led one of a series of revolts in Macedonia in 1908 that triggered the Young Turk Revolution of July 23, 1908. In Constantinople he was hailed as a revolutionary hero. His appointment to Berlin as military attaché at the end of 1908 failed to remove him from the political changes taking place in the capital. During the counterrevolutionary uprising of April 1909, he joined the Army of Deliverance, which marched to Constantinople to restore order, then returned to his post in Berlin. In 1911, after a brief assignment in Scutari at the time of the Albanian uprising, he transferred to Libya, where he commanded Ottoman forces in Benghazi against the Italians. His betrothal to the granddaughter of Sultan ABDÜLMECIT II, Naciye Sultan, was concluded in his absence, presaging a more prominent public role for him in Constantinople.

Enver led the armed CUP coup against the Kamil government in January 1913. He fought for the recapture of Edirne from the Bulgarians during the Balkan War. Enver received multiple promotions and became minister of war in January 1914 and proceeded to reorganize the army by purging the senior officers. He set up a paramilitary intelligence and propaganda organ.

Enver Paşa was responsible for authorizing the passage of German dreadnoughts into the Black Sea in November 1914, effectively committing the Ottoman Empire to war on the side of Germany. As deputy commander in chief of Ottoman forces, he personally led the Russian campaign in Eastern Anatolia that resulted in the earliest and most devastating setback of the entire war for the empire. However, after Russia withdrew from the war, Enver delegated his uncle Halil and brother Nuri to lead the Ottoman armies into the Caucasus, seeking a pan-Turkish union. This strategy was aborted by Ottoman defeats on other fronts.

Following the Ottoman surrender at Mudros, Enver fled abroad with other prominent CUP leaders. In November 1918, he first went to Odessa and was arrested attempting to travel to the Caucasus, possibly to establish a resistance against Allied armies in occupation of Ottoman territories. He managed to flee to Germany. In August 1920, he returned to the Soviet Union. After an audience with the Bolshevik leaders in Moscow, Enver went to Baku and participated in the Congress of Eastern Nations. The Turkish nationalist government in Ankara prevented his entering Anatolia. The Bolsheviks allowed him to go to Turkistan to form an Islamic army to liberate India. Instead, in September 1921, Enver joined the Turkistan resistance movement in Bukhura, which he coordinated signing communiques as "the son-in-law of the caliph." He was killed near Dushanbe, August 4, 1922, as he personally led attacks against the Bolshevik forces.

Enver's reputation as the "hero of liberty" and his notoriety as the dictator of the CUP, though both exaggerated, cast him in history as a controversial figure. A similar hyperbole is the occasional German reference to the Ottoman Empire as "Enverland." Enver personified the eclectic currents prevalent among the Ottoman political elite after 1908. He was sympathetic to the Turkish, and following the Ottoman loss of the Arab provinces, to pan-Turkish ideas. As a member of the royal household and a pious man, Enver was also deeply committed to Ottomanism and the Islamic principles that sustained the Ottomanist ideology.

BIBLIOGRAPHY

There is no comprehensive biographical study of Enver Paşa in Western languages. On his early career, see GLEN W. SWANSON, "Enver Pasha: The Formative Years." *Middle Eastern Studies* 16 (1980): 193–99. ŞÜKRÜ HANIOĞLU reproduced Enver's letters in French, written between 1911 and 1913, and a German translation of his autobiographical notes in *Kendi Mektuplarında Enver Paşa* (Enver Paşa in His Own Letters) (Istanbul, 1989). DANKWART RUSTOW has an extensive entry on Enver in the *Encyclopaedia of Islam*, vol. 2, pp. 698–702. On Enver's adventures in Asia, see MASAYUKI YAMAUCHI, *The Green Crescent under the Red Star: Enver Pasha in Soviet Russia, 1919–1922* (Tokyo, 1991).

Hasan Kayali

Eqbal, Manouchehr   [1908–1977]

Iranian politician.

Born in Mashhad to a prominent Khorasani family, Manouchehr Eqbal pursued his medical studies in France and returned to Iran in 1933. He was minister of health in the 1940s, governor of Azerbaijan in 1950, chancellor of Tehran University in 1954, and prime minister from 1956 to 1960. He then fled Iran for a while, after a fallout with Ali AMINI, who had been appointed prime minister and whose government initiated the prosecution of Eqbal on grounds of bribery and corruption. Eqbal had been under fire from various groups for his blatant rigging of the 1960 parliamentary elections. Having proven his loyalty to Shah Mohammad Reza Pahlavi by passing an anti-communist bill through the parliament in 1948, Eqbal was rewarded with an appointment to UNESCO in 1961 as Iran's representative. He returned to Iran in 1963 as chairman of the National Iranian Oil Company. Eqbal's daughter married Shahriyar Shafiq, the grandnephew of Mohammad Reza Shah Pahlavi.

BIBLIOGRAPHY

AQELI, BAQER. *Iranian Prime Ministers from Moshir al-Dowleh to Bakhtiyar.* Tehran, 1991. In Persian.
ZONIS, M. *The Political Elite of Iran.* Princeton, N.J., 1971.

Neguin Yavari

Eqbal Publishers

Iranian publishing company.

One of Iran's oldest publishing houses, Eqbal was founded in Tehran in 1906 and remains one of the nation's more traditional publishers, both in style as well as in choice of publication. Eqbal published the first Iranian edition of Will Durant's *A History of Civilization* as well as several editions of the Qur'an.

BIBLIOGRAPHY

Fehrest-e Entesharat-e Eqbal (Catalogue of Eqbal Publishers). Tehran, 1964.

Neguin Yavari

Erbakan, Necmeddin   [1926–]

Founder of three political parties and deputy prime minister in several coalition governments in Turkey.

Erbakan was born in the Black Sea town of Sinop. His father was a judge. His family ultimately moved to Istanbul, where he completed middle and secondary schools and graduated with distinction from Istanbul Technical University. He became a faculty member after earning his doctorate and engaging in further study in Germany. He became president of the Union of Chambers of Commerce and Industry in 1969, advocating the interests of the petty bourgeoisie against "big capital" and assuming a militantly anti-Western stance, particularly vis-à-vis the European Economic Community, positions he has consistently maintained ever since.

This engineer-turned politican burst upon the Turkish political scene in 1973 as the head of the National Salvation party (NSP), the first serious party in the republic that openly demanded respect for Islamic piety. In that election, the NSP garnered 12 percent of the vote, enough to turn Erbakan into a major political actor, a role that he retained until the military intervention of 1980. His subsequent efforts as leader of the Prosperity party have been less successful due to the nature of the post-1980 electoral system.

BIBLIOGRAPHY

LANDAU, JACOB M. "The National Salvation Party in Turkey." *African and Asian Studies* 2, no. 1 (1976): 1–57.

Frank Tachau

Erbil, Leyla   [1931–]

Turkish novelist and short story writer.

Born in Istanbul, Turkey, Erbil studied at the Kadiköy Girls School and the Faculty of Literature. She began writing stories while working as a secretary and translator. Her first poetry was published in 1945, but she is known for her stories, which began to appear in various journals in the 1950s.

Breaking away from the traditional techniques of Turkish LITERATURE and the syntax of the Turkish language, Erbil searched for a new narrative voice to depict the existential struggles of the modern individual who clashes with society. Erbil is noted for her ability to observe individuals using different societal perspectives, and her stories are characterized by efforts to depict the multiple dimensions of reality. Among her books are *The Wool Carder* (1960), *At Night* (1968), *A Strange Woman* (1971), *The Old Lover* (1977), and *The Day of Darkness* (1985). She was a founding member of the Turkish Union of Writers in 1974.

BIBLIOGRAPHY

REDDY, NILUFER MIZANOĞLU, ed. *Twenty Stories by Turkish Women Writers.* Bloomington, Ind., 1988.

David Waldner

Eretz Yisrael

Hebrew, meaning "the Land of Israel."

Biblical usage of the term is inconsistent, generally signifying the extent of Israelite sovereignty or habitation rather than a precise geographic entity. By the end of the Second Temple period and the beginning of Talmudic times (0–200 C.E.) "Eretz Yisrael" had superseded "Canaan" and other earlier terminologies denoting the nation of Israel's divinely promised territorial inheritance, and has been retained by Jewish tradition until the present. Its actual borders are defined variously in the Talmud. Since the advent of Zionism the term has been employed more or less interchangeably with PALESTINE, although there has been much vehement disagreement about the extent of the territory described by either of these terms and of present-day Israel's.

Zev Maghen

Ergin, Osman Nuri   [1883–1961]

Turkish historian.

Born in the village of İmran, near Malatya in Ottoman Turkey, Ergin graduated from the Faculty of Literature in 1907. He also studied at religious schools to improve his Arabic. He began to work for the Istanbul municipality, eventually rising to the office of chief secretary. In addition, he worked as a librarian, as a printer, and as a teacher of Turkish, literature, philosophy, history, and sociology at various schools.

Ergin's own research focused on the history of Istanbul and of the municipalities in other Islamic countries and the history of education in the Ottoman Empire and Turkey. Among his major published works are *Local Administration in the Republic and Istanbul* (1933), *The History and Development of Urban Planning in Turkey* (1936), *Five Centuries of Architecture and Housing Movements in Istanbul* (1938), and the five-volume *History of Education in Turkey* (1939–43), all in Turkish.

BIBLIOGRAPHY

IŞIK, İHSAN. *Yazarlar Sözlüğü.* Istanbul, 1990.

David Waldner

Ersoy, Mehmet Akıf   [c. 1870–1936]

Turkish poet and Islamist.

Ersoy was born in Istanbul to a religious Muslim family; his father was a teacher at Fatih Medrese, and his mother's ancestors were from the Uzbek city of Bukhara. He learned Arabic, Persian, and French privately and studied veterinary medicine at the Halkalı Baytar high school, which he finished in 1893. He held various posts as a veterinarian and teacher. In 1908, he began writing and became editor of the monthly Islamist journal *The Straight Path* (which proclaimed the cause of Islam), later called *Fountain of Orthodoxy,* to which he contributed poetry and essays. During the Turkish war of independence, he preached the cause of nationalism in the mosques and local newspapers of the Anatolian provinces.

Later in life, Ersoy would become known as one of the greatest poets in modern Turkish and the leader of the most intellectual of the Islamist movements in Turkey. He opposed nationalist reformers who argued that Turkey must import the West's civilization as well as its technology. He contended that the two were not necessarily linked and that importing the ethics and institutions of another culture would widen the cultural gap between elites and common people. Ersoy advocated an Islamic (not a secular) democracy, with a parliament based on consultative councils, as used by the Prophet Muhammad's followers.

BIBLIOGRAPHY

TOPRAK, BINNAZ. "The Religious Right." In *Turkey in Transition.* New York, 1987.
Yeni Türk Ansiklopedisi (New Turkish Encyclopedia). Istanbul, 1985.

Elizabeth Thompson

Ertuğrul, Muhsin   [1892–1979]

Turkish actor and director in cinema and theater.

Ertuğrul was born in Istanbul, where he attended state-run schools. He began acting in 1909, and in 1911 and 1913 he went to Paris to study theater. Known as the pioneer in all areas of modern Turkish drama, Ertuğrul was the principal man of the stage in Turkey between 1908 and 1923 and the sole movie director in the country until 1939. He received personal support from Atatürk in the development of the theater arts.

Ertuğrul turned the Istanbul Municipal Theater into an influential institution when he was appointed its director in 1927, substituting for the usual vaudeville shows and melodramas foreign classics and innovative new scripts in the Turkish language. When he was appointed director of the state theater and opera in Ankara in 1947, he produced *Kerem,* the first opera composed by a Turk. As director from

1947 to 1958, he opened local theaters in other cities, such as İzmir, Adana, and Bursa.

Meanwhile, Ertuğrul began making films in 1922; his 1935 *Aysel, Daughter of the Marshy Village* is now considered his masterpiece.

BIBLIOGRAPHY

DORSAY, ATILLA. "An Overview of Turkish Cinema from Its Origins." In *The Transformation of Turkish Culture,* ed. by Günsel Fenda and C. Max Kortepeter. Princeton, N.J., 1986.

NUTKU, ÖZDEMIR. "A Panorama of the Turkish Theater under the Leadership of Atatürk." In *The Transformation of Turkish Culture,* ed. by Günsel Fenda and C. Max Kortepeter. Princeton, N.J., 1986.

Elizabeth Thompson

Erzurum

Most important city in eastern Turkey and capital of Erzurum province.

Site of a large military base and, since 1958, Atatürk University, Erzurum is a city of more than 250,000 inhabitants and is located in the Kara Su and Aras valleys, the major thoroughfare between Anatolia and Iran. The city also handles the trade of local products, especially iron, copper, sugar, grain, cattle, and leather. Erzurum was the site of the first nationalist congress in 1919 attended by Mustafa Kemal (Atatürk), which issued a declaration of the Turkish war of independence.

BIBLIOGRAPHY

The Chambers World Gazetteer, 5th ed. New York, 1988, p. 193.

The Encyclopedia of Islam, vol. 2. London, 1965, p. 712.

Elizabeth Thompson

Erzurum, Treaty of

Treaty that ended one conflict in ongoing boundary dispute between the Ottoman Empire and Persia.

For hundreds of years, the eastern border of the Ottoman Empire remained in flux. When Persia (Iran) was strong under the Safavids, the Ottoman border receded toward Lake Van in eastern Turkey; when Persia was weak, the Ottomans were able to push eastward deep into Azerbaijan and toward the Caspian Sea. In 1820, Sultan MAHMUD II went to war with Persia, ruled by FATH ALI SHAH QAJAR. The Persians enjoyed initial success, and in a two-pronged attack, they swept past Lake Van and Bitlis on to

Diyarbekır in the south and Erzurum in the north. On the verge of probable success, the Persian army was struck by a cholera epidemic and sued for peace. The Treaty of Erzurum was signed on July 28, 1823, and by its terms, the war was ended and the status quo restored without alteration. However, the treaty did not prevent further conflicts, and the boundary remained a subject of dispute between Persia and the Ottoman Empire.

BIBLIOGRAPHY

HUREWITZ, J.C., ed. *The Middle East and North Africa in World Politics.* New Haven, Conn., 1975.

SHAW, STANFORD, and EZEL KURAL SHAW. *History of the Ottoman Empire & Modern Turkey.* New York, 1977.

Zachary Karabell

Erzurum Congress

Congress called to assert the integrity of the Ottoman state, 1919.

Named for the city in which it was held, the congress was called immediately after the Ottoman Empire had been on the losing side of World War I; the empire was to be dismembered. It was feared that the local area around Erzurum would become part of an Armenian state. The congress declared the nationalists' intention of defending the sultanate/caliphate against foreign occupiers and appealed to U.S. President Woodrow WILSON's principles of national self-determination. Mustafa Kemal (ATATÜRK) was elected chairman of the congress, and although the Istanbul government declared the congress illegal, ordering his arrest, he escaped. It was here that he made his first declaration of principles that would guide his war to unite Turkey as an independent nation.

BIBLIOGRAPHY

LEWIS, BERNARD. *The Emergence of Modern Turkey.* New York, 1969.

Elizabeth Thompson

Erzurumlu Emrah   [?–1854]

Turkish Ottoman minstrel.

It is believed that Erzurumlu was born in the village of Tanbura, near Erzurum. Although Mehmet Fuat Köprülü believed that he died in 1854, his death has been dated anywhere between 1844 and 1876. Erzurumlu wrote poetry in both prose and syllabic meter. In his poetry, one recognizes the influence of classical poets like Fuzuli and Nedim, as well as themes from Sufism.

BIBLIOGRAPHY

ÖZKIRIMLI, ATILLA. *Türk Edebiyatı Ansiklopedisi*, vol. 2. Istanbul, 1982.

David Waldner

Esad, Mehmet [1789–1848]

Ottoman historian and bureaucrat.

Following his father's profession, Mehmet Esad began his career as a *qadi* (judge). He became the official chronicler of the Ottoman Empire and, in 1827, wrote a famous account of the 1826 destruction of the JANISSARIES called *Üsüs-i Zafer* (The Bases of Victory). He was also editor of *Takvim-i Vekayi*, the first official Ottoman newspaper, established in 1831. In 1846, Mehmet Esad headed the commission on education that designed the first secular school system in the empire.

BIBLIOGRAPHY

SHAW, STANFORD J. *History of the Ottoman Empire and Modern Turkey*, vol. 1. Cambridge, U.K., 1976.
SHAW, STANFORD J., and EZEL KURAL SHAW. *History of the Ottoman Empire and Modern Turkey*, vol. 2. Cambridge, U.K., 1977.

Elizabeth Thompson

Esendal, Memduh Şevket [1883–1952]

Turkish novelist, short story writer, and politician.

Esendal was born in Çorlu to the Karakahyaoğulları family, which had migrated there from Rumelia. After attending elementary school in Istanbul and high school in Edirne, he returned to Çorlu to tend the family farm. He joined the Committee of Union and Progress party in 1906, and during the Balkan War fled to Istanbul, where he held several government jobs. He was Turkey's representative to Azerbaijan in 1920, ambassador to Iran from 1925 to 1930, and ambassador to Afghanistan and the Soviet Union in the early 1930s. Esendal was in the TURKISH GRAND NATIONAL ASSEMBLY from 1939 to 1950 and was general secretary of the REPUBLICAN PEOPLE'S PARTY from 1941 to 1945.

Esendal is perhaps best known for his many short stories, which he wrote in a distinctively direct and realistic style, with careful depictions of daily life. He evoked daily life in Turkey often in a humorous way and with kindliness. With Sait Faik, he is associated with the emergence of the modern Turkish short story form. Esendal also wrote several novels, which resembled his short stories in style.

BIBLIOGRAPHY

Yeni Türk Ansiklopedisi (New Turkish Encyclopedia). Istanbul, 1985.

Elizabeth Thompson

Esfandiary, Fereydun [1930–]

Iranian novelist.

Born in Tehran, capital of Iran, and educated there, in Europe, and in the United States, Fereydun Esfandiary served with the United Nations in the 1950s and thereafter remained in New York City, where he taught at the New School for Social Research. Later, moving to Los Angeles, he lectured at the University of California.

In the late 1950s, Esfandiary turned to writing. Three of his novels dealt with his perception of Iran's ills: *Day of Sacrifice* (1959), *The Beggar* (1965), and *Identity Card* (1966). The last tells the story of a young educated Iranian who returns temporarily to his homeland to find that he is a modern man and thus alien to his societal roots.

Esfandiary broadened his focus from Iranian issues in the 1970s. He became known as a futurist with the three books *Optimism One* (1970), *Up-Wingers* (1973), and *Telespheres* (1977). Therein he sees modern technology as "dehumanizing," school "as obsolete as family," and he asks, "What the hell is so beautiful as Paris?" His mid-1970s futurist projections and forecasts for "the next ten twenty thirty years" did not materialize. Biographical guides in the 1980s cite a change of name for Esfandiary to "FM2030."

Esfandiary's earlier works gave American readers a first glimpse behind the monarchical veneer of Mohammad Reza Pahlavi (ruled 1941–1979) into Iranian society's problems. But his work in this area of Persian LITERATURE has been superseded by more recent expatriate fiction, more deeply Iranian, and more sophisticated in techniques of fiction, for example Nahid Rachlin's *The Foreigner* (1978), *Married to a Stranger* (1983), *Veils: Short Stories* (1992), or Taghi Modarressi's *The Book of Absent People* (1986) and *The Pilgrim's Rules of Etiquette* (1989).

Michael C. Hillmann

Eshkol, Levi [1895–1969]

Israel's Labor party leader; prime minister, 1963–1969.

Born in Kiev, Ukraine, Levi Eshkol immigrated to Palestine in 1914, where he was a founder of Kibbutz Degania Bet and served in the Jewish Legion from 1918 to 1920. He was active in labor politics and Zionism throughout the period of British mandate (1922–1948). For three years, Eshkol headed the settlement department of the Palestine office in Berlin during the period of Nazi rule. He organized immigration and transfers of funds from Germany to Palestine, using the money to establish new settlement projects and the MEKOROT Water Company, of which he was both the founder and the first president. In the same period, he was active in the High Command of the Haganah as the chief financial administrator, organizing arms procurement for the defense organization.

After the establishment of the State of Israel in 1948, Eshkol served in numerous government, JEWISH AGENCY, and cabinet positions including director general of the ministry of defense (1948), where he was instrumental in establishing the Israeli weapons industry; head of the land settlement department of the Jewish Agency (1949), where he coordinated the settlement of the masses of new immigrants arriving in Israel; treasurer for the Jewish Agency (1950–1952); minister of agriculture (1951); and minister of finance (1952), where he was responsible for the implementation of the reparations agreement with Germany from World War II.

In 1963, upon the retirement of David BEN-GURION as prime minister, Eshkol took his post and that of defense minister (with Ben-Gurion's recommendation)—however, Ben-Gurion soon accused him of mishandling state business, especially the government scandal called the LAVON AFFAIR (in which Israeli spies were caught in Egypt but no one in the Israeli cabinet admitted to knowing about the mission). Consequently, Ben-Gurion left the MAPAI party and formed Rafi.

Eshkol continued as prime minister during the period leading to the Arab–Israel War of 1967 and was faced with a divided cabinet over the question of war with Egypt. Because of public pressure, he ceded the defense portfolio to Moshe DAYAN. Eshkol also enlarged the cabinet and brought in members of the right-wing Gahal bloc, establishing a National Unity government, which was retained in the 1969 elections to the sixth Knesset but ended when Gahal broke away in 1970.

BIBLIOGRAPHY

ROLEF, S. H., ed. *Political Dictionary of the State of Israel.* New York, 1987.

Martin Malin

Esnaf

See Guilds

Essaouira

A Moroccan city, located on the Atlantic coast.

Essaouira used to be a Portuguese fortress. It was rebuilt under the rule of Sultan Sidi Muhammad ibn Abdullah in 1765 to attract the caravan trade of the south. The city was designed by the French architect Cournut. It witnessed a period of prosperity during the eighteenth century, followed by a period of stagnation because of competition from other coastal cities. Under the French protectorate, it was named Mogador. Essaouira had a population of sixty thousand inhabitants in 1992. The city is known for its wooden crafts and industrial fisheries.

Rahma Bourqia

Etemadi, Nur Ahmad   [1921–1979]

Prime minister of Afghanistan, 1967–1971.

Etemadi was prime minister and foreign minister (1963–1973) of Afghanistan during the reign of Zahir Shah in the period of constitutional reform. He was also an ambassador to Pakistan (1964; 1976–1978), Italy (1971), and the Soviet Union (1973). He was imprisoned by the Taraki government and executed in 1979.

BIBLIOGRAPHY

ADAMEC, LUDWIG. *Historical Dictionary of Afghanistan.* Metuchen, N.J., 1991.

Grant Farr

Ethiopian Jews

Jews of Ethiopia, many of whom have emigrated to Israel.

In Ethiopia, the Jews referred to themselves as *Beta Israel* (The House of Israel) but were most commonly known as *Falashas* (wanderers, outsiders). In Israel, these same people call themselves Ethiopian Jews, symbolically expressing their equality with other Jews and rejecting the stigma they once held in Ethiopia.

There are 54,000 Ethiopian Jews living in Israel today. Their mass emigration from Ethiopia began in the early 1970s, encouraged by a decree issued by Israel's chief rabbis that the Jews from Ethiopia were "full" Jews (although they still required symbolic conversion to Judaism). In Operation Moses, (which took place during 1984/85), 7,700 Jews were airlifted to Israel from the refugee camps in Sudan. A second large-scale airlift known as Operation Solomon took place in 1991. As the Mengistu Haile Mariam regime was collapsing in Addis Ababa, 14,400 Ethiopian Jews were transferred to Israel.

The majority of the early immigrants to Israel from Ethiopia hailed from the northern province of Tigre and are Tigranian speaking. Today, over 80 percent of Ethiopian Jewry in Israel originate from Gonder, Semien (or Simyen), Woggera, and other areas. They speak Ethiopia's official language, Amharic, which is a Semitic language. The younger immigrants in Israel speak Hebrew. Beta Israel holy books, including the Bible, are written in Geez.

In Ethiopia, the Beta Israel community observed a unique form of Judaism that was based on biblical commandments and was influenced by Ethiopian Orthodox Christianity (which in turn displays remarkable similarities to aspects of Judaism). The Beta Israel did not know the Oral Law; nor were they aware of rabbinic interpretations. They strictly observed rules of purity and pollution. The cornerstone of their religion until this century was monasticism: the monks passing down liturgy, literature, and religious edicts.

In the twentieth century, urged on by visiting Jews such as Dr. Jacques Faitlovitch from Paris, some Beta Israel were exposed to mainstream Judaism. Faitlovitch's pupils, who studied in Europe and other countries, included Taamrat Emmanuel (1878–1956), aide to the Emperor Haile Selassie; Tadesse Yacob (1913–   ), deputy minister of finance in Ethiopia; and Yona Bogale (1908–1987), who acted as teacher and intermediary between Jews in Ethiopia and Israel.

The Ethiopian Jews today are in the process of coming in line with Israeli Judaism, although some *kessoth* (priests) and members of the community do not wish to accept the authority of Israel's chief rabbinate. In 1985, the Ethiopian Jews demonstrated in front of the rabbinate's offices objecting to the ritual immersion they had to undergo for acceptance as "full" Jews. To date, Ethiopian Jews are referred to one particular rabbi for marriage purposes.

In 1992, some Ethiopian Jews organized demonstrations to demand that the Feresmura, Jews who had converted to Christianity in Ethiopia from the nineteenth century on, should be allowed to immigrate to Israel under the LAW OF RETURN (1950). A 1993 government committee decided that certain family members could enter Israel under the Law of Entry.

In Ethiopia, the Beta Israel were primarily agriculturalists and tenant farmers. They also engaged in petty trading and seasonal occupations, such as metalwork and sewing. In Israel, they have been settled almost exclusively in urban areas where they are largely employed in unskilled and often temporary jobs. To date, the majority of Ethiopian Jews in the country live in permanent housing, although many thousands of newcomers live in trailer parks, specially constructed to absorb the large waves of immigrants in the 1990s.

All Ethiopian Jewish children study in regular Israeli schools. Teens attend residential schools. Large numbers of young people have undergone occupational retraining courses. Nearly one thousand young men and one hundred women are currently serving in the Israel defense forces. Several hundred Ethiopian Jews are studying in institutes for higher learning in Israel; many more have graduated from colleges and universities as teachers, social workers, dental assistants, and nurses.

BIBLIOGRAPHY

QUIRIN, JAMES. *The Evolution of the Ethiopian Jews: A History of the Beta Israel (Falasha) to 1920.* Philadelphia, 1992.
WEIL, SHALVAH. "Ethiopian Jews in Israel: a Survey of Research and Documentation." *Jewish Folklore and Ethnology Review* 2 (1989): 28–32.

                                        Shalvah Weil

Ethniké Hetairia

Organization of Greek army officers seeking to take Crete and Macedonia.

In 1894, a group of Greek army officers founded the Ethniké Hetairia with the intent of realizing the ambitions of Greece in Crete and Macedonia, both under the Ottoman Empire. While not a terrorist organization, the group was not above promoting violence to achieve its aims. Within several years of its founding, most Greek army officers were members of the Ethniké Hetairia.

BIBLIOGRAPHY

ANDERSON, M. S. *The Eastern Question.* London, 1966.
SHAW, STANFORD, and EZEL KURAL SHAW. *History of the Ottoman Empire & Modern Turkey.* New York, 1977.

                                        Zachary Karabell

Etoile Nord Africaine

See Star of North Africa

Euphrates Dam

The Keban, Tabaqa, and Atatürk dams on the Euphrates river.

Since 1970, Turkey and Syria have built three major dams on the Euphrates, which as a group will severely limit the river's flow into Iraq. The Keban dam, near Elazığ, was the first to be completed. It supplies electricity to large cities in western Turkey. The TABAQA DAM in Syria is both a major power and irrigation project. The Atatürk (Karababa) dam, near Urfa, is the most ambitious of the three. It is intended to spur development in the Turkish southeast (something the Keban project failed to do) by irrigating nearly 4.5 million acres (1.7 ha), almost three times the area to be irrigated by the Tabaqa.

When all dams are in operation, of the 30 billion cubic meters of water that once reached Iraq, only 11 billion cubic meters will remain. Since Iraq claims that its minimum requirement is 13 billion cubic meters, there will be a shortfall. Since no treaty exists to allocate the water, Iraq has no recourse; in its weakened political position (since the Gulf Crisis of 1990/91) it will be in a poor position to bargain.

BIBLIOGRAPHY

DRYSDALE, ALASDAIR, and GERALD H. BLAKE. *The Middle East and North Africa.* New York, 1985.

John R. Clark

Euphrates River

See Tigris and Euphrates Rivers

Evian Conference

International conference on Jewish refugees from Germany and Austria that met in July 1938 at Evian, France.

The United States initiated the conference shortly after Hitler's annexation of Austria in March 1938 and immediate Nazi persecution of Austrian Jews. In July, thirty-two nations sent representatives to Evian, but Britain insisted that its mandate territory of Palestine not be considered as a place for Jewish immigration. None of the governments was willing to modify its country-by-country immigration quotas, except for the Dominican Repbulic, and the conference concluded that no general territory was available or suitable for Jewish refugees.

One result of the conference was the establishment of a permanent Intergovernmental Committee (IGC) on refugees, which was headed by Lord Winterton, a leading British anti-Zionist. The search for areas suitable for large-scale Jewish resettlement was a failure. In the period after the conference, a few conference countries adopted new and more restrictive immigration regulations—and World War II was started with Germany's invasion of Poland in September 1939, which enlarged the area of Nazi domination.

BIBLIOGRAPHY

LAQUEUR, WALTER. *A History of Zionism.* New York, 1972.
MORSE, ARTHUR D. *While Six Million Died.* New York, 1968.
SACHAR, HOWARD M. *History of Israel: From the Rise of Zionism to Our Time.* Oxford, 1979.

Miriam Simon

Evin Prison

Iranian penitentiary for political prisoners.

Evin Prison, in northwestern Tehran, was a modern prison built in the early 1970s by Mohammad Reza Pahlavi. Equipped with the latest torture devices, it was devoted solely to political prisoners. After the Iranian Revolution of 1979, the prison was replete with members of the opposition, especially from the Mojahedin-e Khalq and myriad leftist organizations.

BIBLIOGRAPHY

ABRAHAMIAN, ERVAND. *The Iranian Mojahedin.* New Haven, Conn., 1989.

Neguin Yavari

Evkâf

See Waqf

Evolués

Term for colonized Algerians who assimilated French culture.

Among the most prominent examples of *évolués* (also *assimilés*) were the YOUNG ALGERIANS (Jeunes Algériens), who wanted full French citizenship. Moderate nationalists such as Dr. Mohamed Salah Bendjelloul and Ferhat Abbas were also considered évolués. Their aspirations were identified in the proposed BLUM–VIOLLETTE PLAN of 1936, which was never enacted by the French parliament.

BIBLIOGRAPHY

AGERON, CHARLES-ROBERT. *Histoire de l'Algérie contemporaine: De l'insurrection de 1871 au déclenchement de la guerre de libération (1954).* Paris, 1979.

Phillip C. Naylor

Evren, Kenan   [c. 1918–   ]

Turkey's president from 1982 to 1989.

Kenan Evren was born in 1917 or 1918 in Alaşehir in the Manisa province of western Turkey. His father was an Ottoman civil servant who had moved the family from Yugoslavia to Anatolia. Evren attended civil schools until 1933, when he entered the military high school at Maltepe, and later was graduated from the war academy in 1949. Promoted to general in 1974, he served as commander of the Aegean forces and then of all land forces, before becoming chief of general staff in 1978. Evren was the leader of the military officers that staged the coup of September 1980 and served as the head of the National Security Council that ruled Turkey until 1983. The council was responsible for dissolving parliament and the existing political parties, suspending the constitution, and declaring martial law; in addition, the officers instituted harsh measures to combat political violence and arrested about 30,000 people. In 1982, as the only candidate, Evren was elected president of Turkey, an office that had previously been ceremonial but was endowed with wider powers by the 1982 constitution. Despite his opposition to Turgut Özal, who formed a civilian government in 1983, Evren cooperated with the new government and is given credit for exerting a stabilizing influence on Turkish politics. His tenure as president ended in 1989.

BIBLIOGRAPHY

SHIMONI, YAACOV. *Biographical Dictionary of the Middle East.* New York, 1991, p. 78.

David Waldner

Exodus

Widely publicized "illegal immigration" ship carrying Jewish refugees to Palestine in 1947.

The *Exodus* was a ship acquired by the Mossad le-Aliya Bet agency in 1946 to carry about 4,500 Jewish refugees from displaced persons camps in Occupied Germany to Palestine in 1947, the year before the British mandate was ended. The ship was called the *President Garfield,* an old 4,000-ton Chesapeake Bay steamer, and it was renamed *Exodus 1947* as it sailed from Marseilles into open waters in July 1947.

When the *Exodus* approached Palestine, the British sent six destroyers and a crusier to divert it to Haifa, claiming illegal immigration and defiance of mandate law. When force was used to remove the passengers, those on board fought in hand-to-hand combat, in which about 100 Jews were wounded and 3 were killed. The story was broadcast worldwide.

The ship surrendered when the British began ramming it to sink it, and since British displaced persons camps in Cyprus were overcrowded to discourage any further sailings or help from the French, the refugees were dragged onto three British deportation vessels and taken back to Marseilles. Witnessed by members of a United Nations (UN) committee in Haifa harbor, their report to the UN recommended the end of the British mandate in Palestine.

For one month the refugees refused to land in France, began a hunger strike, and were then taken in September to Hamburg, Germany. British troops, in view of the world press, again dragged them off the ships. They were sent to displaced persons camps in occupied Germany, where they remained for about a year until they emigrated to Israel in 1948 and 1949.

The *Exodus* became the symbol of the struggle between the British and ZIONISM for the right of free Jewish immigration into Palestine after World War II.

BIBLIOGRAPHY

LAQUEUR, WALTER. *History of Zionism.* New York, 1972.
SACHAR, HOWARD M. *A History of Israel: From the Rise of Zionism to Our Time.* Oxford, 1979.

Miriam Simon

Exxon

See Arabian American Oil Company

Eyalet

See Vilayet

Eyüboğlu, Bedri Rahmi   [1911–1974]

Turkish painter and poet.

Eyüboğlu was born in Giresun-Görele, the son of a *kaimmakam* (local ruler). He attended the Istanbul Fine Arts Academy in 1927 and studied in Paris in

1931/32. From 1937 to his death, he was a teacher at the Fine Arts Academy, while producing paintings, drawings, mosaics, and three books of poetry. His works are most notable for their motifs drawn from Anatolian popular culture.

Eyüboğlu was associated with two important art movements of the mid-century. While painting in a fauvist style in the 1930s he joined the D-Group, which eschewed academicism in art and promoted the latest Western trends. In the 1940s, he and his students formed the Group of Ten, which sought a synthesis between Western technique and Eastern decorative motifs.

BIBLIOGRAPHY

RENDA, GÜNSEL. "Modern Trends in Turkish Painting." In *The Transformation of Turkish Culture,* ed. by Günsel Renda and C. Max Kortepeter. Princeton, N.J., 1986.
Yeni Türk Ansiklopedisi (New Turkish Encyclopedia). Istanbul, 1985.

Elizabeth Thompson

Ezra and Nehemiah Operations

Massive airborne transfer in 1950–1951 of the overwhelming majority of the Jews of Iraq to Israel.

The mass emigration, invoking names of the two organizers of the return of Jews from the Babylonian Exile to the Holy Land some 2,500 years earlier, was made possible by a draft law introduced into Iraq's Parliament on 2 March 1950, permitting Jews to leave the country provided they surrendered their Iraqi nationality. The measure came in the wake of a massive wave of illegal emigration of Jews via Iran, organized by the Zionist underground. Prime Minister Salih Jabr told Parliament, "It is not in the public interest to force people to stay in the country if they have no desire to do so."

The number of emigrants far exceeded original estimates. Whereas immigration authorities in Israel had planned to receive about 300 persons a day—and this with difficulty—the daily influx at its peak reached an average of 1,400. By the end of 1951, Iraqi Jews airlifted to Israel totaled 107,603; some 16,000 others had departed the country by other means—some illegally to Palestine, some legally to countries in the West. By the beginning of 1952, it was estimated that no more than 6,000 (out of a total of some 130,000) Jews remained in Iraq.

BIBLIOGRAPHY

COHEN, HAYYIM J. *Zionist Activity in Iraq.* Jerusalem, 1972. In Hebrew.
MEIR, ESTHER. *The Zionist Movement and the Jews of Iraq 1941–50.* Tel Aviv, 1994. In Hebrew.
REJWAN, NISSIM. *The Jews of Iraq: 3000 Years of History and Culture.* London, 1985; Boulder, Colo., 1986.

Nissim Rejwan

F

Fadan Kharasa Tribe

Kharasa is one of two factions of the Fadan, which is a major tribe in the Anaza confederation of tribes.

The other faction is Fadan Wa'ad. The Kharasa numbered 1,500 *bayt* (household) or *khayma* (tent) in the early 1930s. According to the Ottoman *Salname,* which gives the size of the *khayma* as equal to about five persons, the total number of the Kharasa would have been 7,500 inhabitants. The Kharasa spread in the summer season along the Balikh and the Euphrates rivers in Syria; they are not allowed by the Syrian authorities to cross both rivers to the west. In winter, they go eastward into Iraq, especially during the years of drought. The Kharasa are divided into smaller clans, and they are on the whole warlike tribes.

BIBLIOGRAPHY

KAHHALAH, UMAR RIDA. *Jawla atharityya* (An Archeological Tour). 2nd ed. Damascus, 1984.
———. *Mu'jam qaba'il al-Arab al-qadima wa'l-haditha* (A Dictionary of the Old and Recent Arab Tribes). 5th ed., 5 vols. Beirut, 1985.
ZAKARIYYA, AHMAD WASFI. *Asha'ir al-Sham* (The Tribes of Syria). 2nd ed., 3 vols. Damascus, 1983.

Abdul-Karim Rafeq

Fadhli

Former political division of South Yemen.

The sultanate was situated on the coast of South Yemen northeast of Aden and extended inland to include a portion of the agriculturally productive Abyan region. Its cotton production made Fadhli the most prosperous state, after Lahej (Lahij), in the Western Aden Protectorate. It was one of the nine entities that Britain originally put under "protection" in the nineteenth century, and under Sultan Ahmad ibn Abdullah al-Fadhli, it was one of the six states in 1959 to launch the federation that preceded the short-lived SOUTH ARABIAN FEDERATION.

Robert D. Burrowes

Fahd

See Yusuf, Yusuf Salman

Fahd ibn Abd al-Aziz Al Sa'ud [1921–]

King of Saudi Arabia since 1982.

Fahd uses widely the title Custodian of the two Holy Places, which reflects his special position in Islam of being responsible for the care of the holy cities of Mecca and Medina and for the conduct of the annual Muslim *hajj* (pilgrimage to Mecca). For nearly forty years, he has played a key part in shaping the policies of Saudi Arabia.

Fahd was born in Riyadh, the eleventh son born to King Abd al-Aziz Al Sa'ud (known in the West as IBN SA'UD) and the eldest of seven sons of the king's favorite wife, Hassa bint Ahmad AL SUDAYRI. Fahd and his full brothers form the largest and most cohesive grouping within the Al Sa'ud (House of Sa'ud), the Al Fahd or, in popular Western (not Saudi) usage, the Sudayri Seven. They are thus the dominant faction in a system of government where national politics are essentially family politics. Not only do King Fahd's full brothers hold the two top positions in the key ministries of defense and interior, as well as the important governorship of Riyadh, but his sons and theirs have important roles in the domestic and foreign affairs of the kingdom. While their collective ability and energy are impressive, Fahd may be the most intelligent of the sons of Abd al-Aziz next to the late King FAISAL.

Fahd received the traditional Saudi court education, rote memorization of the Qur'an and mastery of the rudiments of various practical subjects. In middle age, he applied himself to acquiring some knowledge of English, history, and politics. From early adulthood, Fahd's career led rapidly to the exercise of power in key positions. He is the first Saudi king to achieve that position through a career in the bureaucracy. In 1953, just before the death of his father, Fahd had joined the newly established Council of Ministers as the country's first minister of education. In that capacity, he oversaw the creation of a national education system that made possible the enormous expansion of educational opportunities for Saudis at all levels in subsequent decades. In 1958, he helped lead the attempt to force the abdication of his half brother, King Sa'ud. When the older half brother Faisal assumed executive powers as prime minister in 1962, he named Fahd interior minister, confirming a close partnership that would continue until King Faisal's death. Fahd was effective in implementing Faisal's reforms and by the early 1970s had emerged as the most influential prince, already a key voice in foreign-policy issues.

In 1965, the royal family had agreed on Fahd's designation as second deputy prime minister, shortly after it had prevailed on the reluctant Prince KHALID ibn Abd al-Aziz to become crown prince. (Thus a smooth succession was assured when an unbalanced nephew assassinated King Faisal on March 25, 1975.) Khalid and Fahd had formed an effective partnership, with contrasting personalities and qualities. Fahd was, in the Saudi context, a progressive and had made his mark as an able administrator, someone who saw clearly the inevitable challenge of modernization that Saudi Arabia faced and the sorts of reforms required if the kingdom and the Al Sa'ud were to meet the challenge successfully. He enjoyed the exercise of power and worked effectively with bureaucrats and technocrats.

Khalid, who had hoped to avoid the burdens of rule, embodied important qualities that Fahd

King Fahd of Saudi Arabia. (Saudi Arabian Embassy)

lacked—a genuine religious piety and traditional bedouin simplicity of manner that endowed him with a paternalistic image of great appeal to most Saudis. This helped to maintain Saudi Arabia's stability as its conservative society entered the most rapid phase of its economic and social development. Though King Khalid suffered from heart disease, undergoing open-heart surgery both before and after his accession, he played an active role in all major decisions, and Fahd was always careful to defer to the king in his presence. Together they guided the kingdom through a period of great perils—the U.S.–brokered CAMP DAVID ACCORDS between Egypt and Israel, which estranged Saudi Arabia from its principal Arab ally; the IRANIAN REVOLUTION of 1979 that fomented Shi'ite unrest in Saudi Arabia's eastern province (al-Hasa) and helped trigger a profoundly unsettling attempt at a neoconservative Islamic uprising when militants seized the Great Mosque at Mecca; and the outbreak of the IRAN–IRAQ WAR, which threatened to spill over into Saudi Arabia.

When King Khalid succumbed to a heart attack on June 13, 1982, Fahd's accession was smooth, with his next eldest half brother Abdullah immediately confirmed as crown prince and Sultan ibn Abd al-Aziz Al Sa'ud, his next eldest full brother, designated as second deputy prime minister and effectively the next in succession.

Serious challenges have marked Fahd's rule. He became king just as petroleum prices were beginning a downward plunge that would shortly reduce the kingdom's oil revenues more than fivefold. A neo-conservative Islamist movement continues to challenge the Islamic legitimacy of the Al Sa'ud. Israel's 1982 invasion of Lebanon, U.S. failures to provide requested weapons systems, and the Iran–Contra revelations of U.S. arms deliveries to Iran for use in its conflict with Iraq appeared to undermine the wisdom of Fahd's close relationship with Washington and weakened his position in the Arab world. Finally, the Iran–Iraq War presented Saudi Arabia with a constant menace.

In facing these challenges, King Fahd has suffered from disabilities that derive from his personality and style of rule. Rather than embodying the traditional religious and social values associated with Al Sa'ud leadership, Fahd suffers from identification with Western, secular tastes. Because of his progressive secularist image, he is often obliged to defer to the *ulama*—the religious establishment—as in agreeing to impose stricter regulations on the public conduct of Saudis and foreigners. (It was easier for King Faisal to enact far-reaching reforms over the objections of the *ulama,* since his own unassailable piety armed him against their opposition.) Moreover, King Fahd lacks ties to the Arab TRIBES, still a key constituency in Saudi Arabia, and he generally lacks the common touch that characterized King Khalid's relations with his subjects. Fahd's work habits are noncontinuous; he tends to fluctuate between prolonged inactivity and intense application in dealing with the business of state. Finally, Fahd has an easygoing nature and shies away from confrontation.

Despite these drawbacks, Fahd has provided generally effective leadership as king, often surprising those who tend to underestimate him. He has personally supervised an aggressive Saudi oil policy to protect the kingdom's long-term interests. In the GULF CRISIS, his decision to invite U.S. and other non-Muslim forces to enter Saudi Arabia in August 1990, over Crown Prince Abdullah's objections, to defend the kingdom against possible invasion by Iraq and then to liberate Kuwait from Iraqi occupation fatally upset the calculations of Iraq's President Saddam Hussein that Fahd would remain passive. On March 1, 1992, Fahd issued a new basic law that included provision for a long-discussed consultative council (MAJLES) but going beyond what had been anticipated in the scope of proposed governmental changes, including the opening of the royal succession to the grandsons of Ibn Sa'ud.

BIBLIOGRAPHY

HOLDEN, DAVID, and RICHARD JOHNS. *The House of Saud: The Rise and Rule of the Most Powerful Dynasty in the Arab World.* New York, 1981.

LACEY, ROBERT. *The Kingdom: Arabia and the House of Saud.* New York and London, 1981.

LONG, DAVID E. "Fahd bin Abd al-Aziz Saud." In *Political Leaders of the Contemporary Middle East and North Africa: A Biographical Dictionary,* ed. by Bernard Reich. New York, 1990.

NYROP, RICHARD F., ed. *Saudi Arabia: A Country Study.* Washington, D.C., 1984.

Malcolm C. Peck

Fahd Plan

Arab–Israel peace plan (also Fez Peace Plan) proposed by Crown Prince Fahd (1981).

Because the Camp David Accords had failed to address several central issues of the Arab–Israel conflict, Crown Prince Fahd of Saudi Arabia unveiled an eight-point peace proposal on August 8, 1981; it was endorsed in modified form at an Arab summit in Fez, Morocco, on November 25–27. The plan called for Israel's withdrawal from Arab territories occupied in 1967, including East Jerusalem, and the dismantling of Israel's settlements in those territories; guarantees of freedom of worship for all in the holy places; the Palestinian people's right to self-determination under leadership of the Palestine Liberation Organization; indemnity for Palestinian refugees not exercising the right of return; West Bank and Gaza placed under UN control for a transitional period (a few months), leading to an independent Palestinian state with East Jerusalem as its capital; subsequent Security Council guarantee of peace among all states in the area, including the new Palestinian state; and the Security Council guarantee of the above principles.

Jenab Tutunji

Fahum, Khalid al-

Palestinian politician.

Fahum joined the PALESTINE LIBERATION ORGANIZATION (PLO) in its earliest days under Ahmad Shugagri, serving on the PLO's executive committee between 1964 and 1967. In 1970, he joined the

PLO's central committee as an independent member, and in 1971 he was elected chairman of the PALESTINE NATIONAL COUNCIL (PNC). The following year, Fahum led a delegation to Cairo to reconcile differences between Egypt's President, Anwar al-Sadat, and the PLO, and accompanied PLO leader Yasir Arafat to Moscow. In 1973, Fahum was elected head of the PLO's new Central Council, an advisory body to the executive committee.

Although Fahum was not aligned in those years with any particular PLO faction, he became closely associated with the pro-Syrian side of Palestinian politics. This positioned him well in 1982 to help negotiate the withdrawal of Palestinian guerillas from West Beirut, Lebanon. But the crisis within the PLO following the evacuation of Lebanon led to his removal as chairman of the PNC in 1984. Fahum was the only one of Arafat's close associates to join the Syrian-backed challenge to Arafat's leadership of the PLO in 1983 and 1984. Arafat prevailed, and Fahum was sidelined.

BIBLIOGRAPHY

Middle East Contemporary Survey, vols. 7, 10, 11. Boulder, Colo., 1985, 1988, 1989.
QUANDT, WILLIAM, et al. *The Politics of Palestinian Nationalism.* Berkeley, Calif., 1973.
Who's Who in the Arab World 1990–1991. Beirut, 1991.

Elizabeth Thompson

Faisal ibn Abd al-Aziz Al Sa'ud
[c. 1904–1975]

King of Saudi Arabia, 1964–1975.

Faisal was the third son of Abd al-Aziz Al Sa'ud (known in the West as Ibn Sa'ud), born in Riyadh, Saudi Arabia, probably in 1904 or 1905, though some accounts place his birth on April 9, 1906, to coincide with one of his father's important early victories. With no full brothers and no half brothers close to him in age, Faisal grew up in relative isolation. He left the royal court at an early age to study under his maternal grandfather, a prominent religious scholar, which served to reinforce that isolation.

Faisal assumed military, political, and diplomatic responsibilities at a young age. He led Saudi forces in the Asir campaign of 1920 and by 1926 was his father's viceroy in charge of the recently conquered province of Hijaz. This included responsibility for the Muslim holy cities of Mecca and Medina and the annual *hajj* (pilgrimage). He early developed a special, broadly informed expertise in the area of foreign

King Faisal of Saudi Arabia. (© Chris Kutschera)

affairs; this began in 1919 when he represented his father on a diplomatic mission to Europe, the first of the AL SA'UD FAMILY to do so. In 1930, Faisal officially became foreign minister, retaining that position until his death in 1975, with only a brief interruption, thus making him the longest serving foreign minister in the twentieth century.

Faisal's natural intelligence and his success on important state assignments, such as representing Saudi Arabia at the creation of the United Nations in San Francisco in 1945, clearly marked him as the ablest of the sons of Ibn Sa'ud. Yet in 1933, Ibn Sa'ud had the family recognize Faisal's elder brother Sa'ud, the crown prince, as successor despite Sa'ud's obvious lack of intellectual gifts or meaningful preparation for rule. Faisal had doubtless hoped, perhaps expected, that his demonstrated abilities would have secured him the succession, consistent with the well-established Arabian custom of choosing the ablest near relative of the deceased as the new shaykh or emir. Ibn Sa'ud evidently sought to avoid intrafamily rivalries that had fatally weakened the Al Sa'ud during his own father's generation. Though Faisal came to feel contempt for his incompetent elder brother, he insisted in family councils on a scrupulous adherence to the oath of allegiance (*bay'a*) to Sa'ud that he had led the family in swearing. To do otherwise would, in his view, have established a dangerous precedent in undermining the family's rule.

King Sa'ud's reign, 1953–1964, brought nearly constant crisis, with a pattern of events in which the Al Sa'ud called Faisal to assume responsibility for the government, although Sa'ud subsequently reasserted his claim to power. In early 1958, the kingdom was financially bankrupt from Sa'ud's profligacy and at risk because of his ill-conceived challenge to Egypt's

President Gamal Abdel Nasser and radical Arab nationalism. Faisal then assumed executive powers, imposing for the first time fiscal austerity with real limits on princes' pensions and a true budget. He came to a modus vivendi with Nasser, with whom he had earlier been careful to cultivate tolerable relations, though ideologically they were poles apart. By 1959, Sa'ud had forced Faisal out of the government and allied himself with a group of reformist half brothers, the Free Princes, whose embarrassing public split with the rest of the Al Sa'ud and declaration of solidarity with Nasser helped to place the kingdom in real peril.

In 1962, Faisal once again assumed executive powers as prime minister, doing so as a republican coup was about to overthrow the traditional imamate in Yemen and Saudi Air Force officers were preparing to defect to Cairo (Egypt). Faisal revamped the Council of Ministers and established the team of princes that continues to lead Saudi Arabia in the early 1990s. This included the progressive and ambitious FAHD and Sultan ibn Abd al-Aziz Al Sa'ud. They comprise part of the largest and most powerful grouping of full brothers in the family, those born to the favorite wife of Ibn Sa'ud, Hassa bint Ahmad AL SUDAYRI. Fahd at forty-one was both interior minister and, in a new departure, was designated second deputy prime minister behind Prince KHALID, while thirty-eight year old Sultan ibn Abd al-Aziz Al Sa'ud became defense minister, the position he holds today. To counterbalance them, Faisal selected the traditionalist Abdullah who, in contrast both to the king and the Al Sudayri Family enjoyed close ties with the Arab tribes, a constituency whose support was critical to the monarchy. Faisal himself, with his genuine piety and austere morality well established (after sowing a few youthful wild oats), secured the support of the crucial religious establishment. Faisal's care in creating and maintaining balance in the government was key to preserving stability. Thus, when Sa'ud's final attempt to recover his powers led the senior princes, backed by a *fatwa* (ruling) from the *ulama* (religious establishment), to force his abdication in 1964, the government had been put in place that would endure with few changes through King Faisal's own eleven-year rule and then Khalid's seven years as king, with its core still intact in the early 1990s.

The creation of an efficient, stable government in place of the circle of cronies or inexperienced sons on which Sa'ud had heavily relied was typical of the reforms that Faisal enacted. They were meant not to open up the political system in a modern, democratic sense but to enable it to confront the challenges of the twentieth century, so as to preserve the king-dom's traditional values. Thus, Sultan, Fahd, and King Faisal's brother-in-law Kamal Adham, head of the state intelligence service, were given full rein to build up the military and internal security establishments. Bright young technocrat commoners—like Ahmad Zaki YAMANI, who long served as petroleum minister, and Ghazi al-Qosaibi, for many years minister of industry and electricity—began to play significant roles, though without political power, as the bureaucracy began a rapid expansion. Modern public instruction at all levels underwent massive expansion, with girls admitted for the first time, reflecting the king's realization of the necessity of an educated population. The press and radio broadcasting experienced rapid expansion and, against strong conservative opposition, Faisal introduced television—he saw the need to diffuse information rapidly in a modern state and viewed the print and broadcast media as means of promoting national unification.

Faisal met external dangers to the kingdom with reliance on restored prestige and stability at home and on bold initiatives when required. Financial assistance to Yemeni royalists helped to checkmate the radical threat in that quarter, and Nasser's defeat in the Arab–Israel War of 1967 greatly strengthened Faisal's hand in dealing with the Arab nationalist challenge. As oil revenues mounted toward the end of his reign, "RIYAL diplomacy" helped to moderate the behavior of radical recipients of largesse and to strengthen conservative regimes. The new wealth gave substance to Faisal's attempt to promote an international policy based on the conservative values of Islam. In 1970, he took the lead in establishing the ORGANIZATION OF THE ISLAMIC CONFERENCE as an intended alternative to the Arab League (the League of Arab States). Ultimately, however, Faisal knew that Saudi Arabia's security against external threats—principally the Soviet Union, its regional allies, and proxies—could come only from the United States. This dependence placed Saudi Arabia in the painful dilemma of being intimately linked to the principal supporter of Israel. The dilemma became an acute crisis in U.S.–Saudi relations when Faisal led the imposition of the 1973–1974 OPEC (Organization of Petroleum Exporting Countries) embargo after President Richard M. Nixon's decision to resupply massively Israel's armed forces during the Arab–Israel War of 1973. It was typical of Faisal's pragmatic realism that, within months of that crisis, the U.S. and Saudi governments had signed agreements, especially the Joint Commission on Economic Cooperation, that created unprecedented links between the two countries.

In his statecraft, Faisal balanced a fundamental commitment to traditional values with an informed acceptance of the means of creating a strong modern state. He combined a rigorous Islamic view of the world with a sophisticated realpolitik, and he devoted himself unswervingly to the survival of Saudi Arabia. It is likely that, next to his father, Faisal will be remembered as the greatest of the twentieth-century Saudi rulers.

BIBLIOGRAPHY

BELING, WILLARD A. *King Faisal and the Modernisation of Saudi Arabia*. London and Boulder, Colo., 1980.

BLIGH, ALEXANDER. *From Prince to King: Royal Succession in the House of Saud in the Twentieth Century*. New York and London, 1984.

HOLDEN, DAVID, and RICHARD JOHNS. *The House of Saud: The Rise and Rule of the Most Powerful Dynasty in the Arab World*. New York, 1981.

LACEY, ROBERT. *The Kingdom: Arabia and the House of Saud*. New York and London, 1981.

Malcolm C. Peck

Faisal I ibn Husayn   [1889–1933]

King of Iraq, 1921–1933; also known as Emir Faisal, leader of the Arab Revolt against the Ottoman Turks, 1916; king of Syria for a brief period in 1920.

The third son of Sharif Husayn of the Hijaz, Faisal was from a prestigious, wealthy family (Hashimite) that traced its lineage back to the Prophet Muhammad. He spent his early boyhood among the bedouin in Arabia, educated by private tutors, and, at age six, moved to Istanbul, capital of the Ottoman Empire, where he lived during his father's exile until 1908. Faisal completed his education in Istanbul, becoming multilingual and well versed in court etiquette and politics. Life in cosmopolitan Istanbul and his later service as representative from Jidda in the Ottoman parliament, where he was an early spokesman for Arab interests, provided valuable political experience that served Faisal well in his later negotiations with the European powers.

In January 1915, Faisal was sent by his father to Istanbul to determine the political situation of the Hijaz and to contact secret Arab societies in Damascus, Syria, to ascertain if there was support for an Arab uprising against the Ottoman Turks. At first, signs were positive; but at a second meeting in Damascus in January 1916, after these groups had been disbanded by CERNAL PAŞA, the few remaining nationalists indicated via the DAMASCUS PROTOCOL that Husayn should initiate a revolt for Arab independence. Husayn incorporated these ideas in his correspondence with the British. Faisal was less sanguine about British support than was his brother, ABDULLAH IBN HUSAYN, but Ottoman Turkish moves to strengthen their hold on Medina made action more imminent. (The Turks were fighting on the side of the Central powers—Austria-Hungary and Germany—and against the Allies, including Britain and France, in World War I.)

Faisal's note to Cernal Paşa advocated an Arab *ummah* (community). His statement and the cutting of the railroad lines between Damascus and Medina launched the ARAB REVOLT on June 10, 1916. Concern in Cairo that the Arab troops in Arabia needed military training led to the dispatch of the British Colonel Thomas Edward LAWRENCE, who by December 1916 had joined Faisal and suggested to the British that the emir become the field commander of the Hijaz. The suggestion was taken, and, though unable to take Medina, Faisal's troops later occupied Aqaba on July 6, 1917, a victory that provided the Arabs credibility with the British. Faisal was deputized a British general under the command of Gen. Edmund Allenby, commander in chief of the Egyptian Expeditionary Force. Faisal's troops, some 1,000 bedouin supplemented by approximately 2,500 Ottoman ex-prisoners of war, proceeded to harrass the Ottoman Turkish army as the British moved to take Gaza, Beersheba, and Jerusalem.

On September 25, 1918, Allenby ordered the advance on Damascus. As party to the SYKES–PICOT AGREEMENT, Britain attempted to assign organized administration of the city both to the French and to the Arabs, but in the confusion of the British advance and the Ottoman retreat, the Damascus Arabs hoisted their own flag before Faisal and his army had time to reach Damascus. With the aid of Faisal's supporter, Nuri al-SA'ID, pro-Faisal officials controlled the city and were later confirmed by the French. Lawrence asserted that Faisal's men had slipped into the city on September 30–October 1 and had liberated it in advance of the British and Australian troops.

At the Versailles conference in 1919, Faisal was caught between British–French international diplomacy and events in the Middle East that were taking their own course. As the Arab representative to Versailles, Faisal pressed claims for Syrian independence, but under British sponsorship. Discussions with American proponents of Zionism and with Zionist leader Chaim Weizmann elicited Faisal's support for Jewish immigration to Palestine, culminating in the FAISAL–WEIZMANN AGREEMENT signed on January 3, 1919. To the published document, Faisal added a handwritten addendum that Arab support for Jewish aspirations would be conditional upon the achievement of Arab independence. Faisal continued to support Jewish immigration within the context of his later pan-Arab federation programs.

In May, Faisal called for a general congress to be held in Damascus to endorse his position at Versailles. Convened in June, the meeting was dominated by the pre-war Arab nationalist clubs—the primarily Iraqi al-Ahd, the Palestinian Arab Club (al-Nadi al-Arabi), which tried to persuade Faisal to relinquish his support for Zionism, and the al-Fatat (Youth)-dominated Istiqlal party. The congress called for an independent Syria that also would include Lebanon, Jordan, and Palestine. Backed by the British, who wished to exclude the French from the Middle East, Faisal received a grudging acquiescence for an Arab regime from the politically weakened French president, Georges Clemenceau.

Still in session in March 1920, the congress declared Syria (including Lebanon and Palestine) an independent kingdom ruled by Faisal as constitutional monarch. Some Arabs in Palestine proclaimed Palestine a part of Syria, and Basra and Baghdad were declared independent by a group of Arabs in Iraq who wished to be ruled by Faisal's brother, Abdullah. In spite of the international repercussions, Faisal accepted the Syrian draft and allowed Arab nationalists to harass French troops in Syria while he began to negotiate with the forces of KEMALISM in Anatolia who had proclaimed an independent Turkey. As the British withdrew their support from the Arabs in Syria, and a new government in Paris followed a more vigorous policy in Syria, the French ordered their high commissioner in Syria, Gen. Henri-Joseph-Eugène Gouraud, to confront Faisal. Occupying Damascus on July 26, 1920, the French forced Faisal into exile the following day and proclaimed Syria to be under French rule.

A shift in British priorities affected policy after 1920, influenced by an Arab revolt in Iraq against the British occupation and the policies of Winston Churchill, newly appointed colonial secretary, which included leaving Syria to the French and installing Hashimites elsewhere as local rulers who would "reign but not govern" in order to save the expense of full-scale occupation. At the CAIRO CONFERENCE in March 1921, Churchill and his aides proceeded to redraw the map of the Middle East and to plan the installation of Faisal as king of a newly created Iraq.

The British looked to Faisal as a malleable vehicle for their Mesopotamian/Iraqi policy, which was to secure the area and its oil for themselves. He was deemed suitable to both the Sunni and Shi'ite Iraqis because of his Hashimite lineage and his Arab nationalist credentials as leader of the Arab Revolt. Any local candidates, such as Sayyid Talib of Basra, were duly eliminated. The British contrived a plebescite in

July 1921 to authorize Faisal's candidacy. In August 1921, Faisal arrived in Iraq to a lukewarm reception and was proclaimed king.

The leader of the Arab Revolt brought with him to Iraq a coterie of Iraqi (former Ottoman) Arab nationalist army officers who had supported him in Syria and who now took top positions in the new Iraqi administration. Ja'far al-ASKARI became minister of defense; perennial cabinet minister Nuri al-SA'ID became chief of staff of the new Iraqi army; and Ottoman educator Sati al-Husri instituted an Arab nationalist curriculum in Iraqi schools. Faisal's tenure in Iraq was a tightrope walk between nationalism and cordial relations with Britain, without whose financial and military support and advisers he could not rule. Always maintaining his own goals, while remembering the bitter Syrian experience, Faisal worked from 1921 until his death in 1933 to create a modernized, unified country with a centralized infrastructure, to achieve immediate political independence from Britain, and to continue his dream of uniting Arab areas of the Middle East into a pan-Arab union under Hashimite aegis. From the beginning, the British regretted their choice, as Faisal proved to be less docile than they had anticipated.

Throughout the 1920s, Faisal was preoccupied with the fact that Iraq was a British mandate and not an independent state. Faced with local nationalist opposition to himself and to the British presence in the country, he used his considerable personal charisma to garner the support of urban nationalists and tribal leaders in Shi'a areas. Comfortable both in traditional dress meeting with bedouin and in Western-style clothes playing bridge with British officials in Baghdad, Faisal negotiated for independence. He also understood the necessity for British political and military support to ensure the territorial integrity of the new state until Iraq was able to build up its own army and defend its interests against the Persians, Saudis, and Turks, from whom Britain managed to secure Mosul for Iraq.

During treaty negotiations in 1922, delayed by his appendicitis attack, and again in 1927, the king encouraged the anti-British nationalist opposition, all the while advocating moderation by both sides. The result was an agreement signed in 1930 that gave Britain control of Iraqi foreign policy and finances but also resulted, in 1932, in Iraq's nominal independence and admission to the League of Nations.

The Iraqi constitution gave Faisal the power to suspend parliament, call for new elections, and confirm all laws. During his tenure, the king attempted to forge a united Iraq with a nationalist focus instead of the patchwork of disparate religious and ethnic groups. Once independence was assured, Faisal used his prestige and his position as king of an independent Arab state to engage in foreign policy.

Faisal never abandoned his interest in Syria. In contact with the French in Syria over the possibility that a Hashimite such as Abdullah or Ali (especially after the latter lost his throne in Arabia to the Saudis) might be installed there as he was in Iraq, Faisal was also active in local Syrian politics. In 1928 he organized a monarchist party aimed at making him ruler both in Iraq and in Syria. To Faisal, Iraqi independence in 1932 would be but the first step toward an Arab union to include not only Syria and Palestine, but possibly Arabia as well. From 1929 until Syrian elections in 1932, Faisal sent emissaries to lobby Syrian politicians, conducted an intense propaganda campaign to promote his interests, and used the Islamic Congress that met in Jerusalem in 1931 to advance his cause. Plans were made for another congress to meet in Baghdad in 1933, despite British opposition to Faisal's pan-Arab plans. The defeat of his cause in the Syrian elections, anti-Saudi revolts in the Hijaz, and his untimely death put Hashimite unity attempts on hold.

In June 1933, Faisal left for London on a prearranged state visit, leaving an anti-British government in power in Baghdad. He then spent the summer in Switzerland for reasons of health. When word reached him of the crisis with the Assyrian minority in Iraq, Faisal pleaded for moderation. But the exploits of the new Iraqi army that resulted in hundreds of Assyrian civilian deaths were popular in Baghdad, where there were demands for Faisal's resignation. On September 7, 1933, Faisal died of a heart attack in Geneva. He was succeeded by his son, GHAZI IBN FAISAL.

BIBLIOGRAPHY

KEDOURIE, ELIE. *England and the Middle East: 1914–1921*. London, 1978.
MUSLIH, MUHAMMAD Y. *The Origins of Palestinian Nationalism*. New York, 1988.
NEVAKIVI, J. *Britain, France, and the Arab Middle East, 1914–1920*. London, 1969.
SIMON, REEVA S. *Iraq Between the Two World Wars*. New York, 1986.
SLUGLETT, PETER. *Britain in Iraq 1914–1921*. London, 1976.

Reeva S. Simon

Faisal II ibn Ghazi   [1935–1958]

King of Iraq, 1953–1958.

Born in May 1935, Faisal was killed, along with his uncle ABD AL-ILAH IBN ALI and other members of the royal family, on July 14, 1958, in the course of the Iraqi revolution. Faisal's father GHAZI IBN FAISAL had died in an accident in April 1939 when Faisal himself was only three years old. For most of his life, he was overshadowed by his uncle, who acted as regent until he came of age in 1953.

Faisal was educated in the palace in Baghdad and then at Harrow School near London between 1949 and 1952. Although personally popular, he could not escape the stigma that attached to his uncle and the other eminence grise of Iraqi politics, Nuri al-SA'ID—both of whom were stout defenders and major beneficiaries of the close connection with Britain that characterized Iraqi politics in the 1940s and 1950s.

Peter Sluglett

Faisal–Weizmann Agreements

Signed in London, January 3, 1919, between Emir Faisal ibn Husayn ("representing and acting on behalf of the Arab Kingdom of Hedjaz") and Dr. Chaim Weizmann ("representing and acting on behalf of the Zionist Organisation").

The agreement between FAISAL and WEIZMANN was worked out with Col. T. E. LAWRENCE, who acted as both midwife and translator in an arrangement whose immediate purpose was to harmonize the positions of all three parties before the Paris Peace Conference that followed World War I. Its preamble contained remarks about "the racial kinship and ancient bonds existing between the Arabs and the Jewish people," and called for "the closest possible collaboration" between the signatories as "the surest means of working out the consummation of their national aspirations." In its nine articles, the agreement spelled out methods and areas of cooperation between two mutually recognized entities: "the Arab State" and Palestine. The latter was to be governed in a way that would "afford the fullest guarantee for carrying into effect" Britain's BALFOUR DECLARATION. This meant the promotion of large-scale immigration and settlement of Jews and the protection of the rights of "the Arab peasant and tenant farmers," who would also be "assisted in forwarding their economic development." Separate articles assured the free exercise of religion and the keeping of "Mohammedan Holy Places . . . under Mohammedan control." The World Zionist Organization promised to "use its best efforts to assist the Arab State [i.e., the independent GREATER SYRIA to which Faisal was aspiring] in providing the means for developing the natural resources and economic possibilities thereof." In an important proviso, Faisal linked his signature on this agreement to the complete fulfillment of Arab demands as submitted in a memorandum to the British Foreign Office.

The agreement, which remained secret for several years, quickly became inoperative, as neither signatory proved to be in a position to "deliver the goods" to the other. The authenticity of the agreement was challenged by some Arabs during the 1930s when Zionist leaders sought to gain propaganda advantage by publishing the text. Recent historical research has established that the document is genuine enough; thus, only Faisal's motives remain the subject of some debate.

BIBLIOGRAPHY

CAPLAN, NEIL. "Faisal Ibn Husain and the Zionists: A Re-examination with Documents." *International History Review* 5, no. 4 (November 1983): 561–614.
———. *Futile Diplomacy,* vol. 1: *Early Arab–Zionist Negotiation Attempts, 1913–1931.* London, 1983.
PERLMANN, M. "Chapters of Arab-Jewish Diplomacy, 1918–1922." *Jewish Social Studies* 6 (1944): 132–147.
TIBAWI, A. L. "T. E. Lawrence, Faisal and Weizmann: The 1919 Attempt to Secure an Arab Balfour Declaration." *Royal Central Asian Journal* 56 (1969): 156–163.

Neil Caplan

Faiyum village in Egypt. (D. W. Lockhard)

Faiyum

Egyptian desert governorate (province).

Faiyum, southwest of Giza, has an area of about 700 square miles (1,830 sq km) and a population estimated in 1986 to be about 1.5 million. The name comes from a Coptic word, *phiom* (the sea). The oasis is mainly a depression of about 30 miles (50 km) from north to south and about 45 miles (70 km) from east to west. Its abundant water comes from artesian wells and from a channel that branches off the Nile river near Asyut.

Legendary in antiquity for its fertility and in the Middle Ages for its many Christian churches and monasteries of the Copts, it later declined because of Arab and Berber tribal raids. Connected by rail with the Nile valley since 1874, the inhabitants soon came to rely on COTTON as a cash crop; about 700 square miles (1,800 sq km) of irrigated land are under cultivation. Its capital and principal city—called al-Faiyum, el-Fayoum, or Fayyum—had almost 250,000 inhabitants in 1986.

BIBLIOGRAPHY

Coptic Encyclopedia.
Encyclopaedia of Islam, 2nd ed.
HEWISON, R. NEIL. *The Fayoum: A Practical Guide.* Cairo, 1986.

Arthur Goldschmidt, Jr.

Faizi, Ahmad

Ottoman official.

Faizi was a tough, ruthless Ottoman Turkish pasha of Yemen. He fought against the revolt led by the HAMID AL-DIN imams in the first decade of the twentieth century, which ended roughly in a draw.

Robert D. Burrowes

Faiz Mohammad   [1861–1931]

Afghan writer.

Born into a Hazara Sa'id Shi'a family, Faiz Mohammad was educated in Islamic studies in India and Iran. He became historian to the court of Habibullah (1901–1919) and wrote a historical text in Persian called *Torch of History.* His death in 1931 was reportedly caused by a beating he received from Emir Habibullah when he was sent to deal with the Hazaras.

BIBLIOGRAPHY

ADAMEC, LUDWIG. *Historical Dictionary of Afghanistan.* Metuchen, N.J., 1991.

Grant Farr

Faiz Mohammad, Zikria [1892–1979]

Afghan diplomat and poet.

Born in Kabul, Faiz Mohammad was educated at Habibia High School and entered the Afghan foreign service in 1921. He was foreign minister under Nadir Shah (1929–1938) and then served as ambassador to Turkey and Great Britain (1948–1950) and Saudi Arabia (1955–1960). As a poet, he wrote under the pen name Faizli Kabuli. He retired to the United States in 1960.

BIBLIOGRAPHY

ADAMEC, LUDWIG. *Historical Dictionary of Afghanistan.* Metuchen, N.J., 1991.

Grant Farr

Fakhr al-Din I al-Ma'ni

Ruler of the Lebanese Shuf district and founder of a strong Ma'nid emirate.

After the Ottomans invaded Syria in 1515, al-Ma'ni steadily replaced the Tannukhids of the Gharb district as the foremost feudal family of Mount Lebanon. The Tannukhids belonged to the Yamani tribal conglomerate, whose members retained their loyalty to the Mamluks. According to popular tradition, it was Fakhr al-Din's panegyric address to the victorious Sultan Selim in Damascus that won him a preponderant position in the mountain.

BIBLIOGRAPHY

SALIBI, KAMAL. "The Secret of the House of Ma'n." *International Journal of Middle East Studies* 4(1973):272–287.

Bassam Namani

Falasha Jews

See Ethiopian Jews

Falconry

The art of training falcons, hawks, and other game birds to hunt.

Rooted in pre-Islamic Arabia, falconry became a fashionable courtly pastime from the time of Caliph Yazid ibn Mu'awiya (680–683 C.E.) to that of the Ottoman Empire sultans. Also practiced by commoners, falconry's popularity spread from Persia to Morocco. Most prized were the gyrfalcons of Siberia. These Siberian birds were often exchanged as ceremonial gifts among ambassadors. Many treatises were written on the art of training, and the hawk became a common motif in the Islamic arts. Hunting with falcons remains a popular pastime of the wealthy today on the Arabian peninsula.

BIBLIOGRAPHY

"Bayzara." In *Encyclopedia of Islam,* 2nd ed., vol. 1.

Elizabeth Thompson

Family

See Marriage and Family

Family Planning

Used to curb population growth and reduce maternal and infant mortality rates in Turkey.

Turkey's population is largely young and dependent: 62 percent are children between 1 and 14 years of age and women between 15 and 49. Life expectancy for women is longer than for men, but less than in developed countries. It was 66 years for women and 63 years for men in 1992. Although the rate of population growth is declining, it has not yet reached a desirable level. The fertility rate was 4.3 percent in 1978; 3.0 percent in 1988; and 2.5 percent in 1993. In rural and urban settings, it is equal (2.3%); however, there is a relevant difference in regard to regional growth. Although in western provinces, population growth was 1.9 percent in 1993, it remained 4.1 percent in the eastern provinces.

Only 76 percent of women benefited from the assistance of trained personnel during birth, and only 60 percent gave birth in a medical facility. The distribution of women giving birth at home is determined by the educational level of women and their place of residence. This proportion is 59.2 percent in rural and 27.4 percent in urban areas. It takes place up to 19.8 percent in western and 16.9 percent in eastern provinces. Women delivering at home are up to 69.2 percent illiterate, 29.9 percent have attended primary school, and 12 percent have had a high-school education. Delivery at home is performed up to 24.0 percent with the assistance of a midwife and 24.3 percent without any professional help. Until 1960, Turkey followed a strict pronatalist policy. The concept of limiting population growth was introduced via the First Five-Year Development Plan (1962–1967). Starting in 1963, it permitted abortion in the case of endangerment to the mother's life. The plan also oversaw the free distribution of contraceptives and governmental information to families. Following these innovations, the rate of women using some kind of contraceptive reached 56 percent in 1983, rose to 63.4 percent in 1988, and slightly declined to 62.6 percent in 1993. Within this same period, the number of women using modern contraceptives, such as an IUD or birth control pills, increased. However, conventional methods, such as coitus interruptus, still prevail.

A relevant policy change occurred following the third military intervention in 1980. Abortion up to ten weeks on social grounds (meaning simply "on demand") was legalized together with sterilization. In the case of married women, the notarized consent of the husband is compulsory. Abortion can be performed in public and private clinics. Counseling is provided free of charge by governmental mother/child care centers. New legislation was passed on May 27, 1983. Again, educational level plays a determining role. Although only 24 percent of illiterates are using modern family-planning methods, 36 percent of primary school and over 50.5 percent of high school and college graduates are implementing them. Women who do not want more children but do not use any contraceptives have indicated in up to 25 percent of cases that their husband "is not in favor of family planning."

The maternal death rate is very high. It is 30 times higher than in developed countries. The rate was 208 per 100,000 in 1975; it declined to 132 in 1980. The high rate of maternal mortality, similarly the infant mortality rate, can be explained by lack of education, fatalism, unequal distribution of health assistance, the negative approach of certain religious groups, and the low value of women's life.

Next to free governmental medical services, a number of highly efficient nongovernmental organizations, such as the Family Planning Foundation, financed by Vehbi Koç, Turkey's wealthiest businessman, are performing widespread public relations work in order to increase public awareness. The goals for maternal and infant health and family planning in Turkey for the year 2000 are as follows: to reduce the population growth rate to under 2 percent; to diminish regional health disparities by 75 percent; to offer all pregnant women early medical care; to assure that all home deliveries occur with the assistance of qualified health personnel; to reduce the maternal mortality rate by 20 percent; to reduce the infant mortality rate by 20 percent and the child mortality rate by 40 percent. Growing fundamentalism, the demand for a male heir, the increase of de facto, polygamous unions, and the need in rural areas for additional child labor are major factors contributing to the present slow down.

BIBLIOGRAPHY

GENERAL DIRECTORATE OF WOMEN AFFAIRS. *Turkey's National Report for the Fourth World Women Conference.* Ankara, 1994, pp. 23–25.

Nermin Abadan-Unat

Fanon, Frantz   [1925–1961]

French West Indian psychiatrist, author, and ideologue of the Algerian Revolution.

A black man born in 1925 on the French Antilles island of Martinique, Frantz Fanon became the best-known theoretician of the Algerian revolution and, through it, one of the best-known theoreticians of African liberation in general. The child of middle-class parents, Fanon spent the early years of his life attempting to be French. During World War II, however, humiliating experiences of racism in the Antilles and in North Africa and Europe, where he served in the French armed forces, made him increasingly aware of the anomalies confronted by a black man in a world dominated by whites.

After the war Fanon went home to Martinique, but in 1947 he returned to France and entered medical school. He received a degree from the University of Lyons in 1951. In July 1993 he passed his *Médicat de hôpitaux psychiatrique* and, in November 1953, he accepted a position as chief of staff (*chef de service*) in the Blida-Joinville Hospital, the largest psychiatric hospital in Algeria.

While serving at Blida, Fanon treated many patients suffering from the pressures of their colonized status and from the trauma of the revolutionary situation. He came to the conclusion that the resentment that had brought about the Algerian revolution was of the same order as the resentment he had come to feel as a black man in a white world. In 1956, Fanon resigned his medical post and secretly joined the FRONT DE LIBÉRATION NATIONALE (FLN; National Liberation Front). Receiving in January 1957 a "letter of expulsion" from the colonial authorities, he fled to Tunis, where the FLN was beginning to establish its headquarters. There he became an editor of *al Moudjahid*, the official organ of the FLN, served in FLN medical centers, and became a roving ambassador to solicit support for Algeria in African countries. In December 1960, Fanon was diagnosed with leukemia. He died of that illness a year later in Bethesda, Maryland.

Fanon wrote three books. The earliest, *Peau Noire, Masques Blancs* (Black Skin, White Masks), appeared in 1952. It diagnoses the psychologically dependent status of Caribbean blacks and suggests ways for them to transcend that dependency and discover self-possession and authenticity. The second, *L'an V de la Révolution Algérienne* (Year 5 of the Algerian Revolution), was written in great haste in 1959 and is essentially a sociology of the revolution. In it, Fanon describes the transformation of Algerian society brought about by individuals' decisions to revolt. In revolting against colonial oppression, militants also revolt against patriarchal and other oppressions. Out of these individual decisions, a nation of free men and women is born, a process that cannot be reversed. Fanon's last book, *Les Damnés de la Terre* (Wretched of the Earth), was published in 1961. It takes up many of the themes of the preceding works, but with greater urgency. Fanon insists that it is only through violence that colonialism can be defeated and the native overcome his dependency complex. Native bourgeoisies must also be overturned, because they are in a state of permanent dependence upon the West. The Algerian revolution is the model for global revolution, because it represents a peasant revolution led by a genuinely popular party. A fourth book, *Pour la Révolution Africaine* (For the African Revolution), a collection of articles written during Fanon's *Moudjahid* period, was published after his death.

BIBLIOGRAPHY

BULHAN, HUSSEIN ABDILAHI. *Frantz Fanon and the Psychology of Oppression.* New York, 1985.
GEISNER, PETER. *Fanon.* New York, 1971.
GENDZIER, IRENE L. *Frantz Fanon: A Critical Study.* New York, 1973.

John Ruedy

Fao Peninsula

The southernmost tip of Iraq.

The Fao peninsula lies between the SHATT AL-ARAB and BUBIYAN ISLAND. It became the site of the landing place of the submarine cable to India in 1964, of an oil port in 1951, of an offshore oil rig, and of heavy fighting during the Iran–Iraq War (February 1986 to April 1987).

Albertine Jwaideh

Farafra Oasis

Oasis in Egypt's Western desert.

Farafra oasis is roughly equidistant between Egypt's border with Libya on the west and the Nile river on the east; it is on the road between the Dakhla and Bahariya oases. It has been inhabited since ancient times and prospered in the years of early Islam. Later it suffered from raids by the bedouin of Egypt and Cyrenaica, and in 1860 its lands were seized by the Sanusiyya (people of the Sanusi Order). Its one town had about 1,000 inhabitants in 1957 and depended mainly on the sale of dates and olives.

BIBLIOGRAPHY

Encyclopaedia of Islam, 2nd ed.
FAKHRY, AHMED. *The Oases of Egypt.* Cairo, 1974.

Arthur Goldschmidt, Jr.

Faraj, Murad   [1866–1956]

Egyptian Jewish-Karaite author and theologian; Egyptian nationalist and Zionist.

Faraj was born in Cairo and trained as a lawyer; he became a government official during the reign of Khedive Abbas Hilmi (1892–1914) and wrote articles and poems for the two epoch-making newspapers of the pre-1914 era, *al-Jarida* and *al-Mu'ayyad.* He wrote books on Jewish-Karaite topics, on theology and law, biblical exegeses, Hebrew and Arabic philology, medieval Jewish poets who wrote in Arabic, and on current legal issues. He also translated Hebrew works into Arabic.

By the mid-1920s, as a noted author in the field of modern Arabic culture, he advocated Egyptian national unity and interreligious dialogue. His essays, notably *Harb al-Watan* (The National Battle), appealed to Muslim Egyptians to treat their Christian and Jewish compatriots as equals. By the mid-to-late 1920s, Faraj advocated Jewish nationalism, hoping that Zionism would be seen as similar to Egypt's national aspiration. His poetry, the *Divan Faraj,* collected in four volumes (1912–1935), stresses Zionist themes.

BIBLIOGRAPHY

"Faraj, Murad." In *Encyclopedia Judaica.* Jerusalem, 1971.
NEMOY, LEON. "A Modern Karaite-Arabic Poet: Mourad Faraj." *Jewish Quarterly Review* 70 (1979/80): 195–209.
———. "Murad Faraj and His Book, *The Karaites and the Rabbanites.*" *Revue des Etudes Juives* 135, nos. 1–3 (1976): 87–112.
SOMEKH, SASSON. "Participation of Egyptian Jews in Modern Arabic Culture, and the Case of Murad Faraj." In *The Jews of Egypt: A Mediterranean Society,* ed. by Shimon Shamir. Boulder, Colo., and London, 1987.

Michael M. Laskier

Faramushkhaneh

See Freemasons

Farès, Nabile   [1940–   ]

Algerian writer and poet.

Nabile is the son of Abderrahmane Farès, president of the Provisional Executive Council during the transfer of power in 1962. The general theme of Farès's writings expressed a disillusionment with postcolonial Algeria. His novels include a trilogy (*Le champ des oliviers* [1972]; *Mémoire de l'absent* [1974]; *L'exil et le désarroi* [1976]); *Yahia, pas de chance* (1970); *La mort de Salah Bayue ou la vie obscure d'un Maghrébin* (1980); and *Un passager de l'occident* (1971). In addition, *Chants d'histoire et de vie pour des roses de sables* (1978) and *L'état perdu précédé du discours pratique de l'immigré* (1982) are examples of his poetry.

BIBLIOGRAPHY

DÉJEUX, JEAN. *Dictionnaire des auteurs maghrébins de langue française.* Paris, 1984.

Phillip C. Naylor

Farhad, Ghulam Muhammad   [1917–1984]

Mayor of Kabul, 1948–1954.

Born in Kabul in 1917, Ghulam Muhammad Farhad was educated in Kabul and Germany and trained as an engineer. Twenty years after being elected mayor of Kabul, he was elected to the Afghan parliament (1968). He was an active member of the Afghan socialist party Afghan Nation and was the publisher of a newspaper of the same name (1966–1967).

BIBLIOGRAPHY

ADEMEC, LUDWIG. *Historical Dictionary of Afghanistan.* Metuchen, N.J. 1991.

Grant Farr

Farhat al-Zawi

Muslim judge and politician from Tripolitania.

Farhat al-Zawi studied in Tripoli, Tunis, and Paris and was a judge in Zawiya, Tripolitania, as well as a member of the Ottoman parliament from 1908 to 1912. A leader of the Tripolitanian resistance to Italian rule in Libya (1911–1912), he negotiated with the Italians for the region's future (December 1912) and became their adviser, helping to consolidate Italian rule.

BIBLIOGRAPHY

ANDERSON, LISA. *The State and Social Transformation in Tunisia and Libya, 1830–1980.* Princeton, N.J., 1986.
SIMON, RACHEL. *Libya between Ottomanism and Nationalism.* Berlin, 1987.

Rachel Simon

Farhi Family

Dynasty of Jewish financiers in Ottoman-controlled Damascus during the eighteenth and nineteenth centuries.

The Farhis were granted the status of *sarrafs* (bankers) by the authorities in the Ottoman provinces of Damascus and Sidon; they subsequently emerged as the chief financial administrators of these provinces' treasuries.

The most illustrious member of this family was Hayyim Farhi, who in the 1790s entered the service of AHMAD AL-JAZZAR Pasha, the governor of Sidon. There he became responsible for al-Jazzar's financial affairs until the latter's death in 1804. The following year Farhi was involved in the political succession struggle that led to Suleiman Pasha's ascendance to the governorship of Sidon. Given Farhi's assistance to this development, Suleiman allowed him to manage Sidon's financial administration as al-Jazzar had done previously. It was only during the second decade of the nineteenth century under Abdallah Pasha, Suleiman's successor, that Farhi's position declined, eventually resulting in his execution.

Their financial power in Sidon eliminated, the Farhis nonetheless continued to exercise considerable financial influence in Damascus until the early 1830s. In the wake of the Egyptian occupation of Syria and Palestine (1831–1840), the family's status declined temporarily in Damascus. Yet once the Ottomans regained authority in the province, the Farhis once again were partially responsible for running its financial affairs.

BIBLIOGRAPHY

BEN-ZVI, YIZHAK. *Eretz Yisrael and Its Yishuv in the Days of Ottoman Rule.* Jerusalem, 1976. In Hebrew.
ELIAV, MORDECHAI. *Eretz Yisrael and Its Yishuv in the Nineteenth Century, 1777–1917.* Jerusalem, 1978. In Hebrew.
"Farhi." In *Encyclopedia Judaica.* Jerusalem, 1971.
HOLT, P. M. *Egypt and the Fertile Crescent, 1516–1922.* New York, 1967.

Michael M. Laskier

Farhud

Persian word, commonly used in Iraq to refer to the breakdown of civil order in June 1941.

After the defeat of Rashid Ali al-Kaylani's pro-Nazi coup and his flight from Baghdad on June 1 and 2, 1941, Jewish life and property were attacked in what came to be called in Baghdad the Farhud. The looting was started by Iraqi soldiers who had been allowed to roam the streets of Baghdad carrying their weapons. On the second day, when bedouins started pouring into the city across the unguarded bridges, authorities began to worry that the attacks would spread beyond the Jewish community; however, order was finally restored.

The looting and killing had continued for two days while the British army sat on the outskirts of the city, prevented from intervening by order of the British ambassador, Sir Kinahan Cornwallis. Hundreds of houses and businesses were looted. Accounts vary from 120 Jews killed to more than 600; 2,118 injured; and more than 12,000 who lost part or all of their property. An official committee of enquiry reported the lowest figure; but the text of the secret report was published by the chronicler Abd al-Razzaq al-Hasani, who said that a member of the committee reported the largest figures, and orders were given to reduce this figure.

No attempt was made by Iraq to seek out and punish the perpetrators, but some token compensation to the victims was promised.

BIBLIOGRAPHY

AL-HASANI, ABD AL-RAZZAQ. *Al-Asrar al-khafiyya fi thawrat 1941 al-taharruriyya.* Sidon, Lebanon, 1965.
KEDOURIE, ELIE. "The Sack of Basra and the Farhud in Baghdad." In *Arabic Political Memoirs.* London, 1974.
TWENA, ABRAHAM. *Jewry of Iraq: Dispersion and Liberation.* Ramla, Israel, 1977, 1979.
UDOVITCH, A., and M. COHEN. *Jews among Arabs: Contacts and Boundaries.* Princeton, N.J., 1988.

Sylvia G. Haim

Farid, Muhammad   [1868–1919]

Egyptian nationalist leader, writer, and lawyer.

Muhammad Farid, a leader of Egypt's struggle for independence from Britain, came from an aristocratic family of Turkish origin. Trained at the School of Administration (Law), he worked as an attorney for the government of Egypt and later in private practice. A founding member of the NATIONAL PARTY and close friend of Mustafa Kamil, he succeeded him as its president in 1908. He led the party in Egypt and in exile until his death, sacrificing his fortune and his health in defense of the principle that the British must withdraw their forces from Egypt. He espoused parliamentary democracy and economic reforms for Egyptian workers and peasants. Although the National party became deeply split and hence weakened during his presidency, Farid is generally respected by Egyptians for his patriotic courage and self-sacrifice. His memoirs were published in 1978 by the Documentation Center of Modern and Contemporary Egyptian History.

BIBLIOGRAPHY

ABU AL-MAJD, SABRI. *Muhammad Farid: Dhikrayat wa mudhakkirat.* Cairo, 1969.
GOLDSCHMIDT, ARTHUR. "The Egyptian Nationalist Party, 1892–1919." In *Political and Social Change in Modern Egypt,* ed. by P. M. Holt. London, 1968.
———. *The Memoirs and Diaries of Muhammad Farid, an Egyptian Nationalist Leader (1868–1919).* San Francisco, 1992.
AL-RAFI'I, ABD AL-RAHMAN. *Muhammad Farid: Ramz al-ikhlas wa al-tadhiya,* 3rd ed. Cairo, 1962.

Arthur Goldschmidt, Jr.

Farmanfarma, Abd al-Hoseyn Mirza
[1857–1939]

Persian prince and prominent politician. His other titles were Nosrat al-Dowleh and Salar Lashkar.

He was the son of Firuz Mirza and the grandson of ABBAS MIRZA, who had been heir to the throne of Fath Ali Shah, the second monarch of the QAJAR DYNASTY. His mother was Homa Khanum, daughter of Bahman Mirza Baha al-Dowleh, another son of Abbas Mirza.

Abd al-Hoseyn Mirza was educated in the military school in Tehran, run by Austrian officers. He married the daughter of the crown prince and, by his proximity to the throne, gained great influence and wealth. He was an astute and ambitious politician of great resilience in the face of adversity, which was not lacking, as Persia underwent revolution, civil war, foreign invasion, and a change of dynasty in his lifetime.

Farmanfarma first served at the court of the crown prince until he became shah in 1896. He was then made governor of Tehran and minister of war in that year. He was exiled to Iraq when the shah was said to fear him, but he was recalled in 1906 and appointed governor of Kerman, just as the first stirrings of the Constitutional Revolution were beginning.

He became minister of justice, then governor of Azerbaijan. In 1909, he became minister of the interior, then of war, and, later, governor of Kermanshah.

During World War I, his sympathies were with the British in the complicated relations that developed between the government and the belligerents on the one hand and, on the other, between the government and the nationalists. In 1915, he was made minister of the interior, then prime minister. He remained in this post only a few months, then was appointed governor of Fars, which was under British control. This was his last government post. His son, Nosrat al-Dowleh, however, served the new shah, Reza Shah Pahlavi, and was executed in 1937 by a monarch grown suspicious and tyrannical. Abd al-Hoseyn Mirza died in 1939.

BIBLIOGRAPHY

SYKES, ELLA C. *Through Persia on a Side Saddle*. London, 1898.

SYKES, PERCY M. *Ten Thousand Miles in Persia or Eight Years in Iran*. London, 1902.

Mansoureh Ettehadieh

Farouk   [1920–1965]

Egypt's last king, 1936–1952

Farouk, the son of King FU'AD I (reigned 1922–36) and Queen Nazli, and the grandson of Khedive ISMA'IL IBN IBRAHIM (reigned 1863–79), was born in Cairo, on February 11, 1920. Privately tutored until the age of fifteen, Farouk intended to enter a British

King Farouk on an Egyptian postage stamp. (Richard Bulliet)

public school. He was, however, unable to gain admission to Eton and the Royal Military College at Woolwich, but he went to England anyway to pursue his studies. At the Royal Military College he took afternoon classes as an unenrolled student. His formal education was cut short by the death of his father, King Fu'ad, on April 28, 1936. Returning to Egypt, he ascended the throne as a minor and ruled with the assistance of a Regency Council until July 1937.

Upon first coming to power, he enjoyed much local popularity. Young, handsome, and seemingly progressive, he was thought to be an ideal person to foster parliamentary democracy in Egypt. In truth, however, he engaged in the same anti-constitutional practices which had so marked his father's tenure of power. During his reign he constantly plotted against the Wafd, Egypt's majority political party, contended with Britain over monarchical privilege, and intrigued to enhance the sway of the monarchy over the Egyptian parliament. In 1937, shortly after coming to the throne, he removed the Wafd from office. The Wafd had just concluded the Anglo–Egyptian Treaty of 1936, which increased Egypt's autonomy but fell far short of realizing the long-cherished goal of complete independence.

With the onset of World War II, Farouk's clashes with the British intensified. The monarch supported a series of minority ministries, many of which were, in British eyes, insufficiently committed to the Allied war cause. Political tensions came to a head in early 1942 while Germany military forces under the command of General Erwin Rommel were advancing in the western desert toward Alexandria. The British demanded a pro-British Wafdist ministry. When Farouk delayed, the British ambassador, Miles Lampson, on February 4, 1942, surrounded Abdin Palace with tanks and compelled the monarch, under threat of forced abdication, to install the Wafd in office. That day was a defining moment in Egypt's twentieth-century history. It undermined the legitimacy of parliamentary democracy and prepared the way for the military coup of 1952.

The immediate postwar years in Egypt were full of political violence and official corruption. In 1948 the Egyptian army suffered a humiliating defeat in the ARAB–ISRAEL WAR as the state of Israel came into being. During this period, groups opposed to parliamentary government increased their following throughout the country, most notably the Muslim Brotherhood, the Communists, and the Socialists. Within the army an elite of idealistic, young officers organized themselves in the FREE OFFICERS movement. Increasingly, King Farouk came to symbolize all that was wrong with the old order. Outrageously wealthy, he flaunted his wealth in a country wracked by poverty. His penchant for gambling and carousing with women offended many. Learning of the growing opposition to his rule inside the military, he tried to move on his enemies before they turned on him. He did not succeed. On July 23, 1952, the Free Officers, led by Gamal Abdel Nasser, seized power. Three days later, on July 26, 1952, the new rulers exiled the king. Sailing from Alexandria harbor on the royal yacht *Mahrussa,* he was accompanied into exile by his family, gold ingots, and more than two hundred pieces of luggage. His deposition in 1952 effectively brought an end to the rule over Egypt of the family of MUHAMMAD ALI, who had come to Egypt as a military leader in the midst of Napoléon Bonaparte's invasion and had installed himself as Egypt's ruler in 1805. Farouk's infant son, Ahmad Fu'ad, succeeded briefly to the throne, but in June 1953 Egypt abolished the monarchy and became a republic. Farouk continued to lead a dissolute life while residing in Rome. On March 18, 1965, he succumbed to a heart attack in a nightclub.

BIBLIOGRAPHY

GORDON, JOEL. *Nasser's Blessed Movement: Egypt's Free Officers and the July Revolution.* New York, 1992.
VATIKIOTIS, P. J. *The History of Egypt from Muhammad Ali to Sadat.* Baltimore, 1980.

Robert L. Tignor

Farraj, Ya'qub al- [1874–1944]

Palestinian politician.

Born in Jerusalem to a Greek Orthodox family, Farraj attended the first congress of the MUSLIM–CHRISTIAN ASSOCIATION in 1919, where he declined to sign resolutions condemning Zionism and linking Palestine to Syria. With British support, in 1920 he became deputy mayor of Jerusalem, a post he held through the 1930s. Farraj was a leader of the Nashashibi opposition's NATIONAL DEFENSE PARTY (NDA). In 1934 he was appointed acting president of the Arab Executive Committee. He also joined the ARAB HIGHER COMMITTEE in 1936 and the NDP's delegation to London in 1939.

BIBLIOGRAPHY

HUREWITZ, J. C. *The Struggle for Palestine.* New York, 1950, 1976.
PORATH, Y. *The Emergence of the Palestinian-Arab National Movement 1918–1929.* London, 1974.

Elizabeth Thompson

Farrokhzad, Forugh [c. 1934–1967]

A leading modernist female Iranian poet.

Forugh Farrokhzad was the first woman poet in over a thousand years of Persian LITERATURE to present feminine perspectives with recognizably female speakers in lyric verse. In her 150 or so mostly short poems, composed from the mid-1950s onward, she established the female gender and voice in the Persian language.

Farrokhzad is controversial and the most translated twentieth-century Iranian poet. Frank and personal representations of feelings and views in everyday situations, both palpably Iranian and emotionally universal, characterize her verse, for which faith in art and love constitute the spiritual underpinnings.

BIBLIOGRAPHY

Bride of Acacias: Selected Poems of Forugh Farrokhzad (1982) offers over fifty poems in English translation. M. HILLMANN's *A Lonely Woman: Forugh Farrokhzad and Her Poetry* (1987) contains a biographical sketch, analyses of representative poems in translation, and a bibliography.

Michael C. Hillmann

Farsi

See Iranian Languages

Fashoda Incident

Crisis in which both France and Britain, vying for territory in Africa, claimed control over a Sudanese outpost.

At the end of the nineteenth century, the European powers were competing for control of Africa. As the French extended eastward from the Congo, the British expanded south from Egypt. In July 1898, a French expedition commanded by Captain Jean-Baptiste Marchand arrived at the Sudanese outpost of Fashoda on the Nile, some four hundred miles (644 km) south of Khartoum. After British General Herbert Kitchener's victory at Omdurman on September 2, he proceeded to Fashoda on orders from the British prime minister, Lord Salisbury. He arrived on September 19 and met with Marchand. Kitchener claimed the entire Nile valley for Great Britain, and, after several days, both parties withdrew peacefully. The solution to the conflicting claims was later worked out by diplomats in

Britain and France, and it reflected the fact that Britain had an army in Khartoum while France had no appreciable forces in the vicinity. France renounced all rights to the Nile basin and the Sudan in return for a guarantee of its position in West Africa. The Fashoda incident is seen as the high point of Anglo–French tension in Africa.

BIBLIOGRAPHY

ELDRIDGE, C. C. *Victorian Imperialism*. London, 1978.
PORTER, BERNARD. *The Lion's Share*. London, 1984.

Zachary Karabell

Fasi, Allal al- [1906–1973]

Moroccan nationalist politician and writer.

From a prominent Fez family of scholars of Andalusian (Spanish) origin, al-Fasi was an early Moroccan nationalist, involved with the SALAFIYYA MOVEMENT during his education at the Qarawiyyin University. In the 1920s he helped organize the Free School Movement, which established schools to educate Moroccan youths in a modernist Islam tradition rather than according to French colonial ideas, and in 1930 he led protests against the BERBER DAHIR. In 1934 he helped draw up the "Plan of Reforms," a manifesto that demanded radical reforms of the administration and economy of the French protectorate so that Moroccans might benefit from French rule. After his 1937 exile to Gabon, he maintained contact with the founders of the Istiqlal party and at independence in 1956 returned to lead the party, remaining its leader after the split with the Union Nationale des Forces Popularies (National Union of Popular Forces; UNFP) in 1959. The party adopted a strongly nationalist program but was committed to a constitutional monarchical system.

After being minister of state for Islamic affairs (1961–1963), al-Fasi resigned and led the Istiqlal party into opposition, while remaining loyal to the monarchy. He was secretary-general of the party until his death in May 1973. Al-Fasi wrote *Al-Harakat al-Wataniya fi al-Maghrib al-Arabi,* translated by Ahuzen Zaki Nuseibeh as *Independence Movements in Arab North Africa* (1954), and *Al-Naqd al-Dhati* (Self Criticism; 1966).

BIBLIOGRAPHY

JULIEN, CHARLES-ANDRÉ. *Le Maroc face aux impérialismes*. Paris, 1978.

C. R. Pennell

Fasi, Muhammad al- [1908–1991]

Moroccan academic and political leader.

Fasi was educated at Qarawiyyin University in Fez and at the Sorbonne and Ecole des Langues Orientales (School of Oriental Languages) in Paris. He taught at the Institut des Hautes Etudes Marocaines (Moroccan Institute of Higher Studies) (1935–1940); tutored the crown prince, later King Hassan II; and modernized the Qarawiyyin when he served as its president (1942–1944, 1947–1952). A founding member (1944) of the nationalist Hizb al-Istiqlal party, he was held under restriction by the French authorities (1944–1947, 1952–1954). Fasi was minister of national education during the transition to independence (1955–1958). He authored *Contes Fassis* (Tales of Fasi; 1926), *L'Evolution Politique et Culturelle au Maroc* (The Political and Cultural Evolution of Morocco; 1958), and *Chants Anciens des Femmes au Maroc* (Ancient Songs of Moroccan Women; 1967).

BIBLIOGRAPHY

HALSTEAD, JOHN P. *Rebirth of a Nation: The Origins and Rise of Moroccan Nationalism 1912–1914*. Cambridge, Mass., 1967.
WATERBURY, JOHN. *Commander of the Faithful: The Moroccan Political Elite*. New York, 1970.

C. R. Pennell

Fassih, Ismail [1935–]

Persian novelist and translator.

Ismail Fassih was born in Tehran and left Iran in 1956 to study English literature in the United States. Upon his return, he became an employee at the National Iranian Oil Company and taught at the Abadan Institute of Technology. His first novel, *Sharab-e kham* (The Unripe Wine; 1968), treats the life of an employee of the National Iranian Oil Company, Jalal Aryan, who is unwittingly involved in a crime mystery. Fassih's later novels continue the life of this fictitious character and his family in Tehran. In addition to his popular novels, Fassih has published a collection of short stories titled *Namadha-ye dasht-e moshavvash* (Symbols of the Shimmering Desert; 1990). Fassih is now retired and lives in Tehran.

BIBLIOGRAPHY

MOAYYAD, HESHMAT, ed. *Stories from Iran: A Chicago Anthology, 1921–1991*. Washington, D.C., 1991.

Pardis Minuchehr

Fatah, al-

See Fath, al-

Fatat, al-

A clandestine Arab organization that made a significant impact on the development of Arab nationalism.

Al-Fatat was founded in 1911 by a small group of Arabs from Syria, Lebanon, and Palestine in the course of their higher studies in Paris. Initially called Jam'iyya al-Natiqin bi al-Dhad (literally, the "society of those who speak the letter Dad," i.e. Arabic), its name was later changed to al-Jami'a al-Arabiyya al-Fatat (The Young Arab Society). The original aim of al-Fatat was the administrative independence of the Arab lands from Ottoman rule. This meant that the Arab and Turkish nationalities should remain united within the Ottoman framework, but that each should have equal rights and obligations and administer its own educational institutions. Al-Fatat moved its offices from Paris to Beirut late in 1913 and set up a branch in Damascus.

The new environment created by World War I, particularly the Turkish government's execution of prominent Arab nationalists in 1915/1916, made al-Fatat amend its political program and opt for the complete independence and unity of Arab lands. By enlisting Emir Faisal (Faisal I ibn Husayn) in 1915, al-Fatat put itself in direct contact with the family of Sharif Husayn ibn Ali and, through them, with the British. In 1915, al-Fatat and the Iraqi-dominated al-AHD drew up the Damascus protocol, which expressed the Arab nationalists' readiness to join the British war effort against the Ottoman state if Britain pledged to support complete Arab independence and unity. After the war, al-Fatat shifted its attention to the principle of pan-Syrian unity. It reached the height of its political influence during Faisal's short-lived Arab government in Damascus (1918–1920). Although al-Fatat was the backbone of Faisal's government, its founding members preferred to operate clandestinely. They used Hizb al-Istiqlal al-Arabi (Arab Independence party) as a public front for their organization. Differences over Faisal's controversial dealings with the Zionists and the French, as well as the different political priorities of the Iraqi, Palestinian, and Syrian elements that constituted al-Fatat, created serious schisms within the organization. The collapse of Faisal's government in Damascus in the summer of 1920 sealed al-Fatat's fate as a structured political organization. However, many of its members continued to be active in the politics of ARAB NATIONALISM in the generation after World War I.

BIBLIOGRAPHY

ANTONIUS, GEORGE. *The Arab Awakening: The Story of the Arab National Movement.* Beirut, 1960.

KHOURY, PHILIP S. *Urban Notables and Arab Nationalism: The Politics of Damascus 1860–1920.* Cambridge, U.K., 1983.

MUSLIH, MUHAMMAD. *The Origins of Palestinian Nationalism.* New York, 1988.

QASIMIYYA, KHAYRIYYA. *Al-Nashat al-Sahyuni fi al-Sharq al-Arabi wa 'l-Sadah 1908–1918.* Beirut, 1973.

SA'ID, AMIN. *Al-Thawra al-Arabiyya al-Kubra,* vol. 1. Cairo, n.d.

Muhammad Muslih

Fath, al-

Palestinian nationalist movement headed by Yasir Arafat; also known as Fatah.

The name *fath* has a double meaning: it is simultaneously the Arabic word for "conquest" (literally, "opening") and a reversed acronym of *harakat tahrir filastin* (Palestine Liberation Movement).

Although identified for nearly three decades with the leadership of the PALESTINE LIBERATION ORGANIZATION (PLO), al-Fath was separate from and earlier than the foundation of the PLO. It was founded by a group of Palestinian exiles working in the Gulf countries; most of them would be its principal leaders for many years. Most important of these were the engineer Yasir ARAFAT; his friend and colleague Salah KHALAF; Khalil al-WAZIR; Khalid al-HASAN, an employee of the Kuwaiti government, and his brother Hani al-HASAN; in addition to others working in Kuwait, Qatar, Saudi Arabia, and Europe. The founders sometimes date Fath's beginning to 1959, when the Kuwait group was already working together and took over a magazine, *Filastinuna* (Our Palestine). But Fath as such seems to have really been formed in 1962.

The movement has been led from the beginning by a central committee, with occasional general conferences. A revolutionary council was formed early on, but gradually its power was overshadowed by the central committee. (It should not be confused with the "Fath Revolutionary Council," the name adopted by the Abu Nidal organization.) It also created a military wing, operating under the name al-Asifa (the Storm), which began military action against Israel at the end of 1964. During 1965 it continued to claim guerilla operations, though these had little effect upon Israel. Meanwhile, in 1964, the Arab League, with Egyptian prodding, had created the Palestine Liberation Organization under Ahmad

SHUQAYRI, to some extent preempting Fath's constituency.

After the June 1967 Six-Day War, Arafat and other Fath leaders reportedly slipped into the West Bank (from which Fath had previously launched operations) to organize resistance. Failing to successfully pull together a revolt in the newly occupied territories, Arafat and other Fath leaders withdrew and established new training camps in Jordan and Syria.

Fath and other Palestinian guerilla groups were able to increase their military capabilities and training in the camps. Meanwhile, they were also beginning to undermine Shuqayri's leadership of the PLO. In December of 1967, Shuqayri resigned. In January of 1968, Fath convened a meeting in Cairo of most of the guerilla groups and set up a coordinating bureau among them.

On March 21, 1968, Israeli forces raided a Fath base at Karama in Jordan. Forewarned, the guerillas were able to inflict relatively heavy losses on the Israeli attackers, and Karama became a rallying cry for the Palestinian resistance. During the fourth and fifth Palestine National Council (PNC) sessions in 1968 and 1969, the various guerilla groups, including Fath, won larger and larger roles in addition to an amendment to the Palestine National Charter to support armed struggle. At the fifth PNC in February 1969 in Cairo, Fath elected Yasir Arafat the new chairman of the Executive Committee of the PLO. The following year, he was given the title commander in chief as well.

Thereafter, Fath gained greater and greater control of senior PLO positions, with Arafat's close aides Salah Khalaf (known by the nom de guerre Abu Iyad), Khalil al-Wazir (Abu Jihad), Faruq Qaddumi, Khalid al-Hasan, and others taking key posts.

Since 1969 the history of Fath has been closely intertwined with that of the PLO, though the other guerilla movements have often been able to limit Fath's freedom of action. Until after the withdrawal from Beirut in 1982, Fath's positions were sometimes hard to distinguish from the PLO's as a whole, but with each successive split within the PLO (or withdrawal of various rejectionist groups from the PLO leadership), Fath's role as the main pro-negotiation faction became more pronounced.

With the outbreak of the Palestinian Intifada in Gaza and the West Bank in 1967, Fath leaders within the territories became one of the major elements involved in the Unified National Leadership of the Intifada, while Arafat and his Fath colleagues were the main force in pushing the PLO toward recognition of Israel's right to exist. Despite many predictions over the years that Fath would either lose control of the PLO or that Arafat, at least, would be replaced, and

despite the assassinations of Khalaf and Wazir, Arafat and the Fath leadership were the strongest supporters of the declaration of principles with Israel in September of 1993. Fath within the occupied territories, and especially in Gaza, has also become a main rival of the HAMAS Islamist movement.

BIBLIOGRAPHY

The history and organizational structure of Fath are treated in all works dealing with the history of the PLO, as well as biographies of Yasir Arafat. Of particular use are ABOU IYAD (Abu Iyad, Salah Khalaf) with Eric Rouleau. *My Home, My Land: A Narrative of the Palestinian Struggle.* New York, 1981.

COBBAN, HELENA. *The Palestinian Liberation Organization: People, Power and Politics.* New York, 1984.

KHALIDI, RASHID. *Under Siege: PLO Decisionmaking During the 1982 War.* New York, 1986.

WALLACH, JANET, and JOHN WALLACH. *Arafat: In the Eyes of the Beholder.* New York, 1990.

Michael Dunn

Fath Ali Shah Qajar   [1771–1834]

Second monarch of Persia's Qajar dynasty, 1797–1834.

Born Baba Khan, he took the name Fath Ali Shah upon his accession to the throne. He was the nephew of the first shah, AGHA MOHAMMAD QAJAR, and had been designated heir apparent. In 1796, when Agha Mohammad was on his second military campaign to Georgia, Baba Khan was governor of Isfahan; news reached him that his uncle had been assassinated. His right to the throne was immediately challenged by several pretenders who had to be eliminated before he could be crowned in 1797. Fath Ali Shah's reign was marked by wars with Russia—attacks on the Caucasus principalities that had passed out of Persian suzerainty during the several years of turmoil and civil war.

The war with Russia began in 1804 and drew Persia into the European rivalries that are called the Napoleonic Wars. On one side was Britain, nervous of Russian and French designs on India; on the other was France's Napoléon Bonaparte, who was at war with Britain and Russia. The Persian forces were led by Crown Prince ABBAS MIRZA, who was then also governor of Azerbaijan.

Fath Ali Shah needed European aid in his war against Russia, so first he allied himself with the French, then with the British—but each time was abandoned when they changed their policies. Persia suffered a disastrous defeat in 1813 and signed the

Treaty of GOLESTAN. This treaty did not prove final, since the borders between Persia and Russia were not well defined and neither country was satisfied. War resumed in 1824, despite the unwillingness of the shah—who would not send sufficient financial help. Persia was defeated and signed the Treaty of TURK-MANCHAI in 1828. According to this treaty, Persia ceded to Russia all the areas north of the Aras river, paid an indemnity of 5 million *tuman,* accepted other indemnity and capitulatory conditions that weakened the economy, and gave to Russian consuls judicial powers in disputes involving Russian subjects. The Treaty of Turkmanchai, in spirit if not in actuality, became the model for all the future treaties Persia (or Iran) was to conclude with other European nations.

The first premier (*sadr-e azam*) of Fath Ali Shah was Mirza Ebrahim Khan E'temad al-Dowleh, who had helped Agha Mohammad Shah gain the throne; he subsequently grew so powerful that he was feared by the shah, who put him and his family to death. The next premier was Mirza Shafi, a man of modest background. During his ministry, the bureaucracy of the QAJAR DYNASTY and the administration of the country were developed. Iran, disrupted after the fall of the Safavids, was once again strongly centralized and expanded. The capital, Tehran, was developed and endowed with new palaces, mosques, and pleasure gardens.

During the reign of Fath Ali Shah, some attempts at modernizing the army were made to meet any foreign challenge, but none was successful. Modernization was attached to European rivalries and lost ground each time policy shifted. Because of the interest of the European nations, the shah's court was visited by many envoys who have left their accounts of its splendor and extravagance. Nevertheless, the reign of Fath Ali Shah left Persia impoverished and with less territory than he had inherited.

BIBLIOGRAPHY

AVERY, P. *Modern Iran.* London, 1965.
CURZON, G. *Persia and the Persian Question.* 1892. Reprint, London, 1966.
SYKES, P. *A History of Persia.* London, 1951.
WATSON, R. G. *A History of Persia from the Beginning of the Nineteenth Century to the Year 1852.* London, 1866.

Mansoureh Ettehadieh

Fathallah Khan Akbar, Mansur [?–1936]

Iranian politician.

Mansur Fathallah Akbar was the nephew of Akbar Khan, the governor of Rasht. In 1889, he inherited the position of governor from his uncle and was in charge of customs revenues for the provinces of Gilan, Khorasan, and Mazandaran from 1889 to 1892. He joined the ranks of the Constitutionalists (see CONSTITUTIONAL REVOLUTION) and was post and telegraph minister in the first cabinet, formed in 1909. He was minister of war in the infamous cabinet of VOZUQ AL-DOWLEH, when the ANGLO–PERSIAN AGREEMENT was ratified in 1919. In 1920, just before the ascension of Reza Shah Pahlavi, he was made prime minister and minister of the interior. After the coup d'état of 1921, he sought refuge in the British embassy and subsequently withdrew from political life.

BIBLIOGRAPHY

BAMDAD, MEHDI. *Biographies of Iranian Notables in the Twelfth, Thirteenth, and Fourteenth Centuries,* vol. 3. Tehran, 1979. In Persian.

Neguin Yavari

Fatherland

See Vatan

Fatherland and Liberty Society

Ottoman political association.

An organization of junior-level Ottoman officers who sought the reinstitution of the constitution as well as reforms of the military and other state organs, the Fatherland and Liberty Society (Vatan ve Hürriyet Cemiyeti) was founded between 1905 and 1906 in Damascus by younger officers of the Fifth Army, including Mustafa Kemal, and was originally known by the shorter name Vatan (Fatherland). Branches were established in Jerusalem and Jaffa, and membership was extended to provincial bureaucrats. Though the group issued manifestos, their distance from Istanbul, the reluctance of more senior officers to participate, and the lack of a mass following precluded more explicit political activity. In 1906, Kemal organized a branch of the society in Salonika, recruiting officers of the Third Army.

BIBLIOGRAPHY

SHAW, STANFORD, and EZEL KURAL SHAW. *History of the Ottoman Empire and Modern Turkey,* vol. 2: *Reform, Revolution, and Republic: The Rise of Modern Turkey, 1808–1975.* New York, 1977, pp. 264–265.

David Waldner

Fath Jang Durrani

Emir of Afghanistan, 1842.

Fath Jang was officially proclaimed emir of Afghanistan during a period of civil war and British occupation. He was the son of Shah Shuja, who was killed in 1842. When the British left in late 1842, Fath Jang left with them, thereby abdicating the throne.

BIBLIOGRAPHY

DUPREE, LOUIS. *Afghanistan.* Princeton, N.J., 1980.

Grant Farr

Fattin Hamama

See Hamama, Fattin

Fatwa

An opinion on an Islamic legal or religious matter issued by a mufti.

As a legal function, the mufti was required to be a *mujtahid* (one who is capable of deriving law from the textual sources), although this requirement was relaxed after the twelfth century C.E. The opinion of the mufti was solicited by laymen and judges. With the introduction of twentieth-century codes, this function has largely fallen into disuse.

BIBLIOGRAPHY

SCHACHT, JOSEPH. *An Introduction to Islamic Law.* Oxford, 1979.

Wael B. Hallaq

Fawzi, Mahmud   [1900–1980]

Egyptian diplomat and politician.

Fawzi was educated at Cairo University, Egypt; the University of Rome, Italy; the University of Liverpool, England; and Columbia University in New York. His first diplomatic posting was as Egypt's vice-consul to New York and New Orleans between 1926 and 1929. Fawzi served as Egypt's first permanent representative to the United Nations. Following the 1952 revolution, Fawzi was appointed minister of foreign affairs, becoming minister of foreign affairs for the United Arab Republic in 1958. In 1956, Fawzi headed the Egyptian delegation to the UN Security Council debate on the nationalization of the Suez Canal.

In the 1960s, Fawzi served various executive functions. Between 1962 and 1964, he sat on the Presidential Council. In 1967, Gamal Abdel Nasser, Egypt's president, appointed him to the position of special adviser for foreign affairs, and from 1967 to 1968, Fawzi was Nasser's vice president. Following the death of Nasser, Fawzi assumed the position of prime minister, serving under the president, Anwar al-Sadat, until 1972, when he once again became vice president. He retained this post, while serving as the adviser on political affairs to Sadat, through 1974.

BIBLIOGRAPHY

African Who's Who, 1st ed. London, 1981, p. 423.

WUCHER KING, JOAN. *Historical Dictionary of Egypt.* Metuchen, N.J., 1984, pp. 291–292.

David Waldner

Fawzi, Muhammad   [1915–1992]

Egyptian military officer.

Educated at the Staff College and the Military Academy in Egypt, Fawzi led the Egyptian expeditionary forces to Yemen in 1962. He was promoted to general and appointed chief of staff of the Egyptian army in 1964, and commanded joint Syrian–Egyptian forces after the signing of the 1966 Defense Pact with Syria. Following the 1967 Arab–Israel War, Fawzi became the commander in chief of the Egyptian armed forces, and served as minister of defense from 1968 to 1971. Fawzi also played a political role, serving on the Supreme Executive Council of the Arab Socialist Union in 1968.

Fawzi's fortunes took a turn for the worse in 1971 when he was arrested on a charge of allegedly plotting to overthrow the government of Egypt. His fifteen-year prison ssentence was ended by a pardon in January of 1974.

BIBLIOGRAPHY

WUCHER KING, JOAN. *Historical Dictionary of Egypt.* Metuchen, N.J., 1984, p. 292.

David Waldner

Fawzia

First wife of Mohammad Reza Pahlavi, 1939–1949.

Princess Fawzia (or Fawziyya), daughter of King Fu'ad I of Egypt, was Mohammad Reza PAHLAVI's first wife. They married in 1939; their daughter, Princess Shahnaz Pahlavi, was born in 1940. Fawzia apparently could not adjust to the customs of the Iranian court, and the unhappy marriage ended in 1949, after which Fawzia returned to Egypt.

BIBLIOGRAPHY

SAVORY, R. M. "Muhammad Rida Shah Pahlawi." In *Encyclopedia of Islam,* 2nd. ed., vol. 7. Leiden, 1993.

Neguin Yavari

Fayez, Akef al-   [1924–   ]

Jordanian government official; leader of an important bedouin tribe.

Akef al-Fayez is a leader of one of the most important bedouin tribes in Jordan, the Bani Sakhr. He was chief of protocol for tribes in 1946 and has been in government or a member of parliament since. During his most active period in the 1950s and 1960s, he served variously as minister of agriculture, construction and development, defense, communications, and public works. In 1969, al-Fayez was deputy prime minister and minister of interior simultaneously. Elected to the reconstituted parliament in 1984, he was speaker of the lower house of parliament until 1988, when he was appointed to the senate. He is considered to have good relations with Saudi Arabia because of the Bani Sakhr ties with that country. Al-Fayez is viewed as a mainstay of the regime of King HUSSEIN IBN TALAL.

BIBLIOGRAPHY

GUBSER, PETER. *Jordan: Crossroads of Middle Eastern Events.* Boulder, Colo., 1983.

Jenab Tutunji

Faysal ibn Turki Al Sa'ud   [c. 1785–1865]

Ruler of central Arabia for more than a quarter century (1834–1838, 1843–1865).

In 1834 Turki ibn Abdullah was murdered. Faysal, his eldest son, succeeded him and soon consolidated his rule over most of the original Al Sa'ud domain. He acknowledged Abd Allah ibn Rashid as overlord of the dependent emirate of JABAL SHAMMAR in northern NAJD, thus laying the foundation for the Al Rashid dynasty that would briefly eclipse the Al Sa'ud. In 1837 Egypt, which had crushed the Saudi state in 1811–1818 while acting in the name of the Ottoman sultan, again invaded central Arabia, this time to further Muhammad Ali's ambition of a Middle East empire. The next year the defeated Faysal was imprisoned in Cairo, and Khalid, son of "Sa'ud the Great" (1803–1814), ruled as an Egyptian puppet. Faysal's dramatic escape from Egypt in 1843 (probably with the connivance of Muhammad Ali's son, Abbas) led to the rapid reassertion of his rule. He overthrew Abd Allah Thunayyan, who had supplanted Khalid in 1841. Faysal soon took control of Najd, the Saudi state's core, and of al-HASA on the Persian/Arabian Gulf. To the southeast he once again asserted Saudi authority in the Buraymi Oasis area and other parts of northern Oman, but the HIJAZ and its holy cities of Mecca and Medina remained beyond his reach. Throughout the second phase of his rule, Faysal was preoccupied with the rebellious Qasim area of north-central Najd and with recalcitrant tribes, especially the AJMAN.

A follower of the puritanical Wahhabi Islamic reform movement, Faysal ruled in accordance with its austere dictates. His regime, however, lacked the proselytizing thrust of both the eighteenth-century creation and the twentieth-century re-creation of the Saudi realm. In a state with only a rudimentary administrative apparatus he served as imam, leader of the community of the faithful, as well as chief executive of the state and commander in chief of its military forces. At the same time, he allotted considerable power to his three eldest sons. Abd Allah was administrator for the capital of Riyadh and central Najd, Sa'ud and Muhammad governed the southern and northern districts, respectively. In the rebellious Qasim district, Faysal installed his brother, Jiluwi.

Agricultural produce and livestock were taxed, as were Muslim pilgrims crossing Saudi territory. Tribute from Musqat and other territories supplemented tax revenues. Towns and tribes throughout the realm were obligated to provide quotas of men and animals when military emergencies required them. Soldiers were paid largely in the form of booty. Faysal's external relations established patterns for the future, especially in the three-way diplomatic game played with the SUBLIME PORTE and Great Britain. Britain thwarted Faysal's designs on Musqat and Bahrain, but he and they generally cooperated on maritime issues, roughly prefiguring relations between Britain and Saudi Arabia on the Gulf littoral in the twentieth century.

At his death Faysal had regained and consolidated authority over the principal part of the Al Sa'ud patrimony. Although his sons squandered their patrimony, Faysal's long reign reestablished the rule of the Al Sa'ud in central Arabia and thus made possible the restoration under his grandson, Abd al-Aziz ibn Abd al-Rahman (Ibn Sa'ud), in the next century.

BIBLIOGRAPHY

SAFRAN, NADAV. *Saudi Arabia: The Ceaseless Quest for Security.* Cambridge, Mass., 1985.

TROELLER, GARY. *The Birth of Saudi Arabia.* London, 1976.

Malcolm C. Peck

Fayyum

See Faiyum

Fayziyeh Madrasa

One of the main centers of religious training in Iran.

The Fayziyeh Madrasa was established in Qom in 1643 under Safavid patronage and at the behest of leading Shi'a cleric Mawlana Fayz Kashani, after whom it was named. The Qajars paid special attention to the Fayziyeh, which was renovated by order of FATH ALI SHAH QAJAR in 1806 (see QAJAR DYNASTY). The Fayziyeh gained prominence in Iran during the reign of Reza Shah PAHLAVI, whose policy it was to consolidate religious centers on Iranian soil, in an effort to rival the number accumulated in Najaf and Karbala, Iraq. The task of consolidation was supervised by Ayatollah Abd al-Karim Ha'eri of Yazd. Ayatollah Ruhollah KHOMEINI, spiritual leader of the IRANIAN REVOLUTION of 1979, taught at the Fayziyeh. The center also served as the headquarters of the antigovernment uprisings in Qom (1963) that Khomeini incited and that were implemented by the students at the seminary (after which Khomeini was exiled to Iraq).

BIBLIOGRAPHY

MOTTAHEDEH, ROY. *The Mantle of the Prophet.* New York, 1985.

Neguin Yavari

Fecr-i Ati

Ottoman Turkish literary society.

This Ottoman literary society was formed on February 24, 1909, toward the end of the Ottoman Empire. Its goals were to work for the advancement of Turkish language and literature, to enlighten public opinion on literary matters, to provide a forum for discussion and debate, and to forge links with similar groups in the West. The members of Fecr-i Ati regularly stated their opposition to a contemporary literary movement called Edebiyat-i Cedide (The New Literature), but they were united more by what they were opposed to than what they agreed upon, and they did not succeed in producing a countermovement.

Principles that did unify members of Fecr-i Ati were opposition to aesthetic and artistic values external to the individual and a belief in individual freedom for judging beauty. Ironically, it was this faith in individual standards that hastened the breakup of the group, which met for the last time in 1912. Some of the prominent members of the society were Mehmet Fuat KÖPRÜLÜ, Refik Halit, Ali Süha, Fazil Ahmet, Yakup Kadri, Celal Sahir, and Tahsin Nahit.

BIBLIOGRAPHY

ÖZKIRIMLI, ATILLA. *Türk Edebiyati Ansiklopedisi.* Istanbul, 1982.

David Waldner

Feda'iyan-e Islam

A small religious terrorist group active in Iran between 1945 and 1955.

Feda'iyan-e Islam (Devotees of Islam) was founded by Sayyed Mujtaba Mirlawhi, a theology student, who adopted the name Navab Safavi. His followers were mostly youngsters employed in the lower levels of the Tehran bazaar. The group interpreted the Qur'an literally, demanded a strict application of the *Shari'a* (Islamic law), and called for the physical elimination of the "enemies of Islam." Despite ideological affinity with the MUSLIM BROTHERHOOD in Egypt, the two groups had no organizational links. The Feda'iyan-e Islam's victims included Ahmad KASRAVI, the iconoclastic writer, and General Ali RAZMARA, Iran's prime minister in 1951. It also tried to assassinate Husayn Fatemi, Mohammad Mossadegh's foreign minister, and Hoseyn ALA, the prime minister in 1955. After the last attempt, the government destroyed the organization by executing Safavi and his three closest colleagues. Immediately after the IRANIAN REVOLUTION of 1979, some tried to revive the Feda'iyan-e Islam, but other veterans sabotaged the attempt arguing that the organization was now redundant with the Islamic Republic of Iran implementing its original program.

BIBLIOGRAPHY

KAZEMI, FARHAD. "The *Feda'iyan-e Islam*: Fanaticism, Politics, and Terror." In *From Nationalism to Revolutionary Islam,* ed. by Said Amir Arjomand. Albany, N.Y., 1984.

Ervand Abrahamian

Feda'iyan-e Khalq

The Organization of the Iranian People's Feda'i Guerrillas (Sazman-e Cherikha-ye Feda'i-ye Khalq-e Iran), known as the Feda'i or Feda'yan-e Khalq, is the main Marxist guerrilla movement in contemporary Iran.

Feda'iyan-e Khalq (The People's Devotees) was created in the early 1970s by young dissidents from both the TUDEH PARTY and Mohammad Mossadegh's NATIONAL FRONT who felt that their parent organizations, with their conventional political strategies, would never succeed in overthrowing the PAHLAVI regime. These young activists were inspired by the communist leaders Mao Tse-Tung, Ho Chi Minh, and, most important of all, Che Guevara. Some of them received guerilla training from the Palestinians. Their first military exploit was to assault in February 1971 the gendarmerie station in the village of Siyahkal in the Caspian region. This attack, famous later as the Siyahkal incident, acted as a catalyst for the whole revolutionary process in Iran. It prompted others, especially religious radicals such as the MOJAHEDIN-E KHALQ, to follow their example. Disciples of Ayatollah Ruhollah KHOMEINI have admitted that Siyahkal left a "deep impression" on the Iranian population.

In the years following Siyahkal, the Feda'iyan lost all its original leaders and most of its rank and file—either in shoot-outs, under torture, or by firing squads. Most of these martyrs came from the ranks of the intelligentsia—they were teachers, engineers, and university students. By the time of the revolution, the Feda'iyan enjoyed a widespread mystique of revolutionary heroism and martyrdom, but little remained of its armed organization. This little, however, played a part in helping deliver the old regime its coup de grace in the dramatic days of February 1979.

After the revolution, the Feda'iyan grew quickly to become the main Marxist organization in Iran, far outshadowing the older Tudeh party. By early 1981, it had a nationwide structure, its Tehran rallies attracted over 100,000 participants and, with the Mojahedin, its armed cells posed a serious threat to the clerical Islamic Republic. After 1981, however, the Feda'iyan went into sharp decline in part because of a massive government repression and in part because of constant internal fragmentation. Government repression took over 600 Feda'iyan lives. The backgrounds of these martyrs were similar to those before the revolution, with the one minor variation—the new ones included many more high school students.

The main split came over how to deal with the clerical state. One faction, known as the Aksariyat (Majority), viewed the Khomeini regime as intrinsically anti-imperialist and, therefore, potentially progressive. In this respect, they followed a policy similar to the Tudeh; but the other faction, labeled the Aqalliyat (Minority), saw the regime as the executive committee of the petty bourgeoisie, therefore, inherently conservative and even reactionary. Both factions in turn, went through their own splits because of personality conflicts and political disputes over such issues as the Tudeh, the Mojahedin, the Soviet Union, and the 1979–1981 Kurdish revolts. By the early 1990s, there were at least six groups in exile, each carrying the name Feda'iyan and each claiming to keep alive the revolutionary traditions of Siyahkal. Two of the larger groups published monthly newsletters named *Kar* (Work).

BIBLIOGRAPHY

BEHROOZ, MAZIAR. "Iran's Fedayan 1971–88: A Case Study of Iranian Marxism." *The UCLA Journal of Middle East Studies* 6 (1990): 1–39.

TIVA, M. "Chap dar Iran-e Mo'aser" (The Left in Contemporary Iran). *Kankash* 1 (Summer 1987): 179–190.

Ervand Abrahamian

Fedayeen

See Fida'iyyun

Feddan

A square unit of land.

Equal to slightly more than one acre, feddan is an Arabic term for a square unit of land. One of the first reforms instituted by Egypt's Gamal Abdel Nasser was a 1952 land act that limited private holdings to 200 feddans or less and redistributed the excess feddans or larger estates to the hitherto landless peasants (fellahin).

BIBLIOGRAPHY

HOURANI, ALBERT. *A History of the Arab Peoples.* Cambridge, U.K., 1991.

Zachary Karabell

Felafel

Ground beans with spices, fried.

Originally an Egyptian dish, felafel is today popular in Syria, Lebanon, and Israel as well. Traditionally, it is prepared with chickpeas ground into a paste and fried in oil, which is then served in pita bread with salad. Local variations include the use of other beans. In Egypt, felafel is also known as *tamiyya*.

BIBLIOGRAPHY

DER HAROUTUNIAN, ARTO. *Middle Eastern Cookery*. London, 1983.

Zachary Karabell

Fellagha

Term used originally for fugitives and brigands, from the colloquial Arabic of Tunisia.

Fellagha (also *Fallak*) was a term widely used in the French press in Tunisia for the rural-based armed groups that fought against French colonialism in the early 1950s. It was soon taken on and used by the guerrillas themselves. At the start of the ALGERIAN WAR OF INDEPENDENCE (1954–1962), the term was given to the fighters of the National Liberation Front (Front de Libération Nationale; FLN).

BIBLIOGRAPHY

"Fallak." In *Encyclopedia of Islam*, 2nd ed.

Matthew S. Gordon

Fellah

An agricultural worker, or any rural inhabitant, who makes a living cultivating land; also spelled "fallah."

A significant portion of the populations of Middle Eastern countries are fellahin (plural), although there has been a steady decline due to industrialization and urbanization. Countries in the Middle East with significant proportions of fellahin in the labor force include Egypt, just over 50 percent; Morocco and Turkey, about 50 percent; Iran and Iraq, 40 percent; Syria and Tunisia, about 33 percent. Agricultural contribution to gross domestic product is low, however, making the fellahin one of the least affluent segments of society; the least likely to benefit from educational, health, and other public services; and therefore the most susceptible to disease and adversity.

Jenab Tutunji

Feraoun, Mouloud   [1913–1962]

Algerian writer.

Feraoun was born to an impoverished Kabyle family. He received a French education and a teaching degree. Feraoun's publications dealt with Kabyle life as viewed in the novels *Le fils du pauvre* (1950); *La terre et le sang* (1953); *Les chemins qui montent* (1957); and the essays, *Jours de Kabyle* (1954). Feraoun also translated the poetry of the renown Kabyle, Si Mohand. Feraoun's posthumous *Journal, 1955–1962* (1962) chronicled the Algerian war of independence. He was murdered by the colonialist SECRET ARMY ORGANIZATION (Organisation de l'Armée Secrète; OAS). Feraoun belonged to the famous "Generation of 1954" literary figures (composed also of Mohammed DIB, Kateb YACINE, Moulaoud MAMMERI, and Malek HADDAD).

BIBLIOGRAPHY

DÉJEUX, JEAN. *La littérature algérienne contemporaine*. Paris, 1975.

Phillip C. Naylor

Ferit, Damat Mehmet   [1853–1923]

Ottoman politician and grand vizier.

Damat Ferit Paşa rose to prominence first by marrying the sister of future sultan Vahideddin and then by founding the Freedom and Accord party in November 1911. As a revival of the Liberal Union party, the Freedom and Accord party opposed the COMMITTEE OF UNION AND PROGRESS government and demanded an investigation of the Ottoman defeat at Tripoli the same year.

In two terms as grand vizier in 1919 and 1920, Damat Ferit Paşa allied with Sultan Vahideddin and Allied occupiers against the emerging Kemalist national movement, obtaining *fatwas* condemning nationalist leaders to death and inciting the Kurds against Kemalist forces in eastern Anatolia. On 17 October 1920, he resigned under Allied pressure and fled to Yugoslavia. In 1921, the Ankara national assembly condemned him to death in absentia for treason. He died of natural causes on 6 October 1923, the same day the Allies evacuated Istanbul under the Treaty of Lausanne.

BIBLIOGRAPHY

LEWIS, BERNARD. *The Emergence of Modern Turkey*. New York, 1961.
SHAW, STANFORD J., and EZEL KURAL SHAW. *History of the Ottoman Empire and Modern Turkey*, vol. 2. Cambridge, U.K., 1977.

Elizabeth Thompson

Ferman

An imperial edict carrying the Ottoman sultan's tughra, or signature.

Fermans were regulations or communiqués issued on a wide variety of topics in response to appeals from government officials and subjects throughout the empire. They were issued after discussion by top officials at the sultan's palace, or SUBLIME PORTE, often but not necessarily including the sultan himself. The grand vizier handled appeals of a general administrative nature, while the *defterdar* considered fiscal matters and the *kadi-asker* matters of *Shari'a,* or religious law. The sultan's *tughra* would be affixed near the top of the document, which would then be placed in a small bag and sent by courier to the appellant.

With the expansion of government and the increasingly autonomous responsibility of the grand vizier in the nineteenth century, fermans were replaced by *irade,* which means "the sultan's will." The irade was an inscription expressing the sultan's approval that was affixed at the bottom of a document drawn up by the grand vizier. Documents originating personally with the sultan were then called *hatt-i hümayun,* literally "imperial documents."

BIBLIOGRAPHY

The Encyclopedia of Islam. Vol. 2. London, 1965, pp. 803–805.
SHAW, STANFORD J., and EZEL KURAL SHAW. *History of the Ottoman Empire and Modern Turkey.* Vol. 2. New York, 1977.

Elizabeth Thompson

Fertile Crescent

Term used by historians and prehistorians to describe the ancient Near East's agricultural heartland, which produced the Neolithic revolution and the rise of the world's first civilizations.

The Fertile Crescent stretches from the Mediterranean coast north across the Syrian desert to MESOPOTAMIA and then south to the Persian/Arabian GULF. Parts of Egypt, Israel, Lebanon, Syria, Iraq, and Iran are within it.

The first civilization of Sumer and the civilizations of the Bible—Assyria, Akkad, Persia, and ancient Egypt, as well as the Jewish kingdoms of Judah and Israel—all developed in the Fertile Crescent, with cities, agricultural towns and villages, and herders of domesticated sheep and goats. Both ancient Greece and Rome invaded to control the richness of the region, and the Roman Empire continued through the Islamic conquests of the 700s, its Byzantine emperors ruling from Constantinople until the Ottoman Turks conquered the capital in 1453, making it their own capital of ISTANBUL.

Under the Ottoman Empire, the crescent had districts or provinces (VILAYETs) and subdistricts (SANJAKs). After World War I, with the defeat of the Ottomans, Britain and France administered most of it under League of Nations mandates. Beginning in the 1920s, Arab leaders developed various plans for unifying it, and the Hashimites were especially eager to see it ruled by one of their emirs. After World War II, the concept of PAN-ARABISM was championed by Egypt's President Gamal Abdel Nasser and by the Ba'thist political parties of Iraq, Syria, and elsewhere. Today, Fertile Crescent unity is little talked about, but the Islamist political resurgence and the Organization of Petroleum Exporting Countries (OPEC) remind many that common interests and common heritage may yet serve to unite the Arab world, much of which now exists in the Fertile Crescent.

BIBLIOGRAPHY

BRAWER, M., ed. *Atlas of the Middle East.* New York, 1988.
SHIMONI, YAACOV, ed. *Political Dictionary of the Middle East in the Twentieth Century.* New York, 1974.

Zachary Karabell

Fertile Crescent Unity Plans

Post–World War I plans to unify the Arab lands in Asia of the former Ottoman Empire.

After World War I, various plans, differing in source and motivation, were advanced for the unification of that area of Arab Asia known as the Fertile Crescent. This followed the dismemberment of the Ottoman Empire and the sanctioning by the League of Nations of mandates for France and Britain in 1922, to become effective in 1923, covering Mesopotamia and geohistorical or Greater Syria (which included Lebanon, Palestine, and Transjordan). The Fertile Crescent was a conceptual broad arc from Basra to Beersheba, embracing all the mandated territory; it was moderately fertile and, in addition to Arabs, included Kurds, the Druze people, Alawites, and other ethnic minorities.

Well before the collapse of the Ottoman Empire, its Arab provinces in Asia had been edging toward regional autonomy. Such separatist aspirations were submerged in the expectation of a single independent Arab state, ostensibly promised during the

World War I undertakings of Britain and France. By 1919, however, the Syrian national congress urged upon the investigating U.S. King–Crane Commission the reunification of geohistorical Syria as a separate entity. (In March 1920, Faisal, eldest son of Sharif Husayn of Hijaz—who had cooperated with T. E. Lawrence [of Arabia] and British General E. H. Allenby in uniting Arab forces to take Jerusalem and Damascus—was proclaimed king of Syria by the Syrian national congress; he was deposed by the French in July 1920). The Anglo–French repudiation of the congress's resolution and Britain's granting of the throne of Iraq to Faisal after his brief rule in Syria set in motion the first major effort—promoted by Faisal—for the unification of the Crescent. Faisal recognized, however, that the sanction of Britain and France was essential. From neither was it forthcoming. France suspected the project of being inspired by Britain to undermine French influence; for Britain, maintaining the Entente Cordiale outweighed other considerations. Later, the French were to give Faisal momentary encouragement on his visit to Paris in 1931, since, following the signing of the Anglo–Iraqi Treaty of 1930, which looked forward to the termination of Britain's mandate, the French saw possible advantage in Fertile Crescent unity. The project also drew support from the Aleppine People's party and the Syrian monarchists; but the dominant National Bloc in Damascus favored the unification of Greater Syria on its own as a republic. One permanent obstacle to Northern Arab unification, whether under Hashimite auspices or not, was the rooted objection of Ibn Sa'ud, king of Saudi Arabia (1932–1953).

Faisal's final plea for British support in 1933 had received no answer before he died three months later; Nuri al-Sa'id, his prime minister, pursued the cause, but in Iraq and elsewhere, Arab nationalism, which sought the union of all Arabs, exerted a more potent appeal for political theorists, such as the Iraqi Sati al-Husri. Emir Abdullah of Transjordan, Faisal's brother, was meanwhile brooding on his grand design for the unification of Greater Syria with himself as king, while in Syria itself a quite different movement for the cohesion of the "Syrian" people, on a wider interpretation, was being canvassed by the charismatic Antun Sa'ada, a Lebanese-born Christian convinced that "natural" Syria, embracing in his view the whole Crescent (if not more), enjoyed a particularism owed neither to Islam nor to the Arabs but to the ethnic mix within the region's distinctive environment. The aim of the Parti National Syrien (PNS), which he founded, was to unify this Syrian people and defend its separatism. His appeal expectedly attracted non-Muslims; more remarkable was the number of influential Syrian Muslims who grav-

itated into his orbit. In 1938, after arrests by the French for inciting disorder, he fled to South America, returning to the fray in 1947. Before his departure, membership of the PPS was alleged (improbably) to have reached 50,000. All these movements for Arab Federation, as the British authorities called it, were regarded in 1939 by London as subject to insurmountable obstacles—internal rivalries as well as French, Saudi, and Zionist opposition. London's conclusion was to let natural forces take their course.

In July 1940, Emir Abdullah formally launched his Greater Syria plan, finding some support from Syrian ethnic minorities and even from Arab tribal and army factions; but the response of the British government, preoccupied with World War II, was unfavorable. In 1941, the emergence in Iraq of the anti-British Rashid Ali al-Kayani, with the exiled mufti of Jerusalem at his side, and the encouragement of the Axis powers, led to a new call for Fertile Crescent unity; but his briefly successful coup d'état in April was suppressed by British army intervention with Jordanian support. The expected military backing of the Axis had failed to materialize.

Britain's search for a posture that might strengthen its wartime position in the Middle East led in May 1941 to British Foreign Secretary Anthony Eden declaring his nation's "full support for any scheme of [Arab] unity which commanded general approval." Britain's high commissioner in Jerusalem, Lord Samuel, prompted by his Arab adviser, George Antonius, urged active support for Fertile Crescent unity and the abolition of the artificial frontiers imposed on Greater Syria after World War I. The authorities in London remained unmoved.

In December 1942, Emir Abdullah presented a new version of his Greater Syria scheme, in which "cultural union" with Iraq would lead to confederation of the two. The response of the rival Hashimite court in Baghdad was the launching by Prime Minister Nuri al-Sa'id of his so-called Blue Book, an elaborate scheme for solving all Middle East problems, in which a reunified historic Syria would join with Iraq to form the core of an Arab league open to all—the whole scheme resting on an international guarantee. Opposition from Ibn Sa'ud and Emir Abdullah was instant; and Nuri's bid for wider Arab unity was trumped in Cairo where Prime Minister Nahhas announced in March 1943 his intention of consulting all Arab governments with the object of reconciling ideas on Arab unity—a ploy that gathered strength and led eighteen months later to the foundation of the Arab League on Egyptian terms. This was to forebode an end to all Fertile Crescent models, although their proponents by no means yet admitted defeat. Both Emir Abdullah and Nuri continued to propagate their respective schemes, Nuri now toying with a plan for Iraq's merger with Syria, where a number of old-guard politicians and transient strongmen gave him encouragement. Antun Sa'ada, too, returning from exile in 1947, relaunched his own Fertile Crescent vision by organizing from Syria, with undercover support from its President Husni al-Za'im, a coup in Lebanon as a starting point. Za'im betrayed him, and Sa'ada was executed in Lebanon. The zealotry of his PPS partisans was to survive unabated and lead to a final futile coup attempt in Lebanon in 1963.

Further efforts by Iraq to revive its Fertile Crescent project in other modes were made in 1954 by Fadhil al-Jamali, the then prime minister, and again the following year by Nuri al-Sa'id on the basis of the ill-fated Baghdad Pact of 1955. Both were resisted by Syria; and the emergence of Gamal Abdel Nasser as the potent manipulator of Arab resistance to what he saw as continuing British imperialism ended any general Arab acceptance of Iraqi aspirations in the Crescent. In response to Nasser's unification of Egypt and Syria in February 1958, the two Hashimite monarchies laid their jealousies aside and declared the Federal Union of Iraq and Jordan, seeking at the same time to revive the Fertile Crescent concept by detaching Syria from Nasser's embrace. Both initiatives failed, Hashimite rule in Iraq being violently overthrown in the July revolution.

Whether there was ever serious popular enthusiasm anywhere for the Fertile Crescent maneuvers of political leaders is questionable. What mostly animated vocal commoners was independence from the West; political configuration took second place. By the time independence was finally vouchsafed, national particularisms had begun to entrench themselves, as the provisions of the Arab League wisely recognized. Nonetheless, and despite the self-seeking ambitions of rival leaders, Fertile Crescent unity may be seen as a genuine cause, even if the facts made it a lost one. Its revival in the 1990s cannot be excluded in the light of such possible developments as a reconciliation between Syria and Iraq, the disintegration of Lebanon, the weakening of Hashimite control in Jordan, and the ending of superpower confrontation with its divisive effects. Nevertheless, many of the original obstacles remain.

BIBLIOGRAPHY

DAWN, C. E. *The Project of Greater Syria*. Ph.D. diss., Princeton University, 1948.

HOURANI, ALBERT. *Syria and Lebanon*. London, 1946.

HUSSEIN, ABDULLAH IBN. *The Memoirs of King Abdullah of Transjordan*, ed. by P. P. Graves. London, 1950.

KHADDURI, MAJID. *Independent Iraq, 1932–58*. London, 1960.

LONGRIGG, S. H. *Iraq, 1900–1950*. London, 1953.

———. *Syria and Lebanon under French Mandate*. London, 1958.

AL-SAID, NURI. *Arab Independence and Unity*. Baghdad, 1943.

SEALE, PATRICK. *The Struggle for Syria*. London, 1965.

YAMAK, L. *The Syrian Social Nationalist Party*. Cambridge, Mass., 1966.

H. G. Balfour-Paul

Fes, Treaty of

Document providing for the establishment of the French protectorate over Morocco, initialed in Fez March 30, 1912.

The signers to the treaty (also known as the Treaty of Fez) met in Morocco—Eugene Regnault, France's representative in Tangier had negotiated the treaty with the sultan, Mulay Abd al-Hafiz. In addition to clauses that accorded Spain control over the Atlantic coastal zone plus the enclaves of Melilla, Ceuta, and Ifni and that established Tangier as an international city, the treaty spoke of "a new regime" in Morocco based on those "administrative, judicial, educational, financial and military reforms which the French Government judged were necessary to introduce into the territory of Morocco." The treaty also provided for the safeguarding of the "traditional prestige of the sultan [and] the exercise of the Muslim faith."

Only a few weeks later, Abd al-Hafid was forced to abdicate by the new French colonial governor Louis-Hubert Gonzalve LYAUTEY—in favor of his more malleable brother Mulay YUSUF.

The signing of the treaty was the culmination of at least a half century of diplomatic maneuvering to take over Morocco by France, Britain, Spain, and Germany, with other nations including the United States standing by. Since the eighteenth century, systematic piracy and kidnapping had occurred in the Mediterranean, sponsored by CORSAIRS and rulers of the so-called Barbary coast; European and American ships and cargoes were taken and Christian sailors and passengers sold into slavery in the Ottoman Empire and Africa. In the early nineteenth century, the almost unassailable BARBARY STATES were subdued and opened to European concessions. The lure in Morocco became important mineral resources (mainly PHOSPHATES). Within Morocco, decades of political fragmentation had left the ALAWI sultanate all the more vulnerable to European pressures. By the late nineteenth century, in fact, the rivalry between the Western nations was probably all that allowed Morocco to remain independent.

The first of several crises leading to the Treaty of Fes erupted with the signing of the Franco–British agreement of 1904 in which, in effect, France was given free rein in Morocco in exchange for its support of British imperialism in Egypt. The agreement met with opposition from Germany, which had important commercial interests in Morocco. Tensions between the three nations led to the convening of the ALGECIRAS CONFERENCE in January 1906 and the Act of Algeciras in April of that year. The act provided for international supervision over Morocco and, specifically, for French and Spanish control over Moroccan ports, police, and commercial affairs; it sparked off acts of protest and violence against Europeans and European interests within Morocco. French and Spanish troops were sent in on the pretext of preserving order, and through 1907 the French gradually extended their military presence. The reigning Moroccan ruler Abd al-Aziz was forced out of office by his brother Abd al-Hafid, who was recognized in 1909 by the French after his acceptance of the Act of Algeciras.

From 1909 to 1911, French forces in the center and west of Morocco and the Spanish in the north expanded their areas of control. In protest, Moroccan tribal forces marched on the city of FEZ against Abd al-Hafid, giving the French an excuse to seize both Meknes and Fez following their defeat of the tribes. German opposition, which peaked in a symbolic show of force off the Moroccan Atlantic coast in 1911, was defused with an agreement to cede portions of French-controlled Congo to German authority. The signing of the Treaty of Fes followed shortly thereafter. Insofar as French control over Morocco was concerned, however, the treaty was only the first step in a long and difficult campaign for consolidation and colonialism. Moroccan nationalism eventually prevailed, however, when independence was declared in 1956.

BIBLIOGRAPHY

ABUN-NASR, JAMIL. *A History of the Maghrib in the Islamic Period.* London, 1987.
BRIGNON, JEAN, et al. *Histoire du Maroc.* Paris, 1967.
HAHN, LORNA. *North Africa: Nationalism to Nationhood.* Washington, D.C., 1960.

Matthew S. Gordon

Fez

Historical capital of Morocco.

Fez (Arabic, Fas), one of four Moroccan imperial cities, was a historical capital and the economic and cultural center. It declined under the French protectorate

Wool dyers in Fez, Morocco. (Rhimou Berniko)

of 1912, when Rabat became the administrative capital; after World War II, French economic interests were shifted to Casablanca. Fez's prominence is partially due to its location at the juncture of two geographical axes—an East–West route from the Atlantic coast toward Algeria and points east; and the North–South route from the Mediterranean to the Sahara. The plenitude of water from the Fez river as well as numerous nearby springs, rich resources, and productive surrounding plains has encouraged settlement.

Fez was founded in 789 (172 A.H.) on the right bank of the Fez river by Idris ibn Abdallah, who died before his town could be developed. Twenty years later, Idris's son, Idris II, founded another town, al-Aliya, on the left bank of the river. The Berber and Arab population of Fez received a vital population infusion in the early ninth century when refugees from Andalusia (now Spain) arrived in 818 and settled the right bank. Families from Kairouan (Tunisia) settled the left bank around 825. The two rival sides of the city were united under the Almoravid dynasty, which, however, made Marrakech its capital. When the Marinids (c. 1258–1465) took power, Fez became their capital and remained the center of Moroccan political life even when Mulay Isma'il made Meknes his capital and then under the French protectorate. The post–World War II shift from traditional products, leather, textiles, and handicrafts to the mining of phosphates and the export of agricultural produce lessened Fez's economic importance. It must be noted that the transshipment and trade city of Casablanca was developed by Fassi entrepreneurs who moved there with the shift of economic emphasis.

The modern city of Fez had two predecessors: Fas al-Bali, the old Arab city (*madinah*) in the river valley; Fas al-Jadid, the administrative complex built by the Marinids, which encompassed the royal palace, a military complex, the Jewish quarter (*mellah*), and a commercial district located on hills outside the

A portal of the Qarawiyyin mosque in Fez, Morocco.
(Rhimou Berniko)

ramparts to the west. The third city, modern Fez (Nouvelle Ville), was built in European style to the southwest of Fas al-Jadid, and its suburbs stretch out into the surrounding farmland. Fez traditionally housed an array of social and ethnic forces—Berbers, Arabs, Jews, *shurafa, murabits*, artisans, merchants, notables, and the poor. These groups often disputed among themselves and with the governments in power, which often made the city of Fez an independent political entity.

The historical monuments of Fez include the shrine of Idris I, the tomb complex of Idris II, the Qarawiyyin mosque, the Andalusian mosque, the Madrasa of the Attarin, Bou Inaniya Madrasa, and the monumental gates and city ramparts. The Qarawiyyin mosque and university, established in the tenth century by the Fatimids and enlarged by the Alamoravid Sultan Ali ibn Yusuf, became a center of Islamic science and one of the earliest universities ever established. Fez also houses the Sidi Muhammad ibn Abdallah University, established in 1974. Fez's narrow streets forced builders to accent vertical facades of public structures and private dwell-

ings. The result in Fas al-Bali is a unique public architecture. Time and neglect has, however, taken a predictable toll. UNESCO has developed a project to renovate the rapidly decaying Fas al-Bali as an international historic site, but the project has, to date, been halted through lack of funds. Morocco's rapid population growth and the rural migration to urban centers has forced Fez's expansion into suburban residential areas and bidonvilles. According to 1987 figures, the province of Fez has a population of 933,000 people.

BIBLIOGRAPHY

BOULANGER, ROBERT. *Morocco.* Paris, 1966.
CIGAR, NORMAN. *Muhammad al-Qadiri's Nashr al Mathani: The Chronicles.* London, 1981.
JULIEN, CHARLES-ANDRÉ. *Histoire de l'Afrique du nord.* Paris, 1969.
LE TOURNEAU, R. *Fez in the Age of the Marinides.* Norman, Okla., 1961.
LE TOURNEAU, R., and HENRI TERASSE. "Fas." In *Encyclopedia of Islam,* 2nd ed.
TERASSE, HENRI. *History of Morocco.* Casablanca, 1952.

Donna Lee Bowen

Fez

A flat-topped, cylindrical hat of North African origin.

In 1828, Sultan MAHMUD II decreed the fez, or *fas,* the official modern headcovering for men in the Ottoman Empire. Although some religious scholars preferred the traditional turban because it seemed more Islamic, the fez soon became very popular among Middle Eastern men of modern inclination who otherwise adopted Western suits during the nineteenth century.

In 1925, the Republic of Turkey banned the fez as part of its secularization program. The fez was worn in Arab countries until after World War II. It was usually made of red felt and usually had a tassel, and was similar to the TARBUSH.

BIBLIOGRAPHY

"Libas." In *Encyclopedia of Islam,* 2nd ed., vol. 5.
LEWIS, BERNARD. *The Emergence of Modern Turkey.* New York, 1961, 1969.

Elizabeth Thompson

Fez Arab Summit

This conference established, for the first time, an all-Arab proposal for peace with Israel.

This twelfth Arab summit was held in Fez, Morocco, in September 1982 to outline principles for the settlement of the Arab–Israel conflict in the aftermath of Israel's invasion of Lebanon in June 1982. Building on the 1965 peace plan of Tunisia's president Habib BOURGUIBA and the 1981 peace proposals of Saudi Arabia's King FAHD IBN ABD AL-AZIZ AL SA'UD, the summit issued the Fez Declaration, which expressed the Arab consensus on pursuing a peaceful settlement with Israel based on the following: Israel's withdrawal from all the Arab territories occupied in June 1967, including East Jerusalem; the creation of an independent Palestinian state in the West Bank and Gaza with East Jerusalem as its capital, under the leadership of the PALESTINE LIBERATION ORGANIZATION (PLO); international guarantees, drawn up by the United Nations Security Council, for all the states of the region, including the proposed Palestinian state; the withdrawal of Israel from Lebanese territory up to the recognized international borders on the basis of relevant Security Council resolutions, particularly resolutions 425 (1978) and 508 and 509 (1982).

Although the Fez Summit offered a formula for peace between the Arab states and Israel, virtually no progress was made on this issue before the administration of U.S. President George Bush launched the Middle East peace conference in 1991. The significance of the Fez Summit and its declaration lies in the fact that they had forged an all-Arab position on a permanent settlement with Israel, a position that had been evolving since the Arab–Israel war of October 1973.

Muhammad Muslih

Fezzan

Former province of southwest Libya, with an area of about 213,000 square miles (340,800 sq. km).

Fezzan was located south of the former province of Tripolitania, which bordered it approximately along the 30th parallel. The southern part of the former province of Cyrenaica lay to the east. Fezzan had international frontiers with Algeria to the west and with Chad and Niger to the south. The region's chief town and administrative center is Sebha, largely a twentieth-century creation; most other settlements have developed around small but long-established oasis villages. Fezzan is now divided into Sebha, al-Shati, Awbari, Murzuq, Ghat, and al-Jufrah; combined population (1984 census) is some 214,000.

Fezzan is characterized by a series of east–west depressions over artesian waters and oases, some extensive. Widely scattered in the surrounding desert, these oases are the only settled areas. Along the southern and southwestern borders, the land rises toward the Ahaggar and Tibesti massifs of the central Sahara.

Fezzan is approximately one third the distance from Tripoli to Lake Chad and, historically, has been a main artery for caravans between the Mediterranean Sea and central Africa. It has always had a certain Sudanic ethnic and cultural character. Its oases have traditionally provided shade, water, camels, and dates for caravans and, in the past—despite intermittent domination by Tripoli—derived modest prosperity as transshipment centers of the northbound slave trade and the southbound traffic in manufactured goods. In the mid-nineteenth century, the Ottoman Empire imposed direct rule from Tripoli, and the Saharan trade prospered intermittently until its terminal decline at the century's end. In the second half of the nineteenth century, Fezzan became one of several centers of the SANUSI ORDER.

Italy invaded Libya in 1911 and in 1914 briefly occupied Fezzan's main oases. The province was reconquered by Italy in 1929/30 and was designated *Territorio Militare del Sud* (Southern Military Territory), administered from Hon. It had by then become a social and economic backwater, cut off from most traditional trade contacts. During World War II, Free French forces advancing from Chad in 1942/43 expelled the Italians and set up a military administration closely linked with Algeria and Tunisia. Fezzan became one of the three constituent provinces of the United Kingdom of Libya declared independent in December 1951.

Although the poorest and least populous of Libya's three regions, Fezzan gained a certain cachet after the 1969 revolution, because the Libyan leader, Colonel Muammar AL-QADDAFI, had been educated and conceived his revolution there. Since 1969, the infrastructure has been developed and attempts made to promote agriculture with abundant newly discovered water reserves, which are also being piped to northwest Libya. Crude oil has been found in the Murzuq Basin and large quantities of iron ore in the Wadi Shati, but commercial exploitation has been slow. The region still relies on northern Libya for most of its economic and social needs.

BIBLIOGRAPHY

ROSSI, E. *Storia di Tripoli e della Tripolitania* (History of Tripoli and Tripolitania). Rome, 1968.
WRIGHT, JOHN. *Libya, Chad and the Central Sahara*. London and New York, 1989.

John L. Wright

Fida'iyyun

Arabic for suicide squads, shock troops, or commandos.

Although the term *fida'iyyun* is usually associated with modern military operations, it has its roots in medieval Islamic concepts. The Hashashiyyin (Assassin) sects of ISMA'ILI SHI'ISM, a branch of Islam, and were early fighters who conducted guerilla warfare and developed a clandestine organizational structure. More recently, various groups have referred to themselves as fida'iyyun. Examples include the YOUNG TURK revolutionaries of the early twentieth century and Iranian groups such as the Feda'iyan-e Islam.

Since the 1960s, the term has come to refer to Palestinian guerillas conducting sabotage and other military operations against Israeli, and sometimes Arab, targets. After the Arabs' defeat in the Arab–Israel War of 1967, the Palestinian commando groups took charge of the movement to liberate Palestine. The fida'iyyun first came to prominence after their participation in the defeat of Israel's troops at the battle of Karama in Jordan. Other events, such as Jordan's civil war, dubbed BLACK SEPTEMBER by the Palestinians, along with a series of Palestinian attacks in Israel, the Arab world, and Europe, established the fida'iyyun as actors on the international political stage.

Although most factions in the Palestine Liberation Organization (PLO) have moved away from commando activities, the term fida'iyyun is still used. Radical followers of Islamic groups such as the Islamic Resistance Movement, HAMAS, and ISLAMIC JIHAD, operating in the West Bank and the Gaza Strip, consider themselves fida'iyyun. For instance, Hamas's military components are called the Sheikh Izz al-Din al-QASSAM brigades, named after the man whom many Palestinians consider the first Palestinian guerilla. Qassam was killed in 1935, during a battle with British forces in Palestine.

BIBLIOGRAPHY

SMITH, PAMELA ANN. *Palestine and the Palestinians, 1876–1983.* London, 1984.

Lawrence Tal

Fikret, Mualla   [c. 1903–1967]

Turkish painter.

Born in Istanbul, Fikret studied drawing in Germany and then returned to Turkey where he taught art in secondary schools. In 1938, Fikret moved to Paris, where he spent most of the rest of his life. Always living on the edge of poverty, Fikret gained the reputation of a bohemian artist; he was known in Turkey as much for his lifestyle as for his artwork. While in Turkey, he painted landscapes and scenes from life in Istanbul. In France, Fikret shifted to subjects associated with the art of Henri de Toulouse-Lautrec: French saloons, cafes, and prostitutes. In his drawings, Fikret utilized a range of mediums, from watercolors and lead pencils to oils.

Fikret spent the last years of his life living in a small town in the foothills of the French Alps, where he would trade his drawings for a meal or a bottle of wine. Though most of his works are privately held, a collection of his art is found in the Istanbul Art, Painting, and Sculpture Museum.

BIBLIOGRAPHY

BAŞKAN, SEYFI. *Ondokuzuncu Yüzyıldan Günümüze Türk Ressamları.* Ankara, 1991.

David Waldner

Filastin

See Palestine

Filastin

Prominent Palestinian daily newspaper founded in Jaffa in 1911.

Started by a Palestinian Christian, Isa al-ISA, *Filastin* became a daily after 1929, adopting a strong anti-Zionist and Arab nationalist editorial policy. Although not published during part of World War I, it resumed publication thereafter, and Isa ensured that the paper maintained a strong nationalist stance.

Many Christian merchants supported *Filastin* and the Haifa-based *al-Karmil* because they feared Zionist capital competing with those sectors of the economy in which Christians were most active.

BIBLIOGRAPHY

SMITH, PAMELA ANN. *Palestine and the Palestinians, 1876–1983.* London, 1984.

Lawrence Tal

Film

[This entry includes the following articles: Arab Film; Iranian Film; *and* Turkish Film.*]*

Arab Film

Arab film has preserved a record—unparalleled in Arab history—of the Arab world in the twentieth century in all its appearances, sounds, and attitudes.

With the advent of synchronized-sound film, the filmmakers of the Arab world have been able to capture the ways its great singers, such as Egypt's Umm Kulthum and Muhammad Abd al-Wahab and Lebanon's Fayruz, looked and moved as well as sounded. They have made a permanent record of Arab folk music and dances, customs and costumes—village, urban, and bedouin—even as, in many cases, they were vanishing.

Arab film epics, such as *Salah al-Din* (Saladin, 1963), which is a biography of one of Islam's greatest heroes that was directed by one of the Arab world's leading film directors, Yusif Shahin, gave a generation of Arab nationalists vivid images of its heroes. Egypt and Algeria have chronicled their revolutions against Western colonialism with moving images. Lebanon celebrated its gentle poet, Khalil Gibran, in Youssef Maalouf's *Al-Ajniha al-mutakassira* (Broken Wings, 1964).

Despite frequent government censorship, and a weakness for melodrama, Arab filmmakers have, since World War II, used film with increasing honesty to search for their national and cultural identities as Arabs and to depict social and political conditions in the rapidly changing Arab world. *Al-Qahira thalathin,* a story by Najib MAHFUZ, the 1988 Nobel laureate in literature, was turned into the film *Cairo 30* in 1966 by Salah Abu Saif, "the father of Egyptian realism." *Cairo 30,* treating a great Arab city as a developing character, shows how the student protests of the 1930s against the British-controlled royalist regime in Egypt led, ultimately, to Nasser's 1952 revolution.

In 1918, Arab actors from Egypt's Dar al-Salam Company appeared in *Madame Loretta,* directed in Cairo by an Italian, Larrici. The first Arab film, however, was *Ayn al-ghazal* (Gazelle's Eye); it was shot in Tunis by a Tunisian, Shemama Chicly, and written by and starring his daughter, Hayde Chicly.

In 1927, the stage actress Aziza Amir and the writer Wadad Orfy set up in Cairo the first Arab film company. Their first film, *Layla* (1927), which was made with an Egyptian producer, director, and cast, is the first Egyptian film.

Lebanon's first film, *Mughamarat Elias Mabruk* (The Adventures of Elias Mabruk, 1930), directed by Jordano Pidutti, is a comedy about Arab emigrants. Lebanon's Heini Srour, who directed *Layla wa al-Dhi'ab* (Leila and the Wolves, 1984), is one of the Arab world's few women directors.

The leading actress-producer of the Arab world, Egypt's Fatima HAMAMA, made her screen debut as a young girl in *Yawm sa'id* (Joyful Day, 1939–1940), which was directed by Muhammad Karim. In 1957, she acted in Shahin's neorealist *Sirá fi al-Wadi* (The Blazing Sun) with a young Umar SHARIF. In 1988,

Hamama won best actress at the Carthage Film Festival for her *Mother Courage* role as Aisha, an Egyptian widow who always manages to stay one step ahead of catastrophe.

The most prominent Arab director over the last five decades has been Shahin, who was born in Alexandria in 1926 and studied at the Pasadena Playhouse in California. In 1990, he finished his widely praised Alexandria trilogy, consisting of *Alexandria Why?* (1978), *Farewell Bonaparte* (1985), and *Alexandria, Again and Again* (1990).

Morocco's Mohamed Reggab and Mustapha Abdelkrim, Palestine's Michel Khleifi (*Urs al-Jalil,* Wedding in Galilee, 1987), Iraq's Faisal al-Yasiri (*Babel Habibati,* Babylon My Beloved, 1988), and Algeria's well-known actor-turned-director, Mohamed Chouikh (*al-Qal'a,* The Citadel, 1988) are prominent among dozens of directors who have portrayed the Arab world from the vantage point of their native lands. Syria's Mohamed Malas, born in 1948, shot *The Dream* in Palestinian refugee camps in 1980–1981 and released his docudrama of refugees' dreams to critical and popular acclaim six years later.

Lebanon's Maroun Baghdadi, winner of the Jury Prize at the 1991 Cannes Film Festival for *Out of Life* and noted for his vivid film of Lebanon's civil war, *Little Wars* (1982), was killed in 1993 at the age of forty-three by a faulty elevator in Beirut.

Hind Rassam Culhane

Iranian Film

Motion picture industry of Iran.

The strong performances of a host of highly original films from Iran in international film festivals since 1970 have helped Iranian cinema gain distinction.

In 1900, five years after the invention of the motion picture camera, the first moving images were shown in Iran. Mirza Ebrahim Akkas-Bashi, a photographer in the court of Mozaffar al-Din Qajar, the fifth Qajar ruler, purchased film equipment in France, shot some footage of the king reviewing a flower parade in Belgium, and projected it in Tehran to an elite audience at the royal palace. Another pioneer, Mirza Ebrahim Sahhaf Bashi, introduced the new invention to the Iranian public by showing newsreels and comic one-reelers to a paying audience in 1904. When confronted with a rising tide of religious opposition (Islam disapproves of the portrayal of figures in art or the fraternizing of men and women [especially unveiled women] unless family members), he was forced to close his theater. He was followed by Mehdi Russi Khan, a staunch royalist, who stayed in business until the

Constitutional Revolution toppled the Qajar dynasty in 1907.

In 1913, Ardeshir Khan opened the first movie theater with a regular schedule. To appease the Islamic clergy, it did not admit women. In 1928, a rich entrepreneur, Ali Wakili, opened a theater exclusively for women. Other theaters soon started scheduling showings for women only. Next, areas were designated for either men or women within the same theater. Religious fundamentalists were still dismayed and called them *mohebbat-khaneh* (places of illicit romance).

Khan-baba Motazedi, who had received some film training in France, followed the early efforts of cinematographers like Akkas-Bashi and Rusi Khan, documenting several important historical events—including the coronation of Reza Shah Pahlavi and the opening of the Iranian parliament in 1926. In 1931, he shot the first Iranian feature film *Abi o Rabi* (Abi and Rabi), which was basically a series of crude visual gags inspired by a Danish slapstick-comedy series. The film's director was Avanes Ohanian, an Armenian émigré, whose second film, *Haji Agha, Actor-e Cinema* (Haji Agha, the Movie Star), in 1933, was a more indigenous comedy that cleverly questioned the local cultural misgivings about cinema.

Although none of the first Iranian silent films, in competition with lavish foreign talkies, enjoyed commercial success, the first Persian talkie, *Dokhtar-e Lor* (The Lor Girl, 1933), was a huge success. Produced entirely in India to circumvent the religious opposition to the pictorial presentation of women, it was a romantic adventure chronicling the flight of two Iranian lovers to India and their eventual return to a politically stabilized Iran. The man behind the endeavor was Abd-al-Hosayn Sepanta, an Iranian expatriate in India, who wrote the script and played its protagonist. The immense success of *Dokhtar-e Lor* failed to generate a momentum, however. Owing to a climate of political chaos, filmmaking activities in Iran stagnated for more than a decade until, in 1947, Dr. Esmail Kushan, another Iranian entrepreneur with a certain amount of film experience gained in Europe, produced *Tufan-e Zendegi* (Storm of Life), the first Persian talkie to be shot in Iran.

During the 1950s and 1960s, the Iranian cinema became a commercial enterprise lacking any distinction. Disparagingly labeled as Film-farsi (a pun on Farsi, the language of Persia/Iran), the films, made with bankable stars, were moralizing melodramas, routinely punctuated by vulgar musical numbers and brawling scenes. Despite the artistic inferiority of these films, the movie industry in Iran flourished.

Annual domestic film production rose to a peak of eighty-nine films in 1972. A strong audience base of 110 million admissions to 450 theaters viewed 473 films in 1975.

In 1969, the concurrent screening of Daryush Mehrjui's *Gav* (The Cow) and Mas'ud Kimia'i's *Qaysar* marked the creative rebirth of the Iranian cinema. While *Qaysar* was a technically polished Western-style revenge story with high audience appeal, *Gav* was an original and uncompromising experiment using a mode of cinematic discourse unprecedented in Iranian cinema. It showed how the mysterious death of the only cow in an impoverished village disturbs the villagers' collective life; this was so antithetical to the shah's highly trumpeted campaign of modernization that the film was banned and not released in Iran until it won international recognition in foreign film festivals.

Although *Gav* started a movement of socially relevant quality filmmaking, it also alerted the Iranian censors to the works of a thriving group of new filmmakers—including Bahram Bayza'i, Sohrab Shahid Saless, Parviz Kimiavi, Parviz Sayyad, Nasser Taqva'i, Abbas Kiarostami, Amir Naderi, and Bahman Farmanara—who emerged in the early 1970s to form the Progressive Filmmakers Group. The filmmakers' reliance on government financing further complicated the situation. Film production in Iran was largely concentrated in a business-oriented private sector that had little interest in films with uncertain commercial appeal. Consequently, the Progressive Filmmakers had to turn to the government for funding and resort to allegorical devices and symbolic communication to evade the censors. While generating an enthusiastic response among the Iranian intelligentsia and foreign film buffs, their films left the average Iranian moviegoer somewhat alienated.

In Iran, the successful Islamic revolution of 1979, under the Ayatollah Khomeini, appears to have been a mixed blessing for film. The early postrevolutionary years offered a grim prospect. Some 185 movie theaters were burned in the months of rioting leading to the revolution, and a large number of remaining theaters were confiscated and brought under the direct control of newly created government agencies. Film imports were curtailed, and the screening permits of all films in circulation prior to the revolution were revoked. Production, which had averaged sixty films per year in the six years before the revolution, fell to only eleven films per year in the six years after the revolution. Perhaps the most dramatic shift was the introduction of a new set of extremely restrictive censorship codes, principally aimed at creating an "Islamic cinema." Women characters were barred from exposing their hair or wearing clothing revealing their female form on the screen; banned scenes included the depiction of physical love or anything that might offend Islamic sensibilities. Although these codes produced a welcome departure from the fatuous Film-farsis, they also placed tremendous creative shackles on filmmakers trying to probe the new realities of a turbulent postrevolutionary society. Female characters, in particular, could not be portrayed without head scarves—even in the privacy of their homes or in films set before the revolution. Several notable filmmakers left the country, and those remaining had a difficult time adjusting to the new measures of control. These measures begin with approval requirements for the synopsis, script, cast, crew, and filmstock allowance; they continue throughout production, and culminate with a four-tier rating system that practically determines when, where, how long, and with what sort of media publicity an approved film may be screened.

Despite the constraints, by 1986, Iranian cinema had begun a rejuvenation. A new generation of filmmakers emerged, including six women directors, mostly influenced by the Iranian cinema of the 1970s. Curiously, the most celebrated representative of this generation, Mohsen Makhmalbaf, was an Islamic revolutionary with no film training, who followed his early heavy-handed didactic films with a string of bitterly critical ones reminiscent of Italian postwar neorealism.

Iran's government has widened the market for domestic films by curbing the imports and has decentralized the industry to create local film units in some provinces. The policy of support has paid dividends in international film festivals, where Iranian films have become regular staples. Currently, annual production is at an average of 60 films, shown at 275 theaters, with some 80 million admissions. By 1991, the total number of feature films produced during 60 years of filmmaking in Iran surpassed 1,500 titles. In the eyes of many experts, Iranian films now rank among the most interesting.

BIBLIOGRAPHY

AKRAMI, J. "The Blighted Spring: Iranian Cinema and Politics in the 1970s." In *Film and Politics in the Third World,* ed. by J. D. H. Downing. New York, 1987.
ARMES, R. *Third World Film Making and the West.* Berkeley, Calif., 1987.
GAFFARY, F. *Le cinéma en Iran.* Tehran, 1973.
NAFCY, H. "The Development of an Islamic Cinema in Iran." In *Third World Affairs,* ed. by Alta Gruahar. London, 1987.

Jamsheed Akrami

Israeli Film

Motion picture industry, including newsreels, documentaries, dramas, and comedies.

Before World War I (1914–1918), the young world film industry only shot background material in the Middle East, mainly for European and American films or for documentary/news footage. In the immediate postwar period, a number of documentaries were made in Palestine by Yaakov Ben-Dov under the auspices of the ZIONIST organizations.

From the mid-1920s, newsreels were prepared and presented regularly by Natan Axelrod and, for a time, by Baruch Agadati. The first feature films were made in 1932/33; these include Axelrod's *Oded ha-Noded* and, the Polish director Alexander Ford's *Sabra.* In Palestine, before the establishment of the State of Israel (1948), newsreels and documentaries were characterized by propagandistic overtones. Immediately after World War II, topical feature-length films were made there by the American director Herbert Kline with the American novelist Meyer Levin (*The Illegals,* 1946 and *My Father's House,* 1947), and documentaries were made by the South African filmmaker Norman Lourie.

After 1948, Israeli films continued to be primarily documentary and dealt with the challenges faced by the new state—mainly, the absorption of the massive number of immigrants from Europe and the Arab countries (such as Baruch Dienar's *Tent City*), the establishment of an army, reclamation of the desert, and kibbutz life; they depended on financing by the government, public bodies, and organizations. Commercial studios were built—Geva in 1950 and Herzlia in 1951. The earliest of their feature films were inspired by the need to accentuate the positive values of Zionism. The best-known films of the 1950s were *The Juggler* (1953), about a man who goes to Israel after being in the concentration camps, directed by Edward Dmytryk, and *Hill 24 Doesn't Answer* (1955), by the British director Thorold Dickinson, which was based on heroic episodes from the first Arab–Israel War (1948).

In the 1960s, film standards improved, especially when foreign filmmakers shot location features in Israel—*Exodus* (1960), *Cast a Giant Shadow* (1966), *Judith* (1966). With the emergence of a new generation, individual rather than national issues became the concern. Government support encouraged Israeli feature-film production and coproductions with foreign companies. By the end of the 1960s, ten to twelve motion pictures came out each year, up from two to three in the 1950s. The subject matter was mostly drawn from life in Israel, although some were based on Jewish classics. Among the most popular films with Israeli audiences were those dealing—usually humorously—with ethnic differences and the consequent misunderstandings among the nation's varied groups; the main character was often a Jewish immigrant from an Arab country battling with the country's European-style bureaucracy. Best-known was Ephraim Kishon's *Salah Shabbati* (in the U.S., *Sallah,* 1965), featuring Chaim Topol, which attracted a record 1.2 million Israeli viewers—almost half the population. (Topol was the actor who starred in the Broadway musical and U.S. film version of *Fiddler on the Roof,* 1971.)

The most successful of the early Israeli directors were Uri Zohar and Menahem Golan. Golan established an international career with his Cannon Films and Golan/Globus Productions. Television arrived in Israel at the end of the 1960s, so until the mid-1970s Israel had one of the highest movie-going populations in the world, and annual production reached about forty films. The television industry led to a considerable increase in both activity and facilities but a steep drop in the number of movie theaters (as had already occurred in the United States). Israel's television features were most successful in documentary form, but this period also coincided with the establishment of film departments at an academic and professional level in Israel's universities and in special schools. Israeli filmmakers became strongly influenced by European "new wave" concepts; their subject matter was derived from political and social problems and became controversial. Some examples are *But Where Is Daniel Wax* (1972), *Beyond the Walls* (1984), *Avanti Popolo* (1986), and *Ricochets* (1986).

From the 1980s, many Israeli films penetratingly faced the dilemmas raised by the Arab–Israel Conflict which was now presented realistically rather than heroically, and by the relations between Israelis and the Arabs of Israel, as well as with the emerging movement by the Palestinians for a state—all presented with a new sense of understanding.

By the early 1990s, Israel had produced almost 400 full-length films, including five Oscar nominees (by the American Academy of Motion Picture Arts and Sciences) and prizewinners at the Cannes (France) and Locarno (Italy) film festivals. These include *Three Days and a Child* (1967) and *Hole in the Moon* (1965).

BIBLIOGRAPHY

SCHORR, RENEN. "Forty Years of Film-Making." *Ariel* (1988).

Geoffrey Wigoder

Turkish Film

The movie industry in Turkey, as in other countries of the world, has been greatly affected by political climate and economics.

Moving pictures were viewed in the sultan's court soon after the Lumière brothers' first public showing of a film in France (1895). By 1897, the first public screening in Turkey was held at Sponeck's beer house in Constantinople, and a movie theater opened within ten years. Film production was introduced in World War I and was the near-exclusive domain of the Turkish army from that period until just before the founding of the Turkish republic in 1923. The oldest surviving footage shows Sultan Mehmet V visiting Macedonia in the Ottoman Empire. The first known production is a 450-foot propaganda documentary, filmed by a reserve officer, Fuat Uzkinay. Made on November 14, 1914, it shows "patriotic" youths destroying a Russian monument in Istanbul after the empire declared war on Russia. The following year, the army established a film unit (headed by Romanian citizen Sigmund Weinberg), mostly to make documentaries. In 1917, a twenty-year-old journalist named Sedat SIMAVI (the future founder of the newspaper *Hürriyet*) directed the country's first features, *The Claw* (Pençe) and *The Spy* (Casus), under the aegis of the Association for National Defense, headed by Uzkinay.

The first civilian movie company, KEMAL FILM, was established in 1922 by Kemal and Sakir Seden. It launched the career of director Muhsin ERTUĞRUL, who had been trained in filmmaking in Germany. Virtually the only filmmaker in Turkey from 1922 to 1939, Ertuğrul continued to dominate the local cinema until the early 1950s.

He is credited with bringing film out of the silent era and into the eras of talking pictures and color production. *Aysel, Daughter of the Marshy Village,* which he directed in 1935, is considered his masterpiece. Both revered and vilified by Turkish film historians, Ertuğrul was a film pioneer and chronicler of the era of Mustafa Kemal Atatürk, but he is blamed for stunting the development of Turkish cinema by filming only the latest season's stage productions and thereby making film a mere appendage of the theater.

In 1932, the government sought some control over the medium with the issuance of "Instructions Concerning the Control of Cinema Films." Censorship was thus institutionalized and has survived in various degrees since. In the 1930s, operettas and vaudeville were added to the theatrical fare offered in film. Influences of the Soviet cinema were visible, and, in fact, Ankara financed documentaries on Turkey by Soviet directors. Other filmmakers began to offer Ertuğrul some competition, and eighteen new film companies were established in the 1940s. During World War II, a number of Egyptian and U.S. films were imported. Afterward, the director Turgut Demirag, who had been trained in Hollywood and at the University of Southern California, attempted a large-scale nontheatrical production called *A Mountain Tale* (1947).

The first real foray into social realism and rejection of the theater as source material was signaled by Lütfü Ömer Akad's *Strike the Whore* (1949). After single party rule ended in 1950, Akad, aided by the government's provision in 1948 of a tax break on local film productions, led Turkish cinema into its golden era. During this period, many important directors of lasting repute came to the fore, including Atıf Yılmaz and Metin Erksan, who promoted a movie-star culture. For his debut, Erksan directed *Dark World: The Life of Aşik Veysel* (1952), a drama about a blind Anatolian folksinger, which for a long time was banned by censors.

The military coup of May 1960 resulted in a new constitution and an era of free political and artistic expression that revitalized the film industry. Directors such as Yılmaz, Erksan, Ertem Göreç, and Halit Refiğ tackled the issues of women's rights, labor rights, and social injustice, and respected writers began to be drawn to scriptwriting. Erksan's *Arid Summer* (1963), which portrayed the hardships of rural life, won the award for best film at the Berlin Film Festival. By mid-1960s, the heightened public interest in movies prompted producers to churn out numerous low-quality, low-budget films. Comic-book characters, action films, child stars, and soft-core pornographic comedies were popular. As color film came into wide use, production costs climbed and producers took control of film content. Film production hit a peak with 299 films in 1972. That year, Turkey's most famous film star, Türkan Soray, made her directing debut with *The Comeback* (1972). Another notable film of the period was Tunç Okan's *The Bus* (1974), which won several international awards.

By this time, Yılmaz GÜNEY, the son of a sharecropper from Adana, had become popular for the antihero roles he portrayed in films and had started directing. Works such as *Hope* (1970) and *The Herd* (1978) were pivotal to a new generation of directors, such as Tunç Başaran, who developed alternative cinema in the wake of another military coup in March 1971.

Güney served several jail sentences for a string of political and nonpolitical crimes; the last conviction, for killing a prosecutor, brought him a sentence of twenty-four years in prison, during which he wrote screenplays and sent instructions to protégés such as Zeki Ökten and Şerif Gören. Güney's most acclaimed film, *The Road* (1982), was written by Güney and directed by Gören. (Güney escaped from prison in time to do the final edit). The film, which shared the Cannes Film Festival's Golden Palm award with Costa Gavras's *Missing,* placed Turkish cinema in a league with top international films. With this film, Güney also contributed to the global cinematic trend in the 1980s of using prison as a metaphor for society.

By the end of the 1970s, melodramatic "Arabesk" musicals predominated, with popular stars often playing themselves in films that portrayed the plight of poor villagers migrating to the city. Competition from television and video took its toll on the industry; more than half the country's theaters closed during the decade, leaving only 1,200.

The film sector's economic woes were compounded by the coup of September 1980, which imposed tough censorship measures on the arts. In films by Gören, Yılmaz, Ömer Kavur, Kartal, Tibet, Yavuz Turgul, and other directors, the focus shifted increasingly to the individual and to introspective themes, such as women's personal struggles. Kavur's *Motherland Hotel* (1986) exemplifies the move away from social realism and toward psychological drama. By this time, film restrictions were easing, some government support was being given to the industry, and experimental films were beginning to find young, enthusiastic audiences.

By 1992, however, a poor economic climate and a boom in private television channels brought film production down to just thirty-eight features, and the following year only eleven films were released for theaters, although television networks financed some other filmmaking projects. At the same time, foreign-made films were flooding the market, and art-house cinema continued to gain followers as directors again gained control over their films. In 1994, Erden Kıral's *The Blue Exile* earned a nomination in the Academy Awards for best foreign film. In the mid-1990s, more women than ever before joined the ranks of directors. Yeşim Ustaoğlu in *The Trace* (1994) and Tomris Giritlioglu in *A Passing Summer Rain* (1994) typically focused on domestic themes and intimate relationships.

BIBLIOGRAPHY

DORSAY, ATILLA. "An Overview of Turkish Cinema from Its Origins to the Present Day." In *The Transformation of Turkish Culture,* ed. by Günsel Renda and C. Max Kortepeter. Clifton, N.J., 1986.

OZGUÇ, AGAH. "A Chronological History of the Turkish Cinema." *Turkish Review* (Winter 1988).

OZON, NIJAT. "Turk Sinemasi." Istanbul, 1984.

SAYAR, VECDI. "A Brief History of Turkish Cinema." Montreal Film Festival brochure, 1994.

SKYLAR, ROBERT. *Film: An International History of the Medium.* New York, 1993.

Stephanie Capparell

Fils

Word of Greek derivation (follis) used throughout the Middle East at various times to refer to small amounts of money.

Muslim conquerors adopted the word *fals* from its usage for Byzantine copper coins. *Fulus* was used in Persia for copper coins through the eighteenth century and is used today in the colloquial Arabic of Egypt, Morocco and elsewhere as a generic term for money. A *fils* is today a petty coin in Iraq and Jordan.

BIBLIOGRAPHY

"Fals." In *Encyclopedia of Islam,* 2nd ed. Vol 2.

Elizabeth Thompson

Finkenstein, Treaty of

Treaty of cooperation between Napoléon's France and Iran.

The signing of the Finkenstein Treaty in 1807 between representatives of Napoléon Bonaparte and Fath Ali Shah of Iran committed Iran to help France by inciting Afghan revolts against British India, declaring war against Great Britain, and allowing French troops passage through Iranian territory. France in return recognized Iranian suzerainty over Russian Georgia and sent a military mission to Iran headed by Gen. Claude-Matthieu Gardanne.

Farhad Shirzad

Finn, James   [1806–1872]

British diplomat and missionary.

Finn served as British consul in Jerusalem from 1846 to 1862, while simultaneously pursuing missionary work involving the conversion of Jews to Anglican Christianity. With money raised in England, he purchased lands on which prospective converts were employed, despite British regulations prohibiting such land ownership by consuls. Finn also patronized stateless Jews, offering consular protection against the vagaries of Ottoman justice. In the end, heavily in debt for his land purchases, and under attack for his abusive intrusion into Jewish communal life, he was forced into retirement in 1863.

BIBLIOGRAPHY

BLUMBERG, ARNOLD. *A View from Jerusalem, 1849–1858: The Consular Diary of James and Elizabeth Anne Finn.* Cranbury, N.J., 1980.

Arnold Blumberg

Fiqh

Knowledge of Islamic law.

Fiqh literally denotes understanding, particularly of matters not readily grasped. Technically, it means proficient knowledge of SHARIʿA (Islamic law), mainly of the positive legal system (*furuʿ*). A person who possesses this knowledge is a *faqih,* and a student who aspires to become a faqih is a *mutafaqqih.* With the introduction of twentieth-century legal reforms and of Western-style courts, the function of the faqih has become largely obsolete.

BIBLIOGRAPHY

VESEY-FITZGERALD, S. G. "Nature and Sources of the Shariʿa." In *Law in the Middle East,* ed. by Majid Khadduri and Herbert J. Liebesny. Washington, D.C. 1955.

Wael B. Hallaq

Firqat

In Arabic, "division" or "group"; it is used in various parts of the Arab world specifically to refer to a military division.

In Oman's Dhufar Province, the term denotes a body of a few dozen irregular, tribal troops raised to help counter the DHUFAR REBELLION of the 1960s and 1970s. Organized and paid by the government of Oman and trained by military instructors from Britain, the *firqats* (Arabic pl., *firaq*) were largely rebel defectors by the time the uprising was defeated at the end of 1975.

BIBLIOGRAPHY

ALLEN, CALVIN, H., JR. *Oman: The Modernization of the Sultanate.* Boulder, Colo., 1987.

KELLY, J. B. *Arabia, the Gulf and the West.* New York, 1980.

Malcolm C. Peck

Fish and Fishing

All the countries of the Middle East engage in fishing.

Sources of fish and marine animals include the Mediterranean Sea, the Persian Gulf and Gulf of Oman, the Indian Ocean and Arabian Sea, the Red Sea, the Caspian Sea, the Black Sea, the Atlantic Ocean, and the major rivers. The level of activity varies from individual, close-to-shore fishing using rods, nets, and traps to highly industrialized deep-sea fishing and trawling.

Marine fish include carp, whiting, red and gray mullet, bluefish, mackerel, pilchard (sardine), anchovy, and bonito (tuna). Crustaceans and mollusks also are harvested: shrimp, octopus, and squid. Data from the Food and Agriculture Organization for 1989 (the most recent figures available) show annual fishing harvests, in thousands of metric tons of live weight, as follows: Saudi Arabia, 53,391; Qatar, 4,374; Morocco, 520.4; Turkey, 457.1; Yemen, 260.9; Iran, 259.8; Egypt, 254; Oman, 107; Algeria, 99.7; Tunisia, 95.1; United Arab Emirates, 91.2; Israel, 32.7; Iraq, 18.2 (estimate); Bahrain, 9.2; Libya, 7.8; Kuwait, 7.7; Syria, 5.6; Jordan, 5.5; Lebanon, 1.8.

Fish is consumed locally and, where the quantities are sufficient, exported for human consumption or animal feed. It is prepared in a variety of ways, the most common being fried and baked. Shrimp is popular in most Arab cuisines, but mollusks are rarely eaten except by fishermen. Both shrimp and mollusks are not kosher, so observant Jews do not eat them.

Jenab Tutunji

Flapan, Simha   [?–1987]

Israeli historian and political philosopher.

Flapan was one of a handful of Israeli historians who in the 1970s began to challenge the accepted interpretation of Israel's past. In books such as *The Birth of Israel: Myths and Realities* (1987) and *Zionism and the Palestinians 1917–1947* (1979), Flapan sought to explode what he perceived to be historical myths, among them that the Palestinian Arabs left their homes in 1948 on the urging of Arab leaders. Flapan asserted that it was Israeli policy in 1948 to force the Palestinians to flee. Flapan was also an outspoken critic of Israel's treatment of the Palestinians in the West Bank and Gaza.

Zachary Karabell

FLN

See Front de Libération Nationale

FLOSY

See Front for the Liberation of South Yemen

Fly Whisk Incident

Diplomatic cause célèbre of 1827 in which the Algerian ruler, Husayn Dey, struck the French consul, Pierre Deval, with a fly whisk.

The Fly Whisk Incident was caused by friction over Franco–Algerian business transactions dating from the late eighteenth century. In the 1790s, the French government customarily purchased Algerian wheat, most of it through two Jewish commercial families by the names of Busnach and Baqri. By the turn of the century, France owed these Algerian suppliers several million francs.

This debt remained outstanding at the time of Husayn's accession in 1818. It attracted his attention because both the Busnachs and the Baqris owed money to the Algerian government but insisted they could not afford to pay until they had recovered what was owed to them by France. When the French government arranged a financial settlement in 1820 that ignored the claims put forward by successive deys since 1802, Husayn concluded that France and his Jewish debtors had colluded to keep the money from him. In a further irritant to Franco–Algerian relations, the vice-consul at Bône fortified several French trading posts in eastern Algeria in 1825, in direct contravention of existing treaties. Despite Husayn's complaints, the French government took no steps to reprimand its officials.

These tensions exploded in a meeting between Deval and Husayn on April 29, 1827. In the consul's version of the event, the session rapidly degenerated into an exchange of insults culminating with the dey striking Deval three times with his fly whisk and ordering him from the room—an accusation Husayn did not refute but justified on the basis of crude comments made by the consul about Islam and Muslims. Enraged by Deval's behavior, the dey rejected the French government's demand for an apology.

In retaliation, French warships instituted a blockade of Algiers, which Husayn countered by ordering the destruction of French trading posts in the country. The confrontation dragged on for more than two years, but the dey, backed by the Ottoman sultan and encouraged by Great Britain's consul in Algiers, refused to yield. His own corsair captains proved adept at running the blockade, which proved far more damaging to the Marseilles merchants engaged in trans-Mediterranean commerce than to Algerians. By 1828, businessmen from the south of France had begun urging the government to undertake a campaign against Algiers that would restore trade to its previous level. When the dey responded to a French invitation to send a negotiating delegation to Paris in the summer of 1829 by firing on a French vessel, the pressures on the French government to mount an expedition to Algiers peaked. With liberal deputies challenging his power, King Charles X viewed such an undertaking as a means of reasserting royal prerogatives and providing a distraction from domestic issues. The decision to invade Algeria was announced in March; the fleet sailed in May; and Algiers fell in July.

Although the need to avenge the dey's insult gave the monarchy a dramatic issue upon which it seized to rally popular support for an attack against Algeria, this contretemps was not as crucial a cause of the French invasion of Algeria as it has sometimes been portrayed. French commercial interests in North Africa and a last-ditch effort to shore up the monarchy by diverting public attention to an overseas adventure suggest that the encounter between Deval and Husayn was an excuse for, rather than the cause of, the events that followed.

BIBLIOGRAPHY

HAMDANI, AMAR. *La verité sur l'expédition d'Alger.* Paris, 1985.

JULIEN, CHARLES-ANDRÉ. *Histoire de l'Algérie contemporaine: La Conquête et les débuts de la colonisation, 1827–1871.* Paris, 1964.

Kenneth J. Perkins

Food

Middle Eastern food is based on local produce and peasant-style home cooking.

Middle Eastern food preparation has been influenced by Islamic and kosher dietary restrictions and by the native animal and plant resources. Professional restaurant cooking has never significantly influenced Middle Eastern food as it has in Europe and North America. A new influence is the growing popularity of Western food-processing technology such as blenders, food processors, and frozen foods.

Bread, mainly flatbreads such as pita, is a staple food in the Middle East. Other important sources of carbohydrates are wheat in various forms, such as BULGUR, *firik* (immature grains of hard wheat), COUSCOUS, and pasta. Rice is an important grain in all Middle Eastern countries and was originally brought into the region by trade with India and Southeast Asia (including China). Barley, millet, and sorghum are also common grains.

The most important sources of protein in the Middle Eastern diet are the indigenous legumes—lentils, chick-peas, and fava (broad) beans. Sesame seeds are processed for use in pastes, sauces, and oil, whereas nuts such as pistachios, almonds, and walnuts are frequently used in food preparations.

Among animal foods lamb is king. Great flocks of sheep are herded, and the meat is especially important to feast days. Beef and veal are available in Middle Eastern countries, but their popularity is not great, even in the richer countries. In all Middle Eastern cuisines meat is used sparingly, if at all, for daily (non-feast day) meals. Chickens are more common, and they are raised especially for their eggs. Pigeons are a popular meat in North Africa. Among some nomadic Bedouin tribes, camel meat is eaten, but it is almost never found in a market. Middle Easterners are fond of fish, but the small fishing and shellfishing industry and low catch mean that seafood cookery exists only close to ports of origin.

Vegetables frequently cooked and eaten in a Middle Eastern home are eggplant, zucchini, spinach, chard, turnips, squash, carrots, tomatoes, okra, artichokes, and onions. Stuffed vegetables (called DOLMA) are renowned in several of the regional cuisines. Uncooked vegetables, used in pickling and salads, are eaten mainly in Israel, but they are served in restaurants throughout the region. Fruit groves, orchards, and oases mainly produce dates, figs, melons, grapes, apricots, persimmons, and citrus fruits (oranges, lemons, grapefruits, citrons, tangerines, and clementines).

A number of dairy products are made from camel, sheep, and goat milk (as well as some from cow's milk)—yogurt, buttermilk, *labneh* (strained yogurt), *jameed* (dehydrated yogurt), and *kishk* (dried and fermented yogurt and bulgur mixture). A limited variety of cheese is made mostly from goat or sheep milk.

Olive trees are cultivated for table use and for cooking oil. Tunisia is the world's fourth largest producer of olive oil, and Turkey is the second largest producer of table olives. Heading the list of cooking fats is *smen* (or *samneh*)—clarified butter. Olive oil and vegetable oils have increased in popularity, so cornoil and sesame-seed oil are also used alone or added to clarified butter.

Middle Easterners are famed for their sweet tooth, and BAKLAVA, a nut-filled and honey or sugar-soaked phyllo (*filo*) pastry, is known throughout the region.

Water is the beverage of choice in the Middle East, perhaps because of the warm, arid climate. Coffee, tea, mint tea, and a wide variety of fruit juices are drunk on a daily basis. Although drinking alcohol is forbidden in Islam, beer, wine, and aniseed-based distilled liquors are produced (and consumed) in some Middle Eastern countries. Alcohol is not banned by Judaism or Christianity, and wines and liquors are produced in Israel and other countries for both religious and secular use. Generally, alcoholic drinks are not used, so where they are produced it is mostly for export. Soft drinks are produced locally and mineral water is also bottled and drunk.

Middle Eastern food is considered by many nutritionists to be a model diet because of the diversity of nonanimal fats and protein and the rich vitamin and mineral sources in the legumes, vegetables, and fruits. These complement and enrich the complex-carbohydrate base—bread, rice, pasta, and couscous, yielding a healthful balance.

The Middle East can be divided into five culinary regions, each with variations based on ethnicity or national tradition.

First, the Turkish food of today has its roots in the Ottoman Empire's court cuisine that was prepared for the sultan and his aristocracy in Istanbul, as well as the folk cuisines of the countryside. The Ottoman Turks introduced yogurt (a Turkish word for mare's milk), PILAF, and SHISH KEBAB. Lemon juice flavors many dishes and herbs such as parsley, rosemary, mint, and bay leaves are common. Some typical Turkish dishes are *hunkâr beğendi* (sultan's delight), a mashed roasted eggplant dish with grated cheese: *imam bayıldı* (swooning imam, an onion-stuffed eggplant dish; *dolma* stuffed vegetables; and shashlik, a marinated and grilled lamb dish. Armenian food is similar to Turkish food—rice, onions, currants (dried small grapes), and pine nuts being a typical combination.

Second, Levantine food—the cuisines of Syria, Lebanon, Jordan, and the Palestinians—can be grouped together. Arab gastronomes agree that the finest Levantine Arab cuisine, a unique Arab cuisine heavily influenced by Turkish and Armenian cuisine, is found in Aleppo (Syria) and Beirut (Lebanon). A famous preparation is *kibbeh*, a ground lamb and bulgur mixture baked flat in a tray or formed into balls, then stuffed with a pine-nut, meat, and spice mixture; kofta is a grilled or baked ground-meat mixture

seasoned with chopped onions and spices; TABBULA is a parsley and bulgur salad; HUMMUS bi tahina is a chick-pea puree with sesame-seed paste; BABAGHA-NUSH is an eggplant purée; FELAFEL is a fava-bean croquette.

As a nation of immigrants returned from the Diaspora, Israel has an overlay of immigrant food—the food of European Jews and Jews from Muslim lands—on the Levantine food of the Palestinians. Israel's restaurant chefs also experiment with food products new to the region, such as avocado or foie gras.

Third, the food of Iraq, while distinct, has been strongly influenced by Persian (Iranian) and Turkish cookery. Spices such as saffron and turmeric find their way into dishes here more often than in countries to the west of Iraq. Many Iraqi dishes are notable in combining meat or rice with fruit, such as dates. The rice dishes were especially influenced by the ancient empire of Persia. A favorite Iraqi peasant dish is *masguf,* a fresh-water fish from the Tigris river grilled on a wood fire.

The cooking of the Arabian Gulf states—Kuwait, Bahrain, Saudi Arabia, Qatar, Oman, and the United Arab Emirates—is very similar. The cuisine is simple, typically boiled or grilled lamb or mutton served over a mountain of spiced rice. *Fatar,* a mushroom stew, is a typical home preparation. In Saudi Arabia, *quzi* is a whole baked lamb stuffed with rice and spices—and prepared for festive occasions.

Cuisine in Yemen developed in relative isolation when compared to other Middle Eastern cuisines. Hot and spicy foods are popular. Cardamom, coriander, fenugreek, chili pepper, caraway, and garlic are typical seasonings. Barley bread is common and the honey of Yemen is famous throughout the Middle East.

Fourth, Egyptian food is influenced by Turkey, Syria, Greece, Italy, and the MAGHRIB (North Africa). If there is an Egyptian national dish it must be FUL mudammis, a fava-bean puree served with various accompaniments and eaten for breakfast, snacks, or lunch. Flat bread with coarse wheat bran, called *aysh,* is found everywhere in Egypt. Egyptian cuisine is a simple one with mostly peasant-type dishes such as *kashary,* a rice, lentil and macaroni casserole or *muluhkiyya,* a soup made from the mucilaginous vegetable Jew's mallow.

In the Sudan, *kisra,* a bread made from fermented sorghum or millet flour, is a staple food and a source of protein.

Libya, a mostly desert country, has a simple cuisine based on semolina bread (from hard-wheat, *Triticum durum*), dates, and figs. As in all North Africa there are several distinct cuisines; that of the

Berbers with their couscous and that of the bedouin tribes with their dates, yogurt, and goat or camel milk. A typical dish is *bazin,* a semolina and olive oil dough.

In the countries of the Maghrib—Tunisia, Algeria and Morocco—the most common staple food is couscous, prepared with hundreds of variations. Vegetable casseroles, such as *shakshuka* or *ojja,* and stews, TAJIN, are common in the Maghrib, with meats, chicken, and vegetables. In Morocco *bastiya,* a pigeon pie in pastry, is a famed preparation. *Harisa,* a hot-red-chili pepper condiment, is used in the cooking of Algeria and Tunisia.

Fifth, the cuisine of Iran has its roots in the ancient Persian empire. At the center of Persian food is rice and lamb. Fruits are popular and often combined with rice or meat dishes, so sweet-and-sour flavors are common in Persian dishes. Rice dishes such as the steamed CHELOW are popular. Some Persians consider the height of culinary art the proper preparation of *tah chin,* a rice dish of fluffy grains and a golden bottom crust; *chelow kebab,* grilled lamb tenderloin with rice is a simple but delicious dish; *abgusht* are a family of slow-cooked stews in two courses.

The food of Afghanistan is similar to that of neighboring Pakistan, India, Iran, Turkmenistan, and Tajikistan. Afghan food is spiced with *garam masala,* a spice mix of saffron, cinnamon, cloves, and peppercorns (*Piper nigrum*).

BIBLIOGRAPHY

DAGHER, SHAWKY M., ed. *Traditional Foods in the Near East.* FAO Food and Nutrition Paper 50. Rome, 1991.

HALICI, NEVIN. *Nevin Halici's Turkish Cookbook,* trans. by E. M. Samy. London, 1989.

MALLOS, TESS. *The Complete Middle East Cookbook.* New York, 1979.

RODEN, CLAUDIA. *A Book of Middle Eastern Food.* New York, 1974.

WOLFERT, PAULA. *Couscous and Other Good Food from Morocco.* New York, 1973.

Clifford A. Wright

Ford Foundation

Philanthropic organization started by Henry and Edsel Ford with headquarters in Michigan in 1935.

Capitalized with more than 3 billion U.S. dollars, the Ford Foundation sponsors scholarly studies and underwrites seed-money funding for various projects throughout the third world and in the United States. In the Middle East, for example, numerous studies of PALESTINIAN REFUGEE CAMPS, ARAB-ISRAEL CONFLICT and relations, and problems in the occupied territories (INTIFADA) have been sponsored, as well as studies of water and hydropolitics, food shortages, and population control.

BIBLIOGRAPHY

Encyclopaedia Britannica.

Zachary Karabell

Forqan

A secret religious group responsible for the deaths in early 1979 of a number of prominent figures in the Islamic Republic of Iran.

This group took its name from its journal *Forqan* (Sacred Book), published intermittently from 1977 until 1979. Describing itself as the "true followers" of the Qur'an and Ali SHARI'ATI, Forqan called for an "Islam without mullahs" and denounced the regime of Ayatollah Ruhollah Khomeini as a reactionary and clerical dictatorship that had betrayed the principles of egalitarian Islam. The group's leaders, former seminary students, also denounced liberals, such as Premier Mahdi Bazargan, as "bazaar intellectuals." In addition to being a radical and anticlerical group, Forqan was also highly antileftist, denouncing Marxism as an international atheistic conspiracy that was engaged in scheming to dominate the Muslim world. A series of executions in mid-1979 decimated the group.

BIBLIOGRAPHY

"Shenakhti az Goruhe-ye Forqan" (Information about the Forqan Group). *Ayandegan.* May 10, 1979.

Ervand Abrahamian

Forughi, Mirza Mohammad Ali Khan Zaka al-Molk [1877–1942]

Iranian politician.

The son of Mirza Mohammad Hoseyn Khan Zaka al-Molk. Mirza Mohammad Ali Khan inherited the title Zaka al-Molk from his father upon the latter's death in 1908. Originally Iraqi Jews, his family had migrated to Iran and settled in the old quarter of Isfahan. He was elected to the parliament several times, and in 1911 was appointed minister of finance, then head of the supreme court. In 1915, he was named minister of justice and after that served four times as prime minister, finally resigning in 1935. His last appointment as minister of court, came in 1942, the same year that he died.

BIBLIOGRAPHY

BAMDAD, MEHDI. *Biographies of Iranian Notables in the Twelfth, Thirteenth, and Fourteenth Centuries,* vol. 3. Tehran, 1979. In Persian.

Neguin Yavari

Forum

Turkish leftist journal.

Forum was an influential socialist journal published in Ankara in the 1950s by economist Aydın Yalçın and law professor Turhan Feyzioğlu. It was one of the few arenas for intellectual critique of the Democrat party regime in Turkey.

The journal advocated social reform and advanced Keynesian principles of economic growth. Much of the journal was devoted to political criticism. In October 1958, for example, it criticized the government's anticommunism as a pretext inherited from the World War II–era tactics of Hitler and Mussolini for canceling political freedoms. Although some writers were socialist, the journal was avowedly noncommunist. *Forum* was a precursor to the leftist journals that would multiply under the greater press freedoms of the 1960s.

BIBLIOGRAPHY

AHMAD, FEROZ. *The Turkish Experiment in Democracy 1950–1975.* Boulder, Colo., 1977.
DODD, C. H. *Democracy and Development in Turkey.* North Humberside, U.K., 1979.

Elizabeth Thompson

Foucauld, Charles Eugène de   [1858–1916]

French soldier, explorer, and ascetic.

Born in Strasbourg, France, to a famous aristocratic family, Foucauld was a graduate of Saint-Cyr (1876) who led a frivolous life until his assignment to North Africa. Fascinated by the Maghrib (North Africa), Foucauld left his army career and explored Morocco and the Sahara disguised as the servant of a rabbi. This resulted in his book entitled *Reconnaissance au Maroc, 1883–84.* Foucauld gained a deep appreciation of Islam, asceticism, and spirituality, which led

to his entering a Trappist monastery (Christian) to begin a life of contemplation. He later left the Trappists but was ordained a priest in 1901.

Returning to North Africa, Foucauld set up a hermitage in Béni Abbès, Algeria, and in 1905 moved to what became his famous retreat at Assekrem in the desolate Ahaggar (Hoggar) mountains near Tamanrasset. While he failed to convert TWAREG tribesmen to Christianity, he produced a significant ethnographic contribution—a dictionary of their language, Tamahak. Although respected by neighboring Twareg, marauders murdered the priest who had pursued an inspiring spiritual mission while symbolizing a French presence in the deep Sahara.

BIBLIOGRAPHY

PORCH, DOUGLAS. *The Conquest of the Sahara.* New York, 1984.

Phillip C. Naylor

Fourteen Points

See Wilson, Woodrow

Fourth Shore, The

Italy's Fourth Shore (Quarta Sponda) became a key element in the propaganda of Italy's colonialist opinion formers at the turn of the century.

The term *Fourth Shore* implied that Italy needed an overseas colonial extension along the North African Mediterranean that would partner its other three—the Adriatic, Tyrrhenian, and Sicilian. It also reflected the growing concern in Italy, in the wake of the *Risorgimento* of the 1860s, to re-create the splendor of the classical Roman Empire, with Libya as its jewel (after Italy was prevented from annexing Tunisia by France's occupation of that country in 1881).

Once Libya had been conquered—officially by January 1932—Mussolini's Fascist policy toward Libya put the concepts of the Fourth Shore into practice. Libya's supposed agricultural potential was to be realized by the immigration of Italy's excess peasant population from the *mezzogiorno* (the South). After an effective infrastructure would be created, Libya was to become an extension of the Italian mainland itself. This would guarantee Italy's strategic security and make it into a power in North Africa, alongside France and Spain.

Fascist ideology promoted individual family farm units through state-sponsored schemes. Libyans were to become economic collaborators and coparticipants in this process; they were to be transformed into

Muslim Italians, as Italy, after 1937, sought to become "Protector of Islam," in Mussolini's words.

BIBLIOGRAPHY

SEGRE, CLAUDIO G. *Fourth Shore: The Italian Colonization of Libya.* Chicago, 1974.

George Joffe

France and the Middle East

The centuries-old relations between the French and the peoples of the Middle East have been replete with confrontations and contradictions.

Constituents of a Mediterranean world encompassing the Mashriq and the Maghrib, the geographic proximity of the French and the peoples of the Middle East has helped sustain both their affinities and their animosities. In war as in peace, they have had to deal with the problems, as well as the opportunities, of economic life. Some of the ambiguous features of their relationship have derived from their collective links to frequently discordant Greco-Roman, biblical, and Islamic traditions and to no less problematic modern ideologies of social change and nation building. In whatever combination of identities—whether religious, as, for example, Roman Catholic on the one hand, and Muslim, Eastern Christian, or Jewish on the other, or secular, as, for example, French on the one hand, and Ottoman, Turkish, Arab, or Israeli on the other—their encounters have been marked by a bittersweet interaction of words and deeds. Negative images of the "other" have been more often in evidence, particularly on the part of the French, than mutual displays of consideration or acknowledgements of collective achievement.

France's contentious presence in the modern Middle East was shaped in part by distinctive percolations of change among the Western powers. The forces of modernity, which advantaged the West before other parts of the world, enabled the French, as one of Europe's great powers, to exercise an intrusive, frequently aggressive imperialist presence in various parts of the Middle East from Syria to Morocco. However, France itself suffered from constraining imbalances in the modern reconfigurations of power that left it at a disadvantage when confronting rival intrusive presences in the region—Britain's for much of the period, Germany's before and during the two world wars, and that of the United States during and after World War II.

The history of France's involvement with the peoples of the Middle East was also determined by the different ways in which they responded to the challenges of modernization. In some cases, the peoples of the Middle East sought to remove the intrusive features of French influence, as was the case with the Ottoman Empire and Turkey by 1923 and with Egypt by 1956; in others, they sought to secure their independence from French occupation, as in Syria and Lebanon by 1945–1946, in the North African states of Tunisia and Morocco by 1956, and in Algeria by 1962. Their national movements and modernizing administrative polities were shaped by internally developed and externally induced changes. The character of French relations with the relatively unconstrained nineteenth-century Ottoman reformers and their twentieth-century Turkish successors thus differed significantly from their relations with the more dependent mid-nineteenth-century viceroys of Egypt. These, in turn, differed from France's relations with the disfranchised Arab politicians of French

Colons in Oran, Algeria, circa 1958. (André Kaim/J. Cabessa)

mandated Syria during the 1920s and 1930s and with Algeria's revolutionary leaders struggling for independence in the 1950s and early 1960s.

Antithetical undercurrents were never far below the surface in the modern history of Franco–Middle Eastern relations. While the Franks of the Middle Ages had vigorously embraced Europe's Roman Catholic Crusades against the Muslims, sixteenth-century France recognized the strategic usefulness of friendly relations with the Ottomans as a counterweight to the Hapsburgs. The French subsequently developed a commercial preeminence in the Mediterranean over much of the seventeenth and eighteenth centuries as the Ottomans were increasingly drawn into the European-dominated world economy. Expatriate French merchant communities in the Mashriq, the region they called the Levant, traded under the umbrella of the CAPITULATIONS, France having been among the first to enjoy this Ottoman assignment of extraterritorial juridical status to resident foreigners. Yet, the French offset the Muslim policy that had brought them closer to former enemies with a preclusive Roman Catholic policy that harnessed their good relations with the Ottomans to the development of a religious protectorate in the empire, favoring the work of proselytizing Roman Catholic missionaries. By the nineteenth century, the most important corollary to this policy had become their informal, but nevertheless real, support for the political autonomy of the Roman Catholic community of MARONITES in Ottoman Lebanon.

The Ottomans, for their part, had assigned less importance to these contacts with France until the eighteenth century when modernizing changes began to attract the interest of reformers concerned with the fate of the receding empire. Sultan SELIM III, the beginning of whose reign in 1789 coincided with the outbreak of the French Revolution, did not allow the problem of regicide in Europe to distract him unduly from applying, with the help of French advisers, the lessons of the French military sciences to some of the reforms he attempted to introduce.

Postage stamps from Algeria and Tunisia and a French stamp overprinted for Algeria are reminders of the French colonial era in North Africa. (Richard Bulliet)

Picture postcard showing Le Palais des Beaux Arts in Oran, Algeria, circa 1950s. The building is no longer standing. (André Kaim)

However, the sultan's friendship with the French failed to prevent Napoléon Bonaparte from trying in 1798 to gain an advantage in Europe's revolutionary wars by means of a grandiose and abortive scheme pegged to the occupation of the Ottoman province of Egypt, which came to be considered a strategic key to hegemony in the East. In the same vein, by the time the occupation ended in 1802, France had alienated the Egyptians. Their experience was such that French administration, development projects, and scientific advances did not outweigh the adverse effects of the military invasion, or of the political opportunism, cultural arrogance, and colonial aims underlying the occupation. This proved to be an early example of the kind of power relationship that undermined French claims to the exercise of a civilizing mission.

The antithetical features of French interaction with the peoples of the Middle East remained generally pervasive. On the one hand, the history of France's contribution to the betterment of the human condition ensured that accounts of its progressive ideas and sociopolitical experiences received frequent and attentive hearings in the debates on reform that engaged the leading Middle Eastern advocates of change, to many of whom French became a second language. On the other hand, France's imperial interests frequently ran counter to reforms based on the very principles to which the French so eloquently laid claim. The French were not above combining sound investments in Middle Eastern economies with political support for speculative cupidity. As self-interested players in the so-called nineteenth-century EASTERN QUESTION, they not only helped to petrify the extraterritorial privileges they enjoyed, and to encourage continued foreign administration of the public debts in which they had invested, but they also participated in the consolidation of imperial spheres of influence in the Middle East.

The history of French influence in the Middle East was further complicated by unrelenting Anglo–French rivalries. Britain's industrial advantages, combined with the naval superiority it had acquired in the Mediterranean during the Revolutionary and Napoleonic wars, limited France's strategic options and commercial opportunities. Overtaken by Britain at the SUBLIME PORTE, the French tried to refocus their interest during the 1820s and 1830s on links with Muhammad Ali Pasha, the independent-minded and expansionist Ottoman governor of Egypt. They were unwilling, however, to risk a European conflagration by coming to the pasha's assistance in 1840, when Britain and the concert of Europe curtailed his power during the second Syrian war. They reconciled themselves instead to falling back for influence in the Levant on their links with the Maronites of Mount Lebanon, who continued to respond best, though to a narrowly focused Roman Catholic policy. During the nearly two decades of Napoléon III's second empire, and in the aftermath of France's participation in the Crimean War on the side of the Ottomans, French influence among the Maronites equaled that of Britain. During this period the two powers cooperated in an imaginative resolution to the civil strife that had broken out in Lebanon in 1860. In Egypt, France even won an advantage at this time by working for the construction of the Suez Canal. Thereafter, however, three debilitating wars with Germany between 1870 and 1945 left the French at a lasting disadvantage. They had their eyes firmly fixed across the Rhine in 1882 when they failed to act with the British in Egypt, thereby forfeiting to Britain the base from which it was better able to develop its lead.

The French, having once more returned to reinforcing their links with the Maronites after 1870, were subsequently able to use Mount Lebanon as a stepping-stone to a sphere of influence in the Ottoman Empire's Syrian regions. However, they only secured a Pyrrhic victory there in the aftermath of World War I and the defeat of the Ottoman Empire. For one thing, partitioning the empire ran counter to the not inconsiderable capital investments they had made during the later part of the nineteenth century in its overall development. For another, their Roman Catholic policy limited the influence they were able to exercise in Syria and Lebanon over Muslim and non–Roman Catholic Christian constituencies upon whose acquiescence they were dependent. Franco–British alliances in the two world wars did not substantially affect this unfavorable equation. After World War I, Britain limited the imperial expansion of the French to the Lebanese and Syrian mandates, denying them the role in Palestine and the Mosul region that they had been led to expect from the Sykes–Picot Agreement of 1916. By the end of World War II, Britain, backed by the United States, which was even less tolerant of French imperial claims, helped the Lebanese and the Syrians to exclude France altogether from the Levant.

In the aftermath of the war, the French were peripherally involved in the question of Palestine and the Zionists as this problem developed into the Arab–Israel conflict that more directly affected Britain and the United States. Frequently criticized for their failings in the Middle East, the French rarely denied themselves the opportunity to embarrass their "allies" by taking the high ground in their assessments of the problem. French involvement with Zionism, however, reflected their ambiguous relationship to the Jew as "other." This relationship had traversed the spectrum from the offer of assimilation and French citizenship at the time of the French Revolution, to threats of rejection in the turn-of-the-century DREYFUS AFFAIR, to denial of protection against Nazi Germany by Vichy France during World War II. French opportunism, however, was such that France secretly armed and courted Israel for assistance when, for the last time, it joined Britain as a principal actor in the Middle East in the ill-conceived Suez expedition of 1956, a century after the two had concluded the Crimean War as equal partners. Together they made a futile attempt not only to turn the clock back and humiliate Egypt's president Gamal Abdel Nasser, the symbol of changes in an Arab world they could no longer control, but also to belie the lesser roles assigned them in the new global super-power rivalries of the Cold War.

The French had embraced the Suez adventure primarily in the hope of stemming the tide of Arab independence, which had surfaced with revolutionary ardor in 1954 in Algeria, their only remaining North African possession. Their occupation of that region of the Maghrib had begun in 1830 when an opportunist French government swept away the autonomous Ottoman administration of the city of Algiers, whose tradition of privateering had alienated what was then international opinion, and with whom commercial cupidity had brought the French in dispute. Sometimes after they completed the conquest of Algeria, a combination of imperialist pressures and the nineteenth-century scramble for African territories encouraged the French to flank it with a protectorate over Tunisia in 1881 and another over Morocco in 1912.

France's more pervasive domination of North Africa, and the colonization that accompanied it, particularly in Algeria, meant that the French encounter with the peoples of the Middle East was more deeply experienced in the Maghrib than in the Levant. The conquest of the Algerian interior spanned four decades of intermittent campaigning against the resistance of its Muslim Arab and Berber inhabitants. They underwent a more painful and less rewarding experience than that of the Egyptians earlier in the century. The extensive destabilization of their traditional societies eased the way for colonists who were as repressive of the rights of the indigenous majority as they were determined to safeguard their own exclusive rights as French citizens by attaching the most productive region of Algeria to metropolitan France. Always active in French politics, the colons resisted a number of imaginative projects that might have helped them build up a working relationship with their Arab and Berber neighbors. Not surprisingly, after de Gaulle's Fifth Republic wound up the Algerian War in 1962, the whole colon community beat a headlong retreat to France.

The idea of carrying on a bilingual cultural dialogue to find ways of accommodating Islamic and French sociopolitical conduct was more welcome to Tunisian and Moroccan reformers, both before and after the French occupation. They were attracted to accommodation as a way of both assimilating modernizing changes on their own terms and equipping themselves to deal with the French in their midst. The antithetical features of French influence were such, though, that the latter, belittling the validity of compromises with the "other," were generally reluctant to make the necessary concessions in terms of either association or assimilation. The differences between what the French imperialists practiced and what France's social conscience preached did little to smooth the way for modernizing changes in the Maghrib and France; rather, they overburdened the process. In order to move forward and to overcome the impeding French presence, the North Africans pursued costly struggles for independence, while France only recognized their independence in the 1950s and early 1960s after suffering the consequences of its own failures, first in the Indo–Chinese War and then in the Algerian War.

French influence and the problems of working out an accommodation with the "other" did not disappear with the demise of the French empire in the Middle East and North Africa. France and the peoples of these regions continue as long-standing neighbors in the coalescing global village of the end of the twentieth century, where the management of changes has become an even greater challenge, and where socio-economic and political developments have a more immediate ripple effect. France's cultural and socioeconomic experiences have been directed toward European union, while those of the Middle East and North Africa have been directed toward revolution, dictatorship reexamination of fundamental beliefs, and, in the case of Lebanon, which has been overcome by the magnitude of the problems facing it, civil war. In a world of permeable frontiers, differences in the felicity of these two experiences have resulted in the reverse flow of a substantial number of Middle Eastern and North African immigrants to France. Their communal presence there—the result of France's encounter with the people of those regions—has brought home to French society, as never before, the problem of accommodating the "other," a challenge that will doubtless be carried over to twenty-first-century France, as much as the problem of reconciling French-inspired changes to their own traditions will be carried over to the twenty-first-century Middle East and North Africa.

BIBLIOGRAPHY

There is no one study of the whole range of developments involving France and the Middle East, though discussions of different aspects of their interaction may be found scattered among many related works. An impressionist survey of their relationship, drawn from English-language publications, might begin with a compilation titled *Napoléon in Egypt: Al-Jabarti's Chronicle of the French Occupation, 1798,* tr. by Shmuel Moreh (New York, 1993), which includes a French view of the same event and an interpretive extract from EDWARD SAID's *Orientalism*. DAVID S. LANDES's *Bankers and Pashas: International Finance and Economic Imperialism in Egypt* (Cambridge, 1958) is a revealing study based on the papers of a French private banker. Other publications in chronological order of the period they cover and with self-explanatory titles are JOHN P. SPAGNOLO's *France and Ottoman Lebanon, 1861–1914* (London, 1977); PHILIP S. KHOURY's *Syria and the French Mandate* (Princeton, 1987); JACQUES BERQUE's *French North Africa,* tr. by Jean Stewart (London, 1967); and ALISTAIR HORNE's *A Savage War of Peace: Algeria 1954–1962* (London, 1977).

John P. Spagnolo

Franco–Tunisian Conventions

Agreements in which France stipulated the nature of autonomy it was granting Tunisia.

Spurred by the Neo-Destour party of Habib Bourguiba, the Tunisian independence movement gathered steam in the early 1950s. After initial resistance, the French finally conceded Tunisia's right to autonomy in July 1954 when Premier Pierre Mendès-France made a historic announcement to that effect in Carthage, Tunisia. Towards the end of that year, Bourguiba was released from prison and entered into negotiations with the French. On June 3, 1955, the Franco–Tunisian Conventions were signed between Bourguiba and the French, stipulating the nature of Tunisian autonomy. However, Bourguiba's opponents, most notably Salah ben Yousuf, denounced the conventions for not granting independence to Tunisia. Though the Neo-Destour-controlled Congress endorsed the conventions, when France announced its intent to allow Morocco to become independent in the November 1955 DECLARATION OF LA CELLE SAINT-CLOUD, the conventions came under renewed fire in Tunisia. After considerable pressure, France conceded, and Tunisia became independent in March 1956.

BIBLIOGRAPHY

BARBOUR, NEVILLE, ed. *A Survey of North-West Africa.* London, 1959.

MANSFIELD, PETER. *The Arabs.* New York, 1985.

Zachary Karabell

Franjiyya, Hamid   [1909–?]

Lebanese politician.

The son of former deputy Kabalan Franjiyya, Hamid represented the core of the Maronite aristocracy in the government. Elected to the chamber of deputies eight times, he briefly served as minister of foreign affairs in 1943. As a member of the United National Front, Franjiyya resigned his office in 1957 in protest against the Chamoun administration, but continued to represent Maronite interests. Franjiyya negotiated and signed the monetary convention with France.

BIBLIOGRAPHY

Who's Who in Lebanon, 1980–1981. Beirut, 1980.

Mark Mechler

Franjiyya, Sulayman   [?–1992]

President of Lebanon, 1970–1976.

Franjiyya's presidential term is associated with the outbreak of the Lebanese civil war of 1975. He was not initially slated to represent the FRANJIYYA FAMILY in politics. His brother, Hamid FRANJIYYA, was the political leader of this influential Maronite family of northern Lebanon; after Hamid suffered a stroke in the late 1950s, Sulayman was chosen as his successor. Unlike his brother, Sulayman was an uneducated "tough guy" who resorted to violence when it served his family's political interests. He was associated with bloodshed in northern Lebanon that targeted supporters of rival families. To avoid arrest, he fled to Syria where he established contacts with the AS'AD FAMILY that he later utilized.

Franjiyya served in Parliament throughout the 1960s and was active in the centrist (Wasat) bloc, which comprised opponents of the Chehab era. He also held various ministerial positions. He was elected president in 1970 by a one-vote margin. During his administration the Middle East was radicalized, and the Palestine Liberation Organization (PLO) relocated from Jordan to Lebanon after the 1970 clash between Jordan's troops and PLO forces. Franjiyya strongly opposed the presence of armed Palestinians in Lebanon and authorized Lebanon's army to train and give weapons to members of right-wing militias. He aligned himself with the government of Syria for the duration of the Lebanese civil war. He broke off his alliance with Maronite-oriented parties and groups in 1978, when his son, Tony Franjiyya, was killed by gunmen loyal to the Lebanese Forces. Franjiyya succeeded as family leader by his grandson Sulayman Tony Franjiyya.

As'ad AbuKhalil

Franjiyya, Tony   [1942–1978]

Lebanese politican, member of parliament (1970–1978), and militia leader (1975–1978).

In 1970, Tony (Antoine) Franjiyya was elected to the parliamentary seat vacated by his father, Sulayman, when he became president of Lebanon. In parliament, he led the New Central Bloc, a group of deputies loyal to the family. He was minister in several cabinets between 1973 and 1975, and maintained a close personal relationship with Rif'at, the younger brother of Syria's President Hafiz al-Asad. After the Lebanese Civil War broke out in 1975, Franjiyya led the family's small (approximately 1,000 men) Al-Marada (The Giants) militia. When he resisted Bashir JUMAYYIL's drive to incorporate all Christian militias into the Lebanese Forces, he was murdered on June 13, 1978—together with his wife, their daughter, and several others—during a Phalangist commando attack on the family's summer home in the village of Ehden.

BIBLIOGRAPHY

RANDAL, JONATHAN C. *Going All the Way: Christian Warlords, Israeli Adventurers, and the War in Lebanon*. New York, 1983.

Guilain P. Denoeux

Franjiyya Family

The most influential Maronite family in northern Lebanon.

The Franjiyyas are based in the town of Zgharta, in the northern part of Mount Lebanon, a few miles southeast of Tripoli. Unlike most other Maronite families in Lebanon, they have maintained close ties with Syria since the late 1950s. They are long time rivals of the prominent Maronite families of central Mount Lebanon, particularly the CHAMOUNS, EDDÉS, KHURIS, and JUMAYYILS. The Lebanese civil war of 1975–1990 exacerbated many of these rivalries, particularly that with the Jumayyil family. The death on July 23, 1992 of Sulayman Franjiyya, president of Lebanon from 1970 to 1976 and the family's leader for more than three decades, intensified power struggles among the Franjiyyas and raised new doubts regarding the family's political future.

BIBLIOGRAPHY

RANDAL, JONATHAN C. *Going All the Way: Christian Warlords, Israeli Adventurers, and the War in Lebanon*. New York, 1983.

Guilain P. Denoeux

Franklin-Bouillon Agreement

Gave up French claims to Ottoman Turkish region of Cilicia.

Named after the French negotiator, this agreement was concluded between France and Turkey on October 20, 1921. France had suffered a series of defeats at the hands of Turkish nationalist forces, and under the terms of the agreement, it renounced all claims to the southwestern Turkish region of CILICIA. In addition, the province of Alexandretta was made an autonomous region under French administration.

BIBLIOGRAPHY

SHAW, STANFORD, and EZEL KURAL SHAW. *History of the Ottoman Empire and Modern Turkey*. New York, 1977.

Zachary Karabell

Freedom Movement

Islamic nationalist party.

The Freedom Movement (Hizb-e Azadi), a splinter group of the Second National Front, was founded in 1961 by Ayatollah Mahmud Taleqani, Mahdi Bazargan and Yadollah Sahabi. The new group's constituency was made up mainly of Islamically minded technocrats and modernists, with strong ties to the bazaar. The three founders had been active in the Iranian nationalist resistance since the 1940s, when political activity flourished following Reza Shah Pahlavi's forced abdication (1941). They sought to provide a plausible Islamic alternative to the rising stars of secular nationalism and communism, both of which were gaining popularity in Iran after the nationalization of Iranian oil in 1953 by the National Front government of Mohammad MOSSADEGH in 1953. After the June uprisings of 1963 in Qom, led by Ayatollah Ruhollah KHOMEINI, Freedom Movement leaders were imprisoned by the government of Mohammad Reza Shah Pahlavi. The cooperation continued in the 1970s and 1980s, and Khomeini vested Bazargan to lead the provisional government after the success of the Islamic Revolution in 1979. The takeover of the American embassy in Tehran in November 1979 brought about its downfall and in 1980 Bazargan and other Freedom Movement leaders were elected to the Islamic parliament. As with all other members of the loyal opposition, the Freedom Movement was banned from political activity after the fall of the first president of the Islamic Republic, Abolhasan Bani Sadr in 1980, and its newspaper, *Mizan,* was shut down. In April 1985, the Freedom Movement and the National Front urged the United Nations to negotiate an end to the Iran–Iraq War, and in retaliation, government forces attacked its headquarters and prevented Bazargan from running for president in the 1985 elections. After the Islamic Republican party was dissolved in 1987, the Freedom Movement emerged as the only legally recognized political party. The government tolerated its criticism as long as the expression of it was confined to publishing pamphlets and issuing statements.

BIBLIOGRAPHY

CHEHABI, HOUCHANG E. *Iranian Politics and Religious Modernism: The Liberation Movement of Iran under the Shah and Khomeini*. Ithaca, N.Y., 1990.
FEDERAL RESEARCH DIVISION OF THE LIBRARY OF CONGRESS. *Iran: A Country Study*. Washington, D.C., 1989.

Neguin Yavari

Freedom Party

Turkish political party, 1955–1958.

Established late in 1955 by a group of dissident members of the ruling Democrat party, the Freedom party signified rising opposition to the undisciplined economic policies and authoritarian tendencies of the regime of Adnan MENDERES. Prime Minister Menderes reacted to intensifying criticism in the aftermath of destructive riots in Istanbul and other cities in September 1955 by forcing the resignation of the entire government while retaining office himself, thus violating the cardinal principle of collective cabinet responsibility. Composed of some of the most cosmopolitan and intellectual elements of the dominant party, the Freedom party called for effective constitutional guarantees against arbitrary government and greater freedom of association and expression. Ironically, the departure of the dissidents from the Democrat party strengthened Menderes and paved the way for even more dictatorial policies. The Freedom party garnered only 4 out of a total of 610 seats in the election of 1957, while the main opposition REPUBLICAN PEOPLE'S PARTY (RPP) polled 40 percent of the vote and gained 178 seats. Consequently, the Freedom party merged with the RPP in November 1958.

BIBLIOGRAPHY

AHMAD, F. *The Turkish Experiment in Democracy, 1950–1975.* Boulder, Colo., 1977.

FREY, F. W. *The Turkish Political Elite.* Cambridge, Mass., 1965.

Frank Tachau

Free French Mandate

Attempt by France to control Lebanon and Syria.

In June 1941, Free French troops joined British imperial forces in overthrowing the Vichy administration in Damascus. Gen. Charles de Gaulle's envoy to Cairo, Gen. Georges CATROUX, initially offered Syria and Lebanon independence if they would accept Free French rule. But de Gaulle then made independence conditional upon the conclusion of treaties ensuring continued French predominance over the two countries' economic, military, and cultural affairs. Catroux became delegate-general for Syria and Lebanon, a post virtually identical to the earlier office of high commissioner.

Free French officials could not block the integration of Syria and Lebanon into either the sterling area or the Anglo–American Middle East Supply Center. In addition, London pressured the Free French to meet local nationalists' demands, resulting in the restoration of the two countries' prewar constitutions. Elections in July 1943 gave the National bloc control of Syria's national assembly; nationalists captured Lebanon's parliament two months later and immediately took steps to dismantle the mandate. Free French authorities responded by arresting the Lebanese leadership, but massive popular demonstrations forced the prisoners' release. When the government in Damascus adopted a similar program, the Free French first tried to suppress the Syrian nationalist movement but then agreed to a series of negotiations, which culminated in the dual evacuations of April and August 1946.

Fred H. Lawson

Freemasons

A secret fraternal order.

Drawing on guild practices of the masons and deriving its "oriental" origins from the period of Solomon's temple in Jerusalem, the order of Free and Accepted Masons recognizes some six million members worldwide. The order's first Grand Lodge was organized in London in 1717. Incorporating a complex system of secret rituals, rites, and decrees, the society admits members who profess a belief in God, but keep the particulars of their faith private. Members include Muslims, Christians, and Jews. There is no central authority. Freemasonry advocates religious toleration, fellowship, and political compromise, and members work for peace and harmony between peoples.

Freemasonry in the Middle East is traced initially to individuals, most notably Iranians who, serving as diplomats, were invited to join lodges by Europeans and upon their return disseminated the ideology. Masonic lodges in the region were established by Europeans in areas they influenced and were used by the French and the British to cultivate local individuals. Lodges in Calcutta (founded in 1730) attracted Hindus and Muslims, and the philosophy probably entered Iran at this time with Iranian merchants who lived in India.

The establishment in the Middle East of masonic lodges affiliated with the European movement, however, dates from Napoleon's invasion of Egypt, when French soldiers established chapters in Cairo (1798) and in Alexandria (1802). Italian émigrés, after their abortive revolution in Italy (1830), set up Italian lodges, and the British and the Germans became active in the 1860s. In Iran, the first lodge (a nonaffiliated one) was set up in 1858 by an Armenian convert to Islam, Mirza Malkom Khan, and was short lived. The French masonic lodge in Istanbul, L'Union d'Orient, dates from 1865. During the Ottoman period, there were lodges in Beirut and Jerusalem, and the society flourished under the Palestine mandate. Jewish, Christian, and Muslim members support a mutual insurance fund, an old-age home, a library, and masonic temples in Israel. There have been lodges in most Middle Eastern countries at one time or another, depending upon the regime in power.

Although it never attracted many members on the popular level, Freemasonry in the Middle East was a significant component of Middle Eastern reform politics during the latter part of the nineteenth century until World War I. Because it incorporated unique rites, a clandestine apparatus, and a select membership—features familiar in Sufi, *futuwwa,* and other Islamic movements—and was a convenient vehicle for the dissemination of European ideas, it drew Islamic modernists and political activists such as the Egyptian Muhammad ABDUH, the Iranian Jamal al-din al-AFGHANI, and the Algerian ABD AL-QADIR.

Masonic lodges were convenient covers for clandestine activities. Because they were, by and large, Western institutions protected under the CAPITULATIONS, governments could not penetrate them or monitor their activities. Members were also able to draw upon the support of European masons in defense of local members. During the 1870s, the movement was used as a tool by Prince Halim of Egypt who was denied succession and conspired to rule. Khedive Isma'il and his successor, Tawfiq, banished a number of prominent members who were also active in reformist political activities—Ya'qub SANU and Afghani, among others. Ottoman modernists of the Tanzimat period were responsible for Ottoman Sultan Murad V's brief rule in 1876. In Iran, lodges existed sporadically in the nineteenth century and were allowed under Muhammad Ali Shah until 1911 and the end of the constitutional movement. Iranians, Egyptians, and Ottomans met at lodges throughout the Middle East when they traveled, but there is no evidence that any unified political actions emerged.

For the Young Turks, exposed to freemasonry largely in the Balkans and Constantinople (now Istanbul), the lodges were convenient meeting places to bring together Christians and Muslims, and to plan the overthrow of the regime of Sultan Abdülhamit II. The existence of so many Freemasons in the large secular leadership of the Committee for Union and Progress generated polemical literature of a conspiratorial nature against the regime just before Turkey's entry into World War I on the side of Germany.

BIBLIOGRAPHY

ALGAR, HAMID. "An Introduction to the History of Freemasonry in Iran." *Middle Eastern Studies* 6 (1970).
HANIOĞLU, M. SÜKRÜ. "Notes on the Young Turks and Freemasons, 1875–1908." *Middle Eastern Studies* 25 (1989).
KEDOURIE, ELIE. "Young Turks, Freemasons, and Jews." *Middle Eastern Studies* 7 (1971).
LANDAU, JACOB M. "Prolegomena to a Study of Secret Societies in Modern Egypt." *Middle Eastern Studies* 1 (1964).

Reeva S. Simon

Free Officers, Egypt

Clandestine military organization that engineered and executed the coup of July 23, 1952, which began a new chapter in the history of modern Egypt.

The genesis of the Free Officers is much disputed among historians and specialists. Some argue that the group was formed in 1942 after the British ultimatum to King Farouk. Others take the Arab–Israel War (1948) as the starting point. Notwithstanding these differences, general agreement exists on four major points. First, Gamal Abdel NASSER was the undisputed leader of the group from its inception, and his position was never challenged. This fact laid down the foundation of his prominence as the strongman and president of Egypt until his death in 1970. Second, the group did not have an organized file or registry of its membership. It was organized into cells and sections, each with a specific function. The overall command and supervision was provided by a revolutionary committee headed by Nasser.

The organization of the Free Officers reflected a high degree of flexibility that was demonstrated in the frequent movements of individuals into and outside the group. Actually, the first attempt to develop a form of registry was under President Anwar al-Sadat (1970–1981) when he decided to provide a special pension for the Free Officers. Third, the group did not represent an ideologically homogeneous group. Among its members were officers with Islamist inclinations, such as Kamal al-Din Hussein and Abdel Mun'im Amin; others were more or less leftists, such as Khalid Muhyi al-Din and Yusuf Sediq. Lacking a clear ideology, all that the group had was the "six principles," which were their guiding directives after assuming power. The existence of ideological differences within the group was one of the factors that explains the power struggle among the Free Officers after 1952. Fourth, the group, under Nasser, was conscious of retaining its organizational autonomy, resolving not to be absorbed in any other political movement.

As individuals, the Free Officers had contacts with the YOUNG EGYPT party, the MUSLIM BROTHERHOOD, the Democratic Movement for National Liberation, and other communist groups; while, as a group, they maintained a high degree of independence. Nasser believed that they could succeed only if they established a firm independent base within the army. One of the distinct features of the Free Officers is that they were purely military; the group had no civilian members and this has come to affect the nature of the post-1952 political ruling elite.

In the mid-1940s, the voice of the Free Officers was heard for the first time. They began to distribute leaflets, the first of them in 1945 was entitled "The Army Gives Warning." The first open clash with the king took place in the early summer of 1952, when the officers' club in Cairo elected as president General Muhammad NAGUIB, who was the Free Officers' nominee, turning down the king's own candidate.

Between 1949 and July 1952, the Free Officers worked to recruit other sympathetic officers and strengthened their ties with civilians and politicians opposed to the monarchy. During this period too, because most of them were in their early thirties, they looked for a senior officer that could be presented to the public as their leading figure. Finally, they chose Naguib, who was a well-known infantry division commander and had been popular, especially since the Arab–Israel War, among the troops and young officers.

The actual seizure of power took place in the early hours of July 23, 1952, when troops commanded by Free Officers and their supporters occupied and controlled army headquarters, airports, the broadcasting station, telecommunication center, and major roads and bridges in Cairo. The details of what happened on that day show that the plan for seizing power was neither well thought out nor were its parts tightly integrated. Indeed, a combination of coincidence and luck made the operation successful. Within three days, the king abdicated the throne to his infant son and left the country. From then on, the Free Officers became the new rulers of Egypt.

BIBLIOGRAPHY

HAMROUSH, AHMED. *Qissat thawrat 23 Yulyu* (The Story of the 23 July Revolution). 4 vols. Cairo, 1983.
VATIKIOTIS, P. J. *The Egyptian Army in Politics.* Westport, Conn., 1961.

Ali E. Hillal Dessouki

Free Officers, Yemen

Junior officers who led North Yemen's 1962 revolution.

These fifteen or so junior officers were at the center of the planning and execution of the 1962 revolution that overthrew the ZAYDI imamate in North Yemen. Inspired by the Egyptian revolution and the revolutionary Arab nationalism of Gamal Abdel NASSER, they recruited the more prominent senior officers who participated in the successful revolt, only to be upstaged or shunted aside by some of these older figures in the sharp political struggles that followed.

Robert D. Burrowes

Free Republican Party

Turkish political party, 1930.

This short-lived party was founded in August 1930 by associates of Turkey's president, Mustafa Kemal ATATÜRK, at his behest, possibly to siphon off discontent spawned by economic problems and the government's radical reform program. Fethi Okyar, former prime minister and close associate of Kemal, returned from his post of ambassador to France to assume the leadership of the party. It opposed the government's *dirigiste* (paternalistic, state directed) economic policy and emphasized individual rights and freedoms, including freedom of (religious) conscience. It rapidly gained enthusiastic support, especially in the Aegean region. Among its adherents was Adnan MENDERES, leader of the Democrat party of the 1950s, indicating that the Free Republican party was a harbinger of things to come. Contrary to Kemal's image of gentlemanly debates between parties, relations between the new party and the governing People's party were bitter. The latter feared that it might in fact lose power in a free election and accused the Free Republican party of stirring up reaction against Kemal's nationalist reform program. Consequently, the Free Republican party voluntarily dissolved itself after only ninety-nine days, in November 1930.

BIBLIOGRAPHY

FREY, F. W. *The Turkish Political Elite.* Cambridge, Mass., 1965.
KARPAT, K. H. *Turkey's Politics.* Princeton, N.J., 1959.
WEIKER, W. F. *Political Tutelage and Democracy in Turkey: The Free Party and Its Aftermath.* Leiden, 1975.

Frank Tachau

Free United Bloc

Tripolitanian (Libyan) political party (al-Kutla al-Wataniyya al-Hurra) founded in May 1946 by Ahmed and Ali al-Faqih Hassan.

Strongly republican, anti-British, and anti-Italian, the party opposed any Sanusi (Cyrenaican) role in Tripolitanian affairs. It soon split into factions, some of which founded other, smaller parties. Its politics were generally too extreme to attract the wide following it claimed.

John L. Wright

Free Yemenis

Political party of North Yemen in the 1940s.

Founded in Aden in 1944 by such fathers of the modern Yemeni nation-state as Qa'id Muhammad Mahmud al-ZUBAYRI and Shaykh Ahmad Muhammad NU'MAN, the Free Yemeni party (al-Ahrar) was the first major modern expression of constitutional reform and political opposition to the Hamid al-Din imamate in North Yemen. Although their party only existed for a few years, the Free Yemenis led the way from reformism and a constitutional imamate to new, more advanced political ideas (republicanism and revolution), organization (such as the Yemeni Unionists), and action. It could be said that a Free Yemeni movement, more than the party itself, traces an unbroken line from 1944 to the 1962 revolution. However, the Free Yemenis, far from being radical political modernists, were initially the mid-twentieth-century equivalents of the Turkish reformers of the Ottoman Empire during the TANZIMAT period in the nineteenth century. This did not prevent them from playing a major role in the failed 1948 revolution and in laying a big part of the foundation for the successful 1962 revolution.

Robert D. Burrowes

French Foreign Legion

French military unit created by Louis Philippe in 1831 and made up of foreign volunteers.

Deployed only outside metropolitan France, the French foreign legion saw combat first in Algeria. It played a decisive role in the capture of Constantine in 1837 and fought in numerous engagements as the conquest proceeded. Although the legion served in the Crimea, Italy, and Mexico in the 1850s and 1860s, and throughout the French empire later in the century, an encampment established in 1843 at Sidi-bel-Abbès, southwest of Oran, remained its headquarters.

The legion helped check the insurrection of the Walad Sidi Shaykh in western Algeria in 1881 and 1882, but much of its work in that country in the last quarter of the nineteenth century involved efforts to expand French influence into the Sahara as a prelude to linking North Africa with France's possessions south of the desert.

Legionnaires participated in many of the military operations that resulted in the establishment of a French protectorate over Morocco. They formed part of the forces that consolidated French power along the ill-defined southern Morocco–Algeria border during the first several years of the twentieth century and were involved in occupations of the Moroccan cities of Oujda and Casablanca in 1907. Thereafter, they helped maintain security in the areas around both cities. In 1911, a company of the legion was among the troops that lifted a rebel siege of Fez, the sultan's capital, thus paving the way for the inauguration of the protectorate the following year. During the pacification of Morocco's mountainous and desert regions in the 1920s and 1930s, French commanders relied heavily on the legion. Its men also took part in the fighting that ended the rebellion of ABD AL-KARIM in 1925 and 1926.

During World War I, a battalion of legionnaires landed with other Allied soldiers at Gallipoli. After the war, legionnaires were dispatched to the French mandates of Syria and Lebanon. They saw action in the Druze uprising of 1925 and remained on garrison duty in the Levant in the 1930s.

In World War II, units of the legion made up part of the Free French contingent that seized Syria and Lebanon from the Vichy government in 1941. Subsequently attached to the British army in Egypt's Western Desert, they fought in the battle of Bir Hakeim in 1942 and advanced westward with the British following the battle of El Alamein. Other Legionnaires from Sidi-bel-Abbès worked with American and British forces upon their arrival in Morocco and Algeria late in 1942 until the defeat of the Axis in Tunisia the following spring.

After 1954, the legion was heavily involved in French efforts to end the Algerian rebellion. Paratroopers, who had been added to the legion in the late 1940s, were instrumental in breaking up FRONT DE LIBÉRATION NATIONALE (FLN) cells during the 1957 Battle of ALGIERS. A legion paratroop battalion also formed part of the French expeditionary at Suez in 1956. When Algeria acquired independence in 1962, the headquarters of the legion were transferred from Sidi-bel-Abbès to France.

BIBLIOGRAPHY

O'BALLANCE, EDGAR. *The Story of the French Foreign Legion*. London, 1961.

PORCH, DOUGLAS. *The French Foreign Legion: A Complete History of the Legendary Fighting Force*. New York, 1991.

Kenneth J. Perkins

French Report of 1931

One of several studies commissioned by the British after the 1929 Arab–Jewish riots in Palestine.

Lewis French, a British colonial official, concluded in his "First Report on Agricultural Development and Land Settlement in Palestine" that Jewish settlement was not in the best interests of Arab peasants. French recommended laws to control land transfers, because the number of landless Arab peasants was increasing.

French's report contradicted the earlier and controversial HOPE-SIMPSON COMMISSION, which had recommended that Palestinians adopt intensive agricultural techniques to compensate for reduced land ownership. French said that such a plan was economically unfeasible because the local market could not absorb surplus production. The report's recommendations met objections from all sides. Palestinians resisted further government intervention in their lives and claimed the report did not account for their rapidly growing population. The Jewish Agency presented counter evidence that Arab landlessness was not caused by Jewish land purchase. The British filed the report and never acted on it.

BIBLIOGRAPHY

ABBOUSHI, W. F. *The Unmaking of Palestine*. Brattleboro, Vt., 1990.

STEIN, KENNETH W. *The Land Question in Palestine, 1917–1939*. Chapel Hill, N.C., 1984.

Elizabeth Thompson

French Mandate, Syria

See Syria

Frischmann, David   [1859–1922]

Pioneer of modern Hebrew literature.

Frischmann was born in Poland and died in Berlin. As a writer he was versatile and created an enormous body of works—short stories, essays, literary criti-

cism, poetry, translations, and news stories. He was also an editor and publisher. An innovative writer, he is credited with introducing Western standards of aesthetics into Hebrew literature—which he considered provincial at that time.

His stories manifest a sympathy for and portray European Jewish characters who are in conflict with tradition; they often abandon it. His poems express the futility of adapting Judaism to modern European life. He shunned public office and remained apolitical to retain artistic and literary integrity; as a result, he was accused of being against Zionism. However, deeply affected by a visit to Palestine in 1911 and 1912, he recorded his impressions in a book, *Ba-Aretz* (1913). His collected works appear in the seventeen-volume *Kol Kitvei David Frischmann u-Mivhar Tirgumav* (Warsaw, 1922).

Ann Kahn

Front de Libération Nationale

The organizing group behind the Algerian War of Independence; later became the dominant single party of independent Algeria.

The instigators of the Algerian revolution created the National Liberation Front (FLN) in October 1954 as a vehicle for mobilizing Algerians behind the war of independence. As the war went on, the movement spun off various deliberative, executive, and military institutions, creating by September 1958 a Provisional Government of the Algerian Republic. By January 1960 the revolutionary parliament—CONSEIL NATIONAL DE LA RÉVOLUTION ALGÉRIENNE (CNRA)—declared the FLN a single party responsible for carrying out a deeper social and economic revolution.

The Algerian constitutions of 1963 and 1976 confirmed this decision, declaring the FLN the people's monitor of government and the avant-garde of the revolution. By the late 1970s, however, it had grown into a bureaucratized organization of more than 300,000 members, whose principal function was the recruitment and indoctrination of members for support of the government it ostensibly monitored.

The constitution of February 1989 ended the FLN's single-party status, but before newer parties could unseat it, the army seized control of the government.

BIBLIOGRAPHY

ENTELIS, JOHN. *Algeria. The Revolution Institutionalized*. Boulder, Colo., 1986.

John Ruedy

Front for the Liberation of South Yemen

South Yemeni independence movement.

The Front for the Liberation of South Yemen (FLOSY) was a political party established in January 1966 in Britain's Aden Crown Colony and the Protectorate States. The party was forged under heavy Egyptian pressure from a combination of the National Liberation Front (NLF) and the ORGANIZATION FOR THE LIBERATION OF THE OCCUPIED SOUTH (OLOS) in an effort by Egypt to sustain its influence over the course of the campaign against the continued British presence in southern Arabia. When the NLF quickly backed out, FLOSY became nothing more than a renamed OLOS and the political property of Abdullah Ali ASNAJ and Abd al-Qawi MAKAWI. The NLF successfully fought FLOSY to succeed the British in an independent South Yemen in 1967. FLOSY then became a vehicle for opposition from abroad to the regime, and it remained so with decreasing relevance from the late 1960s through the 1970s.

Robert D. Burrowes

Front pour la Défense des Institutions Constitutionelles (FDIC)

Moroccan political group.

Founded in 1963 by Ahmad Rida GUDEIRA, a close confidant of King Hassan, the FDIC attempted to unite promonarchy groups in parliament against ISTIQLAL and the Union Nationale des Forces Populaires (UNFP) during a time of social and economic tensions. Having failed to win a majority in the 1963 parliamentary elections, it split in 1964 into Gudeira's Parti Socialiste Démocratique and the MOUVEMENT POPULAIRE (MP)—the latter had been part of the original FDIC. The failure of the FDIC led the king to assume emergency governing powers in June 1965.

Bruce Maddy-Weitzman

Fu'ad   [1868–1936]

Sultan of Egypt, 1917–1922; king, 1922–1936.

Fu'ad was born in Giza, Egypt, on March 26, 1868, the youngest child of Khedive Isma'il Pasha, who ruled Egypt from 1863 until 1879. Fu'ad left Egypt for Constantinople (now Istanbul) in 1879 at the time of his father's exile. Subsequently, he studied at Geneva, Turin, and the Italian Military Academy, returning to Egypt in 1892. His eligibility for the Egyptian throne was enhanced when the British de-

posed Abbas Hilmi II as khedive of Egypt in 1914 at the beginning of World War I. At the time of Abbas's removal, Britain severed the juridical ties that bound Egypt to the Ottoman Empire, proclaimed a protectorate over the country, and named Fu'ad's elder brother, Husayn Kamil, as the first Sultan of Egypt. When Husayn Kamil died on October 9, 1917, Fu'ad succeeded him to the throne.

Fu'ad reigned in Egypt from 1917 until his death in 1936. He aspired to be a powerful ruler and did much to enlarge the powers of the monarchy. Following the conclusion of the war, Egypt's elite, including Sultan Fu'ad, pressed the British to end the protectorate and to increase the political autonomy of their country. Britain's failure to respond to these overtures set off a powerful protest movement, led by Sa'd ZAGHLUL and his new political party, the WAFD. The political turmoil led to Britain's unilateral proclamation of Egypt's independence on February 28, 1922, subject to the exclusion of a wide range of powers reserved to the British. In the wake of the altered political status of the country, Fu'ad became king of Egypt on March 15, 1922. In 1923 an appointed committee drafted a new constitution for the country. Through the intervention of Fu'ad and the British, the constitution gave far-reaching authority to the monarch. Under its provisions, the crown had the power to designate the prime minister, dissolve the parliament, and postpone sessions of parliament. Additionally, the king controlled charitable and educational institutions and decided upon diplomatic appointments and military commissions.

Armed with its formal, albeit restricted, political independence and a new, sophisticated constitution, Egypt embarked upon an experiment in liberal democracy. Unfortunately, civilian parliamentary government, which lasted until the military ousted the politicians from office in 1952, tended to degenerate into a three-cornered struggle among Egypt's most popular party, the Wafd, the palace, and the British. During these years, the Wafd invariably won any fair electoral contest, but was kept from office through the political manipulations of the palace and the British. Monarchical power reached its apex between 1930 and 1935, after Fu'ad removed the Wafd from office and appointed Isma'il SIDQI as prime minister. Immediately upon assuming power, Sidqi replaced the 1923 constitution with a new one and enacted a new, more restrictive electoral law. Both changes enhanced royal authority. Jealous of the power that Sidqi wielded, Fu'ad removed him from office in 1933 and ruled Egypt through a set of palace appointees. In 1935, under pressure from the British and responding to fears of an impending world war,

Egyptian postage stamp with the portrait of King Fu'ad. (Richard Bulliet)

Fu'ad agreed to restore the 1923 constitution and to hold new elections. Predictably, the Wafd won the 1936 elections. Fu'ad died on April 28, 1936, just months before the signing of the Anglo–Egyptian Treaty, which gave greater political autonomy to Egypt.

Although he was an autocrat and did much to impede the development of parliamentary democracy, Fu'ad was a noteworthy patron of Egyptian education. He played a role in reviving the Egyptian University, which had been founded in 1908 but had languished until Fu'ad and others gave it their support. It was named Fu'ad I University in 1940 and became today's Cairo University in 1954.

BIBLIOGRAPHY

AL-SAYYID-MARSOT, AFAF LUTFI. *Egypt's Liberal Experiment, 1922–1936.* Los Angeles, 1977.
VATIKIOTIS, P. J. *The History of Egypt from Muhammad Ali to Sadat.* Baltimore, 1980.

Robert L. Tignor

Fuad, Mehmed [1815–1869]

Turkish statesman and leading Tanzimat figure.

The son of a well-known poet, Mehmed Fuad Paşa was born in Istanbul in 1815. He studied theology at an early age but entered the new state medical school in 1829, where he mastered French. In 1834, he traveled to Tripoli to serve as an army doctor and, in

November 1837, was appointed to the Translation Bureau to help meet the Porte's increasing diplomatic needs. In 1840, his language skills won him a post as the first secretary of the Turisk embasssy in London. In 1852, following a series of diplomatic posts, he was appointed foreign minister under ABDÜLMECIT I, a position he held until 1853, from 1855 to 1856, and from 1858 to 1860. Fuad served as grand vizier and foreign minister under ABDÜLAZIZ from 1861 to 1862, and again as grand vizier from 1863 to 1867.

Fuad is best known for his leading role in the TANZIMAT period, when a number of Western-style reforms were introduced. As commissioner of education, he proposed a series of reforms for the state school system and collaborated with Ahmed CEVDET on the first work of Turisk grammar published in the empire. These reforms did not come without cost, however, and Fuad was criticized for contributing to the empire's worsening financial situation.

BIBLIOGRAPHY

SHAW, STANFORD J., and EZEL KURAL SHAW. *History of the Ottoman Empire and Modern Turkey.* Cambridge, U.K., 1976.

Jillian Schwedler

Fujayra

One of the United Arab Emirates.

Fujayra is the only one of the seven UNITED ARAB EMIRATES (UAE) whose territory lies wholly on the Gulf of Oman side of the MUSANDAM Peninsula. It consists of two enclaves and three village dependencies totaling 450 square miles (1,166 sq km), with a population of 63,000 (official estimate), making it the third smallest emirate in area and second smallest in population. Most of its territory is in the rugged Hajar Mountains, and most of the population is on the narrow coastal plain, largely in the port and capital city of Fujayra.

Numerically and politically the al-Sharqi tribe dominates the emirate. Its energetic, university-educated ruler is Shaykh Hamad ibn Muhammad al-SHARQI. Like Ajman and UMM AL-QAYWAYN, the other small, poor, oilless emirates, Fujayra has a limited voice in UAE affairs and is heavily dependent on federal (i.e., ABU DHABI) financial largess. In addition to fishing and agriculture, there are some small local industries, including quarrying, that utilize its mineral deposits.

Great Britain granted Fujayra formal recognition as an independent emirate in 1952. From the later nineteenth century, however, it generally enjoyed de facto independence from its Qawasim overlords, the present rulers of SHARJA and RA'S AL-KHAYMA. The long contention of al-Sharqi and al-Qawasim left a legacy of enmity and minor border disputes that still exists.

BIBLIOGRAPHY

HEARD-BEY, FRAUKE. *From Trucial States to United Arab Emirates.* London, 1982.
ZAHLAN, ROSEMARIE SAID. *The Origins of the United Arab Emirates: A Political and Social History of the Trucial States.* London, 1978.

Malcolm C. Peck

Fujayra–Sharja Conflict

Clash over land ownership in the United Arab Emirates (1972).

A few months after establishment of the United Arab Emirates, these two members of the federation clashed over ownership of a tiny parcel of land with a well that had traditionally been used by tribesmen from both. Some twenty lives were lost before federal intervention ended the conflict. The incident underscored the disruptive potential of numerous unresolved border disputes, and the federal government's response reflected its determination to keep them in check.

BIBLIOGRAPHY

ANTHONY, JOHN DUKE. *Arab States of the Lower Gulf: People, Politics, Petroleum.* Washington, D.C., 1975.

Malcolm C. Peck

Ful

Fava-bean mash.

Ful mudammis, a mash of fava beans (the broad bean, a vetch, *Vicia faba*) is considered the Egyptian national dish. There, it is often eaten with bread for breakfast. The peeled fava beans are soaked in water for a day, then covered with fresh water and simmered overnight with onion, some tomatoes, and red lentils, to control the color. Once the *ful* is cooked, it is salted and eaten plain or accompanied by olive oil, corn oil, butter, *smen* (clarified butter), buffalo milk, béchamel sauce, *basturma* (dried beef), fried eggs, tomato sauce, *tahini* (sesame-seed paste), or other ingredients.

Clifford A. Wright

Fuleyhan, Anis   [1900–   ]

Lebanese American pianist, composer, and conductor.

Fuleyhan was born and educated in Brooklyn, New York; he received a degree in music from the Von Ende School of Music in New York City. After teaching piano and composition at Indiana University from 1947 to 1952, he returned to Lebanon to head the Conservatory of Music from 1953 to 1960. He subsequently worked at the Cultural Center in Tunis for two years, and taught for one year (1967–1968) at the University of Illinois. He was a guest conductor of the New York Philharmonic Orchestra on February 10, 1967. He retired to New York City.

As'ad AbuKhalil

Fundamental Pact

An 1857 Tunisian law that increased freedoms for non-Tunisians.

The law was issued by Muhammad Bey (1855–1859) of Tunisia on September 10, 1857. Entitled Ahd al-Aman (Pledge of Security), the Fundamental Pact resulted from an incident involving a Tunisian Jew, Batto (Samuel) Sfez, who was executed on orders of the bey for having blasphemed Islam. The French and British consuls saw in the episode an opportunity to intervene in Tunisian affairs. The two men—Richard Wood of Britain and Leon Roches of France—pressed for the promulgation of reforms that would ensure the security of both Tunisians and foreigners; that would establish MIXED COURTS to handle matters concerning Europeans; and, importantly, that would allow non-Tunisians to conduct business and own property in Tunisia more easily. On the one hand, the law opened the way to greater European economic activity and, on the other, spurred a group of Tunisian notables, led by KHAYR AL-DIN Pasha, to pressure the bey to enact structural reforms that would, in part, place limits upon the powers of the bey's office. The campaign of these notables, backed by the foreign consuls who continued to press for enforcement of the new laws, led Muhammad Bey and his successor MUHAMMAD AL-SADIQ Bey (1859–1882) to draw up a formal constitution.

BIBLIOGRAPHY

ABU AL-NASR, JAMIL. *A History of the Maghrib in the Islamic Period.* London, 1987.
Tunisia: A Country Survey. Washington, D.C., 1988.

Matthew S. Gordon

Futuwwa

Associations of young men who claimed to embody certain virtues and who tried to maintain the distinct identities of their quarters in Cairo. Also, paramilitary youth organizations in Iraq.

In medieval times, the term *futuwwa* (plural, futuwwat) referred to either a specific body of virtues—courage, manliness, chivalry, generosity, truth, honor, self-reliance, altruism—or to informal urban associations of young men who claimed to promote these values. By the early nineteenth century, the word was used in Cairo (Egypt) to refer to a few influential men who acted as informal leaders of their quarters. Their primary function was to protect their quarters against outside threats, other futuwwat, and the government. While they performed good deeds, they also quarreled and were violent among themselves and with police. Some were thugs who preyed on the local populace instead of furthering its welfare.

In Egypt, between Muhammad Ali Pasha's accession to power in 1805 and World War II, their influence declined, mainly as a result of government efforts to centralize authority. After the war, their number and role diminished further, under the combined effects of rapid urbanization, industrialization, expansion of the role of the bureaucracy in the daily life of the people, and the increasing religious and socioeconomic heterogeneity of neighborhoods. The few remaining futuwwat in the older, medieval quarters of Cairo now include a large proportion of toughs engaged in various semilegal and illegal activities.

In another context, the term has been used in Iraq, first in the 1930s and again since the BA'TH party takeover in 1968, to refer to paramilitary youth groups strongly reminiscent of the Hitler Youth of Nazi Germany. In Ba'thist Iraq, the futuwwa is one of three paramilitary youth organizations that belong to the state-run General Federation of Iraqi Youth. It brings together Iraqis aged fifteen to twenty, is strongly hierarchical, and is patterned after the Ba'th party itself. Its members wear uniforms, undergo military training, and participate in various activities and rituals aimed at strengthening the new generation's loyalty to the regime.

BIBLIOGRAPHY

AL-KHALIL, SAMIR. *Republic of Fear.* New York, 1990.
EL-MESSIRI, SAWSAN. "The Changing Role of the Futuwwa in the Social Structure of Cairo." In *Patrons and Clients in Mediterranean Societies,* ed. by Ernest Gellner and John Waterbury. London, 1977.

Guilain P. Denoeux

G

Gafsa Incident

Confrontation between Tunisia and Libya.

In January 1980, during a period of heightened tension between Libya under Muammar al-QADDAFI and Tunisia under Habib BOURGUIBA, Tunisian guerrillas (trained by the Libyan military) crossed into Tunisia and attacked the south-central city of Gafsa. Tunisia responded by severing ties with Libya; in turn, Libya ordered some 10,000 Tunisian workers in Libya to return home.

BIBLIOGRAPHY

PERKINS, KENNETH. *Tunisia: Crossroads of the Islamic and European Worlds.* Boulder, Colo., 1986.

Matthew S. Gordon

Gailani, Ahmad [1923–]

Afghan resistance leader; Sufi pir.

By virtue of being the descendant of the Muslim pir Abd al-Qadir al-Gailani (1088–1166), Ahmad Gailani is the leader of the Qadirya Sufi order. After the Saur revolution, he left Kabul and in Peshawar founded the Afghanistan National Islamic Front, considered one of the moderate Islamic groups in the Afghan war of resistance. In 1992, he returned to Kabul with the other Islamic leaders to participate in forming the Islamic government.

BIBLIOGRAPHY

ROY, OLIVIER. *Islam and Resistance in Afghanistan.* Cambridge, U.K., 1986.

Grant Farr

Galabiyya

See Jellaba

Galata

District of Istanbul on the north bank of the Golden Horn.

A Genoese settlement in the Byzantine era, Galata was officially incorporated into the city of Constantinople (now Istanbul) only in 1840. It continued through the nineteenth century to be the section of Constantinople where Europeans resided. Long the center of international trade and banking in the capital, the district's population and business activity boomed beginning in the Crimean War (1853–1856). Galata and its neighboring district Beyoğlu (formerly Pera) became the modernized center of the city, with many theaters and hotels and the city's first tramway and telephone lines. The famous Galatasaray Lycée, established in 1868, was actually located in Beyoğlu.

BIBLIOGRAPHY

SELTZER, LEON E., ed. *The Columbia-Lippincott Gazetteer of the World*. New York, 1962, p. 655.

SHAW, STANFORD J., and EZEL KURAL SHAW. *History of the Ottoman Empire and Modern Turkey*. Vol. 2. New York, 1977.

Elizabeth Thompson

Galatasaray Lycée

Elite Turkish educational institution in Istanbul.

The school was founded as part of the palace school system for the training and education of palace pages during the reign (1481–1512) of Ottoman Sultan Bayezid II, and was located north of the Golden Horn, near the European district of Istanbul. There were 200 pages in residence who, when completing training at Galatasaray, either went on to higher education at TOPKAPI PALACE or were given appointments in the household cavalry corps. In the seventeenth century the school functioned as a *medrese* but reverted to its original purpose in 1715, and continued as a palace school until it was closed in 1835 during Europeanizing reforms of Mahmud II. The buildings were temporarily allocated to the new medical school from 1838 to 1848, and served as a preparatory school for the military academies in 1862.

The modern history of Galatasaray began in 1868 when it was reorganized as the Imperial Lycée (Mekteb-i Sultani), with support from the French government and modeled after the grand French lycées to provide European education with French as the language of instruction. Turkish and Ottoman classics were also included in the curriculum. The first director was French, but in 1872 he was succeeded by a Christian Ottoman. There were already many foreign schools in Istanbul and elsewhere in the empire providing education for non-Muslim Ottomans; Galatasaray was intended to provide a similar modern education to Muslim as well as non-Muslim boys. The 350 boys in the student body, of various religious and social backgrounds, went on to higher education in the new colleges, especially the School of Government (Mekteb-i Mülkiye), many of them taking up state appointments. In the Republican period, now officially known as the Galatasaray Lycée, the school preserved its prestige, official French support continued, and French was maintained as the language of instruction. Galatasaray graduates remained prominent in public life, still usually via the School of Government, especially in the Ministry of Foreign Affairs, but they also achieved success in the business and cultural circles.

In the 1960s, a primary school was opened to prepare students for the lycée at a separate site in Ortaköy on the Bosporus, and girls were admitted in 1965. Although still a state school, in 1981 it established a Galatasaray Educational Foundation, an endowment to channel private funds, mainly alumni support. In April 1992, during French president Mitterand's visit to Turkey, the two governments agreed to reorganize the school as the Galatasaray Educational Institution and to add facilities for higher education. Accordingly, the Galatasaray University was founded in 1994, envisaged to comprise faculties of Law, Engineering and Technology, Administration, Communication, and Arts and Sciences. The University moved to a new campus built outside the city at Riva, on the Asian shore of the Black Sea. In 1996 there were 500 girls and 1,100 boys enrolled in the primary and lycée divisions, taught by about 100 teachers, one-third French. The University started with 100 students studying French intensively before going on to the various faculties.

BIBLIOGRAPHY

MILLER, BARNETTE. *The Palace School of Mohammad the Conqueror*. Cambridge, Mass., 1941.

I. Metin Kunt

Galib, Şeyh [1757–1799]

Eighteenth-century Turkish Ottoman poet.

The son of a whirling dervish, Galib (Mehmet Esat) received a religious education and then went to work in the Ottoman Chancery. He is considered the last great poet to compose in the classical court style. Among his works are *Divan* and *Hüsn ü Aşk* (Beauty and Love).

BIBLIOGRAPHY

ÖZKIRIMLI, ATILLA. *Türk Edebiyatı Ansiklopedisi*, vol. 4. Istanbul, 1982, pp. 1075–1076.

David Waldner

Galilee

In Hebrew, HaGalil, probably meaning "the circle"; mountainous and comparatively fertile region of northern Israel.

Galilee is bounded by the Mediterranean Sea on the west, the river Jordan on the east, approximately the border in the north, and the JEZREEL VALLEY to the south. A line running from Acre on the coast to the northwest shore of the Kinneret (Sea of Ga-

View of upper Galilee. (Bryan McBurney)

lilee) divides Lower Galilee, reaching an elevation of 1,500 feet (458 m) above sea level, from Upper Galilee, which attains altitudes of 4,000 feet (1,220 m).

Joshua and Deborah conquered the entirety of this area, which in biblical times was alloted to four Israelite tribes and later to the northern kingdom of Israel. Controlled by a series of empires, Galilee became a preeminent Judaic stronghold for some five centuries after the destruction of the Second Temple, and a center of Christianity especially after the sixth century C.E. The region became part of the province of al-Urdun (Jordan) following the Arab conquest (c. 640), then formed a crusader principality, and was later ruled successively by Ayyubids, Mamluks, Ottomans, and intermittently by local potentates such as Zahir al-Umar, Ahmad al-Jazzar and Muhammad Ali of Egypt. Zionist settlement activity, both before and after Britain's Gen. Edmund Allenby's conquest of the area from the Ottoman Turks in September 1918, was slow in penetrating Galilee itself, whose overwhelming Arab majority caused it to be apportioned to the Arab state under partition. Conquered in its entirety by Israel in the 1948 Arab–Israel War, Galilee witnessed a smaller scale Arab displacement than other parts of the country, most of those leaving being Muslim. Since the 1960s the area has been the target of many government settlement and development projects.

Zev Maghen

Galilee, Sea of

Freshwater lake located in northeast Israel.

Measuring 64 square miles (166 sq km) in area, the Sea of Galilee (also Lake Tiberias or Kinneret) is located 680 feet (207 m) below sea level and is formed by waters flowing down from the Jordan River. Deganya, the first Israeli kibbutz, is located on its shore. From the beginning of the British mandate in 1920, the Sea of Galilee was located within the borders of Palestine and, after 1948, the state of Israel. It acts as the principal freshwater source for Israel and supplies the NATIONAL WATER SYSTEM.

BIBLIOGRAPHY

SCHMORAK, M. *Atlas of Israel.* 1961.

Bryan Daves

Galili, Israel   [1911–1986]

Israeli general and politician.

Born in Russia, by 1914 he was growing up in Palestine; he became a leader in the Haganah and its elite wing, the PALMACH. Galili was a member of Israel's KNESSET from 1949 to 1977, first as a MAPAM representative, then as part of the Labor party. He was especially influential during the prime ministry of Golda Meir (1969–1974), when, as minister without portfolio, he helped formulate foreign and defense policy, as well as a domestic program along the lines of the ALLON PLAN.

BIBLIOGRAPHY

ROLEF, SUSAN H., ed. *Political Dictionary of the State of Israel.* New York, 1987.
SAFRAN, NADAV. *Israel: The Embattled Ally.* Cambridge, England, 1981.

Zachary Karabell

Gallei Zahal

Israel's army radio station, created in 1951 to entertain the troops and to bring information on army life to civilians.

The range and level of Gallei Zahal's programs expanded markedly following the ARAB–ISRAEL WAR of 1967. The nonmilitary programs are controlled by the Israel Broadcasting Authority. Many productions have been aimed at young people who are approaching National Service age in the Israel Defense Forces.

Ann Kahn

Gallipoli

Peninsula between the Dardanelles and the Aegean Sea on the European side of the Turkish Straits.

Gallipoli was the site of an unsuccessful WORLD WAR I Allied campaign (1915/16) aimed at defeating the OTTOMAN EMPIRE, opening up a second front against AUSTRIA–HUNGARY and Germany, and opening a supply route to Russia. Britain's First Lord of the Admiralty Winston Churchill proposed this plan, expecting Secretary of War Lord Kitchener to supply the necessary land troops, but Kitchener did not fully support Churchill's plan.

An Anglo–French force (mostly ANZAC [Australia and New Zealand Army Corps]) landed at Gallipoli in April 1915, after four unsuccessful naval attacks; they met a stubborn land defense by the Ottoman Turks. Although suffering enormous losses, the Allies—including Italy by August—nearly succeeded in a breakthrough. Lack of Russian cooperation, faulty intelligence, and skillful tactics on the part of the Ottomans and Germans, however, led to a stalemate, then to Allied withdrawal in January 1916. Churchill became the scapegoat and lost his position.

BIBLIOGRAPHY

MOOREHEAD, ALAN. *Gallipoli.* New York, 1956.

Sara Reguer

Gambetta, Léon   [1838–1882]

French statesman.

Gambetta was minister of war and of the interior in 1870/71 and a deputy in the French parliament from 1869 to 1882. He became premier in November 1881. At that time, the situation in Egypt was becoming critical. A group of army officers and assembly deputies led by Col. Ahmad Urabi were demanding reforms and insisting that the Anglo–French control over Egyptian finances be curtailed. TAWFIQ, the Egyptian khedive, was under intense pressure to concede to Urabi's demands. Perceiving this, Britain and France issued a communiqué on January 8, 1882, known as the Joint Note or the Gambetta Note. The note guaranteed Tawfiq any support he might require to stave off the threat posed by Urabi. Far from helping Tawfiq, the note outraged advocates of national sentiment in Egypt. It made Tawfiq appear a European stooge, and led to the downfall of the moderate ministry of Sharif Pasha and the appointment of Urabi as minister of war. Gambetta's ministry fell at the end of January 1882.

BIBLIOGRAPHY

ANDERSON, M. S. *The Eastern Question.* London, 1966.
Chambers Biographical Dictionary. 1990.

Zachary Karabell

Ganim, Halil

Ottoman opposition politician and newspaper publisher.

A Lebanese Maronite by birth, Halil Ganim served in the Ottoman parliament in 1877/78. When the parliament was closed, he took up exile in Paris, where his prominent opposition newsletter, *La Jeune Turquie,* soon gave its name to the emerging YOUNG TURK movement. In 1895, Ganim collaborated with Young Turk leader AHMET RIZA, also in Paris, in publishing the first major organ of the cause, *Meşveret.* In 1901, he published a book against despotism, *Les sultans ottomans* (The Ottoman Sultans). Ganim was one of a very few Arabs prominent in the Young Turk movement. He lived in Paris for the remainder of his life.

BIBLIOGRAPHY

HOURANI, ALBERT. *Arabic Thought in the Liberal Age 1798–1939.* New York, 1984.
LEWIS, BERNARD. *The Emergence of Modern Turkey.* New York, 1961.
SHAW, STANFORD J., and EZEL KURAL SHAW. *History of the Ottoman Empire and Modern Turkey.* Vol. 2. New York, 1977.

Elizabeth Thompson

GAP

See Southeastern Anatolia Project

Garang, John   [1945–]

Advocate for the rights of the peoples of southern Sudan.

Born into a DINKA family in the southern Sudan, Garang was educated at Catholic mission schools. At the age of twenty-five, he joined a local militia, which, two years later, was integrated into the regular Sudanese army as part of its Southern Command. A captain at the time, Garang was deputy director of military research in the Sudanese army by 1983 and was based in Khartoum. By that time, he had also acquired a B.A. in economics and a Ph.D. in agricultural economics in the United States.

In 1983, he was sent to the town of Bor to negotiate with rebellious southern soldiers. While there, he found himself inside their garrison when it was attacked by troops from the north who had been dispatched by an impatient president, Muhammad Ja'far Numeiri. This incident proved to be the turning point in his career. Determined to respond to the many complaints of the people in the south, in the same year he and a group of other officers and civilians founded the Sudan People's Liberation Movement (SPLM) and the Sudan People's Liberation Army (SPLA), and he became chairman of the first and commander of the second. According to Garang, he was responding to Numeiri's attempts to eliminate the local-government processes in southern Sudan that had been agreed to in Addis Ababa in 1972. Garang favored a federalist relationship between local governments and the government in Khartoum, and he also objected to Khartoum's decision to divide the previously united southern region along ethnic lines. He was most opposed, however, to the imposition in September 1983 of SHARI'A, or Islamic law, on the non-Muslim south. Garang wrote later that in founding the SPLM his aim was "to create a socialist system that affords democratic and human rights to all nationalities and guarantees freedom of religion, beliefs and outlooks." His movement was quickly categorized as being communist and secessionist, although he absolutely denied the validity of both labels.

In mobilizing and training his soldiers, Garang received support from a number of external sources, particularly (until 1985) from Libya, and much of the military training of his men was carried out in Ethiopia. Southern Sudan is landlocked, and Garang's power was very much subject to fluctuating regional and geopolitical alliances. When Numeiri was deposed (1985), he lost Libya's support, and later, with the fall of Mengistu Haile Mariam of Ethiopia (1991), he lost access to that country as a sanctuary and training ground. In the war against a less-than-efficient Sudanese army, the SPLA was never able to achieve superiority; it left the army in control of the larger towns while it operated mostly in the countryside.

Garang also found it difficult to attain political unity among his followers because of the diverse ethnic loyalties and the inevitable personal conflicts with his commanders. Intense debates as to whether or not to make secession the movement's goal also divided them. Garang's struggle reached a critical phase when Numeiri was overthrown (April 1985) and during the following transition period before he was replaced by Sadiq al-Mahdi. At a negotiating session (March 1986) in Ethiopia with all but two of Sudan's major political parties present, Garang agreed to a set of principles designed to pave the way for a national constitutional convention. Garang, however, was not able to make any headway on his major immediate demand that the Shari'a previously imposed by Numeiri be rescinded. The idea of holding a national constitutional convention survived for a few years, but Sadiq's government never fully responded to it. Instead, Sadiq and his followers reverted to Numeiri's tactics by cultivating tribal divisions and other differences among the peoples in the south—for example, by seeking to divide the NUER from the Dinka—and escalating the war.

In 1989, Sadiq was overthrown by a military government committed to the political ideals of the radical National Islamic Front and its leader, Hasan al-TURABI. The new government was even less willing than Sadiq's regime had been to remove the Shari'a laws. Still not seeking secession, Garang then tried to make southern Sudan a world political issue. In this effort, he was helped by U.S. Congressman Mickey Leland, who welcomed him to congressional hearings on Sudan in Washington, D.C. (July 1989), but the initiative was undermined when Leland was killed in a plane accident shortly afterward. In August 1991, Garang had to contend with the rebellion of three of his senior SPLA commanders. A period of uncertainty followed as the government in Khartoum courted the rebels through the provision of arms and food. Southern Sudan was in the international limelight at this time because of severe food shortages and famine, which to a great degree were the consequences of the ongoing civil war. International agencies were allowed to bring food to the area only after extended negotiations, which each of the warring sides tried to use to its advantage.

In the decade from 1983 to 1993, more than one million people in southern Sudan died from starvation and war-related causes. As the war entered its second decade, Garang still had failed to galvanize world opinion in favor of unifying Sudan, retaining substantial independence for southern Sudan. He also faced a government in Khartoum even more determined than ever to impose Islamic laws on the South.

BIBLIOGRAPHY

No biography of John Garang has yet been published. Some of his speeches, with commentaries by the editor, may be found in

GARANG, JOHN. *The Call for Democracy in the Sudan.* Ed. by Mansour Khalid. London, 1987.

Paul Martin

Gardanne Mission

French military mission to Persia, 1807–1808.

The Gardanne Mission's purpose was to train the Persian army along European lines. It consisted of seventy officers and sergeants, led by General Claude-Matthiew Gardanne. The mission was a result of the FINKENSTEIN TREATY of May 1807, in which Iran sought help from France against Russia—while France had visions of using Iran as a stepping stone to British India. The Treaty of Tilsit in July 1807 temporarily ended hostilities between France and Russia, so support of Persia against Russia was no longer a French priority. Persia then negotiated with Britain, agreed to dismiss Gardanne, and signed a preliminary treaty in March 1809 that provided British officers to train the Persian army.

BIBLIOGRAPHY

DANIEL, NORMAN. *Islam, Europe and Empire*. Edinburgh, 1966.

Daniel E. Spector

Gardez

Afghan town.

Gardez is a town of about 20,000 inhabitants, and the administrative center of Paktia province. The town was a stronghold of the Kabul government during the war of resistance (1978–1992), despite several attempts by the Mojahedin to capture it. Gardez is of strategic importance because it controls the route north over the Altamur pass to Kabul.

BIBLIOGRAPHY

ADAMEC, LUDWIG. *Historical Dictionary of Afghanistan*. 1991.

Grant Farr

Gaspirali, Ismail Bey   [1851–1914]

Turkish journalist, educator, and reformer.

Born in the Crimea into a noble family (the Russian form of his name was Gasprinskii), he was a reformer who introduced a new educational method (*usul-i cedid*). He also advocated a single shared identity for all Muslim Turkic peoples of Imperial Russia, hoping to unite them with the motto "unity in language, thought, and action." In 1883, he founded the newspaper *Tercüman*, which was influential throughout the Turkic world; it ceased publication in 1918. Gaspirali intended the language of this newspaper, based on Ottoman TURKISH, to serve as a common literary language for all Muslim Turkic speakers.

BIBLIOGRAPHY

KIRIMLI, SIRRI HAKAN. "National Movements and National Identity among the Crimean Tatars (1905–1916)." Ph.D. diss., University of Wisconsin, 1990.

Uli Schamiloglu

Gaza Strip

Region bordering Israel and Egypt on the Mediterranean Sea under Israeli military occupation since 1967.

The inhabitants of the Gaza Strip are almost all PALESTINIANS with a population estimated at 800,000 (1993). Some 65 percent of these are refugees, descendants of the 250,000 refugees who flooded into the territory in 1948 during the first ARAB–ISRAEL WAR. Few carry passports and everyone is stateless. Arabic is the primary language; Islam is the primary religion, but Arab Christians are also in residence. Eight UN-sponsored PALESTINIAN REFUGEE CAMPS are located in the Gaza Strip.

The boundaries of the Gaza Strip have not changed since 1948—and with only one-fifteenth the area of the WEST BANK, it has one of the highest population densities in the world. The Strip is almost rectangular, bordered by Israel on the north and east and by Egypt on the south. It occupied the southwest corner of Mandatory Palestine under British rule (1923–1948). It has no capital, but its largest cities are Gaza City, Khan Younis, and Rafah. It measures some 28 miles (45 km) by about 5 miles (8 km).

The northern third belongs to the red sands of the Philistian plain; the southern two thirds (south of the main watercourse, the Wadi Gaza) belong to the more fertile sandy loess of the northern NEGEV DESERT

Gaza Beach. (© Yto Barrada)

Palestinian policeman in April 1995, when Yasir Arafat returned to Gaza. (© Yto Barrada)

coast. It is hot and humid in the summer, cooler and humid in the winter, with limited rainfall.

Gaza's economy is small, underdeveloped, and weak, generating 50 percent of its national product from external sources. Under Israeli control, its economy became heavily dependent on wage labor in Israel, where over half of Gaza's labor force has been employed. Israeli military law seriously constrained local economic development. Natural resources, notably land and water, are very limited and diminishing, and no mineral resources exist. Agriculture has always played a large role in the local economy and citrus is the primary agricultural export. Much agricultural produce is used locally. Industry is traditional and rudimentary. Factories are very small and manufacture beverages, tobacco, textiles, clothing, wood products, and plastics.

History. In ancient times the area was inhabited by the Philistines; it is mentioned in the BIBLE as the place of Samson's death; it is the burial place of one of the great-grandfathers of the Prophet MUHAMMAD. The Gaza area was conquered by many peoples, including the Jews (Hebrews), Romans, and Arabs before it became part of the Ottoman Empire. After World War I, when the Ottoman Empire was dismembered, the Gaza region became part of the British mandate over Palestine. In 1947, the mandate disintegrated and resulted in a call for the partition of Palestine into an Arab and a Jewish state. In 1948, the State of Israel was established, which the Arab governments opposed, and war resulted. The State of Israel prevailed and in 1949 an armistice was signed that called for the military administration of the Gaza Strip by Egypt. During the Arab–Israel War of 1956, Israel controlled the Gaza Strip from November until March of 1957, when it reverted to Egypt. Since

the Arab–Israel War of 1967, Gaza has been under Israeli military rule. Israeli policy has been very harsh, particularly since the beginning of the Palestinian uprising (or INTIFADA), which started inside Gaza in 1987. In 1991, the Middle East peace process began with Israel, the Palestinians, and certain Arab states participating. In 1993, an agreement was reached between the Israeli government and the PALESTINE LIBERATION ORGANIZATION (PLO) to implement limited autonomy in the Gaza Strip and in the West Bank town of Jericho.

BIBLIOGRAPHY

BENVENISTI, MERON. *The West Bank and Gaza Atlas.* Jerusalem, 1988.
ROY, SARA. *The Gaza Strip Survey.* Boulder, Colo., 1986.

Sara M. Roy

Gaziantep

Province and city in southern Turkey; known in ancient times as Antep and Aintab.

Located north of Syria's border and east of Adana, the city lies on a tributary of the Euphrates river. Its population increased between 1950 and 1980 from almost 73,000 to about 374,290, making it then the sixth largest city in TURKEY. The province, home to almost 810,000 people in 1980, is rich in pistachios, olives, and tobacco; it has long been a center for animal husbandry and trade. The city is particularly known for its exports of textiles and pistachio nuts.

Gaziantep was the center of resistance to French occupation during the Turkish war of independence; it surrendered to France after a six-month siege in 1921, only to be returned to Turkey later that year.

BIBLIOGRAPHY

Chambers World Gazetteer. New York, 1988.
Yeni Türk Ansiklopedisi. Istanbul, 1985.

Elizabeth Thompson

GCC

See Gulf Cooperation Council

Geagea, Samir [1952–   ]

Lebanese politician and leader of the Lebanese Forces.

A Maronite from Bsharreh in northern Lebanon, Geagea studied medicine at the AMERICAN UNIVER-

SITY OF BEIRUT and the French Faculty of Medicine in Beirut. By the late 1970s, he had become a senior commander of the LEBANESE FORCES (LF) and committed to using force to restore Christian hegemony over Lebanon. When, in December 1985, LF leader Elie Hubeiqa signed the Tripartite Accord on behalf of the Christian community, Geagea denounced it as a surrender to Syria. In January 1986, as chairman of the executive committee of the LF, he challenged President Amin JUMAYYIL and the Phalangist leadership and consolidated his ties with Israel.

After Jumayyil stepped down, Geagea clashed with General Michel AOUN when the latter attempted to curb the militias. Tensions between them culminated in devastating fighting for control of East Beirut's Christian enclave in the first half of 1990. In April 1990, Geagea endorsed the TA'IF ACCORD, largely to neutralize Aoun. After the defeat of Aoun in October 1990 and the normalization of political and security conditions in the country, he became one of the most vocal critics of Syria's power in Lebanon.

By late 1993, Geagea had become a marginal figure in Lebanon's politics because of his past association with Israel, Syria's animosity toward him, and the de facto political neutralization of his militia. More fundamentally he was the target of deep popular resentment against the warlords. Even among Christians, he was largely blamed for the loss of lives and property in East Beirut and was tainted by his participation in the mass killing of Christian rivals, including Tony FRANJIYYA.

BIBLIOGRAPHY

The Lebanon Report. A monthly newsletter published since 1990 by the Lebanese Center for Policy Studies, Beirut.
PETRAN, TABITHA. *The Struggle over Lebanon.* New York, 1987.

Guilain P. Denoeux

Gecekondu

Quasi-legal homes put up by rural-urban migrants around cities in Turkey (Turkish, "put up at night").

In Turkish law, houses could be owned separately from the land they occupy. Walls and roof put up by squatters before a landowner apprehended them, gave them rights that could be overturned only by court order. After 1946, migrants began building such houses, usually on government land. They built overnight to escape police notice, thus presenting a legal fait accompli at dawn. In Turkey's new democracy, politicians avoided prosecuting the squatters for fear of losing votes. Neighborhoods, once established, pressured municipalities to provide water, sewers, electricity, and transportation.

Gecekondus integrated many rural people into urban life. By 1980, half of Ankara's people and a third of Istanbul's were gecekondu dwellers. İzmir, Adana, and Bursa also have extensive gecekondu areas. Attempts to divert migrant flows by building gecekondu-prevention housing in smaller cities or social housing in larger ones failed: The government could never mobilize resources comparable to those of five million gecekondu builders.

BIBLIOGRAPHY

TUMERTEKIN, EVOL. *Urbanization in Turkey.* Istanbul, 1973.

John R. Clark

Gemayel

See under Jumayyil

Genç Kalemler

A Turkish nationalist group and its journal.

Genç Kalemler was founded in 1910/11 in SALONIKA, bringing together a group of writers and poets under the leadership of famous nationalists Ömer SAYFETTIN and Ziya GÖKALP. Theirs was the first organized attempt at TURKISH LANGUAGE reform, born of reaction to the ornate linguistic excesses of the Servet-i Fünun group of the 1890s. They sought to bring written Turkish closer to its spoken form, without the Arabic and Persian grammar and vocabulary of the elite of the Ottoman Empire.

The group also sought to bring realism to what they felt was artificial Ottoman literature—by producing numerous critical essays in its journal and by publishing new stories and poems. Genç Kalemler's pursuit of simple direct language also had a political aim, because it was felt that to rescue the empire, a language understandable to the common people was needed. Genç Kalemler had close ties to the Turkish nationalist COMMITTEE OF UNION AND PROGRESS. The journal was published until the Turkish war of independence after World War I.

BIBLIOGRAPHY

ARAI, MASAMI. *Turkish Nationalism in the Young Turk Era.* New York, 1987.
MANTRAN, ROBERT, ed. *Histoire de l'Empire Ottoman.* Paris, 1989.

Elizabeth Thompson

General Federation of Iraqi Women

Iraqi feminist society.

The first attempt to establish the General Federation of Iraqi Women (al-Ittihad al-nisa'i al-Iraqi) occurred in 1945 as a result of decisions made by the Conference of the Federation of Arab Women in Cairo, whose main objectives were, among others, to promote the interests of Arab women and to coordinate their efforts with those of the international women's movement. The general federation, however, did not become a licensed body until 1954 under the leadership of Asia Tawfiq Wahbi. Prominent members who have led the organization and represented it at international conferences include Azza al-Istarabadi, Batoul Abd al-Ilah Hafiz, Samiha Amin Zaki, Hasiba Amin Khalis, Afifa al-Bustani, and Futuh al-Dubuni.

BIBLIOGRAPHY

DAWOOD, SABIHAH AL-SHAIKH. *Auwal al-tariq: ila al-nahdah al-nisawiyah fi al-Iraq* (The Beginning of the Road to the Rising of Women in Iraq). Baghdad, 1958.

Mamoon A. Zaki

General Federation of Peasants (GFP)

Syrian labor organization.

The General Federation of Peasants (GFP) was created by the BA'TH party in Syria in 1964 to mobilize popular support and establish control over rural affairs. Minister of Agrarian Reform Abd al-Karim al-JUNDI appointed delegates to the GFP, who were to be elected thereafter. At the fourth conference of the federation in 1977, there were 285 delegates, but making up the GFP in 1983 were 3,903 individual unions, with a combined membership of about 408,000. The GFP publishes the weekly newspaper *Nidal al-Fallahin* (Struggle of the Peasants).

BIBLIOGRAPHY

HINNEBUSCH, RAYMOND A. *Authoritarian Power and State Formation in Ba'thist Syria*. Boulder, Colo., 1990.

Charles U. Zenzie

General Labor Confederation of Lebanon

Overall alliance of labor unions and associations in Lebanon.

The role of the confederation was significant before the eruption of the Lebanese civil war of 1975, but the rise of militia activity undermined the effectiveness of civil leaders, especially those who headed nonsectarian groups. The labor leadership posed a challenge to sectarian leaders throughout the civil war and spoke for workers and other "common folk." In May 1992 strikes called by labor leaders toppled the cabinet of Umar Karami, who was held responsible for the dramatic decline of the workers' living standards. The Lebanese government then appointed a client of the government of Syria, Abdallah al-Amin, as minister of labor to intimidate labor leaders. The confederation is now headed by Ilyas Abu Rizq, a moderate Christian activist.

As'ad AbuKhalil

General People's Committees

Libya's ruling cabinet.

The General People's Committees were established in March 1978 in Libya when Muammar al-QADDAFI and the other members of the ruling Revolutionary Command Council formally renounced their government positions. Exercising executive powers, the General People's Committees have a function equivalent to ministerial cabinets.

Lisa Anderson

General People's Congress (GPC)

Ostensibly, Libya's governing body.

Formally the preeminent governing body of Libya, the General People's Congress (GPC) was formed after the March 1977 declaration of the era of the JAMAHIRIYA. Delegates are selected from among district-level basic people's congresses, people's committees, and professional associations. Charged with debating reports from government agencies, the GPC meets infrequently and serves primarily as a sounding board for the head of state, Muammar al-QADDAFI.

Lisa Anderson

General Tunisian Union of Students (UGTE)

Tunisian student union.

The Union Générale Tunisienne des Etudiants (UGTE) was Tunisia's major student group until the government banned it in early 1991 because of its association with the Islamist movement. Beginning in the 1980s, the Islamic Tendency Movement (Mouvement de Tendance Islamique; MTI) actively sought to take over the UGTE. It charged its University Bureau's Mokhtar Bedri with securing Islamist domination at the University of Tunis and provincial colleges through control of the UGTE.

The UGTE Islamist leadership was decimated by numerous arrests, trials, and imprisonments from 1991 to 1992. The government then infiltrated cadres of RCD (government party) candidates into leadership positions in the UGTE. As a result, the UGTE is more nonactivist and pro-government.

BIBLIOGRAPHY

DUNN, MICHAEL COLLINS. *Renaissance or Radicalism? Political Islam: The Case of Tunisia's al-Nahda.* Washington, D.C., 1992.

OUAJAH, LOTFI. "Etudiants: Les dessous du malaise." *Haqa'iq/Réalités,* no. 425 (26 November–3 December 1993): 12–13.

Larry A. Barrie

General Union of Palestine Doctors

Palestinian professional association.

Affiliated with the Palestine Liberation Organization (PLO), the General Union of Palestine Doctors has members in many Arab countries. In the 1980s, its representatives held five seats on the PALESTINE NATIONAL COUNCIL. Palestinian doctors have worked and volunteered in hospitals and clinics run by the Palestine RED CRESCENT SOCIETY, an affiliate of the PLO. (The Red Crescent Society performs functions in various countries of the Middle East similar to those of the Red Cross.) The union has also been referred to as the General Union of Palestine Doctors and Pharmacists and the General Union of Palestine Medical Professionals.

BIBLIOGRAPHY

BRAND, LAURIE. *Palestinians in the Arab World.* New York, 1988.

NASSAR, JAMAL R. *The Palestine Liberation Organization: From Armed Struggle to the Declaration of Independence.* New York, 1991.

RUBENBERG, CHERYL A. "The Civilian Infrastructure of the Palestine Liberation Organization." *Journal of Palestine Studies* 22 (Spring 1983): 54–78.

Elizabeth Thompson

General Union of Palestine Students

International student movement.

In 1959, Palestinian student organizations in Cairo, Alexandria, Asyut, Beirut, and Damascus united to form the General Union of Palestine Students. The union opened branches in several other Arab cities and after 1967 became a constituent of the PALESTINE LIBERATION ORGANIZATION (PLO), with seats on the PALESTINE NATIONAL COUNCIL. It has become one of the most influential of the PLO's mass organizations and is a major vehicle for politicizing and mobilizing young Palestinians.

BIBLIOGRAPHY

BRAND, LAURIE A. *Palestinians in the Arab World.* New York, 1988.

COBBAN, HELENA. *The Palestinian Liberation Organization.* New York, 1984.

NASSAR, JAMAL R. *The Palestine Liberation Organization: From Armed Struggle to the Declaration of Independence.* New York, 1991.

SAHLIYEH, EMILE. *In Search of Leadership.* Washington, D.C., 1988.

Elizabeth Thompson

General Union of Palestine Women

International women's organization.

The General Union of Palestine Women was founded in Jerusalem in 1965 by Palestinian women's organizations from around the Arab world. It has been headquartered since 1969 in Amman, Jordan, and is affiliated with the PALESTINE LIBERATION ORGANIZATION. The union has thousands of members attached to eleven branches. Its goals have been to improve Palestinian women's and family status through its more than ninety women's centers in refugee camps and to stress the duty of women to participate in the liberation movement. In 1976 the Lebanese branch built an orphanage for more than two hundred children from the Tal al-Za'tar refugee camp. Branches in Gaza and the West Bank, Egypt, and Kuwait have focused on education for poor children. The branch in Gaza and the West Bank has a program to aid Palestinian women in Israeli jails.

BIBLIOGRAPHY

BRAND, LAURIE A. *Palestinians in the Arab World.* New York, 1988.

COBBAN, HELENA. *The Palestinian Liberation Organization.* New York, 1984.

Nassar, Jamal R. *The Palestine Liberation Organization: From Armed Struggle to the Declaration of Independence.* New York, 1991.

Rubenberg, Cheryl A. "The Civilian Infrastructure of the Palestine Liberation Organization." *Journal of Palestine Studies* 22 (Spring 1983): 54–78.

Elizabeth Thompson

General Union of Palestine Workers

International labor movement.

The union was launched in 1963 by a group of Palestinian trade unionists in Cairo, who had fled from Jordan in 1957. The union is part of the Palestine Liberation Organization (PLO) and has branches in thirteen Arab countries and several non-Arab countries. In 1969 the union moved its headquarters to Damascus and switched its loyalty from the POPULAR FRONT FOR THE LIBERATION OF PALESTINE (PFLP) to the Fath faction of the PLO. The union's various branches have trained and supported large numbers of fighters (*fida'iyyin*) who fought in the 1973 Arab–Israel war and the LEBANESE CIVIL WAR that began in 1975. Branches also have provided poor relief and facilitated job contracts for refugees and migrant workers.

BIBLIOGRAPHY

Brand, Laurie A. *Palestinians in the Arab World.* New York, 1988.

Rubenberg, Cheryl A. "The Civilian Infrastructure of the Palestine Liberation Organization." *Journal of Palestine Studies* 22 (Spring 1983): 54–78.

Smith, Pamela Ann. *Palestine and the Palestinians, 1876–1983.* London, 1984.

Elizabeth Thompson

General Islamic Conference

See Islamic Congresses

Geneva Peace Conference

Conference called by the United Nations to conclude the Arab–Israel War of 1973.

The December 1973 conference was convened in Geneva, Switzerland, in accordance with United Nations Security Council resolution 338. Its purpose was to settle issues that led to or arose from the ARAB–ISRAEL WAR of 1973. Of the Arab states, Egypt and Jordan participated, but Syria did not. Palestinian representatives were not invited to the opening session. After the opening speeches and ceremony, the conference adjourned and never reconvened. Israel had been reluctant to participate in multiparty conferences where pressures might be exerted for withdrawal from occupied territories and other steps it opposes. DISENGAGEMENT AGREEMENTS were signed in 1974 ending the war between Israel and Egypt and between Israel and Syria.

BIBLIOGRAPHY

Rolef, S. H., ed. *Political Dictionary of the State of Israel.* New York, 1987.

Benjamin Joseph

Gennage, Elias   [1922–   ]

Lebanese economist and professor.

Born in Beirut and educated at St. Joseph University there, Gennage became professor of law and economics at the French law faculty of Beirut. He is the author of several books in French specializing in development economy, including *Economic Growth and Structure in the Middle East* (1958), *Development Economy* (1962), *Economic Planning and Development* (1963), and *Institutions and Development* (1966).

BIBLIOGRAPHY

Who's Who in Lebanon, 1980–1981. Beirut, 1980.

Mark Mechler

Geography

The topography and geography of the Middle East are closely related to the geology and climate of the region.

A zone of mountainous terrain in the north in combination with higher latitudes, lower temperatures, and increased precipitation gives a distinctive character to Turkey, Iran, and parts of the Levantine (eastern Mediterranean) coast. To the south, in North Africa and the Arabian Peninsula, tilted fault-block mountains and volcanoes provide intermittent physical relief to an area largely consisting of plateaus and plains. Unremitting aridity and high temperatures typify the desert that dominates this southern part of the region.

The geology of the Middle East is determined by the movement of continental plates in a northwesterly direction. This movement, in turn, deforms masses of sedimentary strata deposited in Paleozoic times in the ancient Tethyan Sea, which once separated Eurasia and Africa. The African plate is the largest and consists of ancient igneous materials overlain, in part, by a relatively thin layer of more recent sedimentary rocks. With the exception of the folded strata that make up the Atlas and Anti-Atlas mountains in the west of the MAGHRIB (North Africa), the Ahaggar and Tibesti mountains of Algeria and Libya, as well as the highlands of the Ethiopian plateau, are volcanic in nature. The Arabian plate to the east consists of tilted Mesozoic sedimentary strata dipping beneath the Persian/Arabian GULF: These strata overlie pre-Cambrian igneous basement rock exposed by erosion in the Asir mountains along the western shores of the peninsula. The Red Sea, which the uptilted edge of the Asir overlooks, is a continuation of the East African rift valley system and is formed by the moving apart of the African and Arabian blocks. This rift system continues north through the Gulf of Aqaba and forms the valley of the Dead Sea and the Jordan river. It eventually disappears in the downfolded strata of the Biqaʻ (Bekaa) valley of Lebanon.

The heavily folded Zagros mountains bordering the Gulf on its eastern side result from the collision and subduction of the Arabian plate under the Iranian plate. The Persian/Arabian Gulf, which is an inlet of the Indian Ocean along the axis of the subduction zone, has accumulated huge quantities of sediments from the TIGRIS AND EUPHRATES RIVERS, the Karun river, and numerous intermittent streams draining the lands on either side. Within these Tertiary sedimentary strata are found the largest PETROLEUM fields in the world, with deposits in Saudi Arabia, Kuwait, Iran, Iraq, the United Arab Emirates, Qatar, and Oman in descending order of importance. To the northwest, the Turkish plate is sliding westward along a transform fault and colliding with the Aegean plate. These areas of movement create major fault zones subject to severe earthquakes. In Turkey, the Erzincan earthquake of 1992 was typical. Faulting and recent volcanism terminate the northward extension of the rich petroleum fields of the Gulf beyond a few poor deposits near Batman, Turkey.

The northern part of the Middle East is a mountainous extension of the Alpine orogeny. The Pontic mountains paralleling Turkey's Black Sea coast merge with the eastern highlands notable for volcanic Mount Ararat of biblical fame. The Taurus mountains along Turkey's south shore extend eastward as the Anti-Taurus mountains, joining the Zagros mountains running southeast between Iran and Iraq. Another extension forms the Elburz mountains

bordering the Caspian Sea in Iran. Mount Damavand (18,934 ft [5775 m]), the highest peak in the Middle East and North Africa, is part of this range. Still farther east, the Kopet mountains merge with those in Afghanistan and the Hindu Kush.

Great rivers have played their part in the history and development of the Middle East. The White Nile, which rises in equatorial Africa, is joined at Khartoum in Sudan by the Blue Nile, flowing from the highlands of Ethiopia. No precipitation sufficient for human survival occurs from that juncture north to the Mediterranean Sea, and all life in Egypt depends on the use of the combined waters of the two Niles. The Euphrates river and its companion the Tigris both rise in Turkey and join in southern Iraq to form the SHATT AL-ARAB, which empties into the Persian/Arabian Gulf. The area between the two streams, ancient Mesopotamia, was the site of the earliest civilization, Sumer (3500 B.C.E.), and other ancient civilizations based on irrigation farming.

The Mediterranean Sea also has influenced many of the cultural and geographical characteristics of the Middle East. It has served as a major link between Europe, Africa, and southwest Asia since ancient times. The Turkish Straits, composed from north to south of the Bosporus, the Sea of Marmara, and the Dardanelles, are an important waterway joining the Black Sea to the Aegean Sea and the Mediterranean. Bronze Age ships plied these straits and sailed along the coast of Turkey as well as among the Aegean Islands. Early Phoenician traders established sea routes leading to the Straits of Gibraltar and beyond. Ancient Greek ships traveled through the Bosporus to bring grain from the shores of the Black Sea, and Roman triremes linked Italy and Africa. During the Middle Ages, some Arab navigational skills were conveyed to Europeans as Islam was spread. In the nineteenth century, the Mediterranean route was enhanced when the French and Egyptians completed the SUEZ CANAL, joining the Mediterranean Sea to the Red Sea and thus reducing the trip from Europe to India (originally by way of the Cape of Good Hope) by thousands of miles.

The Middle East is composed of four environments, expressed by climate, vegetation, and traditional lifestyle. Well-watered humid and subhumid lands border the Black Sea in Turkey and extend along the Caspian shore of Iran. In these well-populated places, maize (corn), tea, hazelnuts, and rice are important crops.

Mountainous terrain, with remnant forests of pine, cedar, and juniper, rims the Anatolian plateau of Turkey and extends southward into coastal Syria and Lebanon. Similar but drier environments are found in the Zagros and Elburz mountains of Iran. These areas once supported dense growths of mature trees, but with the exception of more remote places in the Taurus mountains, the logger's ax and the charcoal burner's ovens have depleted the forests while nomads' goats have prevented regrowth through overgrazing. The result is either disturbed and impoverished woodlands (French *maquis*) or barren and rocky ground supporting low herbaceous shrubs (French *garrigue*).

The interior plateau of Turkey, the foothills of the Anti-Taurus and Zagros mountains, and the northern portions of Jordan and Israel are semiarid, with grazing or grain production depending on the amount of each year's precipitation. The variance of rainfall on the drier margins of these areas makes permanent rain-fed agriculture difficult. As a result, ancient peoples developed pastoral NOMADISM as a lifestyle that met this challenge. Herds and flocks were moved seasonally to new pastures to avoid overgrazing of sparse vegetation as well as to seek out water sources. Once an important means of livelihood, nomadism has largely been abandoned.

The semiarid steppes merge gradually into true deserts, which dominate southern Israel, Jordan, and Iraq as well as the Arabian peninsula and North Africa west to the Atlas mountains. Saharan conditions extend to the Mediterranean shore of North Africa from Gaza to Sfax in Tunisia, the only exception being a small outlier of Mediterranean climate on the Jabal al-Akhdar (Green Mountain) of Libya. Under desert conditions, agriculture is possible only in scattered oases and along the banks of rivers like the Euphrates in Iraq and the Nile in Egypt.

The narrow rim of Mediterranean climate, which extends north from Gaza through Israel, along the coasts of Lebanon, Syria, and Turkey, is the fourth environment. This same climate is also found from Tunis west to the Atlantic shores of Morocco. The Mediterranean environment is typified by winter rains and hot dry summers, which allow for the production of irrigated vegetables and citrus fruits, as well as various winter grains.

BIBLIOGRAPHY

BEAUMONT, PETER, GERALD H. BLAKE, and J. MALCOLM WAGSTAFF. *The Middle East: A Geographical Study,* 2nd ed. New York, 1988.

BLAKE, GERALD, JOHN DEWDNEY, and JONATHAN MITCHELL. *The Cambridge Atlas of the Middle East and North Africa.* Cambridge, U.K., and New York, 1987.

HELD, COLBERT C. *Middle East Patterns: Peoples, Places, and Politics.* Boulder, Colo., 1989.

LONGRIGG, STEPHEN H. *The Middle East: A Social Geography.* Chicago, 1963. Reprint, New York, 1970.

John F. Kolars

Germany and the Middle East

German involvement in the Middle East developed slowly in the nineteenth century; in the twentieth century, economic and military involvement were at times extensive.

Brief contacts between Prussia and the OTTOMAN EMPIRE occurred before the 1880s. In 1760 Frederick the Great sought an alliance with the Ottomans during the Seven Years' War; and in the 1830s Helmuth von Moltke, later chief of the Prussian General Staff, served as adviser to the Ottoman military in Constantinople (now ISTANBUL).

After 1870, the new Germany was not concerned with the EASTERN QUESTION. BISMARCK, acting as the "honest broker" at the Berlin Congress in 1878, wished to avoid conflict with Austria, Hungary, Britain, and Russia, countries that already had imperialist stakes in the area. German intellectual interest in Iranian culture, language, and poetry had led to a treaty of friendship and commerce between Prussia and Persia (Iran) that was renewed in 1873; the relationship was cautious, however, because Bismarck understood that the area was under the domination of Russia and Britain. He agreed to open a German legation at Tehran in 1885 but would not meet with Naser al-Din Shah when the Iranian ruler visited Berlin in 1889. Similarly, in 1882 Bismarck reluctantly agreed to send military officers to the SUBLIME PORTE after ABDÜLHAMIT II decided to replace France's military advisers with military personnel from Germany.

In this case, Germany's military mission inaugurated a more active political and economic policy toward Turkey that was advocated by Kaiser Wilhelm II, who ascended the throne in 1888 and replaced Bismarck in 1890. Germany's "drive to the East" (*Drang nach Osten*) was the means by which it would achieve imperialist parity with France and Britain through cultural and economic penetration of the declining Ottoman Empire. Advocated by Baron Hatzfeld, Germany's ambassador to Turkey from 1879 to 1881, the policy took into account the possibilities for Germany that resulted from the vacuum created by Britain's loss of prestige in the area after they assumed control of Cyprus (1878), occupied Egypt (1882), and became involved in Ottoman affairs because of the Ottoman public debt. Wilhelm II's visit to the Middle East in 1898, during which he advocated friendship with Islamic peoples, solidified ties between Germany and Abdülhamit II (called by some the Bloody Sultan because of his treatment of the Armenians). Acquiescence to Ottoman sensibilities resulted in lack of official support by Germany for ZIONISM, in spite of an initial favorable reaction to discussions with Theodor HERZL, and for the German TEMPLERS, who had settled in Palestine beginning in the 1860s.

From 1885, Germany's military mission, now under the command of Kolmar Freiherr von der GOLTZ, was responsible for instituting a network of military preparatory schools and reorganizing the Ottoman officer corps on the Prussian model. German advisers worked with Ottoman troops throughout the crises that beset the Sublime Porte before World War I. By that time, despite Germany's diplomatic failures in the Moroccan crises (1905–1906, 1911) and Ottoman defeats in the BALKAN WARS (1912–1913), German officers were teaching and working in Turkey, and Turkish officers were sent to Berlin for advanced training.

Germany's ambassadors to Turkey, von Bieberstein (1897–1912) and Hans von Wangenheim (1912–1915), worked assiduously to open markets for their nation's products. Concessions were granted to a German bank (Deutsche Bank) and an arms merchant (Mauser) to build the BERLIN–BAGHDAD RAILWAY and the HIJAZ RAILROAD; and in 1906 the Hamburg Amerika steamship line sailed the Gulf in competition with ships from Britain. By 1914, Germany's share in the Ottoman public debt reached 22 percent (it had been 4.7 percent in 1888), and it had a 67.5 percent share in Ottoman railway investment. The Deutsche Bank played a major role in the Turkish economy, as did the Deutsche Palästina Bank in Palestine.

Despite Britain's presence in Turkey, Germany's influence, especially in the army, increased throughout the YOUNG TURK period. Disunity in the approach of the Committee of Union and Progress to foreign policy led some to seek different allies as Europe headed toward war. The negotiations of ENVER PAŞA and Mehmet TALAT with Germany resulted in a secret alliance on 1 August 1914. The Ottoman Empire entered World War I in November 1914.

Once the lines of communication between Germany and Turkey were secure, hundreds of German military officers were transferred to Turkey, some in command of Turkish troops, but not as decision makers regarding policy and strategy. As head of the military mission since 1913, General Otto LIMAN VON SANDERS advised the Turks to invade the Ukraine from Odessa; Enver, however, insisted upon the illfated Caucasus campaign. Liman von Sanders commanded the defense of GALLIPOLI in 1915 and intervened successfully in the Armenian deportations at İzmir. Lt. Col. (later Maj. Gen.) Friedrich Kress von Kressenstein, a restraining influence on Cemal Paşa, served in Palestine. Field Marshal Kolmar Freiherr von der Goltz was called back to defend Baghdad in 1915; Lt. Gen. Hans von Seeckt (chief of the Turkish General Staff in 1917), General Erich von Falkenhayn, and Franz von PAPEN (who was ambassador to Turkey during World War II), also fought with the Turkish army.

German Middle East academic specialists were utilized in the war effort. Influenced by predecessors who had been engaged in philological and archaeological research in the Middle East since the latter part of the nineteenth century, some claimed German–Turkish racial affinities. Orientalist Max von Oppenheim directed an Information Service for the East that advocated fomenting Islamic uprisings in Persia, Afghanistan, and Egypt in order to dislodge the British.

In Iran, Germany had no coordinated policy, and as Russia's army moved toward Tehran in 1915, only Wilhelm Wassmuss fought against the British in the south. Germany's competition with Britain in support of Zionist aspirations in order to gain Jewish support became inactive after the United States entered the war.

The defeat of Germany in 1918 and the provisions of the Treaty of Versailles altered Germany's approach to the Middle East. From the Weimar Republic through the early 1930s, official German policy was inherently cautious, more concerned with revising the Treaty of Versailles and not alienating Britain than with taking an active role abroad. Although sympathetic to Zionism, once Germany became a member of the League of Nations (1926), it supported Britain's policy in Palestine and did not take a position on local Arab–Zionist issues. The low-key diplomatic approach, however, did not lessen Germany's economic interest in Turkey, Egypt, and Iran; the latter, due to Reza Shah PAHLAVI's pro-German sympathies, was supplied by German companies with arms, machinery, and regular air service through the 1920s.

Germany's official policy toward the Middle East remained inconsistent through the Third Reich because it was predicated upon ideological, diplomatic, and economic factors that contradicted one another. The Nazi doctrine of racial purity and the search for markets in the Middle East lent themselves to support of the Zionist movement through the HAAVARAH (transfer) agreements as useful tools to rid Germany of Jews. When, after 1937, it was understood that Jewish sovereignty was possible and that a large population of Jews (a circumstance noted after the war in eastern Europe began) might be a base for activity against Germany, Hitler opposed Jewish immigration to Palestine.

Also opposed to Jewish Palestinian immigration were German nationals, including archaeologists, scholars, members of the Palestine Templers, and diplomatic personnel who worked in the area. Both German nationalists looking back to imperial glory and Nazis became disseminators of German propaganda, finding allies in some pan-Arab groups and the military in Egypt, Syria, and Iraq. Max von Oppenheim and German Ambassador to Iraq Fritz GROBBA advocated financial and military support for local anti-British pan-Arab movements as early as 1937. Meetings between pan-Arab nationalists such as Shakib ARSLAN, Hajj Muhammad Amin al-HUSAYNI, and Aziz Ali al-MISRI and German diplomatic officials took place, resulting in a declaration of support in December 1940 but no real aid.

Officially, Germany remained uninvolved in the Middle East, initially leaving the area to Britain. After 1939 and the outbreak of World War II, Germany left the area to Italy, which sought hegemony in North Africa and in the eastern Mediterranean. Italy's losses to the Allies in Greece and in Libya in 1941 sparked a belated interest by Germany, which had planned to turn to the Middle East only after anticipated successes in Russia (Operation Barbarossa).

Last-minute arms deliveries to the pro-Axis Rashid Ali al-KAYLANI government did not prevent Britain's victories in Iraq in June 1941 and in Vichy-ruled Syria in July. Fear that Iran was a potential fifth column because of its economic dependence on Germany, because of the large numbers of German nationals working there, and because it offered a haven for those fleeing the British in Iraq, resulted in Reza Shah's abdication and control of the country by Russia and Britain. A planned pro-Axis FREE OFFICERS' revolt involving Aziz Ali al-Misri and Anwar al-SADAT, among others, in collusion with Abwehr agents infiltrated into Cairo, failed to coordinate with Erwin ROMMEL's advance toward Egypt in the summer of 1942. Berlin provided sanctuary for some pro-Axis Arabs, among them the Jerusalem mufti, who left the Middle East during the war and worked for the German propaganda machine in return for Germany's promise to support Arab independence. After the war, a number of Nazis immigrated to the Arab world.

Two Germanys emerged from the war. East Germany, the German Democratic Republic (GDR), united with West Germany, the Federal Republic of Germany, in 1991. Having followed the policy of the Soviet Union, it never established diplomatic relations with Israel.

From the early 1950s, the Cold War and political obligations to the United States dominated German foreign policy. While blocking international, especially Third World, recognition of the GDR, the Federal Republic strove to balance its economic interests in the Arab world with a commitment to

Israel and the Jewish people forged in reaction to Germany's Nazi past and the Holocaust. Restitution and reparations agreements were signed in 1952, clandestine arms deals were negotiated throughout the 1960s, and diplomatic relations were established in 1965. All Arab states except Morocco, Tunisia, and Libya severed diplomatic ties but had restored them by 1974.

Germany's economic ties in the Gulf grew dramatically in the 1970s through the export of manufactured goods, the recycling of petrodollars through German banks, and the import of almost 50 percent of its oil needs from the region. As the price of oil fell in the 1980s, so did German dependence on Gulf markets. Germany's share in the arms market during the IRAN–IRAQ WAR represented only 1 percent of the total market (France's participation amounted to some 15 percent). German companies' significant but illegal involvement in technology transfers contributed to the development of weapons of mass destruction in Libya and Iraq.

West Germany has expressed support for the Palestine Arabs' right to self-determination and PALESTINE LIBERATION ORGANIZATION participation in negotiations. In 1986 Germany did not join the United States in action against Libya and did not fully support Britain's call for strong reprisals against Libya's and Syria's involvement in terrorism. Unlike the other Western states, Germany did not send troops to the Gulf in 1990–1991. Instead, it contributed minesweepers, pledged some $5.5 billion (which included surplus matériel from East Germany's army), and deployed Patriot missiles to Israel.

[See also: Banks, Turkey; Banks, Palestine; West German Reparations Agreement]

BIBLIOGRAPHY

CHUBIN, SHAHRAM. *Germany and the Middle East: Patterns and Prospects.* New York, 1992.

GROBBA, FRITZ. *Männer und Machte im Orient.* Göttingen, 1967.

HIRSZOWICZ, LUKASZ. *The Third Reich and the Arab East.* London, 1966.

McGARITY, JAMES M. "Foreign Influence on the Ottoman Turkish Army, 1880–1918." Ph.D. diss., American University, 1968.

NICOSIA, FRANCIS R. *The Third Reich and the Palestine Question.* Austin, Tex., 1985.

SIMON, REEVA S. *Iraq Between the Two World Wars.* New York, 1986.

TRUMPENER, ULRICH. *Germany and the Ottoman Empire, 1914–1918.* Princeton, N.J., 1968.

WALLACH, YEHUDA L., ed. *Germany and the Middle East, 1835–1939.* Tel Aviv, 1975.

Reeva S. Simon

Gezira Scheme

A Sudanese agricultural project established by the British.

The Gezira Scheme, located in the plains between the Blue Nile and White Nile of the central Sudan, was the first large-scale irrigated agricultural project established by the British government under the Anglo–Egyptian condominium. When it opened in 1926, it covered 300,000 feddans, of which a third grew cotton. In the 1950s, Sudanese managers replaced the British officials, and the Gezira Board invested a greater share of the profits for social development projects among the tenants. Later extensions quadrupled the area of the scheme, but costs escalated, cotton prices dropped in the world markets, and the tenants and Gezira Board became increasingly indebted. International loans have helped, but they have also increased the country's overall debt burden.

BIBLIOGRAPHY

BARNETT, TONY. *The Gezira Scheme: An Illusion of Development*. London, 1977.

Ann M. Lesch

Gezira Sporting Club

Country club in Cairo.

Long a symbol of British imperialism and insularity in Egypt, the Gezira, as it is usually called, was founded in 1882 and originally limited its membership to high-ranking British civil servants in the Egyptian government and officers of the army of occupation. Between the two world wars, the club's rosters also listed the names of titled European aristocrats wintering in Cairo, members of the diplomatic corps, prominent Levantine Jews and Christians, and Egyptian Muslims and Copts, many of whom were close to the palace. The flavor of the club during its British heyday has been admirably transmitted in memoirs written by former foreign residents of the city, in travel literature, and in such works of fiction as Olivia Manning's *Levant Trilogy*, which is set in Egypt's capital.

The exclusive and exclusionary character of the club was maintained until after World War II, when the tide of nationalism and a rising indigenous bourgeoisie forced its Egyptianization in January 1952. The ethos and structure of the club were further altered during the anti-Western years of the Nasser regime. In the early 1960s, the Gezira was both figuratively and literally truncated when the government, in a tactic calculated as a humiliation, forced it to permanently yield half of its grounds to a politicized athletic institution established to promote sports among the masses called the Ahli, or National Sports Club. Insult was added to injury when the Sadat regime built a suspended highway over the remaining nine-hole golf course and six-furlong racetrack to commemorate its performance in the October War.

Despite its contraction and urbanization, the Gezira still offers most of the sports and games practiced by its founders: golf, squash, bowls, croquet, riding, and even cricket. The last is played almost exclusively by Indian and Pakistani residents of Cairo. Horse racing, one of the club's original raisons d'être, takes place during the winter season. However, polo, which led to the founding of the Gezira as a gift from Egypt's viceroy to the officers of the British army of occupation, is no longer played for lack of grounds, players, and schooled ponies.

With the passing of Nasserism, the Gezira regained a small measure of its colonial grandeur, catering mostly to nouveau-riche Egyptians and a few foreign technocrats.

BIBLIOGRAPHY

GRAFFTEY-SMITH, LAWRENCE. *Bright Levant*. London, 1970.
OPPENHEIM, JEAN-MARC R. "Twilight of a Colonial Ethos: The Alexandria Sporting Club, 1890–1956." Ph.D. diss., Columbia University, 1990.

Jean-Marc R. Oppenheim

Ghab, al-

In Syria, the largest plain of a large trough which also includes the low plains of al-Asharina, al-Ruj, and al-Amq.

Al-Ghab is located between the mountains Jabal al-Ansariyya (al-Alawiyyin) in the west and Jabal al-Zawiya in the east. Its length from south to north is about 56 miles (90 km), its width between 5 and 7.5 miles (8 to 12 km), and its elevation above sea level is between 558 and 656 feet (170 and 200 m). It slightly slopes towards the north like the ORONTES RIVER that traverses it to the northeast of Hama. Its yearly rainfall averages 19.5 to 27 inches (500 to 700 mm), but it receives other sources of water, notably from the Orontes river, which is rejected back into it by the basaltic bedrock of Qarqar in the north. Before 1954, al-Ghab was intersected by swampland, infested by malaria, and covered by reeds used for catching its celebrated catfish.

Within two decades after 1954, the landscape of al-Ghab changed dramatically as a result of the drainage of its swamps, the building of dams, such as the ones at al-Rastan, Maharda, and notably al-ASHARINA, to regulate its irrigation, and the creation by the Syrian government of a number of projects in it. Of its total area of 136,000 acres (55,000 ha), 42,000 acres (17,000 ha) are irrigated by river flooding and dam water, 74,000 acres (30,000 ha) depend on rainfall, and the remaining parts are turned into farms. In 1969, land in al-Ghab was distributed by the government to 11,000 beneficiaries according to the decrees of agricultural reform. To encourage the cultivation of land, fifty-two cooperatives were established there. Other projects include a cattle farm, fisheries, and a sugar factory at the village of Salhab.

BIBLIOGRAPHY

MÉTRAL, FRANÇOISE. "Le monde rural Syrien à l'ère des reformes," In *La Syrie d'aujourd'hui,* ed. by André Raymond. Paris, 1980.
Al-Mu'jam al-Jughrafi li'l-qutr al-Arabi al-Suri (The Geographical Dictionary of Syria). Vol. 1. Damascus, 1990.

Abdul-Karim Rafeq

Ghali, Butros   [1846–1910]

Egyptian diplomat and cabinet minister.

Born in a village near Beni-Suef in Egypt, Butros Ghali went to the reformist Coptic school at Harat al-Saqqayin and the princes' school of Mustafa Fadil. He later studied at the School of Languages, learning Arabic, French, English, Turkish, and Persian, but never earned a *license* or any other degree. He became a clerk for the Alexandria Chamber of Commerce and in 1873 was appointed by the sharif to the head clerkship of the justice ministry. At this time he also helped to organize the Coptic (Lay) Council. When the MIXED COURTS were being established, Ghali helped the justice minister write an Arabic translation of their (mainly French) law code, even though he lacked any legal training.

His work brought him to the attention of Prime Minister Boghos Nubar Pasha, who made him Egypt's representative to the Caisse de la Dette Publique, thus mediating frequently between the Egyptian government and its European creditors. Named deputy justice minister in 1879, he held various responsible posts during the Urabi revolution. Afterward, he mediated between Khedive TAWFIQ and the nationalists, saving many from execution.

Ghali received his first ministerial appointment in 1893 when Khedive ABBAS HILMI II challenged the British occupation by appointing his own cabinet under Husayn Fakhri (without consulting Lord Cromer). He remained finance minister under the compromise cabinet of Mustafa al-Riyad. He served as foreign minister from 1894 to 1910 and continued to mediate between power centers, signing the 1899 Sudan Convention that set up the Anglo–Egyptian CONDOMINIUM AGREEMENT. He represented the cabinet on the bench at the 1906 trial in the DINSHAWAY INCIDENT, concurring in the death sentences on four of the accused peasants and angering Egypt's nationalists.

Khedive Abbas and Sir Eldon Gorst concurred in naming him prime minister in 1908, despite misgivings about having a Copt as the head of Egypt's government. He further angered the nationalists by reviving the 1881 press law and publicly advocating the extension of the Suez Canal Company's concession, policies that he reportedly opposed privately. His assassination by Ibrahim Nasif al-Wardani, a nationalist, in February 1910, set off a wave of Coptic–Muslim confrontations and led to a more repressive government policy against the nationalists.

BIBLIOGRAPHY

Coptic Encyclopedia.
GHALI, IBRAHIM AMIN. *L'Egypte nationaliste et liberale.* La Haye, France, 1969.
HAYKAL, MUHAMMAD HUSAYN. *Tarajim misriyya wa gharbiyya.* Cairo, 1928.
SEIKALY, SAMIR. "Coptic Communal Reform (1860–1914)." *Middle Eastern Studies* 6 (1970): 4.
———. "Prime Minister and Assassin: Butrus Ghali and Wardani." *Middle Eastern Studies* 13 (1977): 1.
AL-ZIRIKLI, KHAYR AL-DIN. *Al-A'lam,* 4th ed.

Arthur Goldschmidt, Jr.

Ghallab, Abd al-Karim   [1919–   ]

Moroccan novelist, short story writer, and journalist.

Ghallab was born in Fez. He studied at the mosque college of al-Qarawiyyin in Fez, then obtained his B.A. in Arabic literature from Cairo university. He is editor in chief and director of the daily *Al-Alam.*

Ghallab is a prolific writer whose publications cover a wide range of topics and interests, some purely literary and others dealing with political and cultural issues. His writings seek to promote nationalist feelings and a deep attachment to Arabic-Islamic culture, with the goal of counteracting the impact of French education that was particularly threatening to Moroccans during the years of French colonialism.

Some of Ghallab's short stories in the collection *Wa Akhrajaha min al-Janna* (1977; He Led Her out of Paradise) criticize the tendency of the upper middle class to express itself in French. Similar concerns are expressed in his novel *Sabahun wa Yazhafu al-Layl* (1984; Morning, then the Night Creeps in). Ghallab's fiction works illustrate and defend his beliefs and values. An active nationalist, he was often at odds with the French colonial power and was imprisoned, an experience that he relates in his novel *Sab'a Abwab* (1965; Seven Gates). Some of his other fiction works, such as *Dafanna al-Madi* (1966; We Buried the Past), reveal his patriotic feelings. Ghallab fervently preaches attachment to the land and its safeguard by Moroccan farmers, as illustrated in his collection of short stories *Al-Ard Habibati* (1971; The Land, My Beloved), his novel *Al-Mu'allim Ali* (1971; Master Ali), and his essay *Fi al-Islah al-Qarawi* (1961; Of Rural Reform).

Ghallab's nationalist positions date back to his student years in Egypt, where he agitated for the independence of the three Maghrib countries, Algeria, Tunisia, and Morocco. Back in Morocco, he joined the ISTIQLAL party and became deeply involved in politics. He was appointed a minister plenipotentiary for the Middle East (1956–1959) and a minister in the government (1983–1985). His writings reflect his political views, ranging from his preoccupation with political governance to Arab unity: *Hadha Huwa al-Dustur* (1962; This Is the Constitution), *At-Tatawwur al-Dusturi wa al-Niyabi bi al-Maghrib min sanat 1908 ila sanat 1978* (1988; The Constitutional and the Legal Development in the Maghrib from 1908 to 1978, 2 vols.), *Ma'rakatuna al-Arabiyya fi Muwajahat al-Isti'mar wa al-Sahyuniyya* (coauthor, 1967; Our Arab Battle with Colonialism and Zionism), *Nabadat Fikr* (1961; The Beat of a Thinking Mind), *Al-Thaqafa wa al-Fikr fi Muwajahat al-Tahaddi* (1976; Culture and Thought in the Face of Challenge), and *Risalat Fikrin* (1968; The Message of a Thinking Mind).

Religious feelings and a pious way of life are also of concern to Ghallab; they are implicit in his fiction and explicitly expressed in his book *Sira al-Madhhab wa al-Aqida fi al-Qur'an* (1973; The Struggle of Ideology and Faith in the Qur'an.)

[*See also:* Literature, Arabic, North African]

BIBLIOGRAPHY

BAMIA, AIDA A. "Ghallab, 'Abd al-Karim." In *Encyclopedia of World Literature in the Twentieth Century,* vol. 5. New York, 1993.

TOUIMI, MUHAMMED B., ABDELKEBIR KHATIBI, and MUHAMMED KABLY. *Ecrivains marocains, du protectorat à 1965. Anthologie.* Paris, 1974.

Aida A. Bamia

Ghanem, Iskander   [1913–   ]

Lebanese officer and commander in chief of the army.

Ghanem's education at the College of the Christian Brothers of Beirut and the military academy of Homs, in Syria, prepared him for military service. He served in the Lebanese army from 1936 to 1966, rising from lieutenant to colonel. In 1966/67 Ghanem was the embassy military attaché in Washington, D.C. He retired in 1969 but was recalled to the army as commander in chief from 1971 to 1975.

BIBLIOGRAPHY

Who's Who in Lebanon, 1980–1981. Beirut, 1980.

Mark Mechler

Ghanim, al-

Merchant family in Kuwait.

The al-Ghanim family traces its roots in Kuwait to the eighteenth century. Together with the Al Sabah, the Al Saqr, and the al-Qatami, the al-Ghanim were among the original Anazi settlers. The family made money first in shipping and trade, but a disaster at sea in 1925 forced them into other occupations. Ahmad al-Ghanim became an agent of the Anglo-Persian Oil Company (APOC) during its negotiations for the Kuwait oil concession. His son Yusuf parlayed the family association with APOC into a contract to supply the company with gravel from Iraq. He later became an APOC agent. During the 1930s, al-Ghanim family income provided the government of Kuwait with two-thirds of its revenues. Yusuf, along with other family members, had to flee Kuwait after the failure of the 1938 MAJLES movement; he returned in 1944 under a general amnesty. By the end of World War II, the al-Ghanim employed 7,000 men, about half the workforce of Kuwait. The family became the top labor and supply contractor for the KUWAIT OIL COMPANY and acquired other agencies and distributorships, including a lucrative arrangement with General Motors. The family owns al-Ghanim Industries, a holding company that ranks among the top companies in the world.

BIBLIOGRAPHY

CARTER, J. R. L. *Merchant Families of Kuwait.* London, 1984.

CRYSTAL, JILL. *Oil and Politics in the Gulf: Rulers and Merchants in Kuwait and Qatar.* Cambridge, U.K., 1990.

Middle East Economic Digest. London.

Mary Ann Tétreault

Ghanim, Fathi   [1924–   ]

Egyptian writer.

Ghanim, born in Cairo, holds a BA law degree from Cairo University. He was a civil servant in the Ministry of Education and editor of *Sabah al-Khayr* (Good Morning), a satirical political magazine, and *Al-Gumhurriyya* (The Republic), a daily newspaper. His novel *The Man Who Lost His Shadow* has been translated into English. Ghanim also published a collection of short stories, *Experiments in Love* (1958).

BIBLIOGRAPHY

VATIKIOTIS, P. J. *A History of Modern Egypt,* 4th ed. London, 1991.

David Waldner

Ghanim, Muhammad

Syrian official in Lebanon.

Ghanim (also called Ghani) is a high-ranking Syrian officer from Qirdaha, the hometown of Hafiz al-Asad. An Alawite, he was appointed head of Syria's intelligence operations in Lebanon—the most influential position for any Syrian in Lebanon. He was dismissed from his position for unknown reasons in the early 1980s. Where he is living today, or whether he is still alive, is not known.

As'ad AbuKhalil

Ghanim, Wahib   [1919–   ]

Syrian physician and politician.

Born to an Alawite family in Antioch, Turkey, Wahib Ghanim received an M.D. from Damascus University. An influential founding member of the executive committee of the BA'TH party, he served as deputy for Latakia in 1954 and minister of health and state in 1954 and 1955. The only Ba'th member in the cabinet, Ghanim resigned from these last posi-

tions under party orders, breaking up Premier Sabri al-Asali's tenuous cabinet.

BIBLIOGRAPHY

Who's Who in the Middle East, 1967–1968.

Charles U. Zenzie

Ghannushi, Rashid   [1941–   ]

Islamist politician; founding member and head of the Islamic Tendency Movement (Mouvement de Tendance Islamique), an offshoot of the Islamic Revival Movement formed in Tunisia in 1979.

Ghannushi entered politics in the 1970s as a member of the Society for the Preservation of the QUR'AN. Along with other leaders of the Islamist movement in Tunisia, he argues for a reintegration of Islam and Islamic law (SHARI'A) in all aspects of national life, including politics. He has been fiercely critical of Westernizing trends in Tunisia and of the secular character of the ruling party, the DESTOUR Socialist party (PSD). To him, the decline of Islamic values and the reliance on Western ideologies and economic-development models have led to social corruption and economic decline in Tunisia and throughout the Islamic world.

In June of 1981, his Islamic Tendency Movement (MTI) filed, without success, for formal recognition. Ghannushi and his party, renamed al-NAHDA (Reawakening) in 1989, attracted a growing number of, in particular, young followers during the 1980s. For his antigovernment activism, he was arrested in 1981 and remained in prison until 1984; he was rearrested in 1987. The issue of his trial and execution, sought by Tunisia's President Habib BOURGUIBA in the fall of 1987, precipitated Bourguiba's overthrow by Zayn al-Abidine BEN ALI. Pardoned by Ben Ali in May of 1988, Ghannushi left Tunisia in April 1989 to begin what he described as a self-imposed exile.

BIBLIOGRAPHY

Tunisia: A Country Survey. Washington, D.C., 1988.

Matthew S. Gordon

Gharb

Moroccan plain.

The Gharb, inhabited by Arab tribes (Banu Malik, Sufiyan, Khlut, and Tliq), is located between Wadi Lukkus, Wadi Sabu, and the Middle Atlas mountains in Morocco. Before colonization, the tribes lived by limited agriculture and pastoralism. Under the French protectorate, the Gharb became a rich region where colons settled and developed different types of agriculture for export.

After independence, the Gharb was subject to intensive development through allocation of irrigated plots of land to peasants and the creation of small exploitation units of industrial agriculture. During this period, the Gharb witnessed an intensive intervention by state agencies, such as national offices of rural modernization and of irrigation and the division of water and forests.

The cities of the Gharb are Mechra Bel Ksiri, Sidi Sliman, Sidi Yahya, and Kenitra. However, except for Kenitra, which is located on the margin of the region, the Gharb has not experienced the development of any major urban agglomeration because of its closeness to big cities like Rabat, Casablanca, and Meknes.

Rahma Bourqia

Gharbiyya

An Egyptian delta province (governorate).

Gharbiyya has an area of 750 square miles (1,942 sq km) and a 1986 population estimated at 2.9 million. It has been an administrative unit since the early days of Islam, and being in Egypt's delta, was a fertile, prosperous province. It has become a major cotton-producing area since the early nineteenth century. Tanta is its capital city.

BIBLIOGRAPHY

Encyclopaedia of Islam, 2nd ed.

Arthur Goldschmidt, Jr.

Gharbzadegi

Persian term meaning "Weststruck."

Coined in the late 1940s and made a household term in IRAN's intellectual circles by writer and social critic Jalal AL-E AHMAD (1923–1969) in a clandestinely published book by the same name (1962, 1964), *gharbzadegi* signals a chief sociological notion and concern among many Iranians in the post–World War II era.

As Al-e Ahmad describes it, throughout the twentieth century Iran has resorted to "Weststruck" behavior—adopting and imitating Western models and using Western criteria in education, the arts, and culture in general—while serving passively as a market for Western goods and also as a pawn in Western

geopolitics. Consequently threatened with loss of cultural, if not Iranian, identity, Al-e Ahmad argues that Iran must gain control over machines and become a producer rather than a consumer, even though once having overcome Weststruckness it will still face that desperate situation, he argues, remains in the West—that of "machinestruckness."

BIBLIOGRAPHY

AL-E AHMAD's influential book is available in three English translations: *Gharbzadegi (Weststruckness)* (1982), *Plagued by the West (Gharbzadegi)* (1982), and *Occidentosis: A Plague from the West* (1984).

Michael C. Hillmann

Ghashmi, Ahmad Husayn   [?–1978]

Yemeni president and soldier.

A career soldier of limited education, al-Ghashmi helped President Ibrahim al-HAMDI consolidate power in the Yemen Arab Republic (YAR) after the 1974 coup. Despite occupying the number two post for three years, al-Ghashmi participated directly in the assassination of al-Hamdi in 1977. He then became YAR president, only to be assassinated himself in June 1978 after eight months in office. Al-Ghashmi was well connected tribally, his brother being the shaykh of the Hamdan tribe, strategically located just to the west of San'a.

Robert D. Burrowes

Ghaydan, Sa'dun   [1929–c. 1985]

Iraqi general and cabinet minister.

Sa'dun Ghaydan was born in Baghdad to a lower-middle-class Sunni Arab family. Being non-political, he made his way up the military ladder fairly quickly. As commander of an armored brigade under Abd al-Rahman ARIF, he was instrumental in ousting Arif in July 1968. At first not a BA'TH party member he was, all the same, made a member of the all-powerful Revolutionary Command Council (RCC). In the mid-1970s he formally joined the party. Between 1968 and 1970 he was commander of the Baghdad garrison and thus indispensible to the regime's survival. In April 1970 he became minister of the interior, in charge of the police and other internal security organs. In July 1979 Saddam Hussein became president and appointed him RCC deputy chairman. In August 1982, following setbacks in the war with Iran, Ghaydan was relieved of all duties to assure that Saddam Hussein had no challengers. Ghaydan died, apparently poisoned, in the mid-1980s.

BIBLIOGRAPHY

BARAM, AMATZIA. "The Ruling Political Elite in Ba'thi, Iraq, 1968–1986." *International Journal of Middle East Studies* 21 (1989): 447–493.

Amatzia Baram

Ghazel

Verse form.

Originally Arabic, the *ghazel* (also known as *gazel* or *ghazal*) form passed into Turkish, Iranian, and Urdu poetry. It is a lyrical poetic mode, usually expressing elegiac love and often eroticism. The form became popular in classical Ottoman poetry.

Elizabeth Thompson

Ghazi ibn Faisal   [1912–1939]

King of Iraq from 1933 to 1939.

The son of King FAISAL I, Ghazi inherited little of his father's sophistication and political understanding. As his father's popularity began to wane at the end of the 1920s, Ghazi began to court a following of his own by identifying himself more or less openly with the opposition politicians and associating with the leaders of the Iraqi army. This continued after his accession, and as the Army high command began to exert an increasing influence on the country's political life (especially after the coup organized by Bakr SIDQI in 1936). Ghazi's relations with the British Embassy, and with Britain's protégé Nuri al-SA'ID, became increasingly strained. While there was no direct evidence linking Nuri to the car accident in which Ghazi was killed, the circumstances surrounding his death always remained obscure. Nuri, Ghazi's cousin ABD AL-ILAH, and Ghazi's estranged wife, Abd al-Ilah's sister Aliya, were long suspected of some form of involvement in it.

Peter Sluglett

Ghazni

Eastern Afghan province and town.

Spanning eastern and central Afghanistan, Ghazni province has a population of about 700,000, most of whom are Tajiks and Hazaras. The provincial capital, the town of Ghazni, has a population of about 30,000 and is approximately 80 miles (129 km) from Kabul on the Kabul-to-Kandahar road.

The town is also the ancient capital of the Ghaznavid dynasty (977–1186), and ruins dating from this period can still be found there.

BIBLIOGRAPHY

ADAMEC, LUDWIG. *Historical Dictionary of Afghanistan.* Metuchen, N.J., 1991.

Grant Farr

Ghazzi, Sa'id al-   [1897–?]

Syrian lawyer and prime minister.

Born in Damascus, married with three children, al-Ghazzi completed his primary education in Damascus and then studied law in Constantinople (now Istanbul) and Beirut. In 1920, he obtained a law degree from the Arab Law Institute in Damascus. In 1928, he was elected deputy of Damascus. Between 1945 and 1956, he held several ministerial positions—such as minister of justice, of finance, of national economy, and of foreign affairs—and was also prime minister.

George E. Irani

Ghetto

Area of a city established by law to be strictly inhabited by Jews.

The term originated in Venice in the sixteenth century although Jews had been segregated from Christians in Europe on and off since the twelfth century. In modern times, the Nazis forced Jews into ghettos—which became characterized by overcrowding and disease—and then systematically "liquidated" the ghettos by transferring the Jews to death camps. In the Middle East, Jews, like other minorities, tended to live with their coreligionists. In Iran (Persia), Yemen, and Morocco, they were restricted to certain areas—called *qa'at al-yahud* or *mellah*—often in economic decline.

[*See also:* Jews in the Middle East]

BIBLIOGRAPHY

LEWIS, BERNARD. *The Jews of Islam.* Princeton, N.J., 1984.

Julie Zuckerman

Ghorbal, Ashraf   [1925–   ]

Egyptian diplomat.

Educated at Washington University in the United States, Ghorbal was the first secretary to the United Nations in Geneva from 1958 to 1962, and an advisor to the Egyptian delegation in New York from 1962 to 1964. When Egypt's embassy in Washington, D.C., was closed following the 1967 Arab–Israel War, Ghorbal became head of the Egyptian interests section of the Indian embassy in Washington, where he served until 1973. In November of 1973, Ghorbal was appointed ambassador to the reopened Egyptian embassy in the United States.

BIBLIOGRAPHY

Africa Who's Who. 1st ed. London, 1981.

David Waldner

Ghorfa

Literally "room" in Arabic; in Tunisia, a room on the ground floor.

In southern Tunisia, seminomadic peoples, primarily of BERBER origin, built fortified food storage complexes arranged like honeycombs on the tops of high hills. These structures were two to six stories high, arranged in an elongated oval with a single entrance barred by a strong gate. The builders periodically lived in these complexes, probably to defend their food supplies from intruders. Examples exist near Tataouine, Ksar Haddada, and Médenine.

BIBLIOGRAPHY

HUREAU, JEAN. *Tunisia Today.* Paris, 1977.

Larry A. Barrie

Ghozali, Ahmed   [1937–   ]

Algerian technocrat; prime minister.

Ghozali studied at an engineering school, the Ecole des Ponts et Chauseés, in Paris. He was the director-general of SONATRACH (1966–1977), Algeria's national hydrocarbons enterprise, and then minister of energy (1977–1979) and of hydraulics (1979). Charged with mismanagement, he quietly returned to prominence as ambassador to Belgium and to the European Economic Community (1984–1988). After the October 1988 riots, he served as finance min-

ister in the Kasdi Merbah government and concluded Algeria's first agreement with the International Monetary Fund. New Prime Minister Mouloud Hamrouche then selected Ghozali as foreign minister (1989). After the aborted June 1991 parliamentary elections, President Chadli BENJEDID replaced Hamrouche with Ghozali, who assumed the difficult task of regenerating the FRONT DE LIBÉRATION NATIONALE (FLN). His immediate efforts failed, as disclosed in December 1991 by the ISLAMIC SALVATION FRONT's (FIS) astonishing success in the first round of the rescheduled elections. This crisis led to the deposition of President Benjedid by a civilian-military High Security Council (HSC). Ghozali kept his position, which intimated his complicity with the coup. In February 1992, he presented a national economic recovery plan founded on privatization, with significant attention given to agriculture.

BIBLIOGRAPHY

EDIAFRIC. *Les élites algériennes.* 2 vols. Paris, 1985.

Phillip C. Naylor

Ghuri, Emile al-   [1907—   ]

A Greek Orthodox Arab from Jerusalem.

Emile al-Ghuri studied political science in the United States in the early 1930s at the University of Cincinnati in Ohio. Upon his return to Jerusalem in 1933, he issued the *Arab Federation,* an English-language weekly that was later closed down by the British authorities in Palestine because of the political line it had adopted. In 1933, he was elected a member of the ARAB EXECUTIVE. Al-Ghuri issued the weekly *Al-Shabab* (The Youth) in 1934 and was later on the staff of the pro-Husayni English-language weekly *Palestine and Transjordan.* Between 1936 and 1939, he was sent on propaganda and fund-raising missions to England, the United States, and the Balkans. He quickly joined the ranks of his country's top political elites, becoming in 1935 the secretary-general of the Husayni-led PALESTINE ARAB PARTY. He later joined the Mufti of Jerusalem, Hajj Amin al-Husayni, in Iraq after the outbreak of World War II. As an active mufti supporter, al-Ghuri was pursued and captured by the British in Iran in September 1941 and allowed the next year to return to Palestine. Until 1944, the British authorities in Palestine prohibited him from engaging in politics. In 1944, he reorganized the Palestine Arab party, which was replaced two years later by a reconstituted Higher Arab Committee. He joined this body of

Palestinian politicians as a member representing it at the LONDON CONFERENCE on Palestine (1946/47) and at several United Nations conferences between 1948 and 1950. Throughout his political career, al-Ghuri enjoyed the support of the mufti and some of his closest associates. He served for many years on the now-defunct Higher Arab Committee and after 1948 represented it in various Arab and international forums. He also occupied a number of senior positions in the Jordanian government between 1966 and 1971. He wrote several books on the Palestinian cause and on Arab nationalism.

Muhammad Muslih

Ghuta Oasis

Green area surrounding Damascus, Syria, irrigated by the river Barada and its tributaries.

Ghuta oasis extends from the eastern slopes of the mountain of Qasiyun overlooking Damascus, the capital of Syria, to al-Marj to the southeast of the city where water decreases, trees disappear, and pastureland and grain farming abound. Mostly fruit and poplar trees are planted in the damp areas of Ghuta nearer to Damascus. The waters of the Barada and its tributaries are distributed in measurements and rotations evolved, accepted, and adhered to by the villagers throughout the centuries. Owing to the rich soil of al-Ghuta and its abundant water, it produces winter and summer crops.

BIBLIOGRAPHY

KURD ALI, MUHAMMAD. *Ghutat Dimashq.* 3rd ed. Damascus, 1984.

Abdul-Karim Rafeq

Giado Concentration Camp

An internment camp for Libyan Jews.

During World War II, Giado was built by the Italian fascist authorities on the Tripolitanian plateau, about 150 miles (240 km) south of Tripoli. It was established after the second British occupation of Cyrenaica, which ended January 27, 1942. The Italians, who had colonized Libya, decided on a "cleaning out" (*sfollamento*) of all Jews from the province. Over 3,000 Jews were taken to internment and labor camps in Tripolitania between May and October. About 75 percent of these were sent to Giado. The camp was administered by Italian officers. The guards included both Italians and Arabs. Rations and sanitary conditions in Giado were very poor, and a typhus epidemic broke out in December 1942.

By the time the British liberated the camp during the North Africa campaign, in late January 1943, 526 of the inmates had died. Others had been shot trying to escape as the Axis forces retreated westward.

BIBLIOGRAPHY

STILLMAN, NORMAN A. *The Jews of Arab Lands in Modern Times.* Philadelphia, 1991.

Norman Stillman

Gibran, Khalil   [1883–1931]

Lebanese author of prose and poetry.

Gibran (Jubran Khalil Jubran) was born at Bshirri in northern Lebanon and in the late 1880s moved to the United States with his sisters. He is known in the West for his book *The Prophet,* and in the Arab world for his contributions to the reformation of the modern usage of the Arabic language. He wrote in prose and poetry, and excelled in both. He ignored the rigid, traditional forms and called for free artistic expressions. Gibran was nonconformist: he opposed the dominance of the clerical establishment and called for the modernization of the Middle East without copying Western models.

Gibran's works in Arabic and in English celebrate individual freedoms and warn against sectarianism and class oppression. His attacks on the religious establishment made him enemies among leaders of the Lebanese church. After his death, however, Lebanese revered his memory and treated him as a cultural icon. Gibran never viewed himself as a Lebanese nationalist, however, but wrote as a Syrian Arab. His experience in the United States led him and other Arab writers and poets to form a literary society, Al-Rabita al-Qalamiyya (Pen's League), which played an important role in the cultural revival in the Middle East in the first two decades of the twentieth century.

As'ad AbuKhalil

Gilboa, Amir   [1917–1984]

Israeli poet.

Amir Gilboa was born in the Ukraine and arrived in Palestine in 1937 as an illegal immigrant. Until 1942, when he joined the Jewish brigade of the British army, he worked in agricultural settlements, stone quarries, and orange groves. As a member of the Eighth Army, he participated in its activities in Egypt, North Africa, Malta, and Italy. At the end of World War II he was active in the transfer of Jewish Holocaust survivors from Europe to Palestine. Gilboa fought in the Israeli War of Independence of 1948 and his experiences play a major role in his poetry. He served as the editor of Massada Publishing in Tel Aviv, published nine volumes of his own poetry and received numerous literary awards, including the Israel Prize for Poetry and the New York University Newman Prize. A collection of his poetry in English translation, *The Light of Lost Suns,* was published in 1979.

Gilboa's early poetry is marked for its figurative expressionism, its prophetic voice, and intense tonality. Repetition, imagination, and colorful carnivalism are characteristic devices. His later poetry combines lyrical expression with nationalistic statements through references to biblical personae and events. The narrative voice often speaks from the excited and naive viewpoint of a child, creating poetic irony and ambiguity.

Zvia Ginor

Giraud, Henri   [1878–1949]

French army officer.

Henri Giraud was a bold French officer, famous for his escapes from Germany during the two world wars. He was promoted by the United States during the CASABLANCA CONFERENCE in early 1943 to replace the intractable Charles DE GAULLE as head of the Free French. Nevertheless, Giraud did not have the political talent nor the presence to compete with his celebrated rival, who out maneuvered him by year's end for sole leadership of the French Committee for National Liberation. Giraud did achieve, however, the liberation of Corsica in September 1943. He retired in 1944 after refusing de Gaulle's offer to be inspector general of the armed forces.

BIBLIOGRAPHY

LACOUTURE, JEAN. *De Gaulle: The Rebel, 1890–1944,* trans. by Patrick O'Brian. New York, 1990.

Phillip C. Naylor

Girgir

A Turkish humor magazine.

Founded in Istanbul in 1972, *Girgir* was originally a page in the *Gün* daily newspaper. Editor Oğuz ARAL turned it into a weekly magazine in 1973; it became one of the top-selling humor magazines in the world by 1980. In the late 1980s, its circulation reached about 450,000. *Girgir* follows a long tradition of popular humor magazines in Turkey dating to 1868/69 when Turkey's first caricature magazines, *Diyojen* and *Letaifi Asarh,* were published.

Girgir specializes in populist, raw humor based on social and political satire. Aral trained its staff of cartoonists, who have created memorable characters, often drawing in a Disneylike style. The magazine was closed for one month in 1981 after the military coup. *Fırt,* a spinoff of *Girgir,* has met moderate success but has failed to capture the popular imagination the way its parent did.

BIBLIOGRAPHY

ŞAHIN, HALUK. "Mass Media in Turkey." In *Turkic Culture: Continuity and Change,* ed. by Sabri M. Akural. Bloomington, Ind., 1987.

Elizabeth Thompson

Giza

A middle Egyptian province (governorate).

West of Cairo, Giza has an area of 32,878 square miles (85,153 sq km) and a 1986 population estimated at 3.7 million. Famous for its three large PYRAMIDS and SPHINX, Giza lagged behind other parts of Egypt in converting to Christianity and then in embracing Islam. Its capital and main city, also called Giza, had some 1.9 million inhabitants, according to the 1986 census estimate. Several of the other towns and villages of Giza province—Duqqi and Imbaba—are suburbs of Cairo, and it has grown rapidly since World War II.

Housing complexes in Giza. (Mia Bloom)

Pyramids of Cheops and Khefren, with Giza skyline in foreground. (Mia Bloom)

BIBLIOGRAPHY

Coptic Encyclopedia.
Encyclopaedia of Islam, 2nd ed.

Arthur Goldschmidt, Jr.

Glawi Family, al-

Powerful Moroccan family of the late nineteenth century.

Originating from the Glawa tribe in the High Atlas mountains in Morocco, the al-Glawi family played an important role in the nineteenth century in linking the tribes of the High Atlas to the Makhzen. Two members of the family contributed to Morocco's recent history.

Madani Glawi (1863?–1918) inherited the chiefdom of Tlwat from his father Mohamed Ibabat, who was an AMGHAR (tribal leader). He built a close relationship with the sultan Mulay Hassan, whom he received in Tlwat in 1893 in the High Atlas. After the sultan gave him the title of caliph (Islamic leader) of Tafilalt, he became a *qa'id* (chief) of the Atlas. His power grew and his authority became widespread when he supported Mulay HAFID against his brother Mulay Abd al-Aziz and became the prime minister of the Cherifian government. Glawi ultimately built a powerful chiefdom in the High Atlas after 1913, when the sultan Mulay YUSUF came to the throne under the French protectorate of Morocco.

Thami Glawi (?–1957), Madani's youngest brother, became pasha of Marrakech in 1909. With French intervention in Morocco, his authority grew even more. After the death of his brother, he inherited his power over the surrounding tribes of Marrakech.

He stayed faithful to the French. When Sultan Sidi Muhammed Ben Yussef (later King MUHAMMED V) returned from exile in 1956, he gave him the *aman* (forgiveness). He died January 23, 1957.

BIBLIOGRAPHY

DEVERDUN, G. "Galwa (sing., glawi)." In *Encyclopédie de l'Islam.* Vol 2.
MONTAGNE, ROBERT. *Les berbères et le Makhzen dans le Sud du Maroc.* Paris, 1930.
PASCON, PAUL. *Le Haouz de Marrakech.* 2 vols. Rabat, Morocco, 1977.

Rahma Bourqia

Glubb, John Bagot   [1897–1986]

British officer who served the Arabs in Iraq during the British mandate and later in Jordan.

Known as Glubb Pasha, chief of staff of the Arab Legion (1939–1956), Glubb belonged to a West Country British family with a long tradition of service to the crown. He followed his father, Major General Sir Frederick Glubb, into the military. Educated at Cheltenham and the Royal Military Academy, Woolwich, Glubb served in France during World War I. He was sent to Iraq in 1920 and served there during Faisal's monarchy for ten years, first in the army and, after resigning his commission in 1926, as a member of the administration of the British mandated territory.

As administrative inspector in Iraq's southern desert, Glubb's main task was to organize the defenses of the bedouin tribes against raids by the Wahabi troops of King Ibn Sa'ud of Saudi Arabia. During this assignment, Glubb acquired his excellent command of Arabic, an intimate knowledge of the bedouin tribes, and a profound understanding of Arab history, culture, and traditions.

In 1930, as Captain Glubb, he was sent to Transjordan to pacify the bedouin tribes, who were also being attacked by the Wahhabi raiders from Saudi Arabia and here, too, he achieved remarkable success. When Glubb joined the Arab Legion—Transjordan's army—it was a tiny force with almost no bedouins in its ranks and was under the command of another Englishman, called Peake Pasha by the legion. As Commander Peake's second-in-command and from 1939 as commander, Glubb developed the Arab Legion from little more than a gendarmerie into the best-trained, most disciplined, and most efficient of all the Arab armies. His most distinctive contribution, however, was the recruitment of bedouins and their transformation from unruly nomads into disciplined soldiers and loyal citizens. Although recruits from the settled areas of Transjordan continued to predominate, the bedouins became the hard core of the Arab Legion and infused it with the fighting spirit for which it became renowned.

A good soldier and organizer, Glubb was also a very subtle politician. As chief of staff of the Arab Legion he needed to be a good politician, because the legion was the mainstay of the Hashimite regime in Amman. Unlike the officers who were posted to the Arab Legion by the British army, Glubb served under contract to the Transjordan government and therefore owed his allegiance to Emir Abdullah. The British government, however, continued to finance the Arab Legion even after Transjordan became independent in 1946; so Glubb had to serve two very different masters; because of his skill as a politician, he managed to sustain this dual loyalty.

In 1948, Glubb commanded the Arab Legion against the new State of Israel, alongside the other regular and irregular Arab armies. Although the Arab Legion was the only Arab army to distinguish itself on the battlefield, Glubb was blamed for the fall of the cities of Lydda and Ramla and for the failure to capture West Jerusalem. Arab nationalists accused him of deliberately curtailing the operations of the Arab Legion in line with a British plan to partition Palestine between Transjordan and the Jews.

After the ARAB–ISRAEL WAR of 1948 and the incorporation of the West Bank into the Hashimite Kingdom of Jordan, Glubb prepared the plans for the defense of the enlarged kingdom. He also played a key role in curbing Palestinian infiltration into Israel, because it generated perpetual tension along the border and provoked military reprisals from Israel. Glubb's aim was to keep the border quiet and avoid clashes with Israel's powerful army.

Arab nationalists, inside and outside Jordan, continued to view Glubb as both the symbol and instrument of British imperial domination over the Middle East. Therefore, having a British chief of staff became an increasing liability for the Hashimite rulers of Jordan as the tides of nationalism swept through the Middle East. In March 1956, Jordan's King Husayn abruptly dismissed Glubb and replaced him with a Jordanian chief of staff. Glubb's dismissal temporarily strained the relations between Britain and Jordan, but it also constituted a turning point on Jordan's path to real independence.

Upon his dismissal, Glubb returned to Britain and became a political writer. His publications include *Story of the Arab Legion*, 1948; his autobiography, *A Soldier with the Arabs*, 1957; *Britain and the Arabs*, 1959; *War in the Desert*, 1960; *The Great Arab Conquests*, 1963; *The Empire of the Arabs*, 1963; *The Course*

of Empire, 1965; *The Lost Centuries*, 1967; *The Middle East Crisis—A Personal Interpretation*, 1967; *Syria, Lebanon, Jordan*, 1967; *A Short History of the Arab Peoples*, 1969; *The Life and Times of Muhammad*, 1970; *Peace in the Holy Land*, 1971; *Soldiers of Fortune*, 1973; *The Way of Love*, 1974; *Haroon al-Rasheed*, 1976; *Into Battle: A Soldier's Diary of the Great War*, 1977; *Arabian Adventures*, 1978; *A Purpose for Living*, 1979; *The Changing Scenes of Life*, 1983. Glubb's most important book is his 1957 autobiography, *A Soldier with the Arabs*.

A British officer who had served under him in the Arab Legion, James Lunt, wrote *Glubb Pasha: A Biography* (London, 1984).

Avi Shlaim

Goeben and Breslau

German ships used by the Ottomans to attack Russia in World War I.

By agreement between the Ottoman Empire and Germany, the German warships *Goeben* and *Breslau* were dispatched to Istanbul in August 1914. The Ottomans took possession of these ships, and at the end of October, the *Goeben* and the *Breslau* attacked Russia's flotilla in the Black Sea, thereby heralding the Ottoman entry into World War I on the side of the Central Powers (Germany and Austria-Hungary).

BIBLIOGRAPHY

FROMKIN, DAVID. *A Peace to End All Peace*. New York, 1989.

Zachary Karabell

Gökalp, Ziya   [1876–1924]

Turkish social and political thinker.

Gökalp was born in the province of Diyarbekır. At the time of his birth, Diyarbekır contained ethnic groups of Kurdish origin, leading some of Gökalp's political opponents to assert that he was of Kurdish lineage. His father, Tevfik, was director of the provincial archives and editor of the official gazette. Gökalp's education incorporated both Western and Islamic values. Along with religious instruction by family elders, he received a secular education in a military junior high school and a state senior high school in Diyarbekır. He then entered the veterinary college in Constantinople (now Istanbul), but was expelled in his second year for his membership in the secret Society of Union and Progress. After a brief imprisonment he was exiled to Diyarbekır, where he continued his avid reading in the natural sciences, philosophy, sociology, politics, and pedogogy, and resumed his study of Islamic philosophy, especially SUFISM.

Gökalp became secretary of the Chamber of Commerce (1902) and the assistant secretary general of the Provincial Council (1904) of Diyarbekır. In 1908 the COMMITTEE OF UNION AND PROGRESS (CUP) appointed Gökalp inspector of its organizations in Diyarbekır, Van, and Bitlis while he continued to serve as inspector of elementary education for the provincial government. In 1910, he became a member of the Central Committee (CC) of the Union and Progress Party and went to Salonika, where he taught sociology at the party school, directed the party's youth department, and continued writing and lecturing. In 1912, after the removal of the CC headquarters to Constantinople, Gökalp was named the first professor of sociology at Darülfünün (now Istanbul University). He was exiled to Malta following dissolution of the last Ottoman parliament in 1919. There he conducted a "one-man university" for the distinguished exiles, many of whom joined the Kemalist nationalist resistance in Anatolia. Upon his release from Malta in 1921, Gökalp returned to Diyarbekır, taught at the secondary school and the teachers' seminary, and continued to publish. He was elected to the Second Grand National Assembly (1923–1927) as a deputy from Diyarbekır, served on the parliamentary committee on national education, and participated in the preparation of the 1924 constitution.

Gökalp did not participate in practical politics in the narrow sense. He was a thinker and writer with a profound sense of responsibility for the public good. He was foremost a social and political theoretician, a public educator, and a formulator of Unionist and Kemalist modernizing reforms. Gökalp was the intellectual leader of modern Turkish nationalism in the transition from the multiethnic Ottoman Empire to the nation-state of the Turkish republic, despite the distance between his thinking and that of the Ottomanist Unionists and the Republican Kemalists. He was the acknowledged mentor of these two movements, although both developed into authoritarian, one-party regimes.

Gökalp's "social idealism" was an attempt at a reconciliation of cultural Turkism, ethical Islam, and European corporatism. His nationalism was based on language, subjective self-identification, socialization, and acculturation in a distinct Turkish culture that was to interact peacefully with other Western cultures. Gökalp called for modernizing reforms in Islamic thought and institutions, the essence of which

was a reduction of Islam—for centuries the state religion of the Ottoman Turkish society—into a body of moral norms and codes of social behavior based on the nonorthodox Sufi (mystic) form of Islam. As a follower of Auguste Comte and Emile Durkheim, Gökalp took a lay attitude toward Islam, both in the narrow sense of separation of state and religion and in the wider sense of primacy of rational, scientific thought over nonsecular thought.

Perhaps the more important influence of European corporatist thought on Gökalp's own thinking was the rejection of the individualism of liberal capitalism (without rejecting capitalism in general) and of the Marxist categories of class struggle and classless society. Gökalp followed Durkheim in believing that society is composed not of egoistic individuals or warring classes, but of interdependent occupational groups working harmoniously for the public good. This approach enabled him to take both a sociological view of society and an ideological stand against liberal and socialist politics. His form of "populism" viewed society as an organic whole and called for political representation of interests through occupational corporations, in which capital and labor were integrated and the social being of the individual was realized.

The racist-fascist Kemalist movement of the 1940s, the fascist Nationalist Action party (1960s–1980), and the Nationalist Work party tried to interpret Gökalp's thought in a fascist manner. Meanwhile, mainstream KEMALISM remained within the confines of Gökalp's corporatism, and his thought continues to dominate Turkish social and political thinking via Kemalism, which remains the official ideology and hegemonic public philosophy of contemporary Turkey.

BIBLIOGRAPHY

GÖKALP, ZIYA. *Principles of Turkism*. Tr. by Robert Devereaux. Leiden, 1963.
———. *Turkish Nationalism and Western Civilization*. Tr. by Niyazi Berkes. New York, 1959.
HEYD, URIEL. *Foundations of Turkish Nationalism: The Life and Teachings of Ziya Gökalp*. London, 1959.
PARLA, TAHA. *The Social and Political Thought of Ziya Gökalp*. Leiden, Neth., 1985.

Taha Parla

Golan Heights

Mountainous Syrian plateau, important militarily as well as because of its water resources.

The Golan Heights (in Arabic, Al Jawlan) has an average altitude of 3,300 feet (1,000 m) and covers an area of approximately 700 square miles (1,800 sq

Golan Heights with Mount Hermon in the distance. (Bryan McBurney)

km) in the southwest corner of Syria. It has a north-south length of 40 miles (65 km) and an east-west dimension varying from 7 to 15 miles (12 to 25 km). Situated between south Lebanon and south Syria, it has elevations that range from 6,500 feet (2,000 m) in the north to below sea level along the Sea of Galilee (Lake Tiberias) and the Yarmuk river in the south.

The word *golan* seems to be related to the Arabic verb *jala* (to circulate or wander about) and to the word *ajwal,* meaning an area that is exposed to dusty winds. After the death of Herod the Great in 4 B.C.E., the Golan must have been given to his son Herod Antipas (died after 39 C.E.), governor of Galilee and Peraea (land east of the Jordan river). The Golan flourished during this period. A large number of towns emerged, including Seleucia, Sogane, and Gamala.

After the defeat of the Byzantine Empire, at the Yarmuk river, all of Syria including the Golan ultimately fell into the hands of Muslim Arabs (633–640). After the Umayyads (661–750), the area fell to the Seljuk Turks, Saladin, the Mongols, the Mamluks, and the Crusaders. It was part of the Ottoman Empire from 1516 until the end of World War I, and, in 1920, France received a League of Nations mandate over modern Syria including the Golan.

Between 1948 and 1967, the struggle between Israel and Syria over their demilitarized border zone was a principal reason behind the ARAB–ISRAEL WAR of 1967 (the Six-Day War), which ended in Israel's capture of the Golan Heights, in addition to the SINAI PENINSULA, WEST BANK, and GAZA STRIP. As a result of the Arab–Israel War of October 1973 and the Israel–Syria disengagement agreement of the following year, Israel returned to Syria about 40 square miles (100 sq km) of the Golan. In December 1981, the Likud-led government of Israel's Prime Minister Menachem Begin extended Israeli law, jurisdiction, and administration to the Golan, an action that was criticized by the administration of U.S. President Ronald Reagan and considered "null and void" by resolution 497, which the UN Security Council unanimously adopted on December 17, 1981.

Prior to its seizure by Israel, the Golan had a population of approximately 130,000 Syrians living in 139 villages and on 61 farms. Today, only about 16,000 people remain in five Arab villages. DRUZE constitute the overwhelming majority of the remaining Syrian population. According to some observers, one reason the Druze community was allowed to remain was the initial attitude of the Israeli government, which assumed that the Syrian Druze would cooperate with Israel like their coreligionists in the Galilee. When attempts to coopt Golani Druze failed, the Israeli government resorted to such measures as curfews, administrative detention, restrictions on the use of water, and efforts to link the daily life of the Golanis to the acquisition of Israeli-citizenship identification cards. In addition, there are now in the

Golan more than thirty-five Jewish settlements with an estimated population of 15,000. Many of these settlements are on the southern approaches above the Sea of Galilee.

In terms of military significance, the Mount Hermon massif (7,300 ft; 2,224 m) in the north is of exceptional geostrategic value because it offers a commanding position overlooking southern Lebanon, the Golan plateau, and much of southern Syria and northern Israel. Conversely, the south Golan has a major weakness because it lacks dominating terrain features. To the east, a range of volcanic hills offers downhill access to Galilee in the west and Damascus in the east. To the west, the Golan plateau overlooks Israeli metropolitan centers. In the mid-1990s, the Israeli army was stationed about 22 miles (35 km) from Damascus, while the Syrian army was stationed about 150 miles (250 km) from Tel Aviv.

The Golan is also important for its regional water sources. This is particularly true of the area of Mount Hermon, where the headwaters of the Jordan river lie. Additionally, the Baniyas spring, a major Jordan river source, is located on the lower slopes of the Golan, thus enhancing the latter's importance. To the south, the sea of Galilee and the Yarmuk river constitute two more important regional water sources.

BIBLIOGRAPHY

Pipes, Daniel. *Greater Syria: The History of an Ambition.* New York, 1992.

Rausch, David A. *The Middle East Maze: A Guide to Israel & Her Neighbors.* Chicago, 1991.

Muhammad Muslih

Goldberg, Leah   [1911–1970]

Hebrew poet, literary critic, translator, educator, and children's author.

Born in Kovno (now Kaunas, Lithuania), Goldberg studied at the universities of Kovno, Berlin, and Bonn. In 1933, she received a doctorate in philosophy and Semitic languages. In 1935, she arrived in Tel Aviv, in British-mandated Palestine, where she published her first volume of poetry, *Tabbe ot Ashan* (1935, Smokerings).

She served on the editorial boards of *Davar* and *Ha-Mishmar* and, from 1952, taught literature at the Hebrew University of Jerusalem. In 1963, she became chair of its department of comparative literature, a position she held until her death.

Leah Goldberg wrote numerous volumes of poetry—unpretentious, delicate, and lyric. Except for the Holocaust, her themes are universal rather than Jewish: childhood, love (especially unrequited), aging, and death. She excelled as a translator into Hebrew of classical European authors—Tolstoy, Gorky, Chekhov, Mann, and Ibsen. She was also a successful children's author of twenty books; in later years she took up art and illustrated her own works.

Ann Kahn

Golden Square

Name given to the four ex-sharifian, pan-Arab Iraqi army officers whose anti-British, pro-Axis politics led to the Rashid Ali coup of 1941 and the war with Britain that followed.

The original "Four" included the leader, Salah al-Din al-Sabbagh, and Kamil Shabib, Fahmi Sa'id, and Mahmud Salman. They organized after the 1936 Bakr Sidqi coup and then joined with three other officers, Aziz Yamulki, Husayn Fawzi, and Amin al-Umari, to form a military opposition bloc to the government. Jamil al-Midfa'i's government in 1938 tried to transfer the officers out of Baghdad, but only succeeded in making them more politically active.

The officers supported the goals of the Jerusalem *mufti* (chief Muslim jurist), Hajj Amin al-Husayni, who arrived in Baghdad and solicited Germany's help to achieve total Iraqi independence from Britain and the pan-Arab goal of Arab unity of the Fertile Crescent. They opposed Prime Minister Nuri al-Sa'id's severance of relations with Germany in 1939. In 1940/41, the officers and the mufti were in contact with the Japanese and the Italians through their missions in Baghdad and supported Rashid Ali al-Kaylani's government (March 31, 1940 to January 31, 1941) as the British pressured Iraq to declare war on Germany. When Rashid Ali resigned, the pro-British regent, Abd al-Ilah, asked Gen. Taha al-Hashimi, who had worked with the Four, to form a government, thinking that he could control the generals. But Taha's weakness and the attempt by the regent to transfer Kamil Shabib out of the capital led them, in collusion with the mufti, to take control of the government in April 1941, with Rashid Ali again as the prime minister.

At the end of the abortive war against Britain in May 1941, the Four fled but were later caught and executed.

BIBLIOGRAPHY

Tarbush, Mohammad A. *The Role of the Military in Politics.* London, 1982.

Reeva S. Simon

Goldmann, Nahum   [1895–1982]

Jewish and Zionist leader.

Born in Lithuania, Goldmann spent most of his formative years in Germany, where he obtained a Ph.D. from Heidelberg University and was active in Ha-Po'el Ha-Tza'ir. He was a co-founder of the World Jewish Congress Israel's in 1936. Goldmann solicited international support for the partition plan, and was offered a seat in Israel's provisional government in 1948, but declined. After the Arab–Israel War of 1967, Goldmann became increasingly critical of the Israeli government and advocated mutual recognition between Israel and the PLO. Goldmann also was instrumental in the planning of the Diaspora Museum, which bears his name in its official title.

BIBLIOGRAPHY

GOLDMANN, NAHUM. *The Autobiography of Nahum Goldmann: Sixty Years of Jewish Life.* New York, 1969.

Julie Zuckerman

Golestan, Ibrahim   [1922–   ]

Iranian writer, photographer, translator, publisher, and filmmaker.

Ibrahim Golestan was born in Shiraz and later studied law at Tehran University. He was a leftist political activist and was imprisoned for his beliefs, which are partly reflected in his fiction. Golestan is a social-realist writer, with a self-reflective prose, who sees life as depressing and bitter. His first collection of short stories, *Azar, mah-e akhar-e payiz* (Azar, the Last Month of Autumn), was published in 1948. He also made a feature film called *Asrar-e ganj-e darre-ye jenni* (Secrets of the Haunted Valley's Treasure, 1974, 1978). In the mid-1970s, Golestan immigrated to England where he now resides.

BIBLIOGRAPHY

MOAYYAD, HESHMAT, ed. *Stories from Iran: A Chicago Anthology, 1921–1991.* Washington, D.C., 1991.

Pardis Minuchehr

Golestan, Treaty of

Treaty in which Iran ceded land to Russia.

The Treaty of Golestan between Iran and Russia yielded the provinces of Georgia, Baku, and Shirvan to Russia after a nine-year war, in 1813. The am-

biguous terms of the accord resulted in renewed hostilities thirteen years later.

Farhad Shirzad

Golestan Palace

A museum built in Tehran, Iran, in 1894, for the Peacock Throne and other royal jewels.

Built in the last years of NASER AL-DIN SHAH Qajar's reign (1831–1896), the Golestan palace, or Rose Garden palace, was a museum for the royal jewels, including the famous Peacock Throne brought by Nadir Shah Afshar (1688–1747) from his expeditions to India. The construction of the palace took five years, with the personal supervision of the shah. In the upheavals of the Tobacco revolt (1891–1892) people resorted to the Golestan palace demanding justice. Subsequently, fearing for the safety of the jewels, the shah moved them to the royal palace, donating, instead, other precious items to the Golestan. The Golestan Palace also includes other chambers, collectively known as *Talar-i Berelian* (or Diamond Chamber). The Golestan is still a museum.

BIBLIOGRAPHY

DEHKHODA, A. *Lughat Nameh.* Tehran.

Parvaneh Pourshariati

Golpayagani, Mohammad Reza   [1899–1993]

Iranian religious scholar; the most senior in Qom.

Golpayagani began his religious studies in his birthplace of Golpayagan, in central Iran, where his father, Seyyed Mohammad Baqer, was a highly respected cleric of Islam. In 1917, he moved to Arak to join the circle of Shaykh Abd al-Karim Ha'eri, one of the most prominent legal authorities of his day within SHI'ISM. When Ha'eri left for Qom in 1922, to reestablish the religious institution in that city, Golpayagani followed him at his invitation and was entrusted by him with the teaching of elementary courses. After the death of Ha'eri in 1937, he graduated to the teaching of jurisprudence, and his lectures, held in the Masjed-e A'zam, would often attract as many as 800 students. He attained still greater influence after the death in 1962 of Hosayn BORUJERDI, Ha'eri's successor, and assumed the major responsibility for administering the complex of colleges and mosques that make up the religious institution in Qom. By then, he had also attained the position of MARJA' AL-TAQLID (source of imitation), an authoritative guide in matters of religious law.

Unbending and rigorous in his understanding of Shi'ite law, he entered the political arena in 1962 with a denunciation of the redistribution of land by the state as contrary to Islam. Despite the conservatism that this implied, he was supportive of the movement inaugurated in 1963 by Ayatollah Ruhollah KHOMEINI, and in 1978, when the IRANIAN REVOLUTION erupted, numerous proclamations condemning the regime of Mohammad Reza Shah PAHLAVI were issued over his signature. He consistently refrained from taking a position on the controversies that plagued postrevolutionary Iran, both because of advancing years and because of a fundamentally apolitical disposition. He died on December 2, 1993 and was eulogized by all the leading figures of the Islamic republic.

BIBLIOGRAPHY

RAZI, MOHAMMAD SHARIF. *Ganjine-ye Daneshmandan* (A Treasury of Scholars). Tehran, 1973.

Hamid Algar

Golshiri, Hushang   [1935–   ]

Iranian writer, critic, and editor.

Hushang Golshiri was born in Isfahan, raised in Abadan, and later returned to Isfahan to study Iranian literature. His most famous novel, *Shazdeh Ehtejab* (Prince Ehtejab, 1968), criticizes the degeneration of an aristocratic family. After this novel was turned into a popular movie, Golshiri was imprisoned for six months. He has also written several collections of short stories, including *Namazkhane-ye kuchek-e man* (My Little Prayer House).

BIBLIOGRAPHY

MOAYYAD, HESHMAT, ed. *Stories from Iran: A Chicago Anthology, 1921–1991*. Washington, D.C., 1991.

Pardis Minuchehr

Goltz, Kolmar von der   [1843–1916]

German general.

Known as Goltz Pasha, von der Goltz was a military adviser to the OTTOMAN EMPIRE's sultan and trained the Ottoman army (1883–1896). He organized military education through government military schools in major urban areas. He returned to the Middle East to command the Ottoman forces in Mesopotamia (1915/16) during World War I. Responsible for the defeat of the British forces at Kut al-Amara in 1916, he died of typhus before Gen. Charles V. Townshend surrendered.

BIBLIOGRAPHY

SHAW, STANFORD, and EZEL KURAL SHAW. *History of the Ottoman Empire and Modern Turkey*. New York, 1977.

Zachary Karabell

Gorchakov, Aleksandr Mikhailovich
[1798–1883]

Russian diplomat.

Born in St. Petersburg, Gorchakov served as Russia's ambassador to Austria-Hungary (1854–1856) during the Crimean War, and was intimately involved with the negotiations leading to the Treaty of Paris. In 1856 he succeeded Count Nesselrode as foreign minister, and in 1870 he repudiated the Black Sea clauses adopted at Paris that had limited Russian naval freedom. Though this repudiation allowed Russia to campaign more vigorously against the Ottomans, it is nonetheless true that throughout his twenty-six years (1856–1882) as foreign minister, Gorchakov worked to preserve the Ottoman Empire as a member of the concert of Europe. In this task, he was often at odds with Russia's minister in Constantinople, Nicholas IGNATIEV. During the Eastern crisis of 1875–1878, Gorchakov sought to limit the scope of the conflict and opposed the creation of Ignatiev's "Big Bulgaria." In the end, Gorchakov's proposal, which allowed for a smaller Bulgaria without access to the Aegean Sea, was adopted at the Congress of Berlin in 1878.

BIBLIOGRAPHY

SHAW, STANFORD and EZEL KURAL SHAW. *History of the Ottoman Empire and Modern Turkey*. New York, 1977.
ANDERSON, M. S. *The Eastern Question*. London, 1966.

Zachary Karabell

Gordon, Aaron David   [1856–1922]

Jewish pioneer in Palestine; philosopher of labor Zionism.

A. D. Gordon was born in Tryano, Russia, and died in Palestine. He was educated in both Jewish studies and Russian secular subjects and spent his early adult life as financial manager of the Guenzburg estate. In 1904, when the estate was sold, at the age of 48, he went to Palestine. He had been influenced by the secular Hebrew language and literary movement, particularly by the essays of AHAD HA-AM. In Palestine, he worked as a farm laborer, and then he and his family participated in a model cooperative agricultural community, Degania, forerunner of the kibbutz.

Although Gordon never affiliated with any of the political parties of LABOR ZIONISM, he published essays that influenced their activities and ideologies. Extolling the virtues of working on the land, Gordon reflected on the distortions in Jewish society caused by the DIASPORA. Jews had not simply been dispersed to many lands but had been denied the opportunities to work in all occupations especially those that might sustain communal vitality. Gordon argued that only through the ideal of physical farm labor, cooperation, and mutual aid in a return to the soil on their own land in their own country would Jews individually and collectively be revitalized.

He was opposed to socialism in its Marxist form and was uninterested in politics but he viewed humanity as part of the cosmos, with national communities forming and embodying a living cosmic relationship. He rejected urban culture as alienated from nature and from creativity. Just as the exile could be ended by bringing Jews to Palestine, so could the exile be banished from the Jewish soul through agricultural labor. The establishment of an agricultural base would provide the possibility for the creation of a just, humane Jewish society, especially with respect to the Arabs. He has said: "Their hostility is all the more reason for our humanity."

BIBLIOGRAPHY

AVISHAI, BERNARD. The Tragedy of Zionism. New York, 1985.

Donna Robinson Divine

Gordon, Charles   [1833–1885]

British army engineer, explorer, and empire builder active in the Crimea, China, and Africa.

Born into a military family on 28 January 1833, Gordon was commissioned in the Royal Engineers in 1852 and two years later fought in the Crimean War. In 1863 he became commander of the Ever Victorious Army, a Chinese ragtag mercenary outfit, which defeated the Taiping rebellion against the Manchu emperor. The popularity he subsequently won in the British press earned him the nickname Chinese Gordon.

It is, however, through his service in Africa that Gordon attained both lasting fame and martyrdom. In 1874 the viceroy of Egypt sent him to the Sudan and equatorial Africa to suppress the slave trade and extend, through exploration, the southern bound-

aries of Egypt's African dominions. In 1877 he continued his antislavery crusade as governor general of the Sudan; frustrated in his efforts, he resigned three years later.

When Muhammad AHMAD, claiming to be the Mahdi (the Muslim messiah), led a revolt in the Sudan that threatened Egypt's and Britain's African interests, Gordon was appointed to lead the evacuation of Khartoum's garrison. Disobeying his instructions, he tried to crush the rebellion but failed in the face of overwhelming odds. Besieged in Khartoum, he chose to make a suicidal stand. The Mahdi's troops stormed the city on 26 January 1885, killing Gordon and most of his soldiers.

BIBLIOGRAPHY

NUTTING, ANTHONY. Gordon of Khartoum: Martyr and Misfit. New York, 1966.

Jean-Marc R. Oppenheim

Goren, Shlomo   [1917–   ]

Chief chaplain of Israel's army, 1948–1968.

Goren was born in Poland and was taken to Palestine with his family in 1925. At twelve he entered Hebron YESHIVA, where he became a prodigy at HALAKHAH (Judaic law).

Goren fought in the first ARAB–ISRAEL WAR of 1948, where he rose to the rank of brigadier general. As first chief chaplain of the new Israel Defense Force, he was responsible for organizing the chaplaincy and establishing the means of religious observance in the service.

Goren wrote numerous halakhic works—of particular note are those dealing with issues arising from modern warfare. In 1961, he received the Israel Prize. From 1968 to 1971, he was Ashkenazic chief rabbi of Tel Aviv and of Israel from 1972 to 1984. He served as head of Ha'Idra, a yeshiva in the old city in Jerusalem.

Ann Kahn

Gorst, John Eldon   [1861–1911]

Anglo–Egyptian and Foreign Office official, 1886–1907; British agent and consul-general in Egypt, 1907–1911.

The Gorst family was mainly from Lancashire, England; it had prospered under Queen Victoria's reign. Gorst (known as Jack to his friends) was born in New Zealand but was raised in London. His father and namesake, Sir John, returned to England from New Zealand after the last Maori War, where he embarked on an erratic career in Conservative party politics. Gorst suffered a painful and unhappy childhood, because an abscess in his pelvis kept him bedridden or wearing a brace for almost seven years. Educated in day schools, at home by tutors, then at Eton and at Trinity College, Cambridge, he earned a degree in mathematics in 1882 and was called to the bar in 1885. Rather than face exclusion, like his father, from the largely aristocratic Tory party inner circle, Gorst entered the diplomatic service in 1885; he was sent to Egypt.

Egypt was still formally under the sovereignty of the Ottoman Empire, but Muhammad Ali Pasha had managed to make it a virtually independent state from 1805 until 1842, when the Ottoman sultan recognized his right to pass the control of Egypt on to his descendants. Because of the building of the Suez Canal and European greed, Egypt became burdened with financial debts. Both France and Britain intervened and, in 1882, British troops occupied Egypt. By 1886, when Gorst arrived, Sir Evelyn BARING, later the Earl of Cromer, was consolidating his power as Egypt's de facto ruler. Gorst learned Arabic well enough to bypass an interpreter and cultivate friendships among the Egyptian Ottoman elite, including Khedive ABBAS HILMI II. Between 1890 and 1904, Gorst distinguished himself at Egypt's ministries of finance and interior. He helped organize and recruit Englishmen to extend British control in Egypt and the Sudan. In 1898 he succeeded Sir Elwin Palmer as financial adviser in Egypt—the most influential post after Cromer's. In 1904, Gorst, now Cromer's heir-apparent, returned to the Foreign Office, especially to act as Cromer's agent there.

In 1907, the Liberal cabinet sent Gorst back to Egypt to reduce Cromer's autocracy and to give selected Egyptians limited responsibility for their internal affairs. This "new policy" of "conciliation" and "moderation" would, the cabinet hoped, diminish Egyptian nationalism and appease hostile critics in Britain and Egypt. By working with the Egyptian ministers and the khedive, Gorst quickly and successfully undermined the nationalists. Unlike Cromer, he did not usually bully the Egyptian Ottoman elite.

Gorst, however, made three major mistakes. First, he alienated the Anglo-Egyptian officials and influential circles in Britain by reducing their influence on the veiled protectorate over Egypt. Second, in 1908, he appointed Butros GHALI, a Coptic Christian, as prime minister to replace the elderly time server, Mustafa Fahmi. Ghali was able but hated by the nationalists for his record and distrusted by many Muslims for his faith. Third, Gorst sought in 1909/10 to extend the Suez Canal Company's concession,

mainly to provide development funds for the Sudan. He lost Ghali and the experiment in limited self-rule to a nationalist assassin, and a defiant Egyptian General Assembly rejected the concession extension.

Gorst's last year as British agent had an element of anticlimax. Despite alarmists who predicted further trouble for the British in Egypt, little or nothing occurred. Although his health deteriorated rapidly, Gorst's control and British influence in Egypt did not. It was enough for the agency to warn, bribe, or deport certain nationalists, suppress so-called seditious periodicals, and indulge in a limited amount of counterpropaganda.

Gorst died of cancer in July 1911, in Castle Combe, England. The khedive, whom he had befriended, rushed to comfort him on his deathbed.

BIBLIOGRAPHY

LUTFI AL-SAYYID, AFAF. *Egypt and Cromer.* New York, 1969.
MELLINI, PETER. *Sir Eldon Gorst: The Overshadowed Proconsul.* Stamford, Conn., 1977.
TIGNOR, ROBERT L. *Modernization and British Colonial Rule in Egypt, 1881–1914.* Princeton, N.J., 1966.

Peter Mellini

Gosn, Hanna   [1907–?]

Lebanese journalist.

Born in Beirut and educated at the American University of Beirut and the Law Faculty of Damascus, Gosn began his career as a lawyer. After one year he left his practice to become associate editor of the *Al-Nida* and *Al-Nahar* newspapers. In 1942, he founded the *Al-Diar* newspaper, which supported Egypt's President Gamal Abdel Nasser in the 1960s. Gosn served as a delegate to the United Nations Organization (UNO) in 1946 and was a UNO press attaché from 1950 to 1951.

BIBLIOGRAPHY

Who's Who in Lebanon, 1980–1981. Beirut, 1980.

Mark Mechler

Government

Exercise of authority over and the performance of functions for a political unit; usually classified by the distribution of power within it.

The modern Middle East is a large and diverse region, the differences well illustrated by the structures and dynamics of government in the area. There are nearly as many types of government as there are states, and many of the systems undergo almost constant change as the need to accommodate domestic and international pressures emerges.

Constitutional government is not deeply rooted or widespread in the Middle East. Israel's democracy rests, in part, on a series of basic laws that provide a framework for governmental action rather than on a formal written constitution, but this does not affect its role as a parliamentary democracy. Iraq and Syria have constitutions with the trappings of constitutional government yet hardly qualify as democratic regimes. Other states have written constitutions, but these rarely provide a clear guide to governmental action. The Republic of Turkey, however, remains a significant exception.

The legislative institutions of Middle East states generally are limited in number and power. In much of the Middle East, the legislatures are rarely representative bodies, although when present they often perform useful functions. In some of the Gulf states, such as Saudi Arabia, Oman, the United Arab Emirates, and Qatar, there exist consultative bodies that generally serve at the pleasure of the ruler but also tend to legitimate the ruler's actions. This function has proven particularly critical in times of crisis and challenge to the regime. In some instances elected (although not in wholly unfettered processes) legislatures are involved in lawmaking and engage in criticism of the regime despite regime-imposing limitations. Such legislatures have existed in Egypt, Iran, Iraq, Jordan, Tunisia, Morocco, Algeria, Syria, and Yemen. Bahrain and Kuwait also have experimented with such systems. The form of legislative dynamic most familiar to Western observers exists in Israel and Turkey (and did exist in Lebanon until the 1975 civil war). Nevertheless, in Israel, the parliament has been a traditionally weak structure in comparison to the cabinet, despite its antecedents in the British model. The Turkish government has been subjected to periodic military interference. In both countries, however, legislatures are freely elected, real political opposition exists, and multiparty competition is the norm. Throughout the rest of the Middle East, political opposition is generally controlled, as are elections.

The politics of the Middle East are dominated mostly by the individuals of the executive branch of government who control the system and its decisions. More often than not, this is a single authoritarian individual, whether by the title of king, prince, general, or president. Most Middle Eastern governments can be classified as authoritarian; the autonomy of their political institutions is limited, and there are serious constraints on personal political freedoms. The individuals' political rights and personal freedoms are not accorded considerable attention in most of the region's systems and are rarely guaranteed. Nevertheless, despite the range and extent of government control over the public sector and formal governmental activity, totalitarian regimes are not a conspicuous regional feature as there is often a clear separation between the public and private sectors, with the private sector insulated from governmental interference.

Authoritarian systems include several major forms of government such as monarchy (absolute or constitutional) with a king, prince, or sultan at its head. The monarchic principle is firmly rooted in Middle Eastern tradition and history. Such leaders—caliphs, sultans, shahs, khedives, shaykhs, and emirs—have held the reins of government in some areas for centuries, often sustaining control through hereditary succession. Monarchies have been seen as legitimate forms of government even if individual monarchs were given to excesses in the assumption or exercise of power. Monarchies were established by the British, or at least with their acquiescence, in Iraq and in Transjordan during their respective mandates. The coup in Iran after World War I shifted dynasties but retained the monarchy until its replacement by the Islamic Republic in 1979. Egypt retained its monarchy until 1952 and Libya until 1969, while Morocco, Jordan, and the Gulf states still maintain the tradition of monarchical rule. Turkey's caliphate-sultanate was terminated after World War I, while the imamate of Yemen survived until the 1950s. The formal change from monarchy to republic does not, however, assure an end to personal control of the affairs of state. On the contrary, often a popular dictator has followed, such as Mustafa Kemal ATATÜRK in Turkey, Gamal Abdel NASSER in Egypt, or Saddam HUSSEIN in Iraq.

A republican form of government was formally established during the French mandate over Syria and Lebanon, and these two states emerged from French control after World War II as republics. Nevertheless, they soon moved in very different directions, with Lebanon retaining at least the form of a republic and Syria establishing a single-person system, which has been dominated by Hafiz al-ASAD since the early 1970s.

Political pluralism is a rare feature in the Middle East, its presence restricted today to Israel and Turkey and, arguably, Lebanon. In Israel, the tradition of proportional representation and coalition government, which originated in the British model for the pre-state Zionist structures in PALESTINE, has helped generate party pluralism. In Lebanon, the NATIONAL PACT of 1943 divided elected and appointive government positions proportionally among the various religious denominational groups. Although it has survived since the French mandate and has been modified various times since, its premise of proportional ethnic and religious representation remains a central feature of Lebanese politics, albeit buffeted by civil war. Turkey is a prominent example of a state that has moved from a one-party to a multiparty system since 1945.

Periodically, suggestions have been advanced for political change and reform as well as for further democratization of the states in the region, but these have rarely advanced beyond the stage of pronouncement, thereby allowing the retention of existing structures and types of government.

Islamic governments (theocracies) have been the exception, not the rule, in the Arab world—Israel is a Jewish state but not a theocracy, Turkey abolished the caliphate in the 1920s and proclaimed itself a secular state. An Islamic government was installed in Iran only after the IRANIAN REVOLUTION and the ouster of the shah in 1979.

The role of ISLAM in government has varied. Most Islamic states are so described because the majority of their populations are Muslim and they utilize elements of Islam to guide their activities. Many of their constitutions include provisions that the state is Islamic, that Islam is the established religion, or that certain officials (generally the head of state) must be Muslim. This is the case in virtually all the Arab states, yet most of their governments, as well as those of Turkey and Iran (until the revolution), are mixtures, and some of the elements of Islam coexist with extensive borrowings from Western and secular conceptions of government and political life. In some states, Islam has been used as a mechanism for achieving and sustaining the legitimacy of the regime; in others it has been a mobilizing force to generate popular opposition to government policies.

The Iranian revolution established a regime in which Ayatollah Ruhollah KHOMEINI and the clerics that supported him dominated the executive, legislative, and judicial branches of government as well as the military, the media, and the REVOLUTIONARY GUARDS, and traditional Islamic law was enshrined as the law of the land. The structure of government was one peculiar to the Shi'a system of Iran, as molded and guided by Khomeini; it achieved its form only after significant internal discord among varying interpreters of the legacy of SHI'ISM. But, that model has not been emulated in other states.

No Arab country has yet formally established an Islamic government, although Saudi Arabia has many of the trappings, including a SHARI'A-based legal system and the king's formal title as Custodian of the Two Holy Mosques.

BIBLIOGRAPHY

BILL, JAMES A., and ROBERT SPRINGBORG. *Politics in the Middle East,* 3rd ed. Glenview, Ill. and London, 1990.
HUDSON, MICHAEL C. *Arab Politics: The Search for Legitimacy.* New Haven, Conn., and London, 1977.
LONG, DAVID E., and BERNARD REICH, eds. *The Government and Politics of the Middle East and North Africa,* 3rd ed. Boulder, Colo., and London, 1994.

Bernard Reich

Grady–Morrison Plan

Plan to solve the Palestine conflict, presented to the House of Commons on July 31, 1946, by Britain's deputy prime minister, Herbert Morrison.

The plan was presented after consultations between British and U.S. officials, among the latter, Henry Grady; but it was in reality a standby British plan for ending the conflict over the future of the British mandate. Its essence was a British trusteeship, under which PALESTINE would be cantonized into four areas, each with autonomy over local (and only local) affairs: Jewish areas, Arab areas, Jerusalem, and the Negev. The Jewish and the Arab areas were each to have an elected legislative chamber. The British high commissioner was to choose a prime minister and a council of ministers from among members of the two legislative bodies. The plan further provided for the admission to Palestine of 100,000 European Jews, survivors of the Holocaust, as soon as it went into effect (as U.S. President Harry S. Truman favored). Future Jewish immigration was to be linked to the country's absorptive capacity.

ZIONISM's proponents in and out of Palestine were opposed to Jerusalem and the Negev becoming separate districts and to the British government having the last word over immigration. The Jewish area would have been about 1,500 square miles (3,885 sq km), considerably less than the 2,600 square miles (6,734 sq km) proposed by the PEEL COMMISSION REPORT in 1937. The plan was also rejected by the ARAB HIGHER COMMITTEE. As political pressures mounted in the United States against endorsement of the plan, President Truman advised British Prime Minister Clement Attlee on August 12, 1946, that no U.S. endorsement would be forthcoming, so the plan never went forward.

BIBLIOGRAPHY

ROLEF, S. H., ed. *Political Dictionary of the State of Israel.* New York, 1987.

Benjamin Joseph

Grand Mosque

Site of an attempt to overthrow the Al Sa'ud dynasty in 1979.

On 20 November 1979, the first day of the Islamic year 1400, Muslim extremists seized the Grand Mosque at Mecca in an attempt to overthrow the AL SA'UD FAMILY. Their leader, JUHAYMAN IBN MUHAMMAD, accused the Al Sa'ud and the state-appointed ULAMA (religious officials) of impiety and hypocrisy, thus directly challenging the source of the government's legitimacy. A member of the important UTAYBA TRIBE, Juhayman emulated the IKHWAN of fifty years before and reflected tribal, as well as religious, disaffection. Government forces retook the mosque after a week of bloody fighting.

BIBLIOGRAPHY

HOLDEN, DAVID, and RICHARD JOHNS. *The House of Saud: The Rise and Rule of the Most Powerful Dynasty in the Arab World.* New York, 1981.

MACKEY, SANDRA. *The Saudis: Inside the Desert Kingdom.* Boston, 1987.

Malcolm C. Peck

Grand Vizier

See Vizier

Grane

Transliterated Arabic word for "little hill."

"Grane" is one phonetic spelling of *qurayn.* It was used by European travelers in the eighteenth century, to refer to the town of Kuwait.

BIBLIOGRAPHY

CRYSTAL, JILL. *Kuwait: The Transformation of an Oil State.* Boulder, Colo., 1992.

Malcolm C. Peck

Graziani, Rodolfo   [1882–1955]

Italian military officer.

Graziani first came to prominence as the conqueror of Tripolitania in 1925, during the second Italo–Sanusi War. In 1929, under the direction of the new governor of Tripolitania and Cyrenaica, Marshal Pietro Badoglio, he completed the conquest of the Fezzan. In 1930, General Graziani was made vice-governor of Libya and military governor of Cyrenaica, and during the next year, completed its pacification using brutal and ruthless tactics. The nomadic population of northern Cyrenaica was herded into detention camps; a wire fence was constructed along the northern Cyrenaican–Egyptian border and the Sanusi *zawiyas* (Islamic religious centers) were destroyed. Graziani's tactics reached their peak with the public execution of the veteran resistance leader, Umar al-Mukhtar, at Soluk on September 16, 1930. Graziani went on to succeed Marshal Balbo as governor of Libya on the latter's death in action in Tobruk in June 1940.

BIBLIOGRAPHY

EVANS-PRITCHARD, E. E. *The Sanusi of Cyrenaica.* Oxford, 1947.

George Joffe

Greater Israel

Hebrew Eretz Yisrael HaShlema—the "whole" or "entire" land of Israel. Phrase designating Jewish national territory within its divinely prescribed and biblically inhabited borders.

These borders are variously defined by the Talmud, depending on the terms of inquiry (legal, historical, messianic). After the 1967 ARAB–ISRAEL WAR, this concept was championed by certain groups and individuals among the socialist left and increasingly the political and religious Zionist right as an impetus and justification for retaining territory conquered in that war.

Zev Maghen

Greater Syria

Pre-1914 name for present-day Syria, Lebanon, Israel, and Jordan.

Until World War I the name Syria generally referred to Greater or geographical Syria, which extends from the Taurus mountains in the north to the Sinai in the south, and between the Mediterranean in the west and the desert in the east. The name was first given by the Greeks to the city of Tyrus (now Tyre)—Sur in Arabic—and then applied by them to the whole of the province.

The early Arabs referred to Greater Syria as Bilad al-Sham; in Arabic *al-Sham* means *left* or *north*. Bilad al-Sham is so called because it lies to the left of the holy Ka'ba in Mecca, and also because those who journey thither from the Hijaz bear to the left or north. Another explanation is that Syria has many beauty spots—fields and gardens—held to resemble the moles (*shamat*) on a beauty's face.

The term Syria, referring to greater or geographical Syria, began to be used again in the political and administrative literature of the nineteenth century. The Ottoman Empire then established a province of Syria, and more than one newspaper using the term Suriyya in its name was published at the time. In 1920, Greater Syria was partitioned by the Allies of World War I into present-day Syria, Greater Lebanon, Palestine, and Transjordan.

BIBLIOGRAPHY

HOURANI, ALBERT. *Arabic Thought in the Liberal Age.* London, 1962.
LE STRANGE, GUY. *Palestine under the Moslems.* Reprint. Beirut, 1965.

Abdul-Karim Rafeq

Greater Syria Plan

Plan for unification of the central regions of the Middle East.

Championed by King ABDULLAH of Transjordan, the Greater Syria plan was the expression of an old dream to unify Syria, Lebanon, Palestine, and Jordan. After Faisal's kingdom in Syria collapsed in 1920, Abdullah tried to unite Transjordan and Syria under his rule, and throughout the 1930s, he kept the dream alive for the Hashimites. Although he received little encouragement from British officials, his ideas revived after World War II and met with the approval of Nuri al-SA'ID of Iraq; certain aspects of the program were incorporated into the Arab League charter in 1945. However, most Syrian leaders, not to mention those of Lebanon and Palestine, were against a Hashimite-led Greater Syria and distrusted Abdullah accordingly. Although the Syrian People's party of Antun SA'ADA supported the scheme, the rest of the Syrian leadership rejected it, including the first president of independent Syria, Shukri al-Quwatli, and his successor, Husni al-Za'im. With the assassination of Abdullah in 1951, the Greater Syria plan lay in ruins, though it was kept alive by Nuri al-Sa'id until his untimely death in 1958.

BIBLIOGRAPHY

LENCZOWSKI, GEORGE. *The Middle East in World Affairs,* 4th ed. Ithaca, N.Y., 1980.
SEALE, PATRICK. *The Struggle for Syria.* London, 1986.

Zachary Karabell

Great Game, The

Phrase coined at the beginning of the nineteenth century, referring to the imperial competition between Britain and Russia over control of southern central Asia.

Thanks in part to Rudyard Kipling, mention of "The Great Game" conjured up images of dashing heroism in the wilds of the Afghanistan mountains. While this romanticism was certainly a part of the game, it was more often played by politicians in London and St. Petersburg than by adventurers in the steppe.

BIBLIOGRAPHY

FROMKIN, DAVID. *A Peace to End All Peace.* New York, 1989.

Zachary Karabell

Greco–Turkish War

Brief war won by Turkey but also benefiting Greece due to great power intervention.

The Greco–Turkish War of 1897 ended in an easy victory for Turkey. It began in April 1897 with clashes across the Greco–Turkish borderline, which at the time ran between Thessaly and Ottoman-held Macedonia. The hostilities ended in May 1897, after the Turkish army had driven the Greeks back deep into Greek territory.

The war grew out of the tension between Greece and Turkey, which was fueled by yet another Greek uprising on the Ottoman-controlled island of Crete. Calling for a more dynamic stance by Greece toward Turkey, the Greek nationalist organization ETHNIKÉ HETAIRIA (National Association) orchestrated an incursion into Turkish territory by Greek irregulars (March 1897), apparently with the knowledge of the Greek government. The irregulars were repulsed by Turkish forces, but the incident led to a break in the diplomatic relations between Greece and Turkey and a massing of their respective armies on the mountainous frontier between Greek Thessaly and Ottoman Epirus and Macedonia.

The Greek army, consisting of two divisions, was unable to capitalize on its early incursions across the Macedonia–Thessaly border and suffered defeats in several battles around the mountain passes between Macedonia and Thessaly south of Mount Olympus. The Greek front collapsed on April 12, 1897, and the Greek forces began to retreat into the Thessalian plain. Within two weeks and with little resistance, the Turkish army controlled all of Thessaly, including its major towns Larissa and Volos. There was relatively little activity on the western front in Epirus, where the Greek offensive was successfully repulsed by the Turkish army.

The war came to an end when the advancing Turkish army scored another two victories in battles on the mountains that divided the Thessalian plain from the rest of Greece, thus consolidating its control over Thessaly. The danger that further Greek territories would fall to the Ottomans prompted Czar Nicholas II to intervene in order to persuade Sultan Abdülhamit to agree to a ceasefire; it was signed by the combatants on May 7, 1897, although the end of the war was not formally agreed upon by the Greek and Turkish governments until November 1897. Because of the involvement of the great powers in the resolution of the conflict, the Ottoman Empire gained very little from its victory except monetary compensation and slight changes in the original borderline that it considered strategically advantageous. The great powers also took the opportunity to oblige both sides to agree to a number of as yet unresolved bilateral issues, such as the free movement of the populations across their borders. Finally, in an important gesture that served to acknowledge Greece's original grievances, the great powers prevailed upon Abdülhamit to accept previously Ottoman-ruled Crete as an autonomous region.

Although the outcome of the Greco–Turkish War of 1897 could have been much more unfavorable for Greece in terms of territorial losses, the result of the war, indirectly, had a catalytic effect on Greek politics, economics, and military policies. Popular distrust of the monarchy increased because Prince Constantine had led the army into war, and there was growing disenchantment with the political elites, who were seen as incapable of shouldering the nation's aspirations. At the same time, the modernization of Greece's armed forces became a major priority. Within twelve years, the political elites were swept aside by the emergence of a new political movement under Eleuthérios VENIZÉLOS, who successfully completed the program of military modernization, as Greece's effective military performance in the 1912–1913 Balkan wars demonstrated.

BIBLIOGRAPHY

CHRISTOPOULOS, GEORGE, ed. *Istoria tou Ellinikou Ethnous* (History of the Greek Nation), vol. 14. In Greek.

Alexander Kitroeff

Greece

Country at southernmost end of Balkan peninsula that has often been engaged in territorial disputes with Turkey.

The official name of Greece, which is also known as Hellas (Ellas in Greek), is Hellenic Republic. Greece has a presidential parliamentary form of government in which the executive branch consists of the president, the prime minister, and the cabinet. The legislative branch is the unicameral Greek Chamber of Deputies (*Vouli*) whose members are elected to a five-year term. The president, who is the head of state, is elected by the parliament to a five-year term.

According to a census taken in March 1991, the population of Greece was then 10,269,074. Greece's territory, which covers 131,944 square kilometers (52,778 square miles), consists of the mainland of the southern tip of the Balkan peninsula and over two thousand large and small islands that contribute to a long coastline estimated at almost 14,000 kilometers (8,694 miles). Greece borders on Albania, the former Yugoslav Republic of Macedonia, and Bulgaria to the north and on Turkey to the northeast. Besides Athens, the capital, the other major cities are Salonika, Patras, Larissa, Ioannina, Heraklion, and Volos. Greece is a mountainous country intersected by narrow valleys, and many of the mountain ranges extend into the sea as peninsulas. The temperate climate is characterized by mild wet winters and dry hot summers. The country is divided into fifty-two administrative departments, and the governor of a department is appointed by the government.

Greece's natural resources are bauxite, lignite, magnesite, crude oil, and marble. Land use is apportioned as follows: 23 percent arable land, 8 percent permanent crops, 40 percent meadows and pastures, 20 percent forest and woodland. Agriculture constituted 12.8 percent of the gross domestic product (GDP) in 1989; the major agricultural products are grains, fruits (especially olives and raisins), vegetables, wine, tobacco, cotton, livestock, and dairy products. The industrial sector includes mining, electricity, and construction. Greece's manufactured goods, which made up 30 percent of the GDP in 1989, are mainly processed foods, shoes, textiles, metals, chemicals, electrical equipment, and cement. Bolstered by the significant tourist industry, the service sector in 1989 was 57 percent of the GDP. Greece's major trading partner for both imports and exports is the European Community.

In Greece, 97 percent of the people are Greek Orthodox, 2 percent are Muslim, and 1 percent are Jewish or some other religion. The official language of the country is Greek, but the Muslim minority speaks Turkish, and there are Slavic speakers in northern Greece whose numbers are estimated to be between ten and twenty thousand or 0.2 percent of the total population. The seven major Greek universities are located in Athens, Salonika, Patras, Crete, Ioannina, Thrace, and the Aegean islands.

The major political parties are currently New Democracy, Panhellenic Socialist Movement, Political Spring, the Communist Party of Greece, and the Greek Left. In 1993, the Panhellenic Socialist Movement, headed by Andreas Papandreou, won the elections and replaced New Democracy, led by prime minister Constantine Mitsotakis, as the governing party. The president Constantine Karamanlis, held his position for a term that ended in 1995.

Greece was formally recognized by the great powers as an independent state in 1830, nine years after the outbreak of the GREEK WAR OF INDEPENDENCE waged against the Ottomans in the Peloponnese, Rumelia, and the maritime islands. From its establishment in 1830, the Greek state pursued the goal of extending its territorial limits to encompass lands adjacent to its original borders that included large Greek populations. Called the Great Idea, this program had as its ultimate (never-realized) goal the incorporation or Istanbul and the Asia Minor littoral within the boundaries of the Greek state. Through diplomatic means or war, Greece's territory was enlarged to include the Ionian Islands (1864), Thessaly and part of Epirus (1881), and southern Epirus, Macedonia, Crete, and the northern Aegean Islands (1913). With the approval of the great powers, Greek troops landed in the Asia Minor port of İzmir in 1919 and occupied the surrounding area, only to find themselves engaged in a full-scale war with the Turkish nationalists. A Turkish victory in 1922 meant that the presence of Greeks in Asia Minor for 3,000 years had come to an end, either through war or the Greco–Turkish exchange of populations agreed upon at the Lausanne Conference (1923), where Greece formally renounced its remaining territorial claims against Turkey, thereby bringing the era of the Great Idea to an end.

In the nineteenth century, Greece's domestic politics were shaped by the government's attempts to balance the demands of the Great Idea with the requirements of a developing state. Until 1864, political activity consisted in the forming and consolidating of a newly modern centralized state. Opposition to that process due to localist and particularist interests on the part of members of the old notable class cost the life of Greece's first governor, Count Ioannes Kapodistrias. The great powers then appointed Otto I, a German prince, to be Greece's monarch (1843). Otto's

entourage of Bavarian advisers helped establish a centralized state apparatus, but a democratic constitution was granted only in 1844, after a revolt against the king. The poor implementation of that constitution and a sense that the king continued to govern autocratically caused another revolt in 1863, which culminated in Otto's replacement by a Danish prince, who became George I. Amendments to the constitution produced one of the most extensive systems of male universal suffrage known in Europe at the time. By contrast, women did not receive the right to vote in national elections until 1952. The democratization of public life and the strengthening of political parties did not affect the continuing importance the state had in initiating economic development because of the location of most Greek entrepreneurs in the diaspora. Two parties dominated Greek politics until the early twentieth century. The one headed by Harilaos Trikoupis favored economic development over territorial expansion whereas the one led by Theodoros Deliyiannes had as its first priority the immediate implementation of the Great Idea. Economic failure (attested by emigration to the United States) and defeat in the GRECO–TURKISH WAR (1897) signaled the bankruptcy of both parties and reflected negatively on the monarchy.

A new era in Greek history was ushered in after the leaders of a military coup (1909) invited Cretan politican Eleuthérios VENIZÉLOS to assume power. Venizelos implemented a liberal, modernizing domestic policy while at the same time vigorously pursuing the goals of the Great Idea; this strategy helped Greece emerge victorious from the BALKAN WARS of 1912/13. Conflict with king Constantine I over Greece's orientation in World War I forced Venizélos, who favored the Allies, to resign, but he became prime minister again in 1917, following Allied intervention in Greece that caused Constantine to abdicate. These events marked the beginning of a major rift in Greek politics between "venizélists" and "royalists" that ended only during World War II. Leading up to this political breach during the interwar period was the social upheaval caused by the influx of 1.5 million refugees from Asia Minor and elsewhere. Urbanization and industrialization were accelerated as a consequence, and the emergence of radical politics was facilitated. Gen. Ioannes Metaxas used the threat of a takeover by the small contingent of communists and labor movement members as an excuse to suspend parliament and democratic freedoms and to establish a dictatorship (1936–1940). The regime ended when Greece, after having repulsed an attack Italy had launched from Albania, was occupied by the Axis powers (1941).

The occupation by Germany, Italy, and Bulgaria during the war had a catalytic effect on Greek society and politics. The repressive measures imposed by the Axis, and the ensuing famine and hardships, favored the development of a radical left-wing resistance movement and tarnished the image of the former royalists and venizélists who had formed an exile government under George II. When Greece was liberated in late 1944, clashes broke out between, on the one side, the left and, on the other, the liberals and conservatives, who were supported by British troops. The conflict culminated in the 1947–1949 Greek civil war, which led to the defeat of the left, especially after the United States had become involved in Greece following the institution of the TRUMAN DOCTRINE (1947). The World War II peace treaty awarded Greece the Dodecanese islands; the British-occupied island of Cyprus thus remained Greece's only outstanding territorial claim.

The aftereffects of civil war and the international climate generated by the Cold War produced a political atmosphere of oppressive anticommunism in Greece. Civil liberties were not fully restored, and leftists (and even liberals) were unable to gain employment in the civil service. All the elections were won by conservative governments until 1963. Having become a member of NATO in 1951, Greece remained closely connected to the United States strategically and militarily. The wartime devastation the country had undergone brought on urbanization and emigration. A clash between the centrist government and King Constantine I (1965) led to a political crisis that ended in the breakdown of the democratic order and the establishment of a dictatorship (1967–1974) by a group of colonels. The military regime collapsed after overthrowing the government of Cyprus and establishing a short-lived nationalist Greek Cypriot regime, thereby provoking the invasion of Cyprus by Turkish troops. The transition to democratic rule in Greece in the post-1974 era was marked by the emergence of two major parties—New Democracy and the Panhellenic Socialist Movement—the legalization of the Communist party, the abolition of the monarchy in favor of a presidential republic by referendum (December 1974), and Greece's entry into the European Community (1981).

Notwithstanding its consolidation of democratic rule domestically after 1974, Greece has continued to be involved in international disputes, primarily with Turkey. The continuing Turkish occupation of the northern part of Cyprus is a constant source of tension between the two countries; their disputes over the air, continental shelf, and territorial waters in the Aegean have similarly presisted. Since the breakup of Yugoslavia, Greece has been locked into a dispute with the former Yugoslav Republic of Macedonia over its decision to adopt the name Macedonia, which Greece claims is a Greek name and whose choice, according to Greece, denotes territorial claims over northern Greece.

[See also: Ankara, Treaty of; Lausanne, Treaty of]

BIBLIOGRAPHY

CLOGG, RICHARD. *A Concise History of Greece.* New York, 1992.
———, ed. *The Struggle for Greek Independence.* Hamden, Conn., 1973.
GREENIDGE, ABEL. *A Handbook of Greek Constitutional History.* New York, 1972.
VAN BOESCHOTEN, RIKI. *From Armatolik to People's Rule: Investigation into the Collective Memory of Rural Greece.* Philadelphia, 1991.

Alexander Kitroeff

Greeks in the Middle East

Greek communities in the Middle East, especially in Egypt, once played a vital economic role.

Once significant, the Greek presence in the Middle East is currently limited to about 6,000 persons in Egypt (primarily in Cairo and Alexandria), and it is much smaller in the Sudan, the Arabian peninsula, and elsewhere in the region. (No official statistics are available to provide reliable figures.)

The geographical proximity of the Middle East to the Greek islands and mainland, the development of Greek maritime trade in the seventeenth century, and the existence of Greek Orthodox patriarchates in Alexandria, Antioch, and Jerusalem ensured that there would be small numbers of Greek merchants and clerics in the Middle East around 1800. Their numbers began increasing subtantially in the nineteenth century, after Muhammad Ali, Egypt's ruler, invited foreign entrepreneurs, including Greeks, to Alexandria to help modernize Egypt. The greatest number of resident Greeks in Egypt's history—99,793 persons, of whom 76,264 were Greek citizens—was recorded in Egypt's annual census of 1927. Constituting the largest of the numerous foreign communities inhabiting Egypt from the mid-nineteenth through the mid-twentieth century, the Greeks were a socially diverse group that ranged in occupation from wealthy bankers and exporters to employees in the service sector and even factory workers. Smaller Greek communities of a few thousand also could be found in Sudan, Palestine, and in cities along the North African coast. The end of the CAPITULATIONS in Egypt (1937) signaled the onset of the decline in numbers of Greeks in Egypt, and the Egyptian Revolution of 1952 accelerated this decrease. The Suez Crisis of 1956 reinforced the trend, although a large part of the Greek community supported Egypt in its claim on the canal. The nationalization measures taken by the Egyptian government in 1963 caused the numbers of Greeks remaining in Egypt to fall to a few thousand.

Spread out across the country, the Greeks in Egypt were formerly to be found even in small towns in the Nile delta and in upper Egypt, and they formed the largest foreign communities in Alexandria, Cairo, Port Sa'id, and Suez. In 1927, out of 99,605 foreign citizens residing in Alexandria, over a third (37,106) were Greek citizens, and the same proportion held for the other major cities. As they had been in Greece, the Greeks in Egypt were Greek Orthodox, and they continued to use their native tongue. With a number of important Greek journals and literary societies based there, Alexandria became a very important Greek literary center in the first three decades of the twentieth century. The Alexandrian Greek poet C. P. Cavafy (1863–1933) gained an international reputation and Alexandrian writer Stratis Tsirkas (d. 1979) enjoys a good reputation in Greece. Like most of the foreigners in Egypt, the Greeks were noted for their cosmopolitanism. Many Greeks were fluent in either French or English, and the wealthier strata of Greek society in Egypt had very close ties with Europe. Several Greeks sat on company boards whose members came from mixed European backgrounds. In the 1930s, more and more Greeks began to acquire a knowledge of Arabic.

As did all the foreign residents, the Greeks benefited from the broad-ranging privileges Egypt provided to the citizens of other countries. Capitulation rights were extended to the Greeks the year after Greece signed a capitulations treaty with the Ottoman Empire (1855); previously, some Greeks had been under the protection of European consuls. Greece agreed to participate in the MIXED COURTS system in 1876. The Egyptian uprising and the British occupation of 1882 that followed it did not affect the status of the Greeks, nor did the outbreak signaling the beginning of the Egyptian nationalist movement (1919), with which many Greeks sympathized. The Greek government was unable to offer the Greeks in Egypt any help in the diplomatic negotiations preceding the end of the capitulations (1937) or the abolition of the mixed courts (1949);

the Greeks had hoped that in regard to these arrangements their traditionally close relationship with the Egyptians would have earned them more favorable treatment than they received.

The Greeks made their greatest impact in Egypt via their role in the banking and cotton sectors. The first group of Greeks brought to Alexandria by Muhamad Ali in the early 1800s were merchants, shipbuilders, and sailors whose activities helped increase commerce and building of the merchant marine in Egypt. The Greek community in Alexandria was unaffected by Egypt's involvement on the side of the Ottomans during the Greek War of Independence (1821–1830), and the number of Greeks in Egypt gradually increased in the following decades, as did their economic strength. The boom in Egyptian cotton production and export in the 1860s, which catapulted the Egyptian economy to new levels and integrated it into the world economy, also further increased the role and economic power of the Greek merchants and financiers, who remained central to the financing, production, and exporting of cotton in Egypt until the eve of World War II. In the 1920s, Greek exporting houses were responsible for 25 percent of all Egyptian cotton exports. The largest of the Greek exporting companies of that period was Choremi, Benachi & Co.; in the banking sector, Greeks such as the Salvago family were well known and influential.

The Greeks in Egypt remained closely identified with issues of Greek nationalism and with Greek party politics. The early settlers had supported the Greek War of Independence and subsequent efforts to incorporate Greek-populated areas within the Greek state. With time, increasing numbers of Greeks returned to Greece to fight as volunteers in the Greek army, especially during the 1912–1913 Balkan War. The wealthiest financed the bulding of schools or philanthropical institutions in their hometowns or villages, and others made contributions that went toward developing the Greek state. For example, the donations of George Averoff helped complete the marble stadium in Athens where the first Olympic games were held in 1896 and made it possible to purchase the battleship *Averoff*, which proved a factor in Greece's victories in the Balkan War.

The Greeks in Egypt created a broad network of communal institutions: schools, hospitals, churches, orphanages, nursing homes, and a variety of leisure and athletic societies, most of them run by the city-based Greek community organizations, which were themselves administered by prominent Greeks in the community. A small and weak institution in the 1800s, the Greek Orthodox patriarchate of Alexandria gradually grew in stature and importance as the numbers of Greeks in Egypt increased.

[*See also:* Levantine]

BIBLIOGRAPHY

KITROEFF, ALEXANDER. *The Greeks in Egypt, 1919–1937: Ethnicity and Class* (St. Antony's Middle East Monographs No. 20). London, 1989.
POLITIS, A. *Hellenism and Modern Egypt*, 2 vols. Alexandria, 1931. In Greek.

Alexander Kitroeff

Greek War of Independence

Aided by the great powers, Greece broke away from the Ottoman Empire to establish a modern state.

The Greek War of Independence began with two uprisings in March 1821. The first was led by Alexander Ipsilanti, a Greek officer in the Russian army, who led an ill-fated attack of Greek rebels into Moldavia from Russian territory. The second uprising took place in southern Greece, in the Peloponnesse, and was to lead eventually to the establishment of the modern Greek state. The uprising in the Peloponnese, launched by Greek military chieftains, spread northward to parts of Rumelia and to the maritime islands off the eastern coast of the Peloponnese. In their clashes with the local Ottoman garrisons, the Greek rebels' object was to capture the fortified towns of the region; Greek vessels proved important in assisting the rebels to lay siege to the coastal forts. By the end of 1821, the Greeks controlled enough territory to be able to convene a meeting of representatives that proclaimed Greece's independence.

The rebels could not, however, sustain the successes they had scored in the first year of the revolt and were soon facing serious military, financial, and political difficulties. Ottoman army units stationed further north marched southward into Rumelia and the Peloponnese and eventually recaptured some of the forts the Greeks had taken. The presence of European philhellenes fighting for the Greek cause did not serve to make less urgent the Greeks' need for more funds and equipment. Although the Greek leaders were able to obtain two loans in London for the purpose of acquiring armaments and equipment, they did so under unfavorable terms. By late 1924, the Greeks had managed to contain the Ottoman counterattack and controlled about half the Peloponnese and parts of Rumelia, but they encountered political dissent within their own ranks. Long-

standing regional and personal ties stood in the way of forming an effective, centralized leadership, and the vision of a liberal, democratic constitution was not shared by all the diverse elements who made up the Greek leadership—that is, the military chieftains, the notables, and the Greeks of the diaspora.

The landing of an Egyptian army in the Peloponnese (1925) in response to the sultan's request for help in suppressing the Greek uprising threatened to put an end to the Greek war of independence. After two more years of hostilities, in which the Greeks had to deal with the Egyptian army's attempt to sweep the Peloponnese and with an Ottoman offensive on the Greek strongholds in Rumelia, the areas under Greek control were considerably contracted, especially after the fall of Athens to the Ottomans in May 1927. At the same time, Britain, France, and Russia had agreed upon a plan to end the war and to grant independence to Greece (i.e., the Peloponnese, Rumelia, and the islands involved in the war, which were to be ruled by a governor appointed by the great powers and acceptable to the Greek leadership). The agreement, formalized by the signing of the Treaty of London (1827), was rejected by the SUBLIME PORTE and by Ibrahim Pasha, the leader of the Egyptian army and navy. As diplomatic initiatives were being examined, a combined British, French, and Russian fleet that had sailed to the Peloponnese to blockade the Egyptian and Turkish navies engaged them in the Battle of NAVARINO (October 1927) and destroyed them completely. This development cleared the way for the implementation of the Treaty of London, and Count Ioannes Kapodistrias, a Greek in the Russian diplomatic service, became Greece's first governor.

Kapodistrias set about building a modern state and dealing with the devastation the war had inflicted. The formerly privileged class of military chieftains and notables resisted the centralization inherent in state building, however, and this resistance was to culminate in Kapodistrias' assassination by one of the military chieftains (1832). The work of establishing the modern Greek state had nevertheless progressed, both domestically and diplomatically. The Treaty of Andrianople (1829) ending the Russo–Turkish War (1828–1829) included an article that proclaimed Greece to be an independent state, and the ambassadors of the great powers delineated the Greek state's boundaries in a document communicated to the Porte in the same year (1829). After the Porte had recognized both the Treaty of Andrianople and the Treaty of London as well as the Greek boundaries, the great powers formally proclaimed Greece to be an independent state in 1830.

BIBLIOGRAPHY

PETROPOULOS, JOHN. *Politics and Statecraft in the Kingdom of Greece 1833–1843.* Princeton, N.J., 1968.

Alexander Kitroeff

Greenberg, Uri Zvi [1894–1981]

Hebrew poet.

Born in Bialykamien in eastern Galicia, Poland, Greenberg was a descendant of prominent Hasidic families both from his mother's and father's side. While he was still very young, his parents moved to Lvov where he received a traditional Hasidic education.

Greenberg's earliest poems, written in Yiddish and Hebrew, were published in 1912. Drafted into the Austrian army in 1915, he served on the Serbian front which he deserted in 1917. The Polish pogroms against the Jews in 1918 made a lasting impression on him. Following World War I, he continued to publish in the same two languages as before; however, upon his emigration to Eretz Yisrael, in 1924, he wrote exclusively in Hebrew. For a number of years after his arrival, Greenberg was a dedicated Laborite and became a regular contributor to the Labor daily, *Davar,* when it was founded in 1925.

Subsequent to the Arab riots in 1929, he abandoned the Labor party and joined the ultra-nationalist Zionist Revisionist Party, which he represented as a delegate to several Zionist Congresses. From 1931 to 1934 Greenberg served as emissary of the Revisionist movement in Warsaw where he edited its Yiddish weekly, *Di Velt.* He returned to Eretz Yisrael in 1936. In his poetry and articles of the period, he harshly criticized moderate Zionists and warned of the impending doom destined for European Jewry.

During Israel's struggle for independence, Greenberg was a sympathizer of the IRGUN ZVAʿI LEʿUMI, pre-Israel's underground resistance movement. Following the establishment of the State of Israel, he was elected to the Knesset as a representative of the Herut party. He served from 1949 to 1951.

Unlike secularist writers, Greenberg viewed Zionism from a religio-mystical perspective. He saw Jewish existence as outside the pale of history and the Jews' return to Zion as nothing less than the fulfillment of their destiny. In his pre-Eretz Yisrael poetry, Greenberg manifests an inordinate preoccupation with what he correctly foresaw as the horrors of the Holocaust, which he interpreted as the culmination of the struggle between Christians and Jews. His poetry is strongly ideological and his sources are almost exclusively Jewish and rooted in the Jewish past.

Among Greenberg's works in Yiddish are: *In Malkhus fun Tselem* (In the Kingdom of the Cross, 1922) which deals with the Holocaust and *Krig oyf der Erd* (War in the Land, 1921). His Hebrew works include *Eimah Gedolah ve-Yareʾah* (1925); *Sefer ha-Kitrug ve-ha-Emunah* (1937); *Min ha-Hakhlil ve-el ha-Kakhol* (1949); *Rehovot ha-Nahar—Sefer ha-Ilyot ve-ha-Koʾah* (1951); and *Be-Fisat ha-Ariq u-ve-Helkat ha-Hevel* (1965). Greenberg was awarded the Israel Prize for Hebrew Literature in 1957.

Ann Kahn

Green Book

The governing philosophy of Libya's ruler, Qaddafi.

The Green Book contains the brief, three-part statement of the THIRD INTERNATIONAL THEORY, the governing philosophy of Muammar al-QADDAFI, ruler of Libya. Designed to be an alternative to both capitalism and communism, the Third International Theory is the theoretical basis for the institutions and policies of the JAMAHIRIYA. The first part, issued in 1976 and titled, "The Solution of the Problem of Democracy: The Authority of the People," discusses the dilemmas of just and wise government and declares the solution to be the rule of the people through popular congresses and committees. Part 2, "The Solution of the Economic Problem: Socialism," which appeared in 1978, calls for the end of exploitation implied by wages and rent, in favor of economic partnership and self-employment. Part 3, "The Social Basis of the Third International Theory," treats social issues, including the importance of family and tribe and the status of women and minorities.

Lisa Anderson

Green Line

Term used to designate the 1949 armistice line after the 1948 Arab–Israel War.

In the 1967 Arab–Israel War, Israel captured control of the West Bank, the Gaza Strip, and the Golan Heights (see ARAB–ISRAEL WAR, 1948 and 1967). The Green Line designates the border between the land that had been considered Israeli territory as of 1949 and the land captured during the 1967 war.

BIBLIOGRAPHY

SACHAR, HOWARD M. *A History of Israel.* New York, 1979.
SAFRAN, NADAV. *Israel: The Embattled Ally.* Cambridge, Mass., 1978.

Bryan Daves

Green Line (Beirut)

See Lebanon

Green March

March of 350,000 volunteers to demonstrate Morocco's claim on Western Sahara.

The background to the Green March was a twofold struggle in the mid-1970s: (1) the sophisticated POLISARIO Front movement for nationalism by the Sahrawi people in the former Spanish colony of Western Sahara, and (2) a series of challenges against King HASSAN II of Morocco, which culminated in two attempted coups in 1971 and 1972. Seeking to claim Western Sahara's mineral resources (mainly phosphates) and spurred by the ideology of a "Greater Morocco," Hassan succeeded in signing the Madrid Accords of November 14, 1975, which ceded the territory from Spain to Mauritania and Morocco.

A month earlier, however, a UN report had rejected Morocco's claims. In response, Hassan announced that he would seek volunteers to march into Western Sahara, in what his state-run press described as a demonstration of the will of the Moroccan people to reclaim its territory. By early November, some 350,000 volunteers had signed up—mostly poor and unemployed, rural and urban, they were organized by regional quota. An enormous effort was launched to provide food and medical care for them. Amid intense diplomatic efforts over Western Sahara's future, and just after initial clashes between Moroccan and POLISARIO troops, the marchers crossed the border at Tarfaya. Tens of thousands reached Umm Deboa, where they halted.

On November 14, the Madrid Accords were signed. The march was recalled on November 18; it had been a successful gamble by Hassan to pressure Spain into reaching an accord with him—and to rally support within Morocco for his claim.

BIBLIOGRAPHY

HODGES, TONY. *Western Sahara: Roots of a Desert War.* London, 1983.

Matthew S. Gordon

Grey, Edward   [1862–1933]

British statesman.

A Liberal member of Parliament from 1885 to 1916, Grey served as Prime Minister Herbert Asquith's foreign secretary (1905–1916). In that capacity, he played a central role in the crisis in Morocco (1905–1906) and the AGADIR CRISIS (1911). He presided over the London negotiations that ended the first BALKAN WAR in 1908. Grey failed to keep the Ottoman Empire from joining the Central Powers in World War I, but he sanctioned the actions of the Arab Bureau in Cairo that resulted in the ARAB REVOLT of June 1916. He was succeeded on 4 December 1916, by Sir Arthur Balfour.

BIBLIOGRAPHY

Chambers Biographical Dictionary. 1990.
SHAW, STANFORD, and EZEL KURAL SHAW. *History of the Ottoman Empire and Modern Turkey.* New York, 1977.

Zachary Karabell

Griboyedov Incident

One of the first major anti-Western incidents that was religiously inspired.

The Griboyedov Incident took place when a Russian mission led by the well-known author Aleksandr Sergeyevich Griboyedov was sent to Iran in 1829. The purpose of the mission was to force the Iranian government to pay the indemnity for its defeat in the recent Russo–Iranian war and abide by the humiliating provisions of the Treaty of TURKMANCHAI. The mission heard that two or more Georgian or Armenian women had been forcibly converted to Islam and brought to the harems of Iranian nobility. In flagrant opposition to Iranian norms, the mission forced its way into the harems and took all the women away, allegedly keeping some overnight. The Iranian *ulama* (religious leaders) reacted by issuing a *fatwa* (legal decree) allowing people to rescue the Muslim women from the unbelievers. The crowd of people then entered the mission and became uncontrollable. When the Russian Cossacks shot an Iranian boy, the crowd retaliated by killing the whole mission, including Griboyedov, with one exception.

BIBLIOGRAPHY

KEDDIE, NIKKI R., and RICHARD YANN. *Roots of Revolution: An Interpretive History of Modern Iran.* New Haven, Conn., 1981.

Parvaneh Pourshariati

Grivas, Georgios Theodoros [1898–1974]

Greek Cypriot political and military leader.

Born in Greece, Grivas served in the Greek army from 1920; he was the organizer of the Greek resistance to the Nazi occupation of Athens in 1944/45. In 1951, he went to CYPRUS at the invitation of Archbishop MAKARIOS II to help in the fight for Cypriot independence from Britain.

In 1954, Grivas founded EOKA (Ethniki Organosis Kipriakou Agonos), a covert nationalist group that used political violence to combat the British. In 1959, he was the general, then commander (1964–1967) of the Greek Cypriot National Guard. After the independence of Cyprus in 1960, Grivas broke with Makarios and supported *enosis* (union) with Greece, founding EOKA B in 1971 toward that end.

BIBLIOGRAPHY

LENCZOWSKI, GEORGE. *The Middle East in World Affairs.* Ithaca, N.Y., 1980.
SHIMONI, YAACOV, ed. *Political Dictionary of the Middle East in the Twentieth Century.* New York, 1974.

Zachary Karabell

Grobba, Fritz Konrad Ferdinand
[1886–1973]

German diplomat, orientalist, and specialist in Middle Eastern affairs during the Weimar Republic and the Third Reich; one of the more important and most controversial European diplomats in the Middle East between the two world wars.

Grobba was born in Gartz/Oder, Germany, where he attended elementary and high school. He studied law, economics, and Oriental languages at the University of Berlin, from which he received his doctorate in law in 1913. Before World War I, he worked briefly as a dragoman trainee in the German consulate in Jerusalem; during the war, he served as a lieutenant in the German army in France and in Palestine.

Grobba joined the legal affairs department of the German foreign ministry in September 1922. In January 1923, he was transfered to Abteilung III, the department responsible for the Middle East. When diplomatic relations were established between Germany and Afghanistan in October 1923, Grobba was named Germany's representative in Kabul with the rank of consul. In 1925, the Afghan government accused him of attempting to help a visiting German geographer to escape from Afghanistan shortly after the geographer had shot and killed an Afghan citizen near Kabul. Grobba denied the charge. A diplomatic crisis between Germany and Afghanistan over Grobba's role ensued, and he was recalled to Berlin in April 1926. From 1926 to 1932, he served again in Abteilung III, where he was in charge of the section for Persia, Afghanistan, and India.

In February 1932, Grobba was named German ambassador to Iraq, a post he held until September 1939, when war caused the break in diplomatic relations between Germany and Iraq. He was also Germany's ambassador to Saudi Arabia from November 1938 until September 1939. From October 1939 until May 1941, Grobba served in the German foreign ministry in Berlin. In May 1941, the foreign ministry dispatched him to Baghdad as German special representative to the pro-Axis government of Rashid Ali al-Kaylani; but he left Baghdad later that month, since the Rashid Ali coup collapsed. In February 1942, Grobba was named foreign ministry plenipotentiary for the Arab States, a job that entailed liaison between the German government and Arab exiles in Berlin, such as Rashid Ali and the mufti of Jerusalem, Hajj Amin al-Husayni. In December 1942, he was named to the Paris branch of the German archives commission, a post he held until his brief return to the foreign ministry in April 1944. He was officially retired from the foreign ministry in June 1944, although he continued to work there until the end of the year. In 1945, he worked briefly in the economics department of the government of Saxony, in Dresden.

Grobba published the following books: *Die Getreidewirtschaft Syriens und Palästinas seit Beginn des Weltkrieges* (Hanover, 1923); *Irak* (Berlin, 1941); and *Männer und Mächte im Orient: 25 Jahre diplomatischer Tätigkeit im Orient* (Göttingen, 1967). The latter constitutes his memoirs of his work and experience in Middle Eastern affairs.

Fritz Grobba was the most influential German diplomat in the Middle East after World War I. He worked for the restoration of Germany's pre–World War I economic and political position in the region, within the context of peaceful coexistence with England. The governments of the Weimar Republic and the Third Reich did not, however, entirely share his ambition for the region. Moreover, lingering wartime animosity coupled with bitter and violent Middle East opposition to Anglo–French imperialism, against the backdrop of Nazi expansionism during the 1930s, created Anglo–French distrust of Grobba. This made him one of the more controversial figures in Middle East diplomacy between the world wars.

BIBLIOGRAPHY

HIRSZOWICZ, LUKASZ. *The Third Reich and the Arab East.* London, 1966.

NICOSIA, FRANCIS R. "Fritz Grobba and the Middle East Policy of the Third Reich." In *National and International Politics in the Middle East. Essays in Honour of Elie Kedourie,* ed. by Edward Ingram. London, 1986.
————. *The Third Reich and the Palestine Question.* Austin, Tex., and London, 1985.

Francis R. Nicosia

Groppi's

Restaurant and pastry shop in Cairo, Egypt.

Located in downtown Cairo, on Tal'at Harb square, Groppi's was known during Britain's occupation of Egypt as a civilized meeting place and palace of oriental delights. Set afire during the riots of January 1952, Groppi's survived but was nationalized by the Free Officers. Still occupying its old location, only Groppi's art-deco decor reminds one of its former renown.

BIBLIOGRAPHY

GOLDSCHMIDT, ARTHUR JR. *Modern Egypt: The Formation of a Nation-State.* Boulder, Colo., 1988.

David Waldner

Gruenbaum, Yizhak　[1879–1970]

Polish Zionist.

Active in the early ZIONISM movement at the turn of the century, Gruenbaum participated in several Zionist congresses before World War I. He was elected to the Polish Sejm (parliament) from 1919 to 1932, when he emigrated to Palestine. He soon became a leader of the JEWISH AGENCY, but he resigned after Lord Moyne's assassination in November 1944. He was Israel's minister of interior in the 1948–1949 provisional government, but he failed to win a Knesset (parliament) seat in the 1949 election. He was a MAPAI (labor party) supporter and an ardent champion of a secular Israeli state.

BIBLIOGRAPHY

Encyclopedia Judaica. New York, 1971.
New Standard Jewish Encyclopedia. New York, 1977.

Zachary Karabell

Gruner, Dov　[1912–1947]

Irgun member executed by the British.

One of twelve Zionists belonging either to IRGUN ZVA'I LE'UMI (IZL) or LOHAMEI HERUT YISRAEL (Lehi) who were executed by the British for committing terrorist acts against the British authority, Gruner was born in Hungary in 1912. He immigrated to Palestine in 1940 and joined the Irgun. During World War II, he served five years in the JEWISH BRIGADE of the British army and was wounded twice while fighting in the Western Sahara and Italy. The raid on a government police station at Ramat Gan (April 23, 1946) in which he was severely wounded and captured was his first Irgun operation. It was an audacious mission in which Irgun men gained entry to the station by posing as Arab petty criminals in order to steal a large cache of weapons and ammunition. No British lives were lost in the attack, but Gruner was condemned to death as a response to the growing campaign of terror that the Irgun, the Lehi, and even the Haganah were mounting against British administrators of the mandate system. The Irgun was kept guessing as to the disposition of appeals to commute the sentence, so that when, without warning, Gruner and three other Irgun men were hanged in Acre prison on April 16, 1947, the Irgun was caught unprepared to carry out its threat to hang British hostages in retaliation. Gruner's refusal to ask for clemency and his rejection at his trial of the British court's authority were dramatized in the Jewish press, and his case came to symbolize for the Jews the struggle against British mandatory rule.

Yaakov Shavit

Guedira, Ahmad Rida　[1926–　]

Moroccan politician and diplomat.

Son of Rida Guedira, an influential politician in the 1950s, Ahmad is known for his liberal political views; like his father, he has close ties to the throne of Morocco. In 1964, he and colleagues founded the Democratic Socialist party, which represented a split within the Front for the Defense of Constitutional Institutions (FRONT POUR LA DÉFENSE DES INSTITUTIONS CONSTITUTIONELLES; FDIC), formed to support the monarchy in 1963. Guedira has, since the early 1960s, held a series of posts for the government, including the ministry of foreign affairs (1963–1964). Since 1977, he has served as a special adviser to the cabinet of King HASSAN II.

BIBLIOGRAPHY

Who's Who in the Arab World. 1990.
ZARTMAN, I. WILLIAM, ed. *Man, State and Society in the Contemporary Maghrib.* New York, 1973.

Matthew S. Gordon

Guest Workers

Turkish citizens who migrate to other countries for the sake of employment.

The Turkish migration to Europe started in the late 1950s, when graduates of Turkish technical schools went to West Germany for additional training. It became a large-scale migration after Turkey's new constitution of 1961 recognized as fundamental the right of citizens to enter and leave the country. It accelerated after the first bilateral agreement was signed between TURKEY and West Germany (October 30, 1961). A series of treaties widened the field of host countries—Austria (May 5, 1964), France (April 8, 1966), Sweden (March 10, 1967), and Australia (October 7, 1967).

Between 1961 and 1975, almost a million Turkish workers went to Western Europe. In 1973, Turkish workers in Europe numbered some 787,000, plus about 450,000 dependents. Since 1974, the return of some 25,000 Turks occurs annually. By 1988, about 2 million Turks were in Europe, with about 34 percent under age 18. (Additionally, some 140,000 were employed in the Middle East, mainly in Saudi Arabia.)

The Turkish migration to Western Europe has undergone six phases: (1) recruitment by invitation, organized by private initiatives (1956–1961); (2) signature of bilateral agreements; start of guest worker programs; out-migration; adjustment to new social and industrial conditions (1963–1967); (3) liquidation of rotation model for workers; consolidation and redefinition of goals; legitimation of illegal (tourist) migrants (1968–1973); (4) energy crisis; stoppage of recruitment; reform of child allowances; increases of family reunions; education a problem for the second generation (1974–1978); (5) extensive associational activities; increased requests for political asylum; visa requirements (1978–1985); (6) encouragement for return migration; demands for political rights; growth of migrant-owned small businesses (1985–). In 1990, Turkish migrants owned some 30,000 businesses in West Germany, providing about 105,000 jobs.

Through the years, Turkish migrants have generated substantial revenue, which, particularly in the 1970s, helped to bridge Turkey's trade deficit. It started with 45 million U.S. dollars in 1964 and has fluctuated another 1.5–2 billion U.S. dollars annually since 1978. Turkey tried to channel some of this revenue into development programs, beginning in 1962. The idea was to promote rural development by securing financial remittance from members who went abroad. It gave priority of migration to cooperative members, which was assumed to be a motivator in modernizing the villages. From 1965 to 1974, almost 1,000 villages were founded, with 38,000 of their members sent abroad. Once they left they did not honor their commitments, and revenue did not flow back. The cooperatives were used merely as a means of moving ahead on the waiting list. The program was frozen in 1966 and phased out in 1974. Other financial initiatives have also proved unworkable, for various reasons. The great bulk of migrants' savings are actually sent as remittances that are used for consumption and investment in Turkey, such as housing, land, small shops, and motor vehicles.

Of the major problems facing Turkish migrants abroad for an indefinite period, the greatest is the education and professional commitment of the children. Turkish children do not always benefit from the host country's educational system—because of restrictions, language difficulties, and discrimination. Turkish women are affected by work in host countries, often becoming economically independent, authoritarian, and responsible for decision making and finances; any or all may cause serious marital tensions.

Emigration clearly provided an alternative for rural Turks to obtain nonagricultural positions, higher wages, and fringe benefits. Dealing with returned migrants, however, was not a strategic factor in Turkey's socioeconomic plans. Also, the dream to return, which was assumed in the 1960s and 1970s, has given way to postponed returns or none—in 1991, 83 percent of Turks living in Germany declared they did not want to return home. Turkey's first large-scale migration has become a route for many people to find a better standard of living and the possibility for upward mobility outside the home country.

BIBLIOGRAPHY

ABADAN-UNAT, NERMIN. *Turkish Workers in Europe, 1960–1975: A Socio-economic Reappraisal.* Leiden, 1976.

Nermin Abadan-Unat

Guicciardi Mission

Mission that recommended independence for Bahrain.

Vittorio Winspeare Guicciardi was sent to BAHRAIN as the personal representative of the United Nations (UN) secretary-general. He headed a good-offices mission to find an acceptable solution to Iran's territorial claims to Bahrain. Guicciardi recommended that Bahrain be given independence as a sovereign Arab state. On May 11, 1970, the UN Security Council adopted Resolution 287, endorsing the mission's recommendation. The state of Bahrain became independent on August 14, 1971, under Emir Isa ibn Sulman al-KHALIFA.

BIBLIOGRAPHY

The Middle East and North Africa, 1991, 37th ed. London, 1991.

Emile A. Nakhleh

Guilds

Organizations of skilled workers or artisans.

The earliest evidence for workers in Middle Eastern urban trades and crafts associating in guilds for their common economic and social benefit dates from the fourteenth century, though there are hints of looser groupings before that time. The Ottoman and Safavid empires and the kingdom of Morocco developed extensive guild systems with each guild being self-governing through a hierarchy of ranks. Government approval or oversight, variously expressed, kept them from being totally independent, however. The goal of the guilds was to ensure a stable level of production and an equitable distribution of work among guild members. The guilds thus constituted a generally conservative force disinclined to change with evolving economic conditions. However, they were often important foci of communal and religious life for their members, as in annual guild-organized commemorations of the martyrdom of Imam Husayn by Shi'ites in Iran. The terms used for guilds include *sinf* (category), *ta'ifa* (group), *jama'a* (society), and *hirfa* (craft). Guilds were commonly subjected to collective taxation administered by the market inspector (*muhtasib*) or other government official. Jews and Christians were members of guilds in some cities, but exclusively Christian or Jewish guilds, like that of the kosher butchers of Aleppo, were rare.

Records of the city of Aleppo mention 157 guilds in the middle of the eighteenth century. Cairo had 106 in 1814. The survival of guilds in the nineteenth and twentieth centuries varied according to country and rate of Westernization. In northern Egypt, for example, guilds had virtually disappeared by the end of the nineteenth century because of the influx of mass-produced European goods and the growing market for labor created by European investment. By contrast, the guilds of Fez in Morocco escaped severe crisis until the worldwide depression of the 1930s. Even so, municipal statistics of 1938 show the continued domination of small-scale craft work. The largest guild, that of the slipper-makers, counted 7,100 members, 2,840 of them employers. There were also 800 tanners, 280 of them employers; and 1,700 weavers, of whom 520 were employers. Altogether the guilds numbered 11,000 members.

The potential for guild political activity had manifested itself from time to time over the centuries, as in occasional revolts by workers in the food trades in Cairo at the end of the eighteenth century. By the time modern political life focused on constitutions and participatory government developed, however, economic forces had diminished the importance of guilds in most areas. Iran, where guilds survive to the present day, provides an exception because of its comparatively late exposure to economic and political influences from Europe. The guilds formed the most cohesive group in the CONSTITUTIONAL REVOLUTION of 1906. In Tehran, separate guilds formed seventy political societies (*anjoman*). The guild leaders lacked a sophisticated understanding of politics, however, so the guilds found themselves barred from political power by the electoral law of 1909. With the advent of the Pahlavi regime in 1926, 230 guilds lost government recognition as corporate entities in an effort to dissipate the coalescence of popular feeling around them; but because the new system of individual taxation proved unworkable, they regained their status in 1948. Many guild members were drawn to the Communist Tudeh party or to the movements led by Mohammad Mossadegh, Ayatollah Khomeini, and other critics of the monarchy. In 1969 the 110 guilds of Tehran had a membership of about 120,000. Guild members played an important role in the demonstrations that led to the Iranian Revolution of 1979.

BIBLIOGRAPHY

LAWSON, FRED H. *The Social Origins of Egyptian Expansionism During the Muhammad Ali Period.* New York, 1992.
MARCUS, ABRAHAM. *The Middle East on the Eve of Modernity: Aleppo in the Eighteenth Century.* New York, 1989.

Richard W. Bulliet

Guinness, Walter Edward   [1880–1944]

British deputy minister of state for the Middle East (1942–1944) and minister resident in the Middle East (1944).

In Cairo, while deputy minister of state, Guinness, known as Lord Moyne, argued that a partition plan for Palestine would not succeed unless both the Jewish and Arab areas were made part of GREATER SYRIA. He proposed creating four states: Greater Syria (comprising Syria, Muslim Lebanon, Transjordan, and the Arab part of Palestine after partition), Christian Lebanon, a Jewish state, and a "Jerusalem state" that would remain under British control. He urged postponement of plans for a Jewish army, favored by Chaim WEIZMANN and Winston CHURCHILL, but agreed to enlarge Jewish settlement police and give them military training.

Lord Moyne presided over a conference of Britain's representatives in the Middle East in the fall of 1944 that did not favor his four-state plan, recommending instead that a southern Syria be created out of Transjordan and the Arab part of Palestine. He was assassinated at Cairo by Jewish terrorists, members of the Stern Gang, on 6 November 1944.

Jenab Tutunji

Guish Tribes

Tribes in the military service of the Makhzen in precolonial Morocco.

The most important of the Guish tries were the Sherarda, Sheraga, and Udayay. Guish tribes were distinguished from the Naiba tribes, which were occasionally recruited to serve the Makhzen militarily. They lived on a plot of land offered by the sultan and did not pay taxes. Most of the administrators of the Makhzen were recruited from the Guish tribes.

Rahma Bourqia

Gülbenkian, Calouste   [1869–1955]

Armenian businessman and philanthropist.

Born in Istanbul, Gülbenkian was educated in France and England. In 1902, he acquired British citizenship, to be eligible for the concession for petroleum fields in Mosul. Later, he transferred this concession to the Iraq Consortium established in 1920 by the United States, France, Britain, and the Netherlands. Because he retained a 5-percent stake in the property and profits of the consortium, he was given the nickname "Mr. Five Percent." Gülbenkian, an enthusiastic art collector, bequeathed his valuable collection to the Gülbenkian Foundation in Lisbon, Portugal, the city in which he died.

BIBLIOGRAPHY

Türk Ansiklopedisi. Ankara, 1971.

David Waldner

Gülek, Kasım   [1910–   ]

Turkish writer and politician.

Born in Adana to a prestigious family, Gülek attended Robert College (now Bosporus University)

and studied politics, economics and law in Paris, Cambridge, New York, and Berlin. He joined Turkey's REPUBLICAN PEOPLE'S PARTY (RPP) and was elected to the assembly twice in the 1940s. While the opposition party ruled from 1950 to 1960, he was his party's general secretary (1950–1959), and he was jailed in 1955 for a speech in which he criticized the DEMOCRAT PARTY. He is credited with holding his party together during the 1950s, representing a younger generation that was dissatisfied with party leader İsmet İNÖNÜ and his old guard.

Known as an intellectual's politician, Gülek was publisher of *Ulus,* the party's newspaper, in the late 1950s, and then *Tatın* in the early 1960s, a paper in opposition to İnönü. In 1969, he became a member of Turkey's senate, a post he held through the 1970s. Gülek has written numerous articles and books on the politics of Turkey.

BIBLIOGRAPHY

AHMAD, FEROZ. *The Turkish Experiment in Democracy 1950–1975.* Boulder, Colo., 1977.

Elizabeth Thompson

Güler, Ara   [1928–1991]

Turkish photojournalist.

Istanbul-born Ara Güler was a pioneer of modern Turkish photography. Influenced by the Magnum school, and especially the work of the French photographer Henri Cartier-Bresson, he started his career as a photographer in 1950 for the magazine *Yeni İstanbul* (New Istanbul). He was the regional photographer for *Life* magazine and for *Paris-Match,* and he also worked for Turkish magazines, including *Hayat* (Life), *Dünya* (The World), and *Hürriyet,* a daily newspaper. In 1962, the photography journal *Camera* devoted a special issue to the work, and in the same year, he was given the nickname "The Master of the Leica."

In addition to many exhibits in Turkey, his work has been displayed in the United States, France, and Germany. The reality of daily life in the farthest corners of Anatolia, the natural beauty of Turkey, and its cultural treasures—all appear in his work. In 1980, a collection of his photographs was published.

BIBLIOGRAPHY

Cumhuriyet Dönemi Türkiye Ansiklopedisi. Istanbul, 1983.
Günümüz Türkiyesinde Kim Kimdir. Istanbul, 1987.

David Waldner

Gülersoy, Çelik   [1930–   ]

Turkish tourism promoter and writer.

Born in Hakkari-Cölemerik in eastern Anatolia, Gülersoy obtained a law degree from Istanbul University and from 1947 to 1961 held a number of professional posts. In 1961 he became legal counsel to the Turkish Automobile and Touring Association, and in 1966 its general director, a post he continued to hold through the early 1990s. He extended the scope of the organization through his broad interests in tourism, historical restoration, and the environment.

Gülersoy restored a number of old houses and monuments in Istanbul, opening a number of them as tourist sites. He led efforts to develop other tourist areas in Turkey as well, while writing more than a dozen books on Turkish history and society, tourism development and practices, parks and historical sites. He has made several cultural films and written scripts for others. In 1979, he won the Sedat Simavi prize for a book on Roman covered markets.

BIBLIOGRAPHY

Günümüz Türkiyesinde Kim Kimdir 1987–1988. Istanbul, 1987.

Elizabeth Thompson

Gulf

Arm of the Arabian Sea and Indian Ocean.

Known as the Persian Gulf, the Arabian Gulf, or the Persian/Arabian Gulf, the waters of the Gulf flow between the Arabian peninsula and Iran (formerly Persia); it is more than 500 miles (800 km) long and as wide as 200 miles (320 km). Fed on the northwestern end by the confluence of the Tigris and Euphrates rivers, called the SHATT AL-ARAB, the Gulf drains to the southeast through the Strait of Hormuz into the Arabian Sea.

A shallow inland waterway, reaching a maximum depth of about 328 feet (100 m), the Gulf has nonetheless been a major trade and marine route between East and West since antiquity. BAHRAIN and Qeshm are the most important islands. Aside from local trade, pearl diving, and some smuggling, the Gulf's importance was dimmed between the fifteenth and nineteenth centuries, when Europeans discovered that they could sail their ships around Africa to reach India and the Asian trade ports.

The SUEZ CANAL opened in 1869, and with the early twentieth-century discovery of PETROLEUM deposits throughout the region, the Gulf returned to strategic and economic importance. In the 1980s, more than 80 percent of Middle East oil exports passed through the Strait of Hormuz to the Indian Ocean. The waters of the Gulf were severely polluted by oil spills and burning oil during the GULF CRISIS of 1990/91.

BIBLIOGRAPHY

RUSTOW, DANKWART. *Oil and Turmoil.* New York, 1982.
SHIMONI, YAACOV. *Political Dictionary of the Arab World.* New York, 1987.

Elizabeth Thompson

Gulf Cooperation Council

An organization formed for economic and security reasons by six states of the Persian/Arabian Gulf and the Arabian peninsula.

Formed in May 1981, the Gulf Cooperation Council (GCC) is a regional organization comprising six family-ruled states: Saudi Arabia, Kuwait, Bahrain, Qatar, the United Arab Emirates, and Oman. The communique issued by the heads of those states in Abu Dhabi on May 26, 1981, emphasized cooperation among the member states, their security concerns, and regional stability. The basic objectives are spelled out in Article 4 of GCC's charter. The GCC secretariat, headed by a secretary-general, is headquartered in Riyadh, Saudi Arabia. Abdullah BISHARA, a Kuwaiti national, has served as secretary-general since the council's inception. The rest of the structure consists of a Supreme Council (heads of the six states), a Ministerial Council (foreign ministers), and a Commission for Settlement of Disputes (to be formed when needed).

In addition to the charter, the GCC also ratified in 1981 a Unified Economic Agreement (UEA) among the member states, calling for trade exchange; the movement of capital and citizens; the coordination of development; technical cooperation; and cooperation in transport, communications, finance, and banking. As a regional organization, the GCC has faced serious challenges regarding threats to GULF security, boundary disputes (especially between Bahrain and Qatar), and the GULF CRISIS, when Iraq invaded Kuwait on August 2, 1990. The GCC is expected to face other challenges in the future—as the Gulf continues to search for stability, security, regional cooperation, and economic development.

BIBLIOGRAPHY

NAKHLEH, EMILE A. *The Gulf Cooperation Council: Policies, Problems and Prospects.* New York, 1986.

The Middle East and North Africa, 1992, 38th ed. London, 1992.

Emile A. Nakhleh

Gulf Crisis

A critical international situation that began on August 2, 1990, when Iraq invaded Kuwait, and that officially ended on February 28, 1991, after a U.S.-led military coalition defeated Iraq and liberated Kuwait.

The reasons for IRAQ's invasion of KUWAIT were primarily financial and geopolitical. Iraq emerged from the 1980–1988 IRAN–IRAQ WAR financially exhausted, with a debt of about eighty billion dollars. Its president, Saddam HUSSEIN, tried to service the debt—and fund Iraq's high-technology defense industry, reconstruction, and food imports—with oil revenue. But oil prices fell between January and June 1990 from twenty dollars to fourteen dollars a barrel. Saddam Hussein charged, with merit, that Kuwait and the United Arab Emirates had exceeded their Organization of Petroleum Exporting Countries (OPEC) quotas, therefore keeping the price of oil low. He claimed that overproduction was encouraged by the United States in order to weaken Iraq, and he considered the Kuwaiti action an act of war. He demanded that the price of a barrel of oil be raised to twenty-five U.S. dollars, that Kuwait "forgive" ten billion dollars in debt incurred during his war with Iran and pay 2.4 billion dollars for Iraqi oil it "illegally" pumped from the Rumayla oil field (the southern tip of which is under Kuwait), and that the Gulf states give Iraq financial aid amounting to thirty billion dollars. Saddam Hussein based these demands on the claim that Iraq's war with Iran and sacrifice of hundreds of thousands of lives was designed to protect the Gulf states from revolutionary Iran.

Saddam Hussein also wanted to lease two uninhabited islands, Warba and BUBIYAN, to provide Iraq secure access to the Persian/Arabian GULF and as possible bases for a blue-water navy. Kuwait was reluctant to negotiate with Iraq, a country of seventeen million with vast potential, because Bubiyan was very close to Kuwait City and because of concerns that the demand was a precursor to Iraqi claims to disputed border territories and, indeed, to all of Kuwait, which Iraq historically considered a part of itself. Kuwait's reluctance to negotiate and its continuing demand for loan repayment were seen as arrogant by Saddam Hussein and shortsighted by others in the region.

Paradoxically, the end of the Iran–Iraq War had left Iraq militarily strong, strong enough to aspire to leadership of the Arab world. Iraq had one million experienced soldiers, five hundred planes and fifty-five hundred tanks, and was developing chemical, biological, and nuclear weapons of mass destruction. Officials in the West and Israel voiced alarm, and Western media criticism of human rights violations, especially against the Kurds in Iraq, made Saddam Hussein suspicious. Fearing an action similar to Israel's destruction of Iraq's nuclear reactor in 1981, he issued a sensational threat on April 2, 1990, to burn half of Israel with chemical weapons if it should attack Iraq. The threat produced an outpouring of support throughout the Arab world, where he was viewed as a blood-and-guts Arab Bismarck ready to take on Israel, which had annexed Jerusalem and the Golan, had invaded Lebanon, had bombed the PALESTINE LIBERATION ORGANIZATION (PLO) headquarters in Tunis, and since 1987, had been suppressing a civilian uprising in the West Bank and Gaza, all without an Arab response. By August Saddam Hussein had used a potent mixture of themes—Western imperialism, Arab impotence, the Palestinian cause, and Islam (later, the poor against the rich)—to tap Arab anger and alienation and to rally the Arab masses.

On the eve of the invasion, the United States gave Saddam Hussein mixed signals. On July 25, United States Ambassador April Glaspie assured him that United States President George BUSH wanted better relations with Iraq and that the United States had no opinion on "Arab–Arab conflicts, like your border disagreement with Kuwait," but she cautioned him against the use of force. There is no evidence that the United States deliberately misled him but, Saddam Hussein ignored a fundamental element of U.S. foreign policy: Oil is a vital U.S. interest, one for which it would go to war.

Saddam Hussein invaded Kuwait on August 2, 1990, to the surprise of most observers. His army occupied the country in a few hours with little resistance, killing hundreds of Kuwaitis and jailing and torturing hundreds more. Soldiers looted schools and hospitals of their equipment and banks of their deposits and bullion.

At the government level, Arab reaction split into two camps. The anti-Iraq group consisted of the Gulf countries (Saudi Arabia, Kuwait, Bahrain, Qatar, United Arab Emirates, and Oman), as well as Egypt, Syria, Morocco, Lebanon, Djibouti, and Somalia. The neutral or pro-Iraq group included Jordan, the PLO, Yemen, Sudan, Libya, Tunisia, Algeria, and Mauritania. The split was reflected in the first voting at an August 3 Arab League meeting of foreign ministers, the majority of whom voted to condemn both Iraqi aggression and foreign intervention. With each passing day, the crisis slipped from Arab League hands, becoming an international confrontation between Iraq and a U.S.-led coalition of twenty-eight countries.

President Bush moved swiftly to galvanize opposition to Iraq. The UN Security Council condemned the invasion on August 2—the day it occurred—and demanded Iraq's immediate and unconditional withdrawal. During the following few days, the Soviet Union and the Islamic Conference Organization joined in the condemnation, and the UN placed economic sanctions on Iraq. Most significant was Saudi Arabia's agreement on August 6 to allow U.S. troops and aircraft on its soil, under the code name Operation DESERT SHIELD, after being shown U.S. satellite photographs of Iraqi troops close to Saudi borders. On August 8 Saddam Hussein formally annexed Kuwait, and the UN reacted by declaring the annexation "null and void." On August 10 the Arab League summit passed resolutions authorizing the use of foreign troops to reverse the annexation. Thus, most nations, willingly or under U.S. pressure, condemned the invasion and demanded Iraq's withdrawal.

Saddam Hussein's response on August 12 was to link the withdrawal of Iraq from Kuwait to Israel's withdrawal from Gaza and the West Bank (including Jerusalem) and Syria's withdrawal from Lebanon. The linkage idea generated support in the Arab world, particularly among Palestinians and their organization, the PLO.

The United States rejected linkage, insisting on unconditional withdrawal and on denying Saddam Hussein any fruits of his invasion. Nevertheless, Bush declared on October 1 at the UN that an Iraqi withdrawal from Kuwait might provide an opportunity "to settle the conflicts that divide the Arabs from Israel." Despite numerous diplomatic missions by world leaders, Saddam Hussein remained intransigent. In November the United States declared that it would double its troop strength in the Gulf from about 200,000 to 400,000—an action that guaranteed an offensive military option—and the UN authorized the use of force to liberate Kuwait. Bush gave Saddam Hussein until January 15, 1991, to vacate Kuwait. When he did not, U.S. and allied forces began air attacks on January 16 on Iraq and on Iraqi positions in Kuwait under the code name Operation DESERT STORM. Some of the air strikes were conducted from Turkey, which had supported the coalition, even though most Turks were against a military confrontation with Iraq. Iraq in turn fired Scud missiles at Tel Aviv, damaging hundreds of buildings and killing several people. Israel uncharacteristically did not retaliate, in deference to U.S. concerns that Israeli involvement in the war would risk the continued cooperation of the Arab partners in the coalition. Instead, the United States sent the Patriot antimissile system to Israel to intercept the Scuds, and a number of nations compensated Israel for the damage. Iraq also fired missiles at Saudi Arabia, and Iraqi troops crossed its borders in late January. In an attempt to break out of its isolation, Iraq offered Iran major concessions regarding the Shatt al-Arab waterway, but fearing Saddam Hussein's ambition, Iran stayed neutral throughout the crisis, even though it exchanged prisoners with Iraq and gave sanctuary to 122 Iraqi combat aircraft.

After another ultimatum from President Bush and a number of unsuccessful diplomatic attempts, the coalition launched ground forces into Iraq on February 23, led by U.S. General Norman Schwarzkopf. Kuwait was liberated four days later, and Iraq, after accepting the relevant UN Security Council resolutions, agreed to a cease-fire on February 28, but not before setting fire to some six or seven hundred Kuwaiti oil wells.

The Gulf crisis, including the war, had enormous consequences for the region. Iraq's infrastucture was destroyed. Middle East Watch charged that the United States and its allies may have deliberately targeted the infrastructure and, in addition, may have bombed civilian residences to encourage Saddam's overthrow, even though such actions are in violation of international law. Neither the United States nor Iraq have been forthcoming about Iraq's death toll, which certainly numbered in the tens of thousands.

Kuwait, of course, suffered the ravages of invasion, occupation, and war. Hundreds of Kuwaitis were killed and tortured. The looting, destruction, sabotage, and liberation cost sixty-five billion dollars, with another twenty-five billion dollars earmarked for reconstruction. Kuwaitis exacted revenge on the thriving community of about 350,000 Palestinians in Kuwait, some of whom had publicly supported the Iraq army. (Others, however, had fought with the Kuwaiti resistance, while most had gone about their daily life.) After liberation, hundreds of Palestinians were tortured and killed. The community lost eight billion dollars and was reduced to about thirty thousand, most of the remainder having resettled in Jordan.

Altogether the Gulf crisis cost hundreds of billions of dollars (one estimate put it at $640 billion). More significant, the crisis produced political divisions—especially involving Kuwait and Saudi Arabia, on the one hand, and Iraq, Jordan, and the PLO, on the other—between not just the governments but also the peoples of the Arab world. These divisions will take a long time to heal.

BIBLIOGRAPHY

FREEDMAN, LAWRENCE, and EFRAIM KARSH. *The Gulf Conflict, 1990–1991: Diplomacy and War in the New World Order.* Princeton, N.J., 1993.

IBRAHIM, IBRAHIM, ed. *The Gulf Crisis: Background and Consequences.* Washington, D.C., 1992.

KHALIDI, WALID. *The Gulf Crisis: Origins and Consequences.* Washington, D.C., 1991.

MARR, PHEBE. "Iraq's Uncertain Future." *Current History* 90, no. 552 (January 1991): 1–4, 39–42.

MATTAR, PHILIP. "The PLO and the Gulf Crisis." *Middle East Journal* 48, no. 1 (Winter 1994): 31–46.

SALINGER, PIERRE, and ERIC LAURENT. *Secret Dossier: The Hidden Agenda behind the Gulf War.* New York, 1991.

SIFRY, MICAH L., and CHRISTOPHER CERF, eds. *The Gulf War Reader: History, Documents, Opinions.* New York, 1991.

Philip Mattar

Gulf of Aqaba

A thin tongue of the Red Sea stretching north from the Strait of Tiran to the Jordanian port of Aqaba and the Israeli port of Eilat.

Nestled between the Sinai and Arabian peninsulas, the Gulf of Aqaba has played a significant role in five wars in the twentieth century.

During World War I, British forces in Egypt had driven the Turkish army back across the Sinai peninsula, but two subsequent attacks on Gaza in 1917 proved to be dismal failures. Meanwhile the Turkish garrison at Medina was keeping the forces of Sharif HUSAYN IBN ALI of Mecca bottled up in the Hijaz, while the Turkish batteries in and around Aqaba kept the Royal Navy out of the narrow channel leading to the port of Aqaba. The Sharif's son, Prince Faisal (who became FAISAL I, King of Iraq), and T. E. LAWRENCE of Arabia enlisted the help of Awda Abu Tayeh, a tribal leader from Syria, who succeeded in capturing Aqaba on July 6, 1917. This allowed the British to transport Prince Faisal and a small bedouin striking force to Aqaba by sea, bypassing the Medina garrison. Prince Faisal was made a general by Gen. Edmund Allenby for the forthcoming drive to Jerusalem. The capture of Aqaba also made possible the political undermining of Turkish power in Syria, as it allowed Prince Faisal to extend the network of his alliances to include the tribes in the Ma'an area north of Aqaba. It also allowed the British, by virtue of the agreement between Sir Henry McMahon and Sharif Husayn, to launch a successful propaganda campaign to win over the bedouin tribes of southern Palestine in the name of Arab independence. In this way, British forces under Allenby found themselves fighting in friendly terrain while the Ottomans were harassed by a hostile Arab population.

Israel has a long coast along the Mediterranean Sea, but Eilat is its only outlet to the Indian Ocean and Africa. Israel invaded Egypt in 1956 partly to secure the right of navigation for its ships through the Strait of TIRAN, off Sharm al-Shaykh. The war resulted in the stationing of the United Nations Emergency Force (UNEF) at Sharm al-Shaykh, along the eastern coast of the Sinai peninsula and along the border with Israel. Egypt's President Gamal Abdel NASSER's request to UNEF to withdraw from these positions, followed by his announcement of the blockade of the Strait of Tiran (although the blockade was never enforced), served as a *casus belli* for the third ARAB–ISRAEL WAR.

Due to the way in which Britain drew the borders of Iraq and Kuwait, Iraq was in need of a secure seaport for importing vital supplies in the event of a war. The Jordanian port of Aqaba, despite its small size, therefore acquired sufficient strategic significance for Baghdad, which then cemented an alliance with Jordan during the Iran–Iraq War of 1980–1988. Aqaba also served as a vital lifeline for Iraq following its invasion of Kuwait and in the course of the subsequent UN embargo. It was the main venue for the import of badly needed food and medical supplies, although Jordan has been accused of allowing some strategic materials to slip through its borders as well.

BIBLIOGRAPHY

ANTONIUS, GEORGE. *The Arab Awakening.* New York, 1946.

BILL, JAMES, and CARL LEIDEN. *Politics in the Middle East.* Boston, 1979.

FROMKIN, DAVID. *A Peace to End All Peace.* New York, 1989.

Jenab Tutunji

Gulf of Oman

A funnel-shaped arm of the Arabian Sea, measuring 350 miles (560 km) in length.

The Gulf of Oman links the Persian/Arabian Gulf to the Indian Ocean and separates Oman from Iran. Two hundred miles (320 km) wide at its outer limit, it narrows to 35 miles (56 km) at the Strait of Hormuz. Most Gulf oil is exported via this strategic waterway.

BIBLIOGRAPHY

LORIMER, J. G. "Oman (Promontory and Gulf of)." In *Gazetteer of the Persian Gulf, Oman, and Central Arabia.* Vol. 2B, *Geographical and Statistical.* Calcutta, 1908–1915. Reprint, 1970.

Robert G. Landen

Gulf of Suez

Maritime inlet that connects the Isthmus of Suez to the Red Sea and; with the Suez Canal, separates the Sinai peninsula from the rest of Egypt.

Almost 200 miles (320 km) long and 12 to 20 miles (20–32 km) wide, the Gulf of Suez is 210 feet (65 m) deep at its deepest point. It is an important passageway for shipping between Egypt and the lands of the Red Sea, the Arabian Sea, and the Indian Ocean, and for ships using the Suez Canal. It contains rich petroleum deposits, which have been utilized on a large scale since the 1960s.

Arthur Goldschmidt, Jr.

Gulf of Suez Petroleum Company

Major oil company in Egypt.

Known as Gupco, the Gulf of Suez Petroleum Company was established in 1965 as a partnership between the Egyptian General Petroleum Corporation and the Amoco-Egypt Oil Company, a subsidiary of Amoco Corporation, USA. The company operates in the Gulf of Suez and in the Western Desert and extracts some one-half of the country's oil output.

Michael R. Fischbach

Gulf Oil Corporation

U.S. oil company that operated in Kuwait and Bahrain.

Gulf Oil was short of petroleum sources in the United States in the 1920s and began to seek exploration concessions in Kuwait and Bahrain. The British government managed to prevent non-British companies from receiving such concessions through their treaties and protectorates in the Persian/Arabian GULF region.

Gulf Oil received its first concession in 1934, through the Kuwait Oil Company, which was jointly and equally owned by Gulf Oil Corporation and British Petroleum (formerly the D'ARCY Exploration Company). In 1975, Kuwait acquired 100 percent of the Kuwait Oil Company. In an effort to reorganize its oil sector in 1980, Kuwait established the Kuwait Petroleum Corporation (KPC). In 1983/84, KPC also acquired the European operations of the Gulf Oil Corporation.

BIBLIOGRAPHY

The Middle East and North Africa, 1991, 37th ed. London, 1991.

Emile A. Nakhleh

Gülhane Decree

See Hatt-i Şerif of Gülhane

Güney, Yılmaz   [1931–1984]

Turkish film actor, writer, and director.

Born the son of a peasant in Siverek, a village near Adana, Güney earned his keep as a boy toting water, caring for horses, and selling *simits* (pretzels) and soda. He attended law school at Ankara University and returned to Adana, where he got a job with Dar Film. He began scriptwriting and acting in 1958, and moved to Istanbul, becoming a popular star by the mid-1960s. Güney directed his first film in 1966, and went on to become the preeminent filmmaker of the era, with more than a dozen more films. His 1970 film *Hope,* about the mystical adventures of a poor carriage driver from Adana, was a turning point in Turkish film, marking the beginning of an era of neorealism. His 1982 *Yol* (The Road) shared the Palme d'Or award at Cannes with Costa-Gavras's *Missing.*

Güney wrote the script for *Yol* while serving a nineteen-year prison sentence for killing a judge in 1974, over a question of honor. The film was directed by Şerif Gören, but Güney escaped from prison in time to finish editing it in France. The film, about five prisoners on home-town leaves, has never been shown publicly in Turkey. Since his death, numerous books have been written about him, and the scripts for all his important films have been published. His films, short stories, and novels reflect his own outspoken Marxism and his preference for outlawed figures on the fringes of society.

BIBLIOGRAPHY

DORSAY, ATILLA. "An Overview of Turkish Cinema from Its Origins." In *The Transformation of Turkish Culture,* ed. by Günsel Renda and C. Max Kortepeter. Princeton, N.J., 1986.

ÖZGÜÇ, AGÂH. "A Chronological History of the Turkish Cinema." *Turkish Review* (Winter 1989): 53–115.

Elizabeth Thompson

Gur, Mordechai   [1930–]

Israeli general and politician.

Educated at Hebrew University in Jerusalem, the Ecole Militaire–Ecole de Guerre in Paris, and Harvard Business School, Gur was a hero of the 1967 ARAB–ISRAEL WAR (commanding a division that took Jerusalem) and then served as Israel's Defense Forces chief of staff from 1974 to 1978. During that time, he coordinated the rescue effort at ENTEBBE (1976) and the LITANI OPERATION in southern Lebanon (1978). During his tenure, he tried to reshape the general staff to be more responsive to field conditions. Active in Labor politics, he served as minister of health (1984–1986). In 1992, he was appointed acting defense miniser by Yitzhak Rabin, the prime minister.

BIBLIOGRAPHY

ELON, AMOS. *The Israelis.* New York, 1981.
Israel: A Country Study. Washington, D.C., 1979.
ROLEF, SUSAN HATTIS, ed. *Political Dictionary of the State of Israel.* New York, 1987.

Zachary Karabell

Guri, Haim   [1923–]

Israeli poet, writer, and journalist.

Guri was born in Tel Aviv and educated at the Hebrew University of Jerusalem and the Sorbonne in Paris. A principal representative of the *Dor ha-Palmah* (the PALMACH generation), he fought in four wars: against the British in prestate Israel and in the ARAB–ISRAEL WARS of 1948, 1967, and 1973. As a Haganah (Israel Defense Force) member sent to rescue survivors of the Holocaust, Guri had his first encounter with DIASPORA Jews, which profoundly affected him and his identity as a Jew. From that time on, the question of "who is a Jew" has significantly influenced his works.

From 1953 to 1970, Guri was a reporter and an essayist for the paper *La-Merhav* for which he covered Nazi war criminal Adolph Eichmann's trial (1961/62). His notes of the trial were published in the book *Mul Ta Ha-Zekhukhit* (Facing the Glass Booth). From 1970 to 1980, he was on the editorial staff of the DAVAR. From 1972 to 1984, he made several documentaries dealing with: the Holocaust

(*The 81st Blow*); Jewish resistance against the Nazis (*Flame in the Ashes*); and the illegal immigration to PALESTINE (*The Last Sea*).

An anthology of his poems, *Heshbon Over* (1988) won him the Israel prize for literature. His novella, *Iskat Ha-Shokolada* (1965; The Chocolate Deal, 1968), takes place in an anonymous European city with a flourishing black market and deals with the state of anarchy among the refugees of the Holocaust after World War II. To date, Guri has published nineteen books, nine of them poetry.

Ann Kahn

Gürpinar, Hüseyin Rahmi   [1864–1944]

Turkish novelist, journalist, and translator.

Born in Istanbul, Gürpinar studied political science and worked as a freelance journalist and translator in a government office of the Ottoman Empire, until he turned to writing in his forties. During World War I, he became famous for his entertaining and realistic novels and short stories. After the war, he moved to an island near Istanbul, where he lived alone with his dog, Kahraman Findik (Hazelnut Hero). He emerged from seclusion to be elected to the TURKISH GRAND NATIONAL ASSEMBLY, serving between 1936 and 1943.

Although Gürpinar was associated with Turkey's elitist Servet-i Fünun (Wealth of Knowledge) literary movement, he eschewed their ornate style and wrote popular novels influenced by French naturalism. He often wrote about the contradictions between tradition and modernity, modern sexuality, adventures, and current events, such as the 1910 panic at Halley's comet and the devastating 1918 worldwide influenza epidemic. Gürpinar often employed humor and caricature, portraying fanatics, charlatans, and gossiping women with wit and psychological insight.

BIBLIOGRAPHY

MITLER, LOUIS. *Ottoman Turkish Writers.* New York, 1988.

Elizabeth Thompson

Gürsel, Cemal   [1895–1966]

Turkish military officer, fourth president of the Turkish republic.

Cemal Gürsel was born in Erzurum, the son of a police officer. World War I broke out while he was studying at the military college in Constantinople (now Istanbul), and he was sent to the front at Çanakkale. After the war, he joined the independence movement led by Mustafa Kemal ATATÜRK. In 1959 Gürsel was appointed commander of the Turkish land forces. In May of 1960, he wrote a letter to the minister of defense protesting Prime Minister Adnan Menderes's use of the army to suppress dissent; in response, he was stripped of his command and placed under house arrest in Izmir. At this point, a group of junior officers invited Gürsel to lead their movement. Gürsel accepted, and on May 27, 1960, he headed a group of thirty-eight officers in a coup that overthrew the civilian government. Gürsel became head of the newly established National Unity Committee, as well as prime minister, president, and commander of the armed forces. An advocate of returning to civilian rule as quickly as possible, Gürsel expelled from the country fourteen younger officers, led by Col. Alparslan Türkeş, who called for continued military rule. In 1961, following the promulgation of a new constitution and election of a new parliament, Gürsel was elected fourth president of the Turkish republic. In 1966, his failing health forced him to resign his office, and he died shortly thereafter.

BIBLIOGRAPHY

SHIMONI, YAACOV. *Biographical Dictionary of the Middle East.* New York, 1991.

David Waldner

Gush Emunim

Zionist movement for the settlement of Eretz Yisrael (the biblical/historical Land of Israel), which includes Judea and Samaria (the West Bank).

Gush Emunim's origins can be traced to the mystical religious Zionist teachings of Rabbi Zvi Yehuda KOOK, from before the Arab–Israel War of 1967, which interpreted the founding of the State of Israel in messianic terms, emphasizing the inherent holiness and wholeness of biblical ERETZ YISRAEL. Following that war, Kook and his followers proclaimed that HALAKHAH (Jewish religious law) prohibits Israel from relinquishing any of the newly captured territory, because it is all part of Eretz Yisrael. After the October 1973 ARAB–ISRAEL WAR, fearing that Israel might cede parts of the territories, a group of Kook's followers established Gush Emunim—initially a pressure group within the National Religious party, it subsequently became an autonomous settlement movement.

From its inception until 1977, Gush Emunim violated government orders in its creation of illegal settlements in the administered territories (sometimes called the occupied territories). The movement's ef-

forts had the overt support of a large segment of Israel's secular population; it also had the covert support of some key government and military personnel. Many of the settlements eventually received government approval.

The years 1977 to 1982 were a period of sharp and conflicting tensions for the movement. With the victory of Menachem Begin and his Likud party in 1977, Gush Emunim had the blessings of Prime Minister Begin and the ruling party. Begin used the movement to further his own settlement objectives; he also signed the Camp David peace accords with Egypt's President Anwar al-Sadat, promising to cede all the Sinai, including Israel's settlements. Many in Gush Emunim joined the movement that tried to prevent the return of the Sinai to Egypt.

That effort was a turning point and, with its failure—coupled with strong government support of the settlement of Judea and Samaria/the West Bank—Gush Emunim underwent a process of "routinization of charisma." Gush Emunim was transformed from a predominantly ideological movement to the more institutionalized, traditional settlement movement. Until 1984, no official leadership had existed but the unofficial leader was the ideologue, Rabbi Moshe Levinger, disciple of Zvi Yehuda Kook and founder of Kiryat Arba and the reestablished Jewish community in Hebron. In 1984, however, the movement decided to appoint an executive secretary and spokesperson, Daniella Weiss, of Kedumim, who still holds that position.

Just as the overt ideological leadership began to recede, the movement was cast into ideological turmoil; in 1984, it split over the arrest and subsequent conviction of the Jewish terrorist underground. Within the movement, some justified the activities of the underground as necessary because Israel's government had not protected Jewish rights adequately in the administered territories. Others denounced the underground's actions as going beyond the limits of legitimate protest.

Despite its institutionalization, Gush Emunim remains a movement rather than an organization; there are no official members. It has varying degrees of support among the Jewish population of Israel, ranging from the staunch support of the new Jewish residents in those administered territories to the staunch opposition of the Peace Now movement and the Palestinian Arabs.

BIBLIOGRAPHY

ARAN, GIDEON. "From Religious Zionism to Zionist Religion: The Roots of Gush Emunim." In *Studies in Contemporary Jewry*, ed. by Peter Y. Medding. Bloomington, Ind., 1986.

LUSTICK, IAN S. *For the Land and the Lord: Jewish Fundamentalism in Israel.* New York, 1988.

NEWMAN, DAVID, ed. *The Impact of Gush Emunim: Politics and Settlement in the West Bank.* London, 1985.

SEGAL, HAGGAI. *Dear Brothers: The West Bank Jewish Underground.* Woodmere, N.Y., 1988. A participant's account of the Jewish underground.

Chaim I. Waxman

Gypsies

A nomadic minority group with distinctive folkways and tribal organization, whose members speak the Romany language.

The term is an alteration of Middle English, "Gypcian," or "Gitane," short for Egyptian. The gypsies arrived in Europe in the fourteenth century from northern India. Legends abound about the origin of the gypsies—one describes them as the degenerate descendants of the priests of Isis in Nubia, Babylonia, and Egypt. The most persistent theory thus far favors India as their place of origin.

Their occupations, predictable for a semisettled people, range from hawking, tinkering, and sporadic seasonal agricultural work to fortune-telling and divination in fairs and circuses. Institutionally, social control is achieved through the Romany Kris, the body of customary law to which all gypsies are subject. Concepts of fidelity, loyalty, cohesiveness, and reciprocity maintain unity among the tribe, and excommunication or ostracism is considered the worst punishment for violators of the law. Today, gypsies no longer defend themselves against persecution from hostile societies, since integration, economic security, and a sedentary mode of life together constitute the benign assault eroding their lifestyles and codes.

Cyrus Moshaver

H

Haaretz

One of the oldest, most respected, and most liberal Israeli newspapers.

Published in Hebrew, *Haaretz* was founded in 1919 in Jerusalem, but its main offices were moved to Tel Aviv in 1922 and have remained there since. The paper was edited by Moshe Glickson until 1937. In 1936, it was bought by S. Z. Schocken and then edited by his son, Gershom Schocken. Because of its private ownership, *Haaretz* enjoyed a wide latitude and early on was a vocal critic of David Ben-Gurion and Israel's government. In recent years, *Haaretz* has been a public forum for debate on the Palestinian issue, attacking Yitzhak Shamir's Likud government, and in particular on Shamir's support for Israeli settlements on the West Bank. Its daily circulation is about 58,000.

BIBLIOGRAPHY

Israel: A Country Study. Washington, D.C., 1979.
New Standard Jewish Encyclopedia. New York, 1977.
SHIPLER, DAVID. *Arab and Jew.* New York, 1986.

Zachary Karabell

Haavarah

The company through which German Jewish immigrants were able to transfer their property and money from Germany to Palestine during the early years of Nazi rule.

Because of currency restrictions imposed by the Nazi government, Jews fleeing Germany needed to demonstrate they had assets of at least £ 1,000 in order to be considered "capitalists" and not subject to immigration quotas. Through an agreement between the Anglo–Palestine Bank and the German Ministry of Economics, the German government allowed Jewish assets in Germany to be used to purchase German goods for use in Palestine; the proceeds of these transactions were distributed to emigrants in Palestine.

BIBLIOGRAPHY

HILLERBERG, RAOUL. *The Destruction of the European Jews.* New York, 1985.

Bryan Daves

Habash, George   [1925–   ]

Palestinian leader and general secretary of the Popular Front for the Liberation of Palestine (PFLP).

Habash was born on 2 August 1925 to Greek Orthodox Christian Palestinian parents in the town of Lydda in central British-Mandate Palestine. His father was a prosperous merchant who specialized in the import and distribution of food products to local retailers. The younger Habash, after excelling in his early studies, completed his secondary education in Jerusalem. After two years as a schoolteacher, he attended the Faculty of Medicine at the American University of Beirut (AUB), receiving his degree with distinction in 1951.

According to Habash himself, he had no interest in politics prior to the dissolution of Palestine in 1948. Significantly, that summer he had returned to Lydda from Beirut to care for his ailing sister. On account of the strict curfew which followed the Israeli occupation of the town, he was unable to procure the required medicines for her. She died and had to be buried in the backyard. Habash also personally experienced the forcible expulsion of the town's population on 13 July 1948. While some sources indicate he immediately volunteered with Arab forces active in Palestine, all agree that in 1949 he helped establish The Partisans of Arab Sacrifice (Kata'ib al-Fida al-Arabi), which attacked Western targets in Beirut and Damascus until it was dissolved by the Syrian authorities in mid-1950.

Upon his return to the AUB, Habash also joined the Society of the Firm Tie (Jam'iyyat al-Urwa al-Wathqa), a student literary club that was undergoing rapid politicization. On the strength of his forceful personality and arguments, he quickly became a leading member of the group, and in 1950 was elected president of its executive committee. In 1951, this committee decided to serve as the nucleus of a new clandestine pan-Arab movement that became known as the Movement of Arab Nationalists (MAN) (Harakat al-Qawmiyyin al-Arab). Habash emerged as its overall leader.

In 1952, Habash left for Amman to develop MAN's Jordanian branch. He opened a people's clinic for the poor, and established the Arab Club to combat illiteracy and serve as a discussion and recruitment center. His activities forced him underground in 1954, but he remained in Jordan until 1958, when he finally fled to Damascus to escape arrest.

During this same period, MAN drew increasingly close to Egypt's Gamal Abdel Nasser, whom it viewed as the best hope for Arab unity. When specifically Palestinian nationalist organizations began to emerge in the 1960s, Habash condemned them as "regionalists" who abandoned general Arab interests and whose guerrilla activities would provide Israel with an excuse to attack the Arab states (and particularly Egypt) before they were ready for the challenge. But when these nationalist groups proved to have considerable appeal among Palestinians, Habash felt obliged to establish the National Front for the Liberation of Palestine (NFLP) within MAN.

Equally important, in the mid-1960s, Habash was also engaged in an ideological battle within MAN against a leftist faction led by Nayif HAWATMA and Muhsin Ibrahim. While Habash could tolerate the vague formulations of Arab socialism produced by Nasser and other Arab nationalists, Marxist-Leninism and its emphasis on class rather than national contradictions was anathema to him.

In a rare display of political flexibility on his part, Habash experienced the stunning Arab defeat of 1967 not as a vindication of his views, but rather as cause for their fundamental revision. The result of this revision was the dissolution of MAN that same year and the emergence of the POPULAR FRONT FOR THE LIBERATION OF PALESTINE, an organization characterized by an equal measure of radical Marxist-Leninism and Palestinian nationalism, with George Habash as its general secretary.

Although the PFLP nearly disintegrated the following year while Habash was in a Syrian prison for sabotaging the Trans-Arabian Pipeline, under his leadership it quickly developed into the most important Palestinian organization apart from the Palestine National Liberation Movement (al-FATH). Its uncompromising stance toward not only Israel, but also the West and conservative Arab regimes, and its insistence that the Palestinian revolution could only succeed as part of a wider regional and international struggle committed to radical social and political change, was consistent with the spirit of the times. And the PFLP's preparedness to pursue its agenda through spectacular actions, most notoriously frequent hijackings of civilian airliners, won it wide support among Palestinian refugees who were eager to shed any residual signs of passivity.

Although Habash has since called a halt to many of the PFLP's most extreme tactics, he remains convinced that in their historical context such actions were both legitimate and necessary. The fact that Israel came to view him as its most dangerous enemy, and that he was vociferously denounced in the West, is for him above all a tribute to his dedication and effectiveness.

In the period since 1967, Habash has worked primarily to steer the PALESTINE LIBERATION ORGANIZATION (PLO) in a radical direction, consistently urging it to participate in political conflicts within the Arab world and reject a political settlement with Israel. In his view, neither Israel nor its Western allies are prepared to reciprocate Palestinian concessions (which are therefore futile), and will respond only to military pressure and regional instability.

As the leader of the radical camp within the PLO, Habash emerged as the main rival to PLO Chairman Yasir Arafat, and at several critical junctures appeared poised to displace him. Whereas Habash contested the leadership of the Palestinian national movement on the basis of a dogmatic strategic vision, Arafat retained it through his extreme tactical flexibility.

Habash, who suffered a near-fatal stroke in 1980, and has remained in poor health since, is today diminished both physically and politically. Although he is said to remain in full control of his intellectual powers and his authority within the PFLP remains supreme, he and his organization have become increasingly marginalized by the rise of the Islamist trend in both Palestinian and Arab politics. While to his followers Habash's vision has been handsomely vindicated by the course of events, such sentiments cannot hide the fact that collectively these events have rendered his vision anachronistic and his program infeasible. The leading Palestinian radical and one of the most influential Arab intellectuals of his generation, Habash will above all be remembered for his single-minded devotion to revolutionary upheaval in Palestine and the Arab world, and the manner in which he put his ideas into practice.

Over the years Habash has given countless interviews, press statements, and speeches. MAN's official weekly, *Al-Hurriyya* (Freedom) and later the official weekly of the PFLP, *Al-Hadaf* (The Target) have published most of these.

BIBLIOGRAPHY

ABUKHALIL, AS'AD. "Internal Contradictions in the PFLP: Decision Making and Policy Orientation." *The Middle East Journal* 41 (1987): 361–378.
GRESH, ALAIN. *The PLO: The Struggle Within: Towards an Independent Palestinian State,* rev. ed. Tr. by A. M. Berrett. London, 1988.
ISMAEL, TAREQ Y. *The Arab Left.* Syracuse, N.Y., 1976.
KAZZIHA, WALID W. *Revolutionary Transformation in the Arab World: Habash and His Comrades from Nationalism to Marxism.* London, 1975.
MOOIS, NADIM. "The Ideology and Role of the Palestinian Left in the Resistance Movement." Ph.D. diss., Oxford University, 1991.

Mouin Rabbani

Habib, Philip Charles   [1920–1994]

U.S. diplomat.

Habib was U.S. President Ronald W. Reagan's special envoy to the Middle East, 1981–1983. In the summer of 1981, he negotiated with Syria for the removal of ground-to-air missiles in Lebanon; in August, he brokered a cease-fire agreement between the Palestine Liberation Organization (PLO) and Israel that lasted until June of 1982.

After Israel invaded Lebanon on June 6 (the 1982 Arab–Israel War), Habib negotiated another series of cease-fires but none lasted. In late 1982, Habib, ignoring Syria, supervised formal negotiations between Israel and the Lebanese government of President Amin Jumayyil, which resulted in the May 1983 agreement ending the war. Implementation of the agreement was contingent on Syrian withdrawal from Lebanon, however, and following Syrian President Hafiz al-Asad's refusal to withdraw, Habib lost favor with President Reagan and, in July 1983, was replaced by Robert McFarlane.

BIBLIOGRAPHY

FINDLING, JOHN, ed. *Dictionary of American Diplomatic History.* New York, 1989.
SPIEGEL, STEVEN. *The Other Arab–Israeli Conflict.* Chicago, 1985.

Zachary Karabell

Habib Allah

An Arabic expression that literally means "the beloved of God."

Habib Allah was applied to the Maronite (Christian) Patriarch Antun Aridah in the early 1940s. In 1941, when the relationship between the patriarch and the French authority in Lebanon deteriorated, the patriarch gave an interview to the Lebanese journalist Iskandar Riyashi in which he stated, "Muslims are not France's slaves." This statement made him popular among Muslims, some of whom chanted "There is no God but God, and Patriarch Aridah is Habib Allah" after attending Friday prayer in the Bani Umayyah mosque in Damascus.

As'ad AbuKhalil

Habibia School

Preparatory high school in Kabul.

Established in 1904 by Amir Habibollah, Habibia was the first public high school in Afghanistan. At first its Islamic curriculum bore similarities to that of the traditional MADRASA, but gradually the school's approach to education was transformed into the British system of education and in the 1960s it adopted the American system.

In addition to being popular with the royal family and among the Afghan elite, the school attracted many students who were to be leaders in the future. Students who did well were given scholarships to study abroad.

BIBLIOGRAPHY

ADAMEC, LUDWIG. *Historical Dictionary of Afghanistan.* Metuchen, N.J., 1991.

Grant Farr

Habibollah Khan   [1871–1919]

Emir of Afghanistan, 1901–1919.

Born in Samarkand, Habibollah was the son of Amir Abd al-Rahman and an Uzbek woman. After being active in his father's administration (1880–1901), he succeeded him to the throne in 1901. He was a successful and well-liked monarch, especially in comparison to his autocratic father. He released prisoners, increased the pay of the army, and invited back political exiles his father had forced out of the country.

His reign has been credited with two accomplishments. A great modernizer who was attracted to Western ideas and technology, he traveled to Europe, brought the first automobiles into Afghanistan, and introduced Western secular education there. He also drew Afghanistan away from British control; for example, he kept Afghanistan neutral during World War I.

He was assassinated on February 20, 1919, while hunting at Kala Gosh in Laghman.

BIBLIOGRAPHY

ADAMEC, LUDWIG. *Historical Dictionary of Afghanistan.* Metuchen, N.J., 1991.

Grant Farr

Habl al-Matin

Influential Iranian newspaper published in Calcutta and Tehran from 1893.

Edited by Seyyed Jamal ad-Din Kashani, *Habl al-Matin* ("The Firm Cord") was noted for its advocacy of Pan-Islamism. It continued publication during various periods of repression. It was said to have one of the largest circulations of the Persian papers published during the Constitutional Revolution.

Farhad Shirzad

Habous

North African term for religious foundation established by the founder from the income of a property and designed for charitable purposes.

Madrasat, mosques, hospitals, shrines of MARABOUTS, public foundations, salaries of *Fuqaha* and *ulama,* and stipends for religious students were set up as *habous* by wealthy men or women and given endowments to ensure their permanence. Habous properties are unalienable because they were used for pious pur-poses. The *hadhir* (administrator) who controlled the collection and distribution of the revenues was under the supervision of the chief *qadi* (judge), who in turn was under that of the ruler. *Ulama* and fuqaha were also given control of great *ahbas.* Under the sultans of Morocco, the chief qadi controlled the habous of Fez and Marrakech. Outside of the Maghrib, the normal word for habous is WAQF (pl., *awqaf*).

BIBLIOGRAPHY

HOURANI, ALBERT. *Islam in European Thought.* Cambridge, U.K., 1991.

Rhimou Bernikho-Canin

Habshush, Hayyim   [?–1899]

Yemenite Jewish writer.

Habshush (also known as Hayyim ben Yahya ben Salim Alfityhi) was a descendant of a rabbinic family in San'a, the capital of Yemen. His craft of copper engraving led to an interest in antiquities and Sabaean inscriptions and, during the 1860s, he guided the scholar Joseph Halévy on his search for Sabaean inscriptions into areas of the Middle East and North Africa unvisited by Europeans. Habshush wrote an account of his travels with Halévy, *Masa'ot Habshush* (The Journeys of Habshush). Its significance lies in its language—a combination of the popular Arabic dialect used in San'a and literary Hebrew. He also authored *Halikhot Teiman,* segments in the history of Yemenite Jewry during the late seventeenth century.

BIBLIOGRAPHY

GRIDI, S., ed. *Shoshannat ha-Melekh* (The King's Rose). Tel Aviv, 1967.
RAZHABI, YEHUDA. "Hayyim Habshush." In *Encyclopedia Judaica.* Jerusalem, 1971.

Michael M. Laskier

Hacene, Farouk Zehar   [1939–   ]

Algerian novelist and short story writer.

Zehar, born in Ksar el-Boukhari, Algeria, left for Europe in 1956 and studied in Switzerland while working at various odd jobs.

Zehar considers himself to be the one who ended the trend of committed literature among Algerian writers. He published a collection of short stories, *Peloton de tête* (Paris, 1965; The Winning Regiment), and a novel, *Le Miroir d'un fou* (Paris, 1979; The

Crazy Man's Mirror), which deal with subjects totally removed from the events of the Algerian war of independence.

Zehar wanted to free himself from the strong hold of tradition on his life without denying his national identity. His short stories reflect a preoccupation with the psychological condition of the human being, the search for an aim and a meaning to life.

BIBLIOGRAPHY

ACHOUR, CHRISTINE. *Anthologie de la littérature algérienne de langue française.* Paris, 1990.
DÉJEUX, JEAN. *Dictionnaire des auteurs maghrébins de langue française.* Paris, 1984.

Aida A. Bamia

Hacettepe University

Public university in Ankara, Turkey.

Founded as a medical school in 1967 (though it sometimes claims spiritual descent from a Kayseri *madrasa*-hospital endowed in 1206), it now comprises the faculties of medicine, dentistry, and pharmacy at its original campus in the city, and the faculties of economics and administrative sciences, engineering, education, fine arts, literature, and science at Beytepe on the outskirts of Ankara, the capital of Turkey. Hacettepe University also includes schools of foreign languages, health administration, health technology, home economics, nursing, physical therapy/rehabilitation, and social work; also four vocational schools, some in neighboring Zonguldak province specializing in woodwork technology. The university also administers the Ankara State Conservatory. English is a heavily used second language of instruction, while some teacher-training programs, especially in the natural sciences, are conducted in German. In 1990 the university had about 2,400 teaching staff and 24,000 students (close to half female). Its state-funded 1991 budget amounted to 327.5 billion Turkish lire, of which 58 billion was for capital investment.

Hacettepe's origins as a medical school explain the wealth of health-related programs. It was the first of two universities founded by Prof. Ihsan Doğramacı, who later headed centralized administration of all university-level education in the country (see YÜKSEK ÖĞRETIM KURULU and BILKENT UNIVERSITY). Hacettepe epitomizes its founder's pragmatic, American style, as opposed to the European approach to university administration, in that the medical school hospital generates considerable income for the university. Revenue also accrues from large-scale furniture manufacture in workshops operated as a side activity. This mingling of academic programs and money-making operations, at best a precarious balance, has remained the exception in Turkish academic life, although by now most universities generate some revenues out of research activities to augment state allocations.

BIBLIOGRAPHY

Higher Education in Turkey. UNESCO, European Centre for Higher Education. December 1990.
World of Learning. 1990.

I. Metin Kunt

Hached, Ferhat   [1914–1952]

Tunisian labor leader and nationalist.

Son of a fisherman from the island of Kerkenna, he began his labor work in the 1930s in Sousse. In 1944, he founded the Association of Free Trade Unions of Southern Tunisia, which in 1946 was incorporated into the powerful General Union of Tunisian Workers (Union Générale de Travailleurs Tunisiens; UGTT). Hashid was selected as the UGTT's first secretary-general and was largely responsible for the close ties between the DESTOUR movement and the union. Well known in the labor movements of Europe and the United States, Hashid was assassinated in December of 1952. It was widely held that a French terrorist organization, the Red Hand, was responsible for his death.

BIBLIOGRAPHY

HAHN, LORNA. *North Africa: Nationalism to Nationhood.* Washington, D.C., 1960.
LING, DWIGHT. *Morocco and Tunisia: A Comparative History.* Washington, D.C., 1979.

Matthew S. Gordon

Haci, Arif   [1831–1885]

Ottoman Turkish composer.

Arif Haci was born in Istanbul, the son of a civil servant. His vocal talents were recognized while he was still in primary school, and he studied with DEDE ZEKAI and MEHMET BEY. At the age of thirteen, he entered the Royal Musical Conservatory. Seven years later, as his reputation as a singer and a composer grew, he became the court chamberlain. Considered the founder of the Turkish Romantic school of music, Haci composed almost exclusively in the *şarki* form; his skilled, lyrical compositions made this ballad form the most important genre of Turkish music. Many of his numerous pieces were never written down; as a result, only 400 survive, many of them collected and published in *Mecmua-i Arifi*. Haci was the father of the violinist Cemil Bey.

David Waldner

Ha-Cohen, Mordechai   [1856–1929]

Zionist activist in Tripoli, Libya; teacher, author, educational reformer, and rabbinical court judge.

Although Ha-Cohen was born in Tripoli, his family had come from Genoa, Italy. His father, Rabbi Yehuda Ha-Cohen, died in 1861 on a trip to Crete. His mother was penniless but refused assistance from the Jewish community or from the Italian consul. She worked as a seamstress, supported her children, and had Mordechai assist by giving instruction in Bible and Talmud. Their poverty made him study, on his own, arithmetic and the literature of the Hebrew Enlightenment (*Haskalah*). He married in 1883, worked as a Hebrew teacher, and when his income was insufficient, taught himself to repair clocks. As his family grew (four boys and nine girls), he studied rabbinic law and worked as a clerk in the court, which gave him a good living. He then devoted more time to intellectual pursuits and writing. His major work was a manuscript entitled *Highid Mordechai,* in which he describes the history, customs, and institutions of Tripolitanian Jewry.

As a reformer, he advocated changes in the educational system that were eventually adopted against the will of the establishment. He supported young Zionists and joined the Zionist club, *Circolo Sion,* when the community leaders opposed it. In 1906, he traveled with Russian-born Jewish scholar Nahum Slouschz throughout Libya and conferred with him on the publication of his manuscript *Highid Mordechai*. He contributed news items to the Italian Jewish paper *Israel* and to Hebrew papers in Warsaw, London, and Palestine.

As a jurist in Tripoli, Ha-Cohen was in conflict with lay and religious leaders on matters of rabbinic law. In 1920, he was appointed magistrate in the rabbinic court of Benghazi, Libya, where he served until his death, August 22, 1929.

BIBLIOGRAPHY

DE FELICE, RENZO. *Jews in Arab Lands: Libya, 1835–1970.* Austin, Tex., 1985.

GOLDBERG, H. E. *Cave Dwellers and Citrus Growers: A Jewish Community in Libya and Israel.* Cambridge, U.K., 1972.

HA-COHEN, MORDECHAI. *The Book of Mordechai: A Study of the Jews of Libya,* ed. and trans. (with introduction and commentaries) by Harvey E. Goldberg. Philadelphia, 1980.

HIRSCHBERG, H. Z. *A History of the Jews of North Africa,* 2 vols. In Hebrew. Jerusalem, 1965.

KAHALON, Y. "La lutte pour l'image spirituelle de la Communauté de Libye au XIX siècle." In *Zakhor Le-Abraham: Mélanges Abraham Elmaleh,* ed. by H. Z. Hirschberg. Jerusalem, 1972.

Maurice M. Roumani

Hadassah

Jewish women's philanthropic organization.

The largest Jewish women's organization in the United States, Hadassah was founded by Henrietta SZOLD and fifteen other women on February 24, 1912. Its stated purpose was to foster Zionist ideals through education in America and to begin public-health and nursing training in Palestine. In Hebrew, the word *hadassah* means myrtle, a hardy plant used to bind and enrich the soil.

In 1913, Hadassah sent two nurses to Jerusalem to set up a maternity and eye clinic. This was the beginning of its continuing involvement in the medical care of the people of Palestine. In 1939, the Rothschild-Hadassah University Hospital, the first teaching hospital in Palestine, opened atop Mount Scopus in Jerusalem. During the Arab–Israel War of 1948, Mount Scopus was designated a demilitarized zone. The hospital was evacuated, and a new center was built in Jewish Jerusalem. After the Arab-Israel War of 1967, the Mount Scopus center reverted to Jewish control.

Hadassah has more than 1,500 chapters, with over 385,000 members and 22,000 associates (male members). Its activities support the Hadassah medical center in Jerusalem and other philanthropic activities in Israel.

BIBLIOGRAPHY

BAUM, CHARLOTTE, PAULA HYMAN, and SONYA MICHEL SONYA. *The Jewish Woman in America.* New York, 1976.

Mia Bloom

Haddad, Malek   [1927–1978]

Algerian novelist, poet, and journalist.

Haddad was born in Constantine and later attended the University of Aix-en-Provence in France. After working as a journalist, he began a literary career that merited inclusion in the distinguished "Generation of 1954" (with Mohammed DIB, Kateb YACINE, Moulaoud MAMMERI, and Mouloud FERAOUN). Themes of exile and engagement characterized his works. He wrote four novels (*La dernière impression,* 1958; *Je t'offrirai une gazelle,* 1959; *L'elève et la leçon,* 1960; *Le quai aux fleurs ne répond plus,* 1961) and published two collections of poetry (*Le malheur en danger,* 1956; *Ecoute et je t'appelle,* 1961). He regretted his inability to compose in Arabic and reflected: "The French language is my exile." During the war of independence, he served on diplomatic missions for the Front de Libération Nationale (National Liberation Front; FLN). He edited the newspaper, *al-Nasr* in Constantine from 1965 to 1968 and became secretary of the reorganized Union of Algerian Writers in 1974.

BIBLIOGRAPHY

DÉJEUX, JEAN. *Dictionnaire des auteurs maghrébins de langue française.* Paris, 1984.

Phillip C. Naylor

Haddad, Sa'd   [1937–1984]

Lebanese military officer and militia leader.

Sa'd Haddad was born in the town of Marj Ayun to a Maronite Christian mother and a Greek Orthodox father. His father was a farmer and a corporal in the Troupes Speciales du Levant during the French mandate (1920–1941). Haddad graduated from the Patriarchal College in Beirut in 1957, and the military academy at Fayadiyya. After the outbreak of the Lebanese civil war in 1975, Major Haddad assumed command of the southern sectors of Lebanon, ostensibly on the orders of the army command in Beirut, though in fact, Haddad's fifteen hundred-strong, predominantly Christian, militia was financed by and under the orders of Israel. In February of 1979, Haddad openly broke with the Lebanese government and declared the land under his control "Free Lebanon."

BIBLIOGRAPHY

HAMIZRACHI, BEATE. *The Emergence of the South Lebanon Security Belt: Major Saad Haddad and the Ties with Israel.* New York, 1988.
New York Times, January 15 and 16, 1984.

David Waldner

Haddad, Tahir al-   [1899–1935]

Trade unionist and journalist.

Tahir al-Haddad was a leading voice of both nationalism and social reform in Tunisia in the 1920s and

1930s. Son of a small shop owner from Tunis, he enrolled at Zaytuna University in 1911, where he took part in student politics and union work. Later, in a series of articles for the nationalist press, he attacked the French protectorate—which had been in effect since 1881—and criticized what he viewed as primitive aspects of Tunisian society. His most significant contributions were two books: *The Tunisian Workers and the Appearance of a Trade Union Movement* (*Al-Ummal al-Tunisiyin wa-Zuhur al-Harakah al-Naqabiyah*), published in 1925, and *Our Women in Islamic Law and in Society* (*Imra'atuna fi-al-Shari'a wa-al-Mujtama*), which appeared in 1930.

BIBLIOGRAPHY

MICAUD, CHARLES. *Tunisia: The Politics of Modernization.* New York, 1964.
SRAIEB, NOUREDDINE. *Algeria, Tahar Haddad: Les Pensées.* Oran, Algeria, 1984.

Matthew S. Gordon

Haddad, Wadi

Activist in the Popular Front for the Liberation of Palestine.

A member of a prosperous Greek Orthodox family from Safed, Palestine, Haddad joined George HABASH in helping to set up a medical clinic for Palestinian refugees in Amman, Jordan after completing medical studies at the American University of Beirut.

With two other founders of the ARAB NATIONAL MOVEMENT (ANM) in Beirut, Ahmad YAMANI (Abu Maher), a former trade union leader, and Abdel Karim Hamid (Abu Adnan), both from Upper Galilee, Haddad became a specialist in military affairs and intelligence matters. He was responsible for planning many of the "special operations" that the POPULAR FRONT FOR THE LIBERATION OF PALESTINE (PFLP) carried out during the late 1960s and early 1970s.

BIBLIOGRAPHY

SMITH, PAMELA ANN. *Palestine and the Palestinians, 1876–1983.* London, 1984.

Lawrence Tal

Hadid, Muhammad   [1906–]

Iraqi government official.

Muhammad Hadid was born in Mosul in what is today northern Iraq, and educated at the American University of Beirut and the London School of Economics. He was a founder of the Iraqi social reformist group Jama'at al-Ahali in 1932 and later of the NATIONAL DEMOCRATIC PARTY, which was prominent between 1946 and 1960. In July 1958, he was appointed minister of finance by Abd al-Karim Kassem. In April 1960, Hadid resigned and retired from politics.

Peter Sluglett

Hadith

Legends and traditions surrounding the Prophet Muhammad.

Hadith is both a singular and collective noun referring to the account(s) of the deeds and/or sayings of the Prophet Muhammad. It also relates to what others are reported to have said or done with the explicit or tacit approval of the Prophet. As an expression of his *sunna* (customary practice) the hadith became the material source of *Shari'a* (Islamic law) second only to the Qur'an.

BIBLIOGRAPHY

ROBSON, JAMES. "Tradition, the Second Foundation of Islam." *Muslim World* 41 (1951): 22–33; also a sequel of three articles by the same author in ibid., pp. 98–112, 166–180, 257–270.

Wael B. Hallaq

Hadj, Messali al-   [1898–1974]

Renowned Algerian nationalist.

Messali al-Hadj was born in Tlemcen and was the son of a cobbler. He received a religious education influenced by the Darqawa sect of Islam and later, in France, enrolled in Arabic language university courses. While serving in the French army from 1918 to 1921, Messali was disturbed by discrimination within the ranks and distressed by the demise of the Ottoman Empire during the post–World War I years. He was attracted by labor politics, which drew him to a French Communist party–affiliated movement known as the Etoile Nord-Africaine (North African Star, ENA). He became its leader in 1926, but the ENA disbanded in 1929. Messali reorganized it in 1933 and distanced it from the French Communists as a new Algerian nationalist organization called the Glorieuse Etoile (Glorious Star—then renamed the Union Nationale des Musulmans Nord-Africans [National Union of North African Muslims]

in 1935). It was dedicated to achieving an Arab Muslim independent state of Algeria. After a sojourn in Geneva, Switzerland, in 1935 with the cultural and political nationalist Chekib Arslan (a Druze leader), Messali placed greater emphasis on Arabism within his movement.

Messali supported the POPULAR FRONT (France) but did not endorse its proposed assimilationist BLUM–VIOLLETTE legislation (which, anyway, never passed in Parliament in 1936). His criticism of France's colonial policy and his agitation in Algeria led to the official dissolution of his movement in January 1937, although Messali responded quickly by forming the PARTI DU PEUPLE ALGÉRIEN (Algerian People's Party, PPA) in March. He was arrested several months later, freed in August 1939, only to be incarcerated again in November. Messali was tried by a Vichy (pro-German French government during World War II) court in March 1941 and sentenced to sixteen years of hard labor. He remained under arrest after the Allied forces landed in North Africa during World War II (late 1942). Messali did not concur with Ferhat Abbas's "Manifesto of the Algerian People" of 1943 but in 1944 agreed to head the Amis du Manifeste et de la Liberté (Friends of the Manifesto and Liberty, AML), an organization that briefly (1944/45) united nationalist movements and called for Algerian autonomy. The announcement in April 1945 of Messali's impending deportation to exile in France heightened tensions but, by that time, Messali's PPA had infiltrated the AML, directing it toward a confrontation with the French colonialists. This was dramatically disclosed in the SÉTIF RIOTS in May when, during the parade celebrating victory in Europe, nationalist placards provoked violence that resulted in 103 European deaths and thousands of retributive Muslim fatalities. The AML disintegrated and the nationalists resumed their separate paths.

In 1946, Messali organized the MOUVEMENT POUR LE TRIOMPHE DES LIBERTÉS DÉMOCRATIQUES (Movement for the Triumph of Democratic Liberties, MTLD). The younger elite, tempered by the Sétif riots, wanted direct action and formed the Organisation Spéciale (Special Organization, OS), which was still linked to the MTLD. The OS paramilitary operations (1947–1950) led to the arrest of its leaders and its demise. The MTLD concurrently faced a Berber crisis, as the Berbers (or Kabylia) believed that the organization was too Arabized, and they questioned Messali's authoritarianism. In 1953, the MTLD split between the centralists and the Messalists over the role of immediate and violent attacks against French colonialism. At first, Messali rejected the centralist position, which soon transmuted into the FRONT DE LIBÉRATION NATIONALE (National Liberation Front, FLN). The FLN's attacks, from October 31 to November 1, 1954, convinced Messali that he had to organize his own military group; it appeared in December as the Mouvement National Algérien (Algerian National Movement, MNA).

During the Algerian War of Independence, the MNA and the FLN's ARMÉE DE LIBÉRATION NATIONALE (National Liberation Army, ALN) campaigned against each other. This fratricide was underscored by the MNA's highly publicized and grievous losses at Mélouza (south of Kabylia) in 1957. Messali's movement lost its credibility (i.e., the BELLOUNIS affair) and its predominant influence over the emigrant community. France intimated a willingness to initiate discussions with the MNA before the Evian negotiations in 1961, but this was generally viewed as a stratagem challenging the FLN's legitimacy.

Even after the war of independence was won by Algeria, Messali remained in exile in France until his death in 1974. He was returned for burial in Tlemcen, the place of his birth. He and his ideas were always viewed as a threat—even after the October 1988 riots and the political liberalization they inspired, a regenerated PPA was denied legal status. Nevertheless, the extensive historical section of Algeria's revised National Charter (1986) could not ignore Messali's commitment and contribution to Algeria's independence.

BIBLIOGRAPHY

AGERON, CHARLES-ROBERT. *Histoire de l'Algérie contemporaine: De l'insurrection de 1871 au déclenchement de la guerre de libération.* Paris, 1979.

HADJ, MESSALI. *Les mémoires de Messali Hadj* (covering the years 1898–1938). Paris, 1982.

NAYLOR, PHILLIP C., and ALF A. HEGGOY. *Historical Dictionary of Algeria,* 2nd ed. Metuchen, N.J., 1994.

STORA, BENJAMIN. *Messali Hadj.* Paris, 1982.

Phillip C. Naylor

Hadramawt

Region of the Arabian peninsula bordered by the Rub al-Khali desert on the north and the Arabian Sea on the south.

The Hadramawt is a mountainous land traversed by a valley and a narrow coastal strip with a hot, arid climate. In 1986 there were 686,000 people living in an area of 155,376 square kilometers (62,150 sq. mi.). Mukalla is the capital, and Shabwa, Huraida, Shibam, Saiwun, Tarim, Inat, and Kabr Hud are important towns.

Agriculture is largely confined to the upper valley, where there is alluvial soil and water from intermittent flooding; the lower valley which runs to the ocean on the east, is largely uninhabited. Newly introduced irrigation and flood control methods are increasing agricultural production. Although dates have typically formed the main crop because of their hardiness, cotton has become an important commodity in recent times. Corn, wheat, and oats are the local grain crops, and tobacco is grown along the coast.

The inhabitants of the Hadramawt have sought their fortunes abroad for centuries. In the modern period, they have been economic middlemen in the European colonial domains spanning littoral East Africa, India, and Southeast Asia—so much so that the economy of the Hadramawt has been heavily dependent on foreign remittances. Indonesia had the most important Hadrami colony until World War II; now it is in the Hadramawt's oil-rich neighbors. The discovery of gold deposits in the 1980s was an important development.

The language of the Hadramawt is Arabic. Outside of literate circles, where modern standard or classical Arabic is the norm, a Hadrami dialect that is close to the former is in general usage. The languages and cultures of the Hadrami diaspora have influenced life in the Hadramawt. Besides its fame as a center for Islamic scholarship, the Hadramawt is noted for its social structure, in which descendents of the Prophet (*sayyid*) have occupied a position of politico-religious and economic paramountcy.

Although the Ottoman government historically claimed the Hadramawt as part of its empire, it did not maintain garrisons or levy taxes in the area. The imam of Yemen exerted some authority, but it is the Kuwaiti and Kathiri ruling houses that have competed for political control over the area in its modern history. The Hadramawt was a British protectorate from the late nineteenth century until 1967, when it became independent under the leadership of the National Liberation Front. It was one of the six governorates of the People's Democratic Republic of Yemen until 1991, when it became part of the Republic of Yemen.

BIBLIOGRAPHY

BERG, LODEWIJK W. C. VAN DEN. *Le Hadhramout et les colonies arabes dans l'Archipel indien.* Batavia, Jakarta, 1886.

BUJRA, ABDALLA S. *The Politics of Stratification: A Study of Political Change in a South Arabian Town.* Oxford, 1971.

Sumit Mandal

Hadrami Bedouin League

Social organization in South Yemen.

Organized in the Hadrami region in 1939, the league was conceived of by Harold Ingrams as a "mixture of [Major John Bagot] Glubb's ideas [as implemented in the Jordanian Arab Legion] and the Boy Scouts." Members of local tribes made up the league, which acted as a police force, a means for spreading education and training, a medical corps, and, most important in Ingrams's view, a mechanism for developing intertribal trust and cooperation.

Manfred W. Wenner

Hadria-Cohen, Elie   [1898–?]

Tunisian educator and politician.

Born in Tunis, Hadria-Cohen received a French education. From 1918 until Tunisia's independence in 1956, he was an active socialist, and from the 1930s he was identified with the Tunisian nationalist movement Neo-DESTOUR. Until 1956, Hadria-Cohen, Albert Cattan, and Segre Moati published *Tunis socialiste,* the main socialist daily newspaper.

BIBLIOGRAPHY

COHEN-HADRIA, ELIE. *Du Protectorat français à l'indépendance tunisienne.* Nice, France, 1976.

Michael M. Laskier

Haffar, Lutfi al-   [1891–?]

Syrian politician.

Born in Damascus to Hasan al-Haffar, Lutfi al-Haffar received a Sunni Islamic education. At the age of fifteen, he founded the secret Arab Renaissance Society. Exiled by the French authorities in 1927, al-Haffar pursued the nationalist cause in becoming a founder of the National Bloc. Serving at different times as minister of finance, education, and the interior, he became prime minister for one turbulent month in 1939. Suspected of the murder of an anti-Bloc political figure, al-Haffar fled to Iraq in July 1940. Al-Haffar served as president of the National party in 1947.

BIBLIOGRAPHY

Who's Who in the Middle East, 1967–1968.

Charles U. Zenzie

Hafid, Mulay   [1876–1937]

Alawi sultan of Morocco, 1908–1912.

After serving as governor of various provinces under his brother, Mulay Abd al-Aziz, Hafid exploited the latter's inability to resist French and Spanish encroachment upon Morocco and launched a bid for power that led him to the sultanate in 1908/09.

Helpless to resist the conquest of northern Morocco by Spain and France, Hafid was pressed by France to sign the Treaty of FES in 1912—widely considered the official beginning of the French protectorate. Hafid was forced to abdicate later that year.

BIBLIOGRAPHY

ABUN-NASR, J. *A History of Maghrib.* Cambridge, U.K., 1976.
BURKE, EDMUND, III. *Prelude to Protectorate in Morocco.* Chicago, 1976.

Matthew S. Gordon

Hafiz, Abd al-Halim   [1929–1977]

Egyptian singer and film actor.

Abd al-Halim Hafiz was a singer known for his work in romantic films. He appeared in more than a dozen films, including *Lahn al-Wafa, Dalila, Banat al-Yawm* (which included Muhammad Abd al-Wahhab's famous song "Ahwak"), the autobiographical *Hikayat al-Hubb,* and *Ma'budat al-Jamahir.*

He was born Abd al-Halim Ali Isma'il Shabana on June 21, 1929, to Ali Shabana and Zaynab Amasha in a village near Zaqaziq in the Egyptian delta province of Sharqiyya. Upon the deaths of his parents shortly thereafter, his maternal uncle took him and his three siblings into his home in Zaqaziq, where Abd al-Halim attended *kuttab* (Qur'an school) and later primary school.

At the age of 18, Abd al-Halim followed his brother Isma'il to Cairo and enrolled in the Institute of Arabic Music. He wanted to study voice and *ud* (oud; a short-necked lute); however, he soon moved to the Higher Institute for Theater Music where he took up the oboe. Upon leaving the institute, he worked as a music teacher in several primary schools for girls and played oboe in the Egyptian Radio orchestra. The oboe, however, was considered a Western instrument and not part of Arabic tradition. Disenchanted, Abd al-Halim returned to his previous ambition of becoming a professional singer.

Among his colleagues at the institute were two young composers, Kamal al-Tawil and Muhammad al-Muji, and the conductor Ahmad Fu'ad Hasan who later established an accomplished and prestigious instrumental ensemble. All three became lifelong colleagues. In 1951, Abd al-Halim performed his first successful song, "Liqa" by Kamal al-Tawil; he also began singing for radio. Shortly thereafter, he signed a two-year contract with Muhammad Abd al-Wahhab to record Abd al-Wahhab's songs and appear in his films.

Along with works by numerous popular lyricists, Abd al-Halim sang the poetry of Abd al-Rahman al-Abnudi, beginning in the early 1960s. At this time, Abd al-Halim sought to change his style from that of ordinary love songs (al-aghani al-atifiyya) to one closer to that of popular folk song. He sought colloquial poetry more colorful and meaningful than the common romantic song lyric. Together, Abd al-Halim and al-Abnudi produced "al-Hawa Hawaya," "Ahdan al-Habayib," and other works that had significant impact on popular song.

Like many other commercial performers, Abd al-Halim was eager for artistic and financial control over his work. In 1959, he and cinematographer Wahid Farid formed their own film company, Aflam al-Alam al-Arabi, and produced, among other works, *Al-Banat wa al-Sayf,* based on three short stories by the well-known writer Ihsan Abd al-Quddus. In 1961, Abd al-Halim and Abd al-Wahhab formed the record company Sawt al-Fann and, in 1963, Aflam al-Alam al-Arabi became Aflam Sawt al-Fann, with Abd al-Wahhab as the third partner.

The beginning of Abd al-Halim's singing career coincided with Muhammad Abd al-Wahhab's shift away from singing to composition. Abd al-Halim's voice differed considerably from that of his famous predecessor: It was mellow and resonant, and his distinctive vocal style was characterized as subtle, with meticulous intonation. He left the impression of extended, almost endless musical phrases. He sang the songs of numerous composers, such as Abd al-Wahhab, Baligh Hamdi, Kamal al-Tawil, and Muhammad al-Muji, all in his own style, in his "confined and fertile vocal space" (al-Najmi, 142). Among his most famous songs are "Safini Marra" (by al-Muji), "Ala qadd al-Shuq" (by al-Tawil), "Ahwak" (by Abd al-Wahhab), and "Qari'at al-Finjan" (by al-Muji, with poetry by Nizar Qabbani).

Abd al-Halim was diagnosed as having schistosomiasis (bilharzia, a parasitic disease of the tropics) in 1939. Debilitating attacks resulting from the disease began in 1955 and ended with his death in 1977.

BIBLIOGRAPHY

MAHMUD, MUHAMMAD. *Hayat wa-aghani Abd al-Halim Hafiz* (The Life and Songs of Abd al-Halim Hafiz). Cairo, 1978.

AL-NAJMI, KAMAL. "Nafikh al-ubu yughanni" (The Oboe Player Sings). In *Al-ghina al-misri* (Egyptian Song). Cairo, 1966.

Virginia Danielson

Hafiz, Amin al- [1920–]

Syrian politician and veteran member of the Ba'th party.

When the Ba'thists started to consolidate their hold on power in the coup of March 1963, al-Hafiz emerged as a prominent Syrian politician. After serving as deputy prime minister and minister of the interior in the government of Salah al-Din al-Bitar, al-Hafiz became chairman of the Revolutionary Command Council in July 1963, after which he served as prime minister from November 1963 to May 1964. He also held the post of president of Syria from 1963 to 1966. In the internal political fighting which became the hallmark of Syrian domestic politics in the 1960s, al-Hafiz took the side of the rural-based regionalist group led by General Salah al-Jadid and Dr. Yusuf Zu'ayyin. As early as January 1965, the regionalists launched a sweeping nationalization program that attacked the entrenched interests of the urban bourgeoisie and put nearly all industry in the hands of the Syrian state. This left-wing group of regionalists was far from being united. In the summer and fall of 1965, internal party strife was brewing. The strife ended with the ouster of al-Hafiz's wing of the Ba'th Party in February 1966, and the ascendance of the neo-leftist Salah al-Jadid faction. Having lost out to al-Jadid, al-Hafiz went into exile in Lebanon in June 1967. From there he moved with Michel Aflaq and other Syrian politicians to Iraq and aligned himself with the orthodox Ba'thists who seized power in Baghdad in July 1968. His embrace of the pro-Iraqi Ba'th wing made his return to Syria a virtual impossibility. In August 1971, he was sentenced to death in absentia. The sentence was commuted to life imprisonment in November of the same year. Al-Hafiz and his Syrian associates formed a loose coalition of anti-Asad politicians who were involved in anti-Syrian activities on behalf of the rival Ba'th wing in Iraq.

Muhammad Muslih

Hafiz, Amin Isma'il al- [1926–]

Lebanese parliamentarian and former head of the Lebanese government.

Hafiz was born to a prominent Sunni Muslim family in Tripoli, Lebanon. His father, Shaykh Isma'il, was a prominent imam (Muslim spiritual leader) and a politician who studied under Shaykh Muhammad AB-DUH and was very active in the Arab revolts in Palestine (1936/37). Amin completed his elementary and secondary studies in Palestine and Lebanon. He holds several degrees in political science, economics, business administration, and international law. He taught banking and economics of Arab countries at the Lebanese University, the American University of Beirut, and the Arab University. Among his students was a prime minister of Lebanon, Rafiq HARIRI. In 1960, Hafiz was elected to the Lebanese parliament and reelected in 1964, 1968, 1972, and 1992.

BIBLIOGRAPHY

Arab Information Center. Beirut.

George E. Irani

Hafiz, Mawlay Abd al-

See Hafid, Mulay

Hafiz, Yasin al-   [1930–1979]

Syrian intellectual.

Born in Dayr al-Zawr to an Armenian Christian mother. His father was Badawi al-Hafiz. In the mid-1960s, Yasin al-Hafiz was a member of the Ba'th Party. He was one of the founders of the Arab Revolutionary Workers Party. In 1975 and 1976, during the Lebanese civil war, he was in Beirut, which he considered the Arab city most open to the West. Among his publications, all in Arabic, are *The Defeat and Defeated Ideology* (an autobiography), *The Historic Experience of Vietnam,* and *Current Issues in Arab Revolution.*

George E. Irani

Haft-sin

A special table prepared in anticipation and celebration of the Iranian New Year (Nowruz) on March 21 on which seven items whose names begin with the Persian letter "s" are put.

One of the most important items on the *haft-sin* table is *sabzi,* wheat or lentil planted almost two weeks in advance in proper plates, which by the new year becomes fresh green shoots several inches high that symbolize spring. On the table are also placed a mirror and candlesticks, a copy of the Qur'an, a bowl of water with a green leaf floating in it, colored eggs, and red fish in a bowl of water, as well as the actual articles of the *haft-sin,* including the sabzi and six items that correspond to the English wild rue, apples, garlic, vinegar, a paste of malt grain, and sumac. When the time of the vernal equinox approaches, the family gatheres around the table and awaits the exact moment of the Nowruz.

BIBLIOGRAPHY

WILBER, D. *Iran: Past and Present,* 4th ed. Princeton, N.J., 1958, pp. 185–187.

Parvaneh Pourshariati

Haganah

See Israeli Military and Politics

Haggiag Family

Prominent North African Jewish family.

The Haggiag family name has several probable origins. According to Mordechai Ha-Cohen, the family originated in Oran, Algeria. In 1555, the family fled to Gharian in south Tripolitania. Others claim the family to be of Berber origin, cave dwellers who inhabited the area of Jabal Nafusa and Gharian. The name may have derived from their pilgrimage to Jerusalem, Safed, and Tiberias, hence the Arabic *haj,* plural *hujjaj,* related to *hajjaj* or *haggiag,* meaning pilgrims. Once the Haggiag settled on the coast of Tripoli, they maintained the name as it is but added surnames, like Pagani and Liluf: One finds, for example, Isacco and David Haggiag Liluf and Abramo Haggiag Pagani.

Hmani (Rahmin) Haggiag was head of the Jewish community of Gharian in 1837 and was a physician. Better known was Rabbi Khalifa Haggiag (died c. 1915). He presided over the Jewish community of Gharian in 1880, served as its spiritual leader, and was a poet and physician-surgeon. He is known to have written poems that appeared in the books of Nahum Slouschz.

Another branch may have come from Tunisia, where they lived as subjects of the bey of Tunis and held French citizenship. Notable were Rabbi Nessim and his son Simeone (born 1882). After the Italian occupation, Simeone's life became intertwined with the destiny of the Jewish community and the economic development of Tripoli. He acquired his education at the Italian school of the Franciscans, in addition to his Jewish studies. He went to the Italian advanced business school and upon graduation joined the company Vadala, which specialized in import/export and banking. He remained until 1911, when the company liquidated assets in Libya.

Simeone assumed the presidency of the Jewish community of Tripoli in the by-elections of 1924, replacing Halfallah Nahum. He was by then a prominent private banker. His tenure lasted until 1926, when disagreements among the council members brought about his resignation. He was then appointed by Italian authorities as commissioner; when in 1929 elections were called and the Haggiag's faction was defeated amid irregularities of voting procedure, the community grew tense and incidents erupted. This led the governor of Libya, Pietro Badoglio, to appoint a non-Jewish Italian, Dr. Alberto Monastero, as administrator of the community in 1929. Until 1938, the eve of World War II, the community was left leaderless.

BIBLIOGRAPHY

ARBIB, LILLO. *Unedited Studies of Surnames of Jews in Libya.* Courtesy of the author, Tel Aviv, 1991.

DE FELICE, RENZO. *Jews in Arab Lands: Libya, 1835–1970.* Austin, Tex., 1985.

HA-COHEN, MORDECHAI. *The Book of Mordechai: A Study of the Jews of Libya,* ed. and trans. (with introduction and commentaries) by Harvey E. Goldberg. Philadelphia, 1980.

ROUMANI, MAURICE M. "Zionism and Social Change in Libya at the Turn of the Century." In *Studies in Zionism*, vol. 8, no. 1. 1987.

ZUARETZ, F., et al., eds. *Yahadut Luv* (Libyan Jewry). Tel Aviv, 1982.

Maurice M. Roumani

Haham

Hebrew for "wise man."

Haham meant "rabbi" in the Ottoman Empire, when used as a title. It came into use during the early sixteenth century, when Spanish Jews expelled from Spain in 1492 resettled in Palestine and other areas under Ottoman control. In the capital of Istanbul, the grand rabbi of the Jewish community was given the honorary title of *haham bashi,* meaning "chief rabbi." Haham became the prevalent title in Arab regions of the empire, replacing the Arabic word for rabbi when used as a title—as for example Haham Jonah ben Isaac.

Jenab Tutunji

Haham Bashi

Chief rabbi of the Ottoman Empire.

Scholarly opinions differ concerning the origins of the office of the chief rabbinate. Upon conquering Constantinople (now Istanbul) in 1453, Sultan Mehmet acknowledged the preeminent position of Moses Capsali as rabbi of Constantinople's Jewish community. The government placed a small police force at Capsali's disposal to enforce his authority. There is no evidence, however, that Sultan Mehmet created the post of Haham Bashi (chief rabbi) or appointed Capsali to such a post at this time. This would have been contrary to established Ottoman practices in the fifteenth and sixteenth centuries. Capsali's position as the rabbi of Constantinople was not necessarily analogous to that of the patriarch of the Orthodox Christians. Rather, contemporary sources indicate that his power did not extend beyond Constantinople and that his successors had even less power. Given Constantinople's preeminence in the fifteenth century, Capsali clearly had substantial power among Ottoman Jews. Nevertheless, when he attempted to spread his powers beyond Constantinople, Salonikan Jewish leaders flatly refused to accept his authority.

Following Capsali's death in 1496 or 1497, Rabbi Elijah Mizrahi emerged as Constantinople's leading rabbi. Although he was a noted legal expert, Mizrahi appears to have lacked a special title or an official representative function. Mizrahi was the Jewish community's acknowledged spiritual leader, but does not appear to have exercised any official representative functions with an official title. Ottoman centralizing tendencies were offset, in the case of the Jews, by the mass influx of diverse groups of Jews after the expulsions from Spain, Portugal, and Italy. They preferred to dispatch special envoys and court favorites, like physician Moses Hamon or merchant Dona Gracia Mendes, to present their case before the imperial authorities when necessary.

The term *haham bashi* and its officeholder gained currency during the nineteenth century in the context of the Ottoman reforms and restructuring of the minority communities as part of the TANZIMAT. The authorities sought to enhance the position of Jews, and formally recognized Jews as one of the "official" communities of the empire. The title of haham bashi was conferred for the first time in 1835 upon Rabbi Abraham Levi. The position was similar in power and stature to the Orthodox and Armenian ecclesiastical heads. The haham bashi was regarded as the civil and religious head of the Jews of the Ottoman Empire and his appointment received official confirmation by the granting of a diploma (*berat*). The hanam bashi of Constantinople served as representative of the Jewish *millet* in all important state functions.

The Jewish community reluctantly accepted the new official. Gradually, the position came to be held by scholars like Rabbi Ya'akov Avigdor (1860–1865) and Rabbi Yakir Geron (1863–1872). In the course of the nineteenth century, the appointment process became the focus of intense communal struggles between the factions supporting reform or modernization and those favoring the status quo ante. Ottoman authorities generally supported the modernizing candidates. The more conservative forces of the Jewish community controlled the rabbinate until 1908.

After the Young Turk Revolution of 1908, Rabbi Hayyim NAHUM was appointed by the government as acting chief rabbi with the new title of "chief rabbi of all the Jews of the capital and its dependencies and of all the Jews resident in the Ottoman Empire." Nahum held this title until 1920. Under the Turkish republic, the preeminence of Istanbul's chief rabbi has continued, although his powers were much diminished by the secularization of all aspects of Turkish society.

BIBLIOGRAPHY

BRAUDE, BENJAMIN. "Foundation Myths of the Millet System." In *Christians and Jews in the Ottoman Empire: The Functioning of a Plural Society,* ed. by Benjamin Braude and Bernard Lewis, vol. 1. New York, 1982.
LEVY, AVIGDOR. *The Sephardim in the Ottoman Empire,* Princeton, N.J., 1992.

Jane Gerber

Haifa

Major city in northwestern Israel.

Established in the late Bronze Age on the edge of the Bay of Haifa on the Mediterranean coast, Haifa

Baha'i temple gardens overlooking the city of Haifa. (Mia Bloom)

Haifa cityscape with the twin Technion Towers and Mount Carmel in the distance. (Mia Bloom)

was part of the Ottoman Empire which ruled Palestine from 1516 until 1918. Haifa's population was predominantly Muslim and Christian Palestinians until Jews began to settle in the city in the late nineteenth century. A number of factors contributed to its economic revival: the Egyptian conquest and reforms of the mid-nineteenth century; the arrival of European steamboats, which began to visit Haifa as their port of call; the immigration in 1868 of German Templers and, after 1880, of European Jews, both of whom introduced modern economic practices and machinery; and the extension of the Hejaz railway to Haifa in 1905. The British conquered Palestine in 1918 and ruled it until 1948. During these thirty years, Haifa experienced expansion and population growth, especially after a deepwater port was opened in 1933. The 1922 census recorded 25,000 people, of whom 6,000 were Jews and 18,000 were Palestinians. As a result of increased Jewish immigration, by 1944 there were about 66,000 Jews and 62,000 Palestinians. There was also a small community of Baha'is, who established their religious center at Mount Carmel. During the Arab–Israel War of 1948, Arab and Jewish forces fought for control of Haifa. Of the city's Palestinian population at this time, only 3,000 remained after the war; the rest were expelled or fled to Lebanon.

Haifa is now Israel's principal port and industrial and commercial center. The city's industries include oil refining, cement, chemicals, electronics, and steel. The city is composed of three sections: port facilities and warehouses at the bottom of Mount Carmel; the business district at the slopes of the mountain; and houses, apartment buildings, and parks on top of the mountain. It also has a maritime museum and two universities. Its 1992 population was about 250,000, of whom 10 percent were Palestinians.

Philip Mattar

Haifa University

Public university in Haifa, Israel.

Opened in 1963 in Haifa, Israel, it was not until the early 1970s that Haifa University became firmly established. With help from Hebrew University in Jerusalem, Haifa University solidified its place as one of the top institutions of higher learning in Israel. Though its enrollment is under 7,000 students, Haifa University has nurtured a disproportionate number of original and often controversial figures, particularly in the humanities and the social sciences. In general, the faculty tends toward the left, and the university has been the seat of innovative studies on such topics as the attitudes of Arabs toward Israelis and of Israelis toward Arabs.

BIBLIOGRAPHY

1991 International Year Book and Statesmen's Who's Who. New Standard Jewish Encyclopedia. New York, 1977. SHIPLER, DAVID. *Arab and Jew.* New York, 1986.

Zachary Karabell

Haigazian College

Armenian academic institution established in Lebanon in 1955 by the Union of Evangelical Armenian Churches and the Armenian Mission Delegation.

Haigazian is a liberal arts college catering mostly to the needs of the Armenian community in Lebanon. Arabic, English, and Armenian literature are taught, as well as political science, economics, sociology, psychology, computer science, and business administration. There are also professors who teach chemistry, physics, and religious studies.

In 1975, Haigazian College had an enrollment of 650 students; by the mid-1990s there were 312 students and 50 faculty. All courses are taught in English and, students are required to take a course on religion. Most of Haigazian's faculty also teach at the American University of Beirut and Beirut University College.

George E. Irani

Haik

Woman's draped, concealing garment.

A *haik* (pl. *hiyak*) is a simple, traditional outdoor costume of Moroccan townswomen, worn at the turn of the century, made of either fine white or coarse lumpy wool, a mixture of silk and wool, or simply cotton. Hiyak are white, with the exception of the black haik of Taroudant, and measure about 5 by 1.6 meters. The haik drapes the woman from head to foot with only the eyes showing.

BIBLIOGRAPHY

BESANCENOT, JEAN. *Costumes of Morocco.* London, 1990.

Rhimou Bernikho-Canin

Haines, Stafford Bettesworth

British captain who established the British base at Aden, 1839.

In the early nineteenth century, an intense competition developed in the Red Sea region among various European powers, Egypt, and the Ottoman Empire. The small village of Aden in South Yemen and its harbor interested some British who were seeking to establish coaling stations and harbors for the trade route to India. Among the strongest supporters for acquiring Aden for miliary as well as commercial purposes was Capt. Stafford Bettesworth Haines. The era's poor communications and the ability of local officers to exercise considerable initiative made it possible for Haines to land troops and take Aden in 1839 for Great Britain.

Manfred W. Wenner

Hajir, Abd al-Hoseyn [1900–1947]

Iranian politician.

Hajir began his political career in the ministry of foreign affairs and then became a clerk at the Russian embassy in Tehran. After holding several ministerial positions, he was appointed prime minister in 1947. In 1949, he was elected to the parliament and also acted as minister of court. Opposed by the popular National Front, his appointments caused mass demonstrations. Hajir was assassinated in Tehran as he was praying in the Sepahsalar Mosque (1949). The murder was attributed to Sayyid Hoseyn Emami of the Feda'iyan-e Islam, a militant Islamic group that accused Hajir of being an Anglophile and having Baha'i affiliations.

BIBLIOGRAPHY

AQELI, BAQER. *Iranian Prime Ministers from Moshir al-Dowleh to Bakhtiyar*. Tehran, 1991. In Persian.

Neguin Yavari

Hajj

Islamic religious pilgrimage.

The pilgrimage to MECCA is the fifth pillar of ISLAM, enjoining every able Muslim who can afford the trip to do so once in a lifetime. The first Muslim hajj was in the year 629 C.E. (7 A.H.), when the Prophet Muhammad gathered his followers in Mecca. A profound spiritual experience in the lives of many Muslims, the hajj has also been, through the centuries, a primary vehicle for commercial and cultural exchange for the entire Muslim world. More than a million Muslims annually make the journey, and there is rising concern over pushing and crushing crowds, which leave dead pilgrims in their wake.

BIBLIOGRAPHY

EICKELMAN, DALE. *The Middle East: An Anthropological Approach*. Englewood Cliffs, N.J., 1981.
"Hadjdj," *Encyclopedia of Islam*, 2nd ed.
HOURANI, ALBERT. *A History of the Arab Peoples*. New York, 1991.
MARTIN, RICHARD C. *Islam*. Englewood Cliffs, N.J., 1982.

Elizabeth Thompson

Pilgrims circling the Ka'ba in Mecca. (Government of Saudi Arabia)

Hajji Baba of Ispahan

Title of the first and most famous of four travel novels about Persia by an Englishman who had spent time there in the British diplomatic corps.

Hajji Baba of Ispahan (1824) by James Justinian Morier (c. 1780–1849) appealed to contemporary interest in things oriental and gave readers a satirical look into Persian society of the early Qajar period (the QAJAR DYNASTY, ruled 1795–1925). Its title character and picaresque narrator is a barber whose desire to get ahead, and cleverness in so doing, leads him from his hometown of Ispahan (formerly Ispahan) to Mashhad, to life with a band of Torkamans (TURKMEN), Tehran, Qom, Karbala, Baghdad, Constantinople (Istanbul), and finally back to Ispahan as a wealthy representative of the shah. In these places and situations—in the bazaar and the royal court and among dervishes and clerics—Hajji Baba satirically depicts Iranian ways and offers entertaining observations on human nature.

Hajji Baba of Ispahan has played a role in modern Persian Literature insofar as its Persian translation in 1905 became a popular model for a type of narrative for which indigenous precedents did not exist. Readers in Iran have even given Morier the ultimate tribute, by alleging that the Persian version was the original and Morier's the translation. They thought the book was so accurate and detailed in its depiction of culture-specific situations and behavior that only an Iranian could have written it.

Michael C. Hillmann

Hajj Ibrahim Family, al–

Prominent Palestinian family from Tulkarm.

The al-Hajj Ibrahim family became large landowners and dominated local administrative posts in Palestine in the late nineteenth century. Although family members sold more than two thousand *dunums* (1,200 acres; 500 hectares) of their land to proponents of Zionism in the 1920s and 1930s, they also became prominent in the Palestinian national movement.

Rashid al-Hajj Ibrahim was an Istiqlal party leader in the 1930s, and in the 1940s he headed the Haifa Chamber of Commerce and founded the Palestine Arab Party.

BIBLIOGRAPHY

KHALAF, ISSA. *Politics in Palestine: Arab Factionalism and Social Disintegration 1939–1948*. Albany, N.Y., 1991.

Elizabeth Thompson

Hajri, Abdullah al-   [?–1977]

Yemeni judge and government official.

A religious, traditional Qadi or judge, al-Hajri sided with the royalists in the Yemen civil war in the 1960s. He then helped pave the way for the republican-royalist reconciliation by switching sides and working to give the republican regime a more conservative cast. As prime minister in 1973, he both secured from his Saudi friends large amounts of state-to-state aid on a regular, annual basis and cracked down harshly on Yemeni leftists. Adviser to the younger, much less conservative President Ibrahim al-HAMDI in the mid-1970s, he was assassinated in 1977.

Robert D. Burrowes

Hakim, Adnan al-   [?–1991]

Lebanese politician.

A Sunni Muslim from Beirut who played a leading role in the LEBANESE CIVIL WAR of 1958, Hakim won a parliamentary seat from Beirut in 1960 and 1968. He is considered an extremist who mobilized the masses following sectarian lines and did not get along with other Sunni politicians, whom he accused of compromising Muslim demands in dealing with the Maronite (Christian) political establishment.

His political career is closely tied to that of the al-NAJJADA party, which was founded as a paramilitary organization in 1946. It emerged from the structure of the Muslim SCOUTS in Syria and Lebanon. Hakim served as the commander of the Beirut section and a vice-president. In the wake of the dissolution of paramilitary organizations in 1949, he revived the organization and became its head in 1951.

The party sought the "propagation of the Islamic heritage" and called for the union of the Arab lands. It cooperated closely with Egypt's President Gamal Abdel NASSER in the 1960s and led a campaign against the pro-Western foreign policies of Lebanon's President Camille Chamoun. The motto of the party is "the Lands of the Arabs are for the Arabs," and it called for the elimination of Western influence and interests from the Middle East.

Al-Najjada's role in the Lebanese civil war of 1975/76 was insignificant because most Muslims were attracted to parties with a more revolutionary agenda. The party was seen as belonging to the past, and Hakim was too old to energize party recruitment as he had done in the late 1950s. His political role in the 1970s and 1980s was limited to his ownership of the Beirut daily *Sawt al-Uruba*.

As'ad AbuKhalil

Hakim, Hasan al-   [1886–?]

Syrian politician.

Born in Damascus the son of Abd al-Razzaq al-Hakim, Hasan al-Hakim founded the People's party in 1924. He was elected minister of education in 1939 and prime minister in 1941–1942. One of few pro-Western Syrians as well as an outspoken Arab nationalist, al-Hakim was reelected prime minister in 1951. He published a two-volume memoir.

BIBLIOGRAPHY

Who's Who in the Middle East, 1967–1968.

Charles U. Zenzie

Hakim, Tawfiq al-   [c. 1898–1987]

Egyptian dramatist, novelist, and man of letters.

Tawfiq al-Hakim was born in Alexandria, and his early life was shaped by his father's frequent moves from job to job and by his ambition that his son should become a lawyer. However, al-Hakim's real interests lay elsewhere; while still a student at the School of Law in Cairo, he wrote some plays (published under a pseudonym) for the Ukasha troupe. When he failed in his legal studies, his father sent him to France to study for a doctorate. Al-Hakim traveled to Paris in 1925, an event that was to be a turning point in his life. Instead of studying law, he immersed himself in European culture, particularly drama, and was strongly influenced by the works of Shaw, Pirandello, Ibsen, and Maeterlinck. Upon returning to Egypt in 1928, he prepared for publication a number of literary projects begun in Paris but also worked for a time as a deputy public prosecutor (*na'ib*) in the Nile delta area and, later, as an official in the ministry of social affairs. In 1943 he resigned his position as a civil servant to devote himself to his writing. Later in life, and particularly during the presidency of Anwar al-Sadat, he became somewhat controversial, partly because of his book *Awdat al-Wa'y* (1974; published in 1985 in English as *The Return of Consciousness*), in which the course of the Egyptian revolution and the status of Egypt's former president Gamal Abdel Nasser was critically reexamined. Only a short time before his death in 1987, he published a series of articles under the title "Hiwar ma'a Allah" (Conversation with God), which aroused the ire of the religious establishment.

The inspiration that al-Hakim had found in France bore fruit when two of his works were published in 1933 to immediate critical acclaim: the play *Ahl al-*

Kahf (People of the Cave) and the novel *Awdat al-Ruh* (Return of the Spirit). The latter was to be the first of a series of partially autobiographical contributions to fiction to be published in the 1930s. While it deals with the life of an Egyptian family during the turbulent years surrounding the revolution of 1919, *Yawmiyyat Na'ib fi al-Aryaf* (Diary of a Provincial Public Prosecutor, 1937; published in English as *The Maze of Justice*, 1989) is a most successful portrait of the dilemma faced by Egyptian rural society in its confrontation with the laws and imported values of Europe, and *Usfur min al-Sharq* (1938; published in English as *A Bird from the East*, 1966) takes Muhsin, the main character in *Awdat al-Ruh*, to Paris.

Ahl al-Kahf was to mark the official beginning of the most notable career in Arabic drama to date. Along with several other plays written in the 1930s and 1940s (such as *Shahrazad* [1934; in English, 1981], *Pygmalion* [1942], and *Al-Malik Udib* [1949; in English, *King Oedipus*, 1981]), it dealt with historical and philosophical themes culled from a wide variety of sources and thus was seen as providing the dramatic genre with a cultural status that it had not enjoyed previously. Al-Hakim's dramatic output is vast and extends over five decades. It includes other plays with philosophical themes, two collections of shorter plays addressing social issues, and a number of works that experiment with dramatic technique (such as *Ya Tali al-Shajarah* [Oh, Tree Climber, 1962; in English, *The Tree Climber*, 1966] and varying levels of language (such as *Al-Safqa* [The Deal, 1956]).

Tawfiq al-Hakim is the major pioneer figure in the development of a dramatic tradition in modern Arabic literature, and he has attained the status of one of the greatest Arab litterateurs of the twentieth century.

[*See also:* Literature, Arabic]

BIBLIOGRAPHY

Long, Richard. *Tawfiq al-Hakim: Playwright of Egypt.* London, 1979.
Starkey, Paul. *From the Ivory Tower: A Critical Study of Tawfiq al-Hakim.* London, 1987.

Roger Allen

Hakim, Yusuf al-   [1883–?]

Syrian barrister, politician, and author.

Born in Lattakia, the son of Dr. Yacoub al-Hakim, Yusuf served as a judge in Lattakia, Jerusalem, Jaffa, Beirut, and Tripoli. He was elected president of the court of appeal and, later, minister of justice. Al-Hakim was a close adviser to Prime Minister Ahmad Nami in his 1926 and later cabinets. He wrote a number of histories of the region.

BIBLIOGRAPHY

Who's Who in the Middle East, 1967–1968.

Charles U. Zenzie

Hakim Family

Prominent Iraqi family of Shi'a religious scholars.

The Najaf-based Hakim family of *ulama* call themselves Tabataba'i SAYYIDS, or "descendents of the Prophet." In the family were Ali Ibn Abi Talib and his elder son, al-Husayn, the second imam of Shi'ism. In the twentieth century the most prominent scholar in the family was Ayat Allah al-Uzma Muhsin ibn Mahdi (1889–1970). He was educated at the *hawza* of Najaf by some of the greatest *mujtahids* of his time—Akhund Khurasani, Muhammad Kazim Yazdi, Muhammad Husayn Na'ini, and others.

Following the death in 1962 of MARJA' AL-TAQLID Husayn ibn Ali Tabataba'i Burujirdi in Iran, Muhsin al-Hakim became the most widely-followed marja' in the Shi'a world, but he never managed to acquire sufficient influence in Qom and thus never became supreme marja' al-taqlid. Under the monarchy Hakim was regarded as a political quietist, but under the revolutionary regime of general Abd al-Karim Kassem (1958–1963) he became very active against the rising influence of the Communist party, which was felt in the Shi'a south as well as in Baghdad. This brought about a number of clashes between the Iraqi Communist Party and Hakim's followers. He also openly criticized Kassem for introducing a secular law of personal status and called upon him to abolish it. At the same time, however, he maintained cordial personal relations with Kassem himself. This is also when he started to sponsor a young and ingenious activist mujtahid, Muhammad Baqir al-SADR (1933–1980) who, in 1957, established the clandestine Da'wa party. Its purpose was to fight atheism and bring people, and in particular the Shi'a masses, back to Islam. As a result of strong criticism leveled by conservative Shi'a *ulama* against this Western innovation, however, in 1962 Hakim forced Sadr to distance himself from the Da'wa, at least in appearance. But Hakim continued to sponsor similar activities performed through traditional channels. He sent some of his and Sadr's disciples as agents (*wukala*) to various parts of Iraq, as well as to Lebanon, to spread the message, and he dedicated great resources to the establishment of libraries, schools, mosques, and other educational activities in and outside of Iraq. Under the first Ba'th rule (1963) of the Arif brothers (1963–1968) relations with the regimes were frosty. The Arifs were regarded by the Shi'ites as extreme Sunni bigots, and Hakim considered their Arab Socialism a deviation from Islam's social teachings. Finally, he had strong reservations about their Nasserist pan-Arabism.

In June 1969, less than a year after it came to power for the second time in Baghdad, the Ba'th regime initiated an unprecedented confrontation with the Shi'a religious establishment. This came as reprisal for Hakim's reluctance to support the regime against the shah of Iran. The Ba'th decided to draft the students of religion, to eliminate the educational autonomy of the *hawzat* (the Shi'a religious universities), and to control the huge funds donated to the Shi'a holy shrines. They also accused Hakim's son Mahdi of espionage and forced him to flee the country. Hundreds of students and teachers had to escape to Iran, and the religious centers of Najaf, Karbala, and Kazimayn quickly deteriorated. Hakim led the doomed struggle and died broken-hearted in June 1970.

Mahdi al-Hakim eventually settled down in London, where he established a Shi'a European political movement, Harakat al-Afwaj al-Islamiyya, and a cultural center, Markaz Ahl al-Bayt. In January 1988 he was assassinated by Saddam Hussein's agents at an Islamic conference in Sudan. His brother, Hujjat al-Islam (later Ayat Allah) Muhammad Baqir, established in Iran in November 1981 the Supreme Assembly of the Islamic Revolution in Iraq (SAIRI), the largest Iraqi Shi'a opposition movement to the Ba'th regime. Supported by Iran, his movement's 4,000-strong military wing, the Badr Forces, participated in operations against the Iraqi armed forces during the Iran–Iraq War. Following the August 1988 cease-fire SAIRI's position in Iran became more precarious, but as long as there is no Iranian–Iraqi peace Hakim can still rely on his hosts for some support. In May 1983 Saddam Hussein imprisoned many members of the al-Hakim family, threatening that unless Muhammad Baqir stopped his opposition activities from Tehran his relatives would be executed. Between 1983 and March 1985 at least eight *ulama* members of the family, including sons, grandsons, and nephews of the late *marja'*, as well as many other Shi'a *ulama*, were executed by Iraq.

BIBLIOGRAPHY

MOMEN, MOOJAN. *An Introduction to Shi'i Islam.* New Haven, Conn., 1985.

Amatzia Baram

Hakimi, Ibrahim   [1871–?]

Iranian politician.

Known as Hakim al-Molk, Ibrahim Hakimi was born to a prestigious family in Tabriz, studied medicine in France, and, upon his return to Iran, was appointed personal doctor of Mozaffar al-Din Shah Qajar. His mistaken medical judgment led to his dismissal. Politically, he emerged on the side of the Constitutionalists and was repeatedly elected to the parliament as the deputy from Azerbaijan. In 1910, he became minister of finance and subsequently held several other cabinet positions. Hakimi was imprisoned in 1921 and refrained from engaging in political activity throughout the shah's reign. Hakimi returned to the political arena in 1941, after the shah's forced abdication, and served three times as prime minister of Iran.

BIBLIOGRAPHY

AQELI, BAQER. *Iranian Prime Ministers from Moshir al-Dowleh to Bakhtiyar.* Tehran, 1991. In Persian.

Neguin Yavari

Halabi, Muhammad Ali al-   [1927–   ]

Syrian prime minister.

Born in Damascus, Muhammad Ali al-Halabi was a member of the Ba'th party leadership, Damascus section. Al-Halabi was general secretary of the Ba'th party in Damascus between 1969 and 1971. In February 1978, he formed a government of twenty-six ministers. Between 1970 and 1980, he was a member of the regional command of the Ba'th party. He chaired the Arab Parliamentary Union in its inaugural session.

George E. Irani

Halakhah

Hebrew for "the path," referring to the Jewish legal system.

Derived from scripture—in which all Jewish law is grounded—expanded in the TALMUD and Codes, and subject to rabbinic interpretation, *halakhah* is binding on all Jews at all times (although secular Jews either ignore it or are ignorant of it). In Israel, the Knesset is the legislature that passes state laws and the State Supreme Court makes decisions about national law, but in matters of JUDAISM—particularly those of ceremony, ritual, marriage, divorce, conversion, and other areas of personal status—halakhah, as interpreted by the rabbinical courts and the chief rabbinate, holds authority for Jews worldwide.

BIBLIOGRAPHY

GILBERT, MARTIN, ed. *The Illustrated Atlas of Jewish Civilization: 4,000 Years of Jewish History.* New York, 1990.
TCHERNOWITZ, CHAIM. *Toldot Hahalakha,* 4 vols. In Hebrew.

Samuel C. Heilman

Halal

Word of Arabic origin denoting the notion of acceptability or lawfulness; applicable to all aspects of life.

In modern usage, the word is applied to meat and poultry, specifically the method of slaughter. Islamic law prescribes the manner and preparation of meat for consumption and may contain certain prohibitions against parts of an otherwise *halal* animal.

Cyrus Moshaver

Halet, Mehmet Sait   [1761–1823]

Ottoman bureaucrat.

A member of the *ulama,* Halet served as the Ottoman ambassador to France between 1802 and 1806. That experience increased his opposition to Sultan SELIM III's westernizing reforms. Halet helped overthrow Selim in 1807. Then, as the most powerful adviser to MAHMUD II, he blocked efforts to reform the JANISSARIES. Supporters of reform secured Halet's dismissal in 1820. He was exiled in 1822 and was murdered the following year.

Elizabeth Thompson

Halicarnassus

See Bodrum

Halikarnas Balıkçısı   [1886–1973]

Turkish novelist and short-story writer.

Born Cevat Şakir Kabaağaçli in Istanbul during the Ottoman Empire, Halikarnas Balıkçısı grew up in Athens, Greece, where his father worked in the Ottoman-Turkish Embassy. A graduate of Robert College (a part of Boğaziçi University), he then studied modern history at Oxford University. Upon his return to Istanbul, he contributed stories, drawings, and caricatures to various magazines. An antimilitary drawing published in a magazine in 1924 resulted in his exile and imprisonment in Bodrum (now part of Turkey). After his release from prison, he decided to remain in Bodrum and adopted the name Halikarnas Balıkçısı, the Fisherman of Halikarnas (Halikarnas is the ancient name of Bodrum).

A humanist and naturalist, he devoted his writing to depictions of fishermen. An important theme of his work is that the roots of modern Western civilization are found in Anatolia, not in Greece—and that modern Turks are the cultural inheritors of all the ancient civilizations of Anatolia.

BIBLIOGRAPHY

ERTOP, KONUR. "Trends and Characteristics of Contemporary Turkish Literature." In *The Transformation of Turkish Culture: The Atatürk Legacy,* ed. by Günsel Renda and C. Max Kortepeter. Princeton, N.J., 1986.

David Waldner

Halil Pasha

Ottoman military officer who commanded the successful Ottoman siege of British forces at Kut al-Amara, Iraq.

During World War I, Britain took KUT AL-AMARA in the September 1915 battle of Kut. Beginning a siege on December 8, 1915, Halil Pasha's Ottoman troops forced the British, led by Sir Charles TOWNSHEND, to surrender on April 29, 1916.

Halil wanted to fortify the Tigris river to prevent a new British campaign, but the forces of the Ottoman Empire were subordinated to German officers, who sent Halil into Persia (Iran) to assist Germany's effort there. The British then recaptured Kut in February 1917, and before Halil could return with his troops, Britain forced the surrender of Baghdad on March 11, 1917.

BIBLIOGRAPHY

SHAW, STANFORD, and EZEL SHAW. *History of the Ottoman Empire and Modern Turkey.* Cambridge, U.K., 1977.

David Waldner

Haluqqah

Hebrew term for "distribution."

Haluqqah is the system under which, in pre-Zionist Israel, Jewish communities, which consisted primarily of the elderly and those who devoted their lives to sacred learning, were supported by charitable contributions from Jews and Jewish communities in the Diaspora. The system became a source of contention between the traditional Orthodox, who wished to preserve it and their communal autonomy, and the Zionists who viewed it as parasitical—saying it hinders the work-incentive—and a barrier to national regeneration and growth.

BIBLIOGRAPHY

RUPPIN, ARTHUR. *Building Israel*. New York, 1949.

Chaim I. Waxman

Halutz

Hebrew for "pioneer"; members of Jewish youth organizations in Europe preparing for pioneer life in Palestine.

The Halutz were members of numerous youth groups established after the 1881 pogroms in Russia. These groups arose independently and under various names—Bilu being the oldest and HE-HALUTZ the largest. They were organized in many European countries, ultimately becoming a worldwide Jewish movement, with Yosef TRUMPELDOR as one of its illustrious leaders.

The goal was to prepare a cadre of Jewish workers, trained in agriculture and various trades, to serve as a vanguard for the resettlement of ERETZ YISRAEL. Hebrew was revived as a modern language for the Pioneers to speak, and most groups leaned toward secular living. The first ALIYAH, members of Bilu, arrived in Ottoman Palestine in 1882. Their numbers increased following the Balfour Declaration in 1917. They drained malarial swamps, planted trees, established agricultural settlements, and realized the need for a defense organization.

BIBLIOGRAPHY

ROLEF, S. H., ed. *Political Dictionary of the State of Israel*. New York, 1987.

Ann Kahn

Halvetiye

Sufi order founded in the fourteenth century.

After the death of its leader, Seyyid Yahya Sirvani, in Baku in 1463 or 1464, the Halvetiye Order split into four branches and became very active, partic-

ularly in Constantinople (now Istanbul) and western Anatolia. The most renowned Turkish poet of the seventeenth century, Mehmet Niyazi-i Misri, who died in 1693, was a member of the Halvetiye. Although primarily a religious order with relatively orthodox beliefs, adherents of the order at times became heavily involved in politics. A Berber offshoot of the Halvetiye, the Tijani order, spread into Turkey in the twentieth century and was particularly influential among the religious opposition.

Elizabeth Thompson

Hama

Ancient town built on the banks of the Orontes river in central Syria.

Hama, is located on the main road between Damascus and Aleppo. It is about 130 miles (210 km) north of Damascus, capital of Syria, and about 94 miles (152 km) south of Aleppo. Hama, like Homs, lies close to the frontier of settlement facing the Syrian Desert. This makes it a flourishing market for the nomadic people and for the villagers in the countryside.

Agriculture in the Hama region profits from the water of the ORONTES RIVER. Water wheels (*norias*), which raise the river water up into canals, help irrigate large stretches of land. About one hundred water wheels are found in the province of Hama, but only twenty of them are in use. Grains and fruits abound in the countryside.

In the 1980 census, the inhabitants of the city of Hama numbered 177,208 out of a total of 475,582

The water wheel at Hama in the Orontes valley. (Richard Bulliet)

inhabitants for the whole province. Earlier, in the census of 1922, the inhabitants of Hama numbered 40,437 out of a total of 69,745 inhabitants for the whole province. The bedouin in the countryside of Hama are not accounted for.

The city of Hama prides itself on a number of ancient monuments. Mosques (the most important of which is the Umayyad Mosque), *khans* (caravansary), and luxurious palaces belonging to the Azm family, which governed in Syria in the eighteenth century, abound in Hama. The countryside has important archeological sites. Castles, some of which were built by the Crusaders and some later on by Saladin, include those of Shayzar, al-Madiq, and Misyaf.

BIBLIOGRAPHY

HARBA, MUHAMMAD, and MUSA, ALI. *Muhafazat Hama.* Damascus, 1985.

al-Mu'jam al-Jughrafi li'l-Qutr al-Arab al-Suri (The Geographical Dictionary of Syria). Vol. 1. Damascus, 1990.

Abdul-Karim Rafeq

Hamadan

One of the most important cities of western Iran.

Hamadan is associated with the ancient Median city of Ecbatana, built in the seventh century B.C.E. It was an important capital of successive pre-Islamic dynasties, being situated on the trade route that linked Mesopotamia with the East. In the medieval period, Hamadan was known as a large commercial city in an agriculturally fertile region. In the seventeenth and early eighteenth centuries, the city was occupied by the Ottoman Empire several times. But in 1732 it finally reverted to Iran.

Hamadan has kept its role as a large commercial city in the modern period. In the nineteenth century, it functioned as a transshipment center for the trade of southwestern Iran with the West. Goods destined for Tabriz, Trebizond (now Trabzon), and the Black Sea were brought to Hamadan. After the development of the Anglo–Indian trade, Hamadan prospered as a result of its location on the trade route via Basra and Baghdad to the east. Although George N. CURZON estimated the population of the city at about 20,000 in 1889, Tumanskii, visiting the city in 1894, had reported that as a result of the Anglo–Indian trade, the population of the city had grown to 40,000 to 50,000 people. The population of Hamadan in 1986 was 272,499 people.

BIBLIOGRAPHY

BOSWORTH, C. E., ed. *An Historical Geography of Iran.* Princeton, N.J., 1984, pp. 131–132.

LEWIS, B., C. PELLAT, and J. SCHACHT, eds. *The Encyclopaedia of Islam,* new ed., vol. 2. Leiden, 1971, pp. 105–106.

Parvaneh Pourshariati

Hamadi, Sabri

Lebanese politician.

Hamadi, a member of one of the most influential Shi'ite families in Lebanon, was born in Hirmil. He received no formal education beyond some elementary schooling in Juniye. He was first elected to parliament in 1925 and was its speaker for much of the 1960s. With Bishara al-KHURI, Hamadi was one of the founders of the CONSTITUTIONAL BLOC. He was a shrewd politician who knew how to exploit the differences among his enemies.

Under Hamadi, the parliament was chaotically structured; appointments within it were made on the basis of total loyalty to him. His cronies from Ba'labak-Hirmil, including some who rarely came to Beirut, where the parliament is located, were on the payroll in key administrative positions. His rule was closely associated with the ascendancy of Chehabism in Lebanon; Hamadi believed that Fu'ad CHEHAB was the best leader in the Arab world.

As a speaker of parliament in the summer of 1970, Hamadi played a crucial role in the presidential election of that year. When Sulayman FRANJIYYA defeated the Chehabi candidate, Ilyas SARKIS, Hamadi initially refused to accept the results. He changed his mind after his advisers and Fu'ad Chehab personally warned him of the dire consequences if Franjiyya's election was not ratified. Franjiyya's armed gunmen were waiting outside the parliamentary hall. Hamadi lost the speakership position that year but served as minister of agriculture under Franjiyya.

As'ad AbuKhalil

Hamadish Brotherhood

Moroccan religious brotherhood.

The brotherhood (often called Hamadsha) was founded in Zerhun near Fez in Morocco by Didi Ali Ben Hamdush in the seventeenth century during the rule of Mulay Isma'il. It is associated with the

Dghoughy brotherhood, founded by Sidi Ahmad Dghoughi. Its celebration, which occurs on the seventh day of the Mulud, is expressed through extravagant practices such as beating the head until it bleeds and eating raw meat.

BIBLIOGRAPHY

CRAPANZANO, V. *The Hamadsha: A Study in Moroccan Ethnopsychiatry*. Berkeley, Calif., 1973.

Rahma Bourqia

Hamama, Fatima [1932–   ]

Egyptian film actress.

Born in Cairo in 1932, Hamama made her film debut in 1939 in the film "A Happy Day." By the 1950s, Hamama was considered the leading star of Egyptian films: her marriage to Umar Sharif in 1953 increased his popularity. Notable films featuring Hamama are "Le Peche" (1967), "Great Love" (1968), and "Lahzat Dha'f" (1971).

BIBLIOGRAPHY

Who's Who in the Arab World 1990–1991, 10th ed. Beirut, 1991.

David Waldner

HAMAS

Palestinian liberation movement.

HAMAS was created in the Israeli-occupied Gaza in December 1987 as the resistance wing of an Islamic revivalist organization, the Association of the MUSLIM BROTHERHOOD. "HAMAS" (zeal, in Arabic) is an acronym for Harakat al-Muqawama al-Islamiyya (Islamic resistance movement).

Prior to the outbreak of the anti-Israeli uprising in the WEST BANK and Gaza known as the INTIFADA in December 1987, the Brotherhood's agenda focused on proselytizing and social purification as the basis for Palestinian socio-spiritual renewal. Hostile to secular nationalist groups within the PALESTINE LIBERATION ORGANIZATION (PLO), the Brotherhood shunned overt acts of anti-Israeli resistance. Israeli authorities quietly assisted the Brotherhood in hopes that it might provide a quieter political alternative to the PLO. The leading figure in the Brotherhood was Shaykh Ahmad Yasin.

Massive popular participation in the intifada prompted the Brotherhood to change tactics and es-

tablish HAMAS, the August 1988 charter of which clearly noted the group's connection with the Brotherhood. Brotherhood leaders argued that the time for vigorous JIHAD had arrived, although political motivations—not losing face as secular groups and the militant religious group ISLAMIC JIHAD struggled against the occupation—were clearly important. The charter called for the total liberation of Palestine from Israeli rule, stating that Palestine is Islamic *waqf* (religious trust) land that must never be surrendered to non-Muslim rule. HAMAS supported the establishment of an Islamic Palestinian state in all of Palestine, as opposed to the PLO's vision of a secular state in the occupied territories.

Israeli authorities struck hard at the HAMAS leadership during the intifada. Shaykh Yasin was arrested in May 1989 and sentenced two years later to life imprisonment. Other important HAMAS figures, such as Shaykh Ibrahim Qawqa and Abd al-Aziz Rantisi were deported. In December 1992, Israel deported 418 members from HAMAS and Islamic Jihad.

HAMAS maintained a difficult relationship with the PLO. It refused to join the PLO-led Unified National Command of the Uprising (UNCU) that emerged to coordinate resistance activity during the intifada. According to an October 1988 agreement between HAMAS and the UNCU, HAMAS operated alongside of but separate from the UNCU. By 1991, HAMAS was pushing for elections to the Palestine National Council, the PLO's parliament-in-exile, which would be held both in exile and in the territories, where its own strength lay. Violence even broke out between HAMAS and secular PLO groups in 1991 and 1992. HAMAS also resolutely opposed the Arab–Israeli peace talks that began in late 1991, and HAMAS activists in the Martyr Izz al-Din al-Qassam Brigades increased the number of armed attacks launched against Israeli targets. HAMAS joined nine other Palestinian groups opposed to the talks in the National Democratic and Islamic Front and denounced the subsequent September 1993 Israeli–PLO accords.

HAMAS accelerated its resistance to the accords after establishment of the Palestinian Authority (PA) in Gaza and the West Bank town of Jericho in 1994. Activists associated with the group mounted a number of attacks on Israeli troops and on civilians as well. In 1995, as serious intra-Palestinian disputes continued, HAMAS and other Islamic militants carried out a number of deadly suicide bombings against Israeli civilians in Israel itself, prompting the PA to crack down on HAMAS activists. HAMAS constituted the most significant challenge to PA rule in the territories.

BIBLIOGRAPHY

ABU-AMR, ZIAD. *Islamic Fundamentalism in the West Bank and Gaza: Muslim Brotherhood and Islamic Jihad*. Bloomington, Ind., 1994.

Michael R. Fischbach

Hama Uprising

See Syria

Hamba, Ali Bash-   [1876–1918]

Tunisian journalist and nationalist.

From a family of Turkish origin, Ali Bash-Hamba earned a law degree in Paris and, in 1905, helped found the reformist organization in Tunisia called the Association of Former Students of al-Sadiqi College. As a leading member of the Young Tunisians, and in an effort to bring their reformist message to a larger audience, Bash-Hamba founded the newspaper *La Tunisien* in 1907. Tensions between the French colonial administration (in place since the French protectorate of 1881) and the Young Tunisians led, in 1912, to the arrest and exile of Bash-Hamba and many of his fellow proponents of nationalism. He died in Istanbul.

BIBLIOGRAPHY

MICAUD, CHARLES. *Tunisia: The Politics of Modernization.* New York, 1964.

Matthew S. Gordon

Hamdi, Ibrahim al-   [1943–1977]

President of Yemen Arab Republic (1973–1977).

Al-Hamdi was born to a *qadi* family in North Yemen. After the revolution that overthrew Imam Yahya in 1962, he entered the army of the newly formed Yemen Arab Republic. He rose rapidly through the ranks, and during the civil war, he became increasingly involved in politics. In the early 1970s al-Hamdi became commander of the Reserves, an elite army unit; in 1972 he was appointed deputy prime minister, and in 1973, deputy commander in chief of the armed forces.

In 1973, al-Hamdi led a military coup against the civilian government of Abd al-Rahman al-IRYANI, which was widely perceived as ineffective. His first government included technocrats and was supported by some of the more conservative tribal elements, including leaders of the Hashid and Bakil confederations.

Upon assuming office, al-Hamdi consolidated his power by methodically reducing the independence of other forces in the country through his "Correction Movement," a nationwide effort to reform the administration, staffing, and operations of all government institutions.

Eventually, the tribal leaders and the more progressive elements (the latter organized into the National Democratic Front) began to oppose al-Hamdi's modernization programs. Political unrest increased in early 1977, amid signs that al-Hamdi desired closer relations with the People's Democratic Republic of Yemen. In October, despite signs that his political situation was improving, he was assassinated.

Al-Hamdi is regarded today as one of the most dynamic and progressive of Yemen's leaders after the civil war of the 1960s, and his role is compared, in meaning and importance, with that of John F. Kennedy in American political history.

Manfred W. Wenner

Hamdi, Osman   [1842–1910]

Turkish painter and archeologist.

Osman Hamdi was born in Istanbul, the son of Ibrahim Edhem Pasha, a grand vizier of the Ottoman Empire. At the age of fifteen, Osman went to Paris to study law but discovered painting and archeology there. He worked in the ateliers of Louis Boulanger and Jean-Léon Gérôme for twelve years before returning home, where he became the first Turkish portrait painter. His paintings show a French orientalist influence in lonely figures often posed near historical monuments.

Osman Hamdi was a leading figure in the founding, in 1883, of the Academy of Fine Arts in Istanbul, which for the first time provided systematic training of young artists in Turkey and exists today as part of the Mimar Sinan University. All the school's teachers were at first foreign, but over time were replaced with Turks. Osman Hamdi was also director of the academy's architecture department and influenced the city's landscape through his promotion of Western styles. Meanwhile, he pursued archeological excavations in the Ottoman territories, and in 1887/88, he discovered Alexander the Great's sarcophagus at Sayda. It and others of Osman Hamdi's finds are housed in the Istanbul Archeological Museum, which he reorganized in 1881.

BIBLIOGRAPHY

RENDA, GÜNSEL. "Modern Trends in Turkish Painting." In *The Transformation of Turkish Culture,* ed. by Günsel Renda and C. Max Kortepeter. Princeton, N.J., 1986.

Elizabeth Thompson

Hamdun, Mustafa

Syrian politician.

Born in Hama of Kurdish descent, Mustafa Hamdun was a relative and a political ally of Akram al-HAWRANI. He was one of three chief conspirators in the February 25, 1954, coup against Adib SHISHAKLI; he made the radio broadcast of the revolt. He was part of the delegation of officers sent to Cairo in January 1958 to pledge Ba'th support to Eypt's President Nasser. Having served as minister of land reform in 1958, Captain Hamdun was later appointed minister of social affairs for the first United Arab Republic.

BIBLIOGRAPHY

SEALE, PATRICK. *The Struggle for Syria: A Study of Post-War Arab Politics, 1945–1958.* London, 1958.

Charles U. Zenzie

Hamedani, Mirza Abu al-Qasem Khan Naser al-Molk   [1865–1927]

Iranian court translator.

The grandson of Mahmud Khan Naser al-Molk Farmanfarma, Mirza Abu al-Qasem Khan was educated at Oxford. Returning to Iran in 1882, he served as court translator under NASER AL-DIN SHAH, minister of finance under MOZAFFAR AL-DIN Shah, and prime minister under MOHAMMAD ALI Shah, who later incarcerated him because of differences they had in regard to policy. Upon the intervention of the British ambassador in Tehran, Naser al-Molk was immediately released, and he remained one of Britain's staunchest supporters in Iran. In 1909, he was appointed Nayeb al-Saltaneh to the Qajar prince and retained that position until 1914, when he became monarch. Naser al-Molk, decorated with the highest British orders, then left Iran for England and returned in 1926 C.E., a year before his death.

BIBLIOGRAPHY

BAMDAD, MEHDI. *Biographies of Iranian Notables in the Twelfth, Thirteenth, and Fourteenth Centuries.* Tehran, 1979. In Persian.

Neguin Yavari

Hamid al-Din Family

A ruling dynasty of North Yemen.

This SAYYID family provided the last dynasty of ZAYDI imams in North Yemen and produced a late, brilliant flowering of the traditional authoritarian political system that had been an important part of Yemeni politics for over 1,000 years. Founded by Imam Muhammad ibn Yahya Hamid al-Din in 1891, the dynasty was consolidated and reached its zenith during the long reign of his son, Imam YAHYA IBN MUHAMMAD HAMID AL-DIN (1867–1948), a reign that began in 1904 and ended with his assassination in 1948. Imam Yahya's son, Imam AHMAD IBN YAHYA, long the crown prince, quickly overturned the 1948 revolution and went on to restore and develop further the institutions and practices of his father until his death in 1962. However, Imam Ahmad was less successful than his father in insulating traditional Yemen from the outside world and modernity. Imam Muhammad al-BADR succeeded his father, only to be overthrown a week later by the 1962 revolution that created the Yemen Arab Republic. A generation later, the Hamid al-Din family remains officially banned from Yemen.

Robert D. Burrowes

Hamina, Mohammed Lakdar   [1934–   ]

Algerian filmmaker.

Mohammed Lakdar Hamina is one of the world's most distinguished directors. Three of his motion pictures have been honored at the Cannes Film Festival: *Le Vent des Aurès* (The Wind from the Aurès, 1966); winner of the grand award, Palme d'Or, *Chronique des années de braise* (Chronicle of the Years of Embers, 1975); and *Vent de sable* (Desert Wind, 1982). Like other postcolonial Algerian directors, Hamina's films explore the promise and paradox resulting from the revolution (1954–1962) and independence.

BIBLIOGRAPHY

NAYLOR, PHILLIP C., and ALF A. HEGGOY. *The Historical Dictionary of Algeria,* 2nd ed. Metuchen, N.J., 1994.

Phillip C. Naylor

Hammamzade İsmail Dede   [1778–1846]

Ottoman Turkish composer.

The most important Turkish composer of the nineteenth century, Hammamzade is also known as Derviş, Ismail, Dede, Dede Efendi, and Ismail Dede. He was born in Istanbul, the son of a provincial notable who had entered the civil service. Hammamzade began to study music with Mehmed Emin at the age of seven. While he was studying Sufism with Ali Nutki Dede, his first musical compositions caught the attention of Sultan Selim III, who became his patron and brought him to the palace. This patronage was continued by Mahmud II. Hammamzade composed over 500 pieces, of which 274 have survived. He wrote in many genres, including *beste, ağir,* and *yürük semai,* as well as more than fifty religious compositions. Two of his most famous orchestral pieces (*fasil*) are *Ferahfeza* and *Sultanı-Yegah.*

BIBLIOGRAPHY

Türk Musikisi Tarihi. Vol. 1. Ankara, 1986.
Yeni Türk Ansiklopedisi. Vol. 4. Istanbul, 1985.

David Waldner

Hammarskjöld, Dag   [1905–1961]

Swedish statesman; United Nations secretary-general, 1953–1961.

After a career as a professor of economics at the University of Stockholm, Dag Hammarskjold joined the Swedish finance ministry (1936–1947) and the ministry of foreign affairs (1947–1953), becoming foreign minister in 1952/53. He was a member of the Swedish delegation to the UNITED NATIONS (UN) and became its secretary-general from 1953 to 1961.

He was instrumental in installing the UN Emergency Force in Sinai and Gaza in the aftermath of the Suez crisis (ARAB–ISRAEL WAR, 1956) and dispatched a UN peace-keeping force to Lebanon in the Lebanese civil war of 1958. When he went to the Congo in 1961 to survey the problem there, he was killed in an airplane crash.

BIBLIOGRAPHY

Chambers Biographical Dictionary. London, 1990.
O'BRIEN, CONOR CRUISE. *The Siege.* London, 1986.

Zachary Karabell

Hammer, Zevulun   [1936–]

Israeli Nationalist Religious party leader, member of the Knesset, and cabinet minister.

Zevulun Hammer was born in Haifa, educated in Israel in the national religious-school system, and did his military service working on a kibbutz. He was instrumental in getting the National Religious party involved in security issues and foreign policy, while assisting those in Gash Emunim to settle the occupied territories. He was first elected to the Knesset (Israel's parliament) in 1969, served as minister of welfare in 1975/76, and was minister of education from 1977 to 1984. He became minister of religious affairs in 1986. In the 1980s, Hammer moderated his views on the West Bank, arguing that domestic unity was more important than holding onto a vision of Greater Israel.

BIBLIOGRAPHY

ROLEF, S. H., ed. *Political Dictionary of the State of Israel.* New York, 1987.

Martin Malin

Hamra Riots

Muslim–Christian riots in Egypt.

In June 1981, continuing intercommunal tensions between Muslims and Coptic Christians in Egypt erupted into violence in Zawiyat al-Hamra, in the Shurabiyya district of Cairo. Seventeen people died and fifty-four were injured. The violence contributed to the government's September 1981 dismissal of the Coptic pope, SHENOUDA III, and banning of the MUSLIM BROTHERHOOD movement.

Michael R. Fischbach

Hamzawi, Rashid al-   [1934–]

Tunisian novelist, playwright, and linguist.

Al-Hamzawi was born in Thala, Tunisia. He received his doctorate from the University of Paris and wrote his dissertation on the Arabic language academy in Cairo. He worked in the Office of Arabization and Translation in Rabat and is presently a professor at the University of Tunis. In addition to his novels, al-Hamzawi has published works on language and translation, particularly in relation to the efforts of the Arab academies to unify Arabic terminology.

Al-Hamzawi's novel *Boudouda mat* (Boudouda Died [Tunis, 1962]) won the Ali al-Bahlawan Prize. It relates the hardships experienced by Tunisians after World War II. Boudouda symbolizes the suffering Tunisian people. The novel also describes rural emigration and the resulting social changes in the cities. Whereas a feeling of optimism pervades the novel, the collection of short stories, *Tarannu* (Tunis, 1975), is pessimistic; the poor and socially disadvantaged seem trapped by their problems.

Al-Hamzawi's plays deal with the corrupt world of politics. In *Al-Shayatin fi'l-qaryal* and *Al-Sarikhun fi'l-sahra'* (The Devils in the Village; Those Who Shout in the Desert [Tunis, 1976]) he searches for the most suitable ideology for Third World countries but refrains from choosing one, preferring to leave the doors open.

[*See also*: Literature, Arabic, North African]

BIBLIOGRAPHY

FONTAINE, JEAN. *La littérature tunisienne contemporaine.* Paris, 1990.
OSTLE, ROBIN. *Modern Literature in the Near and the Middle East, 1850–1970.* London, 1991.

Aida A. Bamia

Hanafi Law School

One of the four approaches to Sunni Muslim law, often called schools.

Though it bears the name of Abu Hanifa al-Nu'man ibn Thabit (died 767), the school in fact owes its doctrine to his two disciples Abu Yusuf (died 798) and Muhammad ibn al-Hasan al-Shaybani (died 805). They laid down the systematic foundations for the work of later Hanafis. In the eighth and ninth centuries, the law school (*madhhab*) was associated with the rationalists (*ahl al-ra'y*), who advocated free legal reasoning not strictly bound by the revealed texts. Although by the eighth century *ra'y*, a form of free reasoning, was largely abandoned in favor of a more disciplined and text-bound reasoning, the Hanafis continued to resort to similar methods of legal argument, notably *istihsan* (juristic preference). After the ninth century, and certainly by the beginning of the eleventh, even *istihsan* was restructured so as to render it subsidiary to the imperatives of the religious texts.

Though the Hanafi school finally came to adopt the mainstream legal methodology and philosophy, it did maintain peculiar characteristics such as its emphasis on the practical aspects of the law. Particularly in the first three centuries of Islam, its followers, more than any other school, were the chief authors and experts on formularies (*shurut*), notarial documents, and the profession and conduct of judgeship (*adab al-qada*).

Among the most important Hanafi authors on positive law after Abu Yusuf and Shaybani are Abu al-Hasan al-Karkhi (died 951), Abu al-Layth al-

Samarqandi (died 985), al-Quduri (died 1036), Shams al-A'imma al-Sarakhsi (died 1096), al-Kasani (died 1191), al-Marghinani (died 1196), Abu al-Barakat al-Nasafi (died 1310), and Ibn Nujaym (died 1563). For these authors, the works of Shaybani, known collectively as *zahir al-riwaya*, remained authoritative; they are *al-Mabsut, al-Jami al-Kabir, al-Jami al-Saghir, al-Siyar al-Kabir, al-Siyar al-Saghir*, and *al-Ziyadat*. The most prominent legal theorists (*usuliyyun*) of the school are Pazdawi (died 1089), Sarakhsi, Nasafi, Sadr al-Shari'a al-Thani al-Mahbubi (died 1346), and Mulla Khusraw (died 1480).

In 1876, the Hanafi law of contracts, obligations, and procedure was codified in the Ottoman law code of Majalla, in an effort to modernize the law and to achieve uniformity in its application. The primary source on which the Committee of the Majalla based its work was Shaybani's collected works, *zahir al-riwaya*, with the commentary on it by Sarakhsi, an eleventh-century Hanafi. In the first few decades of this century, however, the Majalla was superseded by civil codes in all the countries that fell prviously under Ottoman jurisdiction, with the notable exception of Jordan.

In medieval times, the school had a large following in its birthplace, Iraq, as well as in Syria, Transoxania (now Uzbekistan, a former Soviet Republic), the Indian subcontinent, the Mediterranean island of Sicily, and to a lesser extent in North Africa. Later on, the Ottoman Empire declared Hanafism the official doctrine of the state, thus rendering it dominant in all areas that fell under its sway. In modern times, Hanafism still prevails in these regions as well as in Afghanistan, the Balkans, Pakistan, Turkistan, the Caucasus (between the Black and Caspian seas), India, and China.

BIBLIOGRAPHY

MAHMASSANI, SUBHI. *The Philosophy of Jurisprudence in Islam,* trans. by Farhat J. Ziadeh. Leiden, Neth., 1961.
SCHACHT, JOSEPH. *The Origins of Muhammadan Jurisprudence.* Oxford, 1975.

Wael B. Hallaq

Hananu, Ibrahim   [1869–?]

Syrian nationalist.

Ibrahim Hananu was born in Kafr Takharim, a fertile olive-growing area west of Aleppo, to a wealthy rural family of Kurdish extraction. He studied at the prestigious Mülkiye school of public administration in Istanbul. Later he joined the bureaucracy of the Ottoman Empire, only to retire and manage his estates. Having embraced nationalism when the Arab

Revolt broke out in 1916, Hananu joined the Arab army of Faisal I and entered Aleppo with the Allies in 1918. He also joined the secret nationalist society al-Fatat and, with the support of prominent merchants in Aleppo, he founded the League of National Defense and the Arab Club of Aleppo.

Under the influence of Hananu, the Muslim elite of Aleppo gradually assumed an Arab national identity, which was reinforced by the Hananu revolt. Breaking out in the autumn of 1919 in the countryside surrounding Aleppo, the months before French forces occupied the city, the Hananu revolt received aid from the Turkish nationalist movement of Mustafa Kemal ATATÜRK, which was battling the French army of the Levant for control of Cilicia and southern Anatolia. With the withdrawal of Turkish military assistance following the signing of the Franklin-Bouillon Agreement in October 1921, Hananu and his men could no longer sustain a revolt, and their struggle collapsed.

Hananu continued to play an active role in the Syrian national movement. He was one of the founding fathers of the National Bloc, which emerged from the Beirut conference of October 1927, and which steered the course of the independence struggle in Syria until its completion nineteen years later. After his death, Hananu's house in Aleppo was used by Syrian nationalists as a "house of the nation."

Muhammad Muslih

Hanbali Law School

One of the four approaches to Sunni Muslim law, called schools.

The Hanbali Law School takes its name from Ahmad ibn Hanbal (died 854), a major theologian of the ninth century. He was a fierce opponent of the Mu'tazila, a school of religious thought that flourished under the Abbasids. Ibn Hanbal emerged victorious in the *mihna* (inquisition), led by the Abbasid caliph al-Ma'mun and the rationalist theologians against the traditionalists who upheld the doctrine that the Qur'an is not the created but the eternal word of God. Ibn Hanbal's career as a dogmatic theologian, coupled with the fact that he did not elaborate a complete system of law, gave him and his immediate followers the reputation of being a theological rather than a legal school (*madhhab*). Indeed, the school's first complete work on positive law, *al-Mukhtasar,* appeared as late as the beginning of the tenth century, at the hands of Abu Qasim al-Khiraqi (died 946).

Being strict traditionalists, the Hanbalis of the ninth century rejected the rationalist elements of what had by the end of the century become the mainstream legal theory (*usul al-fiqh*). Later Hanbalis, however, gradually adopted the main elements of this theory, and by the eleventh century, their legal theory finally came to accept *usul al-fiqh* as elaborated by the Shafi'i Law School and Hanafi Law School. Thus, it took the Hanbali school nearly two centuries after ibn Hanbal's demise to develop into a full-fledged school of law.

Two centuries later, the celebrated Hanbali jurist and theologian Taqi al-Din ibn Taymiyya (died 1328) even subscribed to a theory of *istihsan* (juristic preference), advocated by later Hanafis and vehemently opposed by early traditionalist Shafi'is and Hanbalis.

There were several figures who dominated the history of Hanbalism. Among the prominent names are al-Khiraqi, Ibn al-Farra, Ibn Aqil, Abd al-Qadir al-Jili (died 1166), Abu al-Faraj ibn al-Jawzi (died 1200), Ibn Taymiyya, and his disciple Ibn Qayyim al-Jawziyya (died 1351), to name only a few. Distinguished as a major figure in Islamic religious history, Ibn Taymiyya was involved in the study of law, theology, philosophy, and mysticism and was engaged in the politics of the Mamluk state. He wrote at length against the Shi'ites, the philosophers, the logicians, and the pantheistic Sufis, though he himself belonged to the mystical school of Abd al-Qadir al-Jili.

Ibn Taymiyya's thought exercised significant influence on Muhammad ibn Abd al-Wahhab (died 1792), who, with the assistance of Ibn Sa'ud, founded Wahhabism, an ideology that has sustained the Saudi state during the last two centuries. Saudi Arabia remains the principal country that applies Hanbali law. However, the writings of ibn Taymiyya and ibn Abd al-Wahhab still continue to influence the Muslim reform and religious movements in the Middle East, from Rashid RIDA (died 1935) to the MUSLIM BROTHERHOOD.

BIBLIOGRAPHY

LAOUST, H. "Le Hanbalism sous le califat de Baghdad." *Revue des Etudes Islamiques* 1 (1959): 67–128.
MAKDISI, GEORGE. "Hanbalite Islam." In *Studies on Islam,* trans. and ed. by Merlin L. Swartz. New York and Oxford, 1981.

Wael B. Hallaq

Hand of Fatima

A folk motif.

European name for the *khamsa* (from Arabic, "five"), the hand with five fingers extended. It can be found today throughout the Middle East in women's jewelry, flat-weaving, embroidery, door-knockers, automobile ornamentation, and so on. Precursors include the Punic "Hand of Baal" and the Roman V-shaped amulets (possibly representing the Roman numeral five), all for protection from the evil eye.

Laurence Michalak

Hani, Nasser al-   [1937–1968]

Career diplomat, foreign minister of Iraq.

After the overthrow of al-Nayif by the Ba'th under Ahmad Hasan al-Bakr, al-Hani, a moderate Nasserist, publicly criticized the new regime. On November 10, 1968, he was assassinated in Baghdad, most probably by Saddam Hussein's National Security Bureau.

Marion Farouk-Sluglett

Hanım

See Khanoum

Hapo'el Hatza'ir

See Labor Zionism

Harakat al-Tajdid

See Movement of Renewal

Haram

Word of Arabic origin denoting that which is unacceptable or outside of lawfulness.

Haram, among other things, governs the lawfulness of various foods and contact with certain animals. In Sunni Islam, the wearing of gold and certain fabrics (such as silk) is also governed by the law. While it is possible for women to wear silk and gold jewelry, men are prohibited from doing so.

Cyrus Moshaver

Haram al-Sharif

See Temple Mount and Haram al-Sharif

Harel, Isser   [1912–   ]

"Little Isser," second and most powerful head of Israeli Mossad, considered the founder of modern Israeli intelligence.

Born Isser Halperin in Russia, he moved with his family to Latvia in 1923 and immigrated to Palestine in 1931, where he was among the founders of Kibbutz Shefayim. He served in the Haganah, and with the British coast guard during World War II. In 1944, Harel was appointed secretary of the "Jewish Department" of the Haganah's Intelligence Services ("Shai"), responsible for counter-espionage and, increasingly, for operations against "dissident" Jewish underground forces such as the Etzel and Lechi. His ruthless successes in the latter sphere particularly endeared Harel to Prime Minister David BEN-GURION, and he quickly rose from Tel-Aviv district commander of Shai (1947) to head of the newly formed General Security Services (Shin Bet or Shabak, 1948–1952), to head of Mossad and coordinator (*memuneh,* "the one in charge") of all five intelligence agencies (1953–1963). While maintaining extensive (and often criticized) internal surveillance, primarily of the pro-Soviet left, Harel developed a powerful international intelligence network. He was largely responsible for the capture of Adolf Eichmann in Argentina in 1961. He left office in 1963 over the German scientists incident, in which Ben-Gurion opposed his activist stance for diplomatic reasons. He briefly coordinated Levi Eshkol's intelligence apparatus in 1966 and later filled a seat in the eighth Knesset (parliament) on the Rafi party list.

Zev Maghen

Harem

Private quarters of a house prohibited to strangers and reserved for women.

From Arabic words meaning "sanctuary" and "forbidden," the word *harem* refers to the female members of a family and their quarters in the home, where only husbands and male relatives can enter. A harem could be simply a special section of a bedouin tent, or, in the opposite extreme, the expanse of rooms and gardens set aside for the Ottoman sultan's harem at Topkapı palace. Strict seclusion of women was generally practiced only by a small elite. Lower-class city women and peasant women routinely left their homes, and the peasants usually did so without a veil.

While European observers since the eighteenth century have exoticized and eroticized the harem as a prison of sexual exploit, actual harems rarely matched this image. Upper-class urban women routinely entertained their women friends, conducted business transactions and legal suits, and pursued literary and other cultural activities from their private residences. The Topkapı harem was at times a powerful wing of the palace's political life. While the Westernized elite in the Middle East largely abandoned sexual seclusion in the twentieth century, it continued to be a sign of prestige among rural notables and an assertion of Islamic identity among others.

BIBLIOGRAPHY

GRAHAM-BROWN, SARAH. *Images of Women.* New York, 1988.
MARCUS, ABRAHAM. *The Middle East on the Eve of Modernity.* New York, 1989.
SHAW, STANFORD J. *History of the Ottoman Empire and Modern Turkey.* Vol. 1. New York, 1976.

Elizabeth Thompson

Hareven, Shulamit   [c. 1931–   ]

Hebrew novelist, poet, essayist, journalist, and activist.

Shulamit Hareven was born in Warsaw, Poland. When World War II broke out, her family was smuggled through Europe and in 1940 settled in Jerusalem, where Hareven still lives. The memory of this escape was responsible for Hareven's belief in self-defense. She served in the Haganah underground and was a combat medic during the siege of Jerusalem in Israel's War of Independence; later she took part in founding the Israel Defense Force radio. In the fifties, she became an officer and worked in the Jewish refugee camps, especially those with Jews from Arab countries. She was military correspondent before and during the Yom Kippur War. Hareven was the first woman member of the Academy of the Hebrew Language.

Hareven published fourteen books of poetry, fiction, and essays. Her first novel, *City of Many Days* (1972), depicts Jerusalem of the British mandate with great compassion, intimate understanding, and poetic richness. Hareven's Jerusalem is a detailed, colorful, and intricate tapestry woven of Arab, British, Sephardic, and European Jewish characters. The novel is also a "coming of age" story of a strong, autonomous woman. Its feminist sensibilities, although ambivalent, represent a first in Israeli literature.

She wrote two novellas set in biblical times, *The Miracle Hater* (1983) and *Prophet* (1989), employing a concise, laconic, biblical style. An avid advocate of human rights, she writes in her essays and articles of Jews and Arabs, new immigrants and Israelis, and declares herself a "selective feminist."

BIBLIOGRAPHY

FELDMAN, YAEL. "Feminism under Siege: The Vicarious Selves of Israeli Women Writers." *Prooftexts* 10 (1990).

Nili Gold

Hariri, Rafiq Baha'uddin al-   [1945–   ]

Saudi businessman, philanthropist, and prime minister of Lebanon.

Born in Sidon, Lebanon, at an early age Hariri helped support his family by working in the orchards. He graduated from the Arab University of Beirut in 1965 and found employment as a mathematics teacher in Jidda, Saudi Arabia. He soon joined a Saudi engineering firm as an accountant and in 1970 founded a small construction company.

His relationship with the Saudi royal family began in 1977, when he completed a palace project in Ta'if for King Khalid ibn Abd al-Aziz Al-sa'ud within the low bid originally proposed and in record time. Henceforth, Hariri was sought for most of the ministry of finance's contracting bids. He became a naturalized Saudi citizen and expanded his global business to include ownership of Paris's Entreprise Oger and the Luxembourg-based Mediterranée Investors Group (MIG).

From early in his financial success, Hariri assisted his native Sidon by offering educational grants and building a hospital and university in nearby Kfarfalous. After the Arab–Israel war of 1982, he aided Lebanon in rebuilding and restoring of essential services to its destroyed capital, Beirut. In 1984 he formed the Hariri Foundation, which extended interest-free loans to thousands of Lebanese students to continue their educations at home and abroad.

Saudi King FAHD designated him a special diplomatic envoy to the 1983 Geneva and Lausanne reconciliation conferences, and Hariri continued to engage in sensitive mediating efforts to bring peace to the Lebanese civil war. This culminated in the active role played by Hariri with Lebanon's parliamentarians to bring about the 1989 TA'IF Agreement, after which he became prime minister, a post he still held in 1996.

Hariri is uncommon as an Arab businessman, because he used his wealth philanthropically rather than ostentatiously, while, at the same time, he remained active in diplomacy and politics.

BIBLIOGRAPHY

MidEast Report. New York, November 15, 1989.

Bassam Namani

Hari Rud

Afghan river.

Beginning in the high mountains of the Hindu Kush in the Hazarajat, the Hari Rud travels west, passing near Herat and turning north at the town of Islam Qala, and then running along the Afghan–Iranian border. It continues north into Turkmenistan and ends in the Turkoman desert.

BIBLIOGRAPHY

ADAMEC, LUDWIG. *Historical Dictionary of Afghanistan.* Metuchen, N.J., 1991.

Grant Farr

Harka

Armed tax collectors.

In precolonial Morocco, *harka* was the armed troop that collected the sultan's taxes from the tribes. The intervals at which collections were made varied according to the strength of central power. Such "fiscal expeditions" were meant to fill the royal treasury while preventing distant tribes from accumulating enough resources to keep horses and buy arms with which to oppose the sultan's authority.

Rémy Leveau

Harkabi, Yehoshaphat [1921–1995]

Professor of international relations; former head of military intelligence.

Yehoshaphat Harkabi held the rank of major general and served as chief of military intelligence from 1955 to 1959. As a professor at the Hebrew University of Jerusalem, he wrote extensively on Arab and Israeli conflict strategies. In *Israel's Fateful Hour* (1988), his self-proclaimed realist assessment of Israeli capabilities led him to advocate the establishment of an independent Palestinian state in the WEST BANK and GAZA STRIP.

Martin Malin

Harkis

Pro-French Algerians during the war of independence (1954–1962); also known as French Muslims.

Harkis is derived from the Arabic *harakat*, meaning "military movement" or "operation." Since the be-

ginning of French colonialism in Algeria in July 1830, local people served as military auxiliaries. During the ALGERIAN WAR OF INDEPENDENCE (1954–1962), approximately 100,000 harkis served France in various capacities (e.g., regular French army, militia self-defense units, police, and paramilitary self-defense units). Their most prominent leader was the Benaïssa BOULAM. After the war, many harkis left for France, but the majority remained in Algeria and faced brutal retributions.

Those in France found inadequate housing conditions (often in isolated relocation camps) and a lack of educational and economic opportunities. This provoked a variety of protests by these forgotten French citizens, ranging from hunger strikes and kidnappings in the 1970s to violence in the 1990s. The French government issued a stamp in 1990 to honor the harkis' contribution, which elicited official protest from Algeria. The population of the French-Muslim community is about 475,000. In France, they remain second-class citizens, are victims of discrimination, and are often confused with the emigrant worker community. It is still unsafe for harki veterans to visit Algeria, but their children and descendants are welcome.

BIBLIOGRAPHY

BAILLET, PIERRE. "Les rapatriés d'Algérie en France." *Notes et etudes Documentaires* (Documentation française), nos. 4.275–4.276 (1976).

STORA, BENJAMIN. *La gangrène et l'oubli: La mémoire de la guerre d'Algérie.* Paris, 1992.

Phillip C. Naylor

Harratin

A group of people in northwest Africa generally of low social status.

In Arabic, hartani (singular); in Berber, ahardan (singular) and ihardanan (plural); in the Twareg dialect, ashardan. The harratin inhabit the oases of the Saharan regions. Ethnically, this population is a mixture of people originating from sub-Saharan Africa and North Africa; they were formerly slaves before being freed. Although they are no longer slaves, they constitute a sort of caste considered by other populations as inferior, below the status of bidan and SHORFA groups in Mauritania. Because of their low status, the harratin seek protection among powerful families for which they work and show respect.

Since land and water are owned by white shorfa and because harratin occupy the lowest position on the social scale, the harratin do not witness any social mobility. They work in less prestigious occupations: When they are sedentaries, they work in agriculture; when they emigrate to the cities, they work as carriers of water, diggers of wells, and ironworkers; and among the nomads they work as shepherds.

In Morocco, the Sultan Mulay Ismail (eighteenth century) recruited his famous army of bukhari from the harratin population of Mauritania. This group had also provided the traditional Moroccan state (Makhzen) with secretaries and functionaries. Families in imperial cities in Morocco such as Fez, Marrakech, and Meknes used to have hartani women under their protection working as servants.

In vernacular language, after the progressive disappearance of slavery, the words *harratin* and *hartani* have replaced the word *'abd* (slave) to mean "black" and have acquired a pejorative meaning.

BIBLIOGRAPHY

COLIN, G. S. "Hartani." *Encyclopédie de l'Islam,* vol. 3.
MOHAMED, ENNAJI. *Soldats, domestiques et concubines. L'esclavage au Maroc du XIXe siècle,* Casablanca, 1993.

Rahma Bourqia

Harriman, W. Averell   [1891–1986]

U.S. diplomat.

While ambassador in Moscow (1943–1946), during World War II (1943–1946), Harriman became concerned with the USSR's involvement in Iran and advocated U.S. support for Iran's shah, Mohammad Reza Pahlavi. In July of 1951, Harriman was U.S. President Harry S. Truman's special envoy to Iran's Prime Minister Mohammad Mossadegh, and Harriman tried unsuccessfully to convince Mossadegh to compromise with Britain over nationalization of the ANGLO–IRANIAN OIL COMPANY. Harriman respected Mossadegh as a genuine nationalist and counseled against intervention by Britain or the United States to remove him.

Harriman was elected governor of New York (1955–1958) but returned to national politics in the Kennedy and Johnson administrations. In 1965, as under secretary of state, he was sent to Jerusalem to inform the government of Israel that the United States intended to sell arms to Jordan. Harriman was later one of the chief negotiators in ending the Vietnam War.

BIBLIOGRAPHY

BILL, JAMES, and WILLIAM ROGER LOUIS, eds. *Mussadiq, Iranian Nationalism, and Oil.* London, 1988.

FINDLING, JOHN, ed. *Dictionary of American Diplomatic History.* New York, 1989.
SPIEGEL, STEVEN. *The Other Arab–Israeli Conflict.* Chicago, 1985.

Zachary Karabell

Harun, As'ad   [1903–?]

Syrian politician and diplomat.

Born the son of Abd al-Wahab Harun in Lattakia, As'ad was educated at the colleges of the Christian Brothers in Damascus, Beirut, and France, receiving a degree in political science. He was appointed Syrian consul in Baghdad in 1937 and, after being imprisoned by the French in 1942, became deputy for Lattakia in 1947. He was elected minister of state in 1954, a position from which he resigned on May 24, 1955. He was appointed minister of public health as a member of the national party in 1956 and was arrested by the new Syrian authorities on July 18, 1966.

BIBLIOGRAPHY

Who's Who in the Middle East, 1967–1968.

Charles U. Zenzie

Hasa, al-

Portion of the eastern province of Saudi Arabia.

Al-Hasa extends from Kuwait in the north to Qatar in the south and is separated from Najd on the west by the Dahna sand belt. It is mostly a sandy plain that gradually slopes to meet the shallow Gulf. The name applies specifically to the world's largest groundwater-fed oasis (also called al-Hufuf), and in Arabic refers to water that percolates to ground level. Virtually all of Saudi Arabia's vast oil wealth is found in al-Hasa; thus it was the first part of the kingdom to experience rapid economic development.

In 1581 al-Hasa came under Ottoman sovereignty, and in 1663/64 the Bani Khalid tribe seized the area, holding it as a loosely organized principality until the AL SA'UD FAMILY and their Wahhabi warriors took it in between 1791 and 1794. In 1871 Ottoman rule was reasserted when internal Al Sa'ud dissention offered an opportunity, and in 1913 Saudi authority was permanently reestablished during Ottoman preoccupation with the first Libyan War. In 1927 King Abd al-Aziz ibn Abd al-Rahman (Ibn Sa'ud) made his cousin, Abdullah ibn Jiluwi, governor of al-Hasa. His and his son's harsh rule entailed repression of the province's large Shi'a population and helped provoke strikes at the ARABIAN AMERICAN OIL COMPANY in 1953 and 1956. In 1979 and 1980 the IRANIAN REVOLUTION stimulated Shi'a unrest, leading the government to improve the economic and social condition of the 300,000 to 400,000 Shi'ites in Al-Qatif and other al-Hasa towns, once disorder had been contained.

BIBLIOGRAPHY

BESSON, YVES. *Ibn Saud, roi bedouin: La Naissance du royaume d'Arabie saoudite.* Lausanne, 1980.
BONNENFANT, PAUL, ed. *La Peninsule arabique d'aujourd-'hui,* 2 vols. Paris, 1982.

Malcolm C. Peck

Hasan, Fa'iq   [1919–   ]

Iraqi artist.

One of Iraq's leading and most influential visual artists during the second half of the twentieth century, Hasan was born in Baghdad and educated in its Institute of Fine Art (which, after 1939, added painting and sculpture to music). He later spent a few years studying art in Paris. In 1950 he established *Jama' at al-Ruwwad* (the avant garde group), also called *Société Primitive*. This was the first art circle in Iraq to be inspired by ancient Mesopotamian and Iraqi themes and which adopted modern styles. Hasan started off with impressionist landscapes but since the 1950s has changed both subject matter and style. While the subject matter of his paintings is local, describing bedouin and other country life, or still life, the style is cubist with strong French influences. Some of his paintings are in the primitive style. He and his group experimented with color planes, and many of his later works are abstract.

Amatzia Baram

Hasan, Hani al-   [1937–   ]

Palestinian politician.

Born in Haifa, Palestine, Hasan was educated at the University of Darmstadt, West Germany, graduating with a degree in construction engineering. He was one of the founding members of FATH, now the most powerful faction in the PALESTINE LIBERATION ORGANIZATION (PLO). He was the European chief of Fath during the ARAB–ISRAEL WAR of 1967 and was the Fath spokesman during Jordan's civil war of September 1970.

In 1974, Hasan became chairman of Fath's Department of Palestinian Political Affairs. He was next appointed deputy to Salah KHALAF (Abu Iyad) in Jihaz al-Rasd in Fath. He managed the establishment of PLO and Fath ties with China, led PLO delegations to China, and requested China's support for the PLO at the United Nations in 1974. Hasan has been a member of both the Palestine National Council and the Central Committee of the Fath Movement.

BIBLIOGRAPHY

Who's Who in the Arab World, 1988–1989.

Lawrence Tal

Hasan, Khalid al-   [1928–   ]

Palestinian politician.

Hasan was born in Haifa, Palestine. Early in his career, he was active in the Islamic Liberation (Tahrir) Party. After working in Kuwait, he joined Yasir ARAFAT and others in founding FATH and was partly responsible for the establishment of Fath's ties with many Arab states. Hasan served on the PALESTINE LIBERATION ORGANIZATION (PLO) Executive Committee from 1969 to 1973. Since then, he has been the head of the PLO Executive Committee Political Department and a member of the Palestinian parliament-in-exile, the Palestine National Council.

BIBLIOGRAPHY

Who's Who in the Arab World, 1988–1989.

Lawrence Tal

Hasani, Taj al-Din al-   [1890–1943]

President of Syria under French mandate.

Al-Hasani was born in Damascus to a North African family. In 1912, he was appointed instructor of religion at the Sultaniyya school in Damascus. Al-Hasani was a member of the Council for School Reform and the General Assembly for the *vilayet* of Syria. He was also an owner of the newspaper *al-Sharq,* which was first published in 1916 with support from the Fourth Ottoman Army. Under the rule of King Faisal I, he was appointed member of the council of state (*majles shura*), the court of appeal, and then judge in Damascus. Al-Hasani taught principles of Islamic jurisprudence (FIQH) at the Institute of Arab Law in Damascus. Under the French mandate, al-Hasani was prime minister from 1928 to

1931 and from 1934 to 1936. He then resigned and traveled to France where he remained until the French appointed him head of the Syrian republic in 1941. He stayed in power until his death in 1943.

George E. Irani

Hashid Tribal Confederation

One of the two major tribal groupings in North Yemen.

Most of the tribes on the highlands of North Yemen have been loosely allied with the Hashid or the BAKIL TRIBAL CONFEDERATION for the past millennium or so. The Hashid confederation—consisting of seven major tribes: al-Usaymat, Idhar, Kharif, Bani Suraym, Sanhan, Bilad al-Rus, and Hamdan San'a—has often been in conflict with the Bakil tribes. In the twentieth century, the Hashid have seemed more united, perhaps better organized and led—and hence stronger—than the Bakil. Shaykh Abdullah ibn Husayn al-AHMAR, the paramount shaykh of the Hashid since just before the 1962 revolution, has been the most powerful and important tribal leader in North Yemen throughout most if not all of the republican era. This is due, in part, to his presumed ability to command a large, loyal following. Both the Hashid and Bakil tribes were early converts to ZAYDISM and over the centuries were counted among the supporters of the Zaydi imamate. The tribes did not always accept the legal role of the imams, however, and they sometimes turned on the imamate when they felt wronged or threatened. For example, the al-Ahmar clan and its followers withdrew support from the imam on the eve of the revolution, and the republic prevailed in the long civil war after 1962 in part because of support from elements of the Hashid.

Robert D. Burrowes

Hashim, Ibrahim   [1888–1958]

Head of the Executive Council and prime minister of Jordan several times, starting in 1933.

Ibrahim Hashim accompanied Emir ABDULLAH IBN HUSAYN to the 1946 negotiations in London to abolish the mandate and renegotiate the Anglo–Jordanian treaty. Thus he was the first prime minister of the newly independent kingdom when the Legislative Assembly (precursor to the parliament) proclaimed King Adbullah a constitutional monarch on May 25, 1946. Hashim was also a leading member of the three-man Crown Council, then the Regency Council, which ruled Jordan briefly between May

and August 1952 following the abdication of King Talal. He was in Baghdad as the deputy prime minister of the joint Jordanian–Iraqi cabinet of the newly formed Arab Federation—a short-lived union between Jordan and Iraq that was formed on February 14, 1958, in response to rising pan-Arab sentiment and to forestall pressures on the conservative monarchies that were likely to result after the planned merger of Egypt and Syria. Hashim was killed during mob violence in Baghdad at the outbreak of the Iraqi revolution in May 1958.

BIBLIOGRAPHY

MADI, MUNIB, and SULAYMAN MUSA. *Tarikh al-Urdun fi al-qarn al-ishrin, 1900–1959.* Amman, 1988.

Jenab Tutunji

Hashim, Joseph

Radio broadcaster and politician in Lebanon.

Hashim, a former teacher of Arabic, holds a graduate degree in Arabic literature. A longtime member of the PHALANGE party, he came into prominence after the Lebanese civil war of 1975 when he took over the Phalange radio station, VOICE OF LEBANON. He was known for his eloquence, and his radio commentaries were published as a book. A close associate of the Jumayyil family, Hashim served as a cabinet minister in the 1980s. Now associated with the moderate faction within the Phalange party, he advocates improved ties with Syria and the Arab world, and opposes the past association of the party with Israel.

As'ad AbuKhalil

Hashimi, Taha al-   [1888–1961]

Iraqi officer, politician, teacher, and author.

Hashimi was born into a Sunni Arab Muslim family of limited means. He attended school in Baghdad and graduated from military college in Constantinople (now Istanbul). He served in the Ottoman army in various capacities and reached the rank of lieutenant colonel. He joined the al-AHD society, formed in 1913 by Aziz Ali al-MISRI. Although the members of Ahd were mostly Ottoman officers of Iraqi origin, Hashimi remained loyal to the Ottomans and did not undertake any activities against them during World War I. He worked with the Faisal government in Syria (1919–1920) as director of defense, then returned to Iraq at the urging of his brother, Yasin al-HASHIMI, who played a leading role in Iraq's politics in the 1920s and 1930s. Hashimi held various civilian posts in the newly established government, including director of the Census Bureau, director of education, and tutor to Prince GHAZI IBN FAISAL. In 1930, he returned to the army, was appointed commander in chief, and then promoted to the rank of general. In 1936 the acting chief of staff, General Bakr Sidqi, executed a military coup against Prime Minister Yasin al-Hashimi. This marked the first military interference in Iraq's modern history.

Hashimi returned to Iraq following a coup launched in 1937. As minister of defense in 1938 and 1939, he acted as an intermediary among the nationalist elements of the army, in particular among the four colonels known as the GOLDEN SQUARE, who played an important role in Iraq's army politics from 1937 to 1941. They espoused the ideas of ARAB NATIONALISM, objected to Britain's constant interference in Iraq's affairs, and wanted to expand and modernize the army. In February 1941, Hashimi became prime minister of Iraq, this time for two months. Having been a compromise candidate, he hoped to resolve the dispute between the regent, who wanted to implement the British government's desire for Iraq to break off diplomatic relations with Italy, and Rashid Ali and the nationalist Golden Square officers, who wanted to pursue a course of absolute neutrality toward the Axis powers and the Allies. On 1 April 1941, Hashimi was forced to resign under pressure from the Golden Square.

In 1941 Iraq experienced its seventh coup since 1936, which led to Rashid Ali's uprising against the British. The failed uprising led to what the Iraqis called the second British occupation of Iraq (the first was during World War I). Hashimi fled to Turkey after the failure of the coup and remained there until the end of World War II. He was permitted to return to Iraq in 1946. In 1951, with a group of politicians, he formed the Nationalist Bloc party, which did not last long because of intense differences among its members. In 1953, Hashimi was appointed vice chair of the Board of Development. He held this position until the board was dissolved after the revolution of 14 July 1958. The board was responsible for preparing and executing general economic and financial plans for the development of Iraq's resources. Among its many accomplishments was the THARTHAR PROJECT, which was primarily designed as a flood control system. Hashimi died in London.

Hashimi is considered a centrist and nationalist in Iraq's politics. He was well liked by young military officers disgruntled with Britain's constant interference in Iraq's affairs; they saw him as defender and protector of their interests. Hashimi taught courses at the military college and at al-Bayt University in Baghdad. He wrote books on such subjects as ancient history, Muslim military leaders, Iraq's geography (including an atlas of Iraq), war in Iraq, and the rebirth of Japan. His two-volume memoirs, published posthumously, are filled with insight, opinions, and information about his role in Iraq's history, as well as the roles of other Iraqi politicians during the monarchy.

BIBLIOGRAPHY

KHADDARI, MAJID. *Independent Iraq 1932–1958: A Study in Iraqi Politics*. London, 1960.

Ayad al-Qazzaz

Hashimi, Yasin al- [?–1937]

Iraqi politician.

Born in Baghdad in the Barudiya zone, Yasin al-Hashimi began life with the name Yasin Hilmi Salman. His father was Sayyid Salman Mukhtar of the Barudiya zone. After graduating from the Military Academy of Istanbul and attaining the rank of general, he joined the al-Ahd organization along with other young officers who sought to serve the interest of the Arabs with the Ottoman Empire. He acquired the name al-Hashimi to emphasize his relation with the royal Hashimite family and as an indication of his loyalty to King FAISAL I. Profoundly influenced by Kemal ATATÜRK, he established the National Brotherhood party. He started his political career as minister of transportation and became a deputy of Baghdad in the Constitutional Assembly in 1924. He held numerous cabinet positions and was prime minister several times. During his tenure as prime minister in 1936, General Bakr SIDQI's militant activities caused the government to fall, and Yasin al-Hashimi was deported to Damascus, where he died in 1937.

Mamoon A. Zaki

Hashimites

See Abdullah ibn Husayn; Faisal I ibn Husayn; Fertile Crescent Unity Plans; Greater Syria Plan; Hussein ibn Talal

Hashim Khan [1886–1953]

Afghan governor and minister of war.

Born into the royal family, Hashim Khan received military training and became military adviser to Amir Habibullah (1901–1919), minister of war (1923), and minister to the Soviet Union (1924–1926). When

ZAHIR Shah came to power in 1933, Hashim Khan looked after the young king as de facto regent.

BIBLIOGRAPHY

ADAMEC, LUDWIG. *Historical Dictionary of Afghanistan,* Metuchen, N.J., 1991.

Grant Farr

Hashomer

Early Jewish defense organization in Palestine.

Hashomer (Watchman) was established in 1909 in Jaffa, Palestine, by Russian immigrants including Yizhak BEN-ZVI to replace Arab guards hired by Jewish landowners. Imitating Arab dress and horsemanship, Hashomer in 1914 grew to forty official members employing up to three hundred guards. During World War I, many joined the JEWISH LEGION. Hashomer established the linkage of soldier and settler identities that has persisted in later Jewish defense forces and military organizations. It disbanded when the Haganah was formed in 1920.

BIBLIOGRAPHY

ROLEF, SUSAN HATTIS, ed. *Political Dictionary of the State of Israel.* New York, 1987.
SCHIFF, ZE'EV. *A History of the Israeli Army.* New York, 1985.
SHAFIR, GERSHON. *Land, Labor and the Origins of the Israeli-Palestinian Conflict.* New York, 1989.

Elizabeth Thompson

Hashomer Hatza'ir

See Labor Zionism

Hasidim

Literally, "pious ones."

In the modern era, Hasidim has come to mean those who identify with a movement founded by Rabbi Israel ben Eliezer (c. 1700–1760), the "Ba'al Shem Tov" or "Besht", the acronym. Originally, it was a mass movement that emphasized mysticism and personal piety, rather than the legalistic learning of elite Judaism. Contemporary Hasidim are generally viewed as ultra-Orthodox. Composed of hundreds of groups, the most widely known are the Lubavitcher and Satmar Hasidim. The Lubavitcher is the largest group, and their spiritual leader resides in Brooklyn,

N.Y., to which they immigrated from the USSR after World War II. Although they officially reject secular Zionism, they are a highly nationalistic group and place great efforts on outreach to nonobservant Jews. By contrast, Satmar Hasidim are adamantly anti-Zionist and anti-nationalist, and they eschew all but purely formal contacts with outsiders.

BIBLIOGRAPHY

MINTZ, JEROME R. *Hasidic People: A Place in the New World.* Cambridge, Mass., 1992.

Chaim I. Waxman

Haskala

Hebrew term for enlightenment.

Haskala is the name of the movement for the dissemination of modern European culture among the Jews. The movement began in the mid-1700s in Berlin with the work of the German Jewish philosopher Moses Mendelssohn (1729–1786). Advocates argued that to achieve emancipation, the Jews must adopt the modern values and social customs of the countries in which they lived. In the mid-1800s, modern European culture for the Jews generally meant German and French culture and secular education, although efforts were made in this period by groups of Jews throughout Europe.

One consequence of this process was the secular use of the HEBREW language to spread the new ideas, leading to an eventual revitalization of the language. Another effect was the creation of a stratum of Jews versed in both the intellectual traditions of modern Europe and traditional Judaism. It was from subsequent generations of these Jews that the ideas of modern ZIONISM originated. Finally, for many Jews, acquiring modern European culture meant the abandonment of traditional Jewish customs, resulting in assimilation.

BIBLIOGRAPHY

ACKERMAN, WALTER. *Out of Our People's Past.* New York, 1977.

Martin Malin

Hassan I   [?–1894]

Emperor of Morocco, 1873–1894.

The favorite son of Sultan Sidi Mohammed, Hassan I was regarded as the last great ruler of pre-colonial

Morocco. As ruler, he resisted foreign influence through control of the local tribes, using both the permanent military units trained by British and French forces and his own status as a political leader of Islam. Through military interventions in the mountains and in the south, he was able to collect taxes and, above all, to prevent the establishment of any potential rival. To reinforce his military power, he created the first military equipment industry in Marrakech and Fez. He was interested in the reforms (TANZIMAT) launched by the Ottoman Empire as long as they were not forced on him.

In 1880, he sought to limit the rights of protection and jurisdiction exerted by foreigners on Moroccan nationals. With British support, he held out against both the French and the Spanish, although neither was pleased that he might remain outside their control. That year he convened the MADRID CONFERENCE, but the meeting failed to resolve diplomatic tensions. Throughout his reign, Hassan I resisted all external pressure, well aware that his forces were not equal to the European forces, and he gave no pretext for military intervention by limiting his contacts with foreigners. His military reforms and his strategy of defending Morocco by playing one tribe against the other while similarly using existing rivalries between the Europeans did not survive long after his death in 1894.

BIBLIOGRAPHY

TERRASSE, HENRI. *Histoire du Maroc des origines á l'establissement du protectorat français.* Casablanca, 1952.

Rémy Leveau

Hassan II [1929–]

King of Morocco, 1961 to the present.

Hassan was the son of MUHAMMED V, king of Morocco. As Crown Prince Mulay Hassan, he graduated from the University of Bordeaux in France. In 1961, when his father died unexpectedly, the 32-year-old playboy prince came to power. The heir of the ALAWITE DYNASTY, which has governed Morocco since the sixteenth century, Mulay Hassan had been well prepared by his father—as early as World War II—to assume the throne. He had also attended the 1942 meeting between Muhammed V and U.S. President Franklin D. Roosevelt.

Since the French had entered North Africa in the eighteenth and nineteenth centuries to end the Corsairs and Barbary piracy in the Mediterranean, they had established a policy of COLONIALISM and protectorates. Hassan had therefore been trained in both Arabic and French and had studied law and economics at the university; he was at ease in both cultures. He was also acutely aware of the ideas and changes that might come to Morocco from outside. Since his adolescence, he was known to favor NATIONALISM, as did many Moroccans of his age. He was said to have some influence on his father, who was more cautious and less brilliant than Hassan. When in 1948 a conflict arose with France's resident general—which had to do with the signing of legal texts presented by French colonial authorities—Hassan was among those who favored a break with France. The consequence was Muhammed V's exile to the French-controlled islands of Corsica and Madagascar. Supporting his father, Hassan participated in the negotiations through intermediaries to reestablish the previous links with the French government and effect Muhammed V's return, which was accomplished in 1955.

In contrast with Muhammed V, who was careful not to offend the parties who had joined the struggle for independence—especially the ISTIQLAL PARTY—Hassan wanted to preserve the autonomy of the monarchy. Designated chief of staff of the Royal Armed Forces, Hassan appeared as the main guarantor of his peoples' destiny. He gathered around himself the former Moroccan officers who had served in the French army, and he ended rebellions in al-Rif, Tafilalt, and Beni-Mellal, which had been provoked by various dissident movements. He also reduced the size of the Liberation Army, born of the Moroccan resistance, since it was almost autonomous in the south; it pretended to be fighting the French and Spanish colonial powers but could easily have offered armed and organized support to any given opposition.

France and Spain recognized Morocco's independence in 1956; by 1958, Hassan's forces prevailed throughout the country and dissidents were no longer a threat to the monarchy. Thus Muhammed V was able to incorporate the various splinter groups of the former nationalist movement within the government. Hassan was sometimes irritated by his father's caution, and he tried to convince him to take back direct control. A change began in May 1960, with Hassan appointed prime minister. When his father died in March 1961, Hassan II had both the experience and the means to put his theories into practice.

The independence of Algeria (July 5, 1962) appeared to be a potential threat to Hassan II's monarchy. It bordered Morocco to the east and south, and Algeria's National Liberation Front (FRONT DE LIBÉRATION NATIONAL; FLN) was known to support the Moroccan left (socialists) against the monarchy. Hassan sought a new legitimacy by mobilizing universal suffrage, which was largely supported by the rural populace. The December 1962 referendum guaranteed Hassan's success with 80 percent approval of his new constitution.

The results of the March 1963 election did not, however, give him similar support. The old Istiqlal had lost its governmental majority and the king's followers were not able to form a political coalition quickly enough. Most of the ministers were defeated and it seemed that the parliament could not easily be governed despite a promonarchy majority. In the meantime, the danger posed by Algeria had faded away. The October 1963 border war and rivalry related to Tindouf had revived in Morocco a strong nationalist feeling, which resulted in support for the monarchy.

Hassan II dismissed the parliament in 1965 and relied mainly on his army for legitimacy. He protected those in the military who had served French and Spanish colonialism, although some of the young officers were not as loyal or as committed as he expected. Tempted by populist idealism, some succeeded in convincing former officers of the French colonial army (who controlled the military organization) to join their project. In July 1971, in Skhirat, General Medbah and General Muhammad Oufkir, among others, faced death after their rebellion failed.

Paradoxically, Hassan would succeed in restoring faith in his monarchy in 1975, when a dispute with Spain (at the time of Spanish dictator Francisco Franco's death) led to the defense of Morocco's position in the former Spanish colony of WESTERN SAHARA. A local nationalistic movement, the POLISARIO, supported mainly by Algeria and Libya, emerged to challenge Morocco. Both Algeria and Libya saw opportunities in the situation—Algeria, especially, under President Houari Boumédienne, wanted to demonstrate its control over the MAGHRIB before the new European Community. Bolstered by petroleum revenues, the growing power of Algeria had the effect of reuniting Morocco under Hassan.

Although Hassan had plans for political pluralism, albeit controlled by the monarchy, his army had been reequipped for possible conflict with Algeria; since they did not want to engage in this fight, they attempted another coup. General Ahmed DLIMI was to be their leader, but the plot was discovered by the home secretary and Dlimi disappeared in an "accident." In the long run, Morocco was to benefit from its tactical building of the "wall" (fortified sand barriers in Western Sahara), and Algeria succeeded in having seventy-five countries recognize the POLISARIO and make it a member of the ORGANIZATION FOR AFRICAN UNITY (OAU).

Hassan managed Moroccan nationalism very cautiously to establish national unity. He found external financial resources by getting Western countries as well as the Arab oil monarchies to support his military efforts and to launch economic development based on a private sector far larger than those of neighboring countries. For that reason, as the Pahlavi dynasty in Iran did (before the Islamist IRANIAN REVOLUTION of 1979), Hassan's monarchy became a major economic actor through the All North Africa association (Omnium Nord-Africain; ONA), not only to find resources but to prevent other North African countries from obtaining power and becoming politically influential. Since Morocco had no oil, Hassan encouraged and often provided an example of an economic-development policy based on modern agriculture (launching a program to irrigate 2.47 million acres [1 million ha]); he also encouraged small and medium-sized manufacturing industries.

In 1984, Hassan signed a treaty of unity with Libya after Libya withdrew its support for the Polisario in the Western Sahara and Morocco agreed to refrain from sending troops to aid the French in Chad. In 1986, Libya abrogated the treaty when Hassan became the second North African leader to meet with an Israeli leader during Prime Minister Shimon Peres's visit to Morocco.

In 1988, international factors continued to prevail over those within Morocco. After Tunisian President Habib Bourguiba had been replaced by General Zayn al-Abidine BEN ALI in November of 1987, a process of realignment occurred among the North African countries. A consequence was the reintegration of Morocco, first at a meeting in Algiers (August 1988), then when the Union of the Maghrib (Union du Maghreb; UMA) treaty was signed in Marrakech, Morocco (March 1989). The treaty marked the end of the Algerian/Moroccan rivalry related to the Western Sahara, but, at the same time, deprived Morocco of a strong factor for internal unity.

The UMA had another hidden aim: to constitute a united front against the growing Islamist political movements in North Africa (an effort to establish Islamic religious regimes). Tunisia appeared the weak link at that time, and it needed support. Political changes nevertheless occurred in Algeria, and their effects were important for Morocco. After the October 1988 riots in Algiers, President Chadli Benjedid controlled the situation by creating a pluralistic political system, open to Islamists, which led to competitive elections. That strategy gave an attractive look to Algerian pluralism in relation to the established Moroccan political system, where the same actors repeated their opposition to the existing power through the years. Algeria was no longer seen as a danger by the people but as an example at a time when the annexation of Kuwait by Iraq (1990) became a military crisis and thus reduced the possibilities of action.

In Morocco, the riots that took place in provincial cities by the end of 1990, the important demonstrations in the capital city at the beginning of 1991, and the reports of deserters leaving the Moroccan army to go to Iraq (by way of Algeria) indicated the gap between Hassan's cautious choice—sending a limited contingent to help the UN coalition forces to defend an oil monarchy—and Moroccan public opinion that favored Iraq's President Saddam Hussein. The Gulf War made visible the differing factions in Morocco.

Hassan II continues to manage the ruling class, which he dominates. His experience in international affairs and his relationships with the personalities in that arena continue to be useful to Morocco. Nevertheless, changes in international, regional, and local situations present a threat to his monarchy—Morocco can no longer be governed as it was in 1961, when the French were still in control and Hassan came to power. Today, the population of his country has doubled and the Islamist political wave is gaining support in Morocco as in other Arab and Islamic countries. His successor is his son.

BIBLIOGRAPHY

Leveau, Rémy. *Le fellah marocain défenseur du trône.* Paris, 1985.
Waterbury, John. *The Commander of the Faithful: The Moroccan Political Elite, a Study in Segmented Politics.* New York, 1970.

Rémy Leveau

Hassana Tribe

A major tribe of the Anaza confederation of Arab tribes who were known for their bravery.

In the second half of the eighteenth century, the Hassana tribe headed towards Syria from Najd, pushed by the Wahhabis. They reached the confines of Homs and Hama and clashed with the Mawali bedouin in control there. The weakened Mawali relinquished their positions and retreated towards Salamiyya and Ma'arrat al-Nu'man. The Hassana numbered 400 *bayts* (households), that is, about 2,000 persons (the *bayt* or the *khayma* (tent), according to the Ottoman *Salname,* included about five persons). The Hassana additionally had 300 *bayts* of followers.

BIBLIOGRAPHY

Kahhalah. "Umar Rida." *Mu'jam qaba'il al-Arab al-qadima wa al-haditha* (A Dictionary of the Old and Recent Arab Tribes). 5th ed., 5 vols. Beirut, 1985.

Zakariyya, Ahmad Wasfi. *Asha'ir al-Sham* (The Tribes of Syria). 2nd ed. 3 vols. Damascus, 1983.
———. *Jawla athariyya* (An Archeological Tour). 2nd ed. Damascus, 1984.

Abdul-Karim Rafeq

Hassi Messaoud

One of Algeria's most important oil-producing basins.

The Hassi Messaoud basin is located east of the Ouargla oasis at the edge of the Sahara. Major PETROLEUM deposits were discovered in 1956, and full production started at the site in January 1958. By Algeria's independence in 1962, reserves at the site were estimated at between 300 and 500 million tons (270–450 million t). Hassi Messaoud and other Saharan hydrocarbon sites became part of French–Algerian bargaining in the events leading up to independence; the Algerian side never wavered from its determination to view the Sahara as part of Algerian territory that could not be handed over to France.

Dirk Vandewalle

Hatay

See Alexandretta

Hatikvah

The Zionist anthem and today the national anthem of Israel.

Written by Naphtali Herz Imber in the 1870s, the poem entitled "The Hope" expresses the Jewish desire to return to Zion. In 1878, Samuel Cohen, a settler of RISHON LE-ZION originally from Moldavia, composed the melody, based on a Moldavian–Romanian folk song.

"Hatikvah" was formally declared the Zionist anthem at the 18th Zionist Congress in 1933. At the Declaration of the State of Israel, it was sung at the opening and closing of the ceremony.

Miriam Simon

Hatim Sultans of Hamdan

Early tribal leaders of North Yemen.

The Hatim sultans were leaders of the Yam tribe, a section of the Hamdan tribal grouping. Control of

SANʿA and much of the north passed into their hands with the loosening of the Sulayhids' grip on that area at the end of the eleventh century. The twelfth century witnessed much competition—from intrigue to wars—as well as truces and alliances between the Hatim sultans in Sanʿa and the ZAYDI imams based to the north in SAʿDA.

Robert D. Burrowes

Hatt-i Hümayun

Ottoman reform edict, the second of the Tanzimat era (1839–1876), when the government enacted a series of measures to create an effective military and civilian bureaucracy and thus preserve the state.

The reform measures decreed by the Ottoman Empire in the 1856 edict Hatt-i Hümayun were part of an evolutionary process rooted in both the Ottoman and Western traditions. Most of the text of the edict focused on the non-Muslim communities (Islam was the state religion) and the announced determination of the government to afford them complete equality and protection before the law. It called for their full participation in government and offered a series of specific measures to assure implementation of the general goal of nondiscrimination. The edict also discussed, more vaguely, the intent of the government to launch an extensive public-works program, eliminate corruption, regularize the financial system, and remove impediments to the development of commerce and agriculture. It restated its commitment to abolish tax farming (ILTIZAM) in favor of direct collection, an unrealized goal of the HATT-I ŞERIF OF GÜLHANE, the first TANZIMAT edict of 1839. It also sought to gain the unachieved goal of publishing an annual imperial budget.

Sultan Abdülmecit I issued the second edict just prior to the convening of the Paris peace conference that followed the CRIMEAN WAR (1854–1856), in which the Ottoman Empire had participated successfully. In its timing and stress, the edict usually has been seen as an Ottoman effort to win international favor. More generally, the edict confirmed the ongoing evolution in Ottoman administrative practices and reaffirmed the commitment of the state to further changes. It continued the process of dismantling the theoretically autocratic Ottoman state that had been based on Muslim ascendancy, erecting instead one based on the rule of law and full equality of all before the law. The edict, in its preoccupation with non-Muslim rights, served to heighten insecurity among Ottoman Muslims, who feared the loss of their nominally privileged position.

BIBLIOGRAPHY

DAVISON, RODERIC. *Reform in the Ottoman Empire, 1856–1876.* Princeton, N.J., 1963.
HUREWITZ, J. C. *The Middle East and North Africa in World Politics: A Documentary Record,* 2nd ed. New Haven, Conn., 1975.

Donald Quataert

Hatt-i Şerif of Gülhane

Ottoman edict that began the Tanzimat era, 1839–1876, when the government sought to reorganize and reform military and civilian institutions.

Hatti-i Şerif of Gülhane (Turkish, Imperial Rescript of the Rose Garden) was not a radical break with the Ottoman Empire's past but the continuation and acceleration of a long evolution of the Ottoman state from an instrument of the monarch's arbitrary power into a modern state. This evolution derived from both indigenous Ottoman roots and borrowings from Western models. The rescript was intended to enhance state power while changing and carefully regulating the relationship between state and subject. A blueprint for change, it sought to implement a series of law codes to replace the arbitrary powers of the sultan. Seeking to assure subjects of equal justice before the law, it called for codes to spell out the rights and duties of government and individual. As part of this effort to assure equality before the law, it also implemented measures giving increased legal rights to non-Muslims (Islam was the state religion). Newly formed councils, subject to executive control, were to implement additional new legislation.

In addition, the rescript abolished tax farming (ILTIZAM), where individuals paid a lump sum to the state and then collected and pocketed the taxes. Instead it decreed direct state collection of taxes. In this way, the rescript sought to give the state greater control over finances while eliminating alternative power sources within the state. It meant to increase government revenues by channeling the tax farmers' share into the state's coffers. This need was particularly great, since the ongoing TANZIMAT reforms—involving a vast expansion of the Ottoman military and state bureaucracy—proved to be extremely expensive. Finally, the rescript called for the principle of equality of obligation for all subjects and for the standardization of military-recruitment methods, regardless of residence or religion.

In common with many programs for change, the rescript's achievements fell short of the goals set. Many Muslims and non-Muslims did not want equality: The Muslims wanted to retain their privileged position in an Islamic state; the non-Muslims were reluctant to lose the benefits gained from intervention by the Great Powers—Britain, France, Prussia, and Russia—on their behalf in Ottoman affairs. The non-Muslims also wanted to avoid military service, thus refusing the equality-of-obligation principle inherent in universal military conscription. Similarly, insufficient resources made it impossible to recruit an adequate cadre of government tax collectors, so tax farming remained in place throughout the nineteenth century. Regardless of its shortcomings, however, the rescript clearly delineated the main paths of change that the Ottoman state pursued for the next eighty years, until its demise after World War I.

BIBLIOGRAPHY

DAVISON, RODERIC. *Reform in the Ottoman Empire, 1856–1876.* Princeton, N.J., 1963.
HUREWITZ, J. C. *The Middle East and North Africa in World Politics. A Documentary Record,* 2nd ed. New Haven, Conn., 1975.

Donald Quataert

Hawadith, al-

Leading news magazine of Lebanon.

In the 1960s and 1970s, *al-Hawadith* was one of the most widely read Arabic-language publications in the Middle East. Its editor, Salim al-Lawzi, bought the magazine in the 1950s and later transformed it into a bluntly political organ. It led an attack against President Gamal Abdel Nasser of Egypt and the Arab regimes after their defeat in the Arab–Israel War of 1967, and later under the control of Arab oil interests. Al-Lawzi's criticisms of the regime in Syria led to his assassination, reportedly at the hands of gunmen employed by that nation's intelligence force, in 1980.

As'ad AbuKhalil

Hawali

Suburb of Kuwait City.

Situated southeast of Kuwait City, Hawali gives its name as well to one of the Kuwait's four governorates. The town was one of several developed for non-Kuwaiti residents as the modern Kuwait City developed in the 1950s and 1960s. It has a much higher population density than Kuwait City, whose residential areas are reserved for Kuwaitis.

BIBLIOGRAPHY

NYROP, RICHARD F. *Persian Gulf States: Country Studies.* Washington, D.C., 1984.

Malcolm C. Peck

Hawar Islands

Group of sixteen small islands off the coast of Qatar; they are claimed by Bahrain.

The Hawar islands are the focus of an ongoing territorial dispute between QATAR and BAHRAIN, which has escalated toward military threats on several occasions in recent years. Hawar is now the most serious boundary dispute in the lower Persian/Arabian GULF; attempts at arbitration have been made by the International Court of Justice and the GULF COOPERATION COUNCIL. Both countries are also contesting the Fisht al-Dibal islet, also located off the coast of Qatar.

BIBLIOGRAPHY

NYROP, RICHARD, ed. *Persian Gulf States: Country Studies.* Washington, D.C., 1985.

Emile A. Nakhleh

Hawatma, Nayif [1935–]

Palestinian activist and guerilla resistance leader.

Born into a Greek Catholic family in al-Salt, Jordan, Hawatma obtained degrees in both politics and economics from Zarqa College and Hussein College in Jordan, from Cairo University, and from the Beirut Arab University. He joined the pan-Arab Movement of Arab Nationalists (MAN) while in Beirut in 1954, and fled Jordan in 1957 following King Hussein's crackdown on leftist activism. His activities on behalf of the MAN in Iraq landed him in prison between 1959 and 1963.

Back in Lebanon in the mid-1960s, Hawatma was one of several MAN activists who began pushing for a more rigidly Marxist-Leninist line within the movement. Hawatma also formed a group dedicated toward armed action in the service of Palestinian liberation, the Vengeance Youth. Although this group was one of several that merged to form the Popular Front for the Liberation of Palestine under the leadership of George HABASH in early 1968, ideological disputes between Habash and Hawatma's leftist faction led the latter to break away and form his own new group in February 1969. He named the new organization the Popular Democratic Front for the Liberation of Palestine, later shortened to the Democratic Front for the Liberation of Palestine (DFLP), and brought the group within the rubric of the PALESTINE LIBERATION ORGANIZATION (PLO).

Hawatma's historical imprint on the PLO has been strong despite the DFLP's small numbers. He has been one of the most ideologically sophisticated leaders in the Palestinian movement. He has carefully analyzed both the relationship between the Palestinian resistance movement and Israel (and Israeli Jews) and, given his Jordanian birth and pan-Arab and Marxist internationalist background, between the resistance movement and the wider Arab world. Hawatma was one of the first Palestinian resistance leaders to call for dialogue with certain leftist elements in Israel and to deal ideologically with a Jewish presence in Palestine. He and the DFLP also advanced a series of carefully-argued theories about the goals of the Palestinian resistance movement. Initially, Hawatma argued that when Palestine was liberated from Israeli control it should not become a separate state, but become part of a larger federated socialist Arab state. In particular, Hawatma believed that the struggle of the Palestinian people against Israeli rule and that of the Jordanian people against the pro-Western regime of King Hussein were inseparable. The DFLP's provocative actions in Hawatma's homeland helped precipitate a disastrous confrontation between the PLO and the Jordanian army in September 1970.

Always a champion of ideological flexibility, by 1973 Hawatma began calling for a phased approach to Palestinian liberation. While still opposed to a separate Palestinian state, he argued for establishing a "national authority" in the West Bank and Gaza in the event of an Israeli withdrawal. The PLO committed itself to this idea in 1974. Hawatma later began speaking of the establishment of a Palestinian state in the occupied territories, once again before this became official PLO policy.

Hawatma has also stood out because of his steadfast rejection of violence directed against targets outside of Israeli-controlled territory. Although committed to armed struggle against Israel, the DFLP eschewed the spectacular airline hijackings and similar acts of international violence carried out by other Palestinian groups.

Hawatma long served as a voice of loyal opposition to Yasir Arafat's leadership of the PLO, particularly since the early 1980s when Arafat began to pursue diplomatic ventures aimed at resolving the Arab-Israeli conflict that Hawatma and others felt compromised cherished Palestinian goals and subsumed them to U.S.-led imperialist domination of the region. Hawatma opposed the 1991 Madrid peace conference and subsequent talks, as well as the 1993 Israeli–PLO accords. He played an important role within the "Damascus Ten," a grouping of Palestinian organizations formed in opposition to the peace talks in 1992, which began calling itself the National Democratic and Islamic Front the following year. However, he always upheld the goal of PLO unity and despite his opposition to the peace accords, never broke with the PLO.

BIBLIOGRAPHY

NASSAR, JAMAL R. *The Palestine Liberation Organization. From Armed Struggle to the Declaration of Independence.* New York, 1991.

Michael R. Fischbach

Hawi, George   [1938–   ]

Former general secretary of the Lebanese Communist party, 1979–1992.

A Greek Orthodox, George Hawi has been a leading figure in the Lebanese Communist party since the early 1970s. He became its general secretary in 1979 and retained that position until 1992. Calls for Hawi's resignation grew from the mid-1980s onward, as a result of personal rivalries, rising confessional tensions between Greek Orthodox and Shi'a members of the party, and criticism of his pro-Syrian policies and lavish life-style. Strong Syrian support nevertheless enabled him to withstand several challenges to his leadership. His position became increasingly precarious following the collapse of communism in eastern Europe in 1989, when the party was split between reformers and backers of Hawi's traditional policies. In June 1992, during the Lebanese Communist Party's Seventh Party Congress, Hawi failed to win reelection as general secretary and was replaced by Farouk Dahrouj.

BIBLIOGRAPHY

HIRO, DILIP. *Lebanon: Fire and Embers.* New York, 1992.

Guilain P. Denoeux

Hawi, Khalil   [1919–1982]

One of Lebanon's best-known twentieth-century poets.

Born in Huwaya, Syria, where his Greek Orthodox Lebanese father was working, Khalil Hawi grew up in Shwayr, Lebanon. He studied philosophy and Arabic at the American University of Beirut, where he received a Bachelor of Arts in 1951 and a Master of Arts in 1955. After teaching for a few years, he obtained a scholarship to enroll at Cambridge University, in England, where he was awarded his Ph.D. in 1959. He then became a professor of Arabic literature at the American University in Beirut. Within a few years, he established himself as one of the leading avant-garde poets in the Arab world. His poetry relies heavily on symbols and metaphors and images, and it frequently has political and social overtones.

An Arab nationalist at heart, he repeatedly expressed his sense of shame and rage at the loss of Palestine in 1948 and at subsequent Arab defeats at the hands of Israel. He was very critical of Arab regimes for their demonstrated lack of pan-Arab solidarity, and he denounced the hedonism, materialism, and corruption that prevailed in Beirut before the civil war broke out. More generally, he lamented what he saw as the Arab world's political and cultural decay, and he expressed deep pessimism about the possibility of a true Arab cultural and political revival. His deeply felt feelings of frustration and powerlessness at the decline of Arab society and culture and at the Arab world's impotence on the international scene are shared by an entire generation of Arab intellectuals confronted with political authoritarianism and the failure of attempts at Arab unity, as well as persistent and costly inter-Arab rivalries.

After 1975, Khalil Hawi experienced the desperation felt by all Lebanese who had to watch their country's slow descent into chaos, internal disintegration, and manipulation by outside powers. He was outraged by Lebanon's inability to stand up to the Israeli army when the latter invaded on June 3, 1982, and he deeply resented the other Arab governments' silence about the Israeli invasion. He committed suicide on June 6, 1982.

BIBLIOGRAPHY

ALLEN, ROGER, ed. *Modern Arabic Literature.* New York, 1987.

BOULLATA, ISSA J. *Modern Arab Poets, 1950–1975.* Washington, D.C., 1976.

HADDAD, FUAD S., ed. *From the Vineyards of Lebanon: Poems by Khalil Hawi and Nadeem Naimy.* Beirut, 1991.

Guilain P. Denoeux

Hawmad, Abd al-Wahhab [1915–]

Syrian politician and criminologist.

Born the son of Mahmoud Hawmad, Abd al-Wahhab Hawmad earned a doctorate of laws and a degree in criminal studies from the University of Paris. A professor at Damascus University and prominent member of the People's party, he was one of the approximately two dozen political figures rounded up in Adib SHISHAKLI's January 27–28, 1954, preemptive coup. His ministerial offices include education (1951), agriculture (1954), justice (1955–56) and education again in 1956. He wrote many articles and full-length works on criminal law.

BIBLIOGRAPHY

Who's Who in the Middle East, 1967–1968.

Charles U. Zenzie

Hawrani, Akram al- [1914–]

Syrian politician and political activist.

Hawrani was born in Hama, an ancient city in the central plain of Syria and a citadel of landed power and rural oppression. In the 1930s, during the French mandate, he tried to mobilize the landless peasants against their feudal lords. When World War II broke out, he went to Iraq, where he joined Rashid Ali al-KAYLANI's 1941 revolt against the British. Having established himself as a champion of agrarian reform, Hawrani was elected to the parliament in 1943, 1947, and 1949. In 1945 he and his *shabiba* (young men) group seized Hama's garrison from the French, and in early 1948 he fought in the Palestine war on the side of Fawzi al-QAWUQJI's Army of Deliverance (*jaysh al-inqadh*). Hawrani held ministerial portfolios in the governments of Hashim al-ATASI and Adib SHISHAKLI. In 1950 he mobilized his followers in the Arab Socialist party, with headquarters in Hama and branches in other centers. Three years later, Hawrani's party merged with BA'TH to form the Arab Socialist Ba'th party, a coalition of the urban middle class (mainly schoolteachers and government employees) and politicized peasants.

Shishakli's heavy-handedness sent Hawrani into exile in Lebanon. In 1954, after Shishakli's fall, Hawrani returned to Syria, and in 1957 he became president of the parliament. He was a strong advocate of the UNITED ARAB REPUBLIC (1958–61); in the central cabinet that Gamal Abdel NASSER created for the union government, Hawrani served as vice president and minister of justice. In 1959 he resigned his cabinet posts, disenchanted with the authoritarianism of Nasser and the unstable structure that he created in Syria. After Syria's secession from the union in 1961, Hawrani opposed subsequent Ba'th efforts to recreate the union and tried to reestablish his Arab Socialist party. The Ba'th officers who engineered the coup of March 1963 (Hafiz al-ASAD, Salah al-Jadid, and others) ordered the arrest of Hawrani. When he was released, he went to Lebanon, where he tried to mobilize Syrians opposed to the Asad regime in the NATIONAL PROGRESSIVE FRONT. In many respects, Hawrani was an agent of social change, an energetic activist who roused the peasants, politicized the army, and shook the foundations of the old order.

[*See also:* Arab–Israel War, 1948.]

BIBLIOGRAPHY

SEALE, PATRICK. *The Struggle for Syria.* New Haven, Conn., 1987.
SHIMONI, YAACOV. *Biographical Dictionary of the Middle East.* New York, 1991.

Muhammad Muslih

Hawza al-Ilmiyya

A Shi'a religious college associated with a major shrine.

The name *Hawza al-Ilmiyya* means "the circle, or territory, of religious learning" and is usually applied to the religious colleges that cluster around major Shi'a shrines. Such colleges are called *madrasas* (see MADRASA).

The most important *hawza* since the last decade of the eighteenth century, and well into the twentieth, was the one in Najaf, replacing KARBALA (both in Iraq). In the 1920s an important hawza was established in Qom (Iran) by Abd al-Karim Ha'iri-Yazdi, after many years of decline of the old madrasas there. Najaf has been in decline since the 1940s due to a decrease in contributions; the decline became more precipitous after the Ba'th regime came to power in Iraq in 1968. Even in the 1950s, however, Najaf had no less than twenty-four different madrasas with some two thousand teachers and students, mostly from Iran. Under the rule of Ayat Allah Ruhollah KHOMEINI in Iran (1979–1989) Qom became the most important hawza. Other hawzat are in Karbala and Kazimayn (Iraq) and Mashhad (Iran). In the early 1970s, a small hawza was established in Damascus, around the tomb of Zaynab, Imam Husayn's sister, by Ayat Allah Hasan al-Shirazi, who had left Iraq due to Ba'thi persecutions. Until the late 1960s there was a small hawza in Samarra, too, but its fate under the Ba'th is not known.

The main role of the hawza is to prepare ULAMA for the Shi'a communities, who are capable of IJTI-HAD, or reinterpreting the QUR'AN and the SUNNA

and re-deducing religious precepts. Until the Ba'th regime "nationalized" the Iraqi hawza there was no set time for graduation, nor were there any formal examinations. Tuition was free, and no salaries were drawn by the teachers. After a few years of studying at the hawza, a student became also a teacher. Save the few most senior scholars, everyone was both teaching and studying.

There are essentially three levels of studies. The first stage, lasting about seven years, consists of the *muqaddimat* (introductions) and the *sutuh* (surface education), which include Arabic grammar, rhetoric, and Aristotelian logic. The next stage is called *al-fudala* (the wise men). It involves the methodology of examining evidence and the primary sources of Islam, and religious jurisprudence pertaining to ritual and social practices. The last stage is *buhuth al-kharij* (external studies). Unlike the previous stages, this one involves lectures to large audiences (150 students and more) by the most eminent *mujtahids.* Among those in Najaf in the 1950s were Shaykhs Muhsin al-Hakim, Abu al-Qasim al-Kha'i, Ali Qani al-Isfahani, Husayn al-Hilli, and Husayn al-Hammani. The lectures involve highly specialized juridical and ritual issues and the philosophy behind them. In the 1960s in Najaf a student could also attend classes in Western philosophies. The general atmosphere at all stages of study is of open debate and inquiry, and much of the class work involves questions and answers. A student may decide his own curriculum at each stage. There are no formal academic demands on the part of the hawza as such, but those who want to become mujtahids keep a very busy schedule. In Iraq until 1969 the government exempted students from military service on condition that they show some ability to study, but the Ba'th regime started to draft them. Economically, the hawzat, much like the individual mujtahids, used to depend mainly on donations from individuals and various funds and bequests, and the mujtahids themselves supported many students and the madrasas. In the late 1970s, the regime in Iraq started to support students, teachers, and madrasas as part of an effort to control the religious universities. In Iran under Khomeini much more government money started to permeate to the hawzat as part of the policy to encourage religious studies.

BIBLIOGRAPHY

BARAM, AMATZIA. "Two Roads to Revolutionary Shi'ite Fundamentalism in Iraq." In *Accounting for Fundamentalism: The Dynamic Character of Movements,* ed. by Martin E. Marty and R. Scott Appleby. Chicago, 1994.
MOTTAHEDEH, ROY. *The Mantle of the Prophet: Religion and Politics in Iran.* New York, 1985.

Amatzia Baram

Hayal

Ottoman Turkish satirical journal.

The magazine *Hayal* (Imagination) was founded in the Ottoman Empire by the noted comic author Teodor Kasap in 1871, with the participation of Greek and Armenian authors. When a caricature of the sultan, ABDÜLMECIT II, appeared in *Hayal* satirizing the ostensible freedoms of the press granted by the Constitution of 1876, Kasap was sentenced to a three-year prison term.

BIBLIOGRAPHY

Cumhuriyet Dönemi Türkiye Ansiklopedisi. Istanbul, 1983.

David Waldner

Hayalı, Küçük Ali   [1886–1974]

Turkish Karagöz (shadow-theater) dramatist.

Born in Istanbul as Mehmet Muhittin Sevilen, Küçük Ali Hayalı was one of the last masters of the traditional theater forms of Karagöz, a drama performed by throwing shadows of puppets or actors on a screen, and ORTAOYUNU, a type of folk theater with set plots performed among the audience.

Hayalı graduated from the Davud Paşa Rüşdiye in 1909 and began to work as a clerk in the post office, a position he held until 1944. He studied with the great Karagöz artists of his time, including Hayalı Saffet and Katip Salih. His first dramatization, performed in a popular quarter in the Fatih neighborhood of Istanbul, established his reputation as a skillful artist. Hayalı devoted himself to preserving this traditional form of drama in the twentieth century without stripping it of its essential characteristics. A collection of his dramas was published in 1969.

BIBLIOGRAPHY

Cumhuriyet Dönemi Türkiye Ansiklopedisi. Istanbul, 1983.
Türk Ansiklopedisi. Ankara, 1975.

David Waldner

Hayari, Ali al-   [1918–   ]

Jordanian general and politician.

Al-Hayari was appointed chief of staff of Jordan's army on April 17, 1957, after his predecessor, Ali Abu Nuwwar, was dismissed by King Hussein Ibn Talal for allegedly plotting to overthrow the monarchy. Three days later, al-Hayari resigned and fled to Cairo, Egypt, where several Jordanian exiles formed a revolutionary council. Pardoned in 1964, he returned to Jordan and served as ambassador to Egypt.

BIBLIOGRAPHY

BE'ERI, ELIEZER. *Army Officers in Arab Politics and Society.* Jerusalem, 1969.
SHWADRAN, BENJAMIN. *Jordan: A State of Tension.* New York, 1959.

Michael R. Fischbach

Hayat, al-

Arabic-language newspaper founded in 1946 by Kamel Mrowa.

The founder of *al-Hayat*, Kamel Mrowa, was assassinated in his office in 1966. The newspaper ceased publication in early 1976 because of the Lebanese Civil War. In 1988, with Saudi Arabia's financial support, *al-Hayat* resumed publication in London and is printed via satellite in Frankfurt (Germany), Cairo (Egypt), Manama (Bahrain), Beirut (Lebanon), Marseilles (France) and New York.

BIBLIOGRAPHY

Information provided by DANIA CHAMI, editorial secretary, *al-Hayat*, London, 1992.

George E. Irani

Haycraft Commission

Appointment by Sir Herbert Samuel, the British high commissioner in Palestine, to investigate the anti-Zionist violence there in May 1921.

The commission, headed by Thomas Haycraft, chief justice of Palestine, which was then under Britain's administration. The group found that Arab violence had been triggered by a May Day demonstration by Jews in Jaffa. Its broader context, however, was the mounting Arab apprehension and fear of Jewish encroachment, with British support, as well as displacement of Arabs by Jews in commerce and labor.

The commission estimated that in Jaffa, where the most serious clashes occurred, 95 died: 47 Jews and 48 Arabs. Of 219 wounded, 146 were Jews and 73 Arabs. Proponents of Zionism viewed the report as pro-Arab, an attempt to justify Jewish immigration restrictions, since it pointed to Jewish immigration and Arab displacement as causes of violence.

BIBLIOGRAPHY

KAYYALI, ABD AL-WAHHAB. *Palestine: A Modern History*. London, 1978.

Encyclopaedia of Zionism and Israel. New York, 1971.

Benjamin Joseph

Haydar, Sa'id   [1890–?]

Syrian lawyer and early Arab nationalist.

Born to a prominent Shi'a landowning family in Ba'albek, Syria, Haydar studied law in Constantinople (now Istanbul) and taught at the Faculty of Law in Damascus after World War I. A delegate to the Syrian Congress in 1919 under King Faisal's government, he helped found al-JAMI'A AL-ARABIYYA al-Fatat, a secret nationalist society. Haydar advocated staunch resistance to the French mandate over Syria (1920–1946), for which he was jailed and exiled in the early 1920s. In 1925 he helped found the PEOPLE'S PARTY in Damascus.

BIBLIOGRAPHY

MUSLIH, MUHAMMAD. *The Origins of Palestinian Nationalism*. New York, 1988.

Elizabeth Thompson

Hayim, Yusef   [c. 1833–1909]

Rabbi of Baghdad.

Born in Baghdad during the Ottoman Empire, Hayim attended the Midrash Beit Zilkha from 1848 to 1853. He became the student of Hakham Abdullah Somekh and his most promising disciple; he married the daughter of Yehuda Somekh, Rahel, and they had children. Hayim belonged to a family of wealthy merchants, which came to be known as *Beit al-Hakham*. As he became well known to the world of Jewish scholars, especially those in the Middle East, his opinions on religious matters were routinely sought. He left a large number of writings (*responsa*), some of which have been published.

When Hayim's father died in 1859, he inherited the place of chief preacher (*darshan*), which he maintained throughout his life. He also wrote poems (*piyyutim*) and hymns (*pizmonim*), some of which are included in the Baghdad prayer book. His principal work, known as *Ben Ish Hai* (a name by which he came to be known) had the status for Baghdad Jewry as the *Shulhan Arukh* had for all Judaism. Philosophically and practically, he was a moderate traditionalist

who assumed that modern Western teachings entering the Middle East by way of the ALLIANCE ISRAÉLITE UNIVERSELLE might be adapted and accommodated.

BIBLIOGRAPHY

BEN YAAKOV, ABRAHAM *History of the Jews in Iraq: End of the Gaonic Period to the Present Time*. Jerusalem, 1965. In Hebrew.

———. *Rabbi Yusef Hayyim of Baghdad: His Life and Writings*. Or Yehuda, Israel, 1984.

Sylvia G. Haim

Haykal, Muhammad Hasanayn   [1923–   ]

Egyptian journalist, author, and politician.

Born to a middle-class Cairo family Haykal went to government schools and attended both Cairo University and the American University in Cairo. He began working as an unpaid reporter for *The Egyptian Gazette* and *Rose al-Yusuf,* covering the battle of El Alamein and the debates in Egypt's parliament. He then became a reporter for *Akhir Sa'a,* winning the King Farouk Prize for investigative journalism for his coverage of the 1947 cholera epidemic. Between 1946 and 1949, he covered the Palestine struggle, interviewing David Ben-Gurion (head of Israel's provisional government and then prime minister) and Jordan's King Abdullah and also meeting Gamal Abdel Nasser, an Egyptian army major who later led a coup and became Egypt's leader. Haykal's assignments were wide-ranging; he also covered the civil war in Greece, the MOSSADDEGH crisis in Iran, and (supported by a U.S. State Department "Leader Grant") the 1952 U.S. Presidential campaign.

Haykal claims to have been on intimate terms with Egypt's FREE OFFICERS before the 1952 revolution; certainly he became closer to Nasser while he was in power than did any other journalist. Editor of *Akhir Sa'a* in the early 1950s, he became editor in chief of *al-Akhbar* in 1956 and of the prestigious but then-fading *al-Ahram* in 1957. He rebuilt this daily into the most influential newspaper in the Arab world. He became Nasser's adviser, confidant, and spokesman and is widely credited with ghostwriting Nasser's *Falsafat al-thawra.* A strong believer in press freedom and scientific management, he made *al-Ahram*'s facilities among the most modern in the world and founded periodicals ranging from the Marxist *al-Tali'a* to the business-oriented *al-Ahram al-Iqtisadi,* as well as a Center for Strategic Studies and a well-stocked research library. His weekly column, "Bi al-saraha" (Speaking frankly) was widely assumed to indicate the direction of Nasser's thinking.

After serving briefly as minister of culture and national guidance in 1970, he broke with Anwar al-Sadat, who succeeded Nasser as Egypt's president, because of Sadat's willingness to seek peace with Israel. Dismissed as editor of *al-Ahram* in 1974, he was barred from publishing articles in the Egyptian press. He went on writing for Lebanese Arabic newspapers and published books in English. Interrogated by the Egyptian police and state prosecutor in 1977–78, he was forbidden to travel abroad, then imprisoned during Sadat's 1981 purge. Although under President Husni Mubarak Haykal has not regained his former influence on policy decisions, he is respected as an intellectual, writer, and possible mediator with other Arab states, such as Libya. His memoirs of events in which he took part should be read with caution. They include *Cairo Documents* (Garden City, N.Y., 1973), *Road to Ramadan* (New York, 1975), *The Sphinx and the Commissar* (New York, 1978), *Autumn of Fury: The Assassination of Sadat* (New York, 1983), *Cutting the Lion's Tail: Suez through Egyptian Eyes* (London, 1986), and *1967: al-Infijar* (Cairo, 1990).

BIBLIOGRAPHY

NASIR, MUNIR. *Press, Politics, and Power: Egypt's Haykal and Al-Ahram.* Ames, Iowa, 1978.
SHEEHAN, EDWARD R. F. "The Most Powerful Journalist in the World." In *The Cairo Documents,* ed. by Muhammed Haykal. Garden City, N.Y., 1973.

Arthur Goldschmidt, Jr.

Haykal, Muhammad Husayn   [1888–1956]

Egyptian author, political leader, and lawyer.

Born to a landowning family in Daqahliyya, Haykal was educated at the Cairo School of Law and at the University of Paris, where he wrote his doctoral thesis on the Egyptian public debt (1912). Homesick for his native village, he also wrote a bucolic fiction, called *Zaynab* (Cairo, 1914), which is usually described as the first modern Arabic novel.

Upon returning to Egypt, he practiced law, wrote for *al-Jarida* of Ahmad Lutfi al-Sayyid (with whom he remained close throughout his life), published a magazine called *al-Sufur* during World War I, and taught at the School of Law. Egypt had become a British protectorate in 1914, and when the nationwide revolution for independence broke out in 1919, he backed the WAFD and Sa'd Zaghlul, one of its leaders, but broke with them in 1921 over negotiations with Britain. At this time, Prime Minister Adli Yakan, Haykal, and other educated Egyptians formed the Constitutional Liberal party (Hizb al-Ahrar al-Dusturiyyin), calling for parliamentary democracy. In 1922, Haykal became editor of its newspaper, *al-Siyasa,* and he later founded an influential weekly edition, *al-Siyasa al-Usbu'iyya.* He continued his literary production with the books *Fi awqat al-faragh* (Cairo, 1925), *Tarajim misriyya wa gharbiyya* (Cairo, 1929), and a touching eulogy of his son who died in childhood, called *Waladi* (Cairo, 1931).

In 1934, when the Constitutional Liberals were competing for popular favor with the Wafd, the palace, and rising Muslim groups, he published *Hayat Muhammad* (Cairo, 1934), an attempt to apply modern scholarship to the biography of the Prophet Muhammad and to reconcile the principles of personal freedom with the teachings of Islam. Increasingly pious, he made the pilgrimage to Mecca (hajj) in 1936, and published *Fi manzal al-wahy* (Cairo, 1937), relating his experience as a pilgrim. He served as Egypt's minister in seven cabinets in the late 1930s and the 1940s and as president of the Senate from 1945 to 1950. He published his last novel *Hakadha khuliqat* (Cairo, 1955) and also his memoirs, *Mudhakkirat fi al-siyasa al-misriyya* (Cairo, 1951–1978, 3 vols.), of which two volumes appeared in his lifetime and the third posthumously. An ambitious man with many talents, he often felt a conflict between secularism and Islam and between the democratic principles of his party and his belief that Egypt should be governed by its most educated citizens.

BIBLIOGRAPHY

SMITH, CHARLES D. *Islam and the Search for Social Order in Modern Egypt.* Albany, N.Y., 1983.
WADI, TAHA UMRAN. *Al-Duktur Muhammad Husayn Haykal: Hayatuhu wa turathuhu al-adabi.* Cairo, 1969.
WESSELS, ANTONIE. *A Modern Arabic Biography of Muhammad.* Leiden, 1972.

Arthur Goldschmidt, Jr.

Hayreddin

See Khayr al-Din

Haytham, Muhammad Ali   [?–1993]

South Yemeni government official.

Haytham was the moderate NATIONAL LIBERATION FRONT (NLF) leader in South Yemen whose removal as prime minister in August 1971 signaled the complete triumph of the NLF's left wing. He went into exile in Cairo where he was the object of two assassination attempts in the mid-1970s. He returned to a minor cabinet post in 1993 in the new government of the unified Republic of Yemen, only to die of natural causes within months.

Robert D. Burrowes

Hazan, Ya'akov   [1899–   ]

Israeli political leader.

Born in Russia, Hazan grew up in Poland and was active there in founding Hashomer Hatza'ir and Hehalutz. Settling in Palestine in 1923, he established, with Me'ir Ya'ari, the Hashomer Hatza'ir kibbutz movement. He played leading roles in the HISTADRUT, as a member of its executive committee. He represented the MAPAM party from 1949 until 1973 in the Knesset.

Martin Malin

Hazara

Ethnolinguistic group in Afghanistan.

Dwelling in the high central mountains of Afghanistan in a region called the Hazarajat, the Hazara number between one and two million. They have distinctive Mongoloid physical features, including the epicanthic fold of the upper eyelid commonly seen in the people of central Asia. Although the Hazaras maintain they are the descendants of the army of the great Mongol conqueror Genghis Khan, scholars now believe them to be descendants of Chaghatai from Transoxiana who entered the area as soldiers under Timur and his son Shah Rukh in the fifteenth century. These soldiers intermarried with local women who were probably Tajiks or Persians. Originally Sunni Moslems, the Hazara were converted to SHI'ISM during the time of the Safavid King Abbas I (1588–1692), when this part of Afghanistan was controlled by Iran. The Hazara speak a dialect of Persian known as Hazaragi, which contains some Turkic and Mongol words.

The Hazaras lived a relatively independent existence until the 1890s, when, during the reign of Abd al-Rahman, they were brought under the sway of Kabul through a series of wars. Looked down upon by other Afghans, the Hazaras are the poorest of the Afghan ethnolinguistic groups. Some have migrated to Kabul and the other major cities, where they work in menial jobs.

During the Afghan war of resistance, the Hazaras were able to expel the government representatives from the Hazarajat, and in 1979 they established a quasi-independent government under a council led by Sayyid Ali Beheshti. By the mid-1980s, however, they came under the control of the Iranian-backed Shi'a groups of Nasr and Pasdaran, and since 1992 Hazaras have played a major role in the fighting for an Islamic government in Kabul.

BIBLIOGRAPHY

ADAMEC, LUDWIG. *Historical Dictionary of Afghanistan,* Metuchen, N.J., 1991.
FARR, GRANT, "The Rise and Fall of an Indigenous Resistance Group: The Shura of the Hazarajat." *Afghanistan Studies Journal* 1 (1988): 48–61.

Grant Farr

Hazarajat

Home of the Hazara people in Afghanistan.

The region in the central mountains of Afghanistan where the HAZARA people live, the Hazarajat includes parts of eight provinces. The area is high in altitude, with inhabited valleys of over 10,000 feet, peaks above 18,000 feet, and no cities or even sizable towns. The roads into the Hazarajat are few and largely unpaved.

BIBLIOGRAPHY

ADAMEC, LUDWIG. *Historical Dictionary of Afghanistan,* Metuchen, N.J., 1991.

Grant Farr

Hazaz, Hayyim   [1898–1973]

Hebrew writer.

Hazaz was born in Sidorvichi, a province of Kiev. His secular and religious education included the study of Russian and Hebrew literature. Hazaz left home at sixteen, and for seven years traveled from one Russian city to another. While in Moscow, during and after the Russian Revolution, he worked at the Hebrew daily *Ha'am.* In 1921, Hazaz settled in Constantinople (now Istanbul) for a year and a half, and subsequently moved to Western Europe. He spent nine years in Paris and Berlin, which replaced pre-Revolutionary Russia as the capital of Hebrew literary activity.

In early 1931, Hazaz left for Eretz Ysrael and settled in Jerusalem. A political activist, he was president of the Israel–Africa Friendship Association from 1965 to 1969. After the Six-Day War (1967), he became an advocate for the LAND OF ISRAEL MOVEMENT, which called for settling the lands captured during the war and permanently incorporating them into the state of Israel.

Hazaz began his writing career while still in Russia publishing a sketch, *Ke-Vo ha-Shemesh* (1918), in *Ha-Shilo'ah* under a pseudonym. Thereafter he published under his own name. The dominant theme of his Russian-period stories is the fate of the *shtetl* in the aftermath of the Russian Revolution. The old world had been turned on its head and its generation became disoriented. Among these stories are *Mi-Zeh u-mi-Zeh* (From This and That, 1924) and *Pirke Mahpekhah* (Chapters of the Revolution, 1924). Another Hazaz story of the revolution is *Shemu'el Frankfurter* (1925), which has as its protagonist the title character, a revolutionary, whose idealism and integrity doom him. Hazaz's first novel, *Be-Yishuv Shel Ya'ar* (In a Forest Settlement, 1930), is set during the Russo-Japanese War and depicts a Jewish family among gentiles. As the story evolves, it becomes clear that while the latter are firmly anchored in their land, the former are manifestly rootless.

His Eretz Ysrael phase began with *Rehayim Shevurim* (Broken Millstones, 1942). While some of his stories continue to recount *shtetl* life, others are located in Eretz Ysrael. One of his major works, *Ha-Yoshevet ba-Gannim* (Thou That Dwellest in the Gardens, 1944), recounts the story of three generations of Yemenite Jews in Eretz Ysrael. *Harat Olam* and *Havit Akhurah* describe the life of German-Jewish immigrants. *Esh Bo'eret* and *Drabkin* are studies of immigrants from Eastern Europe. The first describes the idealism of the *halutzim* (pioneers) who fled Russia and suffered immeasurable hardships to reach Eretz Ysrael, while the second narrative tells of its title hero's disillusionment with Zionism when it fails to fulfill his dreams. Several of Hazaz's protagonists struggle to narrow the gap between their ideals and reality. In *Ha-Derashah* (The Lesson) Yudke, the story's hero, questions the commonly accepted premises of Zionism.

Ya'ish, Hazaz's most elaborate work (4 vols., 1947–52), recounts the life of Ya'ish, a young Yemenite Jew who abandons his mystical beliefs upon arriving in Eretz Ysrael while experiencing external and internal conflicts. In this four-volume opus, Hazaz evinces intimate familiarity with Yemenite culture. *Be-Kolar Ehad* (In the One Collar, 1963) deals with the struggle against the British in Palestine. The heroes, young resistance fighters condemned to death by the British, opt to commit suicide. The story is based on historical fact and raises issues of the Diaspora such as redemption and *Kiddush ha-Shem,* Sanctification of the Name, i.e., sacrificing one's life for the sake of God.

Since Hazaz's linguistic style is rooted in ancient Jewish texts, reflecting a profound knowledge of the Talmud and Midrash, he is not easily understood by the modern Hebrew reader. To overcome this obstacle, a revised edition of all his works was published in 1968, in which Hazaz deleted many archaic words and allusions.

Hazaz was awarded the Israel Prize for Literature in 1953.

Ann Kahn

Hazzan, Elijah Bekhor   [1847–1908]

An important Sephardic scholar, intellectual, and communal leader.

Born in Izmir and raised in Jerusalem, Hazzan traveled to Europe and French North Africa in the early 1870s. He published a philosophical dialogue *Zikhron Yerushalayim* (Livorno, Italy, 1874) on questions of modernity and Jewish identity.

Appointed Hakham Bashi (chief rabbi) of Tripolitania in 1874, he was a leading, but controversial advocate of reforms. He was more successful as the modernizing chief rabbi of Alexandria, where he served from 1888 until his death. He published four volumes of responsa (interpretations), *Ta'alumot Lev* (Livorno/Alexandria, 1879–1902), and a work on Alexandrian Jewish customs, *Neveh Shalom* (Alexandria, 1894).

BIBLIOGRAPHY

STILLMAN, NORMAN A. *The Jews of Arab Lands in Modern Times*. Philadelphia, 1991.

Norman Stillman

Health Care

See Medicine and Public Health

Hebrew

Major official language of the State of Israel.

Hebrew is the national language of the Jewish population of Israel (about 5 million) and the mother tongue of Jews born in the country. For world Jewry (about 14 million) it is the traditional liturgical language and a link to daily life in contemporary Israel.

Hebrew is the original language of the Bible. It has played a central role in the cultural history of the Jewish people for the past three millennia, and has had an important impact on Western culture. Ancient Hebrew names such as Jacob, Joseph, Sarah, and Mary, and old Hebrew words or concepts such as "amen," "hallelujah," "hosanna," "Sabbath," and "Messiah" have survived, resisting translation in many languages and cultures.

Hebrew belongs to the Canaanite group of the Northwestern Semitic or Afro–Asiatic family of languages. During its long history (which follows the historical course of the Jewish people), it has undergone diverse changes and has developed several different layers, from biblical Hebrew to modern Israeli Hebrew.

Biblical Hebrew (BH) is believed to have crystallized over 3,000 years ago, when the Israelite tribes coalesced into a homogeneous political unit under the monarchy in Jerusalem (eleventh–tenth centuries B.C.E.). It emerged as a fully formed literary language whose poetic grandeur is attested by the oldest portions of the Bible, written about that time.

In its early, classical form BH functioned as a living language until the end of the First Temple Period (586 B.C.E.). Due to its prestigious status as the language of the early books of the Bible, it survived as a literary language until the second century B.C.E., as seen in the late books of the Bible, in the Apocrypha, and in the Dead Sea Scrolls. BH was employed centuries later, mainly by the Hebrew poets of medieval Spain (eleventh to thirteenth centuries) and the writers of the Jewish Enlightenment movement in Eastern Europe (late eighteenth and nineteenth centuries). Most important, because praying and reciting the Bible in the original Hebrew have always been central to synagogue worship, contact with BH has never ceased. The preservation throughout the ages of the morphological structure of BH accounts for the relative uniformity in the various historical layers of the language.

The Second Temple Period (516 B.C.E.–70 C.E.) saw the beginning of Jewish bilingualism. Aramaic, another Northwestern Semitic language, closely akin to Hebrew and a lingua franca in the ancient Middle East, became the second language of the Jewish people. The contact between BH and Aramaic (and, to a certain degree, Greek and Latin) gradually resulted in an enriched and quite different kind of spoken Hebrew with a literary counterpart, known as Rabbinic Hebrew (RH). A change in script occurred at that time, the ancient Canaanite alphabet of BH being replaced by the Assyrian square script used in Aramaic.

Well adapted to deal with everyday practical matters, RH was employed in writing down the Mishna (the oral law, 220 C.E.), and for several hundred years it continued to be used together with Aramaic in the Rabbinic literature (the Talmud and the Midrash).

However, its role as a spoken language declined at the end of the second century C.E., following the destruction of Jerusalem and the Judaean state by the Romans (70 C.E.).

For the following 1,700 years, Hebrew fell into disuse as a spoken language in daily use because the diaspora Jews used the vernaculars of their host countries for communication. Nevertheless, Hebrew was by no means a dead language. In their dispersed communities the Jewish people continued to use it as their written language in their liturgical, scholarly, literary, and even practical activities. Writing and copying were greatly aided in the Middle Ages by the introduction of the Rashi script (which survives among Middle Eastern Jews). In addition to the vast, multifaceted religious and secular literature written in Hebrew at that period, hundreds of books were translated into Hebrew, primarily from Arabic and Latin. Each of these literary activities contributed to the growth of the language by enriching its vocabulary and by introducing new syntactic patterns. At the same time, many Hebrew words and expressions were incorporated into the Jewish languages that developed alongside the vernaculars, such as Judeo-Arabic, Judeo-Spanish, and Yiddish.

The search for a new Hebrew idiom, suitable for a realistic literary expression in the modern era, followed the revival of Hebrew culture by the Jewish Enlightenment Movement. Mendele Mokher Seforim (1835–1917) is considered the first modern writer who integrated in his style varied elements from all the periods of Hebrew as well as from Yiddish. His work contributed to the transformation of Hebrew into a flexible modern literary vehicle and helped pave the way for the rise of modern Hebrew literature.

The renaissance of Hebrew as a spoken language in the twentieth century has been closely linked to the national revival of the Jewish people in their forefathers' land. Hebrew was revived thanks to the efforts of a small group of devoted people, led by Eliezar Ben-Yehuda (1858–1922), who in 1881 settled in Jerusalem and pioneered Hebrew usage at home and in school. He published a Hebrew periodical, promoted the coining of new words, and cofounded the Language Committee (1890–1953), which began dealing with language planning issues and set normative measures. Above all, Ben-Yehuda compiled several volumes of the first modern dictionary of ancient and modern Hebrew.

Ben Yehuda's work gained increasing support from the waves of Jewish immigrants and refugees returning to Zion. When the state of Israel was proclaimed in 1948, Hebrew was a functioning modern language, fully established as the living language of the growing

Jewish community in the country. Supervision of its continuous growth was assigned in 1953 to the Academy of the Hebrew Language in Jerusalem.

Since the first days of its rebirth, thousands of new words have been created in Hebrew from its own roots and many of its ancient words have been given new meanings. Influence from other languages on vocabulary and syntax may be discerned as well. Encompassing all areas of life and gaining ever greater flexibility, Hebrew has become the dynamic, vibrant language of modern Israel.

BIBLIOGRAPHY

ORNAN, UZI. "Hebrew Grammar." *Encyclopaedia Judaica.* Vol. 8. 1977.
SAENZ-BADILLOS, ANGEL. *The History of the Hebrew Language.* Cambridge, U.K., 1993.
WALDMAN, NAHUM. *The Recent Study of Hebrew.* Cincinnati, Ohio, 1989.

Ruth Raphaeli

Hebrew University of Jerusalem

Israeli university.

A university in Jerusalem was first suggested by Hermann Schapira in the Hebrew press in 1882–1884 and then at the first Zionist Congress in 1897. The fifth Zionist Congress (1901) passed a resolution that the Zionist Actions Committee should establish a Hebrew college for higher studies. At the eleventh congress (1913), Chaim Weizmann spoke of the related problems. In 1914, an area of land on Mount Scopus was purchased by the Hovevei Zion of Odessa and Y. L. Goldberg. The foundation stones were laid in July 1918 by Weizmann, and the university officially was opened in 1925 by Lord Balfour. The first chancellor and later president was Judah L. MAGNES (1925–1935; 1935–1948), who was succeeded by Selig Brodetsky (1949–1952) and Binyamin Mazar (1953–1961) and then by Eliyahu Elath (1961–1968). Avraham Harman has held the offices since 1968. In 1973, the university had seven faculties (humanities, social sciences, science, law, medicine, dentistry, agriculture) and four schools (education, pharmacy, social work and graduate library sciences). There are approximately 18,000 students, including 3,000 from overseas, and the language of instruction is Hebrew. The Hadassah Hospital serves as the university hospital. The university publishes original and translated works under the auspices of the Magnes Press. The Arab–Israel War of 1948 affected the university, cutting it off from its laboratories, buildings, and libraries on Mount Scopus. In 1954, work commenced on a second permanent site at Givat Ram in the western suburbs of Jerusalem, and a campus opened there between 1955 and 1958. Access to Mount Scopus was reopened after the Arab–Israel War of 1967. The Hebrew University also has other campuses in Ein Kerem and at Rehovot. The student body is being increased beyond 18,000 to accommodate Soviet Jewish emigration.

BIBLIOGRAPHY

Like All Nations? The Life and Legacy of Judah L. Magnes. Albany, N.Y., 1987.

Mia Bloom

Hebron

West Bank city, south of Jerusalem.

Hebron (Arabic, al-Khalil) is an ancient city, holy to both Judaism and Islam, since it is the site of the Machpelah burial cave of the patriarch Abraham and his wife Sarah. Later, in the tenth century B.C.E., David was proclaimed king there when Saul died, and it became his first capital. Above the Machpelah cave is a mosque surrounded by a sacred enclosure (*haram*).

A small Jewish community lived in Hebron throughout the centuries, but the Jews left after the Arab riots of 1929, when 64 Jews were killed. Hebron was within the British mandate of Palestine (1922–1948), was annexed by Jordan in 1950 in the aftermath of the ARAB–ISRAEL WAR of 1948/49, and was occupied by Israel during the ARAB–ISRAEL WAR of 1967. The population estimate (1985) is approximately 75,000, mostly Palestinians. Since 1967, right-wing Israeli settlers began moving into the city and have been a source of tension, especially since the formation of GUSH EMUNIM.

BIBLIOGRAPHY

ROLEF, S. H., ed. *Political Dictionary of the State of Israel.* New York, 1987.

Benjamin Joseph

Hedayat, Sadegh

Iran's most famous and controversial writer.

Born into a prominent Tehran family and receiving a European-style education in Iran, Sadegh Hedayat traveled to Europe in 1926 to undertake his university studies. He returned to Tehran in 1930 without a degree and proceeded to author four collections of short stories and a novella, along with other books and essays on Persian culture and history, in a remarkably productive period until 1942. He became the most famous and controversial writer in Persian literature and the only Iranian writer of fiction with an appreciable audience outside Iran.

Hedayat wrote story after story with tragic endings of alienated, maladjusted protagonists. His writings exude nostalgia for an Indo-European Iranian past; they invoke nationalism, strident anti-Arab sentiments, antipathy toward his fellow countrymen, disgust with the local social and political milieu, and familiarity with contemporary European literature. His masterwork is the novella *Buf-e Kur* (The Blind Owl, 1937, 1941) Iran's most famous piece of fiction, a much translated and still enigmatic, surrealistic narrative of a character out of tune with his times and perhaps deranged. As suggested in M. Hillmann's *Iranian Culture: A Persianist View* (1990), the story may be as much autobiography as fiction.

BIBLIOGRAPHY

A sampling of English translations of Hedayat's short stories appears in *Sadeq Hedayat: An Anthology* (1979), while *The Blind Owl* has appeared in several paperback editions (1957, 1969, and 1989). M. BEARD, *The Blind Owl as a Western Novel* (1990), traces European influences in the novel, while H. KATOUZIAN, *Sadeq Hedayat: The Life and Literature of an Iranian Writer* (1991), offers a biographical sketch and psychological analysis of the writer and his works.

Michael C. Hillmann

He-Halutz

Hebrew for "the pioneer"; umbrella group for various Zionist youth movements throughout Europe and the United States.

From the 1880s in Eastern Europe, various groups of young Jews began to prepare themselves for eventual resettlement in Palestine to create a Jewish community in ERETZ YISRAEL. They stressed manual labor, agricultural proficiency, self-defense, and the speaking of modern Hebrew; they called themselves pioneers (in Hebrew, halutzim). Branches differed over political issues, but all encouraged physical fitness and horticultural studies. Many had already started the New YISHUV and invented the KIBBUTZ and the MOSHAV when the Jewish YOUTH MOVEMENT was eventually financed by the WORLD ZIONIST ORGANIZATION and brought together as a world organization in 1921. A center was established in Warsaw, Poland, and its paper *He'atid* (the Future) was published. The movement reached its high point in 1935 with some 90,000 members, but the Holocaust virtually annihilated it. During World War II, the group assisted in the illegal settlement of Jews in Palestine.

BIBLIOGRAPHY

OPPENHEIM, ISRAEL. *The Struggle of Jewish Youth for Productivization: The Zionist Youth Movement in Poland.* Boulder, Colo., 1989.

Donna Robinson Divine

Hekmatyar, Golbuddin   [1947–   ]

Afghan resistance leader; prime minister of Afghanistan, 1993–1994.

Born in Baghlan in northern Afghanistan to a Kharoti Gilzai Pushtun family, Hekmatyar attended college at Kabul University's faculty of engineering in the 1960s and became active in campus politics. He joined the Muslim Youth movement (1970) and was imprisoned in Kabul (1972–1973) because of his political activities. He was released after the Daud coup (1973) and fled to Pakistan, where he began his antigovernment activities. In Pakistan, he became a leader in the Jami'at-e Islami (1975) but left this group to form his own party, HEZB-E ISLAMI (1978). Having been able to gain the support of Pakistan and other Islamic countries, he turned his party into the most active fighting force in Afghanistan. By the 1980s, Hekmatyar's guerrilla fighters controlled large parts of Afghanistan.

Committed to an Islamic revolution and strongly anti-Western, Hekmatyar is considered one of the more radical and ruthless of the Afghan resistance fighters. His guerillas were accused of fighting with the other Islamic groups as often as they fought the Soviets. Following the 1989 withrawal of Soviet troops, Hekmatyar aligned with Pushtun army officers. In 1992, he returned to Afghanistan to take part in the Islamic government of Afghanistan. He attempted to seize control of the government but was defeated by the troops of Ahmad Shah Mas'ud and Abd al-Rashid Doestam. He was later named prime minister in the government of Burhanuddin RABBANI (1993), but never fully occupied that position; instead he joined other leaders in the attempt to form an alternative government and continued to attack Mas'ud's troops in Kabul.

BIBLIOGRAPHY

ROY, OLIVIER. *Islam and Resistance in Afghanistan.* Cambridge, U. K., 1986.

Grant Farr

Heliopolis

Site of an ancient Egyptian city dedicated to the worship of Ra, the sun god.

Located at 30°08′ N, 31°20′ E, it was also the site of a victory by France over an Ottoman Empire expeditionary force in June 1800. Now called "Misr al-Jadida" in Arabic, it has become a suburb northeast of Cairo, Egypt's capital, that grew up as a result of the construction of a high-speed tram line, starting in 1905, by Baron Empain, a Belgian entrepreneur. It had a population of 100,000 in 1947 and roughly double that number in 1971.

BIBLIOGRAPHY

ABU-LUGHOD, JANET. *Cairo: 1001 Years of the City Victorious.* Princeton, N.J., 1971.

Arthur Goldschmidt, Jr.

Helleu, Jean   [1885–1955]

French diplomat.

Helleu served as minister of France in Rabat, Morocco, (1933–1936) and Tehran, Iran, (1939–1940), among other posts. In 1943, he became delegate-general in Syria and Lebanon. After the Lebanese parliament rejected the French mandate on November 8, 1943, Helleu arrested President Bishara al-Khuri and the entire cabinet, suspended the constitution, and made Emile Eddé president. In the face of widespread strikes and riots, Helleu was recalled.

BIBLIOGRAPHY

Dictionaire de Biographie Française. Paris, 1986.
LENCZOWSKI, GEORGE. *The Middle East in World Affairs.* 4th ed. Ithaca, N.Y., 1980.

Zachary Karabell

Helmand River

Major river system in Afghanistan.

The Helmand River originates in the high mountains of the Hindu Kush range in central Afghanistan and flows to the Sistan desert, where it dissipates. The longest river in Afghanistan (over 2,000 miles; 3,218 km), the Helmand river drains 40 percent of the Afghan watershed. In the 1940s and 1950s, the Helmand Valley Project was initiated as a cooperative venture between the United States and Afghanitan, and a series of dams and canals was constructed to irrigate the arid Helmand valley. Despite problems of salination and poor drainage in some areas, as well as massive

corruption, the project produced beneficial effects since thousands of farmers were relocated from other areas of Afghanistan and given land in this area.

BIBLIOGRAPHY

DUPREE, LOUIS. *Afghanistan.* Princeton, N.J., 1980.

Grant Farr

Helou

See under Hilu

Helwan Iron and Steel Complex

A publicly owned integrated plant producing the vast majority of Egypt's iron and steel.

Located in the town of Hilwan, 16 miles (26 km) north of Cairo, the Hilwan Iron and Steel Complex was designed to use iron ore deposits located at Aswan along with imported coke. Plans to construct the complex were approved in 1954. The plant was financed by the Egyptian government and constructed by a West German firm, the Demag Corporation. Production began in 1958, and, in the 1960s and 1970s, the plant was enlarged with aid from the Soviet Union.

The Hilwan Complex is the best known of Egypt's public sector industries—for its size, its importance in Egypt's metallurgical industry, and for its extreme inefficiencies. The contractor, Demag, has been accused of selling Egypt substandard furnaces, improperly installed. The iron ore from Aswan is of low quality, and the price of imported coke rose after the currency devaluation of 1962. Finally, the oxygen conversion process employed at the plant was obsolete by the time production started. The iron and steel production capacity is low: In 1980, for example, the production of liquid steel was 2 million tons (1,814,000 metric tons) annually.

BIBLIOGRAPHY

NYROP, RICHARD F., ed. *Egypt: A Country Study,* 4th ed. Washington, D.C., 1983.
WATERBURY, JOHN. *The Egypt of Nasser and Sadat: The Political Economy of Two Regimes.* Princeton, N.J., 1983.

David Waldner

Henderson, Loy   [1892–1986]

American diplomat.

During World War II, Henderson was minister plenipotentiary in Iraq and handled United States relations with the oil-producing states. As head of the State Department's Division of Near Eastern and African Affairs in 1945, he opposed the 1947 United Nations Palestine partition plan, claiming that it would damage American prestige in the Arab world. He was ambassador to Iran between 1951 and 1955. Though he was friendly with Prime Minister Mohammad MOSSADEGH, he was fearful of U.S.S.R. influence in Iran and concerned about Mossadegh's ability to handle Tudeh, Iran's Communist party. Thus, Henderson reluctantly supported the Central Intelligence Agency's Operation Ajax, which resulted in Mossadegh's ouster in August 1953. Henderson later represented the United States at the 1956 Suez Crisis conferences.

BIBLIOGRAPHY

FINDLING, JOHN, ed. *Dictionary of American Diplomatic History*. New York, 1989.
SPIEGEL, STEVEN. *The Other Arab–Israeli Conflict*. Chicago, 1985.

Zachary Karabell

Herat

Province and city in western Afghanistan.

Herat, a province in northwestern Afghanistan, has a population of about 700,000. The third largest city in Afghanistan and the major city in the western region, the city of Herat is the provincial capital and has a population of approximately 150,000, most of whom speak Persian although there is also some Turkoman spoken in the north.

Because of its strategic location, Herat has been a fortified town for several thousand years. Mention of it first appears in the Avesta, the holy book of the

The Friday mosque at Herat, Afghanistan. (Richard Bulliet)

Afghan man and his pet owl in Herat. (Richard Bulliet)

Zoroastrians (1,500 B.C.E.), and scholars have conjectured that Herat may be a derivative of Aria, a province in the ancient Persian empire. It was also visited by Alexander the Great, who built Alexandria Ariorum on the site (330 B.C.E.).

During the Afghan war of resistance (1978–1992), the city of Herat saw considerable fighting and suffered significant destruction. Liberated in 1992, it is controlled by Commander Ismail Khan, a leader of the Jami'at-e Islami party.

BIBLIOGRAPHY

ADAMEC, LUDWIG. *Historical Dictionary of Afghanistan*. Metuchen, N.J., 1991.

Grant Farr

Herut Party

The largest conservative political party in Israel.

Founded in 1948, the Herut (Freedom) party was led until 1983 by Menachem BEGIN, a chief protégé of the Revisionist Zionist Ze'ev JABOTINSKY. After several short-lived mergers with other parties, in 1973 Herut became the senior member of the LIKUD bloc, which Begin led to victory in 1977. When Begin retired from public life in 1983, he was succeeded as party leader and prime minister by Yitzhak SHAMIR. Shamir retired after Likud's electoral defeat in 1992 and was succeeded in 1993 by Binyamin (Bibi) NETANYAHU, who defeated several rivals including Moroccan-born David Levy, Ariel Sharon, and Begin's son Ze'ev.

Herut's most prominent program is insistence on the integrity of GREATER ISRAEL, which includes the West Bank and Gaza, with many of its leaders favoring annexation of those areas. It was under the leadership of Begin and Sharon that Israel undertook the 1982 invasion of Lebanon. In domestic affairs, Herut advocated a major reduction in the public sector of the economy, but not much of that was accomplished during its period in power.

BIBLIOGRAPHY

ROLEF, SUSAN, ed. *Political Dictionary of the State of Israel*, 2nd ed. New York, 1993.

Walter F. Weiker

Herzl, Theodor   [1860–1904]

Herzl is considered the founder of political Zionism.

A secular Jew, Herzl earned a doctorate in law in 1884, and worked in the courts of Vienna and Salzburg. After only a year he left the legal profession and began a successful career as a writer and journalist.

As Paris correspondent for the liberal Vienna newspaper *Neue Freie Presse,* Herzl observed and reported on emerging French anti-Semitism. He was court correspondent at the court-martial of Captain Alfred Dreyfus and witnessed the anti-Jewish disturbances by Parisian mobs during the ceremony expelling Dreyfus from the military. Herzl's interest in Jewish affairs was roused by these first-hand observations of French anti-Semitism. Herzl articulated his beliefs in his book, *Der Judenstaat,* which was published in Vienna in 1896.

In order to translate his vision into reality, Herzl had to convince both the international Jewish community and leaders of the great powers. In June 1896, he submitted a proposal to the Grand Vizier whereby the Jews would manage the empire's deteriorating financial affairs. When this proposal was rejected, Herzl requested permission to establish a Jewish state in Palestine that would remain under the suzerainty of the sultan. This too was rejected.

Initial Jewish responses to *Der Judenstaat* were mixed. The Baron Edmond de ROTHSCHILD of London rejected Herzl's appeals for support because of his belief that the Jewish masses could not be organized to implement Herzl's scheme of mass resettlement. In 1897, Herzl established news a weekly, *Die Welt,* in which he lobbied for the convening of a congress of Jewish representatives from around the world. At the First Zionist Congress in Basle, Switzerland, on August 29–31 1897, the Zionist program was adopted by the representatives of world Jewry. The Basle Program, as it came to be known, called for the establishment of "a home for the Jewish people in Palestine secured under public law." It proposed the promotion of Jewish settlement in Palestine, the organization of world Jewry by appropriate institutions, the strengthening and fostering of Jewish national sentiment, and preparatory steps toward gaining the consent of the relevant governments. The WORLD ZIONIST ORGANIZATION was established as the institutional framework for the Zionist program, and Herzl served as its president until his death.

BIBLIOGRAPHY

BEIN, ALEX. *Theodor Herzl: A Biography.* Cleveland, Ohio, 1962.
CHOURAQUI, ANDRE. *A Man Alone: The Life of Theodor Herzl.* Jerusalem, 1970.

Shimon Avish

Herzog, Hayim   [1918–]

Commentator, politician, military man, and Israel's sixth president.

Son of Chief Rabbi Izhak Halevi Herzog, he was born in Dublin, Ireland, and emigrated to Israel in 1935. During World War II, he fought with the British army. And, from the Arab–Israel War of 1948, until 1962, when he retired, he was an Israeli career army officer.

From 1975 to 1978, Herzog was Israel's permanent representative to the United Nations. In 1981, he became a member of the Knesset (Israel's parliament) representing the Ma'arakh party. Herzog published several books on Israel's numerous wars: *Israel's Finest Hour* (1967), *Days of Awe* (1973), and *The War of Atonement* (1974). He served as Israel's president from 1983 to 1993.

Ann Kahn

Herzog, Izhak Halevi   [1888–1959]

First Ashkenazic chief rabbi of Israel.

Izhak Herzog was born in Lomza, Poland. His family moved to England, where his father served as a rabbi in Leeds. In addition to his religious learning, the younger Herzog studied at the University of Paris and University of London, where he completed his doctorate. After serving as a congregational rabbi in Belfast and Dublin for nine years, Herzog became chief rabbi of Ireland in 1925. He helped found the religious Zionist Mizrahi movement in England and testified before the Anglo–American Committee of Inquiry and the United Nations Special Committee on Palestine. Following the death of Rabbi Abraham Isaac Hacohen KOOK, Herzog was elected Ashkenazic chief rabbi of Palestine in 1936. He continued as

Ashkenazic chief rabbi after the establishment of the State of Israel until his death. As Israel's first Ashkenazic chief rabbi, he handled many new and delicate issues in HALAKHAH, Jewish religious law. He was the father of Hayim HERZOG and Ya'acov David HERZOG.

BIBLIOGRAPHY

HACOHEN, SHMUEL AVIDOR. *Yahid be-doro* (*A Unique Individual: The Life of Rabbi Izhak Halevi Herzog*). Jerusalem, 1980.
HERZOG, ISAAC HALEVI. *Main Institutions of Jewish Law*, 2nd ed. 2 vols. London, 1936, 1939.

Chaim I. Waxman

Herzog, Ya'acov David   [1921–1972]

Israeli diplomat; Jewish scholar and orator.

Born in Dublin, Ireland, to Sarah and Rabbi Izhak Halevi Herzog, who was chief rabbi of Dublin (1919), the Irish Free State (1925–1936), Palestine (1936–1948), and Israel's first chief rabbi. Ya'acov's older brother Hayim became a major figure in the Israel Defense Forces; Israel's ambassador to the United Nations; and sixth president of Israel. Ya'acov served as Israel's ambassador to Canada from 1960 to 1963. Known also as a prominent traditional Jewish scholar, he was offered the position of chief rabbi of Great Britain. He accepted another position, however, that of director general of the prime minister's office of Israel, where he served from 1966 until his death. A collection of some of his speeches and articles was published posthumously as *A People That Dwells Alone* (London, 1975).

Chaim I. Waxman

Heskayl, Sasson   [1860–1932]

Iraqi statesman and economist.

Heskayl was born in Baghdad where his father, Hakam Heskayl, was the leading rabbinical authority. After graduating from the Alliance Israélite Universelle, he went to Vienna to study economics and law. His knowledge of foreign languages (French, German, English, Turkish, Persian, Arabic, and Hebrew) enabled him to become chief translator for the *vilayet* of Baghdad upon his return from Europe. In 1908, Heskayl was elected a representative of Baghdad to the Chamber of Deputies in Constantinople (now Istanbul). He spent several years there and was

adviser to the ministry of commerce and agriculture. Upon returning to Baghdad in 1920, he was appointed minister of finance in the first government headed by Abd al-Rahman al-Naqib, retaining that post (with a short interruption) for the next five years. In 1925 he was elected to parliament and was chairman of its finance committee. He died in Paris while undergoing medical treatment.

At the 1921 CAIRO CONFERENCE, which was convened by Winston Churchill, the British colonial secretary, and decided upon the election of Emir FAISAL I as king of Iraq, Heskayl was one of two representatives of the government of Iraq, the other one being Ja'far al-ASKARI. He was knighted in 1923.

During negotiations with the British Petroleum Company, Heskayl demanded that oil revenue be calculated on the basis of gold. His demand was reluctantly accepted. This concession benefited Iraq's treasury during World War II, when the pound sterling plummeted. Some historians maintain that Heskayl's confrontation with the British eventually caused his removal as minister of finance.

[*See also:* Jews in the Middle East]

BIBLIOGRAPHY

BASRI, MIR. *A 'lam al-Yahud fi al-Iraq al-Hadith*. Jerusalem, 1983.
REJWAN, NISSIM. *The Jews of Iraq: 3000 Years of History and Culture*. London, 1986.

Sasson Somekh

Hess, Moses   [1812–1875]

German Zionist.

A committed German Jewish Socialist and a contemporary of Karl Marx and Friedrich Engels, Hess spent much of his life in Paris and is sometimes thought of as the first Zionist Communist. He collaborated with Marx and Engels in 1830s and the 1840s, but he rejected their economic determinism and broke with them after 1848. In 1862 Hess wrote *Rome and Jerusalem,* in which he argued that the Jews, like the Italians, should establish their own state. This book later influenced such proponents of Zionism as Theodor HERZL. Hess believed that anti-Semitism and German nationalism went hand in hand and that with the growth of the latter, a Jewish state was imperative. A firm adherent of peaceful change rather than violent revolution, in *Rome and Jerusalem* Hess extolled the ethics of love, harmony, and cooperation. Once in their own country, Hess claimed, the duty of the Jews was to prepare themselves for a

Socialist "Sabbath of History," which would mark the liberation not just of the Jews but of all mankind.

BIBLIOGRAPHY

ELON, AMOS. *The Israelis*. New York, 1971.
LAQUEUR, WALTER. *A History of Zionism*. New York, 1976.

Zachary Karabell

Hezb-e Islami

Afghan Islamist political party.

The radical Hezb-e Islami, or Party of Islam, was formed in 1977 in Pakistan, as a result of a split from the JAMI'AT-E ISLAMI party. The largest of the two branches of Hezb-e Islami is led by Golbuddin HEKMATYAR; a smaller branch is led by Maulawi Yunis Khalis.

One the best organized, most successful organizations active in the Afghan war of resistance (1978–1992), Hezb-e Islami, which is strongly anti-Western and anti-American, advocates the establishment of an Islamic state and the imposition of SHARI'A in Afghanistan. Because the party was able to gain considerable support from the Pakistani government and other Islamic countries, it received a large share of the international aid given to the fighters of the war of resistance.

BIBLIOGRAPHY

ROY, OLIVIER. *Islam and Resistance in Afghanistan*. Cambridge, U.K., 1986.

Grant Farr

Hezbollahi

An appellation meaning "pertaining to the party of God."

Hezbollahi has gained popular currency in postrevolutionary Iran to designate, usually in a derogatory manner, zealous, often violent supporters of the most radical factions in the Islamic government. The term was first used in this way in 1979, when the Hezbollahi branch—headed by Hadi Ghaffari—of the Islamic Republican party provided the storm troops for breaking up rival demonstrations and gatherings in the early days of the Islamic revolution.

BIBLIOGRAPHY

BAKHASH, SHAUL. *The Reign of the Ayatollahs*. New York, 1986.

Neguin Yavari

Hibbat Zion

First international Zionist organization to be founded; established in the aftermath of the Russian pogroms of 1881/82.

Hibbat Zion was formed in 1884 by Dr. Leo PINSKER, a Russian physician who practiced in Odessa. Its membership combined European Jewish traditionalists—long committed to support the growing scholarly Jewish community in Palestine—with newly recruited secular nationalists from Eastern Europe. Dr. Pinsker had been appalled by the POGROMS and realized that even assimilated Jews could not consider themselves safe in their adopted lands. In his pamphlet *Auto-Emancipation,* Pinsker argued that Jews in the DIASPORA could not afford to remain passive in the hopes of either divine redemption or some voluntary ending of ANTI-SEMITISM. Instead Jews had to liberate themselves by reconstituting themselves as a nation in a land of their own.

Orthodox rabbis joined Hibbat Zion assuming that secular nationalists could be won back to piety. These assumptions were translated into policies: Those who wished to settle as farmers in Palestine and who received financial aid from Hibbat Zion had to observe Judaism and its traditions. For secular nationalists, like Dr. Pinsker, this was a troublesome policy. The enthusiasm initially engendered by the creation of Hibbat Zion waned as the uneasy alliance experienced financial crises and internal disputes. Nevertheless, a few colonies were established and aided in Palestine, such as PETAH TIQVAH (founded in 1878), and the educational aspect of the movement resulted in the Zionist thought and actions of other individuals and groups in Eastern Europe.

BIBLIOGRAPHY

LUZ, EHUD. *Parallels Meet Religion and Nationalism in the Early Zionist Movement (1882–1904)*. Philadelphia, 1988.

Donna Robinson Divine

Hidd

Second largest of six towns on the island of Muharraq in Bahrain.

Hidd's population is nearing 10,000 according to 1990 estimates, with significant growth since 1970. Prior to the oil boom of the 1970s, Hidd was a small village where fishing and pearl diving were the main occupations. Today, wealthy Bahrainis from the capital, Manama, have built second homes and resorts there—the farthest town from the causeway-bridge from the main island of Bahrain.

BIBLIOGRAPHY

The Gulf Handbook, 1978. London, 1978.
The World Factbook, 1992. Washington, D.C., 1993.

Emile A. Nakhleh

Hiddaw, Husayn

Syrian military leader.

Of Druze descent, Husayn Hiddaw was included in the loose coalition of independent officers who were generally opposed to the Ba'th party. In commanding an armored unit in Damascus, Captain Hiddaw made last-ditch attempts to resist Adib SHISHAKLI's February 25, 1954, fall from power. He further attempted to resist the ouster by legal means and also failed at this. He was included in the January 12, 1958, delegation to Cairo to pledge Ba'th support of Egypt's President Nasser in combating the growing communist movement. Hiddaw was also a leader of the March 28, 1962, coup.

BIBLIOGRAPHY

SEALE, PATRICK. *The Struggle for Syria: A Study of Post-War Arab Politics, 1945–1958.* London, 1958.

Charles U. Zenzie

High Commissioner

Position held by the senior official in the mandates created at the end of World War I by the League of Nations.

After their defeat in World War I, Germany and the Ottoman Empire were forced to relinquish control of their colonies to the League of Nations. Under the MANDATE SYSTEM, these territories were then apportioned by the League to Australia, Belgium, France, Great Britain, Japan, New Zealand, and South Africa. Mandates were classified as types A, B, or C, with the areas of the Middle East formerly under Ottoman control designated as class A. The mandatory powers were to use this temporary control to prepare the territories for eventual independence. The role of the high commissioner was to act as the representative of the mandatory government in each territory.

Bryan Daves

High Commissioners, Palestine

The high commissioner was the head of the Palestine government during the period of British rule (late 1917–May 1948).

Except for a short period (December 1917–June 1920) of British military government, PALESTINE was run by a civilian administration headed by a high commissioner, who reported directly to London. Though entrusted by the League of Nations to Great Britain as a mandate, which entailed the "development of self-governing institutions," Palestine was governed as a British crown colony; that is, full power and authority were vested in the high commissioner. His powers included censorship, deportation, detention without trial, demolition of homes of suspects, and collective punishment, powers that were used against both Palestinian and Jewish communities. The high commissioner was assisted by an executive council consisting of a chief secretary, attorney general, and treasurer and an advisory council consisting of British officials and prominent Arab and Jewish appointees from 1920 to 1923, after which its members were all officials. The high commissioner proposed to the Arab and Jewish communities the establishment of self-governing institutions for Palestine, in particular a legislative council, but due to the conflicting political goals of the two communities and Britain's BALFOUR DECLARATION, which favored a Jewish national home in Palestine, such institutions were never established, and the high commissioner continued to exercise sole authority over Palestine until the end of the mandate.

The Palestine government was headed by seven high commissioners, whose names and dates of appointments were as follows:

Sir Herbert Samuel	July 1, 1920
Lord Plumer	August 14, 1925
Sir John Chancellor	November 1, 1928
Sir Arthur Wauchope	November 20, 1931
Sir Harold MacMichael	March 3, 1938
Viscount Gort	October 31, 1944
Sir Alan Gordan Cunningham	November 21, 1945

BIBLIOGRAPHY

PALESTINE GOVERNMENT. *A Survey of Palestine for the Information of the Anglo-American Committee of Inquiry.* 2 vols. Jerusalem, 1946. Reprint. Washington, D.C. 1991.
PATAI, RAPHAEL, ed. *Encyclopedia of Zionism and Israel.* 2 vols. New York, 1971.

Philip Mattar

Hijab

Arabic word for "drape," "screen," or "veil."

Hijab usually refers to the veil traditionally worn by women in Muslim societies. The basis for the wearing of the hijab is chapter 33, verse 53 of the Qur'an, the holy book of Islam, which states that the wives of the Prophet (Muhammad) should be addressed from behind a curtain. In the modern era, the hijab has become highly politicized, with countries such as Turkey outlawing the hijab and countries such as Iran calling for its use.

BIBLIOGRAPHY

RUTHVEN, MALISE. *Islam in the World.* New York, 1984.

Zachary Karabell

Hijaz

Arid mountainous region of Saudi Arabia.

The Hijaz is bounded by the Red Sea on the west, Jordan on the north, and the regions of Najd on the east and Asir on the south. Extending over 620 miles (1,000 km) from north to south and about 185 miles (800 km) wide, it comprises the Saudi districts of Mecca, Medina, al-Bahah, and Tabuk. The name Hijaz suggests the obstacle created by the region's main geographical feature, a broken, rocky escarpment that rises 3,280 feet (1,000 m) or more a few miles from the seacoast. The traditional cities of the Hijaz are Mecca, Medina, al-Ta'if, and Jidda; to these can be added the newly-developing port of Yanbu al-Bahr. These cities account for at least three-quarters of the Hijaz's population of over 4 million.

Southern Hijaz landscape, 1948. (D.W. Lockhard)

The name Hijaz can be traced back to the beginnings of Islam. Rarely completely independent, it was locally governed by native *sharifi* families for almost a millennium until it achieved recognition as a separate kingdom from 1916 to 1925, after which it was incorporated by the Saudis into their realm.

BIBLIOGRAPHY

Encyclopedia of Islam, 2nd ed.

Khalid Y. Blankinship

Hijaz Railroad

Railroad connecting Damascus and Medina.

Built during the reign of Sultan Abdülhamit II, the Hijaz Railroad is 1,308 kilometers (811 mi.) long. It is so named because Medina, its eastern terminus, is located in a western region of the Arabian Peninsula called the Hijaz. Abdülhamit built the railroad to facilitate the movement of the Ottoman army, thus allowing for closer Ottoman control of southern Syria and the Hijaz. In addition, easier movement of religious pilgrims to Mecca, would buttress his claim to be caliph of the Muslims. Additional branches were built connecting the main line to Haifa, Basra, Lydda, and Ajwa, bringing total trackage to 1,650 kilometers (1,023 mi.) in 1918.

The railroad, which cost 4 million Turkish liras (equivalent to about 15 percent of the Ottoman budget), was financed without foreign loans. Arguing that the railroad was essential to the protection of Mecca and Medina, and that it should be financed and operated by Muslims, the Ottoman government raised between one-third and one-fourth of the total cost through contributions from its subjects and donations from Muslims around the world. The remainder was financed by the state.

As the Ottomans began to design and construct the railroad in 1900, they wanted to build the railroad without foreign assistance. Yet because all previous railroads and public utilities had been built and managed by foreigners, their experience was limited. Thus, the goals of speeding construction and limiting costs dictated the use of foreign assistance. Ottoman military officers, led by Mehmed Ali Paşa, supervised the initial engineering and construction, assisted by an Italian engineer, La Bella. But incompetent surveying, maltreatment of workers, and financial problems limited progress in the first six months of construction to the preparation of twenty kilometers (12.5 mi.) of earthwork for tracks. As pressure from Constantinople (now Istanbul) to speed up construction increased, Mehmed Ali Paşa was removed and court-martialed.

His successor, Kazım Paşa, de facto ceded Ottoman control over the technical aspects of construction to a German engineer, Heinrich Meissner. Meissner supplemented his largely foreign staff with Ottoman engineers trained in Europe. Ottoman soldiers pressed into service provided most of the labor force, though foreign workmen also were employed. The railroad reached Medina in August 1908. Over the next six years, facilities including storehouses, switching yards, and repair facilities were constructed.

Passenger service for the pilgrimage began in 1908. In 1914, operations included three weekly passenger trains from Damascus to Medina, and seven weekly trips from Damascus to Haifa. The run to Medina was scheduled to take fifty-six hours, although three days was average; the shorter run to Haifa was scheduled for eleven and a half hours.

During World War I, the Hijaz Railroad was central to the strategy of both the Ottoman army and the Arab army of Sharif Husayn that launched the ARAB REVOLT in 1916. For the Ottomans, a planned invasion of Egypt, defense of the Hijaz, and defense of southern Syria depended on control and extension of the railroad. Unable to confront 25,000 Ottoman troops directly, the Arab army directed raids against the railroad, disrupting service and wresting control of sections from the Ottomans. On October 1, 1918, the Ottoman Hijaz Railroad administration was replaced by an Arab general directorate.

BIBLIOGRAPHY

ISSAWI, CHARLES. *An Economic History of the Middle East and North Africa.* New York, 1982.
OCHSENWALD, WILLIAM. *The Hijaz Railroad.* Charlottesville, Va., 1980.
OWEN, ROGER. *The Middle East in the World Economy, 1800–1914.* London, 1981.
SHAW, STANFORD, and EZEL KURAL SHAW. *History of the Ottoman Empire and Modern Turkey.* Vol. 2, *Reform, Revolution, and Republic: The Rise of Modern Turkey, 1808–1975.* Cambridge, U.K., 1977.

David Waldner

Hikma University, al-

University founded by American Jesuits in Iraq in 1956.

The university was built in Za'franiya, on the southern edge of Baghdad, by American Jesuits. They have been engaged in education in that city since 1932, when they were invited by the Christian hierarchy to open a secondary school—Baghdad College.

Al-Hikma offered degrees in business administration, civil engineering, and literature; instruction was mainly in English. The student body was coeducational, with 95 percent Iraqis; the faculty was about 50 percent Iraqi. Enrollment grew slowly and was approaching 1,000 when the Ba'th government seized the university and expelled the Jesuits in 1968. The students enrolled at the time of nationalization continued their studies until graduation, then the university ceased to exist. The site was transformed into a technical institute.

In 1969, the Jesuits were also expelled from Baghdad College, which continued in existence as a secondary school attached to the Iraqi ministry of education.

BIBLIOGRAPHY

Al-Hikma Yearbook. Baghdad, 1969.

John J. Donohue

Hikmet, Nazim   [1902–1963]

Turkish poet, playwright, and novelist.

Turkey's foremost twentieth-century poet, Nazim Hikmet singlehandedly modernized Turkish poetry and all subsequent Turkish literature. Although his poems were banned in Turkey after 1936 and began to reappear only after his death, since then they have been translated into over fifty languages.

Born in Salonika, where his father worked in the Foreign Service, Hikmet grew up in Istanbul. During the Allied occupation following World War I, he left for Anatolia and, horrified by the famine he witnessed en route, made his way to Moscow. Introduced to Marxism and Russian futurism, he broke with Ottoman literary conventions and in the course of making use not only of free verse but of spoken Turkish and the rich tradition of Turkish folk poetry, he developed a lyric voice at once personal and political. Yet his Marxism proved no more programmatic than his avant-gardism and evolved into a lifelong commitment to social justice, in the same way that his poetic experiments came to include utilizing even Ottoman meters when necessary.

Historically, Hikmet's career coincided with the founding and unsettled early years of the Turkish republic. His revolutionary poetry gained him a wide readership, but his radical politics got him into trouble with the authorities. He spent a total of eighteen years in prison, where he met the peasants and workers who became characters in his epic verse-novel, *Human Landscapes* (1982). Released in a general amnesty in 1950 and forced to flee Turkey, he died in Moscow after thirteen years of permanent exile.

BIBLIOGRAPHY

HIKMET, NAZIM. *Poems of Nazim Hikmet.* Tr. by Randy Blasing and Mutlu Konuk. New York, 1994.

Mutlu Konuk Blasing

Hilal, al–

Monthly magazine founded in 1892 in Cairo by Jurji Zaydan.

Probably the oldest magazine in Arabic. Until World War I, *al-Hilal* was the most important journalistic forum of the Arab *Nahda* (Renaissance) in all its aspects. Later it became a platform for progressive Egyptian literature; after nationalization under Gamal Abdel Nasser, it adapted, increasingly, the *Reader's Digest* model in format and content.

BIBLIOGRAPHY

PHILIPP, THOMAS. *Gurgi Zaidan: His Life and Thought.* Wiesbaden, Ger., 1979.
———. *The Syrians in Egypt.* Stuttgart, Ger., 1985.

Thomas Philipp

Hilla, al–

Central Iraqi town of historical, commercial, and strategic importance.

One of the most important towns of Ottoman Iraq, al-Hilla stands upon both banks of the Euphrates river, adjacent to the ancient city of Babylon, about thirty miles (48 km) below Musayyab (also Musayyib, Musaiyib) and some sixty-five miles (105 km) by the course of the river above Diwaniyya. Surrounded by gardens and fruit trees, al-Hilla is the center of a district producing wheat, barley, and dates in quantities sufficient for export. Construction of the Hindiyya barrage (dam) by Sir William Willcocks in 1913 rectified a deteriorating water supply to the region, which had developed during the second half of the nineteenth century. In addition to its commercial significance, al-Hilla had a strategic importance second only to Baghdad and Basra. Positioned midway between these two cities in the midst of a populous area, it served both military and administrative purposes and afforded a base for operations against insurgents in the surrounding countryside.

Albertine Jwaideh

Hillel, Shlomo   [1923–   ]

Israeli politician.

Hillel, a native of Baghdad, emigrated to Palestine in 1934, and completed high school at Gimnasya Herzliyya in Tel Aviv. In 1945 he was a founder of Kibbutz Ma'agan Michael and the Ayalon Institute, a clandestine Haganah armaments factory. From 1947 to 1951 he worked in Iraq, Syria, Lebanon, Egypt, and Iran as emissary of the Haganah and the immigration authorities. In Iraq, especially, Hillel organized the massive airlift of Jews that became known as Operation EZRA AND NEHEMIA.

After serving in the Knesset (1953–1959), Hillel was Israel's ambassador to Guinea and the Ivory Coast, and a member of Israel's mission to the United Nations (1959–1969). He was minister of police (1969–1973) and subsequently minister of the interior as well (1973–1977). In 1977 he was elected to the Knesset, of which he was speaker from 1984 to 1988. Since 1989 he has been world chairman of KEREN HAYESOD–UNITED JEWISH APPEAL.

Hillel wrote *Operation Babylon* (1987) which was translated into English, French, German, Spanish, Russian, and Arabic.

Nissim Rejwan

Hilmi, Ahmad   [?–1963]

Palestinian politician during British mandate.

Born Ahmad Hilmi Abd al-Baqi in Palestine, Hilmi was active in banking and used his financial leverage for nationalist ends, founding the Arab National Bank in 1930 and later purchasing the newspaper FILASTIN. He used wartime profits from deposits held in the Arab National Bank to invest in Palestine's industry and commerce. Ownership of *Filastin* provided him with a platform from which to air his anti-Zionist, Palestinian nationalist views.

Throughout his life, Hilmi was associated with the ISTIQLAL (Independence) PARTY. This strongly nationalist party was ideologically rooted in Arab nationalism of the World War I era. In April 1936, the general strike in Palestine led to the formation of the ARAB HIGHER COMMITTEE (AHC), of which Hilmi became an independent member. In October 1938, the AHC was outlawed, and Hilmi was arrested and deported to the Seychelles. In 1939, he and Awni Abd al-Hadi urged the AHC to accept the British white paper, which signaled a change in British policy by restricting the levels of Jewish immigration to Palestine. This display of moderation caused the mandate authorities to allow Hilmi to return to Palestine.

In July 1948, the Administrative Council for Palestine was founded in Gaza under the auspices of the Arab League. It was replaced by an all-Palestine government claiming authority over the newly founded state of Israel, the Gaza Strip, and the Jordan-held West Bank. Hilmi was appointed to head the all-Palestine government, which included Jamal HUSAYNI as foreign minister. Although this government was recognized by all the Arab states except Jordan, Hilmi had no authority, and the government was weak and powerless. It was officially laid to rest with Hilmi's death.

[*See also:* Mandate System]

BIBLIOGRAPHY

BRAND, LAURIE A. *Palestinians in the Arab World: Institution Building and the Search for a State.* New York, 1988.

Lawrence Tal

Hilmi, Kasımpaşalı

Ottoman painter.

Hilmi was associated with the realist movement in Ottoman painting of the mid-to-late nineteenth century. He and painters like Ahmet Seker painted landscapes around Constantiniple (now Istanbul), such as Yıldız Palace, and landscapes of distant places, using photographs as models.

Elizabeth Thompson

Hilu, Charles   [1911–   ]

President of Lebanon, 1964–1969.

Hilu was born in Beirut to a MARONITE (Christian) family. He received a French education, earning law degrees from the Jesuit St. Joseph University and the French School of Law in Beirut. He founded the newspaper *L'Eclair du Nord* in Aleppo (1932) and *Le Jour* in Beirut (1934). In the 1930s, Hilu was sympathetic to the ideology of the PHA-LANGE party and was one of its founding members. He later realized that despite his reluctance to cooperate with the Arab world, the narrow sectarian base of the party would thwart his political ambitions. He later presented himself as a moderate Maronite politician who did not oppose good ties with the Arab world.

Hilu was Lebanese minister to the Vatican in 1947 and headed Catholic Action of Lebanon. He held several ministerial positions in the 1950s and 1960s,

and he was serving as minister of education in 1964 when he was elected president. His election was made possible because of his close association with Chehabism; when Fu'ad CHEHAB could not be persuaded to run for another term, Hilu emerged as a candidate who could carry forward the legacy of Chehabism. Chehab later said that his selection of Hilu was one of his biggest mistakes.

Hilu's administration is remembered for allowing the military-intelligence apparatus to control the affairs of the state. Some army officers in the military intelligence bureau had more power than some elected representatives. Hilu is blamed for the increasingly dangerous situation in Lebanon caused by the unwillingness of the state to respond to Israel's attacks and to Palestine Liberation Organization (PLO) activities. Many Lebanese, particularly those living in south Lebanon, thought that he forfeited the sovereignty of southern Lebanese territory. To protect himself against Maronite critics, he solidified his alliance with such conservative Maronite organizations as the Phalange party and the NATIONAL LIBERAL PARTY of Camille CHAMOUN.

The worst crisis of Hilu's administration occurred in 1969, when Lebanese army troops fought with the PLO and its Lebanese allies (in the wake of attacks on them by ISRAEL within Lebanon). Hilu wanted to use heavy-handed methods in dealing with the PLO, but his Sunni prime minister, Rashid KARAME, refused to deal with the PLO, which at the time was the best hope for the restoration of Palestinian rights after the Arabs' humiliating defeat with ARAB–ISRAEL WAR of 1967. The failures of Hilu's administration discredited Chehabism, thereby causing the Chehabi candidate, Ilyas Sarkis, to lose the presidential election of 1970.

Since his retirement, Hilu has lived a quiet life. He continues to make political statements but refrains from taking provocative or extremist stands. He is respected within the Maronite community.

As'ad AbuKhalil

Hilu, Pierre   [1928–   ]

Maronite politician in Lebanon.

Hilu, a wealthy industrialist born in Beirut, is a deputy representing the district of Alay. He was first elected in 1972, and became a cabinet minister for the first time in 1973. He was mentioned as a possible presidential candidate in 1988, but he refused to succeed Amin JUMAYYIL without Muslim support. Hilu is still considered a potential presidential candidate, especially because his ties with Syria have been good over the years. He was one of the few Maronite deputies to seek reelection in 1992.

As'ad AbuKhalil

Hindu Kush Mountains

Main mountain chain in Afghanistan, extending to China; part of the great chain of central Asian mountains.

Beginning west of Kabul, capital of Afghanistan, the Hindu Kush stretch some six hundred miles (965 km) east across the northern tip of Pakistan and Jammu and Kashmir to the Pamir and Karakoram mountains on the border of China. The highest peak is Tirich Mir at 25,260 feet (7,700 m). Both the Indus and Amu Darya rivers spring from the Hindu Kush. It is the main mountain chain in Afghanistan, and during the nineteenth century, it marked the limits of British expansion north of India and the unofficial and often-contested boundary between Russia and Britain in their struggle for hegemony in Central Asia. After World War II, the Hindu Kush divided American from Russian influence in Afghanistan, with the bulk of United States aid flowing south and the bulk of Russian aid going to the north. After the 1979 Soviet intervention and invasion of Afghanistan, the Hindu Kush became one of the main refuges of Afghan guerrillas in their struggle to force the Soviets out of the country.

BIBLIOGRAPHY

DUPREE, LOUIS. *Afghanistan.* Princeton, N.J., 1973.
LENCZOWSKI, GEORGE. *The Middle East in World Affairs.* 4th ed. Ithaca, N.Y., 1980.

Zachary Karabell

Hinnawi, Sami al-

A Syrian colonel who, on August 14, 1949, overthrew his predecessor, Husni al-Za'im, as military dictator of Syria and had him shot.

Hinnawi's coup came barely four and a half months after ZA'IM had staged his military coup, the first in Syria's modern history. Hinnawi collaborated with the PEOPLE'S PARTY, which was disposed towards Iraq. He invited Hashim al-ATASI to form a government. A constituent assembly to draw a new constitution was elected, women voted for the first time, and all the political parties were legalized, with the exception of the Communist party and the rightist SOCIALIST COOPERATIVE PARTY. Atasi then became president

of the republic. Discussions with Iraqi officials to bring about a union between Syria and royalist Iraq were then in full sway. But Syrian republicanists and the army were not happy with the proposed union. On December 19, 1949, Colonel Adib SHISHAKLI overthrew Hinnawi, whom he charged with treason and conspiracy with a foreign power, a reference to the proposed union with Iraq.

BIBLIOGRAPHY

PETRAN, TABITHA. *Syria.* London, 1972.
SEALE, PATRICK. *The Struggle for Syria, 1945–1958,* 2nd ed. London, 1986.

Abdul-Karim Rafeq

Hirsch, Maurice de   [1831–1896]

German–Jewish financier.

Born into an old family of German–Jewish bankers in Bavaria, Hirsch added to his considerable fortune in the 1870s by financing the Balkan railroad between Istanbul and Europe. In 1891, he created the JEWISH COLONIZATION ASSOCIATION and sponsored an unsuccessful plan to resettle Russian Jews in Argentina. The association was funded at over 35 million U.S. dollars, and in addition to colonization, Hirsch promoted education for Jews in Palestine by funding the Alliance Israélite Universelle. His support was sought by prominent advocates of Zionism, including Theodor Herzl.

BIBLIOGRAPHY

Encyclopedia Judaica. New York, 1971.
SACHAR, HOWARD. *A History of Israel.* Oxford, 1977.

Zachary Karabell

Histadrut

Israeli federation of labor.

The Histadrut was founded in 1920, with a membership of 5,000. In 1930 it had 28,000 members; in 1940, 112,000; in 1950, 352,000; in 1960, 689,000; in 1970, 1,038,000; and in 1980 1,417,000. By 1992 it had approximately 1.6 million members.

The Histadrut, which has often been called a state within the state, acts as an umbrella organization for trade unions. It has also played an important role in the development of agriculture, wholesale and retail marketing of food and other products, rural settlement, industry, construction and housing, industry, banking, insurance, transportation, water, health, and social services.

Following the creation of the State of Israel in 1948, the Histadrut handed some of its educational functions as well as its employment exchanges to the government. In recent years, it has sold a number of commercial concerns to the private sector.

In the 1920s, under the British mandate, the Histadrut's role was to help develop the Jewish economy in Palestine. To this end, in 1921 it set up Bank Hapoalim (The Workers' Bank), and in 1923, Hevrat Ovdim (The Workers' Company or Cooperative Federation) was founded. This was to become a holding company for most of the Histadrut's wide range of economic enterprises.

By 1927, when the Solel Boneh construction and industrial group first went bankrupt, the importance of reinvesting profits and maintaining an independent capital base was understood. From the late 1920s onward, economic enterprises were directed toward capital accumulation so as to avoid reliance on outside sources of finance. Solel Boneh, as well as being the largest construction company in the pre-independence period, had investments in industry. Its subsidiary, Koor, owned the Phoenicia glass works, the Vulcan foundry, and other industrial companies. The policy of financial independence was successful until the 1980s, when a number of Histadrut bodies got into serious financial difficulties.

By 1930 the retail cooperative, Hamashbir, the insurance company, Hasneh, and other groups were incorporated into Hevrat Ovdim. The Histadrut had become both a large employer as well as a trade union body. The basic structure has remained unchanged since the 1920s, but attitudes toward profits and dismissing workers have become more pragmatic and less socialist since the late 1980s.

Although about three-quarters of all wage earners in Israel are members of the Histadrut, this includes many who do no more than pay dues to its health fund, Kupat Cholim Clallit, the largest fund in the country. A share of the membership fee is passed on to the Histadrut by the health fund. Members of kibbutzim and other cooperatives are also automatically enrolled, as are those working in Histadrut enterprises. Although far fewer are, therefore, voluntary members, about 85 percent of the labor force is covered by collective labor agreements negotiated by the Histadrut. About forty trade unions, representing a wide range of blue and white collar workers in the public and private sectors, are affiliated. While the Histadrut is highly centralized, professional workers' unions have a high degree of autonomy.

Elections are held every four years on a political party base, and the Labor party and its allies have had a majority since the Histadrut's foundation. Each party, in proportion to its share of the votes cast, nominates delegates to a forum that elects the central committee. The latter consists of members of the ruling coalition alone. Workers' committees at plant level are elected annually or biannually.

The Histadrut and its affiliated organizations (such as the kibbutzim) in 1991 were responsible for about 16 percent of industrial output, and 14 percent of industrial investment in Israel. Exports of these industries came to 1.4 billion U.S. dollars.

In that year, it was also responsible for 80 percent of agricultural output and exports, about 38 percent of the assets of the banking system (through Bank Hapoalim), 9 percent of insurance companies' assets (through Hasneh), the construction of 8 percent of homes being built, as well as large shares of retailing and wholesaling through its producer cooperatives and marketing organizations. It operated most of the country's buses through two large cooperatives and, both directly and through the kibbutzim, had a range of hotels and guest houses. About 70 percent of the population were members of Kupat Cholim Clallit, which provides medical insurance and services through clinics and hospitals. The Histadrut owns the *Davar* daily newspaper and a publishing company and has interests in the shipping and airline industries. Finally through Bank Hapoalim, it has large shareholdings in joint ventures with private sector industry.

During the 1980s, many of the Histadrut's companies and affiliates ran into serious financial difficulties. These included Koor, the kibbutzim, Kupat Cholim Clallit, and Bank Hapoalim. In all these cases, the government provided financial assistance and forced management changes. It remains to be seen if the Histadrut can regain control of these groups by buying shares back from the government or by other means.

The Histadrut's position in Israel has weakened both politically and economically. It has been weakened by grassroots alienation, by the dominance of right-wing parties in the Knesset between 1977 and 1992, and by its own lack of a clear socioeconomic message. It has faced serious financial difficulties in many of its economic enterprises and has had to be bailed out by Likud and Labor governments. The Labor party has distanced itself from the bureaucracy of the Histadrut, which it considers an electoral hindrance. This would have been inconceivable in the first half of the century.

BIBLIOGRAPHY

BROIDO, EPHRAIM. "Jewish Palestine: The Social Fabric." In *Palestine's Economic Future,* ed. by J.B. Hobman. London, 1946.

PREUSS, W. *The Labor Movement in Israel.* Jerusalem, 1965.
RIVLIN, PAUL. *The Israeli Economy.* Boulder, Colo., 1992.
SHALEV, MICHAEL. *Labour and the Political Economy in Israel.* New York, 1992.

Paul Rivlin

Historiography

Development of and trends in historical writing about the Middle East.

The historiography of the modern Middle East developed from three major components: orientalism, the scholarly discipline developed in Europe for studying the languages, religions, and cultures of non-European peoples; reportage on current conditions and affairs conducted by travelers, embassy officials, and missionaries; and from the Middle East itself, studies by scholars writing in either a European language or their national languages. Although the nineteenth- and early twentieth-century Orientalists devoted most of their scholarly energies to premodern literature and medieval history and culture, their eminence as university scholars and the convergence of their findings with more popular, romantic notions of the East as a land of fatalism, fanaticism, sexual irregularity, cruelty, and mystery conferred upon them high authority.

In the formulation of Edward Said in his book *Orientalism*, this convergence of scholarship and exotic romance during the heyday of imperialist endeavor amounted to a consistent pattern of subjugation by which European society mobilized its intellectual and imaginative resources to create an image of a supine, perverse, and religiously benighted East (particularly the Arab Muslim East). This enabled the Europeans to conceive of themselves as being situated on a higher moral and civilizational plane than that of people in the East, and thus it absolved them of any compunctions about imperial domination. Critics of Said's formulation have pointed out that most scholarly Orientalists devoted their careers to learning languages and editing Arabic, Persian, and Turkish manuscripts, and that Oriental studies only occasionally overlapped imperialist enterprise. Nevertheless, Orientalists acted as advisers on Islamic matters for imperialist governments—for example, Snouck Hurgronje (1857–1936) for the Dutch in Indonesia, Carl Becker (1876–1933) for the Germans in East Africa, and entire generations of French scholars in Algeria. During both world wars, Orientalist scholars were enlisted into virtually all European governments' intelligence services, and to some extent the practice continues today.

In the absence of any academic specialty concerned primarily with the modern Middle East, Orientalists schooled in philosophy and medieval studies were the ones relied on for influential books and reports dealing with the recent history and the contemporary affairs of the Middle East. There were, for example, H. A. R. Gibb's *Modern Trends in Islam* (1947) and G. E. von Grunebaum's *Modern Islam: The Search for Cultural Identity* (1962). Although works of this sort were often insightful, they were not seen by their authors as constituting their primary intellectual work. A scholarly discipline specifically devoted to the history and conditions of the modern Middle East was largely lacking until after World War II.

Reportage, the second component of the study of the modern Middle East, was first practiced by a broad diversity of people in the nineteenth century. Travel accounts were written by Orientalists like Edward Lane (1801–1876; *Manners and Customs of the Modern Egyptians,* 1836) and Edward G. Browne (1862–1926; *A Year amongst the Persians,* 1927); by adventurers like Charles Doughty (1843–1926; *Travels in Arabia Deserta,* 1888) and John Louis Burckhardt (1774–1817; *Notes on the Bedouins and Wahabys,* 1830); by missionaries like William Gifford Palgrave (1826–1888; *Personal Narrative of a Year's Journey through Central and Eastern Arabia,* 1865); and by military men like Richard Burton (1921–1890; *Personal Narrative of a Pilgrimage to El-Medina and Meccah,* 1855–1856), not to mention myriad novelists, poets, aristocrats, and tourists. The accuracy and slant of these works varied enormously, but today they constitute a major source for the history of the period, because of their information about both actual conditions and European attitudes.

European diplomats contributed a less colorful but similarly abundant literature in the form of consular reports on conditions abroad and books written either about their experiences or about the history of the country they served in. Notable authors in this vein include the Austrian Joseph von Hammer-Purgstall (1774–1856), who wrote a 10-volume *Geschichte des Osmanischen Reichs* (1827–1835), and the Englishmen John MALCOLM (1769–1833) and Percy SYKES (1867–1945), both whom wrote histories of Persia. Missionaries contributed a similar literature, both in the form of reports and memoirs, but they focused primarily on non-Muslim populations.

After World War II, the study of the modern Middle East slowly gained acceptance as a field of study in history and political science departments, particularly in American universities. Around 1960 several scholars published a small number of broad interpretive works that shaped American studies on the subject up to the 1980s. Among these were Manfred Halpern (1924–   ; *The Politics of Political Change in the Middle East and North Africa,* 1963), Daniel Lerner (1917–1980; *The Passing of Traditional Society in the Middle East,* 1958), John C. Campbell (1911–   ; *The Defense of the Middle East,* 1958), and Bernard Lewis (1916–   ; *The Emergence of Modern Turkey,* 1961). The general ideas in these and similar works underlay the development of Middle East regional or foreign area studies, a distinctively American field of university study devoted to training specialists to help advance U.S. diplomatic and economic interests in the region. The emphasis on secularism, economic and political "modernization," military affairs, and Cold War geopolitics in influential works of this period evolved more directly as a response to governmental needs than was the case with the work of the earlier Orientalists, but the publications themselves were less romantic and imaginative and more in keeping with the general academic social science literature of the period. In Europe, at the same time, scholars in the Orientalist tradition lessened their involvement with current affairs as decolonization removed their countries from direct responsibilities in the region. Indigenous recruitment of new scholars declined, but the number of students of Middle Eastern nationality seeking a European education in this field increased.

The 1979 Islamic revolution in Iran challenged many of the approaches to the Middle East then current. Religion, which modernization theory had seen as a declining force, resumed a central role in the region. A decade later, the Cold War, which had prompted scholars to deal with Middle East politics according to the East–West polarity, dissolved, leaving specialists on the modern Middle East to reconsider their earlier models and definitions. Students of Islamic religion, law, and philosophy, the heirs of the earlier Orientalists, unexpectedly gained notice as commentators on contemporary issues. Whether scholars working on understanding the current of religious reassertion could escape the perils of overgeneralization, Orientalist stereotyping, and subordination to Western political interests remained to be seen, however.

The third component of modern Middle Eastern historiography consists of scholars who are native to the region writing in European or local languages. Some of the most perceptive observers writing in Europe and the United States after World War II were of Middle Eastern family origin; for example, Albert Hourani (1915–1993) was of Lebanese parentage but born in England, and Elie Kedourie (1926–1991) and Majid Khadduri (1908–   ) from Iraq. The earlier, more narrowly Orientalist, phase of studies had been carried out mostly by Europeans.

Historically informative writing in Middle Eastern languages was done throughout the nineteenth and twentieth centuries, however. Although some of it fit into traditional literary genres such as chronicles, local biographical compilations, travel accounts (especially of trips to Mecca or to Europe), and collections of *fatawa,* the influence of European genres was also seen in a growing number of autobiographies and memoirs in the twentieth century and the rise of the novel as a mirror of everyday life.

Scholarship in the European academic style, or something akin to it, appeared gradually in the twentieth century. Turkish scholars like Mehmet Fuat Koprülü (1890–1966) and Ömer Lutfi Barkan (1902–1979), Iranians like Ahmad Kasravi (1890–1946) and Said Nafisi (1895–1966), and Arabs like Abd al-Aziz al-Duri (1919–   ) and Ihsan Abbas (1920–   ) were pioneers who gained international respect but wrote mostly in their native languages. Yet many such pioneers (except for Kasravi) concentrated on premodern projects in the Orientalist tradition and devoted only a portion of their scholarly efforts to modern affairs. A cadre of modern historians and political scientists writing in indigenous languages but adhering to European standards of documentation and argumentation did not appear in most Middle Eastern countries (excluding Israel with its European immigrants) until the 1970s or later.

At the conceptual level, scholarship on the modern Middle East has lagged behind the historiographical pace set by works on other parts of the world. Political and diplomatic affairs dominated historical writing until the 1970s when social and economic history slowly made an appearance, more often relating to pre-modern than to modern topics. The Lebanese economist Charles Issawi (1916–   ) and Israeli historian Gabriel Baer (1919–1982) were among the pioneering figures. Historiography in the Marxist tradition has not had as profound an impact in this area as it has elsewhere in the world, but historians like the Lebanese Hanna Batatu (1926–   ) and the Moroccan Abdalah Laroui (1933–   ), as well as a number of Europeans and Americans, have produced significant works from this standpoint. The influence of Michel Foucault (largely by way of the work of Edward Said) and of various postmodern approaches to history was beginning to be felt in the 1980s.

Yet the modern Middle East has not emerged as a crucial test case for any major school of historiographical inquiry, except, perhaps, for the theory of the rentier state in the field of political science. Hindrances to the development of a more fruitful, innovative historiography in and about the region include a continuing orientation of scholarship toward government needs and policies; a deep and persistent tendency, emanating in part from the Orientalist tradition, to attribute profound cultural uniqueness to the Islamic religion and to see it as the primary constitutive element in society and politics; enormous diversity of language and historical experience within an area loosely and inconveniently denominated the Middle East; and an undervaluation or fear of free historical inquiry within the region's government-controlled educational systems.

BIBLIOGRAPHY

BINDER, LEONARD, ed. *The Study of the Middle East.* New York, 1976.

RODINSON, MAXIME. *Europe and the Mystique of Islam.* Seattle, Wash., 1987.

SAID, EDWARD. *Orientalism.* New York, 1978.

Richard W. Bulliet

Hiyari, Ali al-

See Hayari, Ali al-

Hizb-e Azadi

See Freedom Movement

Hizbullah

Shi'ite political party in Lebanon, also known as Party of God.

Hizbullah was established in 1982 at the initiative of a group of Shi'ite clerics who were adherents of Shaykh Muhammad Husayn Fadlallah. By 1987 the

Hizbullah graffiti on a wall in Beirut, Lebanon. (© Yto Barrada)

party was the second most important Shi'a organization in Lebanon, after AMAL. It has consistently followed the political and theological line of the government of Iran and called (with various degrees of explicitness) for the creation of an Islamic republic in Lebanon. In pursuit of this goal, Hizbullah has coordinated its activities closely with the government of Iran and its representatives in the region. For years the party rejected any compromise with the Christians of Lebanon, Israel, and the United States. This hard-line approach appealed to many Shi'ites, who abandoned the Amal movement to join the Party of God. Those who left Amal tended to be young, radical, and poor.

Hizbullah is headed by the Consultative Council (MAJLES AL-SHURA), consisting of the highest-ranking party officials, some of whom are clerics. Its members' responsibilities include financial, military, judicial, social, and political affairs. The party's operations were geographically organized, with branches in the Biqa' Valley, the South, and the southern suburbs of Beirut. In the late 1980s the Politburo was created to handle day-to-day operations.

Hizbullah gained international attention in 1983 when press reports linked it to attacks against American, French, and Israeli targets in Lebanon and to the abduction of Western hostages in Lebanon. The party continues to deny responsibility for some of those acts. Syria left Hizbullah armed because it considered it to be pursuing a legitimate struggle against Israel's occupation of South Lebanon. The party's armed opposition to Israel's presence resulted in significant confrontations, and Israel's forces killed the party's leader, Abbas al-Musawi, in 1992. In the 1992 election, Hizbullah won eight seats in the parliament; it now participates in the political arena after years of underground existence. The party has been trying to change its image since 1992 and has entered into dialogue with many of its former enemies, both leftists and Christians. It is now headed by Shaykh Hasan Nasrallah.

BIBLIOGRAPHY

KRAMER, MARTIN. *The Moral Logic of Hizbullah.* Tel Aviv, 1987.

As'ad AbuKhalil

Hobeyka, Elie

A leader of the Lebanese Forces.

Elie Hobeyka was a close aide to Bashir Jumayyil, leader of the Maronite Catholic-dominated militias of the LEBANESE FORCES. Hobeyka's name came into prominence following Israel's siege of West Beirut in

1982. On September 16, 1982, with other militiamen, Hobeyka is known to have entered the SABRA AND SHATILA REFUGEE CAMPS, where he participated in the massacre of at least one thousand Palestinians. In 1984, internecine battles erupted between the followers of then-President Amin Jumayyil, who was also head of the PHALANGE party, and the Lebanese Forces led by Hobeyka. In December 1985, Hobeyka and the heads of two other militias, Walid JUMBLATT of the DRUZE-dominated Progressive Socialist party and Nabi BERRI of the Shi'a militia Amal, signed the Damascus Tripartite Agreement. The agreement, engineered by Syria, established strategic, educational, economic, and political cooperation between Lebanon and Syria. This accord placed Lebanon virtually under a Syrian protectorate.

Heavy opposition faced the Damascus agreement, especially in the Maronite and Sunni Muslim communities of Lebanon. President Jumayyil called for the support of Samir GEAGEA, who had replaced Hobeyka as head of the Lebanese Forces in the course of their internal conflicts. Early in January 1986, Hobeyka and his followers were defeated, and Hobeyka had to escape to Paris. He then went to Damascus.

BIBLIOGRAPHY

COLLELO, THOMAS, ed. Lebanon: A Country Study. Washington, D.C., 1989.

George E. Irani

Hoca

A Turkish honorific title from the Persian khwaja.

Hoca has been used variously for religious scholars, teachers, merchants, non-Muslims and people with other statuses in Islamic countries. The Ottomans used it for religious scholars and certain civil bureaucrats. The most famous hoca in the Ottoman Empire was NASRUDDIN HOCA (Juha in Arabic) the folkloric subject of humorous anecdotes who is believed to have lived in fourteenth-century Konya (Turkey).

Today, the title is still used in Turkey for teachers and religious scholars. In India, it is used by the followers of the Agha Khan (*imam,* or spiritual leader, of the Nizari Isma'ili sect of Shi'a Islam). In Egypt, the title is pronounced "KHAWAJA" and has been used primarily for foreign merchants and non-Muslims.

BIBLIOGRAPHY

"Khwadja." Encyclopedia of Islam, 2nd ed. Vol. 4.

Elizabeth Thompson

Hodeida

The major Red Sea port of Yemen since about 1849.

In 1849, the Ottoman Empire, during their second occupation of Yemen, selected Hodeida as their major base and point of entry from the Red Sea. In fact, Hodeida is not a natural deep-water port, and years of ballast dumping have made it incapable of accepting anything but small local ships. The major port activity now takes place at Ra's Khatib, a short distance north of Hodeida; this is a modern facility with wharves, unloading equipment, warehouses, and a transportation infrastructure that can accommodate modern freighters.

Ra's Khatib was constructed by the USSR as part of its foreign-aid program during the 1960s. It remained the key access point to Yemen until 1990, when the Yemen Arab Republic merged with the People's Democratic Republic of Yemen. Then, ADEN, one of the world's best natural harbors, became the primary port and economic capital of the new republic.

Manfred W. Wenner

Hoffman, Yoel [1937–]

Israeli writer and scholar.

Yoel Hoffman was brought to Eretz Yisrael as an infant by his Austro-Hungarian Jewish parents. His mother died a couple of years later and his father entrusted him to a day-care home, whose owner became Hoffman's beloved step-mother when he was seven.

Hoffman studied Hebrew literature and Western philosophy, but wrote his thesis on Far Eastern philosophy. He had lived in a Japanese Buddhist temple where he studied Chinese and Japanese texts with Zen monks. His academic work has ranged from comparative philosophy to interpretations of haiku and Zen koans.

A professor at Haifa University, Hoffman began to write fiction in his late forties. Although chronologically a member of the sixties "Generation of the State," his writing is in the forefront of the Israeli avant-garde of the nineties.

With his first collection of stories, *The Book of Joseph* (1988), Hoffman began his lyrical, experimental literary journey. But only with *Bernhardt* (1989) and *Christ of Fishes* (1991) did his creative genius burst forth. In atomistic texts of unusual typography and poetic rhythms, Hoffman blended Far Eastern with Western philosophy, minimalist aesthetics with unbridled imagination, murmuring of the heart with rationalism, and educated awareness with Nirvana-like trance.

Hoffmann's personae—middle-aged widowers, orphaned children, lonely aunts—often speak or remember in their German mother tongue, transliterated phonetically into Hebrew and glossed in the margins. Reconstructing a culturally and psychologically complex metabolism of loss, Hoffman's work negates boundaries between life and death, self and other, man and woman, human and animal.

BIBLIOGRAPHY

GOLD, NILI. "Bernhardt's Journey: The Challenges of Yoel Hoffmann's Writing." *Jewish Studies Quarterly* 1 no. 3 (1993/1994).
HERZIG, CHANA. "Migovhei Hagaleksiot Umiba'ad Lazekhukhit Hamagdelet" (From the Heights of Galaxies and through the Magnifying Glass). *Iton* 77 no. 113 (1989).
———. "Po'etikat Haperspektivot Shel Y. Hoffmann" (Y. Hoffman's Poetics of Perspectives). *Siman Kri'a,* August 22, 1991, pp. 169–181.

Nili Gold

Hogarth, David George [1862–1927]

British archeologist and intelligence officer.

As head of the Ashmolean Museum at Oxford University in England (1909–1927), Hogarth conducted numerous excavations in the Middle East. During World War I, he served as head of the Arab Bureau in Cairo, Egypt. His name is associated with the 1918 message to Sharif HUSAYN IBN ALI, king of the Hijaz, affirming Britain's intention to honor its war-time commitments to the Arabs. Hogarth was responsible for bringing T. E. LAWRENCE to the Arab Bureau.

BIBLIOGRAPHY

Dictionary of National Biography 1922–1930. London, 1937.
FROMKIN, DAVID. *A Peace to End All Peace.* New York, 1989.

Zachary Karabell

Hojjat al-Islam

See Molla

Holding Companies

Business enterprises for multiactivity firms in Turkey.

Holding companies in Turkey, unlike those elsewhere, are not founded to purchase shares in other companies but instead to maintain active entrepreneurial participation. As a result, all members of the business community are chairmen of multiactivity firms. Turkish holding companies have features that grew out of Turkey's state development after the fall of the Ottoman Empire. Their main characteristics include the following: (1) a strong interdependence between state-building and the development of Turkish business; (2) a background where the majority of entrepreneurs come from small trade or land owning; (3) a business mentality that is primarily commercial rather than industrial; (4) a strong tendency to diversify or to abandon current lines of production; (5) coexistence within the holdings of financial-sector activities, including real estate speculation; and (6) domination of horizontal, rather than vertical, integration.

After the decisive role of the Turkish state, these holding companies distinguish themselves by a continuity of family control. The most striking feature is the centralization of decision making by the mother company, whose board of directors is controlled, sometimes exclusively, by the members of the owner's family—except in the case of joint ventures. Many families at this level try to "professionalize the family" by promoting a first-class education in business administration, often abroad. Skilled managers are also added by marriages to founders' daughters.

Because of few legal requirements for the establishment of Turkish holding companies, a great number were developed—some labeled "slum holdings"—which weakened the bargaining position of both industry and the Chamber of Commerce. Big business, therefore, felt the need to create a new regulatory body, the Turkish Industrialists' and Business Association (TUSIAD). This acts as a lobby for big business and has a strong commitment to market economy and liberalism, including gender equality. Its board has several women, for example Güler Sabancı, a family-appointed heiress to the Sabancı business empire.

The growth of holding companies in Turkey started in the 1970s, reached its present size in 1983, and remains stable through the early 1990s. The dominance of the monopolies within the several business sectors is as shown in the following table.

Turkey's four largest holding companies represent Turkey's four wealthiest businessmen. Their ranking, established by *Fortune* magazine, is as follows: Vehbi Koç, 2 billion U.S. dollars; Sabancı, 1.2 billion; Mehmet Emin Karamehmet, 1.1 billion; Nejat Eczacibaşı, 1 billion.

Koç Holding dominates with the auto industry, durable household equipment, food, housing construction, energy, insurance, and banking. Sabancı

Distribution of Holding Companies by Sector

Product	Market Share %
Margarine	
Unilever-İş	52
Marsa (Sabancı)	20=72
Synthetic Yarn and Filament	
polyester filament	
SASA (Sabancı)	55
Sönmez	10=65
acrylic fiber	
AKSA (Dinçkök)	90
Yalova	10=100
Refrigerators	
Arçelik, Aygaz, Beko	
(Koç)	52
AEG (Profilo)	21
Profilo	26=99
Washing Machines	
Arçelik (Koç)	80.4
Profilo (Kamhi & Alarko)	19.6=100
Television and VCR	
Profilo Sony	
Beko (Hitachi, Nordmende)	9.5
(Koç)	29.4
Phillips (Sabancı)	8.7
Vestel (Polly Peck)	35.0=83
Tires	
Brissa (Sabancı/Japanese)	37
Goodyear (Sabancı)	32
Pirelli	31=100
Automobiles	
TOFAŞ (Koç)	51
Renault (Oyak)	44=95
Pharmaceuticals	
Eczacıbaşı	10.7
Turgut Holding	10.3
Roche (Swiss)	9.4
Bifa (Sabancı)	7.0
Sandoz (Swiss)	5.5
Ciba Geigy (Swiss)	4.4
Pfizer (USA)	4.0=51.3
Detergents	
Temsa (Lever-İş)	40
Mintax	40
Bio-Tursil	13=93

Holding governs 52 firms, which include textiles, autos, tires, insurance, tourism, banking, electronics, computers, and export. Karamehmet Holding controls 14.4 percent of Turkey's banking sector, with additional businesses in cement, textiles, chemicals, processed foods, machinery, and since 1980, exports. Eczacıbaşı Holding dominates pharmaceuticals but also controls sanitary equipment, ceramics, and paper goods.

In addition to the top four, seven corporations have holdings in one or two important fields, such as İş Bankası (est. 1930—Turkey's first private bank) with 65 companies and 20 percent of Turkey's total credit funds. ENKA, a developer/construction firm, has 30 companies in that field, with 50 percent of its 8,000 personnel employed abroad—mainly in Saudi Arabia, Libya, and the former Soviet Union. OYAK, established through Turkey's military pension fund, has mainly invested in the auto industry; this is a unique group, and its affiliation with Renault of France combines a military savings cooperative with multinational production. YASAR represents Aegean capital and concentrates on paint, fertilizer, and food, controlling 45 firms. DİNCKÖK is the giant in the textile industry. ST-FA is Turkey's largest entrepreneurial group, owning 15 firms and functioning mainly abroad, with specialties in highway, bridge, and port construction. PROFILO dominates the household electronics industry with 25 companies; it is mostly owned by the Jak Kamhi and the Alaton groups and is closely affiliated with French Thompson and Italian Olivetti.

BIBLIOGRAPHY

Buğra, Ayşe. "The Turkish Holding Company as a Social Institution." *Journal of Economics and Administrative Studies,* Demirgil Memorium 1, 4 (Winter: 1990): 35–51.

Nermin Abadan-Unat

Holmes, Frank   [1874–c. 1940]

Oil prospector.

Holmes traveled from New Zealand in the 1920s to the Persian/Arabian Gulf to seek oil-exploration concessions on behalf of a prospecting syndicate. He established friendly relations with several Gulf rulers and, in 1923, obtained concessions from Bahrain and from Kuwait and Saudi Arabia to explore for oil in the NEUTRAL ZONE. Holmes's concession in the Neutral Zone lapsed for lack of interest at the time by potential concession buyers. He maintained his concession in Bahrain through a partnership with the GULF OIL CORPORATION.

BIBLIOGRAPHY

Area Handbook for the Persian Gulf States. Washington, D.C., 1977.

Emile A. Nakhleh

Holocaust

Term commonly used in English (Hebrew, shoah) to denote the attempt made by the Third Reich (Nazi Germany, 1933–1945) to annihilate physically the Jews of the world, beginning with those in Europe. Approximately 5.8 million Jews were killed, the overwhelming majority between June 1941 (the beginning of the Nazi invasion of the USSR) and the end of World War II in Europe, May 1945.

Nazi ideology presented the Jews as a satanic, corrupting force in human culture and demanded their "removal," but what that meant was not clarified prior to the Nazi accession to power in 1933. Between 1933 and 1938, German Jews were disenfranchised, and many were deprived of their livelihoods and their homes. At the end of 1938 and in early 1939, just prior to the outbreak of World War II, several statements by Germany's dictator, Adolf Hitler, and others foreshadowed a more radical policy than merely pushing German Jews to emigrate, which had been the Nazi line up to that point and remained so until 1941. No actual plan to murder the Jews was prepared prior to early 1941.

After the Nazi occupation of Poland in September 1939, Polish Jews were herded into ghettoes, deprived of means of subsistence, and exposed to death by hunger and disease on a massive scale. The original German intention (1939–1940) was to expel all Jews into the USSR after concentrating them in an area in southeastern Poland; in 1940, the plan was changed to expel them to Madagascar, a plan never carried out. Germany's mass murder of Jews by shooting began with its invasion of the USSR, by special units (*Einsatzgruppen* and others) and ordinary police battalions, all of whom belonged to the SS, the elite Nazi organization headed by Heinrich Himmler.

In early September 1941, the first experimental gassing (not of Jews) took place at Auschwitz concentration camp (in Poland), followed by other such experiments. In December, gassing of Jews (and some five thousand Gypsies) in mobile vans began at Chelmno, and in the course of the spring of 1942, special death camps to murder Jews were established at Belzec, Sobibor, and Treblinka by teams that had gained experience by murdering close to 100,000 Germans in the so-called euthanasia program designed to "cleanse" the German race of genetically and mentally sick people. From January 1942, mass gassings of Jews began at the Auschwitz-Birkenau complex. From about March 1942 to August 1943, most of the 3 million Polish Jews as well as the Jews of the Baltic States, Slovakia, and Yugoslavia were murdered. Jews from Western and Central Europe were shipped to Auschwitz and elsewhere between July 1942, and October 1944. Jews from the Hungarian provinces were deported and sent to Auschwitz in 1944.

Very little help was provided by the United States and Britain, which closed their doors to Jewish immigration; the USSR was indifferent to their fate. The Nazis received full cooperation from their French, Slovak, and Croatian allies. The mufti of Jerusalem, Amin al-HUSAYNI, fled to Berlin to try to gather Muslim support for the Nazi anti-Jewish policy. A small number of courageous non-Jews in Europe endangered their lives to save Jews, including some churchmen, both Catholic and Protestant. Jewish armed resistance in the Warsaw Ghetto in 1943, lasted for months; it was followed by Jewish rebellions elsewhere in Nazi occupied territory and considerable Jewish participation in underground and partisan resistance all over Europe. From the end of 1944, when the Allied advance moved toward Germany and Poland, Jewish and non-Jewish inmates of concentration camps were force-marched crisscross through Germany; more than half of these people died. Probably some 200,000 European Jews survived the camps; a smaller number survived in hiding or as partisan fighters against the Germans.

BIBLIOGRAPHY

Encyclopedia of the Holocaust. New York, 1990.
HILBERG, RAUL. *The Destruction of the European Jews,* rev. ed. New York, 1985.

Yehuda Bauer

Holy Land

An overall characterization of the area in the Middle East connected with biblical and New Testament narratives.

Centered at Jerusalem, the Holy Land occurs in Jewish biblical and rabbinic literature and later in Christian tradition. The area was extended from modern Israel to Egypt through its association with the family of Jesus derived from the Gospels and to Asia Minor through its connections to the Virgin Mary and Saint John. As the dwelling place of the divine presence, the Holy Land has been, since the era of the Roman emperor Constantine in the fourth century, the location of pilgrimage sites. It began to take on concrete borders with the resurgence of Christian interest in the holy sites and the development of archaeology during the nineteenth century.

BIBLIOGRAPHY

BEN-ARIEH, YEHOSHUA. "Perceptions and Images of the Holy Land." In *The Land That Became Israel: Studies in Historical Geography,* ed. by Ruth Kark. Jerusalem, 1990.
PETERS, F. E. *Jerusalem and Mecca: The Typology of the Holy City in the Near East.* New York, 1986.

Reeva S. Simon

Holy Sepulchre, Church of the

Christian church, said to contain the tomb of Christ, in Jerusalem.

The Church of the Holy Sepulchre is in the Old City of JERUSALEM. Originally a group of separate churches in a single enclosure, in the fourth century Emperor Constantine sought to turn it into an architectural monument; but, it was the Crusaders who gave it its present form, combining its structures into one Romanesque church with a two-story facade. The interior has two principal sections: the rotunda—modeled on the Pantheon—which contains a shrine covering the tomb of Christ, and an Orthodox cathedral. Most Christian sects have appointed chapels and zealously guarded rights within the structure.

Jenab Tutunji

Homeland High Defense Council

Afghan defense organization.

The Homeland High Defense Council was created by the Afghan Marxist government in March 1979 to coordinate the defense of the country against "internal and external enemies." Its formation was a reaction to increased insurgent guerilla activities on the part of the Islamic resistance groups, and particularly to the riots in Herat during which a number of Soviet advisers were killed by angry mobs (February 1979).

BIBLIOGRAPHY

MALE, BEVERLEY. *Revolutionary Afghanistan.* New York, 1982.

Grant Farr

Homs

Syrian city and religious center.

Homs, strategically situated on the Orontes river at the eastern gateway of a pass connecting Syria's central plains to the Mediterranean coast, traces its history back to at least Greco-Roman times. Along with Ba'albak, it was a center of sun worship from the first to the third century C.E. Arab Muslim armies led by Khalid ibn al-Walid captured the city in 637 and converted its massive church of St. John into a mosque. Homs was designated headquarters of one of five Syrian military districts under Mu'awiya. Its inhabitants repeatedly rebelled against the Abbasids before falling under the control of the Tulunids of Egypt (878–944) and Hamdanids of Aleppo (944–1016). Byzantine commanders raided the city throughout the tenth and eleventh centuries, but by the late eleventh century rivalry among competing Saljuq client states shaped politics in the region. Duqaq ibn Tutush turned Homs into a major base of operations against the Crusaders at the beginning of the twelfth century, bringing the city under the direct control of Damascus for the first time. It suffered a series of ferocious attacks from the Zangids of Aleppo in the early twelfth century and provided the linchpin for Nur al-Din Mahmud's defense of Damascus against the Second Crusade.

Salah al-Din ibn Ayyubi captured Homs in 1175, retaining the local Asadi dynasty to block incursions into central Syria from the Crusader strongholds of Tripoli and Krak de Chevaliers (Qal'at al-Husn). After siding with the Mongols at Ayn Jalut, the Asadi ruler al-Ashraf Musa was pardoned by Qutuz, the Mamluk sultan whose successor, Baibars, rebuilt the city's citadel. In 1260, al-Ashraf Musa joined the rulers of Aleppo and Hama to defeat a second Mongol invasion force on the outskirts of the city. With the death of al-Ashraf Musa two years later, Homs vanished under the shadow of the rulers of Hamah and Damascus and continued to be dominated by the Mamluks of Egypt, by Timur, and by a succession of bedouin chieftains before becoming a subdivision (*pashalik*) of the Ottoman governorate of Damascus. The city's inhabitants revolted against the 1831 Egyptian occupation of Syria, prompting Ibrahim Pasha to raze the citadel.

Contemporary Homs is known for being the site of Syria's main oil refinery, as well as of the country's military academy. Several important public sector industrial enterprises, including a massive sugar factory, are located in and around the city. Syria's newest university, al-Ba'th, opened in the southern suburbs in 1979.

Fred H. Lawson

Hone–Bell Proposal

Proposal for independent governance of Aden and the protectorates.

The report prepared in early 1966 by colonial experts Sir Ralph Hone and Sir Gawain Bell laid out an ingenious liberal democratic constitutional framework for ADEN and the PROTECTORATE STATES. It provided a compromise between a federation and a unitary state and between the perceived interests of solitary Aden and those of the several protectorates. It was rendered moot in months by the fast-moving political events that killed hopes for a transfer of authority from Britain to the SOUTH ARABIAN LEAGUE.

Robert D. Burrowes

Hope-Simpson Commission

A British commission of inquiry into economic conditions in Palestine.

The Hope-Simpson Commission was established in the wake of the August 1929 Wailing Wall disturbances. A previous commission, the Shaw Commission, had concluded in March 1930 that the causes for the 1929 disturbances were Palestinian fear of Jewish immigration and land purchases. Because it recommended the curtailment of both, the Labour government of Prime Minister Ramsay MacDonald appointed a commission of inquiry under Sir John Hope-Simpson in October 1930 to investigate land settlement, immigration, and development. His report found that almost 30 percent of Palestinians were landless, presumably because of Jewish land purchases, and that Palestinian unemployment was exacerbated by a Jewish boycott of Arab labor.

The assumptions and recommendations of Hope-Simpson were incorporated in a policy paper called the Passfield White Paper of 1930, which recommended the establishment of a legislative council and restrictions on Jewish immigration and land purchases consistent with the economic absorptive capacity of Palestine.

The recommendations caused a political furor in Great Britain. Chaim WEIZMANN, protesting that the recommendations were inconsistent with the terms of the mandate and a reversal of the British Balfour declaration, resigned as president of the World Zionist Organization and of the Jewish Agency. The Conservative opposition also attacked the tone and content of the recommendations. Under pressure from the Zionists and their supporters, MacDonald issued a letter, known as the MACDONALD LETTER, or Black Letter to Arabs, in February 1931, which in effect reversed the policy of the White Paper of 1930. Consequently, the Hope-Simpson Commission resulted in no permanent change in British policy toward Palestine.

BIBLIOGRAPHY

PALESTINE GOVERNMENT. *A Survey of Palestine for the Information of the Anglo–American Committee of Inquiry.* 2 vols. Jerusalem, 1946. Reprint, Washington, D.C., 1991.

Philip Mattar

Hora

See Dance

Horowitz, David   [1899–1979]

Israeli economist.

Born in Galicia during the Austro-Hungarian empire, Horowitz settled in PALESTINE in 1920 and was a founder of Kibbutz Beit Alfa, which he left in 1925. As a leader of the Israel labor movement, he was active in the economic development of prestate Israel. Horowitz was a liaison for the 1947 UNITED NATIONS SPECIAL COMMITTEE ON PALESTINE (UNSCOP), which recommended partition. He was also a member of the JEWISH AGENCY delegation to the UN in 1948 that accepted the partition of Palestine.

During the Arab–Israel War of 1948, Horowitz was director of the ministry of finance. He helped found the Bank of Israel and became its governor from 1954 until 1971, when he retired. He received the Israel Prize in 1968.

Ann Kahn

Hosayniyeh

Place in Iran where the martyrdom of the Imam Husayn ibn Ali is commemorated.

The commemoration gains fervor during the mourning month of MUHARRAM, on the tenth day of which Husayn ibn Ali, grandson of the Prophet Muhammad and the third imam of the Twelver Shi'ites, was martyred in Karbala (680 C.E.). Traditionally, the Hosayniyeh was different from a mosque in that it was a populist institution and not under the direct jurisdiction of the *ulama.* The most famous of these places was the Hosayniyeh Ershad; it was founded in 1964 by progressive Islamists in Tehran, and its first director was Sayyid Ali Shahcheraqi. According to some scholars, the addition of *Ershad* (guidance) to the name of this Hosayniyeh signified its modernist tendencies and its aim of serving as an inspiration for change in Iranian society. Frequent speakers at the Hosayniyeh Ershad included most future leaders of Iran who took over in 1979, such as the clerics Ayatollah Mortaza Motahhari, Ali Akbar Hashemi Rafsanjani, and Sayyid Javad Bahonar. In 1969, the Hosayniyeh Ershad was taken over by Ali SHARI‘ATI, who was an Islamic modernist and who gave lectures criticizing the reactionary stance of the traditional *ulama* and the despotic regime of Mohammad Reza Shah Pahlavi. In these lectures, which drew huge crowds, Shari‘ati idealized the Islam of Husayn and Abu Zarr, allegedly the first Muslim socialist. Shari‘ati intended to transform the Hosayniyeh into a training center that would serve modern Muslims with its four units devoted to research, teaching, the propagation of Shi‘ism, and publishing and translation. Having alienated both government and clergy, the Hosayniyeh Ershad was shut down in 1972.

BIBLIOGRAPHY

CHEHABI, H. E. *Iranian Politics and Religious Modernism: The Liberation Movement of Iran under the Shah and Khomeini.* Ithaca, N.Y., 1990.

Neguin Yavari

Hoss, Salim al-   [1929–   ]

The most important Sunni politician in Lebanon.

Hoss was born in Beirut. He attended the International College and the American University of Beirut, where he excelled in economics. He later earned a Ph.D. in economics from Indiana University. Hoss taught at the American University for years and did consulting work for the government of Kuwait in the 1960s. Although he was aloof from the political scene in Lebanon he was appointed chair of the state council that monitors banking activities in 1967. As a result he became a friend of Ilyas SARKIS, then governor of the Central Bank.

When Sarkis was elected president in 1976, he appointed Hoss prime minister. He also held that position in the next two administrations (under Amin JUMAYYIL and briefly under Ilyas Hrawi). Although he was considered a political moderate, he was criticized by some Maronite leaders for opposing the president of the republic. In general, however, Hoss remains one of the most widely respected figures in Lebanon; he is seen as one of the few politicians who resisted the temptations of corruption and unprincipled compromises. His views tend to conform to the moderate views of the Sunni political establishment, although he is far less prone to sectarian agitation and mobilization. Hoss ran for parliament in the 1992 election on a platform of "salvation and reform." He is critical of Israel's occupation of Lebanon and has maintained close ties with Syria although he is regarded as less deferent to the latter's wishes than most political leaders in Lebanon.

Hoss has published two books on his experience in government and remains active on the political scene. His integrity and relative independence allow him a degree of political power that other politicians can only envy. Although his power base is Beirut, he is popular in most parts of Lebanon. Although Hoss is committed to a free economic system, in the last several years he has been critical of Western governmental policies toward the Arab–Israel conflict and the situation in Lebanon. In 1988 Hoss served as de facto president in a large part of Lebanon when Amin Jumayyil decided to name the commander in chief of Lebanon's army as president. Hoss, supported by many Lebanese and by Syria, served as acting president until the election of René Mu‘awwad.

As‘ad AbuKhalil

Hostage Crises

Outgrowth of domestic politics in Iran and Lebanon.

In Tehran, Iran, on 4 November 1979, a mob led by radical college students overran the U.S. embassy and took its personnel hostage. They announced that they would not free the diplomats until the United States agreed to extradite the country's former ruler, Mohammad Reza Shah PAHLAVI (1941–1979), to Iran. The shah, overthrown nine months earlier, had been admitted to the United States for cancer treatment two weeks before seizure of the embassy. Within days of the incident, Iran's revolutionary leaders endorsed the demands of the students and supported their claim that the U.S. embassy was a "den of espionage." U.S. efforts to exert diplomatic (UN resolutions), economic (freezing Iran's assets in U.S. banks), and military (an abortive helicopter rescue attempt) pressure on Iran proved unsuccessful in getting the hostages freed; even the death of the shah, in July 1980, had no apparent effect. Only after Iraq had invaded Iran in the fall of 1980 did Tehran indicate a serious interest in resolving the hostage issue. Iran and the United Nations subsequently accepted Algerian mediation; an accord that freed the hostages and established a tribunal to settle outstanding claims was signed in January 1981.

Lebanon. The kidnapping of Europeans and Americans in Lebanon that began in 1984 created a new, albeit less dramatic, hostage crisis. Although Iran denied any complicity in the taking of hostages in Lebanon, it was one of several countries supporting the various militias that had formed during the LEBANESE CIVIL WAR. Because organizations in Lebanon supported by Iran claimed to hold some of the hostages, the United States was convinced that Iran could exert influence to get them released. Iran did play a major role in negotiating the release of a U.S. airliner and its passengers after it had been hijacked to BEIRUT in June 1985.

The successful conclusion of this incident convinced some U.S. officials to undertake secret negotiations with Iran to free other hostages in Lebanon. These negotiations included covert arrangements to sell Iran weapons in exchange for the release of hostages. The weapons sales led to the freeing of two of the hostages over the course of a year during which more Westerners in Lebanon were abducted. Revelations of the arms-for-hostages deals, in October 1986, caused grave embarrassment to the administration of U.S. President Ronald REAGAN and resulted in the resignation of several senior aides. The scandal was compounded by revelations that profits from the secret arms sales to Iran had been diverted to secret accounts to buy weapons for U.S.-backed forces (contras) trying to overthrow the government of Nicaragua. The fallout from the scandal put hostage negotiations on hold for several months. The last U.S. and other Western hostages in Lebanon were not released until 1991.

[See also: Iran–Contra Affair, Iran–Iraq War]

BIBLIOGRAPHY

SICK, GARY. All Fall Down: America's Tragic Encounter with Iran. New York, 1985.
WRIGHT, ROBIN. In the Name of God: The Khomeini Decade. New York, 1989.

Eric J. Hooglund

Hoveyda, Amir Abbas   [1919–1979]

Iranian politician, and prime minister continuously from 1965 to 1977.

Amir Abbas Hoveyda was born in Tehran in 1919 and attended high school in Beirut. He studied political science and economics in Brussels, and upon his return to Iran in 1941, he was assigned a job at the ministry of foreign affairs and stationed in Ankara. In 1958, he became a member of the board of directors of the National Iranian Oil Company. He joined the party of Hasan Ali MANSUR, who was then prime minister, which later became the Iran Novin party. He was appointed as minister of finance in Mansur's cabinet in 1961 and succeeded him to the premiership when Mansur was assassinated in 1965. Hoveyda also inherited from Mansur the de facto chairmanship of the Iran Novin party, which was the majority party in every parliament convened until its dissolution and re-emergence as the shah's Resurgence party in 1974. In 1977, a growing economic crisis led to his fall as prime minister, and he became minister of court. In 1978, after the shah declared martial law, Hoveyda was arrested and imprisoned. When the shah departed from Iran in February 1979, he did not free Hoveyda, although the latter had never opposed him. Hoveyda was summarily tried by the provisional government of the Islamic state and was executed in April 1979.

BIBLIOGRAPHY

AQELI, BAQER. Iranian Prime Ministers from Moshir al-Dowleh to Bakhtiyar. Tehran, 1991. In Persian.

Neguin Yavari

Huda, Nur al-

Lebanese actress and singer.

Born in Turkey, Nur al-Huda (née Alexandra Badran) studied singing and music after graduating from high school. In addition to being a singer, she was also a famous movie actress.

George E. Irani

Hufuf, al-

Saudi Arabian town.

The principal town of the extensive al-HASA oasis in Saudi Arabia's Eastern Province, al-Hufuf has a population of nearly 100,000, most of whom are not organized into tribes and 40 percent of whom are Shi'ites. The Ottomans occupied al-Hufuf from 1871 to 1913, and it was the capital of the Eastern Province until 1952.

John E. Peterson

Huhu, Reda   [1911–1956]

Algerian short story writer, essayist, playwright, and journalist.

Huhu was born in the village of Sidi Uqba, in the Aurès region. He wrote in Arabic but studied

French, which allowed him to translate and adapt literary books from the French. He received most of his education in Algeria.

Huhu lived in Saudi Arabia from 1934 to 1945. While there, he wrote his novella *Ghadat Umm al-Qura* (The Lady of Umm al-Qura [Constantine, 1947]), which he dedicated to Saudi Arabian women. Huhu was a member of the ASSOCIATION OF ALGERIAN MUSLIM ULAMA, founded in 1931 by Abd al-Hamid BEN BADIS. He contributed articles to their papers, *Al-Basa'ir* and *Al-Shihab,* as well as to others. He was assassinated by the French colonial authorities, who feared his militant writings, particularly the impact of his plays performed in Algerian dialect.

Huhu launched a campaign against political, social, and religious corruption in his collection of short stories, *Namadhij Bashariyya* (Human samples [Tunis, 1955]), and also in his conversations with a donkey, in which he freely ridiculed the Algerian politicians who were puppets of the colonial power. Inspired by Egypt's well-known writer Tawfiq al-HAKIM, he titled his dialogues with the donkey Ma'a Himar al-Hakim (With al-Hakim's donkey [Constantine, 1953]). The author's sense of humor slightly attenuated the virulence of his criticism, which was often tinged with biting irony. He had little faith in human nature.

Huhu was a champion of women's rights, taking it upon himself to defend the Algerian woman and her right to freedom. He warned, however, against hasty action on her part, recommending the education of men as a first step in achieving women's emancipation. He spoke freely of love, stressing the nobility of this emotion, particularly in his collection of short stories *Sahibat al-Wahy wa Qisas Ukhra* (The inspiring lady and other stories) [Constantine, n.d.]).

[*See also:* Literature, Arabic, North African]

BIBLIOGRAPHY

BAMIA, AIDA A. "Algerian Literature." In *Encyclopedia of World Literature in the Twentieth Century,* vol. 5. New York, 1993, pp. 12–17.
DÉJEUX, JEAN. *La Littérature algérienne contemporaine.* Paris, 1975.

Aida A. Bamia

Huleh Swamps

Valley and former lake in the upper eastern Galilee region of Israel, known for its marshlands.

The Huleh swamps were a breeding ground for malaria mosquitoes, which infected the people of the region. The Ottoman Empire had declared the area state land but was anxious to raise the standard of living there and increase agricultural productivity. Several Arab entrepreneurs in Beirut won concessions to drain the swamps and develop the land but never implemented any of the proposed projects. In 1934, the PALESTINE LAND DEVELOPMENT COMPANY acquired the Huleh concession and began to drain the land. The JEWISH NATIONAL FUND then increased the number of Jewish settlements in the reclaimed region, including Dafnah, Dan, She'ar Yashuv, Amir, Kfar Blum, and the town of Kiryat Shemonah.

BIBLIOGRAPHY

ORNI, EFRAIM, and ELISHA EFRAT. *Geography of Israel.* Jerusalem, 1966.

Donna Robinson Divine

Human Rights

In the Middle East and the Maghrib, human rights is a concept whose connotations vary by country, religion, and political persuasion.

On paper, by 1991, Algeria, Egypt, Iran, Iraq, Israel, Jordan, Lebanon, Libya, Morocco, Sudan, Syria, Tunisia, and Yemen had all ratified both the International Covenant on Economic, Social and Cultural Rights and the Covenant on Civil and Political Rights. Libya has also adhered to the Optional Protocol to the Covenant on Civil and Political Rights, which recognizes the right of individual petition to the Human Rights Committee. Israel had subscribed to both covenants in 1991 but, prior to that, was subject to humanitarian law standards in the occupied territories under the Geneva conventions. Egypt, Libya, Sudan, and Tunisia have ratified the African Charter on Human and People's Rights. The constitutions of the majority of states in the Middle East reflect the formal incorporation of the international standards, and international human-rights law is taught in the law faculties of most of the abovementioned countries. Israel has neither a constitution nor a bill of rights, but Israeli law protects basic human rights and provides for the democratic process.

In response to claims that international standards were at variance with the traditions of Islam, on August 5, 1990, the member states of the Organization of the Islamic Conference approved what has come to be known as the Cairo Declaration on Human Rights in Islam. Linking human rights and Islamic UMMA (community), the document affirms that "fundamental rights and universal freedoms are an integral part of the Islamic religion and that no one as a matter of principle has the right to suspend them in whole or in part or violate or ignore them in as much as they are binding divine commandments." There follow twenty-five articles covering most of the rights and freedoms enunciated in the international documents, including nondiscrimination on grounds of race, color, language, sex, religious belief, political affiliation, and social status; the protection of civilians during war; and the rights to a clean environment, to education, to health care, to employment, to freedom of movement, and to innocence until proven guilty. Article Number 24 reaffirms explicitly what is repeated throughout the document, "All the rights and freedoms stipulated in this Declaration are subject to Islamic Shari'ah." (SHARI'A is Islamic law.)

In practice, throughout the region, in virtually every category of rights, serious human-rights violations occur. While in the Arab world violations bear characteristics similar to those in other less-industrialized countries—extensive use of physical coercion and torture; arbitrary law enforcement; numerous patterns of discrimination; the persecution of minorities and aliens; and severe controls over the media, freedom of information, and religious expression—the situation is aggravated by the fact that many states in the Middle East control significant economic resources, permitting their governments to use coercive power to even greater effect, as in the case of Iraq's treatment of the Kurds. The status of women in the Middle East is of growing concern to the international human-rights community, although evaluating their condition leads to extended debates on cultural diversity and the attitudes of the women themselves. Western organizations have also focused on the violations of human rights involved in the use of Islamic punishments, such as amputation. In Israel, the most significant human-rights violations occur in the occupied territories of Gaza and the West Bank, where, for the most part, Palestinians live under strict military government and where, especially since the uprising called the INTIFADA (1989), extensive use is made of administrative orders and summary reprisals.

Owing to the range and quantity of human-rights violations, as well as the number of countries involved, it is impossible to indicate a country-by-country balance sheet of violations: Amnesty International and Middle East Watch provide regular reports, but not on all categories. Also, monitoring is handicapped by governmental restrictions on external access to the region and its peoples.

The consciousness of Middle Easterners, with regard to human rights, is beginning to change—as is evidenced by Islamic fundamentalists in Algeria appealing to the international human-rights community. The number and effectiveness of Arab human-rights groups that monitor and publicize human-rights violations in the region are growing, notably in Egypt and Tunisia. Other countries, such as Bahrain, Iraq, Sudan, and Syria must rely exclusively on groups in exile. In Israel, many human-rights organizations exist, active on behalf of generic, Jewish, or Arab causes. Generally, Arab countries assume that human rights are a pretext for Western involvement in Middle East affairs. The limited support for Palestinian claims to autonomy on the part of Western nations reinforced this view: Ultimately, no matter how sympathetic individuals might be to human rights, both Arab and Jew readily give priority to their respective communal needs.

National and ethnic loyalties remain strong determinants of policy and practice. Thus, Islamic fundamentalism, for example, would seem to exclude all but the most self-serving recognition of international human-rights standards. The net picture is, however, of an evolving human-rights profile, as more governments become responsive to international opinion and the work of local activists is seen to appeal to the aspirations of their fellow citizens.

BIBLIOGRAPHY

B'TSELEM. *Violations of Human Rights in the Occupied Territories 1990/1991.* Jerusalem, 1991

DWYER, KEVIN. *Arab Voices: The Human Rights Debate in the Middle East.* Berkeley, Calif., 1991.

Paul Martin

Humayd ibn Ahmad al-Mualla

Minister of planning, United Arab Emirates.

Humayd ibn Ahmad al-Mualla is a younger brother of Ahmad Ibn Rashid al-Mualla, the present ruler of UMM AL-QAYWAYN. He trained at the Police Academy in Cairo, Egypt, and was commander of the police force in his emirate.

Since 1983 he has been minister of planning in the federal cabinet of the United Arab Emirates and chairman of the General Information Authority.

BIBLIOGRAPHY

Persian Gulf Gazette and Supplements, 1953–1972. London, 1987.

Persian Gulf Historical Summaries, 1907–1953. London, 1987.

M. Morsy Abdullah

Hummus

Middle Eastern dish of chickpeas, sesame seeds, and spices.

A staple food of Syria, hummus has become popular in Jordan and Israel as well as throughout America and Europe. It is a pureé of TAHINI, chickpeas, garlic, cumin, and lemon, often garnished with parsley and paprika. It is served with pita bread as an appetizer or a course unto itself.

BIBLIOGRAPHY

DER HAROUTUNIAN, ARTO. *Vegetarian Dishes from the Middle East.* London, 1983.

Zachary Karabell

Humphreys, Francis   [1879–1971]

British diplomat.

Humphreys was the last British high commissioner in Iraq (1929–1932) before Iraqi independence in 1932. In that capacity, he played a central role in negotiating the Anglo–Iraqi Treaty of 1930, which paved the way for independence. Humphreys then served as the first British ambassador to Iraq (1932–1935).

BIBLIOGRAPHY

Dictionary of National Biography, 1971–1980. New York, 1986.

Zachary Karabell

Hunaydi, Ahmad al-

Syrian military leader.

An officer favored by the powerful Adib SHISHAKLI, Ahmad al-Hunaydi continually shifted his political allegiances after Shishakli's downfall, to be counted neither among true Ba'th sympathizers nor in Amin al-Nafuri's group of independent officers. He was sent to Cairo in January 1958 to pledge Ba'th support to Egypt's President Nasser. He later held a ministerial position in the first Syro–Egyptian union.

BIBLIOGRAPHY

SEALE, PATRICK. *The Struggle for Syria: A Study of Post-War Arab Politics, 1945–1958.* London, 1958.

Charles U. Zenzie

Hunchak Party

Armenian-oriented Lebanese political party.

The Hunchak party, organized in Geneva, Switzerland, in 1887, has promoted the dual objective of liberating Turkish ARMENIA and establishing a socialist regime in a unified Armenian homeland. In Lebanon, the party has advocated a planned economy and a just distribution of national income. In 1972, for the first time in its history, the party fielded a joint slate of candidates for parliament with the DASHNAK PARTY. In the world of Armenian politics in Lebanon, ties of Armenian national solidarity supersede ideological considerations that might divide Armenians. During the LEBANESE CIVIL WAR, the differences between the Hunchak and the Dashnak became insignificant.

The Hunchak party achieved a victory in the 1992 election when Yeghya Djerijian, an Armenian (Greek Orthodox, born in 1957) was elected to parliament. He chairs the executive committee of the party.

As'ad AbuKhalil

Hunkâr-Iskelesi, Treaty of

Mutual defense agreement between Russia and the Ottoman Empire.

In February 1833, the Egyptian army of Ibrahim Pasha reached Kutahya in Ottoman Turkey, less than two hundred miles from Constantinople (now Istanbul), seat of the Ottoman Empire. With few options short of capitulation, the Ottoman sultan MAHMUD II sought help from his former enemy, Czar Nicholas I of Russia. Nicholas complied, and Russian troops and ships were dispatched to the Bosporus (Turkish straits). Though the Russian presence did not save the sultan from severe concessions to Ibrahim and his father MUHAMMAD ALI, viceroy of Egypt, it did force Ibrahim to temper his demands and depart from Kutahya. Having helped the sultan, Nicholas demanded payment in the form of a defensive alliance. The Treaty of Hunkâr-Iskelesi, named after the Russian camp, was concluded on July 8, 1833. Concluded for eight years, it bound the sultan to close the Turkish straits to warships in times of war, and it provided for Russian aid if the Ottoman Empire was attacked. Though defensive, the treaty greatly alarmed the other European powers, who believed that it gave the Russians preponderant influence in Constantinople. Britain protested against the treaty and over the next years worked assiduously to reverse this setback to British interests in the Ottoman Empire.

BIBLIOGRAPHY

ANDERSON, M. S. *The Eastern Question*. London, 1966.
HUREWITZ, J. C., ed. *The Middle East and North Africa in World Politics*. New Haven, Conn., 1975.
SHAW, STANFORD, and EZEL KURAL SHAW. *History of the Ottoman Empire and Modern Turkey*. New York, 1977.

Zachary Karabell

Hürriyet

Daily newspaper in Turkey.

Hürriyet (Freedom) is a politically centrist newspaper known for its ardent antifundamentalist stand. In 1990, its managing editor, Cetin Emeç, was allegedly assassinated by Muslim fundamentalist terrorists.

Hürriyet has a circulation of 600,000, with 150,000 copies distributed in Western Europe, making it the most widely read Turkish newspaper outside the country. In Turkey, *Hürriyet*'s readers are typically middle class and high school educated.

Hürriyet was founded in 1948 by journalist and publisher Sedat Simavi, in the early years of Turkey's multiparty politics. It quickly became the top-selling daily in Turkey and remained in that position for about forty years, making it the country's most influential newspaper. Once a gossip paper, it gradually improved its serious news coverage. By the end of the 1970s, the paper maintained an extensive network of domestic bureaus and about a dozen international ones. For three years, until 1991, *Hürriyet* copublished with Bağimsiz Basin Ajansi, an English-language weekly, *Dateline Turkey.*

Hürriyet remained in the Simavi family following the death of the founder in 1953, with his son, Erol, eventually taking sole control. In 1994, the Dogan Group, owner of *Milliyet,* took a controlling share of the newspaper with the purchase of 70 percent of Hürriyet Holding. Of the remaining stake, 15 percent stayed in the Simavi family and another 15 percent was held by various investors.

BIBLIOGRAPHY

Interview with Şevki Adali, former head of Foreign Desk at *Hürriyet.*

Stephanie Capparell

Husayn, Ahmad   [1911–1982]

Egyptian politician.

The son of an agricultural worker in Upper Egypt, Husayn was educated at al-Azhar and in France, where he studied law. A fierce defender of Egyptian nationalism, Husayn founded the political association YOUNG EGYPT (Misr al-Fatat) in 1933. With a program of industrial development and social reform, Husayn attracted followers among students of secondary schools in urban centers, organizing them into a paramilitary organization, the Green Shirts. Husayn was active in antigovernment protests in 1954, which led to his arrest. He was released in 1956 and withdrew from public life.

BIBLIOGRAPHY

GERSHONI, ISRAEL, and JAMES P. JANKOWSKI. *Egypt, Islam, and the Arabs: The Search for Egyptian Nationhood, 1900–1930.* New York, 1986.
VATIKIOTIS, P. J. *A History of Modern Egypt,* 4th ed. London, 1991.
WUCHER KING, JOAN. *Historical Dictionary of Egypt.* Metuchen, N.J., 1984.

David Waldner

Husayn, Husayn al-   [1937–   ]

Shi'a politician in Lebanon.

Husayn was born to a prominent family in Shmistar, near Ba'albak. He first ran for public office in 1964 and was elected to parliament in 1972, when his close association with Imam Musa al-SADR paid off. His political role in the political life of Lebanon was minimal until 1978, when Musa al-Sadr "disappeared" and Husayn assumed the leadership of the AMAL movement. His conflict with other militant factions within the movement began in 1980, when Nabi BERRI (his archrival) took control of AMAL.

With strong backing from Syria, Husayn was elected speaker of parliament in 1984. He held that position until 1992, when Berri was elected to that post. Husayn's showing in the 1992 election was poor, and the candidates of the Hizbullah (Party of God) in his district of Ba'albak achieved great success. The election results weakened his ties with the government of Lebanon, and he has emerged as one of the most bitter opposition figures. He directs his attacks against Prime Minister Rafiq al-HARIRI, whom he accuses of corrupting Lebanon and of profiting from his high office. Husayn has been marginalized in the Shi'ite community by Berri and by the Party of God.

As'ad AbuKhalil

Husayn, Saddam

See Hussein, Saddam

Husayn, Taha [1889–1973]

Egyptian critic and writer of fiction; Egypt's minister of education, 1950–1952.

Born in an Egyptian village in the Nile delta, Taha Husayn's life was transformed at the age of two, when he was blinded by the village barber's attempt to treat ophthalmia. The course of his early education, with its many frustrations and occasional triumphs, is recorded in one of the major monuments of modern Arabic literature, *Al-Ayyam* (1925; published in English as *An Egyptian Childhood,* 1932). In two later volumes under the same title, Taha Husayn traces his transition from the village Qur'an school to the Azhar mosque-university in Cairo (*Al-Ayyam,* 1939; *The Stream of Days,* 1948) and his sense of acute frustration at the kind of education being offered there. The third volume (*Al-Ayyam,* 1967; *A Passage to France,* 1976) describes his transfer to the new secular Egyptian University (now the University of Cairo) from which he obtained the first Ph.D., with a dissertation on the renowned classical Arabic poet, Abu al-Ala al-Ma'arri, whose blindness clearly led to feelings of close affinity between author and subject. In 1915, Taha Husayn traveled to France. Arriving at the University of Montpelier, he hired a young French woman to read to him. The two fell in love and were married in 1917. Husayn moved to Paris in 1915 where he became a student at the Sorbonne and, in 1918, completed a second doctoral dissertation, this one on the famous historian Ibn Khaldun (1332–1406).

Upon his return home, Husayn set himself, both as author and teacher, the task of introducing to his fellow countrymen and, by extension, to the Arab world as a whole, many of the ideas and ideals he had encountered in Europe. Appointed professor of ancient history immediately following his return from France, he assumed the chair of Arabic literature in 1925. It was at this time that he contributed to the newspaper *al-Siyasa* a series of articles on early Arabic poetry, which were to be published later in three volumes as *Hadith al-Arba'a* (1954, n.d., 1957). His lecture references on the debt of ISLAM to Hellenistic ideas were already controversial, but when in 1926 he published in book form *Fi al-Shi'r al-Jahili,* his views on the authenticity of pre-islamic poetry, and suggested that certain stories recorded in the text of the QUR'AN might be fables, he was accused of heresy. He offered to resign but was vigorously defended by the president of the university, Ahmad Lutfi al-Sayyid (1872–1963). Eventually a compromise was reached whereby the work was withdrawn. A revised version, *Fi al-Adab al-Jahili,* was published in 1927, with the offending passages removed but the remainder of his argument expanded.

Taha Husayn was not afraid to provoke and confront controversy during the remainder of his career. Appointed dean of the faculty of arts in 1929, he soon clashed with governmental authorities and was dismissed from that position in 1932 amid strikes and resignations. He now became more active in both journalism and politics while continuing his career as a university teacher, administrator, and writer. In 1938 he published another controversial work, *Mustaqbal al-Thaqafa fi Misr,* laying out a broad and ambitious program of educational reform that involved a process of modernization on the model of Europe. During the 1940s he was accorded increasing recognition as a scholar and writer both in Egypt and abroad; in 1950 he was appointed minister of education in the WAFD government. He was in the process of implementing his reforms when a series of events began that were to culminate in the Egyptian revolution of July 1952.

During the final decades of his life, as the pace of development in the literary tradition that he loved began to accelerate, he became a more conservative figure, bent on preserving the great heritage from what he came to regard as the wilder excesses of some of its contemporary inheritors—not least in the call for literature of commitment that so predominated in the critical environment of the 1950s.

Taha Husayn made several contributions to modern Arabic fiction, of which the novels *Du'a al-Karawan* (1932) and *Shajarat al-Bu's* (1944) and the short-story collection *Al-Mu'adhdhibun fi al-Ard* (1949) are the most notable. It is, however, in the realm of literary criticism that his contribution to modern Arabic cultural life is most significant. He played a major role in the formulation of a modern approach to the issues of Arabic literary history; he applied critical methods to the canon of both poetry and artistic prose through a series of studies on genres and various writers. From his early study of al-Ma'arri, mentioned above, via his work on Abu al-Tayyib al-Mutanabbi (died 965), generally acknowledged as the greatest of the classical poets, to contemporary poets such as Ahmad Shawqi (1868–1932) and Hafiz Ibrahim (1871–1932), it is possible to detect a determined effort to introduce into the world of Arabic literature a critical approach based on a recognizable methodology. In so doing, he laid the groundwork for subsequent generations of critics, most notably his own student, Muhammad Mandur (1907–1965).

Taha Husayn was known during his lifetime as the dean of Arabic literature—the title is appropriate. Not only did he write creative works and critical studies, but his sense of mission led him to play a major role in the difficult process of cultural adjustment and change that the Arab world has had to face during the course of the twentieth century.

[*See also:* Literature, Arabic]

BIBLIOGRAPHY

BRUGMAN, J. *An Introduction to the History of Modern Arabic Literature in Egypt.* Leiden, Neth., 1984.

CACHIA, PIERRE. *Taha Husayn: His Place in the Egyptian Literary Renaissance.* London, 1956.

MALTI-DOUGLAS, FEDWA. *Blindness and Autobiography: "Al-Ayyam" of Taha Husayn.* Princeton, N.J., 1988.

SEMAH, DAVID. *Four Egyptian Literary Critics.* Leiden, Neth., 1974.

Roger Allen

Husayni, Abd al-Qadir al-   [1908–1948]

Palestinian nationalist and military leader.

Abd al-Qadir was born in Jerusalem to a notable family. He was the son of MUSA KAZIM, a major leader of the Palestinian struggle against Zionism. Abd al-Qadir saw military service during the Palestinian rebellion between 1936 and 1939. During World War II, he took part in the Iraqi revolt of Rashid Ali al-Kaylani, a pro-Axis Iraqi politician who replaced Nuri al-Sa'id as prime minister of Iraq in March 1940. After the British crushed al-Kaylani's revolt in 1941, Abd al-Qadir was imprisoned; following his release he went to Egypt. In 1947, Abd al-Qadir managed to return to Palestine where he commanded, together with Fawzi al-Qawuqji, the ARAB LIBERATION ARMY, a poorly-equipped force of some 2,000 volunteers who crossed the Israeli border from Syria in January 1948, under the sponsorship of the Arab League. At the battle of Jabal al-Qastil (April 1948) on the Jaffa–Jerusalem highway, the better-trained and better-armed Haganah forces dealt the Arab forces a decisive blow, reopening the Jerusalem highway, killing Abd al-Qadir, and routing al-Qawuqji's troops. Soon thereafter, the Jewish forces took possession of most of the important Palestinian towns, including the major part of Jerusalem. For the Palestinians, their resistance at al-Qastil remains one of the proudest moments in their modern history, and Abd al-Qadir one of their most honored national heroes.

Muhammad Muslih

Husayni, Ibrahim al-

Syrian military leader.

As leader of the military police in Damascus under President Husni al-ZA'IM, Colonel Ibrahim al-

Husayni was a significant target in Colonel Sami al-HINNAWI's August 14, 1949, backlash coup against Za'im. On his deathbed, Colonel Muhammad Nasir, commander of the air force and a significant anti-SHISHAKLI figure, named al-Husayni as one of his assailants in the politically motivated attack. The accusation was later dismissed. After Shishakli's overthrow in 1954, Husayni became Syrian military attaché to Italy. He returned to Syria in the late 1950s, apparently with U.S. encouragement to counter the perceived growing Soviet influence in Syrian politics.

BIBLIOGRAPHY

SEALE, PATRICK. *The Struggle for Syria: A Study of Post-War Arab Politics, 1945–1958.* London, 1958.

Charles U. Zenzie

Husayni, Jamal al-   [1892–1982]

Palestinian political leader during the British mandate over Palestine.

Jerusalem-born Jamal al-Husayni was secretary of the ARAB EXECUTIVE and the SUPREME MUSLIM COUNCIL. In 1935 he was elected president of the PALESTINE ARAB PARTY, and one year later he became a member of the Higher Arab Committee (HAC). A firm believer in public relations and political lobbying as well as a relative and close aide to the mufti of Jerusalem, he participated as member (1930) and as president (1939) of the Palestinian delegations dispatched to London to discuss Palestinian demands with the British government. He also served on the HAC's delegations to the LEAGUE OF ARAB STATES and the United Nations. He was briefly detained by the British authorities in Palestine for his role in the Jerusalem and Jaffa demonstrations of October 1933. Following the mufti's escape to Beirut in 1937, Jamal secretly joined him and from there he fled to Iraq, then to Iran where he was arrested by the British in 1942 and deported to Rhodesia, now Zimbabwe. Four years later, he returned to Palestine and, after 1947, he served as foreign minister for the All-Palestine Government and later settled in Saudi Arabia where he was adviser to King Sa'ud (1953–1964). Jamal died in Beirut and was buried there. On behalf of the political bodies on which he served during the mandate period, Jamal submitted compromise ideas to the Palestine government and to Jewish representatives concerning a new basis for relations between the government and the Jewish community on the one hand and the Palestinian Arabs on the other hand. The unpublished autobiography of Jamal reveals a feeling of apathy toward the mufti, partly because of the rift between the mufti and Musa al-ALAMI, whose sister Jamal had married.

BIBLIOGRAPHY

Al-Mawsu'a al-Filastiniyya, vol. 2.
PORATH, Y. *The Palestinian Arab National Movement,* vols. 1 and 2. Boston, 1977.

Muhammad Muslih

Husayni, Muhammad Amin al-
[1895–1974]

Palestinian leader during the British mandate.

Born in Jerusalem, Amin al-Husayni (later often referred to as Hajj Amin) was the scion of a very prominent Palestinian Muslim family, which included landed notables and religious officeholders, such as the mufti (Islamic legal expert). He studied in Cairo briefly at al-Azhar University and at the DAR AL-DA'WA WA-AL-IRSHAD of Rashid Rida, the Muslim reformer and precursor of Arab nationalism, and at the military academy in Istanbul. He served in the Ottoman army in 1916, but his loyalty to the Ottoman Empire was shaken by Turkish attempts to impose their language and culture on their Arab subjects. Upon returning to Palestine in 1916, he participated in the British-supported ARAB REVOLT of 1916 against the Turks and worked for the establishment of an independent Arab nation. In 1918 he was elected president of al-Nadi al-Arabi (the ARAB CLUB), a literary and nationalist organization opposed to Zionist claims on Palestine. After participating in a violent anti-Zionist demonstration in 1920, he escaped to Damascus where he worked for the short-lived Arab nationalist government of Emir (later King) Faisal. The first high commissioner of Palestine, Sir Herbert SAM-UEL, pardoned him and appointed him to succeed his brother as mufti of Jerusalem in 1921.

Al-Husayni's political career can be divided into two distinct phases: the Palestine years of 1917 to 1936, when he cooperated with the British while opposing Zionism; and the exile period after 1936, when he became intransigent and cooperated with Nazi Germany.

Palestinian phase. The fundamental explanation of al-Husayni's cooperation with the British can be traced to the politics of the class from which he emerged. The notables were defenders of the status quo and worked with the imperial government to guarantee or enforce stability while representing their society's interests and demands to the ruling power, first the

Ottomans, then after 1917 the British. Before being appointed mufti, al-Husayni assured Samuel that he and his family would maintain tranquillity in Jerusalem. In 1921 he was appointed president of the SU-PREME MUSLIM COUNCIL, giving him control over Muslim courts, schools, religious endowments (WAQF), mosques, and the annual budget. Al-Husayni used his office during the 1920s to extend his influence in religious and political affairs within and beyond Palestine. His rise to power coincided with the decline of the Palestine ARAB EXECUTIVE and with the perception that he had stood up to the Zionists during the 1928/29 WESTERN (or Wailing) WALL controversy and violent riots. (In fact, he neither organized nor led the riots, according to the British SHAW COMMISSION, which investigated the disturbances.)

From 1929 to 1936 al-Husayni cooperated with the British while attempting to change British policy. He opposed militant activities against British rule and sent his secretary to London to propose a representative government. For their part, the British proposed, in the Passfield WHITE PAPERS of 1931, restrictions on Jewish immigration and land purchase, but withdrew the proposal because of Zionist pressure. The mufti convened a general ISLAMIC CONGRESS in December 1931 to excite Arab and Muslim hostility to the Zionists and to caution Britain that support for Zionism would jeopardize her interests in the Arab and Muslim world.

British policy did not change, however. Jewish immigration rose in 1935 to 61,854, which helped radicalize the Palestinian community. The British killing of a revolutionary, Izz al-Din al-QASSAM, further embittered Palestinians, who began to challenge the mufti's ineffective methods. Until 1936 al-Husayni was able to serve two masters: his British employers and his people. But in April 1936 a general strike was declared, and violence spread. The public urged him to assume the leadership of the strike, which protested against Jewish immigration and land purchase and for a national government. His acceptance put him on a collision course with the British.

Exile phase. Several events over the next few years served to radicalize al-Husayni. When the British proposed, in the 1937 PEEL COMMISSION REPORT, to partition Palestine, he rejected the proposal because the Jews, who owned 5.6 percent of the land, would receive 40 percent of the most fertile region, from which most Palestinians would be expelled; the British would get the third holiest city of Islam, Jerusalem; and Transjordan (now Jordan) would be given the rest. Faced with the mufti's refusal to cooperate, the British stripped him of his offices and sought to arrest him.

He escaped to Lebanon in 1937, continued to lead the revolt, and acquiesced (at least) in the assassination of his Palestinian opponents. The revolt was finally suppressed in 1939 after more than three thousand Palestinians had been killed, their leaders exiled, and the Palestinian economy shattered. Al-Husayni became bitter and uncompromising, rejecting the 1939 white papers (as did the Zionist leaders) even though its terms were favorable to the Palestinians. He again escaped, this time to Iraq, where he encouraged a pan-Arab revolt against British rule in 1941. British Prime Minister Winston Churchill approved his assassination, but a British and Zionist mission to assassinate him in Baghdad failed.

Al-Husayni fled to the Axis countries where he conferred with Mussolini and Hitler. He cooperated with the Nazis after Germany promised that the Arab nations would be liberated and given their independence after the war, and he assisted in anti-British and anti-Jewish propaganda campaigns and in recruitment of Muslims for the war effort. He attempted but failed to limit the number of Jews leaving Axis countries for Palestine. His association with the Nazis tainted his career and his cause and limited his freedom of action during the critical period from 1946 to 1948.

In 1946 al-Husayni returned to the Arab world with the aim of continuing his struggle against the Zionists and for establishing an Arab Palestine. But he totally misjudged the balance of forces. He rejected the United Nations General Assembly's partition resolution of November 1947 because it gave the Jews 55 percent of Palestine when they owned only 7 percent of the land. In the civil strife and war that followed, about 725,000 Palestinians fled or were expelled by the Israel defense forces. After the ARAB–ISRAEL WAR of 1948, al-Husayni gradually lost political influence and became a religious Islamic leader, settling first in Cairo and then in Beirut.

Assessment. Though astute, incorruptible, and dedicated to the welfare of his people, the mufti's policies during both phases were a failure. From 1917 to 1936, despite his rhetoric about the ominous threat of Zionism to Palestinian national existence, he cooperated with the British and rejected militant self-defense, preferring petitions, delegations, and strikes. In the meantime, the Zionists' numbers increased from 50,000 in 1917 to 384,000 in 1936.

It was only after 1936 that al-Husayni participated in active measures to stop Jewish immigration, which if unchecked, the Palestinians felt, would result in their expulsion or domination. But by then it was too late: The Zionists had become too powerful, and the British had lost their discretionary authority in the country. Conversely, the Palestinians, especially after the Arab Revolt, were too weak. The mufti did not adjust his demands to the reality on the ground and made no effort to reach an accommodation with the Zionists. His rejection of the 1947 UN resolution was a missed opportunity for the Palestinians and may have unwittingly contributed to their dispossession. However, even had he accepted the resolution, it is unlikely that the establishment of a Palestinian nationalist state would have been allowed because of a 1946/47 agreement (supported by the British) between Emir ABDULLAH IBN HUSAYN and the JEWISH AGENCY to divide Palestine between them.

The overriding factors that frustrated Palestinian nationalists have less to do with the mufti than with the balance of historical forces. The 1897 Basel Zionist program and the 1917 BALFOUR DECLARATION policy, backed by the British military and Western support, gave Palestine's Jewish community time to grow through immigration and land purchase and to establish modern quasi-governmental and military institutions. The Palestinians were a weak, divided, and traditional society and never a match for the British and the Zionists.

BIBLIOGRAPHY

ELPELEG, ZVI. *The Grand Mufti of Jerusalem: Haj Amin al-Husayni, Founder of the Palestinian National Movement.* London, 1993.

AL-HUSAYNI, MUHAMMAD AMIN. *Haqa'iq An Qadiyyat Filastin.* 2nd ed. Cairo, 1957.

KHADDURI, MAJID. "The Traditional (Idealist) School— The Extremist: Al-Hajj Amin al-Husayni." In *Arab Contemporaries: The Role of Personalities in Politics.* Baltimore, 1973.

MATTAR, PHILIP. *The Mufti of Jerusalem: Al-Hajj Amin Al-Husayni and the Palestinian National Movement.* Rev. ed. New York, 1992.

PORATH, YEHOSHUA. "Al-Hajj Amin al-Husayni, Mufti of Jerusalem: His Rise to Power and Consolidation of His Position." *Asian and African Studies* 7 (1971): 212–256.

SCHECHTMAN, JOSEPH B. *The Mufti and the Fuehrer: The Rise and Fall of Haj Amin el-Husseini.* New York, 1965.

Philip Mattar

Husayni, Musa Kazim al-   [1853–1934]

Palestinian politician and nationalist.

Al-Husayni played a major role in the early phase of the Palestinian national movement. Born in Jerusalem to a socially and politically prominent family, he acquired senior positions in the Ottoman imperial bureaucracy in Palestine, Transjordan, Syria, Yemen, and Iraq. After the British occupied Palestine, he was appointed mayor of Jerusalem in March 1918, succeeding his deceased predecessor and brother, Husayn al-HUSAYN. Throughout his political career, Musa Kazim followed a policy of cautious engagement in politics and discreet opposition to the British, who sponsored and supported the Zionist movement. In 1918 he refrained from demonstrating against Zionism after the Jerusalem governor, Ronald Storrs, told him that he must make a choice between political activism and the mayoralty. His circumspect behavior, which was typical of a generation of Palestinian politicians whose political style was shaped by their experience in the Ottoman system of government, did not stop him from fighting for Palestinian nationalism. In 1920, he resigned his post as mayor of Jerusalem and led demonstrations organized against the Jewish National Home policy of the British government. He was elected president of the third Palestinian Arab Congress (held in Haifa in December 1920) and the ARAB EXECUTIVE, a loosely-structured political body formed in 1920 to coordinate the Palestinian national struggle. Husayni led the Palestinian Arab delegations that were dispatched to London to present the Palestinian point of view to the British authorities. His fear of the growing influence of more activist Palestinians prompted him to view with favor proposals for a legislative council. During the 1929 WAILING WALL DISTURBANCES, Husayni signed a manifesto urging his fellow Palestinians not to engage in violence and to arm themselves instead with mercy, wisdom, and patience. Partly as a result of his disappointment with the British pro-Zionist policy, and partly because of the pressure of the action-oriented Palestinian groups that emerged in the late 1920s, he led the 1933 Palestinian demonstrations in Jerusalem. A product of Ottoman times with a penchant for discreetness and a love for senior political posts, Husayni was unable to devise a strategy that would alter the British pro-Zionist policy. The balance of power, which was overwhelmingly in favor of the Zionists and their British supporters, together with internal Palestinian bickering—epitomized by the Husayni–Nashashibi rivalry—put Husayni and his generation of Palestinian nationalists at a decisive disadvantage. He died the "venerable father" (al-ab al-jalil) of the Palestine national movement.

Muhammad Muslih

Husayni, Sa'id al-   [1878–?]

Palestinian politician.

Born to Jerusalem's leading family, the HUSAYNI FAMILY, Sa'id al-Husayni briefly attended the Alliance Israélite Universelle school, where he learned Hebrew. As a local censor of Hebrew newspapers, he became a well-informed opponent of Jewish immigration and land purchases in Palestine, although he supported Jewish immigration elsewhere in the Ottoman Empire. In 1908, 1911, and 1914 he was elected to the Ottoman parliament, advocating administrative reform. Al-Husayni helped found the ARAB CLUB in 1919 and served briefly in 1920 as foreign minister of King FAISAL I in Damascus.

BIBLIOGRAPHY

MANDEL, NEVILLE J. *The Arabs and Zionism before World War I.* Berkeley, Calif., 1976.
MUSLIH, MUHAMMAD. *The Origins of Palestinian Nationalism.* New York, 1988.
PORATH, Y. *The Emergence of the Palestinian-Arab National Movement 1918–1929.* London, 1974.

Elizabeth Thompson

Husayn ibn Ali   [1852–1931]

Arab leader.

Descended from a noble sharifian family of Mecca, the Hashimites, Husayn was the emir of Mecca (1908–1916), king of the Hijaz (1916–1924), and the father of Ali, Zayd, and of King FAISAL I of Iraq and the Emir ABDULLAH of Transjordan, later king of Jordan. In 1893, Husayn moved to Constantinople (Istanbul), seat of the Ottoman Empire, at the bidding of Sultan ABDÜLHAMIT II, and remained there for the next fifteen years. During these years of "gilded captivity," Husayn established himself as the leading candidate for the Meccan emirate, and in 1908, the sultan appointed him to that position. Once in Mecca, Husayn found himself at odds with the YOUNG TURK government in Istanbul. While he sought autonomy for himself and the hereditary office of emir for his sons, the Young Turks and the COMMITTEE OF UNION AND PROGRESS attempted to extend their control over the Hijaz through the construction of the HIJAZ RAILROAD. Husayn's attitude toward Arab nationalism before World War I has been the subject of some dispute. In 1911, he was approached by Arab deputies in the Ottoman parliament as a possible leader of a pan-Arab independence movement. He declined to take active part in their movement. Yet, by 1914, his sons Faisal and Abdullah were actively involved in various secret societies, and in the spring and summer of 1914, Abdullah met with British officials in Cairo. After the outbreak of World War I, Husayn entered into discussions with Britain about the possibility of an Arab revolt led by him against the Ottomans, but he continued to assure the Young Turks of his loyalty. In 1915, he began a correspondence with Sir Henry MCMAHON, the British high commissioner in Cairo. The Husayn–McMahon correspondence established the terms for a British-sponsored Arab revolt, with several critical ambiguities surrounding the status of Palestine. In June 1916, Husayn began the ARAB REVOLT, during which active military leadership passed to his four sons and the British. After the war, he refused to endorse the Versailles Treaty on the grounds that the British had reneged on the Husayn–McMahon correspondence and other wartime promises. At the same time, he came under increasing pressure from Ibn Sa'ud of the Najd in central Arabia. Estranged from the British, who terminated aid to Husayn after 1920, and bitter about the mandates, Husayn declared himself caliph (head of Islam) after Turkey abolished the caliphate in 1924. This ill-advised move alienated Husayn from many of his remaining supporters, and in August 1924, Ibn Sa'ud launched a major assault on the Hijaz. Husayn abdicated, went into exile on Cyprus, and died in 1931 in Amman.

BIBLIOGRAPHY

FROMKIN, DAVID. *A Peace to End All Peace*. New York, 1990.
LENCZOWSKI, GEORGE. *The Middle East in World Affairs*. 4th ed. Ithaca, N.Y., 1980.
MANSFIELD, PETER. *The Arabs*. New York, 1985.
SHIMONI, YAACOV, ed. *Political Dictionary of the Middle East in the Twentieth Century*. New York, 1974.

Zachary Karabell

Husayn ibn Talal

See Hussein ibn Talal

Husaynid Dynasty

See Ahmad Bey Husayn

Husayni Family, al-

Prominent Palestinian Arab family in Jerusalem.

By the late nineteenth century, the family became extremely wealthy owning vast tracts of land, which amounted to about 50,000 dunums, including extensive areas and plantations in Jericho district. The social and political influence of members of the Husayni family was rooted in their ancient status as descendants of the Prophet Muhammad, landowners, delegates to

the Ottoman parliament, mayors and district governors, religious leaders, jurists, and educators. The family's influence also grew from a style of politics based on a delicate balance between the central authority of the Ottoman state and dominance in local Palestinian society. This balancing created a partnership between the central government in Constantinople (now Istanbul) and the urban upper class of the Arab provinces from the mid-nineteenth century until the demise of the Ottoman state in 1917/18. Such partnership contributed to the further ascendance of the Husayni family since it enabled senior members of the family to act as intermediaries between the Ottoman government and local Palestinian society. The British, like the Ottomans before them, had to depend on the Husaynis and other locally influential notables to administer the local affairs of Palestine. The senior members of the family include the following: Musa Kazim al-Husayni (1853–1934) was president of the Arab Executive from 1920 to 1934. Muhammad Amin al-Husayni (c. 1895–1974) was a founder of Palestinian nationalism and the leader of the Palestine national movement until the *nakba* of 1948. Munif al-Husayni (1899–1983) was a close associate of al-Hajj Amin and editor of the Husayni camp's newspaper, *al-Jami'a al-Arabiyya*. Jamal al-Husayni (1892–1982), born in Jerusalem, served as secretary of the Arab Executive and the Supreme Muslim Council, as well as foreign minister for the ALL-PALESTINE GOVERNMENT. Raja i al-Husayni (1902–?) was active from 1945 in the Arab Information Offices, which were organized by Musa al-ALAMI under the auspices of the LEAGUE OF ARAB STATES, served as minister in the All-Palestine government, and later went to Saudi Arabia to work as a senior official in the government. Ishaq Musa al-Husayni (1904–1990), a writer who attained literary prominence on a pan-Arab level, studied Arabic language and literature at the American University in Cairo (1923–1926), Cairo University (1927–1930), and the University of London (1930–1934) where he received a doctoral degree in Semitic languages and literature under the guidance of H. A. R. Gibb, English expert on Arab culture and literature. Ishaq taught Arabic literature at the American University of Beirut, McGill University in Canada, the American University in Cairo, and the Arab League's Institute for Arab Studies in Cairo. He wrote numerous articles and books, the most widely acclaimed being *Memoirs of a Hen* (1943), which won the prize of Dar al-Ma'arif, one of Egypt's most prestigious publishing houses. Dr. Dawud al-Husayni (1904–   ), political activist, played an active role in the PALESTINE ARAB REVOLT, 1936–1939. He was captured by the British in Iraq in 1941 and detained in Rhodesia. Allegedly a coconspirator in the assassination of King ABDULLAH IBN HUSAYN (July 1951) he then served as a member of the Jordanian Parliament (1956, 1962), reportedly as a member of the Executive Committee of the PALESTINE LIBERATION ORGANIZATION (PLO). He stayed in East Jerusalem after the ARAB–ISRAEL WAR of 1967 but was expelled to Jordan by the Israeli authorities in 1968 on charges of hostile political activities. Abd al-Qadir al-Husayni (1908–1948) was a son of Musa Kazim. Unlike most politicians who hailed from notable families, he actually joined the Palestinian commando groups both in the revolt of 1936–1939 and in the ARAB–ISRAEL WAR OF 1948. He died in action (April 1948) at al-Qastal, a mountain along the Jerusalem–Jaffa highway. His son Faysal (1940–   ) established the Arab Studies Center in East Jerusalem in the 1980s. With Fath leanings, he emerged as a local leader of the Palestinian Arabs in the territories occupied by Israel in 1967 and served on the advisory committee of the Palestinian delegation to the Middle East Peace Conference. Faysal is a pragmatist who advocates coexistence between Israel and a Palestinian state in the West Bank and Gaza.

After 1948, the Husayni family was no longer able to retain its dominance over the field of Palestinian politics. This was due to a combination of changes: the dispersal of the Palestinians, the loosening of family ties, the spread of new ideologies, the emergence of new political elites in many parts of the Arab world, as well as the orientation of Palestinian politics and the general weakening of the landowning, scholarly, and mercantile families that constituted a fairly cohesive social class from the second half of the nineteenth century until the end of the British mandate in 1948.

[*See also other members of the Husayni family*]

BIBLIOGRAPHY

MATTAR, P. *The Mufti of Jerusalem.* New York, 1988.
MUSLIH, M. *The Origins of Palestinian Nationalism.* New York, 1988.

Muhammad Muslih

Husayn–McMahon Correspondence

An exchange of letters between Sharif Husayn ibn Ali of Mecca and Sir Henry McMahon, the British high commissioner in Egypt, between 14 July 1915 and 30 March 1916.

The letters, which were not published until 1939, constitute an understanding of the terms by which the sharif would ally himself to Britain and revolt against the Ottoman Turks in return for Britain's support of Arab independence. The sharif asked Britain to support independence of the Arab countries in an area that included the Arabian peninsula, except Aden, and all of Iraq, Palestine, Transjordan, and Syria up to Turkey in the north and Persia in the east. He also asked Britain to support the restoration of the caliphate.

McMahon's reply on October 24, 1915, accepted these principles but excluded certain areas in the sharif's proposed boundaries: coastal regions along the Gulf area of Arabia; the Iraqi province of Baghdad, which would be placed under British supervision; areas "where Britain is free to act without detriment to the interests of her ally France"; and, in Syria, "the districts of Mersina and Alexandretta and portions of Syria lying to the west of the districts of Damascus, Homs, Hama, and Aleppo." The Arabs assumed that at least Arabia, northern Iraq, central Syria, and Palestine, which was regarded as southern, not western, Syria, were part of the area that was to be independent. They started the ARAB REVOLT of 1916, which helped the British to defeat the Turks and to occupy the region. After the war, the Arabs felt betrayed because Britain conceded Syria to France and promised to help in the establishment of the Jewish national home in Palestine. The British claimed that they intended to exclude Palestine from McMahon's pledges.

The interpretations of the letters have been disputed. In addition to deliberate vagueness by the British, who, to obtain French, Arab, and Jewish support during the war, promised more than they could implement, British official oversight and partisan scholars who read into the correspondence interpretations that fit their ideological positions contributed to the confusion.

BIBLIOGRAPHY

KEDOURIE, ELIE. *In the Anglo–Arab Labyrinth: The McMahon–Husayn Correspondence and Its Interpretations, 1914–1939.* Cambridge, U.K., 1976.
MONROE, ELIZABETH. *Britain's Moment in the Middle East, 1914–1956.* Baltimore, 1963.
SMITH, CHARLES D. "The Invention of a Tradition: The Question of Arab Acceptance of the Zionist Right to Palestine during World War I." *Journal of Palestine Studies.* 22, no. 2 (1993): 48–63.

Philip Mattar

Husayn Oweyni   [1900–1970]

Former Prime Minister of Lebanon, 1951 and 1964 to 1965.

A Beirut-born Sunni Lebanese, Husayn Oweyni studied at the Collège Patriarchal Grec-Catholique de Beyrouth. He thereafter began a career as a businessman and settled in Cairo, where he developed commercial interests throughout the Middle East, particularly in Saudi Arabia. In 1937, he returned to Lebanon, where he continued to engage in business activities and became a commercial agent for Saudi Arabian interests. Throughout his life, he remained closely associated with the kingdom.

With time he became progressively more involved in politics as an ally of President Bishara al-KHURI. In 1947, he was elected to parliament as a representative for Beirut and was prime minister for the first time—as well as minister of the interior, foreign affairs, defense, and finance—from February 14 through April 7, 1951. An opponent of President CHAMOUN throughout the latter's tenure (1952–1958), he played a leading role in the 1958 uprising against his government. On October 14, 1958, he was appointed minister of foreign affairs, justice, and planning in the second cabinet (headed by Rashid KARAME) that followed the civil war and General Fu'ad Chehab's election to the presidency. He stepped down almost exactly a year later, however, following Raymond EDDÉ and Rashid Karame's own resignations.

Under President Jean HELLEU, he held the premiership three consecutive times, from February 20, 1964, through July 20, 1965. During that time, he was also minister of defense and of the interior (from February 20 to November 14, 1964). Finally, he was minister of foreign affairs, defense, justice, and the economy, from October 20, 1968, through January 8, 1969, in a cabinet headed by Abd Allah Yafi.

Guilain P. Denoeux

Husayn Pasha   [?–1740]

Bey of Tunisia from 1705 to 1735.

Following the war of 1704/05 with Algeria, Husayn Pasha (also al-Husayn ibn Ali) overthrew Ibrahim Bey and was recognized by the Ottoman Empire as governor of Tunis. While acknowledging Ottoman suzerainty, Husayn won local support for the establishment of hereditary rule; the Husaynids ruled TUNISIA until 1957.

Following years of stable rule, achieved in part by a series of treaties with European states, Husayn Pasha's rule collapsed with an invasion launched by a nephew, Ali Pasha, supported by Algeria. Driven from Tunis in 1735, Husayn was executed in 1740 in Kairouan (al-Qayrawan), north-central Tunisia.

BIBLIOGRAPHY

Encyclopaedia of Islam, 2nd ed.

Matthew S. Gordon

Hüseyin Avni   [1820–1876]

Ottoman soldier and grand vizier.

Hüseyin Avni was *serasker* (commander in chief) of the Ottoman armed forces between 1869 and 1876, except for a term as grand vizier from February 1874 to April 1875. As military chief, he led the coup that deposed the despotic Sultan Abdülaziz on May 30, 1876. Less than a month later, Hüseyin Avni was assassinated by an infantry captain named Çerkes Hasan, apparently in revenge for a personal affront, and perhaps on behalf of his brother-in-law, the deposed Abdülaziz, who had been found dead on June 4.

BIBLIOGRAPHY

LEWIS, BERNARD. *The Emergence of Modern Turkey.* New York, 1961.
SHAW, STANFORD J., and EZEL KURAL SHAW. *History of the Ottoman Empire and Modern Turkey.* Vol. 2. Cambridge, U.K., 1977.

Elizabeth Thompson

Hüseyin Hilmi   [1855–1922]

Ottoman bureaucrat and grand vizier.

A former governor of Yemen, Hüseyin Hilmi was appointed inspector general of Rumelia in 1900 by Sultan Abdülhamit II to quell terrorism and implement reforms in Macedonia. He supported the Committee of Union and Progress after the 1908 revolution, and served as its grand vizier during and after the April counterrevolution of 1909. He was ambassador to Austria-Hungary during World War I.

BIBLIOGRAPHY

MANTRAN, ROBERT, ed. *Histoire de l'empire ottoman.* Paris, 1989.
SHAW, STANFORD J., and EZEL KURAL SHAW. *History of the Ottoman Empire and Modern Turkey.* Vol. 2. Cambridge, U.K., 1977.

Elizabeth Thompson

Husrev, Mehmet Koja   [1756–1855]

Ottoman soldier and grand vizier.

As a lieutenant under Hüseyin, Husrev helped drive the French from Egypt, then served as its last Ottoman governor before the rise of Muhammad Ali. He later reformed the navy while grand admiral (1811–1827), and the army while *serasker* (commander in chief; 1827–1836). As grand vizier in 1839, Husrev supported the proclamation of *tanzimat* reforms. He was ousted the following year during treaty negotiations with Muhammad Ali.

BIBLIOGRAPHY

LEWIS, BERNARD. *The Emergence of Modern Turkey*. New York, 1961.

SHAW, STANFORD J., and EZEL KURAL SHAW. *History of the Ottoman Empire and Modern Turkey*. Vol. 2. Cambridge, U.K., 1977.

Elizabeth Thompson

Hussein, Saddam   [1937–   ]

President of Iraq since 1979.

Saddam Hussein al-Tikriti was born on April 28, 1937, to a Sunni Arab family in Tikrit, Iraq, on the northern bank of the Tigris river. His family (from the village of al-Awjah, near Tikrit) was of poor

President Saddam Hussein of Iraq, 1975. (© Chris Kutschera)

peasant stock; his father died shortly after his birth. His stepfather denied him permission to go to school, so Saddam ran away, seeking refuge in Tikrit in his mother's brother's home. His maternal uncle, Adnan Khayr Allah TALFAH, raised him through adolescence; as a retired army officer and an advocate of ARAB NATIONALISM, a sentiment he imparted to Saddam, he had participated in the short-lived anti-British revolt in 1941, known as the Rashid Ali coup.

In 1956, Saddam moved to Baghdad, where he was impressed by the nationalism that swept Iraq in the wake of Egypt's nationalization of the Suez Canal and the British–French–Israeli attack on Egypt. In 1957, Saddam joined the BA'TH Arab socialist party, which had been founded in Syria in 1947. Dedicated to Arab unity, the party had been popular among students in Jordan, Syria, Iraq, and Lebanon since the early 1950s. From 1957 on, Saddam's life was inextricably bound up with Ba'th.

In 1959, during the presidency of the Iraqi dictator General Abd al-Karim KASSEM, Saddam was a member of a Ba'th team assigned to assassinate Kassem. The attempt failed, and Saddam was wounded in the leg during an exchange of gunfire. He fled Baghdad but later staged a daring escape to Syria, and from there to Egypt, where he joined a number of other exiled Iraqis. It is believed that he became a full member of Ba'th while he was in Egypt.

Kassem's regime ended in February 1963, when a group of Iraqi nationalists and Ba'thist officers brought it down in a violent coup. Kassem was killed; Saddam returned to Iraq with other exiled Iraqis, although he played only a minor role in the Ba'th government that took power. The new regime did not last.

In November 1963, General Abd al-Salam ARIF staged a successful anti-Ba'thist coup and Saddam went underground again. From 1963 to 1968, he worked in clandestine party activities, during which he was captured and jailed, although he managed to escape. In 1966, while still underground, he became a member of the regional command of the Iraqi branch of the Ba'th party. In that position he played a major role in reorganizing the party to prepare for a second attempt at seizing power. He also worked closely with General Ahmad Hasan al-BAKR, a fellow Tikriti, a distant relative, a politician, and a former prime minister under the Ba'th, who was respected by the military. In this period, Saddam was known as a tough partisan and political enforcer, willing to liquidate enemies of the party.

In July 1968, the Ba'th party returned to power after two successful coups that took place in rapid succession. Saddam played an important part in both. Ahmad Hasan al-Bakr became president of the republic; Saddam became vice president of the Revolutionary Command Council (RCC), after some maneuvers to eliminate competitors for the position.

Al-Bakr and Saddam: Dual Role 1969–1979. During these years, Iraq was ruled by al-Bakr, the respected army officer, and Saddam, the young dynamic manipulator and survivor. No major decisions were made without Saddam's consent; in this period, Saddam gradually built the organs of a police state that spread an unparalleled aura of fear and invincibility around himself.

In the 1970s, Saddam had helped shepherd Iraq through major social and economic development, owing to an increase in PETROLEUM revenues. The expansion of social programs included compulsory primary education, a noticeable increase in women participating in the workforce, the founding of new universities, and the availability of medical services. An ambitious industrial program in petrochemicals, steel, and other heavy industry began. The Ba'th party also implemented policies that brought all the social and economic sectors under its control, including the foreign-owned IRAQ PETROLEUM COMPANY (IPC), which was nationalized in 1972.

Saddam and the Ba'th party tended to distance themselves from the West in the 1970s, with strong ties instead to the Soviet Union and Eastern bloc. In 1972, an important Treaty of Friendship was signed between Iraq and the USSR. France was the only Western European country with which Iraq maintained good political and economic relations. Iraq took a hard stand against Israel—attempting to isolate Egypt after the 1978 CAMP DAVID ACCORDS.

The Ba'th party inherited a problem with the Iraqi KURDS, who were struggling for self-determination. After a major revolt for two years, the Kurds had been given special status in 1970, based on self-rule for Kurdish areas. The Kurds revolted again in 1974/ 75. Unable to put a successful end to their revolt, mainly because of help from Iran, Saddam demonstrated his daring style by signing the 1975 ALGIERS AGREEMENT with the shah of Iran. This agreement put an end to Iranian support for the Kurds in return for some modifications of the Iran–Iraq border, along the SHATT AL-ARAB in the south.

Saddam and the War with Iran. The health of President al-Bakr had been deteriorating, reportedly from cancer. Saddam felt that the moment was his to assume total power. On July 16, 1979, al-Bakr was forced to resign and Saddam was "elected" president of the Iraqi republic. Then followed a ruthless purge of suspected challengers. Saddam executed five members of the Revolutionary Command Council and some twenty Ba'th party members. This cleared the

way for the establishment of personal rule and total monopoly of power by Saddam.

Also in 1979, the IRANIAN REVOLUTION established SHI'ISM and an Islamic republic. Iran's new government soon became a political threat to Iraq when it called for an uprising among Iraq's Shi'ite population and the establishment of a regime similar to Iran's. Soon border clashes and claims of border violations by troops from both sides were heard weekly. Some pro-Iranian Shi'ite elements in opposition to Saddam, mainly the al-DA'WA (Religious Call) party, aggravated this situation with internal violence, including two assassination attempts on top Iraqi government members.

Saddam took advantage of Iran's weakness to settle previous scores. In September 1980, he declared that the 1975 Algiers Accord with Iran was null and void. The Iraqi army then crossed the Iranian border and seized Iranian territories, which were later evacuated during the war. The result of Saddam's attack was a bitter and costly war that lasted eight years.

Islamic, Arab, and international mediation efforts to end the war were unsuccessful. Both countries used long-range missiles against cities; during the war Iraq used chemical weapons to ward off Iran's human-wave attacks. Casualties—both military and civilian—mounted on both sides. With the continuation of the war, Saddam adopted a pragmatic stance in international affairs, and the oil-rich Gulf countries provided funds to finance the Iraqi military effort. Then, diplomatic relations with the United States—severed since 1967—were reestablished in November 1984.

Iran unexpectedly announced that it had agreed to a cease-fire in July 1988, after repeated attempts to defeat the Iraqi army near Basra. Peace negotiations continued for months; in the fall of 1990 (after Iraq's August invasion of KUWAIT), in a dramatic action, Iraq accepted the reinstitution of the 1975 Algiers Accord and a rectification of borders between the two countries, as demanded by Iran. By 1992, however, no peace treaty had yet been signed.

The Kuwaiti Adventure. On August 2, 1990, Saddam invaded Kuwait. The invasion was swift and met little resistance, and the Kuwaiti ruling family fled to Saudi Arabia. Iraq had long-standing claims to Kuwait—going back to the days of the Ottoman Empire—but Kuwait's independence had been recognized by Iraq's Ba'thist regime, which had come to power in 1963.

Just before Saddam's invasion, tense relations had existed between Iraq and Kuwait. Differences existed over loan repayments, oil pricing, and the border. Saddam accused Kuwait of stealing oil, by slant drilling from Iraqi oil fields under the border, and of economic warfare, because of Kuwait's oil policy. Saddam annexed Kuwait a few days after the invasion, declaring that country a province of Iraq. The Kuwaiti government called for help to force Iraq's withdrawal. The UN Security Council repeatedly convened for several resolutions, asking Iraq to withdraw and to restore Kuwait's legitimate government. The United Nations agreed to impose an economic blockade on Iraq and, if that did not succeed, to use military force. The role of the United States, Britain, France, and the Soviet Union was pivotal in passing these measures. (See the GULF CRISIS)

Mediation efforts and economic pressures proved unsuccessful, but simultaneously an international coalition of military forces, led by the United States (in accord with the newly cooperative Soviet Union), was deployed to eastern Saudia Arabia. After several months of troop buildup in Saudi Arabia and Saddam's failure to accede to a deadline for withdrawal, the attack began on January 16/17, 1991—beginning with a five-week campaign of air strikes on Iraq, followed by a four-day land campaign. Saddam ordered a retreat from Kuwait when the coalition forces entered southern Iraq. A cease-fire was declared on February 27, 1991, and anti-Saddam uprisings began in some southern Iraqi cities—mainly Basra, Amara, Najaf, and Karbala, spreading throughout the south. Separatist uprisings took place soon after in Iraq's northern Kurdish cities.

Saddam did not waste time in using his army to crush these revolts—he was successful, but only after fierce fighting with insurgents in southern Iraq, resulting in major destruction in the Shi'a cities of the south. The Kurds in the north, faced with Saddam's tanks, left the cities they had occupied and retreated to more secure positions in the high mountains. Many retreated to Turkey and Iran.

The plight of the Kurds was dramatized by the international media, especially in the United States and Europe. As a result, public opinion allowed Western leaders to order military penetration of northern Iraq, to establish secure zones guarded by coalition forces. Safe havens were established to entice Kurdish refugees back. Saddam invited a top-level Kurdish delegation to negotiate with his government in April 1991, but it failed. Saddam then pulled his forces back from Kurdish areas and established his own trade embargo on the north. Inside the Kurdish zone, under the protection of UN forces (mainly U.S., British, and French), the Kurds began to practice genuine self-rule and, in 1992, elected a new Kurdish government.

During his presidency, Saddam has pushed the cult of personality to extremes. Photos of him are everywhere; his speeches have been printed and widely distributed; schools, towns, and the Baghdad airport were named for him. Any criticism of him as head of state has been severely punished. Despite a military defeat, destruction of large parts of the Iraqi economy, and the most widespread rebellion Iraq has experienced since 1920, Saddam's controls prevail. By the end of 1991, although weakened by these events, Saddam's ubiquitous presence once again held sway in Baghdad.

Saddam is married to his cousin Sajida Khair Allah Tulfah and has five children. His two sons, Uday and Qusay, continued to hold high security positions in the mid-1990s.

BIBLIOGRAPHY

HENDERSON, SIMON. *Instant Empire: Saddam Hussein's Ambition for Iraq.* San Francisco, 1991.

ISKANDAR, AMIR. *Saddam Hussein: Le militant, le penseur et l'homme.* Paris, 1980.

KARSH, EFRAIM, and INARI RAUTSI. *Saddam Hussein: A Political Biography.* New York, 1991.

KHADDURI, MAJID. *Socialist Iraq.* Washington, D.C., 1978.

MARR, P. *A Modern History of Iraq.* Boulder, Colo., 1985.

MATAR, FUAD. *Saddam Hussein: The Man, the Cause and the Future.* London, 1981.

MILLER, JUDITH, and LAURIE MYLROIE. *Saddam Hussein and the Crisis in the Gulf.* New York, 1991.

Louay Bahry

Hussein ibn Talal   [1935–]

King of Jordan from 1952.

His Royal Majesty King Hussein ibn Talal is the great-grandson of HUSAYN IBN ALI (Sharif) of Mecca and the grandson of King ABDULLAH IBN HUSAYN, the founder of the Jordanian kingdom (then Transjordan, 1921). It was created out of the collapse of the Ottoman Empire at the end of World War I. Because of the schizophrenia suffered by Hussein's father, Talal, the leadership recognized that Prince Hussein would be the next to assume the throne. Accordingly, Emir Abdullah started instructing the young prince in statecraft at an early age. Hussein became monarch in August 1952, at the age of seventeen, but only after reaching his majority in 1953 did he formally begin his rule.

Despite the family's lack of worldly goods—they could not even buy him a bicycle—Hussein enjoyed a broad but abbreviated education. In Amman, he successively attended a religious school and Kulliyat al-Matran (the Bishop's School); this instruction was supplemented by special tutorials in Arabic and Islam. For his middle prepatory years, he was enrolled

King Hussein of Jordan. (Jordanian Embassy)

in the prestigious Victoria College in Alexandria, Egypt, where he broadened his world view. During this period, the Middle East and Jordan were experiencing momentous events. In 1948, when Prince Hussein was thirteen, Israel was created, and the Arab armies attacked, fighting until 1949. They were defeated, but Transjordan gained possession of the WEST BANK and absorbed a major wave of Palestinian refugees. In 1950, when Prince Hussein was fifteen, the West Bank and Transjordan (also known as the East Bank) were formally joined to create the Hashimite Kingdom of JORDAN.

In 1951, this succession of events began to directly affect the young prince; on July 20, King Abdullah was assassinated. While his father, Talal, temporarily ascended the throne, Prince Hussein was moved to England to join his cousin, Crown Prince Faysal of Iraq, at Harrow, an elite school for future leaders of Britain and the British empire. On August 11, 1952, King Talal was constitutionally removed from the Jordanian throne due to illness, and the crown was passed to his eldest son, Prince Hussein. Since he had not yet reached his majority, the young King Hussein was transferred to Sandhurst, the British military academy, while a regent ruled in Amman. In May 1953, King Hussein returned to Jordan and assumed the throne.

King Hussein has married four times. His first wife was Sharifa Dina, a distant and older cousin from Cairo. They married in 1954; because of incompatibility they divorced eighteen months later. In 1961, King Hussein married the daughter of a British military attaché, Princess Muna, but this union too ended in divorce in 1972. In the following year, the king married a third time, to Alia Tuqan, the daughter of a prominent Nablus, West Bank, family. In 1977, Queen Alia died in a helicopter crash. In 1978, the king married Lisa Halaby, who became Queen Noor, the daughter of Najeeb Halaby, an Arab-American, former chairman of Pan American Airways. The king has by his marriages seven daughters and five sons.

King Hussein enjoys and projects a set of attributes that are crucial to his legitimacy in the minds of the Jordanian people. First, because with T.E. LAWRENCE (of Arabia) they led the ARAB REVOLT against the Ottoman Empire, the Hashimites have a unique claim on the origins of ARAB NATIONALISM. From his speeches and actions, it is clear the king has a strong feeling for and sense of duty toward the larger Arab nation. His vision, though, is not one of a grand political unity. Rather, he thinks that it is incumbent on the Arab states and peoples to cooperate with one another in terms of cultural, social, economic, and strategic matters, which in turn will make the whole Arab nation more than the sum of its parts.

Second, King Hussein is a scion of the family of the Prophet Muhammad. Accordingly, the king has a special relationship to Islam, which he and those around him frequently invoke. This in turn has meaning for more traditional and religious Jordanians. In the age of popular fundamentalism, this legacy is at times an asset that other Arab leaders, King HASSAN II of Morocco excepted, have not possessed. Accordingly, while religious fundamentalism is surging, the movement is relatively more contained in Jordan.

Third, the king and his brother Crown Prince Hasan are perceived as genuinely interested in and, more importantly, capable of delivering socioeconomic development. During the four decades of the king's rule, Jordan has been transformed from a very underdeveloped small state to one that enjoys many features of a middle-income country, including broad availability of drinking water, electricity, and health care, virtually universal education, a sophisticated communications infrastructure, industrialization, and major agricultural projects.

Fourth, Jordanians perceive that they enjoy a relatively high degree of personal freedom and security, especially when they compare their lot to some of their neighbors, especially Iraq, Saudi Arabia, Syria, and the Israeli-administered territories. As long as citizens are not a threat to the state or causing disorder, they can go about life without undue interference. There are limits, however. The king's regime has frequently and severely restricted political freedom. After an absence since 1970, parliament was recalled in the mid-1980s. In 1989, free elections were held accompanied by vibrant debates and a relatively free press; but very considerable power and authority remain with the king.

Fifth, King Hussein's very ability and success at staying on the throne despite adversity and regime challenges create respect. The king is personable, speaks eloquent Arabic, has strength of character and physical courage, and has an attractive family with many children. Jordanians also enjoy seeing the head of their small state dealing as an equal with the leaders of the Middle East and the world.

King Hussein's rule may be divided into three major historical periods. The first twenty years were marked by crises and threats to the throne originating from inside and outside the country: Street riots stimulated by radical Arab nationalism, challenges from his own prime minister in 1956 and 1957, destabilization by larger and stronger Arab states, and the devastating loss of the West Bank to Israel in the ARAB–ISRAEL WAR of June 1967. Soon after, in 1970, the Palestinian guerrilla organizations challenged Jordan in a bloody civil war. Nonetheless, while relying on his loyal military to survive, the king helped put in place the bases for development.

The second phase, starting after the Arab–Israel War of October 1973, is distinguished by quieter internal political conditions, more rapid development fueled by funds (direct grants, loans, individual remittances) derived from the petroleum boom in neighboring states, and improved relations with most of Jordan's Arab neighbors. It was a relatively less radical, regional atmosphere. Despite his problems with the Palestinians and his frequently strained relations with the PALESTINE LIBERATION ORGANIZATION (PLO), the king came to be a respected leader in most Arab capitals. Indeed, he hosted two Arab summits—1980 and 1987—in Jordan.

The third phase is dominated by the end of the Cold War and the alteration of regional relationships. In a sense, King Hussein's decision to disengage Jordan politically and administratively from the West Bank, in response to the pressures from the Palestinian INTIFADA (uprising) of 1987, was a precursor to these changes. More important was the withdrawal of the Soviet Union as an active player in the region (1989/90), the United States's dominance in areas of its perceived interests, and the resulting polarization of the Arab world, so that the 1990/91 GULF CRISIS and war left Jordan (at the time allied with Saddam Hussein's Iraq) and a few other poor Arab states politically, economically, and regionally isolated. Nevertheless, King Hussein continued with the democratization process in Jordan. Most notably, under a mandate from the king, leaders from all political streams wrote a national charter, which defines the general principles for political life in the country. A special general congress made up of 2,000 representatives ratified the document June 9, 1991.

A long-term trend in the king's rule is his moderation and centrism. As a corollary, he does not seek out enemies, he does not try to make enemies or hold grudges against people. Thus after times of internal threat to the regime, he has not executed the challengers. Some were sent to prison or exiled, but in time many were brought back and given positions of some authority. Nor has the king followed radical or overly conservative social, economic, or cultural policies.

The king's relations with the Arab world follow a similar pattern. As the leader of a small state, and in accordance with his perception of Arab nationalism, he attempts to maintain positive relations with the other Arab states. From another viewpoint, King Hussein is following a strategic policy for the survival of his country as he consistently attempts to maintain acceptable ties with some of the strong Arab states; this policy has not always met with success as, for example, during the post–Gulf War period. Finally, he seeks positive relations with the West, with both the United States and European nations. Consequently, in September 1993, he signed the peace accords with Israel.

BIBLIOGRAPHY

DAY, ARTHUR. *East Bank/West Bank: Jordan and the Prospects for Peace.* New York, 1986.

GUBSER, PETER. "Hussein ibn Talal." In *Political Leaders of the Contemporary Middle East and North Africa: A Bibliographical Dictionary,* ed. by Bernard Reich. Westport, Conn., 1990.

———. *Jordan: Crossroads of Middle Eastern Events.* Boulder, Colo., 1983.

HUSSEIN, H.R.M. KING. *Uneasy Lies the Head: The Autobiography of His Majesty King Hussein I of the Hashemite Kingdom of Jordan.* New York, 1962.

JUREIDINI, PAUL A., and R. D. MCLAURIN. *Jordan: The Impact of Social Change on the Role of the Tribes.* New York, 1984.

LUNT, JAMES. *Hussein of Jordan.* New York, 1989.

RUSTOW, DANKWART A. *Hussein: A Biography.* London, 1972.

SATLOFF, ROBERT B. *The Troubles on the East Bank: Challenges to the Domestic Stability of Jordan.* New York, 1986.

VATIKIOTIS, P. J. *Politics and the Military in Jordan: A Study of the Arab Legion, 1927–1957.* New York, 1967.

Peter Gubser

Hut, Shafiq al- [1932–]

Palestinian nationalist, journalist, and intellectual.

Shafiq Ibrahim al-Hut was born in the Manshiyya quarter of Jaffa in British-Mandate Palestine to a wealthy Palestinian Sunni Muslim landowner and citrus merchant. He graduated from Jaffa's elite al-Amiriyya School in 1948, and that same year began a life of exile in Beirut (from where his paternal grandfather had emigrated) as a result of the establishment of Israel.

Al-Hut cut his political teeth in the radical pan-Arabist environment of the American University of Beirut, where he graduated with a B.S. in biology in 1953. Initially a schoolmaster, he joined the leading Lebanese weekly *al-Hawadith* (Events), working first as a correspondent and later as editor. He was subsequently contributing editor to the Lebanese weekly *al-Muharrir* (The Editor).

Al-Hut was a participant in the 1964 Palestine National Council which founded the Palestine Liberation Organization (PLO). That same year he was appointed its representative to Lebanon, a position he held for the next thirty years and that made him an important figure in Palestinian politics and diplomacy. From 1965 to 1967 he was a leader of the internal opposition to then PLO President Ahmad SHUQAYRI (who attempted to exile al-Hut to New Delhi in May 1967), and was linked to the establishment of the Heroes of the Return guerilla group in 1966.

Since 1967, al-Hut has been an independent closely associated with the PLO's al-Fath mainstream. He has also served on the PLO Executive Committee and is widely respected across the Palestinian spectrum for his intellect and skills of expression. Because of his personal opposition to the Israeli–Palestinian Declaration of Principles and his position as a leader of the Palestinian community in Lebanon, in August 1993 al-Hut resigned all his positions in the PLO and became a prominent member of the Palestinian opposition.

A secular pan-Arabist of broadly Nasserist sympathies, al-Hut has published more widely than most Palestinian leaders. He is the author of several books on Palestinian and Arab politics and has written an autobiography. He married the Palestinian writer Bayan Nuwayhid in 1962, and has three children.

BIBLIOGRAPHY

AL-HUT, SHAFIQ. *'Ashrun 'Aman fi Munazamat al-Tahrir al-Filastiniyya: Ahadith al-Dhikriyyat (1964–1984)* (Twenty Years in the Palestine Liberation Organization: A Narrative of Memories). Beirut, 1986

Mouin Rabbani

I

Ibadiyya

The only surviving branch today of the Kharijite schismatic rebels of the seventh century.

The Kharijite movement broke with the fourth caliph Ali in 657 after he agreed to submit his conflict with the governor of Syria, Mu'awiya ibn Abi Sufyan, to arbitration. This action, the Kharijites argued, undermined both the religious and political leadership of Ali. Equally hostile to Umayyad rule by hereditary succession, the Kharijites espoused an ideology of absolute egalitarianism, social austerity, and militant puritanism. The two major Kharijite factions were the Azariqa, who waged a relentless war to overthrow the existing social and political order, and the Ibadiyya, who took a politically quiescent position (*kitman*) during the civil wars of the seventh century.

The Ibadiyya, who derive their name from their founder Abdallah ibn Ibad al-Murri al-Tamimi (died c. 720), were originally based in Basra. Under the early Abbasids in the eighth and ninth centuries, the Ibadiyya took an activist missionary approach (*zuhur*) and spread in the desert frontier regions of north Africa (Tahert), and eastern and southern Arabia (Hadramawt) among tribal social segments. The Ibadiyya developed an elaborate political theory that emphasizes the primacy of religious leadership (imamate), but allows the coexistence of various imams (unlike in Shi'ism). Notwithstanding their acceptance of the Mu'tazili doctrine of the createdness of the Qur'an, the Ibadiyya largely concur with SUNNI ISLAM, particularly the Maliki school on matters of law. The sect survives today in Oman, eastern Africa (Zanzibar), Libya (Jabal Nafusa and Zuagha), the island of Jerba (Tunisia), and southern Algeria (Wargla and Mzab).

BIBLIOGRAPHY

WATT, M. *Islamic Political Thought.* Edinburgh, 1968.

Tayeb El-Hibri

Ibadi oasis of Mzab, Algeria. (Richard Bulliet)

Ibn

Arabic word for son of, descendant of.

In the Middle East, *ibn* is often an integral component of a man's name, where last names do not usually exist. Therefore, *x* ibn *y* defines a person in relation to his father.

Famous medieval Arab and Iberian–Jewish philosophers, authors, historians, geographers, and scientists have been styled in English as Ibn ... ; for example, Ibn Khaldun (1332–1406) wrote a history of Muslim North Africa. More recently, Ibn Sa'ud (1880–1953), king of Saudi Arabia, was actually Abd al-Aziz ibn Faysal ibn Turki Abd Allah ibn Muhammad Al Sa'ud.

BIBLIOGRAPHY

WEHR, HANS. *Arabic-English Dictionary*.

Zachary Karabell

Ibn Musa, Ahmad

Regent of Morocco, 1894–1900.

Sultan Mulai Hassan I was succeeded by his youngest son, ABD AL-AZIZ IBN AL-HASSAN, aged fourteen. As regent, Ibn Musa (known as Ba Ahmad) maintained stability through the control of dissident tribes and counseled cautious diplomacy toward the European powers. Some scholars believe that this caution undermined the sultanate's legitimacy in the eyes of many Moroccans. Ba Ahmad died during a cholera epidemic, leaving the sultanate ruled by a young, untried sultan.

Bruce Maddy-Weitzman

Ibn Nasir, Husayn

Great uncle of Jordan's King Hussein.

Ibn Nasir headed the caretaker governments to oversee elections for the eighth and ninth chambers of deputies in July 1963 and April 1967. After the 1963 elections, when public disturbances died down, he stayed on to form a new cabinet. He was a respected, but not a strong, political figure.

BIBLIOGRAPHY

DANN, URIEL. *King Hussein and the Challenge of Arab Radicalism: Jordan, 1955–1967.* New York, 1989.

Jenab Tutunji

Ibn Sa'ud

See Abd al-Aziz ibn Sa'ud Al Sa'ud

Ibn Tulun Mosque

Ancient mosque in Cairo.

Constructed from 876 to 879 C.E. by Ahmad ibn Tulun, semi-autonomous governor of Egypt for the Abbasid caliphs, this is not only one of Cairo's best-known monuments but is also the best surviving example of religious architecture from that period of Islam. The MOSQUE was erected along with a palace and a government house in a new district known as al-Qata'i (The Allotments), to the northeast of the oldest parts of the city.

Built of brick and rendered with a fine and hard layer of plaster, the mosque comprises a courtyard about about three hundred feet square (92 m), with a fountain-house in the center. The court is surrounded by hypostyle halls covered with a flat wooden roof supported by arcades resting on piers. The prayer hall, on the southeast, is five aisles deep; those on the other three sides are two aisles deep. The mosque, 400 by 460 feet (122 x 140 m) is enclosed in an outer wall 33 feet (10 m) high, with an elaborate cresting adding some 10 feet (3 m) to its height. Beyond the wall on three sides is an outer court (*ziyada*), approximately 62 feet (19 m) broad, enclosed in a somewhat lower wall. In this outer court, opposite the prayer hall, stands the MINARET (tower), the mosque's most distinctive feature. In its present state this tower consists of a square stone base supporting a cylindrical shaft and an elaborate finial; an external staircase winds around the tower. The interior of the mosque is relatively plain, although the arcades are decorated with nook-shafts at the corners of the piers, carved capitals, and bands of geometricized vegetal ornament around and on the underside of the arches and at the top of the walls. Beneath the roof are long wooden planks carved with verses from the QUR'AN written in an angular script.

Most of the architectural and decorative features of the mosque are foreign to Egyptian architecture in the ninth century, although they were common in the religious architecture of Iraq, the Abbasid heartland, and can be seen there in such buildings as the congregational mosques at Samarra, the Abbasid capital where Ahmad ibn Tulun received his training. It is therefore believed that workmen trained in these techniques came to Egypt in the retinue of Ibn Tulun.

The mosque was repeatedly restored and its functions changed. In 1077, the Fatimid vizier Badr al-Jamali restored the mosque and, in 1094, his son al-Afdal added a beautiful stucco MIHRAB (a niche indicating the direction of Mecca) to one of the piers. Under the Ayyubids, who believed that Cairo needed only one congregational mosque, the building fell into disrepair and served as a shelter for North African pilgrims to Mecca and also as a bakery. In 1296, the Mamluk Sultan Lagin, who had taken refuge in the mosque during one of the struggles that eventually brought him to power, restored it extensively; he added a new mihrab, replaced the fountain-house that had stood in the court with the present domed edifice, and reconstructed the minaret, which had also fallen into disrepair.

By the early nineteenth century, the mosque was again deteriorated and, by the middle of that century, it was used as an insane asylum and poorhouse. In 1884, the newly formed Comité de Conservation des Monuments de l'Art Arabe recommended the restoration of the building, and work was soon begun.

BIBLIOGRAPHY

BEHRENS-ABOUSEIF, DORIS. *Islamic Architecture in Cairo: An Introduction.* Leiden, Neth., 1989.
CRESWELL, K. A. C. *Early Muslim Architecture.* Oxford, 1940. Reprint, New York, 1979.

Jonathan M. Bloom

Ibrahim, Abd al-Fattah   [1906–   ]

Prominent Iraqi leftist.

Ibrahim, a native of Baghdad, attended the American University of Beirut. He was founder of Jama'at al-Ahali (AHALI GROUP) in 1932 but split with the group in 1936. Ten years later he founded the National Union Party, which was banned. Best known as a political writer and commentator, he was director-general of petroleum under Abd al-Karim Kassem (1959–1960).

Marion Farouk-Sluglett

Ibrahim, Abdullah   [1918–   ]

Moroccan socialist political leader.

Ibrahim was educated at the Université Ben Youssef in Marrakech and the Sorbonne in Paris. He was a founding member of Hizb al-Istiqlal (1944–1959) and on the editorial committee of *Al-Alam,* the newspaper of the Istiqlal party (1950–1952). He was imprisoned for nationalist activities (1952–1954). After independence from France, Ibrahim served as secretary of state for information (1955–1956) and minister of labor and social affairs (1956–1958). He became prime minister and minister of foreign affairs from 1958 to 1960. In 1959 he helped form UNION NATIONALE DES FORCES POPULAIRES (National Union of Popular Forces; UNFP) from the left-wing of Hizb al-Istiqlal and became leader of the UNFP in July 1972 when its Rabat section became the UNION SOCIALISTE DES FORCES POPULAIRES (Socialist Union of Popular Forces; USFP).

BIBLIOGRAPHY

WATERBURY, JOHN. *Commander of the Faithful: The Moroccan Political Elite—A Study in Segmented Politics.* New York, 1970.

C. R. Pennell

Ibrahim, Izzat   [1942–   ]

Ba'thist politician in Iraq.

Ibrahim was born into an Arab Sunni family, rumored to be of Sabean origin, in al-Dur district of Samarra. His father was an ice vendor. Ibrahim joined the BA'TH party in the late 1950s and was in prison during the 1960s for his political activities. He held several important positions following the Ba'th coup of 1968: minister of land reform (1969–1974) and minister of the interior (1974–1979). In 1979 he became deputy chairman of the Revolutionary Command Council (RCC). Izzat Ibrahim is the constitutional successor to the president of Iraq, Saddam HUSSEIN. His daughter is married to the president's oldest son, Uday.

Ibrahim, an unassuming introvert, is rumored to be in poor health. He is rarely seen on television. In 1973, he headed a special court trying the conspirators who were behind the unsuccessful coup headed by Kzar. As deputy chair of the RCC, he was put in charge of several task forces and special commissions in the Ba'th government. Prior to Iraq's invasion of Kuwait, Ibrahim headed the delegation to negotiate the problems between the two countries.

BIBLIOGRAPHY

HELMS, CHRISTINE M. *Iraq: Eastern Flank of the Arab World.* Washington, D.C., 1984.

Ayad al-Qazzaz

Ibrahim, Muhammad Hafiz   [1871–1932]

Egyptian poet and writer; one of the best-known Arab neoclassicists.

Whereas Ahmad SHAWQI was known as a poet of the court, the "prince of poets," Hafiz Ibrahim was the "people's poet." He was also known as the "poet of the Nile"—an appropriate epithet, since he was born on a houseboat on the Nile river near the town of Dayrut.

Hafiz Ibrahim had a somewhat lonely childhood followed by a long struggle to find a vocation. He went to a modern secular school in Cairo, then to a more traditional Qur'anic school in Tanta. Hafiz also served as an apprentice to several lawyers and later graduated from the Military Academy in Cairo. His military service in the Sudan ended abruptly with a court-martial because of his involvement in an army rebellion. Returning to Cairo, he was unable to find work. This was the beginning of his most difficult years of poverty and unemployment, which lasted until 1911, when he was nominated to head the literary section of the National Library. During these years, Hafiz came into contact with prominent Egyptian nationalists and was popular among them because of his winning balance of earnestness and conversational wit.

Hafiz Ibrahim employed a generally simple, direct, yet fluent poetic diction, adapting traditional forms to speak to new audiences living in a changing world. He reached his audience in two ways: first, he was a master of "platform poetry," reciting his poetry publicly to large groups of listeners; second, he actively contributed poetry to prominent Egyptian newspapers and periodicals. Hafiz Ibrahim was able to address social and political events in verse, giving voice to common Egyptian opinions. His most successful works were his elegies and his occasional poems.

Kenneth S. Mayers

Ibrahim Ethem   [1818–1893]

Ottoman soldier, bureaucrat, and grand vizier.

A lesser Tanzimat reformer with close ties to the future sultan Abdülhamit, Ibrahim Ethem served between 1856 and 1872 as foreign minister, minister of education, and minister of trade. As grand vizier in 1877–1878, he confronted the rebellion in Bosnia and Herzegovina and war with Russia. He is credited with establishing the first modern government printing press outside of Topkapı Palace.

BIBLIOGRAPHY

SHAW, STANFORD J., and EZEL KURAL SHAW. *History of the Ottoman Empire and Modern Turkey.* Vol. 2. New York, 1977.

Elizabeth Thompson

Ibrahimi, Ahmed Taleb   [1932–   ]

Algerian government official.

A medical doctor and son of Bashir Ibrahimi, Taleb Ibrahimi was imprisoned during the ALGERIAN WAR OF INDEPENDENCE, 1954–1962, after serving in the Fédération de France of the FRONT DE LIBÉRATION NATIONALE (National Liberation Front, FLN), a branch of the FLN operating in France. He was released in 1961 and, at the United Nations, represented the Gouvernement Provisoire de la République Algérienne (Provisional Government of the Algerian Republic, GPRA). He was arrested in June 1964 and charged with associating with "counterrevolutionaries" but was freed in January 1965. Under Colonel Houari BOUMÉDIENNE, Ibrahimi was appointed minister of national education (July 1965) and then minister of information and culture (July 1970), where he supervised the inauguration of Algeria's cultural revolution.

After Boumédienne's death (December 1978), Taleb Ibrahimi served his successor President Chadli BENJEDID as a counselor minister and then as foreign minister after the death of Mohamed Benyahia (May 1982) until the formation of the Kasdi Merbah cabinet (November 1988). He then became disaffected and associated with an anti-Benjedid faction within the FLN.

Taleb Ibrahimi authored *Lettres de prison* (1966) and *De la décolonisation à la révolution culturelle* (1973).

BIBLIOGRAPHY

DÉJEUX, JEAN. *Dictionnaire des auteurs maghrébines de langue française.* Paris, 1984.

Phillip C. Naylor

Ibrahimi, Bashir   [1889–1965]

Islamic religious leader in Algeria.

Born in Béjaïa in northeastern Algeria, Ibrahimi became a leading companion to Shaykh Abd al-Hamid BEN BADIS. Ibrahimi was renowned as an orator for the ASSOCIATION OF ALGERIAN MUSLIM ULAMA (Reformist Ulama) and served as its vice president and then its president after the death of Ben Badis. Through his studies in Damascus, he also achieved a great reputation as a scholar of Arabic and Islam while contributing numerous articles to the association's various journals. Ibrahimi was an opponent of French colonialism, as symbolized by the association's support of the FRONT DE LIBÉRATION NATIONALE (National Liberation Front, FLN). After the ALGERIAN

WAR OF INDEPENDENCE, 1954–1962, he questioned the political leadership's use of foreign ideologies and called for the new nation to identify instead with its Arab Islamic traditions. His son Ahmed Taleb Ibrahimi became a government official under presidents, Houari Boumédienne and Chadli Benjedid.

BIBLIOGRAPHY

GORDON, DAVID C. *The Passing of French Algeria*. London, 1966.

Phillip C. Naylor

Ibrahimi, Lakhdar al-   [1934–   ]

Algerian diplomat.

Ibrahimi studied law and political science in Algiers and in Paris. He was independent Algeria's first minister of external affairs in 1962 and 1963. He then served from 1963 to 1969 as Algeria's ambassador to Egypt and Sudan. Since 1970, Ibrahimi has been Algeria's permanent representative to the Arab League, where he has also acted as assistant secretary-general. In the 1980s, Ibrahimi headed the league's efforts to end the Lebanese civil war (1975–1991) leading to the Ta'if (Saudi Arabia) meetings of 1989.

BIBLIOGRAPHY

BUSTROS, GABRIEL, ed. *Who's Who in the Arab World 1988–89*. Beirut, 1989.

Middle East Contemporary Survey 1989. Vol. 13. Boulder, Colo., 1991.

Elizabeth Thompson

Ibrahim ibn Muhammad Ali   [1789–1848]

Nineteenth-century Egyptian general; son of Muhammad Ali Pasha.

The elder son of MUHAMMAD ALI Pasha, the founder of modern Egypt, Ibrahim Pasha was born in Kavala, Anatolia. He and his brother Tusun accompanied their father when he assumed power as Egypt's viceroy for the OTTOMAN EMPIRE in 1805. Ibrahim was assigned various responsibilities that ranged from national finance to the governing of Upper Egypt. Starting his military career in 1816, Ibrahim commanded the expedition sent by Muhammad Ali, at the request of the Ottoman sultan, to Arabia to crush the Wahhabi rebellion. In 1818, Ibrahim Pasha succeeded in what came to be known as the Wahhabi war, destroying their capital (al-Dar'iyah, now Ri-

yadh) capturing their leaders, and restoring Ottoman control over ISLAM's holy cities of Mecca and Medina. Gratified by this success, the Ottoman government (SUBLIME PORTE) named Ibrahim to be *wali* (provincial governor) of the provinces of Hijaz and Abyssinia (today Ethiopia).

In 1822, Ibrahim assisted his brother Isma'il in the invasion of the Sudan and then, in 1824, led the Egyptian army in the name of the Ottoman Empire against a revolt in Greece. By 1826, Ibrahim Pasha was able to capture the Morea (Peloponnesus) and Athens. However, the European powers, despite Muhammad Ali's attempts to reach an agreement with Great Britain, decided to intervene and enforced a blockade on the Morea by the joint naval forces of France, Russia, and Great Britain. In October 1827, the European forces destroyed the whole Egyptian and Ottoman fleet in the battle of NAVARINO, and Ibrahim Pasha was forced to withdraw.

After the Greek war, Muhammad Ali demanded the governorship of Morea and Syria. Denied by the sultan, he declared war on the Porte in 1831 and sent an Egyptian force to Syria under Ibrahim's command. The troops progressed victoriously through Syria, entered Anatolia, and defeated the Ottoman army in the Battle of KONYA in 1832. The Egyptian victory forced the sultan to sign the treaty of Kütahya in which the Porte granted Muhammad Ali the government of Syria and Adana, in what is today southern Turkey. Ibrahim was appointed governor of Syria. During his rule, he attempted to develop the irrigation system and introduced modern industry to the region. However, his enforcement of military service on the Syrians and his strict discipline led to the emergence of anti-Egyptian feelings among the population.

In 1839, the war between the Porte and Egypt was renewed and for the second time Ibrahim Pasha achieved a victory over the Ottomans at the battle of Nisib, and the road to Constantinople (now Istanbul) became virtually open. However, the European powers intervened, demanding the withdrawal of Egyptian troops. Muhammad Ali was forced to ask his son to turn back. The European intervention, headed by Britain, was followed by the LONDON CONVENTION of 1840 in which the European powers forced Muhammad Ali to return Syria and Adana to the Porte.

In 1845, Ibrahim Pasha visited France and England. In April 1848, due to the illness of Muhammad Ali and his inability to rule, Ibrahim Pasha proclaimed himself ruler of Egypt and informed the Sultan of this change. In October of that year, the Porte conferred on him the government of

Egypt. However, a few weeks later in November, Ibrahim Pasha died—even before the death of his father.

BIBLIOGRAPHY

DODWELL, HENRY. *The Founder of Modern Egypt: A Study of Muhammad Ali.* Cambridge, U.K., 1931.
GOLDSCHMIDT, ARTHUR. *Modern Egypt: The Foundation of a Nation-State.* Boulder, Colo., 1988.
MARSOT, AFAF LUTFI AL-SAYYID. *Egypt in the Reign of Muhammad Ali.* Cambridge, U.K., 1984.
AL-RAFI'I, ABD AL-RAHMAN. *Asr Muhammad Ali* (The Age of Muhammad Ali). Cairo, 1930.

Ali E. Hillal Dessouki

Ibrahim ibn Yahya Hamid al-Din
[?–1948]

Opponent of his family's rule over North Yemen.

Son of Imam YAHYA IBN MUHAMMAD HAMID AL-DIN of North Yemen, Ibrahim joined the opposition Free Yemenis in Aden in 1946. Following his father's murder, he joined in the 1948 revolution and was executed on the order of his brother, Imam AHMAD IBN YAHYA HAMID AL-DIN, when the revolution was quickly put down.

Robert D. Burrowes

İbrahim Şinasi

See Şinasi, İbrahim

İbret

Young Ottoman newspaper.

Initially established as a daily newspaper by Aleksan Sarafyan in 1870, *İbret* (Admonition) lasted only one month before being closed. Reappearing as a weekly humor magazine did not resolve the situation. On 13 June 1872, *İbret* reappeared as a daily newspaper, with NAMIK KEMAL as head writer. The paper was more of an intellectual organ than a chronicle of current events and regularly called for the termination of absolutism. Publication was suspended in September 1872, only to be resumed in early 1873. On 5 April 1873, the last issue, number 132, appeared, containing articles about Namık Kemal's controversial new play, *Vatan yahut Silistre.* Following this, the paper was closed for the last time, and the paper's writers were arrested and sent into exile.

BIBLIOGRAPHY

İNUĞUR, M. NURI. *Türk basinida "İz" birakanlar.* Istanbul, 1988, pp. 7, 33–35.

David Waldner

ICA

See Jewish Colonization Organization

İdadi Schools

Ottoman middle or secondary schools.

In the late nineteenth century, İdadi schools provided three years of intermediate and low secondary-level education. Instruction was in Turkish and French. The curriculum included logic, economics, geography, world and Ottoman history, algebra and arithmetic, the physical sciences, and engineering.

In the 1850s the military opened the first provincial İdadi schools in Baghdad, Erzurum, and Sarajevo. The first nonmilitary, state-run İdadi school opened in Constantinople (now Istanbul) in the 1870s. Under the 1869 Regulation for Public Instruction, towns and cities were required to provide one İdadi school for every thousand households. By 1895, about one-third of a total of thirty thousand students attending intermediate school in the Ottoman Empire were enrolled in the fifty-five state and military İdadi schools, the latter being found in every province. The other two-thirds of students attended the seventy MILLET SYSTEM–run İdadi schools or the sixty-three foreign ones, such as American-run Robert College in Constantinople. State-run İdadi schools were financed by taxes. The term "İdadi schools" was changed in 1908 to SULTANI SCHOOLS, and in 1925 in Turkey, to *orta* or middle schools.

BIBLIOGRAPHY

KAZAMIAS, ANDREAS M. *Education and the Quest for Modernity in Turkey.* Chicago, 1966.
LEWIS, BERNARD. *The Emergence of Modern Turkey.* New York, 1961.

Elizabeth Thompson

IDF

See Israeli Military and Politics; Military in the Middle East

Idlib Province

Province in northwest Syria, named after its principal town, Idlib, where the governor resides.

Idlib is north of the mountain Jabal al-ZAWIYA and east of the al-Ruj plain. There were two Idlib's in the past: Lesser Idlib and Greater Idlib. The last was the most ancient, superseded by Lesser Idlib, the present-day town. The region of Idlib is famed for its olive groves and vineyards. Pistachio and cherry trees have recently proven very productive in its hilly countryside. Cotton of high quality and grains are also among the major crops there. Soap making using olive oil and alkaline burnt herb was the most prosperous industry in Idlib in the past, as evidenced by the presence of three hills in the town made up of accumulating ash from soap furnaces. The soap industry moved to ALEPPO, and the hills have been removed.

In the 1952 administrative divisions in Syria, Idlib was part of Aleppo province. Later it became the center of a separate province because of its vast countryside and also because the Aleppo province had become too large. In the administrative divisions of 1982, the province of Idlib had 5 *mintaqas* or *qadas* (sections), 15 *nahiyas* (administrative subdivisions), 6 towns, 16 smaller towns, 411 villages, and 481 farms. The total population of the province, according to the 1980 census, was 352,619 inhabitants, including 51,682 in the town. The province has a number of so-called dead cities dating back to Byzantine times. It also has the well-preserved church of Qalb Lawza and the famous church of Saint Simeon Stylite. The site of historical Ebla has been discovered a few miles from Idlib.

Abdul-Karim Rafeq

Idris I, King of Libya

See Idris al-Sayyid Muhammad al-Sanusi

Idris, Yusuf [1927–1991]

Egyptian author of short stories, plays, and novels.

After a childhood spent in the Nile delta region, Idris moved to Cairo in 1945 to study medicine at Cairo University. He began writing short stories while a student and published several in newspapers before his graduation in 1951. He began to practice medicine but continued his involvement in both political causes and fiction; his first collection of short stories, *Arkhas Layali* (The Cheapest Nights), was published to great acclaim in 1954. In the same year he was imprisoned for his involvement in political activities. Following his release in September 1955, he began writing articles for the newspaper *al-Jumhuriyya*. The late 1950s and the 1960s, until the 1967 ARAB–ISRAEL WAR, became Idris's most productive period—in an amazing outpouring of creativity, he published several short-story collections as well as a number of plays and novels. He gave up medical practice in 1967 and assumed an administrative post in the ministry of culture. As was the case with many Arab authors, the Arab–Israel War had a profound effect on his literary career. Until his death in 1991, poor health, depression, and the demands and distractions of a weekly column in the Cairo daily *al-Ahram* combined to reduce his creative output.

Of the literary genres to which Idris made contributions, it is undoubtedly in the development of the Arabic short story that his key role is most obvious. His mastery of the genre was instinctive, and the brilliance of his contributions was recognized by critics from the outset. From the realistic vignettes of provincial and urban life to be found in the earliest collections, such as *Arkhas Layali* and *Hadithat Sharaf* (An Affair of Honor, 1958), he gradually shifted to more symbolic and surrealistic narratives in collections like *Akhir al-Dunya* (The World's End, 1961) and *Lughat al-Ay-Ay* (Language of Screams, 1965)—many of the stories essentially parables about the alienation of human beings in contemporary society. In these later collections, we still encounter scenes from country life, but the focus has shifted from realistic detail to the symbolic portrait of the inner workings of the mind. Several also show his virtuoso ability to manipulate narrative point-of-view and to incorporate us into the storytelling process. Above all, his command of narrative structure and his use of allusive language has given his contributions to this genre a stature unmatched by any other Egyptian writer—and by very few other Arab litterateurs.

Idris often admitted to writing on impulse, something that may well contribute to his great success in the realm of the short story. This same impulsiveness may explain why his essays in other genres have, for the most part, not met with similar success. While many of Idris's plays have been performed to great popular acclaim, even his most popular and accomplished play, *Al-Farafir* (The Farfoors, 1964), loses cohesion in its lengthy second act. Of his novels, only *Al-Haram* (The Taboo, 1959), with its realistic portrayal of migrant communities in the provinces, manages to sustain a narrative focus through the longer fictional mode.

Idris's craft shows the greatest development and made the greatest contribution in the much-discussed area of language. Coupled to a great storyteller's ability in creating scenes and moods with an allusiveness and economy akin to that of poetry, Idris's narrative style co-opted the riches of the colloquial dialect to create a multitextured descriptive instrument of tremendous subtlety and variety. This colloquial level was his natural choice for dialogue in both plays and fiction, but aspects of the colloquial's lexicon and syntax are also to be found in narrative passages of his fiction. This stylistic feature has not endeared him to conservative critics, but it lent his stories an element of spontaneity and authenticity that contributed in no small part to their popularity. Idris's storytelling style, his lively imagination, sardonic sense of humor, and tremendous concern for the plight of modern life, are at their best in his short stories—many of which rival the very best in that most elusive and self-conscious of literary genres.

[See also: Literature, Arabic]

BIBLIOGRAPHY

ALLEN, ROGER. Modern Arabic Literature. New York, 1987.
KURPERSHOEK, P. M. The Short Stories of Yusuf Idris. Leiden, 1981.

Roger Allen

Idris al-Sayyid Muhammad al-Sanusi

[1890–1983]

Head of the Sanusi order; king of Libya, 1951–1969.

Born in Jaghbub, Cyrenaica, the eastern province of Libya, Idris was the grandson of Muhammad ibn Ali al-Sanusi, founder of the Sanusi order of Islam, and the son of al-Sayyid al-Mahdi al-Sanusi, the leader of the Sanusis in 1890.

During World War I, while the Sanusis were on the Ottoman side fighting the Italians, Idris was training a Sanusi force to fight with the British. In 1916, the British recognized Idris as the leader of the Sanusi order, and in 1920, Italy recognized him as the emir of Cyrenaica. Despite Italy's wishes, Idris also accepted the title of emir of Tripolitania, offered to him by the people of the province. That same year, however, a Sanusi rebellion forced Idris into exile. He fled to Cairo and remained there for twenty years.

When World War II broke out, Idris called all Libyans to fight on the side of the Allies in order to drive out the Italians. He began a Sanusi unit to fight alongside the Allies in their desert campaign. The British recognized Idris's claim to be the head of an independent Cyrenaica, and later he proclaimed himself the region's emir. When Libya became fully independent in 1951, Idris was offered the crown of a united Libya, and he ascended to the throne on 24 December 1951.

The conservative nature of Idris's rule caused a great deal of friction between him and those in Tripolitania, who were more nationalist. In 1963, when the province system was abolished, a unitary regime was established. In 1969, while Idris was abroad, the nationalists, led by Muammar al-Qaddafi, took over the country in a military coup. Idris did not challenge their power and lived out the rest of his days in Greece and Egypt.

BIBLIOGRAPHY

DE CONDOLE, E. A. V. Al-Malik Idris, ahil Libiya: Hayatuhu wa asruh. London, 1989.
WRIGHT, JOHN L. Libya: A Modern History. Baltimore, 1982.

Julie Zuckerman

Idrisids

Descendants of Sayyid Muhammad ibn Ali al-Idrisi living in southwestern Arabia.

The principality of Asir has been important in the politics of southwestern Arabia. It was incorporated into the new state of Saudi Arabia in 1926 when ABD AL-AZIZ IBN SAʿUD AL SAʿUD established a protectorate over the realms of the Idrisi sultanate, as it was known at the time.

In the past, the two major towns of Asir, Abu Arish and Abha, have been the capitals of different families, or clans, accurately reflecting the fact that Asir is really two distinct areas. Geographically, economically, and culturally, much of Asir is a continuation of Yemen and, for most of its history, has been considered a part of Yemen. However, when the imams of Sanʿa or of other towns, such as Saʿda, were weak and ineffectual, local Asiri notables declared their independence and carried on their own domestic and foreign policies. The most recent of these independent notables was Sayyid Muhammad ibn Ali al-Idrisi, a grandson of Sayyid Ahmad al-Idrisi, the native of Fez who founded the religious sect to which the founder of the Sanusi belonged. Idrisi immigrated to Arabia and made his base at Abha; he wrested control of most of Asir from the Ottoman authorities in the early years of the twentieth century. He was able to obtain the support of the Italians in their campaigns for influence in the

Red Sea region precisely because of his connection to the Sanusi, then established in the Italian areas in North Africa.

Idrisi attempted to expand his influence and territory at the expense of the imams of San'a in the period before World War I. Specifically, he attempted to take Shaykh Sa'id, Luhaiya, and Hodeida—Tihama port cities that would have enabled him to add the Yemeni Tihama to his realm. In this effort, he was at times assisted by Italian naval contingents in the Red Sea. During World War I, the British signed an agreement with him in an effort to limit the influence of Yemen, which refused to ally itself against the Ottomans. In return, the British gave him the Yemeni Tihama and other areas, which had to be wrested from Idrisi control by Imam Yahya in the 1920s. After his death, at Sabya, his descendants expanded the influence of the family by taking control of Abu Arish, which had been in the hands of a separate family of sharifs since the eighteenth century. The gradual takeover of Asir by Abd al-Aziz ibn Sa'ud however, ended the separate existence of the Idrisi state, which was reconfirmed in 1930.

Imam Yahya, however, continued to maintain that Asir, and especially its Zaydi and Isma'ili populations, had been illegitimately removed from Yemeni sovereignty; this led, eventually, to a brief war between Yemen and Saudi Arabia, in which the latter emerged the victor. In the treaty of TA'IF (1934) the Yemenis recognized, albeit grudgingly, Saudi sovereignty over Asir, as well as over the Najran oasis. The treaty was renewed every twenty years until the United Republic of Yemen handed Asir over permanently to Saudi Arabia in 1995.

Manfred W. Wenner

Ignatiev, Nikolas Pavlovich [1832–1908]

Russian diplomat.

Born in St. Petersburg, Ignatiev entered the diplomatic service in 1856 and served as ambassador to the Ottoman Empire in Constantinople (1864–1878). He was a zealous pan-Slavist, described by one writer as "brilliant and none-too-scrupulous." In contrast to the Russian foreign minister, Aleksandr GORCHAKOV, Ignatiev worked for the downfall of the Ottoman Empire. He was active in inciting the 1877–1878 Russo–Ottoman War, and is credited with framing the Treaty of San Stefano (1878), which laid the foundation for "Big Bulgaria." However, in the interest of good relations with Britain and Austria, the treaty and Ignatiev's "Big Bulgaria" were jettisoned by Gorchakov at the Congress of Berlin (1878), and with them Ignatiev's career. At the height of his power, Ignatiev influenced the Ottoman government to such an extent that he was referred to as "Sultan Ignatiev."

BIBLIOGRAPHY

ANDERSON, M. S. *The Eastern Question.* London, 1966.
SHAW, STANFORD, and EZEL KURAL SHAW. *History of the Ottoman Empire and Modern Turkey.* New York, 1977.

Zachary Karabell

Ijtihad

Ottoman newspaper.

Published by Abdullah CEVDET, *Ijtihad* (The Struggle), also known as *Içtihat,* advocated modernist views. It appeared monthly between 1904 and 1932. The paper defended the rights of women, and advocated the modernization of the family and the establishment of secular institutions. *Ijtihad* published articles in English and French. It ceased publication upon the death of Cevdet.

BIBLIOGRAPHY

SHAW, STANFORD, and EZEL KURAL SHAW. *Reform, Revolution, and Republic: The Rise of Modern Turkey, 1808–1975.* Vol. 2 of *History of the Ottoman Empire and Modern Turkey.* Cambridge, U.K., 1977.

David Waldner

Ikdam

Ottoman newspaper.

A daily newspaper, published in Constantinople (now Istanbul), *Ikdam* (Perseverance) represented the views of the Ottoman Liberal Union party. Edited by Ahmed CEVDET, *Ikdam* was published between 1894 and 1928. After 1909, the paper opposed the rule of the COMMITTEE OF UNION AND PROGRESS (CUP), and Cevdet was forced into exile in Europe. One of the most important cultural organs of the period, *Ikdam* enjoyed a large audience, printing fifteen thousand copies daily. The issue announcing the reintroduction of the constitution sold over forty thousand copies.

BIBLIOGRAPHY

EMIN, AHMED. *The Development of Modern Turkey as Measured by Its Press.* New York, 1968.

David Waldner

Ikha al-Watani Party

Iraqi political party of the 1930s.

Ikha al-Watani (National Brotherhood) was formed to oppose the Anglo–Iraqi Treaty of 1930. Its principal members were Yasin al-HASHIMI, Rashid Ali al-KAYLANI, and Hikmat SULAYMAN. In 1933 some of its members accepted the 1930 treaty and participated in a government under Rashid Ali (March–October 1933). A second Ikha cabinet under Yasin al-Hashimi was formed in March 1935, but the group disbanded itself shortly afterward.

Peter Sluglett

Ikhlassi, Walid [1935–]

Syrian novelist, short story writer, and dramatist.

Walid Ikhlassi was born in Alexandretta. After the cession of Alexandretta to Turkey in 1939, his family moved to Aleppo. He received his education in agricultural engineering at the University of Alexandria in Egypt. He later became a lecturer at the College of Agriculture at the University of Aleppo.

Ikhlassi was raised in a family preoccupied with religious and national issues. Imbued with nationalistic aspirations during the French mandate, Ikhlassi's writings mainly deal with democracy, freedom, responsibility, alienation, the loss of the self, and the failure of human ideals. The Palestinian diaspora is also a significant theme in his work; he tackled it throughout an entire collection of short stories, *The Time of Short Migrations,* 1970. Although Ikhlassi's first short story, "The Cock," appeared in 1954, his first collection, *Stories* had to wait until 1963. Since then, he has published eight more collections. Some stories have been translated into English, French, Russian, and Persian.

Ikhlassi was the first Syrian novelist to experiment with the nouveau roman. While his first novel, *A Winter of the Dry Sea,* published in 1965, divided the literary critics into conservatives and liberals, his second novel, *The Lap of the Beautiful Lady,* in 1969, pleased the conservative camp for it adhered to traditional rules and practices of fiction. Ikhlassi has published nine more novels. The latest to date is *The Minor Epic of Death* in 1993.

Ikhlassi not only feels comfortable manipulating narrative techniques but also alternating among narrative genres. He believes that the subject matter dictates both the form and the genre to be employed in a certain artistic work. Like his novels and short stories, Ikhlassi's plays show innovation in literary devices and a break with the then dominant realistic mode of expression in favor of a more symbolic, surrealistic, and allegorical mode.

BIBLIOGRAPHY

IKHLASSI, WALID. "The Path." In *Modern Arabic Drama,* ed. by Salma Khadra Jayyusi and Roger Allen. Bloomington, Ind., 1995.

Sabah Ghandour

Ikhwan

An organization created to spearhead the expansion of the modern Saudi state in the second and third decades of the twentieth century.

During the decade following his capture of Riyadh in 1902, ABD AL-AZIZ IBN SA'UD AL SA'UD, better known as Ibn Sa'ud, relied on the townsmen of Najd in central Arabia as the principal source of military manpower, as had earlier rulers. However, early military setbacks and the revolt of the Araif faction of the Al Sa'ud convinced him of the need for a religious revival to reinforce his political legitimacy and for a source of expanded, reliable military manpower. Ibn Sa'ud's innovative solution was to use the revival to sedentarize a large part of the bedouin population by establishing settlements where tribesmen would be instructed in the austere Wahhabi reform interpretation of Islam (based on the teachings of Muhammad ibn Abd al-Wahhab) and would form an expanded military strike force. These cantonments were called *hujar* (sing., *hijra*), in conscious emulation of the first Islamic community under the Prophet Muhammad.

The first hujar were in Najd at Artawiya and Ghat-Ghat, northeast and southeast of Riyadh, respectively. The former was occupied by elements of the Mutayr and the latter by the UTAYBA, two of the most powerful tribes of central Arabia. Although the *ikhwan* (brethren) were intended to supersede tribal loyalties, particular tribes were linked to the various hujar. At the same time the movement split some tribes by converting some to its cause while others resisted proselytization. More than 200 hujar were established, most of them in Najd, organized along similar lines. A mosque and square were at the center where the ikhwan assembled for a raid. Stables were near the square and, extending to a protective mud wall, there were modest houses.

Ibn Sa'ud's assumption that the hujar would support themselves through agriculture and trade proved largely illusory; they remained dependent on the ruler's largess and the percentage of captured booty allotted to them after raids and battles. Religious instruction made the ikhwan literalist and unbending in their interpretation and practice of Islam. They regarded all who did not accept the Wahhabi reform as *mushrikun* (idolators) and, therefore, proper objects of attack. The ikhwan dressed in a distinctively austere fashion, wore the close-cropped beard and mustache attributed to the Prophet, and favored long hair. As the movement grew, it increasingly became a privileged and arrogant group, a military vanguard in the state's expansion and the guardian of its religious purity.

The world outside Arabia first learned of the *ikhwan* as they led Saudi Arabia's attack against the forces of Husayn ibn Ali, Hashimite ruler of HIJAZ. In 1919, ikhwan force defeated Hashimite troops dispatched to recapture the town of Khurma and, in the rout that followed, slaughtered great numbers of them. In 1924 an ikhwan army routed a larger, better-equipped Hashimite army at al-Ta'if, then massacred the town's male population. At that point, with the ikhwan having led the capture of JABAL SHAMMAR to the north of Riyadh, as well as Hijaz, the reconquest of the historical territory of the Al Sa'ud was nearly complete. In 1926 a brass band from Egypt, accompanying the *mahmal* (a decorated litter that bore the *kiswa*, the covering for the sacred KA'BA in Mecca) during the annual pilgrimage procession, was attacked by the ikhwan, to whom music was sacrilegious. This incident led Ibn Sa'ud to ban the ikhwan from Hijaz.

A showdown between the ikhwan and the ruler was precipitated by Ibn Sa'ud's entry into agreements with Britain on demarcation of the boundaries that Saudi Arabia shared with Britain's protectorates Transjordan, Iraq, and Kuwait. Ibn Sa'ud's pragmatic appreciation of Britain's dominant position on his flanks led him to sign the May 1927 Treaty of Jidda, confirming the borders and acknowledging his independence. Signature of the treaty appeared to contravene Ibn Sa'ud's promise at a meeting of ikhwan leaders at Riyadh in January 1927 that the ikhwan would eventually be permitted to carry their military JIHAD into Iraq. At that conference the *ulama* (religious leaders) issued a crucial ruling that jihad should be declared at the ruler's discretion, thereby providing Ibn Sa'ud with a formal excuse for not violating the northern borders and confirming the ikhwan's realization that he would not support their mission beyond the traditional borders of Saudi Arabia. The ikhwan moved toward open rebellion, launching raids into Iraq.

Three men led the rebellion: Faisal al-Dawish, leader of the Mutayr tribe and of the hijra of Artawiya; Sultan ibn Bijad, an Utayba chief and head of Ghat Ghat; and Dhidan ibn Hithlayn, chief of the Ajman tribe. In February 1929 Ibn Bijad, blocked by forces, led by British officers, who earlier had decimated ikhwan raiding parties, turned his wrath against a party of unarmed Najdi merchants, thereby giving Ibn Sa'ud the pretext he needed to move against the rebels. The ruler led a superior force against the rebels, and at Sabila, in March 1929, inflicted a crushing defeat on them. Faisal al-Dawish, having recovered from seemingly mortal wounds, tried again to raise the banner of revolt but was soon compelled to seek refuge with British officials in Kuwait, who then turned him over to Ibn Sa'ud.

The ikhwan movement lasted less than two decades, but in that brief span it spearheaded the conquest of a great part of Saudi Arabia and left a multifaceted legacy that continues to have a profound impact on the kingdom. The hujar permanently sedentarized a large part of Saudi Arabia's bedouin population. The ikhwan became the vanguard of today's National Guard, which continues to recruit its members in tribal contingents. Perhaps most important, its religious fanaticism still lives. Juhaiman ibn Muhammad ibn Saifal al-UTAYBI, leader of the religious militants who in November 1979 seized the GRAND MOSQUE in Mecca, was born in a former hijra of the Utayba tribe while memories of the battle of Sabila were still fresh. In their attempt to overthrow the monarchy, he and his followers consciously emulated the example of the ikhwan to the extent of identifying themselves by the same name and adopting the same dress. Although they failed to promote a general rebellion, it was clear that they acted for a constituency that continues to keep alive the uncompromising faith and fanaticism of the ikhwan.

BIBLIOGRAPHY

HABIB, JOHN S. *Ibn Sa'ud's Warriors of Islam: The Ikhwan of Najd and Their Role in the Creation of the Sa'udi Kingdom, 1910–1930.* Leiden, 1978.
HOLDEN, DAVID, and RICHARD JOHNS. *The House of Saud: The Rise and Rule of the Most Powerful Dynasty in the Arab World.* New York, 1981.
LACEY, ROBERT. *The Kingdom: Arabia and the House of Saud.* New York and London, 1981.
PHILBY, H. ST. JOHN. *Sa'udi Arabia.* London, 1955.

Malcolm C. Peck

Ikhwan al-Muslimin

See Muslim Brotherhood

Ikhwan al-Qassam

See Qassam, Izz al-Din al-

İleri, Celal Nuri   [1877–1939]

Turkish journalist and politician.

Born in Gallipoli, Celal Nuri attended the Galatasaray lycée and law school in Istanbul. He became a prominent writer after 1908 and was a leading spokesman among moderate Westernizers. He advocated adoption of the West's "technical civilization" but argued that the west had not achieved "real civilization," in which Islam was superior. He published several journals, including the newspaper *İleri* from 1918 to 1924, and was a representative in the last Ottoman parliament and the early grand national assemblies of the republican period.

BIBLIOGRAPHY

SHAW, STANFORD J., and EZEL KURAL SHAW. *History of the Ottoman Empire and Modern Turkey.* Vol. 2. Cambridge, U.K., 1977.

Elizabeth Thompson

İlmiyye

The Learned Institution, or hierarchy of religious officials in the Ottoman Empire.

From the early sixteenth century, the İlmiyye became a distinct hierarchy in the Ottoman government. It was headed by the grand mufti, called the SHAYKH AL-ISLAM, in Constantinople (now Istanbul) and extended to the lowest provincial *qadi* (judge) and religious schoolteacher. By the seventeenth and eighteenth centuries, the İlmiyye's top posts were dominated by elite families of Constantinople.

In the nineteenth century, Ottoman reforms undermined the İlmiyye's autonomy and influence by organizing the Ministry of Waqfs in 1834 and, in the TANZIMAT period, introducing secular courts, law codes, and school systems that competed with religious institutions. While ABDÜLHAMIT II increased funding for the İlmiyye, he also furthered its bureaucratization and state control. During World War I, the YOUNG TURKS incorporated all religious courts into the secular Ministry of Justice and religious schools into the secular Ministry of Education. The Shaykh al-Islam was reduced to a consultant. The final blow to the İlmiyye institution was the abolition of the Ottoman CALIPHATE in 1924 and the ensuing secularization of public institutions by Mustafa Kemal (ATATÜRK).

BIBLIOGRAPHY

CHAMBERS, RICHARD L. "The Ottoman Ulema and the Tanzimat." In *Scholars, Saints and Sufis,* ed. by Nikki R. Keddie. Berkeley, Calif., 1972.
The Encyclopedia of Islam. Vol. 3. London, 1971.
REPP, RICHARD. "Some Observations on the Development of the Ottoman Learned Hierarchy." In *Scholars, Saints and Sufis,* ed. by Nikki R. Keddie. Berkeley, Calif., 1972.
SHAW, STANFORD J., and EZEL KURAL SHAW. *History of the Ottoman Empire and Modern Turkey.* Vol. 2. New York, 1977.

Elizabeth Thompson

Iltizam

A form of taxation in the Ottoman Empire, often called tax-farming.

Like other early modern states, the OTTOMAN EMPIRE resorted to taxation to meet state expenses. The Ottomans sold the rights to certain agrarian and commercial tax revenues for a sum that was fixed before collection. Then, for a three-year period, private individuals (*multazim*)—who profited from the difference between the estimated and actual tax yields—collected taxes themselves or subcontracted such collection to others. Administration officials of the *vilayet* (province) system also awarded lucrative iltizam to local elites to win or keep their loyalty. In Egypt, this type of taxation was granted to tribal shaykhs, Mamluks, and the *ulama* (Muslim clergy), until Muhammad Ali Pasha's confiscation between 1812 and 1814.

Abuses were not uncommon as iltizam became widespread, beginning in the seventeenth century. From 1695, contracts for life (*malikane*) gave a privileged group—Istanbul grandees, provincial Janissaries, and gentry—even greater control over these resources. Malikane contracts were retracted during the TANZIMAT period, although iltizam continued throughout the nineteenth century.

BIBLIOGRAPHY

ABDUL-RAHMAN, ABDUL-RAHIM. "The Iltizam System in Egypt." *Journal of Asian and African Studies* 14 (1977): 169–170.
BAER, G. "Iltizam." *Encyclopedia of Islam,* 2nd ed.

Ariel Salzmann

Ilyan, Mikha'il   [1905–   ]

Syrian politician.

Born to a Greek Orthodox landowning family from Aleppo, Syria, Mikha'il Ilyan received his secondary education locally. He joined the NATIONAL BLOC and was elected a parliamentary deputy in 1943 and served as a minister in 1945/46. He became active in the SYRIAN SOCIAL NATIONALIST PARTY in the 1950s and was indicted in December 1956 for his involvement in a coup attempt to restore Adib SHISHAKLI to power.

Ilyan was also closely involved in the 1957 planning of an unsuccessful internal pro-Iraqi coup scheme dubbed Operation Nasr (Victory). Coupled to an invasion by Iraq code-named Operation Sayf al-Arab (Sword of the Arabs), the National Organization of Refugee Syrians that Ilyan was to preside over would be recognized by the Iraqis as the legitimate government of Syria. The plan never took shape.

BIBLIOGRAPHY

SEALE, PATRICK. *The Struggle for Syria.* London, 1965.

Charles U. Zenzie

Imam

Arabic title for Muslim leader.

In Sunni Islam, imam is the title of the prayer-leader in a mosque and may also refer to the mosque leader. In Shi'ism, however, the title refers to the absolute leader of the Muslim community as descended from the Prophet Muhammad through his daughter Fatima and his son-in-law Ali.

Zachary Karabell

Imamzadeh

A Persian word used in a Twelver Shi'ite context to refer both to a descendant of the first eleven imams (who is not himself an imam) and the shrine erected over the tomb of such a person.

A major principle of Shi'a piety is that—like the imams themselves—certain of their descendants are imbued with a special sanctity that can be of great spiritual and even physical benefit to their devotees. Although the practice of making frequent "visitations" (sing., *ziyara*) to saints' tombs was already a well-established feature of Muslim popular religion, by the seventeenth century C.E. the great Shi'a jurist, theologian, and reformer Muhammad Baqir al-Majlisi (d. 1699 C.E.) vigorously encouraged and officially sanctioned pilgrimages to *imamzadehs* as an important means of honoring the imams and thus affirming one's Shi'ism. Today imamzadehs can be found throughout Iran, providing abundant local opportunities for special encounters with holy persons and their blessings (sing., baraka).

[*See also:* Sayyid, Sharif]

Scott Alexander

Immigration

See under Refugees

Imperialism

Direct or indirect control exerted by one nation over the political life or economic life (or both) of other nations.

From the time of its origin around 1300 to its demise after World War I, the OTTOMAN EMPIRE was the primary empire in the Middle East and North Africa. (An empire is a singular political unit—though not a unit necessarily based on territorial contiguity—that incorporates different peoples who were previously self-governing and who retain some institutional autonomy.) In taking over most of the Balkan peninsula, virtually all of the Arab lands, and parts of Anatolia that had majority populations of Greeks, Armenians, or Kurds, the Turkish-speaking armies of the sultans created an empire that included many different linguistic, religious, and ethnic groups. The Ottomans engaged in imperial rivalry to expand their territory. Their rivals were the Holy Roman Empire (later Austria-Hungary), the Russian Empire, and the Iranian state of the Safawids and their successors, which was sometimes called an empire, despite its much smaller size, because it was multilingual, multiethnic, and periodically expansive.

This description of the Ottoman Empire does not differ substantially from the description that could be applied to the Christian European empires established from the sixteenth century onward, except that the Europeans were normally less willing to admit non-Europeans into the ranks of officials. The sultans, like the Russian czars, were primarily motivated by the desire to acquire land and wealth whereas the overseas European empire builders sought raw materials and markets. Thus the latter had a greater impact on the international division of labor than did the former, although this analytical distinction was not necessarily reflected in the attitudes of the imperialists and their subjects.

Despite the substantial similarities between European and Middle Eastern empires, the term *imperialism* is rarely used to describe the underlying principles of the Ottoman Empire. More often, imperialism is defined as a peculiarly European phenomenon embodying military control of non-European peoples; unrestrained exploitation of their economies for the disproportionate benefit of the European home country; feelings of racial, religious, and cultural superiority over the dominated peoples; and, in some regions, the implantation of European colonies or importation of nonindigenous laborers, often as slaves.

Historians in the Marxist tradition have considered economic exploitation by such means as joint-stock companies, forced labor on plantations, and suppression of indigenous manufactures to be the most important aspect of European imperialism. Imperialism, according to this view, is an inevitable stage of a capitalist system that needs to expand in order to survive. Immanuel Wallerstein, whose theories have been particularly influential, portrays imperialism as the imposition upon the entire world of a system through which capitalist Europe made the rest of the world economically dependent and imposed economic underdevelopment by monopolizing resources, reorienting self-sustaining regions toward extraction of primary goods for European manufacturers, and preventing the emergence of viable mixed economies in non-European areas.

Some clear distinctions between the way the Ottomans and the Europeans ran their empires may be noted. The Islamic religion provided a bond for most people under Ottoman rule, whereas European Christianity remained a culturally elitist, minority faith in the parts of the European empires that did not have large colonies of European settlers or where religions of comparable sophistication, such as Islam, impeded religious conversion. Ottoman lands remained comparatively open to trade by foreigners (though not to land acquisition), and the Ottoman government rarely took action to protect its own merchants, as the Europeans commonly did. Finally, the Ottomans administered their territories with a lighter hand than did the Europeans.

In 1800 most subjects of the Ottoman sultan considered it normal to be ruled from a distant capital by means of a rotation of officials and military forces sent from afar and often speaking a foreign language. Napoléon BONAPARTE's propaganda effort in 1798 to convince the Egyptians that they were victims of imperial oppression by foreigners fell on deaf ears. Soon thereafter, however, the Christian peoples of the Balkans, stimulated in part by the exposure of community members to European ideas as a consequence of educational or personal contacts outside Ottoman territories, did begin to see themselves as victims of Ottoman domination.

Through a series of wars and militant movements, they endeavored to gain their freedom and establish independent states with comparative ethnic and religious homogeneity. This struggle roughly coincides with the struggle for independence waged by peoples living under European imperial rule in the Western Hemisphere, and it similarly enjoyed the sympathy and support of the Europeans who espoused the ideals of the French Revolution or were revolted by the idea of fellow Christians being ruled by Muslims. The anti-imperialism of the Balkan secessionists eventually affected the Armenian Christians of Anatolia and more slowly gained headway in Arab nationalist circles after 1900.

European imperialism took three forms in the early nineteenth century: direct military occupation of Algeria by France from 1830 onward, diplomatic pressure on the Ottoman sultans to grant economic and legal privileges to Europeans and non-Muslim minorities, and treaties with rulers and chiefs controlling seaports in the Persian Gulf and southern Arabia designed to ensure British military control of the sea-route to India in return for maintaining the rulers and chiefs in power. In the second half of the century, new forms of European imperialism emerged. Rulers granted concessions to European entrepreneurs for the building of canals, railroads, and telegraph lines; operation of banks; and marketing of primary products. They also sought loans from private European bankers. When Egypt, the Ottoman Empire, and Iran were successively unable to repay these loans, Europeans assumed financial control over customs and other sources of state revenue. In Egypt, fear that Colonel URABI's military rebellion would interrupt these financial controls prompted Britain to suppress the rebellion militarily and commence an occupation in 1882 that would last for seventy years.

Growing European imperialism gave rise to anti-imperialist sentiments that were vented in popular opposition to concessions, as in the TOBACCO REVOLT in Iran in 1891 and in the mobilization of political action around religious symbols and leaders (e.g., in Libya, where the Sanusi Sufi brotherhood spearheaded opposition to Italian occupation after 1911). Anti-imperialism also sparked political movements, most notably the WAFD in Egypt, whose members saw the end of World War I as a possible opportunity to escape British rule. Armenians and Kurds also looked to the peace negotiators to grant them independence from outside control, even if it meant accepting some measure of European protection.

The MANDATE SYSTEM established at San Remo in 1920 to resolve the problems caused by the defeat of the Ottoman Empire extended European imperialism by giving France control of Lebanon and Syria and Britain control of Palestine and Iraq. Legally, the mandate from the League of Nations to France and Britain required them to nurture these territories toward total independence, but these countries' motivation to do so (strongest in Iraq and weakest in Lebanon and western Palestine) was often adversely affected by issues of national interest. In Palestine, in particular, Britain was committed in the terms of the BALFOUR DECLARATION (1917), to fostering the establishment of a Jewish national home. In the eyes of many Arabs and Muslims, the migration of tens of thousands of Jews from Europe to Palestine represented a new form of European imperialism.

Unlike parts of the world rich in raw materials or agricultural products that could not be grown in Europe, most parts of the Middle East and North Africa did not offer great rewards to their imperial masters. Egyptian cotton, Algerian wine, and Iranian oil flowed into international markets, and the Suez Canal was profitable, but the cost of military occupation in the face of rising nationalist hostility and of infrastructure investment, limited though it was in most areas, brought the economic value of imperialism into question. After World War II, the greatly depleted European powers were no longer able to bear the cost, either in money or manpower. One by one, the countries of the Middle East became free of direct imperial control. Only in the most profitable or politically contested countries was the withdrawal of empire accompanied by significant bloodshed. British withdrawal from Palestine in 1947 brought on Israel's declaration of independence and the first ARAB–ISRAEL WAR. The army coup that terminated British control of Egypt in 1952 was followed by the Suez War in 1956 in which Britain, in alliance with France and Israel, attempted to regain control of the Suez Canal. French determination to hold on to Algeria, which had a large French colony, led to a war from 1956 to 1962 that culminated in independence (see ALGERIAN WAR OF INDEPENDENCE).

As direct imperial control waned and overt indirect control in the form of military bases and foreign ownership of oil companies diminished in the 1950s and 1960s, cultural imperialism came to be looked on as a pervasive remnant of the imperialist era. Cultural imperialism was considered to have several components: imposition of Euro-American cultural values and life-styles through market domination by imported consumer goods, motion pictures, and television shows; ideological subversion in the form of secular nationalist political movements philosophically rooted in Western thought; and intellectual domination through the distorted writings and pejorative imaginative constructions of European

Orientalists and their successors in the American academic field of Middle East studies.

Direct imperial domination had evoked a fairly uniform nationalist reaction throughout the region, but the more nebulous concept of cultural imperialism led its proponents in different directions. In Iran, Jalal Al-e Ahmad's concept of GHARBZADEGI or "westoxication" contributed to the explicitly anti-Western character of the 1979 revolution (see IRANIAN REVOLUTION). Other Islamic activist movements have, to varying degrees, shared hostility or suspicion of the West as an imperialist force. Secular intellectuals, on the other hand, have refused to accept Islam as the only alternative to cultural domination by the West. Calls for a decolonization of history and exposure of Orientalist fantasies have come mainly from secularists like Morocco's Abdallah Laroui and the Palestinian Edward Said.

Further stimulus for resistance to Western imperialism came in 1993 from Samuel Huntington's article "The Clash of Civilizations" in the influential journal *Foreign Affairs*. Huntington visualized a future in which an undefined Islamic civilization was destined to conflict with a similarly undefined Western civilization, and he called for the formulation of a strategy that would assure Western victory in such a confrontation. Middle Eastern religious and secular thinkers alike viewed this projection as a portent of continued Western imperial ambition in the post–Cold War era.

BIBLIOGRAPHY

AMIN, SAMIR. *The Arab Nation: Nationalisms and Class Struggle.* Boston, 1979.
BERQUE, JACQUES. *French North Africa: The Maghrib Between Two World Wars.* 1967.
HUREWITZ, J. C. *The Middle East and North Africa in World Politics,* 2nd ed. New Haven, Conn., 1975–1979.
MONROE, ELIZABETH. *Britain's Moment in the Middle East 1914–1971,* new & rev. ed. Baltimore, Md., 1981.
SAID, EDWARD. *Orientalism.* New York, 1979.

Richard W. Bulliet

Imperial Rescript Reform Decree

See Hatt-i Hümayun

Incense

Aromatic gum resins.

Frankincense and myrrh are taken from trees that grow in Dhufar, in Oman, and Hadramawt, in Yemen. Recent archeological discoveries confirm their export from about 3000 B.C.E. through an extensive commercial network. The trade, reaching as far as Rome and India, helped create considerable prosperity and interstate rivalry in southwest Arabia. Exports and prosperity declined when Rome made Christianity its official religion and the use of incense at funerals largely ceased.

BIBLIOGRAPHY

ALLEN, CALVIN H., JR. *Oman: The Modernization of the Sultanate.* Boulder, Colo., 1987.

Malcolm C. Peck

Independence Parties

See under Istiqlal

Indigo

A deep-blue dye important to the Yemeni textile industry.

Yemeni textiles using domestic varieties of indigo have been famous since the first millennium B.C.; indigo has also been used for medicinal purposes. Major trading centers of indigo included Ta'iz, Zabid, Bayhan, and al-Bayda where it was traded through Mocha and Hodeida. Cultivation and dyeing took place in Zabid into the early 1960s and in al-Bayda into the 1970s. Modern dyes and textiles, however, have rendered the traditional methods and industry virtually obsolete.

Manfred W. Wenner

Industrialization

Despite enormous efforts to establish modern industries over more than half a century, manufacturing remains underdeveloped in the Middle East.

There has been a notable failure among Middle East countries to develop viable industries and advance in a way that is comparable to that of the more dynamic Third World countries in Southeast Asia or Latin America. The countries of the region remain dependent on exports of primary produce, and with the possible exception of Turkey, none produce manufactured goods that are competitive in international markets. Indeed, without tariff and quota protection and subsidies, few of the modern industries that have been established could compete even in their own domestic markets.

Yet there is a strong industrial tradition in the Middle East, as the ancient cities of the region served not only as centers of commerce but also as bases for manufacturing. The skills of the craftsmen of cities such as Baghdad in Iraq were renowned throughout the medieval world. Later in the sixteenth century, cities such as Isfahan, Iran, had more skilled artisans than Paris, the major European center of that time, with over half a million workers engaged in manufacturing. The activities encompassed not only fine wool and silk carpet weaving, for which Iran is still famous, but also cotton spinning, cloth production, tailoring, wood carving and furniture manufacture, metalworking in copper and silver, food processing, and decorative arts including very elaborate design work using mosaic tiling.

This manufacturing tradition is certainly comparable to that of East Asia and more advanced than that of Latin America. At the same time, there has not been the debt burden to inhibit development as in the case of Brazil or Argentina, as those Middle Eastern countries with international debts such as Egypt have borrowed from Western governments rather than commercial banks. The price of Middle Eastern debt is more political than financial, and the debts can easily be written down, as was the case with Egypt in acknowledgment of its contribution to the Gulf War effort. Of course for the oil-exporting states of the Persian/Arabian Gulf, the issue since the 1970s has been the management of financial surpluses rather than any problems with debt, and although these fell in value in the 1980s, the stock of Arab-owned overseas investments remains considerable.

The Middle East would appear to have all the necessary prerequisites for successful industrialization given its manufacturing inheritance, artisan skills, and availability of finance. Blessed with both human and financial capital, expectations have been high, yet little has been achieved. What has gone wrong with the industrialization process? Why is the region as vulnerable as ever to the uncertainties of primary produce markets, especially concerning the price of oil? How can the chronic balance of trade deficits caused by complete dependence on imported manufactured goods be overcome?

Undoubtedly the greatest negative factor inhibiting industrialization has been the successive wars, continuous political hostilities, and huge expenditures on armaments, by far the largest in any region of the Third World. Most effort and finance have gone into building military might rather than the development of civilian industry. The follies of the former Soviet Union were mirrored in the Middle East, but in the case of the latter, at even greater cost. At least in the Soviet Union a military industrial complex was established, but Israel was the sole Middle Eastern country to set up successful defense-based industries. In the case of Iraq, despite decades of spending and effort, the military machine was to prove a weak affair when confronted with Western power, and its defense industry now lies in ruins.

The Arab countries in any case have been heavily dependent on imports for most of their military supplies, and the Iraqi military complex, despite the ingenuity and skills of some of its workers, was basically a series of assembly and repair facilities. The local spin-offs were much less than they would have been for civilian manufacturing, and the skills acquired were scarcely relevant to the real industrial needs of the country. Even in Saudi Arabia the offset program, to increase local value added in defense equipment, has merely served to attract scarce manpower from civilian industrial projects, where arguably the high costs of the initial education and training would yield a greater return.

The wars and political tensions in the Middle East have resulted in many investors being put off by the risks and uncertainties. There has been little inward private direct investment, and most major multinational companies are reluctant to establish substantial production facilities in the region. This has been detrimental to both Israel and its Arab neighbors. Capital flight to the safer financial centers of the West has long been a feature of the Middle East, with financial outflows exceeding inflows. Many countries have generous investment incentives, and Egypt has maintained an "open door" policy to attract foreign investment since 1974, but incentives are ineffective unless the local investment climate is favorable, which is not the case.

Not surprisingly, Turkey has experienced the most success with industrialization in recent years, but it is not involved in the major regional conflicts and has its security guaranteed by its membership in the North Atlantic Treaty Organization (NATO). The industrialization drive in Turkey started under Mustafa Kemal (Atatürk) with the establishment of heavy industries in the 1920s and 1930s, such as steelmaking and modern textile plants. These were planned on the Soviet model, being primarily established to serve a protected domestic market. These plants provided the inputs for more consumer-orientated industries such as clothing and household fabrics, and eventually consumer durable manufacturing was developed, including vehicle assembly using domestically produced sheet steel.

Despite the substantial size of the domestic market in Turkey, the import substitution process was run-

ning out of steam by the 1960s, and most of the state-owned industries were sustaining heavy losses. The situation worsened in the 1970s, and it was apparent that a change in policy was needed if industrialization was to progress. This change came in 1980, when economic liberalization measures were introduced freeing prices, reducing subsidies, removing import restrictions, and most importantly letting the exchange rate find its own level in the market. This all but eliminated the black market dealings that had been rife for decades and ended the distortions that had impeded an efficient resource allocation. An export boom resulted, and Turkey moved into balance of payments surplus as a result of flourishing trade with the European Community and exports of manufactured goods to neighboring Middle Eastern countries.

Egypt's industrialization drive under Gamal Abdel Nasser had also faltered by the 1970s, although it was the disastrous Arab–Israel War of 1967 that signaled the end for development planning and economic policies based on Arab socialism. The more favorable outcome of the Arab–Israel War of 1973 from Egypt's point of view gave Egypt's President Anwar al-Sadat an opportunity to make a fresh start, but he was more successful politically than economically. Husni Mubarak has introduced a partial liberalization, but much less sweeping than that of Turkey. Subsidies have been reduced at the behest of the International Monetary Fund (IMF), some price controls removed, and the exchange rate floated. There has been some discussion concerning privatization, but it is difficult to envisage who would be willing to buy the money-losing Helwan steel plant or the other import substitution ventures established by Nasser with Soviet assistance.

The major industrial reform was the abolition of the six state-plan organizations that supervised the 117 public sector companies and their replacement by holding companies that are more commercially oriented. It is hoped to attract foreign participation in these companies, but Egypt is competing with the former communist countries of Europe for the attention of international investors. The economic deterioration in Eastern Europe has resulted in a serious decline in Egypt's cotton textile exports, which were traded under bilateral swaps. Egypt's industries are not yet internationally competitive despite the exchange rate depreciation, the problem being quality as much as price. Yet success in the European Community and other markets is crucial if jobs are to be provided in a country whose population already exceeds 56 million and is increasing at 1 million every eight months. The population pressure has also caused rising food imports, and proceeds from industrial exports could pay for these and reduce external borrowing requirements.

Iran, the other populous Middle Eastern state, has seen its industrial output decline through the 1980s following the disruption caused by the Islamic Revolution and later the eight-year Iran–Iraq War. Many industrialists and managers left after the overthrow of the shah, and the war resulted in severe shortages, which made it difficult for industries to obtain necessary raw materials and imported inputs. It is only since the end of the Gulf War and the efforts of President Hashemi Rafsanjani to improve relations with the West that there is now more optimism about industrial prospects. Manufacturing production remains well below the levels attained in the 1970s, and there is still underutilization of existing capacity, but it is planned to raise steel production from its annual level of 3.5 million tons (3.2 million t) in 1991 to 7 million tons (6.3 million t) by 1996. Both sheet steel and reinforcing bars for the construction industry are produced.

The Islamic Republic of Iran has substantial reserves of copper, and a large smelter was finally opened in 1984 at Sar Cheshmeh, together with a rolling and casting mill. Output averages 145,000 tons (132,000 t) per annum. There is also an aluminum smelter at Arak with a capacity of 45,000 tons (41,000 t) and a further aluminum smelter is being built at Bandar Abbas on the Gulf, to take advantage of Iran's cheap feedstock prices. Around half of the 242,000 tons (220,000 t) of output will be exported to the Far East from 1995 onward, representing part payment to the Japanese contractors who have been involved with the project.

Iran's main industrial efforts, however, have involved the development of petrochemical production. The Shiraz complex produces ammonia, urea, and various nitrates and has a capacity of 850,000 tons (771,000 t). The Bandar Khomeini plant was partially destroyed by the Iraqis before it was completed, but work has started again, and production should exceed 240,000 tons (218,000 t) per annum by 1996. Further petrochemical projects are under construction at Arak for ethylene and at Tabriz. By the end of the decade, Iran should be a significant regional producer of petrochemicals, reducing its dependence on crude oil exports, and bringing much welcome local value added.

Across the Gulf in Saudi Arabia, the buildup of petrochemicals has been a massive undertaking, with the aim of making the kingdom the world's leading producer. Its production already dwarfs that of nearby Iran, with the Saudi Basic Industries Corporation selling over 10 million tons (9.1 million t) of petrochemicals worldwide, in collaboration with the leading multinational oil and chemical companies. Jabal Ali has risen from the desert sands to become the leading industrial complex in the Gulf and the largest in the Arab world. It produces not only a large variety of petroleum derivatives but also fertilizers and steel. The petrochemicals are the feedstocks for plastics, and Saudi Arabia already has a range of downstream manufacturing producing everything from transparent bags and other disposables to heavy durable plastic products.

Apart from Turkey, Saudi Arabia is the only Middle Eastern country to have experienced a considerable degree of industrial success. The Riyadh government took the lead because of the substantial scale of the financing involved, but Saudi Arabia, like Turkey, has a vigorous and growing private manufacturing sector. In Turkey, the comparative advantage lies in its modest labor costs and the adaptability and skills of its people. In Saudi Arabia, the advantage is the abundance of energy and a tradition of trade and commerce, especially in the Hijaz, which favors international dealings. These advantages are found elsewhere in the region, but unless the possibility of continuing conflict is removed, prospects for industrialization and development are certain to remain bleak. It is the two countries that have enjoyed Western protection that appear to have fared best, yet there are other countries in the region with much greater needs at a much lower level of development.

Israel is the most industrialized country in the region, but its record in recent years cannot be considered one of success. Its difficulties highlight the problems of a small state trying to diversify on its own, with a limited domestic market of 4.4 million and virtual exclusion from the markets of neighboring states. Exports to Egypt have been minimal despite the Camp David accords, and trade with other Arab states is impeded by the Damascus boycott. Trade relations with the European Community have been difficult despite a cooperation agreement, and the United States is a somewhat distant market.

Cut diamonds are Israel's largest single industrial export. This industry was established by Jewish refugees from the diamond centers of Amsterdam and Antwerp after World War II and has flourished ever since. Rough diamonds worth around 1.5 billion U.S. dollars are imported annually, mainly from South Africa, and after being skillfully cut they are exported. The stones exported earn around 2 billion U.S. dollars annually, which represents over one-third of Israel's export earnings from manufactured goods. These earnings are welcome, but sales of diamonds are static, and the industry only provides direct employment for a few hundred skilled workers.

Israel's main problem is to provide viable employment for the Jewish migrants from the former Soviet Union, who are highly educated but lack industrial skills. Much of the country's industry is defense related and is very dependent on the financial injections from the United States, which sustain the high level of military expenditure. Defense equipment, including aircraft, is exported to a number of countries, mainly in the Third World, but in the longer term Russian marketing success may undermine these exports. Efforts have been made to build up the civilian electronics industry, including such products as personal computers, but Israel is a relatively high-cost producer, and there is cutthroat international competition. Japanese multinational companies have not invested in Israel, and high technology companies in Israel suffer from their international isolation.

The Maghrib (North Africa) countries, like Israel, have a poor industrialization record, despite enormous effort and much costly, but misguided investment. Algeria has invested the most, especially in hydrocarbon related activities, but its industries compare unfavorably with those of Saudi Arabi. The construction supply sector is badly managed, and socialist planning has been disastrous for truck and tractor assembly. Most consumer durables industries were established to serve the domestic market and are protected from competition by tariffs and foreign exchange rationing. This also applies in the case of Morocco, though there craft-based activities such as traditional wood carving and metalworking are a source of strength.

Tunisia has pursued a more outward oriented industrialization policy and has a number of textile plants that carry out subcontracting work for French garment producers. Food processing is also significant, but like textiles has stagnated in recent years. Despite investment incentives and liberal laws on foreign capital, even in Algeria, there has been little industrial investment from overseas. Incentives it seems are not enough, when the investment climate is so uncertain. Concern over potential conflict and the political environment are the main hindrances to modern industrialization in the Maghrib, but this applies throughout the Middle East.

BIBLIOGRAPHY

ALIBONI, ROBERTO, ed. *Arab Industrialization and Economic Integration.* London, 1979.

EL-NAGGAR, SAID, ed. *Privatisation and Structural Adjustment in the Arab Countries.* Washington, D.C., 1989.

RICHARDS, ALAN, and JOHN WATERBURY. *A Political Economy of the Middle East.* Boulder, Colo., 1990.

TURNER, LOUIS, and JAMES BEDORE. *Middle East Industrialisation.* Farnborough, England, 1979.

WILSON, RODNEY. *The Economies of the Middle East.* London, 1979.

Rodney J. A. Wilson

Infitah

Sadat's program to encourage private investment in Egypt, often called the Open Door policy.

Officially launched with the 1974 "October Paper," which called for relaxing some of the government controls applied under the Arab Socialism of Gamal Abdel Nasser, this policy actually started in 1971 as an effort to attract investment by other Arab countries to rescue Egypt's faltering economy. This policy was accelerated after the Arab–Israel War of 1973 because Egypt needed foreign exchange to finance the importation of materials and parts that would bring its economy back to full production. Egypt hoped also to convert its short-term debt to longer indebtedness under less onerous terms and to attract private investments to increase future income, jobs, and foreign exchange.

Law 43 (1974) activated infitah by giving incentives, such as reduced taxes and import tariffs and guarantees against nationalization, to Arab and foreign investors in Egyptian industry, land reclamation, tourism, and banking. Some of the advisers to Anwar al-SADAT wanted to limit infitah to encouraging foreign investment in Egypt's economy; others hoped to apply capitalist norms to all domestic firms, whether owned by the government or by private investors. Sadat adopted the latter view, causing a deterioration of state planning and labor laws.

Corruption increased under a rising entrepreneurial class of *munfatihin* (those who operate the open door), whose profiteering and conspicuous consumption antagonized many poor and middle-class Egyptians. Their strikes and protest demonstrations erupted almost as soon as the policy was implemented. Sadat's attempt, under World Bank urging, to remove exchange controls and reduce government subsidies on basic foodstuffs led to the January 1977 food riots, but infitah continued. Under Husni Mubarak, the munfatihin have become a distinct interest group that has resisted his efforts to reduce their opportunities for enrichment or to trim their level of consumption. The infitah policy has made Egypt economically dependent on richer Arab countries, Europe, and the United States. It has also widened the economic and social gap between rich and poor, with potentially explosive implications for Egypt's future.

BIBLIOGRAPHY

BAKER, RAYMOND WILLIAM. *Sadat and After: Struggles for Egypt's Political Soul*. Cambridge, Mass., 1990.

COOPER, MARK H. *The Transformation of Egypt*. London, 1982.

HEIKAL, MOHAMED. *Autumn of Fury: The Assassination of Sadat*. New York, 1983.

HENRY, CLEMENT MOORE. "The Dilemma of the Egyptian *Infitah*." *Middle East Journal* 38 (Fall 1984): 4.

HIRST, DAVID, AND IRENE BEESON. *Sadat*. London, 1981.

IKRAM, KHALID. *Egypt: Economic Management in a Period of Transition*. Baltimore and London, 1980.

WATERBURY, JOHN. *The Egypt of Nasser and Sadat: The Political Economy of Two Regimes*. Princeton, N.J., 1983.

Arthur Goldschmidt, Jr.

İnönü, Erdal [1926–]

Turkish politician.

Erdal İnönü was born in Ankara, the son of İsmet İnönü, the second president of the Turkish republic. He studied physics at Ankara University and then received his Ph.D. from California Polytechnic University. After working as a researcher at Princeton University (in New Jersey) and the Oak Ridge (Tenn.) National Laboratory, he returned to Turkey and began teaching at the Middle East Technical University, subsequently becoming president of the university. In 1983, İnönü founded the Social Democratic party (SODEP) and was elected general secretary of the party at its first convention. Barred from entering the 1983 elections, SODEP took part in the 1984 local elections, winning about 23 percent of the vote. In 1985, SODEP merged with the Populist party, and İnönü became head of the newly formed Social Democratic Populist party (SHP). In the 1987 elections, SHP came in second and İnönü entered parliament as head of the largest opposition party. But İnönü's leadership of the Turkish left was contested by Bülent ECEVIT, erstwile leader of the Republican People's party, who formed the Democratic Left party. In the elections of 1991, SHP came in second, with 21 percent of the vote, and entered into a coalition government with Suleyman Demirel's True Path party; according to the terms of the coalition agreement, İnönü was appointed deputy prime minister. In the early 1990s, his control over the SHP was challenged by Deniz Baykal, who subsequently left the party to reestablish the Republican People's party.

BIBLIOGRAPHY

SHIMONI, YAACOV. *Biographical Dictionary of the Middle East*. New York, 1991.

David Waldner

İnönü, İsmet [1884–1974]

Turkish politician and statesman; several times prime minister and the second president of Turkey.

İnönü was born in İzmir, where his father was a judge, and educated in military schools, including the Artillery School in Istanbul and the General Staff College (where he finished first in the class two years behind that of Mustafa Kemal ATATÜRK). In 1912, he became chief of the Ottoman general staff in Yemen and later held the same position in Istanbul. During World War I, the Ottoman Empire joined the Central Powers to fight the Allies; İnönü was sent to fight the British in Palestine and then to the Russian front in eastern Turkey, as chief of staff to Atatürk. In the Turkish war of independence, he continued working with Atatürk. His most distinguished action was in twice defeating the Greeks near the village of İnönü (from which he later took his surname, in the Western style).

In 1922, Atatürk made İnönü foreign minister, so that he could head the Turkish delegation to the Lausanne peace conference. There he gained recognition for his intense and successful work in winning almost all Turkey's demands. He was then made prime minister, an office he held until 1937. He was one of President Atatürk's closest associates, although his views were generally more moderate with regard to the intensity of projected reforms. He fully supported their direction and their basic philosophy, however, and as head of government he vigorously

Portrait of İsmet İnönü on a Turkish postage stamp. (Richard Bulliet)

enforced all the reform laws. For this he acquired a reputation as Atatürk's ruthless henchman, the ideal second man.

İnönü was replaced as prime minister in 1937 by Celal BAYAR for reasons not fully clear; a personal rivalry then continued for many years. When Atatürk died in 1938, however, İnönü became his successor, Turkey's second president. After the strains of World War II, İnönü was faced with demands for multiparty politics; until that time Turkey had been a de facto one-party state under the aegis of the REPUBLICAN PEOPLE'S PARTY (RPP). Based on implicit promises of eventual multiparty democracy, a second party was formed by four RPP rebels, the DEMOCRAT PARTY (DP), in 1946. An early election was called, which the RPP won, partly because the opposition had little time to prepare, but in İnönü's famous declaration of July 12, 1947, he took the statesmanlike position that both parties should have the same privileges. When the Democrats won the 1950 election, rumors surfaced that they would not be allowed to take power, but İnönü stayed true to his word and quietly assumed the role as leader of the opposition, an act for which he won worldwide acclaim. During the 1950s, İnönü led the RPP in the TURKISH GRAND NATIONAL ASSEMBLY, strongly defending Atatürk's policies of secular Western-style government in the face of Democrat policies that many RPP militants saw as a betrayal of KEMALISM.

İnönü's political history made him a target for many Democrats, particularly his rival Celal Bayar, who had become Turkey's third president. As a result of the Democrat government's repressive measures and political shortcomings, the Bayar–Menderes regime was ousted by the armed forces on May 27, 1960. The belief that the military coup was to enable the RPP to return to govern was confirmed for many people when President Cemal Gürsel invited İnönü to form a government despite the RPP having won only a small plurality in the assembly and having run a poor second to the moderate right-wing JUSTICE PARTY (JP) in the Senate. He formed a coalition with the grudging participation of the Justice party, but it fell in May over the issue of amnesty for the ousted Democrats (which the RPP and the military opposed but which the JP supported on behalf of the former Democrats, to whom they considered themselves successors). In June, the commanders again called on İnönü, and his second coalition was formed, with the New Turkey and Republican Peasants Nation party plus some independents.

İnönü's party had little in common with them in terms of programs, and he was faced with strong dissatisfaction within the RPP as well, because of concessions made to his right-wing coalition partners. He also faced criticism because of the RPP's poor vote-getting record since the transition to multiparty politics; this was attributed to a combination of too moderate centrist policies plus his failure to rejuvenate the party with younger successors and those not as closely identified with Atatürk's militant methods. The RPP's poor performance in the 1963 election led to his resignation as prime minister once more, but when other parties could not form cabinets, he was called on a third time, in December 1963, and he formed his third coalition. In the 1964 CYPRUS crisis, İnönü spoke out against the letter sent him by U.S. President Lyndon B. Johnson, which threatened not to defend Turkey from a Soviet attack should Turkey invade Cyprus. Even this did not strengthen his domestic position, and he resigned for the last time early in 1965. Nevertheless, he remained as RPP leader until mid-1972, when the party elected the younger and more leftist Bülent ECEVIT as chairman.

One of İnönü's three children, Erdal, became a politician—the leader of the SOCIAL DEMOCRATIC POPULIST PARTY, starting in the late 1980s, and deputy prime minister in the coalition government in 1992.

BIBLIOGRAPHY

AHMAD, FEROZ. *The Turkish Experiment in Democracy 1950–1975.* Boulder, Colo., 1977.
HEPER, METIN, and JACOB M. LANDAU, eds. *Political Parties and Democracy in Turkey.* London and New York, 1991.
KARPAT, KEMAL. *Turkey's Politics: The Transition to a Multi-Party System.* Princeton, N.J., 1959.
WEIKER, WALTER F. *Political Tutelage and Democracy in Turkey.* Leiden, Neth., 1973.

Walter F. Weiker

Inqilab

An Arabic word that means "coup d'état."

In Lebanon, *inqilab* has occurred twice. In December 1961 the SYRIAN SOCIAL NATIONALIST PARTY sought to seize power. The attempt failed, and the party was subjected to years of harassment and pressure that transformed and radicalized it. The 1961 coup is considered to be the most serious infiltration of Lebanon's army by a political party in modern times.

The second coup had a touch of tragicomedy. In March 1976, Aziz al-Ahdab (a Sunni general in the army), with the support of the Palestine Liberation Organization and Syria, proclaimed a movement to end the Lebanese civil war. The movement lasted for only a few weeks—the warring factions outgunned the power of his weak army base.

As'ad AbuKhalil

Institut d'Egypte

Institute in Cairo, Egypt, for study and promotion of Egyptian culture.

Napoléon Bonaparte founded the Institut d'Egypte in Cairo in 1798. Its members were the elite of the French expedition's Commission des Sciences et Arts, whose massive *Description de l'Egypte* (1809–1826) surveyed all aspects of the Egyptian scene. The institute disappeared when the French evacuated Egypt in 1801.

Inspired by the original institute, Europeans founded the Institut Egyptien in Alexandria in 1859 with Sa'id Pasha's approval. Egyptologist Auguste Mariette was among the forty-odd European founders. The Egyptian scholar Rifa'a al-Rafi al-Tahtawi and Egypt's future prime minister Nubar Pasha were among the seven Middle Eastern founders. The institute maintained a library, sponsored lectures, and published a bulletin and scholarly memoirs. Moved to Cairo in 1880, the institute resumed the Napoleonic name Institut d'Egypte in 1918. When most European residents left Egypt in Gamal Abdel Nasser's day, the membership became mostly Egyptian. Neglected by the government since 1952, when Nasser's coup took place, the institute lacks the funds to keep up its publications, its building on Cairo's central square, and its once impressive library.

BIBLIOGRAPHY

ELLUL, JEAN. *Index des communications et mémoires publiés par l'Institut d'Egypte (1859–1952)*. Cairo, 1952.

Donald Malcolm Reid

Institute for Palestine Studies

Palestinian research and publishing center.

The Institute for Palestine Studies was established in Beirut in December 1963 as the first nonprofit, independent research and publishing center focusing exclusively on the Palestinian problem and the Arab–Israeli conflict. Financed primarily by an endowment, the institute is independent of governments, parties, organizations, and political affiliations.

With branches currently in Beirut, Nicosia, Paris, Washington, and Jerusalem, the institute has striven to accomplish several academic goals over the decades. These have included collecting documents, manuscripts, maps, photographs, newspapers, and books for its library and archives in Beirut, the largest of its kind in the Arab world. The institute was also the first Arab institution to promote the study of the Hebrew language and to translate important Hebrew-language documents in Arabic. The institute continues to publish books and documents relating to the Palestinians and the Arab–Israeli conflict, as well as research journals like *al-Dirasat al-Filastiniyya*, *Revue d'etudes palestiniennes*, and *Journal of Palestine Studies*.

Michael R. Fischbach

Institute of Judicial Studies

A school established in Lebanon as one of the administrative reforms of President Fu'ad Chehab.

The institute prepares candidates for the judiciary after they have passed an examination. The minimum qualifications for entry include the possession of a law degree and an age exceeding thirty-one. After three years of training, the students are appointed as judges.

As'ad AbuKhalil

Intelligence Organizations

Modern information-gathering techniques, as first effected by European colonial powers in the Middle East, and later, those effected by the United States and the Soviet Union after World War II.

Intelligence services in the Middle East originated with the beginnings of European imperialism and colonialism during the nineteenth century. Spies and informers were certainly not new to the region—rulers of the Ottoman Empire had always monitored the activities of their officials—but the notion of systematically collecting, organizing, and evaluating political and strategic data for decision making from both open (overt) and confidential (covert) sources was an innovation.

By the late nineteenth century, the European governments saw political and military intelligence as a more effective means of advancing colonial interests than military force alone. In Algeria, interest in political and ethnographic intelligence peaked during periods of resistance to French colonial rule, but when France saw no direct threat to their rule, interest in intelligence waned. In contrast, since 1904, Morocco's political and social institutions—including its tribal and religious leadership—had been systematically cataloged by the Mission Scientifique au Maroc (the Scientific Mission to Morocco), with the explicit goal of facilitating political intervention. After the Moroccan protectorate was established by France in 1912, the head of the mission became director of native affairs.

Most Western intelligence services compartmentalize their activities: the clandestine collection of data; the analysis of overt and covert sources; counterintelligence blocking an enemy's sources, deceiving an enemy, and reporting against hostile penetration; and covert action. In both the colonial bureaucracies and their postindependence successors in the region, the lines between these activities have often been blurred. The collection of intelligence data sometimes becomes confounded with the supervision, control, and intimidation of populations; and the analysis and reporting of domestic and external threats become subordinate to reassuring insecure rulers or manipulating the information they receive to further careers or factional interests.

The organizational framework of intelligence activities in the colonial era often continued into the initial years of independent Middle East states, and former colonial powers established cooperative arrangements for the training of local intelligence specialists. Thus military and civilian intelligence personnel in Jordan and the Persian/Arabian Gulf area receive training in Britain and French specialist services have provided equivalent training for Morocco and Tunisia. Even in countries that never experienced colonial domination, like the military, intelligence organizations were profoundly shaped by foreign advice and training. Iran's SAVAK was created in 1957 with advice from the U.S. CENTRAL INTELLIGENCE AGENCY (CIA), whose role was supplemented in the 1960s by Israel's counterpart, MOSSAD. Following Egypt's 1952 revolution, the CIA assisted in restructuring the intelligence apparatus; and Soviet-bloc technical assistance replaced Western expertise there after 1956, when Gamal Abdel Nasser led the government. By the 1960s, Soviets and East Germans had begun to play important advisory and training roles in Iraq, Syria, the former People's Democratic Republic of Yemen, and Libya. The Cold War had its players right in the midst of the petroleum-rich Middle East.

Formal training from foreign services notwithstanding, subtle changes occur as intelligence methods and techniques are adapted to local circumstances, which differ in scale and in cultural understanding, depending on authority and governance. First, rival and overlapping services are created to check the authority and autonomy of any one; the result is a high level of factionalism. Some rulers—those of Syria and Iraq provide examples—appoint close relatives to key intelligence posts. Second, the principal task of most services in the region is the

surveillance, control, and frequently the intimidation of their own populations—both domestically and abroad. In some states, such as Iraq and Syria, such surveillance is pervasive and unchecked. Intelligence services in other Middle East countries may be more restrained, although human-rights organizations report abuses in all states of the region. The governments do little to mitigate the people's perception of their intelligence organizations' pervasiveness, because such notions help to suppress dissent. Third, the secretiveness of such services provides formal (diplomatic) deniability for countries' actions against regional rivals—providing arms or refuge to opponents of a neighboring regime, for example—which, if publicly acknowledged, might lead to a major confrontation. Domestic factions can also receive discreet assistance in the same manner. Finally, regional intelligence services opportunistically cooperate with foreign services; for example, during the Iran–Iraq War in the 1980s, the United States provided both sides with intelligence data from the database it was actually amassing for its own purposes.

The political intelligence activities of the superpowers in the Middle East have been primarily concerned with their own rivalries, protecting oil supplies, and—for the United States—guaranteeing the security of Israel. To secure their goals, they have often intervened in the region's domestic and regional politics. For Arab historians, the arch example for such intervention is the role of the British, including T. E. Lawrence (of Arabia) during World War I, in instigating the ARAB REVOLT against Ottoman rule. The British abandoned the Arab cause once their objectives were accomplished. Other examples include U.S.–British cooperation in overthrowing Iran's Prime Minister Mohammad Mossadegh in 1953; and covert U.S. operations against suspected leftist groups in Syria from the late 1940s through 1958. Testimony during the 1987 Iran–Contra hearings in the United States indicates the way covert intelligence activities can elude formal state control and work against declared public policy.

Understanding intelligence organizations and their activities may be difficult, because access to information on them is uneven. The history of Israel's intelligence service is better known than those of other Middle Eastern countries, since many agents have published memoirs and relevant political archives (subject to a thirty-year delay for state papers) are available to scholars. Thus historians can trace the development of Israeli intelligence operations from the early Zionist monitoring of Arab nationalist movements at the beginning of the British mandate in Palestine (1922), to professionalization in the mid-

1930s as an element of Haganah (the Zionist military underground), to its bureaucratic separation into military, domestic, and foreign units following the 1948 establishment of the State of Israel.

Other intelligence services of the region are known primarily through information provided by defectors (Iraq, Iran, Sudan, Egypt, Libya); deliberate leaks; the release of documents during major domestic crises (the trial in Egypt following Anwar al-Sadat's assassination in 1981) or changes of regime (the release of security files on the Iraqi Communist party following the monarchy's overthrow in 1958); and the capture of documents from foreign security services—such as Israel's publication of Jordanian documents seized during the Arab–Israel War of 1967 or the publication of U.S. intelligence documents and diplomatic reports taken from the U.S. Embassy in Tehran.

BIBLIOGRAPHY

The best study of a single Middle Eastern intelligence service is by IAN BLACK and BENNY MORRIS, *Israel's Secret Wars: The Untold Story of Israeli Intelligence* (London, 1991). JAMES A. BILL, *The Eagle and the Lion: The Tragedy of American–Iranian Relations* (New Haven, Conn., 1988), discusses intelligence activities in Iran, while MANSUR RAFIZADEH's *Witness* (New York, 1987) provides an insider's account of SAVAK activities. Many Arabs read GAMAL AL-GHITANI's fictional *Zayni Barakat,* translated by Farouk Abdel Wahab (London, 1988, first published in Syria in 1971), as a metaphor for Egypt's secret services in the 1960s. DALE F. EICKELMAN, "Intelligence in an Arab Gulf State," in *Comparing Foreign Intelligence,* edited by Roy Godson (Washington, D.C., 1988), provides a sociological introduction to the subject.

Dale F. Eickelman

International Debt Commission

Established in 1876 to defend the interests of European creditors when Khedive Isma'il's Egypt went bankrupt.

Britain, France, Austria-Hungary, Italy, and later Russia and Germany had seats on the International Debt Commission, which was usually called La Caisse de la Dette Publique. The Caisse's insistence on putting the interests of European creditors first was a major cause of the deposition of ISMA'IL IBN IBRAHIM and of the Urabist resistance of 1881/82. After the British occupied the country in 1882, their administrators came to see the Caisse as an impediment to necessary financial and agricultural reforms. Britain's entente cordiale with France in 1904, however, removed most of the friction. The weight of external debt on the Egyptian economy lightened between the two world wars, with the importance of the Caisse declining accordingly. During World War II, sterling balances accumulated from Allied expenditures in Egypt essentially eliminated the problem of external debt until the 1960s.

BIBLIOGRAPHY

ISSAWI, CHARLES. *Egypt at Mid-Century.* London, 1954.

Donald Malcolm Reid

International Monetary Fund

An international institution charged with maintaining international monetary stability.

Established in July 1944 at the conference of Bretton Woods, the International Monetary Fund (IMF) provides financing to any of its 150 members experiencing a balance of payments crisis. Each member nation is assigned a quota of funds that can be borrowed and repaid over ten years; this quota can be waived in times of serious crisis. In exchange for this financing, the IMF often demands that borrowers make fundamental changes in their economies to prevent future balance of payments problems. These changes range from stabilization of the exchange rate and of government deficits, to structural adjustment of the economy through privatization of state enterprises and liberalization of trade. Adherence to these measures demands fiscal austerity that has often resulted in political instability. In January 1977 in Egypt, following the reduction in government subsidies for basic consumption goods in compliance with IMF's insistence on the reduction of the public deficit, rioting broke out in Cairo and Alexandria. The army had to be brought in to restore order, and in Cairo alone, seventy-seven people were killed. In January 1984, IMF pressures for cutbacks of consumer subsidies in Morocco led to similar rioting. Following the Islamization policies of Muhammad Ja'far NUMEIRI, the IMF suspended aid payments to Sudan, leaving the country facing a huge debt burden and bankruptcy.

BIBLIOGRAPHY

ADAMS, MICHAEL, ed. *The Middle East.* New York, 1988.
SPERO, JOAN EDELMAN. *The Politics of International Economic Relations,* 4th ed. New York, 1990.
WATERBURY, JOHN. *The Egypt of Nasser and Sadat: The Political Economy of Two Regimes.* Princeton, N.J., 1983.

David Waldner

Intifada

Palestinian Arab uprising.

The Intifada erupted in Israeli-occupied Gaza and the West Bank in December 1987. In broad perspective, it was a continuation of the century-old ARAB–ISRAEL CONFLICT. Its immediate cause was Israel's twenty-year occupation of Gaza, the West Bank, and Arab East Jerusalem. Although the most extensive, the Intifada was not the first manifestation of resistance to the occupation. Resistance began soon after Israel seized the occupied territories during the Arab–Israel War of 1967. From the beginning, the resistance movement had two forms—paramilitary and civil. Israel quickly ended most significant paramilitary activity within areas under its control; from 1967 until the early 1990s, there were only sporadic instances of armed resistance in the West Bank and Gaza. Most Palestinian guerrilla activity occurred outside the occupied territories.

Far more significant was the rise and persistence of civil resistance, which began soon after the 1967 War. Periodically, Palestinian notables and others were arrested and expelled for opposing the occupation policies of Israel in the territories. Among the two thousand Palestinians forcibly deported were the former mayor of East Jerusalem, the president of the Jerusalem *Shari'a* court, and the president of Bir Zeit University.

Palestinian opposition focused on the imposition of military rule in the occupied territories. Under Israeli military government, there was censorship of school texts and other publications; punitive demolition of Arab homes; and the institution of a permit system for travel outside the territories and for constructing new buildings, opening businesses, digging wells, and conducting other routine daily activities. A major cause of Palestinian unrest was the replacement of civilian courts by military tribunals without habeas corpus and the imprisonment of Palestinians for lengthy periods without trial. Various human rights organizations, including those in Israel, protested against the military justice system and the documented cases of torture by Israeli authorities.

Plans for integration of the occupied territories into Israel's economy were also opposed by the Palestinians. These plans included Israeli control and allocation of water resources in the West Bank and Gaza and integration of the electricity grid and road network with those in Israel. Another form of economic integration was employment of approximately half the Palestinian workforce of the territories at the bottom of the Israeli wage scale, in jobs such as construction and agriculture. Because of economic circumstances, many highly educated and skilled Palestinians were forced to accept such employment.

During the twenty years of occupation prior to the Intifada, about half the land in the West Bank was taken over by Israeli authorities and much of it allocated to Jewish settlers. In the decade preceding the Intifada, the substantial increase in the number of Jewish settlers and settlements aroused growing apprehension among Palestinian residents who feared that Israel would absorb or annex the territories, thereby undermining their aspirations for self-determination.

Between 1967 and 1987, a pattern of civic resistance developed that consisted of strikes by merchants, businesses, and schools; demonstrations displaying the Palestinian flag or national colors, which were banned by Israeli authorities; and slogans and chants calling for independence. All these forms of resistance were used during the Intifada. Prior to the Intifada, the most active civil resistance was sparked in 1981 by the Likud government when it established a "civilian administration" in the West Bank whose purpose was to undermine the influence of Palestinian nationalists, especially those representing the Palestine Liberation Organization (PLO). The civilian administration failed because of widespread refusal by Palestinians to cooperate; Israeli attempts to suppress resistance to the civil administration led to bloody clashes with the authorities and even greater resistance.

By December 1987, after more than twenty years of occupation, Palestinian dissatisfaction reached a crisis. The spark that ignited the Intifada was a road accident on December 8, in which an Israeli-driven vehicle killed and seriously wounded several Palestinians returning to Gaza from work in Israel. Reports of the incident spread quickly, resulting in spontaneous protest demonstrations, first throughout Gaza and, within a few days, throughout the West Bank. When Israeli troops arrived to quell the unrest, they were pelted with a barrage of stones and iron bars by hundreds of demonstrators, a large number of whom were children. Children throwing stones at Israeli soldiers soon became a global symbol of the Intifada.

The extent and intensity of the uprising caught Israeli, Palestinian, and Arab leaders by surprise. Few observers expected that it would continue or become so widespread. Shortly after the first spontaneous demonstrations in December, the uprising began to be organized by young representatives of several Palestinian factions in the territories. The Unified National Leadership of the Uprising (UNLU) was an underground organization with delegates representing al-FATH, the POPULAR FRONT FOR

THE LIBERATION OF PALESTINE (PFLP), Democratic Popular Front for the Liberation of Palestine (DPFLP), and the Palestine Communist Organization, all banned by Israeli authorities. Representatives of ISLAMIC JIHAD at times cooperated with the UNLU, although Islamic fundamentalist factions maintained freedom of action and did not submit to the authority of the UNLU. Membership in the UNLU rotated, making it difficult for the occupation authorities to apprehend the leaders. The UNLU represented a new, younger Palestinian leadership, many of whom came from the refugee camps and the working class.

Because of the overwhelming power of the Israeli military, the UNLU avoided using firearms for resistance. Instead, tactics included strikes and demonstrations; extensive posting of illegal slogans, flags, and symbols; boycotting Israeli-made products; resigning from posts in the military government; withholding labor from Israel; and refusing to use Israeli official documents. The UNLU and the fundamentalist factions issued instructions and political pronouncements to the Palestinian population through posters and leaflets called *bayanat*. There were also broadcasts from underground radio stations that moved from place to place.

The objectives of the Intifada were published in bayanat and the political pronouncements of West Bank and Gaza leaders. Initially they called for releasing prisoners, ending the policy of expulsion, ceasing Jewish settlement, and removing restrictions on Palestinian political activity and contacts between those in the territories and the PLO leadership abroad. As the Intifada continued, demands were made to end the occupation and for Palestinian self-determination.

Whereas the Intifada initially galvanized Palestinian society, overcoming divisions among regions, religious groups, political factions, sexes, and social classes, it polarized Israel between those who called for a political solution to the Palestine problem and those who demanded greater use of force to suppress the uprising. The Intifada had a detrimental impact on Israel's economy because it required a great increase in military manpower in the territories and entailed the loss of cheap Arab labor in important sectors of the economy, such as agriculture and construction, and the decline of Israeli markets in the territories.

The Intifada brought the Palestine question to the forefront of international attention, leading to renewed attempts by the United States and Western Europe to find a solution. As a result of the uprising, the PLO gave greater consideration to the views of Palestinians resident in the territories and to the decision in December 1988 to accept the coexistence of Israel and a Palestinian state within the West Bank and Gaza. The Intifada and the 1990 Gulf War were the catalysts that led to the Middle East peace conference that opened in Madrid in 1991.

By the early 1990s, many Palestinians in the territories became impatient with the inability of the UNLU to end the occupation. Economic conditions deteriorated as a result of the periodic strikes; the decline in agriculture, industry, and commerce; and growing unemployment. This disaffection was demonstrated in growing opposition to the peace negotiations and by increasing support for Islamic Jihad and HAMAS (the Islamic resistance movement), militantly fundamentalist groups that called for the establishment of an Islamic state, opposed recognition of Israel, and resorted to the use of guns and other hot weapons in the struggle against occupation. Another manifestation of the loss of credibility by the UNLU was an increase of internecine killing of their fellow countrymen accused of betrayal by Palestinians who resisted the authority of the established leadership.

BIBLIOGRAPHY

LOCKMAN, ZACHARY, and JOEL BEININ, eds. *Intifada: The Palestinian Uprising against Israeli Occupation.* Boston, 1989.

NASSAR, JAMAL R., and ROGER HEACOCK, eds. *Intifada: Palestine at the Crossroads.* New York, 1990.

PERETZ, DON. *Intifada: The Palestinian Uprising.* Boulder, Colo., 1990.

SCHIFF, ZE'EV, and EHUD YA'ARI. *Intifada: The Palestinian Uprising—Israel's Third Front.* New York, 1989.

Don Peretz

Intra Bank

The crash of the Intra Bank, October 1966, was a turning point in the Lebanese economy.

The Intra Bank had under its control assets that exceeded the amount of the budget of Lebanon. The bank was founded by Palestinian businessman Yusuf Baydas, who after the Arab–Israel War of 1948 settled in Lebanon to become one of the wealthiest people in the Middle East. Details of the origins of the bank's crisis are still shrouded in secrecy and mystery, although the role of some Lebanese politicians in launching the war of rumors against Baydas is almost certain. Baydas developed the bank into a major financial institution with holdings in Europe, Africa, and North America. Leftist analysts blame Western financial institutions for the fall of the bank, citing the displeasure of Western capital (and wealthy Lebanese partners) at Baydas's success.

In the 1960s, Lebanese banks, including Intra, faced liquidity problems because they engaged in medium- and long-term investments. The crisis began with a war of rumors against Baydas suggesting that the bank was insolvent; this was untrue. When Baydas appealed for cash from the Lebanese state and from the predominantly Christian Lebanese financial establishment, he was turned down. It was subsequently revealed that the Central Bank itself had led the credit pressure against Intra, under the direction of the President Charles HILU. In a few years, Western banks came to control 60 percent of banking activity in Lebanon. Baydas fled Lebanon and died in exile in Switzerland. The fall of the bank marked the shifting of Arab capital from Lebanon to Europe and the United States.

As'ad AbuKhalil

IPC

See Iraq Petroleum Company

İpekci, Abdi   [1929–1979]

Turkish newspaper editor.

Born in Istanbul, İpekci attended Galatasaray High School and studied law at Istanbul University while beginning his journalism career as a sportswriter, cartoonist, and reporter. At twenty-one, he became editor of the daily *Express,* and four years later took the job that gained him nearly universal respect for the next twenty-five years, editor at MILLIYET, one of Istanbul's leading dailies. İpekci was assassinated in 1979 by Mehmet Ali Ağa, who shot Pope John Paul II two years later.

In İpekci's hands, *Milliyet* became a popular paper that combined slick, attractive presentation with serious news coverage. He was known for maintaining a neutral, but perceptive and reasoned stance in his editorials, although the paper was known to be left-of-center politically. For example, in 1967 İpekci presciently warned against the myth of a communist menace, which he saw as a prelude to a military takeover. As president of the Istanbul Journalists Association (1958–1960) and later, he played a leading role in unionizing journalists and developing a professional code of ethics.

BIBLIOGRAPHY

ŞAHIN, HALUK. "Mass Media in Turkey." In *Turkic Culture: Continuity and Change,* ed. by Sabri M. Akural. Bloomington, Ind., 1987.

Elizabeth Thompson

İpek Film

Turkish film production company.

İpek Film was founded in 1928 by the İpekci brothers, who opened a chain of movie theaters in 1924. It was Turkey's second private film company, after KEMAL FILM, which was organized in 1922. İpek's first film, *The Postman from Ankara,* was directed in 1929 by Muhsin ERTUĞRUL. The company opened Turkey's first sound studio in 1932 but verged on bankruptcy two years later, when Ertuğrul's filmed operetta *Leblebici Horhor* (Horhor, the Chick-pea Vendor) left audiences cold. The following year Ertuğrul produced for İpek what would later be called his masterpiece, *Aysel, Daughter of the Marshy Village.*

The company had a similar experience when it produced Turkey's first color film in 1953, *The Weaver,* which was a flop at the box office. In the 1960s, İpek became the Hollywood-style commercial producer (as opposed to the producer of the emerging avant-garde movement), when Osman Seden began producing star-packed, technically brilliant films.

BIBLIOGRAPHY

DORSAY, ATILLA. "An Overview of Turkish Cinema from Its Origins to the Present Day." In *The Transformation of Turkish Culture,* ed. by Günsel Renda and C. Max Kortepeter. Princeton, N.J., 1986.

Elizabeth Thompson

Iradeh-ye Melli Party

Pro-British political party in Iran, formed in 1943 and dismantled in 1946.

Initially called the Fatherland party, this party was formed in September 1943 in Iran by Sayyed Ziya TABATABA'I. He was a pro-British journalist who had helped Reza Khan's rise to power in his youth and was made premier in 1921 but was subsequently exiled by Mohammad Reza Shah PAHLAVI, the title assumed by Reza Khan as king of Iran. In 1943 Sayyed Ziya revived his old paper *Ra'd* (or Thunder) and called on the *bazaaris* (merchants), *ulama* (clerics), and the tribes to revolt against the military dictatorship of the shah, the "atheistic communism" of Iran's communist-leaning party, the Tudeh, and the corruption of the landed aristocracy. Five months later, Sayyed Ziya renamed the party Iradeh-ye Melli (the National Will). The party had a strong reputation for being pro-British. Included in its program were designs for repeal of all anticonstitutional laws, convening of provincial assemblies, protection of handicraft industries, distribution of state land among peasantry, and formation of a volunteer army. In 1946, the party was dismantled and Sayyed Ziya was arrested by premier Ahmad Qavam as part of the premier's plan for dismantling British influence in the country.

BIBLIOGRAPHY

ABRAHAMIAN, E. *Iran between Two Revolutions*. Princeton, N.J., 1982.

Parvaneh Pourshariati

Iran

Islamic republic in southwestern Asia.

Iran has an area of 636,290 square miles (1,648,000 sq km) and an estimated population of 64 million (1996). It is bounded on the north by the Caspian Sea and the republics of Armenia, Azerbaijan, and Turkmenistan; on the east by Afghanistan and Pakistan; on the south by the Persian Gulf and the Gulf of Oman; and on the west by Turkey and Iraq.

Land and Climate. Iran lies on a high plateau with an altitude of around four thousand feet (1,220 m), surrounded by the Zagros mountains, running from the Armenian border to the shores of the Gulf of Oman, and the Elburz mountains in the north. Great salt deserts in the interior are cut by two mountain ranges in the east. Temperatures reach a low of -15°F (-26°C) in the harsh winters of the northwest and a high of about 123°F (51°C) in the south during the summer, with most of the country enjoying a more temperate climate. Average rainfall ranges from seven feet (2.1 m) in the Caspian region to less than two inches (5 cm) in the southeast.

Population and Education. With an estimated population of 64 million in 1996, Iran is perhaps the most populous country in the Middle East. It has grown at over 3 percent per annum since the 1970s. However, the family planning campaign begun in the mid-1980s has decreased the rate to about 2.5 percent. Iran's population is comparatively young; 45.5 percent of the population was under fifteen years of age in 1986. Over half of Iran's population lives in the cities: in 1986, the capital, TEHRAN, accounted for six million; MASHHAD for over 1.4 million; Tabriz and Isfahan for nearly 1 million each; and Shiraz, Ahvaz, Kermanshah, and Qom for between 500,000 and 800,000 each.

The modern national education system emerged in the 1920s and 1930s, when the influence of the religious establishment was repressed and the control of the rising nation-state over the school system was established. The period from 1956 to 1992 saw the rapid expansion of modern education. The number of students at all levels rose from 1.1 million in 1956 to 7.5 million in 1976, and to 16 million (about 28 percent of the total population) in 1992. Meanwhile, the percentage of the appropriate age group enrolled in primary schools rose from 33 percent in 1956 to 56 percent in 1992, those enrolled in secondary schools leaped from 10 percent to 41 percent, and those in higher education rose from 1 percent to 4 percent. Also in this period the percentage of girls in elementary schools rose from 21 percent of total enrollment in 1926 to 38 percent in 1976 and to 44 percent in 1986; that in secondary schools increased from 6 percent to 35 and to 40 percent; and that in universities leaped from almost none in 1926 to 28 percent in 1976 and to 29 percent in 1986. As a result of the adult literacy campaign and the expansion of primary education, literate population six years of age and over increased from about 15 percent in 1956 to approximately 62 percent in 1986. There are, however, significant differences between males and females, urban and rural populations, age groups, and various regions in the country.

The educational reform of 1966 to 1978 marked the transformation of Iran's school system from the French model to one closely patterned on that of the United States. Schooling was divided into three phases: (1) the primary cycle for ages six to eleven, aimed at mastery of basic skills and knowledge; (2) the middle cycle for ages eleven to fourteen, a period of guidance to discover aptitudes and academic potential; and (3) high school cycle for ages fourteen to eighteen, during which education was diversified and specialized. In this last cycle, either an academic curriculum, preparatory to higher education, or vocational training, preparatory to employment as a middle-grade technician, was instituted.

The structure and organization of the educational system remained virtually intact after the 1979 Islamic revolution. The main goal of educational planners was to shape pupils' behavior according to Islamic values through modification of curriculum and textbooks. Other measures included converting all coeducational schools into single-sex institutions and imposing Islamic dress codes. A major innovation in precollegiate education is a pilot project, introduced in 1992, for restructuring secondary education, reducing it from four years to three years and dividing it into general education (including academic and technical-vocational divisions) and professional education (focusing on specific, practical work-related skills). The twelfth year of high school is redesigned for a college preparatory program, ac-

cepting only high school graduates who pass the entrance examination.

A "cultural revolution" occurred in higher education during the 1980s. In May 1980, over a year after the victory of the Islamic revolution in Iran, the government closed all universities and appointed a panel, the Cultural Revolution Headquarters, to provide a program of reform for higher education in accordance with Islamic values. The universities were reopened in October 1981, and the University Jihad and other militant groups, a mixture of zealot and opportunistic elements, took control of university affairs and purged some eight thousand (about half) faculty members. Following disputes between these groups and the ministry of culture and higher education over reform issues, the Supreme Council of the Cultural Revolution was founded in 1984 to supervise the reconstruction of universities. In the mid-1990s, higher education in Iran consisted of government-sponsored colleges and universities accredited by the ministry of culture and higher education; technical, vocational, and teacher training schools (primarily two-year junior colleges) admin-

istered by the ministry of education and other government agencies; and the Open Islamic University open to any student upon the payment of fairly steep tuition and other fees.

About 80 percent of Iran's population consists of people of Iranian origin, of whom the ethnic Persians are predominant. According to the 1986 census, 82.7 percent of the population (90.9 percent in the urban areas and 73.1 percent in the rural areas) could both comprehend and speak Persian, and another 2.7 percent could understand it. Persians are overwhelmingly Shi'ite Muslims. Azeris or Azerbaijanis form Iran's largest linguistic minority. Estimated at 20 to 25 percent of the population, they are concentrated in the provinces of East and West Azerbaijan, Ardabil, and Zanjan, as well as in and around the cities of Qazvin, Saveh, Hamadan, and Tehran. Iran's second largest ethnolinguistic minority, the Kurds, make up an estimated 5 percent of the country's population and reside in the province of Kurdistan as well as parts of West Azerbaijan and Kermanshahan (Bakhtaran). Most KURDS are Sunni Muslims. The Sunni Baluchi reside mainly in the

Sistan/Baluchistan province and make up 2 percent of Iran's population. Other ethnic minorities include the Sunni Turkmen and the Shi'a Arabs. Also residing in Iran are nomadic and tribal groups, including the Qashqa'is, Bakhtiaris, Shahsevans, Afshars, Boyer Ahmadis, and smaller tribes.

According to the 1986 census, 99.5 percent of the population was Muslim. Followers of the other three officially recognized religions included 97,557 Christians, 32,589 Zoroastrians, and 26,354 Jews. An additional 50,529 were listed as followers of other religions, and 39,753 did not state their religion. The majority of the latter two groups are presumed to be Baha'is, followers of a religion that has not been officially recognized as a faith by the government and has been subjected to persecution since the 1979 revolution.

The Economy. Iran possesses substantial mineral resources. It is estimated that its oil reserves are about 93 billion barrels, some 10 percent of the world total. Iran also possesses the second largest natural gas reserve in the world, estimated at about 20 trillion cubic meters (706.3 trillion cu. ft.), some 15 percent of the world's reserves. Hydropower, coal, and solar energy resources are also significant, and there are substantial deposits of copper, zinc, chromium, iron ore, and gemstones.

The economy of Iran grew rapidly in the 1960s and 1970s. In the period of 1963 to 1976, the total value of goods and services produced yearly (gross domestic product; GDP) grew in real terms by an average annual rate of around 10.5 percent, and per capita income leaped from some $170 to over $2,060 (in constant 1974 prices, per capita income increased from $250 to $1,500). The annual growth rate of the oil sector was about 13 percent in the period 1963 to 1972, quadrupled in 1973/74, then rose more slowly

Zagros mountains near Malayer. (Richard Bulliet)

until 1977. In the period 1963 to 1977, the average annual growth rate of industry was about 15 percent; of the service sector, about 14.3 percent; and of agriculture, about 4.6 percent. With increasing national income came more unfavorable trends in income and wealth distribution. For example, whereas in the period 1959 to 1974 the expenditure share of the top 20 percent of urban households increased from 52 to 56 percent, the share of the bottom 40 percent decreased from 14 to 11 percent.

The 1978 to 1980 period of revolutionary crisis saw the flight of skilled workers and entrepreneurs, the transfer of large sums of capital abroad, and the abandonment of many productive establishments. Under these circumstances, GDP in constant 1974 prices fell from 3.7 trillion riyals in 1977 to 2.5 trillion in 1980, and per capita GDP declined from 108,000 rials to 63,000 riyals. Following a short period of increase in oil revenues and financial recovery, the period of 1985 to 1988 saw an annual GDP decline of 4 percent due to the fall of oil revenues and the heightening of the "tanker war" in the Persian Gulf. The situation changed between 1988 and 1992, when the rise of oil revenues led to an annual growth rate of 7 percent and a gradual increase in GDP. In 1992 agriculture accounted for 24 percent of Iran's GDP, industry for 22 percent, oil for 18 percent, and services for 36 percent. The state owns all heavy industries, many other large industrial establishments, and all major transportation networks and agro-industries, and tightly controls the banking system. Nationalization of large enterprises by the revolutionary government has further expanded the public sector.

Modern industry made its appearance in Iran in the early twentieth century, but it was not until the late 1950s that the government adopted a clear industrialization policy. By the early 1970s the average

Rock-cut tomb at Naqsh-i Rustam. (Richard Bulliet)

annual growth rate of the industrial sector was more than 10 percent. Today, Iran has an industrial base consisting mainly of import-substituting industries that is heavily dependent on imported materials. Steel, petrochemicals, and copper remain Iran's three basic industries. The production of steel reached 3.5 million tons, and that of petrochemical products 2.5 million tons, in 1992. Other important industries include automobiles, machine tools, construction materials, pharmaceuticals, textiles, and food processing. Most of these were nationalized after the 1979 revolution. Vehicle manufacturing companies produced about 50,000 cars, vans, buses, and trucks in 1990. Fifteen cement factories had an output of 15.5 million tons in 1991. Thirty-six sugar refining companies produced 597,000 tons of sugar in 1991. In 1990, over 1,000 textile plants with about 150,000 workers produced 454 million meters (497 million yds.) of fabric. The handmade Persian carpet industry has maintained its traditional importance, and carpet exports amounted to $1.1 billion, 43 percent of the total nonoil export, in 1991.

Only about one-fourth of Iran is potentially suitable for agricultural production. Almost three-fourths of the country receives less than 250 millimeters (9.75 in.) of rainfall per year, and less than half of the crops grown are irrigated. Land under cultivation expanded substantially from the 1960s through the 1980s, reaching some 6 million hectares (14.8 million acres) under irrigation, 7.6 million hectares (18.8 million acres) under rainfall agriculture, and about 8 million hectares (19.8 million acres) in fallow. In 1992 wheat production reached 10.3 million tons, barley 3.1, sugar 7.8, rice 2.4, potatoes 2.7, and onions 1.3 million tons. In 1992 there were an estimated 50 million sheep and goats and 10 million cows and calves.

Mosque and riverbed at the shrine city of Qom during the dry season. (Richard Bulliet)

After the revolution, imports fell from $14.6 billion in 1977 to $10.8 billion in 1980 and $8.2 billion in 1988. Thereafter, the trend changed. By 1991 imports reached about $25 billion, then declined between 1993 and 1995 due to the fall of oil revenues. Germany, Japan, Italy, and the United Kingdom are the main exporters to Iran. Iran has made a considerable effort to increase its nonoil exports, and by 1992 their value was $2.9 billion. However, a steep decline in oil revenues and lack of a coherent and consistent economic policy brought a period of economic hardship in mid-1990s.

Government. Iran is a theocratic republic, a hybrid of the absolute authority of the ruling Shi'a jurist combined with an elected president and parliament, and an appointed chief of the judicial branch.

The ruling Shi'a cleric (VELAYAT-E FAQIH), the supreme spiritual guide, is considered to be the deputy of the twelfth Shi'a imam, the Lord of the Age. His authority includes appointing the head of the judiciary branch, appointing the theologians of the Council of Guardians of the Constitution, and in his capacity of commander in chief of the armed forces, appointing and dismissing all commanders of the armed forces, Revolutionary Guards Corps, and security forces, as well as declaring war. The grand ayatollah, Ruhollah KHOMEINI, served as the supreme guide from 1979 until his death in June 1989; he was succeeded by Ayatollah Sayyed Ali KHAMENE'I.

The president, elected for four years, is the head of the cabinet and the civilian wing of the government's executive branch. President Hashemi RAFSANJANI was elected to his second term in 1993.

The legislative branch consists of two elected assemblies, the Islamic Consultative Assembly (*majles*) and the Assembly of Experts, and two appointed bodies, the Guardian of the Constitution and the Discretionary Council. The *majles* is a body of 270 legislators elected for four-year terms. The twelve Guardians of the Constitution review legislation passed by the *majles* and are empowered by the constitution to veto laws considered to violate Islamic or constitutional principles. The Discretionary Council, created in February 1988 and formally recognized in an amendment to the constitution in July 1989, rules on legal and theological disputes between the *majles* and the Guardians. It is charged with ruling in the best interest of the community, even when such rulings go beyond a strict interpretation of the tenets of Islamic law. The Assembly of Experts functions as a constitutional assembly and determines succession to the position of supreme guide.

The judicial branch consists of regular civil and criminal courts, as well as a special clerical court and

Scene of Ab Ali road through the Elborz mountains.
(Richard Bulliet)

and Revolutionary Guard Corps, with over 530,000 members, are responsible for defense. The 300,000-man army is organized into ten divisions and six brigades. The air force consists of about 35,000 men, with over 400 pilots on active duty and 100 combat aircraft. The 15,000-man navy operates in the Persian Gulf, the Indian Ocean, and the Caspian Sea. It includes two fleets, three marine battalions, and two Russian-made submarines. The 180,000-member Revolutionary Guard Corps is organized into eleven regional commands, with four armored divisions and some twenty-four infantry divisions, as well as air and naval capacities. Second, the police force incorporates revolutionary committees and the rural police force into the urban police force. Third, the suppression of opposition to the regime is the responsibility of the ministry of intelligence and a 100,000-man mobilization corps (*basij*) recruited from veterans of the 1980–1988 IRAN–IRAQ WAR. Ideological–political bureaus have been established in government agencies and in the armed forces to ensure conformity to the regime's rules of conduct. The armed forces and security organizations are under the command of the supreme spiritual guide.

Since the 1979 revolution, various groups, organizations, and factions within the ruling party have reorganized themselves into three major camps. First, those who support the interests of the religious groups (*ulama*) and the bazaar merchants, and who advocate the traditional Islamic jurisprudence, are re-

revolutionary tribunals that hear civil and criminal suits concerning counterrevolutionary offenses. The head of the judiciary is appointed by the supreme guide. The minister of justice functions as a liaison among the judicial, executive, and legislative branches.

Iran is divided into twenty-four provinces (*ostans*) administered by governors (*ostandars*) who are nominated by the minister of interior and appointed by the president. The second level of local government consists of 195 counties (*shahrestans*) under junior governors (*farmandars*). At the third level, 500 districts (*bakhshs*) are under executives (*bakhshdars*), and at the fourth level, 1,581 clusters of villages (*dehestans*) are under headmen (*dehdars*). Villages, the base level, are administered by headmen (*kadkhodas*). Towns and cities have municipal governments with mayors and councils.

The Islamic Republic of Iran has three central organizations to defend the country against foreign aggression, to perform police services, and to suppress opposition to the regime. First, the armed forces

An example of mud-brick architecture in central Iran.
(D. W. Lockhard)

ferred to as conservatives, traditionalists, and rightists. The conservatives fear the cultural penetration of Western lifestyles and hold zealot views on cultural issues such as women's rights, Islamic dress codes, music, movies, television programs, and the media. In the post-Khomeini era, a major shift to the right occurred and the conservative camp prevailed. Second, those who support the cause of the economically deprived (*mostaz'afan*) and advocate a progressive Islamic jurisprudence, distributive justice, and tighter state control of the private sector are called radicals, leftists, followers of Imam Khomeini's line. Receptive to Western progressive ideas and more tolerant on cultural issues, the radicals are nevertheless highly suspicious of "Western imperialism" and Iran's "dependency" on the world capitalist system. The Bureau for Promotion of Unity (Daftar-e Tahkim-e Wahdat), major student unions, and the young Combatant Clerics (Ruhaniyun-e Mobarez) are among the radical organizations. In much of the 1980s the radicals dominated the regime. Third, those who advocate a pragmatic approach—the new middle-class professional and bureaucratic groups— and are concerned with peaceful coexistence in the modern world under a mixed economy are called pragmatists, centrists, or moderates. President Hashemi Rafsanjani has led the centrist camp since its inception in the late 1980s. In the fourth *majles* (1992–1996), conservatives controlled over two-thirds of the seats, pragmatists around one-fifth, and radicals about one-tenth.

The main Islamic opposition to the regime inside the country includes the liberal Iran Freedom Movement (Nahzat-e Azadi-ye Iran), established in the early 1960s under the leadership of Mahdi BAZ-ARGAN, who was prime minister in the provisional revolutionary government in 1979/80. Also organized by Bazargan to fight against frequent violations of human rights in Iran was the Society for the Defense of Liberty and National Sovereignty of the Iranian Nation. Another organization active in Iran is the nationalist Nation of Iran Party (Hezb-e Mellat-e Iran), under the leadership of Daryush Foruhar, who was minister of labor in the Bazargan provisional cabinet. These groups have been outlawed and systematically suppressed by the Islamic Republic. Absence of opportunities for genuine political participation, imposition of a strict Islamic code of conduct, and, above all, shrinking opportunities for higher education and employment have led to increasing alienation of young intellectuals and students.

A number of political groups have been active against the Islamic Republic among the some one million Iranian political and cultural exiles in Europe

Dome of Masjid-e Shah, the Royal Mosque in Isfahan. (Richard Bulliet)

and the United States, including liberal nationalist groups such as the National Front, whose origin may be traced to the period of Mohammad MOSSADEGH, and a number of small groups that advocate the establishment of a secular, Western-style parliamentary system in Iran. Also active are small monarchist groups seeking to resurrect Pahlavi rule through Prince Reza Pahlavi, who has proclaimed himself king in exile. A number of small leftist groups conduct a propaganda campaign against the regime through newspapers and magazines. The most active, militant opposition force has been the People's Mojahedin of Iran (Mojahedin-e Khalq-e Iran). It has waged guerrilla operations and a military offensive against the Islamic Republic from a camp in Iraq near the border with Iran since 1987.

History since 1800. Iran began the nineteenth century under the QAJAR DYNASTY (1796–1925) and the increasing political and economic influence of Russia and Great Britain. After two wars with Russia, the treaties of Golestan and Turkmanchai (now Torkaman) were signed (1813, 1828), and Russia took over the area north of the Araks river. In 1857, following a futile attempt by Persia to reclaim Herat, its former territory in western Afghanistan, the British waged war and forced Iran to give up all claims to British-controlled Afghanistan. To resist the European expansionist schemes, Crown Prince Abbas Mirza initiated a series of military reforms in the 1820s that were continued by more comprehensive reforms of the grand vizier Mirza Taqi Khan Amir Kabir in the mid-nineteenth century. Mirza Hosayn Khan Sepahsalar continued the reforms of his predecessor in the early 1870s.

In the latter half of the nineteenth century, Russia and Britain increased their economic and political domination over Iran. European companies were granted trade concessions that often were disadvantageous to nascent Iranian industries and local merchants. Meanwhile, new ideas of political freedom were being introduced by intellectuals and others who had come in contact with the West. The 1890 grant of a tobacco concession by Naser al-Din Shah to a British citizen was followed by urban riots instigated by the tobacco merchants and the *ulama*. The rebellion eventually forced cancellation of the concession. Many intellectuals and popular religious leaders believed that by reforming the system of government, they could improve the country's economic and social conditions and ensure its political independence. Antigovernment protests were led by a broad alliance of Islamic clergymen, intellectuals, and merchants. On December 30, 1906, the ailing Qajar monarch, Mozaffar al-Din Shah, finally yielded to demands for a constitution. In 1907 Great Britain and Russia divided Iran into two spheres of influence and a neutral zone. With the outbreak of World War I in 1914, Iran declared its neutrality. Nevertheless, Britain and Russia occupied the country, carrying out intrigues and engaging in hostilities against each other on Iran's territory.

In February 1921 a pro-British journalist, Sayyed Ziya al-Din Tabataba'i, and Brigadier Reza Khan staged a bloodless coup and took control of the government in Tehran. With the army as his power base, Reza Khan became the country's monarch in 1925 and founded the PAHLAVI DYNASTY. After establishing the authority of the central government throughout the country in the 1920s, he tried to westernize Iran's economic and social institutions in the 1930s. He replaced the traditional religious schools and courts with a secular system of education and a judicial system based on European legal patterns. He created a modern army and national police force, and his economic reforms included establish-

Storefront in Nishapur, Iran, 1966. (Richard Bulliet)

ing a number of state-owned industrial enterprises and a modern transporting system. The period of his rule (1925–1941), however, was marked by suppression of individual freedoms and political activities.

In August 1941, troops from Russia and Britain invaded Iran and forced Reza Shah to abdicate his throne to his son, Mohammad Reza. In 1946, after the conclusion of the war, the Soviet Union refused to withdraw its forces from Iran. Through a combination of international pressure and internal maneuverings by Prime Minister Ahmad Qavam, Russia's forces finally left in late 1946, and the pro-Soviet autonomous government of Azerbaijan and republic of Kurdistan collapsed (see AZERBAIJAN CRISIS). For much of this period, the young shah and his cabinets were forced to conform to the will of the parliament, which was dominated by the old guard politicians and propertied classes. Following an attempted assassination of the shah on February 4, 1949, the pro-Soviet Tudeh party was outlawed. A Constitutional Assembly convened on April 21, granted the shah the right to dissolve the *majles*.

At the turn of the 1950s, the National Front, a loose coalition of liberal nationalists under the leadership of Mohammad MOSSADEGH, demanded greater control over the British-dominated Anglo-Iranian Oil Company. The oil industry was nationalized, and Mossadegh became prime minister in April 1951. The Soviet-backed Tudeh party strongly opposed the nationalization and the Mossadegh government. In a struggle with the shah over control of the armed forces. Mossadegh resigned, and Ahmad Qavam was appointed premier on July 18, 1952. Three days later, riots broke out in Tehran and major cities; Qavam was forced to resign and Mossadegh was reinstated.

In August 1953 a coup conceived by MI6 and delivered by the CIA ousted Mossadegh; Fazlollah Zahedi became prime minister. The new regime ordered the arrest of supporters of the National Front and the Tudeh party, and placed severe restrictions on all forms of opposition to the government. The 1953–1959 period saw a gradual increase of the shah's power vis-à-vis the old guard politicians, properties classes, and *ulama*. The government signed an agreement with a consortium of major Western oil companies in August 1954, joined the BAGHDAD PACT (later called the Central Treaty Organization, CENTO) in October 1955, and with CIA assistance established an effective intelligence agency (SAVAK) in 1957.

In the early 1960s, under increasing pressure from the Kennedy administration, the shah appointed Ali Amini as prime minister and Hassan Arsanjani as mininster of agriculture. The government initiated a series of social and economic reforms later called the

WHITE REVOLUTION. In January 1963 a national referendum supported six reform measures, including land reform, women's suffrage, workers' sharing up to 20 percent of industrial profits, and the nationalization of the forests. Major urban uprisings protested the referendum and the government's arrest of Ayatollah Ruhollah Khomeini in June 1963. Following a crackdown on rioters, the shah emerged as an autocratic ruler. He allocated oil revenues among state agencies and projects, and he directly supervised the armed forces and security organizations, foreign policy and oil negotiations, nuclear power plants, and huge development projects. The latter half of the 1960s was marked by relative stability and economic development. Iran emerged as the regional power in the Persian Gulf after the withdrawal of British forces in 1971. Following border clashes between Iran and Iraq in the early 1970s, an agreement between the two nations was signed in Algeria in 1975. By the mid-1970s Iran had established close ties not only with the United States and Western Europe but also with the Communist bloc countries, South Africa, and Israel.

Meanwhile, land reform and the rise of a modern bureaucracy eliminated the traditional foundation of the regime: the *ulama,* the bazaar merchants, and the landowning classes. They were replaced by entrepreneurs, young Western-educated bureaucratic elites, and new middle classes discontented with the shah and his policies. The entrepreneurial and bureaucratic elites were unhappy with their lack of political power, the intelligentsia resented violations of human rights, and the *ulama* and the bazaar merchants resented the Western lifestyles, promoted by the state's modernization policies, that contravened Islamic traditions. Under these circumstances, the nucleus of a revolutionary coalition was formed by leaders with ready access to the extensive human, financial, and spatial resources of the bazaar, the mosque, and the school–university networks. They saw an opportunity to challenge the shah after the victory of Jimmy Carter in the U.S. presidential race of November 1976 and his administration's ensuing championing of human rights. As the political upheavals of 1977 to 1979 began, the shah appeared weak and indecisive, whereas the will to power of the charismatic Ayatollah Khomeini, who lived in exile, combined with the substantial political resources of the opposition forces. These circumstances led to the collapse of the Pahlavi regime and to the rise of the Islamic Republic.

In the summer of 1977, a series of open letters written by intellectuals, liberal figures, and professional groups demanded observance of human rights. An article published in the daily *Ettela'at* on January 7, 1978 attacked Ayatollah Khomeini, and violent clashes between religious opposition groups and security forces took place in the city of Qom on January 9. This conflict marked the beginning of a series of religious commemorations of the fortieth day of mourning (a Shi'a rite) for those who had been martyred in various cities. In July and August, riots erupted in Mashhad, Isfahan, and Shiraz. September 1978 began with the first mass demonstrations against the shah's regime. October 1978 marked a new period of mass strikes by government employees. Striking employees brought the oil industry to a standstill on October 31. Mass strikes continued through early November, when a military government was installed by the shah. Serious challenges to that government occurred in December, when the largest mass demonstration—hundreds of thousands of people—was organized in Tehran. The shah left Iran for Egypt on January 16, 1979, and Ayatollah Khomeini returned to Tehran on February 1. Four days later, he appointed Mahdi Bazargan as prime minister of a provisional government. Finally, on February 11, the army's Supreme Council ordered the troops back to their barracks. Military installations were occupied by the people, and major army commanders were arrested.

The April 1979 national referendum sanctioned the declaration of the Islamic Republic of Iran. The national referendum of 2 and 3 December approved the constitution of the Islamic Republic. In January 1980, Abolhasan BANI SADR was elected the first president of the Islamic republic. He was impeached by the *majles* for opposing the ruling clerical establishment and dismissed from the office by Ayatollah Khomeini in June 1981. In July, Mohammad Ali Raja'i was elected president; in August, a bomb exploded in the prime minister's office, killing the new president and Mohammad Javad Bahonar, the new prime minister. In October, Ayatollah Sayyed Ali Khamene'i was elected the third president of the Islamic republic. The *majles* endorsed the radical prime minister, Mir Hoseyn Musavi, who served until 1989. The early 1980s was a period of mounting intellectual conflict, armed struggle, secessionist movements, repression of liberal and leftist forces in the revolutionary coalition, and gradual consolidation of the Islamic republic. It also witnessed the crisis precipitated when Iranian militants took U.S. embassy personnel hostage, Iraq's invasion of Iran's territory, and an "arms for hostages" deal with the United States.

On November 4, 1979, the U.S. embassy in Tehran was occupied by a group of militant students, and sixty-six Americans were taken hostage. The seizure was in response to alleged U.S. interference in Iran's internal affairs and to the U.S. decision in October to admit the shah for medical treatment. President

Carter ordered the freeze of some $12 billion of Iran's assets in the United States on November 14. After 444 days in captivity, the last of the hostages were released on January 20, 1981 as Ronald Reagan was inaugurated president.

The Iran–Iraq War appears to have arisen from a long boundary dispute over the Shatt al-Arab from south of Basra to the Persian Gulf. However, the two nations' rivalry began in the 1960s, when increasing oil revenues and large human resources brought substantial capabilities and hegemonic aspirations. Frustrated by an imposed 1975 border agreement and heartened by Iran's military weakness after the 1979 revolution, Iraq invaded Iran on September 22, 1980. After rapidly occupying large areas of southwestern Iran and destroying the oil refinery at Abadan, Iraq's forces became bogged down in siege warfare. In an offensive of May 1981, Iran recaptured the strategic town of Khorramshahr and its forces entered Iraq. Initiating the "war of the cities," Iraq's forces launched air attacks on Iran's cities in 1984. On September 13, 1986 it was reported that Iran had received 508 U.S.-built TOW missiles in a secret "arms-for-hostages" deal with the United States to intercede for the release of American hostages in Lebanon; this episode became known as the Iran–Contra Affair. After a long pause, the war of the cities resumed in 1988, when Iraq launched missile attacks against Tehran and other cities, and both Tehran and Baghdad came under fire from ground-to-ground missiles. In May 1988, the United States began direct intervention in Persian Gulf affairs by escorting eleven Kuwaiti oil tankers, under the U.S. flag. This action led to increased attacks against oil tankers and merchant ships. On July 3, 1988, the U.S. warship *Vincennes,* stationed in the Strait of Hormuz near Bandar Abbas, shot down a civilian Iranian airliner over the Persian Gulf, killing all 290 people aboard. On July 18, Iran accepted UN Security Council cease-fire resolution 598. The eight-year Iran–Iraq War left about one million casualties and cost several hundred billion dollars in damages and military expenditures.

On June 3, 1989, Ayatollah Khomeini died, and the Assembly of Experts elected President Sayyed Ali Khamene'i as the supreme spiritual guide of the Islamic republic. The change of supreme leadership marked the beginning of a major shift of power from the radical left to the conservative right. On July 28, 1989, Hashemi Rafsanjani was elected the fourth president of the Islamic republic, and was reelected for a second term in 1993. President Rafsanjani's policies for economic, sociocultural, and political reforms were obstructed by the radical faction of the left in the period of 1989 to 1993, and

since then by the rising conservatives on the right. The death in 1994 of Ayatollah Mohammad Ali Araki marked a crisis of leadership in the Shi'a community.

BIBLIOGRAPHY

AKHAVI, SHAHROUGH. *Religion and Politics in Contemporary Iran: Clergy–State Relations in the Pahlavi Period.* Albany, N.Y., 1980.

ASHRAF, AHMAD. "Charisma, Theocracy, and Men of Power in Postrevolutionary Iran." In *The Politics of Social Transformation in Afghanistan, Iran, and Pakistan,* ed. by Myron Weiner and Ali Banuazizi. Syracuse, N.Y., 1994.

———. "From the White Revolution to the Islamic Revolution." In *The Crisis of an Islamic State: Iran After the Revolution,* ed. by Sohrab Behdad and Said Rahnema. London, 1995.

ASHRAF, AHMAD, and ALI BANUAZIZI. "The State, Classes, and Modes of Stabilization in the Iranian Revolution." *State, Culture and Society* 1, no. 3 (1985): 3–40.

BAKHASH, SHAUL. *The Reign of the Ayatollahs: Iran and the Islamic Revolution.* New York, 1988.

BILL, JAMES A. *The Eagle and the Lion: The Tragedy of American–Iranian Relations.* New Haven, Conn., 1988.

GASIOROWSKI, MARK. *U.S. Foreign Policy and the Shah.* Ithaca, N.Y., 1991.

HUNTER, SHIREEN T. *Iran and the World: Continuity in a Revolutionary Decade.* Bloomington, Ind., 1990.

KARSHENAS, M. *Oil, State and Industrialization in Iran.* Cambridge, U.K., 1990.

WRIGHT, DENIS. "Ten Years in Iran." *Asian Affairs* 12 (1991): 259–271.

Ahmad Ashraf

Iran–America Society

Organization to promote cultural ties between Iran and the United States.

Founded in Tehran in 1925 by a distinguished group of Iranians to promote closer ties with the United States, the Iran–America Relations Society met only briefly until its revival in the aftermath of World War II as the Iran–America Society. Its binational cultural and educational centers thrived in several major Iranian cities until the 1970s, when the growth of anti-American sentiment made them obvious targets.

BIBLIOGRAPHY

SALEH, ALI PASHA. *Cultural Ties between Iran and the United States.* Tehran, 1976. Volume commemorating the 200th anniversary of American independence.

Jack Bubon

Iran Bastan Museum

Name of the museum in Tehran built by Reza Shah as a monument to house the historical artifacts of Iran through the ages.

The museum curators attempted to repurchase stone reliefs taken from Takht-e Jamshid and other sites by the colonial powers. Included in its possessions are the genealogies for almost all the imperial dynasties from Achaemenid times to the present.

Cyrus Moshaver

Iran–Contra Affair

U.S. political scandal involving Iran and Nicaragua.

In the early 1980s, the Reagan administration was concerned about the kidnappings of U.S. civilians in Lebanon by Shi'a groups closely allied with Iran. The problem became particularly acute when the Central Intelligence Agency (CIA) station chief in Beirut, William Buckley, was seized and tortured in March 1984. Out of concern for the release of Buckley, who could potentially reveal U.S. intelligence information, and in the belief that it could make contacts with those it believed were "moderates" within the Iranian regime, the U.S. administration launched an operation whereby antitank and antiaircraft missiles were sent to Iran via Israel. This shipment resulted in the release of one U.S. hostage. In January 1986, President Reagan issued a presidential finding giving authority to carry out covert contacts with Iran with the goals of bringing about a more moderate Iranian government, gaining intelligence information on Iran's foreign policy, and gaining the release of the hostages held in Lebanon. U.S. officials traveled to Iran to establish contacts, and further arms shipments were made.

At the same time and in a completely unrelated effort, the U.S. administration tried to figure out ways to bypass a congressional prohibition on U.S. government assistance to the so-called contra rebels who were attempting to overthrow the leftist Sandinista government in Nicaragua. Col. Oliver North of the National Security Council staff and CIA director William Casey devised a plan in which the proceeds from the Iranian sale would fund the contras. This policy violated both the U.S. commitment not to negotiate with terrorists and the prohibition on aiding the contra rebels.

In early November 1986, a Beirut-based magazine reported that there were secret trips by U.S. officials for negotiations with the Iranians. This led to investigations in the United States and exposure of the

operations. President Reagan appointed a special commission under the direction of former senator John Tower to investigate. Later, there was a joint congressional committee formed and a special prosecutor appointed. In the end, only some of those involved were tried and even fewer convicted of any wrongdoing, but it was a political scandal that compromised U.S. credibility with its allies for having violated its pledge not to negotiate with terrorists, sending arms to Iran, and violating a legal ban on providing assistance to the contras. It was never made clear, however, what the president knew and when he knew it as far as illegal activities were concerned.

Bryan Daves

Iranian Languages

Family of languages spoken in Iran and adjacent countries.

The Iranian languages are closely related to those of the Indo-Aryan family, such as Sanskrit, Hindi, and Urdu; both families (the Indo-Iranian and Indo-Aryan languages) are part of the Indo-European language family, which also contains the Germanic, Slavic, Celtic, Romance, and Greek languages. The principal Iranian languages and groups of languages or dialects are discussed below.

The southern and southwestern languages. Modern Persian is the official language of Iran, Afghanistan, and Tajikistan. There are numerous local variants, the most important being the spoken Persian of Afghanistan (Dari) and of Tajikistan (TAJIK). The differences between standard Persian and Dari are not great; but the grammar of Tajik, especially the verbal system, has long been influenced by the neighboring Turkic languages and contains constructions that are foreign to standard Persian. Some of the earliest major Modern Persian texts, written by Persian Jews in the Hebrew alphabet, are in several variants of Persian and contain many archaic features.

Modern Persian is descended from Middle Persian, which is known through documents from the late Parthian and Sassanian periods (from c. 200 C.E.). The earliest examples are on coins from the rulers of Fars and inscriptions from the early Sassanian kings that are written in a local variant of the Aramaic alphabet. The Middle Persian Zoroastrian scriptures were written in a more developed variant of the same script, the Pahlavi alphabet, in which many letters are not distinguished. There is also a large Manichaean literature written in a Syriac script, and a few fragments of Christian texts.

Middle Persian is descended from Old Persian, the language of the Achaemenid inscriptions composed by Darius and Xerxes and their successors (c. 520–340 B.C.E.). It is written in a simple cuneiform script invented by the Persians, rather than the complex cuneiform systems of the Babylonians and Elamites in use at the time.

The languages (dialects) spoken in southern and southwestern Iran in the areas of Bakhtiar, Lorestan, and Fars are all more closely related to Persian than to other Iranian languages.

Kurdish is spoken mainly in western Iran, eastern Iraq, Turkey, and in the southern areas of the former Soviet Union. There are several dialect groups: southern (e.g., Kermanshahi), central (e.g., Sorani, Mokri), and northern (e.g., Kurmanji).

West and east-northeast of Tehran, in Mazandaran, and along the southwestern coast of the Caspian Sea a group of related languages is spoken: Tati, Taleshi, Gilaki, Mazandarani, Semnani, and others. Probably also a member of this group is Zaza or Dimili, spoken in eastern Turkey. All of these languages may be ultimately related to the Parthian language, known through documents and Manichaean texts (c. 1st century B.C.E.–3rd century C.E.).

South of the Central Desert, Dasht-e Kavir, a group of languages referred to as the Central Dialects is spoken: Khuri, Na'ini, the dialect of the Zoroastrians of Yazd and Kerman, and others. These may be related to the ancient Median language, the official language of the Median state (c. 700–560 B.C.E.).

In southeastern Iran there are three related languages in several dialects: Larestani and North and South Bashkardi.

Baluchi is spoken mainly in eastern Iran and Pakistan. It has several dialects.

The northern or northeastern languages. North and northeast of Iran, descendants of the various Scythian or Saka languages are still spoken.

Ossetic, in three dialects, is spoken in the Caucasus. It is the descendant of the old Alanic language(s), of which fragments are known.

PAKHTUN is spoken in Afghanistan, where it is official language, and in northwest Pakistan.

Numerous languages are spoken in Afghanistan, north of the Afghan border with the central Asian republics, and east of the border with Pakistan; none of them have written traditions. The most important are the Shughni group (Shughni, Sarikoli, Yazghulami, Roshani, etc.), Yidgha and Munji (Munjani), Yaghnobi, and Wakhi.

Yaghnobi is descended from a dialect of Sogdian, a Middle Iranian language known from a large corpus of Buddhist, Manichaean, and Christian texts, as well as secular documents (4th–10th centuries, C.E.).

Wakhi is related to the Middle Iranian language Khotanese, spoken in Chinese Turkistan and known from a rich Buddhist literature and secular documents (c. 5th–10th centuries C.E.).

Two other Middle Iranian languages, Bactrian (c. 1st century B.C.E.–c. 4th century C.E.) and Chorasmian (Khwarazmian; c. 3rd–14th centuries C.E.) have no known descendants.

Avestan is the language of the holy scriptures of the Zoroastrians. Old Avestan is very similar to the language of the Indian *Rigveda* and may have been spoken about the middle of the second millennium B.C.E. Young Avestan is similar to Old Persian and may have been spoken throughout the first half of the first millennium B.C.E.

Among the many grammatical features that distinguish the Iranian languages from one another three can be mentioned.

Gender. The distinction between grammatical masculine and feminine has been lost in Modern Persian and Balochi but exists in Kurdish and Pakhtun. For example: Persian, *īn mard/zan āmad*; Pakhtun, *dā saṛay rāyay* (this man came) but *dā šǝja rāyla* (this woman came).

Cases. In many Iranian languages two or more cases are distinguished (in Ossetic, nine). For example: Mazandarani, *per ume* (my father came), *pére sere* ([my] father's house), Baluchi, *ē ā mardē gis int* (this is that man's house), *gisā int* (it is in the house), Pakhtun, *da de saṛī kitāb* (this man's book).

Ergative constructions. In many Iranian languages the past tense of transitive verbs is expressed by a construction that resembles the English passive. This construction was originally used for the perfect tenses, corresponding to the English "I have done." For example: Old Persian, *adam akunavam* (I did) but *manā kṛtam* (I have done); Pakhtun *zǝ rasedǝm* (I arrived) but *dā saṛray me wúlid* (I saw this man).

BIBLIOGRAPHY

SCHMITT, RÜDIGER, ed. *Compendium Linguarum Iranicarum.* Wiesbaden, Germany, 1989.
YARSHATER, EHSAN, ed. *Encyclopaedia Iranica.* London. Articles on individual languages and dialects.

P. Oktor Skjaervo

Iranian Revolution

Islamic uprising in 1979.

The Iranian revolution toppled the regime of Mohammad Reza Shah PAHLAVI, ended twenty-five hundred or so years of monarchy in Iran, and inaugurated the Islamic Republic of Iran, led by Ayatollah Ruhollah KHOMEINI. The revolution had worldwide repercussions. Contradicting all prevailing theories of modernization and industrialization, change came not from the left, but from the religious establishment. The revolutionary potential of Islam had been actualized, and the relationship between religion and the state were altered in all Islamic countries. Iranians of all political affiliations rallied around the banner of Islam, and a politico-cultural transformation was initiated.

Conflicting theories prevail as to the etiology of the Iranian revolution. Those on the left argue for the failure of the shah's economic policies, the vices of dependent capitalist growth, and the imperialist presence of the United States in Iran. More culturally attuned discussions point to the too-rapid pace of modernization and Westernization in Iran and the alienation of the nation's masses. Many, including the shah himself, blame the United States and Britain, who, wary of Iran's impressive growth and development, moved to undo the progress brought about by the Pahlavi regime. These arguments point to the 1973 oil shock, when the shah engineered a huge increase in the price of petroleum produced by OPEC countries, inimical to the interests of oil-importing nations of the west. What is most important is that scholars and political analysts, as well as politicians, of all convictions failed to foresee the imminent revolution.

Although the revolution clearly has long roots in Iran's modern as well as premodern history, such as the constitutional revolution of 1905 to 1911, the governance of the oppositional National Front in the early 1950s, and the clerical uprisings of the 1960s, among the more immediate causes for the revolution in 1979 were galloping inflation, the increased pressure of the international community on Iran to stop human rights abuses, increased migration from rural to urban areas, and agricultural shortcomings. What began as an open letter by Iranian intellectuals seeking freedom of thought and expression was followed by a series of strikes in several Iranian cities, a hunger strike by political prisoners in Qasr prison, and a raid on a prominent ayatollah's residence in Qom and culminated in what has become known to some as the "Black Friday massacre" of September 1978 in JALEH SQUARE in Tehran, where at least five hundred people died. The revolution was on. The shah responded with several desperate attempts at reversing the course of events. Some weeks he spent on compromise, changing prime ministers, granting freedoms, dismissing Baha'i officials, and promising reform. At other times, he punished Iran by imposing martial law, shooting at demonstrators, denigrating the religious establishment, and jailing dissidents.

The shah installed a National Front candidate as prime minister, Shahpur Bakhtiar. On January 16, 1979, the shah left Iran. On February 1, 1979, Khomeini, after years of exile, returned to Iran, having decided to oppose the premiership of Bakhtiar. The shah's much touted armed forces declared neutrality, and the revolution triumphed on February 11, 1979.

BIBLIOGRAPHY

ABRAHAMIAN, ERVAND. *Iran between Two Revolutions.* Princeton, N.J., 1982.
FISHER, MICHAEL M. J. *Iran from Religious Dispute to Revolution.* Cambridge, Mass., 1980.
KALAM, SADEQ ZIBA. *Moqadameh-i bar enqelab-e Eslami* (Introduction to the Islamic Revolution). Tehran, 1993.

Neguin Yavari

Iran–Iraq War

Long, bloody, costly conflict, 1980–1988.

On September 22, 1980, military aircraft from Iraq mounted a surprise attack on military airfields throughout Iran in an attempt to destroy Iran's air force on the ground. A day later Iraq's forces crossed the border in strength, igniting what was to develop into one of the longest, bloodiest, and costliest armed conflicts in the post–World War II era. By the time the war ended on August 18, 1988, there was neither victor nor vanquished; only a million casualties, untold economic dislocation, and widespread destruction on both sides.

Exactly what drove Iraq's leader, Saddam HUSSEIN, to the extreme move of invading a neighboring state will probably never be known. The standard explanation views the invasion as an expression of Hussein's aggressive personality and his unbridled regional ambitions. These ranged from the occupation of Iran's territories (SHATT AL-ARAB waterway and the oil-rich province of KHUZISTAN), through the infliction of a decisive defeat on the Iranian revolution, to the desire to make Iraq the preeminent Arab and Gulf state. It has even been suggested that by defeating Iran, Hussein hoped to become the most influential leader of the nonaligned movement.

Conversely, the invasion has been viewed as an excessive reaction by Hussein to the threat posed to his personal rule by the revolutionary regime in Tehran. Coming to power in January 1979 on the ruins of the Pahlavi dynasty, which had ruled Iran since the 1920s, the Islamic republic, led by Ayatollah Ruhollah KHOMEINI, sought to substitute its own version of an Islamic order for the status quo in the Persian gulf.

Since this meant, first and foremost, the subversion of the nationalistic, secular BA'TH regime in Baghdad, and since his attempts to contain Iran's pressures by emergency measures short of war came to naught, Hussein was forced to conclude that he had no alternative but to resort to arms.

The reluctant nature of Iraq's invasion was clearly reflected in its strategy. Instead of dealing a mortal blow to Iran's army and trying to topple the revolutionary regime in Tehran, Hussein sought to confine the war by restricting his army's goals, means, and targets. His territorial goals did not go beyond the Shatt al-Arab and a small portion of Khuzistan, in southern Iran. The invasion was carried out by less than half of Iraq's army, five of twelve divisions. Also, the initial strategy avoided civilian and economic targets in favor of military targets. Only after Iran struck nonmilitary targets did Iraq respond in kind.

No less important, Hussein failed to grasp the operational requirements of his campaign. Rather than allow his forces to advance until their momentum was exhausted, he voluntarily halted their advance a week after the onset of hostilities and announced his willingness to negotiate a settlement. This decision proved catastrophic, turning what had been conceived as a brief campaign, at the most, into an eight-year war.

Iraq's limited campaign saved Iran's army from defeat and gave Tehran time to reorganize and regroup; it also devastated the morale of Iraq's army, and hence its combat performance. Above all, it did nothing to endanger the revolutionary regime, or to drive Ayatollah Khomeini to moderation. Instead of seeking a quick accommodation, the authorities in Tehran seized the initiative and moved onto the offensive.

In January 1981, Iran launched its first major counteroffensive. Although this attack was contained in one of the largest tank battles of the war, by the time 1981 was over, Iran had dislodged Iraq from most of its strongholds in Khuzistan.

In one of his wisest strategic moves, Hussein withdrew from areas of Iran still under Iraq's control and redeployed along the border. Citing Israel's invasion of Lebanon on June 6, 1982 he announced that his troops would be completely withdrawn from Iran within ten days. This move, however, failed to appease Tehran, and on July 13, 1982, following a bitter debate within Iran's leadership, a large-scale offensive was launched toward Basra, the second most important city in Iraq.

The war now became a prolonged exercise in futility, reminiscent of the trench warfare of World War I, in which human-wave attacks were launched by Iran against Iraq's formidable lines, only to be repulsed at a horrendous human cost.

In February 1986, after nearly four years of costly attacks, Iran gained its first significant foothold on Iraq's territory by occupying the Fao peninsula at the southern tip of Iraq and holding it despite desperate counterattacks.

By this time, the specter of a victory by Iran had gathered a most unlikely group to ensure that Iraq did not lose the war. The Soviet Union and France armed Iraq, and the United States provided vital intelligence support and economic aid; numerous companies in Europe built Iraq's nonconventional weapons; the Arab Gulf monarchies financed Iraq's war effort; and a million Egyptian workers serviced Iraq's overextended economy.

Meanwhile, Iran, starved of major weapons systems and subjected to an economic blockade, was showing signs of war weariness. Iraq's air and missile attacks on Iran's cities, the exorbitant human toll, and the economic dislocations gave rise to great frustration as shortages of basic commodities worsened, and a black market and corruption flourished. Discontent grew among the poor, the mainstay of the regime's support, and the number of war volunteers dropped sharply.

As early as mid-1982, a loose coalition of military and political figures began to question the logic of taking the war into Iraq. As national spirits fell, these skeptical voices became increasingly influential, but they could not sway the aged Ayatollah Khomeini, who would not budge until Iraq's regime was overthrown.

In April 1988, Hussein ordered his troops to move onto the offensive, after nearly six years on the defensive. Within forty-eight hours of fierce fighting, Iraq recaptured the Fao peninsula, signaling the final reversal in the fortunes of the war.

In May, Iraq drove Iran from Salamcheh (east of Basra), and a month later dislodged Iran from the Majnun islands, which it had held since 1985. In early July, Iraq drove the rest of Iran's forces out of Kurdistan, and later that month gained a small strip of Iran's territory on the central front.

The mullahs in Tehran desperately urged their spiritual mentor to drink from the "poisoned chalice" and order the cessation of hostilities. On July 18, 1988, Iran accepted Security Council Resolution 598 on a cease-fire. A month later the guns fell silent.

BIBLIOGRAPHY

CHUBIN, SHAHRAM, and CHARLES TRIP. *Iran and Iraq at War*. Boulder, Colo., 1988.
KARSH, EFRAIM. *The Iran–Iraq War: A Military Analysis*. Adelphi Papers no. 220. London, 1987.
KARSH, EFRAIM, and INARI RAUTSI. *Saddam Hussein: A Political Biography*. New York, 1991.

KING, RALPH. *The Iran–Iraq War: The Political Implications.* Adelphi Papers no. 219. London, 1987.

Efraim Karsh

Iran Novin Party

Political party created in Iran in 1963 to support government's reform program.

Iran Novin (New Iran) party was created as a "majority" or government party in 1963 by Muhammad Reza Shah PAHLAVI in place of the Melliyun (National) party, a royalist party, in order to maintain the semblance of a two-party system. The other was the MARDOM or People's party. The establishment of the Iran Novin party coincided with the period of a government-sponsored modernization and reform program known as the WHITE REVOLUTION or the "Revolution of the Shah and the People" (1963–1979). The party platform represented the shah's program of reform, which included land reform, sale of state-owned factories in order to implement the land reform, enfranchisement of women, nationalization of forests and pastures, formation of literacy corps, and implementation of profit-sharing schemes for industry workers. The party chairman, Hasan Ali Mansur, a royalist from a rich land-owning family, was at the same time appointed as prime minister. After Mansur's assassination in 1965, the chairmanship, as well as the premiership, was given to Amir Abbas HOVEYDA, who served until 1975, the longest tenure in the post. Some of the party leaders, including Hoveyda, were suspected of having Freemasonic ties, often associated with the British in Iran. Hoveyda controlled the party thoroughly.

In the late 1960s, the Women's Party of Iran Novin was created in order to enroll women in the political process. The official organ of the Iran Novin party was the daily *Neda-ye Iran-e Novin* (or Voice of New Iran) with an approximate circulation rate of five thousand in 1970. The New Iran party was dissolved in March 1975 when the shah decided to create a single-party system with the establishment of the RASTAKHIZ (or Resurgence) party, with Hoveyda as secretary-general of the new party.

BIBLIOGRAPHY

ARJOMAND, S. *The Turban for the Crown.* New York, 1988.
KEDDI, N. *Roots of Revolution: An Interpretive History of Modern Iran.* New Haven, Conn., 1981.
LENCZOWSKI, G., ed. *Iran Under the Pahlavis.* Stanford, Calif., 1978, p. 452.

Parvaneh Pourshariati

Iranology

Iranians have been reconstructing their long-lost ethnic inheritance.

From the middle of the nineteenth century, Iranians eager to learn about their ancient history and culture had to turn to European scholars, many of whom had served as leading diplomats in the court of the Qajar dynasty. Iranology thus came to be linked with sociopolitical affairs and exerted a tremendous influence upon subsequent generations of educated Iranians, particularly the nationalists. Early in the twentieth century, for example, the Iranian solar calendar—with its Zoroastrian month names and link to the pre-Islamic past—was adopted in place of the Islamic lunar one with Arabic month names, although years were still counted from the *hijra,* the Prophet MUHAMMAD's flight to Medina in 622 C.E. Iranianists, particularly Edward G. BROWNE, ardently supported religious and political freedom as advocated by Iranian "constitutionalists," while Indian Parsis provided financial and educational aids to fellow Zoroastrians of Iran, particularly in Yazd and Tehran.

During World War I, S. H. Taqizadeh and a few others—notably the German scholar Oskar Mann—published the journal *Kaveh* in Berlin. *Kaveh* became a nationalistic model for the literary and political fields and greatly influenced later generations. A few years later, the German Iranianist Ernst Herzfeld founded in Tehran the Society for the National Monuments (*Anjoman-e Athar-e Melli*), and taught the Pahlavi (or Middle Persian) language to a select group (Ahmad KASRAVI, Sadegh HEDAYAT, Mohammad Taqi Bahar, and Rashid Yasemi) who published New Persian versions of works written in Pahlavi, or Middle Persian. Herzfeld also started archeological investigations at PERSEPOLIS and at other sites and aided the Frenchman André Godard in building the Iranian Archeological Museum (*Muze-ye Iran-bastan*) in Tehran in the form of the palace of Khosrow at the ancient city of Ctesiphon. Herzfeld was also instrumental in planning various monuments in close imitation of Persepolitan buildings; the mausoleum of Ferdowsi in Tus (MASHHAD), for instance, resembles the tomb of Cyrus in PASARGADAE.

In the fields of history and linguistics, Arthur Christensen's *L'empire de Sassanides* and the three volumes of *The History of Ancient Iran (Tarikh-e Iran-e Bastan)* by Moshir al-Dowleh Pirniya (1932–1933) profoundly influenced the Iranian state and society. They helped to revive (sometimes erroneously by the Academy or *Farhangestan*) ancient terms from Old Persian, coin new ones (e.g., "airplane," "officer"), and give currency to ancient Iranian names (e.g., "Cyrus," "Cambyses").

In the mid-1930s, the Iranian government officially requested foreigners to use *Iran* instead of the more common *Persia,* while the Afghans revived the ancient term *Ariyana* (used for east Iran) as the title of their country, the name of the Afghan journal of history, and the Afghan national airline.

In the political sphere, some leftist Iranians (particularly poets) tried to exonerate Mazdak, the fifth-century religious reformer, as a venerable founder of social equality, while others, influenced by the Germanic school, favored pan-Iranism—the gathering of all people with Iranian heritage under one banner in "Greater Iran." In the realm of religion, Ebrahim Poure Davoud and his followers propagated Avestan teaching and presented ancient Iranian ideas favorably while denouncing Arab influence upon Iranian society. Consequently, with the coming of the Islamic Republic, a reaction set in and the positions became reversed. Today a more balanced view is gaining ground that considers Iranian heritage—both Islamic and ancient—as the valid inheritance of the Iranian people.

BIBLIOGRAPHY

There is no study of the subject, but references of diverse quality are scattered in a variety of publications: M. BOYCE, *Zoroastrians: Their Beliefs and Practices* (London, 1979); A. HABIBI, "Aryana," in *Encyclopedia Iranaica,* vol. 2 (1987); S. HEDAYAT, *Nirangestan* (Tehran, 1934); E. HERZFELD, *Zoroaster and His World* (Princeton, N.J., 1948); I. SADIQ, "Anjoman-e Athar-e Melli," in *Encyclopedia Iranica,* vol. 2 (1987); and R. YASAMI, introduction to translation of Arthur Christensen, *L'Iran sous le sassanides* (Tehran, 1938).

A. Shahpur Shahbazi

Iraq

Very important Middle Eastern country.

The Republic of Iraq, officially governed by the BA'TH political party, is in actuality controlled by Saddam HUSSEIN. As president of the country and head of the party's Revolutionary Command Council (RCC), Hussein controls a highly organized regime dominated by loyal Ba'th party members or personal favorites. Membership in the hierarchically organized party (from local cell increasing in size to the major political divisions of Iraq) has become less important than personal linkage to Hussein or his family.

According to the official 1987 census, the population of the country was approximately 17.5 million people living in an area of some 172,000 square miles (445,480 sq km) bordered on the south by Kuwait and Saudi Arabia, on the west by Jordan and Syria, on the north by Turkey, and on the east by Iran. Its major rivers, the Tigris and the Euphrates, combine in the south near Basra and flow as the Shatt al-Arab into the Persian/Arabian Gulf.

The capital of Iraq is BAGHDAD (pop. 3,844,608). The other key cities are BASRA (pop. 1,540,000), Iraq's gateway to the gulf; and MOSUL (pop. 1,220,000), major center in the north and historically a trading entrepôt linked with Aleppo. KIRKUK (pop. 535,000), also in the north, is the site of major oil reserves. The holy cities of Shi'ism, al-NAJAF and KARBALA, are located at the Euphrates river, southwest of Baghdad. Under Ba'th rule, the country was divided into 15 provinces or governates with 3 autonomous regions in the north.

Aside from the heavily irrigated land between the two rivers (ancient Mesopotamia) near Baghdad, and the marshes of southern Iraq, the area to the west of the capital is an extension of the Syrian desert. To the east and north of Baghdad are the ZAGROS mountains, ancient land of the Assyrians, which are inhabited by the KURDS in the north of the country bordering Turkey.

The Iraqi climate is one of extremes; summer temperatures can exceed 109 degrees F (43 degrees C), in the shade, while frost can occur in the winter. There is scanty rainfall, except in the northeast, the only area where crops can grow without irrigation.

Iraq's nationalization of petroleum in the early 1970s and its rapid increase in output of crude oil made it the world's second largest oil exporter after Saudi Arabia (1979 and 1980 averaged 3.3 million barrels per day [b/d], producing revenues of 21.3 million dollars and 26.3 million dollars respectively). Much of this income was invested in military expenditures, construction, and the development of chemical and nuclear capabilities.

After petroleum, dates are Iraq's major export (1988/89: 411,000 tons; 373,000 metric tons). Hussein's goal was to make Iraq self-sufficient in food production. To that end, in the late 1980s there was some privatization in agriculture, but after the GULF CRISIS of 1991, the state resumed control of agricultural output, wheat and barley being the major crops.

Water supply, electricity, and building materials industries located in Baghdad were destroyed along with 90 percent of the country's infrastructure during the war in 1991. They are slowly being repaired.

In August 1990 the United Nations Security Council imposed economic sanctions on Iraq as a

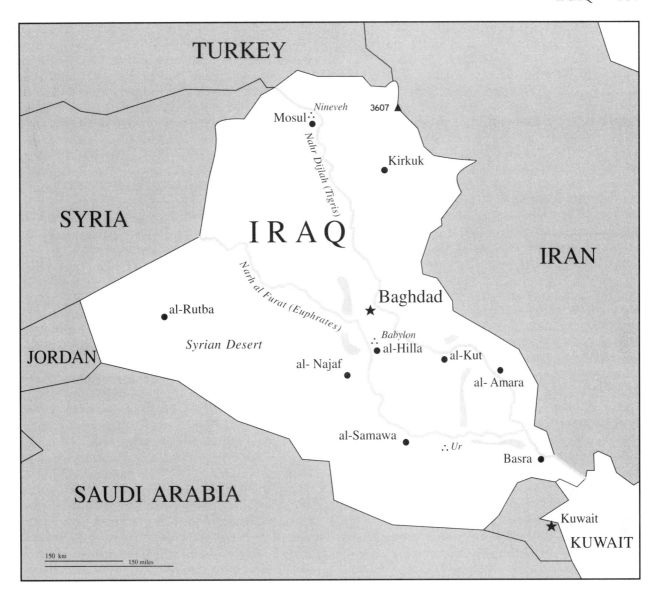

result of Iraq's invasion of Kuwait in August 1990. These forbade the sale or transshipment of Iraqi oil or the import of commodities except for medical supplies and food. Iraqi assets abroad were frozen.

The official language of Iraq is Arabic. Most Iraqis are Arabs and Muslims. Approximately 60 percent of the Arab Muslims follow Shi'ism and are concentrated in the south, and 40 percent are Sunnis. There are groups of Christians, mainly of the Nestorian (Assyrian) Church, and some Jews, a remnant of the Jewish population that left Iraq in 1950/51. The Kurds, who are Sunni Muslims, are not Arabs, speak Kurdish, and live in the northern part of Iraq, now concentrated near the Turkish border. Other minorities include the YAZIDIS of the north, and the MARSH ARABS in the south.

By the mid-1960s more than 60 percent of Iraq's population lived in urban areas. Primary through secondary education has been a priority. Baghdad University has expanded, and branches at Basra and Mosul have become independent universities.

Iraq, the area the Greeks called Mesopotamia (the Land Between the Two Rivers), was conquered by the Ottoman Empire in 1517 from the Safavi Persians. Laid waste by the Mongols in the thirteenth century, and bypassed in the fifteenth century once the Portuguese found alternative sea routes to the East, Iraq remained a backwater province until the mid-nineteenth century. Virtually ignored by Istanbul, the territories were ruled by independent Mamluk and tribal chiefs. Sulayman Pasha (1780–1802) and Da'ud Pasha curbed the power of the Kurdish chiefs and the MUNTAFIQ tribes of the south and brought Karbala and Basra under Ottoman rule.

The period of the *Tanzimat* (Ottoman Empire reform) initiated new interest by Istanbul in the area.

MIDHAT Paşa was sent to restore centralized Ottoman authority in the provinces of Baghdad, Basra, and Mosul. During his short tenure (1869–1872), the process of modernization was initiated through land registration, road construction, the establishment of newspapers, and the institution of government schools that enabled Iraqis to attend the military academy and the law school in Istanbul and join the civil service. International trade increased with the opening of commercial steamship traffic on the Tigris and the opening of the Suez Canal in 1869. Under the Young Turks, there was some support for the Committee of Union and Progress, but local nationalist groups developed as well. Iraq sent deputies to the Ottoman parliaments, and Iraqi Ottoman military officers were well represented in the pre–World War I Arab nationalist societies. Men such as Nuri al-SA'ID, Ja'far al-ASKARI, and Yasin al-HASHIMI played a variety of prominent roles in the Arab Revolt, the Syrian government of the Hashimite Emir Faisal ibn Husayn, and the post-war government of Iraq.

With the declaration of war in 1914, Britain's India Office, in charge of Persian/Arabian Gulf policy, advocated and carried out the invasion of Mesopotamia via Basra, which was taken in 1914. The British were stopped at Kut and only managed to conquer Baghdad in 1917, placing the city under military occupation headed by Sir Arnold WILSON and Sir Percy COX. Policy made in Cairo, however, determined the fate of post-war Iraq.

The British were awarded the area as a mandate at the SAN REMO CONFERENCE in 1920, and, at the CAIRO CONFERENCE, created the modern country of Iraq from the Ottoman provinces of Baghdad, Basra, and Mosul. Despite a revolt in 1920 against foreign rule, the British placed their wartime ally, Faisal ibn

Remains of pre-Islamic Sasanid palace at Ctesiphon. (D. W. Lockhard)

Husayn (FAISAL I) on the throne of a constitutional monarchy with a representative system of government. Through an indirect presence via British advisers, Britain's Royal Air Force, and an Anglo–Iraqi treaty (first signed in 1923 and renewed in 1930), the British thought to retain control of Iraq with its oil and strategic significance. Throughout his reign (1921–1933), Faisal worked for Iraqi independence and membership in the League of Nations, which were achieved in 1932. A newcomer to Iraqi politics, he had to balance the political aspirations of local Iraqi nationalists and the advocates of pan-Arabism who accompanied him back to Iraq from Syria and who formed the political parties that either fought or supported the treaty and the British.

Independence and Faisal's death in 1933 led to new political alignments. Animosities between Sunni rulers and Shi'a tribesmen continued, as did problems with land tenure, creation of the infrastructure, and minorities issues (Assyrians and Kurds). Political parties formed around personalities vying for power who used the army's massacre of Assyrian civilians in 1933 and incited tribal revolt in 1935 to their own political advantage. Yasin al-Hashimi's anti-British IKHA AL-WATANI (National Brotherhood Party) opposed Nuri al-SAID, who had seen Iraq to independence. By 1936 a coalition of army officers and the socialist-leaning AHALI GROUP resulted in a military coup led by Hikmat SULAYMAN and Gen. Bakr SIDQI that initiated a period of instability. Eight cabinets dominated by factions of Iraqi army officers governed Iraq from 1936 until the British re-occupied the country in 1941.

Arab nationalism, inculcated in the army and in the schools by Sati al-Husri, Muhammad Fadhil al-JAMALI, and Sami SHAWKAT throughout the 1920s and 1930s, was supported by Faisal's heir, GHAZI IBN FAISAL, who ruled from 1933 until 1939. The creation of pan-Arab clubs, such as al-Muthanna and the FUTUWWA youth movement, made Baghdad a center for pan-Arabism and a haven for exiled Palestinians, led by Jerusalem mufti (Muslim religious leader) Hajj Amin al-Husayni, and Syrians who joined Iraqi army officers under the direction of the pan-Arab GOLDEN SQUARE to plan a revolt against the British as a first stage in the establishment of a pan-Arab state. Anti-Jewish sentiments increased because of events in Palestine and Germany's influence in Iraq. Ghazi's death and the outbreak of World War II in 1939 led to negotiations between Iraqis, the mufti and the Axis powers (Germany, Italy, and Japan) for military and financial aid. Tensions with the British increased as prime ministers Nuri al-Sa'id and, later, Rashid Ali al-KAYLANI refused to declare war on Germany.

Vessels and huts of Marsh Arabs in Iraq during the 1950s. (D. W. Lockhard)

A group of Marsh Arabs in southern Iraq, 1973. (© Chris Kutschera)

When, on April 1, 1941, Rashid Ali, backed by the military, seized control of the government and refused the British passage for their troops on Iraqi soil, FAISAL II and his uncle, Abd al-Ilah, acting as regent for the young king, fled with al-Sa'id to British lines. The abortive war with Britain that followed in May resulted in a decisive defeat for the Iraqis, which led to a FARHUD (pogrom) against the Jewish population of Baghdad and a second British occupation.

From 1941 through 1958, the government was controlled by the regent and al-Sa'id, who emerged as the major political figure throughout the period of the monarchy. Wartime prosperity, oil royalties, and the emergence of a Shi'a middle class did not alleviate the growing economic and social problems caused by urbanization and the perpetual factionalism in Iraqi society. Anti-British sentiment, exacerbated by negotiations for the renewal of the treaty and growing dissatisfaction with the government's showing in the ARAB–ISRAEL WAR of 1948, led to riots (*wathba*) and the emigration, by 1951–1952, of most of the Jewish population (c. 150,000) to Israel.

Until 1958, al-Sa'id controlled politics in Iraq, allowing and shutting down political parties as the situation dictated. As income from oil exports increased, economic programs and flood control projects were initiated. Egyptian president Gamal Abdel Nasser's popularity and competition with al-Sa'id for leadership in the Arab world led al-Sa'id to use American and British support for the short-lived BAGHDAD PACT as a means to achieve Middle Eastern unity under Iraqi aegis, a possibility that both Faisal before his death and al-Sa'id in the 1940s had envisioned. The Suez Crisis (1956) led to more anti-British riots and dissatisfaction at Iraq's pro-Western orientation.

The Free Officers, who overthrew the monarchy on July 14, 1958 and killed the royal family and al-Sa'id, were led by Abd al-Karim KASSEM and Abd al-Salam ARIF. Initially inspired by Nasser, Kassem

(in power from 1958–1963) broke with the West, withdrew from the Baghdad Pact, and garnered support from the Kurds and Iraqi Communists. Kassem's crackdown on the Communists, the suppression of political parties, and the Kurdish rebellion led by Mullah Mustafa BARZANI led to Kassem's overthrow in 1963 by a coalition of the Ba'th party allied with Abd al-Salam Arif, who took control of a pan-Arab nationalist government only to die in a helicopter crash in 1966. He was succeeded by his brother, Abd al-Rahman ARIF.

On July 17, 1968, Arif was overthrown by a Ba'th-led coup. Ousting his allies from power by the end of July, Ahmad Hasan al-BAKR became president of a People's Democratic Republic in Iraq, whose goal

Euphrates river at Hilla. (D. W. Lockhard)

was to achieve a united Arab state under a socialist system. Controlled by a Revolutionary Command Council with executive, legislative, and judicial powers, the Iraqi national command of the Ba'th party, which had broken with the Syrian Ba'th by this time, was hierarchically organized by cells within provinces, with party leaders and increasingly men from Bakr's hometown of Tikrit appointed to top positions in the government bureacracy and the military. An Iraqi–Soviet Friendship Agreement in 1972 inaugurated USSR military and diplomatic support.

Not a party to armistice agreements with Israel, Iraq led the REJECTION FRONT, which eschewed negotiations with Israel and supported splinter Palestinian groups. Accommodation with the Kurds was achieved in 1970, however, war was renewed in 1972 and continued intermittently throughout the 1970s and 1980s.

The enormous wealth from oil royalties that increased substantially throughout the 1970s enabled the regime to raise substantially the Iraqis' standard of living. Schools, hospitals, land reform, major construction projects, and the creation of a Soviet-advised military made Iraq a competitor with Iran for leadership in the Gulf.

In 1979 Bakr resigned for reasons of ill health. Saddam Hussein took over as president. As deputy to President Bakr, his cousin, Hussein had used his position as head of the Ba'th party intelligence apparatus to consolidate his position in the party, and, by 1980, to become sole leader. Inculcating a cult of personality on the Stalin model, Hussein emerged as

Iraqi Kurds on horseback, 1955. (D. W. Lockhard)

father of the country, benevolent provider, military savior against Iran, and scion of newly Arabized ancient Mesopotamia. By the end of the 1980s, Hussein ignored the Ba'th ideology but retained the party structure as a useful means to control the country.

Once in power, Hussein embarked on two disastrous military adventures: the war with Iran (1980–1988) and the invasion of Kuwait (1990–1991). During the IRAN–IRAQ WAR, Hussein turned his attention to threats from within Iraq and ameliorated the wartime economic hardships with some privatization of agriculture and business, resuming relations with the United States in 1986, and promising elections (held with pre-approved candidates in 1989), leading the West to perceive a moderating tilt in his policy.

The lack of a peace treaty with Iran meant that the army could not demobilize, and the enormous cost of the war led Saddam to invade Kuwait in 1990. His miscalculation of the American response in 1991 resulted in the virtual destruction of Iraq's infrastructure, United Nations sanctions against the regime, and rebellions by Kurds and Shi'ites against a regime that consists of Hussein, family members, and close advisers.

BIBLIOGRAPHY

BARAM, AMATZIA, *Culture, History, and Ideology in the Formation of Ba'thist Iraq.* New York, 1991.

BATATU, HANNA. *The Old Social Classes and the Revolutionary Movements in Iraq.* Princeton, N.J., 1978.

DANN, URIEL. *Iraq under Qassem.* New York, 1969.

FAROUK-SLUGLETT, MARION, and PETER SLUGLETT. *Iraq Since 1958.* London, 1990.

MARR, P. *The Modern History of Iraq.* Boulder, Colo., 1985.

SIMON, REEVA S. *Iraq Between the Two World Wars.* New York, 1986.

SLUGLETT, PETER. *Britain in Iraq 1914–1932.* Oxford, 1976.

Reeva S. Simon

Iraqi–Iranian Boundary Agreement of 1937

Accord regulating use of waterway, Shatt al-Arab, by Iran and Iraq.

The SHATT AL-ARAB waterway, resulting from the confluence of the Tigris and Euphrates rivers, forms the southern part of the boundary between Iraq and Iran. As the only major river access to the Persian/ Arabian Gulf for these two countries, it is strategically vital, and it has been the source of much conflict. In July 1937, the first of a succession of disputes was settled in an agreement that granted Iran four miles (6.4 km) of the Shatt al-Arab near the Iranian ports of Abadan and Khorramshar, with Iraq retaining control of the rest. The border was drawn at the low-water mark on the Iranian side. In addition, the two countries agreed to joint upkeep of the waterway, and vessels of war were permitted entry into either Iraqi or Iranian ports through the Shatt al-Arab. The treaty was the cause of rioting in Iraq when the government of Hikmat Suleyman fell some months later, but Iran was not satisfied either. Although both countries were allowed rights of navigation, Iraq still controlled the greater portion of the waterway. The uneasy accord lasted until 1969, when Iraq attempted to seize unilateral control of the Shatt al-Arab. In response, Iran abrogated the 1937 agreement.

BIBLIOGRAPHY

AL-IZZI, KHALID. *The Shatt al-Arab Dispute.* London, 1981.
MANSFIELD, PETER. *The Arabs.* New York, 1985.
RUBIN, BARRY. *Paved with Good Intentions: The American Experience in Iran.* New York, 1981.

Zachary Karabell

Iraq Petroleum Company

Successor to Turkish Petroleum Company.

The Iraq Petroleum Company (IPC) was organized in 1928 from the remains of the Turkish Petroleum Company (TPC). In 1927, TPC discovered the large KIRKUK field in the Kurdish Mosul region of Iraq. Seven years later, IPC completed a crude oil pipeline with termini in Tripoli, Lebanon, and in Haifa, then in the British mandate of Palestine. Its oil exports reached 1 million tons per year by the end of 1934, but revenues remained modest until the 1950s.

Iraq's militant oil policy can be explained by the country's dependence on pipelines to move crude oil to market, and by its history of bitter conflicts with IPC. The IPC pipeline to Haifa, vulnerable to sabotage, was severed during the Arab–Israel War (1948), and the pipeline through Syria was blown up during the Arab–Israel War (1956). Shipments of crude through the IPC pipeline in Syria were halted for three months in 1966/67 because of a dispute over transit fees between IPC and the government of Syria. This was a preview of the relative ease with which transit countries were able to halt the flow of crude oil through IPC-owned pipelines following the imposition of sanctions by the United Nations in response to Iraq's invasion of Kuwait in August 1990.

Iraq's conflicts with IPC began during the negotiations over the original TPC concession. The government had demanded a 20 percent equity share in the company to give it some influence on management policies, including production levels. The TPC partners resisted giving a share to Iraq and called upon their home governments, then engaged in carving the Ottoman Empire into mandates for themselves, to help them. Needing British support to prevent the Mosul *wilayet* from being lost to Turkey, the government of Iraq reluctantly signed an agreement giving TPC a concession until the year 2000 and omitting the provision for an equity share for itself.

The most serious dispute between Iraq and IPC was over the laggardly development of Iraq's oil resources. IPC concentrated on developing its fields in Mosul, which depended upon the limited capacity of vulnerable pipelines to transport crude to markets. Development of the southern oil fields, close to the gulf where export via tanker was possible, did not occur until the 1950s. Iraq was convinced that IPC's foreign ownership was responsible for this delay, although other factors, such as the RED LINE AGREEMENT, are also likely explanations. IPC's foreign owners agreed to revise their concession agreement in 1952 to conform to the new industry standard of 50–50 profit sharing without the rancor that accompanied these negotiations in Iran. IPC also went along with another industry standard in 1959 and 1960, unilaterally reducing the prices paid to host governments for crude oil. This prompted Iraq to join four other oil-exporting countries to found the ORGANIZATION OF PETROLEUM EXPORTING COUNTRIES (OPEC) in 1960.

Negotiations between the government of Iraq and IPC in the early 1960s were beset by the inability of each side to understand the reasons behind the positions taken by the other. In December 1962 Iraq's Public Law 80 (PL 80) called for respossession of more than 99 percent of IPC's landholdings, including its share of the southern oil fields. The law also established the Iraq National Oil Company (INOC). PL 80 allowed Iraq to preserve its income stream from IPC, which retained its producing properties in Kirkuk, but also initiated a protracted struggle with IPC over the law's legitimacy. After intensive negotiations, IPC regained control of the southern oil fields in a new agreement initialed in 1965 but lost these rights after passage of PL 97 in August 1967, which gave INOC exclusive rights to develop all the territory expropriated under PL 80. IPC threatened to sue purchasers of oil from the disputed fields. INOC developed the disputed fields by itself and disposed of production through barter agreements, in order to circumvent the IPC ban on crude sales.

Following the 1968 coup and the installation of the al-BA'TH party, the government of Iraq moved rapidly toward nationalization. Continued conflicts over IPC's production rates, and company demands to be compensated for losses it had sustained as the result of PL 80, led to PL 69 (1 June 1972). This law nationalized IPC and established a state-owned company to take over its operations in Kirkuk. In response, IPC extended its embargo to cover oil from Kirkuk. The immediate impasse between Iraq and IPC was resolved in an agreement reached in February 1973, in which substantial concessions were made by both sides. However, by the end of the year, Iraq had nationalized all foreign oil holdings, including all of the remaining properties of IPC.

BIBLIOGRAPHY

MARR, PHEBE. *The Modern History of Iraq*. Boulder, Colo. 1985.
ORGANIZATION OF PETROLEUM EXPORTING COUNTRIES. *OPEC Member Country Profiles*. Vienna, 1980.
PENROSE, EDITH T. *The Large International Firm in Developing Countries: The International Petroleum Industry*. Cambridge, Mass., 1968.

Mary Ann Tétreault

Irbid

Largest city in northern Jordan.

Located 53 miles (85 km) north of the capital city, Amman, Irbid is the third largest city in JORDAN (pop. 385,000 in 1992) and the traditional administrative capital for the northern province.

Known during the Roman Empire as Arbila, Irbid was counted among the ten towns of the Decapolis—a commercial federation of towns in Judea, Jordan, and Syria during the first century B.C.E.

When reconsolidating their rule over Jordan in the nineteenth century, the Ottoman Empire's representatives in Damascus made Irbid the seat of the subgovernorate of Ajlun, the first district in Jordan to be ruled directly by the Turks. As such, Irbid became the home of some of Jordan's first public institutions. Irbid continued to serve as the capital of Ajlun during the emirate of Transjordan and of today's governorate of Irbid.

As an administrative and commercial center, Irbid has undergone considerable population growth, particularly since the 1950s. Irbid is also home to YARMUK UNIVERSITY, one of Jordan's three public universities.

BIBLIOGRAPHY

Statistical Yearbook 1992. Amman, Jordan.

Michael R. Fischbach

Irgun Zva'i Le'umi (IZL)

Jewish resistance organization (1937–1948).

For the most part, Irgun Zva'i Le'umi (National Military Organization) operated without the authority of the JEWISH AGENCY—as did a smaller, more fanatic group, the LOHAMEI HERUT YISRAEL (Lehi). The IZL derived from a split in the Haganah (1931) that developed as a repercussion of the Arab riots in 1929. By demonstrating the inability of both the British Mandate police and the Haganah to protect isolated Jewish settlements, the Arabs' attacks had led to the forming of Haganah-bet, a more militant wing of the Haganah. With escalated violence from Arab groups, however, some Haganah-bet members concluded that a single Jewish militia would be a more effective defense and rejoined the original Haganah; Haganah-bet members who had been Revisionists or sympathized with the REVISIONIST viewpoint, as well as nonmember sympathizers, founded the Irgun Zva'i Le'umi (1937).

The IZL was particularly attuned politically with Betar, the youth wing of the Revisionist movement, and in the years preceding World War II it drew recruits from secret Polish Betar cells, which the Polish government helped to equip and train as part of an arrangement it had made with the Revisionists to facilitate the transfer of Polish Jews to Palestine.

The IZL engaged in retaliatory attacks against the Arab violence that erupted following the recommendation of the PEEL COMMISSION for the partitioning of Palestine (July 1937). When IZL member Shlomo Ben Yosef was captured during such an attack, sentenced to death, and hanged (June 29, 1938), he became the first IZL martyr. After his execution, the IZL stepped up its terrorist activity to deter the Arabs and to demonstrate its military strength and the YISHUV's own objection to partitioning.

The IZL helped bypass restrictive quotas by arranging for the illegal emigration from Eastern Europe and smuggling of about two thousand Jews into Palestine. The WHITE PAPER of May 1939 limiting Jewish immigration caused much of the IZL's terrorist activity to be directed at British targets, but when England declared war against Germany (September 1939), the IZL voluntarily suspended its anti-British operations. Some IZL members initially joined the British army, and later on (after September 1944) others fought in the JEWISH BRIGADE. IZL commander David Raziel was killed (May 1941) in

Iraq while on a British intelligence mission prompted by the pro-Nazi revolt of Rashid Ali al-Kaylani.

Menachem BEGIN accepted command of the IZL at a point (November 1943) when the group was planning to resume terrorist activities to fight Britain's closed-gate policy, which appeared to ignore the plight of European Jewry. The IZL severed all formal ties with the Revisionist party in January 1944, thus becoming an autonomous underground organization and political entity. On February 1, 1944, Begin issued a Proclamation of Open Warfare against the British in which he called for an end to the truce between the Jews and the British administration in Palestine and demanded that the British immediately withdraw and declare a sovereign Jewish state in western Palestine. From 1944 to 1948, the IZL carried out approximately two hundred operations against British army and government installations and other unpredictable targets while also continuing to retaliate against Arab violence. The most infamous operation, the blowing up in Jerusalem of a wing of the KING DAVID HOTEL that served as the British military headquarters (July 22, 1946), killed ninety-one people and injured forty-five, many of them civilians. In its most sensational operation, "the Great Prison Escape" (May 4, 1947), IZL men broke into the Acre fortress prison and freed forty-one IZL and Lehi members as well as many other Jewish and Arab inmates. On July 29, 1947, the IZL thoroughly alienated public opinion within Palestine and abroad when, adhering to its "hanging-for-hanging" policy, it hanged two British sergeants it had taken hostage in retaliation for the execution of three IZL men. The continuous assaults on the British were designed to pressure the mandate authorities to conclude they could no longer rule in Palestine and to depart.

Like many other paramilitary nationalist groups, the IZL was often opposed by compatriots who abhorred its methods; members of IZL was steadily hunted down and either dispersed or executed by its declared enemies. British forces exiled several hundred IZL prison inmates to detention camps in East Africa (October 21, 1944). The assassination of Lord Moyne (November 6, 1944) by Lehi resistance fighters strengthened the resolve of the Jewish Agency, under pressure from the British, to rid Palestine of armed dissenters, especially the IZL. In a campaign called "the Season," the Haganah relentlessly pursued, interrogated, and turned over to the British wanted IZL men. By eschewing reprisals against the Haganah and in effect sitting out the Season, the IZL avoided setting off a violent internal struggle between the Haganah and the IZL and Lehi groups. The IZL's restraint earned it a measure of respect from the Yishuv, and the end of the Season coin-

cided with the end of World War II (May 1945), which also ended the overriding need for cooperation with the British.

Despite the constant friction between them, the IZL and the Haganah subsequently (Fall 1945) joined with the Lehi to form the Jewish (or United) Resistance Movement, whose purpose it was to pressure the British into leaving Palestine. The IZL's bombing of the King David Hotel, however, caused the movement to break up (August 1946), and the IZL continued operating independently. The IZL obtained resources through ongoing propaganda efforts in Palestine and abroad. It set up sympathetic organizations in Europe and the United States (e.g., in the U.S. the Hebrew Committee for National Liberation, headed by Hillel Kook, known as Peter Bergson) with whose help it purchased arms, raised funds, and recruited members. IZL agents abroad also carried out anti-British operations, such as the bombing of the British Consulate in Rome (October 31, 1946).

The United Nation's partition resolution of November 29, 1947, caused the IZL, which opposed the division of Palestine into two states, to deploy for a military struggle against the Arabs, who also refused to accept partitioning. On April 9, 1948, IZL men, together with a force of Lehi men, launched an attack on Dir Yassin, a small Arab village near Jerusalem; what had been conceived as an easy operation that would result in the flight of the Arabs and control of the village turned into a mass killing of civilians when the attackers met with sustained, unexpected Arab resistance. On April 25, 1948, an IZL force of six hundred attacked JAFFA, which had been designated part of the Arab state but which the Jews were determined to capture because it afforded the Arabs access to unprotected Jews in the city of Tel Aviv and on the Tel Aviv–Jerusalem road. The Haganah gave up its own plans for taking Jaffa (by encirclement and isolation) to assist the IZL in the four-day battle, after which the city surrendered, and all but three thousand of the seventy thousand Arab residents took flight. Whether the Haganah's more circumspect strategy would have succeeded in taking Jaffa has remained a controversial issue. Controversy also marked the IZL's unsupervised role in Jerusalem, where nine hundred IZL men fought unsuccessfully (May 1948) to establish Jewish sovereignty over the Old City.

On June 1, 1948, Begin signed an agreement with the military leaders of the new Jewish provisional government to dismantle the IZL. IZL members were permitted to join the Israel Defense Forces (IDF), and the IZL, in turn, pledged to turn over all its military equipment to the IDF. The arrival from France (late June 1948) of the ALTALENA, a ship carrying recruits and arms for the IZL, disrupted the process of reconciliation and led to an armed clash between the IZL and the IDF. The assassination of the UN mediator Bernadotte by Lehi men (September 16, 1948) produced outrage throughout the world and caused Prime Minister BEN-GURION to order the unconditional dissolution of the IZL and the Lehi (September 20, 1948). The Irgun Zv'ai Le'umi, numbering five thousand members at the time of its dissolution, was subsequently converted by Begin into the HERUT (Freedom) party, which garnered 11 percent of the Knesset seats in the first elections of 1949 and eventually drew back into its ranks many former Revisionists.

Participants in the IZL cause regarded themselves as fighting a battle for national liberation that forced the British to withdraw from Palestine. Most historians have not concurred in this view, although the IZL's operations probably did effect an earlier withdrawal than might otherwise have been the case. The annulment of the partition plan was another IZL goal, but the IZL was too insignificant a military force to change the balance of power or the official policy of the parties involved. Ideologically, the IZL considered Ze'ev JABOTINSKY its founder, leader, and teacher and maintained the tenets of Revisionism in most respects except for the major one of armed struggle against the British, which Jabotinsky opposed. Over the years, IZL propaganda revealed an intensification of the group's Anglophobia, and Britain came to represent for the IZL a pro-Arabic imperialist power; the IZL sought political support from France and the United States in its efforts to oust Britain from Palestine. According to its propaganda, the attitude of the IZL toward the Arabs of Palestine was that they were entitled to equal civil rights so long as they accepted Jewish sovereignty over all of Palestine.

BIBLIOGRAPHY

A detailed history of the Irgun Zva'i Le'umi can be found in DAVID NIV's *Battle for Freedom: The IZL,* 6 vols. (1975–1980; in Hebrew). See also TREVOR N. DUPUY's *Elusive Victory: The Arab–Israeli Wars, 1947–1974,* rev. ed. (Fairfax, Va., 1984) and J. BOWYER BELL's *Terror Out of Zion: Irgun Zvai Leumin, Lehi and the Palestine Underground* (New York, 1985). The story of the IZL is extensively documented within the context of the history of the Yishuv during the 1940s and the Jews' struggle against the British in Palestine. See also the many memoirs written by former IZL members and biographies of Begin.

Yaakov Shavit

Irrigation

See Water

Iryani, Abd al-Rahman al-

Second president of the Yemen Arab Republic.

Al-Iryani served as head-of-state of the YEMEN ARAB REPUBLIC from the overthrow of President Abdullah al-SALLAL in late 1967 until the bloodless coup led by Ibrahim al-HAMDI in mid-1974. The head of a famous family of jurists and teachers, Qadi al-Iryani's pre-1962 efforts qualify him as a father of the modern Yemeni republic, and his tenure as head of state was most notable for the republican-royalist reconciliation that ended the YEMEN CIVIL WAR and for the drafting and adoption of the 1970 constitution. A traditionally trained QADI (judge) who held to some modern ideas, he bridged the old imamate and the new republic; indeed, some called him the "republican imam" and claimed that this was the key to the successful transitional role he played. He spent most of his exile in Syria, was invited by the regime to return to Yemen in 1982, and made annual visits to his native land after that time. Although referred to as "president" in English, his actual title was chairman of the Republican Council during his tenure.

Robert D. Burrowes

Isa, Isa al-   [1878–1950]

Palestinian politician and newspaper publisher.

Born to a Greek Orthodox family in Jaffa, Isa Da'ud al-Isa attended Orthodox schools in northern Lebanon and the American University in Beirut. From 1911 to the 1940s, he was publisher and editor of FILASTIN in Palestine. After World War I, he became a top player in King Faisal's court in Damascus, Syria, and went on to play a prominent role in the moderate Nashashibi faction from the 1920s through the 1930s. He died in Lebanon.

BIBLIOGRAPHY

KHALAF, ISSA. *Politics in Palestine.* Albany, N.Y., 1991.
PORATH, Y. *The Palestinian Arab National Movement.* London, 1977.

Elizabeth Thompson

Isa Family, al-

Prominent Palestinian family from Jaffa.

A Greek Orthodox family of landowners, businessmen, and politicians, the al-Isas became most known in the twentieth century as publishers of the long-lived newspaper FILASTIN. Brothers Yusuf and Isa

Da'ud ISA, who both attended the American University of Beirut, Lebanon, founded the newspaper in 1911. Leaders of the Nahda al-Urthuduksiyya (Orthodox Club) before World War I, they were also active in the anti-Zionist movement. Isa's son Raja became editor of *Filastin* in 1951 and of the *Jerusalem Star* in the 1960s. He is now a publisher and owner of the Jordan Distribution Agency in Amman, Jordan. Another member of the family, Michel al-Isa, headed a battalion in defense of Jaffa against the Israelis in the 1948 Arab–Israel War.

A second prominent branch of the al-Isa family is based in Beirut, Lebanon. Elias al-Isa was a wealthy contractor in the early twentieth century from Bsous. His son Emile is a retired banker, and his son Raymond is an architect and engineer.

BIBLIOGRAPHY

KHALAF, ISSA. *Politics in Palestine.* Albany, N.Y., 1991.
SHAFIR, GERSHON. *Land, Labor and the Origins of the Israeli-Palestinian Conflict.* New York, 1989.
Who's Who in the Arab World, 1990–1991. Beirut, 1991.
Who's Who in Lebanon, 1986–87. Beirut, 1986.

Elizabeth Thompson

Isawiyya Brotherhood

Religious brotherhood.

The Isawiyya brotherhood, or Isawa, was founded in Meknes, Morocco, in the sixteenth century by Shaykh Muhammad ben Isa al-Sufyani al-Mukhtari, known as Shaykh al-Kamil (the perfect master). The brotherhood is found all over Morocco and Algeria and has extended its influence to other Muslim countries like Libya, Syria, and Egypt. Each year during the three days following the Mulud, members hold a celebration in Meknes where music, ecstatic dances, and extravagant rituals are collectively performed. Because it preaches renouncement, Isawa recruit their disciples mostly among poor social categories.

BIBLIOGRAPHY

MICHON, J. L. "Isawa." In *Encyclopédie de l'Islam,* vol. 4.

Rahma Bourqia

Isfahan

One of Iran's largest and oldest cities.

Isfahan is located in the west central part of the country. Very little is known of its history before the Sasanian period; yet, due to its geographical position at the intersection of many important roads, it is presumed to have been an important cultural and financial center. It is said that some of the Achaemenids used Isfahan, at one point referred to as Gaba or Gi, as their residential area; Isfahan probably became important after Arabs captured it in 642 and made it the capital of the province of al-Jibal. Thereafter, it experienced a history of great successes and defeats, depending on the ruling dynasty. Toghril Beg, who founded the Seljuk dynasty, designated Isfahan as the capital of his domain during the eleventh century and the city grew in magnificence, size, and population throughout the reign of this dynasty. After the fall of the Seljuks, the city declined markedly. It had its most notable surge in growth and import in 1598 when Shah Abbas I the Great, made Isfahan his capital city, and by investing in its sanitation and architecture, turned it into one of the most beautiful cities of the seventeenth century. After the fall of the Safawids, the city experienced another wave of decline. Its population was subjected to much injustice and social, political, and economic uncertainties. Many of the struggling powers, in order to prove their legitimacy, attacked Isfahan and tried to capture it; they hoped to establish themselves as the new heads of state and to reign in the same glamour that their Safawid predecessors had enjoyed. As a result, in the years following the fall of the Safawids the residents of the city were subject to a number of mass killings until the Qajar dynasty was able to bring Iran under its unified control. Once more, the city began to grow in population, and its economy recovered as political stability was strengthened, most notably during the reign of the PAHLAVI DYNASTY. In modern times, Isfahan played a significant role during the 1979 Islamic revolution. Isfahan is ornamented by many famous architectural landmarks such as Meydan-i Shah (Royal Square), Masjid-i Shah (Royal Mosque), and Masjid-i Shaykh

The Friday mosque in Isfahan. (Richard Bulliet)

Lotfollah (Lotfollah Mosque). The census of 1985 estimated the population of Isfahan to be 1,121,200.

BIBLIOGRAPHY

Asar-i Milli-i Isfahan. Tehran, 1974.
Isfahan. Tehran, 1967.

Farhad Arshad

Isfahan University

Public university in Isfahan, Iran.

Established in Isfahan in 1949 as part of an effort to install public institutions of higher education in the provinces of Iran, Isfahan University had 3,654 students by 1970/71. It has faculties of administrative sciences and economics, educational sciences, engineering, foreign languages, letters and humanities, and pure sciences, with 350 teachers and 10,200 students, as of 1990. The Isfahan University of Medical Sciences, with faculties of medicine, dentistry, and pharmacy and a school of nursing, had 250 teachers and 4,916 students as of 1990.

BIBLIOGRAPHY

SAMII, A., M. VAGHEFI, and D. NOWRASTEH. *Systems of Higher Education: Iran.* New York, 1978, pp. 5–7.

Parvaneh Pourshariati

İshaq, Adib [1856–1885]

Arab intellectual.

A Syrian Christian by birth, İshaq was educated in French schools in Damascus and Beirut. Emigrating to Egypt, İshaq became the editor of the noted journal *Misr.* While he has been described as an early promoter of Arab nationalism, İshaq avidly supported the Ottoman Empire as a viable political community. Inspired by liberal thought of France, İshaq wrote extensively about the nature of freedom and society. In his view, there were several layers of social organization in the Middle East, each of which defined itself differently. There was an "Arab" identity shared by those who spoke Arabic, an "Ottoman" identity shared by those who acknowledged the sultan as sovereign, and even an "Eastern" identity shared by those who felt besieged by the West. These layers were not mutually exclusive; they overlapped, and it was possible for one individual to hold to more than one of these identities.

BIBLIOGRAPHY

HOURANI, ALBERT. *Arabic Thought in the Liberal Age 1798–1939.* New York, 1983.
VATIKIOTIS, P. J. *The History of Egypt.* 3rd ed. Baltimore, 1985.

Zachary Karabell

Iskenderun

See Alexandretta

Islah Party

Yemeni political party.

The Islah party was formed in 1990, soon after the People's Democratic Republic of Yemen and the Yemen Arab Republic united to form the Republic of Yemen. Although widely characterized as Islamist, the Islah party is actually a coalition of the HASHID TRIBAL CONFEDERATION, the MUSLIM BROTHERHOOD, some prominent businessmen, and a few other small groups. In May 1993, the party won the second-largest bloc in the country's first democratic parliamentary elections, gaining fewer seats than the General People's Congress (GPC) but more than the Yemeni Socialist Party (YSP) (the former governments of North and South Yemen, respectively). Islah nevertheless remained marginalized until 1994, when civil war brought about the demise of the GPC–YSP partnership and the exile of many YSP leaders. A new government was formed based on a coalition between the GPC and Islah, dramatically increasing Islah's political strength as many of its leaders were appointed to prominent cabinet positions.

BIBLIOGRAPHY

DRESH, PAUL, and BERNARD HAYKEL. "Stereotypes and Political Styles: Islamists and Tribesfolk in Yemen." *International Journal of Middle East Studies* 27 (November 1995): 405–431.

Jillian Schwedler

Islah Taleban Party

A conservative political party in Iran that supported Reza Khan's coming to power as shah and helped support his policies.

An heir to the Moderate Party (or *Firqeh-ye I'tidal*), a conservative party which supported the aristocracy and the traditional middle class, the Islah Taleban

(Reformers) party was established in 1910. Like its predecessor, the Islah Taleban was a conservative party led by prominent clerics, merchants, and landed aristocracy. The party was instrumental in paving the way for Reza Khan's assumption of power as the king of Iran. Almost unanimously, the party supported a bill introduced by the Revival Party that deposed the QAJAR DYNASTY and proclaimed Reza PAHLAVI the king (shah) of Iran. With three other political parties, the Reformers formed the alliance system that Reza Shah used for implementing his policies. The leading members of the party were instrumental in passing a new law in the parliament calling for universal adult male suffrage. But in the semifeudal conditions of the country in the early twentieth century, this law extending the vote to the uneducated rural masses only helped strengthen the elite. The famous Iranian poet Mujammad Taqi Bahar wrote of the law in 1944 that "it continues to plague the country even today."

BIBLIOGRAPHY

ABRAHAMIAN, E. *Iran between Two Revolutions*. Princeton, N.J., 1982.

Parvaneh Pourshariati

Islam

The religion of nearly one-fifth of the world's population.

Geographically Muslims are primarily centered on the Asian and African continents with minorities in Europe and North and South America. The historical beginning of Islam (*Islam,* an Arabic word with the sense of "submitting oneself to the will of God") goes back to the year 610 when Muhammad, the Prophet of Islam, first preached its message in the town of Mecca in the Arabian Peninsula. In an environment that was primarily polytheistic and pagan, Muhammad called for the worship of the one God (*Allah*), creator of the universe, and warned of the coming of a Judgement Day when all will be rewarded or punished according to their deeds in this life. Islam did not conceive of itself as a new religion but as a reaffirmation of the monotheistic message of previous revelations transmitted through various prophets.

On the eve of Islam, Mecca was ruled by an oligarchy of merchant families who sought to maintain the status of Mecca as a center for pagan pilgrimage in order to attract a parallel commercial traffic to the city. Against the stout rejection and hostility of Meccans, Muhammad turned to the neighboring city of Medina, which proved receptive for the new mes-

Entrance of the Qadimayn mosque, a Shi'a shrine in Baghdad. (Richard Bulliet)

sage. In 622, Muhammad secretly traveled from Mecca to Medina in an episode that became known as the *hijra* (migration), which marks the beginning of the Islamic lunar calendar, and there set out organizing the new Islamic community. In the successive years the Prophet gradually became accepted by neighboring tribal communities who embraced the new religion, while Mecca eventually also joined the Islamic fold in 630. When he died in 632, Muhammad left behind an Islamic state whose influence covered most of the Arabian Peninsula. Under the rule of his immediate successors, the Rashidun caliphs (the "Rightly Guided Caliphs"), the Islamic state scored a series of decisive victories, which ended the rule of the Persian Sasanid empire in the east and seriously crippled the power of the Byzantine empire by wresting from it the affluent provinces of Syria and Egypt. With the coming of the Umayyad dynasty (661–750), which shifted the capital of the caliphate to Damascus, the Islamic expansion continued until it eventually covered the region stretching from Spain in the west to the borders of India in the east. It was under the Abbasid dynasty (750–1258), however, centered in Baghdad, that Islamic civilization reached the zenith of its intellectual and scientific floresence.

Theology and Rituals. Belief in the absolute oneness of God constitutes the foundation of the Islamic faith. This belief is succinctly articulated in the Islamic profession of faith (the *shahada*), "There is no god but God and Muhammad is His messenger." Utterance of this statement marks the point of conversion of an individual to Islam. A Muslim believer is expected to also practice four other elements of ritual, which together with the credo form the "five pillars of Islam." These rituals are: prayer (*salat*) five times a day (at dawn, noontime, afternoon, sunset, and evening), fasting the month of Ramadan, paying a fixed annual sum of alms (*zakat*), and—for those who are capable physically and financially—undertaking a pilgrimage to Mecca (*hajj*) once in a lifetime. Ritual ablution (*wudu*) constitutes a crucial prerequisite to the performance of prayer in Islam.

While the rhythm of Islamic rituals differs substantially from those of Judaism and Christianity, the moral message of Islam overlaps with that of other religions. One is exhorted to lead an upright life and to refrain from committing murder, adultery, stealing, and harmful (physical or verbal) treatment of others. In an additional nuance, however, Islam characterizes unfair acts inflicted by one onto others as a wrong done to one's self (*zulm al-Nafs*). The individual must constantly struggle against his or her physical inclinations and personal ambitions. Pride, ego, envy, greed, and the constant pursuit of material and social power are some of the negative side effects of human nature and one's interaction with others. But while Islam does not call for celibacy and total detachment from the world, it emphasizes a sober and restrained attitude toward prosperity and pleasure. The individual's effort to control instinctual and impulsive feelings is labeled in tradition as *jihad* (struggle), a term that also refers to the community's political and military struggle against injustice and aggression.

Aside from the rituals, the nature of the Islamic religious belief is further elaborated in a set of elements known as "the pillars of the faith." These are summarized in the Islamic doctrine as: belief in God, the angels, earlier revelations and prophets, the Day of Judgment, and the reality of fate (*al-qada wa'l-qadar*). Muslims are encouraged to join together and unite in a binding tie that fulfills the Qur'anic exhortation, "And hold fast to, all together, by the Rope (which God stretches out for you), and be not divided among yourselves." (3:103). The community of believers, *jama'a* (congregation), is viewed as the basic unit of social organization, which along with other communities across the Islamic world come together to form the *umma,* the world community of Islam. No lines of difference in the community are recognized. Piety and charitable deeds are the only marks of social honor. The Qur'an states, "O you people, we have created [all of] you from a male and a female, and we have made you into different nations and tribes [only] for the purpose of identification—otherwise, the noblest of you in the sight of God is the one who is the most righteous." (49:13). Toward other religions Islam calls for tolerance and dialogue. It views biblical religions, Ju-

daism and Christianity, as ancestor religions (*ahl al-kitab*, People of the Book), which at their inception conveyed the same monotheistic message of Islam, and similar moral injunctions. Under various influences, however, the biblical messages were critically transformed, thereby requiring a renewal through the Islamic message. This perception is particularly important for understanding the Islamic rejection of the Christian doctrines of the Trinity and Incarnation. Jesus, in Islam, is one prophet in a long line that starts with Noah and Abraham, passes through Moses and David, and concludes with Muhammad. Muhammad described his own role in light of previous revelations as the last brick completing the historically developing edifice of prophecy.

The Qur'an and Islamic Law. The Qur'an (recitation), the holy book of Islam, is considered by Muslims the word of God transmitted to Muhammad through the angel Gabriel. Between the years 610 and 632, Muhammad pronounced various verses of the Qur'an in various contexts, both in Mecca and Medina. The 114 chapters (*suras*) of the Qur'an, which constitute the only sacred text in Islam, are hence divided into Meccan and Medinan chapters. The Meccan chapters are on the whole shorter than the Medinan and contain a warning thrust. Meccan verses are imbued with images of eschatology, vividly describe Judgement Day, and call on mankind to observe nature and the universe as a system of signs that point to the Creator. The later Medinan verses, by contrast, are longer and mostly provide detailed descriptions of aspects of Islamic ritual and law. Issues such as marriage and divorce procedures, inheritance law, and contracts are all discussed, and often in specific terms. However, whether in the Meccan or Medinan chapters, the one theme that recurs throughout is the Qur'anic description of the lives of previous prophets, their religious experiences and confrontation with tyrants and rejectionists, and the eventual resolution of these stories with the downfall of the enemies of divine truth and the rescue of the minority of believers.

The Qur'an forms the basis of Islamic law. In situations where the Qur'an provides only a general guideline, Muslim jurists turn to the HADITH (the sayings of the Prophet), and descriptions of the Prophet's behavior (SUNNA, custom), as an authoritative source for issuing judgement. Interest in compiling *Hadith* started only well after the Prophet's death in 632, and various scholars emphasized the importance of the oral transmission of these statements. By the ninth century, as the chain of Hadith narrators extended considerably, scholars set themselves to examining the veracity of Hadith reports by scrutinizing the reputations of Hadith narrators mentioned in the chain of reporting (*isnad*). Two compendia of Hadith that resulted from such examinations, by the scholars Muslim ibn al-Hajjaj (d. 875) and Muhammad ibn Isma'il al-Bukhari (d. 870), have since been considered the most reliable testaments (*sahih*) on Hadith and *Sunna*. In view of the diversity of the sources of Islamic law, the medieval scholar Muhammad ibn Idris al-Shafi'i (d. 819) proposed a formula outlining the process by which a legal opinion can be adduced. According to al-Shafi'i's system, known as *usul al-fiqh* (the Foundations of Jurisprudence), which has represented the overarching legal framework ever since, a jurist (*faqih*) must first turn to the Qur'an for legal judgement. If the Qur'an does not address the matter in question or contains only a general principle, then he must turn to Hadith evidence. If neither the Qur'an nor Hadith address the issue, one is exhorted to investigate the possibility of reasoning a judgement on the basis of analogy (*qiyas*) to a situation that the Qur'an or Hadith covers specifically. Finally, if qiyas proves impossible, the issue must be submitted to a consultative assembly of scholars who should work out a judgement resting on a consensus (*ijma*) that becomes symbolic of the consensus of the Islamic community.

Islamic Trends. On the whole the Islamic community is divided between the Sunni and Shi'a sects (SUNNI ISLAM represents roughly 85 percent, and Shi'a Islam the rest). While the two agree on religious essentials, such as definitions of faith and matters of ritual, they mostly differ on political and historical points and some juridical issues. SHI'ISM rests on the historical belief that Ali ibn Abu Talib, the fourth caliph of Islam (656–661), and his posterity (the Alid branch of the extended Hashimite family of the Prophet) are the rightful successors to the Prophet. This is not merely a political point, but one with significant religious implications. Ali was the cousin of the Prophet and father of his only grandchildren, Hasan and Husayn, through his marriage with the Prophet's daughter Fatima. Ali's familial proximity is considered a mark of social and religious affinity that is unique among the early companions (*sahaba*) of the Prophet. Shi'a tradition also specifically states that the Prophet designated Ali as his political successor and imparted to him the power of interpreting the Qur'an and other aspects of religious knowledge. This unique religious knowledge was hence transmitted, according to Shi'a thought, down a line of his descendants, through his son Husayn, who represented—each in his day and age—the holder of the special religious knowledge (*ma'rifa*) transmitted through his predecessor by a covenant (*wasiyya*). The

Alid descendants were hence considered *imams,* both religious masters and the rightful leaders of the community. Following the occultation of the twelfth imam (873), Shi'ism considers that the authority of religious knowledge was transmitted to Shi'a religious scholars, who upheld this particular system of religious interpretation.

In contrast, Sunni Islam recognizes no unique right for the descendants of Ali to political leadership and does not credit them with exclusive religious knowledge. Various companions of the Prophet, in Sunnism, are considered comparable in religious merit without attention to kin ties with the Prophet's family (the Hashimites), while the degree of qualification of the first four caliphs (Abu Bakr, Umar, Uthman, and Ali) to caliphal (and religious) leadership is acknowledged according to that order of succession. Whereas the imam in Shi'ism commands a binding role in matters of religious interpretation and the juridical field, in Sunnism religious authority rests in the institution of the *ulama* (religious scholars), and the *Shari'a* (law), which comprises Hadith, some of which are relayed by Ali, but the majority of which are relayed on the authority of other companions of the Prophet. Today, the main centers of Sunni religious learning are found in Egypt (the Azhar University), Tunisia (Zaytuna), and Morocco (Qarawiyyin), while the centers of Shi'a spirituality are found in Iraq (al-Najaf) and Iran (Qom).

The mystical trend, better known as Sufism, represents a current common to both Sunnis and Shi'ites. Sufism represents a path of spirituality that emphasizes the contemplation of existence, renouncement of the world, and attachment to the experiences of saintly figures and prophets (primarily Muhammad). Themes of divine love, pursuit of a transcendent consciousness, asceticism, inner satisfaction, and admiration for nature are some of the recurrent themes in Sufi poetry and testaments. The leading lights of Sufi thought are: Junayd (d. 910), Hallaj (d. 922), al-Ghazali (d. 1111), Ibn al-Arabi (d. 1240), Jalal al-Din al-Rumi (d. 1273), and perhaps the earliest of all, the female mystic Rabi al-Adawiyya (d. 801). While Sufism originally developed largely as an expression of personal experiences, several Sufi scholars eventually outlined systematic descriptions of the Sufi path, the method by which one trains one self to partake in such contemplative exercises, and the nature of the relation between the spiritual guide and his disciple (*murid*). In early medieval times, juristic and orthodox scholars tended to distance themselves from Sufi figures, but starting in the twelfth century, largely due to the writings of al-Ghazali, the two currents started to reconcile. By the nineteenth century, Sufi movements, known as *tariqa*s, were popular all over the Islamic world: the Mawlawiyya and Naqshbandiyya (in the Ottoman Empire and Central Asia), the Qadiriyya (Iraq), the Rifa'iyya (Egypt), and the Tijaniyya and Sanusiyya (North Africa). Sufi movements in the modern period assumed various political roles, sometimes strengthening the religious legitimacy of governments, and at other times mobilizing their networks in the anti-colonial struggle.

Islamic Modernism. The growth of European colonial economic and political dominance of the Islamic world in the nineteenth century elicited various responses from various Islamic regions. Europe's economic and technological progress at the time generated a debate in the Islamic world as to how a similar experiment could be successfully applied in the Islamic world. A range of Muslim thinkers from various countries, Jamal al-Din al-AFGHANI (Iran), Muhammad ABDUH (Egypt), Rashid RIDA (Lebanon), and KHAYR AL-DIN al-Tunisi (Tunisia) concurred on the need for the Islamic community to open its doors for ideas and scientific disciplines developed in the West in order to strengthen the ability of Islamic societies to defend against outside domination. Invariably they agreed that the rigidity that was pervasive in Islamic society, institutions, and governments had little to do with the earliest traditions of Islam, which propelled the scientific and intellectual achievements of medieval Islamic civilization. To effect a renewal, these scholars argued the need to return to the pristine roots of Islamic thought, which encourage the pursuit of scientific inquiry and foster the mission of human progress. Western patterns, ranging from the secular system of primary and secondary school education to the parliamentary form of government, became popular goals of the new reformist generation. The most daring change that took place in this period was the adoption by some states, such as the Ottoman Empire and Egypt, of considerable sections of the Western legal codes alongside the traditional Islamic legal code (*Shari'a*). In areas such as commercial law, where the circumstances of international markets had become too complex to be sufficiently addressed by the *Shari'a,* the Western code was imported intact. Similar changes were also introduced in the spheres of criminal and civil law. The Islamic laws of personal status and succession, however, underwent little or no alteration. This trend of reconciling the basic rules of the Islamic *Shari'a* with new civil statutory laws has continued into present times, as has the debate between the Islamic modernists seeking a contemporary reading of classical Islamic ideas, and traditionists in favor of a singular reliance on the letter of the *Shari'a.*

BIBLIOGRAPHY

ALI, AYED AMEER. *The Spirit of Islam: A History of the Evolution and Ideals of Islam.* London, 1974.
BULLIET, RICHARD. *Islam: The View from the Edge.* New York, 1994.
COULSON, J. *A History of Islamic Law.* Edinburgh, 1971.
ENAYAT, HAMID. *Modern Islamic Political Thought.* Austin, Tex., 1982.
ENDRESS, GERHARD. *An Introduction to Islam.* New York, 1988.
ESPOSITO, JOHN. *Islam: The Straight Path.* Oxford, 1988.
HADDAD, YVONNE Y., and JANE I. SMITH, eds. *Muslim Communities in North America.* New York, 1994.
MARTIN, RICHARD C. *Islam: A Cultural Perspective.* Englewood Cliffs, N.J., 1982.
MORTIMER, EDWARD. *Faith and Power: The Politics of Islam.* New York, 1982.
POSTON, LARRY. *Islamic Da'wah in the West: Muslim Missionary Activity and the Dynamics of Conversion to Islam.* Oxford, 1992.

Tayeb El-Hibri

Islamic Amal

Radical movement of Lebanese Shi'a militants that split from AMAL.

The split from AMAL occurred when Nabi BERRI, AMAL's leader, joined the Karame government of Lebanon in 1982. Islamic Amal, led by Husayn Musawi, was based in Ba'albak. It may have been responsible for the bombings of the U.S. and French compounds that had been set up for the peacekeeping force in Beirut after Israel's withdrawal from the city's edge. The attacks were in response to the peace forces' perceived support of moves by the government of Lebanon against Shi'a forces and population centers.

Islamic Amal did not engage in independent activity after the bombing incidents, and its members apparently joined similar movements. Musawi, who became active in Hizbullah, was killed in southern Lebanon by Israeli forces in 1991.

Jenab Tutunji

Islamic Congresses

Muslims, either of a certain faction or in general, convening to promote solidarity and interaction among Muslim peoples and states.

Although the concept of Muslim solidarity is intrinsic to the faith of ISLAM, it took no organized form until modern times. In the course of the twentieth century, Islamic congresses have emerged as the structured expression of that concept. Some of these congresses have evolved into international Islamic organizations, which promote political, economic, and cultural interaction among Muslim peoples and states.

The idea of Muslims convening in congresses first gained currency in the late nineteenth century, in the Ottoman Empire. The advent of easy and regular steamer transport accelerated the exchange of ideas among Muslims and made possible the periodic assembling of representatives. The idea also appealed to Muslim reformists, who sought a forum to promote and sanction the internal reform of Islam. Such an assembly, they believed, would strengthen the ability of Muslims to resist the encroachments of Western imperialism.

A number of émigré intellectuals in Cairo first popularized the idea in the Muslim world. In 1900, one of them, the Syrian Abd al-Rahman al-Kawakibi, published an influential tract entitled *Umm al-Qura,* which purported to be the secret protocol of an Islamic congress convened in Mecca during the pilgrimage of 1899. The imaginary congress culminated in a call for a restored Arab CALIPHATE, an idea then in vogue in reformist circles. Support for such a congress also became a staple of the reformist journal *al-Manar,* published in Cairo by Rashid RIDA. The Crimean Tatar reformist Ismail Gaspirali (Russian, Gasprinski) launched the first concrete initiative in Cairo in 1907, where he unsuccessfully worked to convene a general Islamic congress.

Kawakibi's book, Rida's appeals, and Gaspirali's initiative all excited the suspicion of Ottoman authorities. The Ottoman Turks believed that a well-attended Islamic congress would fatally undermine the religious authority claimed by the theocratic Ottoman sultan-caliph and, in particular, feared the possible transformation of any such congress into an electoral college for choosing an Arab caliph. Steadfast Ottoman opposition thwarted all the early initiatives of the reformers.

With the final dismemberment of the Ottoman Empire after World War I, a number of Muslim leaders and activists moved to convene general Islamic congresses. In each instance, they sought to mark their causes or their ambitions with the stamp of Islamic consensus. In 1919, Mustafa Kemal Atatürk convened an Islamic congress in Anatolia to mobilize pan-Islamic support for his military campaigns. During the hajj (pilgrimage) season of 1924, Sharif Husayn ibn ali of the Hijaz summoned a pilgrimage congress in Mecca to support his claim to the caliphate—a maneuver that failed to stall the relentless advance of Ibn Sa'ud (ABD AL-AZIZ IBN

SA'UD). Following Ibn Sa'ud's occupation of Mecca, he convened his own world congress during the pilgrimage season of 1926. The leading clerics of al-Azhar in Cairo convened a caliphate congress there in 1926 to consider the effects of the abolition of the caliphate by Turkey two years earlier. The congress was supported by King FU'AD, who reputedly coveted the title of caliph, but no decision issued from the gathering. In 1931, Amin al-Husayni, the mufti of Jerusalem, convened a general congress of Muslims in Jerusalem to secure pan-Islamic support for the Arab struggle against the British mandate and Zionism. In 1935, pan-Islamic activist Shakib Arslan convened a congress of Europe's Muslims in Geneva to carry the protest against imperialism and colonialism to the heart of Europe. Each of these congresses resolved to create a permanent organization and convene additional congresses. But all such efforts were foiled by internal rivalries and the intervention of the European powers.

With spreading post–World War II political independence for Middle East states, several Muslim leaders offered new plans for the creation of a permanent organization of Muslim states. After the partition of India, Pakistan took a number of initiatives in the late 1940s and early 1950s but soon encountered stiff opposition from Egypt, which gave primacy of place to PAN-ARABISM and the Arab League. When Egypt's President Gamal Abdel Nasser transformed pan-Arabism into a revolutionary doctrine, Saudi Arabia sought to counter him by promoting a rival pan-Islamism, assembling congresses of Muslim activists and ULAMA (Islamic clergy) from abroad. In 1962, the Saudi government sponsored the establishment of the Mecca-based Muslim World League, which built a worldwide network of Muslim clients. Beginning in 1964, Egypt responded by organizing large congresses of Egyptian and foreign *ulama* under the auspices of al-Azhar's Academy of Islamic Researches in Cairo. These rival bodies then convened a succession of dueling congresses in Mecca and Cairo, each claiming the sole prerogative of defining Islam. In 1965/66, Saudi Arabia's new king, Faisal (son of Ibn Sa'ud), launched a campaign for an Islamic summit conference that would have balanced the Arab summits dominated by Egypt. President Nasser of Egypt, however, had sufficient influence to thwart the initiative, which he denounced as a foreign-inspired Islamic pact, designed to defend the interests of Western imperialism.

Israel's 1967 defeat of Arab armies and its annexation of Jerusalem eroded faith in the brand of Arabism championed by Egypt—inspiring a return to Islam. This set the scene for a renewed Saudi initiative. In September 1969, following an arsonist's attack against the al-Aqsa Mosque in Jerusalem, Muslim heads of state set aside their differences and met in Rabat, Morocco, in the first Islamic summit conference. King Faisal of Saudi Arabia took this opportunity to press for the creation of a permanent organization of Muslim states. The effort succeeded, and, in May 1971, the participating states established the ORGANIZATION OF THE ISLAMIC CONFERENCE (OIC; *Munazzamat al-mu'tamar al-islami*). The new organization, headquartered in Jidda, Saudi Arabia (pending the liberation of Jerusalem), adopted its charter in March 1972.

The OIC eventually earned a place of some prominence in regional diplomacy, principally through the organization of triennial Islamic summit conferences and annual conferences of the foreign ministers of member states. The OIC's activities fell into three broad categories. First, it sought to promote solidarity with Muslim states and peoples that were locked in conflict with non-Muslims. Most of its efforts were devoted to the causes of establishing a state of PALESTINE and of recapturing Jerusalem, although it supported Muslim movements from Eritrea (incorporated into Ethiopia in 1962) to the Philippines. Second, the organization offered mediation in disputes and wars among its own members, although its effectiveness was greatly limited by the lack of any force for truce supervision or peacekeeping. Finally, the OIC sponsored an array of subsidiary and affiliated institutions to promote political, economic, and cultural cooperation among its members. The most influential of these institutions was the Islamic Development Bank, established in December 1973 and formally opened in October 1975. The bank, funded by the wealthier OIC states, financed development projects while adhering to Islamic banking practices.

The OIC represented the culmination of governmental efforts to organize Muslim states. But it did not end moves by individual states to summon international congresses of *ulama,* activists, and intellectuals. Saudi Arabia and Egypt, realigned on the conservative end of the Islamic spectrum, increasingly cooperated in mounting large-scale Islamic congresses. Their rivals—Iran, Libya, and Iraq—did the same. Divisive events, such as the war between Iran and Iraq (1980–1988), the killing of several hundred Iranians in Mecca during the pilgrimage season of 1987, the Iraqi invasion of Kuwait in 1990, and the Arab–Israel peace talks that began in 1991 produced congresses and countercongresses, each claiming to express the verdict of united Islam. Leaders of Muslim opposition movements also met in periodic congresses, sometimes on the safe ground of Europe. Less than a century after Kawakibi's fantasy, a crowded calendar of congresses bound together the world of Islam as never before—but it remains uncertain whether these often competing institutions bridge the differences between Muslims or serve to widen them.

BIBLIOGRAPHY

The genesis and early history of the Islamic congresses are the subject of MARTIN KRAMER's *Islam Assembled: The Advent of the Muslim Congresses* (New York, 1986). The wider stage is set by JACOB M. LANDAU's *The Politics of Pan-Islam: Ideology and Organization* (Oxford, 1990). REINHARD SCHULZE's *Islamischer Internationalismus im 20. Jahrhundert: Untersuchungen zur Geschichte der Islamischen Weltliga* (Leiden, Neth., 1990) is a detailed case study of a major international Islamic organization, the Muslim World League. HASAN MOINUDDIN's *The Charter of the Islamic Conference* (Oxford, 1987) examines the constitutional foundation of the OIC. The most recent activities of the OIC, and many other Islamic congresses, are the subject of an annual chapter in the *Middle East Contemporary Survey,* commencing with volume 5 (1980–81).

Martin Kramer

Islamic Jihad

Palestinian liberation movement.

Islamic Jihad emerged from the Islamic revivalist tradition of the association of MUSLIM BROTHERHOOD in the Israeli-occupied Gaza Strip. Rather than pursue the Brotherhood's policy of the gradual Islamization of Palestinian society as the basis for future liberation from Israeli occupation, certain militants in the 1970s began arguing for a more active, armed, Islamic response to the occupation much as secular groups associated with the PALESTINE LIBERATION ORGANIZATION (PLO) had undertaken. Sources of inspiration included such militant historical figures as Shaykh Izz al-Din al-Qassam in Palestine and Sayyid Qutb in Egypt, as well as the revolutionary movements spawned by Muhammad Abd al-Salam Faraj in Egypt (the Jihad Organization) and the Ayatollah Ruhollah Khomeini in Iran. What tied these traditions together was their belief in active struggle (*jihad*) in the service of Islam as opposed to mere preaching.

It is believed that Islamic Jihad emerged as an actual organization in 1980. Two early leaders were Shaykh Abd al-Aziz Awda, deported by Israeli authorities in November 1987, and his successor, Fathi Abd al-Aziz Shiqaqi, himself deported in August 1988. Shiqaqi operated in Lebanon thereafter until his assassination in Malta in October 1995. One of Islamic Jihad's first dramatic acts against the Israeli occupation was an attack on a group of soldiers in

Jerusalem in October 1986, followed by a series of well-planned attacks on Israeli targets in late 1987. These helped to precipitate the Palestinian uprising against Israeli rule in the occupied territories known as the INTIFADA.

Islamic Jihad has operated as a clandestine group of activists who seek the total liberation of all of Palestine through armed struggle rather than a mass-based organization like the Muslim Brotherhood, although its activities were severely hampered by Israeli repression during the Intifada. Jihad operated alongside of but separate from the PLO's Unified National Command of the Uprising during the Intifada. Jihad activists were among the 418 Palestinians from the territories deported by Israel in December 1992.

Jihad opposed the Israeli–Palestinian peace talks, which began in 1991, as well as the subsequent 1993 Israeli–PLO accords. In 1992, it joined the "Damascus Ten," a grouping of Palestinian organizations opposed to the peace talks, which changed its name to the National Democratic and Islamic Front in 1993. Jihad continued to attack Israeli targets even after establishment of a Palestinian National Authority (PNA) in Gaza and the West Bank town of Jericho in 1994, promoting considerable friction between it and the PNA leadership.

BIBLIOGRAPHY

ABU-AMR, ZIAD. *Islamic Fundamentalism in the West Bank and Gaza: Muslim Brotherhood and Islamic Jihad.* Bloomington, Ind. 1994.

Michael R. Fischbach

Islamic Republic of Iran

See Iranian Revolution

Islamic Revolution

See Iranian Revolution

Islamic Salvation Front

Algerian Islamic political party.

The Islamic Salvation Front (*Front Islamique du Salut,* FIS) is Algeria's largest Islamic political party. Founded in February 1989 by a large group of Algerian religious leaders, the FIS calls for the establishment of an Islamic state based on the SUNNA and the QURʾAN. It is headed by Abassi al-Madani, a university professor, and Ali Belhadj, a radical imam.

Since their imprisonment in June 1991, Abdel-kader Hachani has served as the provisional leader. The principle structures of the party are the Majlis al-Shura, a consultative body of some forty religious leaders, and the National Executive Bureau.

The FIS has been Algeria's most highly-mobilized party. It has gained substantial financing from local businessmen and Saudi Arabian sources. With solid support from the young, urban unemployed, it won the most votes in Algeria's last two elections. In the June 1990 elections for regional and municipal assemblies, it garnered 55 percent of the vote and an absolute majority of the seats. In the first round of National Assembly elections in December 1991, the FIS won 188 of the 430 seats and was poised to win an absolute majority in the second round. The Algerian army staged a coup d'état in January 1992, arrested thousands of FIS members, and declared the party illegal. Since then, the party has been in a state of disarray, its entire leadership imprisoned, and its activities repressed.

Bradford Dillman

Islamic University of Medina

Saudi Arabian institute of Islamic studies.

The Islamic University of Medina was founded in 1961 to provide scholarly training in Islamic studies on a par with that found elsewhere in the Muslim world. Beside the Saudi students, many foreigners receive instruction to help them become imams (spiritual leaders) of mosques in their own countries. In 1992, the university employed 383 faculty and had 2,449 students. The library possessed 334,000 volumes in addition to 26,000 manuscripts.

BIBLIOGRAPHY

The World of Learning 1993. Rochester, N.Y., 1992.

Khalid Y. Blankinship

Ismaʿil, Abd al-Fattah [?–1986]

Yemeni government official.

From North Yemen, Ismaʿil emigrated to Aden for work as a young man. He became coruler of the PEOPLE'S DEMOCRATIC REPUBLIC OF YEMEN (PDRY) with his rival Salim Rabiyya Ali from mid-1969 to mid-1978. Ismaʿil served during this period as head of the regime's evolving political machine. He was an insistent, dogmatic proponent of "scientific socialism" and is regarded as the father of what became a well-developed ruling party, the YEMENI SOCIALIST PARTY (YSP). He ousted Salim Rabiyya in 1978 and led the PDRY until his own ouster in 1980. He returned from his Moscow exile in 1984, only to die in Aden in the intraparty blood bath of January 1986.

Robert D. Burrowes

Isma'il, Abd al-Qadir   [1906–   ]

A founder of Jama'at al-Ahali an Iraqi populist reform group in the 1930s.

Isma'il was born in Baghdad. A lawyer and journalist, he left Iraq after Rashid Ali's failed coup in 1941 and took refuge in Syria, where he joined the Communist party. He was a member of its Central Committee in Syria (1948–1958) and subsequently in Iraq (1959–1963). In Iraq he pounded the influential AHALI GROUP.

Marion Farouk-Sluglett

Isma'ilia Canal

Artificial waterway in Egypt.

The canal at first linked the Cairo *khalij* (interior waterway) with the NILE RIVER and then was modified in 1866 to link Cairo's port on the Nile, Bulaq, and central Cairo with the SUEZ CANAL at Ismailia on Lake Timsah. In 1912, the Cairo portion was filled in and the canal reconnected with the Nile at a point north of the city. The canal has played a diminishing role in conveying people and goods, relative to modern Egypt's railroads and motor transport.

BIBLIOGRAPHY

ABU-LUGHOD, JANET. *Cairo: 1001 Years of the City Victorious.* Princeton, N.J., 1971.

Arthur Goldschmidt, Jr.

Isma'il ibn Ibrahim   [1830–1895]

Modernizing viceroy of Egypt, reigning from 1863 until his deposition in July 1879.

Born in Cairo, Isma'il was educated at the Qasr al-Ayni Princes' School established by his grandfather, MUHAMMAD ALI Pasha, and at the Saint-Cyr Military Academy in France. He served briefly on the council for the sultan of the Ottoman Empire in Istanbul and then chaired the corresponding vice-regal council in Cairo.

Upon succeeding his uncle, Muhammad Sa'id Pasha, in 1863, he started a policy of national modernization in Egypt by ordering the construction of factories, irrigation works, public buildings, and palaces. Many traditional Cairo and Alexandria neighborhoods and buildings were razed to facilitate the Europeanization of these cities. His reign marked the inauguration of many Egyptian cultural institutions, including the Cairo Opera House, the National Library (Dar al-Kutub), the Egyptian Museum, the Geographical Society, and various primary, secondary, and higher schools, such as DAR AL-ULUM. The Suez Canal was completed during his reign; its 1869 inauguration occasioned a gala celebration attended by many European leaders.

Isma'il also established Egypt's system of provincial and local administration and convened the MAJLES SHURA AL-NUWWAB, the country's first representative assembly. He reorganized the national and SHARI'A (Islamic law) courts, established the MIXED COURTS, created the postal service, and extended railroads and telegraph lines throughout Egypt. He sent explorers to the African interior and armies to complete Egypt's conquest of the Sudan. Egypt became more independent of the Ottoman Empire. Since Isma'il obtained the title of *khedive* (Persian for "little lord"), he gained permission to pass down his khedivate according to the European rules of succession and the right to contract loans without first obtaining permission from Istanbul. His industrial, military, and construction projects proved costly, and he indulged in other extravagances having no long-term value to Egypt, such as his many palaces and extensive luxuries that he bought for his wives and mistresses or bestowed upon Europeans he wished to impress.

At first, Isma'il paid for his program with revenues derived from the expanded output of Egyptian COTTON, for which demand boomed during the American Civil War. Later, when European industrialists could buy cotton from other sources, Isma'il raised taxes and took loans from European bankers at increasingly unfavorable terms. Unable to repay them, he resorted to unorthodox financial measures—such as the 1871 Muqabala loan and the sale of his government's Suez Canal shares in 1875—finally conceding to European control over Egyptian state revenues and disbursements through the 1876 Caisse de la Dette Publique.

In 1878 he surrendered much of his power to the DUAL CONTROL of a "European cabinet" that included English and French ministers. Financial stringencies ensued, leading to an uprising by Egyptian army officers who had been put on half-pay, causing the European cabinet to resign. European creditors and their governments suspected Isma'il of engineering the uprising to regain his absolute rule. In July 1879, their envoys in Constantinople persuaded the sultan to replace him with his eldest son, TAWFIQ. Isma'il left Egypt and lived out his life in exile. Although ambitious for Egypt's development and his own reputation, his achievements were eclipsed by his fiscal misrule, which led in 1882 to the British occupation.

BIBLIOGRAPHY

HUNTER, F. ROBERT. *Egypt under the Khedives, 1805–1879: From Household Government to Modern Bureaucracy.* Pittsburgh, Pa., 1984.
SCHÖLCH, ALEXANDER. *Egypt for the Egyptians!* London, 1981.

Arthur Goldschmidt, Jr.

Isma'ili Shi'ism

Islamic movement that split from the Twelver Shi'a over the successor of the sixth imam, Ja'far al-Sadiq (d. 765).

Some believed that Ja'far had appointed his son, Isma'il as his successor, but Isma'il predeceased Ja'far, thus making his brother, Musa, their father's successor. However, supporters of Isma'il maintained that his son, Muhammad, should become IMAM.

The Isma'ili movement, whose followers are generally known as seveners of Isma'ilis, spawned several subdivisions, including the Fatimids, the Assassins, the Tayyibis, and the Nizaris. The Fatimids developed from a group of Isma'ilis who had maintained their movement in secret from the time of Ja'far's death until about the mid-ninth century. This group believed that Isma'il had not really died but had gone into occlusion, and that Muhammad, the seventh imam, would reappear as the MAHDI. The Fatimids founded Cairo in 969 C.E. and were wiped out in 1021 after their sixth caliph, al-Hakim, died. Al-Hakim's followers consolidated in the mountains of Syria and are known as DRUZE.

Outside Egypt, the Isma'ili movement was propagated by Hasan-i-Sabbah, from his mountain fortress of Alamut in northern Iran in 1090 C.E. The movement he founded was known as the Assassins because of their use of hashish (users of hashish are called *hashshasheen* in Arabic. Hasan's followers were notorious for murdering their enemies as a form of intimidation, from whence assassin was coined. After Hasan's death, the followers of the movement came to be known as Nizari Isma'ilis, named for Nizar, an heir to the Fatimid caliphate whose claim was usurped in a palace coup, and whose namesake succeeded Hasan, claiming descent from the Fatimid Nizar. The Nizar Isma'ili rule at Alamut ended with the Mongol conquest of 1256. Survivors kept the movement alive, however, settling in Azerbaijan and India. In 1840, their imam took the title Agha Khan, which continues until today. His followers, known as Khojas, are located mainly in Gujarat, Bombay, and East Africa, with others scattered around the world, including a small group based at Salamiyya, Syria.

Jenab Tutunji

Israel

Officially, the State of Israel (Hebrew, Medinat Yisrael), a democratic republic with a parliament-cabinet form of government, established by proclamation May 15, 1948.

Israel is a small state in both population—estimated at 5.2 million in 1993—and size—encompassing some 8,019 square miles (20,770 sq km). It is located on the eastern coast of the Mediterranean Sea, bordered on the north by Lebanon and on the east by Syria and Jordan. In the south, from a short coastline on the Gulf of Aqaba, Israel's border runs northwestward to the Mediterranean along the SINAI PENINSULA of Egypt. The WEST BANK and GAZA STRIP territories have been under Israel's administration since the 1967 ARAB–ISRAEL WAR. In 1981, Israel extended its law and jurisdiction to the GOLAN HEIGHTS, also taken from Syria in 1967.

Israel extends 260 miles (420 km) south from the northern border with Lebanon and Syria to Eilat on the Gulf of Aqaba, and east from the Mediterranean for 60 miles (100 km) to the Rift Valley, through which the Jordan river flows. The southern half of Israel, mostly desert, is known as the NEGEV—an area of arid flatlands and mountains. North of the Negev is a highland region with a series of mountain ranges that run from the Sea of Galilee in the north to Judea and Samaria (the West Bank) in the south, divided by the Plain of Esdraelon (some 300 feet [90 m] below sea level). A narrow but fertile coastal plain, three to nine miles (5 to 15 km) wide, along the Mediterranean shore is where most Israelis live and most of the industry and agriculture are located, including the citrus crop.

About 90 percent of Israel's people live in urban areas, and the three largest cities—JERUSALEM, TEL

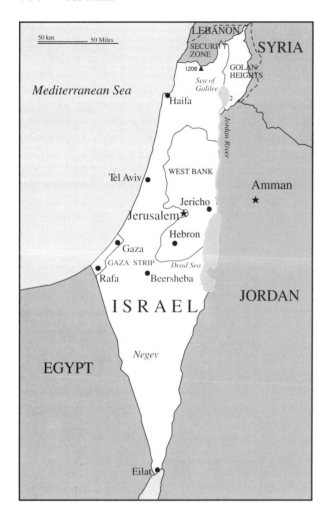

the DEAD SEA. In January, the coldest month, temperatures average 48° F (9° C) in Jerusalem and 57° F (14° C) in Tel Aviv. Israel has almost continuous sunshine from May through mid-October. The Khamsin, hot dry dusty wind, sometimes blows in from deserts in the east. Almost all the rainfall occurs between November and March, and great regional variations exist. In the driest area, the southern Negev, the average yearly rainfall is only one inch (25 mm). In the wettest area, the hilly parts of upper Galilee, average annual rainfall is forty-two inches (1,080 mm). Snow also falls sometimes in the hills.

Israel has six administrative districts—Central, Haifa, Jerusalem, Northern, Southern, and Tel Aviv. Elected councils are the units of local government, responsible for such services as education, water, and road maintenance.

Economy. At its independence in 1948, Israel was a poor country with only a little agricultural or industrial production. The economy has grown substantially, and today Israel enjoys a relatively high standard of living, despite limited water and mineral resources. Human resources (large numbers of educated immigrants) plus financial assistance from Western nations (especially the United States and Germany) contribute to Israel's economic well-being. The nation's main trading partners are the United States, Great Britain, Germany, France, Belgium, and Luxembourg.

About 50 percent of Israel's businesses are privately owned, and some 25 percent are government owned. The Histadrut (General Federation of Labor), a powerful organization of trade unions, also owns some 25 percent of businesses, farms, and industries. Service industries account for about 67 percent of Israel's net domestic product (NDP) and

AVIV, and HAIFA—account for some 25 percent of the population.

Jerusalem is Israel's capital and largest city; it is the spiritual center of Judaism (the Jewish religion) and also a holy city for Christianity and Islam. West Jerusalem, the newer part of the city, is inhabited mainly by Jews. East Jerusalem—captured by Israel from Jordan in 1967—is inhabited mainly by Arabs.

Tel Aviv serves as the country's commercial, financial, and industrial center and houses some government agencies. Haifa, on the Mediterranean, is a major port city, the administrative and industrial center of northern Israel. BEERSHEBA is considered the capital of the Negev region. In the 1950s, Israel's government began creating "development towns," to attract industry to lightly populated areas and to provide homes for new immigrants.

Israel has hot dry summers and cool mild winters, although the climate varies from region to region, partly because of altitude. In August, the hottest month, the temperatures may reach 98° F (37° C) in the hilly regions and as high as 120° F (49° C) near

Roman aqueduct at Caesarea. (D. W. Lockhard)

The Judean hills. (Mia Bloom)

employ about 65 percent of workers, many of whom are employed by the government or by government-owned businesses. Government workers provide many of the services needed by Israel's large immigrant population—housing, education, and vocational training. Tourism is also a major service industry. Manufacturing accounts for about 23 percent of Israel's NDP and employs about 22 percent of its work force—factories produce such goods as chemical products, electronic equipment, fertilizer, paper, plastics, processed foods, scientific and optical instruments, Textiles, and clothing. The cutting of imported diamonds is a major industry. Government-owned plants manufacture equipment used by Israel's armed forces.

Agriculture accounts for about 4 percent of Israel's NDP and employs about 5 percent of its workers. Agriculture employed a much larger percentage of Israel's work force until the mechanization of much of the work. Important agricultural products are citrus and other fruits, cotton, eggs, grain, poultry, and vegetables. The government develops, helps finance, and controls agricultural activity, including fishing and forestry. Israel produces most of the food needed to feed its people, and agricultural exports provide enough income to pay for necessary food imports. Water drawn from the Jordan irrigates large amounts of land, farmed mostly by advanced technological methods.

The Dead Sea is Israel's leading mineral source, yielding bromine, magnesium, potash, and table salt. Potash, used chiefly in fertilizers, is the most important mineral. phosphates, copper, clay, and gypsum are mined in the Negev. Israel is poor in energy sources, having no coal deposits or hydroelectric power resources and only small amounts of crude oil

and natural gas; crude oil and coal are imported to meet energy needs.

Population. When Israel was established in 1948, it had about 800,000 people. In 1993, Israel's population numbered about 5.2 million; about 83 percent are Jews. Between 1948 and the 1990s, more than 2 million Jews migrated to Israel, many to escape persecution in their home countries. In 1950, the Knesset (parliament) passed the LAW OF RETURN, which allows any Jew, with a few minor exceptions, to immigrate to Israel and apply for citizenship. Israel's Jewish population shares a common spiritual heritage but has a diverse ethnic heritage—each group has its own cultural, political, and recent historical background. The two main groups are the ASHKENAZIM—who came from the countries of central and eastern Europe—and the SEPHARDIM—who came from the countries of the Middle East and around the Mediterranean. At the time of independence, most of Israel's Jews were Ashkenazim; as a result, the political, educational, and economic systems are primarily Western in orientation. The massive migration of Jews from the former U.S.S.R., which began in the *glasnost* era of Mikhail S. Gorbachev (late 1980s), brought more than 185,000 in 1990 and hundreds of thousands in subsequent years—Soviet Jews becoming the largest ethnic group in Israel as of the 1990s.

Arabs make up nearly all the remaining 17 percent of Israel's population. Most are Palestinians whose families remained after the independence of Israel and the 1948 ARAB–ISRAEL WAR. Arab and Jewish Israelis have limited contact, live in separate areas, attend separate schools, speak different languages, and follow different cultural traditions.

Israel has two official languages—Hebrew and Arabic. Many Israelis also speak English, and many Ashkenazic Jews speak Yiddish, a Germanic language spoken since the Middle Ages by Jews in central and eastern Europe. Because of the DIASPORA, Israelis also speak a great many other languages, reflecting their diverse histories.

Religion. About 20 percent of Israeli Jews observe the religious principles of Judaism and are classified as Orthodox, while an additional 50 percent observe some of the principles some of the time; the rest (30 percent) tend to be secular. Orthodox Israelis hold that Jewish religious values should play an important role in the shaping of government policy, but secular Israeli Jews seek to limit the role of religion in the state.

Of Israel's non-Jewish population, about 76 percent are Muslims, the largest group of which are

SUNNI. Another 14 percent of the non-Jews are Arab Christians, mostly Roman Catholic and Eastern Orthodox. Of the remaining 10 percent, the majority are DRUZE, but there are also some BAHA'I and other small religious communities. All faiths are guaranteed religious freedom by law.

Education. Education has a high priority in Israel. One of the first laws passed there established free education and required school attendance for all children between the ages of five and fourteen. Attendance is now required to age sixteen. Adult literacy is estimated in excess of 97 percent. The Jewish school system instructs in Hebrew, and the Arab/Druze school system in Arabic; both are government-funded systems.

Israel has a number of internationally recognized institutions of higher education—the Technion, Haifa University, Hebrew University of Jerusalem, Tel Aviv University, Ben-Gurion University, Bar Ilan University, and the Weizmann Institute of Science.

The Arts. With a population drawn from more than 100 countries, Israel is rich in cultural diversity and artistic creativity. In music, dance, theater, films, literature, painting, and sculpture, many artists work within the traditions of their own ethnic groups. Others have blended various cultural art forms to create a uniquely Israeli tradition. The arts not only reflect Israel's immigrant diversity, they also draw upon Jewish history and religion and address the social and political problems of modern Israel. The arts are actively encouraged and supported by the government.

Publishing is a major industry—the number of books published per person in Israel is among the highest in the world. Most Israeli authors write in Hebrew, and some have achieved international fame; the novelist and short-story writer Shmuel Yosef AGNON shared the 1966 Nobel Prize for literature. Other renowned authors include Hayyim Nahman BIALIK, Saul TCHERNICHOVSKY, Amos OZ, and A. B. YEHOSHUA. Israel's newspapers are published daily in Hebrew, with others available in Arabic, English, French, Polish, Yiddish, Russian, Hungarian, and German.

The Israel Philharmonic Orchestra performs throughout the country and on frequent international tours, as does the Jerusalem Symphony, the orchestra of the Israel Broadcasting Authority. Israeli and international artists tour as well, and almost every municipality and small agricultural settlement has a chamber orchestra or jazz ensemble. Folk music and folk dancing, drawing from the cultural heritage of the many immigrant groups, are very popular, as is the theater. Among the museums are the Israel Museum in Jerusalem, which houses the DEAD SEA SCROLLS and an extensive collection of Jewish religious and folk art; located on the campus of Tel Aviv University is the Museum of the Diaspora. ARCHEOLOGY is an important pursuit, and archeological remains are on display throughout the country.

Government. Israel has no written constitution; instead it follows "basic laws" passed by the Knesset (parliament). Legislative powers are vested in this unicameral body of 120 members, elected for a term not to exceed 4 years. The Knesset passes legislation, participates in the formation of national policy, and approves budgets and taxes. All Israeli citizens 18 years or older may vote. Voters do not cast ballots for individual candidates in Knesset elections, but instead vote for a party list, which includes all the candidates of the political party. The list may range from a single candidate to a full slate of 120 names. Elections are national, general, equal, secret, direct, and proportional in nature. A party's seats in parliament are approximately proportional to the share of the votes it receives in the national election.

The prime minister—the head of government—is normally the leader of the party that controls the most seats in the Knesset and must maintain the support of a majority of the Knesset to stay in office. He or she selects, forms, and heads the cabinet, which is Israel's senior policymaking body, composed of the heads of each government ministry as well as other ministers; appointments to the cabinet must be approved by the Knesset. The president—the head of state—is elected by the Knesset to a five-year term and may not serve more than two consecutive terms. The powers and functions are primarily formal and ceremonial; actual political power is limited. The president's most important task is selecting a member of the Knesset to form a government. The political composition of the Knesset has, so far, determined this selection, but different combinations of parties might at some point gain the support of the Knesset, thereby giving the president the choice of which person actually forms the cabinet.

Since 1948, Israel's governments have been coalitions of several political parties—the result of several factors: the intensity with which political views are held; the proportional representation of the voting system; and the multiplicity of parties. These factors have made it all but impossible for a party to win an absolute majority of seats. Despite the constant need for coalition governments, they have proven remarkably stable. Political life in Israel was dominated since the mandate period by a small and relatively cohesive elite, which held positions in government and other major institutions. The strength of the Israel Labor party until 1977 helped to stabilize the political situation. Between 1977 and 1983, Prime Minister Menachem BEGIN's political skills had the same effect. Rigorous party discipline exists in the Knesset.

The judiciary comprises both secular and religious court systems.

History. The independence of the State of Israel in 1948 was preceded by more than a half century of efforts by Zionist leaders to establish a sovereign state as a homeland for dispersed Jews. The desire of Jews to return to their biblical home was voiced continuously and repeatedly after the Romans destroyed Jerusalem in 70 C.E. and dispersed the population of Roman Palestine. Attachment to the land of Israel (ERETZ-YISRAEL) became a recurring theme in Jewish scripture and literature. Despite the ancient connection, it was not until the founding of Zionism by THEODOR HERZL toward the end of the nineteenth century that practical steps were taken toward securing international sanction for large-scale Jewish resettlement in Palestine. Small numbers of Jews had always remained in the area or returned to it throughout the centuries, mainly (but not always) Orthodox scribes and scholars. The BALFOUR DECLARATION in 1917 asserted the British government's support for the creation of a national home for the Jewish people in Palestine, but Britain was granted a League of Nations mandate for Palestine after World War I that lasted until after World War II.

In November 1947, international support for establishing a Jewish state led to the adoption of the United Nations (UN) PARTITION PLAN, which called for dividing mandated Palestine into a Jewish and an Arab state and for establishing Jerusalem as an international city under U.N. administration. Violence between the Arabs and Jews erupted almost immediately. On May 15, 1948, the State of Israel proclaimed its independence. Armies from neighboring Arab states entered the former mandate lands to fight Israel in the ARAB–ISRAEL WAR of 1948. In 1949, at Rhodes, Greece, four armistice agreements were negotiated and signed—between Israel and Egypt, Jordan, Lebanon, and Syria. Peace was not achieved, however, although Israel remained a state.

After Egypt had nationalized the Suez Canal and formed a United Military Command with Syria and Jordan, Israel invaded the Gaza Strip and the Sinai peninsula in October 1956 in concert with French and British operations against Egypt concentrated near the canal. At the conclusion of the 1956 ARAB–ISRAEL WAR, Israel's forces withdrew (March 1957) after the United Nations established an Emergency

Force (UNEF) along the Egyptian side of the 1949 armistice line and on the Strait of TIRAN to ensure passage of Israel-bound ships. In 1966 and 1967, terrorist incidents and retaliatory acts across the armistice demarcation lines increased. In May 1967, after tension had developed between Syria and Israel, Egypt's President Gamal Abdel NASSER moved armaments and troops into the Sinai and ordered withdrawal of UNEF troops from the armistice line and from Sharm al-Sheikh at the Strait of Tiran. Nasser then closed the strait to Israel's ships, blockading the Israeli port of Eilat at the northern end of the Gulf of Aqaba. On May 30, Jordan and Egypt signed a mutual-defense treaty.

In response to these events, Israel's forces attacked Egypt on June 5, 1967. Subsequently, Jordan and Syria joined in the hostilities of the 1967 Arab–Israel War. After six days of fighting, Israel controlled the Sinai peninsula, the Gaza Strip, the Golan Heights, the West Bank, and East Jerusalem. On November 22, 1967, the UN Security Council adopted Resolution 242, which called for the establishment of a just and lasting peace; Israel's withdrawal from territories occupied in June 1967; the end of all states of belligerency; respect for the sovereignty of all states in the area; and the right to live in peace within secure recognized boundaries.

Waterfall in the Banyas. (Mia Bloom)

In the spring of 1969, Nasser initiated the WAR OF ATTRITION between Egypt and Israel along the Suez Canal. The United States helped to end these hostilities in August 1970, but subsequent efforts to negotiate an interim agreement to open the Suez Canal and achieve disengagement of forces were unsuccessful.

On October 6, 1973 the Yom Kippur (the most holy day of the Jewish year), Syrian and Egyptian forces attacked Israeli positions along the Suez Canal and in Golan. Initially, Syria and Egypt made significant advances but Israel recovered on both fronts, pushing the Syrians back beyond the 1967 cease-fire lines and crossing the Suez Canal to take a position on its west bank. This 1967 war was followed by renewed and intensive efforts toward peace. The United States and the Soviet Union helped achieve a cease-fire based on Security Council Resolution 338, which reaffirmed U.N. Security Council Resolution 242 as the framework for peace and called, for the first time, for negotiations between the parties to achieve it.

The cease-fire did not end the clashes on the cease-fire lines. The United States helped the parties to reach agreements on cease-fire stabilization and military disengagement. On March 5, 1974, Israel's forces withdrew from the Suez Canal, and Egypt assumed control. Syria and Israel signed a disengagement agreement on May 31, 1974, and the United Nations Disengagement and Observer Force (UNDOF) was established as a peacekeeping force in the Golan. Further U.S. efforts resulted in an interim agreement between Egypt and Israel in September 1975, which provided for another withdrawal by Israel from the Sinai, a limitation of Egypt's forces therein, and three observation stations staffed by U.S. civilians in a UN-maintained buffer zone between Egypt's and Israel's forces.

The Sea of Galilee seen through a mountain pass. (Mia Bloom)

In November 1977, Egypt's President Anwar al-SADAT launched an initiative for peace. Sadat recognized Israel's right to exist and established the basis for direct negotiations between Egypt and Israel. This led to meetings at the presidential retreat of Camp David, Maryland, when U.S. President Jimmy Carter helped negotiate a framework for peace between Israel and Egypt and for a comprehensive peace in the Middle East (known as the CAMP DAVID ACCORDS)—with broad principles to guide negotiations between Israel and the Arab states. An Egypt–Israel Peace Treaty was signed in Washington on March 26, 1979, by Prime Minister Menachem BEGIN and President Sadat, with President Carer signing as witness. They agreed that negotiations on a transitional regime of autonomy for the West Bank and Gaza would begin one month after ratification. Under the peace treaty, Israel returned the Sinai to Egypt in April 1982. In 1989, the governments of Israel and Egypt concluded an agreement that resolved the status of TABA, a resort area in the Gulf of Aqaba.

Israel's border with Lebanon had been quiet since the 1948 war, compared to its borders with other neighbors. After the 1970 JORDANIAN CIVIL WAR, the Palestinians were expelled from Jordan and most went to southern Lebanon, so hostilities against Israel's northern border increased. In March 1978, after a series of such border clashes, the Israel Defense Forces were sent into Lebanon during the ARAB–ISRAEL WAR of 1978. Israel withdrew its troops after the passage of UN Security Council Resolution 425, calling for the creation of the UN Interim Force in Lebanon (UNIFIL), a peacekeeping force.

In July 1981, after additional fighting between Israel and the Palestinians in Lebanon, U.S. President Ronald Reagan's special envoy, Philip C. HABIB, helped secure a cease-fire. In June 1982, however, Israel invaded Lebanon in the ARAB–ISRAEL WAR of 1982 to fight the forces of the PALESTINE LIBERATION ORGANIZATION (PLO). In August 1982, the PLO withdrew its headquarters and some forces from Lebanon relocating in Libya. With U.S. assistance in May 1983, Israel and Lebanon reached an accord to withdraw Israeli forces from Lebanon; however, in March 1984, Lebanon, under pressure from Syria, abrogated the agreement. In June 1985, Israel withdrew most of its troops from Lebanon. A small residual Israeli force and an Israeli-supported militia remained in southern Lebanon in a "security zone," regarded by Israel as a necessary buffer against attacks on its northern territory.

Until the election of May 1977, Israel had been ruled by a coalition government led by the labor alignment or its constituent parties. From 1967 to

1970, the coalition government included all of Israel's parties but the Communist party.

After the 1977 election, the LIKUD (Union) bloc came to power, forming a coalition with Menachem Begin as prime minister. The Likud retained power in the election in June 1981, and Begin remained prime minister. In 1983, Begin resigned and was succeeded by his foreign minister, Yitzhak SHAMIR. New elections were held in 1984. The vote was split among numerous parties, and neither Labor nor Likud was able to attract enough small-party support to form a coalition. They agreed to establish a broadly based government of national unity. The agreement provided for the rotation of the office of prime minister and the combined office of deputy prime minister and foreign minister midway through the government's fifty-month term. During the first twenty-five months of the unity government's rule, Labor's Shimon PERES served as prime minister, while Likud's Shamir held the posts of deputy prime minister and foreign minister. Peres and Shamir exchanged positions in October 1986.

The November 1988 elections resulted in a similar coalition government. Likud and Labor formed another National Unity Government (NUG) in January 1989 without providing for rotation. Again Shamir became prime minister and Peres deputy prime minister and finance minister.

That government fell in March 1990, after a no-confidence vote, precipitated by disagreement over the government's response to a U.S. peace initiative. Labor party leader Peres was unable to attract sufficient support to form a government, and Shamir then formed a Likud-led coalition government, which included members from religious and right-wing parties; it took office in June 1990. After Iraq's invasion of Kuwait in the summer of 1990 and the GULF CRISIS of 1991, a new peace initiative by the United States led to Arab–Israel peace conferences—with much emphasis on the Palestinian problem.

In the 1992 Knesset election, the Labor party, under the new leadership of Yitzhak RABIN, secured the largest number of seats in parliament and Rabin soon formed a coalition government. The new government began to alter the nature and direction of Israeli policy, seeking to restore the concepts of Labor Zionism to the center of Israeli politics. The focus of attention was foreign and security policy.

The Madrid Peace Conference of 1991 inaugurated a series of multilateral discussions focusing on functional issues, including refugees, arms control, water, economic development and the environment, as well as bilateral negotiations that convened in Washington, D.C. In the spring of 1993, Israel and the PLO began secret negotiations in Norway that led to the signing, in September 1993, of a Declaration of Principles that provided for Palestinian autonomy in Jericho (a city of the West Bank) and the Gaza Strip. It also provided for continued negotiations between Israel and the PLO to establish the basis for the future relationship between Israel and the Palestinians.

BIBLIOGRAPHY

ARIAN, ASHER. *Politics in Israel: The Second Generation.* Chatham, N.J., 1989.

KLIEMAN, AARON S. *Israel and the World After 40 Years.* Oxford, 1989.

LIEBMAN, CHARLES S. and ELIEZER DON-YEHIYA. *Civil Religion in Israel: Traditional Judaism and Political Culture in the Jewish State.* Berkeley, Calif., 1983.

MEDDING, PETER Y. *The Founding of Israeli Democracy, 1948–1967.* New York and Oxford, 1990.

REICH, BERNARD. *Historical Dictionary of Israel.* Metuchen, N.J. and London, 1992.

———. *Quest for Peace: United States-Israel Relations and the Arab-Israel Conflict.* New Brunswick, N.J., 1977.

REICH, BERNARD, and GERSHON R. KIEVAL. *Israel: Land of Tradition and Conflict,* 2nd ed. Boulder, Colo., 1993.

———, eds. *Israeli Politics in the 1990s: Key Domestic and Foreign Policy Factors.* Westport, Conn., 1991.

SACHAR, HOWARD M. *A History of Israel: From the Rise of Zionism to Our Time.* New York, 1976.

SAFRAN, NADAV. *Israel: The Embattled Ally.* Cambridge, Mass., 1981.

Bernard Reich

Israel, Political Parties in

Political parties have always been important in Israel, though in recent years their role has declined.

Among the factors accounting for both the strength and the decline are (1) the electoral system, (2) the extension of party influence into all levels of government during much of the early period of the state, (3) the complex crosscutting of major political issues, (4) the intensity of Israeli democracy, and (5) social, economic, and political modernization. The combination of these factors has often resulted in considerable political immobilism.

The electoral system in Israel has led to both centralization of control within many parties and to frequently extreme fragmentation of the party system. In regard to the former, the country is structurally a single constituency, with voting entirely by party lists and in which each party's candidates for the KNESSET run on a single nationwide list. The position of each candidate on the party's list is determined by the party's central organization, making party loyalty and rising through the ranks the major potential qualifications for individual political advancement. This has been modified in recent years by several phenomena. One is the coming of modern campaign techniques such as television, which has made it possible for new but glamorous entrants into politics to affect a party's electoral fortunes. Another is the emergence of hitherto underrepresented groups like Oriental Jews, who have used arenas like local mayoralties to challenge a party's central leadership. The two major parties, the Israel LABOR PARTY and the LIKUD, have responded by broadening their process of selection of party leaders and Knesset candidates through a series of primary elections involving all of the parties' members. Reform has not, however, gone to the point where local or regional parties have been formed or where the policies of local branches of the major national parties act independently of their centers.

Another aspect of party activity is a legacy of earlier practices. In the prestate period and the early years of the state, the importance of political parties was also enhanced by the fact that they were given a role in various governmental activities including employment, education, and immigrant absorption. While many of these functions were later taken over by the government, elections in nongovernmental organizations like the HISTADRUT (the General Confederation of Trade Unions) and the JEWISH AGENCY continue to be contested in the framework of candidate lists submitted by the major political parties.

The extreme fragmentation of the party system is the result of another feature of the electoral law, one of the world's lowest thresholds for winning a Knesset seat. Until 1992, it was possible to win a Knesset seat with slightly less than 1 percent of the votes cast, with the result that popular personalities and representatives of narrow views on particular issues have often been prominent in the Knesset. This has lead to the situation that, at no time in the history of Israel, has there been a single party with a Knesset majority, so that it has always been necessary to form complex and fragile coalitions. This meant that governing could be only by lowest common denominator and with few bold initiatives to solve the many problems that the country has faced. The only exceptions have been two periods (1967–1969 and 1984–1988) when circumstances all but necessitated national unity governments formed by the members of all electoral blocs. When the threshold was raised to 1.5 percent in the 1992 election, it had some effect: Only 10 of the 26 parties that ran won Knesset seats.

The importance of small parties has also been magnified by the complexity and multiplicity of Israeli political issues. The political parties can be basically divided into three major blocs, but there are also sharp divisions within each one, and there are always parties that fit only partly into any bloc. The three are (1) the Labor Alignment, a group of parties that are generally socialist in domestic politics as well as conciliatory and compromising on the Palestinian issue; (2) the Likud bloc, generally antisocialist as well as the proponents of a hard line on the Palestinian issue and a vision of a GREATER ISRAEL, which would give up none of the territories won during the ARAB–ISRAEL WAR (1967); (3) the religious parties, which have held the balance of power in every government in Israel's history and some of whose members have made coalitions with both Labor and Likud in exchange for the furtherance of orthodox religious interests.

What has been called the intensity of Israeli democracy has been reflected in the fact that each bloc is made up of several groups. Each of these at one time or another has been a separate political party that ran candidates for the Knesset and each of them considers itself still to be distinct. The result is that there has been what seems a never-ending series of marriages and divorces, and even though both the Alignment and Likud have been fairly well established for some time, most of the numerous factions within each insist on keeping their own names. Thus, the Labor Alignment consists of factions including the MAPAI PARTY (1930–1968), MAPAM (1948–   ), the RAFI PARTY (1965–1968), AHDUT HA'AVODAH (1919–1968), and the Israeli Labor party (1968–   ). Likud consists of the former HERUT PARTY (1948–1983) and the LIBERAL PARTY OF ISRAEL (1961–   ). Parties that have at one time or another been included in the religious camp are the NATIONAL RELIGIOUS PARTY, SHAS, TAMI, and the United Torah Judaism. In addition to all of these, there have been numerous parties that did not fit neatly into any of these categories and were frequently formed as protest or reform movements: the DEMOCRATIC MOVEMENT FOR CHANGE (1976–1980), the CIVIL RIGHTS MOVEMENT (1973–   ), SHINUI (1977–   ), TEHIYA (1979–   ), MERETZ (1992–   ), and TZOMET (1992–   ).

Finally, the role of political parties has been diminished by aspects of social, political, and economic modernization. These include an increasingly scrutinizing electorate, a large increase in the number of Israelis who consider themselves independents, and the frequent dissatisfaction with all of the traditional political parties. The result is that many new parties and movements, a few of which were named above, have frequently received sizable votes even in their initial ventures into the electoral fray. These dissat-

Election Results 1949–1992

	Socialist	Non-Socialist	Religious	Other
First Knesset (1949)	65 (MAPAI 46) (MAPAM 19)	21 (Herut 14) (Liberals 7)	16 (single-list)	18 (Communist 4) (Arab 2) (Other 12)
Second Knesset (1951)	60 (MAPAI 45) (MAPAM 15)	28 (Herut 8) (Liberals 20)	15 (NRP 10) (Aguda 5)	17 (Communist 5) (Arab 1) (Other 11)
Third Knesset (1955)	59 (MAPAI 40) (MAPAM 9) (Ahdut Ha'Avodah 10)	28 (Herut 15) (Liberals 13)	17 (NRP 11) (Aguda 6)	16 (Communist 6) (Arab 4) (Other 6)
Fourth Knesset (1959)	63 (MAPAI 47) (MAPAM 9) (Ahdut Ha'Avodah 10)	25 (Herut 17) (Liberals 8)	18 (NRP 12) (Aguda 6)	14 (Communist 3) (Arab 5) (Other 6)
Fifth Knesset (1961)	59 (MAPAI 42) (MAPAM 9) (Ahdut Ha'Avodah 8)	34 (Herut 17) (Liberals 17)	18 (NRP 12) (Aguda 6)	9 (Communist 5) (Arab 4)
Sixth Knesset (1965)	63 (MAPAI 45) (MAPAM 8) (Rafi 10)	26 Likud (single-list)	17 (NRP 11) (Aguda 6)	14 (Communist 4) (Arab 4) (Other 6)
Seventh Knesset (1969)	56 Israel Labor party (single-list)	26 Likud (single-list)	18 (NRP 12) (Aguda 6)	20 (Communist 4) (Arab 4) (Other 12)
Eighth Knesset (1973)	51 Israel Labor party (single-list)	39 Likud (single-list)	15 (NRP 10) (Aguda 5)	15 (Communist 5) (Arab 3) (Other 7)
Ninth Knesset (1977)	32 Israel Labor party (single-list)	43 Likud (single-list)	17 (NRP 12) (Aguda 5)	28 (Communist 5) (Arab 1) (DMC 15) (Other 7)
Tenth Knesset (1981)	47 Israel Labor party (single-list)	48 Likud (single-list)	10 (NRP 6) (Aguda 4)	15 (Communist 4) (Tehiya 3) (Tami 3) (Other 5)
Eleventh Knesset (1984)	44 Israel Labor party (single-list)	41 Likud (single-list)	12 (NRP 4) (Shas 4) (Aguda 2) (Morasha 2)	23 (Communist 4) (Arab 2) (Tehiya 2) (Shinui 2) (Civil Rights Movement 3) (Other 6)
Twelfth Knesset (1988)	39 Israel Labor party (single-list)	40 Likud (single-list)	18 (Shas 6) (NRP 5) (Aguda 5) (Other 2)	23 (Communist 5) (Arab 3) (Civil Rights Movement 5) (Tehiya 3) (Shinui 2) (Other 5)
Thirteenth Knesset (1992)	56 (Israel Labor party 44) (Meretz 12)	32 Likud (single-list)	16 (Shas 6) (NRP 6) (United Torah Judaism 4)	16 (Communist 3) (Arab 2) (Tzomet 8) (Other 3)

isfactions are also reflected in the estimate that party membership has fallen from 18 percent of the electorate in 1959 to 8 percent in 1984.

BIBLIOGRAPHY

ARIAN, ASHER. *The Elections in Israel.* 1969, 1973, 1977.
———. *Politics in Israel. The Second Generation.* Chatham, N.J., 1985.
ARONOFF, MYRON J. *Power and Ritual in the Israel Labor Party.* Armonk, N.Y., 1993.
PENNIMAN, HOWARD, ed. *Israel at the Polls: The Knesset Elections of 1977.* Washington, D.C., 1979.

Walter F. Weiker

Israel Aircraft Industries

Major Israeli corporation.

Israel Aircraft Industries (IAI) was founded as a publicly owned company in 1966. It was originally planned as a maintenance center for the Israeli air force and Israel Aircraft Industries. To this end it took over the Bedek Aviation Company, which had been set up in 1953 to carry out aircraft repairs and overhauls. Bedek is now one of IAI's main divisions. Other divisions, subsidiaries, and joint ventures are involved in aircraft production and development, electronics, aircraft equipment, drones (unmanned aircraft), missiles, helicopters, and satellites.

IAI is one of Israel's largest firms, with 17,100 workers at the end of 1991, a large share of whom are professionals involved in research and development. In 1991, sales came to 1.6 billion U.S. dollars and net profits to 22 million U.S. dollars.

IAI suffered a major set back in 1987 when the Lavi jet fighter project was cancelled. The project had largely been funded. This was part of a trend toward lower defense procurement both in Israel and, since the end of the Cold War, worldwide. As a result, IAI has suffered from falling demand for its products and incurred losses in 1992.

BIBLIOGRAPHY

Ministry of Finance, Government Companies Authority. *Accounts of Government Companies Year to March 1992.* Jerusalem, 1993. In Hebrew.

Paul Rivlin

Israel Bonds

Method of alleviating economic situation.

In September 1950, Prime Minister David Ben-Gurion convened a conference to discuss Israel's eco-

nomic situation. The prime minister proposed that an Israel bond issue be floated in the United States as a means of opening up a new source of needed funds. Ben-Gurion visited the United States in May 1951 to launch the Israel bond drive. In time, other countries joined the drive: Sales in Latin America began in 1951, in Canada in 1953, and in western Europe in 1954. By 1967, Israel bonds were sold in over thirty countries. There are four types of bonds, or development issues. The third development issue, sold in 1967, consisted of savings bonds, which matured in twelve years at 160 percent of face value, and a 4 percent fifteen-year coupon bond. Eighty-five percent of Israel bonds are sold in the United States, and over one billion dollars worth of bonds have been sold since 1951. The bonds are sold through volunteer Jewish organizations, like B'nai B'rith, and all branches of the Zionist movement.

BIBLIOGRAPHY

FEDERAL RESEARCH DIVISION, LIBRARY OF CONGRESS. *Israel: A Country Study,* 3rd ed. Washington, D.C., 1991.

Mia Bloom

Israel Defense Forces

See Israeli Military and Politics; Military in the Middle East

Israeli Arabs

See Arabs of Israel

Israeli Invasion of Lebanon (1978)

See Litani Operation

Israeli–Lebanese Armistice   [1949]

Agreement between Lebanon and Israel at the conclusion of the Arab–Israel War of 1948.

In 1948, Lebanon participated in the first ARAB–ISRAEL WAR with a contingent of at least 2,000 soldiers. During the war, armistice efforts were undertaken by UN mediator Dr. Ralph J. Bunche. In March 1949, following the example of Egypt, the Lebanese government concluded an armistice agreement with Israel. Lebanon was eager to sign the armistice with Israel, given its weak military status—also, some members of the Christian community in

Lebanon opposed fighting a war against the Jewish state.

BIBLIOGRAPHY

KHOURI, FRED J. *The Arab–Israeli Dilemma.* Syracuse, N.Y., 1985.

George E. Irani

Israeli Military and Politics

Essential components of a state under constant military threat since its formation.

Civil-military relations in Israel are totally different from those in the Arab world. Israel is a full-fledged democracy, and a complex society, and has highly developed political organizations and structures, as well as a fiercely free press. With one of the largest armies in the Middle East (400,000, including reservists), it has been a nation in arms from 1948 to 1979. Since the peace treaty with Egypt, it is still a garrison state; security arrangements with Palestine and Syria undergird the importance of the military in Israel's domestic politics.

Most remarkable is how Israel has sustained a democratic, pluralistic culture in the midst of adversity and of unceasing arms races. In fact, the Arab world has quadrupled its arsenal as Israel has shrunk its own. The nucleus of the Israel Defense Forces (IDF) directly evolved from the Haganah and later transferred its authority from the Jewish Agency to the new government of Israel. The IDF was shaped by Israel's first prime minister and defense minister, David BEN-GURION, who emphasized civilian control over the military and through his personal domination institutionalized these relationships.

Ben-Gurion sought to make the IDF a model for nation building and envisioned its officer corps as the quintessence of Israeli's elites, who would become involved in settlement and integration of over a million immigrants and refugees from Europe and the Arab countries. He established a military pioneer unit called NAHAL, an frontier army to protect the eastern and southern borders of Israel.

The five major wars and mini-campaigns that Israel fought between 1948 and 1992 considerably changed the military institution, the nature of the IDF, and its relationship to civilian authority. To begin with, the process of professional organization and autonomy brought an end to the nation building volunteer efforts. Between 1948 and 1956, the senior officer corps was composed mainly of PALMACH and British army and Haganah veterans, but a new group was created by Chief of Staff General Moshe DAYAN: the paratroopers. Observing the exhaustion of the military after 1949, and the threat at the eastern, northern, and southern borders, these paratroopers created a new aggressive spirit of warfare, a new model army. The first generation of Palmach veterans included General Yigal ALLON and four chiefs of staff—Generals RABIN, BAR-LEV, Elazar, and Eitan—as well as Ariel SHARON and Mordechai GUR. These military men were involved in border raids and retaliation, challenging the unstable armistice that was constantly violated by Egypt, Jordan, Syria, Lebanon, and now Israel. Fighting on enemy territory and short lines of supply characterized the raids of the 1950s that culminated in the 1956 Suez war, in which the professionals and aggressive military personnel played a key role in the training, education, and professionalization of the IDF.

National security was the exclusive province of Prime Minister David Ben-Gurion (1947–1953, 1954–1963). During his administrations, IDF involvement in domestic affairs was broad, because domestic issues were viewed as security issues. The high command's decisions and tactics crossed civil–military boundaries. Politics, ideology, and security concerns clearly were shared by the government and the military.

With the growth of complex organizations and the further professionalism of the IDF, as well as the 1963 retirement of Ben-Gurion, the boundaries between civil and military relations had to be redefined. Civilian authorities dealt with direct issues of national security, such as strategic planning, operations, force structure, and procurement of weapons. In the latter area, the military gained considerable influence; each branch of the military emphasized the type of weapon with which it won the last war to procure a greater part of the budget. Israel's military, like that in America and Western Europe, strongly lobbies for all its interests: procurement, promotion, development, structure, compensation, pensions. These issues were clearly undergirded by the Defense Ministry.

Since the 1970s, civil–military relationships have been "fusionist." The boundaries between civil and military relations, however clearly defined, were blurred, and the army, now free of ideology, moved into traditional bureaucratic politics, securing more for its organization. This was especially true of the IDF, the quintessence of Israel's security. The strength of Israel's army and the stability of its society have given Arab countries the impetus to sign pragmatic peace arrangements and treaties with Israel.

The involvement of institutionalized civil–military relations in national security is directly connected with operations. Operations carried out by an aggressive army sometimes go beyond civil military authority. The case of Lebanon is a good example. In 1982, Defense Minister Ariel Sharon acted as a super chief of staff and conducted the war in Lebanon far beyond the goals of Prime Minister Menachem BEGIN and his government. The consequences of this war clearly demonstrated that aggressive military operations breaking political and strategic boundaries—such as the unnecessary war with Syria, and the unnecessary occupation of Beirut—reveal the traditional tensions between military and civilian authorities. Although the Lebanon case is unique, nevertheless revealed that not respecting and overextending the civil–military boundaries, especially by the military, can bring strategic disasters and political failure.

The war in Lebanon taught that civilian control cannot be dictated by military operations and options. And this goes both ways. Defense ministers like Ben-Gurion and Sharon have created their own strategies and imposed them on the military. Ben-Gurion was in total control of the government and of national consensus. National consensus was disrupted by the war in Lebanon, with serious implications for civil–military relations. Civilian control cannot always depend on a strong military man (Ben-Gurion, Sharon, or Rabin), as the ARAB-ISRAEL WAR of 1967 demonstrates. Prime Minister Levi ESHKOL procrastinated for three weeks regarding the Egyptian challenge, which energized the IDF's high command for the 1967 war.

Another factor that affects civil–military relations is the extraordinary role played by former generals in politics. Dayan, Allon, Bar-Lev, Sharon, Etan, Gur, and many more have not only become senior politicians and in some cases defense ministers (Ezer Weizman and Sharon, as well as Prime Minister Rabin) but also have joined government bureaucracy, there are many generals serving as directors of ministries, public utilities, and some of the largest conglomerates in the private sector. The military export industry is run by retired generals. Some have been heads of research and strategic institutes. In fact, the culture and language of Israel have been tremendously influenced by the IDF "Pentagonese" and specific military jargon.

Civil–military relations, fusionism, and the cooperation/conflict between these institutions are directly related to national consensus. From 1948 until the Egyptian peace treaty, there was national consensus on matters of security in both society and the military. The military still follows Ben-Gurion's concept of security: only a Jewish state is safe for Israel. Occupation of Arab peoples should be temporary, and a Greater Israel should be unacceptable. This consensus was disrupted after the LIKUD Party came to power in 1977, with Menachem Begin's concept of Judaea and Samaria as the seat of Israel's past kingdoms. The consensus was further disrupted with the rise of nationalist religious radicalism, which is the dominant force in Israel's West Bank settlements. The clash between Beautiful Israel and Greater Israel has now split society and politics, disrupting the historical consensus. The militant ideologies of Greater Israel are challenging the historical role of the IDF.

The clashes between the IDF and the settlers and between Palestinians and Israelis have been widened and enhanced since the 1993 Oslo Declaration of Principles. The army will play a greater role in securing the removal, if not the ouster, of settlers from Palestinian territory. Already clashes have begun between the army and the settlers. The army dislikes being in charge of securing a few settlers in a place like Hebron by means of a large military force. This does not mean the officer corps will act independently because of its frustrations with the settlers, but it certainly exacerbates tensions between reserve officers who are settlers and active-duty officers of the IDF. This tension will widen as the Palestine issue is settled. It will certainly leave scars on Israel, as will the whole peace process. Here is a case where civilian control is challenged by organized, militant societal forces, as the IDF becomes involved in the dispute between the government (which has embarked on negotiations for peace) and the settlers (dedicated to a Greater Israel). The army's function will become much more complicated, in view of the fact that it has both to defend the government from the settlers and the settlers from Palestinian terrorists, who are growing in number. However, there is no danger of a military takeover. It will be the IDF's role, as well as the role of security services, to protect the government and society from militants. This will not change the relationship between civil and military; rather, it demonstrates the strength of the fusionist relationships.

BIBLIOGRAPHY

LISSAK, MOSHE, and DAN HOROWITZ. *Origins of the Israeli Polity.* Chicago, 1978.

LUTTWAK, EDWARD, and DAN HOROWITZ. *The Israeli Army.* New York, 1975.

PERI, YORAM. *Battles and Ballots.* New York, 1982.

PERLMUTTER, AMOS. *Military and Politics in Israel.* London, 1969.

———. *Politics and the Military in Israel: 1967–1977.* London, 1977.

SCHIFF, ZEEV. *A History of the Israeli Army (1870–1974).* New York, 1974.

———. "Three Weeks That Preceded the War." *Ha-Aretz,* October 4, 1967.

———. "Young Officers of Zahal," *Ha-Aretz*, September 18, 1963.

Amos Perlmutter

Israel War of Independence

See Arab–Israel War (1948)

Istanbul

Largest city of Turkey; capital of the Byzantine and Ottoman empires.

Istanbul is the only city in the world straddling two continents (Europe and Asia). Its situation at the southern end of the Bosporus Strait and on the Golden Horn (an inlet of the Bosporus bisecting the European side) provides the city with excellent harbors. When the Ottoman sultan Mehmet II conquered the city in 1453, he took the title "Master of the Two Seas and Lord of Two Lands," glorifying his new capital at the junction of land routes from Asia and Europe, and of sea routes from the Black Sea and the Mediterranean (through the Dardanelles Strait). Until London and Paris rose to become capitals of world powers in the early nineteenth century, Istanbul was widely regarded as the natural capital of the world because of its unique setting, size, and fabulous wealth.

Istanbul's roots date to a short-lived Mycenean settlement in the second millennium B.C.E. and the foundation of Byzantium as a Megaran colony in the seventh century B.C.E. The city rose to greatness when the Roman emperor Constantine I chose this "New Rome" as his capital in 324 C.E. renaming it Constantinopolis and extending its area over seven

Boats docked at a quay on the Golden Horn, 1952. (D.W. Lockhard)

hills on the peninsula between the Golden Horn and the Sea of Marmara. The most imposing Byzantine monuments of the city date from the reigns of early emperors who followed Constantine: Theodosius II (r. 408–450) built new walls for the enlarged city; Justinian (r. 527–565) gave final form to the great cathedral of St. Sophia; and, throughout its eleven centuries as capital, the city was continuously adorned by other fine examples of Byzantine architecture. The last efflorescence of Byzantine culture came after the city was regained from Latin rule (1204–1261) and is best represented by the fourteenth-century church of St. Savior in Chora, decorated with remarkable mosaics and frescoes. Both St. Sophia and St. Savior were converted into mosques after the Ottoman conquest, and into museums during the republican era.

By the mid-fifteenth century, the once mighty Byzantine Empire had shrunk to such an extent that

The Golden Horn of Istanbul, with Fatih mosque in the distance, 1952. (D. W. Lockhard)

Aerial view of the city showing the Golden Horn and the Atatürk Bridge. (Robin Bhatty)

it held only the city and its immediate environs, surrounded on all sides by the rising Ottoman state. When Mehmet II ascended the Ottoman throne in 1451, he focused his energy and resources on the conquest of the city, using the project as a means of uniting various Ottoman factions. He constructed the Rumeli hisar Castle on the European shore of the Bosporus at the narrowest point of the strait, directly across from the Anadolu hisar fortress, built fifty years earlier by his great-grandfather, Bayazid I, in a failed attempt to capture the city. The new castle weakened the city by blocking any aid from Europe via the Black Sea. Mehmet II also cast the largest cannon of the period, to be used in attacking the formidable defenses of Theodosius, and moved galleys overland to float them on the Golden Horn, the entrance to which he had blocked with an immense chain. This epic struggle ended when the last Byzantine emperor, Constantine XI, died defending the city, which finally fell into Ottoman hands 29 May 1453.

The city that Mehmet II captured had much diminished from its earlier splendor, and he set about rebuilding his prize. To populate his city, he moved

Taksim Square in modern-day Istanbul. (Mia Bloom)

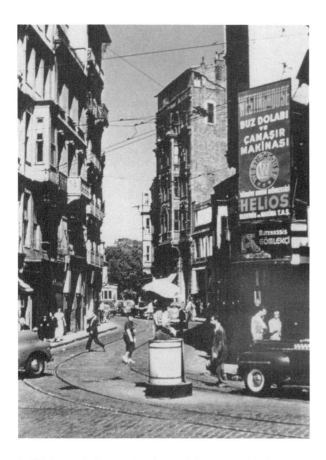

Istiklal Caddesi, a major thoroughfare in Istanbul. (D.W. Lockhard)

Turks, Greeks, Armenians, and Jews from various parts of the Ottoman domain. Trading privileges were renewed for Genoese merchants who lived in their compound in Galata, across the Golden Horn. Two palaces were built in quick succession, the newer of which, Topkapı, served Mehmet II's successors until the nineteenth century. A vast covered market was built as the focus of the city's immense trade, and a *külliye,* a complex of colleges situated around a mosque, was constructed on the site of the patriarchal buildings that had fallen into disrepair. Viziers and pashas were asked to build similar complexes in various parts of the city. Within a century, after further construction by Bayazid II and Süleyman the Magnificent, Istanbul had regained a size and splendor befitting the capital of a vast empire that was, at the same time, a great trading center. It had a cosmopolitan population that reflected its international status and the multiethnic character of the empire. Of the two Greek names of the city, Kustantaniyye remained an official designation, but the colloquial *eis ten polein,* Turkified as Istanbul, was firmly established as the city's name.

As an imperial capital, Istanbul was under the direct authority of the sultan and policed by his household troops. There were, however, qadi magistrates in both the walled city proper and its three outer districts: Eyüp, at the end of the Golden Horn; Galata, including both the northern area across the Golden Horn and the European shore of the Bosporus; and Üsküdar, extending north along the Bosporus on the Asian side. In the seventeenth century, Pera, located on the heights above Galata, became the site of European embassies and merchants' mansions, leading to the Europeanization of the city's municipal administration, architecture, banking, and

Dolmahbahçe Palace. (Mia Bloom)

The Turkish nationalist movement that defeated the aggression against Anatolia had been directed from Ankara, hitherto a second-rate city on the Anatolian plateau. After victory, the sultanate and the caliphate were abolished (in 1922 and 1924, respectively), and the Turkish republic (founded in 1923) chose Ankara as its capital, because it was both easier to defend against foreign powers and untainted by the Ottoman past. During the occupation, Istanbul saw an influx of White Russians fleeing Bolshevik rule. Most of these Russians, along with many of the local Greeks and Armenians, left in the early years of the republic. Istanbul became much more Turkish, albeit at the cost of a reduced population. The prewar population level was regained only after 1950 and was followed by an explosive rate of growth. Much of this new growth was due to the migration of the rural poor to the industrializing urban areas. Istanbul's population in the mid-1990s is approximately 10 million.

Greater Istanbul has covered a large area ever since it was rebuilt by the Ottomans. The population was concentrated in the walled city and across the Golden Horn in Galata; fishing villages along the Bosporus became fashionable summering suburbs, expanding with the advent of steam ferry service. Railway lines constructed late in the nineteenth century led to the further development of European and Asian suburbs along the Sea of Marmara. With the population explosion, the city has suffered the breakdown of transport, electricity, gas, and water supply. Temporary shantytowns have been gradually transformed into permanent tenements that are unsightly as well as unclean and unsafe. In older quarters of the city, graceful wooden houses have given way to blocks of characterless apartments. Nevertheless, this ancient capital of two great empires is so rich in its architec-

trading. By the middle of the century, the sultans and the Ottoman establishment had begun to build palaces and mansions to the north, effectively shifting the political and economic center away from the old city. In the last days of the Ottoman Empire, the city and its suburbs had a total population of about 900,000: 560,000 Muslims, 205,000 Greeks, 73,000 Armenians, 52,000 Jews, and several thousand Europeans, according to a 1914 census.

During World War I, the Ottoman capital was successfully defended at the Dardanelles (Gelibolu/ Gallipoli). Despite this victory, the city suffered not only the typical wartime deprivations but also occupation by the Allied powers after the armistice. Istanbul was the only defeated capital to be subjected to occupation, primarily because of its strategic position and the international importance of the Turkish Straits, but perhaps also because the Allies wished to humiliate this Muslim capital and the sultan–caliph.

Interior of Topkapı Palace in Istanbul. (Mia Bloom)

The Aya Sofya in Istanbul. (Mia Bloom)

Rumeli Hisar fortress with suspension bridge over the Bosporus connecting Europe and Asia. (Mia Bloom)

tural heritage, and the setting of the city is so extraordinary, that Istanbul remains one of the great cities of the world. Two bridges across the Bosporus connect the European and Asian suburbs, and a new business center has developed further to the north. Istanbul has begun to regain its historical role as the region's international trading and financial capital.

BIBLIOGRAPHY

CELIK, ZEYNEP. *The Remaking of Istanbul: Portrait of an Ottoman City in the Nineteenth Century.* Seattle, Wash., 1986.
FREELY, JOHN. *Istanbul Blue Guide.* New York, 1987.
KARPAT, KEMAL. *Ottoman Population, 1830–1914.* Madison, Wis., 1985.
MANSEL, PHILIP. *Constantinople: City of World's Desire, 1453–1924.* London, 1995.

I. Metin Kunt

Istanbul International Festival

Annual series of concerts and performances by internationally renowned artists.

Organized for the first time in 1973 by the Istanbul Culture and Art Foundation, the festival takes place in June and July in various indoor and outdoor venues in Istanbul. Ballet, opera, symphonies, jazz, blues, folk dancing, and other performances are presented by artists from many countries.

BIBLIOGRAPHY

Cumhuriyet Dönemi Türkiye Ansiklopedisi. Istanbul, 1983.

David Waldner

Istanbul Technical University

Oldest engineering college in Turkey.

Istanbul Technical University (ITU) is one of the oldest engineering colleges in the world; it traces its foundation to 1773, when the Ottoman Empire established a military engineering school in Constantinople as part of a modernization effort. In 1884 a separate department in the school was set up for civilian students. That department was transferred to the Ministry of Public Works in 1909 and was spread over several campuses in Istanbul until 1920, when its present campus was established on a hill overlooking the Turkish Straits. After Turkey was proclaimed a republic in 1923, additional departments were added to provide training in railroad construction, electro-mechanics, civil engineering, and architecture. In 1944 the school was reorganized and named Istanbul Technical University. It provides instruction in thirty branches of engineering in eleven departments. Students usually acquire a B.S. degree in four years.

BIBLIOGRAPHY

Büyük Larousse sözlük ve ansiklopedisi, vol. 2. Istanbul, 1993.

Niyazi Dalyanci

Istanbul University

Largest and oldest public university in Turkey.

Founded in 1900 and reorganized in its present form in 1933, Istanbul University now comprises the faculties of letters, science, law, economics, forestry, pharmacy, dentistry, political science, business administration, veterinary science, engineering, and two faculties of medicine, as well as schools of fisheries, journalism, paralegal studies, and tobacco specialist education. With 2,600 teaching staff and 40,000 students (17,000 female) in 1990, it is Turkey's biggest university. Its 1991 budget, state-funded, amounted to 497.5 billion Turkish lire, of which 90 billion was for capital investment.

Istanbul University sometimes claims descent from the complex of eight MADRASA (religious schools) colleges endowed by Mehmed II soon after the conquest of Constantinople (now Istanbul), and the foundation date of 1453 is therefore adopted. A university in the European sense, however, was first proposed in the era of TANZIMAT, the Ottoman Empire's reform period in the 1860s. After some abortive attempts, the university was launched in 1900, incorporating some newly established faculties and some colleges founded in the previous two decades. After the establishment of the Republic of Turkey in 1923, the staff as well as the programs of Istanbul University were viewed from Ankara, the capital, with some suspicion of resistance to republican reform. Finally, in 1933, a complete overhaul of the academic programs and a purge of the staff brought it in line with republican thinking. This era of reestablishment was facilitated by the influx of large numbers of German and other European scholars, many of them Jewish, fleeing Nazi intimidation of persecution. The refugee scholars were especially active in the fields of law and economics, but other programs, including Islamic studies, benefited from a substantial European presence.

In spite of the government's attempts to promote ANKARA UNIVERSITY during the 1950s, Istanbul University was the country's oldest, biggest, and still most prestigious academic establishment. Its academic staff and students were in the forefront of protest against what amounted to majority dictatorship under the government of Adnan MENDERES. Its legal experts were influential in the preparation of the liberal 1961 constitution, promulgated after the young officers' coup of 1960. Istanbul and Ankara universities remained the most highly politicized academic institutions in the 1970s. Armed clashes between the nationally organized right wing and various factions of the Marxist left rendered certain faculties of the university incapable of a normal academic program. The inability of governments, let alone university authorities, to deal with this unbearable degree of political violence facilitated the 1980 military takeover of the Turkish government. The centralized and authoritarian university regime brought about by the Higher Education Council (YÜKSEK ÖĞRETIM KURULU) was also justified by the unacceptable level of violence of the late 1970s.

BIBLIOGRAPHY

Higher Education in Turkey. UNESCO, European Centre for Higher Education. December 1990.
World of Learning. 1990.

I. Metin Kunt

Istiqlal Party, Libya

Political party of Tripolitania, Libya, 1948–1952.

Istiqlal (Independence party) was founded in 1948 by Salim al-MUNTASIR, former leader of the United National Front of Libya, from which many members were drawn. One of several political parties that briefly flourished under the British military administration at a time of intense debate about the future of LIBYA, the Istiqlal's influence belied a small following. It came under the patronage of a powerful lobby advocating renewed Italian rule in Tripolitania, activity the British authorities eventually suppressed. The party was a divisive element in Tripolitanian politics at a time when most of the province's leaders were trying to make a coherent case for Libyan unity and independence. It was one of four Tripolitanian political groups whose views on Libyan independence were heard by the United Nations in 1949. Like all other officially sanctioned parties, the Istiqlal was suppressed as a result of the disturbances that followed the first postindependence elections of February 1952.

BIBLIOGRAPHY

WRIGHT, JOHN. *Libya.* London and New York, 1969.

John L. Wright

Istiqlal Party, Morocco

Leading party in the Moroccan nationalist movement, 1946–1956, and chief competitor of the monarchy for political preeminence during the first post-independence decades.

Istiqlal was founded in 1943 by the core leadership of the banned PARTI NATIONAL. Headed by Ahmad Balafrej and Allal al-Fasi, it drew its strength from the traditional bourgeois elites of the northern cities, particularly FEZ, the emerging national bourgeoisie, and more leftist urban professionals. Its charter, issued on 11 January 1944, demanded independence from France with a constitutional monarchy under the sultan. The publication of the charter and the resulting arrest of Balafrej provoked serious urban unrest in January–February 1944. Al-Fasi returned to Morocco in 1946, after nine years in Gabon, and assumed undisputed leadership of the party. By 1950, Istiqlal's membership was 100,000. After 1951, Istiqlal supported the sultan against the French authorities. In 1952, the party was suppressed following riots in Casablanca, but it played an important role in the negotiations for independence (1953–1956).

Istiqlal assumed a dominant position in the initial postindependence Moroccan governments, but internal splits and competition from the palace prevented it from establishing lasting dominance. In 1959, Istiqlal was weakened by the secession of some of its more dynamic leaders (e.g., Prime Minister Abdullah IBRAHIM, Mehdi BEN BARKA, Mahjoub BEN SEDDIQ, and Muhammad al-Basri), who formed the

UNION NATIONALE DES FORCES POPULAIRES (UNFP), which favored far-reaching social reforms and vigorous development programs through nationalization of key economic sectors.

The monarchy refused to acquiesce to Istiqlal's efforts to reduce its powers. From the end of 1962 to 1977, King Hassan II repelled challenges to his rule and consolidated his political supremacy. Like the other opposition parties, Istiqlal was harnessed into service by Hassan during the mid-1970s in support of his Western Sahara policy. In Istiqlal's case, that was hardly unexpected, since it had been the original standard-bearer of the claim of historical rights to "Greater Morocco" (which in the doctrine's purest form included all of Mauritania and parts of Algeria, Senegal, and Mali, as well as the Spanish enclaves of CEUTA and Melilla.

Fasi died in 1974, while in Romania to explain the king's western Saharan policy; Muhammad BOUCETTA replaced him as secretary-general. Boucetta and other Istiqlal leaders were co-opted into the government in 1977, but following the 1984 elections, Istiqlal returned to opposition ranks. Although no longer the leader of the nationalist movement, Istiqlal maintained a significant place in the political landscape, thanks in part to its affiliated labor confederation, the UNION GÉNÉRALE DES TRAVAILLEURS MAROCAINS, and its influential daily newspapers, *Al-Alam* and *L'Opinion*. In May 1992, with the UNION SOCIALISTE DES FORCES POPULAIRES (USFP), the Parti du Progrés et du Socialisme (PPS), the rump Union Nationale des Forces Populaires (UNFP), and the tiny Organisation pour l'Action Démocratique et Populaire (OADP), Istiqlal formed the "Democratic Bloc" (*al-kutla*) to press for constitutional and electoral reform. Istiqlal won forty-three seats in Parliament in the direct balloting portion of the 1993 elections, a gain of nineteen seats from 1984, but only eight seats in the indirect portion of the vote, a decline of nine seats. Along with the USFP, Istiqlal was now roughly equal in size to the pro-palace Union Constitutionelle and the MOUVEMENT POPULAIRE as the largest parliamentary factions. They refused the terms offered to them for joining a new government, and thus remained in opposition.

Bruce Maddy-Weitzman

Istiqlal Party, Palestine

Important political party established in Palestine, August 1932.

The party's creation was spurred by the Husayni–Nashashibi split, which had almost paralyzed the Pal-

estinian national movement. Its founders, most of whom hailed from the Nablus area, called for the adoption of new methods of political action, including noncooperation with the British mandate authorities and nonpayment of taxes. The party also called for total Arab independence, pan-Arab unity, the abrogation of the mandate and the BALFOUR DECLARATION, and the establishment of Arab parliamentary rule in Palestine.

After reaching its maximum degree of influence, especially among the young and the educated, in the first half of 1933, the party began to decline very rapidly. Among the factors responsible for its decline were the active hostility of the Husayni camp, the lack of financial resources, and the differences between the pro-Hashimite and pro-Sa'udi elements within the party. A distinctive mark of the party was its espousal of the idea that British imperialism was the principal enemy of the Palestinians; thus the party urged them to focus their struggle not simply on ZIONISM, but on British colonialism as well.

BIBLIOGRAPHY

PORATH, YEHOSHUA. *Emergence of the Palestinian Arab National Movement: 1918–1929*. London, 1974.

Muhammad Muslih

Istiqlal Party, Syria

The Independence party, officially founded in Damascus on February 5, 1919.

Also known as Hizb al-Istiqlal al-Arabi (Arab Independence party), the party was established after the demise of the Ottoman Empire and during the Arab kingdom of Syria under FAISAL IBN HUSAYN. Its core members were drawn from the committee of the secret Arab society al-FATAT (Young Arab Society). The founding members of the Istiqlal were Sa'id HAYDAR, As'ad Daghir, Fawzi al-Bakri, Abd al-Qadir al-Azm, Salim Abd al-Rahman, Fa'iz al-Chehabi, and Muhammad Izzat Darwaza, its secretary who was at the same time the secretary of al-Fatat. They decided to come into the open and form a political party under a new name. Al-Fatat continued to exist as the mother party of the Istiqlal, which was considered its spokesman. Members from the other Arab secret society, al-Ahd (the Covenant), also joined the Istiqlal. Party adherents, known as al-Istiqlaliyun (the Independentists), were active in the towns of Syria, where the party had branches during the early years of the French Mandate. Istiqlal also included Palestinian members, who were active against the British mandate authority in Palestine, 1923–1948.

Istiqlal called for Arab unity and independence; it was secular rather than religious. Faisal had supported it financially and politically while he ruled Syria (1918–1920). The party supported the Great Syrian Revolt of 1925 and party members supported the PALESTINE ARAB REVOLT of 1936–1939. It is not known whether the Syrian party was still functioning in 1936.

BIBLIOGRAPHY

DARWAZA, MUHAMMAD IZZAT. Mi'atam Filastiniyya (One Hundred Palestinian Years). Damascus, 1984–1986.

KHOURY, PHILIP. Syria and the French Mandate: The Politics of Arab Nationalism, 1920–1945. Princeton, N.J., 1987.

———. Urban Notables and Arab Nationalism: The Politics of Damascus, 1860–1920. Cambridge, U.K., 1983.

MUSLIH, MUHAMMAD. "The Rise of Local Nationalism in the Arab East." In The Origins of Arab Nationalism, ed. by R. Khalidi et al. New York, 1991.

Abdul-Karim Rafeq

Italy in the Middle East

The Italian presence in North Africa loomed large in the nineteenth and twentieth centuries.

Modern Italian dreams of an empire along the southern rim of the Mediterranean long predated the achievement of Italian reunification. As early as 1838, Giuseppe Mazzini, the great theoretician of the *Risorgimento*, had argued that Tunisia, the key to the central Mediterranean, would have to belong to Italy. By 1861, with the first achievement of the *Risorgimento* of an independent Italian kingdom, some were already looking toward the recovery of former territory from the Roman Empire and for a Mediterranean role for the new nation. By the mid-1860s, there were public expressions of concern over the danger of Italy being excluded from the region altogether by powers such as France and Great Britain.

The opening of the Suez Canal in 1869 and the recovery of Papal Rome the following year spurred Italian mercantilist and classical dreams. On the one hand, they wished to benefit from the commercial advantages offered by empire, on the other, many Italians wished to re-create the greatness of classical Rome. The latter sentiment was particularly acute as far as Tunisia was concerned, where there were already 25,000 Italians in the Regency by 1881. Furthermore, Italian aspirations had been lulled into a false sense of security by a twenty-year-long treaty with the Beylik after 1868. The French annexation of Tunisia as a protectorate in 1881 came, therefore, as a very unpleasant surprise.

As a result, Italy rushed to join other European powers in trying to carve out a colonial empire in Africa during 1882, as part of the scramble for Africa. Italian troops landed at Assab, on the Red Sea coast, and in 1882 began the process of creating a colony in Eritrea—an attempt that was to last fourteen years—and of establishing its presence in Somalia. Italian attempts to occupy Ethiopia, however, were to be unsuccessful, culminating in the catastrophic Italian defeat at Adwa in 1896.

However, by the start of the twentieth century, Italian self-confidence had been restored and attention was being directed toward North Africa once again. The new wave of Italian colonial interest was signaled by the Italian–French agreement of December 1902, which recognized Italian interests in Libya. Peaceful penetration began thereafter, as Italian commercial houses and banks began to appear along the Libyan coast. In 1911, Italy declared war on the Ottoman empire in Libya and invaded the coastal regions.

A concerted intellectual and journalistic effort conducted in Italy persuaded public opinion that a colony in Libya would be a worthwhile endeavor: Not only would it recreate the dream of imperial Rome (frustrated by France's annexation of Tunisia in 1881) but it was believed that Libya was potentially very fertile. It was argued as well that Tripoli was still the crucial endpoint of trans-Saharan trade and, thus, a source of immense wealth. Such arguments were opposed by the socialists, who saw the national crusade for Libya as a diversion from the essential task of revivifying Italy itself.

In reality, however, there were immense pressures building up inside Italy for the development of settler colonies as demographic growth threw into stark relief the problems faced by poverty-stricken regions. Only Libya was left as a potential destination for Italy's excess population, apart from migration to the Americas. As a result, the illusory claims of journalists over the potential offered by Libya were reinforced by the hard realities of domestic economic crises.

The difficulties of establishing a firm grasp on Libya, after the 1911 invasion, were revealed by the two Italo–Sanusi wars, and it was only in 1932 that the new colony was declared pacified. Italy soon discovered that Libya's agricultural potential was a myth, and the new colony turned out to be a constant drain on the metropole's resources. By 1942, 110,000 Italians resided in Libya, of whom 40,000 were involved directly in agriculture; the development of an infrastructure and of colonial settlement had cost the vast sum of 1.8 billion Italian lire, and Italy had little to show for its colonial experiment.

Nonetheless, Libya had been molded into the Fascist vision, which, during the 1930s, had in addition sought to avenge the defeat of Aduwa in Ethiopia. The definitive military pacification of Libya had occurred directly after the Fascists had come to power in Rome, in October 1922. Libya was also seen by the Fascist party as an ideal testing ground for their ideas of racial development, where Libyans were to become Italian Muslims and Italy, under Mussolini, would become the protector of the Muslim world. All these ambitions were to be destroyed by Allied victory in Libya in 1943.

The one other major Fascist experience in Africa was to be the Italian attempt, once again, to conquer Ethiopia. Despite Italian military superiority, the conquest was never completed. It also led to Italy's ostracism by the League of Nations. Finally, the Italian presence there was ended during World War II by British troops, who restored the emperor, Haile Selassie Miriam, to his throne.

Italy's African experiences have, however, left some traces on the modern scene. In 1935, France offered concessions over Libya's southern international border as part of a complex attempt to satisfy Italian claims in Tunisia and in Nice—as well as trying to prevent Italy from joining Nazi Germany as an ally. Although the proposal was never realized, it still remains to bedevil modern international relations, as a result of the competing claims between Libya and Chad to the Aozou Strip.

BIBLIOGRAPHY

NYROP, R. F., et al., eds. *Libya: A Country Study*. Washington, D.C., 1979.

WRIGHT, JOHN. *Libya*. London, 1969.

———. "Libya: Italy's 'Promised Land.' " In *Social and Economic Development of Libya*, ed. by E. G. H. Joffe and McLachlan, K. S. Wisbech, U.K., 1982.

———. *Libya: A Modern History*. London, 1982.

George Joffe

Ivanov

See Russi Khan

IZL

See Irgun Zva'i Le'umi

Izlane

Short poems (songs) of Middle Atlas Berber-speaking peoples (plural of izli; izri, izran in the Rif).

Composed by men or women at festive gatherings, izlane seldom are longer than two lines and are usually sung, accompanied by a drum or clapping.

Though the subject is often love, and the objective is often a thinly veiled courting of someone present, many other subjects may be dealt with, including current events, sometimes morality and religion, and not infrequently mordant commentaries on important issues and persons.

Thomas G. Penchoen

İzmir

Second largest city in Turkey; seaport on the Aegean Sea.

İzmir, formerly known as Smyrna, is situated at the head of a long bay which provides the city with an excellent harbor. With mountains in the Aegean region of western Anatolia stretching east to west, the river valleys from the Anatolian plateau leading to the Aegean Sea allow easy communication with a considerable hinterland. Due to these advantages, the city has been an important trading center over a very long period of time: its origins go back to the third millennium B.C.E.; it maintained its prominence during Hittite, Greek, Roman, and Byzantine domination. In the fourteenth century Smyrna was held by the Turkish Aydın principality, and when Aydın, as well as other Anatolian Turkish emirates, was incorporated into the rising Ottoman state at around 1400, it became an Ottoman city.

In late medieval times Byzantine Smyrna was only one of several ports along the Aegean coast of Anatolia; it continued in Ottoman hands in this restricted role, with Bursa as the main international market of Anatolia and a number of Aegean ports serving the local export trade. Changes in the nature of international trade from around 1600, the growing share of Aegean and Anatolian exports in overall trade, and an increase in Asian caravan trade coming to Anatolia led to a shift in Ottoman policy. The empire decided that it would be easier to control trade if it were concentrated in one location, and so promoted İzmir as the main Aegean port for the increasing trade with Europe. Many Ottoman statesmen invested in the city's infrastructure, building waterworks, fountains, trade emporia, and markets. From a small town of about 5,000 people, İzmir grew to a population of about 100,000 by the end of the seventeenth century, including hundreds of Dutch, English, and French merchants who displaced Italians as the leading traders in Anatolian and Asian exports. İzmir's population also included a sizeable proportion of local non-Muslims, many employed by European merchants. With this elevation in its position, İzmir eclipsed not only other Aegean ports but also surpassed Bursa as the leading trade center in Anatolia, and even diverted some of the traditional caravan trade of Aleppo. With its Frankish Street along the quay and its cosmopolitan population, seventeenth-century İzmir became a prototype of the great nineteenth-century international ports such as Shanghai and Alexandria.

In the early nineteenth century İzmir's European trade was disrupted first by the Revolutionary and Napoleonic Wars and then, in the 1820s, by the war of Greek independence, but industrializing Europe's demand for Anatolian raw cotton and wool soon brought trade to much higher values. Dried fruits (raisins and figs), tobacco, olive oil, animal hides, too, were exported at unprecented levels. The city's population increased considerably, attracting not only foreigners but also an influx of population both from Anatolia and the Aegean islands. The first railroad to be built in Anatolia was laid between İzmir and Aydın to facilitate the exports of its rich hinterland. Just before World War I, İzmir and its vicinity had a total population of 210,000, of which 100,000 were Muslims, 74,000 Greek, 10,000 Armenian, 24,000 Jewish, and about 2,000 Europeans.

After the defeat of the Ottoman Empire in 1918, the victorious allies allowed the Greek occupation of the city and its hinterland, more to enforce a dictated peace settlement than for the purpose of supporting a justifiable Greek claim. But the Greek invasion in fact served to spark the nascent Anatolian Turkish resistance, and the Turkish war of independence ended with the recapture of İzmir in September 1922. The city was devastated by a huge conflagration as the Greek forces and population withdrew to the Aegean; its burgeoning industry was wrecked and its foreign trade sharply declined. The republic, however, indicated its determination to restore İzmir's prominent commercial role by holding its first national congress there in 1923 to set economic policy, and by creating a vast park in the central area flattened in the conflagration to become the setting for an annual international fair. Although it became a much more Turkish city than in Ottoman times, Muslims immigrating from Crete, Aegean islands, and Salonika replaced the earlier Greek population and helped to preserve a relatively cosmopolitan outlook; the city also quickly regained its accustomed role as the port with the largest exports, though second to Istanbul in imports.

From the 1950s İzmir experienced a significant degree of industrialization, adding import substitutes in the automotive and food processing sectors to its traditional textile production. Rapid urban growth has been faster than in other cities of Turkey, except Istanbul, so that just recently İzmir passed Ankara as the second largest city, with a population of about 2,500,000. Beyond its commercial importance, İzmir serves as the focus of a hinterland rich in classical and Turkish cultural heritage. Classical sites of the highest importance, such as Ephesus, Pergamum, and Sardis are within easy reach, as are cities and towns such as Manisa, Aydın, Birgi, and Tire, important centers of the Muslim-Turkish past.

BIBLIOGRAPHY

ANDERSON, SONIA. An English Consul in Turkey, Paul Rycaut at Smyrna, 1667–1678. Oxford, 1989.
FRANGAKIS-SYRETT, ELENA. The Commerce of Smyrna in the Eighteenth Century. Athens, 1992.
GOFFMAN, DANIEL. İzmir and the Levantine World, 1550–1650. Seattle, 1990.
KARPAT, KEMAL. Ottoman Population, 1830–1914. Madison, Wis., 1985.

I. Metin Kunt

İzmir Economic Congress

Turkish economic summit meeting, 1923.

Convened in February 1923 during a recess in the Lausanne Peace Conference, the İzmir Economic Congress consisted of more than 1,100 Turkish delegates representing agriculture, trade, artisans, and labor, as well as top political leaders, including Mustafa Kemal Atatürk. The resolutions adopted were referred to as the Economic Pact (*Misak-i Iktisadi*), signifying that the government considered them as important as the previously promulgated TURKISH NATIONAL PACT (*Misak-i Milli*), which enunciated the goal of political independence. These resolutions proclaimed the intention of developing the nation's economy by relying on the free activity of Turkish entrepreneurs. Foreign capital was to be welcome provided it adhered to Turkish law. Monopolies were opposed. Thus, the congress inaugurated a phase of reliance on private enterprise. This phase ended after the consolidation of the republican regime and the onset of the worldwide depression in the late 1920s. It was replaced by a concerted policy of state initiatives on the economy, including ownership and operation of major enterprises.

BIBLIOGRAPHY

BIANCHI, R. Interest, Groups and Political Development in Turkey. Princeton, N.J., 1984.

Frank Tachau

Izzeddine, Jado   [1926–   ]

Syrian military officer.

Born to a Druze family in Aleppo, Izzedine graduated from the Homs Military Academy in 1947. He was associated with Amin al-NAFURI's "liberation" faction of officers in the period after the government of Adib Shishakli, and in January 1958 was part of a delegation sent to Cairo to pledge BAʿTH support for President Gamal Abdel NASSER. In March 1960, he was appointed minister of state for presidential affairs in the United Arab Republic.

BIBLIOGRAPHY

HOPKINS, ED. "Military Intervention in Syria and Iraq." Master's thesis, American University of Beirut, 1970.

Charles U. Zenzie

J

Jabal al-Akhdar, Libya

Eastern "green mountain" region.

An area of Libya in the hinterland of the eastern city of Benghazi, with mountains of nearly thirty-three hundred feet (1,000 m). It is one of the few parts of Libya with relatively good rainfall (98–118 in./yr; 250–300 cm/yr) but with difficult terrain and soil conditions, characterized by grain cultivation with modest yields and livestock grazing.

BIBLIOGRAPHY

ALLAN, J. A., ed. *Libya since Independence: Economic and Political Development.* New York, 1982.

Laurence Michalak

Jabal al-Akhdar, Oman

Massif in the western Hajar mountains of Oman.

The "Green Mountain," blessed with significant vegetation, rises to about 10,000 feet. It is part of the once nearly inaccessible area of Oman proper to which minority groups fled in early historical times. One of those groups was the Ibadi Muslim sect, whose followers still comprise the majority of Oman's population. Jabal al-Akhdar was the last stronghold of the Ibadi imamate in 1959.

BIBLIOGRAPHY

ALLEN, CALVIN H., JR. *Oman: The Modernization of the Sultanate.* Boulder, Colo., 1987.

HELD, COLBERT C. *Middle East Patterns: Places, Peoples, and Politics.* Boulder, Colo., 1989.

Malcolm C. Peck

Jabal, Badawi al- [1905–1981]

Pen name of Muhammad Sulayman al-Ahmad, a Syrian poet of high reputation in the Arab world.

He was born in the village of Difa in the district of al-Haffa, in Latakia province, to Sulyaman al-Ahmad, the head of a distinguished Alawite family. His pen name was given to him, according to the compiler of his poetry, Midhat Akkash, by the editor of the Damascus newspaper *Alif Ba,* apparently in 1920. The editor liked the poetry, but because the poet was not well known, the editor agreed to publish the poetry under the pseudonym of Badawi al-Jabal, a reference to the cloak (*aba'a*) and the headband (*iqal*) the poet wore at the time—like a *badawi* (bedouin) coming from *al-Jabal* (the Alawite mountain).

Badawi al-Jabal practiced politics and poetry at an early age. As a nationalist, he joined the National block, and later on the NATIONAL PARTY. He was imprisoned by the French mandatory authorities in Syria, and in 1939 he sought refuge in Baghdad. While there, he taught Arabic at the University of Baghdad and also supported the revolt of Rashid Ali al-KAYLANI against the British in 1941. Upon returning to Syria, he was apprehended by the French authorities in 1942. Later on, he was twice elected to parliament, in 1943 and 1947. In the 1950s, he became minister of health. The defeat of the Arabs in the 1967 ARAB–ISRAEL WAR was a great shock to him; he wrote much poetry inspired by it. He adhered to the old school of Arabic LITERATURE and poetry, which upholds the classical mode. His poetry was also influenced by a mystical orientation. Selections from his poetry were published in Damascus in 1968 by Midhat Akkash. A full anthology appeared in Beirut in 1978 with an introduction by Akram Zu'aytir.

BIBLIOGRAPHY

JAYYUSI, SALMA KHADRA. *Modern Arabic Poetry, an Anthology*. New York, 1987.

Abdul-Karim Rafeq

Jabal al-Khalil

Group of mountains surrounding the town of Hebron (Khalil), about twenty miles (32 km) south of Jerusalem.

Jabal al-Khalil forms the tallest and southernmost part of the mountain ridge extending north to Tiberias. The ridge was where most villages of Palestine were concentrated in the nineteenth century. While agricultural cultivation increased under Jordan's rule between 1938 and 1967, many villagers of the relatively congested and unindustrialized Jabal al-Khalil migrated for work to the east bank of the Jordan river. Since the 1967 Arab-Israel war, Jabal al-Khalil has been part of the Israeli-occupied WEST BANK and the site of a growing number of Israeli settlements like Qiryat Arba.

BIBLIOGRAPHY

MIGDAL, JOEL. *Palestinian Society and Politics*. Princeton, N.J., 1980.
SHAFIR, GERSHON. *Land, Labor and the Origins of the Palestinian Conflict 1882–1914*. New York, 1989.

Elizabeth Thompson

Jabal Druze

A volcanic massif in southern Syria, between the plain of Hawran and the Eastern desert.

This mountain region has a curved, cone-like surface, its highest peak rising to 5,915 feet (1,803 m). On the west, the basalt upland is surrounded by lava, which tapers into the fertile plains of Hawran and Jawlan, famed since Roman times for their abundance in grain. The western slopes of the mountain receive an average annual rainfall of about 11.7 inches (300 mm). The soil is especially suitable for vine and fruit trees.

The term Jabal Druze was first applied to the Shuf region of Mount Lebanon where the people of the DRUZE community predominate. Under the Mamluk sultanate (1260–1517), some Druzes, suffering from Mamluk punitive expeditions against them, took refuge in Jabal Hawran. After the Qaysi–Yamani war at Ayn Dara in Lebanon in 1711, the Yamanis, most of whom were Druzes, who were overpowered in the fighting, fled to Jabal Hawran, where they formed the bulk of the Druze community. Later on, more Druzes fled from Mount Lebanon to the Hawran in the wake of the 1860 events, when punitive measures were taken against them. Others went there during World War I to avoid Ottoman Empire conscription and the famine. Because of this considerable Druze settlement in Jabal Hawran, it became known in the latter part of the nineteenth century as Jabal Druze. In the 1930s, Jabal Druze was also referred to as Jabal al-Arab to avoid the sectarian term of *Druze* and also in recognition of the nationalist role played by the Druzes, headed by Sultan al-Atrash, in leading the Great Syrian Revolt against the French (1925–1927).

BIBLIOGRAPHY

LEWIS, NORMAN. *Nomads and Settlers in Syria and Jordan, 1800–1980*. New York, 1987.

Abdul-Karim Rafeq

Jabal Nablus

Group of low mountains in the region of the city of Nablus, in the West Bank area of Israel.

Located about thirty miles north of Jerusalem, Jabal Nablus forms the northern edge of the Central Highlands that extend south to Hebron (al-Khalil). The region, dotted with hillside agricultural villages, has been known particularly for its olives and olive oil soap. For much of the Ottoman era, Jabal Nablus was ruled as part of Damascus province, and dominated for centuries by the TUQAN FAMILY. The area became known in Palestinian folklore as Jabal al-Nar (Mountain of Fire) for its resistance to Britain's rule in the mandate period (1922–1948). Since 1967, it has been part of the Israeli-occupied West Bank.

BIBLIOGRAPHY

AL-ABASI, MUSTAFA. *Tarikh al-Tuqan fi Jabal Nablus*. (History of the Tuqans in Jabal Nablus). Shefa Amr, 1990.
GRAHAM-BROWN, SARAH. "The Political Economy of Jabal Nablus, 1920–48." In *Studies in the Social and Eco-*

nomic History of Palestine in the 19th and 20th Centuries, ed. by Roger Owen. London, 1982.

Elizabeth Thompson

Jabal Shammar

Two mountain ranges located in Saudi Arabia.

Jabal Shammar covers an area of 100 square miles (260 sq km) south of the Nafud Desert in northern Najd. Sufficient rainfall supports grazing animals, and the area has a large cluster of oases and agricultural villages, the largest being Ha'il and Jofar. In the nineteenth century, the population consisted mainly of SHAMMAR and Beni Tamim tribespeople. The political center of the Jabal area is Ha'il, formerly ruled by the AL RASHID FAMILY of the Shammar Bedouin, which is now an administrative center (emirate) under the government of Saudi Arabia.

Eleanor Abdella Doumato

Ja'bari, Muhammad Ali   [1900–1980]

Palestinian politician.

Born in Hebron (al-Khalil) and educated at al-Azhar in Cairo, Shaykh Muhammad Ali Ja'bari began his career as a chief clerk in a *shari'a* (Muslim law) court. He was mayor of Hebron from 1940 to 1976, when he was ousted in an election by Fahd Kawasmeh, a Palestine Liberation Organization (PLO) supporter, apparently because of his long-standing ties with the Jordanian ruling house. Ja'bari had supported Hashimite rule in Palestine since the 1930s, and delivered support for Jordan's annexation of the West Bank at the 1948 Palestinian Congress at Jericho (the JERICHO CONGRESS). In the 1950s, he held several ministerial posts in Amman, Jordan.

BIBLIOGRAPHY

SAHLIYEH, EMILE. *In Search of Leadership.* Washington, D.C., 1988.
SMITH, PAMELA ANN. *Palestine and the Palestinians 1876–1983.* London, 1984.

Elizabeth Thompson

Ja'bari Family

Prominent Palestinian family from Khalil (Hebron).

The Ja'bari family dominated political posts in the Khalil district from the 1940s to the 1970s. They rose to prominence in Palestinian politics through their support of Jordanian rule in the West Bank. In the 1970s and 1980s, the family's political support declined as their cooperation with the governments of Israel and Jordan came under increasing criticism.

BIBLIOGRAPHY

SAHLIYEH, EMILE. *In Search of Leadership.* Washington, D.C., 1988.
SMITH, PAMELA ANN. *Palestine and the Palestinians 1876–1983.* London, 1984.

Elizabeth Thompson

Jabarti, Abd al-Rahman al-   [1753–1825]

Egyptian historian and scholar.

Best known as the foremost Egyptian Muslim chronicler of Napoléon Bonaparte's invasion and occupation of Egypt from 1798 to 1801. His family was originally from the village of Jabart on the Red Sea coast, but al-Jabarti himself was born in Cairo to a wealthy family whose economic base included *iltizam*s (tax farms) and a *waqf* (religious endowment). Both he and his father were educated at al-Azhar University.

Al-Jabarti's studies included medicine and arithmetic, but his main scholarly activity was writing histories of Egypt. His principal works were *Aja'ib al-Athar fi al-Tarajim wa al-Akhbar* (Wondrous Seeds of Men and Their Deeds), *Muzhir al-Taqdis bi Dhahab Dawlat al-Faransis* (The Demonstration of Piety in the Demise of French Society), and *Tarikh Muddat al-Faransis bi Misr* (History of the French Presence in Egypt).

There is debate over whether *Tarikh Muddat al-Faransis* is an earlier version of *Muzhir al-Taqdis.* Both are short works dealing only with the period of French occupation. *Tarikh Muddat al-Faransis* appears to be an eyewitness account of the events, probably written in 1798; *Muzhir al-Taqdis* was probably completed in 1801. *Aja'ib* is a longer work covering Egyptian history from 1688 to 1821 in four volumes. There are also questions about the relative dating of the first three volumes of *Aja'ib,* which include the events of the French occupation, and *Muzhir al-Taqdis.* The parts of *Aja'ib* relevant to the French occupation are now thought to have been completed in 1805 or 1806, after *Muzhir al-Taqdis.* The issue of the relative dating of the two works is considered important because *Muzhir al-Taqdis* is more critical of the French than *Aja'ib,* which, if it were indeed written after *Muzhir al-Taqdis,* suggests that it could have been a "revisionist" work reflecting the real opinions of al-Jabarti, as opposed to "official" versions of the events related in the other works.

Although al-Jabarti is a key figure in late eighteenth- and early nineteenth-century Egyptian history, historians have reevaluated the period itself. In particular, they question the idea that the French invasion marked the definitive onset of modernity in the Middle East. Both historians Peter Gran and Kenneth Cuno argue, from otherwise different perspectives, that the French invasion is best understood as an event in the larger processes of Egyptian history. In the same vein, the nature of al-Jabarti's histories has been reexamined. Jack Crabbs, for example, argues that al-Jabarti was an outstanding, but typical, medieval Egyptian historian who happened to have recorded extraordinary events. In contrast, Gran claims that al-Jabarti's accounts of the French invasion, and his historiography in general, were cultural manifestations of a nascent capitalist transformation already underway before the first European attempts to colonize the region. But aside from such issues, there is general consensus that al-Jabarti's histories were the best account of the French invasion from an Egyptian or Arab perspective, and generally above the standards for accuracy and detail common in late Ottoman historical writing. Al-Jabarti remains one of the principal sources for historians interested in early modern Egypt.

BIBLIOGRAPHY

AYALON, DAVID. "The Historian al-Jabarti and his Background." *Bulletin of the Society of Oriental and African Studies* 23 (1960): 217–249.

CRABBS, JACK. *The Writing of History in Nineteenth-Century Egypt: A Study in National Transformation.* Detroit, 1984.

CUNO, KENNETH. *The Pasha's Peasants: Land, Society, and Economy in Lower Egypt, 1740–1858.* Cambridge, U.K., 1992.

GRAN, PETER. *Islamic Roots of Capitalism: Egypt, 1760–1840.* Austin, Tex., 1979.

AL-JABARTI, ABD AL-RAHMAN. *Napoleon in Egypt: Al-Jabarti's Chronicle of the French Occupation, 1798.* Tr. by Shmuel Moreh, introduction by Robert L. Tignor. Princeton, N.J., 1993.

Walter Armbrust

Jabha al-Wataniyya, al-

Tripolitanian nationalist movement.

The political movement, al-Jabha al-Wataniyya (United National Front), was established by Tripolitanian notables during the British military administration of Tripolitania after World War II to oppose the return of Tripolitania to Italian trusteeship. Instead they advocated the resolution that eventually prevailed: the independence of all the provinces of Libya together under the leadership of the emir of the SANUSI ORDER.

Lisa Anderson

Jabir I

See Al Sabah, Jabir I al-Sabah

Jabiri, Ihsan al-   [1880–?]

Syrian politician.

Ihsan al-Jabiri was born in Aleppo, Syria, to Abd al-Kader al-Jabiri. He was educated at the Institute of Laws in Istanbul, where he received his doctorate of laws, and in Paris, where he earned an advanced law degree. He served his hometown as mayor, then was chamberlain to Faisal in 1918, when he was establishing himself as king of Syria; consequently, Jabiri was exiled by the French mandate authorities when they ousted the kingdom in the early 1920s. He returned to serve, as a member in the NATIONAL BLOC, as administrator of Latakia in 1939. He was also elected parliamentary deputy of Aleppo in 1954.

BIBLIOGRAPHY

KHOURY, PHILIP S. *Syria and the French Mandate: The Politics of Arab Nationalism, 1920–1945.* Princeton, N.J., 1987.

Charles U. Zenzie

Jabiri, Sa'dallah al-   [1893–1946]

Syrian politician.

Born to a Sunni Islam notable family, Sa'dallah al-Jabiri was educated in law at Istanbul. He was a very early advocate of Arab nationalism, leading the Red Hand Society (an Alleppo offshoot of the Damascus-based Iron Hand). He fought in World War I for the Ottoman Empire. He fled to Egypt after the war and returned in 1921 to join Ibrahim HANANU's revolt against the French mandate troops in northern Syria.

Jabiri joined the NATIONAL BLOC in 1928, was elected parliamentary deputy in 1928, 1936, and 1943, and served as minister from 1936 to 1939, in 1944, and in 1946.

BIBLIOGRAPHY

KHOURY, PHILIP S. *Syria and the French Mandate: The Politics of Arab Nationalism, 1920–1945.* Princeton, N.J., 1987.

Charles U. Zenzie

Jabotinsky, Vladimir Ze'ev [1880–1940]

Founder and leader of the Revisionist movement.

A central figure in the Zionist movement during the period following Herzl's death (1904) until his own death in 1940, Jabotinsky was a man whose uncommon gifts—as orator, thinker, journalist, poet, linguist, and translator—and charismatic personality attracted a large following and touched off numerous controversies. As political crusader, movement organizer, diplomat, and propagandist, he traveled continuously throughout the world while at the same time maintaining a life as a creative writer. Among other works, he wrote the historical novel *Samson the Nazarite,* which first appeared in Russian in 1926, and he translated poetry from Italian, Czech, English, and Hebrew into Russian.

Born in Odessa on October 5, 1880, he studied law, sociology, history, and philology from 1898 to 1901, first in Bern and then in Rome where the national-unification struggle of the Italian people made a strong impression on him. During this period he also launched his career as a journalist, serving as correspondent for two Russian dailies. He spent one more year of formal study (1907–1908) in Vienna researching the issues surrounding nationality and minority rights. On his return to Odessa from Rome, he became a popular writer of feuilletons and wrote verse plays and poetry; until 1914, his prolific writing continued to span literary, political, and theatrical as well as Jewish subjects.

By the time of the Russian pogroms of 1903 and 1904, Jabotinsky had already become well known in Russian Zionist circles, and he aligned himself with Jews who promoted the idea of a Jewish self-defense corps. As a delegate to the Sixth Zionist Congress in Basel (1903), he opposed Herzl's UGANDA PROJECT, but regretted his stance when, during World War II, European Jews could not emigrate to Palestine. In 1904 in St. Petersburg, he became associated with new Zionist publications that instructed Jews on Zionism's political goals. He was a fiery orator who criticized Russian socialists, liberals, and members of the intelligentsia for ignoring the pogroms. Beginning in 1905, he traveled widely throughout the Russian provinces, attacking the antinationalist, anti-Zionist attitudes of Jewish assimilationists and members of the socialist Bund. His strong impact on audiences and readers made Zionist leaders view him as the rising star of Russian Zionism. In 1906, he had a major role in forming the Helsingfors program, in which the national and political activity of a united Jewish party in multinational Russia was seen as a prerequisite to the founding of a national Jewish state in Palestine, rather than an end in itself.

A proponent of a Hebraist renaissance in which Hebrew would be the living language in the Diaspora as well as in Palestine, Jabonitsky contributed articles to a Hebrew weekly (1908–1909), completed a favorably received translation of Bialik's poems into Russian (1910), and sometimes lectured in Hebrew. He promoted the idea that Hebrew should be the language of all instruction in Russia's Jewish schools, helped bring to fruition CHAIM WEIZMANN's 1913 proposal for a Hebrew university in Jerusalem, and in 1923 realized a longtime ambition of publishing Hebrew dictionaries and textbooks.

Jabotinsky made a first, brief trip to Palestine (1908) while he was in Turkey reporting on the Young Turks' revolution. In 1909, he was appointed head of the Turkish Zionist press network by the WORLD ZIONIST ORGANIZATION and brought many Turkish Jews into the Zionist fold. After Turkey declared war on the Allied Powers (1914), Jabotinsky, who had previously favored a unified Ottoman Empire, became convinced that the empire's imminent dissolution constituted a historical opportunity for Zionism. In advocating support for the Allies, however, he drew opposition from Zionist leaders throughout Europe and even in Palestine (which was then part of the Ottoman Empire) because they feared the consequences of associating with the Allies or because they were dead set against helping the detested tsar of Russia. In 1915, Jabotinsky proposed that a JEWISH LEGION be formed to fight alongside British soldiers in conquering Palestine. Disregarding the opposition of many Zionist groups, Jabotinsky persisted in campaigning for the legion, which he envisioned as cementing a political and military alliance between the British and the Zionists. The creation of the legion was announced in 1917, and the three battalions it comprised were recruited from Jewish volunteers in England, America, and (later) Palestine. During the summer of 1918, the legion, in which Jabotinsky served first as a noncommissioned officer and later as a lieutenant, played a minor role in the operations of General Allenby's army in Palestine.

Once the war ended, the British immediately disbanded the Jewish Legion, dashing Jabotinsky's hope that it would be converted into a permanent Jewish defense force. In 1918, Jabotinsky worked with the Zionist Commission in Palestine and was appointed to head its political department in January 1919. His activism, however, alarmed moderate Zionists and he was discharged from the commission in February 1919. Following Arab riots in Jerusalem in April 1920, Jabotinsky was arrested (under an article of the Ottoman code) for supplying a Jewish defense force with arms and sentenced to fifteen years in prison, but he was released after three months.

In the early nineteen-twenties, Jabotinsky became an increasingly harsh critic of what he deemed the anti-Zionist policies of the British mandate administrators and the conciliatory responses of the World Zionist Organization, headed by Chaim Weizmann. He went along with Weizmann's acceptance of the 1922 White Papers but later regretted having tendered this support, which he depicted as having been extracted from him under the pressure of events. These differences, coupled with the storm of indignation that greeted news of his unilateral agreement in September 1921 with Maxim Slavinsky, a representative of the Ukrainian anti-Bolshevik government in exile, led to his resignation from the Zionist Executive.

Throughout his life, Jabotinsky was identified with publications that functioned as his mouthpiece, allowing him to make his case and conduct his political crusades. In 1923, he wrote for the Zionist Russian weekly *Rassvyet,* which later became a leading Revisionist weekly and which also published his novels. In 1928 he took over the editorship of the daily paper *Doar Hayom,* turning it into the first Revisionist publication in Palestine. His unceasing excoriation in the paper of the anti-Zionist policy of the British administration and the inaction of the Zionist Executive caused the Palestine administration to suspend the paper's publication (1930) until it renounced Revisionist control.

In April 1925, Jabotinsky founded a new political movement, the World Union of Zionist Revisionists, whose name referred to the founders' goal of revising the programs, plans, and methods of the World Zionist Organization to accord with the new situation of world Jewry. In the same year, he also founded Betar, a movement comprised of youths who he foresaw could be equipped with the ideals and training that would be required in the new Jewish state. At first Jabotinsky yielded to the view of the Revisionist cofounders that the movement should act as an opposing force within the general structure of the World Zionist Organization while retaining the right to conduct its own propaganda campaigns. Jabotinsky tried but failed to influence that body to adopt the Revisionist program. The Revisionist proposals were consistently stymied both in the Zionist congresses and in the Yishuv, and often provoked

hostility and fierce conflict, sometimes taking the form of violent clashes, especially between the Betar and Jewish Socialists. By 1935, determined to conduct independent political activities unhampered by the threat of discipline from the World Zionist Organization, Jabotinsky and a majority of the Revisionist membership seceded and formed the New Zionist Organization (NZO).

Between 1925 and 1939, Jabotinsky's activities centered around building up the membership of the Revisionist movement (and later the NZO) through an arduous schedule of lectures, meetings, and writings. His frequent trips to Western capitals and centers of Jewish population in Poland and the Balkans were often simultaneously dictated by diplomatic missions. In 1925 he considered the goal of Zionism to be to obtain British support for creating conditions conductive to Jewish settlement in Palestine on both sides of the Jordan. The attainment of a Jewish majority through the unfettered flow of Jewish immigrants to Palestine and the guaranteeing of security for the Yishuv was an essential part of this goal. This position alienated many Zionists who were content to give the process of building a Jewish homeland time and who sought avenues for coexistence with the Arab population. To the Palestinian administrators, Revisionist propaganda was the direct cause of eruptions of Arab violence, after the Arab riots of 1929 Jabotinsky was barred from reentering Palestine, where he had settled in 1928. Believing that the Jews' and the Arabs' interests were mutually exclusive, Jabotinsky never held out much hope for negotiating with Palestinian Arabs. He developed a theory of the "iron wall," according to which the fait accompli of a dominating Jewish political entity would force the Arabs to grant the Jews in Palestine full recognition and to accept their sovereignty. Jabotinsky maintained that Palestinian Arabs were entitled to the full civil rights of a national minority, but that the state's national policy and national character would be determined by the Jewish national majority.

In spite of his constant criticism of British anti-Zionist policies, Jabotinsky retained a pro-British orientation. He believed that as long as Zionist goals in the long run meshed with Britain's own interests, the burden was on Zionists to apply consistent moral pressure on Britain to live up to what he saw as the promises to Jews inherent in the BALFOUR DECLARATION and the mandate agreement. Until 1937, he advocated meeting Arab violence with restraint, but thereafter he began favoring limited retaliation as a means of persuading Britain to suppress the Arab revolt. In the late nineteen-thirties, Jabotinsky encouraged the illegal immigration to Palestine of several thousand European Jews, regarding it not only as a means of rescue but also as a way for the YISHUV to declare its readiness to violate the immigration restrictions imposed by the British.

Self-defense capabilities played a significant role in Jabotinsky's view of the Jews' relationship to the British and to the rest of the world. After World War I, Jabotinsky advocated restoring the Jewish Legion, and with the outbreak of World War II he propagandized for help in building a Jewish army as a way of proving that the Jews were a faithful ally to the British in their time of need, and also as a means of forging a place for the Jews at the peace table and on the world stage. This emphasis on building a fighting force also antagonized many Zionists who had a strong distaste for all suggestions of militarism.

In 1933, Jabotinsky initiated the drive to impose an international economic boycott against Nazi Germany, in the hope that such a concerted action might overthrow Hitler's newly installed regime. He vigorously objected to the Jewish Agency's agreement with Nazi Germany to allow German Jews to withdraw their money from Germany in the form of goods and believed the Jews in Palestine would refuse to buy goods obtained on such a basis. In retrospect, Jabotinsky's characteristic urgency seemed particularly suited to the desperate situation of the Jews in Europe at the time, but the need for this urgency was not generally recognized. In 1934, Jabotinsky achieved few tangible results with a program that entailed petitioning governmental and institutional leaders of England, reminding them of the Jews' mass distress, and appealing to them to honor the promise of sixteen years before to help rebuild a Jewish national homeland in Palestine. A determined opponent of the long-awaited PARTITION PLANS that was announced in the Peel Report (1937), in 1935, Jabotinsky reaffirmed the need for an organized mass migration of a million Jews from Europe to Palestine under a ten-year plan.

Among Zionists, Jabotinsky's most bitter enemies were socialists and members of the Labor party, a fact that Jabotinsky attributed to the irreconcilable differences between himself and these adversaries. Jabotinsky was discouraged by the determination of the Labor party in Palestine to preserve its own interests exclusively and to reject the development of industry and private enterprise. He welcomed the contributions of the middle class settlers, insisted that labor disputes be settled by national arbitration rather than strikes, and disparaged what he saw as the Jewish laborites' promotion of class war at a time when he considered the Yishuv to be badly in need of an influx of capital. On its side, the Labor wing branded him a reactionary—a demagogue

with fascistic tendencies who condoned the exploitation of workers. In 1934, Jabotinsky tried to effect a truce with the members of the Labor party in order to put an end to the physical clashes that had become commonplace between them. At a meeting with David Ben-Gurion, he arrived at a compromise agreement in regard to the issues that separated them, but the members of the Histadrut rejected the agreement in a special plebescite in 1935, shortly before the Revisionists seceded from the World Zionist Organization. Jabotinsky died in 1940 while traveling in the United States in an attempt to gain support for establishing a Jewish army. Following his instructions that as long as there was no Jewish state, he be buried wherever he died, he remained buried in New York until 1964, when Prime Minister Levi Eshkol contravened a decision of Ben-Gurion's and allowed his remains to be brought to Israel for burial.

A man to whom leadership came naturally and who was the ideological mentor for several political movements, including the IRGUN ZVA'I LE'UMI (IZL), Jabotinsky imprinted his own personality so strongly on Revisionism that it came to be known as the Jabotinsky movement, and the force of his personality was a major factor in increasing the movement's numerical and political strength. Respected and liked even by some of his longtime adversaries, Jabotinsky has been described as one of the great Zionist leaders after Herzl, a profound thinker, and the driving force behind the birth of the Jewish Brigades, the Haganah, and the IZL. He has been credited with foreseeing the full consequences to the Jews of the rise of Nazism and trying to orchestrate rescue efforts in the form of large-scale evacuations of Jews from Europe to Palestine. His effectiveness in disseminating the idea of a Jewish state and in promoting its realization has also been recognized. The subject of numerous commentaries, his teachings have attained canonical status.

For his Zionist adversaries and other observers who resisted his magnetism, however, Jabotinsky was a disquieting phenomenon—one of a species of nationalist-fascists leaders who sprang up in Europe between the two world wars and was a sworn enemy of socialism and the labor movement and an impetuous statesman. His disregard for the aspirations of Palestinian Arabs, which derived from personal prejudice and a politically expedient approach to the problem of a Jewish homeland, has been regarded by many as his greatest failing.

BIBLIOGRAPHY

For a complete bibliography of Jabotinsky's writings, see ISRAEL JEVAROVITCH, *The Writings of Ze'ev Jabotinsky: A*

Bibliography (in Hebrew; Tel Aviv, 1977). Selections from Jabotinsky's works have been published, but there is no complete edition and no annotated edition. An annotated edition of Jabotinsky's letters was published in 1992. Many books were written about Jabotinsky during his life and after his death. Two comprehensive biographies have been written by admirers: J. B. SCHECHTMAN's *Vladimir Jabotinsky's Story* (2 vols.; Silver Spring, Md., 1956–1961) and SHMUEL KATZ's *Jabotinsky: A Biography* (in Hebrew, 2 vols.; Tel Aviv, 1993). See also RAPHAELLA BILSKI, *Ben-Hur, Every Individual Is a King: The Social and Political Thought of Ze'ev (Vladimir) Jabonitzky* (in Hebrew; Tel Aviv, 1988); O. K. RABINOWICZ, *Vladimir Jabotinsky's Conception of a Nation* (1964); and YAACOV SHAVIT, *Jabotinsky and the Revisionist Movement 1925–1948* (London, 1988).

Yaakov Shavit

Jabr, Salih   [c. 1896–1957]

Iraqi politician.

Jabr was born in al-Nasiryya, in southern Iraq, to a Shi'a Muslim family of limited means. He learned to speak Turkish early in life. During the British occupation of al-Nasiryya, he worked for the British revenue officers as a petty clerk and learned to speak English. In the early 1920s, Jabr graduated from Baghdad Law College. He was appointed judge shortly after graduation because the government of Iraq was dominated by Sunni Muslims and the demand for educated Shi'ites was great. His professional and public career advanced rapidly. He was elected a deputy senator; appointed governor of several provinces; and served as minister of education, justice, finance, social work, the interior, and foreign affairs numerous times. During the Rashid Ali uprising, Jabr was governor of Basra. Because he sided with the regent and helped him to escape from Iraq, he was dismissed as governor, arrested, released a short time later, and allowed to go to Iran. With the collapse of the uprising, he returned to Iraq and was appointed minister of the interior.

On March 29, 1947, the regent invited Jabr to form a new government and appointed him prime minister, the first Shi'ite to hold this post. The regent hoped that Jabr, being a Shi'ite, would secure support for the revision of the Anglo–Iraqi Treaty of 1930. The treaty gave Britain numerous privileges, including the right to have two military bases in Iraq over the next twenty-five years. Many Iraqis were not enthusiastic about Jabr and did not welcome him. The nationalists resented him for his support of the British during the Rashid Ali uprising and for sending hundreds of people to prisons and detention camps when he became minister of the interior after the uprising. The leftists disliked him for marrying the daughter of al-Jaryan, one of the largest landlords in southern Iraq.

Jabr announced a sweeping and ambitious program for his government. On the domestic scene, he called for social, economic, and cultural development. On the international scene, he called for a revision of the Anglo–Iraqi Treaty of 1930, ratification of the Iraq–Transjordan Treaty, and the signing of the Turkish–Iraqi Agreement. As prime minister, Jabr proved to be less liberal than his predecessors. His term in office was marred by violent demonstrations. In less than six months in office, he banned the two moderately Left parties and put their leaders, Kamil Chadirchi and Abd al-Fattah Ibrahim, on trial. Three leaders of the Communist party were sentenced to death. The Portsmouth Treaty—the revision of the Anglo–Iraqi Treaty of 1930—was signed in January 1947. Public dissatisfaction and resentment among the masses led to what came to be known as the Wathba uprising. Violent demonstration erupted against Jabr for several weeks in Baghdad and across Iraq. Virtually every element of Iraq's society—students, teachers, lawyers, doctors, artisans, members of parliment and of political parties—demanded his resignation. Several people lost their lives.

The Wathba uprising underlined the people's resentment of and dissatisfaction with the government and its foreign connections. Several factors contributed: the nationalist resentment over the continuous British interference in Iraq's affairs; the British role in creating the problems in Palestine by the establishment of Israel; and the high cost of living and inflation aggravated by a bad crop year. The Wathba forced Jabr to resign on January 27, 1947. He fled to his home on the Euphrates, then later to Jordan and England. The succeeding government repudiated the treaty.

Jabr was rehabilitated and became minister of the interior in the government of Tawfiq al-Suwaydi in 1950. During his term in office, he introduced a law permitting Iraqi Jews to leave the country, provided they gave up their nationality and property. Over 130,000 Jews left the country.

In 1951, Jabr formed a conservative party, Hizb al-Umma al-Ishtiraki (National Socialist party), to challenge Nuri al-Sa'id. The principles of the party were democracy and nationalism. But in reality, the party was neither democratic nor nationalist, drawing its members largely from tribal and feudal elements. Most of the support came from the Middle Euphrates—Jabr's birthplace—and from the Shi'a community.

Jabr died of a heart attack while giving a speech opposing Prime Minister Nuri al-Sa'id.

[*See also*: Ezra and Nehemia Operations]

BIBLIOGRAPHY

KHADDURI, MAJID. *Independent Iraq 1932–1958: A Study in Iraqi Politics.* London, 1960.
MARR, PHEBE. *The Modern History of Iraq.* Boulder, Colo., 1985.

Ayad al-Qazzaz

Jabri, Rashad [1910–?]

Syrian engineer and politician.

Born in Damascus to Tal'at Jabri, Rashad received a degree in mechanical engineering from Manchester College in the United States. A prominent member of the People's party, he became administrator for Damascus in 1950 and went on to become deputy of Damascus and minister of public works in 1954. Jabri was elected president of the Engineer's syndicate in 1955, and was later appointed minister of agriculture in 1956.

BIBLIOGRAPHY

Who's Who in the Middle East, 1967–1968.

Charles U. Zenzie

Jabri, Shafiq al- [1898–?]

Syrian educator.

Shafiq al-Jabri was born in Damascus. He was educated at the Lazarist College of Damascus from 1904 to 1913. In 1914, he became a writer in Jaffa (then in Palestine). Al-Jabri returned to Syria to direct the Faculty of Arts at the Syrian University from 1918 to 1946. He published a number of literary articles and collections of poetry and was a member of the Arab Language Academy.

BIBLIOGRAPHY

Who's Who in the Arab World.

Charles U. Zenzie

Jacobite Church

See Christians in the Middle East

Jadid, Ghassan [?–1957]

Syrian military leader and politician.

Born in Latakia of Alawi descent, Ghassan Jadid was a leading officer loyal to the SYRIAN SOCIAL NATIONALIST PARTY (PPS). After Adib Shishakli's downfall in 1954, the party attempted to retain some control over military affairs by assassinating Adnan al-MALKI, deputy chief of staff of the army. Jadid, then a major, had been dismissed from the army two weeks prior to the murder, but as secretary-general of the party, he was indicted on June 29, 1955, for his involvement. He and other PPS leaders fled to Beirut and conceived the ill-fated 1956 plot to restore Adib Shishakli to power in Syria. Jadid was assassinated by a fellow Syrian in Beirut on February 19, 1957, eight days before the death sentence for the major conspirators was handed down.

BIBLIOGRAPHY

SEALE, PATRICK. *The Struggle for Syria: A Study of Post-War Arab Politics, 1945–1958.* London, 1958.

Charles U. Zenzie

Jadirji, Kamil

See Chadirchi, Kamil

Jaffa

An ancient port on the central coast of the eastern Mediterranean, south of modern Tel Aviv, Israel.

Jaffa, also known as Joppa, became an important entrepôt in the nineteenth century when the local rulers constructed walls, planned markets, established a central mosque, and built a road leading to Jerusalem. Occupied by the Egyptian Ibrahim Pasha in 1831, Jaffa prospered because the Egyptians encouraged trade, immigrated to the city, and relaxed restrictions against minorities. With the return of Ottoman rule after 1840, the port became a stop for steamships plying the eastern Mediterranean and, after the opening of the Suez Canal in 1869, for ocean-going liners. The port was expanded to accomodate grain, olive, and citrus exports. Jaffa was linked to Jerusalem by road and rail to serve pilgrims and tourists. German Templer and American colonies were established near the city.

The population expanded from 5,000 in the mid-nineteenth century to nearly 40,000 in 1914, of whom 15,000 were Jews. They made Jaffa the center for the first and second ALIYAH until the develop-

Ships beached off Jaffa, 1880. (Arnold Blumberg, Towson State University Media Services. From Sir Charles Wilson, *Picturesque Palestine, Sinai and Egypt.* London, 1884.)

Ibrahim Pasha's army camped outside Jaffa, 1841. (Arnold Blumberg, Towson State University Media Services. From William Henry Bartlett, *Walks in and About the City of Jerusalem.* London, 1844.)

ment of Tel Aviv just to the north of Jaffa. The city was deserted during World War I because the port was closed, citizens were conscripted into the Turkish army, and the Turks forced many of the inhabitants to leave the city. Under the British mandate, as Tel Aviv developed into an almost exclusively Jewish city, Jaffa expanded. Its population, the majority of whom were Arabs, reached more than 30,000 in 1922.

A center of opposition to Zionism, Jaffa suffered during the strike called during the 1936 to 1939 Arab rebellion. The rebellion paralyzed the port; it did not recover, and the port of Tel Aviv replaced it. Most of the Jews left Jaffa at that time.

Riots broke out after the United Nations decision to partition Palestine in 1947 and, in the fighting that ensued, the Jews took the city (May, 1948). Most of

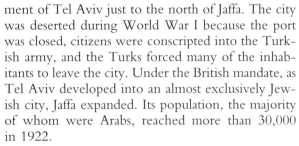

Artists' quarter in Jaffa. (Mia Bloom)

Marina at the port of Jaffa. (Miriam Simon)

Ottoman clock tower at an intersection in Jaffa. (Miriam Simon)

the 65,000 Arabs abandoned the city—only 4,000 remained. A large number of Jewish immigrants were housed in the city, and in 1950, Jaffa was incorporated into the Tel Aviv municipality.

In the 1960s, reconstruction of Jaffa was undertaken with the planting of gardens, renovation of old buildings, and the creation of an art and tourist center in the area of Jaffa Hill.

BIBLIOGRAPHY

KARK, RUTH. *Jaffa: A City in Revolution, 1799–1917.* Jerusalem, 1990.

Reeva S. Simon

Jaffa Riots

Violent outbreak between Arabs and Jews in Jaffa, leading to the 1936–1939 Palestinian Arab Revolt.

The Arabs of Palestine had been part of the Ottoman Empire, as were the Zionist Jewish settlers at the turn of the century. With the advent of World War I, the political climate changed in the Middle East—the Ottoman Empire was dismembered by the winning side, and the League of Nations awarded Britain the mandate over Palestine (1922–1948). Because of promises the British had made to both the Jews and

the Arabs, both sides felt that eventually they would have a sovereign state in the region. The Arabs had helped the British militarily; in return for that help and for the petroleum that had been found throughout the region, the British were willing to create Arab states within their jurisdiction, such as Iraq under Faisal I ibn Husayn.

Palestine was the only area in the large Arab and Islamic region that might not conform to the pan-Arabist ideal. In the 1920s and 1930s, various agreements concerning a Zionist state coexistent with or next to an Arab state were rejected by the Arab representatives. Nevertheless, with European anti-Semitism focused by Nazi Germany in the 1930s and 1940s, Palestine was one of the only places that Jewish refugees might be saved from the Holocaust. As increasing numbers of Jews came into Palestine, at the port of Jaffa, the Arab inhabitants became frustrated and fighting broke out.

The April riots in Jaffa followed fighting in a number of cities, and a rumor circulated that several Arabs had been killed in nearby Tel Aviv. In four days of rioting, Arab rioters killed some nine to twenty Jews, but a similar number of Arabs were killed by police. Several months later, the British retaliated by blowing up 237 Arab houses in Jaffa and displacing 6,000 residents. This was followed by the PALESTINE ARAB REVOLT and General Strike of 1936, led by the Arab Higher Committee; it was directed against both the British and the Zionists.

BIBLIOGRAPHY

HIRST, DAVID. *The Gun and the Olive Branch.* London, 1977. Reprint, London, 1984.
MATTAR, PHILIP. *The Mufti of Jerusalem.* New York, 1988.
ROLEF, S. H., ed. *Political Dictionary of the State of Israel.* New York, 1988.
SYKES, CHRISTOPHER. *Crossroads to Israel 1917–1948.* Bloomington, Ind., 1965.

Elizabeth Thompson

Jaghbub

Desert oasis deep in the Cyrenaica region of Libya.

Jaghbub served as the headquarters of the Sufi SANUSI ORDER of Islam, from 1856 to 1895. From this strategic center, a large network of Sanusi lodges was established throughout the northeastern Sahara. The tomb of the order's founder, Sidi Muhammad ibn Ali al-Sanusi (died 1859), is located there.

Will D. Swearingen

Jalalabad

Small city in eastern Afghanistan.

Jalalabad had a population estimated at 56,000 as of 1979, before the Soviet intervention in Afghanistan (1979–1988). During that civil war of Afghanistan factions and Soviet troops, Jalalabad was a vital link in the black-market arms trade from Peshawar, Pakistan, through the Kunar valley to Afghan guerillas.

During the nineteenth century, Jalalabad was the northern line of defense for the British during the first Afghan war (1840–1842).

BIBLIOGRAPHY

Webster's New Geographical Dictionary. 1988.

Zachary Karabell

Jaleh Square

Site of a mass killing of civilians in Iran.

The incident at Jaleh Square took place on Friday, 8 September 1979, in Tehran, on the eve of the IRANIAN REVOLUTION. Martial law had been declared on 7 September, and in the Jaleh Square, situated in the *bazaari* residential area in eastern Tehran, government forces clashed with demonstrators and, unable to disperse them, shot into the crowds. Over five hundred people were killed, and the incident, known afterward as the "Black Friday massacre," was a watershed in the confrontation between the government and the people of Iran.

BIBLIOGRAPHY

ABRAHAMIAN, ERVAND. *Iran between Two Revolutions.* Princeton, N.J., 1982.

Neguin Yavari

Jallud, Abd al-Salam   [1944–   ]

Libya's second in command.

A childhood friend of Muammar al-QADDAFI, Abd al-Salam Jallud has been the second most powerful figure in Libya since the military coup that brought Qaddafi to power on September 1, 1969. Like Qaddafi a graduate of the Libyan military academy, he was a captain when he joined in planning the coup against the Libyan monarchy; upon its success, he was promoted to major and made the de facto deputy chair of the ruling Revolutionary Command Council. He was the country's premier until 1977, when the establishment of the JAMAHIRIYA was pro-

claimed; in 1979, both he and Qaddafi resigned their formal government positions, but they remained in full control of the affairs of state.

Jallud is considered more pragmatic, less ideological, a more skilled negotiator, and less impervious to temptations of the flesh than Qaddafi. Although his loyalty has been the subject of much speculation, there has been no confirmed evidence of a serious rift between these old friends.

Lisa Anderson

Jalluli Family

A family important in the commercial elite of nineteenth-century Tunisia.

The Jalluli family was influential at the bey's court, and thus secured ILTIZAM (tax farms), monopolies, and supply contracts. They were also *qa'id*s of SFAX, and thereby responsible for the collection of taxes and security in that city.

Important members of the family in the nineteenth century were Mahmud (d. 1839), Muhammad (d. 1849), and Hassunah. In the 1830s Mahmud made his fortune as a corsair. Between 1805 and 1808, he had been chief customs collector, one of the most lucrative concessionary posts; he was also a prominent figure at the bey's court under Hammudah Pasha (ruler of Tunisia, 1777–1814). Muhammad ran the *qiyada* of Sfax for a number of years. In 1829, the Jallulis saved the government of Husayn Bey from bankruptcy. In 1864, Hassunah gained the *qiyada* of Sfax. Following the insurrection of 1864, the family was regarded by Muhammad al-Sadiq Bey as a stabilizing force.

The Jallulis' tradition of state service continued into the twentieth century. Many Jallulis are prominent in Tunisia's commercial and political elite.

BIBLIOGRAPHY

BROWN, L. CARL. *The Tunisia of Ahmad Bey, 1837–1855.* Princeton, N.J., 1974.

PERKINS, KENNETH J. *Historical Dictionary of Tunisia.* Metuchen, N.J., 1989.

Larry A. Barrie

Jamahiriya

In Libya, "rule of the masses."

This new word was coined by Muammar al-QADDAFI and adopted by the Libyan GENERAL PEOPLE'S CONGRESS in 1977 as part of the country's official name: the Socialist People's Libyan Arab Jamahiriya. It is designed to convey the abolition of "government" and the beginning of the "era of people's authority" in Libya.

Lisa Anderson

Jamal al-Din al-Afghani

See Afghani, Jamal al-Din al-

Jamali, Muhammad Fadhil al-   [1903–   ]

Iraqi educator, diplomat, and prime minister.

A Shi'ite born in Kazimayn of a lower middle-class family, Jamali had a religious education, studying in al-Najaf. He attended the newly established Teachers Training College in Baghdad, and was sent to the American University of Beirut, receiving a B.A. in 1927. He did post-graduate work at Teachers College, Columbia University, in New York, where he wrote on the problems of bedouin education. He returned to Iraq in 1932 and served in the ministry of education until 1942.

Touring Europe in 1937, he made arrangements for an Iraqi delegation to attend the Nuremburg rally the following year. His admiration of Germany was expressed in a published comparative study of education—*Ittijahat al-Tarbiyya wa al-Ta'lim fi Almaniya wa Inkiltera wa Faransa* (Modern Ways of Training and Culture in Germany, England, and France), and in the institution of the *futuwwa* (paramilitary) youth movement in Iraq. In the late 1930s, he also invited teachers from Syria and Palestine to write textbooks and teach in Iraq.

Jamali encouraged Shi'ites to attend the Teachers College and used his position as director-general in the ministry of education to spread schools to the rural south and to provide scholarships for Shi'ites to study abroad. Not being directly involved in Prime Minister Rashid Ali al-Kaylani's government, he retained his post in the ministry of education after 1941.

From 1942 until the end of the monarchy in 1958, he served in various posts for the ministry of foreign affairs, including Washington, D.C., the United Nations, and the Arab League, except for a brief tenure as prime minister from September 1953 to April 1954. Jamali served during a period of disastrous floods. Dissatisfaction with his flood relief program and his involvement in the regent's intervention in Syrian politics led to a change of government.

After the revolution of 1958, Jamali was tried by the revolutionary military tribunal and spent three years in prisons, after which he moved to Tunis, Tunisia.

BIBLIOGRAPHY

SIMON, REEVA S. *Iraq Between the Two World Wars.* New York, 1986.

Reeva S. Simon

Jamal Pasha

See Cemal Paça

Jamalzadeh, Mohammad Ali   [1892–?]

Iranian short story writer.

Mohammad Ali Jamalzadeh was born in Isfahan, Iran, and studied in Tehran, Beirut, and Paris. From 1916 to 1930, he worked for the Iranian embassy in Berlin and participated with a group of Iranian intellectuals there to publish the journal *Kaveh.* Jamalzadeh is known as the pioneer of Iranian short stories in the Western style. In 1921, he published *Yeki bud yeki nabud* (Once upon a Time), a collection of six stories with a simple and flowing narrative style characteristically distinct from classic Iranian written prose. Later, Jamalzadeh moved to Switzerland as the representative for the International Employment Agency in Geneva. His autobiographical work, *Sar-o tah yek karbas* (Cut from the Same Cloth), was published in English as *Isfahan Is Half the World: Memories of a Persian Boyhood* in 1983.

BIBLIOGRAPHY

MOAYYAD, HESHMAT, ed. *Stories from Iran: A Chicago Anthology, 1921–1991.* Washington, D.C., 1991.

Pardis Minuchehr

Jami'a al-Arabiyya, al-

Palestinian newspaper.

A Jerusalem weekly established in 1927 and edited by Munif al-Husayni of the prominent HUSAYNI FAMILY, *Jami'a al-Arabiyya* was a mouthpiece for the mufti (canon lawyer of Jerusalem) Amin al-Husayni. In 1928, it inaugurated a campaign calling for enforcement of Muslim ownership of the Western (Wailing) Wall and for protection of the al-Aqsa mosque. In the 1930s, its anti-British, pan-Arab ideology was expressed by a map of the Arab world printed on the back page of each issue.

In the 1930s, the paper led a long campaign against renewed Jewish immigration after the rise of the Nazi government in Germany. A pro-Italy editorial written by Munif al-Husayni in 1935 caused a furor among opposition parties.

BIBLIOGRAPHY

MATTAR, PHILIP. *The Mufti of Jerusalem.* New York, 1988.
PORATH, Y. *The Emergence of the Palestinian-Arab National Movement 1918–1929.* London, 1974.

Elizabeth Thompson

Jami'at-e Islami

Afghan Islamist political party.

Jami'at-e Islami, Islamic Society, began in Kabul in 1971. It was conceived as a group whose mission was to fight the increasing secular and leftist trends in Afghanistan. In 1975, the party moved its headquarters to Peshawar, Pakistan, and became a political and guerilla resistance organization dedicated to the overthrow of the Afghan Marxist government. In 1978, Burhanuddin Rabbani became its leader. Advocating the establishment of an Islamic government in Afghanistan and strict adherence to SHARI'A, the Islamic law, Jami'at has connections with other international Islamist movements, including the Muslim Brotherhood and the Jami'at-e Islami of Pakistan.

During the war of resistance (1978–1992), the Jami'at was generally allied with the other Islamist parties, but it was considered one of the more moderate ones. In part because Rabbani is a Tajik, Jami'at's greatest following is to be found among Tajik, and other non-Pushtun Afghans, although there are also Jami'at adherents among some Pushtun commanders. The Jami'at party consequently dominates much of northern Afghanistan and numbers among its commanders Ahmad Shah Mas'ud, who controls the Panjshir valley north of Kabul, and Isma'il Khan, who controls Herat province.

In 1992, the Jami'at party returned to Kabul along with the other resistance groups to take part in the government. In 1993, Rabbani became president of Afghanistan in a rotating presidency, but he refused to leave office when his term expired in June 1994. With its hold on the presidency and with access to the military capability of Ahmad Shah Mas'ud, Jami'at continues to control Afghanistan, but opposition from other groups, particularly those of HEKMATYAR and Doestam, makes its leadership shaky.

BIBLIOGRAPHY

FARR, GRANT. "The Failure of the Mujahedin." *Middle East International* 476 (1994): 19–20.

Grant Farr

Jamil, Naji

Syrian military officer.

Born to a Sunni Islam family in Dayr al-Zawr province, Naji Jamil became an air force officer and head of the military police in Syria. As a non-Alawi officer of the BA'TH party, he was active in the rise of President Hafiz al-Asad. He became Syria's deputy defense minister in 1977 and was retired from the post the following year.

BIBLIOGRAPHY

SEALE, PATRICK. *Asad: The Struggle for the Middle East.* Los Angeles, 1988.

Charles U. Zenzie

Jandali, Farhan   [1910–?]

Syrian physician and politician.

Born in Homs to Sa'dallah al-Jandali, Farhan received a doctor of medicine degree from Berlin University and specialized in ophthalmology. He practiced in the city of his birth and, as a member of the People's party, was elected deputy of Homs in 1947. Jandali was appointed minister of national economy and then of education in the politically turbulent year of 1950.

BIBLIOGRAPHY

SEALE, PATRICK. *The Struggle for Syria: A Study of Post-War Arab Politics, 1945–1958.* London, 1965.

Charles U. Zenzie

Jangali

A nationalist and reformist movement in Iran in the early twentieth century.

The Jangali movement was formed in the forests (*jangal*) of northwestern Iran. Its members, under the leadership of Mirza Kuchek Khan and Ehsan Allah Khan, were intent on eradicating foreign influence in the country.

The Jangalis were active in the constitutional revolution of 1905–1911, and their aim was to restore the sovereignty and autonomy of Iran under a broad Islamic framework. They established a revolutionary council, Ettehad-e Eslam (Islamic unity), published a newspaper called *Jangal,* and enlisted the help of Ottoman and German military advisers. The Jangalis stole from the rich landowners of Gilan to give to the poor and to support their movement. The 1917 Bolshevik revolution in Russia enhanced their standing in Iran. The movement spread to Mazandaran, another Caspian province, and in 1918 the Jangalis nearly took Qazvin. In that year, the British signed an agreement with Mirza Kuchek Khan, in which Britain would recognize Jangali autonomy in Gilan in return for a cessation of hostilities between the two camps and the expulsion of all German and Ottoman Jangali advisers. The agreement was seen as a compromise by the more radical faction of the movement under the leadership of Ehsan Allah Khan, and their split enabled the Cossack Brigade, dispatched from Tehran, to temporarily quell the uprising. Following the Russian revolution of 1917, Russian troops invaded Rasht, the capital of the province of Gilan, in 1920, and Mirza Kuchek Khan proclaimed the Socialists Republic of Gilan. The Soviet–Iranian treaty of 1921 stopped Soviet aggression in the country; the Soviets withdrew their troops and Reza Khan, later to become the first Pahlavi monarch, obliterated the Jangalis by October 1921. Mirza Kuchek Khan was executed, and Ehsan Allah Khan fled to the USSR.

BIBLIOGRAPHY

SAVORY, R. M. "Djangali." In *Encyclopedia of Islam,* 2nd ed. Leiden, 1983.

Neguin Yavari

Janissaries

Military corps in the Ottoman Empire's army from late fourteenth century to 1826.

The term *janissary* is the anglicized form of the Turkish *yeni çeri* (new troops). The Janissary Corps was established in the early years of the reign of Murad I (1360–1389). Its foundation reflected the growing complexity of the OTTOMAN EMPIRE and the sultan's need to have under his direct control a regular and well-disciplined infantry force that could be used against both foreign and domestic military challenges. The Janissaries constituted the central element within a new military establishment known as *kapıkulu* (also *kapukulu,* "slaves of the [sultan's] gate"). The corps' first recruits were from the ranks of young Christian prisoners of war; they were converted to Islam, taught Turkish, and given a rigorous military training. At the end of the fourteenth century, to supplement the numbers of prisoners, the Ottomans instituted the *devşirme* (collecting) recruitment system—a periodic conscription of Christian boys from the Balkans and Anatolia. During the fifteenth and sixteenth centuries, the *devşirme* was the main source of new recruits for the corps. The system insured that the janissaries, having severed their bonds with their families and previous lives and having been forced to celibacy, would have no other loyalties but to their comrades in arms and the sultan. Superbly trained and equipped with the most modern arms, they became the most effective fighting organization of the time, and they played the leading role in the vast Ottoman military conquests of the fifteenth and sixteenth centuries. Conscious of their power, the janissaries often intervened in affairs of state and mutinied to secure their interests. Controlling them was a constant challenge to Ottoman rulers.

The janissaries were organized as a corps, known as *ocak* (hearth), comprising three divisions. The tactical unit was the *orta* (company), which varied in size. In its final form, the corps consisted of 196 companies. The *ocak* was commanded by a general officer, known as the *ağa* of the janissaries (*yeniçeri ağası*), who was assigned a special residence and headquarters in the capital. He was also in charge of police duties and the maintenance of public order throughout most of the quarters of Istanbul, the Ottoman capital. The janissaries were closely affiliated with the Bektashi order of dervishes.

At the end of the sixteenth century, the Janissary Corps began to admit untrained, mostly Muslim-born, recruits. The *devşirme* was now used less frequently, but it continued to be employed, although with increasing irregularity, until the beginning of the eighteenth century. The admission of untrained recruits marked the beginning of the janissaries' decline as a fighting force and their growing corruption—a trend closely connected to wider processes of general decline within the empire. The basic regulations that had preserved the special character of the corps for some two centuries were now treated with growing laxity, until they were abandoned altogether. The janissaries were allowed to marry and have families; then, in order to support their dependents, they were permitted to engage in gainful activities. Over the years, an ever-increasing number of janissaries gave up the practice of living at the barracks and training regularly, until the corps became largely a poorly trained and undisciplined militia. Commissions were sold to the highest bidders, and numerous civilians seeking to enjoy tax exemptions and other privileges bought their way into the corps. Consequently, the numbers of the janissaries steadily increased from 12,000 in the early sixteenth century to 140,000 around 1820. The great majority of these men were not soldiers, but shopkeepers, artisans, porters, and followers of other trades, who rarely performed any military duties but zealously defended their privileged position. Identified with large segments of the urban population, they became a powerful caste resisting change.

The janissaries consistently opposed attempts to introduce military reforms, because those required training and submission to discipline. They also objected to any attempts to create a new military force that might replace them or threaten their privileged position. Consequently, due to janissary opposition, throughout most of the eighteenth century, the European-style military reforms adopted by Ottoman rulers could be introduced only in the relatively small, technical military branches, such as the artillery, the bombardiers, and the Ottoman navy.

In the last decade of the eighteenth century, Selim III (ruled 1789–1807) hesitatingly introduced a new infantry corps known as the NIZAM-I CEDIT. The janissaries, however, objected to the new force, and they eventually led a coalition of conservative forces that overthrew Selim and abolished his reforms (May 1807). An attempt by the grand vizier, BAYRAKDAR (Alemdar) Mustafa Pasha, to reintroduce the Nizam-i Cedit was also foiled by the janissaries, and Bayrakdar himself was killed (November 1808).

Following Bayrakdar's death, Mahmud II (ruled 1808–1839) concluded a pact with the janissaries, known as *Sened-i Ita'at* (Deed of Obedience), promising not to introduce military reforms in return for a janissary commitment not to intervene in political affairs. However, the Greek War of Independence that broke out in 1821 (lasting until 1830), with the possibility of European intervention, confronted the Ottoman Empire with new and dangerous challenges. The janissaries proved ineffective against the Greek insurgents, and the sultan was forced to enlist the support of his governor of Egypt, Muhammad Ali Pasha, with his new European-style, modern army. The ineffectiveness of the janissaries contrasted poorly with the discipline and good performance of the Egyptian troops, creating thereby a general public mood more favorable to military reform. Capitalizing on these changes, early in 1826, Mahmud proposed a plan (the *Eşkinci/Eşkenci* project) to reform a small segment of the Janissary Corps and transform it into a regular, modern, European-style force. Although most of the senior officers approved the plan, a short while after its implementation the janissaries once again rose in rebellion. The sultan, however, had taken precautions against such a possibility. With the support of the *ulama* (body of Islamic scholars) and the general public, loyal forces, including artillery and naval units, quickly suppressed the re-

bellion with considerable bloodshed (June 15, 1826). Mahmud seized the opportunity to abolish completely the Janissary Corps and the Bektashi order affiliated with it.

Thus came the end to an institution that had existed for almost five centuries and that had become a hallmark of Ottoman power in both its greatness and decline. The suppression of the janissaries made a great impression on contemporaries in the Ottoman Empire and abroad. It became known in Ottoman history as the Beneficial Event (VAKA-I HAYRIYE). It also cleared the way for comprehensive, European-style military and administrative reforms that, in the long run, affected every aspect of society and extended the life of the Ottoman Empire into the twentieth century.

BIBLIOGRAPHY

GIBB, HAMILTON, and HAROLD BOWEN. *Islamic Society and the West*, part 1. London, 1950.

LEVY, AVIGDOR. "The *Eşkenci* Project: An Ottoman Attempt at Gradual Reform (1826)." *Abr-Nahrain* 14 (1974): 32–39.

SHAW, STANFORD J., and EZEL KURAL SHAW. *History of the Ottoman Empire and Modern Turkey*. Cambridge, Mass., 1976–1977.

UZUNÇARŞILI, İSMAIL HAKKI. *Osmanlı Devleti Teşkilâtından Kapukulu Ocakları I: Acemi Ocağı ve Yeniçeri Ocağı* (The Kapukulu Corps in the organization of the Ottoman state, vol. I: The Acemi Corps and the Janissary Corps). Ankara, 1943.

Avigdor Levy

Japan and the Middle East

Japan's main concern is to secure an oil supply without jeopardizing relations with the United States.

In the 1990s, Japan relied on petroleum from the Persian/Arabian GULF and estimated that more than 70 percent of its national consumption comes from that region. Given an expected decline in oil production outside the Middle East, Japan's dependence on Gulf producers is expected to increase and, therefore, Japan has a vital interest in securing good relations. In the past, however, this has caused problems in Japan's relations with the United States, especially in the 1970s and 1980s. For example, during the oil embargo (1973–1978) by the Organization of Petroleum Exporting Countries (OPEC), Japan took a pro-Arab position in the interpretation of UN Security Council Resolution 242, which called for Israel's total withdrawal from all the territories taken and occupied in the 1967 ARAB–ISRAEL WAR. This

Japanese-built suspension bridge in Istanbul. (Mia Bloom)

pro-Arab stance strained Japan's relations with the United States, then Israel's strongest ally.

Japan's relations with Iran since the Iranian Revolution of 1979 is another case in point. Tokyo maintained good relations with Iran's rulers in Tehran, even when the United States tried to isolate Iran during the U.S. embassy hostage crisis (1979–1981) and during the final stages of the IRAN–IRAQ WAR (1980–1988). Japan's desire to court Middle East oil producers, such as Iran and Saudi Arabia, thus came into direct conflict with its policy of support for its most important ally, the United States.

BIBLIOGRAPHY

KATUKURU, KUNIO, and MOTOKO KATAKURA. *Japan and the Middle East.* Tokyo, 1991.

Kazuo Takahashi

Jarallah Family

Prominent Palestinian family from Jerusalem.

The Jarallahs belonged to Jerusalem's old Muslim elite, and were counted among the city's *ashraf* or descendents of the Prophet Muhammad. Family members held religious posts in Jerusalem for hundreds of years and emerged at the end of the nineteenth century among the local Ottoman bureaucratic-landowning class, although less influential than the Husaynis and Nashashibis.

In 1921, Husam al-Din Jarallah, a graduate of al-Azhar, received the highest number of votes in an election for mufti (canon lawyer) of Jerusalem. But

the rival Husaynis organized a petition campaign and succeeded in placing their candidate, al-Hajj Amin al-Husayni, in the post. Husam nonetheless served as chief justice of the religious courts, and in 1948 was finally appointed mufti by Jordan's King Abdullah, to replace the anti-Hashimite Husayni. While Husam al-Din was a pro-Hashimite moderate, other family members took stronger stands against Zionism. Hasan Jarallah, for example, in 1918 helped found an organization that took violent action against Arabs who sold land to Jews, called Jam'iyyat al-Ikha wa al-Afaf (Association of Brotherhood and Purity).

BIBLIOGRAPHY

MATTAR, PHILIP. *The Mufti of Jerusalem.* New York, 1988.
MUSLIH, MUHAMMAD. *The Origins of Palestinian Nationalism.* New York, 1988.

Elizabeth Thompson

Jarash

Jordanian town and archeological site.

Lying 29 miles (47 km) north of Jordan's capital city, Amman, the ruins at Jarash are some of the most famous in the Middle East and, along with PETRA, one of Jordan's two main tourist attractions.

Founded as part of Alexander the Great's empire (c. 334 B.C.E.), Jerash became a thriving Roman provincial city during the first to third centuries C.E. It was one of the ten cities of the Decapolis, a commercial federation in Roman Syria. After its decline from shifting trade routes, Jarash lay in ruins until about 1884, when the Ottoman Empire introduced CIRCASSIANS (Muslims from the Caucasus mountains fleeing Russian rule).

The first European to report on Jarash's Roman ruins was the German Ulrich J. Seetzen in 1806. Serious restoration and archeological work began in the 1920s on the city's amphitheater, forum, colonnaded road, temples, churches, and other buildings, which now offer one of the best examples of provincial architecture from the Roman Empire. The 1991 population was about 21,600.

BIBLIOGRAPHY

HARDING, G. LANKESTER. *The Antiquities of Jordan,* 2nd ed. Amman, 1967.
SHOWKER, KAY. *Fodor's Jordan and the Holy Land.* New York, 1984.
Statistical Yearbook 1991. General Statistics Department, Jordan.

Michael R. Fischbach

Jarida, al-

Egyptian liberal daily newspaper.

Edited by Ahmad Lutfi al-SAYYID from 1907 to 1914, *al-Jarida* was the first Egyptian journal to be owned by a limited-liability corporation. Read by many Egyptian intellectuals, it served as the organ of the Umma party and was also a pioneer in Arabic literary criticism, social reform, and feminism. Among its contributors were Muhammad Husayn HAYKAL, Taha HUSAYN, and Malak Hifni NASIF. It claimed to reflect purely Egyptian interests and to be independent of British, Ottoman, or khedivial influences. Unwilling to submit to wartime press censorship, it closed in 1915.

Arthur Goldschmidt, Jr.

Jarring, Gunnar   [1907–?]

Swedish diplomat.

Jarring was Sweden's representative to the United Nations (1956–1958), and Swedish ambassador to the United States (1958–1964) and the Soviet Union (1964–1973). Between 1967 and 1971, he was also the UN special representative to the Middle East. In the aftermath of the ARAB–ISRAEL WAR (1967), Jarring shuttled between the Arab capitals and Jerusalem in an unsuccessful attempt to forge a consensus on the proper implementation of UN Resolution 242. The Jarring talks were then broken off and were resumed at the end of 1969, but the inability of Israel and Jordan to agree on the status of Jerusalem led to a breakdown in negotiations. Again in his capacity as UN envoy, Jarring participated in the diplomatic dance that resulted in the cease-fire initiative of U.S. Secretary of State William ROGERS in July 1970, after which the Jarring mission was suspended yet again. It was finally terminated in the spring of 1971, after the Israelis indicted Jarring for entering into unauthorized peace negotiations with Egypt's president, Anwar al-SADAT.

BIBLIOGRAPHY

SAFRAN, NADAV. *Israel: The Embattled Ally.* Cambridge, U.K., 1981.

SHIMONI, YAACOV, ed. *Political Dictionary of the Middle East in the Twentieth Century.* New York, 1974.

SPIEGEL, STEVEN. *The Other Arab–Israeli Conflict.* Chicago, 1985.

Zachary Karabell

Jassy, Treaty of

Ended war between Russia and Ottoman Empire.

In 1787, Russia and Austria went to war against the Ottoman Empire. After four years of intermittent warfare, Empress Catherine II of Russia and Sultan Selim III decided to terminate the conflict. Russia was under pressure from Prussia and Britain to end the war, and the Austrians had already concluded a separate peace by August 1791. The Treaty of Jassy was signed on January 9, 1792, after months of negotiations. While Russia renounced its claim to Bessarabia and Moldavia, it finally obtained legal possession of the long coveted khanates of the Crimea. In addition, the sultan ceded the Russians the territory between the Bug and Dneister rivers, including the Ottoman fortress of Ochakov.

Russian commercial rights to the Turkish straits were also affirmed. The treaty had at least two major consequences. After Jassy, it was clear that Russia had supplanted Austria as the major rival to the Ottomans. This transition was already apparent at the time of the Treaty of KUÇUK KAYNARJA in 1774, but Jassy marked its completion. In the nineteenth century, it was Russia that posed the single greatest threat to the integrity of the Ottoman Empire. For the Ottomans, Jassy acted as a spur to domestic reform. This tendency was also evident prior to Jassy, but in the aftermath of the treaty, Selim III enacted a series of extensive reforms that ultimately had serious repercussions for Ottoman society. Embassies and consulates were opened in the major European cities, and Selim began to restructure the Ottoman military along European lines. For these reasons, Jassy is often cited as a watershed in the history of the Eastern Question.

BIBLIOGRAPHY

ANDERSON, M. S. *The Eastern Question.* London, 1966.

HUREWITZ, J. C., ed. *The Middle East and North Africa in World Politics.* New Haven, Conn., 1975.

LEWIS, BERNARD. *The Emergence of Modern Turkey.* New York, 1961.

Zachary Karabell

Javid, Mehmed

See Cavit, Mehmet

Jawahiri, Muhammad Mahdi al-   [1900–]

The leading neoclassical poet of modern Iraq.

Al-Jawahiri, born in al-Najaf, became a teacher in the 1920s. His poetry brought him to the notice of

King Faisal I, who became his patron and protector. Closely associated with the Communist party, al-Jawahiri became president of the Journalists' Association after the Revolution of 1958, and was Iraq's ambassador to Czechoslovakia until 1963. He returned to Iraq in the early 1970s but went into exile in Damascus a few years later. He is famous for his forceful revolutionary poetry.

Peter Sluglett

Jawdah, Michel Abu

Newspaper columnist in Lebanon.

Jawdah started his career with the daily *al-Nahar*. Soon promoted to daily columnist, he expressed moderate and politically independent views that made him one of the most influential columnists in the Arab world. His writings were often directed at corruption and foreign policy mismanagement in the Arab world. Jawdah's criticisms of the Syrian's regime in the 1970s led to his kidnapping and torture, reportedly by members of a pro-Syria militia in Lebanon. He clashed frequently with the government of Sulayman FRANJIYYA. After *al-Nahar*'s editor, Ghassan TWAYNI, became heavily involved in political affairs, Jawdah assumed the editorial responsibility for the paper, which became less and less influential over the years as other newspapers (like *al-Hayat* and *al-Safir*) came to prominence.

As'ad AbuKhalil

Jawdat, 'Ali

See Ayyubi, Ali Jawdat al-

Jazira, al-

Plateau in Syria situated between the Tigris and the Euphrates rivers.

It is bounded on the north and east by the TAURUS and ZAGROS mountains, on the west and southwest by the SYRIAN desert, and on the southeast by Mesopotamia. The plateau of al-Jazira rises from 656 to 1476 feet (200–450 m) from the southeast and to the northwest. It includes a number of mountains, among which are Jabal Abd al-Aziz and Jabal Sinjar, the latter of which has an elevation of 4790 feet (1460 m). These mountains give rise to a number of rivers, the most important of which are the Balikh, the Khabur, and Tharthar. Dry-terraced valleys, known as WADIs, multiply in al-Jazira.

Al-Jazira had great importance historically. Across it, lines of communication connected Mesopotamia (now Iraq) with Anatolia and Syria, and Armenia and Persia (now Iran) with Syria. Several market towns and cities on the banks of the Khabur, the TIGRIS, and their tributaries were established in al-Jazira. In the last few decades, al-Jazira was transformed from pasture land frequented by nomads to a developing agricultural land profiting from the rivers' waters and producing principally grains. The establishment by Syria of the TABAQA DAM on the Euphrates was intended to promote agriculture. The discovery of oil in al-Jazira and its inclusion in the railway network linking it to the Syrian seaports promise to make it a major economic region. The present-day province of al-Hasaka in Syria was earlier known as the province of al-Jazira.

Abdul-Karim Rafeq

Jazira, al-

Newspaper of Saudi Arabia.

Al-Jazira is printed daily in Arabic at Riyadh, the capital of Saudi Arabia. It is one of the nation's eleven key dailies (three of which are published in English).

Les Ordeman

Jazrawi, Taha al-   [1938–   ]

Iraqi government official.

Taha al-Jazrawi was born in Mosul, Iraq, to a working-class Arabized Kurdish family. In 1959, he was dismissed from the army by the regime of Abd al-Karim KASSEM, because of his BA'TH leanings. In 1966, he became a member of the Ba'th party's regional leadership, and after the Ba'th takeover in 1968, he supervised the purging of the army. Since 1969, al-Jazrawi has been a member of the Revolutionary Command Council; since 1972, he has commanded the Ba'th militia. He is one of the ideological hard-liners among Saddam HUSSEIN's entourage, always toeing Hussein's line. Between 1979 and 1991 he was first deputy prime minister, following which he was appointed vice president. Excluding Hussein's family, by early 1992, al-Jazrawi was still one of the few most powerful individuals in Ba'thi Iraq; his power base rests in the city of Mosul and in the party apparatus.

BIBLIOGRAPHY

BARAM, AMATZIA. "The Ruling Political Elite in Ba'thi Iraq, 1968–1986. *International Journal of Middle East Studies* 21 (1989): 447–493.

Amatzia Baram

Jazzar, Ahmad al-

See Ahmad al-Jazzar

JDC

See Joint Distribution Committee

Jebhe-ye Azadi-ye Afghanistan

Afghan political organization.

The Jebhe-ye Azadi-ye Afghanistan, also called the Hezb-e Azadi-ye Afghanistan (the Front for the Freedom of Afghanistan), was a clandestine organization formed to fight the Afghan Marxist government in the early 1980s. The group was composed mostly of Shi'ites, particularly Qizilbash, but the identity of the membership was kept secret. The Jebhe led an unsuccessful antigovernment demonstration in the Chendawal district of Kabul in 1979. Later, most of its members joined the Shi'a party Harakat-e Islami of Shaykh Mohseni.

BIBLIOGRAPHY

FARR, GRANT. "The New Afghan Middle Class as Refugees and Insurgents." In *Afghan Resistance: The Politics of Survival,* ed. by Grant Farr and John Merriam. Boulder, Colo., 1984.

Grant Farr

Jebhe-ye Melli

See National Front, Iran

Jebhe-ye Nuristan

Afghan political organization.

The Jebhe-ye Nuristan (the Nuristan Front) was established in 1979 in the Afghan area of Nuristan to fight the government agents of the Democratic Republic in Afghanistan. Having successfully revolted in the Pech valley, Nuristan remained relatively free of government interference. By 1984, the major po-litical parties in Peshawar had taken over the fighting and local fronts such as the Jebhe-ye Nuristan had disappeared.

BIBLIOGRAPHY

ROY, OLIVIER. *Islam and Resistance in Afghanistan.* Cambridge, U.K., 1986.

Grant Farr

Jedda Agreement on Yemen

See Yemen Civil War

Jellaba

A traditional man's long robe; in Egyptian Arabic, gallabiya.

The original version is ankle-length and unadorned, loose-fitting with slightly flared sleeves that curve under the arms to join side gores that contain vertically slit pockets.

Designed to be worn over a shirt, the jellaba is often made of striped cloth, usually cotton. Jellabas are most commonly seen in Egypt and Sudan, particularly in rural areas.

Jenab Tutunji

Jerba

See Djerba

Jericho

Modern West Bank town under Israeli occupation since 1967, resting on the ruins of the ancient city.

Jericho dates archeologically to about 9000 B.C.E. It is best known from the Bible as the city conquered by Joshua (c. 1400 B.C.E.) leading the Hebrew tribes and as the site where Zacchaeus spoke with Jesus from a tree.

Jericho is about 15 miles (22.5 km) northeast of Jerusalem, and some 825 feet (250 m) below sea level. The 1985 population estimate was 8,000 (not counting the PALESTINIAN REFUGEE CAMPS). After the Ottoman Empire was defeated and dismembered in World War I, Jericho became part of the British mandate over PALESTINE, which began in 1922. The town became a winter resort. When Israel became a state in 1948, Jericho fell under Jordanian rule after the first ARAB–ISRAEL WAR. The UN Relief and Works Agency built three large Palestinian refugee camps near it and, shortly before the Arab–Israel War of 1967, the population of the city and the camps was estimated at 80,000. Almost all the inhabitants of those refugee camps became refugees yet again in 1967, crossing the Jordan river into Jordan. On September 13, 1993, Israel and the Palestinian Liberation Organization signed an agreement under which Jericho, along with the Gaza Strip, became an area of Palestinian autonomy.

BIBLIOGRAPHY

KHALIDI, WALID. *From Haven to Conquest.* Washington, D.C., 1971.
SACHAR, HOWARD M. *A History of Israel.* New York, 1979.

Benjamin Joseph

Jericho Congress

Arab conference held in the wake of the establishment of the State of Israel.

Held in Jericho on December 1, 1948, the Jericho Congress was convened in response to the establishment of the State of Israel and the corresponding loss to the Arabs of most of Palestine. This provided the legal basis for the union of central Palestine (the West Bank and East Jerusalem) with Transjordan (East Bank). The conference was presided over by Shaykh Muhammad Ali JA'BARI, mayor of Hebron, and included leaders from Jersualem, Hebron, Bethlehem, Nablus, and Ramallah, as well as representatives of refugees from Israeli-occupied cities and towns. It was attended by 1,000 delegates, including mayors, tribal chiefs, MUKHTARS, and military governors from all over Palestine. The conferees voted unanimously to request unity with Jordan; proclaimed ABDULLAH IBN HUSAYN to be king of all Palestine; affirmed faith in the unity of Palestine; called for the return of Palestinian refugees to their homes; called on Arab states to continue the fight to save Palestine; and asked King Abdullah to hold elections for legitimate Palestinian representatives for consultations on affairs of Palestine. It was understood that the union would not compromise Arab rights to Palestine. The conference also repudiated the ALL-PALESTINE GOVERNMENT in Gaza sponsored by the ARAB HIGHER COMMITTEE. On December 7, the Jordanian cabinet under Tawfiq Abul-Huda approved the resolutions, and parliament ratified them December 13. The Jordanian election law was amended, doubling the number of seats in the lower house of parliament to forty, designating half for representa-

tives from the West Bank and Jerusalem and the other half from Jordan. Elections to the new, expanded parliament were held in 1950, and unity was ratified unanimously on April 24, 1950.

Egypt strongly opposed the union. Syria criticized it but did not oppose it outright. Britain approved of the congress and its resolutions. Israel's recognition of the union was implicit in the armistice agreement between the two countries. The United States granted *de jure* recognition on January 31, 1949.

BIBLIOGRAPHY

DANN, URIEL. *King Hussein and the Challenge of Arab Radicalism: Jordan, 1955–1967.* New York, 1989.

Jenab Tutunji

Jernegan, John [1911–]

American diplomat.

John Jernegan entered the foreign service in 1936. After several posts in the Middle East, he became deputy secretary of state for Near Eastern Affairs during President Dwight D. Eisenhower's administration (1953–1961). He was then appointed ambassador to Iraq (1958–1962). There he attempted to stabilize relations with the government of premier Abd al-Karim KASSEM, who was perceived by Jernegan as dangerously pro-Communist.

BIBLIOGRAPHY

LENCZOWSKI, GEORGE. *The Middle East in World Affairs.* 4th ed. Ithaca, N.Y., 1980.

Zachary Karabell

Jerusalem

The core of Judaism, the cradle of Christianity, and the third holiest site of Islam; in the twentieth century, the capital of Israel and the political center of Palestinian nationalism.

Located in the Judaean mountains, on the watershed between the Judaean hills and the Judaean desert, Jerusalem (in Hebrew, Yerushalayim; in Arabic, Bayt al-Muqaddas or al-Kuds al-Sharif) overlooks the Dead Sea to the east and faces Israel's coastal plain to the west. It has warm, dry summers and cool, rainy winters.

Jerusalem was the Jewish national and religious center after its conquest by King David (c. 1000 B.C.E.) from the Jebusites until the destruction of the

Temple Mount and Haram al-Sharif. (Mia Bloom)

second Jewish temple (70 C.E.) and the rebellions against Roman occupation, which resulted in the Jews' exile from the city and their dispersion. The western wall of the temple complex was the only remnant to survive destruction and has been the focus of Jewish veneration since that time. As the scene of the last ministry, death, and resurrection of Jesus, Jerusalem emerged as one of the five original Christian patriarchates and has remained a center of Christian pilgrimage since the reign of the Roman emperor Constantine, when it was rebuilt as a Christian city. After the Muslim conquest (638 C.E.), the construction of the al-Aqsa mosque and the Dome of the Rock on the TEMPLE MOUNT (Haram al-Sharif) to commemorate the Night Journey of the Prophet Muhammad focused Muslim attention on the city, which, by the period of the Crusades, had become the third holiest city of Islam.

Conquered by the Ottomans in 1517, Jerusalem remained a backwater town in the province of Syria until the nineteenth century, when Europeans and Ottomans refocused on its religious significance. During the brief reign of Ibrahim Pasha (1832–1840), relaxed restrictions against the *dhimmi* (non-Muslim) population and renewed interest by Western Christians in the Holy Land resulted in an increase in tourism, the installation of European consulates, the beginnings of biblical archeology, and the establishment of Protestant institutions adjoining those of the Latin, Greek, Coptic, Armenian, and other Christian denominations. Communal conflicts over the religious jurisdiction of the Christian holy places led to the Crimean War (1854–1856), after which the keys to the Church of the HOLY SEPULCHRE were entrusted to the NUSAYBA FAMILY.

The city plan at the time remained as it was when it was rebuilt by the Romans as Aelia Capitolina. Walled, with a system of principal streets, it was dominated by the holy sites and divided into Muslim, Christian, Jewish, and Armenian residential quarters with mazelike streets, bazaars, churches, synagogues, and mosques. It was the residence of Muslim notables and, later, members of the Ottoman official class. The KHALIDI, NASHASHIBI, and HUSAYNI families played important roles in local politics and Muslim religious administration.

The majority in the city since the mid-nineteenth century, the Jewish population was composed of Middle Eastern and Sephardic Jews who had lived there since ancient times or who had migrated after the expulsion of Spanish Jewry in 1492, and of Ashkenazi Jews who began to immigrate to Jerusalem during the early nineteenth century. The SEPHARDIM were craftsmen, teachers, and petty merchants; among them the Navon, Amzalak, Antebi, and Valero families became important as translators, bankers, merchants, and intermediaries for Europeans (and, after 1882, for the Zionists and Ottoman rulers). The non-Zionist ASHKENAZIM, including some Hasidim (called *haredim* in the late twentieth century) were dependent upon philanthropy from abroad to support them while they lived a life of full-time study.

In the 1860s, at the invitation of British Consul James Finn and philanthropist Sir Moses Montefiore, who donated money for the construction of residential areas outside the walls, Jews, some Muslims, and the Russian Orthodox Church began to build new neighborhoods along the roads to the Old City. As it developed, the New City became primarily Jewish and the Old City, except for the Jewish Quarter, was primarily Muslim and Christian.

In 1873 Jerusalem was placed under direct rule of Constantinople (now Istanbul), and during the reign of ABDÜLHAMIT II, who championed its Islamic sig-

A café in East Jerusalem. (Bryan McBurney)

The Western Wall. (Mia Bloom)

nificance, it underwent major expansion. A municipal council, dominated by Muslims, was established. Jerusalem became a major provincial city with new courts, a modern water system, mosques, and public offices. New residential and commercial construction, both inside and outside the walls, was undertaken by the local population and by Europeans who established banks and built schools, hospitals, and hospices. Roads were paved, the city was linked by rail, and Ottoman secondary schools were set up close to new Muslim neighborhoods. The visit to Jerusalem by Kaiser Wilhelm of Germany (1898) heralded the city's emerging importance in the Ottoman Empire.

In 1917 Jerusalem was occupied by the British army under the command of General Edmund Allenby; it later became the capital of the Palestine mandate (1922–1948). The New City expanded with the development of additional Arab and Jewish neighborhoods. The British improved the water supply system, paved roads, planted gardens, and encouraged the repair and construction of buildings. The population of the city rose from just over 91,000 in 1922 to almost 133,000 in 1931.

Jerusalem also became the center of both Zionist and Palestinian nationalist institutions. The establishment of the Supreme Muslim Council in Jerusalem (1922), headed by the Jerusalem mufti, Muhammad Amin al-HUSAYNI (who now also controlled the considerable *waqf* income that under Ottoman rule had gone directly to Constantinople) and elections to the Municipal Council reflected the competition between the Husaynis and the Nashashibis for control of the Palestinian nationalist movement. Mayors were Arab notables active in the nascent Palestinian nationalist movement; Musa Kazim al-Husayni, Raghib al-Nashashibi, Husayn al-Khalidi, and Mustafa al-Khalidi.

With the Arab and Jewish populations governed by the British under separate systems, the Zionists developed economic, social, educational, and political institutions of their own, including the Hadassah Hospital and the Hebrew University in Jerusalem. By 1944, according to the American Committee of Inquiry, the Jewish population in the city was 97,000; the Muslim population, 30,630; and the Christian population, 29,350.

Jerusalem's religious significance, its occupation by a Christian power, and the conflicting political claims of Zionist and Arabs heightened international awareness of the Arab–Zionist conflict. The Wailing Wall (Western Wall) incident of 1929 and the paralysis of the city by riots, strikes, and deportations in the 1930s led to plans that opted for continued British rule or for the internationalization of the city under UN administration (UN Resolution 181). These were rejected by Arabs and/or Jews. Subsequent unilateral political solutions by Israel or Jordan were not recognized by the international community.

During the ARAB–ISRAEL WAR of 1948, Jerusalem was divided into Arab and Jewish sectors, despite proposals for its internationalization supervised by the UN Trusteeship Council and the establishment of the Palestinian Conciliation Commission. After bitter fighting, the Old City was conquered by the Arab Legion, resulting in the destruction of the Jewish Quarter. The war ended with a de facto division of Jerusalem: the Old City and East Jerusalem, in Arab hands, and the New City (West Jerusalem) under Israel's control. Access between the two sectors was via the Mandelbaum gate.

East Jerusalem was officially incorporated into Jordan in 1950 and, throughout the period of Jordanian

Outdoor café on the Midrachov in West Jerusalem. (Mia Bloom)

Section of the Chorva synagogue in Jerusalem. (Mia Bloom)

rule, despite protestations by mayors Arif al-Arif and Ruhi al-Khatib, remained subordinate to Amman. Requests to establish an Arab university in Jerusalem were denied. Many of the Palestinian elite left the city; they were replaced by notables from Hebron invited to the city by Jordan. Though the city expanded northward, plans to incorporate the neighboring villages in the direction of Ramallah never crystallized. Hotels and a royal palace were constructed. Christians were allowed to visit East Jerusalem on Christmas. Jews were denied access to their holy places; Jewish sites were desecrated; and throughout Jordan's rule, the Islamic character of the Old City was intensified. Its economy was almost totally dependent on tourism.

West Jerusalem came under Israel's control. In 1950, Israel proclaimed Jerusalem as its capital even though almost all governments maintained embassies in Tel Aviv, where the real work of the state was done. Institutions such as the Hebrew University and Hadassah Hospital, which had come under Jordan's rule, were rebuilt in West Jerusalem.

In the Arab–Israel War of 1967, Israel occupied East Jerusalem, immediately declared the city reunified, and placed it under its legal and administrative jurisdiction; it thus effectively annexed the city, a procedure formally completed in 1980. The population was 74.2 percent Jewish. Under the administration of Mayor Teddy KOLLEK (1965–1992), all barriers dividing the city were removed; the Jewish Quarter in the Old City was renovated and resettled; and the open space opposite the Western Wall was enlarged. The city underwent a major beautification program that included a ring of parks around the Old City. New neighborhoods and high-rise apartment buildings house a population employed in the government, education, medical, and cultural sectors, and in industrial zones at the periphery of the city. Jerusalem is the seat of the government of the State of Israel, and the site of the KNESSET, Supreme Court, Chief Rabbinate, and the offices of many Jewish institutions.

Since 1967, Muslim and Christian holy places have been under the jurisdiction of their respective religious authorities, with the Temple Mount under the administration of the *waqf* and *Shari'a* courts. Jerusalem Palestinians may choose to become citizens. Although most do not, they are nevertheless eligible to vote in municipal elections and to receive the benefits of Israel's health and social welfare programs.

In 1967, Jerusalem began to expand its boundaries from the airport in the north to a mile from Bethlehem in the south, and from the Pisgat Ze'ev in the east to Mount Herzl in the west. The aim was to prevent the redivision of the city and to establish Israel's strategic presence south, north, and northwest of the city. Empty land between the old Hebrew University on Mount Scopus and West

Jerusalem cityscape facing the Mount of Olives. (Mia Bloom)

Friday market at Damascus gate in Jerusalem. (Mia Bloom)

Jerusalem was built on, and new suburbs were constructed in areas that before 1967 had been part of the West Bank. These, and some Arab suburbs in northern Jerusalem, were incorporated into the city. The acceleration of construction benefiting Jews under the LIKUD governments resulted, by the mid-1980s, in 12 percent of the Jewish population of Jerusalem residing in new suburbs beyond the 1948 armistice line (Green Line). These neighborhoods, some of which were constructed on confiscated lands, are considered illegal "settlements" by the Palestinian Arabs, some of whom consider Jerusalem's borders to be the pre-1967 municipal borders under Jordan's rule, while others regard both East and West Jerusalem as Palestinian territory. At the same time, construction for Palestinians, limited by Israel's government but funded by Palestinians working in the Persian Gulf and outside the region, has expanded villages and Arab neighborhoods in order to change

the demographic distribution and to prevent complete encirclement by the expanded city (i.e., Greater Jerusalem).

The unification of Jerusalem in 1967 revived the religious and political competition for control of the city. Some of the new Israeli neighborhoods have been settled by *haredi* Jews, for whom Jerusalem is the center of their religious worldview that calls for strict observance of the Sabbath. Their opposition, at times violent, to secular traffic through these neighborhoods has renewed the religious–secular conflict in Israel. Haredi votes enabled the Likud candidate, Ehud Olmert, to become mayor of Jerusalem in 1993 and to place haredi members on the Municipal Council. Through immigration and natural increase, the haredi population will soon exceed that of the secular Jewish residents of the city. For the Jewish religious nationalists, who also have a presence in these neighborhoods and have bought or leased housing in Palestinian neighborhoods in the Old City or in villages such as Silwan that have Jewish historic significance, Jerusalem is holy land never to be relinquished.

The more than 2,000 Muslim endowments in the city—including Islamic schools, colleges, mosques, welfare services, commercial enterprises, and the repair of Islamic holy sites—have been funded by the Jerusalem waqf, which has benefited from monies contributed by the governments of Jordan and Saudi Arabia, and by private individuals. The signing of the Declaration of Principles (DOP) in 1993 has accelerated contributions to ensure the Islamic character of Arab Jerusalem. With the growth of HAMAS presence during the intifada, Jerusalem has become a focus for religious opposition to Israeli rule of the city. Despite Palestinian claims for control of waqf and the appointment of religious functionaries, the

Old City of Jerusalem surrounded by Süleyman's walls and dominated by the Tower of David. (Shep and Myra Waldman)

West Jerusalem's Yemin Moshe area. The King David Hotel is at the center, and a flurry of building construction is apparent in the surrounding area. (Shep and Myra Waldman)

Israel–Jordan treaty (1994) maintains Jordan's role in Islamic religious affairs in Jerusalem.

The unification of Jerusalem afforded the opportunity to resuscitate it as the focus of Palestinian nationalism that had lain dormant throughout Jordan's rule. It has become the Palestinian religious, cultural, and intellectual center, and, through the establishment of the Arab Studies Society (1979) by Faisal al-Husayni at New Orient House, the site of Palestinian archives collected to build and transmit Palestinian nationalism. As the intifada effectively split the city once again into Arab and Jewish sectors, and with the PALESTINE LIBERATION ORGANIZATION's Algiers declaration (1988) of an independent Palestine with Jerusalem as its capital, Palestinian strategy to bring about a two-state solution of the Arab–Israel conflict proceeded apace. After the signing of the DOP, Faisal al-Husayni was given responsibility for assessing municipal functions of a Palestinian part of the city, and the New Orient House began to play the de facto role of a municipal institution with national functions.

According to the DOP, Jerusalem is to be discussed in the final status negotiations in 1996. With the papacy's official recognition of Israel in 1995, the Christian role in the conflict over Jerusalem has receded to consideration of access to and the safeguarding of the Christian holy places. Palestinian political interests have become an active issue, with Jerusalem residents voting in the first elections for the Palestinian Authority. For Jews and Israelis, Jerusalem is the irrevocable religious and national capital of Israel; for Palestinians, the city is the capital of Palestine; and for Muslims, it is a holy part of Muslim territory not to be relinquished. How the city is governed, the final delineation of its borders, and how religious jurisdiction is settled are yet to be resolved.

BIBLIOGRAPHY

BEN-ARIEH, Y. *Jerusalem in the Nineteenth Century: The Emergence of the New City.* Jerusalem, 1986.
———. *Jerusalem in the Nineteenth Century: The Old City.* Jerusalem, 1984.
BENVENISTI, MERON. *The West Bank Data Project: A Survey of Israel's Policies.* Washington, D.C., 1984.
DUMPER, MICHAEL T. "Jerusalem's Infrastructure: Is Annexation Irreversible?" *Journal of Palestine Studies* 23 (1993): 78–95.
FRIEDLAND, ROGER, and RICHARD HECHT. *To Rule Jerusalem.* Cambridge, U.K., 1996.
HALPERN, JEFF. *Between Redemption and Revival: The Jewish Yishuv of Jerusalem in the Nineteenth Century.* Boulder, Colo., 1991.
IRANI, GEORGE E. *The Papacy and the Middle East: The Role of the Holy See in the Arab–Israeli Conflict 1962–1984.* South Bend, Ind., 1986.
KRAEMER, JOEL, ed. *Jerusalem: Problems and Prospects.* New York, 1981.
TIBAWI, A. L. *Jerusalem: Its Place in Islam and Arab History.* Beirut, 1969.

Reeva S. Simon

Jerusalem Post

Israel's major English-language daily newspaper.

It was founded as the *Palestine Post* in 1932 by Gershon Agran, and between 1955 and 1974 it was edited by Ted Curie. During Britain's mandate, the *Post* was highly critical of British administration, particularly of the 1939 WHITE PAPERS ON PALESTINE, and it served as the unofficial organ of the Jewish Agency. After Israel's independence in 1948, the *Post* leaned toward the labor movement; in recent years, it has become generally supportive of the LIKUD party. Along with HAARETZ, it frequently attacked the policies of Likud prime minister Yitzhak SHAMIR. It has also paid particular attention to U.S.–Israeli relations.

BIBLIOGRAPHY

New Standard Jewish Encyclopedia. New York, 1977.
SHIPLER, DAVID. *Arab and Jew.* New York, 1986.

Zachary Karabell

Jeunes Algériens

See Young Algerians

Jewish Agency

Established in 1929 in an effort to enlist non-Zionist Jewish support for the national home in Palestine.

The League of Nations mandate for Palestine, awarded in the Treaty of SÈVRES (1920), mentioned a Jewish agency, which was expected to provide Britain with advice and aid in discharging its duties as the mandatory power. For Zionist leaders, Britain's endorsement of the idea of a Jewish national home in Palestine constituted both an achievement and a challenge. This long-desired international recognition created expectations that masses of Jews would go to live in Palestine and that sufficient capital would be invested to accommodate an expanded population. Given these expectations, British Zionist leader Professor Chaim WEIZMANN realized that ZIONISM needed a larger number of advocates than those enrolled as members of the WORLD ZIONIST ORGANIZATION (WZO).

Although World War I had brought together Zionists and non-Zionists in shared efforts to relieve suffering, such cooperation proved temporary. The determination of postwar priorities deepened divisions between the two groups. While Zionists considered the needs of Palestinian Jewry paramount, non-Zionists emphasized reconstruction of Diaspora Jewish communities, thereby undermining Zionist efforts to transfer Jews from the Diaspora to Palestine.

With respect to the goal of meeting the financial requirements of the Jewish settlement in Palestine, it was necessary to mobilize funds from Jewish philanthropists in the United States and Britain; there was no easy way to overcome the resistance of many prominent and successful Jews in these countries to the idea of Jewish nationalism. Following World War I, several organizations were established to try to attract broad-based Jewish support for Palestinian Jewry to increase the annual revenues donated to the World Zionist Organization. In fairly quick succession, the World Zionist Organization created the Preparation Fund, the Restoration Fund, and finally in 1920, the Foundation Fund. Notwithstanding sustained fund-raising campaigns, the revenues generated were disappointing and, according to Weizmann and other Zionist leaders, would continue to fall below expectations as long as financial contributions were separated from financial control.

After several years of deliberations, the sixteenth congress of the World Zionist Organization created the Jewish Agency and accepted the principle of parity in membership between Zionists and non-Zionists on its three governing bodies—the 224-member council, the administrative committee, and the executive. The president of the World Zionist Organization was to serve as Jewish Agency head unless opposed by 75 percent of the council. Of the non-Zionists on the council, 40 percent were American, and many had international reputations. The nature of the agency's economic and social mission allowed both non-Zionists and Zionists to participate without compromising or altering their own divergent founding principles. Economic aid could be provided to Palestinian Jewry either on the grounds that it was a community in distress or as a means to building the infrastructure of a Jewish state. But parity in the agency was not sustained. Because the agency never created effective links with non-Zionist philanthropic organizations, non-Zionists continually lost positions to Zionists and the balance of political alignment shifted in favor of the Zionists.

The Jewish Agency initially opened offices in Jerusalem, London, and Geneva; during World War II, an office opened in New York City. Its political department conducted negotiations with the Palestine government, with Britain, and with the League of Nations, effectively functioning as a foreign office. YISHUV policies (those of the Palestinian Jews) regarding Palestine's Arab population were hammered out among the agency's top leaders. The agency supervised the transfer of Jewish capital from Germany to Palestine in the 1930s, along with the immigration of thousands of Jews—legal and illegal—from Nazi-dominated Europe. The agency also assumed partial control over the Yishuv's defense forces; at the end of World War II, the agency helped prepare Palestine's Jewish population for war (the Arab–Israel War of 1948) by uniting, at least for a short period, the Haganah, Irgun, and LEHI.

After the State of Israel was established in 1948, the agency consigned its major policymaking responsibilities first to the provisional government and subsequently to the ministries of state. In the first years of statehood, the agency undertook primary responsibility for the settlement of Israel's mass immigration from Europe and the countries under Islam. Although a government ministry was created to manage the process of immigrant absorption, the Jewish Agency retains control over organizing the rescue of Diaspora Jews in danger. Some authority pertinent to agricultural resettlement also resides in agency offices. Hoping to intensify the commitment of world Jewry to Israel's charge as a Jewish state, the agency expends a large portion of its budget on education and related cultural activities. Finally, as the agency is still an important vehicle for transferring financial conditions from Diaspora Jews to Israel, it has continually struggled with the problem of how to give Jews who raise money for Israel influence over the flow of expenditures.

BIBLIOGRAPHY

HALPERN, BEN. *The Idea of the Jewish State.* Cambridge, Mass., 1961.
STOCK, ERNEST. *Partners and Pursestrings: A History of the United Israel Appeal.* Lanham, Md., 1987.

Donna Robinson Divine

Jewish Brigade

Established by the British war cabinet in 1944 as the only Jewish military unit to fight the Axis powers.

The Jewish Brigade represented the culmination of efforts by Jews in both Palestine and the United States to create an independent Jewish fighting force. In 1939, Jews in Palestine began to volunteer for military service, and after repeated pressure from the JEWISH AGENCY and other Jewish organizations, in 1942 the British agreed to form a Palestine Regiment. The Palestine Regiment was sent to serve in the Middle East, although its responsibilities there were primarily restricted to guard duty.

Finally, in September 1944, the British created the Jewish Brigade (in Hebrew Ha-Hayil) out of the Palestine Regiment, a field artillery regiment, and other auxiliary service units. The men, numbering approximately 5,000, were placed under the command of a Canadian-born Jew, Brigadier Ernest Frank Benjamin of the Royal Engineers, and they continued their training with the Eighth Army in Italy. In early 1945, the soldiers of the Jewish Brigade saw their first fighting at Alfonsine, and in April 1945 they led the offensive across the Senio River.

As they moved into northern Italy, the Jewish soldiers met Holocaust survivors for the first time; thereafter they provided them with food, clothing, and assistance immigrating to Palestine. They continued these activities in Belgium, Austria, Germany, and Holland and also assisted the Allied authorities in searching for Holocaust survivors.

In 1946, the Jewish Brigade was disbanded, partly because of increasing tension between the YISHUV and the mandatory authorities.

BIBLIOGRAPHY

RABINOWITZ, L. *Soldiers from Judea.* 1945.

Bryan Daves

Jewish Colonial Trust

Financial organ of the Zionist movement.

The Jewish Colonial Trust (JCT) was established in England in 1899. The first Zionist Congress (1897) had created the Zionist Organization; the JCT was one of two subsidiaries subsequently set up in order to promote Jewish settlement in Palestine. The JCT was in charge of banking operations and of colonization projects in Palestine. It set up the Anglo–Palestine Bank, which virtually became the official bank of the Jewish national home, as a subsidiary. By 1936 it was the second largest bank in Palestine (after Barclay's). The other subsidiary, the JEWISH NATIONAL FUND, was responsible for the purchase of land that was to become the inalienable property of the Jewish people.

Jenab Tutunji

Jewish Colonization Association

Philanthropic organization (also known as the ICA) founded in 1891.

Baron Maurice de HIRSCH founded the ICA to assist Jews in Europe and Asia to flee persecution and go to countries in the Western Hemisphere. He initially endowed it with ten million dollars as a joint stock company, and the amount was eventually increased fourfold. The ICA assisted Jews by establishing agricultural settlements; most of these were in Argentina but there were also some in Brazil. It also helped Jewish farmers in Canada and the United States and provided assistance to Jews who were still living in Russia and the newly created states of Eastern Europe after World War I. In Palestine, the ICA took over the support and consolidation of colonies Baron de Rothschild had created.

Since Israeli statehood, the ICA has helped support settlements as well as research and training in agriculture. It also works with the Hebrew Immigrant Aid Society and the JOINT DISTRIBUTION COMMITTEE in providing relief aid.

BIBLIOGRAPHY

WINSBERG, D. *Colonia Baron Hirsh: A Jewish Agricultural Colony in Argentina*. Gainesville, Fla., 1964.

Bryan Daves

Jewish Legion

Jewish volunteers in the British army during World War I.

In 1917, on the urging of Russian Zionist Vladimir Jabotinsky, several Jewish battalions were formed in the British Army. Proponents of Zionism believed that if they supported Britain in World War I, it would reflect favorably on their aspirations for a national home in Palestine. Commanded by Lt. Col. John Henry Patterson, the Jewish Legion, as this force was called, participated in Edmund Allenby's campaigns in Syria in 1918. One of its members was David Ben-Gurion, who became the first prime minister of Israel in 1949. Following World War I, the Jewish Legion acted as a Jewish self-defense force in Palestine under the command of Jabotinsky. After the Jewish–Arab riots in April 1920, Jabotinsky and other leaders of the legion were arrested and sentence to prison. After the even more severe riots in May 1921, the Jewish Legion was disbanded by the high commissioner, Sir Herbert Samuel. However, its members later formed the core of the Jewish army in Palestine, the Haganah.

BIBLIOGRAPHY

FROMKIN, DAVID. *A Peace to End All Peace*. New York, 1989.
SHIMONI, YAACOV, ed. *Political Dictionary of the Middle East in the Twentieth Century*. New York, 1974.

Zachary Karabell

Jewish National Council

See Va'ad Leumi

Jewish National Fund

Land purchase and development fund of the Zionist Organization of America.

The Jewish National Fund (JNF), or Keren Kayemeth LeIsrael in Hebrew, was set up in 1901. Its primary aim was to buy land in Palestine for the "eternal possession" of the Jewish people. The con-cept of public ownership was based on the Biblical injunction that the land of Israel belongs to God and that it may be leased for forty-nine years.

Funds raised by Jews all over the world were used to buy land in Palestine for Jewish settlements. The first land was bought in 1904 at Kefr Hittim in Lower Galilee. The first forest was planted by the JNF in 1908, and this has became a major activity of the JNF after the establishment of the State of Israel. By 1960 the JNF had 637,000 acres (258,000 hectares) of land, and control of these was passed to a body set up by the government of Israel.

Paul Rivlin

Jews in the Middle East

A people whose origins are in the Fertile Crescent in the ancient Near East.

The collective memory of the earliest Jewish history dates back to the second millennium B.C.E. and is

Representation of Sephardic Jews in Tiberias, 1875. (Arnold Blumberg, Towson State University Media Services. From Louis Lortet, *La Syrie d'Aujourd'hui*. Paris, 1884.)

Jewish money changers in Baghdad. (Richard Bulliet)

preserved in the patriarchal narratives of the book of Genesis in the Bible. The remainder of the Hebrew Bible recounts the evolution and vicissitudes of JU-DAISM and Jewish national life in Canaan (present-day Israel and parts of Egypt and Jordan). By the time of the Roman occupation and the destruction of the Second Jewish Commonwealth by the Romans in 70 C.E., Jews were living in much of what is now called the Middle East and some moved into the western Roman Empire—Europe. The foundations of post–Second Temple Judaism were then laid by the rabbis of Roman Palestine and Parthian and Sassanian Babylonia, who canonized the Scripture, redacted the liturgy, and created the TALMUD and Midrash.

With the conquests of Islam in the seventh and eighth centuries, the majority of world Jewry at that time was brought under Muslim Arab rule. Not only were the demographic centers of world Jewry located in the Middle East and the Maghrib (North Africa), but during certain periods, such as the height of medieval Islamic civilization (in the ninth to thirteenth centuries) and the Ottoman revival of the Middle East (during the fifteenth and sixteenth centuries), the creative centers of Jewish life were to be found there rather than in Christian Europe.

In the later Middle Ages, the quality of Jewish life in the Middle East declined precipitously as a direct result of an overall radically transformed economic, social, and intellectual climate within the lands of Islam. During this period, the general attitude toward non-Muslims hardened, and the laws of differentiation (Arabic, *ghiyar*) were enforced with greater consistency than in earlier times and with increasing vigor. Over the centuries, Jews throughout the Middle East found themselves increasingly confined by law or custom to overcrowded ghetto-like quarters, called by various names: the *mellah* in Morocco, the

qaʿat al-Yahud in Yemen, the *mahallat* in Iran, and the *harat al-Yahud* in most other places.

The arrival of the SEPHARDIM—Jewish exiles from Spain, Portugal, and Sicily at the end of the fifteenth century—and the Ottoman conquest of much of the Middle East in the early sixteenth breathed new life into Oriental Jewry—demographically, intellectually, and economically. Judeo-Spanish (called LADINO) became the language of Jews in the coastal urban centers from Tangier to Istanbul. Some of the Sephardic elite (along with other non-Muslims such as Greeks, Armenians, and Levantine Christians) acted as intermediaries between European commercial interests and local populations. The great majority of Jews, like the great majority of Muslims, were poor.

In the nineteenth century, Middle Eastern Jews and Christians who worked for European consular or mercantile interests began to take increasing advantage of the foreign protection that was available under the CAPITULATIONS (Turkish, *imtiyazat*). At the same time, they came to enjoy an improved civil status in the Ottoman Empire under the nineteenth-century TANZIMAT reforms. They also eagerly began to avail themselves of the benefits of modern Western educations provided by foreign cultural and religious missionaries. From 1862 on, the ALLIANCE ISRAÉLITE UNIVERSELLE served as the main propagator of the French language and European-style education among Jews from Morocco to Iran. By 1900, more than 100,000 students had studied in Alliance schools. The Alliance gave these Jews a new self-image, created new expectations within them, and aroused a sense of international Jewish solidarity. It produced cadres of Westernized Jews, who had a distinct advantage of opportunity over the largely uneducated Muslim masses as the Middle East was drawn into the modern world economic system. In addition to so-

A synagogue in Istanbul. (Mia Bloom)

A Jewish jewelry maker displays his wares in San'a, Yemen. (Mia Bloom)

cioeconomic mobility, the Alliance contributed to physical mobility. Jews with education moved within the region from areas of lesser economic opportunity such as Morocco, Syria, and the Turkish Aegean isles to areas of greater opportunity such as Algeria and Egypt. Others emigrated to Europe and South America. Jews from Iraq established considerable colonies in India, Burma, Hong Kong, and Shanghai. Several families rose to the heights of international wealth and prominence, such as the Sassoons, the Kadoories, and the Ezras.

The Alliance also further alienated Jews from the Muslim societies around them and heightened their receptivity to French colonialism in the Maghrib, Syria, and Lebanon, as well as to a strong European presence generally. With the exception of a few individuals, such as Ya'qub Sanu, the father of modern Arab theater and political journalism in Egypt, and Albert Carasso, prominent in the Young Turk movement, most Jews did not take part in the intellectual and political currents developing in the Islamic world. Only in Iraq were there even a handful of Jewish writers who used literary Arabic as their medium of expression.

A small but widespread stratum of Jews was touched by the Hebrew-language revival of the mid-to-late nineteenth-century HASKALA (Jewish Enlightenment) in Europe. European books and newspapers in Hebrew then circulated throughout the Middle East and North Africa, and through this literature, Jews of the region became aware of all the currents sweeping some of the rest of the Jewish world, including religious reform, migratory movements, and ZIONISM.

From its very earliest days, Zionism made modest, but not insignificant, inroads into most of the major urban Jewish communities of the Middle East. Much of the sympathy for the movement was passive and philanthropic, rather than politically active. Zionism aroused considerable popular enthusiasm among Middle Eastern Jews, however, in the wake of the 1917 BALFOUR DECLARATION, the Allied victory in World War I, and the SAN REMO CONFERENCE. In 1917, for example, thousands of Jews gathered in Cairo and Alexandria in support of the Balfour Declaration, and similar scenes greeted Chaim WIEZMANN and the ZIONIST COMMISSION when they passed through Egypt the following year. In a burst of semi-messianic enthusiasm, several hundred Jewish families emigrated from Morocco to Palestine between 1919 and 1923, much to the chagrin of French colonial authorities. About 1,000 Iraqi Jews and smaller numbers from both Syria and Libya also settled in Palestine at this time, and there had been a steady stream of Jews from Yemen, totaling several thousand from 1880 to 1929, when the iman of Yemen issued an edict to stop the emigration.

The initial, outward ardor for Zionism soon subsided considerably due to opposition from the colonial authorities, members of the Jewish upper class, and, most importantly, the growing Arab and pan-Islamic nationalist movements. With rare exceptions, such as Sasson Heskayl, who served as Iraq's first finance minister, Joseph Alsan Cattaoui, who served as Egypt's minister of finance in 1923 and communications in 1925, or Léon Castro, who was editor of the Egyptian Wafd party's French-language daily *La Liberté,* most Jews in the Muslim world were studiously apolitical, especially in the Arab countries. From the time of the Western Wall riots of 1929, Arab nationalism became increasingly anti-Zionist, and despite frequent disclaimers, nationalist leaders and the masses seemed to be increasingly unable to differentiate between Jews and Zionists. In the 1930s and 1940s, the growing admiration among Arabs for German national socialism and Italian fascism, accompanied by the adoption of their anti-Semitic rhetoric, also helped ensure that Jews would find no place in the society that the Arab nationalist camp wanted to create. The strong Axis sympathies of the government and national leaders of Turkey resulted in social and legal discrimination of nonethnic Turks, and this also affected many Jews.

World War II further affected the Jews of the Muslim world as it affected their coreligionists everywhere. Not only did Hitler and Nazi Germany pose a threat to world Jewry, but each Jew's own experience helped give rise to a heightened Jewish consciousness and esprit de corps. For example, Iraqi Jewry had been harmed by the violent pogrom known as the FARHUD, which occurred at the end of the short-lived pro-Axis regime of Rashid Ali in June 1941; Jews in Italian Libya and the French Maghrib had suffered a wide range of humiliations, exactions, and internment under anti-Jewish colonial rule while the Arabs looked on with indifference; Jews in Egypt could only wonder at what might have befallen them if King Farouk had been able to welcome German General Erwin Rommel and his Afrikakorps into the country as he had hoped to do. Throughout the Muslim world, Jews had heard the Mufti Hajj Muhammad Amin al-Husayni broadcast from Berlin, calling upon Arabs to "kill the Jews wherever you find them, for the love of God, history and religion."

The postwar years witnessed a renewed surge of pan-Islam and Pan-Arabism on the one hand and Jewish nationalism on the other. A rapid chain of events then totally undermined the weakened underpinnings of Jewish life in the Arab countries. Major anti-Jewish riots occurred in Egypt and Libya in November 1945. In December 1947, following the UN vote to partition Palestine, riots devastated the Jewish communities of Aden, Bahrain, and Aleppo. With the establishment of the State of Israel in May 1948, highly restrictive administrative measures were imposed on Jews in Egypt, Syria, and Iraq both during and after the first ARAB–ISRAEL WAR in 1948. Between 1949 and 1967, the majority of the 800,000 Jews in the Arab countries became refugees, who fled or emigrated to Israel. During this period, half of Turkey's 80,000 Jews and about a third of Iran's 100,000 Jews departed for Israel, but others, including nearly half of Maghribi Jewry, went to France.

In the early 1990s, Jews of Middle Eastern origin—the EDOT HA-MIZRAH—comprise more than half of Israel's Jewish population. The Jewish community in Turkey, although generally comfortable and stable, has dwindled to about 20,000. Iranian Jewry flourished until the Iranian Revolution of 1979 and the rise of Ayatollah Khomeini's Islamic republic; during the 1980s, there was mass emigration to Israel, Europe, and the United States. By 1989, the Jews remaining in Iran were only about 22,000. Of the small number of Jews who remain outside Israel in the Arab world, only Morocco's 5,000 Jewish citizens enjoy genuine freedom and relative security.

BIBLIOGRAPHY

COHEN, HAYYIM J. *The Jews of the Middle East, 1860–1972.* New York, 1973.
DESHEN, SHLOMO, and WALTER P. ZENNER, eds. *Jewish Societies in the Middle East: Community, Culture and Authority.* Lanham, Md., 1982.
LEWIS, BERNARD. *The Jews of Islam.* Princeton, N.J., 1984.
STILLMAN, NORMAN. "Fading Shadows of the Past: Jews in the Islamic World." In *Survey of Jewish Affairs 1989,* ed. by William Frankel. Oxford, 1989.
———. *The Jews of Arab Lands: A History and Source Book.* Philadelphia, 1979.
———. *The Jews of Arab Lands in Modern Times.* Philadelphia, 1991.

Norman Stillman

Jezreel Valley

Hebrew, Emek Yizre'el; Arabic, Marj ibn Amer; fertile alluvial plain of the river Kishon in northern Israel.

The largest in Israel after the Jordan valley, the plain extends roughly twenty miles (32 km) from the base of Mount Carmel in the northwest, southeastward along the Samarian range to the foot of Mount Gilboa, and eastward along the hills of Lower Galilee to Mount Tabor. Total area is about ninety-six square miles (249 sq km).

Named for the ancient Israelite city Yizre'el ("May God give seed"), the valley boasted dense habitation and consistent royal residence and witnessed many a decisive battle from biblical times until the crusader period, after which it degenerated into swampland. Shortly after the establishment of the British mandate over Palestine, the JEWISH NATIONAL FUND purchased large tracts of the valley, which were drained and settled.

Zev Maghen

Jibril, Ahmad [1935–]

Palestinian guerilla leader.

Born at Ramla, Palestine, Jibril (also Abu Jihad) served in Syria's army and was the national chess champion of Syria in 1956. He left the army in 1958 and formed the Palestinian Liberation Front in 1961. The organization began military operations in 1965, and after the Arab–Israel War (1967) was briefly part of the Popular Front for the Liberation of Palestine (PFLP), headed by George HABASH. Jibril withdrew his group from the PFLP and formed the Popular Front for the Liberation of Palestine–General Command (PFLP–GC), a nonpolitical organization that did not join the Palestine Liberation Organization, although he had been a member of al-Fath's Central Committee. He was a member of the rejectionist front with George Habash and the secretary-general of the Palestinian Liberation Front.

The PFLP–GC concentrates its guerilla operations across Israel's northern border. It was suspected of involvement in the bomb explosion aboard Pan American flight 103 above Lockerbie, Scotland, in December 1988.

BIBLIOGRAPHY

Who's Who in the Arab World, 1988–1989. 9th ed. Beirut.

Lawrence Tal

Jidda

The second largest city of Saudi Arabia.

With a population estimated at 1.5 million, Jidda is the largest city of HIJAZ. Its prosperity dates from its designation by the early Islamic state as the port of nearby Mecca. After being occupied by the first

The Old Sea gate amid the streets of modern Jidda. (Richard Bulliet)

Saudi state in the early nineteenth century, it was restored to nominal Ottoman authority by Muhammad Ali in 1811. The last city in the short-lived Hashimi kingdom of Hijaz to resist the Al Sa'ud, Jidda finally surrendered after a long siege in 1925. An important city because it is the commercial and banking center of the country, Jidda is also the site of the Islamic port of Jidda, Saudi Arabia's largest port, and King Abd al-Aziz Airport, through which most of the pilgrims pass during the annual hajj. The centuries-old immigration of Muslims from around

A house in Jidda. (Richard Bulliet)

Street scene in modern Jidda. (Richard Bulliet)

the world makes Jidda one of the most cosmopolitan of Saudi Arabia's cities.

John E. Peterson

Jidda

Small rocky islet off the west coast of Bahrain; used primarily as a penal colony.

Through the years, according to eyewitnesses and statements by Amnesty International and other human-rights organizations, many of Bahrain's political prisoners were held in Jidda, a government security zone. About one mile (1.6 km) by half a mile (0.8 km), Jidda is located next to the island of Umm Na'san, which is personally owned by the ruler of Bahrain and the site of his game preserve.

BIBLIOGRAPHY

NAKHLEH, EMILE A. *Bahrain: Political Development in a Modernizing Society.* Lexington, Mass., 1976.

Emile A. Nakhleh

Jifri, Muhammad Ali

Campaigned for independence from Britain of south Arabian protectorates and Aden.

Muhammad Ali was the best-known member of a south Arabian SAYYID clan that was prominent in the 1950s and 1960s in the campaign for independence for Aden and the Protectorate States. He helped found the SOUTH ARABIAN LEAGUE (1950–1952), which followed a reformist and relatively conservative program—and was later funded by Saudi Arabia.

Manfred W. Wenner

Jihad

An Arabic word that literally means "struggle."

In an Islamic legal context, the term *jihad* is most often used to refer to a martial campaign in the cause of religion and is therefore frequently translated as "holy war." According to classical Muslim legal theory, the only kind of lawful military conflict is jihad and a jihad can only be used to fulfill at least one of two main objectives. The first is the effective spread of Muslim ideals and values into a region of society unmoved by the call to Islam. The second is defense of the Muslim community from external threats. In addition to discussing the conditions necessary to establish these objectives, Muslim teachings on jihad

also deal with important related issues such as the immunity of noncombatants, ethical restrictions on the applications of destructive force, and the circumstances warranting armistice. In fact, the doctrine of jihad is probably best understood as being similar to the "just war" theory in Western Christian contexts. Over the course of the twentieth century, jihad discourse has been polarized by modernists like Muhammad Shaltut (died 1963) who argue that, in the modern era, offensive jihad should only take the form of a peaceful propagation of Islam, and revolutionary Islamist groups such as ISLAMIC JIHAD, HAMAS, and HIZBULLAH, which maintain that Muslims around the world are obliged to use any available means to fight against the forces of Western imperialism.

Scott Alexander

Jiye Power Plant, al-

A major power plant in Lebanon.

With al-Dhuq, al-Jiye is one of the two major power plants in Lebanon. Direct hits and lack of fuel during the Lebanese Civil War of 1975 left the plant inoperative for years. The European Investment Bank financed the installation of three 60-megawatt units at al-Jiye and at al-Dhuq under a 1977 program. In 1981, Israel's bombing of the Zahrani petroleum refinery, which provided fuel to al-Jiye, severely diminished the electric power supply of the country. Israel's 1982 invasion severed the lines to this power plant.

As'ad AbuKhalil

Jizan

A Red Sea port and capital of the province of the same name in southern Saudi Arabia.

The region is also known as al-Mikhlaf or Asir Tihama. It was held by the Al Sa'ud, the Egyptians, the Ottomans, and the Khayrat and Idrisi families until the 1920s, when it was incorporated into the Saudi realm.

John E. Peterson

Jizya

A poll tax.

Several poll taxes were levied throughout the Middle East from the time of the Muslim conquests (seventh century). Caliph Umar II (717–720 c.e.) established the principle that they should be levied only on non-Muslims. Islam exempted women, children, and the disabled or unemployed from the tax.

In 1855, the Ottoman Empire abolished the tax, as part of reforms to equalize the status of Muslims and non-Muslims. It was replaced, however, by a military-exemption tax on non-Muslims, the BEDEL-I ASKERI.

BIBLIOGRAPHY

"Djizya." *Encyclopedia of Islam,* 2nd ed.
LAPIDUS, IRA. *A History of Islamic Societies.* New York, 1988.
LEWIS, BERNARD. *The Emergence of Modern Turkey,* 2nd ed. New York. 1968.

Elizabeth Thompson

Jma'a Tribal Council

North African Berber political unit.

In precolonial North Africa, Jma'a represented the highest political authority in the tribe, led by an *amghar* (chief). During periods of war, the amghar became the chief of war (amghar n-l-baroud). Each subtribe had its representative in the Jma'a. In the contemporary period, although some villages still have a Jma'a, its functions have been, however, reconciled to the management of collective social events.

Rahma Bourqia

John XIX   [1928–1942]

113th Coptic patriarch of Egypt

The successor of Cyril V (1874–1927), John had an uneventful patriarchate. He had been chosen by Cyril to be the *abuna* (archbishop) of the Ethiopian Orthodox Church but declined the offer. For many years metropolitan (chief bishop) of the Egyptian provinces of Behariya and Minufiyya, in 1892 he went into exile after a dispute with the Coptic Community Council but eventually regained its favor for his part in reforming the church's handling of bequests and administration of educational institutions. As patriarch, John established near Cairo a theological college to improve their education. He appointed the abuna and several bishops of the church in Ethiopia.

[*See also:* Copts]

BIBLIOGRAPHY

MEINARDUS, OTTO F. A. *Christian Egypt: Faith and Life.* Cairo, 1970.

SHOUCRI, MOUNIR. "John XIX." In *The Coptic Encyclopedia,* vol. 4, ed. by Aziz S. Atiya. New York, 1991.

Donald Spanel

Johnson, Lyndon Baines   [1908–1973]

U.S. president, 1963–1969.

Johnson succeeded to the presidency after the assassination of John F. Kennedy in November 1963. Although a long-time member of the U.S. House of Representatives (1937–1949) and U.S. Senate (1949–1961), and a most effective legislative leader, he had little experience in foreign affairs. With an escalating war in Vietnam, the Middle East had low priority for him.

He was unable to persuade Egypt to limit its armament program; to balance USSR arms sales to Egypt, Syria, Iraq and elsewhere, Johnson authorized increased military sales to Israel and to conservative Arab regimes, particularly to King Hussein ibn Talal of Jordan. When Egypt blocked the Strait of Tiran to Israeli shipping in May of 1967, Johnson denounced the act as illegal. During the Arab–Israel War of June 1967, Johnson kept the United States neutral, although American sympathies were clearly with Israel. Through his ambassador to the United Nations, Arthur Goldberg, Johnson gave crucial support to UN Resolution 242, passed in November 1967, which has been the keystone of Arab–Israeli diplomacy since then. In 1968, Johnson declined renomination for another term.

BIBLIOGRAPHY

SAFRAN, NADAV. *Israel: The Embattled Ally.* Cambridge, Mass., 1981.
SPIEGEL, STEVEN. *The Other Arab-Israeli Conflict.* Chicago, 1985.

Zachary Karabell

Johnson–Crosbie Committee Report

A 1930 survey in Palestine.

The Johnson–Crosbie committee collected data from 25,573 Palestinian Arab families in 104 villages. The report calculated that Arab peasant debt per family averaged 27 Palestinian pounds, the equivalent of a year's income. It also found that the average cultivator held a mere 56 dunums (33 acres; 14 ha) whereas 75 dunums (45 acres; 19 ha) were required for basic economic maintenance. The survey was conducted by William Johnson and Robert Crosbie, officials in the British administration in Palestine.

BIBLIOGRAPHY

KHALAF, ISSA. *Politics in Palestine: Arab Factionalism and Social Disintegration 1939–1948.* Albany, N.Y., 1991.

Elizabeth Thompson

Johnston Plan

Development plan for the Jordan river.

This comprehensive plan was drawn up by U.S. Special Ambassador Eric Johnston in 1953, for regional development of the Jordan river system. The hope was that it would reduce regional conflicts by promoting cooperation and economic stability. The two major riparians—Israel and the Kingdom of Jordan—had their own plans for water development, but each objected to the other's plan. Eric Johnston and his commission attempted to reach a unified plan through negotiations that dealt with water quotas, use of Jordan water for outside the water-basin area, use of the Sea of Galilee (also called Lake Tiberias or Lake Kinneret) as a storage area, incorporating the Litani River into the Jordan system, and international supervision.

Negotiations lasted from 1953 to 1955 and the Unified Plan was negotiated, with Eric Johnston playing the key role in pushing the compromises along. The Unified Plan was accepted by the technical committees of the League of Arab States (Arab League) and Israel. Israel's government informed the United States that it would accept the plan, but in October 1955, the Arabs decided not to ratify it. In fact, there has been implementation of the Johnston Plan on the part of Israel and separately by Jordan.

BIBLIOGRAPHY

GRUEN, GEORGE. *Water and Politics in the Middle East.* New York, 1964.
REGUER, SARA. "Controversial Waters: Thirty Years of Exploitation of the Jordan River, 1950–1980." *Middle Eastern Studies,* Spring 1993.

Sara Reguer

Joint Distribution Committee

Charitable organization that assists Jews in distress.

The Joint Distribution Committee (JDC) was established in 1914 by a committee of relief agencies, including the American Jewish Relief Committee (affiliated with the American Jewish Committee), the Central Relief Committee (part of the Orthodox movement); and the People's Relief Committee (affiliated with American labor groups).

Initially, the JDC assisted Jews in central and eastern Europe before, during, and after World War I, and later it helped reconstruct the Jewish communities in those regions. Before and during World War II, the JDC worked to rescue Jews from Nazi-occupied Europe; after the war, it assisted in the resettlement of displaced persons. Thereafter, the JDC focused its attention on helping the Jews of central and eastern Europe and the Jewish communities in Muslim countries. In 1991, it helped the Israeli government airlift nearly 15,000 Ethiopian Jews from Ethiopia to Israel.

BIBLIOGRAPHY

HANDLIN, O. *A Continuing Task: AJDC 1914–1964.* 1964.

Bryan Daves

Jordan

A small Arab kingdom east of the Mediterranean Sea and Israel.

Jordan is bordered on the north by Syria, on the east by Iraq, on the south by Saudi Arabia, and on the west by Israel and the West Bank. The Gulf of Aqaba, an extension of the Red Sea, abuts its southernmost tip. To the west, it shares the Dead Sea (an inland salt lake) with Israel and the West Bank. Jordan is a

Dead Sea terrace on the west flank of the Jordan valley. (D.W. Lockhard)

crossroads in the region: The hajj (Islamic pilgrimage) route from Turkey and Syria passes through Jordan to western Arabia (the Hijaz) to the holy city of Mecca. A major trunk road runs from Iraq to Jordan's only port, Aqaba. Oil pipelines, now nonfunctioning, were built from Iraq and Saudi Arabia across Jordan to Mediterranean ports. Prior to the establishment of the State of Israel (1948), Jordan (as Transjordan) was the transit route from Palestinian ports to Iraq, Saudi Arabia, and the Persian/Arabian Gulf. With a population that is about 50 percent Jordanian Arabs and 50 percent Palestinian (refugees), and a location between Israel and the powerful Arab states, Jordan is frequently buffeted by Middle Eastern and international political currents.

Geography and Climate. Jordan's landmass, almost 38,000 square miles (90,649 sq km), is marked by three distinct geological systems—the Jordan rift valley, the Transjordan plateau, and the Arabian/Syrian desert. At 1,302 feet (397 m) below the level of the Mediterranean Sea, the Jordan valley contains the Dead Sea, the lowest surface point on the planet (the lowest actual point being beneath the ocean). Since the 1960s, the Jordanians have developed a sophisticated irrigation system in the valley, because it receives little rain. Given the topography and low rainfall, most of Jordan is a classic desert, with only 3 percent arable (partly under irrigation) and 1 percent forested. The Jordan valley is, however, warm in winter, so off-season fruits and vegetables can be produced for temperate markets. To the east of the rift valley, the Transjordan plateau runs like a wedge from the Syrian border to Ma'an in the south of the country. The plateau is composed of broad rolling plains, cut by precipitous valleys or wadis (streambeds that have water only during the rainy season). Rain-fed agriculture and animal husbandry are prac-

ticed here. To the east and south of the plateau, lies the Arabian/Syrian desert, a wasteland only sparsely populated by bedouin.

Jordan possesses few natural resources; its only significant mineral deposits consist of phosphates, which are mined, and potash, which is extracted from evaporation of Dead Sea water. Jordan has very few petroleum deposits and no coal. Its important rivers are the Yarmuk (shared with Syria and Israel), the Jordan (shared with Israel and the West Bank), and the Zarqa. Except for the small oasis of Azraq in the northeastern desert, Jordan has no natural freshwater lakes. An artificial lake was established behind the Talal dam on the Zarqa river.

Jordan has a pleasant warm climate with little humidity, but also little precipitation. In the winter in the capital of AMMAN, the average high temperature is 52° F (11° C) and the average low is 40°F (4.4°C); in the summer they are 86°F (30° C) and 64°F (18°C). In the northern part of the Transjordan plateau, precipitation averages 25 inches (64 cm), but in the southern part it falls to an erratic 10 to 14 inches (25–36 cm), barely enough to raise a wheat crop. The desert and the Jordan valley receive 0–10 inches (0–25 cm) of rain. Typical of the eastern Mediterranean, the precipitation falls only during the late autumn, winter, and early spring—the rainy season.

The People, Language, and Religion. Jordan's population of 3.6 million (1992 estimate), lives largely in the fertile highlands of the Transjordan plateau. Smaller numbers live in the Jordan valley, where they practice agriculture or mining, and in the desert, where they herd sheep, goats, and camels or enlist in the military. About 50 percent of the population are

Bedouin tents dwarfed by rugged valley terrain outside Amman, 1940s. (D.W. Lockhard)

Section of the ancient caravan city of Petra. (Richard Bulliet)

Jordanians who originate from the land east of the Jordan river. Most of the balance have their origins in Palestine. Many arrived as refugees in Jordan following the establishment of the State of Israel and the 1948 and 1967 Arab–Israel Wars. Other Palestinians moved to Jordan beginning in the 1950s. As a result of the 1990/91 Gulf Crisis and war, about 300,000 Palestinians with Jordanian citizenship moved from Kuwait back to Jordan, where they increased the population by 9 percent. While relations between the refugees and other Jordanians are relatively amicable today, Palestinian guerrilla organizations did conduct an unsuccessful civil war against the Jordanian regime in 1970. Both groups are of Arab stock and think of themselves as part of the larger Arab nation.

In terms of minorities, about 5 percent of the population are Arab Christians, mostly Greek Orthodox. They have positive relations with the Muslim majority and hold responsible and high level positions in business, industry, commerce, banking, and government. Ethnic minority groups are even smaller; among these are Armenian Christians and

Circassian Muslims. Some Circassians are royal palace guards.

The official language of Jordan is Arabic. Throughout the Arab world, although the written language is virtually the same, spoken dialects have developed. The Arabic spoken in Jordan conforms to the general eastern Mediterranean dialect; however, one finds some variations in the spoken language between the rural and urban regions, the older and younger generations, and the Jordanians and Palestinians. The influence of modern communications and education is causing many of these differences to be tempered or to disappear. Among the ethnic minority groups, Arabic is spoken in public but their mother tongue is often spoken at home.

Islam is Jordan's official religion. Ninety-five percent of the population are of that faith and almost all are SUNNI Muslims. The government supports the established religion through its ministry of Awqaf (WAQF) and Islamic affairs. (Religious pluralism is also officially countenanced; the state recognizes and respects the rights of religious minorities.) Islam deeply affects the lives and behavior of many Jordanians. Praying five times a day, attendance at mosque on Fridays (Sabbath), tithing, fasting during Ramadan, and the Hajj to Mecca are aspired to and practiced by many. The wave of popular Islamic fundamentalism that has affected the Middle East since the 1970s has had its influence in Jordan. Some practice their religion more diligently and demonstrably. Islamic classes and discussions, including informal and formal organizational activities, are popular; some women follow the religious dress code characterized by modest long coats and head scarves.

Jordan is a highly urbanized country. Seven out of every ten Jordanians live in towns of 5,000 or more; the balance resides in villages and encampments. With the return of the Palestinian Jordanians from Kuwait in 1990/91, many of whom settled in Amman, well over 1 million people now live in that city. In the 1970s, there was a great contrast between urban and rural living standards. Urbanites enjoyed basic services, such as drinking water and electricity in their homes, with schools and clinics in close proximity to their residences. By the late 1980s, those differences had substantially, but not entirely, disappeared. In urban areas, 99 percent have electricity in their residences; in the rural areas, the figure is 81 percent. For drinking water, the figures are 92 percent and 78 percent respectively. In terms of living space, while there are certainly some crowded quarters in the urban regions, they do not approach the crowded conditions often associated with third-world countries. About 10 percent of the people reside in PALESTINIAN REFUGEE CAMPS, where living conditions are congested. In rural areas, around 25 percent live in stone and mud houses; a diminishing number (less than 5 percent) follow the traditional life of the Arab bedouin, living in tents and tending camels, sheep, and goats.

Jordan is substantially overpopulated, given its limited natural resources, because of the substantial influx of Palestinian refugees and the very high birth rate. This is a major reason for the degree of urbanization in the country. Low rainfall and a growing population put pressure on the very limited water supply. Some significant cuts in irrigation have already occurred and more are expected. In addition, as of the 1990s, some 60 percent of the population are below 20 years of age—a heavy burden on the economy and service sector, especially in education.

Economy. Jordan's economy is highly skewed by its growing population and its dependence on the economies and politics of the Middle East. From the period of its gradual independence from Great Britain in the late 1940s and early 1950s, development has been the watchword of Jordan's economy. Beginning from a modest base, it grew by 11 percent per year from 1954 to 1967. During this period, Jordan received considerable economic and financial assistance first from Britain and later from the United States. After a period of decline caused by wars, civil strife, and international and regional constraints, it recommenced steady growth in 1974. This was stimulated by substantial aid and remittances from the oil-rich states of the region, plus a period of relative stability in Jordan and the region. By the mid-1980s, along with the Middle East economy generally, growth slowed to the point of stagnation. In 1988, the Jordan dinar, considered to be overvalued by international financial circles, was devalued by 40 percent. This economic decline was exacerbated by the 1990/91 Gulf Crisis and war. Among other things, Jordan lost most of the remittances from the returned Jordanians who had been working in the Persian/Arabian Gulf states as well as the direct financial aid from those countries.

In terms of both labor force and share of gross national product (GNP), Jordan's economy is dominated by the service sector (over 60 percent in both categories), followed by mining and manufacturing, construction, and agriculture. The service sector overshadows the economy because of the country's relatively large population, high birth rate, number of government employees in both the civilian and military sectors, and the government's successful efforts at extending essential services throughout the country. The mining and manufacturing sector is composed of five large companies—phosphate mining, potash extraction, fertilizer and cement facilities, and an oil refinery—as well as many small factories and artisans. Agriculture, which is usually important in developing countries, claims less than ten percent of both GNP and the labor force in Jordan.

History. Throughout most of recorded history, Jordan (formerly Transjordan) was not a distinct geographical or political entity. Rather it was usually just a provincial area of a larger state or empire. The exceptions might be the biblical Moabite kingdom centered in what is now KARAK, the Nabatean trading state ruled from its unique capital carved out of the rose-colored stone cliffs of PETRA, and the Crusader state led by Renard de Châtillon, who built a large citadel in Karak. Otherwise, the area was ruled successively by the Hittites, Egyptians, Assyrians, Babylonians, Persians, Israelites, Greeks, Seleucids, Ptolemies, Romans, Byzantines, and the Muslim dynasties (Umayyads, Abbasids, Fatimids, Ayyubids, and Mamluks). In 1518, the Ottoman Empire established control in the region that would endure until the last days of World War I.

Rock-cut temple at Petra. (Richard Bulliet)

After World War I, Transjordan came under the British-sponsored rule of King FAISAL I in the short-lived United Syrian Kingdom. In July 1920, France drove Faisal out of Syria and took control of most of the Arab kingdom, while Britain continued to claim Transjordan, as prescribed in the most secret French–British SYKES–PICOT AGREEMENT. In the meantime, Faisal's brother, Emir ABDULLAH IBN HUSAYN, arrived with an entourage of followers in the fall of 1920. In 1921, British Colonial Secretary Winston Churchill accepted Abdullah as the ruler of Transjordan under the League of Nations mandate for Britain (while Faisal was made ruler of Iraq). Emir Abdullah, with the crucial cooperation and financial help of Britain, established the basic institutions of the state—a government, parliament (Council of Notables, later replaced by the Legislative Council), a constitution (the Organic Law), and the military (the Arab Legion). After World War II, in 1946, an Anglo–Jordanian treaty was signed, to be revised in 1948—after which the emirate of Transjordan became the Hashimite Kingdom of Jordan and Abdullah was crowned king.

In 1948, Jordan, along with other Arab states, declared war on the newly declared State of Israel. In 1949, at the end of the war, Jordan was in military possession of the WEST BANK. Following considerable political maneuvering and parliamentary elections on the East Bank (of the Jordan river—the old Transjordan) and the West Bank, the two entities were coupled via a parliamentary vote as a unitary kingdom. On July 20, 1951, angered by Jordan's secret negotiations with Israel, a Palestinian assassinated King Abdullah in Jerusalem's Haram al-Sharif, one of the holiest Islamic shrines. He was succeeded by his son TALAL. By constitutional means, Talal was removed from the throne in 1952 due to mental illness. He was succeeded by his son, HUSSEIN IBN TALAL, who was then a minor. King Hussein did not take up his duties until he reached the age of eighteen in 1953.

Jordan's history during King Hussein's reign may be divided into three major periods. The first two decades were marked by internally and externally generated crises and threats to Hashimite rule and the very existence of the country. Radical ARAB NATIONALISM stimulated street riots, challenges to the regime from Jordan's prime minister in 1956 and 1957, destabilization by larger and stronger Arab states, and the devastating loss of the West Bank to Israel in the ARAB–ISRAEL WAR of June 1967. In addition, the Palestinian guerrilla organizations confronted Jordan in a bloody civil war in 1970. Nonetheless, while relying on his loyal military to survive, King Hussein and his circle helped put in place the bases for social and economic development.

The second phase, starting after the ARAB–ISRAEL WAR of October 1973, is distinguished by quieter political conditions within Jordan, rapid development fueled by funds (direct grants, loans, individual remittances) derived from the oil boom in neighboring states, and improved relations with most of Jordan's Arab neighbors in a relatively less radical regional atmosphere. Despite Jordan's problems with the Palestinians and its frequently strained relations with the Palestine Liberation Organization (PLO), the country became an accepted player and the king came to be a respected leader in most Arab capitals. Indeed, Jordan hosted two Arab summits—1980 and 1987—in Amman.

The third phase is dominated by the end of the Cold War and the alteration of regional relationships. In a sense, as a precursor to these changes, King Hussein decided to disengage Jordan politically and administratively from the West Bank, in response to the pressures from the Palestinian INTIFADA (uprising), which began in 1987. More important was the withdrawal of the Soviet Union as an active player in the region (1989/90), the United States's ensuing dominance in areas of its perceived interests, and the resulting polarization of the Arab world.

The 1990/91 GULF CRISIS and war left Jordan (then allied with Saddam Hussein's Iraq) and a few other poor Arab states politically, economically, and regionally isolated. On the domestic level, though, Jordan continued its gradual democratization process; its parliament had been recalled in 1984 after a hiatus that began in 1970, and in 1989, elections (generally considered to be the freest in the Arab Middle East) were held. Subsequently, under a mandate from King Hussein, leaders from all political streams wrote a national charter that defines the general principles for political life in the country. They include democracy, pluralism, and the recognition of the legitimacy of the Hashimite throne. A special general congress, of 2,000 representatives, ratified the document June 9, 1991. Jordan fully embraced the United States-sponsored Middle East peace process and, along with other Arab states and the Palestinians, participated in direct negotiations with Israel beginning in 1991. In September 1993, Jordan signed the peace accords with Israel.

BIBLIOGRAPHY

DAY, ARTHUR. *East Bank/West Bank: Jordan and the Prospects for Peace.* New York, 1986.
GUBSER, P. "Jordan: Balancing Pluralism and Authoritarianism." In *Ideology and Power in the Middle East,* ed. by P. Chelkowski and R. Pranger. Durham, N.C., 1988.
———. *Jordan: Crossroads of Middle Eastern Events.* Boulder, Colo., 1983.

JUREIDINI, PAUL A., and R. D. McLAURIN. *Jordan: The Impact of Social Change on the Role of the Tribes*. New York, 1984.

KHADER, BICHARA, and ADNAN BADRAN, eds. *The Economic Development of Jordan*. London, 1987.

LUNT, JAMES. *Hussein of Jordan*. New York, 1989.

SATLOFF, ROBERT B. *The Troubles on the East Bank: Challenges to the Domestic Stability of Jordan*. New York, 1986.

SHLAIM, AVI. *Collusion across the Jordan: King Abdullah, the Zionist Movement and the Partition of Palestine*. London, 1988.

VATIKIOTIS, P. J. *Politics and the Military in Jordan: A Study of the Arab Legion, 1927–1957*. New York, 1967.

WILSON, MARY C. *King Abdullah, Britain and the Making of Jordan*. Cambridge, U.K., 1987.

Peter Gubser

Jordan Cooperative Organization

Umbrella association for the cooperatives of Jordan.

In 1968, the Jordan Cooperative Organization (JCO) replaced the Jordan Cooperative Union, Jordan Cooperative Training Institute, Cooperative Auditing Union, and the government's Cooperative Development Department as the governing organization for Jordanian cooperatives. Its board is elected by these cooperatives, whose membership is, in turn, drawn from the general population. These businesses operate in the tradition of cooperatives in free-market economies. In terms of function, Jordan's cooperatives may be categorized as agricultural, consumer, producer, and handicraft. The JCO provides credit, banking, administrative, technical, training, and auditing services. Despite Israel's military occupation of the WEST BANK, the JCO maintains personnel and limited services in that region.

BIBLIOGRAPHY

GUBSER, PETER. *Jordan: Crossroads of Middle Eastern Events*. Boulder, Colo., 1983.

Peter Gubser

Jordanian Civil War

Internal strife between the Jordanian army and Palestinian guerillas.

Between 1967 and 1970, Palestinian guerilla groups established a strong presence in Jordan. By the summer of 1970, their attacks against Israel and activities within Jordan posed a significant threat to the stability, if not to the existence, of the Jordanian monar-chy. As a complicating factor, in the aftermath of the Arabs' defeat in the 1967 ARAB–ISRAELI WAR, Iraq's troops were stationed in Jordan. They, along with a strong Syrian military presence just north of Jordan's border, constituted an additional security threat.

In June 1970, Palestinian guerillas and the Jordanian army clashed in the capital, Amman, but fighting ceased after an agreement was struck allowing the guerillas to continue their presence. In September, another round of clashes erupted with serious new complications. The Popular Front for the Liberation of Palestine (led by George Habash) hijacked four airplanes, forcing three to land in Jordan with their hostages. As this international outrage was being sorted out, the fighting between the guerillas and the Jordanian army escalated. In mid-September, Jordan's King Hussein ibn Talal appointed a military cabinet—signaling his intent to seriously confront the guerillas. Iraq's troops, by minor repositioning, indicated they would not interfere; but on September 19, as many as 200 Syrian tanks invaded. For a time, Jordan seemed to be asking either the United States or Israel to help defeat this Syrian force. On September 22, the Jordanian air force joined the battle, turning the tide decisively in Jordan's favor. Because of internal Syrian politics and direct communications between King Hussein and Hafiz al-Asad, then Syrian air force commander, Syrian fighter planes did not join the battle. Subsequently, Jordan's army defeated the Palestinian guerillas on the ground.

With considerable assistance from Egypt's President Gamal Abdel Nasser, King Hussein and Yasir Arafat (head of the Palestine Liberation Organization [PLO] and al-Fath) signed a peace accord in Cairo, dated September 27, that called for the withdrawal of the Palestinian guerillas from Jordan. During the following months, Jordan's army undertook extensive and harsh mopping-up operations; as punishment for its actions against the politically favored Palestinian guerillas, Kuwait and Libya ended financial aid, and Syria closed its border and airspace to Jordanian traffic. Although Jordan suffered economically and politically for its defeat of the Palestinian guerillas, it eventually renormalized relations with the Arab world, especially after the October 1973 ARAB–ISRAEL WAR.

BIBLIOGRAPHY

DAY, ARTHUR. *East Bank/West Bank; Jordan and the Prospects for Peace*. New York, 1986.

GUBSER, PETER. *Jordan: Crossroads of Middle Eastern Events*. Boulder, Colo., 1983.

SATLOFF, ROBERT B. *The Troubles on the East Bank: Challenges to the Domestic Stability of Jordan*. New York, 1986.

Peter Gubser

Jordanian Option

A term used to describe the foreign policy of the Israeli Labor party; a preference for reaching a settlement with the Hashimite rulers of Jordan rather than with the Palestinians.

The origins of the Jordanian Option can be traced to the contacts between the JEWISH AGENCY (the official link between the Jews in Palestine and the British mandate authorities) and King Abdullah of Jordan, which culminated in a secret agreement to partition Palestine between themselves in 1947. After the attainment of Israel's independence, on May 15, 1948, Israeli leaders saw the survival of the Hashimite monarchy in Jordan as essential to their own nation's security.

After Israel captured the West Bank of the Jordan river during the 1967 ARAB–ISRAEL WAR, Labor party leaders opposed the creation of a Palestinian state and strove, unsuccessfully, for a territorial compromise with Jordan. The Jordanian Option ceased to be Israel's official policy following the rise to power of the Likud party in 1977. Later, whether in opposition or as the Likud's coalition partner, the Labor party continued to advocate the Jordanian Option. By cutting the links between Jordan and the West Bank in July 1988, Jordan's King Hussein announced, in effect, that a Jordanian Option no longer exists—if it ever did.

BIBLIOGRAPHY

SHLAIM, AVI. *Collusion across the Jordan: King Abdullah, the Zionist Movement, and the Partition of Palestine.* New York, 1988.

Avi Shlaim

Jordanian Press Agency

The official government-owned news agency, established in 1965.

The agency provides national news and official transcripts to Jordanian newspapers, radio and television, government departments and international subscribers. The agency operates a teleprinter that transmits in Arabic and English, and also provides a photo service.

BIBLIOGRAPHY

GUBSER, PETER. *Jordan: Crossroads of Middle Eastern Events.* Boulder, Colo., 1983.

Jenab Tutunji

Jordan Phosphate Mining Company

One of the largest employers in Jordan.

Jordan is the world's third-largest exporter of phosphates, the country's most important natural resource and its principal export commodity. Established in 1930, the company mines and sells phosphates extracted from its three mines. In 1988, 7 tons (6.5 t) were mined, of which 6 tons (5.5 t) were exported.

BIBLIOGRAPHY

The Middle East and North Africa 1991, 37th ed. London, 1991.

Abla M. Amawi

Jordan River

River that forms the boundary between Israel and Jordan; it flows south from Syria to the Dead Sea.

The Jordan river rises from the confluence of three major springs and streams located on the southern and western slopes of Mount Hermon (Arabic, Jabal al-Shaykh). The largest is the Dan and the other two are the Hasbani (Hebrew, Nahal Senir) and the Baniyas (Hebrew, Nahal Hermon) streams. The streams unite about four miles (6.5 km) south of the Lebanon–Israel border. These springs usually provide 50 percent of the water of the upper Jordan, the rest coming from surface runoff in the rainy winter months. The discharge flows into the northern end of the Ghor, which is the valley of the Dead Sea (and the northern extremity of the Great Rift valley that runs south to Africa, ending at Mozambique).

Jordan river viewed from the Allenby (King Hussein) bridge. (D.W. Lockhard)

The upper Jordan river flows swiftly through the Hula valley, additional water coming to it from minor springs and Wadi Barayghit (Hebrew, Nahal Iyyon). Four miles (6.5 km) south of the Jordan's outlet from Lake Hula, the water course deepens and the river runs for ten miles (16 km), plunging 850 feet (270 m). The central Jordan river begins north of the Sea of Galilee (also called Lake Tiberias or Lake Kinneret), leaving the southern exit of the lake where it meets up with a few more streams but, most importantly, with its main tributary, the YARMUK RIVER. The Yarmuk originates in the eastern rift and forms the border between Syria and the Kingdom of Jordan as it flows westward to enter the Jordan river six miles (9.5 km) south of the Sea of Galilee at 985 feet (295 m) below sea level. The lower Jordan river flows southward, dropping to 1,310 feet (395 m) below sea level, emptying into the Dead Sea, a great salt lake whose surface level is the lowest point on the earth's surface.

The water of the Jordan is freshest at the headwaters and becomes more saline as it enters the Sea of Galilee; the salinity rises rapidly as it moves south to the Dead Sea. Agriculture depends in part on water quality (freshness) and in part on soil quality (organic matter and minerals). Over the years, and after much intensive study and advice, during the British mandate (1922–1948), the Zionists in Palestine determined that the northern Negev desert had very fertile soil and that all it needed was a good supply of water. At that time, the only large-scale development plan for the Jordan river was carried out by the Zionist leader and hydroelectric engineer Pinhas Rutenberg; even that was limited by the British mandate administration to the erection of just one power station to supply hydroelectric power to Palestine west of the Jordan. All Rutenberg's plans for irrigation and electrification of the area east of the Jordan river came to nothing.

When the State of Israel came into existence in 1948, plans were drawn for the diversion of water from Jisr Banat Yakub, on the upper Jordan, to be taken via massive pipelines across the Jezreel valley and south along the coastal plain, terminating in Beersheba, where it could be used most effectively. When work began on this diversion scheme in 1952, Syria complained to the United Nations that this violated the demilitarized zone agreement of the 1949 armistice (which ended the 1948 ARAB–ISRAEL WAR). Israel was ordered to cease construction, and U.S. Special Ambassador Eric Johnston was appointed to devise a scheme for regional development of the Jordan river system. Johnston's Unified Plan, worked out from 1953 to 1955, was never formally ratified by the League of Arab States (Arab League) but has been implemented by Israel and by the Kingdom of Jordan in separate schemes.

Israel has constructed the Cross Israel Water Carrier (see NATIONAL WATER SYSTEM), which was its original idea, but the carrier was started at the northern end of the Sea of Galilee—a costly modification, considering that the water had to be pumped up to the level of the Jezreel valley. Across Israel, the government built smaller pipelines radiating out over the farmland to bring water for irrigation. The entire system forms a water grid, easily controlled and measured; it was completed in 1964.

The Kingdom of Jordan has constructed the East Ghor project, hooking up a pipeline to the Yarmuk above Adassiya, which parallels the flow of the Jordan river. The pipeline is on a much higher level than the river, just below the high ridges, and the radiating smaller pipelines thus, by gravity, flow to the rich Jordan valley soil, irrigating the farms. The final stage of the project, under Jordan Valley Authority control (created in 1973), was completed in 1980 when the pipeline reached the Dead Sea.

Jordan wants to construct a high dam at Maqarin, farther up the Yarmuk, both for better control of winter floods and for hydroelectricity. Israel objects to this project since it would lessen its supply of water.

After the 1967 ARAB–ISRAEL WAR, new issues complicated an already complex situation, since Israel took and occupied the west bank of the Jordan and Jerusalem. Discovering the existence of the huge aquifer under the spine of the mountains of Judea and Samaria (the WEST BANK), Israel began to pump winter floodwaters into the aquifer—to use it as a better water-storage area than the Sea of Galilee. Israel refuses to allow the Palestinians of the West Bank to drill deeply for new wells lest they tap this vital storage area.

Another complication is connected with the supplying of the Jordan's water to the occupied West Bank territory: Should this be computed as an unofficial percentage going to the Kingdom of Jordan or to Israel? If it is supplied by Israel, then Israel should get a larger share of the Jordan waters.

Hydropolitics are vitally important to both Israel and the Kingdom of Jordan as they reach the point where they use almost all their available water and yet have rapidly growing populations. Unless there is a major technological breakthrough, hydropolitics may precipitate the next war.

BIBLIOGRAPHY

NAFF, THOMAS, and RUTH C. MATSON, eds. *Water in the Middle East, Conflict or Cooperation?* Boulder, Colo., 1984.

ORNI, EFRAIM, and ELISHA EFRAT. *Geography of Israel.* Jerusalem, 1973.

REGUER, SARA. "Controversial Waters: Thirty Years of Exploitation of the Jordan River, 1950–1980." *Middle Eastern Studies,* Spring 1993.

Sara Reguer

Jordan Times

Jordanian English-language newspaper.

The *Jordan Times,* a daily newspaper, was founded in 1976 by the Jordan Press Foundation, which also publishes the widely circulated Arabic-language daily, *al-Ra'i.* Until the late 1980s, the *Jordan Times* was the only Jordanian newspaper published in English. In 1988 the editors were dismissed because of royal displeasure with their editorial policies.

BIBLIOGRAPHY

GUBSER, PETER. *Jordan: Crossroads of Middle Eastern Events.* Boulder, Colo., 1983.

Jenab Tutunji

Joseph, Dov [1899–?]

Israeli lawyer, member of the Knesset, and cabinet minister.

In 1918 Joseph joined the Jewish legion, serving in Palestine. He settled in Jerusalem, where he became an attorney. In 1948 he was in charge of the defense of Jerusalem while the city was under siege. As a member of the Knesset (Israel's parliament) from 1949 to 1959, Joseph held a variety of cabinet posts including minister of supply and rationing (1949–1950), minister of communications (1950–1951), minister of trade (1951–1952), and minister of state (1952–1953). He was minister of justice from 1961 to 1965. Prior to 1948, Joseph was active in the leadership of the World Zionist Organization and the Jewish Agency.

Martin Malin

Jubayl, al-

A small port on the Gulf coast of Saudi Arabia.

Al-Jubayl traditionally served the Najdi hinterland, especially the Qasim district. The kingdom's Second Five-Year Development Plan (1975–1980) teamed al-Jubayl with Yanbu on the Red Sea coast in an ambitious industrial development scheme, involving crude oil refining, petrochemical complexes, and steel-manufacturing industries, linked by trans–Saudi Arabian oil and gas pipelines. The development of the two sites was envisaged as taking ten years and costing in excess of 70 billion dollars. Jubayl was to be the bigger of the two industrial developments, with three petroleum refineries, six petrochemical plants, an aluminum smelter, and a steel mill, as well as support industries, an industrial port, and a city of 100,000 inhabitants.

John E. Peterson

Judaism

The religion of the Jewish people.

Judaism developed out of scripture (the Torah) and an oral tradition of legal and ethical conduct as inscribed in the Talmud, codes, mystical literature, and rabbinic commentaries. Although traditional Jews assume that Judaism has remained unchanged from the revelation at Sinai to the present, most scholars agree that it has been transformed by the vicissitudes of Jewish history since the days of the Bible.

A significant turning point in Judaism occurred when the wandering Israelites entered into the Promised Land and later when they built their Holy Temple in Jerusalem. For much of this time, the religion was essentially a temple cult, organized around regular ritual sacrifices and a series of three pilgrimages to Jerusalem, and practiced by a people ruled by kings, guided by prophets, and ministered to by priests.

After the Babylonian destruction of the First Temple in 586 B.C.E. and even more so following the Roman destruction of the Second Temple in 70 C.E., Judaism became a religion of exile. Replacing the temple and temple rites were synagogues, regular prayer, and an emphasis on the lifelong study of sacred texts in the Torah. Rabbis and teachers replaced the priests and prophets, and Jewish community leaders, the kings. This new Judaism was a more portable religion, appropriate to a wandering people. Moral and ethical laws became central, but ritual praxis, governed by strict codes and guided by rabbinic interpretation of the law, was also crucial. The Torah became the focus of Judaism, the YESHIVA its most important sanctuary, and a return to the Promised Land Zion and a rebuilding of the temple in Jerusalem remained abiding hopes and part of the promise of messianic redemption.

The DIASPORA has led to a nuancing of Jewish tradition into distinct customs. Among the most outstanding have been the custom variations between Sephardic Jews, whose expatriation occurred in the Middle East, North Africa, and the Iberian Peninsula, and Ashkenazic Jews, who trace their origins to France and the German-speaking countries but who emigrated ultimately to almost all of Europe and later to the Americas. Sephardic Jews and Ashkenazic Jews share a belief in Scripture and a dependence on the Talmud, but they have evolved variations in custom and ritual praxis based upon their varying ethnic experiences and the disparate rabbinic authorities by whom they have been guided over the years. Nevertheless, many of the rabbis and their commentaries have, through time, acquired a religious legitimacy that supersedes these differences. Thus, for example, Rashi, an eleventh-century Ashkenazic exegete, and Maimonides, a twelfth-century Sephardic rabbinic codifier, are recognized by all Jewish traditions to be authoritative interpreters of Judaism.

By and large, Judaism defines a Jew as someone born of a Jewish mother or someone who has submitted to religious conversion. Although there is debate about what constitute the minimal requirements of conversion, the *halakhic* (Judeo-legal) minimum requirement consists of circumcision for males, immersion in the waters of a ritual bath (*mikveh*), a period of Torah study, and a commitment to be bound by all the laws of Judaism. During the twentieth century, some non-Orthodox Jews have expanded this religious definition to include children of either a Jewish father or mother and do not require a commitment to keep all the laws. The definition is a crucial one in Israel, which guarantees full citizenship rights to all Jews.

Through most of the period of the Diaspora, Judaism has tended to focus on matters of praxis more than on principles of faith, because, it was argued, the former better guaranteed the religion's continuity while insuring the integrity of belief. Since the eighteenth century and especially in the twentieth century, however, a large-scale move away from praxis has occurred. A result of religious reform and social changes that brought Jews out of their status as pariahs and into the mainstream of Western societies, this development has led to a Judaism that focuses more on its moral and ethical principles and on some vague notions of ethnicity than it does on ritual praxis. Accordingly, in contemporary Judaism, those who strictly maintain traditions, ritual praxis, and time-honored Jewish codes of conduct now constitute a growing minority.

Although the principles of Jewish faith have been the subject of much discussion and debate among Jewish philosophers and rabbinic commentators, among the most commonly cited essentials are thirteen principles listed by Maimonides. These include a belief in a single Creator, a unique and everlasting God, who is incorporeal, who existed before time be-

gan and will last after it has passed, and who alone is worthy of worship. It also includes a belief in the utterances of the prophets, and especially the words of Moses; a conviction that the entire Torah was divinely revealed to Moses at Sinai and passed on intact to the Jewish people, who may not replace it with another set of teachings; and a belief that God is omniscient and that He creates all life, rewards the good, and punishes the bad. Finally, it includes a faith in the promise of messianic redemption. In the same way that only a minority of Jews today abide by all the rules of Jewish law and praxis, so is it likely that only a few Jews today hold all of the thirteen beliefs.

Although Judaism has demonstrated a remarkable capacity to survive the vicissitudes of Jewish history and the vagaries of existence in the Diaspora, including persecution and pogrom (most recently during the European Holocaust), some observers are anxious about its future in the context of an open society like America's and that of a secular state like Israel, the two largest population centers of Jewry today. Pointing to a decline in numbers of Jews in America as well as a diminution of Jewish education, practice, and faith, these observers argue that Judaism's days as a vital religion are numbered in America and throughout the Diaspora. On the other hand, looking at Israel's large-scale redefinition of Jews as secular Israelis, other observers worry no less about the future of the religion in the Jewish homeland. To some of these observers, the answer to these anxieties is to press for the coming of the Messiah. To others, the answer is a revitalization of Jewish education and a return to Jewish tradition.

BIBLIOGRAPHY

FINKELSTEIN, L. *The Jews.* New York, 1971.
GLATZER, N. N. *In Time and Eternity: A Jewish Reader.* New York.
HEILMAN S., and S. M. COHEN. *Cosmopolitans and Parochials.* Chicago, 1990.

Samuel C. Heilman

Judea and Samaria

See West Bank

Judeo-Arabic

The various forms of Arabic spoken or written by Jews from before the rise of Islam to modern times.

Like all Diaspora Jewish languages, Judeo-Arabic is distinguished from its non-Jewish cognate, Arabic, in the use of the Hebrew alphabet, a significant number of Hebrew and Aramaic loanwords and elements, and its own distinguishing grammatical, syntactical, and phonological forms.

In the Middle Ages, written Judeo-Arabic, which depending upon the subject matter ranged from Classical to Middle Arabic in style, became a primary medium of Jewish intellectual creativity for theologians, philosophers, grammarians, lexicographers, and legal scholars, and was also the primary medium of correspondence. Only for poetry (which in Islamic society is considered the supreme national art form) was Hebrew the principal language of expression. Owing to the decline of Hellenistic humanism after the High Middle Ages and the increased social isolation of Jews within the context of a larger Arab world after the thirteenth century, the regional varieties of modern Judeo–Arabic that emerged in the late fifteenth century were characterized by their vernacular nature.

During the nineteenth and early twentieth centuries, Judeo-Arabic books and newspapers were published from Morocco to India (where there was an Iraqi Jewish mercantile colony). Many of the books were translations or adaptations of European popular literature and, in some instances, works of HASKALA Hebrew writers. By the 1920s, Judeo-Arabic publication was declining in many places as French became the main language of high culture for many Jews, because of the ALLIANCE ISRAÉLITE UNIVERSELLE schools. Nevertheless, it remained the spoken language for the great majority of Jews until their mass exodus to Israel in the mid-1950s. Judeo-Arabic is dying out among the second and third generations born in Israel, France, and the Americas, who tend to speak their national languages (Hebrew, French, and English, Spanish, or Portuguese).

BIBLIOGRAPHY

STILLMAN, NORMAN A. "Language Patterns in Islamic and Judaic Societies." In *Islam and Judaism: 1400 Years of Shared Values,* ed. by S. Wasserstrom. Portland, Oreg., 1991.
———. *The Language and Culture of the Jews of Sefrou, Morocco: An Ethnolinguistic Study.* Manchester, U.K., 1988.

Norman Stillman

Jufayr, al-

A former British naval base located near Mina Sulman, Bahrain's major port, in Manama.

After independence in 1971, Bahrain agreed in a series of letters to lease Jufayr to the United States to provide homeport facilities for the U.S. Navy's Command Middle East Force (COMIDEAST-FOR). During the Arab–Israel War of 1973, Bahrain responded to domestic and Arab criticism of this arrangement by canceling the homeport agreement with the United States. A new agreement was negotiated in 1977, however, and the small U.S. naval presence in the Persian/Arabian Gulf expanded dramatically in the late 1980s and, of course, during the 1990/91 Gulf crisis, when Iraq attempted to annex Kuwait and a coalition of UN forces massed in the Gulf region. The Jufayr agreement was always a very sensitive issue for Bahrain's ruling family, and the Bahraini press has not been allowed to discuss the issue on grounds of national security. The agreement was also a major source of tension between the government and the opposition in Bahrain's National Assembly in the early 1970s.

BIBLIOGRAPHY

NAKHLEH, EMILE. *The Persian Gulf and American Policy.* New York, 1982.

Emile A. Nakhleh

Juhaiman al-Utaybi

See Utaybi, Juhaiman al-

Jumayyil, Amin   [1942–]

President of Lebanon, 1982–1988.

A lawyer by training, Jumayyil is noted for his oratorical skills in Arabic. A moderate who was not active in the Phalange party, founded by his father, Pierre Jumayyil, he concentrated on his political career after being elected to parliament in 1970. Jumayyil was named president in 1982 after the assassination of his brother Bashir, through consensus among the various political factions, key Arab states, and Western powers. He based his policies on his alliance with the United States, which ultimately led to the unraveling of his presidency. Under pressure from Syria, he abrogated the U.S.-brokered 1983 security agreement with Israel. On 17 February 1984, the last of the multinational force withdrew from Beirut. Without support, Jumayyil was a lame duck president. He remained in office until the end of his term in 1988.

Majed Halawi

Jumayyil, Bashir   [1947–1982]

President of Lebanon, 1982.

Fluent in Arabic, English, and French, Jumayyil studied at Jesuit schools and earned degrees in law and political science. Charismatic and iron-willed, under his command he unified the Lebanese Forces, the cornerstone of the Christian political–military apparatus during the civil war in Lebanon. Jumayyil's forthright, militant nationalism and the social programs he inaugurated gained him wide-ranging support within the Christian community and established him as the preeminent Christian political force in the country. On 23 August 1982, Bashir Jumayyil was elected president of Lebanon, an event that affronted a significant majority of the country's Muslim population. He was subsequently assassinated on 14 September 1982.

Majed Halawi

Jumayyil, Pierre   [1905–1984]

Lebanese nationalist; founder of al-Kata'ib (Phalange) party.

Jumayyil was born in Bikfayya, Mount Lebanon, into a Maronite family. He completed his education at Jesuit schools and obtained a degree in pharmacy. In 1936 Jumayyil attended the Berlin Olympics, where he was impressed by the youth movement of the National Socialist (Nazi) Party. He decided, upon his return to Lebanon, to form a similar group, al-Kata'ib (the Phalange). Initially, al-Kata'ib stood at the divide between the two main currents of Christian public opinion: that of Emile Eddé, which favored the consolidation of France's hegemony in Lebanon, and that of Bishara al-Khurd, which called for Lebanon's independence with close ties to the Arab world.

After a failed attempt in 1951, Jumayyil was elected deputy from Beirut in 1960. He had led the opposition to President-elect Fu'ad Chehab, the candidate of the consensus between President Gamal Abdel Nasser of Egypt and the United States that ended the 1958 civil war; nevertheless, he joined a four-member national reconciliation cabinet that was formed on 24 September 1958. He subsequently participated in most cabinets formed by Chehab and by his protégé successor, Charles Hilu.

In 1968, Pierre Jumayyil entered into al-Hilf al-Thulathi (Tripartite Alliance) with former President Camille Chamoun and Deputy Raymond Eddé, gradually distancing himself from Chehab. In 1970, the Hilf candidate, Sulayman Franjiyya, was elected president.

Jumayyil staunchly opposed Nasserism and Arab nationalism. He was particularly hostile to the armed Palestinian fighters in Lebanon. The Kata'ib repeatedly clashed with Palestinian fighters in the early 1970s. In January 1975, Jumayyil denounced the Palestine Liberation Organization for sowing anarchy in Lebanon, and the following month demanded a referendum on Palestinian presence in the country. The Ayn al-Rimmani incident of April 13, 1975, which ignited Lebanon's civil war, occurred between Kata'ib members and Palestinian fighters.

During the Lebanese civil war, with the Kata'ib as his base, Jumayyil was at the center of the Christian right camp. He played a key role in obtaining the introduction into Lebanon of troops from Syria, who initially helped the Christians to achieve a reversal of the successes of the Palestinian–leftist alliance. His relations with Syria, however, deteriorated as the Kata'ib's military cooperation with Israel, which culminated in Israel's invasion of Lebanon in 1982, grew ever stronger.

During the civil war, Jumayyil worked with the traditional Muslim leadership to create a right-wing Christian–Muslim alliance. With the failure of these efforts, he began advocating political decentralization, which many considered a call for the de facto partition of Lebanon. At the time of his death, Jumayyil was a minister in the National Unity government of Rashid Karame.

Majed Halawi

Jumblatt, Kamal   [1917–1977]

Lebanese Druze politician.

Kamal was the son of Fu'ad (assassinated when Kamal was a boy) and Nazira Jumblatt. A bright young man, he showed deep interest in academic matters and distanced himself from the political affairs of the DRUZE community, of which his mother was the political leader. He studied at St. Joseph

University and attended the Sorbonne. As a student Jumblatt was far from the radical politics with which he was later associated. He was sympathetic to the French mandate in his youth but became a supporter of Bishara al-KHURI after independence. His first prominent political role was in 1952, when he was instrumental in the formation of the opposition block that worked for the ouster of President al-Khuri.

Over the years, Jumblatt became identified with socialist and pro-Palestinian politics. He initially tried to mobilize non-Lebanese Druzes, and he founded the PROGRESSIVE SOCIALIST PARTY in the late 1940s. The party, however, gradually lost its non-Druze leaders and became a political tool for Jumblatt political leadership. Jumblatt was inconsistent: he championed secularization of politics in Lebanon while cultivating sectarian support among Druze followers, and he promoted socialist policies while remaining a large landowner. He emerged as a prominent pan-Arabist in 1958, when he was one of the key leaders of the popular uprising against the rule of Camille CHAMOUN. He became a staunch supporter of Camal Abdel Nasser.

In his political career, Jumblatt maintained the roles of both insider and outsider. He held ministerial posts in cabinets beginning in the 1940s, although he always spoke as the representative of the antiestablishment. In the 1960s, Jumblatt formed a loose coalition of leftist and Muslim organizations and parties to champion support for the Palestine Liberation Organization (PLO) in Lebanon and to call for major reforms of the political system in Lebanon. By 1975, Jumblatt had become one of the most effective and popular leaders in the country. He headed the LEBANESE NATIONAL MOVEMENT (which comprised leftist and Muslim organizations) and aligned himself with the PLO. His conflict in 1976 with the regime in Syria over the future course of the LEBANESE CIVIL WAR OF 1975, which Jumblatt wanted to end with a decisive victory for his coalition, led to his death the following year at the hands of assassins believed to be working for Syria.

Although Jumblatt's critics question his motivations during the civil war (he was often accused of frustration at not being able to run for president, an office reserved for Maronites), he succeeded in playing a role that far exceeded the historical role of the JUMBLATT FAMILY. Some say that he solidified the ties between the Druze and Arabism, at the same time that others within the community wanted him to focus more on the affairs of the community.

As'ad AbuKhalil

Jumblatt, Walid [1945–   ]

Lebanese Druze politician.

Like his father, Kamal, Walid Jumblatt did not seek the political leadership of the DRUZE community or of the JUMBLATT FAMILY. It was thrust upon him in the wake of his father's assassination in 1977. Jumblatt studied at the American University of Beirut. In his first years as leader, he was uncomfortable with his new role and merely followed the path of his father. However, he quickly made peace with the regime in Syria. He later abandoned his father's policy and decided to focus more on the affairs of the community, abandoning Kamal's pan-Arab vision. Following Israel's 1982 invasion of Lebanon, Walid reorganized the PROGRESSIVE SOCIALIST PARTY, making it a purely Druze fighting force. He led the defense of the predominantly Druze mountain areas against the encroachments of the Maronite-led Lebanese Forces. His stand within the community was strengthened when he allowed his militias to fight an all-out war against the Lebanese Forces, aided by some Palestine Liberation Organization factions. The fighting (in what became known as the war of the mountains in 1983) was accompanied by bloody massacres, committed by both sides.

Jumblatt survived a 1982 assassination attempt that soured his relationship with the regime of Amin JU-MAYYIL. He later formed the nucleus of the opposition to Jumayyil after the agreement of 17 May 1983 between Israel and Lebanon, which was rejected by Syria. Jumblatt dissolved his militia after the election of Ilyas Hrawi as president in 1989. He ran in the 1992 elections and won. His party also won another seat in Parliament, bringing their total to ten. Jumblatt was named minister for the affairs of the displaced peoples in 1994.

As'ad AbuKhalil

Jumblatt Family

Prominent Druze family in Lebanon.

The Jumblatts are one of two rival DRUZE family confederations in Lebanon (the other being the Yazbaki). The family is traced to a Kurdish family of Janbulad (and to the chieftain Ali Janbulad from Aleppo), Syria; they came to Lebanon in the seventeenth century after a failed rebellion against the Ottomans. With the support of Prince Fakhr al-Din II, the family was invited to settle in the SHUF.

After their conversion to the Druze religion, the extinction of the Ma'nid dynasty enabled them to become shaykhs of the Shuf. They extended their feudal domain south of the Shuf, coming to rival in power, and later forming the opposition to the Chehab dynasty. In the nineteenth century, the Jumblatt family became one of the most prominent political (zu'ama) families in Lebanon. In the twentieth century, the history of the family is indistinguishable from the history of the Druze in Lebanon. In the 1920s during the French mandate, the political leadership of the family was assumed by Nazira Jumblatt, who succeeded her husband Fu'ad after his assassination. She cooperated with the French authorities to prevent the Druze from defying the mandate government.

The political prominence of the family was boosted by the emergence of Kamal Jumblatt (Nazirah's son), who, until his death in 1977, dominated Lebanon's political life. The nature of the Jumblatt leadership changed when Kamal promoted progressive and socialist policies that extended his leadership beyond the confines of the Druze family confederation. He also succeeded in marginalizing, perhaps more than at any other time in the modern history of Druzes in Lebanon, the role of the Yazbaki ARSLAN FAMILY. This was especially true under the leadership of the highly ineffective Prince Majid, whose close association with Maronite leader Camille CHAMOUN discredited him, particularly after the outbreak of the Lebanese civil war of 1975. Kamal emerged as the spokesperson of the leftist/Muslim coalition that he had helped to found before the outbreak of civil war. The death of the Yazbaki shaykh al-aql (the highest religious authority among the Druzes) also helped the Jumblatt family, whose shaykh al-aql became the religious leader of all Druze in Lebanon, thereby unifying, for the first time in modern times, the religious leadership of the community.

As'ad AbuKhalil

Jumhuriyyah, al-

Cairo daily newspaper.

The first editor of al-Jumhuriyyah, which was founded in 1953 and is owned by the Egyptian government, was Anwar al-SADAT. Usually more leftist than al-Ahram or al-Akhbar, al-Jumhuriyyah does not compete effectively against them. Its circulation was 650,000 in 1992.

Arthur Goldschmidt, Jr.

Jundi, Abd al-Karim al-

Syrian military officer and politician.

Born in Sulamiya of Ismai'li descent, Jundi received a military education and rose to become a colonel in the Syrian army. He was a key figure in guiding the leadership of the Ba'th party from 1962, as a member of the secret and internal military committee. He served as minister of agrarian reform in 1965 and chief of military intelligence in 1966.

BIBLIOGRAPHY

HINNEBUSCH, RAYMOND A. Authoritarian Power and State Formation in Ba'thist Syria: Army, Party, and Peasant. Boulder, Colo., 1990.

Charles U. Zenzie

Jundi, Khalid al-

Syrian military officer and statesman.

Educated at the military staff college and member of the Ba'th party, Khalid al-Jundi served as president of the General Syrian Workers' Federation from 1965 to 1967. In 1967 he was military attaché to China, until his arrest in July 1968.

BIBLIOGRAPHY

Who's Who in the Middle East, 1967–1968.

Charles U. Zenzie

Jundi, Sami al-   [1924–   ]

Syrian dentist and politician.

An early Ba'th leader in Sulamiya in the 1940s, Sami al-Jundi was selected as director general of information from 1958–1961. In 1963, he founded the Socialist Unionist party and served as minister of culture and national guidance. Finishing a brief stint as minister of information in 1964, he was appointed ambassador to France until 1968. Arrested in that year, he fled first to Lebanon, then to Europe.

BIBLIOGRAPHY

Who's Who in the Middle East, 1967–1968.

Charles U. Zenzie

June War

See Arab–Israel War (1967)

Justice Party

Turkish political party.

The Justice party (JP) was founded in early 1961 by the former chief of the general staff, Ragip Gümüspala and ten associates, four of whom had been active in the DEMOCRAT PARTY (DP). The JP was created as a continuation of the DP and absorbed the latter's provincial party organization. Three groups comprised the JP in the early years and vied for its leadership: a group of officers centered around Gümüspala; a right-wing group led by Gökhan Evliyaoğlu; and a liberal wing, which succeeded in making Süleyman Demirel head of the party in 1964. The JP received 43.8 percent of the vote in the October 1961 elections and formed a coalition government with the Republican People's party (RPP) that lasted until May 1962. In the October 1965 general elections, the Demirel-led JP received 53 percent of the vote and 240 out of 450 seats in the National Assembly. The JP also won the 1965 and 1969 elections, but despite a rapidly growing economy, expanding political instability led the military to threaten to intervene. On March 13, 1971, the Demirel government resigned.

When civilian politics resumed in 1973, Demirel refused to form a coalition with the RPP, and the JP became the main opposition party. In 1975, Demirel formed a coalition government, known as the Nationalist Front, with three other parties and independents. Although the coalition lasted more than two years, members of the coalition seldom cooperated, preferring to work to infiltrate supporters into the bureaucracy. In addition, during these years, the JP became associated with the extremist right-wing positions of one of its partners, the Nationalist Action party. The 1977 elections were held among increasing street violence. Following the elections, the RPP formed a minority government that lasted less than one month, and Demirel attempted to form a government. The second JP-dominated Nationalist Front government lasted only through 1977. The JP formed a third government in December 1979: It was in power at the time of the Black September coup. One of the first acts of the new military government was to close down all existing parties, putting an end to the JP. In 1983, the True Path party was established as a continuation of the JP.

Like the DP, the Justice party won support from peasants in the wealthier regions of the country, commercial farmers, and the business community. In addition, the party won the votes of many workers and residents of the squatter districts of the cities, but in the 1970s, the RPP began to win the loyalty of these two groups. Like the DP, the JP sought to expand the private sector but also intervened widely in the economy through the public sector, controls over trade, and other regulations. Through 1970, the JP pursued a policy of import-substituting industrialization. Beginning in 1970, the government attempted to reorient the economy toward exporting, a move resisted by many industrialists.

Despite similarities with the DP, a number of changes in Turkey prevented the JP from replicating its predecessors' electoral success. First, the proliferation of smaller parties made it necessary to form coalition governments in the 1970s. Second, the RPP made many inroads into the urban coalitions that had supported the DP in the 1950s and the JP in the 1960s. Third, in 1967, a more militant workers' union was formed, which refused to cooperate with the government. Fourth, small-business men in the party were alienated by JP policies that favored large-business men, particularly in Istanbul. Many small-business owners supported the National Order party, led by Necmeddin ERBAKAN, which captured a portion of JP votes. Fifth, the JP continued the DP policy of closely allying with the West. But, particularly after American condemnation of the Turkish intervention in Cyprus in 1974, many people criticized the JP for being too close to the West. Finally, in the 1960s, rising tensions led to escalating political violence. All of these factors combined to make it more difficult for the JP to form stable governments than it had been for the DP.

BIBLIOGRAPHY

AHMAD, FEROZ. *The Making of Modern Turkey.* London, 1993.

LEVI, AYNER. "The Justice Party, 1961–1980." In *Political Parties and Democracy in Turkey,* ed. by Metin Heper and Jacob M. Landau. London, 1991.

SHERWOOD, W. B. "The Rise of the Justice Party in Turkey." *World Politics* 20 (1967/68): 54–65.

David Waldner

K

 ——

Ka'ba

In Islam, the most sacred sanctuary, the center of the Muslim world.

The Ka'ba (also Kaaba) is a cubic stone structure that stands at the approximate center of the Mosque of the Sanctuary of Mecca and is revered by Muslims as the unique shrine of the one true God, and thus the most sacred spot on earth. It is in the direction of this shrine that Muslims everywhere face when engaging in their obligatory five daily prayers. The Ka'ba is also one of the main destinations of pilgrims who come to circle the structure as one of the rites of either the HAJJ (the yearly mass pilgrimage to

The Ka'ba shown on a Saudi Arabian postage stamp. (Richard Bulliet)

Mecca) or the *umra* (a shortened version of the hajj that can be performed at any time of the year). Usually covered by a black brocade cloth decorated with gold embroidered passages from the Qur'an, the Ka'ba measures some fifty feet (15 m) high with a facade of about forty feet (12 m) and three remaining walls of about thirty-five feet (11 m) in length. The principal external features of the building are two silver- and gold-plated doors forming a single entryway, a waterspout, and the famed Black Stone encased in silver and identified by tradition as the shrine's celestial cornerstone, brought to earth by the angel Gabriel. The Qur'an attributes the construction of the Ka'ba to Ibrahim (Abraham), the great ancestral monotheist of Islam, and his son Isma'il (Ishmael) (2:127). Legend has it, however, that the Arab peoples descended from Isma'il forgot the original monotheistic charter of the Ka'ba and gradually transformed it into a temple housing idols representing 360 divinities. Accordingly, after conquering Mecca for Islam (c. 630 C.E.), the Prophet Muhammad is said to have made it his first order of business to cleanse the Ka'ba of its idolatrous trappings and rededicate it to Allah. Today the interior of the Ka'ba is furnished only with a number of suspended oil lamps. At least once yearly, the doors are unlocked and the interior is swept, washed, and perfumed by special functionaries. Also, on special occasions, select pilgrims are granted the honor of entering and being permitted to pray within the shrine itself.

Scott Alexander

Kabak, Aaron Abraham   [1880–1944]

Hebrew novelist.

Born near Vilna (now Vilnius, Lithuania), Kabak studied at universities in Berlin and Switzerland and settled in Palestine in 1911. He left in 1914 but returned in 1921. As a teacher at Jerusalem's Rehaviah Gymnasium (secondary school), he had great influence on the literary and educational dynamics of the city.

In 1905 Kabak wrote the first Zionist novel in Hebrew, *Levaddah* (By Herself). His *Shelomo Molkho* (1928–1929), a three-volume work about the sixteenth century pseudo-messiah, was the first historical novel in Hebrew. *Ba-Mish'ol Ha-Zar* (In the Narrow Path), written in 1937 after his return to Orthodox Judaism, describes the teachings of Jesus of Nazareth, the Jew. Although he retained its Jewish content, Kabak modernized the Hebrew novel by ridding it of its hitherto conventional protagonists, motifs, and settings.

Ann Kahn

Kabbara, Sami

Syrian journalist and politician.

Sami Kabbara earned a Ph.D., and served as secretary-general of the chamber of deputies from 1932–1934. Later, he held positions as an independent—including deputy for Damascus in 1947, minister of justice in 1949, and minister of the interior in 1950 and 1951. He was indicted on December 22, 1956, for his involvement in the pro-Iraqi coup attempt led by the Syrian Social Nationalist party (PPS) against the Syrian regime. During much of his political career, Kabbara was publisher of the newspaper *al-Nidal.*

BIBLIOGRAPHY

Who's Who in the Middle East, 1967–1968.

Charles U. Zenzie

Kabul

Afghan city and province.

Because Kabul, the largest city in Afghanistan and the national capital, saw intense fighting, its population decreased greatly after 1992 and is now about 1.5 million. Kabul province has a population of about 2 million.

Kabul province is located in a Pushtu-speaking region, but the citizens of the city of Kabul for the

A royal tomb in Kabul, Afghanistan. (Richard Bulliet)

most part speak Persian. Strategically located both with regard to north-south and east-west trade routes, Kabul has been a major city for thousands of years; the oldest reference to it is found in the Rig Veda (1500 B.C.E.). Kabul became the capital of Afghanistan in 1775, when Timur Shah moved his court to the city from Kandahar. Kabul has withstood two British invasions, including the destruction of the covered bazaar in 1843, in retaliation for the defeat of the British at the hands of the Afghans in 1842. Since 1992, much of the city, including Kabul University, has been destroyed by the fierce fighting between rival Islamic political groups.

BIBLIOGRAPHY

ADAMEC, LUDWIG. *Historical Dictionary of Afghanistan.* Metuchen, N.J., 1991.

Grant Farr

Kabul University

Afghan university.

Founded in 1932 during the reign of Nadir Shah, Kabul University began as a medical school with Turkish and French faculty. By 1963, it had eight faculties, including faculties of law and political science, natural sciences, economics, home economics, education, engineering, and pharmacy.

In 1959, dormitories were built at the university to house students from rural or outlying areas. A quota system was imposed in 1964 that fixed the urban to rural ratio at 60 percent to 40 percent, so as to increase the number of Pushtu-speaking students receiving higher education. In the late 1960s and early 1970s, Kabul University became the center of political activity, although the government officially banned such activity on campus in 1968. Many of the future leaders of Afghanistan, from both the left and the right of the political spectrum, began their political careers by engaging in campus politics during this time. Since 1992, the intense fighting between Shi'a and Wahhabi groups around the campus has largely destroyed the university. It has been closed since 1992, and most of the faculty have fled.

BIBLIOGRAPHY

FARR, GRANT. "New Afghan Middle Class: Refugees and Insurgents." In *Afghan Resistance: The Politics of Survival,* ed. by Grant Farr and John Merriam. Boulder, Colo., 1984.

Grant Farr

Kabylia

Berber-speaking area in northern Algeria east of Algiers (from Dellys east along the coast past Bejaia, thence south to the environs of Borj-bou-Arreridj); the term is also applied to Arabic-speaking areas as far east as Skikda.

Kabylia, probably derived from the French Kabylie, is based on the Arabic *qabila* (tribe; pl., *qbayl*). The population of the BERBER-speaking area (western Kabylia) is estimated at 4 million to 5 million. Traditionally it is divided into two parts: the Djurdjura Mountains (highest point 2,305 m/7,565 ft.) separating "Great" Kabylia, to the north and centering on the regional capital, Tizi-Ouzou, and "Small" Kabylia, to the south and east. Population density in this very hilly and not very fertile region is often above 250 inhabitants per square mile. Though the area produces much of the nation's olive oil and dried figs, the agricultural economy cannot support the population. A great many Kabyles therefore migrate both within Algeria and to the manufacturing centers of France.

Tizi-Ouzou, the only city of any importance in the area, is its commercial and cultural center. In 1980 it was the main site of violent student-led demonstrations protesting the government's suppression of Berber cultural events. Since then, and despite the strong opposition of the Muslim fundamentalists, Kabyles have been able to obtain greater recognition for their cultural traditions and language: *tamazight* (Berber for "the Berber language") was recognized as one of the languages of the country in 1989, and a Berber culture curriculum has been developed at the University of Tizi-Ouzou.

Thomas G. Penchoen

Kach

See Kahane, Meir

Kadishman, Menashe   [1932–   ]

Israeli sculptor and artist.

Born in Tel Aviv during the British mandate over Palestine, Kadishman studied with Rudi Lehmann and Moshe Sternschuss in Tel Aviv but spent the 1960s in London, where he studied and worked. He returned to Israel in 1972, influenced by the avant-garde developments in art during the 1960s and 1970s.

Kadishman is continuously redefining art, whether expressed in minimalist sculptures—reflecting a defiance of gravity by the juxtaposition of opaque and transparent materials—or in "painting" nature, such as at the 1978 Venice Biennale where he painted the backs of sheep blue. He has exhibited extensively in Israel, Europe, and the United States.

Ann Kahn

Kadoori Family

Jewish family from Iraq, whose members have been successful in business and charitable ventures.

The Kadoori family name is derived from al-Khidr (Khidr Ilyas), Arabic for the prophet Elijah, who is particularly revered in Iraq. In the nineteenth and twentieth centuries, the family operated out of Basra, Iraq, and had business connections in Bahrain, where a branch still exists today. It is believed that they were originally pearl merchants.

The first to emigrate from Baghdad were the two brothers Eliahu (Sir Ellis, 1865–1922) and Eliezer (Sir Elly, 1867–1944)—sons of Saleh (Silas, died 1876) and his wife Rima. They first went to Asia as employees of the Bombay firm of David Sassoon & Sons, but they soon built their own business empire in Shanghai, China. Their philanthropic work concentrated mainly on education and they founded schools in Iraq and India as well as a synagogue in Oporto, Portugal. Sir Ellis left money for an agricultural school to serve all the communities of Palestine, but during the British mandate (1922–1948) the authorities decided to split the money to set up two separate schools—one in Galilee for Jews and one in Tulkarm for Arabs.

Sir Elly married Laura Mocatta (in whose London home King Faisal of Iraq would stay). They had two sons, Lawrence (born 1899) and Horace (born 1902), who reestablished themselves in Hong Kong after World War II, and who formed a financial base that included China Light and Power, Hong Kong's electric company. Their charitable works are aimed at helping refugees in Hong Kong.

BIBLIOGRAPHY

Who Was Who. 1941–1950.

Sylvia G. Haim

Kafiristan

See Nuristan

Kafiyya

A large headscarf.

In the nineteenth century, the kafiyya was worn mainly by bedouin and peasants of both sexes in the Arabian peninsula, Iraq, Syria, and Palestine.

The kafiyya's distinctive red or black and white checked design has become a symbol of Palestinian nationalism. Because the scarf is often wrapped around the head and face, it is used to conceal identity by Palestinian youths in Israel, the West Bank, and Gaza, especially during the Intifada.

BIBLIOGRAPHY

"Libas," *Encyclopaedia of Islam,* 2nd ed.

Elizabeth Thompson

Kafr al-Sheikh

Egyptian Delta province (governorate).

Kafr al-Sheikh, in the Nile DELTA region, has an area of 1,327 square miles (3,437 sq km) and an estimated 1986 population of 1.8 million. Its capital and principal city, also called Kafr al-Sheikh, had an estimated 104,200 inhabitants in 1986.

BIBLIOGRAPHY

Europa World Yearbook, 1994, vol. 1. London, 1994, p. 1024.

Arthur Goldschmidt, Jr.

Kafr Kasim

Israeli Arab village; site of a curfew incident in 1956.

On the eve of the 1956 Arab–Israel War, October 29, 1956, Israeli border police shot and killed forty-nine Israeli Arabs—workmen, women, and children—who were returning to Kafr Kasim, for the violation of a curfew of which they were not aware. A commission of inquiry was formed on November 1, 1956, which established the extent of responsibility and compensation.

Eight of the eleven military personnel brought to trial were convicted of murder and given sentences of up to seventeen years. All were released by 1960 through a partial pardon.

BIBLIOGRAPHY

HIRST, DAVID. *The Gun and the Olive Branch.* London, 1977. Reprint, 1984.
ROLEF, SUSAN HATTIS, ed. *Political Dictionary of the State of Israel.* New York, 1987.

Elizabeth Thompson

Kahana, Kalman   [1910–?]

Israeli leader.

Born in Galicia, Kalman Kahana was educated at the Berlin Rabbinical Seminary and at the universities of Berlin and Wurzburg. In 1938, he moved to Palestine, where he joined the Po'alei Agudat Israel movement and ultimately became the movement's president. He was a member of the Knesset and later, in the 1960s, served as the deputy minister of education.

Bryan Daves

Kahan Commission

Israeli commission investigating the massive loss of life at Sabra and Shatila refugee camps.

The Kahan Commission, officially the Commission of Inquiry into the Events at the Refugee Camps in Beirut, was set up by Israel's government in response to public outrage following the killing of an estimated 700 to 800 Palestinian men, women, and children in the SABRA AND SHATILA REFUGEE CAMPS on the outskirts of Beirut by right-wing Christian militiamen belonging to the Lebanese Phalange party, the National Liberal party, and renegade Major Haddad's Army of Free Lebanon. These events occurred in territory under Israel's control during its 1982 invasion of Lebanon, and the perpetrators were allies of Israel. The three-man commission was chaired by Yitzhak Kahan, president of the Supreme Court; the other members were Aharon Barak, a Supreme Court justice, and retired army general Yona Efrat.

The commission issued its report on February 7, 1983. It noted that the Phalange had secured the permission of Maj. Gen. Amir Drori, of the Northern Command, to enter the camps. This was approved by Israel's chief of staff, Lt. Gen. Rafael Eitan, and Minister of Defense Ariel Sharon. The commission found that Israel's commanders bore indirect responsibility for the mass killing of civilians by not anticipating what might happen, disregarding the fairly obvious danger, and not acting soon enough to halt the killing. The chief of staff, the director of military intelligence, General Drori, and Division Commander Gen. Amos Yaron were found guilty of breach of duty. The commission found that Sharon bore personal responsibility and recommended that the prime minister consider removing him from office. It also recommended that the director of military intelligence, Gen. Yehoshua Saguy, be fired, and General Drori disciplined.

BIBLIOGRAPHY

BILL, JAMES, and CARL LEIDEN. *Politics in the Middle East.* Boston, 1979.

Jenab Tutunji

Kahane, Meir   [1932–1990]

Rabbi who founded the Jewish Defense League in the United States and the Kach party in Israel.

Born in New York, Meir Kahane was active in several youth movements before he became a rabbi in Howard Beach, New York, and a writer for Jewish nationalist journals. He founded the Jewish Defense League (JDL) in 1968 to combat anti-Semitism and to help Jews protect themselves and their community. The JDL soon was the most militant Jewish self-defense organization, running into difficulties with the U.S. government because of its use of strong-arm and often armed tactics. In 1971, Kahane moved to Israel, where his Kach party quickly became a major proponent of inducing Arabs to leave the West Bank voluntarily or expelling them. He ran for the Knesset unsuccessfully in 1973 and 1977. He won a seat in 1984, but in 1988 Kach was outlawed on the grounds that it was racist. Kahane was assassinated in New York in November 1990, allegedly by a Palestinian Arab, though no one has been convincted of the crime. The Kach movement has been continued by his followers.

Walter F. Weiker

Kaid, Ahmed   [1927–1978]

Algerian officer and government minister.

Kaid was born near Tiaret. He attended the French military school at Hussein-Dey and then the Normal School for teacher training in Algiers. Before the Algerian War of Independence (1954–1962), he aligned with the moderate nationalist Union Démocratique du Manifeste Algérien (UDMA) of Ferhat Abbas. He joined the Front de Libération Nationale (FLN) and rose to assistant chief of staff of the Armée de Libération Nationale (ALN). Kaid sided with Ahmed Ben Bella–Houari Boumédienne faction after the war. He was elected to the National Assembly and served as minister of tourism (1963). He resigned in 1964, though he retained his seat on the Central Committee of the FLN. After Boumédienne's coup, he became minister of finance (1967) and then was chosen to head FLN. He resigned in 1972, critical of the party's bureaucracy and of the Agrarian Revolution. In March 1976 while in France, he publicly criticized the Boumédienne government. Given his anti-Boumédienne position, suspicion rose over his death, reportedly from a heart attack. Thousands attended his funeral in Tiaret.

BIBLIOGRAPHY

OTTAWAY, DAVID, and MARINA OTTAWAY. *Algeria: The Politics of a Socialist Revolution.* Berkeley, Calif., 1970.

Phillip C. Naylor

Kairouan

See Qairawan

Kalakani, Abd al-Majid   [1939–1980]

Afghan political leader and poet.

Born in the town of Kalakan in Kabul province, Kalakani attended Kabul University. He was active in campus politics in the late 1960s and early 1970s and founded a leftist political party, Eternal Flame. The party started by Kalakani, who was a Tajik, was popular among non-Pushtun minorities. Sometimes referred to as the Afghan Che Guevara because of his charismatic style and Maoist politics, Kalakani was arrested and executed in Kabul in 1980.

BIBLIOGRAPHY

ADAMEC, LUDWIG. *Historical Dictionary of Afghanistan.* Metuchen, N.J., 1991.

Grant Farr

Kalat

Afghan city; city and former state of Pakistan.

The capital of Zabul province, Kalat, is located on the highway from Kabul to Kandahar and has a population of about 6,000, most of whom are Gilzai Pushtuns. The city was occupied by the British during the second Anglo–Afghan war (1878–1879).

Kalat is also a city in the Baluchistan province of Pakistan, which, during the nineteenth century, was a semiautonomous Brahui state.

BIBLIOGRAPHY

DUPREE, LOUIS. *Afghanistan.* Princeton, N.J., 1980.

Grant Farr

Kalem

Ottoman humor magazine.

Kalem (Pen) first appeared in August 1908; it was established by Celal Esat and Salah Cimcoz. The sophisticated wit of the magazine made it popular among the Ottoman literati. Featuring some of the best authors of the period, *Kalem* was written half in Ottoman Turkish and half in French and included illustrations and caricatures drawn by CEMIL CEM, short stories, anecdotes, and literary articles. Among the regular contributors were Izzet Melih DEVRIM, SÜLEYMAN NAZIF, and AHMET RASIM. The magazine was closed down in 1911.

David Waldner

Kalemiyye

Ottoman hierarchy of scribes, clerks, and accountants headed by the reis ül-küttap.

Aside from the sultan's own staff, the kalemiyye (scribal institution) was one of three powerful bureaucracies in the Ottoman government, the others being the SEYFIYYE (military) and ILMIYYE (religious). From 1794, the kalemiyye was headquartered in the Sublime Porte, and while the grand vizier was nominally its head, the *reis ül-küttap* held the real power. In the early nineteenth century, the major Tanzimat reformers emerged from the kalemiyye, the most prominent of them Mustafa Reşid Paşa, who was reis ül-küttap in 1827–1830. In 1835, the kalemiyye was joined with the sultan's imperial bureaucracy. Later renamed the mülkiyye, it would be reformed several times during the nineteenth century, as former patronage systems were replaced with regular salaried employees and formal departments and ministries were organized. It would come to include the finance, commerce, interior, foreign affairs, and other ministries.

BIBLIOGRAPHY

MANTRAN, ROBERT, ed. *Histoire de l'empire ottoman.* Paris, 1989.
SHAW, STANFORD J. *History of the Ottoman Empire and Modern Turkey.* Vol. 1. Cambridge, U.K., 1976.
SHAW, STANFORD J., and EZEL KURAL SHAW. *History of the Ottoman Empire and Modern Turkey.* Vol. 2. Cambridge, U.K., 1977.

Elizabeth Thompson

Kalischer, Hirsch   [1795–1874]

Rabbi and precursor of Zionism.

Born in western Poland in a region acquired by Prussia in 1793, Kalischer was aware of nationalist struggles from an early age; perhaps sensitizing him to the misery of European Jewry. He was engaged early in his career in a defense of traditional Judaism against the Reform movement. Subsequently, he began to argue that the redemption would only come after action was taken by the Jewish people on their own behalf. He elaborated these ideas in *Derishat Tziyon* (1862; Seeking Zion), a book about modern Jewish agricultural settlement in Palestine.

Kalischer was successful in persuading the Alliance Israélite Universelle, a French organization for the international defense of Jewish rights, to found an agricultural school in Jaffa, Palestine in 1870. He made numerous visits to wealthy Jews in Germany to recruit their support for Jewish settlement in Palestine.

BIBLIOGRAPHY

HERTZBERG, ARTHUR. *The Zionist Idea.* New York, 1979.

Martin Malin

Kallas, Bahij   [1907–   ]

Syrian military officer.

Born in Hama in 1907, the son of Fareis Kallas, Bahij Kallas attended the Syrian military academy. An equestrian enthusiast, he became colonel and commander of the Syrian army in the 1945 revolution. He later became Husni al-ZA'IM's second in command at the time of his successful coup (March 1949). Colonel Kallas increasingly sided with his old Hama ally Akram al-HAWRANI, in the face of Za'im's growing relationship with the Barazi family, who were traditional enemies of Hawrani.

BIBLIOGRAPHY

Who's Who in the Middle East, 1967–1968.

Charles U. Zenzie

Kallas, Khalil

Syrian politician.

Along with his brothers Nakhle and Bahij, Khalil was a longtime supporter of Akram al-HAWRANI, a powerful military leader from his native Hama. He became Syria's minister of economics in 1955, minister of economics and commerce in 1962, and minister of national economy in 1963.

BIBLIOGRAPHY

Who's Who in the Middle East, 1967–1968.

Charles U. Zenzie

Kalvaryski, Chaim Margaliut- [1868–1947]

Land-purchase agent and adviser on Arab–Jewish relations in Palestine.

Kalvaryski was born in Poland and emigrated to Palestine in 1895, after completing studies in agronomy in France. Between 1900 and 1922, he served as an administrator of the Jewish Colonization Association in the Galilee, helping to acquire extensive areas for Jewish settlement. Beginning in 1913/14, he became involved in political discussions with Arab nationalists in Beirut and Damascus. Between 1923 and 1927, Kalvaryski was employed by the Palestine Zionist Executive as an adviser on Arab affairs. Despite controversies over his methods and doubts about his financial management, he was recalled to head the Joint Bureau of Jewish Public Bodies that was formed to coordinate relations with the Arabs following the 1929 Palestine riots.

Kalvaryski was a member of the palestine government's first Advisory Council (1920–1923), of the *Va'ad Le'umi* (National Council of the Jews) beginning in 1920, and was active in Jewish groups promoting binationalism and rapprochement with the Arabs of Palestine and the neighboring countries. He also devised several of his own peace plans, which he discussed with Arab leaders.

Kalvaryski's articles and speeches were published in various Hebrew newspapers and periodicals and in a collection entitled *Al Parshat Darkeinu* (At the Parting of Our Ways; Jerusalem, 1939).

BIBLIOGRAPHY

CAPLAN, NEIL. "Arab–Jewish Contacts in Palestine After the First World War." *Journal of Contemporary History* 12, no. 4 (1977): 635–668.
———. *Futile Diplomacy,* 2 vols. London, 1983, 1986.
COHEN, AHARON. *Israel and the Arab World.* New York, 1970.

Neil Caplan

Kamal, Ahmad [1849–1923]

The first prominent Egyptian archeologist and Egyptologist.

Ahmad Kamal Pasha studied under Heinrich K. Brugsch (1827–1894), a German archeologist, a scholar of hieroglyphics and demotic Egyptian, and director of the short-lived school of Egyptology in Cairo in the 1870s. Kamal made his career in the Egyptian Antiquities Service and helped open professional Archeology and Egyptology to Egyptians (they were dominated by Europeans). His long campaign succeeded when immediately after his death, the department that evolved into today's Faculty of Archeology of Cairo University was established.

BIBLIOGRAPHY

DAWSON, WARREN R., and ERIC P. UPHILL. *Who Was Who in Egyptology,* 2nd ed. London, 1972.

Donald Malcolm Reid

Kamil, Kıbrıslı Mehmet [1832–1913]

Ottoman grand vizier.

The son of a military officer, Kıbrıslı Mehmet Kamil was born in Nicosia on the island of Cyprus (in Turkish, *Kıbrıs*). He graduated from the military academy in Cairo and served as adjutant to Abbas Paşa. Between 1860 and 1879, he held various positions in the Ottoman provincial bureaucracy, rising to the position of governor of Kosovo and Aleppo. In 1879, he became a cabinet minister, serving for short periods as minister of education and of religious foundations until becoming grand vizier on 25 September 1885, replacing Küçük Sait Paşa who became a rival and regular replacement. Between 1885 and 1891, he successfully stabilized Ottoman finances while encouraging foreign investment in Ottoman railroads and industries. In 1895, at the start of a second stint as grand vizier, he fell into the sultan's disfavor and was sent into exile, serving eleven years as governor of İzmir. Although an opponent of the Committee of Union and Progress, he was appointed grand vizier for a third time on 5 August 1908, serving until 14 February 1909. During this period, when Abdülhamit II was still sultan, Kamil Paşa worked to balance the budget, reorganize the bureaucracy and armed forces, and put an end to the millet system and the privileges enjoyed by foreigners according to the CAPITULATIONS.

BIBLIOGRAPHY

SHAW, STANFORD, and EZEL KURAL SHAW. *Reform, Revolution, and Republic: The Rise of Modern Turkey, 1808–1975.* Vol. 2 of *History of the Ottoman Empire and Modern Turkey.* Cambridge, U.K., 1977.

David Waldner

Kamil, Mustafa   [1874–1908]

Egyptian nationalist leader, orator, and editor.

Mustafa Kamil, the son of an army officer from an ethnic Egyptian family, was educated in government schools, the French School of Law in Cairo, and the University of Toulouse, France, where he received his law degree in 1895. A strong opponent of the British occupation of Egypt, he soon became closely associated with Khedive ABBAS HILMI II and with Ottoman Sultan ABDÜLHAMIT II, both of whom supported him materially as well as morally in his campaigns to persuade European governments and peoples to demand the evacuation promised by successive British governments. He also worked closely with Muhammad FARID and other Egyptians to form a secret society, initially under the aegis of the khedive, to inculcate resistance to the British among the people of Egypt. This society, known from its inception as *al-Hizb al-Watani* (the National party), became a public political party, open to all Egyptians, in December 1907. He also founded a popular daily newspaper, *al-Liwa* (The Banner), in 1900, which became the official party organ, and a boys' school that bore his name. He wrote many articles for the French press, for *al-Muayyad* under Shaykh Ali Yusuf, and for *al-Liwa,* as well as a book on the Eastern Question called *al-Mas'ala al-Sharqiyya,* in which he strongly supported the Ottoman Empire. He delivered many stirring speeches in French and in Arabic, of which the best remembered was translated into English as "What the National Party Wants." He died of tuberculosis (but some think he was poisoned) in the 34th year of his life, and his funeral was the occasion for a

massive demonstration of popular grief. Remembered as a fervent patriot and occasional supporter of pan-Islam, he called for the British evacuation of Egypt and a constitutional government but showed little interest in economic or social issues.

BIBLIOGRAPHY

GOLDSCHMIDT, ARTHUR. "The Egyptian Nationalist Party, 1892–1919." In *Political and Social Change in Modern Egypt,* ed. by P. M. Holt. London, 1968.
RIDWAN, FATHI. *Mustafa Kamil.* Cairo, 1946. Rev. ed., 1974.
AL-SAYYID, AFAF LUTFI. *Egypt and Cromer.* London, 1968.
STEPPAT, FRITZ. "Nationalismus und Islam bei Mustafa Kamil." *Welt des Islams* 4 (1956): 241–341.

Arthur Goldschmidt, Jr.

Kanafani, Ghassan   [?–1972]

Palestinian writer and political activist.

A native of Acre, Palestine, Kanafani published the ARAB NATIONAL MOVEMENT's official organ, *al-RA'I* (Opinion), with George Habash. Kanafani was also a prominent spokesman and ideologue for the Popular Front for the Liberation of Palestine. Believed by Israel's intelligence service, Mossad, to have been involved in planning terrorist operations, Kanafani was assassinated by a hit team from Israel who detonated a car bomb outside his home in Hazmiyeh, near Beirut, killing him and his seventeen-year-old niece, Lamis Najem. Kanafani's Danish wife, small son, and daughter escaped unhurt. Kanafani's successor, Bassem Abu Sharif, also was targeted by Israel's intelligence; he lost the sight in one eye and several fingers when a letter bomb exploded in his Beirut office.

At his death, Kanafani had already established himself as a prolific writer and commentator. Among his best-known works is *Rijal fi al-Shams* (1963; Men in the Sun), based on his traumatic experiences as a refugee. Some of his other books include *The Middle of May, The Land of Sad Oranges,* and *That Which Is Left Over for You.*

BIBLIOGRAPHY

COOLEY, JOHN K. *Green March, Black September: The Story of the Palestinian Arabs.* London, 1973.

Lawrence Tal

Kanbar, Ahmad   [1911–   ]

Syrian journalist and politician.

Son of Muhammad Kanbar, Ahmad founded the daily newspaper *al-Nazir* in his hometown of Aleppo.

He was elected deputy for Aleppo in 1947 and was appointed minister of public works in 1951, then minister of the interior from 1952 to 1954. Kanbar wrote a number of political articles as a member of the People's party.

BIBLIOGRAPHY

Who's Who in the Middle East, 1967–1968.

Charles U. Zenzie

Kandahar

Afghan city and province.

Located in southern Afghanistan, the province of Kandahar has a population of approximately 700,000, most of whom are Durrani Pushtuns. The city of Kandahar is the provincial capital and the second largest city in Afghanistan, with a population of about 200,000. Centrally situated on trade routes and a major link between the Iranian plateau and the Indian subcontinent, Kandahar has been an important city for thousands of years.

Kandahar has played a major role in the history of Afghanistan. All of the Afghan kings and many of the other leaders of Afghanistan have come from the tribes in the Kandahar area. The capital of Afghanistan from 1747 to 1775, the city of Kandahar is still an important cultural and political center for the western Pushtun tribes. The British occupied the city twice and suffered one of their greatest defeats at the battle of Maiwand (1880).

During the war of resistance (1978–1992), Kandahar was the scene of intense fighting and much of the city was destroyed. Almost half of the population of the province fled to neighboring Pakistan during the war, but most subsequently returned.

BIBLIOGRAPHY

ADAMEC, LUDWIG. *Historical Dictionary of Afghanistan.* Metuchen, N.J., 1991.

Grant Farr

Kanık, Orhan Veli   [1914–1950]

Turkish poet.

Born and educated in Istanbul, Kanık was the son of a conductor of Turkey's Republican Symphony Orchestra. He worked for many years as a translator of French poetry in the Turkish ministry of education. He wrote poetry, at first, using traditional forms but in 1941 was a founding member of the Garip

(Strange) movement. This was a reaction to the stylized clichés and sentimentality of the traditional poetry in Turkish literature; Garip used free verse and colloquial Turkish language. His poetry treats aspects of the daily life of impoverished people, mixing lighthearted depictions of their dreams and struggles with calls for peace and freedom.

BIBLIOGRAPHY

ERTOP, KONUR. "Trends and Characteristics of Contemporary Turkish Literature." In *The Transformation of Turkish Culture: The Atatürk Legacy,* ed. by Günsel Renda and C. Max Kortepeter. Princeton, N.J., 1986.
GALIN, MUGE, ed. *Turkish Sampler: Writings for all Readers.* Bloomington, Ind., 1989.

David Waldner

Kaniuk, Yoram   [1930–   ]

Israeli novelist and journalist.

Yoram Kaniuk was born in Tel Aviv. His family was deeply involved in the cultural life of "the first Hebrew city": His father was one of the founders of the Tel Aviv Museum, and his mother was one of the city's prominent teachers. He served in the Haganah, the underground army of Jewish Palestine, an experience that informs much of his writing. After fighting in Israel's War of Independence, Kaniuk traveled to Europe and the United States, seeking respite from the physical and emotional trauma of war. An accomplished painter when he arrived in New York in the early 1950s, he soon shifted his attention to writing and evolved a prose style that was, from early on, enriched by his painterly sensibilities.

Kaniuk has written twelve works of fiction and several children's books and has been widely translated. He has been active as a journalist and lecturer, commenting on political events as well as the broad cultural scene. Some of his work, such as *The Acrophile, Rockinghorse,* and *The Story of Aunt Shlomzion the Great,* is obviously autobiographical. Much of it has a surreal quality, drifting between different planes of reality, rich with imagery that is both dense and dazzling. His fictional world is inhabited by characters whose comic dimension compensates for their grimness. Kaniuk's novels, especially those that deal with the Holocaust—*Adam Resurrected* and *The Last Jew*—and with the moral implications of political decisions—*Confessions of a Good Arab* and *His Daughter*—have been widely read and applauded in Israel.

BIBLIOGRAPHY

RAMRAS-RAUCH, GILA. *World Literature Today* 54 (Spring 1980).

SHAPIRO, ZEVA. *World Authors, 1985–1990*. New York, 1995.

Zeva Shapiro

Kanna, Khalil [1911–]

Iraqi conservative politician active during the 1940s and 1950s in the Hashimite regime.

A Sunni Arab and Baghdadi lawyer, Kanna was connected, in his youth (the early 1930s), with the activities of al-Ahali, a moderate group of intellectuals with reformist and Socialist inclinations. In the early 1940s, he was involved in Rashid Ali's pro-Axis nationalist movement. The British arrested and interned him, but he returned to the political arena in 1946. Kanna married a niece by marriage of Nuri al-SA'ID, the strongest and most prominent member of the old, conservative ruling elite in Iraq. In 1949 he was appointed to the Higher Directorate of Nuri al-Sa'id's Constitutional Union Party. Later he served as Minister of Education and Minister of Finance in various governments under Nuri al-Sa'id. After the 1958 revolution, Kassem's Revolutionary Court sentenced Kanna though he was later released and exiled.

BIBLIOGRAPHY

GALLMAN, WALDEMAR J. *Iraq under General Nuri: My Recollections of Nuri al-Said, 1954–1957*. Baltimore, 1964.

Michael Eppel

Kanun

See Qanun

Karabagh

Region of historic Armenia, autonomous district in the former Soviet Azerbaijan, proclaimed an independent republic in 1992; also known as Nagorno-Karabagh.

The easternmost range of the Armenian upland, the region of Karabagh (called Artsakh in Armenian) had been continuously governed by Armenian noble families since the Middle Ages. The area was regarded as a marshland of the ancient Armenian kingdom, and its population was noted for its martial traditions. Protected by the rugged terrain, these highland areas remained outside the direct political control of the Muslim states established in the CAUCASUS region after the breakup of the caliphate and the entrance of the Turkic tribes into the surrounding lowlands to the east. With their privileges renewed by successive rulers of the area from the Mongol through the Safavid era, the Armenian population, under the immediate governance of its native princes, led a separate existence in the isolation of their mountain fastnesses.

Armenian control of the region began to break down in the early eighteenth century. By 1813, when the area was annexed by Russia in accordance with the Treaty of Golestan, the Armenian feudal dynasties had lost their hold. Karabagh was made part of the province of Elizavetpol (Ganja), which, along with Baku province, held the great bulk of the Azeri-Turkish population of the Caucasus. When AZERBAIJAN was declared an independent republic in 1918, its government laid claim to both provinces and thereby incorporated Karabagh within its borders. While the region's population was almost completely Armenian, it was cut off from the Republic of Armenia, which did not succeed in resolving the disputed status of the district. Unrest marked the entire period of the independent republics in the Transcaucasus, as the Armenian population of Karabagh resisted Azerbaijani rule while the Baku government enforced its authority through the use of arms.

The problem remained for the Soviet regime to solve. While Moscow recognized Karabagh as part of Soviet Azerbaijan, the Armenian-populated part, mainly an upland area, was designated an autonomous *oblast* (district) in 1923—hence, the current Russian designation Nagorno-Karabagh, meaning Mountainous Karabagh. Separated from Soviet Armenia by an eight-kilometer-wide corridor, the Armenian population of Karabagh, while severely repressed for its expressions of nationalism, continued to seek unification with Armenia. In 1988, during the Gorbachev era in the Soviet Union, the Armenians of Karabagh began to press Moscow to respond to their appeals. While Soviet authorities procrastinated, the appeals resounded in Armenia in mass protests, which became known as the Karabagh Movement. The protesters beseeched Moscow to permit the Armenians of Nagorno-Karabagh to transfer the jurisdiction of their autonomous district from Soviet Azerbaijan to Soviet Armenia.

The Karabagh movement proved to be the first of many nationalist crises faced by the Soviet regime in its final years. In Azerbaijan, the Armenian effort at unification engendered hostility and rejection, leading to mob violence in a number of Azeri cities, and eventually degenerated into small-scale warring in and around Nagorno-Karabagh. With the dissolution of the Soviet Union, the government of Azerbaijan abolished the separate status of Nagorno-Karabagh. The district parliament subsequently pronounced the area independent of Azerbaijan and, on January 6, 1992, declared it a sovereign republic. In so doing, the Republic of Mountainous Karabagh found itself in a state of war with Azerbaijan. After initial Azeri military successes in 1992, the Karabagh Armenians turned the tide by going on the offensive in March 1993. They established a common border with Armenia and created a buffer zone by occupying the regions surrounding Karabagh. A cease-fire signed in May 1994 ended active hostilities. Negotiations under the auspices of the Organization for Security and Cooperation in Europe (OSCE) were still going on in 1996.

BIBLIOGRAPHY

OLCOTT, MARTHA B. The Soviet Multinational State: Readings and Documents. Armonk, N.Y., 1990.

SAROYAN, MARK. "The 'Karabagh Syndrome' and Azerbaijani Politics." Problems of Communism (Sept.–Oct. 1990): 14–29.

SUNY, RONALD GRIGOR. Looking toward Ararat: Armenia in Modern History. Bloomington, Ind., 1993.

WALKER, CHRISTOPHER J., ed. Armenia and Karabagh: The Struggle for Unity. London, 1991.

Rouben P. Adalian

Karabekir, Kazım

Officer in the Ottoman army and Turkish politician.

Karabekir played a prominent role as commander of the Ottoman garrison in Baghdad (1917), then as commander of the eastern Anatolian–Caucasus front (1918). In April 1919, he took command of the 18,000-man 15th Army corps headquartered at Erzurum. From this position, he joined other military commanders in supporting Mustafa Kemal (ATATÜRK) Pasha's efforts to organize nationalist resistance against the World War I allies and the invading Greek army in western Anatolia. Returning to Ankara after a successful military campaign, Karabekir became a leader of the opposition against Mustafa Kemal in the Grand National Assembly (July 1921). Reacting against secularizing reforms (specifically, abolition of the caliphate), Karabekir and such military colleagues as Ali Fuat Cebesoy, Hüseyin Rauf Orbay, and Refet Bele resigned their military commissions and formed the opposition PROGRESSIVE REPUBLICAN PARTY. In 1926, Karabekir was among those implicated in a plot against Mustafa Kemal; he was acquitted by the court, however. In his memoirs, suppressed in 1933, Karabekir claimed that he, not Kemal, had been the real initiator of the Anatolian Turkish nationalist resistance in 1919. In 1946, in a show of nonpartisanship, the REPUBLICAN PEOPLE'S PARTY had him elected chairman of the Grand National Assembly (parliament).

BIBLIOGRAPHY

SHAW, S. J., and E. K. SHAW. History of the Ottoman Empire and Modern Turkey, vol. 2. Cambridge, U.K., 1977.

Frank Tachau

Karacan, Ali Naci   [1896–1955]

Turkish journalist and publisher.

Born in Istanbul, Karacan attended Galatasaray Lycée. He began working as a reporter at a young age, before World War I, first at Tasvir-i Efkar and then at the oppositional paper Ikdam. Later, he worked as an editor for famous newspapers like Vakit. He was co-founder, in 1918, of Akşam, with well-known journalists Salıh Rifki Atay and Kazım Şinasi Dersan. In 1935, Karacan became editor of Turkey's newly founded leftist daily Tan.

Karacan's greatest success was founding the daily paper MILLIYET in 1950. Karacan and his son Ercüment quickly carved a place among a number of new newspapers of the period, including Simavi's Hürriyet, founded two years before. Carrying the slogan "Independent Political Newspaper" on its masthead, Milliyet matched Hürriyet's slick style, but also managed to appeal to intellectuals with a well-respected staff of writers. Under the editorial leadership of Abdi İpekci, it became an influential player in Turkey's political arena in the 1960s and 1970s. By then, the Karacan family, including grandson Ali Naci Karacan, controlled a publishing syndicate that included printing and book and magazine publishing companies.

BIBLIOGRAPHY

ORAL, FUAT SÜREYYA. Türk Basin Tarihi 1919–1965 (The History of the Turkish Press 1919–1965). Istanbul, 1965.

Elizabeth Thompson

Karagöz

See Theater

Karaites

Religious sect that was formed in Babylonia in the eighth century C.E.

The Karaites hold to a literal interpretation of scripture, rejecting Talmudic and rabbinic interpretations that are based on an oral tradition. In twentieth-century Israel, there are two small communities of several hundred persons in Galilee and Jerusalem. The Jewish status of Karaites is ambiguous; in Israel, they have the option of holding identity cards that label them either as "Karaite" or "Karaite-Jew."

BIBLIOGRAPHY

BIRNBAUM, PHILIP, ed. *Karaite Studies*. New York, 1971.

Samuel C. Heilman

Karak

A small provincial capital in the central part of Jordan.

During the Bronze Age, starting about 2400 B.C.E., the region surrounding Karak supported sedentary agriculturalists. Semitic tribes settled there in 1200 B.C.E. and, in 850 B.C.E., the great King Mesha consolidated what came to be known as the Moabite kingdom. Then, atop a small mountain, Karak was settled and fortified. Nearby on the plains of Mo'ata, the first battle between the Arab Muslims and the Byzantine Empire was fought in 629 C.E.. The Crusader Renauld de Châtillon ruled the broad region east of the Jordan rift from the massive fortress he built at Karak.

After World War I, Karak was a southern province of the short-lived United Syrian Kingdom. Following its demise at the hands of the French in July 1920, the local tribal shaykhs declared the Karak region to be the independent Arab Government of Moab. In 1921, it became part of the Hashemite Emirate of Transjordan. Today, Karak is an agricultural market town of 40,000 people and the government center for the Karak district of Jordan. The majority are Sunni Muslim, but a significant minority are Christian. One of Jordan's institutions of higher education, the University of Mu'ta, is located nearby in the village of that name.

BIBLIOGRAPHY

GUBSER, PETER. *Politics and Change in al-Karak, Jordan: A Study of a Small Arab Town and its District*. London, 1973.

Peter Gubser

Karakul

Afghan sheep.

Karakul is the name of a breed of short-tailed sheep raised in the north of Afghanistan, largely by Turko-mans and Uzbeks. Introduced into Afghanistan from Central Asia during World War I, the sheep are generally a solid color: black, gray, or brown. The skins of the newborn sheep have tight curly fleece and are valued for making hats and women's coats. Historically, Karakul skins have been one of Afghanistan's major exports.

BIBLIOGRAPHY

DUPREE, LOUIS. *Afghanistan*. Princeton, N.J., 1980.

Grant Farr

Karam, Yusef [1822–1889]

Lebanese hero known for his opposition to Ottoman rule in Lebanon.

Born to a Maronite family in Ehden, north Lebanon, Karam had an eclectic education. He wrote and spoke fluent Arabic, Syriac, Italian, French, and English. He also learned the art of fighting and horse riding.

In 1841, he participated in his first battle against the Ottomans to lift the siege against the town of Deir al-Kamar. At the age of twenty-three, he succeeded his father as governor of Ehden. During the conflicts between Maronite Christians and Druze from 1840 to 1845, he was appointed by the Ottomans to become governor of the Christian district headquartered in Jounieh. In 1860, Karam refused the Ottomans' offers that he lead a small contingent of Lebanese soldiers. Exiled from Lebanon by the Ottomans, Karam returned in 1864, but he was exiled again in 1867 and died in Italy in 1889.

George E. Irani

Karama, Battle of

Battle in Jordan valley in which Yasir Arafat and his al-Fath faction successfully resisted Israel's forces, March 1968.

After the ARAB–ISRAEL WAR of 1967, although repeated artillery shelling by Israel had driven Palestinian refugees from the Jordan valley to the Biqa' and Marqa refugee camps outside Amman, there were still 25,000 to 35,000 refugees in Karama. In early March 1968, information on an impending attack by Israel had come from Arafat's agents in the occupied territories and Jordan's intelligence services under the command of Col. Ghazi Arabiyyat. The Palestinians and Jordan's army decided to take a stand. President Gamal Abdel Nasser of Egypt offered to send air power, but Jordan's King Hussein refused because he feared another disaster like that of 1967.

On March 21, about 15,000 troops began the assault from Israel in three armored brigade formations using M-48 Patton tanks. Their main columns hit the Shuna–Karama area near the King Abdullah Bridge, north of the Dead Sea and Ghor Safi. A smaller attack took place in neighboring al-Himma, but Jordan's army command believed that the main thrust was taking place in Karama. Jordan's artillery stopped Israel's tank column at the Allenby Bridge, near the crossroads of the main road from Shuna to Karama. Palestinian commandos (fida'iyyun) were able to destroy several of Israel's tanks and armored cars, and engaged Israel's airborne troops entering the town of Karama. The town was destroyed after fierce fighting between Israel's troops and approximately 200 to 300 Palestinian commandos. Israel admitted losing 21 soldiers, but the Palestinians claimed the real figure was over 200.

The significance of the battle lay in the fact that, for the first time, Palestinian fighters had successfully engaged Israel's army, scoring a major symbolic victory. Although Jordan's military sources indicated that Jordan's troops did the bulk of the fighting, King Hussein allowed Yasir Arafat and al-FATH to take credit for the victory, thus boosting the prestige of the PALESTINE LIBERATION ORGANIZATION (PLO). After Karama, thousands of young Palestinians flocked to the PLO's guerrilla wings and began paramilitary training.

BIBLIOGRAPHY

COOLEY, JOHN K. *Green March, Black September: The Story of the Palestinian Arabs.* London, 1973.

Lawrence Tal

Karame, Abd al-Hamid   [1890–1947]

Lebanese politician; prime minister (1945).

Karame was born into a prominent Sunni family of Tripoli, whose scions traditionally held the office of mufti of the city. He himself served in that post until France's mandatory power replaced him with a man more agreeable to them. A socially conservative and very devout man, he vehemently opposed the creation of Greater Lebanon in 1920. During the 1920s and 1930s, Karame repeatedly clashed with the authorities, demanding the annexation of Tripoli and its hinterland to Syria. Although he was the dominant political figure in Tripoli, he never developed a national base, and thus failed to pose a real challenge to France. A pragmatic politician, he established a

close relationship with Britain in the early 1940s, when he joined the movement for Lebanon's independence, reconciling himself to the concept of Lebanon as an entity separate from Syria. Although Karame initially supported President Bishara al-Khuri, under whom he served as prime minister between January and August 1945, he eventually became the leader of an opposition group first called the Independent Bloc and, after April 1946, the Reform Bloc. Following his death in 1947, his son Rashid inherited his political mantle.

[*See also:* Karame, Rashid.]

BIBLIOGRAPHY

HUDSON, MICHAEL C. *The Precarious Republic: Political Modernization in Lebanon.* Boulder, Colo., 1985.
ZAMIR, MEIR. *The Formation of Modern Lebanon.* Ithaca, N.Y., 1985.

Guilain P. Denoeux

Karame, Elie   [1940–]

Lebanese doctor and politician.

Elias Constantin Karame was born September 15, 1940, in Beirut to a Maronite Catholic family. His father Constantin was a medical laboratory owner. Karame was educated at the Jesuit institutions in Beirut and obtained degrees in medicine at the Faculté Française de Médecine and the Université de Paris. Karame also conducted medical research at the Hormonology Research Foundation in Paris. In 1971, he was elected to the politburo of the Lebanese PHALANGE party (Hizb al-Kata'ib), and in 1981 he was elected vice president of the party. In September 1984, following the death of Pierre Jumayyil, party founder and president, Elie Karame was elected to succeed him.

BIBLIOGRAPHY

Who's Who in Lebanon, 1990–1991. Beirut, 1990.

George E. Irani

Karame, Rashid   [1921–1987]

Lebanese politician; prime minister at various times from the 1950s through the 1980s.

Karame, the son of Abd al-Hamid Karame, received a law degree from Cairo University in 1947. He was elected deputy for Tripoli in 1951 and remained a member of parliament until his death. A staunch Arab nationalist and an advocate of political and social reforms, he gained influence through patronage and his ability to function within a confessional political system.

Karame became prime minister in 1955 but resigned in 1956 to protest President Camille Chamoun's refusal to sever diplomatic relations with France and Britain in the wake of the Suez crisis. He became a major opponent of the Chamoun regime and was a leader of the uprising against Chamoun in 1958. After the Lebanese civil war (1958), President Fu'ad Chehab appointed him prime minister. Karame held the premiership regularly under both Chehab (1958–1964) and his successor, Charles Hilu (1964–1970).

In the late 1960s and early 1970s, Karame supported the presence of armed Palestinians in Lebanon and a radical restructuring of the country's political system. Such positions brought him into conflict with key Maronite politicians, including President Sulayman Franjiyya. In June 1975, when he appeared to be the only politician who might overcome the growing polarization in the country, President Franjiyya appointed him prime minister; he resigned in June 1976.

After Israel's invasion of Lebanon in 1982, Karame emerged as a leading opponent to President Amin Jumayyil's government. With Druze leader Walid Jumblatt and former President Franjiyya, he founded the NATIONAL SALVATION FRONT in July 1983. In April 1984, Jumayyil bowed to pressures and appointed him prime minister of a government of national unity. Although he formally remained premier until he resigned in May 1987, his authority was limited. He was assassinated on 1 June 1987, when a bomb exploded aboard his helicopter.

BIBLIOGRAPHY

HUDSON, MICHAEL C. *The Precarious Republic: Political Modernization in Lebanon.* Boulder, Colo., 1985.

PETRAN, TABITHA. *The Struggle over Lebanon.* New York, 1987.

Guilain P. Denoeux

Karaosmanoğlu, Yakup Kadri   [1889–1974]

Turkish politician and writer.

Karaosmanoğlu was born in Cairo to a powerful Ottoman Turkish dynasty that had once owned much land in the Aydın–İzmir region. At the age of six his family returned to Turkey, and he attended military school in Manisa and high school in İzmir, where he first met the influential language reformer Ömer Sayfettin. He returned to Cairo for two years, studying French literature there. In 1908, he went to Istanbul for the first time, where he joined nationalist circles influenced by Ziya GÖKALP and helped found the TURKISH LINGUISTIC SOCIETY in 1932.

He is best known perhaps for cofounding *Kadro* (Cadre) in 1933, a journal that established an influential current in Turkish politics, mixing Marxist, corporatist, and nationalist views. *Kadro*'s reform philosophy, of economic liberation from imperialism and elite leadership of the masses, influenced some members of Turkey's Republican People's party. Karaosmanoğlu would advance similar views again in the early 1960s, as editor of that party's official journal *Ulus*. He resigned from the party in 1962, saying it was deviating from Atatürk's principles.

Karaosmanoğlu was also a leading novelist, focusing on themes of social justice and relations between the elite and peasantry.

BIBLIOGRAPHY

LEWIS, BERNARD. *The Emergence of Modern Turkey.* New York, 1969.

SHAW, STANFORD, and EZEL K. SHAW. *History of the Ottoman Empire and Modern Turkey.* New York, 1977.

Elizabeth Thompson

Karbala

Site of sanctuary honoring Husayn's martyrdom.

Karbala is the name of a plain located in Iraq, approximately fifty-five miles south-southwest of mod-

Interior courtyard of the Abbas mosque in Karbala. (© Mark Dennis)

Front of the Abbas mosque. (© Mark Dennis)

ern Baghdad and close to the west bank of the Euphrates. The plain is the recorded site of the infamous mass killing, in 680 C.E. (A.H. 61), of the prophet Muhammad's grandson Husayn ibn Ali and his small band of supporters by the forces of Yazid ibn Mu'awiya, the second Umayyad caliph. According to tradition, the decapitated body of Husayn was buried in a spot not far from the battlefield. As a result, Karbala and its environs quickly became known as Mashhad al-Husayn (the tomb shrine of Husayn), and today it is still one of the principal pilgrimage centers for Twelver Shi'ite Muslims, who revere Husayn as one of the great imams, or divinely inspired leaders, of the Muslim community. Each year, for example, beginning on the first and culminating on the tenth of the Muslim month of MU-HARRAM, large numbers of pilgrims gather at the shrine complex at Karbala and perform solemn passion plays and other commemorations of Husayn's great martyrdom (other Twelver Shi'ites around the world do the same). According to the common belief of Twelver Shi'ites, Husayn's suffering and death constitute a source of redemption for all who are sincerely devoted to Husayn and his fellow imams.

Many Twelvers believe that such practices as ritual visitation to Karbala as well as to other sacred tombs are excellent means of realizing this devotion to the imams and the salvific blessings it entails. Throughout its long history, Karbala has generally prospered as a richly endowed pilgrimage site. A few notable exceptions to this sanctuary's history of good fortune include its destruction by the Abbasid caliph al-Mutawakkil in 850 C.E. (A.H. 236), its storming and looting by the *muwahhidun* in 1801 C.E. (A.H. 1215), and the widespread devastation it suffered as a consequence of the confrontation after the Gulf War between Iraq's Republican Guard and Shi'a rebel forces in March 1991.

Scott Alexander

Kariz

See Qanat

Karmal, Babrak [1929–   ]

President of Afghanistan, 1980–1986.

Babrak Karmal was a founder of the Marxist movement in Afghanistan and the country's third Marxist president (1980–1986). He was born in Kamari, near Kabul, into the family of an army officer, Mohammad Hossayn. His father became a general and was at one time governor of Paktika province. Karmal received his secondary education in Kabul at Nejat School, sometimes called Amani Lycée because it was founded by King Amanollah, which had a German curriculum and German teachers. He graduated in 1948 and entered Kabul University in 1951; he had failed the entrance examination on his first attempt. At the university he became active in student politics and in the Afghan Communist movement. Known as a gifted orator, he adopted the name Karmal, which in Persian means "friend of labor," in 1954.

From 1953 to 1956, Karmal was arrested for his political activism but was well treated in jail because of his family connections. In 1965 and 1969, during the period of constitutional reforms (1963–1973), he was elected to the Afghan parliament. He was a founding member of the People's Democratic party of Afghanistan (PDPA) in 1965. When the party split into two factions in 1967, he led the PARCHAM (flag) faction. Karmal's background in the Kabul elite put him at odds with other members of the Marxist movement in Afghanistan.

At the time of the Saur Revolution (April 1978), the two rival factions of the PDPA united and swept into power. Karmal was elected vice-chairman of the Revolutionary Council and deputy prime minister. In July 1978, the Parcham members of the party were purged, and Karmal was named ambassador to Czechoslovakia. On December 27, 1979, he returned to Kabul with the Soviet forces and became president of Afghanistan in January 1980, soon after President Hafizullah AMIN was killed. Karmal was unable to unite Afghanistan or to win the trust of the resistance fighters, and the country spiraled into civil war during his term. In 1986, in part because of his failing health, he was replaced by strongman NAJIBULLAH.

Although he was a gifted orator, Karmal was never an effective leader. He was more a thinker than a doer, more an ideologue than a politician. In addition, his aristocratic urban background often worked against his Marxist rhetoric, especially in a country like Afghanistan, which is mostly rural and largely populated by peasants. He spoke only Persian, the language of the aristocracy, rather than Pakhtun, the language of the rural people. He was never able to consolidate his hold on Afghanistan, and throughout his presidency he depended heavily on Soviet troops to protect his government from the Islamic insurgents.

[*See also:* Communism in the Middle East.]

BIBLIOGRAPHY

ARNOLD, ANTHONY. *Afghanistan's Two-Party System: Parcham and Khalq.* Stanford, Calif., 1983.
MALE, BEVERLEY. *Revolutionary Afghanistan.* New York, 1982.

Grant Farr

Karp Report

Examined irregularities in the conduct of police investigations of violence by Israeli settlers against Palestinian inhabitants in the occupied territories.

The Karp Report was issued in 1984 by a committee of Israeli jurists headed by Judith Karp. The committee was appointed by Attorney General Yitzhak Shamir in 1981 when a group of Israeli law professors expressed concern over the deterioration of the rule of law in the territories occupied by Israel. The committee examined seventy cases, fifty-three of which had been left unsolved, in which Israeli settlers were charged with various forms of harassment of Palestinian residents in the Hebron region who refused to sell their land.

The report found that police inquiries into the complaints lodged by Palestinians had been inade-

quate and criticized the police for failing to seriously investigate charges. It also faulted the separation between the regular and military police for impeding the inquiry process. The report advised a reassessment of the instructions given to Israeli soldiers for opening fire on civilians.

The committee's findings were controversial, with the Right charging that the investigation had failed to examine cases in which Palestinian Arabs had gone unpunished for attacks on Jews. Karp resigned after the Likud-led government neglected the report's findings.

Martin Malin

Kars

City and province in northeastern Turkey near the Armenian border.

The capital of a mountainous and forested province rich in salt deposits and known for textiles and carpets, the city of Kars has a population of more than seventy thousand. The city and province were captured by Russia from the Ottomans three times in the nineteenth century and ceded to Russia from 1878 to 1921. The local Armenian population, partly supplanted by Muslim refugees during the nineteenth century, controlled the city for much of the years 1918–1920, until Turkish nationalist forces captured it. By 1921, most of the non-Muslim population had disappeared.

BIBLIOGRAPHY

Encyclopaedia of Islam. Vol. 5. Leiden, 1986.

Elizabeth Thompson

Kasap, Teodor   [1835–1905]

Turkish Ottoman journalist, dramatist, and publisher.

Teodor Kasap, the son of a manufacturer, was born in Kayseri, Turkey. When he was eleven, his father died and he moved to Istanbul, where he was apprenticed to a Greek merchant and studied at a Greek school. While working in the merchant's store, he met a French officer who had come to Turkey during the Crimean War. Under the patronage of this officer, he went to France in 1856 to complete his studies. Upon his return to Istanbul, Kasap gave private French lessons, through which he entered the Istanbul literary circuit.

On November 24, 1870, Kasap published the first issue of the first Ottoman humor magazine, DIYOJEN. *Diyojen* quickly became famous for its caricatures and high-quality articles; among the regular contributors were NAMIK KEMAL and EBÜZZIYA TEVFIK. *Diyojen* also featured translations from French literature: Kasap's translation of Alexandre Dumas's *The Count of Monte Cristo* was one of the first Turkish translations of a French novel.

The caustic humor that was featured in *Diyojen* led the government to order it temporarily closed after only four issues. Kasap eventually published 183 issues of *Diyojen* before it was ordered permanently closed in 1873. Following this, he published two other magazines, *Cingirakli Tatar* and *Hayal* (both in 1873), and a daily political newspaper, *Istikbal* (1875). In 1877, Kasap was sentenced to three years in prison for a cartoon criticizing censorship of the press that appeared in *Hayal*. He was released from prison on the condition that he cease publishing *Hayal* and *Istikbal*; upon his release, he went into exile in Europe. Following a stay in Europe of several years, he was pardoned by Sultan Abdülhamit II and allowed to return to Istanbul where he was employed in the sultan's private library.

In addition to his publishing and journalistic activities, Kasap is known for his plays. His first play, "Pinti Hamit," was performed at the Gedikpaşa Theater in 1873; this was followed by "Iskilli Memo" in 1874 and "Para Meselesi" in 1875. The first two were based on plays written by Molière, the last, on a play written by Alexandre Dumas. Kasap believed that Turkish theater had to draw upon local sources and customs; his play "Iskilli Memo" was based on Turkish folk theater (ORTAOYUNU). He was opposed to unreflective adoption of Western theatrical genres, and he defended local traditions of drama: "Theater, like civilization, does not enter a country from the outside, but must come from within."

BIBLIOGRAPHY

ÖZKIRIMLI, ATILLA. *Türk edebiyati ansiklopedisi.* Vol. 4. Istanbul, 1982.
Türk ansiklopedisi. Vol. 32, Ankara, 1982.

David Waldner

Kashani, Abu al-Qasem   [1882–1962]

Iranian religious leader and political activist, important for his role in the events of 1945–1955, the postwar decade.

Born in Tehran, Kashani was taken at an early age by his father to al-Najaf in Iraq, where he began his formal religious education in Islam. With his father, he fought against the British in the battle of KUT AL-AMARA in 1916. Hostility to British imperialism was destined to remain the chief emphasis of his political life. Kashani also participated in the anti-British uprising of 1921, as a result of which he was compelled to return to Persia (Iran). He remained politically inactive until 1941, when the British forces occupying Iran arrested him for alleged contacts with agents. Released in 1945 (after World War II), he was placed under house arrest in 1946 for opposing a new press law.

In 1948, he organized demonstrations that called for volunteers to fight the Zionists in Palestine (Israel was established in May 1948) and also began collaborating with the militant organization FEDA'IYAN-E ISLAM. In 1949, he was exiled to Beirut on charges of involvement in a failed attempt on the life of the shah, Mohammad Reza Shah Pahlavi. He returned in triumph in 1950 and was elected to the *majles* (Iran's legislature), where he worked with Mohammad Mossadegh in bringing about the nationalization of the Iranian oil industry. From the fall of 1952 on, relations between the two men declined, and Kashani stood aside when Mossadegh was overthrown by the U.S.-sponsored royalist coup of August 1953. Kashani nonetheless resumed his own oppositional activities in 1954 and was arrested anew in 1955. He was released in January 1956 and, intimidated by the death of his son under questionable circumstances, remained politically inactive until his death in March 1962.

BIBLIOGRAPHY

RICHARD, YANN. "Ayatollah Kashani: Precursor of the Islamic Republic?" In *Religion and Politics in Iran*, ed. by N. R. Keddie. New Haven, Conn., 1983.

Hamid Algar

Kashif al-Ghita Family

A family of Shi'a ulama and mujtahidun originating in the Shi'a holy city of al-Najaf in southern Iraq.

The founder of the family, Ja'far ibn Khidr al-Najafi (1743–1812), was an *alim* (sing. of *ulama*) who wrote the *fiqh* (Islamic jurisprudence) textbook *Kashif al-Ghita* (The Uncoverer of the Error), from which the family surname was derived. In 1807, he led the defense of Najaf against the raiding Wahhabi, a Sunni fundamentalist and purist movement led by emirs of the house of Al Sa'ud, based in Najd.

Ja'far's sons, Shaykh Musa ibn Ja'far (1766–1827), Shaykh Ali ibn Ja'far (d. 1837), and Shaykh Hasan ibn Ja'far (1776–1848), were *mujtahidun* (senior Shi'a religious authorities empowered to issue religious decrees based on primary sources; singular *mujtahid*) in Najaf, where they were involved in political developments. Shaykh Musa ibn Ja'far Kashif al-Ghita mediated between the Ottoman Empire and the Persians during the 1820s.

The most prominent scion of the Kashif al-Ghita family in the twentieth century was Muhammad Husayn Kashif al-Ghita (1877–1954), who received the title and status of *marja* (supreme religious authority). He was the author of numerous books on religious topics, printed in Arabic and Persian, and had adherents throughout the Shi'a world. In his books he showed the need for Islamic unity and espressed his views about the ideal Islamic society. He maintained a correspondence with the Maronite intellectual Amin Rihani. He traveled to Hijaz, Syria, and Egypt, and lectured at al-Azhar University in Cairo. In 1909, he published a book, *al-Din wa al-Islam aw Dawa al-Islamiyya* (Religion and Islam or The Islamic Call), which called for a revival of Islam and its purification from recent trends of extremism and superstition.

During the 1920s and 1930s, Muhammad Husayn was an active Shi'a politician in Iraq. In the period of unrest and tribal rebellions (1934–35), he formulated the Shi'a demands, but refused—due to the strife among the Shi'a tribes and politicians—to commit himself to the tribal rebellion under Abd al-Wahid Sikkar, which was backed and manipulated by Sunni Baghdadi politicians of the Ikha al-Watani party. Starting from the late 1930s, he introduced moderate reforms and modernization in his *madrasa* (religious college) in Najaf.

In 1931, Muhammad Husayn Kashif al-Ghita attended the Muslim Congress in Jerusalem—the first Shi'a mujtahid to take part in a Muslim Congress—and led the prayers at the opening ceremony at the al-Aqsa Mosque.

Following World War II Muhammad Husayn began to warn against the dangers of communism. In 1953, he held talks with the British and American ambassadors on the communist influences among young Shi'ites in Iraq.

BIBLIOGRAPHY

AL-MAHBUBA, JA'FAR AL-SHAYKH BAQIR. *Madi al-Najaf wa Hadiriha,* vol. 4. Al-Najaf, 1955.

MOMEN, MOOJAN. *An Introduction to Shi'i Islam.* New Haven, Conn., 1983.

NAKASH, YIZHAK. *The Shi'is of Iraq.* Princeton, N.J., 1994.

Michael Eppel

Kashrut

See Kosher

Kasim, Abd al-Ra'uf al-   [1932–   ]

Syrian educator and politician; prime minister, 1980–1987.

Born in Damascus during the French Mandate over Syria, the son of a *mufti* (jurist and interpreter of Islamic law), Abd al-Ra'uf was educated in architecture at the universities of Istanbul and Geneva. He became dean of the Faculty of Fine Arts at the Syrian University from 1964 to 1970.

He served as governor of Damascus in 1979/80, then held the position of prime minister under Syria's President Hafiz al-ASAD, from 1980 to 1987.

BIBLIOGRAPHY

SEALE, PATRICK. *Asad: The Struggle for the Middle East.* Los Angeles, 1988.

Charles U. Zenzie

Kasravi, Ahmad   [1890–1946]

Iranian writer and reformer.

Born into a religious family in Tabriz, Kasravi received a religious education and for a brief time was a preacher. As a young man, he joined the Tabriz branch of the reformist Democrat party, which had acquired a reputation in the national assembly for being anticlerical. Kasravi was expelled from the party in 1917 for his opposition to a growing trend among Tabriz Democrats to emphasize provincial concerns over national concerns. In 1921, he moved to Tehran, where he spent the remainder of his life working as a social reformer, activist, and historian. Kasravi was one of the most prolific and influential writers of early twentieth-century Iran. His important works include *History of Iran's Constitutional Revolution, An Eighteen-Year History of Iran, Shi'igari,* and *Piramun-e Islam* (all of them in Arabic). Kasravi often criticized the Shi'a clergy in his writings, especially in the two latter works, both of which were condemned by some clergy. He was assassinated by a member of the radical FEDA'IYAN-E ISLAM.

BIBLIOGRAPHY

KASRAVI, AHMAD. *On Islam and Shi'ism.* Translated by M. R. Ghanoonparvar. Costa Mesa, Calif., 1990.

Eric J. Hooglund

Kassallah

Commercial and agricultural center of eastern Sudan.

Founded in 1840, Kassallah grew rapidly, and within a few decades became the most important commercial and agricultural center in eastern Sudan. During the Mahdiya revolt, its Turko–Egyptian defenders withstood the siege by the Mahdists from 1883 until 1885, when the garrison surrendered after the MAHDI had captured Khartoum. In 1894 the Italians, who had occupied Eritrea, captured the town; they did so again for a few months in 1940, before Kassallah was liberated by Allied forces under British command. As the gateway to Eritrea and Ethiopia and the entrepôt for the rich agricultural lands in the Gash River delta of the Sudan, Kassallah became the center for road and rail traffic between Port Sudan and Khartoum. Its strategic location has made it the sanctuary for the thousands of refugees who have fled from the Eritrean–Ethiopian war since the mid-1960s. The influx of refugees has swollen the population beyond any accurate assessment, but Kassallah has become the largest city in the Sudan after the Three Towns (Khartoum, Khartoum North, and Omdurman).

Robert O. Collins

Khatmiyya mosque in Kassallah, Sudan, in 1987. (© Chris Kutschera)

Kassem, Abd al-Karim   [1914–1963]

Leader of the leftist nationalist 1958 revolt in Iraq; president and prime minister of Iraq, 1958–1963.

Kassem (also Qasim) was born into a poor Baghdad family. His father, a carpenter, was a Sunni Arab and his mother was a Kurdish Shi'ite. After finishing high school, he taught for one year in a primary school before changing careers and joining the military college of Iraq from which he graduated in 1934. As part of an Iraqi military unit, he participated in the first ARAB–ISRAEL WAR, 1948/49. Like other officers of his generation, he retained a bitterness about the defeat, which he attributed to the weakness and corruption of the Arab monarchies.

In 1952, the Egyptian monarchy was overthrown by nationalist officers and a republic was established. Reverberations from that coup soon reached Baghdad. The Iraqi military was not only disgusted with corruption in the Baghdad regime but was still bitter over the failed anti-British military coup of 1941 and the repression of nationalists that followed.

In Iraq, after the Egyptian revolution, junior officers began to organize underground cells. Kassem joined this clandestine organization in 1955 and, because of his seniority and his respected professional reputation, soon became chairman of the Central Committee of the Free Officers, as they called themselves.

On July 14, 1958, these officers staged a successful coup, which resulted in the killing of the royal family and the Prime Minister Nuri al-Sa'id—and the proclamation of a republic. General Kassem became president and prime minister, and his fellow officer and colleague Abd al-Salam Arif became deputy prime minister. In a very short time, relations between the two men soured over differences relating to Iraq's policy toward Egypt's President Gamal Abdel Nasser. Arif advocated an immediate rapprochement with Nasser and an eventual joining of the United Arab Republic (Egypt and Syria); Kassem wanted to keep his distance from Nasser.

As prime minister, Kassem took several anti-Western steps in foreign policy. He let Iraq's membership in the BAGHDAD PACT lapse, he restored diplomatic relations with the Soviet Union, and he signed an arms agreement with that country. In domestic policy, he began an agrarian reform program and passed progressive legislation giving women additional rights in matters of divorce and inheritance.

In 1961, Kassem issued Law Number 80, which stripped the foreign-owned Iraq Petroleum Company (IPC) of 99.5 percent of its concessionary territory. For a time, he allowed open activity by political parties; however, his lenience toward the Communist party led to serious dissatisfaction among the population and the army.

Criticism of his policies toward Nasser and the Communists exacerbated the rift between him and Arif, who was arrested (on charges of attempting to kill Kassem) and imprisoned. In March 1959, Iraqi nationalist officers attempted a coup in Mosul. In response, the Communists and their allies took to the streets in Baghdad and elsewhere, which resulted in mass killings in Mosul and Kirkuk in July 1959 (that Kassem did little to prevent).

Besides facing opposition from Arab nationalists and the Ba'th party, Kassem had to confront a renewal of KURDISH REVOLTS for separatism. After returning to Iraq in 1958, Mustafa Barzani, the renowned Kurdish leader, staged a revolt in 1960 which lasted (off and on) until 1963, further weakening Kassem and his legitimacy. Kassem also had political problems within the Middle East: In May 1961, Britain ended Kuwait's protective status, making that country independent. Relying on vague historical claims, Kassem announced that Kuwait was an integral part of Iraq but sent no troops to back up his claim. British troops were, however, dispatched to Kuwait to defend it, although these were eventually replaced by forces from the League of Arab States. Thus Kassem became isolated from his Arab League neighbors.

During these events, the Arab nationalists and Ba'thists had been organizing and undertook a successful military coup in Baghdad. On February 8, 1963, Kassem was arrested and executed the following day. Arif became president of the republic, with a Ba'thist as prime minister and a civilian government, after annulling the military law that had been in force since 1958.

BIBLIOGRAPHY

DANN, URIEL. Iraq under Qassem: A Political History, 1958–1963. Jerusalem, 1969.
KHADDURI, MAJID. Republican Iraq. London, 1969.

Louay Bahry

Kasztner Affair

Dramatic and highly politicized slander trial in Israel from January 1954 to June 1955.

Gossip journalist Malkiel Grunwald stood accused of defaming Dr. Rudolf Kasztner, director of public relations for the ministry of commerce and industry and hero of Holocaust rescue efforts on behalf of Hungarian Jewry. Kasztner's role in the failed 1944 negotiations to "buy" the survival of Hungary's Jews from Adolf Eichmann was portrayed by the defense as collaboration with the Nazis in exchange for the freedom of a handpicked few of Kasztner's friends and relatives who were transported to Switzerland as an agreed-upon "good faith" gesture. According to defense counsel Shmuel TAMIR, whose HERUT party's political agenda was to associate Kasztner's "war-crimes" with the Jewish Agency and by extension with MAPAI party, it was to ensure this "delivery" that Kasztner kept from Hungarian Jewry the truth about its expected fate and encouraged Palestinian Jewish parachutists to surrender to the authorities. He was also disparaged for testifying on behalf of one of his Nazi interlocutors, Kurt Becher, at the Nuremberg trials after World War II. Grunwald was acquitted. Reverberations of the trial led to the resignation of Prime Minister Moshe Sharett's government in June, 1955. Kasztner was assassinated in March of 1957 by three youths associated with the extreme right, ten months before Israel's Supreme Court overturned the ruling in the Grunwald case.

Zev Maghen

Katagan

Afghan city.

Katagan, also Qatagan or Qataghan, is a city in northern Afghanistan near the border of Uzbekistan. It has a population of approximately 10,000 and is in a mixed Uzbek–Tajik area. The city is a major trading center, famous for its horses.

BIBLIOGRAPHY

DUPREE, LOUIS. Afghanistan. Princeton, N.J., 1980.

Grant Farr

Kata'ib Party

See Phalange

Kattani, Muhammad ibn Abd al-Kabir al-
[?–1909]

Idrisi sharif; head of the Kattaniya Sufi brotherhood; anticolonial leader in the period of the Moroccan Question.

As head of the KATTANIYA BROTHERHOOD, in 1904 Muhammad al-Kattani led the notables of Fez in opposition to France's reform plan presented to Morocco's sultan Abd al-Aziz. Disappointed with the sultan's acquiescence to French pressure, in 1907–1908 he led demonstrations at Fez in favor of deposing Abd al-Aziz and proclaiming Abd al-Hafid as sultan. He also sought to impose conditions on the latter when he assumed the throne, committing him to a program of unwavering opposition to European rule.

In 1909, Kattani's unrelenting public attacks on Abd al-Hafid led to the former's arrest and execution. Subsequent generations of Moroccan nationalists have, however, viewed him as a hero for his staunch opposition to French colonial rule.

BIBLIOGRAPHY

BURKE, EDMUND, III. *Prelude to Protectorate in Morocco: Precolonial Protest and Resistance, 1860–1912* Chicago, 1976.

LAROUI, ABDULLAH. *Les origines sociales et culturelles du nationalisme marocain (1860–1912)*. Paris, 1977.

Edmund Burke III

Kattaniya Brotherhood

A Moroccan Sufi order, formally intended to enhance the spirituality of its adherents, which played a major political role in the early twentieth century.

The Kattaniya brotherhood (in Arabic, *tariqa*) was founded in Fez, Morocco, in 1890 by Muhammad ibn Abd al-Kabir al-KATTANI—known popularly as Muhammad al-Kabir. Al-Kabir was inspired by the Sufi doctrines and practices of the established Darqawi *tariqa*.

The Kattani family, known for its scholars and jurists, claimed descent from the Prophet Muhammad through Morocco's Idrisi dynasty. The Kattaniya rapidly gained adherents in Fez, Meknes, and Morocco's rural regions, but the brotherhood was condemned by reformist *ulama* (religious scholars). In 1909, Muhammad al-Kabir fled Fez to sanctuary with a neighboring tribe when the new ruler, Sultan Mulay Abd al-Hafid (ruled 1908–1912), ordered his arrest and closed all Kattaniya ZAWIYAS (Islamic compounds). Pursued and beaten, he was executed soon after he was brought back to Fez.

Once the French protectorate was established (1912–1956), the Kattaniya again flourished under Shaykh Muhammad Abd al-Hayy al-Kattani—a scholar, popular religious leader, implacable foe of the ALAWITE DYNASTY, and a beneficiary of French colonial rule. In 1953, Abd al-Hayy joined other antinationalists in calling for the deposition of Sultan Muhammad V, and the Kattaniya brotherhood rapidly collapsed.

BIBLIOGRAPHY

DRAGUE (SPILLMAN), GEORGES. *Esquisse d'histoire religieuse du Maroc.* Paris, 1951.

Dale F. Eickelman

Katznelson, Berl [1887–1944]

Pioneer Labor Zionist.

Berl Katznelson was born in Belorussia and went to Palestine in 1909. He became a farm laborer and a friend of A. D. Gordon. In World War I, he was in the Jewish Legion with David Ben-Gurion and Yitzhak Ben-Zvi. With them, and as a theoretician in Labor Zionism, he created the platform for bringing together the several Labor Zionist (socialist) parties into a unified framework. He was a founder of AHDUT HA-AVODAH in 1919, the HISTADRUT labor organization in 1920, and the MAPAI political party in 1930. In 1925, he founded the Histadrut's daily newspaper, *Davar,* which he edited until 1936, and its publishing house, Am Oved.

Central to Katznelson's outlook was the notion that ZIONISM would not be achieved without socialism because of the need to direct investment. He called his socialism "constructive" to signal both its preference for the interests of the workers and its priority for building the infrastructure necessary in a state. During World War II, the knowledge of the Holocaust changed his rigid stance against the Arabs and inclined him toward compromise.

BIBLIOGRAPHY

SHAPIRA, ANITA. *Berl: The Biography of a Socialist Zionist.* Cambridge, U.K., 1981.

Donna Robinson Divine

Kawakib, al-

Egyptian magazine.

Established in 1952, *al-Kawakib* is a weekly film magazine published by the Dar al-Hilal publishing company. Its circulation is estimated at 86,000.

Michael R. Fischbach

Kawakibi, Abd al-Rahman al- [1854–1902]

Central figure in the development of Arab nationalist thought.

Abd al-Rahman al-Kawakibi was born in Aleppo but grew up in Antioch, where he studied a variety of subjects in Arabic, Turkish, and Persian under the supervision of a prominent scholar related to his mother. He then returned to Aleppo and served as an editor of the Ottoman-sponsored newspaper *al-Furat* during the latter half of the 1870s. In 1878, he founded the city's first privately published Arabic-language newspaper, the weekly *al-Shadaba*. He played active roles in the then newly-estalished Chamber of Commerce, the municipal administration, and the government-owned Tobacco Corporation. His outspoken advocacy of programs to help the poor won him the nickname Abu al-Du'afa (Father of the Weak). His willingness to challenge the authorities eventually brought him into conflict with the provincial governor, who arrested him for sedition and confiscated his property. An appeals court ordered his release but refused to return his possessions, so around 1898 he emigrated to Egypt and entered the service of the Khedive Abbas Hilmi II. He died in Cairo.

Al-Kawakibi is best-known for two short treatises, written in Aleppo but first published in Cairo. The first, *Umm al-Qura* (The Mother of Towns, i.e., Mecca), appeared in print in 1899 under the pseudonym al-Sayyid al-Furati. Structured in the form of a discussion among twenty-two Muslims planning to set up a secret society to revitalize the Islamic world, the book's thesis is that Islam will remain incapable of resisting the intellectual and political challenges emanating from Europe unless the leadership of the faith (*khalifa*) is returned to the Arabs from the (Ottoman) Turks. If a new khalifa were to be established in Mecca and were accorded authority only in religious matters, then the political position of all Muslims would be greatly strengthened. Despite its controversial if not explosive argument, this book went virtually unnoticed until it was serialized in Rashid Rida's journal *al-Manar* in 1902/3.

The second treatise, *Taba'i al-Istibdad wa Masari al-Isti'bad* (The Attendants of Despotism and the Destruction of Subjugation), is a spirited critique of tyranny in all its myriad forms: political, intellectual, economic, spiritual, and national/racial. For al-Kawakibi, each of these despotisms can be traced to earthly rulers' refusal to acknowledge the rule of Allah. Bringing an end to tyranny thus entails recognizing the supremacy and oneness of God (*tawhid*). But in order to prevent despotism from reemerging, governments must be made fully accountable to the people and wealth must be distributed equitably. Al-Kawakibi thus presents a program for social reform which is sharply at variance with that advocated by contemporaneous Islamic thinkers, who generally considered both democracy and socialism to be antithetical to Islam. There are indications that al-

Kawakibi outlined several other writings during his years in Aleppo, but the notes for these works were seized and destroyed by the Ottoman police.

Fred H. Lawson

Kayhan

Iranian newspaper.

Kayhan, published since 1942, is the second-longest-running evening newspaper in Tehran. Its original proprietor, Mustafa Mesbahzadeh, currently publishes an opposition newspaper called the *London Kayhan* in London. From its inception until 1953, *Kayhan*'s editor, Abdolrahman Faramarzi, gave the newspaper a critical bent. After the fall of the Mossadegh government in 1953 and the consolidation of Pahlavi rule, *Kayhan*'s new editor, Amir Taheri, toned down its criticisms and refrained from meddling in politics. Following the Iranian revolution in 1979, *Kayhan* was put under government control with a representative from the office of the leader of the revolution on its board. In its post-1979 phase, *Kayhan* is marked by a radical Islamic stance on political and cultural issues. Hoseyn Shari'atmadari is the newspaper's current editor.

Neguin Yavari

Kaylani, Abd al-Rahman al- [1841–1927]

First prime minister of Iraq.

Scion of an ancient aristocratic family, al-Kaylani was the head of the Qadiri (Sufi) mystical order, established by his ancestor, Abd al-Qadir al-Kaylani (or al-Jilani) (1077–1166). He was also the *naqib al-ashraf* (a noble title denoting responsibility for the genealogical records listing the descent of a city's families from the Prophet; the title conveys the status of titular head of those families) of Baghdad.

Sir Percy Cox, British Civil Commissioner after World War I, regarded the Kaylani family as the most aristocratic and monarchial in Baghdad, and suggested that Abd al-Rahman al-Kaylani be made emir of Iraq. In November 1920, al-Kaylani was appointed president of the Iraqi Council of Ministers, the nucleus of the future Iraqi administration. In 1921, as a candidate for the planned throne of Iraq, al-Kaylani objected to the choice of Faisal ibn Husayn of Hijaz as king of Iraq, but gradually resigned himself to the idea, realizing that the British insisted on Faisal. Al-Kaylani resigned from the Council of Ministers on Faisal's accession in August 1921. Subsequently he was appointed by Faisal as head of the cabinet and became the first prime minister of Iraq. Al-Kaylani conducted talks with Britain about the ANGLO–IRAQI TREATIES and also objected to the Mandate. In 1922, as the official representative of Iraq, al-Kaylani signed the treaty with Britain but on condition that it would be ratified by the Constituent Assembly.

BIBLIOGRAPHY

BATATU, HANNA. *The Old Social Classes and the Revolutionary Movements of Iraq.* Princeton, N.J., 1973.

Michael Eppel

Kaylani, Rashid Ali al- [1892–1965]

Four-time prime minister of Iraq in the 1930s and 1940s and a symbol of Arab nationalist resistance.

Rashid Ali al-Kaylani (also al-Gilani) was born in Baghdad in 1892. Although a member of one of the oldest local families, Rashid Ali's personal circumstances were quite modest, as a family disagreement had deprived his father of the stipend from the Qadiriyya WAQF to which he was entitled as a Kaylani family member.

In 1924 he was appointed minister of justice in the cabinet of Yasin al-Hashimi, probably his closest political colleague; they were cofounders, in 1930, of Hizb al-IKHA AL-WATANI (Party of National Brotherhood), which spearheaded the opposition to the Anglo–Iraqi treaty of that year. By 1933, however, when the treaty had taken effect, both men acquiesced to the new situation, and Rashid Ali accepted his first premiership (March 20–October 28).

Out of office between October 1933 and March 1935, Rashid Ali and Hashimi spent much of this period encouraging the Middle Euphrates tribes to rebel against the governments of Ali Jawdat al-AYYUBI and Jamil al-Midfa'i. By March 1935, they had succeeded to the extent that Jawdat and Midfa'i could no longer form cabinets; Hashimi became prime minister and Rashid Ali minister of interior in a government that lasted until the coup d'état by Bakr Sidqi in October 1936.

By the late 1930s, Britain and France had become increasingly unpopular in the Arab Middle East. In addition, while pan-Arab nationalism had little following in Iraq outside the officer corps, anti-British—and to some extent pro-Axis—feeling was heightened by the combination of the general weakness of the institutions of the state after the death of King Faisal I; the existence of widely shared aspirations for independence from Britain; the arrival of Hajj Amin al-Husayni, the mufti of Jerusalem, in Baghdad in October 1939; and the fact that a small clique of nationalist officers, the so-called GOLDEN SQUARE, had come to exercise a pivotal influence on Iraqi politics.

Rashid Ali became the chief political ally of the nationalist officers of the Golden Square and became prime minister in March 1940 after the fall of Nuri al-SA'ID's fifth ministry. Sa'id, unpopular because of his staunch support for Britain, considered, somewhat overoptimistically, that Rashid Ali, who had opposed the Anglo–Iraqi treaty, was both less compromised than himself and better able to resist the Golden Square's more extreme demands.

Under the terms of the 1930 treaty, the Iraqi government agreed to allow the transit of British troops across its territory in time of war. Britain sought to take advantage of this provision in June 1940, and permission in principle was given in mid-July. However, in spite of requests from Britain, Iraq refused to break off relations with Italy when Italy declared war on Britain in June 1940, and in consequence, the Italian legation in Baghdad developed into a center of anti-British intrigue. In addition, in August 1940 Rashid Ali and the mufti entered into secret negotiations with Berlin.

Matters rapidly came to a head, since Rashid Ali, who had the support of most of the armed forces, would not yield to British pressure to resign because of his refusal to allow troops to land in Iraq and pass through the country to Palestine in November 1940. By January 1941, he had been forced to step down as prime minister, but he returned to power on April 12. In consequence, the regent Abd al-Ilah, Sa'id, and other pro-British politicians fled to Transjordan (now Jordan).

British troops landed at Basra a few days later; while this showed that Britain meant business, it became clear that Rashid Ali and his government enjoyed widespread popular support. Given the balance of forces, the defeat of the Iraqi army by British troops after the thirty days war (May 1941) was very much a foregone conclusion. The much-heralded German support never materialized, and Rashid Ali fled the country with some of his closest supporters, reaching Germany in November 1941. He stayed there until May 1945, subsequently taking refuge in Saudi Arabia, where he remained until 1954.

After the overthrow of the Iraqi monarchy, Rashid Ali returned to Baghdad in September 1958, apparently hoping that his previous services to the state would be properly acclaimed. When adequate recognition was not forthcoming, he set about inciting rebellion among the tribes of the Middle Euphrates in a quixotic attempt to unseat the government of Abd al-Karim Kassem. He was arrested in December 1958, tried and condemned to death, but subsequently pardoned by Kassem. He died in Beirut on August 30, 1965.

Peter Sluglett

Kaymakam

See Qa'immaqam

Kayyali, Abd al-Rahman   [1887–?]

Syrian physician and politician.

Born to a Sunni Muslim family in Aleppo in 1887, Kayyali received an M.D. from the American University of Beirut. He joined the National Bloc party and was first elected to parliament in 1928. He was returned to this post in 1936, 1939, 1943, and 1946; he also held the offices of minister of education and minister of justice from 1936 to 1939. He was again justice minister from 1943 to 1947, when he doubled as minister of public works. Kayyali represented Syria at the United Nations in 1948 and was president of the al-Watani party from 1949 to 1958.

BIBLIOGRAPHY

Who's Who in the Middle East, 1967–1968.

Charles U. Zenzie

Kayyali, Fakhir al-

Syrian politician.

A member of the National party, Fakhir al-Kayyali became minister of national economy in 1954 under Sabri al-Asali. He was returned to that position later that year in the cabinet of Faris al-Khuri. Along with other National party members, he resigned from his post as minister, a collective move that destroyed al-Khuri's coalition. He served as minister of public works under the returning Sabri al-Asali beginning in 1956.

BIBLIOGRAPHY

Who's Who in the Middle East, 1967–1968.

Charles U. Zenzie

Kaza

The smallest administrative unit in the Ottoman Empire.

A subdivision of a SANJAK or LIWA, the *kaza* was traditionally, but not always, the area of a qadi's (judge's) jurisdiction. Kaza can also refer to the judgment of a qadi. The term is still used for local districts in Turkey but has been abandoned elsewhere.

BIBLIOGRAPHY

SHAW, STANFORD J. *History of the Ottoman Empire and Modern Turkey*, vol. 1. New York, 1976.

Elizabeth Thompson

Keban Dam

Dam built on the Euphrates river in eastern Turkey.

In 1974, near the provincial capital city of Elazığ (1980 population about 143,000), the Keban Dam was opened by Turkey's Prime Minister Bülent Ecevit, after eight years of construction. A future prime minister, Turgut OZAL, had been an engineer on the project. When it was completed, the Keban Dam was the world's eighteenth-tallest dam at 680 feet (207 m); it created Turkey's third-largest lake.

The Keban Dam is part of Turkey's SOUTHEASTERN ANATOLIA PROJECT, a long-term hydroelectric program designed to increase the country's electrical generating capacity by 45 percent. It includes two other dams—one on the Tigris river and a second, the Atatürk Dam, completed in 1990, on the Euphrates. The project is intended to increase irrigable land in the region by 700,000 acres (283,000 ha) and to stimulate the economy of the region, largely inhabited by Kurds. The project has been a source of political tension with Syria and Iraq, since both depend on the same rivers for water.

BIBLIOGRAPHY

Turkey: A Country Study. Washington, D.C., 1988.

Elizabeth Thompson

Kececizade, İzzet   [1785–1829]

Ottoman Turkish poet.

The son of a chief military judge, İzzet Kececizade received a religious education and became an Islamic scholar (*molla*). He was appointed qadi of Galata at a young age but lost this position due to a dispute with Sultan Mahmud II, who, according to tradition, had İzzet killed. Considered the last great pre-Tanzimat poet, his *Gülsen-i aşk* (Garden of Love) was Sufi inspired. He is also known for his satires, especially *Mihnet-kesan* (The Sufferers), which uses puns and satire to attack court life.

BIBLIOGRAPHY

MITLER, LOUIS. *Ottoman Turkish Writers: A Bibliographical Dictionary of Significant Figures in Pre-Republican Turkish Literature*. New York, 1988.

David Waldner

Kedourie Family

See Kadoori Family

Keinan, Amos   [1927–   ]

Israeli writer and satirist.

Keinan was a regular columnist for the dailies *Yediot Aharonot* and *Ha-Aretz* in Israel. He achieved renown through his caustic, satirical column, "Uzi and Shoti," that appeared in *Ha-Aretz* from 1950–1952. His first stories were published in *Alef* in 1949. Keinan's writings are often pessimistic and voice an exaggerated sense of fear of destruction.

Among his works are *Shoah II* (Holocaust II; 1975); *Ba-Derekh Le-Ein Harod* (On the Way to Ein Harod; 1984), describing the destruction of Israel; *Mi-Tahat La-Perahim* (Under the Flowers; 1979), an anthology of short stories describing attitudes toward death during war; and *Sefer Ha-Satirot* (Book of Satires; 1984), a compilation of satires from 1948–1984. A collection of his plays was published in 1979.

Ann Kahn

Kel, Hasan   [1874–1929]

Ottoman Turkish actor and theater director.

Born to a poor Istanbul family, Kel was a yogurt seller who improvised comic routines to attract customers. His improvisational skills were eventually displayed on the stage with Küçük Ali in the suburb of Kadıköy.

Later, Kel founded a theater company with Ağa Effendi, where he popularized his role of an inept servant. Kel also founded a theater company and directed its performances.

BIBLIOGRAPHY

Türk Ansiklopedisi. Ankara, 1974.

David Waldner

Kemal, Namık

See Namık Kemal

Kemal, Yaşar

See Yaşar Kemal

Kemalettin Bey   [1870–1927]

Turkish architect.

Kemalettin was born in Constantinople (now Istanbul), capital of the Ottoman Empire, into a middle-class family; his father was a naval captain. After graduating from the School of Civil Engineering in 1891, he became the assistant to the German architect A. Jasmund, who designed the Sirkeci railroad station in Turkey. Kemalettin then went to Germany where he studied at the Charlottenburg Technische Hochschule. Upon his return to Constantinople in 1900, he began to work as chief architect in the ministry of war, and to teach at the School of Civil Engineering. He was a founder of the First National Architectural Movement in the early part of the twentieth century. The style developed by him and his contemporary Vedat Bey has been termed Ottoman Revivalism, because it incorporated the architectural elements of the classical Ottoman period over basically neo-Renaissance structures. When in 1909 he was appointed to the architectural department at the ministry of religious foundations, he began to apply his ideas of a national architecture. Architects trained under his guidance at the ministry helped to spread his vision throughout the Ottoman Empire.

At the ministry, Kemalettin was responsible for the restoration of historical monuments and the design of new buildings. Over the next decade, he built new mosques, mausoleums, office buildings, prisons, hospitals, schools, and train stations. His buildings were characteristically symmetrical with reference to the entrance, while protrusions at the two ends and at the central axis served to highlight this symmetry. These protrusions were often towers covered with domes, in the classical Ottoman style. He emulated Renaissance architecture by dividing his facades into three sections separated by continuous molding; he used different window orders in each section to render the three sections as distinct entities. The facades had rich carvings, tile panels, and carved moldings, composed in careful symmetry.

One of Kemalettin's most important works is a complex of 124 apartment houses and 25 shops. These buildings replaced 7,500 houses that had been destroyed in the fire of 1918. The first examples of reinforced concrete construction in the country, the apartments received natural light and ventilation from the central courtyards, around which they were built to enhance social interaction. These apartments quickly became popular among the elite.

Kemalettin's influence did not wane with the establishment of the Republic of Turkey in 1923. Although the new government wanted to distance itself from its Ottoman heritage and identify more strongly with the West, it had no choice but to recruit the best architects of the previous decade to design its new public buildings. Kemalettin was called in to design the portal of the new Turkish Grand National Assembly building and to complete the design of the Ankara Palace Hotel across from the new parliament building. In addition, he designed a series of housing projects for civil servants. Thus, architecture in Turkey's first decade was in many ways an extension of the nationalist architecture of the final years of the empire.

By the last days of Kemalettin's life, his vision of architecture came under attack. His last project, a 1926 commission to design a teacher's college, was criticized by foreign, particularly German, consultants, who preferred the less ornate forms of international architecture, as influenced by the Bauhaus school. If the national school had previously been seen as ornate, it was now considered ponderous. In the 1930s, the Second National Architectural Movement began to focus on Ottoman civil, not religious, structures. But Kemalettin Bey did not live to see this transition.

BIBLIOGRAPHY

SEY, YILDIZ. "To House the New Citizens: Housing Policies and Mass Housing." In *Modern Turkish Architecture,* ed. by Renata Holod and Ahmet Evin. Philadelphia, 1984.

YAVUZ, YILDIRIM. "Turkish Architecture during the Republican Period (1923–1980)." In *The Transformation of Turkish Culture: The Atatürk Legacy,* ed. by Günsel Renda and C. Max Kortepeter. Princeton, N.J., 1986.

YAVUZ, YILDIRIM, and SUHA ÖZKAN. "The Final Years of Ottoman Empire," and "Finding A National Idiom: The First National Style." In *Modern Turkish Architecture,* ed. by Renata Holod and Ahmet Evin. Philadelphia, 1984.

David Waldner

Kemal Film

Turkish film production company.

Founded in 1922 by two brothers, Kemal and Şakir Seden, Kemal Film was the first private film production firm in Turkey. That same year, it produced two silent films by the leader of Turkish theater, Muhsin ERTUĞRUL: *A Love Tragedy in Istanbul* and *The Mystery of the Bosphorus/Father Light*. While filming the latter, however, a group from the Bektaşi

Sufi sect (of Islam) heard the film was against their teaching and raided the studios. Kemal Film continued working with Ertuğrul as director through the 1930s, however.

Kemal Film met rising competition as the number of production companies increased in the 1940s and 1950s. It signed director Lütfi Ömer Akad, Turkey's first world-class director, in the 1950s. Akad made what many consider his masterpiece, *In the Name of the Law,* with Kemal Film in 1952. Osman Seden, owner of Kemal Film in the 1950s, was a screenwriter who moved into directing with his 1955 *They Paid with Their Blood.* He became known for technically beautiful films packed with stars, but short on plot.

BIBLIOGRAPHY

DORSAY, ATILLA. "An Overview of Turkish Cinema from Its Origins to the Present Day." In *The Transformation of Turkish Culture,* ed. by Günsel Renda and C. Max Kortepeter. Princeton, N.J., 1986.

ÖZGÜÇ, AGAH. "A Chronological History of the Turkish Cinema (1914–1988)." *Turkish Review* (Winter 1989): 53–115.

Elizabeth Thompson

Kemalism

The official present-day political ideology of the Republic of Turkey.

Kemalism refers variously to Mustafa Kemal ATATÜRK's (1881–1938) thought; the ideology and regime of the single-party period (1920–1950) in the Republic of Turkey; the official Turkish political ideology to date (semi-official in the 1961 constitution, fully official and imperative in the 1982 constitution); the principles of national education and citizenship training; the hegemonic public philosophy in contemporary Turkey; and finally to the name of the persistent Turkish personality cult.

Kemal derived his legitimacy from the commandership in chief of the successful war of independence (1919–1922), which ended up in the foundation of the republican Turkish nation-state on the ruins of the Ottoman Empire (1299–1922). No less importantly, this legitimacy was reinforced by his extreme qualities of charismatic leadership. Kemal and his followers, after abolishing the sultanate and the caliphate, proceeded to build up an authoritarian, single-party state, with discernable totalitarian characteristics in certain ideological and institutional spheres. The Kemalists implemented, alternately gradually and forcefully, a series of radical reforms in the political, legal, educational, and cultural fields, including adoption of

Western legal codes (some liberal, such as the Swiss civil code; some fascistic, such as the penal and labor codes); latinization of the Ottoman alphabet; adoption of the Western calendar and units of measurement and imposition of Western clothing and headwear; the closing down of social and associational institutions of Islamic sects; unification of education in the sense of prohibiting schools of religious instruction and creating a new system of secular national education; and disestablishment of Islam in general beyond the narrow laicist sense of separation of religion and politics, but at the same time bringing religion under the control and supervision of the state through a Directorate of Religious Affairs.

The main thrust of these reforms was Westernization and secularization of the society, based on a rejection of the Ottoman Islamic past and on a synthesis of Western values with the virtues of old, original, Turkish "national character," not excluding a tertiary element of the purified, pre-Arabic-Persian-Ottoman version of Islamic morality. Many of these reforms constituted the completion of a long process of Westernist modernization, some inaugurated by the "Re-Ordering" (TANZIMAT, 1838) and the First and Second Constitutional periods (1876 and 1908), some others formulated by Ziya GÖKALP and partially implemented by the Unionists (1908–1918). Whether the Kemalist reforms constitute a revolution or radical reform is the subject of an ongoing debate, but the Kemalists identified themselves as "transformist" (*inkilapi*).

Partly impressed by the Westernist reformist and laicist character of "cultural Kemalism," most interpreters—Turkish and foreign alike—have designated Kemalism as a tutelary democracy overlooking or playing down the severely anti-democratic essence of "political Kemalism" both as an ideology and as a regime. This standard interpretation of Kemalism has also been partly guided by an imputation of false causality, in the sense that the development of the single-party regime after the end of World War II into a sort of multiparty parliamentary system (1946–1950), as a result of external pressures, was attributed to the unfolding of the internal dynamics of the first thirty formative years of the Turkish republic. As a matter of fact, this rootless parliamentarianism has been thrice interrupted by military coups (1960, 1971, 1980) of varying degrees of violence—all declared to be staged, among but above all other things, in the cause of Kemalism.

Kemalism was an early brand of those "third way" (*tertium genus*) ideologies and regimes of the post–World War I world of late-modernizing capitalist countries which were to borrow further elements, especially in the 1930s and early 1940s, from the full fascisms of interbellum Europe. Kemalism was anti-socialist and anti-Marxist, anti-liberal but not anti-capitalist; that is, it was corporatist capitalist. It belonged more to the solidaristic species of corporatism formulated by the Turkish social and political thinker Ziya Gökalp, only later assuming partial fascistic overtones in certain ideological and institutional spheres. The Kemalist single-party regime rested on a class alliance of civilian-military petite bourgeoisie, big landowners, a nationalistic commercial bourgeoisie, and an incipient and subordinate industrial bourgeoisie, which it was the explicit ideology of the Kemalists to create and strengthen through neo-marcantilist policies of economic statism (etatism). This developmentalist objective required accelerated capital accumulation through labor policies which provided a cheap and disciplined labor force for private enterprises, for state economic enterprises, and for joint ventures between the two and through fiscal policies that called for transfer of resources from the agricultural countryside to industry and the urban centers, especially after the Great Depression.

The Kemalist regime, aiming at the creation of a bourgeois society without liberal politics, was not a de jure but a de facto dictatorial regime. Mustafa Kemal Atatürk, as the "greatest father" (*Ata-Türk*) of the nation, as the "eternal chief" of the single party, as the president of the republic, as the effective head of the executive branch (in breach of the 1924 Constitution that formally called for a sort of cabinet system) which governed in accordance with his directives, sat at the apex of this system. The parliamentary facade but thinly veiled the fact that the legislature (the Grand National Assembly) was regularly "packed" by Atatürk and his lieutenants, second-degree electors rubber-stamping the candidates handpicked by the former. The parliament, in Kemal Atatürk's own words, was coterminous with the parliamentary group of his REPUBLICAN PEOPLE'S PARTY.

In other words, Kemalism was a plebiscitary, Bonapartist-charismatic "chief-system" in whose ideology the identity of the charismatic leader, the nation and its will, the state, and the party was emphatically expressed. Opposition, pluralism, and freedom of press and association, among others, were suppressed in the name of "transformationism" as against the over-stretched category of reactionary forces. This attitude and its attendant formal and informal arrangements were to leave a durable imprint on the political culture, political-legal regime, and institutional structures of contemporary Turkey—the most recent fortification of which was to be made after the 1980 military coup in the form of the 1980 Constitution, the new Political Parties Act, the Higher Education Act, the Associations Act, and so forth. Certain liberalizations of the 1950s and 1960s had already been reversed immediately after the semi-coup of 1971, restorationist reorderings and preparations of which were to culminate in the systemic overhauling executed by the 1980 coup.

The Kemalist ideology is summed up by, but cannot be reduced to, the Six Arrows: (1) Republicanism, meaning antimonarchism rather than democratic res publica; (2) Nationalism, aiming at linguistic and cultural identity-building rather than being an expansionist or irredentist political program; with a less known second face that has racist undertones (3) "Peopleism," not in the common sense of populism but one which postulates a unified, indivisible, harmonious "whole people"; (4) Statism/etatism; (5) Laicism; and (6) "Transformism," meaning radical, especially cultural, reformism in contradistinction to both revolutionism and evolutionism—all seminally formulated by Gökalp, subsequent distortions notwithstanding.

Technically a rightist ideology, Kemalism in the Turkish context, however, proved to be very pervasive and all-embracing, thanks to characteristics typical of most "third way" ideologies, which try to "reconcile the incompatibles" in order to have a catch-all appeal. Hitherto all Turkish political groups, from the extreme right to the center, and more interestingly, to many gradations of the left, have professed (and had to profess) allegiance to Kemalism. Its appeal to the right and center parties is more opaque in view of its authoritarian, "above-parties" and "above-classes," corporatist context. It has been and continues to be very functional in this sense, being the "grund-norm" of political legitimacy in Turkish politics, reproduced by the intelligentsia and forcefully guarded by the military. As for the left, most have incorrectly taken Kemalism's developmentalist statism for a form of state socialism, its anti-imperialism for a kind of anti-capitalism, and some of its political reforms for a variant of bourgeois revolution (that would mechanically lead into a socialist revolution)—forgetting the profoundly anti-democratic character of political Kemalism. This consensus, surviving the 1990s despite the foregoing, excludes only a very marginal sector of academe and the non-authoritarian left, as well as the fringes of the fundamentalist—but not the orthodox, statist-religious right. The former is excluded for obvious reasons; the latter less because of the authoritarian aspects of Kemalism than for its, in their view, excessive Westernism. It should also be noted that the much-spoken-of revival of Islam in Turkey in the last decade was not initiated by the fundamentalist groups—certainly one of the beneficiaries—but by the military (1980–1983) and civilian (1983–) governmental policies of granting religion a far greater domain of legitimacy than hitherto seen in the history of the Republic of Turkey. The military-imposed Constitution of 1982 provided for compulsory courses on "religious culture and morality" in elementary and secondary education "under the control and supervision of the state." This constituted the first significant deviation from the otherwise intact Kemalist orthodoxy of Turkish establishment politics. In breaking, in this instance, with the classical Kemalist principle of laicism, which has excluded religious instruction from the national education and citizenship training system, the military sought to add Islam to Kemalism in its program of depoliticization, control, and ideological manipulation of Turkey's youth and society, paralleling measures it has taken in many other spheres.

Works on Kemalism, interchangeably called Atatürkism, are legion. Attempts at differentiating the two are polemical and unfounded; Atatürk and his followers baptized their own ideology as Kemalism. A great many of these works, however, are hagiography or are based on secondary or tertiary evidence, whether they be belletristic or academic. In academe, too, Kemalism remains the social scientific official ideology—the obvious contradiction in terms notwithstanding.

BIBLIOGRAPHY

The soundest sources for understanding Kemalism are the party documents (especially for the 1923–1945 period) and the declarations and writings of Atatürk himself. A seminal study on the 1923–1931 phase of Atatürk's Republican People's party is METE TUNÇAY's *Türkiye Cumhuriyeti'nde Tek-Parti Yönetimi'nin Kurulmasi* (1981). The first critical textual analysis of Atatürk's collected speeches and statements is TAHA PARLA's *Atatürk'ün Natuk'u* (vol. 1, 1991) and *Atatürk'ün Söyler ve Demecleri* (vol. 2, 1991). For the political ideology of the Kemalist single-party period (1930–1950), see T. PARLA, *Tek-Parti Idoolouci* (vol. 3, 1991). A full-scale theoretical and comparative reassessment of the Kemalist regime and reforms is T. PARLA, *Kemalist Reüm ve Reformlar* (vol. 4, 1991). (The last four studies are collectively titled "The Official Sources of Turkish Political Culture.") For the overarching institutionalization of Kemalism at the level of constitutions, see T. PARLA, *Türkiye'de Anavasalar* (1991).

Taha Parla

Kemani, Sadi İsilay   [1899–1969]

Turkish composer and violionist.

Kemani, born in Istanbul, was trained as a violinist by his father. At the age of eight he began performing with the group of musicians who entertained the patrons in his father's coffee shop. His presence as a violinist was a novelty; traditional Oriental instruments accompanied the musicians' singing. Their music was written in the monophonic form called *makam*. Kemani was noted for his ability to integrate the violin into traditional Turkish music. His compositions totaled about forty, and he gave recitals both in Turkey and abroad. Kemani died in Istanbul.

BIBLIOGRAPHY

Buyuk Larousse sozluk ve ansiklopedisi, vol. 11. Istanbul, 1993.

Niyazi Dalyanci

Kennedy, John Fitzgerald   [1917–1963]

U.S. President, 1961–1963.

Born in Brookline, Massachusetts, he was the son of Joseph P. Kennedy, first chairman of the U.S. Securities and Exchange Commission and ambassador to Britain from 1937 to 1940. After a Harvard education, Kennedy served in World War II, then became a congressman (1947–1953) and a senator (1953–1960) from Massachusetts. As a senator, Kennedy supported Algeria's independence from France. After taking office as president in 1961, Kennedy initially supported Egypt's President Gamal Abdel Nasser, whom he saw as a progressive leader favoring nationalism and socialism—one who might keep the Arab world out of the USSR's orbit.

Nasser's conflict with Saudi Arabia over the YEMEN CIVIL WAR undermined Kennedy's policy, however. While attempting to woo Nasser, Kennedy strengthened U.S. ties with Israel and approved the sale of Hawk antiaircraft missiles to Israel in 1962. Kennedy was assassinated on November 22, 1963, in Dallas, Texas. He was the author of *Why England Slept* (1940) and *Profiles in Courage* (1956, Pulitzer Prize).

Zachary Karabell

Kenter, Müşfik   [1932–   ]

Turkish actor and director.

Born in Istanbul, Kenter graduated from the Ankara State Conservatory in 1955. After working in the State Theater, he founded a theater company with his sister Yıldız KENTER, called the Kent Actors, which performed at the Karaca and Dormen the-

aters. He won the İlhan İskender award for his play *Salincakta İki Kişi* (Two People on a Swing) in the 1959/60 season.

BIBLIOGRAPHY

Türk Ansiklopedisi. Ankara, 1974.

David Waldner

Kenter, Yıldız   [1928–   ]

Turkish actress and director.

Yıdız Kenter, born in Istanbul, is the older sister of Musfik KENTER. After graduating from the Ankara State Conservatory in 1948, she won recognition for her work in small theaters in Ankara and soon began to perform in Turkey's State Theater. In 1959/60, she and her brother left the State Theater to form their own performance company, the Kent Actors. She has twice won the prestigious İlhan İskender award—for her role in the play *Salincakta İki Kişi* (Two People on a Swing) in the 1959/60 season, and for her play *Nalinlar* (Clogs) in the 1961/62 season.

BIBLIOGRAPHY

Türk Ansiklopedisi. Ankara, 1974.

David Waldner

Keren Hayesod

Fund-raising agency for Israeli development.

The Keren Hayesod, or the foundation fund, was established by the Zionist Conference in 1920 to raise funds for Jewish settlement and development in Palestine. The nonprofit agency uses its funds to encourage business development in partnership with the private sector. In the United States, it operates as part of the United Jewish Appeal and coordinates fund-raising in other countries.

Paul Rivlin

Kerman

A province and its capital city in south-central Iran.

The province of Kerman (also known as Kirman) is in south-central Iran. The construction of the town of Kerman probably began in pre-Islamic times. When Marco Polo visited the city in 1271, it had become a major trade emporium linking the Arabian/Persian Gulf with KHORASAN and Central Asia. Subsequently, however, the city was sacked many times. The present city of Kerman, 661 miles (1,064 km) southeast of Tehran, and the capital of modern province of Kerman, was rebuilt in the nineteenth century to the northwest of the old city. But the city did not recover until the twentieth century. Carpet weaving is one of the main industries of the city, and the carpets produced there are renowned internationally. A number of modern establishments such as textile mills and brickworks have also been constructed there in modern times. The province's mineral wealth includes copper and coal. The population of the city in 1986 was 287,284. The total population of the province in 1986 was 1,622,958.

BIBLIOGRAPHY

FISHER, W., ed. *The Cambridge History of Iran.* Vol. 1. Cambridge, U.K., 1968, pp. 100–102.
Islamic Republic of Iran Today. Tehran, 1987, pp. 35, 323.

Parvaneh Pourshariati

Kessar, Israel [1933–]

Israeli trade union leader; member of the Knesset.

Working first as a teacher and with new immigrants, Israel Kessar then worked in the ministry of labor. He began serving as secretary-general of the HISTADRUT, the Israeli trade union, in 1984. He was elected to the Knesset (Israel's parliament) in the same year. Kessar was cooperative with the government's economic programs, while fighting to keep real wages from falling too steeply and guarding against policies that would increase unemployment.

Martin Malin

KGB

Primary security and intelligence organization in the USSR.

After Josef Stalin's death, the KGB was created in 1954 as the USSR's primary security and intelligence organization. It was organized into four Main Directorates, with the First Main Directorate responsible for Soviet clandestine activities abroad. Files released after the demise of the Soviet Union (1991) revealed that in the 1970s and 1980s, the KGB provided weapons, funding, and technical advice to the POPULAR FRONT FOR THE LIBERATION OF PALESTINE (PFLP), a Marxist group led by George HABASH.

BIBLIOGRAPHY

WIECZOWSKI, JOSEPH, ed. *Modern Encyclopedia of Russian and Soviet History.* New York, 1981.

Zachary Karabell

Khaddam, Abd al-Halim [1932–]

Syrian political leader.

Born in 1932 to a Sunni family of modest means from the coastal town of Jabla, just north of Banyas, Abd al-Halim Khaddam became active in Ba'th party politics while attending secondary school in Latakia in the late 1940s. During his student days, he forged a fast friendship with another young firebrand, Hafiz al-ASAD. After graduating from the Faculty of Law at Damascus University, he practiced law and taught school before devoting himself to a career inside the party apparatus. He married into a prominent Alawi family in 1954.

By 1964, Khaddam had become governor of the troubled city of Hama, whose citizenry rose in rebellion against the Ba'th-dominated regime that April. He was governor of Qunaitra when the Israelis overran the Golan three years later. He then served as governor of Damascus city, before assuming the post of minister of the economy and foreign trade during the turbulent final years of the Salah Jadid period (1966–1970). When his old friend Hafiz al-Asad seized power in November 1970, Khaddam was promoted to the post of foreign minister. President al-Asad entrusted him with the thankless duty of negotiating the May 1974 disengagement agreement with Israel and with the difficult task of mediating among rival Lebanese factions during the tense period between the outbreak of the civil war in April 1975 and Syria's intervention in the conflict the following June. He was also given the delicate assignment of lobbying Arab leaders to reject the Egyptian–Israeli peace initiative of 1977/78 and the tricky role of emissary between Damascus and Tehran during the uncertain months immediately following the 1978/79 Iranian revolution.

When President al-Asad fell ill at the end of November 1983, Khaddam was appointed to the six-person committee charged with keeping affairs of state in order. Four months later, in a move clearly intended to counterbalance the influence of the president's ambiguous brother Rif'at, al-Asad named him to be one of Syria's first three vice presidents, forcing him to relinquish the foreign ministership. Shortly thereafter, one of his sons married a daughter of the venerable al-Atasi clan in a lavish ceremony at the

Damascus Sheraton Hotel. By the mid-1990s, his evident astuteness and longevity made him the most likely candidate to succeed Hafiz al-Asad as president of the republic.

Fred H. Lawson

Khal, Yusuf al- [1917–1987]

Lebanese poet; founder of the poetry review Shi'r.

A Protestant born in Tripoli, Lebanon, Yusuf al-Khal was educated in literature and philosophy at the American University at Beirut. After World War II, he spent several years in the United States, where he worked as publishing director at *al-Huda,* a New York–based magazine catering to Lebanese emigrants. The years spent at AUB and in the United States provided him with a great familiarity with Western (particularly Anglo-Saxon) literature, and he even edited an anthology of American poetry.

Back in Lebanon, he became a leading figure in an emerging group of young modernist Lebanese poets who were determined to break away from the traditional poetic forms that had prevailed in the Arab world since al-NAHDA, the cultural awakening of the late nineteenth century. In January 1957, drawing on his experience as a journalist and publisher, he founded the poetry review *Shi'r,* which remained a rallying point for avant-garde Arab poets—including Khalil HAWI, ADONIS, and Badr Shakir al-SAYYAB—until it ceased to exist in the early 1970s.

In *Shi'r,* al-Khal pressed for the opening up of Arab poetry to the influence of the new poetic current emanating from the West. He advocated making colloquial Arabic the basis of literature as a way of reviving and widening the appeal of Arabic poetry, which, he thought, would otherwise be condemned to die out slowly. His own poetry was written in a language that aproached that of everyday conversation. Its rhythm and skillful manipulation of images and sounds established him as the most prominent Lebanese member of the group of poets belonging to the free verse movement. Unlike many of his contemporaries, however, he always refrained from mixing poetry and politics; he even condemned "engagement literature," which he saw as a source of cultural decay.

BIBLIOGRAPHY

ALLEN, ROGER, ed. *Modern Arabic Literature.* New York, 1987.
BOULLATA, ISSA J. *Modern Arab Poets, 1950–1975.* Washington, D.C., 1976.

Guilain P. Denoeux

Khalaf, Abd al-Hadi [1945–]

An advocate of political reform in Bahrain.

A former Bahraini professor with a doctorate from a European university, Khalaf was a member of the leftist-reformist bloc that ran for election to the National Assembly of BAHRAIN in 1973. It was rumored at the time that he belonged to the National Liberation Front, which demanded political participation. Although elected to the National Assembly, he was later disqualified for misrepresentation of age. The minimum was thirty years of age, and Khalaf was then twenty-nine.

BIBLIOGRAPHY

NAKHLEH, EMILE A. *The Persian Gulf and American Policy.* New York, 1982.

Emile A. Nakhleh

Khalaf, Salah [1933–1991]

Palestine Liberation Organization leader, also known as Abu Iyad.

Born in Jaffa to a religious Muslim family, Khalaf fled to Gaza during the 1948 Arab–Israel War. After 1951, he attended the University of Cairo, where he joined Yasir ARAFAT's Palestinian Students Union. He and Arafat founded the al-FATH organization in Kuwait, where Khalaf was working as a schoolmaster in the 1960s. Khalaf played a leading role in the fighting of BLACK SEPTEMBER in 1970, participated in the LEBANON CIVIL WAR in the late 1970s, and was linked to several violent incidents in the 1970s and 1980s. By the late 1980s he had emerged as the second most powerful leader of the PALESTINE LIBERATION ORGANIZATION (PLO), in charge of intelligence and security.

Khalaf was killed January 14, 1991, in the Tunis suburb of Carthage at the villa of Abu al-Hol (the Fath security chief). The gunman was Hamza Abu Zaid, a guard stationed at the villa. Khalaf had married the daughter of a wealthy Palestinian businessman, with whom he had six children. He was author of a widely read memoir, *My Home, My Land,* written with Eric Rouleau.

BIBLIOGRAPHY

BECKER, JILLIAN. *The PLO: The Rise and Fall of the Palestine Liberation Organization.* London, 1984.
LIVINGSTONE, NEIL, and DAVID HALEVY. *Inside the PLO.* New York, 1990.

Elizabeth Thompson

Khal'atbari, Mohammad Vali Khan Sepahsalar-e Tonekaboni [1848–1926]

Iranian prime minister.

Mohammad Vali Khan Sepahsalar-e Tonekaboni was appointed commander in chief of Mohammad Ali Qajar's forces in Azerbaijan, following the unrest in that province after the bombardment of parliament by the shah in 1908. He joined the ranks of the constitutionalists, however, and became caretaker of the first parliament elected after the defeat of the royalist forces in 1909. He resigned in 1910 and was elected to parliament. Later that year, he was reinstalled as prime minister. Accused of collaboration with Mohammad Ali Shah, Mohammad Vali Khan was again forced to resign. In 1914, he became prime minister for the third time, with the new title of "sepahsalar," and agreed to several major concessions to British and Russian interests in Iran. His premiership did not last for more than a few months. After a brief governorship of Azerbaijan, Sepahsalar was briefly imprisoned along with several political dignitaries, following the coup d'état of 1920. Arthur Millspaugh's relentless efforts to collect a considerable sum in back taxes from Sepahsalar, along with the death of his son, Sa'd al-Dowleh, brought about his suicide in 1926.

BIBLIOGRAPHY

KHAL'ATBARI, AMIR ABDOLSAMAD. *Sepahsalar-e Tonekaboni: Mohammad Vali Khan Khal'atbari*, ed. by M. Taffazoli. Tehran, 1983.

Neguin Yavari

Khaldunniyya

Tunisian educational society.

Khaldunniyya was founded by the Young Tunisians in 1896 and named in honor of the fourteenth-century Tunisian intellectual Ibn Khaldun. Intended to acquaint Tunisians who were illiterate in European languages with the contemporary Europen world, it offered instruction in Arabic in a wide variety of subjects. The organizers of the Khaldunniyya especially sought to reach ZAYTUNA UNIVERSITY students in order to enhance their still largely traditional curriculum.

BIBLIOGRAPHY

JULIEN, CHARLES-ANDRÉ. "Colons français et Jeunes Tunisiens (1882–1912)." *Revue française d'histoire d'outre-Mer* 54 (1967): 87–150.

Kenneth J. Perkins

Khalid, Khalid Muhammad [1920–]

Egyptian religious teacher and essayist.

A teacher at al-Azhar, Shaykh Khalid published many works on political, religious, and social themes. Influenced by the teachings of Jamal al-Din al-Afghani and Muhammad Abduh, Khalid participated in the second generation of Egyptian nationalism on the eve of World War II in alliance with the WAFD. His experiences during this period led him to denounce the theocratic tendencies of the MUSLIM BROTHERHOOD, to defend the need for a parliamentary regime, and to promote a popular social and economic agenda.

Khalid's first book, *Min Huna Nabda* (From Here We Begin), appeared in 1950; in this book, and in his writings in the press, he appealed for a social democratic society that would blend Islam and Marxism. Khalid's liberal attitude could be best summarized in the slogan "freedom, intellect, and progress." Among his other works are *Citizens, Not Subjects*; *Democracy Forever*, and *We Human Beings*. In the 1980s, Shaykh Khalid adopted a more conservative, pro-Saudi line in his writings.

BIBLIOGRAPHY

ABDEL-MALEK, ANOUAR, ed. *Anthologie de la litterature arabe contemporaine*. Paris, 1965.
BASHUR, RASHID L., ERNEST N. MCCARUS, and ADIL I. YACOUB, eds. *Contemporary Arabic Readers*. Ann Arbor, Mich., 1967.

David Waldner

Khalid ibn Abd al-Aziz Al Sa'ud [1912–1982]

King of Saudi Arabia, 1975–1982.

Khalid was born in Riyadh, the seventh son of King Abd al-Aziz Al Sa'ud (known as IBN SA'UD in the West), the founder of modern Saudi Arabia. Khalid's only full brother was Muhammad ibn Abd al-Aziz AL SA'UD, two years his elder. It is ironic that Khalid, a modest and retiring man surrounded by brothers ambitious to exercise power, was fated to be king during seven of the most turbulent and dangerous years of his country's history.

Khalid received the prescribed education for a royal Saudi prince of his day—rote memorization of the Qur'an and limited study of several practical subjects, together with firsthand observation of court politics. He did not pursue an overtly political career but, from early adulthood, played an important part in family councils and by his thirties had become part of the small circle of princes that would guide Saudi Arabia's affairs. Of all his brothers, he was, perhaps, the closest to the aloof FAISAL. When only nineteen, he acted as viceroy in Hijaz during Faisal's absences, accompanied Faisal to the United States in 1943, and was deputy prime minister in the cabinet that Faisal, acting as the Saudi prime minister, appointed in October 1962. Following Faisal's accession as king in November 1964, the senior princes and he pressed the reluctant Khalid to become crown prince. After several months of resistance, Khalid yielded to their pressure.

The selection was a wise one that served the country well when King Faisal was assassinated ten years later. Khalid was demonstrably neutral in the politics of the AL SA'UD FAMILY and represented to many family members a desirable check to putting excessive power in the hands of FAHD, crown prince under Khalid, and his full brother Sultan ibn Abd al-Aziz AL SA'UD, next but one in the succession. More importantly, his qualities of character were perfectly matched to the needs of the kingdom. Khalid's moral reputation was spotless, his tastes were simple, and his piety was genuine while lacking any fanatical edge. He exhibited none of the arrogance associated with many of the Al Sa'ud and in contrast to several, especially his brother Muhammad, he possessed an equable temperament. Thus he frequently acted as an effective conciliator and mediator, a vital role in a society where all significant decisions are reached by consensus. Moreover, his obvious attachment to traditional bedouin values strengthened the Al Sa'ud's links to the still important tribal element in Saudi society, and his old-fashioned fatherly manner connected the ruling family more firmly to the population for whom he was a comforting presence.

All this proved critically important during a reign that encompassed Saudi Arabia's most rapid phase of economic and social development, the outbreak of the LEBANESE CIVIL WAR, the CAMP DAVID ACCORDS between Egypt and Israel, the IRANIAN REVOLUTION, the seizure of the GRAND MOSQUE in Mecca by Sunni Muslim ultraconservatives attempting to overthrow the Al Sa'ud, the Soviet occupation of Afghanistan, and the outbreak of the IRAN–IRAQ WAR. All these events had represented severe threats to the kingdom. In the West, Khalid's retiring nature was mistakenly interpreted to suggest indecisiveness or passivity. In fact, although Fahd saw to the day-to-day conduct of affairs—an arrangement that suited both Khalid's inclinations and his delicate health—Khalid's authority was never in doubt. It was Khalid who acknowledged the legitimacy of some complaints that those who seized the Grand Mosque had raised and sought to address them. Following the

1979–80 disturbances among the long mistreated Shi'ites of the eastern province (al-Hasa), he launched a major new development project in the principal Shi'a area and made a personal visit, the first time a reigning Saudi monarch had done so. His 1976 tour of the other conservative Gulf Arab states to discuss common security concerns initiated the process that led to creation of the GULF COOPERATION COUNCIL in 1981. Khalid's so-called interim rule eased Saudi Arabia through a critical period and paved the way to a smooth succession by King Fahd upon his death in June 1982.

BIBLIOGRAPHY

BLIGH, ALEXANDER. *From Prince to King: Royal Succession in the House of Saud in the Twentieth Century.* New York, 1984.

HOLDEN, DAVID, and RICHARD JOHNS. *The House of Saud: The Rise and Rule of the Most Powerful Dynasty in the Arab World.* New York, 1981.

Malcolm C. Peck

Khalidi, Ahmad al-Samih al- [1896–1951]

Palestinian educator, scholar, and social reformer.

A pioneer in the field of education, Amad al-Samih al-Khalidi established *Lajnat al-Yatim al-Arabiyyah al-'Ammah* (Arab Public Orphanage Committee), and an institute for educating the sons of Palestinian martyrs in Dayr Amre in Jerusalem. From 1925 to 1948, al-Khalidi was the principal of the Arab College in Jerusalem, a teacher training academy and one of the leading public secondary schools in mandate Palestine. His written works include *Anximat al-Ta'lim* (Systems of Education, 1933, 1935), the unpublished *Tarikh al-ma'ma'ahid al-Islamiyyah* (A History of Islamic Institutions), and *Ahl al-'Ilm wal-Hukm fi rif Filastin* (Men of Learning and Leadership in the Rural Areas of Palestine, 1968). After the Arab–Israel War of 1948, he went to Lebanon where he founded a school for Palestinian children.

Muhammad Muslih

Khalidi, Husayn Fakhri al- [1894–1962]

Palestinian politician who hailed from a prominent Arab family.

Born in Jerusalem, Husayn Fakhri al-Khalidi studied medicine in Beirut. He joined the department of health in Aleppo during the short-lived rule (1918–

1920) of King Faisal ibn Husayn (1885–1933) in Syria. He was elected mayor of Jerusalem in 1934, the last time that the city's mayor was elected by the entire population. The following year he founded the Reform Party (Hizb al-Islah). He was elected member of the Arab Higher Committee, a Palestinian political body formed in 1936 to direct the Palestinian national struggle. Al-Khalidi was then exiled by British authorities to the Seychelle Islands along with other nationalist leaders. In 1946 he was a member of the reconstituted Arab Higher Committee. As a senior politician, al-Khalidi participated in the London (St. James) Conference of 1939, and after 1948 he served as Jordan's foreign minister in the cabinets of Fawzi al-Mulqi (1953) and Samir Rifa'i (1955). In April 1957, al-Khalidi was appointed prime minister of Jordan, but his cabinet lasted only one week. Al-Khalidi spent the rest of his life in Jericho where he wrote articles for the Jerusalem daily *al-Jihad* and authored a book entitled *The Arab Exodus (al-Khuruj al-Arabi)*. Al-Khalidi's unpublished autobiography illuminates many aspects of Arab and Palestinian politics.

Muhammad Muslih

Khalidi, Walid   [1925–   ]

A Palestinian intellectual and major Arab strategist and statesman.

Walid Khalidi has devoted much of his life to research and writing on the Palestine question. In 1963 he co-founded the Institute for Palestine Studies, an independent non-profit Arab research and publication center. He has taught at the American University in Beirut, as well as at Oxford and Harvard, and has been a research associate at the Center for International Affairs and the Center for Middle East Studies at Harvard University. He has written and edited several articles and books including *From Haven to Conquest* (1970); *Conflict and Violence in Lebanon: Confrontation in the Middle East* (1979); *Before Their Diaspora, A Photographic History of the Palestinians 1876–1948* (1984); *All That Remains: The Palestinian Villages Occupied and Depopulated by Israel in 1948* (1992). A consummate expert on the Palestinian question and the Arab–Israeli conflict, he played an important role in shaping the Palestine Liberation Organization's peace strategy toward Israel, and was a member of the Jordanian delegation to the peace talks with Israel (1991/92). Despite Khalidi's role in developing PLO policy, he has never been affiliated with the PLO.

Muhammad Muslih

Khalidi, Yusuf Diya al-   [1842–1906]

Scholar and son of a prominent Palestinian Arab family in Jerusalem.

Yusuf Diya al-Khalidi had a long record of public service in the Ottoman Turkish administration, having been a vice-consul at the Russian Black Sea port of Poti, a deputy in the first Ottoman Parliament, and mayor of Jerusalem in the 1890s. Well-versed in French and English, as well as in Arabic, Turkish and Kurdish, al-Khalidi was a talented orator who held liberal views, which put him at odds with the heavy-handed regime of Sultan ABDÜLHAMIT II. His extensive readings and his travels in Europe enabled him to put Zionism in perspective. In a prophetic letter that he wrote to Zadok Kahn, the chief rabbi of France in 1899, he expressed his understanding for the Jewish longing for Palestine, but he also warned that Palestine was already inhabited by non-Jews and that its Arab inhabitants would fight against the Zionist program. Among the works he wrote was the first Arabic–Kurdish dictionary.

BIBLIOGRAPHY

SHIMONI, YAACOV. *Biographical Dictionary of the Middle East.* New York, 1992.

Muhammad Muslih

Khalidi Family, al-

Muslim Arab family from Jerusalem; members claim descent from Khalid ibn al-Walid, the Muslim commander who conquered Syria in 636 C.E.

To a large extent, the prominence of the al-Khalidi family grew out of the religious and educational standing of its senior members, some of whom held positions of authority in the Ottoman, British, and Jordanian governments. Ruhi Yasin al-Khalidi (1864–1913) was elected from Jerusalem to the Ottoman Parliament in 1908 and 1912 and served as vice president of the parliament in 1911. Ruhi's published works include *An Introduction to the Eastern Question* (1897), *The Ottoman Coup and the Young Turk Society* (1909), and *Arab Research in Chemistry* (1953). Al-Shaykh Khalil al-Khalidi (1863–1941), born in Jerusalem, was an authority on Islamic manuscripts, including science and *Shari'a* law, and became president of the Shari'a Court of Appeal. His published works include *The Khalidi Literary Selections* and *My Trip to al-Maghrib and Andalusia*. Al-Shaykh Raghib al-Khalidi, founded Khalidiyya Library in 1900 in Jerusalem. The library houses a large collection of medieval Arab manuscripts. Dr. Husayn Fakhri al-

Khalidi (1894–1962) was born in Jerusalem but joined the Department of Health in Aleppo during the short-lived rule of Faisal I in Syria. He later became ministry director of Public Health in the Palestine government. He was elected mayor of Jerusalem in 1934, and the following year he set up the Reform party and continued to be active in the Palestine national movement. Moving to Jordan after 1948, he became foreign minister in 1953 and 1955, and two years later he became prime minister. Ahmad Samih al-Khalidi (?–1951), born in Jerusalem, was active in the field of education, especially through the Arab College of Jerusalem and the Institute of the Sons of the Martyred in Day Amre. He edited numerous books on education and Islamic history. His unpublished works include *A History of Islamic Institutes* and *A History of Jerusalem*. Walid KHALIDI founded the INSTITUTE FOR PALESTINE STUDIES.

BIBLIOGRAPHY

AL-AWDAT, YA'QUB. *Min A'lam al-Fikr wa al-Adab fi-Filastin.*

SHIMONI, YA'COV. *The Arabs of Palestine.* New Haven, Conn., 1956.

Muhammad Muslih

Khalifa, Abdullah ibn Ahmad al- [?–1849]

Joint second ruler with Sulman; joint third ruler with Khalifa; and fourth ruler of Bahrain, 1796–1843.

Abdullah was a son of the first ruler of BAHRAIN, Shaykh Ahmad, and the brother of the second ruler, Shaykh Sulman. Abdullah took charge of commercial activities at Muharraq after the al-Khalifa conquest of the Bahraini islands in 1796, causing thirty years of rivalry with his brother Sulman and his descendants, who ruled from the adjacent port of Manama (now the capital, on the main island, Bahrain).

Abdullah's supporters carried out a series of raids along the Arabian coast, disrupting regional trade and prompting the emigration of several prominent clans from Bahrain to other ports. He negotiated a secret agreement with the commander of Egyptian forces in 1839, whereby he would accept Egyptian suzerainty under Muhammad Ali Pasha in exchange for recognition as sole ruler of the islands. His move toward Egypt prompted the British resident to propose British annexation of Bahrain, but the situation was defused by Egyptian withdrawal.

Abdullah was driven out of Muharraq in 1843 by a coalition of tribes led by his grandnephew Muhammad (who became the fifth ruler that year); he took refuge in Dammam (now in Saudi Arabia). From

there he attempted to recapture Muharraq on several occasions, with the assistance of Wahhabi forces in al-Hasa and Qatar, and with occasional support from the Persian governors of Bushire (Bushehr) and Nabund (Nay Band; Naband); such moves were repeatedly blocked by the British. In early 1849, Abdullah traveled to Musqat in the hope of forming an alliance with Oman, but he died before it could be concluded, and Shaykh Muhammad ibn Khalifa ruled Bahrain until 1868, when the British caused him to flee into exile and pronounced his brother Ali ruler.

BIBLIOGRAPHY

LAWSON, FRED H. *Bahrain: The Modernization of Autocracy.* Boulder, Colo., 1989.

Fred H. Lawson

Khalifa, Ali ibn Khalifa al- [?–1869]

Sixth ruler of Bahrain.

When, in the summer of 1868, his brother Shaykh Muhammad, the fifth ruler, fled the islands in the face of a British flotilla, the British commander pronounced Ali ruler and razed Muhammad's redoubt at MUHARRAQ. The Persians immediately complained that this action compromised their sovereignty, a claim London parried by reiterating its long-standing recognition of BAHRAIN's independence. While these two governments debated Bahrain's formal status, the exiled Muhammad mobilized dissident members of the KHALIFA FAMILY for an attack on the islands. The local people, incited by Muhammad ibn Abdullah (Ali's cousin and the son of the fourth ruler, Abdullah), rose in open rebellion as the al-Khalifa landed in September of 1869—resulting in the death of Ali and the sacking of Manama (Ali's capital on the main island, Bahrain).

When the fighting ended, Muhammad ibn Khalifa was imprisoned by his cousin Muhammad ibn Abdullah, who declared himself seventh ruler at his capital, Muharraq.

BIBLIOGRAPHY

LAWSON, FRED H. *Bahrain: The Modernization of Autocracy.* Boulder, Colo., 1989.

Fred H. Lawson

Khalifa, Hamad ibn Isa al- [1866–1942]

Ninth ruler of Bahrain, 1932–1942.

After quietly supporting the expansion of British administration on the islands of BAHRAIN, Hamad collaborated in suppressing both the merchant-based reform movement of 1921/22 and subsequent anti-British riots by rural laborers. He was appointed acting ruler in May 1923, when his father Shaykh Isa was removed by the British resident, who convened a special congress of Bahraini notables to approve the transfer of power. Hamad then consolidated his position as ruler by deporting a group of Isa's prominent supporters to India, and he engaged the Briton Charles BELGRAVE to serve as his permanent adviser. In the mid-1920s, Hamad negotiated aircraft-basing arrangements and the first petroleum concession (Bahrain's oil was not discovered until 1932), thus providing the ruling family with a secure source of revenue, independent of the island's merchants. These contracts dramatically improved the position of the KHALIFA FAMILY, relative to the local commercial elite, enabling the regime to parry the 1938 reform movement and survive the disruptions in regional trade during World War II.

BIBLIOGRAPHY

LAWSON, FRED H. *Bahrain: The Modernization of Autocracy.* Boulder, Colo., 1989.

Fred H. Lawson

Khalifa, Hamad ibn Isa al-

Heir apparent as al-Khalifa ruler of Bahrain.

Eldest son of Isa ibn Sulman al Khalifa, the emir of the state of BAHRAIN, Shaykh Hamad enjoys the position of heir apparent, according to the terms of the 1973 constitution. He studied at the military academy at Mons, Belgium, and was appointed commander of Bahrain's national guard when it was created in mid-1968. Shayleh Hamad has served as minister of defense in every cabinet since independence, August 14, 1971.

BIBLIOGRAPHY

LAWSON, FRED H. *Bahrain: The Modernization of Autocracy.* Boulder, Colo., 1989.

Fred H. Lawson

Khalifa, Isa ibn Ali al-

Eighth ruler of Bahrain, 1869–1923.

This governor of the al-Khalifa territories in QATAR was appointed ruler of BAHRAIN at the end of 1869, by the British authorities in Bombay, in an attempt

to end the bitter rivalry between the Sulman and Abdullah factions of the KHALIFA FAMILY in the Bahrain islands—which had disrupted regional affairs for about seventy years. In 1878, however, intrafamily fighting resumed when dissident members joined the AL THANI in razing the port of Zubara (Qatar).

When Qatari forces launched a series of raids on Bahraini ships and settlements at the beginning of 1879, Isa entered into secret negotiations with the Ottoman Empire's governors of Basra (Iraq) and al-Hasa (Arabia) to provide troops to defend the islands. These talks alarmed the British resident in the Gulf region, who in 1880 forced Shaykh Isa to sign a formal treaty pledging himself and his successors "to abstain from entering into negotiations or making treaties of any sort with any State or Government other than the British without the consent of the said British Government." This document, in conjunction with a second treaty concluded in 1892, consolidated al-Khalifa rule and made Bahrain a British protectorate.

Isa's reign saw the constant expansion of local trade, accompanied by growing friction between the indigenous merchants and entrepreneurs from India, who also operated under British protection. Isa resisted continual British attempts to take charge of the customs administration, leading the political agent appointed to Manama (the capital) in 1904 to suggest his demotion to the post of governor of Muharraq (Bahrain's second city). The proposal was not adopted, but by 1920 the British administration controlled virtually all aspects of local politics. When opposition to Britain erupted in 1923, the resident demanded that Isa abdicate in favor of his son Hamad. Isa refused but was outmaneuvered by the British—who convened a special congress of the islands' notables to approve the transfer of power to Hamad that May.

BIBLIOGRAPHY

FARAH, TALAL TOUFIC. *Protection and Politics in Bahrain 1869–1915.* Beirut, 1985.
LAWSON, FRED H. *Bahrain: The Modernization of Autocracy.* Boulder, Colo., 1989.

Fred H. Lawson

Khalifa, Isa ibn Sulman al-   [1933–   ]

Eleventh ruler of Bahrain, 1961–

Isa became ruler of BAHRAIN on December 16, 1961, upon the death of his father. He had served as president of the Manama municipal council, supervising the creation of a free-trading area at the

KHALIFA, SULMAN IBN AHMAD AL- 1007

capital's port, following the anti-British disturbances during the mid-1950s. He was designated heir apparent in January 1958 and accompanied his father on an official visit to Saudi Arabia in February, which produced a treaty confirming the marine borders of both countries.

Shaykh Isa assumed greater responsibly for Bahrain's internal and external affairs during the next two years, as his father suffered a series of debilitating heart attacks. Isa also took charge of the KHALIFA FAMILY council, enabling him to decide how oil revenues should be divided among the members and supporters of the clan. He was thus well positioned to accede to the rulership following his father's death in November 1961.

As it became clear during the late 1960s that the smaller Arab states in the Persian/Arabian Gulf region would be incapable of forming a political union in the wake of Britain's withdrawal from the area, Shaykh Isa began establishing an autonomous government apparatus for Bahrain: He declared it an independent state on August 14, 1971, and took the title of emir, at the same time decreeing that elections would be held for a constitutional assembly in 1972, over the objections of several senior members of the ruling family. He approved the constitution in June of 1973 and presided over subsequent parliamentary elections. When his brother, the prime minister, submitted the cabinet's resignation in 1975—in the face of growing criticism of the regime's domestic and foreign policies on the part of its parliament—Isa dissolved the assembly and reinstated the cabinet as the legislative body. He generally epitomizes the pragmatic wing of the al-Khalifa, consistently supporting the gradual introduction of new technology and social services, while at the same time conciliating the family's more conservative shaykhs.

BIBLIOGRAPHY

LAWSON, FRED H. *Bahrain: The Modernization of Autocracy.* Boulder, Colo., 1989.

Fred H. Lawson

Khalifa, Khalifa ibn Sulman al-

Third ruler of Bahrain, 1825–1834.

When Shaykh Sulman ibn Ahmad died in 1825, several of his sons conspired with the ruler of Oman to oust their uncle, Shaykh Abdullah from ruling the port of Muharraq. Civil war was avoided when Abdullah agreed to recognize Khalifa ibn Sulman as coruler in Manama (now the capital of BAHRAIN). An Omani flotilla nevertheless sailed against Bahrain in

September 1828, accompanied by warships of the BANU YAS TRIBE from Abu Dhabi. This force blockaded and shelled Manama and, in early November, the Banu Yas landed at Jufayr (the port area of Manama), where they were defeated by the al-Khalifa. The Omanis maintained the blockade for two more weeks, but they finally retreated in the face of an outbreak of cholera on their ships. Abdullah seized the opportunity to regain a predominant position within Bahrain by leading a counterattack against Omani shipping in the Persian/Arabian Gulf, although Shaykh Khalifa retained his post as ruler of Manama until his death. Then Abdullah became the fourth ruler of Bahrain.

BIBLIOGRAPHY

LAWSON, FRED H. *Bahrain: The Modernization of Autocracy.* Boulder, Colo., 1989.

Fred H. Lawson

Khalifa, Muhammad ibn Khalifa al-

Fifth ruler of Bahrain, 1843–1868.

Muhammad seized power after forming a coalition of dissident tribes from BAHRAIN and the Arabian Wahhabis that ousted his great-uncle Abdullah. Persistent conflict between his allies and the forces loyal to Abdullah (based in al-Hasa, Arabia, and in Qatar) culminated in a large-scale raid by his supporters on the Qatar ports of Doha and Wakra in 1867. This convinced Britain to intervene to end the fighting between the Sulman and Abdullah branches of the KHALIFA FAMILY in 1868. The severity of the reparations exacted by the British pushed Muhammad into a temporary alliance with Abdullah's grandson, and their combined forces captured MUHARRAQ in 1869, after razing MANAMA (now the capital). This campaign prompted Britain to reoccupy the islands and exile to India both Muhammad and his primary opponents.

BIBLIOGRAPHY

LAWSON, FRED H. *Bahrain: The Modernization of Autocracy.* Boulder, Colo., 1989.

Fred H. Lawson

Khalifa, Sulman ibn Ahmad al-

Second ruler of Bahrain, 1796–1825.

During the final years of the eighteenth century, the KHALIFA FAMILY came into conflict with the Al Sa'ud family (of Arabia) for control of the prosperous ports along the QATAR coast. In an effort to dissuade the Al Sa'uds from capturing Zubara, Shaykh Sulman ordered his followers to abandon that port in 1796 and relocated their commercial activities to the BAHRAIN islands. He then took charge of trading at Manama (now the capital on the main island, Bahrain), precipitating thirty years of rivalry with his brother Abdullah, who ruled the port on the adjacent island of MUHARRAQ. Competition between these two branches led Sulman to increase taxation on the merchants and farmers in his domain, which convinced some of them to emigrate to other ports during the 1820s.

BIBLIOGRAPHY

LAWSON, FRED H. *Bahrain: The Modernization of Autocracy.* Boulder, Colo., 1989.

Fred H. Lawson

Khalifa, Sulman ibn Hamad al-   [1894–1961]

Tenth ruler of Bahrain, 1942–1961.

Sulman was designated heir apparent during his father's lifetime, and he succeeded to rule in February 1942, when Britain's strategic position in Asia was being severely threatened by the advancing Japanese during World War II. London announced that spring that military installations on the islands of BAHRAIN would be upgraded and that inactive oil wells were to be plugged. (Britain held a protectorate over Bahrain from 1820, which had been expanded during the early twentieth century; petroleum had been discovered in 1932.)

The augmented British presence strained local food supplies, prompting Sulman to make repeated appeals to the government of British India to accelerate shipments of staples to his country. He presided over the establishment of the Merchants' Advisory Committee, to deal with wartime smuggling, and supervised a marked expansion in the scale of the central administration. Opposition to these developments sparked a liberal movement for nationalism during the 1950s, which was suppressed by the coordinated efforts of the Bahrain security services and the British authorities. He prepared his son Isa to rule during the late 1950s, because he was suffering from heart disease. He died in November 1961.

BIBLIOGRAPHY

LAWSON, FRED H. *Bahrain: The Modernization of Autocracy.* Boulder, Colo., 1989.

Fred H. Lawson

Khalifa Family

Ruling family of the State of Bahrain, 1782–present.

Just after 1700, the al-Khalifa, a prominent Kuwait-based trading clan, within the broader Banu Utub confederacy, became involved in pearl fishing in the waters around the BAHRAIN archipelago (of thirty-three islands in the Persian/Arabian Gulf). When its members left Kuwait, some sixty years later, they attempted to establish themselves on the islands but were forced to move on by tribes from Oman holding the archipelago on behalf of the shah of Persia. The Khalifa family and its allies then settled at Zubara, on the northwestern coast of the QATAR peninsula. When a Kuwaiti fleet captured the Bahraini fort at Manama (now Bahrain's capital), in 1782, the clan moved onto the islands and took charge of removing the Omani garrison. Senior al-Khalifa shaykhs have ruled Bahrain since that time, creating a protectorate over the islands by treaty with Britain (1880); they gave up all claim to their former territories in Qatar in 1913 and, under Shaykh Isa ibn Sulman, created the independent State of Bahrain on August 14, 1971.

BIBLIOGRAPHY

LAWSON, FRED H. *Bahrain: The Modernization of Autocracy.* Boulder, Colo., 1989.

Fred H. Lawson

Khalifa–Qatari Wars

Series of conflicts from the eighteenth through the twentieth centuries contesting the al-Khalifa claim to Qatar.

When the al-KHALIFA clan of the BANU UTUB confederacy pulled out of Kuwait around 1760, its members first attempted to settle on the islands of BAHRAIN, in the Persian/Arabian Gulf, but were forced to move on by the tribes from Oman garrisoning the archipelago on behalf of the shah of Persia. The KHALIFA FAMILY and its allies then established themselves at Zubara, on the northwestern coast of the QATAR peninsula. When the al-Khalifa succeeded in capturing Bahrain in 1782, their leader Shaykh Ahmad continued to reside at Zubara, entrusting the islands to his eldest sons, Sulman and Abdullah.

The rising prosperity of the ports of Manama and Zubara in the ensuing decade prompted the AL SA'UD FAMILY of Arabia to move against Zubara in 1795/96. The al-Khalifa attempted to thwart this drive by abandoning Zubara and retreating to Bahrain; deprived of booty, the Al Sa'ud turned their attention toward Kuwait. Zubara was not reoccupied by the al-Khalifa until 1799, and by the early 1800s control of the area was contested by the AL THANI and al-Sudan, allies of the Al Sa'ud based at Doha, on the eastern coast of Qatar.

Cross-channel raiding persisted until 1880, however, when the British resident at Bushire (Bushehr, Persia, now Iran) imposed a treaty upon the al-Khalifa, prohibiting its leaders from engaging in any but "friendly" relations concerning "business of minor importance" with their neighbors. An accord between the British and the Ottoman Empire, signed in 1913, committed the British to preventing the al-Khalifa from annexing any part of the Qatar peninsula, while the outbreak of World War I prompted the resident to conclude a pact with the Al Thani, promising British assistance in repelling any attack on its territory. These agreements effectively terminated al-Khalifa intervention on the Arabian peninsula but left indeterminate the status of the HAWAR ISLANDS, situated just off the Qatari coast. Despite a 1939 British ruling awarding sovereignty of these sixteen islands to Bahrain, skirmishes erupted around the archipelago in 1978, 1982, 1986, and 1991. Bahrain had proclaimed its independence from Britain in 1971.

BIBLIOGRAPHY

KELLY, J. B. *Britain and the Persian Gulf 1795–1880.* Oxford, 1968.
LAWSON, FRED H. *Bahrain: The Modernization of Autocracy.* Boulder, Colo., 1989.

Fred H. Lawson

Khalis, Mohammad Unis [1919–]

Afghan resistance leader.

The leader of one branch of the HEZB-E ISLAMI party, Unis Khalis was born in 1919 in Gandamak among the Khugiani Pushtun and studied Islamic law and theology. He fled Afghanistan in 1973 at the time of the coup led by Muhammad DAUD. At first he joined the Hezb-e Islami party led by Hekmatyar, but he left to form his own party of the same name in 1978. During the war of resistance (1978–1992), his men fought in the Khugiani area, and Khalis, despite his advanced age, often accompanied them.

In 1992, he returned to Kabul with the other Islamic leaders to play a role in the attempt to form an Islamic government. He is strongly Muslim and anti-Western and opposes universal suffrage as well as the participation of the Shi'ites in Afghanistan politics.

BIBLIOGRAPHY

ROY, OLIVIER. *Islam and Resistance in Afghanistan.* Cambridge, U.K., 1986.

Grant Farr

Khalkhali, Mohammed Sadeq [1927–]

The notorious "hanging judge" of the early years of the Islamic revolution of Iran.

Ayatollah Mohammad Sadeq Khalkhali was born in 1927 in Azerbaijan, in northwestern Iran. A disciple of Ayatollah Ruhollah Khomeini in Qom from 1952 to 1964 and a vociferous anti-shah activist and member of the radical Feda'iyan-e Islam group, Khalkhali was imprisoned in 1963. After the revolution of 1979, he was the most famous spokesman for Feda'iyan-e Islam (Devotees of Islam). As a Khomeini loyalist, he was appointed president of the Islamic revolution government court in 1980, where he hunted down opponents of the Islamic republic. In April 1980, he was appointed by President Bani Sadr to head an anti-narcotics campaign. His numerous, swift executions, however, led to his dismissal in December. Ironically, his resignation was brought about because he was unable to account for fourteen million dollars seized through drug raids, confiscations, and fines. He was instrumental in the impeachment of President Bani Sadr in June 1981. He also served as deputy to the Islamic parliament in the first, second, and third *majles*. He was a member of the first experts' assembly, charged with drawing up the constitution of the Islamic republic. Over the past decade, Khalkhali, an embarrassment to the government, has had only a marginal presence in Iranian public life.

BIBLIOGRAPHY

BAKHASH, SHAUL. *Iran under the Ayatollahs.* New York, 1984.

Neguin Yavari

Khamene'i, Ali [1939–]

Leader (rahbar) of the Islamic Republic of Iran: successor to the constitutional functions of Ayatollah Ruhollah Khomeini.

Born in the northeastern Iranian city of Mashhad, Khamene'i began his advanced studies in Islam in 1958, with a year's attendance at courses on Islamic jurisprudence at al-NAJAF, in Iraq. He received the bulk of his training in Qom (Qum), where he studied with ayatollahs Damad, Ha'eri, Tabataba'i, and—

most importantly—KHOMEINI. During the uprising in Iran of June 1963, inspired by Khomeini, Khamene'i acted as liaison between Qom and his native city of Mashhad; he was jailed twice for this in 1964. Released in 1965, he resumed propagating the revolutionary vision of Khomeini in Mashhad while teaching the Qur'an and Islamic law. These activities earned him further periods of imprisonment as well as banishment in, 1968, 1971, 1972, 1975, and 1978.

After the triumph of the IRANIAN REVOLUTION in February 1979, Khamene'i emerged as a key figure in the elite of clerical activists that founded the Islamic Republican party and came to dominate the Iranian parliament during its first postrevolutionary term. In July 1979, he was appointed undersecretary for defense in the Mehdi Bazargan cabinet, becoming acting minister of defense after Bazargan's resignation. Among the most determined opponents of Abolhasan BANI SADR, the first president of the Islamic republic, Khamene'i played an important role in the events leading to his dismissal in June 1981. On June 27, while delivering the Friday sermon at Tehran University, Khamene'i almost fell victim to one of the numerous assassinations of leading government figures that followed the disgracing of Bani Sadr.

When Mohammad Ali Raja'i, the next president, was assassinated in August 1981, Khamene'i was appointed head of the Islamic Republican party and, on October 2, 1981, was elected president of the Islamic republic. He was elected for a second term, with an overwhelming majority, on August 16, 1985. After the death of Ayatollah Khomeini on June 4, 1989, Khamene'i was swiftly chosen as his successor, despite his lack of seniority in the learned hierarchy of Iranian SHI'ISM; this choice was ratified by popular vote in August 1989, with the modifications to the constitution necessitated by this. He has since led the country in effective collaboration with President Hashemi RAFSANJANI.

BIBLIOGRAPHY

BAKHASH, SHAUL. *The Reign of the Ayatollahs: Iran and the Islamic Revolution.* New York, 1984.

Hamid Algar

Khan

Arabic term meaning highway way station or urban warehouse for merchants.

Roadside khans, where caravans found lodging, flourished in Anatolia, Syria, and Iran from the thirteenth century. Khans were also built in cities by governments and private traders to provide storage, lodging, and trading facilities for both local and long-distance merchants. They formed the backbone of the magnificent bazaars in Middle Eastern cities today. By the early twentieth century, their architectural form was modified to resemble the modern office building.

BIBLIOGRAPHY

CEZAR, MUSTAFA. *Typical Commercial Buildings of the Ottoman Empire and the Ottoman Construction System.* Istanbul, 1983.

Elizabeth Thompson

Khanjar

A slightly curved, very sharp, double-edged dagger that tapers from the middle to a point.

A *khanjar* can be between twelve and forty-two inches long. The hilt is made of horn, bone, wood, plastic, or ivory and has a T-shaped crown. Today it is a purely ceremonial part of the traditional male Arab costume, sheathed in a wooden scabbard covered in silver or brass and attached to a belt. Both scabbard and hilt usually are decorated with finely tooled metal, sometimes encrusted with gems.

Jenab Tutunji

Omani man sporting a khanjar in his belt. (Richard Bulliet)

Khanoum

An honorific applied to the wife of a titled man or officer during the Ottoman period.

In Turkish, *hanım*, the word for "lady," is a title for upper-class married women. In some parts of the Middle East, particularly in Iran and Egypt, *khanoum* is used to address married women in much the same way "madam" is used in English, but it is becoming less common, especially among younger people.

Jenab Tutunji

Kharg, al-

The capital of a district of the same name in Saudi Arabia.

Al-Kharg is situated in the southern Najd region of Saudi Arabia, not far from Riyadh. The Arabian American Oil Company (ARAMCO) built a model farm at al-Kharg for King Abd al-Aziz (Ibn Sa'ud), thereby marking the beginning of al-Kharg as an agricultural center. A Saudi army base is located nearby.

John E. Peterson

Kharga Oasis

Egypt's largest oasis.

The oasis is located in Lower Egypt, Western Desert at 25° 30′ N, and 30° 35′ E. The town of al-Kharga (al-Kharija in classical Arabic) is the capital of Egypt's New Valley (al-Wadi al-Jadid) province (governorate). The 1976 population was estimated at some 27,000.

BIBLIOGRAPHY

VIVIAN, CASSANDRA, and NIGEL RYAN. *Islands of the Blest: A Guide to the Oases and Western Desert of Egypt.* Maadi, Egypt, 1990.

Arthur Goldschmidt, Jr.

Kharg Island

Island off the coast of Iran in the Persian Gulf.

Kharg Island is the site of major Iranian petroleum and petrochemical installations, and, connected by pipelines to the oil fields in Abadan, serves as one of its most important oil-loading terminals. The island was briefly held by the Dutch in 1753 and fell for a while under British control in 1838. Kharg Island was repeatedly attacked in the course of the Iran–Iraq War, which lasted from 1980 to 1988.

BIBLIOGRAPHY

SA'IDIAN, ABDOLHOSEYN. *Da'erat al-ma'aref-e sarzamin va mardom-e Iran* (Encyclopedia of the Land and People of Iran), 3rd ed. Tehran, 1984.

Neguin Yavari

Khartoum

Capital of Sudan.

The Three Towns—Khartoum, Omdurman, and Khartoum North—together comprise the political, commercial, and administrative center for Sudan. Located where the Blue Nile and White Nile join to flow north toward Egypt, the capital city is the largest urban complex in the country. Its population of 850,000 in 1980 more than doubled to over 2 million by 1990, as the result of the influx of migrants

A street in Khartoum, circa 1985. (© Chris Kutschera)

A mosque in Khartoum, 1987. (© Chris Kutschera)

from drought areas in the west and displaced persons from the war-torn south.

Khartoum, the political capital, means "elephant trunk" in Arabic. It was a small village called al-Jirayf, on the south shore of the Blue Nile, before the Turko–Egyptian conquest of 1821. The invading force established a small garrison there, which became the government center after 1824. The government encouraged the residents to replace their straw huts with permanent brick houses; built a dockyard, military storehouse, barracks, and large mosque; and encouraged commerce by steamer on the Nile and overland to the west and east. A telegraph line linked Khartoum to Egypt by 1874 and, later, to the Red Sea coast and the west. The Mahdiyya forces captured Khartoum on January 26, 1885, which signaled the demise of Turko–Egyptian rule and was dramatized by the death of the British officer Charles Gordon on the steps of the Turkish governor-general's palace.

Khartoum was neglected during the Mahdist period (1885–1898), but it was restored as the capital when Anglo–Egyptian forces reconquered the Sudan in 1898. Those forces seized Khartoum and Omdurman on September 1, 1898. During the Anglo–Egyptian condominium (1898–1956), the British rebuilt Khartoum and constructed a series of stone government buildings along the Nile waterfront, flanking the imposing governor-general's house.

Since independence, the principal government offices, embassies, European-style hotels, airport, offices, shops, and villas have been located in Khartoum; so has the University of Khartoum (known until independence on January 1, 1956 as Gordon Memorial College).

Omdurman, located on the southern side of the junction of the White and Blue Niles, served as the capital of the Sudan during the Mahdist period.

Omdurman is a sprawling residential area with traditional-style housing: The wealthier areas have stone and brick villas with courtyards and gardens hidden from the street by high walls, and the poorer areas consist of mud-brick huts in walled-off compounds along dirt roads. The parliament building, television and radio stations, and major academic institutions such as Omdurman Islamic University and al-Ahfad College for Women are located there. The headquarters of the leading political parties and religious movements, notably the Ansar and its Umma party and the Khatmiyya brotherhood and its Democratic Unionist party, are in Omdurman. The skyline is dominated by the silver-colored dome of the Mahdi's tomb, destroyed by British gunboats in 1898 but rebuilt in the 1940s.

Khartoum North, located on the north bank of the Blue Nile, is the newest section of the Three Towns. Known originally as Qubbat Khujali, it was the site of an encampment of the Khatmiyya during the Turko–Egyptian period. When the railway from Egypt reached the capital in 1899, its terminus was placed in Khartoum North. Spurs to Port Sudan in the east and to Sennar, farther south, opened in 1909. The railway was extended west to al-Ubayd in 1911. Although Khartoum North was not the headquarters for the railway, its location at the junction of those lines provided a base for the rapid growth of industry and residential areas. The main manufacturing industries are located there as well as extensive middle-class and squatter housing areas.

BIBLIOGRAPHY

HALL, MARJORIE, and BAKHITA AMIN ISMAIL. *Sisters under the Sun.* London, 1981.
HOLT, P. M., and M. W. DALY. *The History of the Sudan.* Boulder, Colo., 1979.

Ann M. Lesch

Khartoum Arab Summit

A meeting of Arab states to formulate a unified response to Israel's occupation of Arab lands after the Arab–Israel War of 1967.

In a unique display of solidarity, leaders of the United Arab Republic and twelve other Arab states met in Khartoum, Sudan, to agree upon a response to Israel's occupation of Arab lands. The conference, which lasted from 29 August to 3 September 1967, resulted in the decision that Arab states would not recognize, negotiate with, or make peace with Israel. Furthermore, the nations of the conference agreed to offer continued support to the Palestinians and to

Arab countries affected by Israel's invasion. Such support was primarily financial; Saudi Arabia, Kuwait, and Libya donated nearly 400 million U.S. dollars in aid to Jordan and the United Arab Republic.

The Arab leaders at Khartoum also decided to end the oil embargo that had been placed on the United States and Britain for their support of Israel. Oil production would henceforth be used as a positive resoruce to strengthen the Arab economies, especially those damaged by the Arab–Israel conflict. Finally, the Khartoum Arab Summit attempted to resolve inter-Arab strife; Saudi Arabia and Egypt agreed that they would work to end civil conflict in Yemem.

[See also: Arab–Israel War (1967)]

Karen A. Thornsvard

Khartoum University

Prominent institution of higher learning in Sudan.

Ironically, it was Lord KITCHENER of Khartoum, whose army had destroyed the MAHDIST STATE in the Sudan in 1898, who established Gordon Memorial College, not only in the memory of General Charles George Gordon, who died at Khartoum in 1885, but also to found a formal seat of learning in the Sudan. His appeal to the British public raised more than £100,000, and Kitchener proudly opened the college on November 8, 1902. During its first half-century Gordon Memorial College was slowly transformed from a secondary school to a college with ever increasing sophistication not only in its curriculum but also in its faculty and students. Most of the graduates during these years became the civil servants the British administration needed to modernize the Sudan.

Its function as a vocational training institute was symbolically and substantively changed when the college was affiliated with London University in 1945 to grant equivalent degrees in a wide range of subjects. The reality of its transformation was confirmed in 1951, when Gordon Memorial College and the Kitchener School of Medicine were combined as the University College of Khartoum. Upon independence in 1956 the University College became the University of Khartoum. Since then it has expanded to include numerous research institutes and a variety of schools, and the student body has become increasingly politicized. Because the campus lies in the heart of Khartoum, faculty, staff, and particularly the students have played a significant role in the political life of the Sudan.

Robert O. Collins

Khashoggi, Adnan   [1935–   ]

Saudi businessman.

Khashoggi is from a prominent Meccan family of Turkish origin; his father was physician to King Abd al-Aziz ibn Abd al-Rahman. Adnan attended Victoria College in Egypt, where he was a classmate of Hussein ibn Talal, who became King Hussein of Jordan, and studied briefly in the United States before beginning his commercial activities. His interests range from Arab tourism in Israel to ventures in Africa to banking in South Korea. However, he is most widely known for his role as a middleman in the Iran–Contra scandal and for his alleged involvement in the attempt to conceal the wealth of Ferdinand Marcos, former president of the Philippines. As a result of his involvement in the Iran–Contra scandal, most of his assets, including his American and Swiss bank accounts, have been frozen. Khashoggi's daughter, Nabila, married Muammar al-Qaddafi, ruler of Libya, in 1987.

BIBLIOGRAPHY

PETERSON, J. E. *Historical Dictionary of Saudi Arabia.* Metuchen, N.J., 1993.

Les Ordeman

Khatib, Ahmad al-

Politician in Kuwait.

Al-Khatib earned an M.D. degree from the American University of Beirut on one of Kuwait's first government scholarships. While private physician to Abdullah Salim Al Sabah, emir of Kuwait, from 1950 to 1965, he gained prominence as leader of the nationalist opposition. In 1963 he was elected to the first National Assembly, where he led the Nationalist Bloc. He was again elected to the 1985–1986 Assembly (but not the 1992 Assembly).

BIBLIOGRAPHY

CRYSTAL, JILL. *Oil and Politics in the Gulf: Rulers and Merchants in Kuwait and Qatar.* Cambridge, U.K., 1990.

Malcolm C. Peck

Khatib, Kan'an al-

Royal poet in Saudi Arabia in the 1970s.

Kan'an al-Khatib served Saudi Arabia's King Faisal ibn Abd al-Aziz Al Sa'ud, who encouraged poets and wrote poetry himself. As royal poet, al-Khatib gave recitations at official functions. He was also a valued confidant, conversationalist, and sympathetic listener for the king.

BIBLIOGRAPHY

LACEY, ROBERT. *The Kingdom: Arabia and the House of Saud.* New York, 1981.

Malcolm C. Peck

Khatibi, Abdelkabir   [1938–   ]

Moroccan sociologist, literary critic, and novelist.

Khatibi, born in al-Jadida, Morocco, received a doctorate in sociology from the Sorbonne in 1965. He is both a professor of sociology at Muhammad V University in Rabat and a researcher at the Centre de Recherche Scientifique de Rabat.

Khatibi writes in French. One of his early works was a play titled *La Mort des Artistes* (The Death of the Artists), presented at Paris in 1963. Whether he is writing essays or novels, Khatibi's attitude is characterized by the double identity resulting from his double culture that is perceived positively, as revealed in his book *Amour Bilinque* [Montpellier, 1983], translated by Richard Howard as *Love in Two Languages* [Minneapolis, 1990]). The diversity of the Maghrib is studied and analyzed with lucidity and realism in *Maghreb Pluriel* (Paris, 1983).

Khatibi's first work of fiction was *La Mémoire Tatouée* (Paris, 1971), a highly autobiographical novel. Another of his novels, *Un Eté à Stockholm* (Paris, 1990), explores human relations within the context of love. This theme is also the subject of a collection of poetry, *Dédicace à l'Année Qui Vient* (Montpellier, 1986).

Khatibi's well-known *La Blessure du Nom Propre* (Paris, 1974) reveals his interest in the popular culture of Morocco. It is a remarkable trait in his writing that no matter how removed his philosophical thinking is from his culture, he almost unfailingly links it to his Arab Islamic roots and elevates it to a universal precept. This is obvious in his *Le Livre de Sang* (Paris, 1979) and *Ombres Japonaises* (Montpellier, 1988), where he studies the seductive power of the narrative based on the *Arabian Nights*. His study of the concept of the false prophet in his play *Le Prophète Voilé* (Paris, 1979) uses examples from Arab Islamic history.

Some of Khatibi's writings reveal his interest in the political situation of the Arab world today, particularly the Palestinian problem. Although he blasts Zionism in *Vomito Blanco* (Paris, 1974), his *Le Même Livre* (Paris, 1985) stresses the similarities between Arabs and Jews in a correspondence with his Jewish friend Jacques Hassoun.

The long list of Khatibi's publications demonstrates his prolific production as well as the varied nature of his writings. Certain themes predominate, however, such as the question of identity resulting from the bilingual situation in Morocco. He approaches many of his themes from the perspective of sociology. His writings cover a wide range of topics, some purely literary, such as *Le Roman Maghrébin* (Paris 1958), *Ecrivains Marocains, du Protectorat à 1965. Anthologie* (Paris, 1974), and *Figures de l'Étranger* (Paris, 1987).

Khatibi is also interested in art and has written on calligraphy in *L'Art Calligraphique Arabe* (Paris, 1976; coauthor, Mohammed Sijilmassi) and painting in *La Peinture de Ahmed Cherkaoui* (Casablanca, 1976; coauthor, M. el-Maleh Maraini).

BIBLIOGRAPHY

GONTARD, MARC. "La littérature marocaine de langue française." *Europe* (June–July 1979): 102–116.
TCHÉHO, ISAAC CELESTIN. "Maghreb pluriel, africanité et internationalisme chez Abdelkébir Khatibi." *Notre librairie* 95 (1988): 50–54.
———. "Quelques aspects de la pluralité chez Abdelkébir Khatibi." *CELFAN Review* 6, no. 1 (1986): 5–9.

Aida A. Bamia

Khatisian, Alexander   [1876–1945]

Prime minister of Armenia, 1919–1920.

Khatisian was born in Tbilisi. After completing his education at the state school in Tbilisi, he studied medicine in Moscow, Kharkov, and Germany. Upon his return to Tbilisi, however, Khatisian turned his attention from medicine to politics, and after holding various posts in the city administration, he became mayor of Tbilisi (1909–1917). Politically, he was aligned with the Russian Constitutional Democrats (Kadets).

From 1915 to 1917, Khatisian was president of the Armenian National Council. In 1917 he moved to Alexandropol (now Leninakan) in Yerevan province, where he was elected mayor. During the very short-lived Democratic Federative Republic of Transcaucasia, declared independent on 22 April 1918, he was minister of finance. By early June, the Transcaucasian Federation had been broken up into Georgia, Armenia, and Azerbaijan.

Khatisian was minister of foreign affairs in the first Armenian cabinet. He also served briefly as minister of welfare, minister of the interior, and acting prime minister. After national elections were held in June 1919, and the (ARF) swept the majority of seats in Parliament, he was called upon in August to form a new cabinet, in which he was both prime minister and minister of foreign affairs. He served through May 1920. Khatisian's final service to the independent republic was as chief negotiator with the Nationalist Turks who, by imposing the Treaty of Alexandropol, sealed the fate of the republic in late November/early December 1920. Khatisian spent his remaining years in Paris, where he wrote his memoirs and one of the main sources on the history of the era, *Hayastani Hanrapetutian Dsagumn u Zargatsume* (The Creation and Development of the Republic of Armenia).

BIBLIOGRAPHY

HOVANNISIAN, RICHARD. *Armenia on the Road to Independence, 1918.* Berkeley, Calif., 1967.
————. *The Republic of Armenia: The First Year, 1918–1919.* Berkeley, Calif., 1971.
————. *The Republic of Armenia: From Versailles to London, 1919–1920.* Berkeley, Calif., 1982.

                                            Rouben P. Adalian

Khattabi, Muhammed ibn Abd al-Karim al-   [c. 1880–1963]

Moroccan leader of resistance to Spanish and French colonial conquest.

Muhammad ibn Abd al-Karim al-Khattabi was born in the RIF mountains, a Berber region of northern Morocco, sometime in the 1880s. His father was appointed QADI of the largest and most powerful tribe of the central Rif, the Banu Waryaghal (Aith Waryaghar in Berber) by Sultans HASSAN I and Mulay ABD AL-AZIZ, although neither had much influence over day-to-day affairs in the region. His father, like many other people in the area, also had an association with the Spanish military in the enclaves of Melilla and Alhucemas island, the latter immediately off-shore from the village of Ajdir, where the Khattabi family lived. The Spanish authorities hoped to use their influence with him, and with other local notables, to ease their path in occupying the northern zone of Morocco.

Abd al-Karim's early life was a mixture of Moroccan and Spanish influences. He studied at the Qarawiyyin University in FEZ, where he was influenced by teachers of the SALAFIYYA MOVEMENT. In 1907 he went to Melilla where he became, in rapid succession, teacher, military interpreter and qadi, and finally qadi qudat (chief judge) of the Moroccan

community in the Spanish enclave. He also wrote and translated articles for *El Telegrama del Rif*, the local newspaper. In 1913, the year after the joint Franco–Spanish protectorate was declared over Morocco, he was decorated for his services to Spain.

During World War I, this relationship with the Spanish authorities broke down because of Abd al-Karim's impatience with Spanish cooperation with France and his corresponding sympathy for Germany, despite his desire to marry the benefits of European technical modernization with Islamic reform. In 1915 he was arrested and imprisoned in Melilla on suspicion that his German sympathies had taken the form of subversive activities. Although he was released quite quickly, the Spanish authorities never regained his trust or sympathy.

In 1919, as the Spanish army began a slow march westward from Melilla toward the central Rif, his father broke relations with the Spanish garrison in Alhucemas island and joined a slowly growing resistance movement centered in the Banu Waryaghal. At the same time, Abd al-Karim left Melilla and returned to Ajdir. This resistance movement was based upon an unstable unity between the various tribal subdivisions and depended on the continued functioning of customary legal and political systems. When his father died—or was murdered—in 1920, Abd al-Karim succeeded in taking the leadership of the resistance and secured a more stable unity by insisting on the imposition of the SHARIʿA. At the same time he trained a military nucleus using European methods and weapons.

This military nucleus enabled him to defeat the Spanish forces in the eastern part of the Spanish protectorate in July 1921. He went on to set up a government in the central Rif that united his two aims of modernization and Islamic reform. In February 1923 he received *bayʿa*s (formal declarations of allegiance) from various central Rifi tribes that justified his leadership in terms of fulfilling requirements for the caliphate—justice, unity, order, and the preservation of *Shariʿa*—and referred to him as imam. On other occasions he referred to himself as *amir al-muʾminin*, a title that, despite its caliphal connotations, reflected not so much a claim to universal leadership as a statement of the religious nature of his movement. The official title of the Rif state was *al-Dawla al-Jumhuriyya al-Rifiyya* (The State of the Rifi Republic), although the Rifis themselves referred to it as *al-jabha al-rifiyya* (the Rifi front) reflecting its temporary nature. The confusion of titles reflected the fluidity of the political structures in the Rif. Nevertheless, they were strong enough for Rifi forces to again defeat the Spanish in northwestern Morocco in 1924 and the French in 1925, before the combined strength of the two European armies put an end to his state.

After his surrender in May 1926, Abd al-Karim was exiled on the French island of Réunion, where he stayed until 1947. In that year he escaped from a ship taking him back to France while it was traveling through the Suez Canal. He spent the rest of his life in Egypt, where he became the titular leader of the North African Defense League, the umbrella organization for Maghribi nationalists. He refused to return to Morocco at independence in 1956 saying that, since there were still foreign (American) troops on Moroccan soil, the country was not truly independent. He died in Cairo in 1963.

Abd al-Karim has been described by both French colonialist and modern Moroccan nationalist writers as a typical example of Berber resistance to outside authority. But others have seen him as a great guerrilla leader, part of a tradition including China's Mao Tse Tung and North Vietnam's Ho Chi Minh. Abd al-Karim himself situated his ideological stance in religious and nationalist terms. Despite the clear religious feeling of his followers, he told Léon Gabrielli, a French intelligence officer, that he specifically rejected the label of a JIHAD, saying that such medieval concepts were not relevant to the modern world. In an interview in the Egyptian Islamic journal al-Manar after the war, however, he admitted that he had made use of religious sensibilities as a rallying cry, although he presented himself in the context of the Salafiyya movement and modern Moroccan and Arab nationalism, and blamed his defeat on the opposition of the tariqas (Sufi religious brotherhoods), particularly the Darqawiyya, that was one of the biggest in the Rif, and on the failure of many of his supporters to accept his long-term political objective of replacing tribal systems with central government control and the absolute rule of the Shari'a. It is true, however, that other tariqas did support him, and in fact, the Rif was too small and too poor to resist the combined force of two European armies.

BIBLIOGRAPHY

There is no biography in English of Abd al-Karim, although there are plenty of accounts of the war. DAVID M. HART's The Aith Waryaghar of the Moroccan Rif, an Ethnography and History (Tucson, 1976) has a long chapter on Abd al-Karim. LÉON GABRIELLI, a French intelligence officer who took part in the campaign, provided a personal portrait in Abd el-Kaim et les événements du Rif 1924–1926 (Casablanca, 1956). J. ROGER-MATHIEU's Mémoires d'Abd-el-Karim (Paris, 1927) was compiled by this French journalist after interviewing Abd al-Karim on his way to exile in Réunion. It was rushed and is inaccurate. A book by a Moroccan historian, GERMAIN AYACHE, Les Origines de la Guerre du Rif (Paris and Rabat, 1981) contains details about Abd al-Karim's family background and social environment but only takes the story up to the very beginning of the war. The interview in al-Manar is in vol. 27, no. 8 (1925–1927): 630–634.

C. R. Pennell

Khawaja

A personal title of Persian origin.

Khawaja has been used in many senses throughout the Islamic lands. It has long been used in Egypt and the Levant to designate foreign merchants (often Persian) and as a polite form of address for non-Muslims. Its variant, *hoca* or *hoja*, is used by Turks, Iranians, and others for religious scholars and teachers.

Elizabeth Thompson

Khawr

A Gulf Arabic-Persian word meaning "natural harbor"; but it has also been used in place names.

One of Qatar's towns is named al-Khawr. Khawr al-Udayd is a gulf outlet that borders on the disputed boundary between Qatar and Abu Dhabi (U.A.E.)—through which Saudi Arabia was given access by Abu Dhabi to the Gulf. Jabal al-Khawr is a mountain range in Oman that separates the coastal section of the country from the interior.

BIBLIOGRAPHY

NYROP, RICHARD, ed. *Persian Gulf States: Country Studies.* Washington, D.C., 1985.

Emile A. Nakhleh

Khayr al-Din   [c. 1822–1890]

Prime minister of Tunisia (1873–1877) and grand vizier of the Ottoman Empire (1878–1879).

Khayr al-Din, a Circassian from the Caucasus Mountains, was sold as a slave in Constantinople at a young age; he was then resold to an agent of the bey of Tunis. As a teenager he arrived as a Mamluk at the court of Ahmad Bey. After receiving an education at the military school established by Ahmad Bey, Khayr al-Din rose through the military ranks to cavalry commander (*fariq*). He spent the years 1853–1857 in Paris arguing Tunisia's position against Mahmud ibn Ayad, who had defrauded the government of millions of dinars. Under Ahmad Bey's successor, Muhammad Bey, Khayr al-Din served as minister of marine (*wazir al-bahr*) from 1857 to 1859. He later presided over the Majlis al-Akbar (Great Council), a parliamentary body established in 1860.

In conflict with Prime Minister Mustafa KHAZNADER (his father-in-law), whose ruinous policy of incurring foreign loans was just beginning, Khayr al-Din resigned in 1862 and spent the next seven years in Europe. In response to his European experience, and in hopes of reforming the political system in Tunisia, he wrote *The Surest Path to Knowledge Concerning the Condition of Countries* (1868). In it he discussed the economic superiority of the West and offered a practical guide for improving the political system in Tunisia. He saw the ULAMA as the key guarantors of the political system who would ensure that the SHURA ideal of Islam would be upheld, and urged them to fulfill this role.

Khayr al-Din returned to Tunisia in 1869 in order to preside over the International Debt Commission. In his new political capacity, he conspired to discredit and replace Khaznader as prime minister. Faced with mounting pressures from foreign consuls and the disastrous state of Tunisia's finances, the bey retired Khaznader in 1873 and made Khayr al-Din prime minister. As prime minister, Khayr al-Din had to contend with the machinations of foreign consuls (particularly those of France, Britain, and Italy), the press campaign of his father-in-law to discredit him, his Mamluk rivals, and the economic downturn of the mid-1870s. Furthermore, he had lost faith in the pact of security of 1857 and the constitution of 1861. He realized that these liberal reforms were merely camouflage behind which Khaznader had been able to hide his ambition to become the wealthiest and most powerful member of the bey's government, and that they had been implemented to enhance foreign influence in Tunisia. Having witnessed first-hand Europe's aggressive intentions toward Africa, as well as the machinations of the foreign consuls in Tunis, Khayr al-Din had come to perceive that Europe was the paramount threat to Tunisia's existence and that the reincorporation of Tunisia into the Ottoman Empire was perhaps the country's one hope to avoid being occupied.

Khayr al-Din's disillusionment with constitutionalism led him to conclude that reforms should be directed to a wise elite in cooperation with an enlightened *ulama*. These two groups could limit the arbitrariness of absolutist rule and implement principles of justice and freedom according to the *Shari'a* (Islamic religious law). He then advocated a selective incorporation of those elements of Western civilization compatible with Islam. His final goal was the implementation of the Islamic concept of *maslaha* (the public good).

To help him introduce his reforms, Khayr al-Din appointed his Circassian and military school colleagues to positions of authority. He was also supported by Muhammad BAYRAM V, whom he appointed to direct the Hubus Administration, the government press, and *al-Ra'id al-Tunisi*, the official gazette of the government.

Khayr al-Din tackled administrative, financial, and tax reform, and ended the expensive MAHALLA military taxation expeditions against the tribes. To improve the country's economy, he expanded land under cultivation from 60,000 to 1 million hectares (132,000–2.2 million acres), reformed the customs system to protect Tunisia's handicraft and other industries, and launched public works projects such as paving the streets of Tunis. He founded SADIQI COLLEGE in 1875, and established a public library (al-Abdaliya). He briefly instituted a complaint box for citizens and sought to introduce a mixed judicial system to prevent foreign efforts to protect minorities in Tunisian courts. In his attempts to limit tyranny, he tried to persuade the bey to acquiesce to Ottoman claims of sovereignty and to restrictions on his arbitrary rule.

Khayr al-Din's efforts turned MUHAMMAD AL-SADIQ Bey against his reformist minister. Khayr al-Din's support of the Ottomans in the Russo-Turkish War of 1877 provided the bey with an excuse to dismiss him. Complicating his pro-Ottoman stance and loss of the bey's confidence were economic and financial difficulties, intrigues of foreign consuls and of the bey's favorite, Mustafa ibn Isma'il, and Khaznader's vilification campaign. All of these factors finally forced Khayr al-Din to resign on 2 July 1877. He went into self-imposed exile in Constantinople, where, because of his pro-Ottoman viewpoint, he was rewarded with a brief appointment as Ottoman grand vizier in 1878/1879. After his removal as grand vizier, Khayr al-Din retired to private life and spent his final years in Constantinople, where he died.

Khayr al-Din's legacy in Tunisia proved an inspiration for later reformers such as the young Tunisians. Sadiqi College was the most enduring of his accomplishments. Young Tunisians and later Tunisian nationalists, including Habib BOURGUIBA, were educated there.

BIBLIOGRAPHY

ANDERSON, LISA. *The State and Social Transformation in Tunisia and Libya, 1830–1980.* Princeton, N.J., 1986.

KHAYR AL-DIN AL-TUNISI. *Surest Path: The Political Treatise of a Nineteenth-Century Muslim Statesman.* Cambridge, Mass., 1967.

———. *Kheredine, homme d'état: Documents historiques annotés*, Vol. 1. Ed. by Mohamed-Salah Mzali and Jean Pignon. Tunis, 1971.

KRAIEM, MUSTAPHA. *La Tunisie précoloniale*, 2 vols. Tunis, 1973.

SMIDA, MONGI. *Khereddine: Ministre réformateur, 1873–1877*. Tunis, 1970.

Larry A. Barrie

Khayr-Eddine, Mohammad

Algerian nationalist.

Mohammad Khayr-Eddine was a member of the Association of Reformist Ulama. He supported Ferhat Abbas's MANIFESTO OF THE ALGERIAN MUSLIM PEOPLE (1943) and represented the FRONT DE LIBÉRATION NATIONALE (FLN; National Liberation Front) in Morocco during the Algerian War of Independence. He also served in the National Assembly (1962–64). Khayr-Eddine joined other dissidents (Abbas, Ben Youssef BEN KHEDDA, Hocine LAHOUEL)) in 1976 and signed the "New Appeal to the Algerian People," a declaration denouncing the government and policies of Colonel Houari BOUMÉDIENNE.

Phillip C. Naylor

Khaz'al Khan   [c. 1880–1936]

Shaykh of Muhammara, independent tribal chieftain in Iran.

In 1897, Khaz'al became chief to the Muhaysin, a powerful Arab tribe whose territory, mostly in Persia (now Iran), extended into Iraq. Confirmed as marchwarden by the weak Qajar shah, he expanded his sway over the Ka'b and other local tribes. As de facto ruler of Khuzistan, with a potential army of 20,000 tribesmen, he was courted as a strategic ally by the British; when oil was discovered at Masjed Soleyman in 1908, Khaz'al granted them the necessary rights of way for a pipeline to the Persian/Arabian Gulf and port facilities at Abadan. In the 1920s, however, after Reza Shah Pahlavi came to the throne and began centralization—which was also seen to be in Britain's interest—Khaz'al's British patrons were unwilling to support him and defy the shah. The Iranian army, having subjugated neighboring Luristan, advanced on Khuzistan; in 1925, Khaz'al was arrested at Muhammara (now Khorramshahr) and kept in Iran's capital, Tehran, until his death.

BIBLIOGRAPHY

BURRILL, R. M. "Khaz'al Khān." In *Encyclopaedia of Islam*. Vol. 4, 2nd ed. Leiden, 1978.

John R. Perry

Khaznader, Mustafa   [1817–1878]

State treasurer (1837–1861) and prime minister (1861–1873) of Tunisia.

Mustafa Khaznader was born Georges Kalkias Stravelakis, on the island of Chios. In 1821, during the Greek rebellion against the Turks, he was seized, taken to Constantinople, and sold into slavery. In 1827 he was sent to Tunis, where he was sold again. He converted to Islam and took the name Mustafa.

Mustafa became a close friend of Ahmad ibn Mustafa, future bey of Tunis. When Ahmad became bey in 1837, he named Mustafa *khaznader* (state treasurer). (His long tenure in this office led to the use of Khaznader as his surname.) The centralization of governmental authority under Ahmad Bey and the combination of an increasingly complex tax structure and a rudimentary tax collection apparatus obliged the government to farm out the various taxes in ILTIZAM.

Mahmud ibn Ayad, the top tax farmer, conspired with Khaznader to fleece the government of millions of dinars by transferring funds to France and acquiring French citizenship. In 1852, having transferred the equivalent of 50 million francs, he fled to France and acquired French citizenship; he was unable to secure citizenship for Khaznader. The latter's involvement in the affair apparently did not lessen the bey's ultimate faith in his finance minister.

Khaznader built up a powerful patronage network through his own marriage into the bey's family and marriage of his children into prominent political and business families. He encouraged Ahmad Bey in his reforms because these enabled him to profit from new tax farms and other financial ventures. Under Muhammad Bey (1855–1859) and MUHAMMAD AL-SADIQ Bey (1859–1882), Khaznader supported the reforms of the FUNDAMENTAL PACT (1857) and the constitution of 1861 because these sought to restrict the power of the bey and increase the power of his ministers.

Between 1859 and 1869, Khaznader and his associates virtually ran and ruined the Tunisian state. The Grand Council, established as a kind of Parliament to implement the 1861 Constitution, was staffed with his cronies. Beginning in 1863, Khaznader floated a series of foreign loans that bankrupted the government by 1868. To pay for these loans, he authorized the doubling of the personal income tax, the *majba*. When this went into effect in 1864, there arose a widespread tribal revolt. It was severely repressed, the constitution was suspended, and Khaznader ran the state even more firmly. But in the long term, his financial policies destroyed the state's financial viability. Bad harvests, famines, and epidemics compounded Tunisia's financial plight and led to the International Finance Commission of 1869, set up by foreign creditors to ensure that Tunisia paid its debts.

Khaznader's son-in-law KHAYR AL-DIN used his position on this commission to discredit Khaznader and to force the bey to dismiss him. In 1873, Muhammad al-Sadiq Bey reluctantly agreed to retire Khaznader and confiscate some of his wealth. In his place, the bey appointed Khayr al-Din prime minister. During the latter's tenure of office (1873–1877) Khaznader continually attacked him and sought his removal. Finally, in 1877, the bey discharged him. Khaznader's triumph was short-lived, however; he died the following year.

BIBLIOGRAPHY

BARRIE, LARRY A. "Tunisia: The Era of Reformism, 1837–1877." Master's thesis, Harvard University, 1966.
BROWN, L. CARL. *The Tunisia of Ahmad Bey, 1837–1855.* Princeton, N.J., 1974.
GANIAGE, JEAN. *Les Origines du protectorat français en Tunisie (1861–1881).* Paris, 1959.

Larry A. Barrie

Khider, Mohamed   [1912–1967]

Algerian revolutionary.

The son of a poor family from Biskra, Khider was born in Algiers, the capital of Algeria, and became a bus driver/fare collector. He joined the Etoile Nord Africaine (Star of North Africa, ENA) of Messali HADJ and the PARTI DU PEUPLE ALGÉRIEN (Algerian People's party, PPA). He favored armed rebellion against the French, although he tried to reconcile Messalists and centralists of the MOUVEMENT POUR LE TRIOMPHE DES LIBERTÉS DÉMOCRATIQUES (Movement for the Triumph of Democratic Liberties, MTLD). As a cofounder, Khider was known as an historic chief of the FRONT DE LIBÉRATION NATIONALE (National Liberation Front, FLN). During the Algerian War of Independence (1954–1962), he served with the "external" FLN and in 1956 was involved with initial French government contacts. He was seized along with other historic chiefs (Ahmed BEN BELLA, Hocine AIT AHMAD, Mohamed BOUDIAF, and Rabah

BITAT) in the infamous skyjacking of an Air Maroc airplane in October 1956.

After the war, he became secretary-general of the FLN but later disagreed with Ben Bella concerning the relationship between the party and the army in independent Algeria. Thereupon, he resigned and went into exile but kept a substantial sum of the party funds (to be used by the Algerian opposition), which was invested in a Swiss account. Khider was assassinated in Madrid in 1967, but the Algerian government failed to recover the funds. Khider's reputation was later officially rehabilitated in 1984.

BIBLIOGRAPHY

HORNE, ALISTAIR. *A Savage War of Peace: Algeria, 1954–1962.* New York, 1987.

Phillip C. Naylor

Khobar, al-

Port of Saudi Arabia.

Located in the Eastern Province, on the Gulf coast of Saudi Arabia, al-Khobar was founded in 1923, as a fishing and pearling village, by members of the Dawasir tribe fleeing from Bahrain. It thrived as a terminal for the first crude oil that was shipped from Saudi Arabia to Bahrain for refining, until a deep-water port was constructed at nearby al-Dammam. A causeway and four-lane highway link Bahrain and Saudi Arabia at al-Khobar. The unofficial census of 1974 counted 48,817 inhabitants, making al-Khobar the twelfth largest city (by population) in Saudi Arabia.

Les Ordeman

Kho'i Najafi   [?–1993]

Shi'a cleric.

Ayatollah Abu al-Qasim Musavi Kho'i Najafi was one of the highest ranking Shi'a *ulama* and *marja' al-taqlid* (source of emulation) until his death. He lived in al-Najaf, Iraq, voiced his opposition to Ayatollah Khomeini's doctrine of *velayat-e faqih* (vice-regency of the legist) in 1983, and was generally opposed to clerical involvement in political affairs.

BIBLIOGRAPHY

ABRAHAMIAN, ERVAND. *Iran between Two Revolutions.* Princeton, N.J., 1982.

Neguin Yavari

Khomeini, Ahmad   [1945–1995]

Second and youngest son of Ayatollah Ruhollah Khomeini

Hojjat al-Eslam Ahmad Khomeini played a minor role in the prerevolutionary stage of clerical politics in Iran. It was his older brother, Mostafa Khomeini (1930–1977), who accompanied their father to exile in Iraq and was among his closest aides. Ahmad, who graduated from a national Iranian high school before embarking on a religious education, gained prominence only after his brother's death and the victory of the Iranian revolution of 1979. He initially supported the presidency of Abolhasan Bani Sadr but withdrew his support in 1981 when Bani Sadr was warming up to leftist and other opposition groups in Iran. After his father's death in 1989, Ahmad withdrew again to the margins of political life in Iran. A few weeks prior to his sudden death of a heart attack in March 1995, Ahmad had for the first time since 1989 directly criticized the government of President Ali Akbar Hashemi Rafsanjani. "Seventeen years have passed since the revolution," Ahmad wrote in a widely distributed pamphlet in Tehran, "and we can no longer blame our ills and shortcomings on the United States." Ahmad's son, Hojjat al-Eslam Hasan Khomeini, is entrusted with his father's legacy.

BIBLIOGRAPHY

BAKHASH, SHAUL. *The Reign of the Ayatollahs.* New York, 1984.

Neguin Yavari

Khomeini, Ruhollah   [1902–1989]

Leader of the Iranian revolution of 1979.

Ayatollah Ruhollah Musavi Khomeini was born in Khomein, Iran, in 1902. His birth certificate, however, registered under the last name Mostafavi, erroneously records his year of birth as 1900. Khomeini's great-grandfather, Sayyed Din Ali Shah, of Neyshabur, a town in the northeastern Iranian province of Khorasan, resided in Kashmir, India. Din Ali Shah's son, Sayyed Ahmad, traveled to al-Najaf and Karbala, holy Shi'ite cities in present-day Iraq, between 1824 and 1834, and from there took residence in Khomein, a town in central Iran. Ayatollah Khomeini's father, Mostafa, was a cleric and owned property in Khomein. Ayatollah Khomeini received his early religious education in Khomein as a student of Akhund Molla Abolqasem, Aqa Shaykh Ja'far, Mirza Mahmud Eftekhar al-Olama, Mirza Mehdi

Da'i, Aqa Najafi, his brother-in-law, and Ayatollah Morteza Pasandideh, his older brother. Ruhollah Khomeini left for Arak, a religious center in central Iran, in 1920. In 1922, when Ayatollah Abd al-Karim Ha'eri left Arak for Qom and founded the Feyziyeh religious seminary, Khomeini accompanied him and studied at the seminary there with Ha'eri, Mohammad Taqi Khonsari, and Sayyed Ali Yasrebi Kashani. In 1929, Khomeini went to Tehran to marry Khadijeh Saqafi, the daughter of a prominent ayatollah. Their first son, Mostafa, was born in 1930 and died under mysterious circumstances in 1977 in Iraq; three daughters, Sediqeh, Farideh, and Fahimeh, and another son, Ahmad, who died in 1995, followed.

Ayatollah Ha'eri died in 1937, and by that time, Khomeini, who had completed his formal education in 1928, had established himself as one of the more active and prominent religious scholars of Qom. Ha'eri was succeeded by Ayatollah Hosayn Borujerdi. Khomeini also studied with Borujerdi, serving as his special assistant. Borujerdi's primary preoccupation, however, was the expansion and strengthening of the Feyziyeh and preserving its autonomy from governmental supervision. To do so, Borujerdi generally assumed an apolitical and quietist stance throughout his tenure as director of the Feyziyeh. Khomeini, for instance, did not openly participate in the oil nationalization process of the early 1950s. With the death of Borujerdi in 1962, however, activist *ulama* at the Feyziyeh openly pursued an oppositional stance regarding the Pahlavi government and its efforts at Western-style modernization, secularization, and centralization of the state.

Khomeini's first direct involvement with the political affairs of the country took place in October 1962, when the government of Mohammad Reza Shah PAHLAVI, under the premiership of Asadollah Alam, passed a law to form representative local councils throughout the country. Khomeini expressed his opposition in letters to the prime minister and the shah, objecting to its inclusion of women as voters and the permissibility of non-Muslim representatives. Threatened with nationwide protests organized by the *ulama*, the government backed down, and the local-council law was suspended.

What distinguished Khomeini from his peers, and made for his ultimate victory, was his wider view on politics and the scope of his anti-regime activity. Rather than focusing solely on particular government laws and actions, Khomeini chose to attack the pillars of the regime's worldview. Throughout his political life, he consistently attacked, on a conceptual level, the government's strong pro-West stance, its neglect of Islamic beliefs, corruption, uneven distribution of income, and the shah's close alliance with Israel.

In January 1963, Mohammad Reza Shah launched the WHITE REVOLUTION, which included a land-reform decree, guidelines for the nationalization of forests and pastureland, and the establishment of a literacy corps to provide elementary education in remote villages. The revolution was perceived as instigated by the United States and as inimical to Iran's traditional and Islamic societal norms; agitation arose in Qom and other Iranian cities. Khomeini was arrested, along with several other prominent clergymen, on June 5, 1963 after delivering a fiery sermon denouncing the shah and his pro-Zionist, pro-American, and anti-Islamic stance. Khomeini was incarcerated in Tehran and released under pressure from other prominent clerics ten months later. In July 1964, Khomeini again was in the vanguard of the religious opposition, decrying the shah's decision to grant diplomatic immunity to all U.S. military representatives and their families residing in Iran. Khomeini was reincarcerated and exiled to Turkey. In 1965, he was allowed to take up residence in al-Najaf, Iraq, a Shi'a shrine city with an important religious seminary. While in exile, Khomeini continued to draw a large mass of supporters among Iranian clerics and the traditional middle class, never losing an opportunity to criticize the shah and his policies: in 1971, when the monarchy lavishly celebrated its twenty-five hundredth anniversary, and in 1975, when a single-state party, the Rastakhiz, was inaugurated.

In the late 1960s and early 1970s, while in al-Najaf, Khomeini formulated his concept of VELAYAT-E FA-QIH, or the governance of the jurist. Essentially, the doctrine called for an Islamic government run by the clergy and modeled on the Qur'an and the early period of Prophetic rule. *Velayat-e faqih,* led by jurists, also called for active opposition to all non-Islamic states. Apart from his network of supporters inside Iran, including Mahdi BAZARGAN, Mortaza MOTAH-HARI, and Mahmud Taleqani, Khomeini spent these years fostering his ties with oppositional groups abroad, such as Islamic student associations led by the likes of Ibrahim YAZDI, Sadeq QOTBZADEH, Abolhasan BANI SADR, and Mostafa CHAMRAN, all of whom rose to prominence after the revolution of 1979.

In January 1978, when the first anti-shah protests occurred in Iran, Khomeini had access to a well-established and influential infrastructure inside Iran. Rejecting all pleas for compromise, including Bazargan's request for cooperating with the shah's newly announced reform plans, Khomeini only heightened his anti-shah declarations. In October 1978, under pressure from the Iranian government, President Saddam Hussein of Iraq expelled Khomeini to Paris. There, Khomeini not only enjoyed attention from the Western press, but also gained access to wider

communication with Iran. In January 1979, the shah, having failed at quelling the revolution, left Iran and in his place installed a prime minister from the oppositional group, the National Front. Khomeini returned to Iran amid widespread celebrations on January 31, 1979. He refused to acknowledge the sovereignty of the prime minister, Shahpur Bakhtiar, and on February 11, 1979, the Islamic republic of Iran was established after a national referendum. Bazargan was appointed by Khomeini to lead the provisional government. After the revolution, Khomeini gradually became known as the leader of the revolution (*rahbar-e enqelab*) and as Imam Khomeini, a title once reserved for the twelve infallible leaders of the Shi'a community, descendants of the first Shi'a imam, Ali ibn Abi Talib, cousin and son-in-law of the Prophet Muhammad. In 1980, the victorious Ayatollah Khomeini was selected as *Time* magazine's man of the year.

Khomeini's policies in the initial phases of the revolution were marked by subtle compromises undertaken to consolidate the revolution. Political opposition was tolerated, and a non-cleric Abolhasan Bani Sadr emerged as the leader's choice for the nation's first president. The eight-year war with Iraq (1980–1987), severing diplomatic ties with the United States, international isolation, instances of armed struggle by the internal opposition, and factional strife within Islamic circles in Iran combined to radicalize the imam's political decisions. In 1987, he only agreed to the UN-sponsored cease-fire with Iraq after he was repeatedly informed by Iranian officials of the country's inability to further maintain the war effort.

The success of the Islamic revolution of 1979, uncontestably engineered by Ayatollah Khomeini himself, not only toppled the Pahlavi regime in Iran, but also bore far-reaching implications for the Islamic world at large. Islamic revolutionary groups exist today in virtually all Islamic nations, inspired in their struggle against Westernization, secularization, and economic subordination by the example set by Ruhollah Khomeini.

Khomeini died on June 5, 1989. Although he had, in 1983, designated an old ally, Ayatollah Hosayn Ali Montazeri, as his successor, the nomination was later repealed, and he died without an heir. Ayatollah Ali Khamene'i was the choice of the nation's ruling *ulama*, and he functions presently as Iran's vali-ye faqih.

BIBLIOGRAPHY

BAKHASH, SHAUL. *The Reign of the Ayatollahs.* New York, 1984.

FISHER, MICHAEL M. J. *Iran from Religious Dispute to Revolution.* Cambridge, Mass., 1980.

KHOMEINI, RUHOLLAH MUSAVI. *Velayat-e faqih: Hokumat-e*

Eslami (Governance of the Jurist: Islamic Government). 1976.

PASANDIDEH, MORTEZA. *Khaterat-e Ayatollah Pasandideh* (Memoirs of Ayatollah Pasandideh). Ed. by Mohammad Javad Moradinia. Tehran, 1995.

Neguin Yavari

Khorasan

Province in northeastern Iran.

Today the northeasternmost province (*ostan*) of Iran, with its capital at MASHHAD, in the medieval period Khorasan (also Khurasan) comprised a much wider region, covering parts of present-day central Asia as well as Afghanistan.

Khorasan is dominated by a zone of mountain ranges, a continuation of the Alborz mountains in northern Iran, running roughly northwest to southeast. In northern Afghanistan they connect to the Paropamisus and Hindu Kush. Khorasan is bounded in the north by the steppes and deserts of Turkemenistan in the former USSR. To the south lie extensive landlocked deserts, such as the Dasht-e Kavir and Dasht-e Lut. Khorasan receives adequate rainfall only in the more northerly mountain zone, where there is a relatively flourishing agriculture and pastoral economy, and the population is quite dense. The southern region typically has an oasis pattern of life sustained by wells and irrigation systems called QANATS (underground canals).

Khorasan's strategic position as a corridor between the steppe and the settled, civilized parts of the Middle East endowed it with a rich cultural and political history up until the modern period. Through Khorasan armies of Alexander the Great of Macedonia (356–323 B.C.) passed to Bactria (now the Balkh district in Afghanistan) and India, and Turkish people moved into the Middle East. In the pre-Islamic times, Khorasan was one of the four great provinces of Persia, as Iran was then called. In the early Islamic period, Khorasan was culturally and economically backward, relative to western Persia, but from the 800s onward, its socioeconomic and cultural significance grew. Then the Turkic Oghuz invasion of Khorasan in the eleventh century and the Mongol onslaught in the thirteenth century devastated the region and instigated its decline. Some believe that "Khurasan never recovered its cultural and intellectual position within Persia." In the fourteenth century, however, Khorasan prospered once again and witnessed a period of political stability and abundant cultural and artistic life. In the sixteenth century, when Iran became officially a Shi'a country under the Safavid dynasty, the shrine of the Imam Ali al-Rida (a spiritual leader who tried to bring Shi'ites and Sunnis together) at Mashhad grew in importance. The city of Mashhad (the name means *shrine*) also grew as a result, becoming thenceforth the principle city of Khorasan.

In the second half of the eighteenth century, parts of Khorasan passed into the hands of the Durrani Afghan chief Ahmad Shah for a short period of time. But from the late eighteenth century onwards, Khorasan was fully restored to the newly established dynasty in Persia, the Qajars. As a result of continuous wars with the UZBEKS (Ozbegs) and TURKMENS, however, life in the northern regions of Khorasan continued to be precarious. Commerce and agriculture declined, and many Persians were carried off as slaves by the central Asian emirates. Only Russian intervention and annexation of Khiva in 1873 and crushing of the Turkmens in 1881, actions motivated by Russian political ambitions, finally rectified this situation. The Persian government was no longer able to withstand Russian pressure. The Russians also annexed the Merv oasis, once part of Khorasan, in 1884.

Meanwhile, relations with the emirs of Afghanistan continued to deteriorate. Yet another superpower intervention, this time British, put a halt to this hostility. Herat, also a part of Khorasan, was finally ceded to Afghanistan after a brief war between the Qajar ruler Naser al-Din Shah and the British in 1856–57. The boundary dispute between Iran and Afghanistan was not finally settled until 1934–35.

Variegated political and cultural influences on Khorasan have created a heterogeneous population in the region, including tribes such as Turkmens, Kurds, Baluch, Arabs, and others besides the important Iranian substratum. The census of the province gave its population as 2½ million. Mashhad in 1986 was the second largest city in Iran with a population of 1,466,000 inhabitants.

BIBLIOGRAPHY

LEWIS, B., C. PELLAT, and J. SCHACHT, eds. *The Encyclopaedia of Islam.* Vol. 4. Leiden, 1965, pp. 55–59.

Parvaneh Pourshariati

Khoury, George-Paul [1910–?]

Syrian lawyer.

Born in Damascus to Nicolas al-Khoury in 1910, George-Paul attended the University of Damascus and received a licentiate of laws. He served as the Syrian representative to agricultural fairs in Istanbul and Beirut in 1954 and as director of the Agricultural Bank in 1955.

BIBLIOGRAPHY

Who's Who in the Middle East, 1967–1968.

Charles U. Zenzie

Khraief, Bechir   [1917–1983]

Tunisian novelist and short story writer.

Khraief, born in Nefta, is considered the father of fiction writing in Tunisia. He first worked in trade, selling fabrics during the day while attending night school. His occupation gave him an excellent insight in the life of the Tunisian people and enhanced the realism of his writings. When Khraief went into teaching, he looked back on those years as the best of his life. His writings reveal his strong attachment to his Tunisian roots. Like other writers of his generation, Khraief published his writings first in the journal *Al-Fikr* (founded in 1955).

Khraief, noted for his realistic approach, simple style, and use of dialect in dialogue, gives a truthful and interesting depiction of Tunisian life while shying away from philosophical themes. His efforts to endow his short story "Al-murawwid wa'l-thawr (The trainer and the bull), in his collection *Mashmum al-full* (Smelling the Arabian jasmine [Tunis, 1971]), with a specific theme failed. Another story in the same collection, "Khalifa al-aqra'" (Khalifa the bald), reveals his skill as a fiction writer.

Khraief's writings provided a panorama of Tunisian life in its different settings. His novel *Al-dajla fi arajiniha* (Dates on the branch [Tunis, 1969]) reveals various aspects of desert life, although he often uses too many details, a weakness that characterizes some of his other works. *Iflas aw hubbak darbani* (Being penniless or your love hit me [Tunis, 1959]), on the other hand, paints a picture of the ZAYTUNA UNIVERSITY circles as well as of the middle class when Tunisia was undergoing the social transition from a traditional to a modern society.

Motivated by the same nationalist feeling that influenced his fiction, Khraief wrote two historical novels, *Barq al-layl* (Night's lightning [Tunis, 1961]) and *Ballara* [Tunis, 1992]), which was published posthumously.

[See also: Literature, Arabic, North African]

BIBLIOGRAPHY

BACCAR, TAOUFIC, and SALAH GARMADI. *Ecrivains de Tunisie: Anthologie.* Paris, 1981.
FONTAINE, JEAN. *La littérature tunisienne moderne.* Tunis, 1989.

Aida A. Bamia

Khrimian, Mkrtich   [1820–1907]

Patriarch of Constantinople, 1869–1873; catholicos of all Armenians, 1892–1907.

Born in the city of Van, Khrimian joined the church in 1845, after the death of his wife and child. He was ordained a *vardapet* (celibate priest) in 1854. He began publishing the periodical *Ardsvi Vaspurakan* (The Eagle of Vaspurakan) in 1855 and a year later returned to Van as the prior of the monastery of Varak. In 1858 he resumed publication of *Ardsvi Vaspurakan.* In 1862 he became prelate of Daron and prior of the monastery of Surp Karapet.

Khrimian was ordained a bishop in 1868 and elected Armenian patriarch of Istanbul in 1869. Because of his efforts to document the exploitation of the Armenian populace and to register official complaints with the Sublime Porte, he was forced to resign in 1873. Five years later, he led an Armenian delegation that hoped to appeal to the conferring powers at the Congress of Berlin. Unsuccessful, Khrimian returned to Istanbul and delivered the homily for which he is most remembered, the "Sermon of the Iron Ladle," in which he stated that each power at Berlin took a share of the contents of a great soup bowl with an iron ladle, whereas he had only a paper petition and thus could bring nothing back to the Armenian people. It marked a turning point in Armenian political consciousness.

In 1879 Khrimian was elected prelate of the Armenians in Van. Suspected of associating with Armenian resistance groups, he was recalled to Istanbul and in 1890 was exiled to Jerusalem. In 1892 he was elected catholicos (supreme patriarch) of all Armenians at Echmiadzin. Khrimian's refusal to obey the Russian imperial edict of 1903, which authorized seizing the properties of the Armenian church, galvanized the Armenian communities of Russia to protest the decision, resulting in the eventual rescinding of the edict in an effort to reduce the turmoil in the Transcaucasus.

BIBLIOGRAPHY

WALKER, CHRISTOPHER J. *Armenia: The Survival of a Nation.* New York, 1980.

Rouben P. Adalian

Khrushchev, Nikita S.   [1894–1971]

Soviet politician; premier of the USSR, 1958–1964.

Before the Communist revolution, Khrushchev, son of a Russian villager, worked in the Ukrainian coal region of Donbas. He joined the Communist party in

1918 and rose rapidly through its ranks. After Stalin's death in 1953, Khrushchev became first secretary of the CPSU, retaining this position until 1964, when he was ousted by opponents led by Leonid Brezhnev.

In contrast to Stalin, Khrushchev adopted the policy of peaceful coexistence with the West. However, in the Middle East, he engaged in political competition with the United States. Arguing the advantages of "scientific socialism" and offering military and economic assistance, Khrushchev hoped to persuade the neutralist leaders of Egypt, Syria, Iraq, and Algeria to join the USSR in an anti-Western "zone of peace," as he called it. While several accepted Soviet assistance, no Arab leader took seriously Khrushchev's ideological arguments. Consequently, Moscow established relatively close relations with several Arab states and supported them in the 1956 war with Israel but was not able to sway them from their independent course.

BIBLIOGRAPHY

SMOLANSKY, OLES M. *The Soviet Union and the Arab East under Khrushchev.* Lewisburg, Pa., 1974.

Oles M. Smolansky

Khulayfawi, Abd al-Rahman

Syrian politician; prime minister 1966, 1971/72, 1976–1978.

A Sunni Islam military officer in the al-BA'TH party, Major General Abd al-Rahman Khulayfawi was included in the early inner circle of Syria's President Hafiz al-ASAD. He served as Syria's prime minister in 1966, 1971/72 (resigning for health reasons in December 1972), and from August 1976 through March 1978.

BIBLIOGRAPHY

HINNEBUSCH, RAYMOND A. *Authoritarian Power and State Formation in Ba'thist Syria: Army, Party and Peasant.* Boulder, Colo., 1990.

Charles U. Zenzie

Khuri, Bishara al [1890–1964]

Prime minister of Lebanon under the French mandate; first president of independent Lebanon (1943–1952).

Khuri, born into a Maronite family, studied law in Paris. After spending World War I in Egypt, he returned to Lebanon and in 1922 was appointed secretary of Mount Lebanon. He served as prime minister in 1927–1928 and 1929. During the 1930s, his rivalry with Emile EDDÉ dominated Maronite politics. Khuri strove to develop good relations with moderate SUNNI circles, gambling that since they had opposed the establishment of Greater Lebanon, they would abandon their demand for unity with Syria if the Christians asserted their independence from France. He created the CONSTITUTIONAL BLOC Party in 1934 and cooperated closely with a group of Sunni politicians, led by Riyad al-SULH.

After being elected president of the republic in 1943, Khuri chose Sulh as prime minister, and they concluded the oral agreement known as the NATIONAL PACT. It defined the terms of the Maronite–Sunni partnership that provided the framework of Lebanon's politics until the outbreak of the LEBANESE CIVIL WAR in 1975. In 1947, Khuri rigged the parliamentary elections in an effort to obtain passage of a constitutional amendment that would allow him to run for reelection in 1949. After 1949, he faced a powerful coalition including the Druze leader Kamal JUMBLATT and the Maronite politicians Pierre JUMAYYIL, Camille CHAMOUN, and Raymond EDDÉ. In September 1952 a general strike compelled Khuri to step down.

BIBLIOGRAPHY

HUDSON, MICHAEL C. *The Precarious Republic: Political Modernization in Lebanon.* Boulder, Colo., 1985.

SALIBI, KAMAL. *The Modern History of Lebanon.* New York, 1965.

Guilain P. Denoeux

Khuri, Khalil al- [1923–]

Lebanese politician.

A Maronite Catholic, Khuri was the son of Bishara al-KHURI, the first president of the independent Republic of Lebanon. Born in Beirut on June 1, 1923, he completed his law degree at the Jesuit-administered St. Joseph University. In 1960, 1964, and 1968, he was elected as parliamentary representative of the District (Qada') of Aley in the Shuf mountains. In December 1965, he was elected president of the CONSTITUTIONAL BLOC, a political party established by his father. Between January and November 1969, he served as minister of social affairs.

BIBLIOGRAPHY

Who's Who in Lebanon, 1990–1991. Beirut, 1990.

George E. Irani

Khutba

Sermon delivered from an elevated pulpit (minbar) by a khatib, or Muslim preacher, at Friday prayers and at special celebrations.

The Friday *khutba* precedes the noon prayers that bring local Muslim communities together at the mosque. The *khatib* usually follows a formula in which he admonishes those present to be pious, conducts a prayer on behalf of the faithful, and recites part of the Qur'an.

The khutba has also traditionally included an expression of loyalty to the sovereign. This practice has at times carried political significance, as in 1953, when the French deposed the Moroccan sultan Muhammed V. Many khatibs refused to invoke the name of his French-appointed replacement and even suspended prayers, a protest that ultimately led to his return and the independence of MOROCCO in 1956.

Khatibs also address public issues, and many governments today circulate suggested themes on public health, political issues, and other topics for the weekly khutba. In recent years, the khutbas of famous religious leaders have been distributed directly to the faithful on cassette tape, thereby reaching a wide audience, often across national boundaries.

BIBLIOGRAPHY

ANTOUN, RICHARD T. *Muslim Preacher in the Modern World.* Princeton. N.J., 1989.

EICKELMAN, DALE. *Knowledge and Power in Morocco: The Education of a Twentieth-Century Notable.* Princeton, N.J., 1985.

"Khutba." *Encyclopedia of Islam,* 2nd ed., vol 5.

Elizabeth Thompson

Khuzistan

A province in southwestern Iran with its capital at Ahvaz.

The Iranian province of Khuzistan is in a fertile southwestern region of alluvial plains made by two rivers, Karkheh (or Kerkheh) and Karun. It is situated between the Zagros mountains and the sea. On the north Khuzistan borders Lorestan (Luristan) governorship; in the south, the Persian Gulf. The Iran–Iraq border forms the western part of its boundaries, and on the east lies the Hindiya or Hindijan river.

Khuzistan's climate is hot and very humid in the summer due to a lack of altitude—averaging only 32.80 ft (10 m) and in the south and 328 feet (100 m) in the central parts of the region; the southerly inclination of the land (which makes it susceptible to maximum effects of the sun); the hot winds from the Syrian desert and Saudi Arabia; and the lack of snowcovered mountains, forests, or open water to ease the effect of these winds. In spite of its heat and humidity, Khuzistan has always been amply provided with water by the Karkheh, Diz, and Karun rivers, and noted from earliest times for its prosperity. Thriving agriculture produces plentiful grain, rice, sugarcane, citrus fruits, melons, and dates, as well as cotton. The Persian/Arabian Gulf provides abundant seafood.

Arabs form a substantial portion of the Khuzistani population. The local Arab Shi'a dynasty of the Musha'sha (who established their rule in the region for a short period in the fifteenth century and acted as powerful governors of the region until the nineteenth century), and other Arab tribes such as the Banu Ka'b and Banu Lam (who imigrated from Arabia and the lower course of the Tigris in the eighteenth and nineteenth centuries), have been the cause of the alternative name Arabistan, especially for the western parts of the province. In 1925, under Reza Shah Pahlavi, the name of the region was established as Khuzistan.

The prosperity of Khuzistan declined after the eighteenth century primarily beause of Iran–Arab hostility, damage to agriculture by migrations and nomadism, raiding of trade caravans, especially by the Banu Lam, and, finally, lack of central authority.

Prosperity returned to Khuzistan in the twentieth century because of various factors: the discovery of oil at Masjed Soleyman in 1908; the construction and growth of the Abadan oil refinery by the 1950s; the construction of the Trans-Iranian railway in 1938; the construction of the Muhammad Reza Pahlavi dam on the Diz river in 1962 (which provided the region not only with hydroelectricity but also with water for market gardening and other agricultural projects on a large scale); the development of the natural gas industry (which exported 8.7 billion cu. m of natural gas to the USSR in 1973), and, finally, the development of Khorramshahr (or Khurramshahr) as one of the major ports-of-entry on the Persian/Arabian Gulf. The IRAN-IRAQ WAR (1980–88) was largely fought in Khuzistan, causing extensive damage.

BIBLIOGRAPHY

LEWIS, B., C. PELLAT, and J. SCHACHT, eds. *The Encyclopaedia of Islam.* Vol. 5. Leiden, 1986, pp. 80–81.

Parvaneh Pourshariati

Khyber, Mir Akbar   [1925–1978]

Afghan Marxist leader.

Born in 1925 in Logar province, Mir Akbar Khyber graduated from military high school in 1947. He was imprisoned for his political activities in 1950, and spent the next five years in jail. He became a leading member of the Parcham faction of the People's Democratic party of Afghanistan and the editor of its newspaper, *Parcham*. His assassination in April 1978 sparked a major demonstration that led to the Saur revolution.

BIBLIOGRAPHY

ARNOLD, ANTHONY. *Afghanistan's Two-Party Communism: Parcham and Khalq*. Stanford, Calif., 1983.

Grant Farr

Khyber Pass

Pakistani pass into Afghanistan.

The Khyber Pass begins about ten miles (16 km) outside the Pakistani city of Peshawar in the Northwest Frontier Province and ends on the Afghan border at Torkham. Because it is the main connection between Afghanistan and the Indian subcontinent, the route through the Khyber Pass constitutes one of the major means of access to Central Asia. The pass, which narrows at one point to 200 yards (183 m) and reaches an altitude of 3,500 feet (1,068 m) is situated in the Afridi Tribal Areas, where the government has little authority; as a result, kidnapping and smuggling are common occurrences along the route. The treaty of Gandamak (1879) gave control of the pass to the British, who built a narrow-gauge railroad from Peshawar to Torkham.

BIBLIOGRAPHY

ADAMEC, LUDWIG. *Historical Dictionary of Afghanistan*. Metuchen, N.J., 1991.

Grant Farr

Kianuri, Nur al-Din   [1916–   ]

First secretary of Iran's Tudeh party, 1978 to 1983.

Nur al-Din Kianuri was born in the village of Nur in Mazandaran. His grandfather was Ayatollah Fazlollah NURI, the famous arch-conservative clerical leader executed during the CONSTITUTIONAL REVOLUTION.

Kianuri's father, however, was a prominent proconstitutionalist, later killed in a street shoot-out. Kianuri received his schooling in Tehran, studied architecture in Germany during the late 1930s, and joined the faculty of Tehran University in 1941. He became a member of the TUDEH PARTY, Iran's Communist organization, in 1942 and was elected to its central committee in 1948. In the mid-1940s, he married Maryam Firuz, the head of the Tudeh women's organization. Maryam Firuz is the daughter of Prince Nasrat al-Dowleh (Farmanfarmayan), a wellknown QAJAR DYNASTY aristocrat killed by Reza Shah PAHLAVI.

Kianuri fled Iran after the 1953 coup and spent over twenty-six years in exile—mostly in East Germany. He was elected first secretary of the Tudeh party in late 1978, because he headed the wing of the party that supported the Iranian Revolution—a policy favored by the then Soviet Union. In 1983, however, when the Tudeh criticized the Islamic Republic of Iran for prolonging the war against Iraq, much of the their leadership, including Kianuri, were arrested and tortured into "confessing" that they were spies and traitors plotting to overthrow Ayatollah Ruhollah KHOMEINI. Although most of his colleagues were executed, Kianuri and Maryam Firuz were released in 1991 without any explanation.

BIBLIOGRAPHY

"Bozorgmard-e Tarikh-e Mo'aser-e Iran" (The Great Man of the Contemporary History of Iran). *Rah-e Tudeh*, March 11, 1983.
KIANURI, NUR AL-DIN. *Khatirat-e Nur al-Din Kianuri* (The Memoirs of Nur al-Din Kianuri). Tehran, 1993.

Ervand Abrahamian

Kiarostami, Abbas   [1940–   ]

Iranian film director.

Abbas Kiarostami, perhaps postrevolutionary Iran's most influential and famous film director, was born in Tehran. He graduated from Tehran University's School of Fine Arts, where he studied painting. His films have won wide critical acclaim in the west. In 1986, his *Where Is My Friend's House* won the Bronze Leopard Award, as well as the Award of the International Confederation of Cinema Newspapers at Locarno Film Festival in Switzerland. In 1995, again at Locarno, Kiarostami, dubbed "the Magnificent," won the first jury prize for *Under the Olive Trees*, his first commercial success.

BIBLIOGRAPHY

ROTH, LAURENT. "Kiarostami le magnifique" (Kiarostami the Magnificent). *Cahiers du cinema* 493 (July–August 1995): 67–114.

Neguin Yavari

Kibbutz

Voluntary, communal settlement, unique to Israel.

Originally the kibbutz (plural: kibbutzim) was agricultural, but since the 1970s there has been a move to industrialize. In 1991, approximately 127,000 people lived on 270 kibbutzim.

The kibbutz dates back to 1909 when the first *kvutsa*, or small commune, was founded at Deganya on the south shore of the Sea of Galilee. The kvutsa (plural: *kvutsot*) functioned as a large family. After World War I, a new influx of Jewish immigrants into Palestine resulted in the creation of larger settlements. These were known as kibbutzim and the first was set up at Ein Harod in the Galilee in 1921. No significant distinction, other than size, remains between kvutsot and kibbutzim.

The kibbutzim have played a very significant role in the development of Israeli society. Many early members came from Socialist Zionist youth movements in Eastern Europe. In conformity with the ideas of Aaron David GORDON and Ber BOROCHOV, these pioneers proposed redeeming the land of Israel and transforming the Jewish people. Redeeming the land would result from transforming swamps and deserts into agricultural land and creating rural settlements. The Jewish people would do this with their own hands and would thus regain their direct association with the land and would become workers again. This was of crucial ideological importance: Diaspora Jews were generally forbidden to own or farm land. They became traders and took on other urban occupations and thus became either members of the bourgeoisie or employees.

The kibbutz offered a radical change in Jewish sociology. Jews became farmers on land owned by the Jewish people as a whole. Through the kibbutzim and their affiliated organizations in the workers' economy, they played a vital role in the development of the pre-state Jewish community (YISHUV) and then in the State of Israel. The kibbutzim also played a vital role in the defense of the Yishuv and then of the state. They were often deliberately located on the borders to act as defense points, and their members have played a disproportionately large role in the armed forces.

The kibbutz is run by its members, through meetings of its members and through a secretariat and committees. The governing principle, which still applies to most kibbutzim, is the socialist motto: from each according to his ability, to each according to his need. Work is organized by the kibbutz and each member is assigned a job; rotation of jobs is also a fundamental principle. Members may request particular jobs; these requests are met in accordance with the needs of the kibbutz as a whole and in line with the need to meet the requests of other members. As the population of the kibbutzim has aged, so they have started industries and other commercial services such as guest houses.

Consumption is also organized on a communal basis. There is a communal dining room, which acts as the central meeting place on the kibbutz. Members are provided with the main services (health, education) either directly by the kibbutz or on a local basis in coordination with the relevant authorities. The kibbutz, through its elected committees, organizes such services as entertainment, counseling, absorption of newcomers, and help for the elderly.

Nurseries are provided for babies and young children in order to free mothers for work and to provide the children with a communal framework to grow up in. A primary school is often located on the kibbutz and older children usually go to a regional kibbutz school, where they mix with others from neighboring non-kibbutz settlements and towns. There has been a move away from communal accommodation for young children, which was a feature of many kibbutzim in the early days. Most young children now live with their parents.

Members have a small budget, which can be spent on the kibbutz and, on a limited basis, outside. In recent years there have been many changes in economic and social arrangements in the kibbutzim. On some, the dining room is hardly used; on many, telephones and television in members' homes have weakened or changed the social climate. A few kibbutzim are trying to introduce private incomes, which would be a major ideological break, both with the past and also with other kibbutzim.

The kibbutzim belong to different movements, each of which are politically affiliated and which provide a wide range of services to them. The kibbutz is obliged to accept decisions of the movement and this has at times caused frictions.

One of the most important aspects of the kibbutz movement is the mutual guarantee: through the movement, each kibbutz helps to support the others. In the late 1980s, as many kibbutzim and their affiliated organizations (such as regional, agricultural processing plants) ran into severe financial difficulties, the effects spread from financially weaker to stronger kibbutzim through the operation of the mutual guarantee. In 1992, the government wrote off 400 million shekels of debt, which the kibbutzim owed to the banks. As part of the rescue plan, many kibbutzim reduced consumption and reorganized their economic enterprises. In some cases, this reorganization involved going into partnership with the private sector and the sale of shares in kibbutz companies on the stock exchange.

There are three main kibbutz movements. Ihud Ha-Kvutsot ve Hakibbutzim (The Union of Kvutsot and Kibbutzim) was founded in 1951, a union of a kvutsot and a kibbutz movement. It was associated with the MAPAI political party, which is now the Labor party. It can be described as a liberal socialist movement: young children always lived at home on its kibbutzim and personal freedom was maximized within the communal context. In 1980 it joined with Ha-kibbutz Ha-Meuhad to form TAKAM (The United Kibbutz Movement).

Ha-kibbutz Ha-Meuhad was founded in 1927. Its kibbutzim tended, in the 1920s and 1930s, to be larger than those of Ihud. It encouraged membership from outside the youth movements so as to integrate as wide a section of the population as possible. Its first kibbutz was Ein Harod.

Hakibbutz Ha-artzi shel Ha-Shomer Ha-Tza'ir (The National Kibbutz of the Young Guard) was founded in 1927. It is a left-wing movement based on class struggle and the creation of a socialist society. Its first kibbutz was founded at Bet Alfa in the Galilee in 1922.

Kibbutz Ha-Dati (The Religious Kibbutz Movement) was founded in 1935 to combine religious practice with communal living. Its socialism is based on biblical concepts of social justice and human relations.

BIBLIOGRAPHY

LEON, DAN. *The Kibbutz.* Oxford, 1964.
NEAR, HENRY. *The Kibbutz Movement, A History,* vol. 1. Oxford, 1992.
SPIRO, M. E. *Kibbutz: Venture in Utopia.* New York, 1963.
VITELES, H. *A History of the Cooperative Movement in Israel.* Vol. 2. *The Evolution of the Kibbutz Movement.* Vol. 3, *An Analysis of the Farm Sectors of the Kibbutz Movement.* London, 1968.

Paul Rivlin

Kibbutz Movement

Association representing agricultural collectives.

The movement (Ha-Tnu'ah Ha-Kibbutzit Ha-Meuhedet; acronym, TAKAM) is an association comprising three of the four federations of agricultural collectives in Israel that operated in Palestine before independence, including Hever Ha-Kvutzot, Ha-Kibbutz Ha-Meuhad, and Ha-Kibbutz Ha-Artzi. The consolidation of the separate KIBBUTZ federations, to an extent, reflected both bureaucratic realignments since the 1948 independence of Israel and the changing balance of political party power in the election arena.

The kibbutz is a socialist community without private ownership and was first improvised in 1909 at Degania, in Ottoman Palestine, by young Jewish immigrants devoted to the establishment of a highly egalitarian society. Theirs was a small agricultural community, concentrating on a single crop. After World War I, immigrants from Europe and Russia brought ambitious schemes for an organization based on the Bolshevik Revolution, postulating that Palestine might only be developed by an all-embracing commune of Jewish workers. In 1921, they founded the first large kibbutz in the JEZREEL VALLEY at Ein Harod, with a diversified crop base and, eventually, with industries.

In 1924, a third form of collective was founded at Beit Alpha, by Ha-Shomer Ha-Tza'ir (Young Guard), rooted in egalitarian principles and the possibilities for self-fulfillment in a small community. An association of religious (Orthodox Jewish) kibbutzim, Ha-Kibbutz Ha-Dati, has not affiliated with the all-embracing kibbutz movement federation.

BIBLIOGRAPHY

DREZON-TEPLER, MARCIA. *Interest Groups and Political Change in Israel.* Albany, N.Y., 1990.

Donna Robinson Divine

Kikhya, Rushdi al-   [1900–1988]

Syrian politician and founder of the People's party.

Born in Aleppo, where he was elected deputy in 1936, 1943, 1947, 1949, and 1954. In 1948, together with other Aleppo leaders such as Nazim al-QUDSI and Mustafa BARMADA, al-Kikhya formed the PEOPLE'S PARTY. This party represented the interests of the business community in Aleppo and northern Syria. It won the support of the prominent ATASI FAMILY of Homs against the head of the NATIONAL BLOC headed by Shukri al-Quwatli and other notables from Damascus. In August 1949, al-Kikhya was appointed minister of interior in the cabinet headed by Hashim al-Atasi. In December 1949, he was elected speaker of the Syrian parliament. In September 1954, following the overthrow of the Shishakli dictatorship, the People's party participated in the first free elections in post-independence Syria. Al-Kikhya firmly believed in the union of Iraq and Syria under Hashimite rule.

BIBLIOGRAPHY

SEALE, PATRICK. *The Struggle for Syria: A Study of Post-War Arab Politics, 1945–1958.* New Haven, Conn., 1986.

George E. Irani

Kikhya Family

Political family of Cyrenaica (Libya).

Umar Mansur al-Kikhya was educated at the Ottoman Empire's capital, Constantinople. His first official post under the Turkish administration of CYRENAICA was as *kaimmakam* (district officer) of Gialo oasis. In 1905, the sultan gave him the title of pasha, and in 1908 he was one of three Cyrenaican representatives in the Ottoman parliament. After the 1911 Italian invasion of Libya, he went into exile in Egypt and practiced law in Alexandria to raise funds for the resistance in Libya. In 1920, he returned to Cyrenaica and became native-affairs adviser to Governor Giacomo di Martino. At a time when Italy was trying to put a Cyrenaican constitution and an elected parliament into effect, Umar Mansur acted as liaison between the Italian authorities and the head of the Sanusi Order, Sayyid (Emir) Idris. He was particularly active in the negotiations leading to the accord of al-Rajma in October 1920. When, however, these arrangements broke down in 1923 and Emir Idris al-Sanusi went into exile, Umar Mansur was tried on charges of misleading the Italian government and spent many years in prison and in exile.

After the Allies liberated most of North Africa during World War II, the British brought Umar Mansur back to Benghazi, where he began to campaign for the recognition of Idris as ruler of a self-governing Cyrenaican emirate, assisted by and formally allied to Great Britain. His was an important voice in keeping international public opinion aware of the Cyrenaican case at a time when it could easily have been ignored. On the declaration of Cyrenaican autonomy in July 1949, Umar Mansur was appointed head of the emir's *diwan* (royal court). In November 1949, he became prime minister of the first Cyrenaican government after his son, Fathi, had resigned as the designated prime minister. He also held the interior, foreign affairs, defense, and education portfolios. Although he initiated a vigorous program, he came into increasing conflict with the younger opposition leaders grouped around the OMAR MUKHTAR CLUB, largely on the emotive issue

of a purely Cyrenaican independence (which Umar Mansur and others of his generation favored) or the independence of a united Libya. Opposition to his administration also grew within the sole legal political organization, the Cyrenaican National Congress, and in March 1950 he was forced to resign. He was appointed president of the upper house of the all-Libyan parliament, the Senate, in March 1952, but was dismissed in October 1954 for his public criticism of the new base-leasing agreement with the United States.

Omar Mansur's son Fathi first entered public service as justice secretary in the new British military administration in Cyrenaica in 1943. In July 1949, Fathi had been named prime minister of the first Cyrenaican government, which took office in September, during his absence abroad. Fathi never took office, however, resigning on the grounds that his powers would have been too restricted. He returned to his law practice in Egypt.

In 1949, Hajj Rashid al-Kikhya was president of the Cyrenaican Legislative Assembly and was one of seven Cyrenaican representatives on the preparatory committee of twenty-one Libyan members, set up in July 1950, to decide the composition of the Libyan National Assembly and to draft the constitution.

BIBLIOGRAPHY

KHADDURI, MAJID. *Libya: A Study in Political Development.* Baltimore, 1963.
PELT, ADRIAN. *Libyan Independence and the United Nations.* New Haven, Conn., 1970.

John L. Wright

Kilometer 101 Talks

Negotiations at the end of the Arab–Israel War of 1973.

In October 1973, Israel's forces had surrounded Egypt's Third Army. Gen. Aharon Yariv of the Israel Defense Forces and Gen. Abd al-Ghani al-Gamasi of the Third Army met at kilometer 101 on the Cairo–Suez road to discuss a cease-fire and relief for the Egyptians. Though they made substantial progress, U.S. Secretary of State Henry Kissinger helped to conclude the talks in November and devised his own settlement in the form of the Sinai Agreements in 1974.

BIBLIOGRAPHY

O'BRIEN, CONOR CRUISE. *The Siege.* London, 1986.

Zachary Karabell

Kimche, David [1928–]

Israeli diplomat and writer.

Kimche was born in London and immigrated to Israel in 1948. He was educated at the Hebrew University in Jerusalem (Ph.D.) and the Sorbonne in Paris. In 1980 he was appointed foreign minister director-general under Prime Minister Menachem Begin; he was the Israeli delegate at Khalde, outside Beirut, Lebanon, in the December 1982 talks with the Lebanese and Americans discussing Israel's withdrawal from Lebanon following the ARAB–ISRAEL WAR of 1982.

He was a journalist with the *Jerusalem Post* and a guest lecturer at Tel Aviv and Bar Ilan universities. Kimche is also the author of numerous books, among them are *The Secret Roads, Both Sides of the Hill,* and *The Afro–Asian Movement.*

Ann Kahn

King Abd al-Aziz University

See Umm al-Qura University

King–Crane Commission

A U.S. commission of inquiry sent to Syria and Palestine in 1919 to investigate the wishes of the populace regarding the political future of the territories.

U.S. president Woodrow Wilson opposed British and French plans to annex territories conquered from the Ottomans during World War I. The proposed League of Nations provided a formula, the mandate system, that would allow these territories to be taken over temporarily, until they were guided to self-determination, by the power to whom the mandate was awarded. The covenant of the league stipulated that "the wishes of these communities must be a principal consideration in the selection of a mandatory power." At the Council of Four, the United States proposed an Allied commission consisting of representatives from France, Great Britain, Italy, and the United States to ascertain the wishes of the inhabitants of Syria, Palestine, and Iraq. The British and French, at odds with each other and interested in dividing up the spoils of war, declined to join. President Wilson then sent two U.S. representatives, Henry C. King and Charles R. Crane, to interview Syrians and Lebanese regarding Syria and Palestinians and Jews regarding Palestine. The two envoys spent June and July 1919 in the region but did not go to Iraq.

The King–Crane Commission found that the inhabitants of Syria and Palestine opposed being placed under a mandate, which they perceived as a disguised form of colonial rule. They wanted independence for a united Greater Syria, including Lebanon and Palestine, with Faisal as king; but if they had to accept tutelage, their first choice of guardian would be the United States, which had no history of imperialism, and their second would be Great Britain. The Syrians were opposed to any French rule.

The King–Crane Commission also looked into Zionist claims and demands, which it had initially supported. It concluded that Zionist leaders anticipated "complete dispossession of the present non-Jewish inhabitants of Palestine, by various forms of purchase." General opposition to Zionism led the King–Crane Commission to recommend limiting Jewish immigration, reducing the Zionist program, and giving up on the project of a Jewish commonwealth in Palestine.

The British and French ignored the report and occupied and divided up the territories between themselves. As the British historian Elizabeth Monroe points out: The "report came to nothing because of Wilson's failure to grasp that consultation is a virtue only if the consulting authority has the will and the ability to act on what it finds."

BIBLIOGRAPHY

HUREWITZ, J. C. *British–French Supremacy, 1914–1945.* Vol. 2 of *The Middle East and North Africa in World Politics: A Documentary Record,* 2nd rev. ed. New Haven, Conn., 1979.

MONROE, ELIZABETH. *Britain's Moment in the Middle East, 1915–1956.* Baltimore, 1963.

PALESTINE GOVERNMENT. *A Survey of Palestine for the Information of the Anglo–American Committee.* 2 vols. Jerusalem, 1946–1947. Reprint, Washington, D.C., 1991.

SMITH, CHARLES D. *Palestine and the Arab–Israeli Conflict.* New York, 1988.

Philip Mattar

King David Hotel

Famous hotel in Jerusalem.

The King David hotel served as the British military and administrative headquarters during the Palestine mandate period (1922–1948). On July 22, 1946, it was blown up by the Irgun, a Jewish underground organization. Two other Jewish organizations, Haganah and Lehi, had collaborated in planning the attack but pulled out at the last minute. Ninety-one people, mostly British officials, were killed.

While publicly condemned, the bombing was a forceful statement of Zionist intent to win statehood after World War II. The hotel was rebuilt and still houses tourists on King David Street.

BIBLIOGRAPHY

SACHAR, HOWARD M. *A History of Israel.* New York, 1982.

Elizabeth Thompson

King Fahd University for Petroleum and Minerals

University in Saudi Arabia.

The King Fahd University for Petroleum and Minerals was founded in 1964 to train engineers for the petroleum industry. It is based in Dhahran, the home of ARAMCO. It has an enrollment of about three thousand students, to be increased by 1997 to fifty-five hundred undergraduates and seven hundred graduate students. It offers bachelor of science degrees and programs of higher studies.

Jean-François Seznec

Kings' Alliance

Brief alliance (1957–1958) of monarchs of Middle Eastern countries in opposition to Egypt's President Nasser.

During the late 1950s, a period which the scholar Malcolm Kerr labeled the "Arab Cold War," two distinct blocs formed in the Middle East. One revolved around Egypt's president, Gamal Abdel NASSER, while the other was a coalition of monarchical states. For many years after World War I, the ruling house of Saudi Arabia had been hostile to the Hashimite rulers of Iraq and Jordan, but with the threat of Nasserism looming over them, the monarchs of these countries buried their old animosities and formed a loose coalition known as the Kings' Alliance toward the end of 1957. King Sa'ud of Saudi Arabia, King Hussein of Jordan, and King Faisal II of Iraq with his minister Nuri al-Sa'id and the regent Abd al-Ilah formed the main core of this coalition. The alliance was never more than symbolic at best, and the July 1958 revolution in Iraq that ended the lives of Nuri and Faisal ended the Kings' Alliance as well.

BIBLIOGRAPHY

KERR, MALCOLM. *The Arab Cold War.* London, 1970.
LENCZOWSKI, GEORGE. *The Middle East in World Affairs,* 4th ed. Ithaca, N.Y., 1980.

Zachary Karabell

King Sa'ud University

The oldest, largest, and probably the most prestigious of Saudi Arabia's universities.

King Sa'ud University opened in 1957 as the University of al-Riyadh. Though its main campus is located in Riyadh, there are several other campuses as well. The name was changed in 1982 to commemorate King Sa'ud's role in founding the university. As the flagship university of the Saudi system, King Sa'ud University offers virtually all important specializations in both arts and sciences. The language of instruction is Arabic, except for engineering and medicine, which are taught in English. In 1992, the university employed 2,765 faculty and had 31,321 students, while the library possessed over 1 million bound volumes as well as nearly 15,000 manuscripts.

Khalid Y. Blankinship

King Talal Dam

Dam in northern Jordan.

Built on the Zarqa river from 1972 to 1978, the King Talal Dam originally held 76 million cubic yards (58 million cu m) of water for irrigation, urban use, and as a power source for a 5 megawatt generator. The dam was raised in 1983, increasing its capacity to 118 million cubic yards (90 million cu m) of water.

BIBLIOGRAPHY

The Middle East and North Africa 1991, 37th ed. London, 1991.
NYRUP, RICHARD F., ed. *Jordan: A Country Study.* Washington, D.C., 1980.

Michael R. Fischbach

Kinneret, Lake

See Galilee, Sea of

Kirkbride, Alec Seath   [?–1978]

British colonial administrator.

Kirkbride, who had lived in Egypt since he was nine years old, enlisted in the British armed services in 1916 and spent his entire service career in Arab countries. At the beginning of 1918, he was posted to the Arab army, commanded by Emir Faisal ibn Husayn. This put him in touch with a number of experts on the Middle East, such as Wyndham Deedes, T. E. Lawrence, and D. G. Hogarth.

Kirkbride left the army in April 1921 and was posted as the British representative in the southern town of Karak in Transjordan. He first dealt with Emir ABDULLAH IBN HUSAYN during 1922 and 1923, when Abdullah negotiated with the British to recognize his claim for independence while ensuring that Transjordan would be excluded from the provisions of the Balfour Declaration. Throughout his service in Transjordan and Jordan, Kirkbride helped Emir Abdullah to negotiate with Britain's colonial office.

When Jordan became independent in 1946, Kirkbride was the first British minister accredited there. He continued his close involvement with King Abdullah, and after the king's assassination in 1951, he remained as ambassador and helped ensure the legitimacy of the succession of Abdullah's son Talal. In December 1951, Kirkbride established the first British ministry in Libya. He retired from public service three years later.

BIBLIOGRAPHY

KIRKBRIDE, SIR ALEC SEATH. *Crackle of Thorns: Experiences in the Middle East.* London, 1956.
———. *From the Wings: Amman Memoirs, 1947–1951.* London, 1976.

Jenab Tutunji

Kirkuk

A city in northeastern Iraq at the foot of the Zagros mountains.

Historically a Kurdish city, Kirkuk today has an Arab plurality. According to the 1977 census, the population was 535,000, though it had fallen to 175,000 by 1990. The city is in the heartland of the Kurdish region; the Kirkuk oil field, the largest oil field in Iraq, is also the center of the Iraqi petroleum industry. Refineries and major oil pipelines lead from Kirkuk to Syria, Lebanon, and Turkey.

Reeva S. Simon

Kisakürek, Necip Fazıl   [1905–1983]

Turkish Islamist publisher and writer.

Born in Istanbul, Kisakürek began his writing career at a Kemalist monthly youth magazine in the late 1920s. He wrote for other magazines, like Sedat Simavi's *Yedigün* (Seven Days), and in 1936 started his own arts and ideas journal, *Ağaç,* which he published for one year. Kisakürek also published three volumes of poetry in those years and began writing plays about materialism and despair in modern life. Although his works in this period expressed the mystical turn of mind that would later inform his Islamist politics, in the 1930s, he joined Western-influenced artistic movements like the D-Group.

In 1945, he became editor of *Büyük Doğu* (Great East), an Islamist magazine whose anti-Westernization message carried influence particularly in rural areas. From 1950, the ruling Democrat party provided financial support to the magazine, but in a twist of politics, Kisakürek was jailed in 1952 in a crackdown on politically oriented Islamist publications. He resumed publication of *Büyük Doğu* and turned it into a daily paper in 1957. In the 1960s and 1970s, he alternatively lent his influence in religious circles to the National Salvation Party and to the neofascist National Movement Party of Colonel Alparslan Turkeş. Kisakürek continued writing plays (several of which were made into films), poetry, and political memoirs in the 1960s and 1970s.

BIBLIOGRAPHY

AHMAD, FEROZ. *The Turkish Experiment in Democracy.* Boulder, Colo., 1977.

Elizabeth Thompson

Kisch, Frederick Hermann   [1888–1943]

British career officer; director of the Political Department and chairman of the Palestine Zionist Executive (PZE), 1923–1931.

Kisch was born in India, the son of a British civil servant. He served in military intelligence in Paris during and after the World War I peace conference (1919–1922). In 1923, Kisch's Anglo–Jewish background was put to use in efforts at improving the tense relations in Palestine between the *Yishuv* (Palestine's Jewish community) and the British mandate administration. Another of his priorities as PZE chairman was to convince both his superiors and local Jewish leaders of the importance of devoting more attention and funds to dealing with Arab–Jewish relations. He cultivated contacts with Emir Abdullah of Transjordan and others; supported C. M. Kalvaryski's attempts to organize a pro-Zionist Arab movement in Palestine; and sought to influence Arab opinion through press subsidies. He frequently criticized the British attitude of encouraging "extremist" Arab leaders while discouraging those who might have taken a more "moderate" view of Zionism. Throughout his tenure, he enjoyed the complete confidence of Dr. Chaim Weizmann, president of the Zionist Organization, and was seen by many as "Weizmann's man" in Palestine.

After leaving his Zionist post in 1931, Kisch resided and worked in Haifa and continued to advise the Yishuv on security matters. In 1938, he published an edited version of the extensive diaries that he had kept during his period as political secretary and chairman of the PZE. In addition to detailing the day-to-day complexities of Anglo–Zionist and Arab–Jewish relations, his *Palestine Diary* (London, 1938; reprinted New York, 1974) offers a colorful portrait of the political parties and personalities of the Yishuv during a formative period of its development.

Kisch returned to active military service in World War II as an army engineer with the rank of brigadier. He was killed while inspecting a minefield in Tunisia.

BIBLIOGRAPHY

BENTWICH, NORMAN, and MICHAEL KISCH. *Brigadier Frederick Kisch, Soldier and Zionist.* London, 1966.
CAPLAN, NEIL. "Britain, Zionism and the Arabs, 1917–1925." *Wiener Library Bulletin* 31 (1978): 4–17.
———. *Palestine Jewry and the Arab Question, 1917–1925.* London, 1978.

Neil Caplan

Kissinger, Henry [1923–   ]

American diplomat.

The son of a Jewish schoolteacher, Kissinger was born in Fürth, Germany. He and his family fled in 1938, settling ultimately in New York. He entered the City College of New York, but his studies were interrupted by World War II. During the war, Kissinger served with army intelligence, and subsequently worked with the U.S. occupation forces in Germany. In 1947, he enrolled at Harvard, where he earned his Ph.D. As a scholar, Kissinger contributed to the realist school of international relations, which argued that foreign policy should be based on rational calculations of state interests, not on ideals of freedom and democracy. He published two works on foreign policy, and became associate director of the Center for International Studies at Harvard University and a frequent contributor to the influential periodical *Foreign Affairs*.

In November 1968, President-elect Richard Nixon appointed Kissinger his national security ad-

viser. Nixon and Kissinger agreed on the need to transfer authority over foreign policy from the State Department and Congress to the president; the National Security Council was to be the mechanism for realizing this. In accordance with this plan, Kissinger did not support Secretary of State William P. ROGERS' 1969 Middle East peace plan, even after Egypt's President Gamal Abdel Nasser acepted it as a framework for negotiations. Indeed, for much of Nixon's first term, the Middle East was clearly a marginal area. Kissinger suggested that a prolonged stalemate "would move the Arabs toward moderation and the Soviets to the fringes of Middle East diplomacy."

In 1973 the ARAB–ISRAEL WAR moved from the periphery to center stage of American strategic interests. Kissinger, appointed secretary of state that September, was determined to use the war to start a peace process. He immediately realized that if either Israel or the Arabs achieved a decisive victory, it would be difficult to reach a compromise solution during peace negotiations. His strategy was therefore to seek a return to the prewar situation, thereby preventing either side from winning the war while creating momentum for a peace process.

Negotiations commenced immediately following the cease-fire of October 22, 1973. Kissinger believed it would be a mistake to seek a comprehensive settlement that could not be attained and, by leading to frustrated expectations, would result in an enhanced role for the Soviet Union in the Middle East. Instead, he elected to pursue a "step-by-step approach": achieving more modest goals that, by producing results, would create the momentum needed to tackle the bigger issues. In January 1974, Kissinger began the first episode of his "SHUTTLE DIPLOMACY": a series of flights between Tel Aviv and Aswan over six weeks, during which he hammered out the terms of Sinai I, a disengagement agreement separating the armies of Israel and Egypt. In May 1974, Kissinger undertook a similar round of shuttle diplomacy between Damascus and Tel Aviv to reach a disengagement agreement between Syria and Israel. In the winter of 1975, as President Gerald Ford's secretary of state, he embarked on a third round of shuttle diplomacy during which he negotiated Sinai II, which called for further withdrawal of Israel's troops into the Sinai desert.

BIBLIOGRAPHY

KISSINGER, HENRY. *Years of Upheaval.* Boston, 1982.
SCHULZINGER, ROBERT D. *Henry Kissinger: Doctor of Diplomacy.* New York, 1989.

David Waldner

Kitchener, Horatio Herbert   [1850–1916]

First earl of Khartoum, British field marshal, and colonial administrator in the Sudan, 1899–1900, and in Egypt 1911–1914.

Herbert Horatio Kitchener was born in Ireland, the second son of Henry Horatio Kitchener, an eccentric Anglo–Irish landowner. Educated at home, then in Switzerland (where he became fluent in French), and at the Royal Military Academy, Woolwich, England, Kitchener was commissioned in 1871 into the Royal Engineers. He devoted most of the rest of his life to sustaining the British Empire in Egypt, the Sudan, South Africa, and India. He never married.

While working on land surveys in Palestine, Cyprus, and the Sinai peninsula between 1874 and 1883, he learned Arabic and acquired a passion for porcelain and old furniture. He joined the reconstituted Anglo–Egyptian army in 1883, after Britain had occupied the country in 1882 because of Suez Canal debts and the Urabi revolt. He participated in Lord Wolseley's tardy expedition of 1885 that failed to rescue the hapless British General Charles ("Chinese") GORDON at the siege of Khartoum in the Egyptian Sudan. He also helped delimit the territory of the sultan of Zanzibar and served as governor-general of the Eastern Sudan before returning to the Anglo–Egyptian army as adjutant general in 1888.

Kitchener's exploits in battle against the Mahdi and his followers and his reputation as a methodical and penurious military organizer captured the attention of the British public and ruling elite. He was promoted to *sirdar* (commander in chief) of the Anglo–Egyptian army in 1892. Under control of the Foreign Office and Lord Cromer, Kitchener brilliantly organized the River War campaigns of 1896–1898, which ousted the followers of the Mahdi from the Sudan. His desecration of the Mahdi's remains failed to harm his extraordinary popularity in England, and the bemustached Kitchener of Khartoum became the symbol of Great Britain at her imperial zenith.

At Fashoda, in 1898, he repulsed France's efforts to control the Nile's headwaters. In South Africa, he organized the ruthless crushing of the Boers. Then, while commanding the Indian Army, he deviously wrecked the political career of India's viceroy, Lord Curzon. When Sir Eldon Gorst (the former British foreign office agent and consul-general in Egypt) died in 1911, the Liberal government sent Kitchener back to Egypt as agent and consul-general, with instructions to keep Egypt quiet while seeing to its economic health.

Kitchener was regal in style, where Gorst had been self-effacing. Egypt was relatively quiet politically during Kitchener's tenure, and he worked to improve the lot of the Egyptian *fellah* (peasant) and extended the irrigation system. He banned nationalist newspapers and excluded certain Egyptian leaders, including Sa'd Zaghlul, from office. At least two attempts by nationalists to assassinate him failed. He cut Khedive Abbas Hilmi II's finances, trying, unsuccessfully, to force him to abdicate. As the Ottoman Empire waned, he kept Egypt "neutral." Hoping to bring it and the Sudan under formal British control, he sought to end the CAPITULATIONS and opened anti-Ottoman discussions with various Arab leaders, especially the son of Sharif Husayn ibn Ali of Mecca.

When World War I began, British Prime Minister Herbert H. Asquith insisted Kitchener join the British cabinet as war minister. He grasped the nature of modern war, but his popularity and prestige were not enough to compensate for his deficiencies as a politician, administrator, and organizer. He died midway through the war.

BIBLIOGRAPHY

MAGNUS, PHILIP. *Kitchener: Portrait of an Imperialist*. London, 1958.
ROYLE, TREVOR. *The Kitchener Enigma*. London, 1985.

Peter Mellini

Kléber, Jean-Baptiste   [1753–1800]

French general.

Kléber accompanied Gen. Napoléon Bonaparte to Egypt in 1798, and was placed in command of the expeditionary force of France after Napoléon's departure in 1799. Kléber then negotiated the terms of the French evacuation with Britain's Admiral Sidney Smith, but when the British government refused the terms, Kléber attempted to reconquer Egypt. He defeated an Anglo–Turkish army at Heliopolis in 1800 and took Cairo, but was then assassinated by an Egyptian.

BIBLIOGRAPHY

ANDERSON, M.S. *The Eastern Question*. London, 1966.
Chambers Biographical Dictionary. Cambridge, U.K., 1990.

Zachary Karabell

Klibi, Chadli   [1925–   ]

Tunisian diplomat.

Klibi was educated at Sadiqi College in Tunis and the Sorbonne in Paris. He started his professional career as a professor and journalist in the early 1950s. He served in a number of capacities in the ruling Destour Socialist party. His first position in government was as director general of Tunisian radio and television. He went on to hold a number of other positions, including secretary of state for information and cultural affairs, mayor of Carthage, secretary of state for cultural affairs, minister of cultural affairs, and minister of information.

Bryan Daves

Knaz, Yehoshua [1937–   ]

Israeli novelist and critic.

Yehoshua Knaz was born in Petah Tiqvah, a small rural town not far from Tel Aviv. He studied philosophy and Romance languages at the Hebrew University and went on to the Sorbonne, where he studied French literature.

Coming of age toward the end of the British mandate, during the years of Israel's struggle for autonomy, he provides sensitive insights into the dilemmas confronting his generation in his early novels. In *Heart Murmur,* Knaz chronicles the lives of a group of young recruits whose adjustment to army life is complicated by the fact that they are new immigrants from highly diverse backgrounds. In *Musical Moment,* he probes the surface of everyday life, offering deftly constructed fragments of experience that reflect the mood of the period of austerity that followed establishment of the State of Israel. In his highly acclaimed novel, *The Way to the Cats,* Knaz re-creates the charged environment of an old-age home—a dehumanizing institution that exploits the psychic weaknesses and physical infirmities of its effectively captive inhabitants. Loneliness, a pervasive theme in Knaz's work, permeates this novel. Its often grotesque characters are rendered with painstaking detail so that the reader recognizes counterparts beyond this closed circle of age, illness, and inevitable decay.

Knaz has been on the staff of *Haaretz,* one of Israel's leading newspapers, writing on theater and literature. Three of his novels have appeared in English.

Zeva Shapiro

Knesset

The parliament of Israel.

A unicameral legislature containing 120 members, the Knesset is elected for a term of 4 years, but a majority of its members may call a new election

The Knesset in Jerusalem, seen from a distance. (Mia Bloom)

before the expiration of its term. As the supreme locus of power, it can pass laws on any topic without being subject to checks and balances including judicial review (except for procedural matters). The Knesset can also change the several Basic Laws, which serve as a substitute for a constitution. But changing these laws requires a greater number of votes, in contrast to simple majorities for ordinary legislation. The Knesset chooses the prime minister and the cabinet and can dismiss the government through a no-confidence vote (a process that has never succeeded). It also elects the nonpartisan and politically powerless but symbolically important president of the state. In addition to legislative duties, it has broad investigative powers. The Knesset meets twice yearly and must be in session for no less than eight months. It normally does not meet on Fridays or Sundays out of respect to Israel's Muslims and Christians. The deputies enjoy a wide scope of legislative immunity, which applies to many of their personal actions as well as to those directly connected to their legislative duties.

The Knesset is organized into several major committees: Law, Constitution, and Justice; Finance; Foreign Affairs and Security; Immigration and Absorption; Economics; Education and Culture; Interior Affairs and Environment; Labor and Welfare; State Control; and the House Committee, which together with the speaker sets the agenda and resolves disputes about the jurisdiction of functional committees. Most of the Knesset's work—putting legislation into final form and conducting investigations—occurs in committee. The Knesset also frequently holds full-scale public debates on important issues. Almost always spirited and not infrequently filled with animosity and sometimes violence, the advent of television has helped make the debates a focus of great public attention. The grounds around the Knesset building are also one of the favorite sites for Israel's numerous political demonstrations.

The legislative process is similar to those in most other countries. After a first reading, a bill is sent to the applicable committee where it may be studied and amended, after which it is referred back to the full Knesset for second and third readings.

The structure of the Israeli government can be described as a classical parliamentary system, and therefore the Knesset has little of the political independence found in a system with separation of powers. All committees are made up according to the distribution of party strength within the Knesset, and the deputies are restrained by their parties under tight discipline, except on what are called matters of conscience, such as religious matters. The individual roles of Knesset members are enhanced in that they may introduce private bills, may question members of the government who are obliged to reply within specified time periods, and may present motions for debate of subjects that are not on the agenda presented by the government. However, it is rare that these actions have a significant impact.

Much of the subordination of Knesset members to their parties comes because of the Israeli electoral system. The entire country is a single constituency in a proportional representation system. Voting is by party lists only, and the placement of all of a party's candidates into positions on the lists is done by the central party organization. Among attempts at various electoral reforms has been a proposal to have at least some percentage of Knesset members elected from separate constituencies, but it has not been successful to date. There was more success on the matter of the electoral threshold, which until the 1992 election required a party or an individual candidate to poll only 1 percent of the votes to gain representation in the Knesset. The usual result was the presence of numerous minuscule parties, some consisting of a single individual. This created a situation that complicated the coalition-building that has been necessary throughout the history of the state—there has never been a time when a single party had a majority in the Knesset. When the threshold was raised to 1.5 percent in 1992, the number of parties comprising the legislature dropped markedly.

These structural characteristics also strengthen the role of the executive at the expense of parliamentary independence. It has been estimated that 95 percent of the bills are introduced into the Knesset by the government. Knesset debate on them, both in committees and on the floor, seldom leads to any outcome other than that desired by the coalition members. Although the Knesset usually includes most of Israel's important political leaders—and despite the fact that many are often very capable, outspoken, and hardworking—very few Israeli political leaders have based their rise in politics on Knesset membership.

BIBLIOGRAPHY

ARIAN, ASHER. *Politics in Israel. The Second Generation.* Chatham, N.J., 1985.
Encyclopedia Judaica. Vol. 10.
ROLEF, S. ed. *Political Dictionary of the State of Israel.*

Walter F. Weiker

Koç, Vehbi [1901–1996]

Turkish businessman.

Born in Ankara, Koç entered trade in 1917 at a grocery store in Karaoğlan. In the 1920s he founded his own company, and accumulated businesses steadily, emphasizing assembly industries for import substitution, including cars and trucks. By the 1970s he was called the wealthiest man in Turkey. Koç's group sales doubled in the 1970s to $1.1 billion, profiting particularly from increased demand for consumer goods. In 1987, he controlled 117 firms. Koç Holding A.S. remained in the early 1990s the largest of an elite group of conglomerates that dominate Turkey's private economy. These companies have benefited from government ties and foreign capital.

Koç remained a member of the original state RE-PUBLICAN PEOPLE'S PARTY through the 1950s, when many businessmen were attracted to the new Democrat party and its call for free enterprise. But he resigned from his party in 1960, opposing the growing violence between the two, which harmed the business environment. After the military coup of 1960, Koç advocated strong government against anarchy, although in the 1970s he opposed efforts by the employers' union to allow government to intervene in collective bargaining. As a leading member of the Turkish Industrialists and Businessmen's Association (TÜSIAD), he advocated social reform in conjunction with promoting Turkey's entrance into the European Economic Community. His son Rehmi M. Koç has taken over as chairman of the vast Koç Holding A.S., which in 1991 employed some 35,500 people.

BIBLIOGRAPHY

BIANCHI, ROBERT. *Interest Groups and Political Development in Turkey.* Princeton, N.J., 1984.

Elizabeth Thompson

Kochi

Afghan pastoral nomads.

Kochi is the term generally used to describe the pastoral nomads in Afghanistan (*koch* means "pack" in Pushtu). The nomads move their sheep from high summer pasture in the central mountains of Afghanistan to winter pasture in the lower plains that surround the mountains. These Afghan nomads, most of whom are Pushtun or Baluchi, are estimated to number as many as two million, although no accurate count has been done.

BIBLIOGRAPHY

DUPREE, LOUIS. *Afghanistan.* Princeton, N.J., 1980.

Grant Farr

Koçu, Reşat Ekrem   [1905–1975]

Turkish historian.

While born in Istanbul, Koçu attended grade school in Bursa before graduating from the School of Literature in Istanbul in 1931. For most of his career, he taught history in high schools while writing histories, historical novels, and children's books. He also published many articles on Turkish history in daily newspapers. He was particularly associated in the 1950s with the journal *Türk Düşüncesi* (Turkish Thought), which sought to rationalize the eclectic borrowing of Western ideas since the TANZIMAT (reforms).

Koçu is mostly associated with the *Istanbul Encyclopedia,* the first volume of which he published in 1947. By 1975, he published eleven volumes, up to the letter G. The encyclopedia presents a highly original and broad view of the city and its history, although it is sometimes flawed by its lack of references. Koçu's major book on history was *The Janissaries,* published in 1964.

BIBLIOGRAPHY

Türkiye'de Dergiler Ansiklopediler. Istanbul, 1984.

Elizabeth Thompson

Kol, Moshe   [1911–]

Israeli cabinet minister and political leader.

Moshe Kol was founder of the Progressive party in 1932, which later became the Independent LIBERAL PARTY, for which he served as chairman of the executive committee. He also was minister of development and tourism (1965) and minister of tourism (1969).

Martin Malin

Kollek, Teddy   [1911–]

Israeli politician; mayor of Jerusalem, 1965–1993.

Born in Hungary, Teddy Kollek moved in 1934 to Palestine, where he was an active supporter of David BEN-GURION in the formative years of the State of Israel. In 1935, he became a founding member and also a resident of Kibbutz Ein Gev. In 1942, he was recruited by the Jewish Agency to serve as an intelligence officer in Istanbul, where he helped maintain contact with Jewish communities in Europe, both in areas outside of Nazi territory and those under Nazi control. Much intelligence of importance to the Allied cause came through this channel, as did the initial news about the Holocaust and the destruction of European Jewry. After returning from Istanbul, in the summer of 1943, Kollek continued to work for the intelligence branch of the Jewish Agency. He was frequently sent to Cairo by Re'uven Shiloah, head of intelligence for the Jewish Agency's political department. When in Egypt, Kollek arranged for stolen British weaponry to be smuggled back to Palestine so that it could be used by the Jewish Defense Force in Palestine.

In the 1940s his principal contribution to the Jewish nationalist movement was the acquisition of armaments, primarily in the United States, where he worked for the Haganah mission to the United States from 1947 to 1948. After returning to Jerusalem following World War II, Kollek was sent back to the United States to work with Abba Eban as an officer in the newly established Israeli embassy in Washington. He was primarily responsible for liaison with American Jewish groups and the U.S. State Department. In 1949, he was made head of the United States desk of Israel's foreign office.

Shimon Peres first recommended that Kollek run for the office of mayor of Jerusalem in 1965. He wanted Kollek to represent his new party, RAFI, which was primarily made up of supporters of David Ben-Gurion who were unhappy with MAPAI. Although Kollek did not want the position, he accepted the assignment to bolster the political support of Ben-Gurion. Kollek won the election and served as mayor of Jerusalem until he was defeated in 1993 by Ehud Olmert. One of Kollek's initiatives as mayor involved the establishment of the Jerusalem Foundation, whose goal was to raise money for the beautification and cultural enhancement of Jerusalem.

The Jerusalem Foundation was an enormous success, and was instrumental in building parks, stadiums, buildings, roads, and any number of cultural and recreational initiatives.

Although Kollek was offered a number of other positions over the years, including the position of minister of tourism, head of the Weizmann Institute, head of the Jewish Agency, and others, he remained as mayor of Jerusalem.

BIBLIOGRAPHY

KOLLEK, TEDDY. *For Jerusalem: A Life.* New York, 1978.
SACHAR, HOWARD M. *A History of Israel: From the Rise of Zionism to Our Time.* New York, 1981.

Gregory S. Mahler

Kol Yisrael

Israel Broadcasting Authority, an offshoot of the British-run Palestine Broadcasting Service, based in Jerusalem.

A department of the prime minister's office until 1965, Israel radio was thereafter placed by the Knesset (parliament) under the supervision of Kol Yisrael and its board of directors, and has since developed an increasingly diversified program schedule. Kol Yisrael currently broadcasts on seven networks in some twelve languages besides Hebrew.

Zev Maghen

Komitas   [1869–1935]

Armenian composer and ethnomusicologist.

Komitas (originally named Soghomon Soghomonian) was born in Kütahya, in central Anatolia. Orphaned at the age of eleven, he was placed at the Echmiadzin seminary in 1881 to develop his musical talents. Upon completing his education in 1893, he was appointed choirmaster in the cathedral church of Echmiadzin. He was ordained a celibate priest (*vardapet*). Komitas continued his musical education in Berlin (1896–1899), studying composition and conducting.

Though he composed works for the piano and the string quartet, and a cappella church music, Komitas's principal contribution to Armenian music came from his lifelong devotion to collecting and transcribing Armenian folksongs—he gathered more than 3,000 songs. In 1910 Komitas settled in Istanbul, where he trained a group of students in Armenian melody and formed a choir that performed the folk compositions

he had arranged for four parts. Komitas also identified the ethnomusical characteristics specific to Armenian folk composition and presented his findings at European ethnomusicological symposia. He won recognition as the principal Armenian national composer and was a member of the International Musical Society.

Komitas was among the 200 prominent figures of the Armenian community of Istanbul arrested on the night of 24 April 1915. He was the only member of this group to escape execution, rescued through the appeals of the International Musical Society. His experiences left Komitas's mind unhinged, however. He was taken to Paris in 1919, and spent the rest of his life in an asylum there.

Rouben P. Adalian

Komiteh

Any of several armed revolutionary groups formed in the early days of the Iranian Revolution.

Officially merged with the regular armed forces in 1991, the Komitehs (Islamic Revolutionary Committee) grew out of the small units of revolutionaries that mushroomed in mosques throughout Tehran in 1978 (see IRANIAN REVOLUTION). They were institutionalized by an official decree from Ayatollah KHOMEINI in 1979 and in 1983 were further institutionalized by parliament. The Komitehs sought to eliminate drug trafficking and other illegal activities, including those of opposition groups. Setting up checkpoints throughout the country to enforce Islamic regulations, Komiteh members arrested people for sacrilegious acts such as consumption of alcohol, nonobservance of proper Islamic attire, and extramarital relationships.

BIBLIOGRAPHY

IRAN RESEARCH GROUP. *Iran 89/90.* Bonn, 1989.

Neguin Yavari

Konya

Capital of Konya province, Turkey.

Konya is the leading grain-producing region of Turkey. Called Iconium by the Romans, Konya flourished from 1150 to 1250 C.E. as the capital of the Seljuk sultanate of Rum. Mystic poet Celaleddin Rumi's tomb (died 1273) is the richest of Konya's many monuments. The population in 1990 was 509,208.

BIBLIOGRAPHY

CAHEN, CLAUDE. *Pre-Ottoman Turkey*. New York, 1968.

John R. Clark

Konya, Battle of

Victory of Egyptian forces over the Ottoman army in December 1832.

An army sent by Egypt's Muhammad Ali and led by his son Ibrahim Paşa occupied Konya on November 21, 1832, after sweeping through Palestine and Syria during the previous year. On December 21, outside of Konya, Ibrahim Paşa defeated the army sent by Sultan Mahmud II and led by Mehmet V Reşat, opening the way for conquest of all of Anatolia. Russian, British, and French intervention forced an Egyptian retreat to Syria and Cilicia, which was formalized in an agreement in March 1833.

BIBLIOGRAPHY

MARSOT, AFAF LUTFI AL-SAYYID. *Egypt in the Reign of Muhammad Ali*. New York, 1984.

Elizabeth Thompson

Kook, Abraham Isaac Hacohen

[1865–1935]

Religious Zionist theoretician.

Born in Latvia, Kook's early education was in the local *cheder* (Jewish day school). His father was a scholar who gave him a great love for Eretz Yisrael, the Land of Israel. He then studied privately with several well-known Jewish scholars and, later, in the yeshiva in Volozhin. In addition to the traditional Talmud, he studied literature, philosophy, and *Kabbalah* (Jewish mysticism), during his young adult years; he also began writing on Talmudic literature, philosophy, and poetry. He served as a rabbi in Lithuania from 1888 to 1904 and immigrated to Palestine in 1904, where he was appointed rabbi of Jaffa. His enthusiastic support of Zionism, which he perceived as part of messianic redemption, antagonized much of the rabbinic leadership, whose members opposed, on religious grounds, both the notion and the movement. In 1914, he traveled to Europe and, prevented from returning by the outbreak of World War I, assumed the temporary position of rabbi in a London congregation; there he also attempted to establish a movement for spiritual renewal, Degel

Yerushalayim (Flag of Jerusalem), which was to supplement the secular Zionist movement. He returned to Palestine after the war, was appointed chief rabbi of Jerusalem and, when Palestine's rabbinate was established in 1921, he was selected as the Ashkenazic chief rabbi.

Kook's personal warmth and his interaction with all Jews, regardless of their degree of religiosity, as well as his attribution of holiness to all participants in the Zionist endeavor, became legendary and won him admiration even among the most secular Zionists; they mistook his individual acceptance of them as acceptance of their secularism in principle, however. Although firmly entrenched in traditional learning, he was also well versed in modern Western thought. He manifested simultaneously the sensitivity of the mystic and the intellectual sharpness that took cognizance of the rational. As a communal rabbi, he was attuned to contemporary difficulties and attempted to accommodate his rabbinic decisions to both his interpretation of religiolegal decision making and the contemporary situation. This was, at times, another source of tension in his relations with various Orthodox Jewish sects. Another manifestation of his relatively modern perspective was his view of higher Jewish education. He established a school, the yeshiva Mercaz Harav, which was unique in its incorporation of Bible studies and Jewish thought with traditional Talmudic studies, to promote a deep commitment to Zionism. The yeshiva was small and remained so after his death, when it was headed by his son, Rabbi Zvi Yehuda Kook, and his son-in-law, Rabbi Shalom Natan Ra'anan. It became a major institution only after the Arab–Israel War of June 1967.

Although Kook's voluminous writings are available in Hebrew, only some few have been translated into English. These are his *The Lights of Penitence; Lights of Holiness; The Moral Principles; Essays, Letters, and Poems* (translated and with an introduction by Ben Zion Bokser, New York, 1978). *Rabbi Kook's Philosophy of Penitence* is by Alter B. Z. Metzger (New York, 1968), and *Rav A. Y. Kook: Selected Letters* is translated and annotated by Tzvi Feldman (New York, 1986).

Chaim I. Waxman

Kook, Zvi Yehuda [1891–1982]

Lithuanian-born rabbi, teacher, and leader of Gush Emunim, the religious Zionist settlement movement.

Kook was born in Kovno, Lithuania, the son of Rabbi Abraham Isaac Kook. The family immigrated to Palestine in 1904, and Zvi studied in yeshiva (Jewish religious school) in Jerusalem. Later, he administered his father's yeshiva, Mercaz Harav. When his father died, in 1935, he began editing his father's extensive writings. He retained his father's mystical tradition and devotion to Zionism.

After the Arab–Israel War of June 1967, Kook's messianic approach to Zionism attained new levels of political significance. He advocated that Israel keep all the territories captured in that war, which made him a nationally known figure instead of the relatively quiet scholar he had been. He became the spiritual leader of the dominant nationalist wing of the religious Zionist movement. Following the October 1973 Arab–Israel War, he led the settlement movement called Gush Emunim into the new administered territories and opposed the evacuation of settlers from the Sinai, as was agreed by Israel and Egypt in the Camp David Accords.

Most of his writings, which include traditional essays on the Talmud and volumes on contemporary public issues, were edited by students and published posthumously. Among the latter is the two-volume work *Mitokh ha-Torah ha-Goelet* (From the Redeeming Torah), edited by Chaim Avihu Schwartz (Jerusalem, 1983, 1984), and *Le-Hilkhot zibur* (On the Laws of Community) (Jerusalem, 1987).

Chaim I. Waxman

Koor Industries

Major Israeli industrial conglomerate.

Koor Industries was founded by the HISTADRUT in 1944, and until 1958 it was part of the Solel Boneh group. Its main areas of activity are building materials, electronics, telecommunications, and chemicals.

Koor's biggest component is Tadiran, one of Israel's largest companies, a producer of electrical, electronic, and telecommunication equipment. It also owns Telrad, another major telecommunications producer. Other large companies in the group include the Nesher cement company and Soltam, an armaments firm, which has incurred financial losses as a result of declining military purchases. Among the older companies in the group are Phoenicia, a glassmaking company, and Koor's metal production subsidiary.

Between 1987 and 1989, Koor suffered a major financial crisis and accumulated losses of 845 million U.S. dollars. In 1989 alone, its losses came to 303 million U.S. dollars. After protracted negotiations between Hevrat Ovdim, the government, and the banks of Israel and abroad to whom Koor was in debt, the company was rescued by a government loan, made on condition that it implement a radical restructuring program. This involved reducing the labor force, selling subsidiaries, and closing unprofitable production lines. Koor's workforce fell from 31,000 in 1987 to about 17,000 in 1992. It has shares in 35 companies, compared with 130 in 1989.

In 1991 and 1992, Koor's financial position improved and its net profits in 1992 came to 375 million shekels. It has raised funds on the stock exchange and has been able to repay debts owed to the banks.

Given that the company was owned by the Histadrut, this posed serious ideological problems, but reforms were implemented. Koor's admission to the manufacturers' association of private sector employers in 1992 was an indication of the extent of these changes. It remains one of the largest industrial groups in the economy, although its share in total industrial output has declined sharply from about 25 percent in the early 1980s to about 8 percent in 1992. In that year, Koor's sales came to 6.1 billion shekels ($2.5 billion), of which 1.8 billion shekels ($725 million) were exports. Its operating profits equaled 630 million shekels. Koor is now considering investments in the tourist and retailing sectors.

Koor's shares are owned by the Israeli bank, Hevrat Ovdim, the government of Israel, and others. In 1993 the government sold shares that it acquired in exchange for loans made to Koor.

BIBLIOGRAPHY

HEVRAT OVDIM. *Economic Report 1992*. Tel Aviv, 1992. In Hebrew.
KLEINMAN, EPHRAIM. "The Histadrut Economy of Israel: In Search of Criteria." *Jerusalem Quarterly* 41 (1987).

Paul Rivlin

Koprülü, Mehmet Fuat   [1890–1966]

Turkish literary scholar, historian, and statesman.

Born in Istanbul during the last decades of the Ottoman Empire, Koprülü was descended from a family of viziers and taught at the Ottoman University (reorganized as Istanbul University) from 1913 to 1943. He was a prolific scholar, best known for his many fundamental contributions to the study of Turkish and Ottoman classical and folk literature, religion and political and institutional history. Koprülü was also prominent in public life. He was elected to the TURKISH GRAND NATIONAL ASSEMBLY in 1935, representing Kars and, later, Istanbul until 1957. He was a cofounder of Turkey's new opposition DEMOCRAT PARTY in 1946; following the party's

1950 electoral victory, he served as foreign minister (1950–1956), except for a brief period as a minister of state and deputy prime minister (1955).

BIBLIOGRAPHY

TANSEL, F. A. "Memleketimizin Acı Kaybı" (Our Country's Painful Loss). *Belleten* 30 (1966): 621–636.

Uli Schamiloglu

Koran

See Qur'an

Kordofan

Province of the Democratic Republic of Sudan.

Kordofan, which lies west of the BAHR AL-ABYAD, consists of black clay plains that support grasslands in the south; arid, treeless flatlands in the central part; and desert in the northern reaches. In the south, less than 100 miles west of the Bahr al-Abyad, are the Nuba mountains, home of the Nuba. On the plains roam the Baqqara, cattle-owning Arabs who migrate from south to north with the rains. In the arid north live the Kababish, camel-owning Arabs who also migrate with the rains. Their herds and gum arabic are marketed in the provincial capital of al-Ubayd, Umm Ruwaba, al-Nahud, and al-Rahad. Although Kordofan was the heartland of the Mahdist movement in the last two decades of the nineteenth century, the Tijanniyya *tariqa* (fraternity), as well as indigenous Sudanese Sufi orders (the Majdhubiyya, the Idrisiyya, and the Khatmiyya), are well represented.

Robert O. Collins

Korea and the Middle East

Korea has been in contact with the Middle East since the seventh century C.E.

Korea's relations with the Middle East began as early as the seventh century, when, during the Silla kingdom, it is recorded that the rulers employed mercenaries from Persia (now Iran). A statue of a soldier with Middle Eastern appearance still guards the tomb of one of the Silla rulers in the ancient capital of Kyonju. Ancient Persians were not the only Middle Easterners who fought in Korea; during the Korean War (1950–1954), Turkey sent 23,000 troops as part of the UNITED NATIONS forces defending South Korea.

Since the cease-fire in 1953, both Koreas (the Democratic People's Republic [North] and the Democratic Republic [South]), have competed for diplomatic recognition throughout the world, including the Middle East. North Korea's strength is based on its arms industry; large quantities of North Korean weapons have been exported to the Middle East, including missiles to Iran, Syria, and Libya. South Korea has made its presence felt in the region by sending skilled workers and engineers to the Persian/Arabian Gulf to construct industrial plants, often outbidding Japanese and European rivals. South Korea is also attracting investment from Saudi Arabia in its petroleum refining industry, for its own domestic market as well as for export to the newly industrialized East Asian economies—the world's fastest growing oil market.

BIBLIOGRAPHY

EMBREE, AINSLIE T., ed. *Encyclopedia of Asian History.* New York, 1988.

Kazuo Takahashi

Kosher

In Judaism, dietary regulations for daily life.

Yiddish, from Hebrew *kasher,* "proper" or "fit." The laws of *kashrut* (dietary laws) define foods fit for use, those that are kosher for Jews. They are mentioned in numerous verses of the Bible (especially in Deuteronomy), but they were interpreted for daily use by the sages of the TALMUD (in the commentaries called the Mishnah, c. 200 C.E., and in the Gemarah, commentaries on the Mishnah). They went into effect, for the most part, during the early Diaspora, and they helped establish both a religious and a folk sense of community among a dispersed nation. Those who traveled, who were engaged in international trade, or who were dispossessed from century to century could seek others who shared a sense of proper food handling.

The laws of kashrut define how to kill, handle, and prepare meat and dairy products. They define which animals may be considered food at all—and which parts of kosher animals may be used. For example, fish without fins and scales may not be eaten and; animals without horns and cloven hooves may not be eaten. Animals that eat carrion are unfit, as is the eating of meat with dairy products. Vegetables, fruits, and grains are never unfit. Thus, out of necessity, many Jews who travel without kosher food available become vegetarians in order to keep the kashrut tradition.

BIBLIOGRAPHY

FISHBANE, MICHAEL. *Judaism.* New York, 1987.

GILBERT, MARTIN, ed. *The Illustrated Atlas of Jewish Civilization: Four Thousand Years of Jewish History.* New York, 1990.

Zachary Karabell

Kosygin, Aleksey Nikolayevich
[1904–1980]

Premier of the USSR, 1964–1980.

Kosygin joined the Communist party in 1927 and held various party positions during the 1930s. From 1940 to 1960, he was deputy chairman and from 1960 to 1964, first deputy chairman. He became a full member of the Politburo in 1948, was removed in 1953 but reinstated in 1960.

After Premier Nikita S. Khrushchev's removal in 1964, Kosygin became premier; for much of the next ten years, he, Nikolai Podgorny, and Leonid BREZHNEV governed the USSR. Kosygin was a moderating influence on the other Soviet leaders and worked for good relations with the Middle East. He provided aid to Syria, Iraq, and Egypt. In addition to encouraging Egypt's President Gamal Abdel Nasser, Kosygin concluded a treaty of friendship with Ba'thist-run Iraq in 1972.

BIBLIOGRAPHY

LENCZOWSKI, GEORGE. *The Middle East in World Affairs,* 4th ed. Ithaca, N.Y., 1980.

Zachary Karabell

Kovner, Aba [1918–1988]

Organizer of Vilna ghetto revolt, World War II partisan leader, and acclaimed Hebrew poet.

Born in Sevastopol, Russia, and raised in Vilna, Kovner joined ha-Shomer ha-Tza'ir and planned immigration to Eretz Yisrael (Palestine) but was prevented by the outbreak of World War II. After his wartime resistance activities, Kovner helped organize clandestine Jewish refugee immigration to Eretz Yisrael (the *brikha*), and was briefly imprisoned by the British in Egypt. Returning to Israel, he joined the *Givati* brigade and fought in the War of Independence (Arab–Israel War, 1948). Books of Kovner's poetry, which focuses on themes of the Holocaust and Zionism, were published in Israel in the 1940s (reprinted from partisan newsletters),

1950s and 1960s. In 1970 he was awarded the Israel prize.

Zev Maghen

Krim, Belkacem   [1922–1970]

Algerian revolutionary leader.

A Kabyle (a BERBER group), he was born near Dra-el-Mizan and was an employee of the Mirabeau mixed commune. In 1945 he joined Messali al-Hadj's PARTI DU PEUPLE ALGÉRIEN (PPA) and then the Organisation Spéciale (OS). Following the assassination of a forest ranger in 1947, Krim was always on the run from French authorities. In 1954 he assisted in the organization of the COMITÉ RÉVOLUTIONNAIRE D'UNITÉ ET D'ACTION (CRUA) which led to the formation of the FRONT DE LIBÉRATION NATIONALE (FLN) and became one of the nine "historic chiefs" of the revolution (the ALGERIAN WAR OF INDEPENDENCE, 1954–1962). During the Gouvernement Provisoire de la République Algérienne (GPRA) years, he served as war minister (1958), vice president of the Council of Ministers (1958), foreign minister (1960), and minister of the interior (1961). He was the chief FLN negotiator with the French, resulting in the EVIAN CONFERENCE (March 1962). He opposed Ahmed BEN BELLA and was eventually forced to leave Algeria, given his opposition to Houari BOUMÉDIENNE, who took over the government in June 1965. In 1969 he organized in opposition the Mouvement Démocratique de Renouveau Algérien. He was assassinated, probably by Boumédiennist agents, in Frankfurt in 1970. Krim was officially rehabilitated in 1984.

BIBLIOGRAPHY

HORNE, ALISTAIR. *A Savage War of Peace: Algeria, 1954–1962.* 2nd ed. New York, 1987.

Phillip C. Naylor

Kubba, Muhammad Mahdi

Iraqi nationalist and government official.

Muhammad Mahdi Kubba was born to a Shi'a trading family of Samarra in Iraq. He espoused a form of pan-Arabism more common among Iraqi Sunnis, serving as vice-chairman of the nationalist Muthanna club between 1935 and 1941 and chairman of Hizb al-Istiqlal (Independence party) between 1946 and 1959. A deputy in the 1950s,

Kubba was a member of the Presidency Council between the revolution of 1958 and February 1959. His memoirs, *Mudhakkirati fi Samim al-Ahdath 1918–1958*, were published in 1965.

Peter Sluglett

Kubbara, Sami   [1904–?]

Syrian politician and parliamentarian.

In 1928, Kubbara obtained a law degree from the Syrian University and in 1930 a doctorate in law in France. In 1932, he returned to Paris and became president of the Syrian Arab Association. He established and edited the newspaper *al-Nidhal* (1939). Kubbara was elected deputy of Damascus in the Syrian parliament (1947) and between 1949 and 1951 held a ministerial position in the cabinets headed by Nur al-Din al-ATASI and Khalid al-Azm. In 1956, Kubbara was accused of plotting to unite Syria with Iraq and was condemned to death; this sentence was later commuted to forced labor. In March 1963, Kubbara was released but barred from political activity.

George E. Irani

Kuchek Khan-e Jangali   [1888–1921]

Iranian revolutionary fighter.

Mirza Kuchek Khan-e Jangali was born in Rasht, Iran. He attended religious school in Tehran and was in contact with Russian revolutionaries in Baku and Tbilisi. He cooperated with the constitutional revolution of 1905–1911 but he espoused a religious pan-Islamist worldview. From 1909 to 1911, he collaborated with the constitutionalists in fighting the despotic Qajar monarch, Mohammad Ali Qajar. In 1913, Mirza Kuchek Khan was exiled to Tehran, where he frequented political and pan-Islamist religious meetings. In 1914 he returned to his native Gilan and rose in rebellion against the central government with the help of Ottoman and German military advisers. The movement's official organ, *Jangal,* was published in 1917. Following the Bolshevik revolution of 1917 and the Anglo–Persian Agreement of 1919, Mirza Kuchek Khan sided with the Russian Bolshevik regime and, in 1920, proclaimed the Socialist Republic of Gilan. The Soviet–Persian Agreement of 1921 reversed all czarist policy in Persia, and Mirza Kuchek Khan was hence deprived of Soviet support. He was ex-

ecuted in 1921. During the lifetime of the Gilan republic, he initiated a land-reform policy and was intent on eradicating foreign influence, even that of the Russians, in Iran. Mirza Kuchek Khan was also a poet and wrote under the pen name of "Gomnam," which means "unknown."

BIBLIOGRAPHY

FAKHRA'I, EBRAHIM. *Sardar-e Jangal Mirza Kuchek Khan* (Mirza Kuchek Khan, the Warrior of Jangal). Tehran, 1965.

Neguin Yavari

Kuçuk Kaynarja, Treaty of

Treaty ending Russo–Ottoman War, 1774.

In an effort to conquer the northern shore of the Black Sea, Catherine the Great of Russia (1762–1796) was following in the footsteps of the Muscovite czars and of Peter the Great. She won her first war against the Ottoman Empire (1768–1774), and the Treaty of Kuçuk Kaynarja is generally regarded as the most important agreement concluded by the two states. It set the tone for Russia's subsequent Ottoman policy and provided a general framework in which bilateral relations were conducted well into the twentieth century.

Territorial Provisions. Russia returned to the Ottoman Empire some of the provinces captured during the war—Bessarabia and the principalities (Wallachia and Moldavia) on the western shore of the Black Sea, as well as Georgia and Mingrelia in the Caucasus. Istanbul undertook to govern these territories fairly and leniently. Russia retained the strategic fortresses of Kinburn (situated at the mouth of the river Dnieper), Yenikale, and Kerch (located on the eastern tip of the Crimea). In addition, a large section of the Black Sea coast from the river Bug to the fortress of Azov, as well as the Kabarda region in northern Caucasus, were annexed to Russia. Lastly, the Crimean Tartars who, in 1475, had accepted Ottoman suzerainty were granted independence. These territorial changes established Russia as a Black Sea power and created a means for expansion into the eastern Balkans and the Caucasus.

Diplomatic Provisions. Russia was granted permission to establish permanent diplomatic representation in Istanbul. Its ambassador was allowed to open a Greek Orthodox church, which was placed under St. Petersburg's protection. Moreover, the Ottoman authorities undertook to facilitate Russian nationals' travel to the holy places.

Economic Provisions. To help foster Russian trade, St. Petersburg was granted the right of "free and unimpeded" commercial navigation in Turkish waters, including the Straits. Russian subjects were permitted to engage in commerce in the territory of the Ottoman Empire, enjoying the same rights and privileges as the merchants of such favored states as France and Great Britain. Similar courtesies were accorded to Ottoman subjects in Russia.

Religious Provisions. St. Petersburg claimed subsequently that the treaty had established Russia as the protector of the sultan's Greek Orthodox subjects, enabling it to intervene in the internal affairs of the Ottoman Empire. Since Istanbul and London disagreed, the relevant sections of the treaty deserve a closer look. As noted, permission to open the embassy included a provision for the construction in Istanbul of a Greek Orthodox church (Article 14). The ambassador was allowed "to make, upon all occasions, representations . . . in favour of the new church" and the Ottoman authorities promised "to take such representations into due consideration . . ." (Article 7). Moreover, some of the territories occupied by Russia during the war, inhabited mainly by a Greek Orthodox population, were returned to the Ottoman Empire on condition of improved governance, including freedom of Christian religion. Finally, and importantly, Istanbul undertook explicitly "to protect constantly the Christian religion and its churches" in its territory (Article 7). Turkish failure to abide by these provisions implicitly entitled Russia to intervene in the affairs of the Ottoman Empire.

The very favorable terms that Russia had secured under the treaty of Küçük Kaynarja reflected the decisive victory scored against the weakening Ottoman Empire. Nevertheless, St. Petersburg was not entirely satisfied with its gains: the Turks had not been completely dislodged from the northern shore of the Black Sea; the Crimean state had remained independent (it was annexed by Russia in 1783); and Russian naval vessels had not been granted permission to sail through the Straits. Attempts to resolve these and other problems were undertaken by Catherine as well as by her successors.

BIBLIOGRAPHY

HUREWITZ, J. C. *The Middle East and North Africa in World Politics: A Documentary Record.* Vol. 1, 2nd ed. New Haven, Conn., 1975.

MARRIOTT, J. A. R. *The Eastern Question: A Study in European Diplomacy,* 4th ed. London, 1940.

SHOTWELL, JAMES T., and FRANCIS DEAK. *Turkey at the Straits: A Short History.* New York, 1940.

Oles M. Smolansky

Kudsi, Nazim al-   [1906–   ]

Syrian lawyer-politician, born in Aleppo, from landowning, scholarly Sunni family.

During the French mandate, Nazim al-Kudsi was one of the leaders of the Nationalist Youth (al-Shabab al-Watani), an elitist organization that began to take shape in Damascus at the encouragement of Fakhri Bey al-Barudi, a Damascene notable. Al-Kudsi's class origin and the advanced Western education he received in Beirut and Geneva enabled him to acquire a number of political positions: leader of the Aleppo-based People's party; member of the Syrian parliament; foreign minister and prime minister for brief intervals in 1949, 1950, and 1951; president of the Syrian parliament from 1951 to 1953 and from 1954 to 1957; and president of Syria following the dissolution of the Egyptian–Syrian union in 1961. Following the Ba'th coup of March 1963, al-Kudsi withdrew from political life and left Syria to live in Lebanon and France.

Muhammad Muslih

Kufta

A meatball.

Kufta is a ground meat, onion, parsley, and spice mixture popular in Turkey, Syria, Lebanon, Jordan, and among Palestinians. The meat is molded around a skewer and then grilled. Kufta can also be baked or braised.

Clifford A. Wright

Küleli Incident

Plot to depose Sultan Abdülmecit.

In the late 1850s, a small group called the Society of Zealots organized at the Küleli army barracks in Constantinople (now Istanbul) in protest of unpaid military stipends, the lavish spending of ABDÜLMECIT I, and recent reforms such as concessions made to non-Muslims. The group consisted of students and army officers led by Shaykh Ahmed, a madrasa teacher at the Sultan Beyazit mosque. The conspirators plotted to depose or, if necessary, assassinate Sultan Abdülmecit, but they were discovered and forty of them were arrested in September 1859. Widespread support for the group prevented further arrests. The incident is often cited as the first protest against Ottoman absolutism, followed by the Young

Ottoman movement in the next decade. The Society of Zealots is also considered a forerunner of Ottoman political parties and the first modern attempt at military intervention in politics.

BIBLIOGRAPHY

DAVISON, RODERIC H. *Reform in the Ottoman Empire 1856–1876.* Princeton, N.J., 1963.
LEWIS, BERNARD. *The Emergence of Modern Turkey.* New York, 1961.
SHAW, STANFORD J., and EZEL KURAL SHAW. *History of the Ottoman Empire and Modern Turkey.* Vol. 2. Cambridge, U.K., 1977.

Elizabeth Thompson

Kurd Ali, Muhammad   [1876–1953]

Syrian historian, literary critic, and educator.

Muhammad Kurd Ali was a man of letters who began his career during the Ottoman Empire as a pioneer journalist and then devoted his mature years to scholarship as a historian, literary critic, and memoirist. His writings embraced a wide range of subjects, but he paid special attention to the historical achievements of Arab–Islamic civilization and to a comparison of those achievements with the ascendancy of Western Europe.

Kurd Ali's father was from a long-established Damascene (Syria) family of Kurdish ancestry, while his mother's family was Circassian (from the Caucasus region of Russia). The family was of modest means. Kurd Ali's upbringing took place during a period of intellectual ferment in Damascus. Therefore, he was the beneficiary of a considerable range of educational opportunities, both formal and informal. After completing his secondary studies at a standard government school, he spent two years at the Lazarist school in Damascus where he acquired fluent French and began a lifelong appreciation of French literature and culture. He was also profoundly influenced by his personal contact with the Damascus circle of religious reformers and studied under their most prominent member, Tahir al-Jaza'iri. In addition, he was a friend of Rashid RIDA and an admirer of Muhammad ABDUH, whose lectures he attended at Cairo's venerable institution of Islamic learning, al-Azhar University. Kurd Ali's outlook was further shaped by two lengthy visits to Europe (1908 and 1913), which convinced him that Western society possessed certain attributes that were worth emulating.

In 1901, Kurd Ali took up residence in Cairo, where he honed his journalistic skills in the lively Egyptian press, writing and editing for such well-known publications as *al-Muqtataf* and *al-Mu'ayyad.* He founded his own journal, *al-Muqtabas,* in 1906 and transferred it to Damascus in 1909. It was as the publisher, editor, and principal correspondent of *al-Muqtabas* that Kurd Ali rose to prominence in Damascene society. *Al-Muqtabas* was an outspoken reformist journal that addressed such sensitive issues as Ottoman misrule, the stagnation of the Islamic world, and the special role the Arabs had to play in the revival of Islam. Despite his criticism of the Ottoman government, Kurd Ali favored Syria's continued affiliation with the empire. During World War I, he supported the government by serving on the editorial board of an Ottoman-sponsored newspaper, *al-Sharq.*

Following the Ottoman defeat and the establishment of a separate Syrian state, Kurd Ali abandoned political journalism. Although he served two terms as Syrian minister of education (1920–1922 and 1928–1931), he generally eschewed politics and devoted his energies to scholarship. He played a leading role in the establishment of the ARAB ACADEMY OF DAMASCUS in 1919 and served as its director until his death. Modeled on the Académie Française, the Arab Academy facilitated the publication of classical and contemporary works in Arabic and generally sought to encourage a public interest in literature. Kurd Ali's personal contributions to this endeavor were substantial. He edited several classical texts, compiled a six-volume history of Syria (*Khitat al-Sham*), and wrote other works on literature and on the achievements of Arab-Islamic civilization. He also published four volumes of memoirs.

Kurd Ali's historical studies were intended not only to inform readers about the past but also to demonstrate the positive achievements of Arab-Islamic civilization. He believed that European progress was generated by the rediscovery of ancient knowledge during the Renaissance, and he argued that Arab Muslims must become aware of the achievements of their ancestors in order to experience their own awakening and renewal.

BIBLIOGRAPHY

KURD ALI, MUHAMMAD. *Memoirs of Muhammad Kurd 'Ali: A Selection,* trans. by Khalil Totah. Washington, D.C., 1954.
PELLAT, CHARLES. "Muhammad Farid Kurd 'Ali." In *The Encyclopaedia of Islam.* 2nd ed.
SEIKALY, SAMIR. "Damascene Intellectual Life in the Opening Years of the 20th Century: Muhammad Kurd 'Ali and al-Muqtabas." In *Intellectual Life in the Arab East, 1890–1939,* ed. by Marwan R. Buheiry. Beirut, 1981.

William L. Cleveland

Kurdish

See Iranian Languages

Kurdish Revolts

A nearly century-long series of revolts to achieve independence.

A sense of Kurdish nationalism had already developed before World War I, and it was given hope for success by Woodrow Wilson's support for the concept of self-determination. But the results of the peace settlement—a redrawing of the borders of the Ottoman Empire that did not provide for a Kurdish homeland in eastern Anatolia and the Mosul region of Iraq—sparked revolts beginning in 1925 by the Kurds against the new states.

In Iraq there were intermittent uprisings against the monarchy (1921–1958). After the coup in 1961, the Kurds supported the new government, but when Kassem turned against them soon after he took power, Mullah Mustafa BARZANI and his PESH MERGA led a full-scale rebellion that lasted until 1966, at which time an agreement was reached with the Bazzaz government (it was never implemented). Full-scale war returned in 1969, after the Ba'th took power; paused in 1970, when the Kurds were granted autonomy, and resumed shortly thereafter, with Iranian and Is-raeli support, until the ALGIERS AGREEMENT of 1975. The Ba'th reached an understanding with the shah of Iran, who agreed to stop his support of the Kurdish rebellion in Iraq, and thus effectively eliminated the Kurdish threat there. The Iraqi government initiated military offensives and instituted a resettlement plan, transferring an estimated one third of the Iraqi Kurdish population to the south, away from the Iranian border. Fighting resumed in 1985 during the IRAN–IRAQ WAR, resulting in a major 1988 Iraqi military offensive that included the use of poison gas against several Kurdish villages. Hostilities broke out again during the GULF CRISIS of 1990/91. When, however, the U.S.-led coalition did not back the rebellion, Baghdad regained control of most of the north. The Kurds retreated to Iran and to Turkey, which were less hospitable. In the wake of the devastating Iraqi attacks on the Kurds, the United States and its allies in April 1991 supported the establishment of a Kurdish enclave above the 36th parallel.

In Iran the situation was quiescent until the Kurds attempted, with Soviet encouragement, to set up an independent Kurdish republic in Mehabad in 1946. This action was defeated by the shah's armed forces. Relations with the Iranian government returned to their previous state, but they subsequently became closer when the Shah supported the Kurdish rebellions in Iraq. In 1979/80, another rebellion broke out in Iran after the accession to power of Ayatollah Khomeini when the Shi'a Islamic regime attempted to end the semiautonomous status of the Iranian Kurds. During the Iran–Iraq War, Iranian Kurds received aid from the government of Iraq. Though the Iranian Kurdish rebellion was crushed in 1982, sporadic fighting has persisted.

In Turkey the Kurds constitute the largest ethnic minority and have been the focus of the government's Turkification policy, which has attempted to impose the Turkish language and culture on the Kurds. Called "mountain Turks," the Turkish Kurds initially worked for cultural autonomy through the Turkish political parties. In the 1970s, with the establishment of the Kurdish Workers' party (PKK), a more activist approach was employed, first with attacks against rival Kurdish groups. Though temporarily neutralized by the military coup in 1980, armed attacks against Turkish civilian and military officials in Kurdish areas of Turkey resumed in the late 1980s and have persisted. In 1992 Turkey began a major offensive in Kurdish areas of eastern Anatolia and in Iraqi territory to suppress and isolate members of the PKK.

Though Kurdish revolts have occurred throughout the twentieth century, they have been unsuccessful in establishing an independent Kurdistan. Political rivalries and linguistic and cultural differences among Kurds living in Iraq, Turkey, and Iran have forestalled a united attempt at independence.

BIBLIOGRAPHY

McDOWELL, DAVID. *A Modern History of the Kurds.* London, 1996.
O'BALLANCE, EDGAR. *The Kurdish Struggle.* New York, 1996.

Reeva S. Simon

Kurdistan

The land of the Kurds.

Kurdistan does not have boundaries on any map, but it extends over five Middle Eastern states: Turkey, Iraq, Iran, Syria, and parts of the former Soviet Armenia. It is a 620-mile (1,000 km) strip of land and, stretching from the southeast to the northwest, extends from Hamadan (Iran) to the Gulf of Iskenderun (or Alexandretta, Turkey). Its width varies from about 150 miles (250 km) to 250 miles (400 km) between Mosul and Mount Ararat. The heart of Kurdistan is two long chains of mountains, the Taurus and the Zagros, with many summits towering over

Mountains of Kurdistan, April 1955. (D.W. Lockhard)

9,800 feet (3,000 m), while Mount Ararat reaches 16,900 feet (5,157 m).

Two long rivers, the Tigris and the Euphrates, have their sources in Kurdistan, which is also watered by two huge lakes—Van, in Turkey, and Urmia in Iran. Despite its harsh climate, Kurdistan is very fertile and rich in natural resources, particularly petroleum. SULAYMANIYA has long been considered the "capital" of Iraqi Kurdistan, with DIYARBEKIR in Turkey and Mahabad in Iran.

BIBLIOGRAPHY

NIKITINE, BASILE. *Les Kurdes.* Paris, 1956.

Chris Kutschera

Kurds

People of Aryan origin who live in an area that embraces the highlands of eastern Anatolia and the northwest Zagros mountains.

Approximately 25 million Kurds have been living for millennia in the region they call KURDISTAN, which is divided today among five countries: Turkey (10–12 million), Iraq (4 million), Iran (6–8 million), Syria

(1.5 million) and the Caucasus of the former Soviet Armenia (500,000).

History. Scholars debate whether the Kurds belonged originally to a group of Iranian (Indo-European speaking) populations living around Lake Urmia, who migrated westward in the seventh century B.C.E.; others emphasize the indigenous character of the Kurds living in the Taurus and Zagros mountain ranges since antiquity. Clearly, they have always been seen by their neighbors as a people apart, as documented by the medieval geographer Abu Ishaq al-Farsi some thousand years ago.

Their history becomes clear after the conquest of Tikrit by Islam, when Caliph Omar's troops prevailed in 637 C.E. Arab chronicles detail KURDISH REVOLTS against their successive masters; they also tell of the rise of Kurdish dynasties—the Shahdids (Shaddadids of Arran and eastern Armenia, c. 951–1174), the Hasanwayhids (Rawwadids of Azerbaijan, early tenth century), and the Merwanids (Marwanids of central and eastern Anatolia, 983–1085).

The Zands of Persia (1750–1794) were the last Kurds to form a dynasty before European intervention in the affairs of the Ottoman Empire. Playing upon the rivalry between the Ottoman Turks and

Two Kurds in eastern Turkey pose in traditional garb, 1952. (D.W. Lockhard)

Kurds in northern Iraq. (D.W. Lockhard)

the Persians, the Kurds always managed a measure of autonomy. After World War I and the demise of the Ottoman Empire, Kurdistan was apportioned to Syria, Iraq, and Turkey—while the Caucasus region had been within Russia from the beginning of the early 1800s.

Kurdish Culture. Despite the influence of the neighboring cultures and the displacements of populations, and despite the campaigns of open or covert assimilation, Kurdish identity has always asserted itself around the Kurdish language (an Iranian language), although the majority of the population is illiterate. Kurdish is not a dialect of Persian as some writers have claimed but an Indo-European language of the western Indo-Iranian branch, which also includes Baluchi, Tajiki, and Persian. Kurdish (or Kurdi) is characterized by a distinct grammar and syntax and by its own rich vocabulary.

Linguists working in France at the Paris-based Institut Kurde have been editing a dictionary of 50,000 words. There are two main Kurdish dialects, the Kurmandji, spoken in Turkey and in the northern part of Iraqi Kurdistan, and the Sorani, used in Iran and in southern Iraqi Kurdistan. Since the Kurdish people are subjected to national borders, the Kurdish language is written in three different types of characters—the Latin, or Roman, alphabet in Turkey and Syria; the Arabic alphabet in Iraq and Persia; and the Cyrillic alphabet in the former Soviet Union. Although, or because, Kurds are forbidden by many governments of the region to study their own language at school, they demonstrate a passion for their own idiom that led to a "hypertrophy of the folklore": There is a Kurdish proverb or saying for every situation; daily life inspires popular songs (love and death, but also war and hunting); stirred by the feats of their leaders, poets have written epics that are memorized and transmitted from generation to gen-

eration—one of these is Ahmad Khani's *Memo Zin,* the Kurdish *Romeo and Juliet.*

Religion. Most of the Kurds practice SUNNI ISLAM, save for some districts of Turkey and the southern part of Iranian Kurdistan where they practice SHI-'ISM (which, in Iran, negatively affects their relationship to the Kurdish national movement). SUFISM is traditionally very strong in Kurdistan—after the demise of the principal Kurdish feudal leaders, the Kurdish revolts of the late nineteenth century and early twentieth century were led by religious shaykhs belonging to one or another of the great dervish orders—the QADIRIYYA ORDER, and the NAQSHBANDI.

Observing a tolerant Islam, marked by survivals from ZOROASTRIANISM, such as the celebration of the new year (*Nowruz*) on March 21, the Kurds have coexisted for centuries with a number of minorities (Yazidis, around Jabal [mount] Sinajar; Jews, who lived in Badinan, Iraq, until the 1950s; and NESTORIANS—Christian Assyrians—by far the largest group). This coexistence was mostly peaceful, but it was marred by some conflicts that contributed to a negative reputation in the West for the Kurds. In 1846, Emir Badr Khan had invaded the Nestorian districts, provoking a violent reaction in Europe and

Female Kurdish freedom fighter in Iraqi Kurdistan, circa 1974. (© Chris Kutschera)

a punitive Ottoman expedition that led to his capture. At the end of the nineteenth century and during World War I, the Kurds participated in the Turks' mass killing of the Armenians. In February 1918, Simko, the leader of the Kurdish revolt in Iran, assassinated the Mar Sham'un, the Nestorian patriarch—an act that was condemned by other Kurdish leaders, like the Barzani family.

Anthropology, Ethnography, Sociology. At the beginning of the twentieth century, Kurdish society was not very different from the Kurdistan in eighteenth or nineteenth century European travelers' "narratives": Feudal chiefs were living in castles in relative luxury, while peasants lived in natural caves or in mud huts, cultivating wheat and barley, tobacco and rice; most Kurds were nomads or seminomads, spending the summer with their herds of sheep and goats in the mountains, migrating back with them to the lowlands in the winter. The big tribes—the Herki, the Jaf, and the Shikak—were known by the number of tents (1,600 tents for such a tribe, and so many guns for one tent). The Kurds were living outside the towns, inhabited mainly by Turkish soldiers, officials, and merchants plus Jews, and the Armenians and some other Christian minorities (Nestorians, Chaldeans, Jacobites, and so on).

Only in the second half of the nineteenth century did the Kurds start settling down in the cities and in their own villages. For many centuries, DIYARBEKIR, SULAYMANIA, and Bitlis were the only big Kurdish cities (unlike Kirkuk, Erbil, Ruwanduz, Amadiya, Mardin, and Urmia, inhabited by "outsiders"). Land tenure was conservative, with aghas owning the land—sometimes several villages—on which the poor peasants were working and paying a rent of as much as half the crop. Traditional Kurdish society has been seriously eroded by the exploitation of petroleum in Kirkuk and by Saddam Hussein's wars in Iraqi Kurdistan; by the policy of systematic destruction of the tribal system by the Pahlavi shahs of Iran; and by Turkey's policy of repression and assimilation. Most Kurds live now in the villages and in the big cities of Kurdistan, while a number of them have looked for shelter in Istanbul, Tehran, Baghdad, or Western Europe.

BIBLIOGRAPHY

BOIS, THOMAS. *Connaissance des Kurdes.* Beirut, 1965.
GHASSEMLOU, ABDUL RAHMAN. *Kurdistan and the Kurds.* Prague, 1965.
NIKITINE, BASILE. *Les Kurdes, étude sociologique et historique.* Paris, 1956.
VAN BRUINESSEN, MARTIN. *Aghas, Shaikhs, and State.* London, 1992.

Chris Kutschera

Kurush

See Qirsh

Kütahya, Peace of

An 1833 pact granting Ottoman Empire territories, including Egypt, to Muhammad Ali Pasha and his son, Ibrahim Pasha.

In 1831, MUHAMMAD ALI Pasha, the Ottoman governor of Egypt, attacked Syria, also part of the Ottoman Empire. Commanded by his son Ibrahim Pasha, Muhammad Ali's forces were successful. The empire's sultan, Mahmud II, responded to this rebellion, only to be soundly defeated by Ibrahim near Konya on December 21, 1832. Ibrahim continued his advance through Anatolia and occupied Kütahya in early February 1833. With Ibrahim so near Constantinople (now Istanbul), seat of the empire, Mahmud turned in desperation to Russia. Czar Nicholas I sent Russian ships to the Bosporus in late February, and Russian troops encamped at Hunkâr-Iskelesi soon after. At this point, the other European powers intervened. Egypt's ally France pressured Ibrahim to settle with the sultan, and Britain wished to defuse the crisis before Russian troops became involved in hostilities. On orders from his father, Ibrahim demanded the provinces of Syria and Cilicia, as well as Crete and Egypt for his father. At the end of March 1833, an agreement was concluded between Ibrahim and the sultan's representative, Mustafa Raşit Paşa. Ibrahim and Muhammad Ali were granted the aforementioned territories, and the Egyptian army then withdrew from Kütahya. The Peace of Kütahya was not an official treaty, but rather a pact between the sultan and his vassal. It concluded the First Egyptian Crisis and left Muhammad Ali in an extremely strong position, so strong that Britain's foreign minister, Lord Palmerston, was determined that he would not be allowed to maintain that position permanently. Eight years later, in the Second Egyptian Crisis, Muhammad Ali lost much of what was gained at Kütahya. After the First Crisis, Russia and the Ottoman Empire signed a mutual-defense agreement, the Treaty of HUNKÂR-ISKELESI.

BIBLIOGRAPHY

ANDERSON, M. S. *The Eastern Question.* London, 1966.
SHAW, STANFORD, and EZEL KURAL SHAW. *History of the Ottoman Empire and Modern Turkey.* New York, 1977.

Zachary Karabell

Kut al-Amara

Town in Iraq.

Kut al-Amara is approximately one hundred miles (160 km) southeast of Baghdad on the left bank of the Tigris, opposite the mouth of the Shatt al-Hayy, the old canal connecting the Tigris with the Euphrates. The name Kut al-Amara, often shortened to Kut, derives from the Hindi word *kot*, meaning fortress.

Kut al-Amara's main claim to fame—or rather notoriety—is the decimation of several thousand British and Indian Allied forces stranded there during World War I by the advancing Turkish forces on April 29, 1916, after a five-month-long siege. The whole affair boiled down to a miscalculation on the part of the British commander, Major General Charles Townshend, who thought he could take Baghdad. Repulsed at Ctesiphon by the Turkish forces in late November 1915, Townshend was forced to retreat to Kut. In the end, after all attempts to redeem the situation failed, the Allied forces surrendered. According to the records, approximately two thousand Allied soldiers lost their lives during the siege, and almost twelve thousand were taken as prisoners of war.

BIBLIOGRAPHY

MILLAR, R. W. *Kut: The Death of an Army.* London, 1969.

Karen Pinto

Kutla al-Wataniyya al-Hurra, al-

See Free United Bloc

Kuttab

Basic school in Islamic education.

The *kuttab* was originally attached to a mosque, and the school taught children and new converts to be true believers of Islam. In the morning, students would recite and memorize passages from the QUR'AN. In the afternoon, they would learn to write, study Islamic prayers and rituals, and, particularly in the Arab East, study Arabic grammar and poetry.

Beginning in the mid-nineteenth century, secular studies were introduced in many kuttabs, especially in cities, where they faced competition from new Western-style primary schools. In 1926, the Republic of Turkey abolished the kuttabs and instituted secular education and society.

Throughout the Middle East, most religious education is now taught in government schools, but kuttabs have remained an important vehicle of rural education, particularly in Saudi Arabia and Egypt.

BIBLIOGRAPHY

"Kuttab." *Encyclopaedia of Islam,* 2nd ed.

Elizabeth Thompson

Kuwait

Arab country situated at the northern end of the Persian/Arabian Gulf.

Land and People. The country's official name is Dawlat al-Kuwait, or State of Kuwait. *Kuwait* is the diminutive for the Arabic for "fort," probably of the type associated with a sixteenth-century Portuguese structure. Located at the northern tip of the Persian Gulf, Kuwait covers an area of 7,800 square miles (20,202 sq. km) and shares borderland of almost 300 miles (483 km) with Iraq and Saudi Arabia. Largely flat, its landscape rises to almost 1,000 feet (305 m) in the southwest. The most prominent geographical feature is Kuwait Bay, a large natural harbor. Kuwait has only a few oases, and its brackish groundwater has necessitated the construction of enormous desalting facilities to provide adequate drinking water. The enormous petroleum reserves, conservatively estimated at 92 billion barrels, constitute Kuwait's only significant natural resource.

From late spring to early fall, Kuwait is hot and humid, with temperatures regularly reaching 110°F (44°C) and, on occasion, 120°F (49°C). Moderate, pleasant weather characterizes most of the rest of the year, with temperatures falling to 45°F (7°C) and, on rare occasions, below freezing in winter. Although the scant rainfall averages just over three inches (8.2

Aerial view of Kuwait landscape with water towers in distance. (Richard Bulliet)

cm) annually, specific rainfalls range from virtually nothing to over twelve inches. Winds exaggerate the effects of both heat and cold and sandstorms are common.

Before the Iraqi invasion of August 1990 (see GULF CRISIS), Kuwait's population was officially estimated at 2,120,302, with Kuwaiti citizens accounting for less than one third of the total. Most of the expatriate population had come from other Arab countries. Most of the Palestinians, who at 400,000 represented by far the largest immigrant community, had emigrated to Kuwait after the 1948 and 1967 Arab–Israel wars. In 1993, the population totaled 1.40 million, and the government was determined to prevent the percentage of Kuwaitis, then about 43 percent, from falling significantly below half of the total. The Palestinians played a key role in developing both Kuwait's public and private sectors, but primarily because of their flight at the time of the Iraqi invasion and secondarily because of their expulsion later on, their number was reduced to no more than 30,000 to 40,000. Kuwait has increased the number of Egyptians and South Asians in the expatriate workforce, which continues to represent about 80 percent of Kuwait's economically active population. All native Kuwaitis are Muslim; 85 percent are Sunnis and the balance are Shi'ites. The great majority of resident non-Kuwaitis are also Muslim. The nomadic population has dwindled to a tiny minority, and virtually all of the population is contained in the coastal conurbation that extends from Kuwait Bay to the port of Mina Sa'ud in the south.

History. Kuwait's history dates from the third millennium B.C.E. when the area was part of a highly developed culture based on maritime commerce and linked to ancient Sumer. Its modern history begins in the early eighteenth century when several clans of the al-UTUB tribal grouping, claiming association with the great Anaza tribal confederation to which the Al Sa'ud belong, left famine-stricken central Arabia and settled on the northern Gulf coast. The Al Sabah emerged as the dominant clan, and were formally established as rulers in 1756; they directed Kuwait's affairs in consultation with members of the other clans, who, like them, had become merchants. Throughout the eighteenth and nineteenth centuries, Al Sabah proved adept at the kind of maneuvering that was necessary for a small, weak state to survive next to powerful Saudi and Rashidi neighbors and in the arena of Ottoman and British imperial rivalry. In 1899, Mubarak AL SABAH ("Mubarak the Great") reached a secret agreement with the British, which was amplified and made formal in 1914, whereby Great Britain assumed responsibility for Kuwait's security and foreign relations, although domestic governance remained in Kuwaiti hands. This arrangement continued until the 1914 treaty was abrogated by mutual agreement in 1961. British advisers helped create and run an administration that evolved into the modern bureaucracy of independent Kuwait. Another British legacy is Kuwait's borders, which were essentially determined at the UQAYR CONFERENCE (1922), when the country's territory was greatly reduced compared to what it had been under Mubarak. Another part of the British legacy,

Colonel Imad Adrasi, liaison officer between Iraq and the United Nations, stands in 1993 by a marker designating the Iraq–Kuwait border. (© Mark Dennis)

Iraq's limited access to the Persian Gulf, had fateful consequences for Kuwait.

Economics. Before the discovery of oil, the prosperity of Kuwait's merchants and the welfare of most its population depended on maritime trade, especially pearling. Oil was found in 1938, just as the Japanese introduced cultured pearls, thereby ruining the market for Gulf pearls. Oil production began after World War II through the KUWAIT OIL COMPANY (KOC), which was jointly owned by British Petroleum (formerly the Anglo–Iranian Oil Company) and the American-owned Gulf Oil Corporation. The Kuwaiti government assumed complete ownership of the KOC in 1976 (retroactive to 1975), and in 1977 it completed the nationalization of all concessionaires. In 1946, 5.9 million barrels were produced, and in 1972 daily production peaked at over 3.8 million barrels. The country's annual income rose from under $1 million in 1946 to just under $18 billion by 1980. By the early 1980s, Kuwait's astute overseas investments, primarily in Europe and in the United States, were yielding as much income as did the export of crude and refined oil products.

The accumulation of great wealth led to the creation of the Middle East's first full-fledged welfare state. Kuwaiti citizens receive comprehensive welfare services, medical benefits, and free education beginning with kindergarten and up through the University of Kuwait and vocational schools. For the most part, the benefits of the welfare system have also been available to resident aliens, although to a lesser extent since the 1990–1991 Gulf Crisis. To ensure the prosperity of Kuwaitis after the end of the oil era, the government established the Reserve Fund for Future Generations in 1976. Also with a view to the future, it has tried to diversify the country's economy, but the lack of other significant resources, a very small domestic market, and the lack of complementarity with other Gulf economies has largely stymied such efforts. Even before independence, Kuwait, driven by both philanthropic and political motives, had established a foreign aid program. The principal instrument of the extensive program, which benefited both Arab and non-Arab developing countries, was the KUWAIT FUND FOR ARAB ECONOMIC DEVELOPMENT. Since the Desert Storm conflict, however, economic and political considerations have caused Kuwait to greatly curtail its foreign aid program.

Kuwait's oil revenues declined severely as a result of the oil glut in the mid-1980s, but income from investments and large financial reserves made the problem manageable. The Iraqi occupation and the Desert Storm operation that ended it were very costly for Kuwait in economic terms. Kuwait's financial contribution to the allied military effort formed the greatest part of this expense. This outlay and the cost of replacing physical infrastructure were the main factors responsible for reducing Kuwait's foreign exchange reserves from the prewar amount of about 100 billion dollars to perhaps 30 billion dollars. Less financially draining but more politically unsettling were the losses of several billion dollars' worth of investments after the war through gross mismanagement in the Kuwait Investment Office, long a leading symbol of Kuwait's financial strength and acumen. Such a disastrous financial performance, added to the government's continuing failure to come to grips with the consequences of the collapse in 1982 of the SUK AL-MANAKH, an unofficial stock market, shook Kuwaitis' confidence in the government's ability to manage the country's wealth.

Government and Politics. Kuwait's dynastic, patriarchal system of government is in the hands of the Al Sabah family. In this century, succession has been confined to male descendants of two sons of Mubarak the Great, known as the Al Salim and the Al Jabir. British protection and oil wealth gave the ruling family dominance over the great merchants with whom power had been more equally shared in earlier times.

The constitution of 1962 confirmed the hereditary power of the Al Sabah, but it also established a National Assembly with the potential for curtailing the rulers' power. The emir and the cabinet hold executive power and share legislative power with the assembly, which can override the ruler's veto with a two-thirds vote. The limitation of the electoral franchise to 15 percent of the Kuwaiti population (women are excluded from voting by enforced custom) has generated a certain cynicism about the efficacy of parliamentary government which was reinforced by the ruler's lengthy suspension of the assembly in 1976 and in 1986. Parliamentary government has nevertheless survived. The earlier assemblies had a strong Kuwaiti and Arab nationalist component; the spokesman for the Nationalist Bloc (no formal parties are permitted) was the redoubtable Dr. Ahmad al-KHATIB. Later assemblies had a more conservative complexion with a strong Islamist representation. Following the suspension of the assembly in 1986, the government permitted only the election of a national council that lacked legislative powers. The traumatic events during the period from 1990 to 1991 persuaded many Kuwaitis of the need for greater government accountability and compelled the emir to agree to a parliamentary election, which he set for October 5, 1992. In January 1992, the government lifted the prepublication censorship of the press.

The 1992 election marked a significant political watershed for Kuwait. Antigovernment candidates won thirty-five of the fifty seats, and nineteen of these candidates ran on Islamist platforms. Although the new sixteen-member cabinet contained six opposition members, twice the previous highest number, the key portfolios of defense, interior, foreign affairs, and information remained in Al Sabah hands. The prime minister's office, moreover, was still reserved for the Al Sabah heir apparent. At the same time, the new assembly addressed difficult and controversial issues, such as modification of Kuwait's restrictive requirements for citizenship, the need for stronger penalties to deter corruption among government officials, and repeal of the secrecy law that has prevented those outside the Al Sabah ruling circle from being able to scrutinize important government documents. In reaction to the scandal involving the Kuwait Investment Office, the assembly is pressing for a law to be enacted that would require biannual reports from public investment companies. The working relationships of Islamist and secularist members in the assembly, who cooperated with each other in the electoral campaign, are also significant, because this successful interaction may provide insight into the prospects for such relationships elsewhere in the Arab world.

Foreign Relations. Kuwait's foreign relations have undergone a profound shift in recent years. For the first two and a half decades after gaining independence in 1961, Kuwait used its oil revenues to deflect actual and potential threats; a prime example of this "checkbook diplomacy" was the financial aid disbursed to Iraq during that country's war with Iran. The corollary to this strategy was an accommodationist policy in the Arab world, which included strong support of the Palestinian cause, and a neutralist international stance, which included an insistence on the exclusion of U.S. military forces from the Gulf. The Iranian threat, which in 1987 led Kuwait's government to request that American warships escort Kuwaiti oil tankers in the Gulf, was the first great departure from the earlier policy. Dependence on the West (especially on the United States) for the country's basic security was confirmed by the events that followed the Iraqi invasion. In the aftermath of the Gulf Crisis, most Kuwaitis felt that they had been stabbed in the back not only by those Arab countries that supported Iraq's aggression but also by those that did not support military action against Iraq. This feeling makes Kuwait's effective reintegration in the Arab world a slow and difficult process.

BIBLIOGRAPHY

CRYSTAL, JILL. *Kuwait: The Transformation of an Oil State.* Boulder, Colo., 1992.
———. *Oil and Politics in the Gulf: Rulers and Merchants in Kuwait and Qatar.* New York, 1990.
EGLIN, DARREL R., and JAMES D. RUDOLPH. "Kuwait." In *Persian Gulf States: Country Studies,* ed. by Richard F. Nyrop. Washington, D.C., 1984.
GRAZ, LIESL. *The Turbulent Gulf: People, Politics and Power.* New York, 1992.
SALIBI, KAMAL. *A History of Arabia.* Delmar, N.Y., 1980.

Malcolm C. Peck

Kuwait City

Capital of Kuwait.

Ancient settlements existed in the vicinity of the present city on the southeastern edge of Kuwait Bay, but the origins of modern KUWAIT appear to date to a settlement established in the mid-seventeenth century by the Bani Khalid tribe. Early Western maps generally identify that settlement as Grane, the phonetic spelling of the local pronunciation of Qurayn (Arabic for either "hillock" or "little horn," both of which describe features of the coast). In the last third of the eighteenth century, the name being used for the settlement was the present one, which refers to a "little fort" on the site. By that time, the Banu Utub, a group of migrating clans driven from central Arabia by drought, had settled in the area. Soon thereafter, the clans chose the Al Sabah to be the ruling clan, and all the subsequent rulers of Kuwait have been drawn from the Al Sabah dynasty.

In the latter part of the eighteenth century, Kuwait began to enjoy modest prosperity as a port that could be used as an alternative to Basra, which was

Kuwait City skyline. (Richard Bulliet)

Modern apartment complex rebuilt after the Iraqi occupation and the 1991 Gulf War. (Richard Bulliet)

then under Ottoman control. In the nineteenth century, it developed into a significant entrepôt and was the home port of large trading vessels that sailed as far as India and East Africa. Shipbuilding became a major industry, as did pearl fishing, which employed some 700 ships and 15,000 men by the early twentieth century. This commercial success generated steady expansion in the town, whose population reached about 30,000 by 1900 and was just under 100,000 by 1947, on the eve of the era of oil-fueled growth.

With the influx of sudden oil wealth in the 1950s, the town was transformed. A master plan drawn up by a British firm in 1952 imposed a paradigm that reflected current city planning in the West, with little thought given to Kuwait's specific past or to the model of the historic Arab Islamic city in general. Most of the old town was razed and became the modern city's central business district, which is surrounded by a series of concentric ring roads connected by roads radiating outward. Five gates and a brief segment of wall remain from the defenses of the old town; a green belt was created to replace the rest. Residential areas were developed to the southeast and industrial sectors to the southwest. Planned neighborhoods contained large plots with detached villa-style houses for Kuwaiti citizens as well as shopping areas and mosques. Some links to the city's past were retained, such as the ruler's Dasman Palace and the eighteenth-century Khalifa mosque. Between 1960 and 1964, the Kuwait Ministry of Public Works hired the Palestinian–American architect and city planner Saba George Shiber to improve upon the previous efforts. His influence is visible in the handsome architecture that has characterized Kuwait City's later phases of development. The handsome National Assembly building, the spacious interna-

tional airport, and the dramatic water towers on the seafront are among the more striking examples of a new idiom that suggests something of Kuwait's past. An inevitable accompaniment of rapid growth was significant traffic congestion, which the city addressed by implementing ambitious road and multistory parking-facility projects.

At the last census (1985), Kuwait City proper (also known as al-Kuwait), had a population of 44,335. However, the metropolitan area is a conurbation that stretches some twenty-five miles across the south coast of Kuwait Bay and contains roughly two-thirds of the country's population, estimated at just over 2 million before the Iraqi invasion of August 1990 and about 1.4 million in late 1993. To the west is al-Shuwaikh, site of the country's largest port, the main university campus, and the Shuwaikh industrial area, where factories and workshops are located. To the east is Hawali, the largest, most densely settled of Kuwait's suburbs and home to many expatriate workers and their families, particularly Palestinians in the years before their flight and expulsion in 1990 and 1991.

The Iraqis inflicted extensive damage on buildings and infrastructure in the city. American firms played a large role in the city's reconstruction, which cost about 20 billion dollars.

BIBLIOGRAPHY

BONINE, MICHAEL E. "The Urbanization of the Persian Gulf Nations." In *The Persian Gulf States: A General Survey,* ed. by Alvin J. Cottrell. Baltimore, 1980.
CRYSTAL, JILL. *Kuwait: The Transformation of an Oil State.* Boulder, Colo., 1992.
WHELAN, JOHN, ed. *Kuwait: A MEED Practical Guide.* London, 1985.

Malcolm C. Peck

Kuwait Fund for Arab Economic Development

Organization (KFAED) set up in 1961 to extend foreign aid to Arab, Islamic, and third-world countries, primarily in Asia and Africa.

The Kuwait Fund for Arab Economic Development was the first foreign-aid vehicle of its kind in the Arab world. Kuwait's foreign aid included the Levant, North Africa, sub-Saharan Africa, the Arabian peninsula, India, and China and compared favorably with the most generous of all Organization for Economic Cooperation and Development (OECD) countries. In the 1960s and 1970s, Kuwait's total foreign aid disbursements, which included considerably more than KFAED grants and loans, exceeded 5 percent of the country's gross national product (GNP).

By 1989, KFAED's capital was more than $2 billion. From 1962 to 1984, the organization had disbursed about $4 billion for 280 loans. In the late 1980s, Kuwait's foreign aid in general and KFAED'S loans in particular decreased significantly. For example, in 1987/88 KFAED made only 22 loans totaling approximately $150 million.

Before the 1990/91 Gulf Crisis, one of three channels of Kuwaiti foreign aid was KFAED; the other two were the General Board for South Arabian and Gulf States and direct loans from the country's reserves. Of the three channels, KFAED has the most formalized structure and operates according to the procedures of the World Bank. KFAED loans, which supported economically sound projects, compared favorably with other loan-granting institutions in terms of interest rates. The projects that received KFAED loans over the years included sugar manufacturing and railroad development in Sudan, phosphate production and tourism expansion in Jordan, and dredging and improvement of the Suez Canal. Whereas most of KFAED's loans from 1962 to 1972 were extended only to Arab countries, by 1974, with an amendment to its charter, KFAED was authorized to extend loans to non-Arab developing countries.

BIBLIOGRAPHY

The Middle East and North Africa, 1991, 37th ed. London, 1991.

Emile A. Nakhleh

Kuwait National Industries Company

Kuwait company founded in 1960 to spark industrialization.

The Kuwait National Industries Company was established as part of the country's initial drive for industrialization outside the oil sector. The government is a major owner of the company, which has a controlling interest in such construction enterprises as cement works, a brick-making plant, and a metal pipe-manufacturing plant.

BIBLIOGRAPHY

CRYSTAL, JILL. *Kuwait: The Tranformation of an Oil State.* Boulder, Colo., 1992.

Malcolm C. Peck

Kuwait National Petroleum Company

A government-owned firm created in 1962.

The Kuwait National Petroleum Company (KNPC) refines oil, liquefies gas, and markets its operations locally. When nationalized in 1975, the KUWAIT OIL COMPANY (previously owned by Gulf Oil Corporation and British Petroleum) was placed under the jurisdiction of the KNPC. In 1980, the KNPC and other related companies were made part of the KUWAIT PETROLEUM COMPANY.

BIBLIOGRAPHY

CRYSTAL, JILL. *Kuwait: The Transformation of an Oil State.* Boulder, Colo., 1992.

Malcolm C. Peck

Kuwait Oil Company

State-owned oil company.

Established in 1934 under the joint ownership of the GULF OIL CORPORATION and British Petroleum, Kuwait Oil Company (KOC) received the first oil concession in that year. For years, KOC was the principal company to hold concessions in mainland Kuwait, beginning operations in 1935. Petroleum was not discovered until 1938—a powerful well at the Burgan (Burqan) oil field, today one of the largest and most productive. Later, KOC discovered and operated more fields.

Kuwait's goal was to control its oil industry and, in 1975, the government bought the entire stock of KOC, including its refinery and other installations. British Petroleum and Gulf Oil continued to provide technical expertise for access to oil supplies and fees. By 1980, about 50 percent of KOC's work force, including administrators, were Kuwaitis. Although the external activities of the business were assigned to the KUWAIT NATIONAL PETROLEUM COMPANY (KNPC), primary responsibility for domestic oil and gas exploration and production was assigned to KOC. The KOC fields accounted for almost 50 percent of Kuwait's oil production, roughly 2 to 3 million barrels per day before the 1990 invasion of Kuwait by Iraq. In 1980, Kuwait's government reorganized its oil industry by creating the KUWAIT PETROLEUM COMPANY (KPC), whose main task was to coordinate the activities of the four existing companies: the KOC, the KNPC, the Petroleum Industries Company (PIC), and the Kuwait Oil Tankers Company (KOTC). Despite centralization, KOC continues to specialize in and be responsible for exploration, drilling, and production.

BIBLIOGRAPHY

The Middle East and North Africa, 1991, 37th ed. London, 1991.

Emile A. Nakhleh

Kuwait Petroleum Company

National oil company of Kuwait.

The Kuwait Petroleum Company (KPC) was created on January 27, 1980. It initially included oil properties that the government had acquired through the nationalization of foreign and domestic private investments in oil operations based in Kuwait. From the start, KPC was a fully integrated company, owning exploration, production, and refining facilities acquired from the KUWAIT OIL COMPANY (KOC) and Aminoil, an additional refinery as well as overseas and domestic marketing acquired from the KUWAIT NATIONAL PETROLEUM COMPANY (KNPC), an oil tanker company, and wholly owned and joint ventures in petrochemicals.

KPC's first chairman was Kuwait's oil minister, Shaykh Ali Khalifa. Together with a small group of advisers, he launched an ambitious program designed to make KPC the "eighth sister," a new oil "major" that would be both multinational and vertically integrated. Such a strategy would enable Kuwait to maximize oil income while reducing its vulnerability to losses arising from normal fluctuations in the prices of crude oil.

KPC established a foreign exploration subsidiary, the Kuwait Foreign Petroleum Exporting Company (KUFPEC), in April 1981. By mid-1994, KUPFEC held exploration, development, and production rights in eleven countries in the Eastern Hemisphere. In 1982, KPC acquired Santa Fe International, an exploration, engineering, and construction firm based in Alhambra, California. Its decision to offer a premium for outstanding Santa Fe shares initiated domestic criticism of the company that continues today. The Santa Fe purchase was also troubled by a profit-eroding slide in oil prices that began shortly after it was completed; a conflict with U.S. Interior Secretary James Watt over Kuwait's rights to explore for and produce oil on land leased by Santa Fe from the U.S. government (resolved in Kuwait's favor in 1985); and conflicts over refinery modernization projects between Santa Fe's construction subsidiary, C. F. Braun, and KPC refining affiliates in Kuwait and Europe. C. F. Braun was sold to Brown and Root in 1989. That year, Santa Fe's exploration and production assets in the North Sea were split off into an independent company, Santa Fe Exploration.

Undaunted by domestic criticism, Ali Khalifa embarked on an ambitious series of downstream acquisitions beginning in 1983, when KPC purchased refining and marketing operations from Gulf Oil in several European countries. KPC's European holdings, managed by its subsidiary Kuwait Petroleum International (KPI), were expanded by further acquisitions. The largest was KPI's 1990 purchase of Mobil Italia, which more than doubled the company's marketing outlets in Italy and gained it a large refinery in Naples. Meanwhile, KPI initiated negotiations for marketing and refining facilities in eastern Europe and the Far East.

The quality and locational disadvantages of Kuwait crude had led KNPC to invest in a high-technology refinery at Shuaiba as early as the 1960s, when KNPC was still a joint state–private sector firm. KPC invested heavily in modernizing two of its Kuwait-based refineries, MINA AL-AHMADI and Mina Abdullah. Its tanker arm, the Kuwait Oil Tanker Company (KOTC), modified existing tankers to carry light products from Kuwait's sophisticated refineries to Europoort in the Netherlands, where extensive tankage and blending facilities were constructed on the site shared with the old Gulf refinery to tailor products for individual markets. KPC's overseas and domestic operations became closely integrated, thereby increasing overall efficiency and profitability. Its multinational vertical integration also increased national autonomy by reducing Kuwait's dependence on third-party crude oil sales as its primary source of oil income.

The August 1990 invasion of Kuwait by Iraq severed the connection of KPC's Kuwait-based production and refining to its overseas refining and marketing outlets (see GULF CRISIS). By the end of the year, however, most KPC overseas affiliates were once again profitable through use of crude and products purchased on the open market. All of KOTC's ships escaped confiscation by Iraq, thus providing another source of income for Kuwait's government in exile.

KPC's overseas affiliates did more than generate income for Kuwait during the occupation by Iraq. They were also concrete evidence of the community of interests between Kuwait and the host governments of the affiliates. All of KPC's operations were run from London during the occupation, a process facilitated by the British government, which exempted them from taxation during this period. KPI's London headquarters was used as a base by Kuwaitis mobilizing popular support for the liberation of Kuwait from Iraq.

Ali Khalifa led KPC throughout the occupation, but he did so as finance minister rather than as oil minister, a position from which he had been removed in June 1990 in response to domestic and foreign criticism of Kuwait's persistent production in excess of its ORGANIZATION OF PETROLEUM EXPORTING COUNTRIES (OPEC) quota. After liberation, Ali Khalifa continued to be criticized, especially for his alleged role in the Kuwait Investment Office's losses of nearly 5 billion U.S. dollars in Spain. The financial operations of KPC subsidiaries also came under scrutiny. Investigators found that top officials of KOTC had embezzled millions of dollars from the company. Although managing director Abd al-Fattah al-Badr and two other KOTC employees managed to flee the country before they were arrested, one of his subordinates and Ali Khalifa were charged and brought to trial.

The domestic political conflict over the running of KPC is embedded in a broader conflict over Kuwait's investment policy. Domestic interests favor diversification out of oil, whereas government leaders have concentrated resources in oil by pursuing a strategy of multinational vertical integration through KPC. Critics deplore not only the economic vulnerability that results from concentrating investment in a single industry but also the political vulnerability that comes from investing abroad, where properties can be expropriated. This position received indirect support from a 1993 World Bank report recommending extensive privatization of state assets, including parts of KPC. KPC's defenders point to the integral role of oil in supporting the state and the population of Kuwait, and the benefits that the company's overseas investments brought throughout the occupation, in the form of human as well as financial support for liberation.

Despite the threat that Iraq's sabotage of Kuwait's oil fields represented to the long-term economic vitality of Kuwait, this danger was quite easily dealt with through mostly technical means. In contrast, the threat of internal disarray and conflict over KPC policy cannot be met by technology. Under the fourth oil minister since June 1990, KPC's remarkable venture into the world of the major oil companies is still unappreciated by most Kuwaitis. Until the fundamentally political conflicts over KPC's strategy are resolved, the company will remain acutely vulnerable to critics at home.

BIBLIOGRAPHY

AARTS, PAUL W. H., and GEP EISENLOEFFEL. "Kuwait Petroleum Corporation and the Process of Vertical Integration." OPEC Review 14, no. 2 (1990).
CRYSTAL, JILL. Oil and Politics in the Gulf: Rulers and Merchants in Kuwait and Qatar. New York, 1990.
TÉTREAULT, MARY ANN. The Kuwait Petroleum Corporation and the Economics of the New World Order. Westport, Conn., 1995.

Mary Ann Tétreault

Kuwait Planning Board

An independent body established in 1962 and attached directly to the Council of Ministers.

The prime minister served as the Kuwait Planning Board's chairman, and the minister of finance was its deputy chairman. Other cabinet members served on the board along with four prominent Kuwaitis from the private sector. The board was vested with comprehensive powers to enable it to set general economic, social, and population policy as well as to establish development programs and oversee their implementation. It carried out its mandate in a series of five-year plans, the first of which was adopted in 1967. The board outlined broad, long-term goals that included the creation of a diversified economy, the assurance of an equitable distribution of wealth, and the training of human resources for the development of specialized skills.

In conjunction with the Kuwait Municipal Council and other agencies, the board played a significant role in overseeing the planning of modern KUWAIT CITY. The board's Central Statistical Office published the *Statistical Abstract,* also known as the *Statistical Yearbook,* and other information on Kuwait's economy. These functions were assumed by the Ministry of Planning in 1974, following the board's termination.

BIBLIOGRAPHY

BONINE, MICHAEL E. "The Urbanization of the Persian Gulf Nations." In *The Persian Gulf States: A General Survey,* ed. by Alvin J. Cottrell. Baltimore, 1980.
ISMAEL, JACQUELINE S. *Kuwait: Dependency and Class in a Rentier State.* Gainesville, Fla., 1993.

Malcolm C. Peck

Kuwait University

Established in October 1966 to enable Kuwaiti men and women to receive a university education at home; the university became integral to Kuwait's assertion of national sovereignty.

At the time it opened in 1966, with 31 faculty members and 418 students, Kuwait University was divided into the College of Sciences, Arts and Education, and the College for Women. By 1990, there were more than 900 faculty and over 17,000 students in eleven colleges, or faculties, on four campuses. The colleges of science, engineering, and graduate studies are at Khaldiya, as is the university's administration; the colleges of commerce, economics, and political science and the Language Center are at Adaliya; the College for Women is in Keifan; and the colleges of law, arts, and medicine are at the new campus in Shuwaikh. The College of Arts (liberal arts) has the largest faculty and almost 5,000 students; the College of Sciences has the next largest faculty and over 3,000 students. Nearly 500 students are enrolled in the College of Medicine, and between 300 and 400 students in the College of Allied Health Sciences and Nursing. All these schools, including the science laboratories, have state-of-the-art facilities. The quality of faculty and students is high by Arab-world standards.

Generally organized along the same lines as American universities, Kuwait University operates on a semester basis and uses the course unit. Arabic is the language of instruction for most faculties, but English is used in the College of Science, Energy and Petroleum, the College of Medicine, and the College of Allied Health Sciences and Nursing, as well as in certain courses in other colleges. Tuition is free in all of the colleges, and most other services are either free or provided for nominal fees.

Although a major objective of the university is to produce Kuwaiti instructors who can teach in the nation's educational system, Kuwaitis remain in the minority on the university's faculty. Kuwaiti students make up about two-thirds of the students in the university; most of the non-Kuwaiti students come from other Arab countries. The faculties are coeducational, and, by the late 1980s, 60 percent of all entering students and 66 percent of the Kuwaiti students were women. The College for Women has provided a segregated education for the daughters of conservative families.

From its inception, Kuwait University has had a pragmatic, community-oriented mission, which is especially reflected in its Center for Community Service and Continuing Education, whose programs include business administration, computer sciences, and languages. By the 1987/88 school year, the center was serving 3,200 students. The university sponsors more than a dozen specialized publications, including *The Arab Journal for the Humanities* and *The Journal of Gulf and Arabian Peninsula Studies,* as a means of furthering its objective of promoting the study of Arab civilization and history and the Gulf–Arabian Peninsula area.

From 1990 to 1991, the Iraqi occupiers of Kuwait used Kuwait University as a prison. They ransacked its buildings and stole or destroyed most of its equipment, but within a year of Kuwait's liberation the physical damage had been repaired. The numbers of faculty and students were close to prewar levels by the 1993–1994 academic year.

BIBLIOGRAPHY

Kuwait: Facts and Figures, 1988. Kuwait Ministry of Information, n.d.
Kuwait University: General Undergraduate Catalog, 1991–1993.
SAPSTED, DAVID. *Kuwait.* London, 1980.
Welcome to Kuwait and Kuwait University. Kuwait University, 1992.

Malcolm C. Peck

Kuzbari, Haydar al-

Syrian military officer.

Affiliated with a Damascus industrialist bourgeois class that was opposed to the sweeping nationalizations of Egypt's President Gamal Abdel Nasser, Haydar al-Kuzbari led a 1961 coup against the United Arab Republic with Abd al-Karim Nahlawi. This action was indicative of the growing polarization of the Syrian military in the face of Nasser's differences with the Ba'th party. Al-Kuzbari was arrested after both the 1962 and 1966 coups.

BIBLIOGRAPHY

HINNEBUSCH, RAYMOND A. *Authoritarian Power and State Formation in Ba'thist Syria: Army, Party, and Peasant.* Boulder, Colo., 1990.

Charles U. Zenzie

Kuzbari, Ma'mun al-   [1914–   ]

Syrian lawyer and politician.

Al-Kuzbari completed his secondary studies at the Christian Brothers school. In 1937, he obtained a law degree from the Université Saint-Joseph (Beirut) and in 1945 a doctorate in law from the Université de Lyon in France. Between 1951 and 1953 he served as director general of the Ministry of Finance. In 1953 and 1954, al-Kuzbari was elected deputy of Damascus. He then filled the posts of minister of justice, of education, of labor, and of social affairs in the cabinets headed by Sabri al-ASALI (1955, 1956–58) and Sa'id al-GHAZZI (1955–56). In 1961, after the breakup of the UNITED ARAB REPUBLIC (UAR), he went to Holland to participate in an international lawyers' conference. That same year he was appointed prime minister and held the ministries of defense and foreign affairs in the first government following the split between Syria and Egypt. In 1962, al-Kuzbari became president of Syria, a post he held until his fall from power in March 1963. He is the author of several books and a holder of medals from Egypt and Jordan. He married Yasar Abed al-Khoja and had two children.

George E. Irani

Kzar, Nazim [1935?–1973]

Iraqi Ba'th party leader.

Nazim Kzar was born in Kut al-Amara, a town on the Tigris in the southern part of Iraq, home of al-Mi'dan, a wretched and poverty-stricken people. His father, a poor man of obscure origin, was probably a member of the Sabaean community and apparently became a Shi'ite during his youth.

Kzar received his elementary education in Kut al-Amara then entered the technological institute in Baghdad. He joined the Ba'th party in 1959 while he was still a student and was able to climb the ranks of leadership. After the 1963 coup, he masterminded the mass killing of Communists, Kurds, and Nasserites, among others. In 1969, Kzar was appointed chief of security police, and in 1973, he attempted to lead a coup to overthrow Saddam Hussein but was captured and executed.

BIBLIOGRAPHY

KHADDURI, MAJID. *Socialist Iraq*. Washington, D.C., 1978.

Mamoon A. Zaki

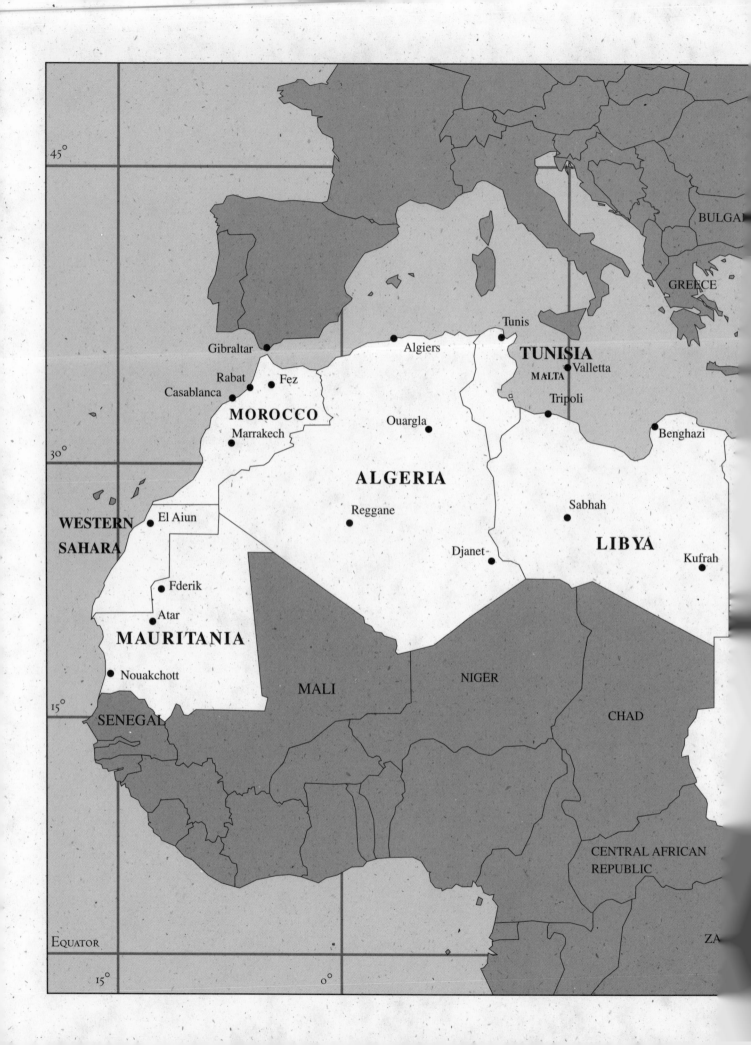